# Classical and Romantic Performing Practice

# Classical and Romantic Performing Practice

Second Edition

CLIVE BROWN

## OXFORD
UNIVERSITY PRESS

Oxford University Press is a department of the University of Oxford. It furthers the University's objective of excellence in research, scholarship, and education by publishing worldwide. Oxford is a registered trade mark of Oxford University Press in the UK and certain other countries.

Published in the United States of America by Oxford University Press
198 Madison Avenue, New York, NY 10016, United States of America.

© Oxford University Press 1999, 2025

All rights reserved. No part of this publication may be reproduced, stored in a retrieval system, or transmitted, in any form or by any means, without the prior permission in writing of Oxford University Press, or as expressly permitted by law, by license, or under terms agreed with the appropriate reproduction rights organization. Inquiries concerning reproduction outside the scope of the above should be sent to the Rights Department, Oxford University Press, at the address above.

You must not circulate this work in any other form
and you must impose this same condition on any acquirer.

Library of Congress Cataloging-in-Publication Data
Names: Brown, Clive, 1947– author.
Title: Classical and romantic performing practice / Clive Brown.
Description: Second edition. | New York, NY : Oxford University Press, 2025. |
Includes bibliographical references and index. |
Identifiers: LCCN 2023053745 (print) | LCCN 2023053746 (ebook) |
ISBN 9780197581629 (paperback) | ISBN 9780197581612 (hardback) |
ISBN 9780197581636 (epub) | ISBN 9780197581650
Subjects: LCSH: Performance practice (Music)—History—18th century. |
Performance practice (Music)—History—19th century.
Classification: LCC ML457 .B76 2025 (print) | LCC ML457 (ebook) |
DDC 781.4/3—dc23/eng/20231121
LC record available at https://lccn.loc.gov/2023053745
LC ebook record available at https://lccn.loc.gov/2023053746

DOI: 10.1093/oso/9780197581612.001.0001

Paperback printed by Marquis Book Printing, Canada
Hardback printed by Bridgeport National Bindery, Inc., United States of America

*To Dorothea, who will not read this book, but without whose encouragement it would never have been finished.*

*This second edition is also dedicated to the University of Music and Performing Arts (Universität für Musik und darstellende Kunst), Vienna. After I 'retired' to Austria in 2017, Professor Johannes Meissl, with the support of Rektorin Ulrike Sych, made it possible for me to continue working with highly talented young musicians, as a part-time member of staff. Their support, and that of many other colleagues, has been a key source of inspiration and motivation for undertaking the challenging task of incorporating twenty-five years of research and experience into this extensively revised edition.*

# Contents

| | |
|---|---|
| *Acknowledgements* | xi |
| *About the Companion Website* | xiii |
| Introduction: Past and Present: Perspectives and Prospects | 1 |
| 1. Accentuation in Theory | 7 |
|    Categories of Accentuation | 9 |
|       Metrical Accent | 10 |
|       Structural and Expressive Accent | 23 |
| 2. Accentuation in Practice | 36 |
|    Slurred Figures | 37 |
|    Dissonance and Chromatic Notes | 46 |
|    Note Pitch | 48 |
|    Note Length | 49 |
|    Syncopation | 49 |
|    Beaming | 52 |
|    Final Notes | 59 |
|    Other Factors | 60 |
|    Agogic Accent | 61 |
|    Percussive Accent | 72 |
| 3. The Notation of Accents and Dynamics | 75 |
|    Italian Terms and Abbreviations as Accents | 80 |
|       *Forte (f, for; ff, etc.)* | 80 |
|       *Forte-piano (fp, for:po:, ffp, mfp)* | 86 |
|       *Sforzando (sforzato, forzato, forzando, sf, sfz, sff, fz, ffz)* | 98 |
|       *Rinforzando, Rinforzato (rf, rfz, rinf, rfp)* | 110 |
|          *rf* as Accent | 123 |
|          *Rinforzando* as "Strengthened" | 129 |
|    Signs as Accent Markings | 134 |
|       The *Staccato* Mark (¦.) | 137 |
|       The Hairpin (> or ▷) | 147 |
|       *Le Petit Chapeau* (∧) | 156 |
|       The Short *Messa di voce* (<>) | 167 |
|       The Horizontal Line (– ∸ ∸) | 169 |
|    The Box (▭) | 179 |

| | |
|---|---|
| 4. Articulation and Phrasing | 181 |
| 5. Articulation and Expression | 217 |
|    *Staccato,* *Legato,* and *Non-Legato* (or *"Non-Staccato"*?) | 218 |
|    Unmarked Notes Implying Slurs | 233 |
|    *Sciolto,* *Spiccato,* and *Non Legato* | 241 |
|    Implied *Non Legato* or *Non-Staccato* | 253 |
|    Heavy and Light Performance | 257 |
| 6. The Notation of Articulation and Phrasing | 265 |
|    Dots and Strokes as Articulation Marks | 265 |
|       The Functions of Articulation Marks | 274 |
|       Musical Context as a Guide to Execution | 290 |
|    Other Articulation Marks | 299 |
|    Slurs and Articulation | 301 |
|       The Nuanced Slur and the Slur as *Legato* | 305 |
|       The Long Phrasing Slur | 314 |
|    Articulated Slurs | 317 |
| 7. Articulation and String Bowing | 341 |
|    The Action of the Bow Arm | 344 |
|    The Right Arm in 18th- and 19th-Century Teaching | 351 |
|    Mid-18th-Century Bowstrokes | 355 |
|    The Impact of Viotti and His Disciples | 380 |
|    A Divergence of Bowing Practices | 393 |
|    A Controversy about Bowstrokes in Beethoven | 414 |
|    Orchestral Bowing in the Mid- to Late-19th Century | 419 |
|    The Absorption of Franco-Belgian Techniques into German Practice | 422 |
|    Bowstrokes in the Later 19th and Early 20th Centuries | 434 |
| 8. Tempo | 444 |
|    Choice of Tempo | 445 |
|    Late-18th-Century and Early-19th-Century Tempo Conventions | 453 |
|    Late-18th-Century Tempo | 462 |
|    Beethoven's Tempo Preferences | 465 |
|    The Impact of the Metronome | 469 |
|    19th-Century Tempo Conventions | 476 |
| 9. Alla Breve | 481 |
|    Tables of Metronome Tempos | 492 |
| 10. Terms of Tempo and Expression | 507 |
|    Slow Tempo Terms | 511 |
|    Intermediate Tempo Terms | 520 |
|       *Andante* as a Relative Tempo Direction | 529 |
|       The Changing Connotations of *"Andante"* for Tempo and Performance | 531 |

| | |
|---|---|
| Moderately Fast Tempo Terms | 534 |
|    *Moderato* and *Allegro Moderato* | 535 |
|    *Maestoso* | 537 |
|    *Allegretto* | 540 |
| Fast Tempo Terms | 541 |
|    *Vivace* | 541 |
|    *Allegro* | 542 |
| Other Terms Affecting Tempo and Expression | 546 |
|    *Amoroso* | 546 |
|    *Animato; Animoso, Con anima* | 547 |
|    *Cantabile* | 548 |
|    *Diminuendo* | 550 |
|    *Dolce* | 553 |
|    *Espressivo* | 555 |
|    *Morendo, Smorzando, Perdendosi, Calando* | 556 |
|    *Sostenuto* | 557 |
| **11. Tempo Modification** | **559** |
| Types of Tempo Modification | 562 |
|    Modification of Tempo over a Steady Beat | 564 |
|    *Tempo Rubato* as Arhythmical Embellishment | 580 |
| Modification of the Basic Pulse | 582 |
| The Endorsement of Conspicuous Tempo Modification | 606 |
| Tempo Flexibility in Orchestral Performance | 613 |
| **12. Notated Ornaments** | **626** |
| *Appoggiaturas* and *Grace-Notes* | 629 |
|    The *Appoggiatura* | 638 |
|    The *Grace-Note* | 655 |
|    Anticipatory Notes | 668 |
| The Trill | 668 |
|    Trill Beginnings | 670 |
|    Trill Endings | 684 |
| The Turn (*Doppelschlag*) | 692 |
|    Accenting Turns | 692 |
|    Connecting Turns | 696 |
| The Notation of Turns and Trills | 700 |
|    Direct and Inverted Turns | 710 |
| **13. Improvised Ornamentation and Embellishment** | **713** |
| Improvised Ornamentation in 18th-Century Theory and Practice | 715 |
|    Vocal Ornamentation | 718 |
| The Performance of Recitative | 738 |
|    Recitative Accompaniment | 747 |
| Improvised Ornamentation in Songs | 754 |

Changing Attitudes towards Vocal Ornamentation 759
Improvised Ornamentation in 18th- and Early-19th-Century
   Instrumental Music 771
The *Fermata* 788
Improvised Embellishment: Correct and Beautiful Performance 800

14. Asynchrony, Arpeggiation, and Flexible Rhythm 832
    Asynchrony 832
    Arpeggiation 840
    Rhythmic Flexibility 861
       Dotted Notes and Triplets 862
       Over-Dotting 873
       Agogic Nuance 882

15. Sliding Effects 888
    Terminology 888
    Types of Vocal *Portamento* and Their Execution 889
    Types of Instrumental *Portamento* and Their Execution 897
       String Instruments 897
       Wind Instruments 907
    Sliding Effects in Late-18th- and Early-19th-Century Practice,
       and Their Reception 910
    Sliding Effects in the Orchestra 926
    Sliding Effects in the Later 19th Century 930

16. Trembling Effects 953
    The Notation of Trembling Effects 953
    Terminology and Types of Trembling Effects 957
       Sympathetic Trembling on String Instruments 967
       Trembling Effects with the Bow 968
    Pulsating Effects on Wind Instruments 972
    Vocal Trembling Effects 977
    Speed and Amplitude 980
    Changing Aesthetics in the Musical Application of Trembling Effects 986
       The Late 18th and Early 19th Centuries 986
       The Mid 19th Century 997

*Bibliography* 1019
*Index* 1039

# Acknowledgements

It is a pleasant, but also a daunting task to acknowledge the assistance I have received in writing and bringing this new edition to publication. For everyone whom I mention by name, there have been many others who have contributed something to my knowledge and experience. Almost everyone with whom I have ever worked closely, either as a scholar, teacher, or performer, has had some impact on my thinking and insights. I am grateful to all of them, even those whose names I no longer remember. People who were particularly important for my work on the first edition are gratefully acknowledged there, and I will not repeat their names here.

In the UK, at the beginning of this century, we began to develop the concept of PhDs, in which the rigorous intellectual demands of scholarship and the skills of performance were inextricably combined. Supervising practice-oriented PhD students in Leeds, Vienna and Leiden, has contributed significantly to my gradually developing understanding of historical performing practices. I have also had the pleasure and stimulation of performing in concerts with many of them. I am glad to pay tribute to their influence on my thinking then and now, naming them in chronological order: Neal Peres Da Costa, David Milsom, Heng-Ching Fang, George Kennaway, Ilias Devetzoglou, Martin Pickard, Peter Collyer, Sarah Potter, Miaoyin Qu, Kate Bennett Wadsworth, Jung-Yoon Cho, Masumi Nagasawa, Johannes Leertouwer, Alexander Nicholls, Emma Williams, Laura Granero, Francesca Piccioni, and Darija Andzakovic. In recent years, I have also collaborated very fruitfully with Neal Peres Da Costa in several research projects, as well as making experimental recordings of Brahms Violin Sonatas with him. It has also been inspiring to perform with Mikayel Balyan in the past few years, without whose encouragement I would not have had the confidence to record sonatas by Beethoven and Krufft with him, based on the performing practice research for my 2020 Bärenreiter edition of Beethoven's Violin Sonatas.

I am grateful to many other people who have provided valuable insights, or provoked me to rethink my understanding of historical sources (some perhaps without realizing it). Some of them have supplied information and stimulated my thinking; others have prompted my awareness of still unanswered—often unanswerable—questions during our practical work together. They are listed here in alphabetical order: Boris Atanasov, Chiara Banchini, Sebastian Bausch, Cecilia Bernadini, Sylvie Brély, Diego Castelli, Avishai Chameides, Beth Chen, Luca Chiantore, Barry Cooper, Will Crutchfield, Johannes Gebauer, Anselm Gerhard, Stefan Gottfried, Peter Hanson, Peter Holman, Bruno Hurtado-Gosalvez, Peter van Hyghen, Kai Köpp, Johannes Leertouwer, Robert Levin, Sébastian Levy, Aldo Mata, Richard Maunder, Mimi Mitchell, Leonardo Miucci, Markus van der Munckhof, Guido de Neve, Marten Noorduin, Olga Paschenko, Joe Puglia, Constance Ricard, Rudolf Riedel, Jane Rogers, Léna Ruisz, Shunske Sato, Leila Schayegh, Keiko Shichijo, Jan Schultsz, Paulina Sokołowska, Philipp von Steinaeker, Richard Sutcliffe, John Thwaites, Dorothea Vogl, David Watkin, Robin Wilson, Douglas Woodfull-Harris, Hed Yaron-Meyerson, Daniel Yeadon.

I wish also to record my gratitude to all the other talented performing musicians—too many to acknowledge by name—with whom I have had the opportunity to work during the past quarter century. Whatever I may have contributed to their understanding of Classical and Romantic musical notation has been amply repaid by the impulse they have given me to re-evaluate constantly the implications of historical evidence.

As indicated in the dedication, the opportunity to continue working on a regular basis with highly skilled young musicians in Vienna, has been an important stimulus to my motivation during the past five years, and a key factor in persuading me to undertake this major revision. I am grateful to all those who have welcomed and encouraged my continuing efforts to incentivise knowledge-based experimentation and innovation in the performance of our priceless legacy of beautiful music.

Finally, I thank Jacqueline Pavlovic and all those at Oxford University Press who have steered this book through the process of publication.

# About the Companion Website

www.oup.com/us/ClassicalandRomanticPerformingPractice

This book features a companion website that provides the full original source quotations for translated passages throughout the book. The reader is encouraged to consult this resource in conjunction with the book.

# Introduction

## Past and Present: Perspectives and Prospects

During the three decades that have elapsed since I began work on the first edition of this book, much more research into the performing practices of the late 18th and 19th centuries has been undertaken and published. This new edition incorporates my own research over the last twenty-five years, some of which appeared in individual articles, and I have drawn gratefully on the research of others, either published or communicated to me directly. One of the most far-reaching changes that has occurred during the interim has been the ever-increasing accessibility of documentary sources and early recordings on the Internet. In the 1980s and 1990s I was heavily dependent on physical archives, working in libraries and collecting relevant material on handwritten file cards. The subsequent digitization of books, newspapers, and periodicals, as well as printed and manuscript music, has transformed documentary research. Word searching in digital archives allows the discovery of information that would previously have been difficult, if not impracticable to locate. Furthermore, the substantially augmented accessibility of aural evidence, in the form of acoustic recordings and piano rolls, enables enhanced insights into the relationship between musical notation, the written word, and the realities of performance. In this new edition, therefore, references have been given wherever possible to sources that are currently available online.

My understanding of the historical evidence and its relevance for contemporary practice has been greatly advanced by the opportunity to work experimentally with many talented performers. This practical work, much of it undertaken together with my practice-led PhD students in Leeds, Vienna, and Leiden, and with gifted young musicians at the University of Music and Performing Arts in Vienna, as well as other conservatories internationally, has provided an invaluable laboratory in which the implications of documentary and aural evidence could be collaboratively tested and evaluated.

* * *

This book has no pretensions to comprehensiveness. My aim has been to focus on key issues that help us to understand the intentions, expectations, or tacit assumptions of late-18th- and 19th-century composers, to investigate the extent to which these intentions, expectations, and assumptions may be implied or specified by their notation, and, above all, to identify some of the constantly changing conventions of performance that informed the experience and practice of composers and executants alike.

While a broad range of major issues is examined, some significant matters, such as details of playing technique on individual instruments, methods of conducting, the physical conditions of music-making, and so on, are considered only where there are special insights to offer. The technical specifications of instruments, and the changes that took place in these during the period, though important for re-imagining the textures and tone colours with which 18th- and 19th-century composers were familiar, are referred to solely where they are directly relevant to questions of performing style.

There are other self-imposed restrictions. At the end of the 20th century, much heat was generated by philosophical and aesthetic debate about the ways in which theoretical knowledge of historical performing practice might be utilized in the modern concert hall and recording studio, and these are still live issues. I do not seek to engage directly in that debate, although my standpoint on certain issues may become to some extent apparent. I am firmly convinced that dogmatism is seldom, if ever, appropriate in matters of musical performance. Taste is in a constant state of flux, and, as Joseph Joachim believed: "It may be taken as self-evident that all rules applying to the art of performance are not of unbending strictness."[1]

What was written about performance during the Classical and Romantic periods is merely the palest reflection of what was done; it cannot offer more than hints of the intentions or expectations that lay behind a composer's notation, but it shows incontrovertibly that the only unintended and unenvisaged way to perform the music of the Classical and Romantic periods is to adhere as strictly as possible to the literal meaning of the notation as it has been generally understood since the mid-20th century. The more performers understand about the potential but unspecified implications of the notation, the more likely they are to render the music in the spirit of its creators.

\* \* \*

---

[1] Joseph Joachim and Andreas Moser: *Violinschule* (Berlin, 1905), ii, 95.

Performing practices and musical styles are continually changing, but there are times when change occurs more rapidly, often in conjunction with substantial political and social upheaval, as happened towards the end of the 18th century and again at the beginning of the 20th century. During the intervening decades, a canon of "great music" was established. At the same time, musical notation became more complex. Composers sought to convey their expectations in increasing detail, and the authority of the notated text, as the perceived repository of the composer's will, increased, while the executant's scope for individuality in the creation of a musical performance gradually diminished. Already during the later 19th century, there was a growing tendency to criticize deviations from the strict letter of the notation: for instance, in the reaction against un-notated asynchrony in piano playing, and in the avoidance of turned endings to trills, unless specifically indicated. During the 20th century, the authority of the text was also manifest in a progressive narrowing of the circumstances in which the use of un-notated practices, such as prosodic appoggiaturas in vocal music, expressive portamento, rhythmic freedom, and tempo flexibility, was regarded as acceptable. Vibrato, on the other hand, came to be seen as an aspect of tone colour, instead of an expressive ornament, and its continual, rather than expressive use was thus regarded as acceptable. Recording was an increasingly significant factor in these changes: it discouraged conspicuous deviations from the notated text that might be criticized as unwarranted, and prioritized a clean, objective performing style. This attitude was reinforced during the second half of the century by the growing availability and use of Urtext editions, in which editors have sometimes explicitly and misleadingly equated composers' intentions for the notation with their expectations for its translation into sound.

* * *

The artistic upheavals of the early 20th century were transformative in many respects. They were manifest not only in radically new styles of composition, but also in rapidly changing attitudes towards the performing practices of canonical repertoire. The first decades of the century witnessed a growing belief that, when performing earlier music, "modern modes of expression", as one writer put it in 1925, were superior to older traditions; championing the use of continuous vibrato, he asserted that performing practice "follows the law of progress in common with other arts and sciences."[2] A similar

---

[2] W. E. Bell-Porter: *The Musical Times*, lxvi (1925), 1021. (See Ch. 16 for a fuller quotation.)

attitude is apparent in Carl Flesch's writings, performing, and teaching. In 1929, arguing for the rehabilitation of Spohr's "Gesangsszene" Concerto into the concert repertoire, Flesch proposed the rejection of all Spohr's known performing practices, even though many of them were specifically indicated in the composer's notation. He insisted: "If we want to bring Spohr's compositions to new life, we must use contemporary means of expression for their rendition." Having explicitly rejected Spohr's bowing and fingering practices, with their implications for specific types of articulation, portamento, and vibrato, Flesch asserted: "Only that which is essential—the Spohrian spirit—must be rescued and brought unscathed into our own time."[3] For Flesch, the "spirit" evidently had nothing to do with Spohr's aural intentions. In practice, of course, musicians had almost always adapted their performance of older music to the expectations of contemporary listeners (Carl Czerny wrote something similar about performing Beethoven's music less than 20 years after the composer's death),[4] but Flesch's typically modernist rejection of every aspect of earlier practice, not only in Spohr, but in all pre-20th-century repertoire, was different in kind: it was ideological.

Another factor that may have militated against the preservation of some of the practices and expressive freedoms associated with Classical and Romantic music was the spreading influence of popular music during the early 20th century—at that time usually referred to indiscriminately as jazz—which was promoted by the growing availability of gramophone records. In 1929, "jazz" was perceived as having "in the few years of its hotly controversial existence, become triumphantly dominant, from the millionaire's salon to the criminal's den."[5] Elitism encouraged classical musicians to respond to this phenomenon by deliberately avoiding the un-notated liberties of their predecessors, many of which continued to have parallels in popular music performance.

*　*　*

Working with highly gifted musicians, both on modern and on period instruments, has convinced me of the immense benefits that can accrue from awareness of the rejected or forgotten historical practices that were once regarded as an essential aspect of beautiful performance. There is always a delicate balance between performance style and the expectations of the

---

[3] Carl Flesch: *Die Kunst des Violinspiels* (Berlin, 1929), ii, 179.
[4] See Ch. 4, pp. 183–184.
[5] Felix Apold: 'Die Jazzmusik', *Signale für die musikalische Welt*, lxxxvii (1929), 428.

audience, and the synergies between 18th- and 19th-century performers and listeners, which depended on shared experience, can never be reproduced; but the expressive practices that lay at the heart of that interaction, which involved significant deviation from the musical notation, have not lost their essential value, since they are rooted in fundamental human emotional responses. These subtle, though often substantial discrepancies between the written text and its execution were regarded as indispensable for the effective realization of the composer's conception, and were expected to vary from musician to musician and performance to performance. Composers, performers, and pedagogues repeatedly insisted that the necessary divergences from a strict rendition of the notated text could not be adequately prescribed. In the early 1820s, Anton Reicha concluded the preface to a collection of his piano trios with the comment: "the greatest achievement in performance is to sense and understand the composer's intentions, for which no signs exist."[6] Despite the proliferation of signs and performance instructions that occurred during the 19th century, this situation scarcely changed. As Otto Klauwell explained in 1883, notation can indicate "only measurable quantities, multiples and fractions of a fundamental unit";[7] thus the composer "has no option but to leave it to the performer's discretion how far, in one way or another, to deviate from the literal meaning of the musical symbols. In my opinion, what is usually called the **Art of Performance**, consists in understanding and utilizing these necessary deviations, these various kinds of rubato, which are of course only to be read between the lines."[8] Prominent composers and performers echoed these remarks. Carl Reinecke observed: "There still remains much to be read between the lines which no composer can convey by signs, no editor by explanations";[9] and Joseph Joachim regretted that late-19th-century Franco-Belgian violinists "adhered too strictly to the lifeless printed notes when playing the classics, not understanding how to read between the lines."[10]

The creative energy that can result from sensitive employment of these practices—not as an attempted recreation of the past, but as a contemporary expression of feeling—can invest the well-known masterpieces of the

---

[6] Anton Reicha: Six Grands Trios Concertants pour Piano, Violon et Violoncelle op. 101 (Paris, [1824]), 1.
[7] Otto Klauwell: *Der Vortrag in der Musik* (Berlin and Leipzig, 1883), 1.
[8] Klauwell: *Der Vortrag*, 2f. Boldface in the original.
[9] Carl Reinecke: *Die Beethoven'schen Clavier-Sonaten*, 2nd edn (Leipzig, 1897), 126.
[10] Andreas Moser: *Joseph Joachim. Ein Lebensbild*, 2nd edn, 2 vols. (Berlin: Verlag der Deutschen Brahms-Gesellschaft, 1908–10), ii, 292. For further discussion of these issues see Ch. 13.

Classical and Romantic periods with more of the emotional depth envisaged by their creators; it can give them the freshness of new music and it can also reveal unexpected beauties in less familiar repertoire.

\* \* \*

The first decades of the 21st century have seen a widening recognition that many of the assumptions about what constitutes stylish performance of Classical and Romantic music, which we have inherited from the protagonists of early-20th-century aesthetics, have no connection whatsoever with the messages its notation was expected to convey to performers at the time of its composition. Nevertheless, many of those assumptions remain central to the training and professional activities of mainstream classical musicians, to the requirements for success in competitions and orchestral auditions, and to the critical norms of many music journalists. Despite the growing engagement with historical practice that has developed since the last decades of the 20th century, therefore, there is still much scope for a more adventurous approach to the interpretation of late-18th- and 19th-century notation. This implies a greater degree of spontaneity in performance, which poses substantial challenges, but also new creative opportunities for the art of sound recording. It is, in my opinion, vital for the future of classical music that we attempt to regain the free, creative spirit and emotional commitment that Classical and Romantic composers expected to be perceived between the lines of their notation and which the most accomplished performers brought to the music of their own day.

# 1
# Accentuation in Theory

Effective accentuation is a fundamental aspect of musical performance; but the relationship between theory and practice in its application is far from straightforward. 18th- and 19th-century theorists laid out the principles of correct accentuation, often in great detail, but many of them acknowledged that, in practice, skilled musicians might often modify, or even break the rules for the sake of beautiful, expressive performance. During the 20th century, however, distinctions between "correct" and "beautiful" performance narrowed.[1] The revolutionary cultural changes that occurred during its early decades resulted in a widespread disparagement and active rejection of previous artistic attitudes and traditions in favour of a new "modernist" aesthetic. As Carl Flesch asserted in 1923: "In the past decades, all the arts have undergone tremendous changes, so that it only seems natural if musical interpretation is influenced and adapted to contemporary feelings."[2] In the emerging cultural environment of the 20th century, the musical text assumed much greater primacy than in previous centuries; "correct" performance of the [Ur]text, as it was understood at that time, gradually became a principal duty of the performer, and substantial departures from its literal meaning, which would once have been regarded as necessary for a "beautiful" performance, came increasingly to be seen as unwarranted license and tastelessness; and this view, to a large extent, remained current at the beginning of the 21st century.

Misconceptions about the teaching of pre-20th-century theorists, and its relationship to the practice of contemporaneous performers, have been widespread during the past century. Recordings of Classical repertoire, especially since the 1960s, imply a widely held notion that performance in the Classical period was characterized by a rather rigid observance of hierarchical metrical accentuation. This view was propounded in an unsophisticated form by

---

[1] For further discussion of these concepts see Ch. 13.
[2] Carl Flesch: *Die Kunst des Violinspiels* (Berlin, 1923), i, 30.

Fritz Rothschild,[3] on the basis of examples given by Johann Abraham Peter Schulz and other 18th-century authors, taking little account of the cultural context or the corpus of theoretical writing that qualifies these early attempts at a scientific analysis of musical procedures. An insufficiently critical evaluation of the sources may have tended to encourage the rhythmically stiff and inexpressive performances of late-18th-century music that became typical during the later 20th century. In addition, the paucity or absence of accent markings in 18th-century scores and their increasing frequency in 19th-century music has tended to engender a false idea among non-specialists that differentiated accentuation for structural or expressive purposes became more prevalent with the passage of time. There is no good reason to believe that this is the case. The inclusion of more frequent and detailed performance instructions is not necessarily evidence that the effects they specify were being more often employed than before; it is likelier to be an indication that composers increasingly regarded individual patterns of expressive accentuation as integral to the character of particular pieces of music, and no longer wished to entrust this vital ingredient of expression entirely to the experience or whim of the performer. Nevertheless, the more comprehensive notation of accents that developed during the 19th century generated its own problems. The meaning of signs and written instructions varied from time to time, place to place, and composer to composer, leading to confusion about their significance that has persisted to the present day. Even the most precise of composers, however, did not expect that they could indicate every nuance of performance so exactly that they provided an unmistakable guide to beautiful performance, which always depended on inspired liberties with the notation. The contrast between the sparsity of performance instructions in most 18th-century music and their abundance in many later 19th-century compositions is striking, but it is questionable whether their profusion made the composer's expectations clearer for the performer. Richard Barth asserted, less than a quarter century after Brahms' death, that people no longer understood how he expected his works to be performed; and Natalie Bauer-Lechner recalled that Mahler, repeatedly frustrated by misunderstanding of his immensely detailed markings, exclaimed: "One would almost be tempted not to write down any instructions for tempi or expressive dynamic signs at all, and to leave it up to each performer to decide

---

[3] Fritz Rothschild: *The Lost Tradition: Musical Performance in the Time of Mozart and Beethoven* (London, 1961).

for himself how he understands the work on closer examination and how he expresses it."[4] Nevertheless, every insight into the messages composers expected to convey by their instructions, or lack of them, can be a valuable stimulus towards a freer, more creative response to their notation.

## Categories of Accentuation

Throughout most of this period, accents were seen as falling into several basic categories. At a fundamental, almost subliminal, level was the accentuation connected with the metrical structure of the music, which was integral to the relationship between melodic figuration and harmony change, and the positioning of dissonance and resolution; this was variously known as grammatical or metric accent, or, in England, simply as accent. Superimposed upon this basic framework was a level of accentuation that was designated rhetorical, oratorical, or expressive accent or, by some English writers, emphasis.[5] Some theorists further subdivided this type of accentuation. Heinrich Christoph Koch described two kinds of expressive accent, which he called *oratorical* and *pathetic*, the latter being an intensified version of the former. A few theorists regarded accentuation whose function was to define the extent and subdivision of musical phrases (here referred to as structural accent) as a distinct category,[6] but it is not always possible to see where the dividing line between this and expressive accent occurs. Most writers made no firm distinction between accentuation that emphasized phrase structure or rhythmic features, thus clarifying the rhetorical meaning of the music, and accentuation that was essential to its emotional content (since phrase structure and rhythm are inextricably linked with expression), yet it seems clear that this sort of notion lay behind the tripartite division of Koch and others.

Similar analyses of functionally different types of accentuation continued to be made in the following century, modified, however, in response to changes in musical style. Mathis Lussy broadly adhered to a three-part categorization, identifying metric, rhythmic, and pathetic accentuation as counterparts to instinct, intelligence, and emotion respectively. Yet by

---

[4] Kurt Hoffmann: *Johannes Brahms in den Erinnerungen von Richard Barth* (Hamburg, 1979), 31. Natalie Bauer-Lechner: *Erinnerungen an Gustav Mahler* (Leipzig, Wien, and Zürich, 1923), 168.

[5] E.g., by John Wall Callcott: *A Musical Grammar* (London, 1806); and John Jousse: *The Theory and Practice of the Violin* (London, 1811).

[6] This type of accentuation was described by, among others, Schulz, Türk, Fink, and Lussy.

that time, there were, as Lussy put it, in registering his disagreement, "certain modern theoreticians" who rejected the teaching of metric accent altogether.[7] Perhaps the most radical rejection of the received notion of metrical accent came from Hugo Riemann, who arrived at the view that it was almost entirely irrelevant to the accentuation demanded by musical phrasing. In an essay in 1883 he regretted that the old grammatical accent system had been constantly reproduced, even in his own earlier writings, and wished to replace it with a *crescendo-decrescendo* system, related to phrase structure.[8] Riemann's theories, which seem to have been strongly influenced by 19th-century practice, enjoyed considerable prestige in the late 19th century and, in some quarters, well into the 20th century, but they did not displace the concept of metrical accent in conventional theory teaching.

## Metrical Accent

Between the middle of the 18th century and the end of the 19th, most theorists were broadly agreed about the nature and function of metrical accent. Analyses of this type of accentuation took several forms, and the terminology employed is diverse; but (apart from a few differences discussed below) there was a general consensus about the arrangement of accented and unaccented beats in most species of metre. Fundamental to the system, and still expounded in conventional modern theory teaching, was the age-old concept of rhythmic arrangement by twos and threes, where, in duple metres, the beats are alternately accented and unaccented and, in triple metres, the first of each group of three beats receives a greater degree of metrical accent than the others. These principles were also seen to operate in subsequent subdivisions of the beat, thus producing patterns of duple or triple grouping in smaller note values. From the various permutations of twos and threes all the commonly used metres were derived.

While the fundamental patterns of alternation of strong and weak were generally agreed, however, there was rather more diversity of opinion with respect to the relative degree of strength or weakness each beat should

---

[7] Mathis Lussy: *Le Rythme musical, son origine, sa fonction et son accentuation* (Paris, 1883), 33 (footnote).
[8] Carl Wilhelm Julius Hugo Riemann: 'Der Ausdruck in der Musik', *Sammlung musikalische Vorträge*, i, no. 50 (Leipzig, 1883), 47.

receive. Many writers of practical instruction manuals contented themselves merely with explaining how strong and weak beats were distributed in different metres, without making any distinction between greater or lesser accentuation of strong beats according to their position in the bar. More theoretically minded authors went further, elaborating a hierarchical system in which some accented beats received more stress than others. The precise pattern of this differentiated accentuation was determined by the metre. In the early 1770s, J. A. P. Schulz explained it thus:

> Duple [even] time has two principal time-units, the first of which is long, the second short: [Ex. 1.1a] If, however, these notes are divided into smaller values, such as quarter-notes in Alla breve time, for example, the first note of the second time-unit receives more emphasis and the quarter-notes themselves behave like time-units [ Ex. 1.1b]
>
> If the bar is divided into still smaller values such as eighth-notes, each of these will have a different degree of emphasis. E.g.: [Ex. 1.1c]
>
> This last example shows clearly the difference between the long and the short notes in duple time.
>
> In triple [uneven] time the unequal value of notes is illustrated by the following example: [Ex. 1.1d]
>
> How to play these notes in respect of their different weights and the accents placed upon them will easily be understood from what has been said about duple time.
>
> In fast movements, or in time signatures where the number of notes can be divided by three, such as 12/8 or 6/4 and in all similar cases, the first note of three is invariably emphasized thus –⌣⌣, and the emphasis on other time-units depends on whether they are even or uneven. E.g.: [Ex. 1.1e].
>
> After what has been said of the inner value of time-units, surely no proof is required to show that, as regards accentuation, 6/4 is essentially different from 3/2, and 6/8 from 3/4, despite the fact that both metres contain the same number of identical note values. The following table will show the difference clearly: [Ex. 1.1f].[9]

---

[9] Johann Abraham Peter Schulz: 'Takt' in Johann Georg Sulzer (ed.), *Allgemeine Theorie der schönen Künste*, 1st edn (Leipzig, 1774), ii, 1136f.

Ex. 1.1 a–f. Sulzer: *Allgemeine Theorie*, 1st edn, ii, 1136f.

Similar hierarchical principles were constantly reiterated during the 19th century, though not wholly unchallenged. Adolph Bernhard Marx mused in 1855:

> we may content ourselves with merely marking the greater divisions (parts, sections, phrases) or we may proceed to define in detail the bars and members of the bar, distinguishing the more important with stronger accents.

It may be asked how far this detailed accentuation is to be carried? In my 'Theory of Composition' I have already drawn attention to the charm that rests in this 'play of the accents,' and also to the danger of producing a fragmentary effect by obtrusion of subordinate features. This danger can easily be illustrated to the eye by a variegated accentuation, such as: [Ex. 1.2]

Where is the medium between an undefined and an exaggerated accentuation?[10]

Ex. 1.2  Marx: *Die Musik des neunzehnten Jahrhunderts*, 462.

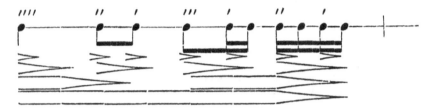

Hugo Riemann, however, was apparently the first theorist fundamentally to question the relevance of hierarchical metrical accent to musical performance.

Nevertheless, as the most penetrating expositions make clear, the system was not, in practice, so neatly logical as certain writers would have liked to make it. Not all the ways in which composers used common time (C), for instance, could be reconciled with a single conception of that metre in relation to its *tempo giusto*[11] and accentual characteristics. In addition, Schulz and Kirnberger, together with other theorists, some of whom were probably influenced by their approach,[12] and others who were not,[13] insisted

---

[10] Adolf Bernhard Marx: *Die Musik des neunzehnten Jahrhunderts und ihre Pflege: Methode der Musik* (Leipzig, 1855), 462.

[11] See Ch. 8.

[12] E.g., Daniel Gottlob Türk: *Klavierschule oder Anweisung zum Klavierspielen für Lehrer und Lernende mit kritischen Anmerkungen* (Leipzig and Halle, 1789); 2nd rev. edn (Leipzig and Halle, 1802), and, in England, August Frederic Christopher Kollmann: *An Essay on Musical Harmony* (London, 1796), 73. Kollmann was certainly influenced by Johann Philipp Kirnberger: *Die Kunst des reinen Satzes in der Musik*, i (Berlin and Königsberg, 1771), ii (Berlin and Königsberg, 1776–79), trans. D. Beach and J. Thym as *The Art of Strict Musical Composition* (New Haven, 1982); he quotes him on p. 77.

[13] E.g., François-Joseph Gossec, Joseph Agus, Charles-Simon Catel, and Luigi Cherubini: *Principes élémentaires de musique arrêtés par les membres du Conservatoire, suivis de solfèges* (Paris, [?1798–1802]), and other French writers.

that there was an important distinction between a true quadruple metre and one which was merely derived from two bars of duple metre with the bar-line removed. Schulz explained that the true c (*Viervierteltakt*) was accented as in: Ex. 1.3a not Ex. 1.3b, the latter accentuation belonging properly only to the c that resulted from two bars of combined $\frac{2}{4}$ (*zusammengesetzter Viervierteltakt*).[14]

Ex. 1.3 a–b. Sulzer: *Allgemeine Theorie*, 1st edn, ii, 1135.

(a)
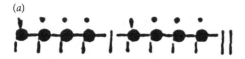

(b)

Some writers, though, regarded this distinction as dubious. Leopold Mozart categorized all even time as duple and all uneven as triple, regarding the division of even time into four quarter-notes as essentially a means of making the even time-measure more comprehensible to the pupil, adding: "That even time is essentially only duple, a good composer must know best."[15] Half a century later Callcott too argued that, notwithstanding the notion (held by some French and German musicians) that common time was a simple rather than a compound measure, there were really no grounds for recognizing quadruple metres as in any essential way different from duple ones; he took the view that c was only distinguished from $\frac{2}{4}$ "by the omission of the alternate Bar".[16] Callcott seems even to have questioned the value of establishing a hierarchy among the accented notes within the bar, being content merely to recognize the normal distribution of accents on the first note of groups of two and three; in this respect he stands closer to the practical approach of many authors of instrumental methods.

---

[14] Schulz: in *Allgemeine Theorie*, ii, 1135. Kollmann repeated this in his *Essay*, 72.
[15] Leopold Mozart: *Versuch einer gründlichen Violinschule* (Augsburg, 1756), 28 (footnote).
[16] Callcott: *Musical Grammar*, 257.

In fact, even those writers who attempted the most extensive classifications of the differences between the various types of metre were conscious that, in practice, many factors modified the strict operation of these rules. Tempo, above all, was crucial in determining the frequency and weight of metrical accents. Callcott observed: "every species of measure may be subdivided by Accents, according to the degree of quickness in which it is performed."[17] Even Schulz, having detailed the difference between a genuine ₵ metre and one that really consisted of combined bars of 2/4, admitted that "in performance, especially in slow pieces, it [genuine 4/4] is often confounded with the combined [type] and divided into two parts, each of two quarter-notes."[18] And later in the 19th century, Marx articulated a generally held view when he made the observation that speed determines the extent to which a hierarchy of accents is intelligible.[19]

In the early part of the period there were also some rather basic disagreements about the metrical accentuation of triple time. A considerable number of important 18th-century and early-19th-century writers maintained that in certain triple metres the third beat was emphasized more than the second. Schulz's example of accentuation in 9/8 (Ex. 1.1e) shows that he regarded this to be the case in that metre too. Johann Peter Milchmeyer asserted that "in a three-four metre, the first and third quarter-notes are the strong beats and the second the weak beat", but he cautioned that in 3/8 only the first beat received the emphasis.[20] G. S. Löhlein seems also to have regarded a stress on the third beat in 3/4 as normal,[21] giving the example shown in Ex. 1.4; while Rousseau[22] and Castil-Blaze,[23] among French authors, and Charles Burney[24] and Callcott,[25] among English ones, maintained a similar position. Burney, however, qualified his observation that in triple time "the *first* and *last* are accented, the *second* unaccented", with the comment: "if the *third* note in triple time is accented in serious music, it is always less forcibly marked than the first". Türk, while apparently recognizing a subsidiary stress

---

[17] Callcott: *Musical Grammar*, 44.
[18] Schulz: 'Takt' in *Allgemeine Theorie*, ii, 1135.
[19] Adolf Bernhard Marx: *Allgemeine Musiklehre: Ein Hülfsbuch für Lehrer und Lernende in jedem Zweige musikalischer Unterweisung* (Leipzig, 1839), 135.
[20] Johann Peter Milchmeyer: *Die wahre Art das Pianoforte zu Spielen* (Dresden, 1797), 7.
[21] Georg Simon Löhlein: *Anweisung zum Violinspielen* (Leipzig and Züllichau, 1774), 53.
[22] Jean Jacques Rousseau: *Dictionnaire de musique* (Paris, 1768).
[23] François Henri Joseph Castil-Blaze: *Dictionnaire de musique moderne* (Paris, 1821).
[24] Charles Burney: 'Accent' in Abraham Rees (ed.), *Cyclopaedia* (London, 1819) (no pagination).
[25] Callcott: *Musical Grammar*, 41.

on the third beat as normal, remarked, perhaps thinking of such pieces as polaccas and chaconnes, that "in some cases the second is internally long and therefore the third is short".[26] In a similar manner, the authors of the Paris Conservatoire's *Principes élémentaires de musique* recognized the possibility of a metrical accent occurring on either or neither of the last two beats.[27]

**Ex. 1.4** Löhlein: *Anweisung zum Violinspielen*, 53.
The signs above the symbols for unaccented and accented are indications for up- and down-bow.

It seems likely that such conceptions were related partly to the old practice of beating time in triple metre with an uneven tactus (a two-beat downbeat followed by a one-beat upbeat) and partly, perhaps, to its association with specific dance types in which those sorts of accentuation were characteristic. Towards the end of the 18th century, as the uneven tactus disappeared and the relationship between art music and dance music weakened, the idea that the third beat in triple metres might have a regular metrical accent seems largely to have died out. The new orthodoxy was that the third beat in triple metres required the least metrical accent. In the 1840s, François Habeneck stated that "In a bar with three beats, the first beat is always strong, the second is sometimes strong and sometimes weak. The third beat is always weak".[28] The proposition that the natural metrical accentuation of triple metres was strong-weak-weaker is found in many 19th-century German sources: Fink described it thus in the 1830s,[29] and Moritz Hauptmann's almost metaphysical analysis of metre and rhythm, in his highly respected treatise *Die Natur der Harmonik und der Metrik* (1853), led him to propose this scheme as an essential aspect of triple metre.[30] Hauptmann's approach may well have been responsible for the similar views expressed by Arrey von Dommer (1865)

---

[26] Türk: *Klavierschule*, 92.
[27] Gossec et al.: *Principes*, 44.
[28] François Habeneck: *Méthode theorique et pratique de violon* (Paris, [1842]), 109 (footnote).
[29] Gottfried Wilhelm Fink: 'Accent' in Gustav Schilling (ed.), *Encyclopädie der gesammten musikalischen Wissenschaften* (Stuttgart, 1835–38).
[30] Moritz Hauptmann: *Die Natur der Harmonik und der Metrik* (Leipzig, 1853).

and Hauptmann's pupil Oscar Paul (1873).[31] Dommer's description of the third beat in ¾ as "completely accentless, completely upbeat"[32] certainly indicates a very different concept of triple metre from that which had been widely held at the beginning of the century.

In reality, much in the more elaborate expositions of metrical accentuation had scant relevance to practical music-making, since such things as different varieties of common time or differently accented triple metres were not prescribed for the performer by the time signatures composers gave to their works; they were, at best, only recognizable from the nature of particular pieces of music. It is this fact that seems to be acknowledged when, in its discussion of triple time, the *Principes élémentaires de musique* stated that in ¾ an accent may fall on the second or third beat "through the nature of the melody".[33] A more practical rather than theoretical approach is evident in Johann Samuel Petri's 1782 treatise on practical music-making. Having stated that in all triple metres "the first beat is good, the second bad, and the third mediocre, or sometimes also good",[34] he went on to illustrate how this might be affected by the distribution of shorter note values (Ex. 1.5).

**Ex. 1.5** Petri: *Anleitung zur praktischen Musik*, 2nd edn, 162.
Petri uses g. (*gut*) for strong, s. (*schlecht*) for weak, and m. (*mittelmässig*) for medium accentuation.

---

[31] Oscar Paul: 'Accent' in *Handlexikon der Tonkunst* (Leipzig, 1873), 13.
[32] Arrey von Dommer: 'Accent' in *Musikalisches Lexicon* (Heidelberg, 1865), 13.
[33] Gossec et al.: *Principes*, 44 (footnote).
[34] Johann Samuel Petri: *Anleitung zur praktischen Musik*, 2nd edn (Leipzig, 1782), 162. This does not appear in the 1st edn of 1767.

As implied by differences of opinion among theorists, and complaints about the casualness of composers in choosing the correct metre, much depended, in practice, on the knowledge and stylistic sensitivity of the performer, which was acquired far less from awareness of theoretical writings than from direct musical experience. In this respect the borderline between metrical and structural accent becomes blurred.

While the performer was ideally expected to be aware of the metrical scheme that provided the framework for the composer's musical ideas, it was nevertheless acknowledged by many writers throughout the period that it was unnecessary, indeed inartistic, to make purely metrical accentuation obtrude upon the listeners' perceptions, except in special cases (for example, dances and marches) where distinct accentual patterns were an essential feature of the genre. Elsewhere, the metrical accentuation was generally expected to be conveyed to the listener by the melodic and harmonic structure of the music, without any necessity for the performer to contribute an obvious accent. Referring to the accents that fall on the strong beats, Johann Friedrich Schubert commented in 1804: "These require no accentuation on the part of the singer, since they accent themselves through their inner strength."[35] It may be noted, however, that some thirty years later G. W. Fink, though he warned in general against excessive stressing of metrical accents, made quite the opposite point about accents in singing, saying: "The metrical accents in vocal compositions, where they generally coincide with the long syllables [of the text], should least of all be neglected."[36]

The necessity of subordinating metrical accent to the accentuation required by the shape of the phrase and the expressive content of the music was often stressed by writers throughout the period. In England in 1770, John Holden, having remarked that "In the performance of music, there is a certain emphasis, or accent laid on the beginning of every measure, which distinguishes one species of time from another", observed: "There is no occasion to make the beginning, or emphatical part of the measure, always stronger, or louder than the rest, though it is sometimes best to do so."[37]

---

[35] Johann Friedrich Schubert: *Neue Singe-Schule oder gründliche und vollständige Anweisung zur Singkunst* (Leipzig, [1804]), 134.
[36] Gottfried Wilhelm Fink: 'Accent' in Gustav Schilling (ed.), *Encyclopädie*, I, 36.
[37] John Holden: *An Essay towards a Rational System of Music* (Glasgow, 1770), 32.

And Johann Friedrich Reichardt cautioned his reader against interpreting Quantz's instructions for metrical accentuation too literally:

> Also, it would be extremely faulty if the accentuation of the notes—about which Herr Quantz says so much—were always to be marked with a particular pressure of the bow. This [accentuation] is nothing more than the slightest weight, with which anyone with a correct feeling for the beat plays, which, of his own accord, without thinking about it, he will give to the stronger beats, just as children on their coloured fiddles already give it to the notes on which, if left to themselves, they will stamp with their foot. If the child does not get this right, he should not learn music.[38]

At the beginning of the 19th century, Heinrich Christoph Koch referred similarly to the metrical accent as an "almost unnoticeable stress",[39] and Gottfried Weber, a musician of a younger generation, made much the same point almost twenty years later when he cautioned that "This is not to say, of course, that the first half of a bar must always be more weighty and stronger (more forte) than the following half, for we are speaking here of an internal weight, which the feeling of every listener naturally attaches to the first part of every bar."[40]

Johann Nepomuk Hummel's description of metrical accent, too, seems to emphasize the essentially notional quality of strong and weak beats, rather than suggesting that the performer will automatically deliver them more strongly:

> The parts of the bar are divided into heavy (good) and light (bad). By the former are to be understood those parts upon which our feelings naturally bestow a degree of weight. Thus, the latter pass by our ear, so that, in comparison with the former, they appear light and unimportant.[41]

---

[38] Johann Friedrich Reichardt: *Ueber die Pflichten des Ripien-Violinisten* (Berlin and Leipzig, 1776), 28f.
[39] Heinrich Christoph Koch: 'Accent' in *Musikalisches Lexikon* (Frankfurt-am-Main, 1802), 50.
[40] Gottfried Weber: *Versuch einer geordneten Theorie der Tonsezkunst* (Mainz, 1817), 97.
[41] Johann Nepomuk Hummel: *Ausführliche theoretisch-practische Anweisung zum Piano-Forte-Spiel*, 1st edn (Vienna, 1828), 60; 2nd rev. edn, 50.

During the Galant and Classical periods, however, there seems to have been a significant distinction between melody and accompaniment with respect to metrical accentuation. It arises from the characteristic textures of this music, in which accompanying parts and bass were so often given regular patterns of repeated notes: the so-called *Trommelbass*. As with so much else in the study of performing practice, it is important to distinguish here between the conventions that applied primarily to solo performance and those that were germane to ensemble or accompaniment. The metrical structure of the music, seen from the point of view of the composer, is intimately connected with such things as phrase structure, the rate of harmonic change, and the fullness or lightness of texture at any given point. To a large extent these factors will, as J. F. Schubert remarked, cause the strong beats of the metre to "accent themselves through their inner strength";[42] and this evidently lay behind Weber's and Hummel's comments. But many writers pointed out that when instrumentalists played repeated patterns of accompaniment figures, they had to ensure that the accents were placed strictly in accordance with the music's metre unless this were expressly countermanded by the composer's markings. Thus Quantz advised the cellist that "If in a Presto, which must be played in a very lively fashion, several eighth-notes, or other short notes, appear upon the same pitch, the first in each measure may be stressed by pressure on the bow".[43] And Leopold Mozart gave a similar example of an "ordinary accompaniment to an aria or concert piece, where, for the most part, only eighth-notes or sixteenth-notes appear" (Ex. 1.6).[44]

Ex. 1.6 Mozart: *Versuch*, 258.

In these types of accompaniment it would clearly be out of place either to make absolutely no kind of metrical accent, or to place the stronger

---

[42] See p. 17.
[43] Johann Joachim Quantz: *Versuch einer Anweisung die Flöte traversiere zu spielen* (Berlin, 1752), 217.
[44] Mozart: *Versuch*, 257.

accents on metrically weaker beats, except in special circumstances, or where the composer has indicated something particular. It may well be the case that rhythmic or expressive accent in the melody will contrast with the metrical accentuation of the accompaniment. From time to time, however, the accompanying parts will also have melodic material and will then be likely to make freer use of non-metrical accent, in accordance with the general principles discussed below. In more intricately textured works, such as string quartets, all parts in the ensemble may alternate between the observance of metrical accentuation in accompaniment figures and the application of expressive accents in melodic passages. As is evident from later 19th-century discussions of accentuation, this type of differentiation weakened during the Romantic period when, in many types of music, the distinction between melody and accompaniment became less clear-cut.

Before looking at the factors that were seen to modify the principles of metrical accentuation, it may be useful to note one situation in which, during the Classical period, it was felt by many to be especially undesirable that the hierarchy of strong and weak beats should be emphasized by the solo performer. This was in passagework with relatively fast-moving equal notes. Koch observed that in this case the metrical accent "must be so finely modulated that it is barely perceptible, otherwise a tasteless and limping style of performance results".[45] Burney considered that in "very rapid divisions, ascending or descending the scale in notes of equal length, no regard is had to accents".[46] And Milchmeyer similarly instructed that "in a run of several bars the ear should not be able to distinguish any strong or weak beat from the beginning to the end"; though, apparently contradicting himself, he added that "in triplets and in upwards and downwards passages of four, six, and eight notes in both hands one mostly strikes the first notes a little more strongly and in passages of four sixteenth-notes, or in slow tempo of two eighth-notes, one changes the finger on the first note very often, in order to give the melody its true accent".[47] J. F. Schubert commented: "In passagework it is difficult to prescribe where the accents have their proper place; this must be entirely a matter of feeling and taste",[48] and Bernhard Romberg made a

---

[45] Koch: 'Accent' in *Musikalisches Lexikon*, 51.
[46] Charles Burney: 'Accent' in Abraham Rees (ed.), *Cyclopaedia*, i (London, 1802), no pagination.
[47] Milchmeyer: *Die wahre Art*, 7f.
[48] Schubert: *Singe-Schule*, 134.

22  CLASSICAL AND ROMANTIC PERFORMING PRACTICE

similar point when he observed that in rapid passages "it is only requisite to make a few notes prominent, here and there, in order to deprive the passage of its otherwise monotonous effect".[49] Hummel, Carl Czerny, and Manuel García were among those who gave illustrative examples of this kind of selective accentuation (Ex. 1.7a–c). García explained that the accent "(according to the artist's instinct) is placed on any one sound selected in passages of equal notes. This is done to avoid monotony".[50] As in other aspects of accentuation, however, tempo was seen as important in determining the frequency with which accents were appropriate in passagework.

Ex. 1.7a  Hummel: *Anweisung*, 1st edn. 436; 2nd edn, 450.

Ex. 1.7b  Czerny: *Pianoforte-Schule*, iii, 9.

---

[49] Bernhard Heinrich Romberg: *Violoncell Schule* (Berlin and Posen, 1840), 128.
[50] Hummel: *Anweisung*, 1st edn, 436; 2nd edn, 450; Carl Czerny: *Vollständige theoretisch-practische Pianoforte-Schule* op. 500, 3 vols. (Vienna, 1839), iii, 9; Manuel García, *École de Garcia. Traité complet de l'art du chant*, ii (Paris, 1847), 26.

Ex. 1.7c  García: *École*, ii, 26.

## Structural and Expressive Accent

After considering metrical accentuation, Koch continued with a discussion of what he called oratorical accentuation. He began his treatment of the subject with an analogy between the nature and purpose of accentuation in speech and music which is typical for the period:

> Just as in speech, particularly if the speaker speaks with feeling, certain syllables of the words are marked by a special emphasis, by which the content of the speech is mainly made clear to the listener, so in the performance of a melody, which has a definite feeling, it is necessary to execute certain notes with a conspicuous manner of performance if the feeling which it contains is to be clearly expressed.[51]

Like other theorists of his time, Koch observed that these expressive accents, which he divided into oratorical and pathetic (apparently making a distinction only of degree rather than kind between them), are much more evident in performance than the metrical accents. Using an analogy with painting, he continued: "They are at the same time the highest lights and impressions of the tone-picture, and in performance the ear will be made aware of the more definite meaning of the melody through these accents." He further remarked:

> They are distinguished from the metrical accent not only through the above-mentioned more prominent performance, but also through the fact that they are not confined to any specific part of the bar, but are

---

[51] Koch: 'Accent' in *Musikalisches Lexikon*, 49; see also Türk: *Klavierschule*, 335; Hummel: *Anweisung*, 1st edn, 429; 2nd edn, 441.

merely contained in the ideal concept of the composer, which he has portrayed in notes, from which the taste of the performer must discover it. Of this type are the accents with which the notes marked * in the following extract must be performed, if the melody is not to sound as lame and insignificant as that of many a schoolboy's monotonous recitation of his catechism [Ex. 1.8].[52]

Ex. 1.8  Koch: 'Accent' in *Musikalisches Lexikon*, 51.

These accents represent a larger-scale structural feature of the music than that defined by metrical accentuation. In the given examples, Koch's accents come exclusively on metrically strong beats, because this is required by a melody of that type, though the oratorical accents could be less regularly distributed if the melody so required. Koch's failure to differentiate clearly between the accentuation necessary to articulate the phrase structure and that required to bring out the emotional content of the music reflects the widely prevalent view of the time, that music was fundamentally a language whose principal purpose, like that of poetry, was to express something more than the mundane material of common speech; the intelligible delivery of a phrase and its emotional weight, therefore, were inseparable.

Other late-18th-century and 19th-century writers seem to have been more acutely conscious of a distinction in function between structural and

---

[52] Koch: 'Accent' in *Musikalisches Lexikon*, 52.

expressive accentuation (and articulation), but the recognition that the latter types of accentuation should operate at a significantly more obtrusive level than metrical accentuation appears to have been general. In the 1830s, G. W. Fink advised against too much regularity: "because a too-symmetrical and scrupulously regular, mechanical beat introduces a stiffness into the performance which equates with crudeness. As a rule, therefore, the metrical accents should not be applied anything like so sharply and strongly as the rhythmical and above all the sectional accents [*Einschnittsaccente*][53] of the rhythmic segments".[54] And in a similar vein Arrey von Dommer observed in 1865:

> A correct oratorical accentuation must always fundamentally be a correct metrical one, despite many liberties for the sake of the particular expression. Yet it reaches beyond the simple regularity of the metrical accentual pattern, appears already as a higher artistic freedom and is a more essential part of expressive performance. One can deliver a passage with absolutely correct metrical accentuation and still play very stiffly and vapidly if the animation through oratorical accentuation is lacking.[55]

Thus, the harmonic and melodic structure of a well-written piece could be seen as virtually sufficient in itself to convey the metrical pattern of the composition to the listener so long as performers were responsive to that pattern in their choice of accentuation; there was no need for the metrical regularity of the music to be stressed. Only those notes that were important for the shape of a phrase or the expressive content of a melody were expected to receive a distinct emphasis. Although individual structural and expressive accents would often occur on metrically strong beats, the accentual pattern of a melody in performance would rarely, if ever, conform exactly with the theoretical hierarchy of beats, for the accentual relationships required by the phrase structure would override the small-scale metrical patterns with, for instance, a greater emphasis on the strong beat of one bar than another, or

---

[53] The term *Einschnitt*, frequently employed by musical theorists of this period, has no entirely satisfactory English equivalent. The word means literally a cut, incision, or notch and was used in this context to describe the notional or real articulations which separate the 'phrases' in a musical 'sentence'.
[54] Fink: 'Accent' in Schilling (ed.), *Encyclopädie*, i, 36.
[55] Arrey von Dommer: 'Accent' in *Musikalisches Lexicon*, 10.

more stress on the second half of a $\frac{2}{4}$ or $\frac{4}{4}$ bar than on the first. Frequently, too, the expression might require more accent on so-called weak beats than on strong ones. Schulz gave an example of displaced stress in $\frac{3}{4}$, where the first beat of a bar in which the phrase began was a rest (Ex. 1.9).

Ex. 1.9 Sulzer: *Allegemeine Theorie*, ii, 1137.

Türk qualified his explanation of metrical accent with the observation that the initial note of each section of melody "must be given an even more marked emphasis than an ordinary strong beat", and added that even among these more prominently stressed beats there should be a hierarchy, according to whether they were the beginning of a main section or only a unit within the larger phrase. He illustrated his meaning with an example (Ex. 1.10), noting that the greater the number of crosses the greater the emphasis, and that

> However necessary it may be to emphasize the initial note of a segment or section, according to the aforementioned rule; it is equally necessary to restrict this to noticeably marking only the initial notes which fall on strong beats. The *a* marked with o, in the sixth bar, must therefore not be struck quite as strongly as the following *b natural*, although the idea as a whole is to be presented more strongly than the preceding one.[56]

Ex. 1.10 Türk: *Klavierschule*, 336.

---

[56] Türk: *Klavierschule*, VI, §14, 336.

Türk's concern that the upbeat should not be stressed in this context would undoubtedly have been endorsed by other theorists; but there were circumstances in which, even if nothing were indicated by the composer, some 18th-century musicians might have thought it appropriate to accent a note that would normally be seen as an upbeat. Quantz, for instance, had advised that "in merry and quick pieces the last eighth-note of each half bar must be stressed with the bow"[57] and gave an example in which such a treatment was to be applied to the $g^2$, the second $e^2$, and the $f^1$. (Ex. 1.11a). Leopold Mozart, too, advocated a similar procedure, instructing: "in merry pieces the accent is usually applied to the highest note to make the performance really lively"[58] (Ex. 1.11b).

Ex. 1.11a Quantz: *Versuch*, Tab. XXII, Fig. 7.

Ex. 1.11b Mozart: *Versuch*, 260.

It is questionable whether, in practice, Türk would have expected the performer literally to apply the predominantly *decrescendo* pattern of phrasing indicated in Ex. 1.10 to other melodies any more than he would have anticipated slavish adherence to the theoretical hierarchy of metrically stronger and weaker beats in the bar (except perhaps in repeated accompaniment figures). His example certainly cannot be taken to prove that, as a general principle, late-18th- and early-19th-century melodies were expected, either absolutely or relatively, to have the most prominent accent on the first strong beat of each major melodic segment. Yet it seems possible that

---

[57] Quantz: *Versuch*, 190.
[58] Mozart: *Versuch*, 259.

"downbeat" rather than "upbeat" treatment of the first part of a phrase was regarded as normal in the majority of circumstances at that period. A generation later it was still possible for August Leopold Crelle to state that, as a rule, "The first note of the figure never sounds too early, and is given proportionately more weight than the others. The middle of the figure has a measured movement, and the end of the figure decreases in strength and increases in speed."[59]

Examples from other sources suggest, however, that even if Türk's illustration and Crelle's advice represented the most usual approach to the accentual shaping of a melodic figure during the Classical period (in the absence of contrary markings by the composer), it would have been neither unknown, nor considered unmusical for a performer to shape an unmarked melody differently; it is precisely this latitude that blurs the distinction between structural and expressive accentuation. In the case of Türk's example, for instance, the expressive impact of the melody could be changed by giving it the dynamic shape shown in Ex. 1.12, with its implications of a quite different accentuation.

Ex. 1.12

A careful 18th-century composer, for instance Mozart, might mark such accentuation where he regarded a particularly emphatic rendition of it as integral to the expression (Ex. 1.13), but the absence of such a marking in the music of his less meticulous contemporaries, or even of Mozart himself, may not necessarily be an indication that this type of treatment would be contrary to the composer's conception. The melodies shown in Ex. 1.14, for instance, may well have elicited an 'upbeat' accentual pattern from many contemporary performers, although the composer did not mark it. In all these cases, as in Mozart's K. 454, the increase of harmonic tension (dissonance) suggests more accentual weight, even without a dynamic marking. Theoretical support for this type of approach is provided by Hummel, who

---

[59] August Leopold Crelle: *Einiges über musikalischen Ausdruck und Vortrag* (Berlin, 1823), 54f.

gave several examples in his piano method where he considered such accentuation appropriate (Ex. 1.15; + indicates a slight accent, ^ a more emphatic one).

Ex. 1.13  Mozart, Violin Sonata K. 454/ii.

Ex. 1.14a  Mozart, Symphony in D K. 504/ii.

Ex. 1.14b  Haydn, String Quartet op. 55/2/ii.

Ex. 1.14c  Beethoven, String Quartet op. 18/6/ii.

30  CLASSICAL AND ROMANTIC PERFORMING PRACTICE

Ex. 1.15 a–d. Hummel: *Anweisung.* (*a*) 1st edn (1827), 431; 2nd edn (1828), 443; (*b*) 432/444; (*c*) 432/444; (*d*) 434/447.

It must always be borne in mind that the overwhelmingly prevalent 18th-century view was that details of this kind could generally be left to the taste of skilled performers, whose treatment of a melody would be determined by their responses to such internal musical signals as harmony, melodic shape, and so on (as discussed further below). On the other hand, it is conceivable that the modern performer's instinct to apply this sort of upbeat treatment to passages in 18th-century music, where no dynamic instructions are given, may be the anachronistic product of musical conditioning by a tradition that only became established during the 19th century.

In short, there was general agreement during the Classical period that, within broadly defined parameters, fine and knowledgeable performers would accent a melody according to their perception of its distinctive character, rather than rigidly emphasizing the metrical accent indicated by the time signature. Consequently, rather more flexibility is likely to have been approved in practice than the stricter theorists seem to imply. Türk provided two musical examples to show that $\frac{12}{8}$ and $\frac{6}{8}$ are essentially different and that a piece of music appropriate to the one cannot properly be written in the other (Ex. 1.16).[60] But his examples also illustrate that even if they were "incorrectly" written in the other metre, the skilful player, responding to the nature of the melody, the texture and harmonic structure of the music, and so on, would almost certainly seize upon the sense of the piece and give it an appropriate accentuation and phrasing. Many composers were clearly felt by their more theoretically-minded contemporaries to reflect too little on the metre in which their conceptions could best be expressed. Nevertheless, it can scarcely be doubted that thoughtful composers strove hard to find the metre that most closely fitted the predominant accentual characteristics of their ideas. Instances of the same theme notated in different metres in Beethoven's sketchbooks may well reflect his search for the most appropriate pattern and intensity of metrical stress for a particular phrase. A similar motive may also lie behind the re-scoring of whole movements in different metres by, for example, Mozart and Mendelssohn.[61]

**Ex. 1.16** Türk: *Klavierschule*, 96.

The continuing elaboration and systemization of a hierarchy of metrical accent appropriate to each metre, in a stream of 19th-century theoretical works, especially by German authors, seems distinctly at odds with the increasingly free approach of the more experimental musicians of that period; but such theoretical elaborations were, to a considerable extent, the result of a desire to endow *Musikwissenschaft* with the dignity of a historico-scientific discipline. Indeed, there were few 19th-century theorists who did not acknowledge, at least in parentheses, that

---

[60] Türk: *Klavierschule*, 96.
[61] See Ch. 8.

the rigid hierarchy of metrical accent was overridden in practice by the requirements of the musical context. It seems probable that while, with minor modifications, theoretical understanding of metrical and structural accentuation remained constant throughout the period, practical application of that theory diverged ever further from it, in line with developing musical aesthetics. Just as the music of the late 18th century and early 19th century was characterized, in general, by distinct and regular rhythmic patterns, so the coincidence of metrical and structural accentuation was correspondingly more frequent, and there was often a rhythmic counterpoint of metrically accented accompaniment figures with more freely accented melodic lines.

This situation is nicely summed up by J. A. P. Schulz's treatment of the subject, which could in many respects have come from a traditional theorist at any point during the period. It is worth quoting at length, for the clarity with which it highlights the complexity of the interaction between the varying types of accentuation. He explained:

> the accents of the melody must be made apparent. The notes which fall on the strong beats of the bar will be reckoned first among these. Of these the first note of the bar receives the most prominent pressure, so that the feeling of the beat is constantly sustained, without which no one will understand the melody. After the first beat of the bar the other strong beats of the bar are marked, but less strongly. Hereby, however, the distinction which the phrase divisions make between the beats must be well observed. The first note of a bar which is only a part of a phrase cannot be so strongly marked as when it begins the phrase or when it is the principal note of a phrase. Those who do not observe this, but constantly mark the first note of the bar with equal strength in every piece, ruin the whole piece; for by this, since they are in this respect too clear, they damage the clarity of the whole, in that they are thereby prevented from marking the phrase divisions appropriately, which is of the greatest importance. This will become clearer from what follows. The weak beats will only be marked when a new phrase begins on them, as will be shown hereafter.
>
> Secondly, those notes in every phrase which require a particular emphasis are reckoned among the accents. As in speech many words merely serve to connect, or depend upon the principal word of the phrase, which

the speaker pronounces without noticeably raising his voice, so that he might be able to make the principal word all the more audible: so also in every melodic phrase there are principal and auxiliary notes which should be well distinguished from one another in performance. Often, and particularly in pieces that have a single type of note throughout, the principal notes coincide with the aforementioned accents of the bar. In such pieces, however, where there is greater variety of melody, the principal notes almost always stand out from the ordinary notes and should be marked with particular emphasis. They can be recognized by the fact that they are in general longer or higher than the preceding and immediately following notes; or that they are raised or lowered by a ♯ or ♭ which is foreign to the prevailing key; or that they are free clashing dissonances; or that they prepare a dissonance which is tied to them; they fall mostly on the strong beats of the bar except when a new phrase division begins with them, or when the composer in order to make himself more emphatic decides on a syncopation and allows it to come in a beat too early; in such cases they also occur on the weak beat of the bar, and in the latter case are most easily recognizable by their added length, as in the fifth and sixth bars of the following example: [Ex. 1.17]. All notes marked + are so many main notes of this phrase, that should be performed far more emphatically than the rest. [...]

This may be sufficient to make those who wish to perform a piece clearly aware of the accents in it. One can easily grasp that their observation gives performance, apart from clarity, a great light and shade, especially if a differentiation of emphasis is also made between the main notes, in that one always requires more or less emphasis than another, like the main words in speech. Through this occurs the fine shadings of strong and weak, which the great virtuosos know how to bring into their performance. But to say where and how this ought to happen is so difficult, and for those who do not have their own experience and a fine sensitivity, so inadequate, that we regard it as superfluous to dwell further upon it.[62]

---

[62] Schulz: 'Vortrag' in *Allgemeine Theorie*, ii, 1249f. A broadly similar understanding of the principles of accentuation is shown in the article 'Accent' in Nicolas Etienne Framery, Pierre Louis Ginguené, Jerome Joseph de Momigny, and Charles-Joseph Panckoucke (eds.): *Encyclopédie Méthodique. Musique*, i (Paris, 1791), 5–12.

Ex. 1.17 Sulzer: *Allgemeine Theorie*, 1st edn, ii, 1249.

In the 19th century several important composers strove to produce music in which accentuation was liberated from what they saw as the restrictions of metre; in such music, structural and expressive accentuation occurred with increasing frequency on beats that were metrically weak, and the distinction between free melody and metrically more regular accompaniment became far less common. Symptomatic of this attitude is Liszt's comment, in the preface to the collected edition of his symphonic poems, "that I wish to see an end to mechanical, fragmented up and down playing, tied to the bar-line, which is still the rule in many places, and it is only the phrase-based style of performance, with the prominence of special accents and the rounding off of melodic and rhythmic nuances, that I can acknowledge as appropriate".[63] His statement is not essentially in conflict with the opinion expressed by earlier writers, at least with regard to melody, but taken in conjunction with the style of much of his music and that of the mature Wagner, for instance, it becomes clear that it embodies a substantial difference in practice. Even composers closer to the Classical tradition such as Schumann and Brahms, sought to escape the fetters of rhythmic regularity and an over-rigid phrase structure. This was undoubtedly, to some extent, a conscious reaction against the

---

[63] *Liszts Symphonische Dichtungen für grosses Orchester*, 3 vols. (Leipzig: Breitkopf & Härtel, [1856]), i, 1.

predominantly symmetrical phraseology that underlay much early Romantic music, by composers such as Spohr, Weber, Marschner, and Mendelssohn, where it sometimes seems to contrast with their increasingly expressive harmonic idiom. A similar tendency can be seen in the approach to phrasing in many mid- to late-19th-century editions of earlier music, such as Ferdinand David's *Die höhe Schule des Violinspiels* and Hugo Riemann's editions of the Classics, or in discussions of phrasing by later 19th-century writers such as Mathis Lussy. It seems that these musicians frequently envisaged structural and expressive accentuation as running contrary to the metrical accentuation where, in many cases, earlier musicians may have seen them as coinciding.

# 2
# Accentuation in Practice

In his discussion of oratorical accentuation Koch stated that although the notation of his day was "complete and precise" in showing pitch and duration in music, "the things by which its spirit must be made palpable in performance can never fully be represented by signs". He nevertheless took the view that, since it is an "established thing that the lively representation of the melody of a piece of music depends for the most part on the correct performance of the oratorical and pathetic accents",[1] a more sophisticated system for prescribing which notes should be accented, and in what degree would be highly desirable. He did not believe that his contemporaries were anything like careful enough in marking the accentuation they required in their music. In this he was entirely in agreement with Türk, who, in his *Sechs leichte Klaviersonaten* of 1783, had made use of a sign (^) to indicate accentuation where he felt that it was not necessarily obvious, explaining in his *Klavierschule*: "For I still believe that the accent which is so essential to good execution can, in certain cases, be as little left to the discretion of the performer as, for example, the extempore use of *forte* and *piano*, or of one of the essential ornaments."[2] A couple of years later, this sign was endorsed by G. F. Wolf, who described it as an accent that "is expressed by a gentle pressure, not an attack [Stoß], with a noticeable lingering on the note."[3]

Discussion of the subject by 18th-century writers makes it abundantly clear that the relative scarcity of accent signs at that time carries no implication that expressive accents were not envisaged where they are not specifically marked. As with much else in the music of that period, even the more painstaking composers indicated only the music's most prominent and essential expressive features, and many seem to have neglected even to do that; thus, it was left to the executant to supply most of the accentuation necessary for a fine and tasteful performance. Despite the vastly increased

---

[1] Koch: 'Accent' in *Musikalisches Lexikon*, 51–53.
[2] Türk: *Klavierschule*, 338.
[3] Georg Friedrich Wolf: 'Zeichen' in *Kurzgefasstes muskalisches Lexikon* (Halle, 1792), 221.

use of various forms of accent markings by composers of succeeding generations,[4] accomplished 19th-century performers would still have been expected to contribute much accentuation and phrasing that was not indicated by the composer. Louis Spohr, for instance, distinguishing like many of his contemporaries between "correct performance" and "beautiful performance", instructed that the former required a minute observance of all the composer's performance markings, but that "the accentuation and separation of musical phrases" were among those that the executant was expected to achieve through "his own additions".[5] To a greater or lesser extent, Spohr's identification of the requirements for beautiful performance remains valid for all conventionally notated music. Many of the situations in which subtle unmarked accentuation was expected in 18th-century music have parallels in later music, despite the increasing use of an expanding range of accent marks. Composers such as Mendelssohn and Brahms, whose instincts were more firmly rooted in the Classical tradition, avoided the painstaking annotation of performance markings that was typical of other composers, from Schumann to Mahler.

Illustrations of tasteful accentuation in theory and instruction books provide examples of the circumstances in which 18th- and 19th-century musicians envisaged accents where none were indicated; but as well as giving guidance for the placement of metrical and structural accents through specific examples, some theorists catalogued general circumstances in which, unless the composer specified something different, a structural or expressive accent was generally needed.

## Slurred Figures

During the 18th century and throughout the 19th, there was a strong association between accentuation and the first of a group of slurred notes. Despite the unqualified endorsement of this practice by many theorists, however, the association was clearly not quite as obligatory as it sometimes appears from their writings. As is often the case, theorists tended to reiterate rules that were expounded by earlier authors, whether or not these accurately represented the notational habits of their contemporaries. Although some degree of

---

[4] See Ch. 3.
[5] Louis Spohr: *Violinschule* (Vienna, [1833]), 195.

accentuation at the beginning of slurred groups will frequently be appropriate in late-18th-century music and often, too, in 19th-century music, there will be many situations in which slurs have no such implications, for composers had already begun to use them in various, quite different ways during the second half of the 18th century.[6]

Authors of 18th- and early-19th-century treatises were broadly agreed about the execution of slurred groups, but individual treatments of the matter reveal some interesting differences of detail. Leopold Mozart taught that "if in a musical composition two, three, four, and even more notes be bound together by the half-circle, so that one can see from this that the composer does not want such notes to be separated, but to be performed singingly in a slur, the first of such connected notes must be somewhat more strongly stressed, but the remainder slurred on to it quite smoothly and increasingly quietly".[7] The musical examples which precede this statement consist of a four-bar passage repeated thirty-four times with different patterns of slurred and separate notes, and with slurs beginning frequently on metrically weak beats. He later insisted that a degree of lengthening was integral to this accentuation.[8] In Löhlein's 1774 *Anweisung zum Violinspielen*, the first explanation of the slur says simply that the notes so marked must be "performed in one bowstroke and softly connected to each other".[9] But when explaining patterns of stress in a melody, by means of an underlaid text, he observed: "when two notes come on one syllable [. . .], both notes will be played in one bowstroke, but the first receives a special pressure because the syllable will be enunciated on it, and the other is, as it were, passed over."[10]

Many writers, especially in the earlier part of the period (when very long slurs were extremely rare), considered this type of accented and nuanced execution appropriate to slurred groups of any length. The 1791 revised edition of Löhlein's *Clavier-Schule*, for instance, referred without reservation to slurred groups "of which the first note always receives a somewhat stronger pressure."[11] Türk gave examples of up to eight notes in a slur for which he instructed: "the note over which the slur begins, will be very lightly (hardly

---

[6] For more extensive and general discussion of the range of meanings of slurs, see Ch. 6.
[7] Mozart: *Versuch*, 135.
[8] See below, "Agogic Accent".
[9] Georg Simon Löhlein: *Anweisung zum Violinspielen* (Leipzig and Züllichau, 1774), 32.
[10] Löhlein: *Anweisung*, 53.
[11] Löhlein: *Clavier-Schule, oder kurze und gründliche Anweisung zur Melodie und Harmonie* (Leipzig and Züllichau, 1765), 5th edn, ed. Johann Georg Witthauer (Leipzig, 1791), 18.

noticeably) accented."[12] Those Classical writers who made a distinction based on the length of the slurred group, generally taught that, as a rule, groups of up to three or four notes should certainly be treated in this manner whereas longer slurred groups might not be. Asioli merely instructed that in groups of three or four slurred notes: "The first sound should be more emphatic and resonant than the others."[13] In keyboard playing, Kalkbrenner, like Hummel, Czerny, and Moscheles, similarly taught that "Two or three slurred notes can only be performed on the piano by leaning on the first and shortening the last"[14] (Ex. 2.1); and Crelle in 1823 emphatically characterized the accentual element in slurred pairs by instructing "while the first note enters strongly, the second etc. is weaker, and the last one is barely audible, almost like a breath", which he illustrated with his figures 36 and 37 (Ex. 2.2).[15] It was in the context of piano playing that Brahms and Joachim discussed this aspect of performance in 1879, though rather with respect to articulation at the end of the slur than to accent at the beginning.[16] In 1833 the cellist J. J. F. Dotzauer, in contrast to the pianists, instructed that "The first of the two slurred eighth-notes in No. 14 is somewhat emphasized, but not too much, otherwise it could easily make it seem as if, instead of the second eighth-note, there were a sixteenth-note and a rest"[17] (Ex. 2.3). And in the 1850s, the violinist Charles de Bériot also recommended a small accent at the beginning of slurred groups, but no break between them.[18] It seems clear that string players, and also wind players, who could control the decay of the sound, approached the execution of the final note of short slurred figures differently from keyboard players, who could only control the initial impulse. But all these generalized instructions might, as their authors would undoubtedly have been the first to acknowledge, be overridden by particular musical circumstances.

---

[12] Türk: *Klavierschule*, 355. Türk's instruction was repeated verbatim thirty years later in Friedrich Starke: *Wiener Pianoforte-Schule* (Vienna, 1819), i, 13.

[13] Bonifazio Asioli: *Principj elementari di musica* (Milan, 1811), 45; trans. as *A Compendious Musical Grammar [. . .] by Bonifacio Asioli [. . .] translated with considerable additions and improvements by John Jousse* (London, [1825]), 108, where this sentence is given as "The accent is given to the first; the others are played with an equal degree of force."

[14] Fréderic (Friedrich Willhelm) Kalkbrenner: *Méthode pour apprendre le piano-forte à l'aide du guide mains* op. 108 (Paris, [1831]), 13.

[15] Crelle: *Einiges*, 93.

[16] See Ch. 6.

[17] Justus Johann Friedrich Dotzauer: *Violoncell-Schule für den ersten Unterricht* (Vienna, [1833]), 19 (Exercise on 36).

[18] Charles de Bériot: *Méthode de violon* (Paris, [1857/8]), 88.

Ex. 2.1 Kalkbrenner: *Méthode*, 13.

Ex. 2.2 Crelle: *Einiges*, 93.

Ex. 2.3 Dotzauer: *Violoncell-Schule*, 36.

Slurs that begin on metrically weak beats will often imply a displacement of accent. Milchmeyer, making no qualification about the length of slurs, observed: "in the legato style, finally, everything hangs on the slurs and the expression which the composer wished to give to the piece; here one very often makes the weak beat strong and changes the finger on it."[19] Türk had also given examples of slurs beginning on weak beats, where he required accentuation of the first note, though none of his examples exceeded four notes (Ex. 2.4).[20] Philip Anthony Corri, too, expounded the general proposition

---

[19] Milchmeyer: *Die wahre Art*, 8.
[20] Türk: *Klavierschule*, 355.

that the first note of a slur, even, as he observed, were it to occur on a weak beat, would require emphasis.[21]

**Ex. 2.4**  Türk: *Klavierschule*, 355.

The association of accent with the beginning of a slur continued in theory books throughout the 19th century, even when composers were making much greater use of explicit accent and dynamic markings. But the association became increasingly out of touch with composers' practices, for a distinction between the symbol as an indication for *legato* and as a sign for the accentuation and phrasing of short figures was rarely made with clarity either by composers or theorists. Nevertheless, Mathis Lussy could still maintain without qualification in 1883 that "Every time the last note of a bar is the *beginning* of a *slur*, of a beat, it is strong. Every time the first note of a bar is the *end* of a *slur*, of a beat, it is weak."[22] The contemporaneous Mendel *Lexikon* was more cautious about implying an inevitable link between the beginning of a slur and accent; it gives the example illustrated in Ex. 2.5, commenting that it "shows a shift of the accent, which is designated by the phrasing slur and also for greater certainty by sf and >".[23] Many other practical and theoretical considerations indicate that, in 19th-century music especially, the application of accent to the beginning of a slur, however discreet, is by no means always appropriate.

**Ex. 2.5**  Mendel: *Musikalisches Conversations Lexikon*, i, 14.

---

[21] P. A. Corri: *L'anima di musica* (London, 1810), 72.
[22] Lussy: *Le Rythme musical*, 33.
[23] Hermann Mendel: 'Accent' in *Musikalisches Conversations-Lexikon* (Berlin, 1870), i, 14.

The weight of late-18th- and early-19th-century authority behind the idea that the first note of a short, slurred group should receive greater accent, and that the subsequent notes under the slur should become progressively quieter, need not be considered to exclude other possibilities in particular circumstances. Asioli, for instance, extending the principle that ascending phrases increase in volume and descending phrases decrease in volume, instructed that in slurred ascending passages one should "begin the passage *piano* and reinforce the sound to *forte*".[24] (This does not, of course, necessarily exclude a slight emphasis on the first note in relation to the one immediately following.) A more important ambiguity in the slur-emphasis relationship occurs with string bowing. Here the principal accentuation or dynamic high point of the phrase may not always be intended to coincide with the beginning of the slur; this was particularly the case in works by string-playing composers. Sometimes, even in 18th-century music, a composer would take care to indicate the disparity between the slurring (bowing) and the accentuation, as did Vogler in his melodrama *Lampedo* (Ex. 2.6).

Ex. 2.6  Vogler: *Lampedo*, unpaginated (p. 58) urn:nbn:de:tuda-tudigit-44513 http://tudigit.ulb.tu-darmstadt.de/show/Mus-Ms-1097a/0058.

With less fastidious composers it will be rash to assume a coincidence of slur beginning and accent as a matter of course where no alternative is indicated. This is increasingly true of 19th-century music, though at least from the 1830s careful composers would seldom have left such things to chance.[25] In music from that period, however, there are many problematic cases of transition between the earlier use of the slur predominantly to articulate short figures, and its later widespread employment as a less specialized indication for *legato*. Even in the case of short slurs in string music, especially when the composer was a string player, there may well be a tension between the slur as a bowing instruction and the slur as an indication for an accent-*decrescendo* delivery. Dotzauer, in his *Violoncell-Schule*, for instance,

---

[24] Asioli: *Principj*, 45.
[25] See Ch. 3, for instance Ex. 3.64.

cautioned the student to make an accent within a slur where this was necessary to maintain the integrity of the metre, observing, with respect to Ex. 2.7: "On account of the metre the third of the slurred notes must be somewhat staccato, otherwise it could easily give the effect of triplets."[26]

Ex. 2.7 Dotzauer: *Violoncell-Schule*, 33.

Only in the case of slurred pairs were pianists more or less agreed throughout the period that a distinctive treatment was called for; and it was solely with respect to paired notes that Franklin Taylor (a pupil of Clara Schumann) unreservedly employed the term "slur", observing: "When two notes of equal length in quick or moderately quick tempo are joined together by a curved line they are said to be *slurred*, and in playing them a considerable stress is laid on the first of the two, while the second is not only weaker, but is made shorter than it is written, as though followed by a rest."[27] But even where only two notes were joined in this way he remarked that there were exceptions, writing: "When the curved line is drawn over two notes of considerable length, or in slow tempo, it is not a slur, but merely a sign of legato"; and, in contrast to earlier writers such as Kalkbrenner and Czerny, he remarked that the sign indicated *legato* rather than a slur "if it covers a group of three or more notes" (Ex. 2.8a). In Taylor's view, an exception occurs where the curved line is extended to "end upon an accented note, then an effect analogous to the slur is intended" (Ex. 2.8b).[28]

---

[26] Dotzauer: *Violoncell-Schule*, 18 (Ex. on p. 33). It is noteworthy here that he evidently uses the term *abgestossen* (often signifying simply *staccato*) solely to mean accented, since shortening the third note would have the opposite consequence, by enhancing the triplet effect.

[27] Franklin Taylor: 'Phrasing' in George Grove (ed.), *A Dictionary of Music and Musicians*, ii, 706ff. (He is here referring to piano music. For further discussion of the articulation of slurred pairs see Ch. 6.)

[28] Taylor: 'Phrasing' in Grove, *Dictionary*, ii, 707.

Ex. 2.8 a–b. F. Taylor: 'Phrasing' in Grove, *Dictionary* 1st edn, ii, 708.

Another exception to accenting the beginning of slurred pairs, at least in some musicians' practice, seems to have been the performance of "scotch snap" or "Lombard" rhythms. Several writers mention that the accent should occur on the second note of each pair. Ignaz Kürzinger, in 1763, explained that such figures should be played "in a special way; the first must be swallowed up very quickly, as it were, the second, because it is dotted, must be expressed as if the first were barely there, which the teacher can demonstrate better than it can be described."[29] Pietro Lichtenthal, discussing musical accent, gave the illustration shown in Ex. 2.9.[30] Similarly Justin Heinrich Knecht, after explaining the accentuation of long-short dotted figures, remarked: "if, however, the dot stands after the second note of a figure of two notes or after the second and fourth notes of a figure of four notes, so the accent and the weight fall on the second and fourth notes; on the other hand, the first and third notes are quickly dispatched, as follows" (Ex. 2.10).[31] Dotzauer was even more explicit about shortening and lightening the first note of such figures, commenting on the passage in Ex. 2.11: "The sixteenth-note before the

---

[29] Ignaz Franz Xaver Kürzinger: *Getreuer Unterricht zum Singen mit Manieren, und die Violin zu spielen* (Augsburg, [1763]), 65.

[30] Pietro Lichtenthal: *Dizionario e bibliographia della musica* (Milan, 1826), 'Accento musicale', i, 6ff. (Fig. 2 in vol. Ii, unpaginated [following p. 300]).

[31] Justin Heinrich Knecht: *Knechts allgemeiner musikalischer Katechismus*, 4th edn (Freiburg, 1816), 34.

dotted eighth must be treated as if it were a grace-note."[32] An aural manifestation of this practice can be heard in the Klingler Quartet's 1911 recording of the Minuetto from Mozart's String Quartet K. 421, where the reverse-dotted figures in the Trio section are played very much in this manner, almost certainly reflecting an unbroken 18th-century tradition.

Ex. 2.9 Lichtenthal: 'Accento musicale' in *Dizionario*, Fig. 2 in vol. ii, unpaginated (following p. 300).

Ex. 2.10 Knecht: *Katechismus*, 34.

Ex. 2.11 Dotzauer: Violoncell-Schule, 19 (music example on p. 41).

Nevertheless, in this respect as in many others, there were contrary opinions among the theorists. Türk, echoing C. P. E. Bach, stated that in these figures: "The first (short) note, of course, is to be accented but the emphasis should be only a very gentle one";[33] while J. F. Schubert, who gave these figures as an example of "light performance" (*leichter Vortrag*)[34] (Ex. 2.12a), felt that a very gentle accent on the first note might be appropriate "in certain cases, if the *Affekt* or expression of the text requires it", but that neither

---

[32] Dotzauer: *Violoncell-Schule*, 19 (music example on p. 41).
[33] Türk: *Klavierschule*, 363; Bach: *Versuch über die wahre Art das Clavier zu spielen*, i (Berlin, 1753), 128.
[34] For the concept of "heavy and light performance" see Ch. 5.

note of the figure should be especially accented or significantly shortened, "so that the performance does not degenerate into cheekiness" (Ex. 2.12b).[35] A further exception, in some musicians' opinions,[36] was when rising two-note figures, particularly rising semitone appoggiaturas, required a *crescendo* treatment.

Ex. 2.12  a–b. J. F. Schubert: *Neue Singe-Schule*, 132.

(a)

(b)

## Dissonance and Chromatic Notes

One of the chief reasons for stressing an appoggiatura was its dissonance. There was a widely held view in the 18th century that all dissonances implied a special degree of emphasis. Quantz advised strengthening chromatic notes, explaining that the degree of accent was determined by the intensity of the dissonance; and he detailed three classes of dissonance, according to the intensity of accent required.[37] Leopold Mozart was among the musicians who instructed that accentuation was required on a dissonant note, or on one that prepares a dissonant interval, and on a chromatic note, or a melody note that occurs over chromatic harmony.[38] Similar advice was repeated by

---

[35] Schubert: *Singe-Schule*, 132.
[36] For instance, Domenico Corri (see Ch. 12).
[37] Quantz: *Versuch*, 195 and 228.
[38] Mozart: *Versuch*, 256.

J. F. Schubert in 1804; he observed that notes belonging to a foreign tonality should be accented, so long as they were not too short (Ex. 2.13), and he added: "the more foreign or distant the tonality, the more emphasis the note which prepares or makes evident the tonality must receive".[39] Türk made much the same points about dissonances, notes preparing a dissonance, or chromatic notes that required accentuation; but having stated that the harder a dissonance is, or the more dissonant notes there are in a chord, the more strongly the harmony should be emphasized, he very sensibly cautioned: "But this rule cannot and ought not always be followed to the letter, because too many changes might then ensue".[40]

**Ex. 2.13** J. F. Schubert: *Neue Singe-Schule*, 133.

The association of dissonance and accent continued throughout the 19th century. Frédéric Kalkbrenner required that "all notes foreign to the key and those which bear an accidental should be well marked".[41] Bernhard Romberg, having instructed that a descending scale should diminish in volume, added: "Only if, in the descending scale, a note that does not belong to the key in which the music is written occurs at the end, will this note require a stronger accent, and there are very few cases in which it would not have to be emphasized."[42] A musician of the next generation, Manuel García, also insisted on accenting dissonances in singing, stating: "The accent should always be laid on notes that, requiring nice and delicate intonation, are difficult to seize, for instance, dissonances; in this case the accent should be accompanied by prolongation."[43]

---

[39] Schubert: *Neue Singe-Schule*, 133.
[40] Türk: *Klavierschule*, VI, §32, 351.
[41] Kalkbrenner: *Méthode*, 12.
[42] Romberg: *Violoncell Schule*, 127.
[43] García: *École*, ii, 26.

## Note Pitch

Just as a dissonance was to be emphasized because, by its very nature, it gave prominence to the beat on which it occurred, so a particularly high or low note, especially if it were separated by a considerable interval from the preceding note, was likely to require a more forceful delivery. Thus, Leopold Mozart advised accenting particularly high or low notes following a leap. He also suggested emphasizing high notes in lively pieces, even on a weak beat (see Ex. 1.11b), but cautioned against doing so in slow or sad ones, because in those "the upbeat must not be played *staccato*, but must be sustained and performed in a cantabile manner".[44] Türk and J. F. Schubert gave similar advice (Ex. 2.14a–b).[45] Kalkbrenner and Henri Herz reflect general opinion in suggesting that the highest note of an ascending phrase or phrase unit should be played louder than its neighbours, and that, whereas an isolated low note might be played loudly, one that came at the end of a descending phrase would normally be very gently delivered unless the composer specified the contrary, or unless, as Romberg instructed, some other factor, such as dissonant harmony, also exerted an influence.[46] Kalkbrenner warned, however, that "The high notes of the piano should never be attacked in an abrupt or harsh manner".[47]

Ex. 2.14a  Türk: *Klavierschule*, 337.

Ex. 2.14b  Schubert: *Neue Singe-Schule*, 133.

---

[44] L. Mozart: *Versuch*, 260.
[45] Türk: *Klavierschule*, 337; Schubert: *Singe-Schule*, 133.
[46] Henri Herz: *Méthode complète de piano* op. 100 (Mainz and Anvers, 1838), 20.
[47] Kalkbrenner: *Méthode*, 12.

## Note Length

Similar principles were applied to long and short notes within a phrase. According to Leopold Mozart, a note distinguished from the surrounding ones by greater length would be emphatic.[48] Kirnberger stated simply: "Longer note values are always performed with more weight and emphasis than shorter ones".[49] Philip Corri observed: "Emphasis should be generally placed on the longest and highest note of a sentence, and a note that is dotted among equal notes".[50] Hummel likewise commented: "If after a short note occupying the accented time of the measure, a longer note should succeed on the unaccented time, the latter usually requires an emphasis",[51] while Czerny insisted that, in general, long notes be strongly accented.[52] Later in the century, Lussy continued to promulgate this notion, commenting that a long note that follows several shorter ones "acquires great force".[53]

## Syncopation

The rule of accenting individual syncopated notes that occur in an otherwise unsyncopated melody seems closely related to the principle that long notes should be more emphatic than short ones. The degree of emphasis appropriate to a particular syncopated note would, of course, depend on its length, prominence, or function. Syncopation was, however, often described as a displacement of the metrical accent. John Jousse expressed the conventional view, commenting: "When syncopated notes happen the Emphasis lays on them contrary to the Rules of Accent".[54] Knecht was more explicit: "Although its first half comes on a weak part of the bar, one commonly gives [the beginning of] a syncopated note a stronger emphasis than its second half which comes on a strong part of the bar, even if there is no accent sign above or below it".[55] Leopold Mozart, from the practical viewpoint, advised the violinist that

---

[48] Mozart: *Versuch*, 256.
[49] Johann Philipp Kirnberger: *Die Kunst des reinen Satzes in der Musik*, ii (Berlin and Königsberg, 1776), 116.
[50] P. A. Corri: *L'anima di musica*, i, 72.
[51] Hummel: *Anweisung*, 1st edn 130; 2nd edn 442 (footnote).
[52] Czerny: *Pianoforte-Schule*, iii, 5.
[53] Mathis Lussy: *Traité de l'expression musicale: Accents, nuances et mouvements dans la musique vocale et instrumentale* (Paris, 1874), 95.
[54] Jousse: *Theory and Practice of the Violin*, 43. See also Callcott: *Musical Grammar*, 44.
[55] Knecht: *Katechismus*, 28.

in playing a given passage that included a syncopation (Ex. 2.15), "You must not forget to attack the middle note rather more strongly with the up stroke; and to slur the third note smoothly on to it with a gradual fading away of the tone".[56] In the context of tempo rubato,[57] therefore, where syncopation might continue for some time, the metrical accent in the melody could be at odds with that of its accompaniment for an extended period.

Ex. 2.15  Mozart: *Versuch*, 80.

Yet, although most authorities seem to have agreed about the accentuation of syncopated notes, a few authors suggested that, in certain circumstances at least, syncopated notes might receive the accent on the part of the note that occurred on the normal metrical strong beat. In the original edition of his *Violinschule* Leopold Mozart unreservedly condemned this practice. Discussing ties, he gave the example shown in Ex. 2.16a, commenting:

> It is bad enough that people exist who flatter themselves greatly on their art and who yet cannot play a half-note, yea, hardly a quarter-note without dividing it into two parts. If one wished to have two notes, one would certainly write them down. Such notes must be attacked strongly and, with a gradual dying away, be sustained without after-pressure; just as the sound of a bell, when struck sharply, by degrees dies away.[58]

And in his consideration of performance style in general, he returned to this point, observing: "the notes that are divided by the bar-line must never be separated; neither must the division be marked by an accent, but must merely be attacked and quietly sustained; not otherwise than if it stood at the beginning of a quarter-note."[59] He illustrated the point with the example shown in Ex. 2.16b. But in his 1787 revision of the book, he added an additional footnote to one passage of syncopation (Ex. 2.16c): "This is the only case in which it is customary to mark the division of the notes by a perceptible

---

[56] L. Mozart: *Versuch*, 80.
[57] See Ch. 11.
[58] Mozart: *Versuch*, 44 (footnote).
[59] Mozart: *Versuch*, 260.

after-pressure of the bow. That is to say: when several such notes follow each other in a quick tempo."[60]

Ex. 2.16 a–c. Mozart: (*a*) *Versuch*, 44; (*b*) *Versuch*, 261; (*c*) *Versuch*, 3rd edn, 84.

(*a*)

(*b*)

(*c*)

Schulz also recommends this kind of treatment for successive syncopations, commenting on one of his examples (see Ex. 1.17): "The syncopated notes in the seventh bar are certainly not real main notes; but one only wanted to show here that one has to perform such notes like main notes, namely firmly and emphatically, and the second half of them will be strengthened with a jerk in order to make the strong beat of the bar felt."[61]

Some early-19th-century authors also seem to suggest this as a legitimate way of performing syncopation. Romberg illustrated something similar, giving the original notation and its proposed execution (Ex. 2.17). The vertical strokes over the tie evidently imply accent rather than shortening, as was common in German usage,[62] and he instructed that "in playing the third and fifth eighth-note, a slight jerk be given to the bow".[63] Baillot, too, described a similar treatment of syncopation (Ex. 2.18) as the first of three principal styles of performing such figures, commenting that one made it "By swelling the note and accelerating the speed of the bow right up to the end of the note, but lightly".[64]

---

[60] Leoold Mozart: *Versuch*, 3rd edn (*Dritte vermehrte Auflage*), 84 (footnote).
[61] Schulz: 'Vortrag' in *Allgemeine Theorie*, ii, 1249.
[62] See Ch. 3, "The Staccato Mark".
[63] Romberg: *Violoncell Schule*, 38.
[64] Pierre Marie François de Sales Baillot: *L'art du violon: Nouvelle méthode* (Paris, 1835), 135.

Ex. 2.17 Romberg: *Violoncell Schule*, 38.

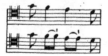

Ex. 2.18 Baillot: *L'Art du violon*, 135.

Such approaches to the performance of syncopation are at odds with modern orthodoxy, which, like Leopold Mozart's earlier handling of the subject, stresses that it is always bad style to accent the second half of the note. It is possible, however, despite Mozart's explicit prohibition of that practice, that in the 18th and 19th centuries there was a greater tendency to press on the second half of an isolated syncopation when dissonance occurred at that point; and Baillot's and Romberg's discussions of the subject indicate that (except in keyboard playing, where such an effect was impossible) this kind of treatment may not infrequently have been made a feature of the passage.

## Beaming

Beaming may sometimes have served, to a certain extent, to indicate phrase groupings and therefore accent, as illustrated by Türk (Ex. 2.19), especially in passages of unslurred notes or within a general *legato* context. It was, however, a very uncertain way of showing accent or phrasing, since only eighth-notes and faster note values have beams, and in many contexts there is little scope for modifying the beaming from conventional groupings. Nevertheless, there are numerous occasions where Classical and Romantic composers evidently used this device with the deliberate intention of showing where the accents or phrase divisions were to fall. This notational practice was described and illustrated by Schulz as a means favoured by some composers for indicating where phrases should be separated (see Ex. 4.4). In many cases such peculiarities of notation have been ironed out in later editions, even so-called critical editions.

Ex. 2.19  Türk: *Klavierschule*, 355.

There were, however, various circumstances that might induce a composer to use this type of notation. J. C. Bach commonly separated the first of a group of eighth- or sixteenth-notes to indicate where a *forte* was followed by a subito *piano*, for instance in *Cefalo & Procris* (Ex. 2.20); and this practice seems to have been followed by many of his contemporaries. In such cases the meaning was precisely opposite to that of the breaks in beaming that indicated the end of one phrase and the beginning of another, since it made the note following the interruption in the beaming weaker rather than stronger than the separated note.

Ex. 2.20  J. C. Bach: *Cefalo & Procris* (autograph MS, 137r), Terzetto Violin 1 & 2, bassi.

Many early-19th-century writers explicitly acknowledged that the first note of groups that are beamed together, contrary to the usual conventions, should receive an accent. Callcott gave an example from Haydn to illustrate how a composer might employ this device (Ex. 2.21).[65] Beethoven used modified beaming on many occasions where it evidently has implications for both accent and phrasing (Ex. 2.22); but there are other occasions where inconsistency of notation (caused partly by a conflict between convenient shorthand and intentionally irregular beaming) confuses the issue: in the first movement of his Fifth Symphony, for instance, the separation of the three-note figure (Ex. 2.23a) from the first note of the bar does not always seem to be significant, though at times it certainly is (Ex. 2.23b).

Ex. 2.21 Callcott: *Musical Grammar*, 44.

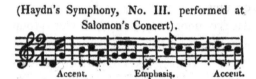

Ex. 2.22 a–b. Beethoven: (*a*) *Chorfantasie* op. 80; (*b*) String Quartet op. 132/v.

---

[65] Callcott: *Musical Grammar*, 44; also in Jousse, *Theory and Practice of the Violin*, 43.

ACCENTUATION IN PRACTICE 55

Ex. 2.23 a–b. Beethoven: Fifth Symphony op. 67/i (autograph).

Weber often used irregular beaming to clarify phrasing. Sometimes this implied accent on the first note of a beamed group, as when he beamed pairs of notes contrary to the normal notational convention, or sometimes it merely showed where a phrase should be articulated, particularly when accompanying voices (Ex. 2.24). Schubert, too, evidently considered abnormal beaming to be significant. In the autograph of the Andante of his String Trio D. 581, for instance, he clearly began by writing separate eighth-notes in the viola and cello parts but then, having altered the first occurrences, subsequently wrote them with a beam from metrically weak to strong beats to displace the accent. In bars 14–15 of the cello part, he even wrote the beam across the bar-line. That Schubert wanted to reinforce the irregular accentuation is suggested by the simultaneously occurring accents in the violin melody in bars 5 and 6 (Ex. 2.25). Among later composers who used modified beaming, sometimes across a bar-line, with evident implications of accent and phrasing, were Schumann, Brahms, and Tchaikovsky (Ex. 2.26). An example from Tchaikovsky is particularly interesting because it shows how, in the string parts, the slurring seems to have limited implications for phrasing, because the change from fours to pairs, as comparison with the flutes suggests, is merely to permit the players to use more bow for the *crescendo*.

Ex. 2.24  Weber: Mass in E flat J. 224, Credo.

Ex. 2.25  Schubert: String Trio D. 581/ii (autograph).

Ex. 2.26a  Schumann: Piano Quintet op. 44/i.

Ex. 2.26b  Brahms: String Quartet op. 51/2/i.

Ex. 2.26c  Tchaikovsky: *Symphonie pathétique* op. 74/i.

In the early 19th century, A. E. Müller linked the beaming of triplets in threes, and sextuplets in sixes with their accentuation, saying that "in triplets the first of the three notes is gently accented while in sextuplets only the first of six notes" (Ex. 2.27).[66] Gottfried Weber, on the other hand, somewhat pedantically insisted that a beam joining six notes together as a sextuplet was only appropriate where metrical accentuation falls on the first, third, and fifth notes (Ex. 2.28).[67]

Ex. 2.27  Müller: *Klavier und Fortepiano Schule*, 16.

Ex. 2.28  G. Weber: *Versuch*, 87.

## Final Notes

The rule that musical units should generally begin powerfully and progressively decline in force was outlined by Crelle, as mentioned earlier, and many other musicians of the period. The majority view implies that in most contexts the final note of a phrase, though receiving the appropriate metrical accent, would be unlikely to have an expressive accent. But an occasional dissenting opinion can be found; Kalkbrenner, for instance, observed that "the first and last notes of a passage should be more marked than the rest".[68] Hummel's examples of appropriate accentuation show some final notes gently accented, some more forcibly accented, and some without any accent.[69]

---

[66] August Eberhard Müller: *G. S. Löhleins Klavierschule oder Anweisung zum Klavier- und Fortepiano Schule [. . .] ganz umgearbeitet und sehr vermehrt* (Jena, 1804), 16. This book, though nominally the 6th edn of Löhlein's *Klavierschule*, is in fact an entirely new treatise.
[67] Gottfried Weber: *Versuch einer geordneten Theorie der Tonsetzkunst [. . .]* (Mainz, 1817), 87f.
[68] Kalkbrenner: *Méthode*, 12. This may be related to the habit of early-19th-century French string players delivering the final notes of a phrase, even when they were the resolution of a dissonance, forcibly and with vibrato, which was criticized by German musicians. See Ch. 12, p. 655.
[69] Hummel: *Anweisung*, 2nd edn, 441–48.

There seems to have been one important exception to the principle enunciated by Crelle and others, and it may have been quite widespread. Philip Corri, writing about keyboard playing, agreed with the majority view when he noted that "the final note of a phrase [is] never to be played with emphasis unless marked"; but he added: "N.B. this rule is quite reversed in singing as the last note should be sung with firmness and sustained long".[70] Here he was echoing an aspect of the teaching of his father, Domenico Corri,[71] and perhaps a principle of the 18th-century Italian school.

## Other Factors

Other criteria for the performer to apply emphasis where none was specifically notated were given by musical writers throughout the period; each author had slightly different advice to offer, sometimes of a generalized nature and sometimes applied to specific examples. Manuel García recommended that the first note of every repetition of a similar figure should be distinguished by greater weight (Ex. 2.29a); he felt that this was particularly applicable to passages of dotted notes (Ex. 2.29b), and that in certain circumstances the short note of the figure, too, should be accented (Ex. 2.29c). He also suggested that use might be made of the so-called *contra-tempo* (Ex. 2.29d).[72]

**Ex. 2.29** (*a*) García: *École*, ii, 26; (*b*) García: *École*, ii, 26; (*c*) García: *École*, ii, 30; (*d*) García: *École*, ii, 26.

---

[70] P. A. Corri: *L'anima di música*, 73.
[71] Domenico Corri: *The Singers Preceptor* (London, 1810).
[72] García: *École*, ii, 30.

Ex. 2.29 Continued

J. F. Schubert had given similar counsel a couple of generations earlier, remarking: "In very special cases the notes which fall on the weak beat [may be accented]." He gave two examples (Ex. 2.30), but added: "In the case of (b) one would do well to observe that the notes marked with ∧ must only receive a gentle emphasis, otherwise the melody could easily become bizarre. One always does better not to accent notes of this kind if one cannot rely on one's taste or if they are not specifically marked *f* or *pf* [poco forte] by the composer".[73] Schubert also made another point, which he regarded as relevant to some of the vocal music of his period: he noted that whereas the principal rule for singers was to take account of the words in accenting the melody, there were cases where the composer had evidently subordinated the words to the melody, and in these cases the singer should take care to adapt his accentuation to the melody rather than the words.

Ex. 2.30 J. F. Schubert: *Neue Singe-Schule*, 134.

## Agogic Accent

There were several ways in which accents would have been realized in performance during this period, and the sort of accentuation that would have

---

[73] Schubert: *Singe-Schule*, 134.

been regarded as appropriate to varying contexts is often difficult to determine. As Koch remarked: "the manner in which the emphasis of these notes is brought out is really easier to feel than to describe"; but he went on to identify the principal aspects of accentuation, including the statement that it "consists partly in a certain emphatic lingering, whereby it appears as if one remains a moment longer on such an accented note than its specific duration requires".[74]

The question of what Koch meant by lingering is related to the vexed problem of inequality, and the extent to which related procedures may have been applied during this period. It is important to distinguish, however, between:

1. "inequality" as a term for a technique applied to specific note values, or types of passages, in particular circumstances, as occurred in French and French-influenced music;
2. the rendition of certain notes in performance, according to well-established conventions, with different values from the written ones, for example, dotted rhythms and some triplet patterns;[75]
3. the convention of elongating the first note under short slurs, especially slurred pairs, and regaining the lost time by hurrying the following note or notes, which, as recordings show, survived until the early 20th century;
4. a more or less obvious deviation from notated values that may have been applied from time to time by performers, following the dictates of their own taste, for expressive purposes.

The last two of these encompass what Riemann designated the agogic accent, but they are also directly related to the matter of *rubato* in its various meanings.[76]

Sources from the Classical and Romantic periods contain numerous references to what Koch described as "emphatic lingering". But before examining more closely what may have been implied by these references it is necessary to consider the German terminology, in which "internally long" (*innerlich lang*) and "internally short" (*innerlich kurz*) were used for strong and weak beats respectively. There has been a degree of uncertainty

---

[74] Koch: 'Accent' in *Musikalisches Lexikon*, 50.
[75] See Ch. 13, "The Variable Dot".
[76] See Ch. 11.

and confusion about whether the nomenclature implied a real chronometric lengthening of the notes that fell on the strong beats. It seems clear, however, that, for the most part, the terminology (which derives from that of poetry) is not to be understood as indicating that all strong beats, which were by definition internally long, would have been expected to be lengthened in duration, even to a minimal degree, although this may easily be inferred from some mid-18th-century authors, such as Friedrich Wilhelm Marpurg, who remarked: "Experience teaches that if two notes of a similar genre, e.g. two quarter-notes, are sung one after the other, even though they are sung at different intervals, one will still be heard by the ear a little longer than the other."[77] Koch, who began by paraphrasing Marpurg's remark, was at pains to explain that he did not consider "long" in this context to mean actually of longer duration; in his *Versuch einer Anleitung zur Composition*, commenting on the relationship between stressed and unstressed in pairs of consecutively sounded notes, he observed that "one of them will be perceived by the hearing as longer (that is really to say, with more emphasis), and that therefore it expresses more inner worth than the other".[78] In the early 19th century, Gottfried Weber adopted a more explicit terminology for his discussion of metrical accentuation, writing of internal weight rather than length.[79]

In the middle of the 18th century, however, a type of unequal performance similar to, but almost certainly freer than the French *notes inégales*, was current among German and Italian musicians. Quantz, working in Friedrich II's Berlin, where French practice was particularly influential, made detailed recommendations about lengthening notes that, according to the rules of metrical accent, fall on the internally long beats; though, as in the French tradition, this was limited to specific circumstances. He stated that "the quickest notes in every piece of moderate tempo, or even in the Adagio, although to the eye they appear to have the same value, should nevertheless be played a little unevenly", and instructed that the stressing and lengthening must be given to the first, third, fifth, and seventh note of each figure (assuming the figure starts on the beat). Exceptions to this rule occurred if the notes had staccato marks, if several notes were repeated at the same pitch, if more than two notes came under a slur, or in eighth-note passagework in a gigue. In the case of passagework in instrumental music that is too quick to permit

---

[77] Friedrich Wilhelm Marpurg: *Kritische Briefe über die Tonkunst*, I (Berlin, 1760) (letter 13, §2), i, 99.
[78] Heinrich Christoph Koch: *Versuch einer Anleitung zur Composition*, ii (Leipzig, 1787), 273.
[79] Weber, *Versuch*, §104, 97.

unequal execution, the first of each group of four notes was to receive this treatment; but he observed that singing was exempt from this rule "because every note in this kind of vocal passagework must be clearly articulated and marked by a gentle puff of air from the chest; thus no inequality occurs".[80] Quantz's account does not make it clear how pronounced a lengthening he expected, though he stated that it should not be as much as if the note were dotted. There seem to be no direct rejections of this aspect of Quantz's teaching in the three or four decades during which his book remained a respected source of authority, unless we take J. F. Reichardt's caution against constantly marking "the accentuation of the notes—of which Herr Quantz says so much",[81] as a criticism of his approach (although Reichardt does not appear to direct this at unequal execution). Nevertheless, since other German writers failed to reiterate Quantz's instructions, it seems probable that his highly stylized description of the technique, tied rather to metrical than expressive accent, is not representative of normal practice throughout central Europe, even at the time the book was published, and that, by the 1770s at any rate, few musicians would have consciously employed unequal performance in the formalized way he described.

Yet, while there is no clear evidence in other sources known to me that inequality was employed as a matter of rule in the late 18th or 19th century, there are indications that performers were in the habit of spontaneously converting patterns of equal notes into unequal patterns. Sometimes, it is clear that this occurred through slovenliness or lack of skill, similar to that implied by Türk when he complained that the phrase marked *a* in Ex. 2.31 often came out as one of the three versions marked *b*.[82]

Ex. 2.31 Türk: *Klavierschule*, 102.

Rhythmic irregularity of this kind, resulting from carelessness, or what the expert regarded as poor musical judgement, undoubtedly occurred throughout the Classical and Romantic periods. In the mid-19th century, for instance, Manuel García felt it necessary to comment, after explaining the

---

[80] Quantz: *Versuch*, 105.
[81] Reichardt: *Ueber die Pflichten*, 28.
[82] Türk: *Klavierschule*, 102.

desirability of strongly accenting dotted notes: "Much as we acknowledge the necessity of strongly over-dotting the above examples [see Ex. 2.29c], and others of a similar character, we reprobate the habit of dotting notes of equal value."[83]

There is abundant evidence, however, that during the whole of this period, agogic accentuation of diverse kinds was seen as a vital aspect of stylish and expressive performance. Leopold Mozart, whose *Violinschule* was published just four years after the appearance of Quantz's book, although he gives a rather different account of where and how he wished the performer to lengthen notes beyond their written value, agreed with Quantz about the necessity for stressing the metrically strong beat and about lengthening as well as stressing the first note not only of slurred pairs, but also of all short, slurred figures. Rather than prescribing stressing and lengthening only for the fastest notes in a piece, he also envisaged an element of lengthening being applied to longer notes. Mozart wrote nothing about lengthening un-slurred notes, but his instructions make it clear that, where slurs were concerned, he regarded a degree of inequality as obligatory in a tasteful performance. Discussing the bowing patterns applicable to a figure in sixteenth-notes in C meter, he stated: "The first of two notes in one bowstroke is made somewhat stronger and also sustained somewhat longer; the second however is slurred onto it quite quietly and somewhat later. This manner of performance cultivates good taste through a singing style; and through the holding back it hinders hurrying."[84] Later, he insisted:

> The first of two, three, four, or even more notes, slurred together, must always be stressed more strongly and sustained a little longer; but those following must diminish in tone and be slurred on somewhat later. But this must be carried out with such good judgement that the bar-length is not altered in the smallest degree. The slight sustaining of the first note must not only be made agreeable to the ear by a nice apportioning of the slightly hurried notes slurred on to it, but must even be made truly pleasant to the listener.[85]

He applied this principle even to slurs including notes of different value, explaining in his next paragraph: "Similarly, when uneven notes come

---

[83] García: *École*, ii, 30.
[84] Mozart: *Versuch*, 123.
[85] Mozart: *Versuch*, 145.

66 CLASSICAL AND ROMANTIC PERFORMING PRACTICE

together in a slur, the longer notes must definitely not be made too short, indeed, they should rather be held a bit too long, and such passages played in a singing manner with sound judgement, in the style described in the preceding paragraph."[86] A representative selection of his examples of the sorts of slurred figures that required this treatment suggests a type of rhythmic flexibility that seems very alien to musicians brought up with the rhythmic strictness of the 20th century (Ex. 2.32); its closest modern equivalent would be certain kinds of jazz performance.

Ex. 2.32 a–h. Mozart: *Versuch*, 136–43. (*a*) Examples 2b & c; (*b*) Examples 4a & b; (*c*) Example 5b; (*d*) Example 7b; (*e*) Examples 8c & d; (*f*) Example 20b; (*g*) Example 21.a; (*h*) Examples 32a & b.

(*a*)

(*b*)

---

[86] Mozart: *Versuch*, 145.

ACCENTUATION IN PRACTICE 67

**Ex. 2.32** Continued

(c)

(d)

(e)

(f)

(g)

(h)

A few years later, Löhlein, in the accompanying explanation to one of the practice pieces in his violin treatise, instructed that in a passage of sixteenth-notes, where two are slurred and two are separate: "The first of the slurred notes receives a special pressure and is sustained somewhat longer than the notation requires; the other is delivered more weakly and shorter; the third and fourth are played with a short staccato in the middle of the bow"[87] (Ex. 2.33). This instruction was retained in later editions, including the fourth of 1797, which was extensively revised by J. F. Reichardt. From this and other evidence it seems likely that there was a widespread tendency to apply agogic accent to the first note of slurred pairs and short slurred figures throughout the 18th and 19th centuries.

**Ex. 2.33** Löhlein: *Anweisung zum Violinspielen*, 78 [Vivace].

By no means all discussions of accentuation in the second half of the 18th century are as explicit as those of Quantz and Mozart with respect to the circumstances in which lengthening should occur. Indeed, many musicians seem to have regarded agogic accent as a resource that performers might introduce at their own discrimination. Thus, comparison of Domenico Corri's versions of vocal music with the original published editions reveals many instances where slurred pairs that were originally notated with equal note values become dotted, but also others where this is not so, or even where Corri suggests reverse dotting (short-long).[88]

Towards the end of the century, and in the early years of the 19th century, writers—while continuing to insist that the technique of lingering on accented notes was an essential aspect of expressive performance—treated the matter in a generally freer manner; it was no longer to be applied by rule, but rather according to the individual performer's creative conception. In this respect, attitudes reflect changing musical aesthetics and concepts of Romantic individualism, as found in the writings of Jean Paul Richter, W. H. Wackenroder, E. T. A. Hoffmann, and others. It is typical of this freer attitude

---

[87] Löhlein: *Anweisung*, 79.
[88] See Ex. 13.3, which compares Corri's version of J. C. Bach's "Nel partir bell'idol mio" with the original.

that in 1804 J. F. Schubert, having discussed various situations in which expressive accentuation is appropriate, added: "It is still to be noted about the notes which should be accented, that from time to time they are also dwelt on longer".[89] Elsewhere in the book, however, he advised:

> It is to be observed of the accented notes that they must be performed emphatically with strength and receive an imperceptibly longer value than their specified one; but the correct tempo or specified duration of a bar may not be altered. The worth over and above its proper value which the emphasized beat receives is taken from the following beat (in a few cases also from the preceding). Also, in particularly emotional passages the equality of the beat will often be restored only in the following bar.[90]

Some twenty years later, Crelle implied the possibility of lengthening as a concomitant of accent in a rather roundabout way when he asserted: "The rule that weight does not hurry has even wider application. It is not limited to the metre alone, but also applies when notes have more weight than others for other reasons, which can also have nothing to do with the metre."[91] His recommendations also contain explicit advice for rhythmic flexibility, which will be considered below. At about the same time, Ignaz Moscheles, in the introduction to his Studies op. 70, remarked that in performing passagework, each element in the figuration should be "performed with a moderate accentuation which should be distinguished not so much by power as by a barely perceptible lingering on the first note."[92] And a couple of decades later, García, discussing tempo rubato, unambiguously linked the practice of lingering with accentuation. He observed: "This prolongation is usually conceded to appoggiaturas, to notes placed on long syllables, and those which are *naturally salient in the harmony*. In all such cases, the time lost must be regained by accelerating other notes. This is a good method for giving colour and variety to melodies"[93] (Ex. 2.34). After discussing accentuation in general, he commented: "We may likewise observe, that both accent and prolongation follow nearly the same laws."[94]

---

[89] Schubert: *Singe-Schule*, 134.
[90] Schubert: *Singe-Schule*, 102.
[91] Crelle: *Einiges*, 61.
[92] Ignaz Moscheles: *Studien für das Pianoforte* op. 70 (Leipzig: Probst, [1827]), 5.
[93] García: *École*, ii, 24.
[94] García: *École*, ii, 27.

Ex. 2.34 García: *École*, ii, 24.

The ability to employ agogic accentuation appropriately and effectively continued to be regarded throughout the 19th century as an essential aspect of more advanced artistry. Arrey von Dommer, for instance, comparing declamatory speech and music, stated:

> For the sake of this special, enhanced expression, the oratorical accent allows a freer treatment of the simple metrical accents in respect of the accentuation of the beats, and in addition there may be deviations from the strict regularity of tempo, because single notes that are to be particularly emphatically brought out may well be held a little bit longer; others that must be subordinated may well be somewhat shortened.[95]

Some revealing examples of this type of agogic accentuation may be found in the meticulously annotated text of Rode's Seventh Violin Concerto given by Spohr in the section on advanced performance in his *Violinschule*. Comparison with the original notation shows that whereas in his verbal commentary Spohr sometimes recommended lingering on one musically more important note among a group of equal-length notes, he also occasionally specified lengthening by altering the note values of Rode's original text. In almost all the many examples of lingering specified in Spohr's commentary the player is required, in accordance with the conventions of *tempo rubato* at that time, to regain the time lost on the emphasized note, or notes, from the following ones.[96] Later in the 19th century, Hugo Riemann, who used an elaborate system of signs to indicate performance instructions as precisely as possible in his editions and pedagogical material, adopted the sign ∧ to mark agogic accents, where he required "a slight lingering on the note"[97] (Ex. 2.35). Aural evidence of this kind of emphatic lingering can be heard in early recordings, especially those made by older artists; and its very noticeable application by some of the greatest performers of the second half of the 19th century shows that words such as "slight" and "imperceptible" had a quite different implications for musicians at that time. Joseph Joachim's 1903

---

[95] Dommer: 'Accent' in *Musikalisches Lexikon*, 16f.
[96] See Ch. 11 and also Ex. 13.45.
[97] Hugo Riemann: *New Pianoforte-School/Neue Klavierschule* (London, [1897–1910]), pt. 1, 17.

recordings confirm his contemporary reputation as a master of rhythmic subtlety, but the extent of his departures from the strict letter of the notation are substantial. So too, for instance, are those of Carl Reinecke, and the much younger Marie Soldat, but their very substantial rhythmic freedom never obscures the sense of a steady fundamental tempo.[98]

Ex. 2.35a  Schubert: *Moments musicaux* op. 94 no. 1 (Brunswick, Litolff, [c. 1890]).

Ex. 2.35b–c  Haydn: Piano Sonata No. 39/ii (Hob.XVI:47) (London, Augener, [c. 1930]).

---

[98] For more detailed discussion see Ch. 13 and especially Ex. 13.47.

## Percussive Accent

The percussive element in accentuation is infinitely variable, from a powerful explosive attack to the slightest hint of emphasis. In mid-18th-century music any of these degrees of accentuation may be appropriate, even where the composer has not marked an accent, though in later music more powerful accents will very seldom have been envisaged unless indicated. The quality of attack is substantially conditioned by the nature of the medium; a vocal accent, depending to a considerable extent on the pronunciation of consonants, is quite different from the accent of a pianist, on the one hand, or a violinist, or wind player on the other. Nevertheless, the intensity of accent will principally relate to the character of the music. Charles de Bériot wrote informatively on this in the mid-19th century. Like many musicians of his and earlier generations, he believed that instrumentalists should seek to emulate the human voice as closely as their instrument permitted, commenting at the beginning of his discussion "On pronunciation by the bow" [De la prononciation de l'archet]:

> We cannot repeat too often that the performer will not be perfect until he can reproduce the accents of song in their most delicate forms.
>
> By the song we mean not only the music, but also the poem of which it is the brilliant ornamentation—without which the melody would be nothing more than a vocal exercise.
>
> It is then of the highest importance for the singer to articulate clearly the words which he undertakes to interpret.
>
> The clearness of the pronunciation depends entirely on the degree of force given to the consonants which begin each syllable. It is by means of this little percussion, in which the consonant seems to chase the vowel, that the singer makes himself understood even with a bass voice by the most distant of his auditors in a large room. It is well understood that the degree of intensity of this pronunciation should be in harmony with the spirit of the piece.

Having discussed the accentuation appropriate to various types of dramatic music, he continued:

> These are the varied and diverse shades of expression which the violinist should render, giving to his bow a soft pronunciation for calm and serene music, and employing it with graduated force in passionate music. This accentuation gives to the instrument the prestige of words: we say that the violin speaks in the hands of the master. [...]
>
> But just so much as pronunciation is, in itself, a precious quality, so much does it degenerate if employed in a systematic manner. It is for the good

ACCENTUATION IN PRACTICE    73

taste of the artist to use these means with discernment, and in such a way as to vary the effect: avoiding on the one hand too much softness, on the other too much power.[99]

He explained his wedge signs, indicating different gradation of attack and decay of the sound (Ex. 2.36a) then proceeded to give a series of "Examples of shading showing pronunciation of the bow from the softest sounds to the most energetic" with four examples which he considered required successively greater percussive accent, using the horizontal wedge to mark the appropriate place for the accents to be applied (Ex. 2.36b).[100]

**Ex. 2.36** a–b. Bériot: (*a*) *Méthode*, 200; (*b*) *Méthode*, 201.

[99] Bériot: *Méthode*, 200.
[100] Bériot: *Méthode*, 201.

Bériot's comments applied largely to accents that had not been specified by the composer. Where composers marked accents, they employed a range of instructions that attempted to show different types and degrees. These are considered in the next chapter; but the piecemeal growth of a compendium of accent markings and instructions, together with the varying usages of different composers, often makes it difficult to be certain what is implied without a close study of their individual practices.[101]

In fact, there was considerable diversity of practice and diversity of opinion about what constituted a tasteful application of accentuation where nothing was marked in the musical text. A passage in Dommer's discussion of accentuation reveals these tensions, but it is unclear whether his criticisms represent a conservative, academic standpoint, or merely reflect the untypical practices of some contemporaneous performers:

> The cases in which the player must bring out the [grammatical] accents or not are impossible to specify in detail; but at all times he must feel the accent, even in the freest performance and when he does not mark it at all. For a performance that shows that the player is either not at peace with himself about the grammatical order of accents, or that he has no natural feeling for rhythm and beat, can become unbearable, because he is blurred, unsteady, unmarked and powerless. And on the contrary, the manner in which some players use the accentuation for all sorts of little effects and embellishments is no less unpleasant; virtuosos, who are nothing more than such, often enjoy introducing hesitations, shifts in the accent and the accentuation of weak beats, etc., where it is not at all necessary, in order to appear clever and to cover up their fundamental ordinariness through piquant gimmicks. But nothing more is achieved than an unnatural exaggeration and a violation of the right feeling of every musically educated listener.[102]

---

[101] For discussion of Carl Czerny's innovative employment of an exceptional range of accent marking in his own compositions see Clive Brown: 'Czerny the Progressive' in Leonardo Miucci, Claudio Bacciagaluppi, Daniel Allenbach, and Martin Skamletz (eds.), *Beethoven and the Piano. Philology, Context and Performance Practice*, Musikforschung der Hochschule der Künste Bern, xvi (Schliengen: Argus, 2023), 15–39.
[102] Dommer: 'Accent' in *Musikalisches Lexikon*, 16.

# 3

# The Notation of Accents and Dynamics

In the middle of the 18th century, expressive accentuation and dynamic nuance was largely at the discretion of the performer; few composers indicated more than the most important dynamic contrasts and accents in their music. J. A. P. Schulz remarked in 1774 that dynamic marks "are often put there only so that very crude improprieties may not be committed [. . .]; they would, if they were really adequate, often have to be put under every note of a piece".[1] For the effectiveness of their music in this respect, composers relied on the performer's taste and experience in applying generally understood principles of phrasing and accent. To a great extent, therefore, stylish accentuation and dynamic shading depended on the executant's recognition of the phrase structure of the music, its character, and so on. Even in the early 19th century this was seen to present considerable difficulties for the average performer; it was felt to be so subtle and variable that, as Schulz had implied, it could only be learned effectively from observing great musicians.

The markings employed in mid-18th-century music to indicate the contrasts and accents that composers regarded as essential were few and, as a rule, sparingly introduced. These instructions might encompass *fortissimo*, *forte*, *mezzo forte*, *poco forte*, *piano*, and *pianissimo*, and from time to time, composers who were especially concerned to achieve a quite specific effect, such as Gluck, might employ less common terms like *piano assai* where something particularly arresting was required (Ex. 3.1).

---

[1] Schulz: 'Vortrag' in Sulzer (ed.): *Allgemeine Theorie*, ii, 1254.

Ex. 3.1 Gluck: *Semiramide reconosciuta*, Act II, Scene iii. Österreichische Nationalbibliothek, Cod. mus. 17.793, repr. in *Italian Opera 1640–1770* (New York, Garland, 1982), 131.

The additional dynamic shading and accentuation supplied by performers, partly in accordance with established conventions and partly according to their individual tastes, was an important aspect of the criteria by which, in the case of solo parts, their quality as artists would be judged. In orchestral playing, too, the ideal was certainly a well-controlled and aptly nuanced performance, but since this demanded uniformity of expression among all the players it necessitated control by the director if, in addition to observance of the composer's markings, anything other than the phrasing-off of appoggiaturas and the application of similar simple and universally accepted conventions were expected. Thus, instructions were even more necessary here than in solo music. J. F. Reichardt's discussion of *crescendo* and *diminuendo* in the orchestra illustrates the growing feeling, in the last quarter of the 18th century, that composers needed to specify their requirements more fully:

> If the composer wants to have it absolutely precisely performed, he will do well to include all these different gradations exactly under the notes where they should occur. [...] Or he must come to an understanding with his orchestra on particular occasions, namely that every whole or half bar should become to a degree brighter or darker, or whatever may be agreed. From time to time, however, precise specification will nevertheless be necessary so that one player does not get louder more quickly than another. [...] The composer may, therefore, merely write *pp.* in the first bar, in the second *cresc.* and in the ninth *ff.*; in any case he may also add the sign ⟶ and the orchestra will make the second bar *p.* the third *poco p.*

the fourth *rinf* the fifth *poco f.* the sixth *mf.* the seventh *più f.* the eighth *f* and the ninth *ff*.[2]

Reichardt's assumption that performances would commonly be under the composer's direct control also hints at one reason why such markings were relatively infrequent in mid-18th-century music, which was seldom written with a view to publication. In practice, very few composers in the 1770s or 1780s took the sort of care with their scores that Reichardt recommended, and very few orchestras seem to have achieved his ideal. This is reflected in his comments about "loud and soft and their various nuances", where he remarked:

> This is, for our feelings, what the attractive force of the moon is for the sea: it will just as surely cause ebb and flow in us. The majority of orchestras only recognize and practise *forte* and *piano* without bothering about the finer degrees or the shading of the whole. That is to say they paint the wall black and white: it is all very well if it is beautiful white and beautiful black, but what does it say? It is difficult, extraordinarily difficult, to get a whole orchestra to do that which already gives a single virtuoso much trouble. But it is certainly possible: one hears this in Mannheim, one has heard it in Stuttgart.[3]

The idea that orchestras were only just learning to produce effective dynamic contrasts at that time is supported by C. G. Neefe's report in 1783 that Kapellmeister Cajetano Mattioli in Bonn "first introduced accentuation, instrumental declamation, careful attention to *forte* and *piano*, all the degrees of light and shade in the orchestra of this place".[4] Reichardt's treatment of the subject also implies that matters were not helped by confusion about the meaning of some of the terms employed at this period. He stated that such markings as *m.v.* (*mezza voce*) and *f.v.* (*fatto voce*—occasionally used as a synonym for *mezza voce*) were sometimes taken to mean the same as *mf* (*mezzo forte*) and sometimes even the same as *fz.* (*forzato*).[5] In fact, in

---

[2] Reichardt: *Ueber die Pflichten*, 65–67.
[3] Reichardt: *Ueber die Pflichten*, 59.
[4] Christian Gottlob Neefe: in *Magazin der Musik*, i (1783), 377.
[5] Reichardt: *Ueber die Pflichten*, 68.

the period around 1812, Beethoven used *mezza voce*, clearly with dynamic implications (*mezzo forte* was not among his standard markings); though of course, it may also have had expressive connotations.[6] And Asioli included *mezza voce* among the terms indicating a dynamic between *f* and *p*.[7] Reichardt might have added *pf* to his list of ambiguous abbreviations; it might have stood either for *più forte* or *poco forte*, both of which he had employed in his treatise. Türk gave both possibilities for *pf*, stressing in a footnote that it could not mean soft-loud, as suggested in some unidentified sources.[8] When this marking stood for *poco forte* (rather than *più forte*), it clearly indicated a dynamic level between *p* and *f*; but where it stood in relation to *mf* in composers' usage remains uncertain. Galuppi used it in *Antigone* between *piano* and *fortissimo*, probably to indicate a *crescendo* in something approaching Reichardt's manner (Ex. 3.2). It gradually fell out of general use. Brahms's idiosyncratic employment of *poco f* or *pf* seems likely to have involved an expressive element, perhaps implying the character of a *forte*, but with a dynamic level closer to *mf*.

**Ex. 3.2**  Galuppi: *Antigone*, Act I, Scene iii, 30v. https://s9.imslp.org/files/imglnks/usimg/e/ec/IMSLP362956-PMLP585978--Rari_6.2.15-_Antigona_Atto_Primo.pdf.

The situation was further complicated by the employment of the same terms to indicate either an absolute dynamic level, an accent, or a dynamic nuance. *Rinforzando*, for instance, was sometimes synonymous with *crescendo*, sometimes designated an accent on a single note, and sometimes indicated an emphatic style of performance for a phrase or passage. As Reichardt's remarks and Galuppi's practice suggest, a composer might also use a sequence of apparently abrupt dynamic levels to indicate a progressive *crescendo* or *decrescendo*. Terms such as *smorzando, morendo, calando, decrescendo*, and *diminuendo* might be used as synonyms, or they might have particular and specific connotations; *calando*, for example, could be

---

[6] For instance in the Allegretto ma non troppo of the String Quartet op. 95 and the Adagio espressivo of the Violin Sonata op. 96.
[7] Asioli: *Principj*, 43.
[8] Türk: *Klavierschule*, 116.

synonymous with *decrescendo*, but like *diminuendo* it might also imply a slackening of tempo. It was not until the last decade or so of the 18th century that the convention of indicating a gradual increase or decrease of volume (and sometime speed) by terms such as *cresc. decresc., dim.*, or by "hairpins" became commonplace.

Rapid diversification of musical style in the late 18th and early 19th centuries progressively weakened the relationship between, on the one hand, clearly recognizable categories of music, or conventions of notation and, on the other, particular types of accentuation and dynamic shading. Schulz had already complained about this with respect to "heavy and light" performance styles in the 1770s.[9] Many composers, especially in the German sphere of influence, came increasingly to regard accentuation and dynamic nuance as integral to the individuality of their conceptions and were unwilling to entrust this merely to the performer's instinct. During the 19th century, a growing number of performance instructions of all kinds was devised to show finer grades or types of accents and dynamic effects.

Pierre Baillot, from the vantage point of the fourth decade of the 19th century, was well aware of the consequences attendant on the development of a more individualistic, expressive, dramatic style in composition during the second half of the 18th century; he was also conscious that, concomitant with the growing reliance on notated dynamic and accentual detail, there was decreasing awareness of the conventions that had governed dynamic nuance and accent in earlier music. He remarked:

> This tendency towards the dramatic style was to give rise to the need to increase the number of signs and to notate every inflection, in order to correspond more closely with the wishes of the composer. This is what modern composers have done, and this is what makes music written before this era much more difficult to perform and interpret well: we stress this point in order that students may not be in any way discouraged at the prospect of the large number of works where the absence of signs makes an appeal to their intelligence which is bound to turn out to their advantage if they will only take the trouble to deepen their studies.
>
> The abundance of signs is favourable to music in that it can prevent many misinterpretations and serve as a guide for those who cannot do without

---

[9] See Ch. 5.

them, but it could end up extinguishing the genius of the performer who especially likes to explore and be creative in his own way.[10]

Baillot's final comment emphasizes an important aspect of Classical and Romantic musicality: that the composer's text was always recognized as indicative, rather than prescriptive. Many of the ambiguities and contradictions in the usage of specific terms and signs reflect the limitations of musical notation and instructions, which throughout the period were recognized as being incapable of conveying the subtleties and refinements that were necessary to achieve a beautiful performance. The following discussion, therefore, is concerned more with a range of possibilities than with precise meaning. Even the most fastidious composers were forced to recognize that, however many instructions they provided, it was impossible to communicate their own conception of a beautiful performance.[11]

## Italian Terms and Abbreviations as Accents

The following discussion of individual terms and signs looks at theoretical explanations and at different ways in which these instructions were used in the music of the period. A comprehensive examination of the practices of individual composers is beyond the scope of this chapter, but a cross section of examples illustrating differences in usage is offered.

### *Forte (f, for; ff, etc.)*

Although *f* was most commonly used to indicate a general dynamic level, it also occurs sometimes on single notes that required a particular accent. The implications of this marking must, at first, have been wider than they later became, when other instructions for accent had come into use. Where *f* was the only accent instruction employed by the composer, as was often the case in the mid-18th century, it would have had to be deduced from

---

[10] Baillot: *L'art du violon*, 162.
[11] See, e.g., Mahler's comment, quoted in Ch. 1, pp. 8–9.

the musical context whether it implied a sharp, heavy, moderate, light, rapidly decaying, or more sustained accent. In scores where other accent indications do not occur, *f* may well have been used to designate the kind of accent that would later have been indicated by *sf*. This is suggested by versions of Gluck's *Orfeo ed Euridice*. In the first printed edition (Paris, Duchesne, 1764), the overture has *f* on the first violins' whole-notes in bars 6–10, while at the same place in the 1774 version (Paris, Lemarchand, 1774), the marking is *sf*. A third alternative is found in J. C. F. Rellstab's contemporary piano score of the work, which has *rf*, sometimes used as a lighter accent than *sf*.

Where it was used in conjunction with other accent markings, *f* may be presumed generally to have had a more specific meaning. The instructions *sf*, *fz*, *rf*, *mfp*, *fp*, and *ffp*, as well as several graphic signs, were increasingly employed to indicate accents that might once have been implied simply by *f*. Sometimes, as in Salieri's *Der Rauchfangkehrer*, *ff* might even be used as an accent within a *forte* dynamic (Ex. 3.3). Where a composer used a range of accent markings, *f* alone, in a *forte* context, may have implied a weighty but not sharp execution, though there seems not to be explicit theoretical support for such an assumption. Some composers, especially those who employed *sf* rather than *sfp* within *piano* passages without any implication of a *forte* continuation, may also have used *f*, instead of *sf*, when the *forte* was meant to continue beyond the initial attack.

**Ex. 3.3** Salieri: *Der Rauchfangkehrer* (autograph), Act II, no. 6, 124v. Österreichische Nationalbibliothek, Vienna Mus. Hs. 16611. Violin 1, Herr von Bär (bass), and Bassi.

It is less common to find *f* used primarily to indicate accentuation after the widespread adoption of *sf* and *fz*, but some 19th-century writers continued to list it specifically as an accent marking, and it is sometimes encountered in this sense in 19th-century music, particularly in the music of composers who employed a wide range of accent markings. Schumann, for instance, used a series of *fs*, apparently to ensure an equally weighty performance of successive chords in his Violin Sonata op. 105 (Ex. 3.4), perhaps recalling such instances as the succession of *ffs* in the first movement of Beethoven's Violin Sonata in C minor op. 30 no. 2, or a weighty cadence in the String Quartet op. 59 no. 3 (Ex. 3.5). Beethoven occasionally used *f* with accent connotations in his early works (Ex. 3.6); in compositions of his middle and especially of his last period, where he sought to define expressive nuances with ever greater precision, he used it more often, seemingly to obtain an emphatic but less explosive execution than would have been elicited by *sf*, for example in the final movements of the string quartets op. 127 and op. 131, or the first movement of op. 130 (Ex. 3.7). In this type of usage, too, Schumann followed Beethoven (Ex. 3.8). Another explanation of repeated *f* markings in some circumstances may have been that they were needed to counteract the strong–weak relationships arising from the music's metrical framework (Ex. 3.9), or to prevent the normal *diminuendo* effect implied by the phrase structure. This seems likely to have been a factor in William Sterndale Bennett's use of repeated *fs* in his overture *The Naiads* (Ex. 3.10).

Ex. 3.4  Schumann: Violin Sonata op. 105/i.

NOTATION OF ACCENTS AND DYNAMICS 83

Ex. 3.5 a–b. Beethoven: (*a*) Violin Sonata op. 30/2/i; (*b*) String Quartet op. 59/3/i.

Ex. 3.6 Beethoven: String Quartet op. 18/5/iii.

Ex. 3.7 a–c. Beethoven: (*a*) String Quartet op. 127/iv; (*b*) String Quartet op. 131/vii; (*c*) String Quartet op. 130/i.

(*a*)

(*b*)

**Ex. 3.7** Continued

(c)

**Ex. 3.8** Schumann: Violin Sonata op. 121/ii.

86  CLASSICAL AND ROMANTIC PERFORMING PRACTICE

Ex. 3.9  Beethoven: String Quartet op. 18/4/iv.

An idiosyncratic use of *f* within *forte* or even *fortissimo* contexts can occasionally be found in some of Weber's music, where it seems rather to have dynamic than accentual implications. In his E flat Mass J. 224, for instance, he frequently used this means, especially in contrapuntal passages, apparently to advise the singer or instrumentalist that their line should be particularly prominent. Instances of this kind might prompt performers to consider whether, when an isolated *f* or *ff* occurs, it implies an accent or is merely a reminder of the prevailing dynamic.

## Forte-piano (*fp, for:po:, ffp, mfp*)

The marking *fp* is likewise susceptible of different interpretations in 18th- and 19th-century music depending on the other accent markings employed. Where a composer did not use the marking *sfp* or *fzp*, the dynamic and accentual implications of *fp* may range from a sharp and powerful accent to a relatively gentle emphasis. A *forte* sustained for a definite length of time and followed by a sudden *piano* may sometimes be intended by *fp*.

Many composers juxtaposed *forte* and *piano* to show that a single beat or a group of notes should be played *forte*, perhaps with a *decrescendo*, before returning to *piano*, but not to indicate a short, sharp accent. Others undoubtedly saw *fp* as a means of indicating an accent within *piano* passages, where *f* alone could easily be confused with a dynamic marking that applied to the whole of the following passage. On occasion, composers, for example

J. C. Bach,[12] made the meaning of an *fp* clearer by their beaming of the notes. The same notational device was still used in the 19th century, for instance by Weber (Ex. 3.11). Among those who appear to have regarded *fp* and *fzp* primarily as a means of indicating rapidly decaying accents was Joseph Haydn. In a copyist's score of his opera *Armida* he made a note: "The composer asks that, in the following and similar places [see Ex. 3.12], in order to achieve his intention and true expression, the initial impact of the forte should be of the shortest duration in all the parts, thus therefore as if the forte immediately seems to disappear."[13] Such an interpretation seems appropriate for many occurrences of this instruction in Haydn's music. An instance in the String Quartet op. 17 no. 4 (Ex. 3.13) is particularly interesting because of the discrepancy between the placement of the dynamic markings in the upper strings and the bass, where *p* comes one note earlier; the explanation is surely that Haydn and all his contemporaries recognized that slurred pairs of this kind would always be played with a rapid *decrescendo*.

**Ex. 3.10** Bennett: *The Naiads*.

---

[12] See Ex. 2.20.
[13] Karl Geiringer: *Joseph Haydn* (Potsdam, 1932), plate facing 114.

Ex. 3.11 Weber: *Der Freischütz*, Act I, 'Introduzione'.

Ex. 3.12 Haydn: *Armida*.

Ex. 3.13 Haydn: String Quartet op. 17/4/i.

Haydn and other late-18th-century composers used *fp* in both these ways, and the difference is sometimes evident from the way the *f* and *p* are written, though it is impossible to tell this from most printed editions. In Mozart's autographs the distinction between the two usages is generally made clear (though not entirely consistently) by his manners of writing. Where the *forte* and the *piano* are intended to apply to separate beats or notes it is usually *f:p:*, and where he intended a *forte* followed rapidly by *piano*, he wrote *fp*: (Ex. 3.14). An interesting use of *fp* by Mozart occurs in *Don Giovanni* (Ex. 3.15), where the combination of a *staccato* mark with *fp* seems clearly intended to indicate that the *forte* applies only to the first note of a group of eighth-notes. The *staccato* mark together with *fp* in the violins may be intended to clarify the extent and nature of the attack, while the *staccato* marks alone on half-notes in the violas (also in cello/bass) seems to specify a similar, perhaps lighter accent. It seems unlikely, in view of the relationship with the vocal part, that the *staccato* marks indicate any significant shortening of the notes.[14]

---

[14] The traditional term "staccato mark" is retained for the various forms of dots and strokes, despite its ambiguity in modern usage. As explained in Chapter 6, these signs are by no means always to be seen as an instruction to shorten notes.

Ex. 3.14 a–b. (*a*) Mozart: String Quartet K. 575/i; (*b*) K. 575/iii.

(*a*)

(*b*)

**Ex. 3.15** Mozart: *Don Giovanni*, Act II, Scene vii (autograph).
Vn. 1 & 2, viola, Leoprello, bassi.

[Molto allegro]

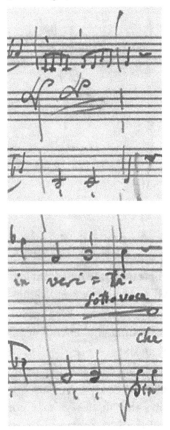

A few 18th-century composers sought greater precision in the degree of accentuation by using *mfp* for a less powerful accent. Mozart used it quite often, and it is also found in Salieri's music. Whether Salieri, for instance, saw these markings essentially as accents, with a rapid decay of sound, however, is less clear. In the autograph of *Der Rauchfangkehrer*, he employed *mfp* and *fp* in several ways: a fast decay after the initial accent seems implied by Ex. 3.16a, while the line after the *mf* in Ex. 3.16b is probably intended to specify the duration of the *mf* before a *subito p*. Some composers, for instance Beethoven and Schubert, might indicate a louder attack with *ffp*. Examples of even greater specificity, together with the use of dynamic markings such as *fff* and *ppp*, are already encountered in the early 19th century. Schubert used the latter occasionally, perhaps to indicate the use of a soft pedal on the piano, and Dussek, in 1806, in the autograph of his String Quartet op. 60 no. 2 marked *ppp* then *pppp* at the end of the Adagio pathetico (in the printed parts it is only *pp* in both places).

**Ex. 3.16** a–b. Salieri: *Der Rauchfangkehrer.* (*a*) Act I, no. 1, 2v (autograph); (*b*) Act I, no. 5, 17v (autograph). Violin 1.

As a wider range of markings was adopted by composers who were anxious to designate different types and degrees of accentuation, it would seem logical that *fp* should have been employed primarily to indicate a rapid falling-away of sound after the initial loudness, but probably without a sharp accent. This was certainly the way Meyerbeer used it. A footnote in the score of *Les Huguenots* echoes Haydn's instruction of more than sixty years earlier: "Each note marked *fp* should be sounded loudly only at the first instant, then dying away afterwards."[15] The fact that Meyerbeer felt it necessary to specify this interpretation of the marking, however, indicates that this usage may not have been universal, even towards the middle of the 19th century. In fact, among Meyerbeer's contemporaries, there seems often to have been a degree of unclarity about the effect indicated by *fp*. Instances in Spohr's *Faust* imply that he may have envisaged a more gradual decrease of volume than that required by Meyerbeer (Ex. 3.17). The same conclusion may be drawn from some of Schumann's uses of the marking, as in the Trio op. 80, where, if the violin is to correspond with the piano, an abrupt decrease in dynamic would hardly be appropriate (Ex. 3.18).

---

[15] Meyerbeer: *Les Huguenots*, 1st edn (Paris, Schlesinger, 1836), 100.

NOTATION OF ACCENTS AND DYNAMICS 93

Ex. 3.17 Spohr: *Faust*, no. 5.

Ex. 3.18 Schumann: Piano Trio op. 80/i.

It is also probable that *fp* may sometimes have been seen as little different from, or synonymous with, *sf/fz* or *sfp*. In Schumann's First Symphony, though *sf* occurs quite frequently, there is no use of *sfp*; here, *fp* seems to supply its function. Schumann's subsequent symphonies use both markings freely, but the distinction is not always clear, as, for example, in his Third Symphony (Ex. 3.19a), where *sfp* and *fp* are used simultaneously. Comparison of the first and second versions of Schumann's D minor Symphony (1841 and 1851) suggests a change in his practice (assuming that he did not require a different effect in 1851). In the fifth bar of the first movement, for example, the earlier version has *fp* where the later one has *sfp* and *sf* (Ex. 3.19b).

Ex. 3.19 a–b. Schumann: (*a*) Third Symphony op. 97/i; (*b*) Fourth Symphony op. 120/i (1851 version).

**Ex. 3.19** Continued

Schumann's older contemporary Spohr also mixed *fp* and *fzp* in a similar manner. In *Faust*, where he did not employ *fzp*, Spohr often used *fz* and *fp* simultaneously in different parts, the former on notes followed by rests and the latter to specify the ensuing *piano* in a continuing part (Ex. 3.20). Mendelssohn's employment of *sfp* and *fp* in the Scherzo of his D minor Piano Trio, and elsewhere, certainly suggests that he did not see a very significant distinction between the two markings, although the former probably represented a sharper accent (Ex. 3.21).

96  CLASSICAL AND ROMANTIC PERFORMING PRACTICE

Ex. 3.20  Spohr: *Faust*, no. 7.

Ex. 3.21  Mendelssohn: Piano Trio op. 49/ii.

At times *fp* was used, apparently, without any obvious implication of accent, simply to obtain an abrupt decrease of volume at the end of a loud passage, for instance by Liszt and Brahms (Ex. 3.22 a–b).

**Ex. 3.22a** Liszt: *Eine Faust Symphonie*, i, 'Faust' (strings).

98 CLASSICAL AND ROMANTIC PERFORMING PRACTICE

Ex. 3.22b Brahms: Second Symphony op. 73/i.

*Sforzando* (*sforzato, forzato, forzando, sf, sfz, sff, fz, ffz*)

The abbreviations *sf*, or *sfz*, and *fz*, standing for *sforzando, sforzato, forzando*, or *forzato*, were generally regarded as synonymous, and most composers habitually employed only one or the other in their autographs. Mozart, Cherubini, Beethoven, Mendelssohn, Liszt, Schumann, Berlioz, and Wagner are among those whose standard marking is *sf* or *sfz*; Haydn, Spohr, Schubert, Chopin, Dvořák, and others employed *fz*. Because of the vagaries of engravers, this distinction is not always apparent in original or later printed editions; but it is evident from surviving autographs. Some writers explicitly stated that *sf* and *fz* were synonymous.[16] Over time, a wider range of terms began to be employed for different grades of accentuation. One late-19th-century writer even suggested a distinction between *sf* and *sfz*, writing: "The metrical accent is only indicated in the notation for particularly prominent notes by *sf* (*sforzato* = intensified) and *sfz* (*sforzando* = very intensified)."[17]

Where a composer employed *f*, *fp*, *sf*, or *fz* as accents, the last two will generally have implied, as the meaning of the Italian word suggests, the sharper attack. During the early part of the period, *sf* or *fz* occurring in a *piano* dynamic was sometimes used to signify a powerful accent followed by a *forte* continuation. On other occasions, particularly where a composer did not use *sfp* or *fzp*, an immediate return to the prevailing dynamic after an *sf* or *fz* in a *piano* passage was evidently envisaged. Haydn used *fz* (sometimes *sf* in printed editions) in this way, although very sparingly in works up to the 1770s, and even in late works he occasionally used *fz* in *piano* sections where he did not expect a *forte* continuation (Ex. 3.23). Unlike Mozart, he never adopted *fzp* (*sfp*) as a regular marking to show whether a return to the prevailing dynamic was required.

**Ex. 3.23** Haydn: Symphony No. 104/iv (autograph).

---

[16] E.g., Muzio Clementi: *Introduction to the Art of Playing on the Pianoforte* (London, 1801), 9; Dotzauer: *Violoncell-Schule*, 13.
[17] Richard Scholz: *Die Vortragskunst in der Musik* (Hannover, [1892]), 23.

100  CLASSICAL AND ROMANTIC PERFORMING PRACTICE

Mozart was quite systematic in this respect as in so many others. When he wanted an *sf* within *piano*, he generally cautioned the performer to return to the original dynamic by writing *sfp* (Ex. 3.24a). Other late-18th-century composers, for example Piccinni and Sacchini, adopted a similar use of *sfp*. Sometimes, however, Mozart wrote *sf*, where he evidently envisaged a *forte* continuation until the next *p* (Ex. 3.24b).

**Ex. 3.24a**  Mozart: String Quartet K. 589/iv (autograph).
[Allegro assai 6/8]

**Ex. 3.24b**  Mozart: *Don Giovanni* (Gugler, 317) (Act 2, no. 7), Leporello: "Ah pietà signori miei" (autograph).

NOTATION OF ACCENTS AND DYNAMICS 101

Beethoven, in earlier works, though he sometimes used *sfp* to clarify his intentions, often, like Haydn, used *sf* in quiet music, where he undoubtedly intended an immediate return to *piano* (Ex. 3.25a). Until around 1803, he seems generally to have used *sfp* mostly where the previous marking was *forte* and he required an abrupt decrease to *piano* after the *sf* (Ex. 3.25b). By the time of the op. 59 quartets, however, he marked *sfp* regularly in *piano* passages (Ex. 3.25c) or sometimes indicated the position and extent of a *decrescendo* by means of ⟩ (Ex. 3.25d).

Ex. 3.25a  Beethoven: String Quartet op. 18/4/i. The dynamics are the same in the other parts.

Ex. 3.25b  Beethoven: String Quartet op. 18/4/ii.

Ex. 3.25c Beethoven: String Quartet op. 59/1/i, Allegro (autograph). The passage begins *p dolce*.

Ex. 3.25d Beethoven: String Quartet op. 131/i, Adagio ma non troppo e molto espressivo.

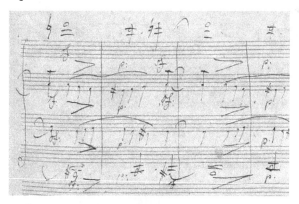

With respect to the weight of accent implied by *sf* or *fz*, there were conflicting opinions in the late 18th and early 19th centuries. Koch observed that composers used *sf* only in cases where the note should be heavily accented,[18] and Milchmeyer remarked: "*forzato, fz* as strong as possible, or as strong as the instrument will take".[19] Several composers at that period sought to differentiate between stronger and more gentle accents. Reichardt proposed *rf* (an abbreviation of *rinforzato*) to indicate accentuation at a dynamic between *poco piano* and *poco forte*,[20] and some early-19th-century composers began to employ both *sf* and *fz* to convey different degrees of accent; but there was no universal agreement about their meaning. Carl Gollmick, writing around 1830, seem to have recognized *fz* as a slighter accent than *sf*, observing: "one

---

[18] Koch: 'Accent', *Musikalisches Lexikon*, 54.
[19] Milchmeyer: *Die wahre Art*, 53.
[20] See pp. 123–124.

finds the term *forzando* in few treatises, but it exists in *compositions*" (in a footnote he refers to Carl Czerny's use of *fz* in his op. 235), adding: "If one takes it to mean the same as *sfz* it is redundant. If one takes it as less intense, then the newer sign ∧ perfectly performs its function."[21]

In the absence of autographs, it is difficult to be sure how far the markings in an edition correspond with the composer's intentions, since engravers were often careless about which punch they selected for stamping *staccato* marks or performance instructions onto the plates. In Czerny's case, however, quite a few carefully corrected proofs survive in which he retained the differences; but even without these, the use of accent instructions in his numerous works provides a reliable impression of his practice. He used *fz* and *ffz*, together with *sf* and *rf*, as differentiated accent signs throughout most of his career. In earlier works he also employed *sff*. In his Piano Sonata op. 7, for instance, he used *sff* alongside *sf, fz, and rfz*, but in his Piano Sonata op. 57 he used only *fz, ffz*, and *rf*; and for some time after that, *sf* is scarcely found in editions of his works. (In the *Grand Polonaise Brillante* op. 118 *sf* is used exclusively, but this may have been the engraver's choice of punch, because *fz* is used exclusively in the *Sonate Militaire et Brillante* op. 119). In Czerny's Piano Sonata op. 124 and the three works entitled *Grande fantaisie en forme de Sonate*, opp. 143, 144, 145, however, *sff* occurs as well as *ffz* alongside *sf*, and *rf*, and more occasionally *fz* (Ex. 3.26a–b). In later works all these instructions except *sff* are used with evident deliberation (Ex. 3.26c). From his usage of them, and on logical grounds, it seems that Czerny expected the following hierarchy of accents in ascending order of force: *rf, sf, fz, sff, ffz*; but in his didactic publications he never explained this.

**Ex. 3.26a** Carl Czerny: Grande fantaisie en forme de Sonata op. 143 (Leipzig, Probst [c. 1827]), 3. (Proof copy corrected by Czerny. University of Rochester, Eastman School of Music, Sibley Music Library.)

---

[21] Carl Gollmick: *Kritische Terminologie* (Frankfurt-am-Main, 1833), 3.

**Ex. 3.26b**  Carl Czerny: Grande fantaisie en forme de Sonata, op. 145 (Leipzig, Probst [c. 1827]), 3 (Proof copy corrected by Czerny.)

**Ex. 3.26c**  Carl Czerny: Huit Nocturnes Romantiques, op. 604 no. 1 (Mainz, Schott [1843]), 5.

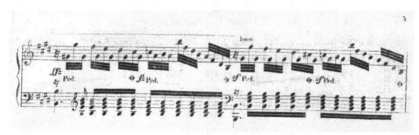

Brahms too employed *sf*, *fz*, *ffz*, *sff*, and *rf*. Clara Schumann's pupil Fanny Davies recalled that he "was most particular that his marks of expression (always as few as possible) should be the means of conveying the inner musical meaning".[22] It is not surprising, therefore, that he was much more sparing of accent markings and performance instructions than Czerny. Brahms's practice, however, was not consistent: in the Piano Quintet op. 34, for instance, he used *fz* and *ffz*, as well as *rf*, but not *sf*; yet in the Variations on a Theme of Haydn op. 35, he used *sf* and *rf* (Ex. 3.27a), but not *fz*; and in the String Sextet op. 18 he used *sf* and *fz*, both very infrequently (Ex. 3.27b). Curiously, Brahms very occasionally used *sff*, perhaps as an equivalent of *ffz*; it occurs already in the First Piano Sonata op. 1 and the Scherzo op. 4 but also recurs, for example, in the *Triumphlied* op. 55, the Third Symphony op. 90, and the Intermezzo op. 118 no. 6. He used *ffz* more frequently, but still sparingly, for instance in the Serenade op. 16, Sextet op. 18 (Ex. 3.27c), *Ein deutsches Requiem* op. 45 (just once, for the piccolo, on page 142 of the 1st edition score), Alto Rhapsody op. 53, Fourth Symphony op. 98, Cello Sonata op. 99, and String Quintet op. 111. In the String Quintet op. 88 he replaced *sf* with *rf* in the autograph (Ex. 3.27d), but since the first edition contains additional *sf*s he seems to have changed his mind again (Ex. 3.27e).

---

[22] Fanny Davies: 'Some Personal Recollections of Brahms as Pianist and Interpreter' in *Cobbett's Cyclopedic Survey of Chamber Music* (London, 1929), i, 182.

NOTATION OF ACCENTS AND DYNAMICS  105

Ex. 3.27a  Brahms: Variations on a Theme by Jos. Haydn op. 56, p. 65. *sf* and *rf*.

Ex. 3.27b  Brahms: String Sextet op. 18, i (1st edn).
[Allegro ma non troppo]

Ex. 3.27c  Brahms: String Sextet op. 18, iii (autograph): *ffz*.
[Allegro molto]

106  CLASSICAL AND ROMANTIC PERFORMING PRACTICE

**Ex. 3.27d**  Brahms: String Quintet op. 88 (autograph): *rf* (*sf* deleted).
[Grave ed appassionato]

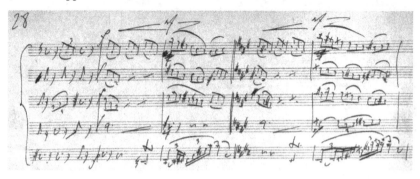

**Ex. 3.27e**  Brahms: String Quintet op. 88 (1st edn).

The frequency with which individual composers used these accent markings, as well as their repertoire of other accent markings, will be a clue to the type of accentuation they wished to indicate by them. Beethoven's very frequent employment of *sf* in all sorts of dynamic contexts suggests that, together with *sfp*, it was a relative accent—its intensity depending on the prevailing dynamic or dramatic situation—whereas *ffp*, *fp*, and *mfp* clearly indicate absolute dynamic levels. Yet the interpretation of *sf* as a light accent in the music of Beethoven or his contemporaries, even within *piano* contexts, is unsupported by any theoretical discussion of *sf* at that period. In Beethoven's case there is no reliable evidence from the composer himself or from his contemporaries to determine whether his *sfs* were meant to cover the whole range of accents from the slightest to the most powerful, leaving lighter phrasing accents that he might have indicated with > (though he rarely did) to the discretion of the performer, or whether he intended them to denote weighty or even explosive accents (which may well be thought to fit his musical personality). Starke's *Wiener Pianoforte Schule*, to which Beethoven contributed pieces, gave the definition "Sforzando, (*sf, fz*) strong, performed forcefully".[23] Junghanss's contemporaneous treatise defined it as "performed strongly, the note is given sharply", warning only that it should not be so strong "that it becomes unpleasant".[24] Hummel too wrote that it should be "played sharply".[25] Among Beethoven's Viennese contemporaries, Anton Eberl made similarly frequent use of *sf* in his compositions, and Franz Weiss (violin in Schuppanzigh's quartet) also used *fz* rather frequently at all dynamic levels in his string quartets, although he also used >, apparently as a lighter accent, or an accent with *decrescendo*.

Some composers used more complex combinations of these markings, choosing a variety of accent and dynamic instructions for different instruments or voices to obtain the desired effect. Cherubini, who rarely left any ambiguity about the dynamic consequences of his *sf*, shows notable fastidiousness in this respect (Ex. 3.28a). He apparently regarded *sf* as having an absolute dynamic level: in the scherzo of his String Quartet in E flat, for instance, he used the direction *mz.sf* (*mezzo sforzando*) in *piano* passages (Ex. 3.28b).

---

[23] Friedrich Starke: *Wiener Pianoforte-Schule* (Vienna, 1819), 20.
[24] Johann Christian Gottlieb Junghanss: *Theoretich-praktische Pianoforte-Schule* (Vienna, [1820]), 43.
[25] Hummel: *Anweisung*, 2nd edn, 57.

Ex. 3.28a Cherubini: Requiem in C minor, "Pie Jesu".

Ex. 3.28b  Cherubini: String Quartet no. 1/iii.

Schubert may have taken a similar view, for he not only employed > very regularly as an accent sign but also used both *sf* and *sff*, implying a graduated scale, with *sf* as a middle ranking accent. Spohr, however, seems to have regarded *fz* as a relative dynamic marking. Thus, in his 1813 opera *Faust*, he used it in *piano* passages, where a powerful accent seems unlikely (Ex. 3.29a). A variable dynamic level seems also to be envisaged in Ex. 3.29b, where *fz* is used both in *forte* and *piano*, paired in the latter with >.

Ex. 3.29a  Spohr: *Faust*, no. 5.

Ex. 3.29b  Spohr: String Quartet op. 82/2/iv (autograph).
[Allegro]

Schumann used *sf* quite often but, since he utilized an even more extended range of accent markings, it is probable that his intentions were more narrowly conceived, although they were undoubtedly not consistent throughout his career. Schumann's *sf* seems, for the most part, to be a rather powerful accent; he was sparing of its use in *piano* passages, where *fp*, >, and <> are more common. A few prominent 19th-century composers, including Weber, Meyerbeer, and Verdi, employed *sf/fz* even more rarely, apparently preferring the accent mark > as an equivalent.[26]

## *Rinforzando, Rinforzato (rf, rfz, rinf, rfp)*

The implications of this instruction, most often used in an abbreviated form, are particularly problematic. There are essentially three potential meanings: (1) a progressive increase in volume; (2) an accent on a single note; (3) an emphatic delivery (but not necessarily *crescendo*) applying to a group of notes.

The first of these was already established in Italian opera in the 1750s, where *rinforzando* was often written out in full. It was still being taught to students at the Milan Conservatory as a form of *crescendo* in the early 19th century. Asioli's *Principj Elementari di Musica* (1811), written as a dialogue for the students, for their "daily repetition", included the following exchanges: "Q[uestion]. Where does *rinforzando* or *crescendo* occur? A[nswer]. After the *piano*. Q. Where does *diminuendo* or *smorzando* occur? A. After the *forte*."[27] And later: "Q. How is a succession of ascending sounds such as *Do Re Mi Fa Sol La Si Do* to be performed? A. It will begin *piano*, or even *forte*, but always *rinforzando*."[28]

The second category of *rinforzando*, written as an abbreviation (usually *rf* or *rinf*), was already current by the 1770s.

The third does not emerge as a clear concept until the 19th century, although in 1791, the violinist Francesco Galeazzi, in his list of signs, defined <> as "Rinforzando", explaining it simply as *crescendo* to *forte* followed by

---

[26] See "The Hairpin".
[27] Asioli: *Principj*, 44. The reference to *rinforzando* and *crescendo* as "To swell gradually the sound from *piano* to *forte* and *fortissimo*" is retained in John Jousse: *A Compendious Musical Grammar [...] by Bonifacio Asioli [...] translated with considerable additions and improvements by John Jousse* (London, [1825]), 105f.
[28] Asioli: *Principj*, 45.

*decrescendo* to *piano*.²⁹ The usage of *rf*, *rfz*, or *rinf* by some late-18th- and early-19th-century composers often gives the impression that they expected the instruction to apply in a similar manner to Galeazzi's definition, or simply as an increase in intensity, to a group of notes rather than a single one.

A distinction between *rinforzando* and *rinforzato* in Italian, the one meaning "strengthening" and the other "strengthened", which is obscured in the abbreviated forms, was undoubtedly a factor in this diversity of usage. While many non-Italian writers made no distinction between the two words, some specifically associated *rf* as an accent with the word *rinforzato*, including Reichardt and Koch,³⁰ while others specifically identified the difference, such as a reviewer of Koch's *Lexikon* who asserted that *rf* "Should only be used as an abbreviation of *rinforzando*, not *rinforzato*, thus meaning "a gradual increase (*cresc.*) of a single note".³¹ In the early 1780s, however, G. F. Wolf equated *rinf.* with *Rinforte*, explaining it as "somewhat strong",³² as did J. P. Milchmeyer in 1799.³³ Around the same time, A. E. Müller, having defined *rf (rinforzando)* as "reinforced" (*verstärkt*) and *sfz* or *fz (sforzato/forzato)* as "very strong" (*sehr stark*), inconsistently added a footnote, explaining the two terms: "the former signifies a gradual strengthening of one and the same note, the latter a sudden accentuation of it." But he concluded: "Most composers, however, do not make a sufficiently precise distinction in their writing."³⁴ Some twenty years later, August Swoboda defined *rinforzando* as "strengthening, swelling" and *rinforzato* as "strengthened".³⁵ In England at a similar date, J. F. Danneley also distinguished between *rinforzando* and *rinforzato*. He regarded the former as indicating "strengthening of sound" and remarked of the latter: "strengthened; it is thus abbreviated R.F. and is placed over such notes as should be forcibly accented".³⁶ Hugo Riemann made a similar distinction

---

[29] Francesco Galeazzi: *Elementi theorico-practici di musica con un saggio sopra l'arte di suonare il violino [. . .]*, 2 vols (Rome, 1791–96), i, 47.
[30] Koch: 'Rinforzato', *Musikalisches Lexikon*, 1260.
[31] Anon.: *Allgemeine musikalische Zeitung*, vi (1803–4), 43.
[32] Georg Friedrich Wolf: *Unterricht in Klavierspielen. Zweite, ganz umgearbeitete Ausgabe.* (Halle, 1784), 9, §96, 83.
[33] See p. 130 footnote.
[34] Müller: *Klavier- und Fortepiano Schule*, 29.
[35] August Swoboda: *Allgemeine Theorie der Tonkunst* (Vienna, 1826), 141.
[36] John Feltham Danneley: *Dictionary of Music* (London, 1825), 'Rinforzando' and "Rinforzato". No pagination.

more than half a century later, giving the definition "*Rinforzando* (Ital. 'becoming stronger') a strong *crescendo*; *rinforzato*, 'strengthened', is almost identical with *forte assai*, an energetic *forte*".[37] But since composers rarely provided more than *rf or rinf*, these definitions remain in the realm of pure theory. To have determined which of them might most closely suit the passage in question, performers depended on knowledge of the composer's practice or, failing that, on the context and their own instincts. What these efforts to refine the terminology demonstrate is a failed attempt to reconcile conflicting usage, as the following discussion of composers' practices shows.

In scores of the 1750s to 1770s, *rinforzando* is mostly found in contexts that show it to be essentially synonymous with *crescendo*. At that time, both those terms were of recent usage. Niccolò Jommelli, for instance, did not yet employ either of them in the 1743 autograph score of his first version of *Demofoonte*, where he used a succession of terms such as *piano, poco forte, più forte*, and *forte assai* to indicate a gradual increase in volume. In the autograph of his 1753 setting of *Demofoonte*, however, both *rinforzando* and *crescendo il forte* occur. He evidently did not regard the two term as identical; quite often he marked *crescendo il forte* in the strings at the same time as *rinforzando* on sustained notes in wind instruments. This usually occurs over several bars, as in the overtures of his 1753 and 1764 settings of *Demofoonte*.[38] Occasionally he marked *rinforzando* in string parts where he evidently wanted a rapid increase of volume; this intention is demonstrated by a passage in the 1764 version, where at the same time as *rinforzando* in the strings, he indicated *pia:* and *for:* for successive half notes in the horn parts (Ex. 3.30a). A similar use of *rinforzando* over a single bar in string parts also occurs, for instance in the printed score of *L'Olimpiade* (1783), where it surely indicates a particularly rapid and powerful *crescendo*. (Ex. 3.30b).

---

[37] Hugo Riemann: *Musik-Lexikon* (Leipzig, 1882), 772; 5th edn (1900), 949.
[38] Jommelli: *Demofoonte* 1753 version (autograph): Bibl. del Cons. di Musica S. Pietro a Majella, Naples (I-Nc):Rari 1.7.1. 1764 version part autograph: Württembergische Landesbibliothek, Stuttgart (D-Sl): HB XVII 240a–c. Online.

NOTATION OF ACCENTS AND DYNAMICS 113

**Ex. 3.30a** Nicollò Jommelli: *Demofoonte* (1764 version: Württembergische Landesbibliothek, Stuttgart (D-Sl): HB XVII 240a–c), Act I, Scene ii, p. 56. [Allegro]

**Ex. 3.30b** Jommelli: *L'Olimpiade*, Act I, Scene i, in *Recueil des opéra[s] composés par Nicolas Jomelli à la cour du Sérenissime duc de Wirtemberg* (Stuttgart, 1783), Act 1, p. 28.

The terminology for indicating dynamic nuance was evolving rapidly at this period. In a manuscript score of Baldassare Galuppi's *Anfione* (dated 1780),[39] a three-bar *crescendo* is indicated in the overture by *à poco a poco*

---

[39] Galuppi: *Anfione*, Bibliothèque nationale de France, Musique (F-Pn): D-4295. Online.

*il f* in the violins, with *cresc.* in the other instruments; this is the only use of *cresc.* in the piece, but there are several occurrences of *rinf* in other numbers, always from *p* to *f* in a single bar. J. C. Bach, who had worked in Italy for more than a decade before moving to London, also employed both *rinf* and *cresc.* in very similar musical contexts to Italian composers. In a manuscript copy of Bach's *L'Endimione* (1772), a three-bar sequence, *p, rf, fmo* in strings, occurs together with *p, cresc.*, and *f* in timpani.[40] In the autograph score of his cantata *Cefalo e Procri* (1776) he used *rinf* in contexts where it is clearly intended to indicate a *crescendo*, for instance, several times in Procri's A major aria, where it leads rapidly from a *piano* dynamic to *f* (Ex. 3.31a). He generally used *crescendo* where the increase in volume begins a few bars before the *f*, but on one occasion in the concluding D major Terzetto in this cantata, he used the two terms in very similar circumstances, suggesting that the distinction between them was not substantial (Ex. 3.31b).

**Ex. 3.31a** J. C. Bach: *Cefalo e Procri* (autograph), Aria Procris.
[Andante]
Violin 1.

**Ex. 3.31b** J. C. Bach: *Cefalo e Procri*. Terzetto (no tempo term given, but clearly Allegro).
Vn 1.

---

[40] J. C. Bach: *L'Endimione* Overture. Darmstadt Univ. BRD DS Mus.ma 57, 23r. Online.

Boccherini marked *rinf* quite often in the context of an increasing dynamic in earlier works, where he generally used only *f*, *p*, *rinf*, and *dolce* as dynamic markings. He began to mark *crescendo* with increasing frequency during the 1770s, when this newer marking and *rinf* occur in very similar, sometimes identical contexts (Ex. 3.32). In later works, *rinf/rf*, sometimes preceded by *poco*, appears less prominently among a greatly increased repertory of dynamic and expressive markings, but seems always to retain the character of a rapid and intense *crescendo*.[41]

Ex. 3.32 a–b. Boccherini: Quintet in D minor op. 17 no. 5, 1st edn (Paris: M. De la Chevardiere, n.d.[c. 1775]).
1st movement Vn1 (the Vn 2, playing in 3rds with Vn 1 has the same dynamic markings).
[Allegro moderato]
(*a*) bb. 5–9; (*b*) bb. 49–52.

(*a*)

(*b*)

Among younger Italian composers, Luigi Cherubini continued using *rinf* in a similar manner. It often occurs in the final bars of a passage that had earlier been marked *cresc.*, evidently to ensure that the increase of volume continues (and intensifies) right up to the point of arrival at *fortissimo*. An example from his overture to *Anacréon* provides clear proof of its function as an intensification of a continuing *crescendo*; in bar 76 of the Allegro he marked *cresc. poco a poco* and in bar 82 *rinf*, but the piccolo, coming in at bar 80, is marked *cresc.* in bar 82, as are the alto and tenor trombones in bar 86 at the same time as *cresc.* in timpani, preceding *ff* in bar 88 (Ex. 3.33).

---

[41] Loukia Myrto Droopoulou: *Dynamic, Articulation and Special Effect Markings in Manuscript Sources of Boccherini's String Quintets* (diss., University of York, 2008), https://etheses.whiterose.ac.uk/14119/1/495873.pdf.

116   CLASSICAL AND ROMANTIC PERFORMING PRACTICE

**Ex. 3.33**  Cherubini: Ouverture *Anacréon* (Paris [c. 1803]), bb. 80–86. [Allegro]

Haydn, who for most of his life was very sparing with dynamic instructions, rarely used *rinforzando*, but, where he did, he evidently intended it as a brief intensification of volume, as in the final movement of his String Quartet op. 71 no. 2, where it marks the transition from *sempre più piano* to the return of the principal theme (Ex. 3.34).

NOTATION OF ACCENTS AND DYNAMICS 117

Ex. 3.34 Haydn: String Quartet op. 71/2/iv.
[Allegretto]

Among Haydn's younger contemporaries, Dussek employed the instruction frequently; in contexts that unambiguously indicate *crescendo* (Ex. 3.35a), it sometimes appears among a complex of dynamic and expressive instructions, as an intensification for very short figures (Ex. 3.35b). Dussek's usage is in line with Clementi's definition: "to swell 2, 3, or 4 notes",[42] and with J. B. Cramer's similar explanation.[43] In their compositions, both Clementi and Cramer certainly employed it in this way.

Ex. 3.35a Dussek: String Quartet No. 1 in G major (Breitkopf & Härtel, [c. 1806]), 1st edn.
Violin 1 (These dynamics supplement the markings in the autograph score).
[Rondo: Tempo di Polacca quasi Andante]

---

[42] Muzio Clementi: *Introduction to the Art of Playing on the Piano Forte* (London, 1801), 9.
[43] John Baptist Cramer, *J. B. Cramer's Instructions for the Piano Forte* (London, [c. 1812]), 45.

Ex. 3.35b  Dussek: Piano Sonata op. 64, "Le retour à Paris" (Paris, Pleyel, [1808]), 2nd movement.

By the 1820s most musicians employed only *crescendo* or ⟨, to specify an increase in volume. Beethoven, however, continued using *rinforzando* as well as *crescendo*. He may have become aware of its implications already during his early years in Bonn, perhaps encountering it in the music of the Maestro di Capella, Andrea Luchesi, who used both terms, for instance in his Sei Sonate per il Cembalo con l'accompagmento di un violino (1772). A reference to *rinforzando* in a performance by the prince-archbishop's court orchestra in 1791, in which Beethoven played viola, might describe a special effect, or might simply be a synonym for *crescendo*: "the performance could not be more precise than it was. Such a close observation of the *piano*, the *forte*, the *rinforzando*, such a swelling, and gradual increase of the sound, and then a decrease, from the greatest strength to the quietest volume—formerly, this was heard only in Mannheim."[44] Certainly, Beethoven employed the term throughout his career to mean an increase in volume that was not synonymous with *crescendo*. This is strongly suggested by an alteration in the autograph of his Violin Sonata op. 24; he originally wrote *cres:* in the violin part, but before adding the dynamic in the piano part, changed it to *rinf:* (Ex. 3.36a). Other instances where he evidently envisaged a more emphatic treatment of a phrase than if he marked *cres.* occur in the Rondo of the same sonata (Ex. 3.36b) and in the Piano Sonata op 26 (Ex. 3.36c), where the placing of the instruction clearly indicates that it applies only to a particular line in the texture. In the Adagio of the "Waldstein" Sonata he used it in circumstances that leave no doubt about its function as a powerful *crescendo* (Ex. 3.36d). Sometimes, however, he employed *rinforzando* for a longer passage, as in the

---

[44] Anon.: 'Noch etwas vom Kurköllnischen Orchester', *Musikalische Realzeitung*, 1791, 376.

Allegretto ma non troppo of the String Quartet op. 95, where he could hardly have intended a progressive *crescendo*; in that case, he marked a four-bar thematic passage in the cello *rinforzando*, while the other parts remained *piano*, and despite the 1st violin taking over the theme immediately after the cello, no further dynamic is marked until *crescendo* several bars later (Ex. 3.36e). In the last movement of the same quartet, the cello is also marked *rinforz.* for a melodically important figure, but without an obvious *crescendo* implication (Ex. 3.36f).

**Ex. 3.36a** Beethoven: Violin Sonata op. 24/i, b. 51ff (autograph).
[Allegro]

**Ex. 3.36b** Beethoven: op. 24/iv b. 99f., 1st edn (Vienna, Mollo, [1801]).
[Rondo: Allegro ma non troppo]

**Ex. 3.36c** Beethoven: Piano Sonata op. 26/i. (The autograph is not extant, and the 1st edn marks *rf*, but Beethoven almost certainly wrote *rinf* as usual. The 1860s *Gesamtausgabe* however printed *sf*.)
[Andante con variazioni]

**Ex. 3.36d** Beethoven: Piano Sonata op. 53/ii.
[Adagio molto]

**Ex. 3.36e** Beethoven: String Quartet op. 95/ii.
[Allegretto ma non troppo]

Ex. 3.36f Beethoven: String Quartet op. 95/iv.
[Allegretto agitato]

Nevertheless, Beethoven's late string quartets contain passages in which intensification of *crescendo* seems to be envisaged (Ex. 3.37a–c). But inconsistencies abound (especially on the part of copyists or engravers). In the *Missa solemnis*, the first edition score and the 1860s *Gesamtausgabe* replaced Beethoven's *rinforz* with *rf*. This was already noted in 1876, together with many other places where printed editions (including 1st editions and the *Gesamtausgabe*) obscured Beethoven's *rinforzando* instructions by printing *rf* as if it were an accent on a single note.[45]

Ex. 3.37a Beethoven: op. 135/iii.

[45] Anon.: *Leipziger Allgemeine musikalische Zeitung*, xi (1876), 469f.

**Ex. 3.37b** Beethoven: String Quartet op. 127/ii. Copyist's score with Beethoven's corrections.
[Adagio molto espressivo]

**Ex. 3.37c** Beethoven: String Quartet op. 132/iii (autograph).
[Molto adagio]

During the 19th century, the use of *rinforzando* to indicate a special kind of swell in volume becomes increasingly rare, but it was still occasionally used simply as a synonym for *crescendo*. A Viennese translation and revision of Pleyel's and Dussek's *Méthode* stated that "*Rinforzando* (strengthened) is very often used instead of *crescendo*",[46] and a journal report on a new keyboard instrument, the Melodica, observed that "the mechanism permits a pleasant *rinforzando* and *decrescendo*".[47] Although increasingly fewer composers employed it in that sense, Rossini's use of *rf* in the overture to his final opera *Guillaume Tell* indicates that he regarded it as an intensification of *crescendo*. In the Allegro, after 38 bars of *p* and *pp*, three bars of *cresc.* is followed by three of *rf*, leading to *ff*. This is marked in the 1829 full score, but the piano reduction in the contemporaneous vocal score merely gives six bars of *crescendo*, with continuation lines.[48] Even Donizetti still, very occasionally, used the term in that way, for instance in the sequence *crescendo a poco a poco—rinforzando—f* in the overture to *Anna Bolena* (1830). In the 1830s, August Gathy could still define *rinforzando* simply as "reinforcing, continually stronger; now one, now several notes, indeed bars",[49] and Henri Herz, in his 1838 *Méthode*, explicitly stated: "The *rinforzando* is a more abrupt *crescendo* because of the shorter space in which it is confined."[50] A few composers continued using it in this sense. Joachim Raff, for instance, in his Phantasie für Pianoforte op. 119, employed the instruction *rinforzando assai* for a one-bar transition from *p* to *f* and, later in the piece, *rinforz.* following ⋖ where he probably expected an intensification of the increase in volume.[51]

Although some theorists continued to acknowledge that *rinforzando*, strictly speaking, indicated a progressive increase in volume, this was not, by the middle years of the century, how most composers used it. The function of the rapidly swelling *rinforzando* was superseded by ⋖ or terms such as *crescendo molto*, and by the second half of the century, many musicians no longer seem to have understood this aspect of earlier practice.

### *rf* as Accent

Some 18th-century composers used *rf* or *rinf* not as an instruction for getting louder, but solely as an accent on a single note. Reichardt stated explicitly

---

[46] *Pleyel's Clavier-Schule* (Vienna, Steiner, [c. 1815]), 38.
[47] Anon.: *Allgemeine musikalische Zeitung*, xxiii (1821), 712.
[48] Rossini: *Guillaume Tell*, full score (Paris, Trupenas, 1829).
[49] August Gathy: *Musikalisches Conversations-Lexikon Encyklopädie der gesammten Musik-Wissenschaft für Künstler, Kunstfreunde und Gebildete* (Leipzig, Hamburg, and Itzehoe, 1835), 381. This definition was retained in the 3rd edn, 1871, 326.
[50] Henri Herz: *Méthode*, 17.
[51] Joachim Raff: Phantasie für Pianoforte op. 119 (Kistner, [1866]), 6 and 8 (on IMSLP).

in 1776 that *rinforzato (rf.)* "should signify nothing more than a small pressure, an accent, on the note on which it stands".[52] Several sources from the beginning of the 19th century show that Reichardt's understanding of *rf* had gained currency among some German musicians. J. H. Knecht, like many authors, failed to appreciate the significance of the Italian words, writing: "*Rinforzando* abbreviated *rinf.* or *rf.*, strengthened, applies only to a single note to which one should give a strong emphasis"—he made no mention of a *crescendo* element—while "*sforzato*, abbreviated *sf.* or *sfz.*, forcefully strengthened, is applied to a single note, to which one must give a forceful but only briefly lasting emphasis".[53] As implied by Müller's definition,[54] some authorities simply saw *rf/rinf* as a less powerful accent than *sforzato*, and thus Koch complained:

> Various composers mark the notes which should be accented with the word *rinforzato* (strengthened), which is shown in abbreviated form as *rf.* Who will not have noticed, however, that the notes thus marked are for the most part accented too strongly and stridently and that one mixes up the *rf* as an abbreviation for *rinforzato* with the *sf* as an abbreviation for the word *sforzato* (exploded), which the composer only uses in cases where the note should be heavily accented, not with the gentler kind of accent which is under discussion here.[55]

F. J. Fröhlich, too, viewed the distinction between the two terms as one of degree rather than kind, giving the following definitions: "sf, sforzato, sforz, forzando, exploded, seize the note strongly, rinforzando, rfz. less".[56] In the 1830s a contributor to Schilling's *Encyclopädie*, following Koch, stated: "The only difference between *sforzando* and *rinforzando* is a higher degree of intensity in performance; while the latter needs only a gentle pressure or accent on the note, the former requires a very strong one."[57] This difference was still recognized later in the century by Dommer, who defined *rinforzato, rf, rfz* as "firmly accented, though not so powerfully as *sfz* (*sforzando, sforzato*). One must therefore distinguish between the two kinds of attack".[58] Fétis in 1834, however, simply equated *rf* with *sf*, and *fz* as accents over one or more notes, without any comment about their relative strength.[59]

[52] Reichardt: *Ueber die Pflichten*, 68.
[53] Knecht: *Katechismus*, 50f.
[54] See p. 111.
[55] Koch: 'Accent', *Musikalisches Lexikon*, 54.
[56] Franz Joseph Fröhlich: *Vollständige theoretisch-praktische Musikschule* (Bonn, 1810–11), i. 50.
[57] Anon.: 'Sforzando' in Schilling (ed.), *Encyclopädie*, vi, 362.
[58] Dommer: *Musikalisches Lexikon*, 733.
[59] François-Joseph Fétis: *La musique mise à la portée de tout le Monde*, 2nd edn (Paris, 1834), 39.

In the absence of further evidence, it remains uncertain whether Reichardt was the first to propose the use of *rf* simply as an accent, but he certainly used it with that meaning in his own compositions, which were quite widely known. In the printed score of his Cantata *Ariadne auf Naxos* (1780), *rf* occurs frequently (Ex. 3.38a); in that work he did not employ either *sf* or *fz*, but he used *fp*. For a short figure where an Italian composer might have employed *rinforzando* he writes *p cresc sin all fortiss*. In his very late Piano Sonata in F minor he still used *rf* occasionally (Ex. 3.38b), but also, more rarely, *sf*, presumably as a stronger accent. In other works, he employed a range of signs to convey various kinds of accentuation.

**Ex. 3.38a** J. F. Reichardt: *Ariadne auf Naxos* (Leipzig, 1780), 22.
[Mit Ernst und Nachdruck]

**Ex. 3.38b** Reichardt: Grand Sonate in F minor (Leipzig, Breitkopf & Härtel [c. 1812]).
[Larghetto (5 flats)]

Among Reichardt's younger contemporaries, Haydn's pupil Ignaz Pleyel used *rinf* very frequently in contexts where it can only be understood as an accent, and since he often used *fz* too, it was clearly a less powerful one. In Pleyel's works, *rinf* usually occurs in *piano* passages, whereas *fz* is most often used in *forte*. Many instances make it clear that he did not regard *rinf* as a synonym for *crescendo* (Ex. 3.39a–b). Another composer of a younger generation who used *rf* in the sense of an accent less powerful than *fz* was George Onslow. Carl Czerny, too, evidently regarded it as a relatively light accent.

Ex. 3.39a  Pleyel: String Quartet op. 2 no. 1, B 307 (Mannheim, Götz, c. 1788).

Ex. 3.39b  Pleyel: 8e Livre de Quatuors, Quartet 1, B 353 (Paris, Imbault, c. 1791).

Brahms also used *rf* as an accent on individual notes. Like Onslow and Czerny, he clearly used it as a relatively gentle accent, as on the first page of his Piano Sonata op. 1, where *rf* and *sf* appear in close proximity (Ex. 3.40a). He doubtless derived this usage from his Hamburg teacher Eduard Marxen (Ex. 3.40b). The abbreviation *rf* occurs throughout Brahms's works until at least as late as the Double Concerto op. 102, where he made a revision in the Stichvorlage, substituting *rf* for *sf* (Ex. 3.41a–b), but it becomes less frequent in later works, where he used *sf* almost exclusively as an accent abbreviation, apparently leaving it to the sensitivity of the performer to give it the appropriate degree of attack. Exceptional uses of the abbreviation *rinf.* occur in his Piano Trio op. 87, where he evidently intended it to apply to several bars in the strings against a particularly weighty piano texture (Ex. 3.42a), and in the

Clarinet Quintet op. 115, where he evidently expected it to elicit extra weight on a three-note figure (Ex. 3.42b).

Ex. 3.40a  Brahms: Piano Sonata op. 1 (Leipzig, Breitkopf & Härtel [1854]), i. [Allegro]

Ex. 3.40b  Eduard Marxen: Capriccio op. 47 (Hamburg, Schuberth, 1841).

128    CLASSICAL AND ROMANTIC PERFORMING PRACTICE

**Ex. 3.41a**  Brahms: Double Concerto op. 102/i/309ff. Copyist's score with Brahms's revision of *sf* to *rf*.
[Allegro]

**Ex. 3.41b**  1st edn score p. 48.

**Ex. 3.42a**  Brahms: Piano Trio op. 87/i/139ff.
[Allegro]

**Ex. 3.42b**  Brahms: Clarinet Quintet, op. 115/i, 1st edn, p. 57.
[Allegro]

Saint-Saëns, who utilized *rf* occasionally, seems initially to have regarded it as an accent or emphasis somewhat less strong than *sf*, to judge by its occurrence in his Six Bagatelles op. 3, where he also used both instructions.[60] Somewhat later, however, his understanding of the term seems to have changed. He occasionally used the abbreviation *rinf* in contexts where it apparently indicated a progressive increase in volume, for instance, in the string parts of his Piano Quintet op. 14 during a *cresc.* in the piano part,[61] and in his Album pour Piano op. 72, in the first of four bars leading from *f* to *ff*.[62] The shift in theoretical explanation of *rinforzando* is nicely encapsulated in a late-19th-century revision of Cramer's piano treatise, which states: "*Rinforzando (rf, rfz)* strengthened. Stands over single notes";[63] whereas Cramer's original had "Rinforzando, Increase the sound of several notes, this sign ⎯⎯ is often times substituted."[64]

### *Rinforzando* as "Strengthened"

During the 19th century the ambiguity of this term discouraged many composers from using it at all, since there were other instructions or signs that fulfilled its potential functions more clearly. In the 1833, Carl Gollmick directly addressed this ambiguity, commenting:

> About the meaning of the *rinf.* most doubts prevail, since almost all textbooks and dictionaries contradict each other, and every musician uses it in his own way. Many take it as synonymous with *sforz.*, as reinforced; other as more moderate than that; some, like *crescendo*, as strengthening, others as a more intensive *crescendo*; and again others as constantly lively, strong. Since there are sufficient signs for sudden and less sudden accentuation on the individual note, as well as for the sudden and less sudden *crescendo*, the definition of *rinf.* in Milchmeyer's Clavierschule, as continuously lively, strong, leading a lively conversation as it were—for which we do not yet have an adequate sign—might be most appropriate.

---

[60] Saint-Saëns: Six Bagatelles op. 3 (Paris, Richault [1856]), on pages 12 and 23.
[61] Saint-Saëns: Piano Quintet op. 14 (Paris, Maho [1865]), 53.
[62] Saint-Saëns: Album pour Piano op. 72 (Paris, Durand [1884]), 12.
[63] *Praktische Pianoforte Schule . . . von J. B. Cramer. Neueste umgearbeitet und vervollständigste Ausgabe* (Leipzig, [c. 1872]), 39.
[64] Cramer: *J. B. Cramer's Instructions*, 45.

A footnote to the last sentence states: "In my compositions that have been published so far, all occurrences of *rinf.* are to be understood in this latter sense."[65] Later in the same decade, after defining *Rinforzando* as "strengthening" [verstärkend], a contributor to Schilling's *Encyclopädie* provided a somewhat convoluted explanation:

> [*Rinforzando*] means that one or, depending on the nature of the melody, several notes, even bars, are played with greater tonal strength, and that they should receive a certain sharpened accent or emphasis. The word should literally be synonymously with *crescendo*, and only *sforzando* (see that) should signify sudden accentuation of a note; but these are often confused, and in recent times *rinforzando* is used almost more than *sforzando* for this short *forte*, which only extends to the one or two notes above or below which it is located. The expression *rinforzato*, which is only the participle of the passive form of the verb *rinforzare*, and must therefore be translated as strengthened, has exactly the same meaning in music as *rinforzando*, the participle of the active form.[66]

Schumann and Liszt apparently understood *rinf.* like Gollmick, as "continuously lively, strong". Schumann used it quite liberally in earlier works, but with decreasing frequency in later ones. It appears in his Concert ohne Orchestre op. 14, but in his revision of this composition as Dritte Grosse Sonate he expunged it (Ex. 3.43a–b). In Carnaval op. 9, Schumann employed both the word and the abbreviation *rfz*, using the latter as an accent marking, and the contexts in which he used *rfz* suggests that he regarded it as stronger than *sf* (Ex. 3.43c).

Ex. 3.43a Schumann: Concert ohne Orchester op. 14, 1st edn (1836) bb. 8–11. [Allegro brillante]

---

[65] Gollmick: *Kritische Terminologie*, 2. Gollmick was, in fact, mistaken in the attribution of his preferred meaning to Milchmeyer, who wrote: "Rinforte [sic], rf. always stronger, gradually stronger" (*Die wahre Art*, 53).
[66] a.: 'Rinforzando' in Schilling (ed.): *Encyclopädie*, vi, 8.

NOTATION OF ACCENTS AND DYNAMICS    131

Ex. 3.43b  2nd revised edn as Dritte grosse Sonate (1853) bb. 8–11.
[Allegro]

Ex. 3.43c  Schumann: *Carnaval* "Florestan".
[Passionato]

Liszt's early piano piece "Harmonies poétiques et religieuses" contains three occurrences of *rinforz.*, all of which indicate a more emphatic delivery than the surrounding bars, but not necessarily a *crescendo* (Ex. 3.44a–c). In his *Années de pèlerinage*, *rinforzando* occurs frequently in contexts where it seems to imply intensity rather than *crescendo*. In "Orage", its first appearance might imply increasing volume, but later, within an extended section marked *fff*, Liszt employs both *rinforz.*, where *crescendo* can scarcely be envisaged, and *rfz*, apparently regarding the latter abbreviation, like Schumann, as a very powerful accent on a single note (Ex. 3.45a). In the earlier version of "Au bord d'une source", *rinforz.* occurs in conjunction with a *diminuendo* sign (Ex. 3.45b).

Ex. 3.44  a–c. Liszt: "Harmonies Poétiques et Religieuses" (Leipzig, Hoffmeister, [1835]).

(a)
[Agitato assai]

**Ex. 3.44** Continued

(b)
[Adagio religioso]

(c)

**Ex. 3.45a** Liszt: *Années de pèlerinage* II "Orage".
[Più moto]

**Ex. 3.45b** Liszt: "Au bord d'une source", in *Album d'un voyageur* (1841).
[Allegretto]

Comments in a review of a new edition of Mozart's *Don Giovanni* in 1870 indicate that some later 19th-century musicians still saw the instruction as applicable to a group of notes; referring to Mozart's use of *sf*, the reviewer stated: "here *sf* is evidently employed in a similar sense to that in which recently the word *rinforzando* has sometimes been used to denote the emphatic highlighting of a whole series of notes."[67] At the end of the century, Puccini still used it in this sense in *Tosca* (Ex. 3.46).

**Ex. 3.46** Puccini: *Tosca* (Full score, Ricordi, 1900), Act II, p. 317.
[Andante lento appassionato]

[67] F. Faisst: 'Mozart's Don Giovanni' [ed. Bernhard Gugler], *Neue Berliner Musikzeitung*, xxiv (1870), 122.

## Signs as Accent Markings

Signs designating various types of accents, proposed and used to a limited extent by such composer-performers as Veracini and Geminiani in the earlier part of the 18th century, failed to gain currency. It was not until the last decades of the century that a significant number of composers began to adopt signs for accents. During the 19th century a growing number of signs began to be used alongside the established Italian terms and their abbreviations; but here too there were many ambiguities, and scrutiny of individual composers' practices reveals considerable divergence of usage. With the introduction of a wider range of such markings, the problem of understanding the conventions for applying accentuation and dynamic nuance where none was marked was largely superseded by the problem of recognizing what composers intended to convey by their various performance instructions.

The number of signs introduced during the last few decades of the 18th century and the first half of the 19th century was considerable. A glance at treatises published during this period reveals a mixture of signs that became widely adopted and others that failed to gain acceptance and are seldom encountered in music of the period. The accent signs proposed and employed during these years reflect the growing preoccupation of composers and theorists with conveying ever finer levels of expressiveness to the performer. It was accepted in the 18th century that the metrical accentuation was often overridden by the accentuation necessary to shape and characterize a melody (rhythmic accentuation), and many theorists stressed that recognition of this type of accentuation was vital to correct performance. Thus, late-18th- and early-19th-century composers became increasingly concerned to specify rhythmic and expressive accentuation more precisely.

One important factor was the rapid expansion of music printing, much of which was aimed at an amateur market. In these circumstances, composers were receptive to methods of indicating their envisaged emphases in a melody. Since this generally necessitated a degree of accent less powerful than such markings as *fp*, *sf*, or *fz* might suggest, several graphic signs and instructions were proposed and employed. Most of these either failed altogether to gain currency or, after a period of sporadic use, achieved more widespread acceptance, though often with significantly different implications from those originally envisaged. In 1776, Reichardt had suggested ▶ to indicate where a stress should fall. He considered that it should "merely signify that a note, whether alone or with several in one bowstroke, should be brought out with a somewhat stronger pressure of the bow. Its form shows, at the same time, the increase of pressure. This has the same effect as a small point of light in painting" (Ex. 3.47a).[68] Reichardt used it in some of his own scores (Ex. 3.47b), but it seems not to have been adopted by others, despite Koch's sponsorship of it in his widely read *Lexikon*.[69]

Ex. 3.47a J. F. Reichardt: *Ueber die Pflichten*, 82.

Ex. 3.47b J. F. Reichardt: *Brenno* [comp. 1797/8, published 1801–2. Act 1, p. 17. [Allegro con brio]

Domenico Corri's use, in the 1780s, of a similar sign ◄ above a note, to show that "particular strength is to be given to it",[70] was probably independent of Reichardt. Türk proposed ∧ to denote an accent less intense than

---

[68] Reichardt: *Ueber die Pflichten*, 81.
[69] Koch: 'Accentuiren' in *Musikalisches Lexikon*, 53.
[70] Domenico Corri: *A Select Collection of the Most Admired Songs, Duetts, &c.*, 3 vols. (Edinburgh, [c. 1782]), i, 8.

would have been implied by *sf*. He described it in his 1789 *Klavierschule*,[71] explaining that he had already used it in his *Sechs leichte Klaviersonaten* of 1783. G. F. Wolf adopted this sign as a "gentle pressure" (*sanften Druck*) in the third edition of his *Unterricht*, published the same year as Türk's treatise,[72] and it was also used by J. F. Schubert in his *Singe-Schule* of 1804.[73] A generation later, Hummel, perhaps influenced by Türk, used ʌ and + in his piano method (Türk, like Schulz, had also used + as a sign for marking rhythmic accents),[74] explaining the former as a more pronounced accent than the latter.[75] The sign ʌ was not, however, used to any great extent by composers at this stage, although an inverted form (v) occurs occasionally as an accent sign in Haydn's later works. An example can be found in the autograph of the String Quartet op. 77 no. 1, though it is not entirely clear what kind of accent the sign was meant to convey and whether it was derived from Türk's sign (Ex. 3.48). At about the same time, the short *decrescendo* sign (>) was also beginning to be used by some composers, including Haydn, as a means of specifying accentuation. Before the general adoption of any of these various accent signs, however, the *staccato* mark (either stroke, dot, or wedge, but most commonly stroke) was often used not only to indicate separation but also, sometimes, simply to indicate accent.

Ex. 3.48 Haydn, op. 77 no. 1/ii.

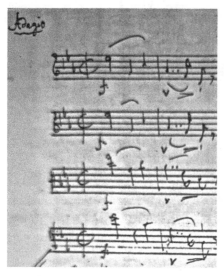

[71] Türk: *Klavierschule*, 337.
[72] Wolf: *Unterricht im Klavierspiel. Erster Theil. Dritte, verbesserte und vermehrte Auflage* (Halle, 1789), 4, §14, 38.
[73] Schubert: *Singe-Schule*, 133f.
[74] See Exx. 1.10 and 1.17.
[75] Hummel: *Anweisung*, 2nd edn, 441 (footnote).

## The *Staccato* Mark (∣.)

The accent element in *staccato* was discussed by theorists at an early stage, but the *staccato* mark's multiple functions were never clearly differentiated. Sometimes it seems to have been used merely to shorten a note, sometimes to indicate both shortening and emphasis, sometimes to indicate accent without shortening, and sometimes merely to indicate that notes should not be slurred.[76] This agglomeration of functions was acknowledged in Walther's early-18th-century consideration of the term, in which he derived the word's two alternative forms, *staccato* and *stoccato*, from different roots. He observed:

> Staccato or Stoccato is almost synonymous with spiccato, indicating that the bowstrokes must be short without dragging and well separated from each other.[77] The first derives from staccare, separate, detach, and this word from taccare, stick and dis[taccare]; or better from attaccare, attach, stick to, and instead of the syllable at-, dis-, or s- signify ent- [in German]. The second [of these terms] however derives from stocco, a stick, and means pushed, not pulled. The sign for this, when the word staccato or stoccato are absent, is a little stroke over or under the note, thus: ∣ .[78]

Agricola's 1757 revised version of Tosi's treatise on singing used the *staccato* mark unequivocally as a sign for accent without any implication of separation, instructing the pupil that a clear marking of the beat was necessary "not only for the sake of clarity but also for an all the more secure maintenance of steady tempo",[79] and illustrated this with an example (Ex. 3.49a). So, too, did Leopold Mozart (Ex. 3.49b).[80] But strokes indicating accent may easily be confused with the diametrically opposite usage, alluded to by Schulz and Türk, where they signified only the shortening necessary at the end of a musical phrase to separate it from the following one, in which case the note would generally be performed very lightly.[81]

---

[76] For further discussion of these signs as articulation, rather than accent marks, see Ch. 6.
[77] See Ch. 5 and Ch. 7 for further discussion of the various implications of *spiccato*.
[78] Johann Gottfried Walther: 'Staccato' in *Musicalisches Lexicon* (Leipzig, 1732), 575.
[79] Johann Friedrich Agricola: *Anleitung zur Singkunst* (Berlin, 1757), 129.
[80] Mozart: *Versuch*, VI, §8, 116.
[81] See Exx. 4.6 and 6.16.

Ex. 3.49a  Agricola: *Anleitung zur Singkunst*, 129.

Ex. 3.49b  Mozart: *Versuch*, 116.

Reference to the accent properties of the vertical stroke can be found in many 18th- and 19th-century sources. Thomas Busby, having observed in his *Dictionary* that notes marked with strokes "are to be played in a short, distinct, and pointed manner",[82] also commented that a dot, too, "when stationed over a note, implies that such a note is to be played in a strong and striking manner".[83] Where a distinction was made between dot and stroke it was predominantly the latter that was seen by the majority of early-19th-century German musicians as inherently having the more pronounced accent function. Knecht, echoing Vogler, instructed that notes with strokes should be "staccatoed long and sharply" and that those with dots should be "tipped briefly and daintily".[84] At least one French string method, the Paris Conservatoire *Méthode de violoncelle*, approached Knecht's view, observing: "When the [bow]stroke requires that each note be hammered (*martelé*), they are separated as in the second example [Ex. 3.50]. If the sign is lengthened a little on the note in this manner, the bow is lengthened a little more; but if there are only dots, one makes the bowstroke very short and far from the bridge, so that the sound is round and the attack [*martellement*] is soft to the ear."[85]

Ex. 3.50  Baillot et al.: *Méthode de violoncelle*, 128.

---

[82] Busby: *A Complete Dictionary of Music*, 52.
[83] Busby: *Dictionary*, 60.
[84] Justin Heinrich Knecht: *Knechts allgemeiner musikalischer Katechismus*, 4th edn (Freyburg, 1816), 48. This was repeated, word for word, in Matthäus Zeheter and Max Winkler: *Vollständige theoretisch-praktische Generalbass- und Harmonielehre* (Nördlingen, 1845), 28.
[85] Pierre Marie François de Sales Baillot, Jean Henri Levasseur, Charles-Simon Catel, and Charles-Nicolas Baudiot: *Méthode de violoncelle du Conservatoire* (Paris, 1804), 128.

Fröhlich referred to strokes as indicating "the more powerful staccato" and dots as indicating "the gentler one".[86] In the *Violinschule* of Mendelssohn's and Schumann's colleague Ferdinand David, accented on-string *martelé* bowstrokes were associated with *staccato* strokes, while *staccato* dots were used to indicate the lighter elastic *staccato* bowstrokes.[87] This interpretation was followed by many German authors. Louis Schubert stated in his *Violinschule* that the stroke requires "a degree of accent much stronger than the dot".[88] Among other writers who echoed David's usage, not necessarily referring to string playing, was Dommer, who noted that the wedge-shaped, pointed mark indicated "the real short and sharp staccato", while the dot signified "a gentler, rounder, less pointed staccato";[89] Hermann Mendel, observing that *staccato* was indicated by dots or strokes, commented: "These latter commonly serve as accentuation";[90] and Riemann remarked: "When staccato marks are distinguished in two forms, namely • and |, the | indicates a sharp, the • a light staccato."[91] In the pedagogic tradition of German violin playing, the Joachim and Moser *Violinschule* of 1905 also lent authority to that interpretation. In England this notation was adopted, for instance, by J. M. Fleming in his *Practical Violin School* of 1886.[92]

In France, however, a rather different view of the two forms of *staccato* mark became normal during the 19th century despite the treatment of *staccato* in the 1804 *Méthode de violoncelle*. From at least Baillot's *L'art du violon* (1835) onwards, the French seem generally to have regarded the stroke (wedge) as not only shorter, but also lighter than the dot. Such an interpretation is suggested by many mid-19th-century references, for example the definition of *Piqué* in the *Dictionnaire de musique* endorsed by Halévy in 1854, which commented that such passages were marked with strokes (*point allongé*) and that these notes were to be "equally marked by dry and detached strokes of the tongue or bow".[93] In *L'art du violon* Baillot used the dot to indicate sharply accented *martelé*, where the bow remains in contact with the string, and strokes (wedges) for light, elastic bowstrokes.[94] And Emile Sauret,

---

[86] Fröhlich: *Musikschule*, iii, 49.
[87] Ferdinand David: *Violinschule* (Leipzig, 1864), esp. ii, 37ff.
[88] Louis Schubert: *Violinschule nach modernen Principien* op. 50 (Brunswick, [1883]), ii, 34 (with German, French, and English texts).
[89] Dommer: 'Abstossen' in *Musikalisches Lexicon*, 5.
[90] Mendel: 'Bewegung' in *Musikalisches Conversations-Lexikon*, i, 608.
[91] Riemann: *New Pianoforte School/Neue Klavierschule*, 17.
[92] J. M. Fleming: *The Practical Violin School for Home Students* (London, 1886), 249, 251.
[93] Escudier (frères): *Dictionnaire de musique théorique et historique* (Paris, 1854), ii, 127.
[94] Baillot: *L'art du violon*, esp. 92f.

among other French string players, followed him in associating the dot with *martelé*.⁹⁵ The description of the two marks in the early-20th-century *Encyclopédie de la musique* reflects this French usage (though the association of the dot with *martelé* is not explicit), indicating the persistence of this disparity between French and German practice: the stroke (*point allongé*) was described as betokening that the note "ought to be separated, struck very lightly, almost dryly [. . .] depriving the note of three-quarters of its value"; whereas the dot (*point rond*) meant that "these notes ought to be lightly quitted, however, in a less short, less dry manner than with the stroke".⁹⁶

Outside France, Baillot's system rather than David's was also adopted by some influential pedagogues. The Viennese violinist Jacob Dont, for instance, used dots to designate a *martelé* bowstroke (*gehämmert*) and strokes (wedges) to signify that notes should be played with a springing bow (*mit springendem Bogen*) in his 1874 edition of exercises from Spohr's *Violinschule*;⁹⁷ and the Czech violinist Otakar Ševčík made a similar use of these signs in his extremely influential teaching material, thus helping to perpetuate the confusion to the present day.⁹⁸ On the other hand, Fétis explained in 1864: "When the notes must be forcefully detached [. . .], they are surmounted by elongated dots. If they must be detached lightly, the dots above them are round."⁹⁹

Many 18th- and 19th-century German composers continued employing vertical strokes in contexts where the principal purpose seems to have been accentual.¹⁰⁰ The fact that Haydn did not expect performers always to see it as necessarily shortening the note is shown by occasions such as the first movement of Symphony no. 91, where he added the word *staccato* to ensure that Oboe 2 shortened the notes to correspond with the notation in Violin 2 (Ex. 3.51).

---

⁹⁵ Emil Sauret: *Gradus ad Parnassum du violiniste* op. 36 (Leipzig, [c. 1890]), 5.
⁹⁶ Albert Lavignac and Lionel de la Laurencie: *Encyclopédie de la musique et dictionnaire du Conservatoire* (Paris, 1920–31), pt. 2, 'Technique-esthetique-pédagogie', 335.
⁹⁷ Dont: *Zwölf Uebungen aus der Violinschule von L. Spohr mit Anmerkungen, Ergänzungen des Fingersatzes der Bogen-Stricharten und der Tonschattierungszeichen* (Vienna, 1874). Spohr himself had not intended any springing bowstrokes in these exercises.
⁹⁸ Ševčík: *Schule der Violine-Technik* op. 1 (Leipzig, 1881), *Schule der Bogentechnik* op. 2 (Leipzig, 1895), etc.
⁹⁹ François-Joseph Fétis: *Manuel des principes de musique* (Paris, 1864), 67.
¹⁰⁰ The question where and when a distinction between dots and strokes was intended in 18th- and early-19th-century music is addressed in Ch. 6.

NOTATION OF ACCENTS AND DYNAMICS 141

Ex. 3.51 Haydn: Symphony no. 91/i.
[Allegro assai]

Similar instances occur at the beginning of Haydn's Symphony no. 102 (see Ex. 6.24), and in Mozart's *Don Giovanni* (see Ex. 6.23). Elsewhere in Mozart's opera, ׀ corresponds with *fp* and seems not to indicate shortening (above Ex. 3.15), and in another number from the opera Mozart ensured that the sign would not be taken as shortening the note by also writing *Ten[uto]* (Ex. 3.52a). In Mozart's Symphony no. 41 the bold strokes over the tied whole-notes in the viola and bass (Ex. 3.52b) may have been intended merely to ensure that players did not assume that ties were meant to continue throughout this passage; but they may also suggest an accent, slightly stronger than the normal metrical accent, at the beginning of each new note. In the music of Mozart's pupil Süssmayr, too, strokes seem sometimes to be used essentially as accents (Ex. 3.53).

Ex. 3.52a  Mozart: *Don Giovanni* Act 1 no. 6.
[Allegro di molto]

Ex. 3.52b  Mozart: Symphony no. 41 K. 551/iv.

NOTATION OF ACCENTS AND DYNAMICS    143

**Ex. 3.53** Süssmayr: *Der Spiegel von Arcadien*, no. 50, MS score in Staatsbibliothek zu Berlin, mus. ms. 21 533; pub. in fac. in the series *German Opera 1770–1800* (New York and London, Garland, 1986).

Beethoven's Piano Sonata op. 53 contains a passage in which strokes could scarcely have been intended to signify anything other than accents (Ex. 3.54a),[101] although elsewhere, it is clear that he did expect shortening. Other instructive evidence that Beethoven's *staccato* marks were perceived as accents in some contexts occurs in the Trio section of the Scherzo of his Septet. In a copy of the 1st edition, ∧ has been added in pencil above *staccato* strokes (Ex. 3.54b); and these accent signs are also printed in a Peters edition of the score from about 1870 (Ex. 3.54c).

**Ex. 3.54a** Beethoven: Piano Sonata op. 53/iii.
[Rondo Allegretto]

**Ex. 3.54b** Beethoven: Septet op. 20/iv [Allegro molto e vivace]. 1st edn (Vienna, Hoffmeister) pl. no. 108 (copy in ÖNB stamped Philharm[onische]. Gesellschaft in Laibach).
[Allegro molto e vivace]

---

[101] Sandra P. Rosenblum: *Performance Practices in Classic Piano Music* (Bloomington, IN, 1988), 183. She cites this passage as an example of *staccato* marks used as accents, but assuming a theoretical distinction between dot and stroke conflates form with function, remarking: "where composers seem to have intended an accent or a metrically accented note, the printed sign should be a stroke or a wedge".

Ex. 3.54c Beethoven: Septet op. 20/iv (Leipzig, Peters, c. 1870) plate number 5960, p. 45.

Where later 19th-century German composers used both forms of *staccato* mark, the stroke seems generally to have been intended as much to indicate accent as to specify shortening. G. F. Kogel, the 19th-century editor of Marschner's *Hans Heiling*, explained that Marschner used the *staccato* stroke to designate "notes that ought, with short, powerful bowstrokes, to be most especially strongly (*sfz*) made to stand out".[102] A similar type of execution appears to be implied by Schumann's use of strokes (printed as wedges), for instance in the first movement of his "Rhenish" Symphony, where a particular passage is always marked in this way (Ex. 3.55a), while only dots are used for *staccato* in the rest of the symphony. The autograph of "Reiterstück" from Schumann's *Album für die Jugend* provides a good example of the composer's use of ׀ together with ∧ and • as a graduated series of accent/articulation marks in keyboard writing (Ex. 3.55b).

Ex. 3.55a Schumann: Third Symphony op. 97/i.

---

[102] G. F. Kogel (ed.): Preface to Marschner's *Hans Heiling*, full score (Leipzig, Peters, c. 1880).

**Ex. 3.55b** Schumann: *Album für die Jugend*, "Reiterstück". These distinctions in the autograph were not retained in the edition.

Brahms also made a distinction between dots and strokes, and although Kogel (writing in the 1880s) considered that the stroke as used by Marschner was "an obsolete form of notation", Brahms, who was quite conservative in his attitude towards notation, seems clearly to have associated strokes with this kind of sharp, accented *staccato* (Ex. 3.56a–b).[103] Dvořák, too, made use of them in a similar way (Ex. 3.57).

---

[103] See Ch. 6, p. 289 and Ex. 6.22.

146　CLASSICAL AND ROMANTIC PERFORMING PRACTICE

Ex. 3.56 a–b. Brahms: (a) First Symphony op. 68/i; (b) Clarinet Quintet op. 115/i.

Ex. 3.57 Dvořák: String Quartet op. 80/iv.

Amongst other composers who certainly used the stroke and the dot in this manner was Wagner, at least in some of his late works.[104] His orthography in the autographs is often unclear, nor does it always correspond with the earliest printed editions, but where Wagner is known to have overseen the publication of a work (i.e., in the case of his later operas), it may be conjectured that some of the differences result from alterations at proof stage. Among more recent composers, Schönberg seems to have inherited this tradition, for he explained in the preface to his Serenade op. 24: "In the marking of the short notes a distinction is here made between hard, heavy, staccatoed and light, elastic, thrown (spiccato) ones. The former are marked

[104] But see Ch. 6.

with |,▼ the latter by •."[105] Elgar, too, evidently considered the stroke to have accentual qualities (Ex. 3.58).

Ex. 3.58 Elgar: First Symphony op. 55/ii.

## The Hairpin (> or ▷)

Apart from the *staccato* stroke, the earliest accent sign to be widely and permanently accepted was >, which seems to have developed from the sign for *decrescendo* shortly after that became current. The signs ⟨ and ⟩ as graphic illustrations of *crescendo* and *decrescendo* began to be regularly used only from about the 1760s, though something similar had been proposed by Italian composers, such as G. A. Piani and Francesco Veracini several decades earlier. By the 1780s, > was being employed by many composers as an accent sign. Mozart, however, had little interest in using it either as an accent sign or as an indication for *decrescendo*, and it is found very rarely in his compositions. Haydn began to utilize it in works of the 1790s, including the op. 71 and op. 74 string quartets, but did not employ it often. Beethoven used it sparingly in his earlier works, and even in later compositions it is far less common than *sf*. Other late-18th- and early-19th-century composers adopted the sign more extensively, either as an equivalent for the effect many of their contemporaries would have indicated by *sf* or *fz*, or as a slighter accent than implied by these markings. Early and frequent use of the sign, as both *decrescendo* and accent, can be found in G. J. Vogler's music (see Ex. 2.6), and it is commonly encountered in the music of Vogler's pupils Weber and Meyerbeer. It occurs frequently, too, in music by Cherubini, Süssmayr, Dussek, Spohr, Rossini, and Schubert. For almost all composers born after 1800 it was a standard sign.

---

[105] Arnold Schönberg: Serenade op. 24 (Copenhagen and Leipzig, W. Hansen, 1924).

Its occurrences, however, reveal problematic aspects of its usage. It is often difficult to determine whether it is intended to be purely accentual (i.e., indicating a note with greater emphasis than its unmarked neighbours), whether it denotes merely *decrescendo* (requiring no more than a decrease in volume from the previously prevailing dynamic), or whether it signifies a combination of both these things. The difficulty is compounded by ambiguous orthography on the part of composers and, where autographs are not to hand, the evident unreliability of many early editions.

Beethoven's employment of this sign usually suggests that he saw it literally as a short *decrescendo* "hairpin", although evidently with enhanced emphasis at the beginning (Ex. 3.59a–b), reflecting the typical agogic treatment of such figures as described by Leopold Mozart.[106] In works of Beethoven's early and middle periods, it is difficult to find clear examples where he might have intended it to signify an accent on a single note. In the String Quartet op. 131, where > occurs quite often over single notes, it usually seems to signify a rapid *decrescendo* rather than an accent; only near the beginning of the Adagio ma non troppo e semplice in the fourth movement may Beethoven have envisaged it as an accent sign (Ex. 3.60a). Presumably, since he freely used *sf*, it was meant to indicate a lighter degree of expressive weight. It is questionable whether the use of the sign in the Vivace of op. 135 indicates an accent or merely a *decrescendo* (Ex. 3.60b).

**Ex. 3.59** a–b. Beethoven: (*a*) *Chorfantasie* op. 80; (*b*) Piano Trio op. 97.

---

[106] Mozart: *Versuch*, 123.

**Ex. 3.60a** Beethoven: String Quartet op. 131/iv. 1st edn parts, Violin 1.

**Ex. 3.60b** Beethoven: String Quartet op. 135/ii. 1st edn parts, Violin 1.
[Vivace]

The problems of distinguishing between > as accent, as accent plus *decrescendo*, or purely as *decrescendo* continued well into the 19th century. This was exacerbated in the case of composers such as Schubert, Bellini, and others, who often wrote large "hairpins" in contexts that suggest a rapidly decaying accent rather than a gradual *decrescendo*. In Schubert's case a relationship between the size of the "hairpin" and the intensity of the accent, perhaps resulting from the subconscious reflection of his feelings in his handwriting, often appears plausible, though it would be injudicious to press that hypothesis too far. It is interesting to note that the meaning of this sign remained a matter of some uncertainty as late as 1841, when a writer felt it necessary to explain that it need not always mean *decrescendo*, but could often mean simply accent, commenting: "Very frequently *decrescendo* signs (>) occur even on short notes, by which, however, the composer only wishes to show that the notes should be performed more markedly. That this is really the case, is shown by the use of this sign also in *piano* passages."[107]

Wagner's notation of the sign usually leaves no doubt about its accent meaning, and when he also required a distinct *decrescendo* he often used both the short and long versions of the sign (Ex. 3.61). In works up to about 1880, Brahms also made his intentions clear by combining > with a longer *decrescendo* sign (Ex. 3.62a). In later works, however, although Brahms continued to use the short form of the sign to denote an accent, such double signs are rare; but it has been persuasively argued that the *decrescendo* and accent meanings appear often to be subsumed in the same long version of the sign (Ex. 3.62b).[108]

---

[107] Anon.: 'Einiges über die Pflichten des Violoncellisten als Orchesterspieler und Accompagnateur,' *Allgemeine musikalische Zeitung*, xliii (1841), 133.
[108] Paul Mies: 'Ueber ein besonderes Akzentzeichen bei Johannes Brahms' in Georg Reichert and Martin Just (eds.), *Bericht über den internationalen musikwissenschaftlichen Kongress Kassel 1962* (Kassel, 1963), 215–17. For other implications of the longer "hairpin" see Ch. 11, pp. 599–605.

Ex. 3.61 Wagner: *Parsifal*, Act III, rehearsal numbers 255f.

Ex. 3.62a Brahms: Piano Sonata op. 1/i. 1st edn.
[Allegro]

Ex. 3.62b Brahms: Clarinet Quintet op. 115/i. 1st edn parts Violin 1.

The other major issue with this sign is what degree of accent it might imply; in particular, whether it calls for a slighter accent than *sf/fz* or *rf* (when used solely as an accent indication), or whether it is synonymous with one or other of them. Haydn certainly seems, sometimes at least, to have regarded it as synonymous with *fz*, for instance in the Finale of Symphony no. 104, where the two markings appear to be interchangeable (see Ex. 3.23). In the music of Vogler, Weber, and Meyerbeer, > seems rather consistently to have been used as a graphic equivalent of *sf/fz*. It is listed as such by one of their contemporaries, the cellist J. J. F. Dotzauer (a leading member of Weber's orchestra in Dresden), who considered it to be merely an abbreviation for *rinforzando* or *sforzando* on a single note. For Dotzauer, all these directions simply meant that the note should be strengthened (*verstärkt*)

NOTATION OF ACCENTS AND DYNAMICS    151

to an unspecified degree.[109] Although Weber did not entirely avoid *fz* he employed it rarely, but not apparently as a more powerful accent; its occasional appearances in *Der Freischütz* are often in conjunction with > in circumstances that make it highly improbable that a distinction between the two accent markings was intended. Weber certainly used > purely as an accent, even when the sign, as so often with Schubert, was boldly written and might be perceived as a *decrescendo* "hairpin". The use of > exclusively to mean an accent is nicely illustrated by an instance in the score of *Der Freischütz* (Ex. 3.63).

**Ex. 3.63**  Weber: *Der Freischütz,* no. 15 (autograph).

In Meyerbeer's case, the correspondence between *sf* and > is confirmed, in *Les Huguenots* for instance, by his occasionally supplementing > with an instruction such as *poco sfz* or *dolce sfz*. These are the only occasions in *Les Huguenots* where he used the term *sf/sfz*; it never occurs alone (Ex. 3.64). However, Meyerbeer often combined > with another marking, such as *fp* or even ʌ, and the intention of the sign in such circumstances is not always clear. Verdi is among later 19th-century composers who preferred to use > rather than *sf*; it appears in all sorts of contexts in his music but seems often to suggest a quite powerful accent.

**Ex. 3.64**  Meyerbeer: *Les Huguenots,* Act 2, no. 18. 1st edn score, p. 481.
[Allegro con spirito ben mosso]

[109] Dotzauer: *Violoncell-Schule,* 13.

In the music of these composers, > probably indicates an accent of variable strength, from a full-blooded *sforzando* to a gentle emphasis, depending on the context and on any other qualifying expressions. Many composers, on the other hand, evidently regarded > as having a more restricted meaning, and quite definitely as specifying a level of accent inferior to *sf*. The largest body of opinion in the first half of the 19th century regarded it as indicating one of the slightest degrees of accent. Philip Corri used > in his pianoforte method to mark the notes on which the expressive stress, which according to English usage he calls emphasis, should fall in a melody.[110] And Hummel, apparently equating > and ^ (at least in terms of strength), observed that "The emphasis sign (^ or >) is used both in *piano* and *forte* passages, and makes the note above which it is placed stand out a little from the others."[111] Both these musicians saw it as appropriate to any dynamic. Later theorists increasingly considered it to be less powerful than ^, and more appropriate in *piano* passages than in *forte* ones. Having designated ^ as a somewhat less powerful accent than *sf*, Gollmick observed: "The sign > already signifies only an accent and belongs more to a gentler style of performance."[112] Wagner described his ideal performance of a passage in Weber's *Der Freischütz* "gently melting away without the usual *sforzando* on the only delicately inflected [Ex. 3.65a]. The violoncello, too, softens the usually violent impulse of the [Ex. 3.65b] above the tremolo of the violins, to the merely quiet sigh that was intended."[113] It seems highly questionable whether this was, in fact, what Weber intended, but Wagner's use of > implies that this was how he envisaged its execution in his own operas.

Ex. 3.65 a–b. Wagner: "Ueber das Dirigiren", in *Gesammelte Schriften*, viii, 367.

(a)

(b)

Schubert, who often employed *sf*, and sometimes *sff*, and who very frequently used >, undoubtedly intended it primarily to indicate where the expressive stress

---

[110] P. A. Corri: *L'anima di musica*, 72.
[111] Hummel: *Anweisung*, 2nd edn, 55.
[112] Gollmick: *Kritische Terminologie*, 4.
[113] Richard Wagner: 'Ueber das Dirigiren' in *Gesammelte Schriften*, viii, 367.

in the melody should fall. Sometimes he reinforced the message of the slurring with > and sometimes he overrode it (Ex. 3.66). The basic meaning of this sign for Schubert is tellingly illustrated by instances in *Alfonso und Estrella* where > and <> in the orchestral parts are clearly intended to support the lightest of (unmarked) emphases in the vocal line and to add subtle contrasting accentuation (Ex. 3.67). Such passages imply that, for Schubert, > corresponded with the normal degree of emphasis that a good singer would naturally give to the stressed syllables of the text or to musically important notes.

Ex. 3.66 a–b. Schubert: (*a*) Piano Trio D. 898/ii; (*b*) Symphony in B minor D. 759/ii.

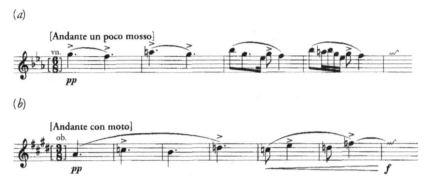

Ex. 3.67 Schubert: *Alfonso und Estrella*, no. 11.

Spohr's use of the accent in his Concertante for violin, cello, and orchestra WoO. 11 (1803) suggests that in his early works he saw it, like Weber and Meyerbeer, as an accent mark that was relative to the prevailing dynamic and that could signify anything from a light emphasis to a fairly powerful accent; it occurs not only in *piano* contexts, but also simultaneously with *fp* in parts

154  CLASSICAL AND ROMANTIC PERFORMING PRACTICE

doubled at the octave and even with *fz* (Ex. 3.68a–b). In later works, Spohr apparently saw it as a lighter accent than *fz*, often with a quite distinct element of *decrescendo* (see also Ex. 3.29b).

**Ex. 3.68**  a–b. Spohr: Concertante WoO. 11. Autograph, Kassel Landesbibliothek, 269 fol Mus. (*a*) p. 37; (*b*) p. 41 (on the first occurrence of this passage [p. 17], he used *fz* in all parts except timpani).

(*a*)
[Allegro]

**Ex. 3.68** Continued

(b)

By the second half of the 19th century the acceptance of other signs into common usage tended to fix > towards the middle of a wider hierarchy of accents; but its meaning remained quite variable. The systematic discussion of accents in the early-20th-century *Encyclopédie de la musique* supports its position as a middle-ranking accent. It was categorized there as necessitating a "stronger attack [than the preceding note] followed immediately by a decrease in tone."[114] Yet Riemann perpetuated the notion of the equivalence

---

[114] Lavignac et al.: *Encyclopédie de la musique*, pt. 2, 335.

of > and *sf*, commenting: "A > over a note requires a stronger tone (accent, *sforzato*)."[115]

Much depends on the number of different accent markings a composer chose to employ. In the music of Brahms, who generally scorned the newer accent signs,[116] a variety of treatments will be appropriate; in Schumann's, Wagner's, Dvořák's, and Bruckner's works, and those of many of their contemporaries, however, where several of the accent signs discussed below are encountered, its meaning will be more firmly located in a hierarchy of markings.

Another question mark over the use of this sign in the late 18th and early 19th centuries concerns whether any distinction was meant between the > and the ▷. On the whole this seems unlikely; but Rossini's use of the two forms (in the autograph of *La gazza ladra*, for instance) sometimes hints at an apparent difference between the one as a *decrescendo* and the other as an accent. Like so many other notational subtleties, however, the distinction, if it were intended, appears not to have been consistently pursued, and it seems much more likely that the change in the symbol, by the omission of the inessential line, came about as a natural process of simplification, particularly when composers or copyists were writing at speed. An occasionally encountered specialized meaning of > was, when used successively (i.e., >>>>), a trembling effect.[117]

## *Le Petit Chapeau* (^)

The meaning of this sign also varied from time to time and composer to composer.[118] As mentioned above, it was used by Türk and Wolf in the 18th century to designate the notes upon which expressive stress should fall, and adopted in the instruction books of J. F. Schubert and Hummel in the early 19th century. In all these cases it was clearly meant to designate a relatively gentle accent, though Hummel used + to indicate an even lighter one. In

---

[115] Riemann: *New Pianoforte School*, 17.
[116] See Ch. 6.
[117] See Ch. 16.
[118] *Le petit chapeau* (the little hat), the name given to this accent in Lavignac et al.: *Encyclopédie de la musique*.

1808 G. W. Fink listed ∧ along with *f. sfz. p.* and > as one of what he designated "nuanced expressive accents";[119] he failed to discuss the degree or type of accent implied by the sign, but since he listed it after *sfz* and > it is probable that he regarded it as slighter than those accents. In practice, however, ∧ was scarcely employed in the early 19th century. One reason for this, at least in music for string instruments, may have been the fact that when signs for down- and up-bows began to be adopted, the sign for the latter was often written as ∧ rather than ∨ until at least the middle of the century; and occasionally ∧ was used for down-bow.[120]

Meyerbeer was one of the first prominent composers to use ∧ regularly as an accent sign, but its significance in his music is not altogether clear. In many instances it appears to be a less powerful accent than >. In *Les Huguenots*, whereas > is equivalent to *sf*, and sometimes occurs with the qualification *poco sfz*, ∧ is, on occasion, combined with the term *dolce sfz* (Ex. 3.69a). It is often found, too, in *piano* passages where a gentle accent seems to be implied (Ex. 3.69b). A particularly revealing instance occurs when it is used in a vocal part with the additional instruction "mark each of the six notes but without force"[121] (Ex. 3.69c); and at a later point in the opera, it occurs with the instruction "Very soft (with plaintive expression)", being superseded by > with the advent of a *crescendo* (Ex. 3.69d). Yet, elsewhere, Meyerbeer used it where a stronger accent seems called for (in *Le Prophète*, for instance, where it is found in conjunction with the instruction *martelé*)[122]; and it is difficult to see what is meant in *Les Huguenots* when a figure is first given with ∧ on each note and then with both ∧ and > on each note (Ex. 3.69e). It may be significant for the type of accent Meyerbeer envisaged that he very often combined it with the instruction *tenuto*, suggesting that the perceptible *decrescendo* effect associated with > was not required.

---

[119] Gottfried Wilhelm Fink: 'Ueber Takt, Taktarten, und ihr Charakteristisches', *Allgemeine musikalische Zeitung*, xi (1808–9), 226. Probably *p.* was a misprint for *fp*.
[120] In Christian Heinrich Hohmann: *Praktische Violin-Schule* (Nürnberg, [1849]), 8th edn, 1865, p. 5, various now obsolete bow direction signs are given, which, confusingly, also include ⊓ for up-bow and ⊔ for down-bow.
[121] Meyerbeer: *Les Huguenots*, 1st edn full score (Paris, Schlesinger, [1836]), 335.
[122] Meyerbeer: *Le Prophète*, 1st edn full score (Paris, Brandus and Troupenas, [1849]), 739.

158   CLASSICAL AND ROMANTIC PERFORMING PRACTICE

Ex. 3.69 a–e. Meyerbeer: *Les Huguenots*, 1st edn score. (*a*) No. 5, p. 129f; (*b*) No. 8, p. 261; (*c*) No. 12A, p. 335; (*d*) No. 27, p. 828; (*e*) No. 27A, pp. 847 and 848f.

(*a*)

NOTATION OF ACCENTS AND DYNAMICS 159

**Ex. 3.69** Continued

(b)

**Ex. 3.69** Continued

(c)

(d)

(e)

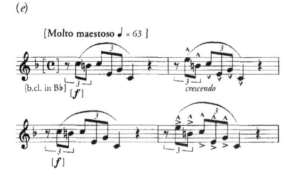

During the middle decades of the 19th century, ^ began to be more widely used. Spohr, who did not use it in earlier works, employed it in the additional music that he wrote for an 1852 London production of his 1813 opera *Faust*, apparently as a light accent, since it occurs only in *piano* and *pianissimo*

contexts. Like Meyerbeer and Spohr, Verdi may have regarded ^, which occurs sometimes in combination with slurs and sometimes alone, primarily as a lighter accent than >, especially in works from the 1860s onwards. It seems occasionally to be intended to counter the normal tendency to phrase off the metrically weaker beats, for instance in some passages in the Requiem (Ex. 3.70a). But Verdi does not appear to have considered the difference in meaning between > and ^ to have been very pronounced, and he sometimes mixed the two signs indiscriminately, as in the "Libera me" from the abortive *Messa per Rossini* of 1869 (Ex. 3.70b).

Ex. 3.70 a–b. Verdi: (*a*) Requiem; (*b*) *Messa per Rossini*.

(*a*)

(*b*)

By that time, however, there appears to have been a growing tendency to see ^ as a relatively powerful accent. In the 1830s, Henri Herz had stated that ^ "indicates, in general a degree of intensity inferior to *sforzando*",[123]

---

[123] Herz: *Méthode*, 17. In the Italian edition, however, the sign is given as > not ^.

while Carl Gollmick stated: "The newer sign ∧ requires a stronger pressure on the individual note, but less harsh than *sfz*."[124] Gollmick also suggested that if *forzando* indicated a slighter accent than *sf* "then the newer sign ∧ does the job perfectly."[125] Yet, revealing continuing confusion in his *Handlexikon* of 1857, Gollmick first defined ∧ as the same as *sf*, then defined *sfz* as "extremely strong and forced out [. . .]. Also often the sign ∧. Therefore not the same as *rinforzando*."[126] Carl Czerny, in the 1840s ranked it among the stronger accents, stating, in a discussion of Liszt's usage, that "the upright sign (∧) implies a higher degree of power than the horizontal (>), and, in general, all the performance signs used by Liszt are to be taken into account, since they are still the surest point of reference for those who have not had the opportunity to hear him themselves."[127] Whether other composers used ∧ in this sense or whether they saw it as indicating a relatively gentle emphasis was evidently linked with their view of >, and those composers who used > instead of *sf* will probably have favoured the lighter interpretation of ∧. In 1892, Richard Scholz could still explicitly identify > as "the stronger" and ∧ as "the weaker accent".[128]

For Schumann, as for Liszt, the sign normally denoted a degree of accent greater than >. This is suggested in his *Album für die Jugend*, where the piece "Fremder Mann", which is marked *Stark und kräftig zu spielen* (to be played strongly and powerfully), has mostly ∧ in *forte* and > in *piano* sections; and in "Jägerliedchen", where both signs occur in close juxtaposition, the former evidently implies the heavier emphasis (Ex. 3.71a). The sign does not appear in Schumann's First Symphony, but in the Second he used it, in conjunction with repeated *fs*, evidently to designate a weighty accent. The sign occurs more often in the Third Symphony, but in the second movement it is used, somewhat puzzlingly, over a *staccato* dot in a piano passage. That Schumann did not regard it as synonymous with *sf* is clearly indicated by its use in the Violin Sonata op. 121 (Ex. 3.71b). Since Schumann appears not to have used *rf* as an accent mark, it seems possible that, if not always quite consistently, he was in general agreement with Gollmick's earlier opinion about the ranking,

---

[124] Gollmick: *Kritische Terminologie*, 4.
[125] Gollmick: *Kritische Terminologie*, 3.
[126] Carl Gollmick: *Handlexikon der Tonkunst* (Offenbach am Main, 1857), 84f.
[127] Carl Czerny: *Die Kunst des Vortrags der älteren und neueren Klavierkompositionen oder Die Fortschritte bis zur neuesten Zeit. Supplement oder 4$^{ter}$ Theil zur grossen Pianoforte-Schule* (Vienna, 1846), 29.
[128] Scholz: *Die Vortragskunst*, 23.

in descending order of strength, of *sf*, ^, and >. As with Meyerbeer, however, the form of the sign may also have implied a different type of accent from >.

Ex. 3.71a  Schumann: *Album für die Jugend*, "Jägerliedchen".

Ex. 3.71b  Schumann: Violin Sonata op. 121/i.

Berlioz's use of ^ is similarly ambiguous; it has been suggested that its difference from > lies in the *decrescendo* element,[129] but this is not always clear, for instance when the two signs are used in fast music, in which any perceptible, or even notional *decrescendo* would be impossible (Ex. 3.72). Dvořák evidently intended the sign normally to be used in a forceful context; in his Violin Sonata it occurs in *ff* passages while > occurs in *f* passages (Ex. 3.73a). Its implication of greater strength for Dvořák is also suggested by a passage in his String Quartet op. 106, where the viola part is evidently meant to be more prominent than the violin (Ex. 3.73b).

Ex. 3.72  Berlioz: *Les Troyens*, "Danse des esclaves".

---

[129] Macdonald: 'Two Peculiarities of Berlioz's Notation', *Music & Letters*, 1 (1969), 32.

164  CLASSICAL AND ROMANTIC PERFORMING PRACTICE

Ex. 3.73 a–b. Dvořák: (*a*) Violin Sonata op. 57/i; (*b*) String Quartet op. 106/i.

A revealing example of Bruckner's employment of ∧ can be found in his Third Symphony, where the autograph clearly shows him using ∧ over a succession of notes in the wind instruments while the strings simultaneously have a repeated down-bow signs together with the instruction *Streicher*

*sämmtlich alles abwarts gestrichen* (all strings play everything down-bow); the down-bows were evidently an afterthought, as can be seen from the violin parts, where Bruckner originally wrote ∧ (Ex. 3.74). The same combination of down-bow and ∧, this time in the same part, occurs in Dvořák, in a passage where the accents change to > with the *diminuendo* (Ex. 3.75a). In the Adagio ma non troppo of String Quartet op. 106 (Ex. 3.75b), the use of ∧ in cello and > in the other three parts is clearly to bring out the bass more strongly. But the implications of Dvořák's rather lavish use of dynamic signs can often be unclear, for instance the conglomeration of markings in the 1st violin part of the String Quartet op. 96 (Ex. 3.75c) which appear in the first edition of the parts; in the score the ∧ is omitted, but even without it the combination remains ambiguous.

Ex. 3.74 Bruckner: Third Symphony, i, Mäßig bewegt ♩ = 66.

**Ex. 3.75a**  Dvořák: String Quartet op. 106/i, Violin 1.
[Allero moderato]

**Ex. 3.75b**  Dvořák: *String Quartet* op. 106/ii (p. 28).
[Adagio ma non troppo]

**Ex. 3.75c**  Dvořák: *String Quartet* op. 96/i.
[Allegro ma non troppo]

The tendency of later 19th-century composers to employ ^ as similar to *sf* is also suggested by scrutiny of Wagner's scores. His view of ^ as a powerful accent is implied by his use of it in *Siegfried* to represent a very strong stroke of the anvil, while v indicated "a weaker one" and | "a lighter stroke".[130] In *Parsifal*, Wagner employed ^ in conjunction with *sf*;[131] in *Die Walküre* the sign

---

[130] Wagner: *Siegfried*, Act I, Scene iii (Schott miniature score, 382).
[131] Wagner: Rehearsal nos. 74–75 (Schott miniature score, 180).

(inverted in the printed edition) is accompanied by the instruction "heavy and held back".[132] Whether this is related to Hugo Riemann's employment of ∧ as an indication for agogic accent is a moot point; Riemann seems to have been isolated from other theorists in defining the difference between > and ∧ as being that the latter requires "a slight lingering on the note".[133] The *Encyclopédie de la musique* expressed the orthodox opinion of the late 19th century when it observed that in contrast to >, which required a *decrescendo*, a note marked with ∧ "should be accented, marked strongly, with firmness".[134] Curiously, perhaps, this logical interpretation of ∧ (although it is scarcely possible on the piano on longer notes) seems seldom to be an explicit factor in its execution.

### The Short *Messa di voce* (< >)

The short *crescendo-decrescendo* sign, which derives from the *messa di voce*, is common in some 19th-century composers' music. From his earliest period, Beethoven liked to use this expressive nuance over short phrases or long notes, and occasionally in the late works it appears in association with shorter notes where there would scarcely be time to execute a real *crescendo-decrescendo* (Ex. 3.76). Since he also used the term *rinforzando*, he evidently did not regard it as synonymous with that term, as Galeazzi did (above pp. 110–111).

Ex. 3.76 Beethoven: String Quartet op. 135/i.

---

[132] Wagner: *Die Walküre* Act I, Scene i (Schott miniature score, 81).
[133] Riemann: *New Pianoforte School*, 17.
[134] Lavignac et al.: *Encyclopédie de la musique*, pt. 2, 335.

Many later composers, perhaps taking the hint from Beethoven's usage, or from violinists such as Campagnoli or Pierre Rode, or deriving it directly from the typical 18th-century treatment of the *Abzug*, began to employ this sign over shorter notes, purely as a type of accent.[135] That it was seen entirely as a special kind of accent by composers such as Schumann (who used it extensively) is indicated by its inclusion in piano music (Ex. 3.77; see also Ex. 3.37). It is quite frequently used in string music by Mendelssohn, Brahms, Bruch, and Elgar, where it seems generally to require a warm but not too powerful accent (Ex. 3.78a–c).

Ex. 3.77 Schumann, *Lied* op. 101/4.

Ex. 3.78a Bruch: Violin Concerto in G minor op. 26/ii.

Ex. 3.78b Elgar: Violin Sonata op. 87/i.

---

[135] Its concomitant implications for trembling effects in string playing are considered below, Ch. 14, where further examples are given.

Ex. 3.78c Elgar: String Quartet op. 83/ii.

It could be associated with trembling effects in singing and on instruments that were capable of it, as is made explicit in the Joachim and Moser *Violinschule*.[136] It also had agogic as well as accentual implications, as Andreas Moser instructed in relation to Rode's third Caprice.[137] In Brahms's music, however, it may also indicate lingering without restitution, for Fanny Davies, who had direct knowledge of Brahms's playing, recalled that <>

> often occurs when he wishes to express great sincerity and warmth, applied not only to tone but to rhythm also. He would linger not on one note alone, but on a whole idea, as if unable to tear himself away from its beauty. He would prefer to lengthen a bar or phrase rather than spoil it by making up the time into a metronomic bar.[138]

It may well also have encouraged other expressive practices such as piano arpeggiation and sliding effects. As with so many other practices, however, only the most necessary places were marked. Anton André, having explained his use of <> in his *Lieder*, pointed out that any other expressive note might similarly be lingered on longer than its notated value and given a *messa di voce* treatment.[139]

## The Horizontal Line (- ¬ ´)

The use of these signs by composers is rare before the middle of the 19th century, although they are mentioned in instruction books at an earlier date.

---

[136] See Ch. 11, p. 567.
[137] Joseph Joachim and Andreas Moser: *Violinschule*, 3 vols. (Berlin, 1905), iii, 7. See Ex. 11.1.
[138] Fanny Davies: 'Some Personal Recollections' in *Cobbett's Cyclopedic Survey*, i, 182.
[139] Anton André: 'Bemerkungen über den Vortrag meiner Lieder und Gesänge.' (Offenbach, 1822).

Herz's *Méthode* includes the explanation "If the execution of a single note requires to be heavily accented this sign ÷ is employed."[140] This form of the sign is also listed by Hamilton among other accent markings, but simply with the collective explanation that they all denote "stress or marked accent on any single note or chord".[141] Although neither author stated that the combination of a dot with the line might specify not only stress, but also a degree of separation between the note so marked and the following note, this seems to be implied by its form; the dot indicates *staccato* yet its combination with the line suggests greater length than would be indicated by the dot alone. However, the line (without dot) would also have had deep-rooted implications of stress because of its association with the sign for a strong syllable in poetry. It also became a graphic equivalent for the word *tenuto*, which in 18th- and early-19th-century usage sometimes (perhaps usually) involved an accentual element. In C. P. E. Bach's music, *tenuto* could also indicate the use of the Clavichord *Bebung* (repeated pressure on the key to produce a trembling effect), for instance; C. F. Cramer, having heard Bach perform the second of his *Sonaten für Kenner und Liebhaber* of 1779 (Ex. 3.79), referred to "his *tenuto*, which is fundamentally nothing less than the *Bebung* [...], which he is also accustomed to mark with dots (. . . . ) over the notes".[142]

Ex. 3.79 C. P. E. Bach: Sonaten für Kenner und Liebhaber 1st book no. 2, p. 12.

Two decades earlier, Samuel Petri associated *ten.* not only with length, but also with accentuation; he explained it as signifying "that one should deliver the note very strongly and hold it as long as its time value specifies."[143] The term's association with accentuation remained current into the 19th century. In 1826, August Swoboda wrote: "Often one finds the syllable *ten.*, which is the first syllable of *tenuto* (to hold, sustain), above a note, and by this it is indicated that the tone should be marked with a special emphasis." Accentuation, rather than merely holding the note full length, was surely how

---

[140] Herz: *Méthode*, 17.

[141] James Alexander Hamilton: *A Dictionary of Two Thousand Italian, French, German, English and other Musical Terms*, 4th edn (London, 1837), 87 (107 in the 5th edn).

[142] Carl Friedrich Cramer: 'Einige Gedanken über Aufführung von Concertmusik', *Magazin der Musik*, i (1783), 1217. His commentary on R[obert] Bremner's preface to Schetky's op. 6.

[143] Petri: *Anleitung zur praktischen Musik*, 1st edn, 26; 2nd edn, 148.

Anton André understood *ten.*, for in his four volumes of *Lieder und Gesänge* it frequently occurs on the first syllable of a two- or three-syllable word. Swoboda also alluded to an effect that seems similar to the one described by Cramer, stating: "By *ten.* it is often also understood that one should make the vibrations of a note audible, i.e. make them felt by the ear."[144]

A. B. Marx, including ‒ among signs that indicate "a greater degree of intensity", instructed that the performer "is, at the same time, to linger over each sound";[145] and Czerny equated ‒ on notes separated by rests, with dots under a slur, observing: "In these cases the keys must be struck with more than the usual emphasis, and the notes must be held for almost more than their usual value. To express the special holding of a single note, some composers put ‒ above the note."[146] Such an interpretation would nicely fit Schumann's use of it in "Winterzeit 2", as notated in the autograph of his *Album für die Jugend* (Ex. 3.80a) or in the third movement of his "Rhenish" Symphony, where it occurs in close juxtaposition with *portato* sixteenth-notes (Ex. 3.80b). Brahms, however, among other composers, continued to employ dots and a slur, even over notes separated by rests, to indicate the type of *portato* illustrated in the example from Schumann's symphony. In his Horn Trio Brahms used a more curious (? shorthand) version of the same thing, putting a slur and dot over single notes (Ex. 3.81).[147]

Ex. 3.80 a–b. Schumann: (*a*) *Album für die Jugend*, "Winterzeit 2"; (*b*) Third Symphony op. 97/iii.

---

[144] Swoboda: *Allgemeine Theorie*, §95, 44.
[145] Marx: *Allgemeine Musiklehre*, 138f.
[146] Czerny: *Pianoforte-Schule*, i, 144.
[147] See Ch. 11 for the association of *portato* notation with piano arpeggiation.

**Ex. 3.81** Brahms, Horn Trio op. 40/i. bb. 249–56 (autograph). [Andante]

The Mendel & Reissmann *Lexikon* associated the sign with accent and a degree of sostenuto,[148] and Riemann described it as requiring "*a broad kind of playing, but yet with, separation of the single tones* (portato, non legato)",[149] while the *Encyclopédie de la musique* described both ⁒ and ʌ as instructions to "attack the note heavily and weightily, and quit it immediately in a detached manner".[150]

The horizontal line without a dot was often used, in combination with a slur, to clarify the difference between slurred *staccato* and *portato* for string players, both of which were conventionally marked with dots under slurs during the 18th and much of the 19th century.[151] Ferdinand David, who employed – to indicate an on-string bowstroke, occasionally used lines under slurs in his own later compositions and, somewhat sporadically, in his annotated editions of the classics. In his *Dur und Moll* op. 39, however, he also included a note to No. 13, stating: "The notes marked <> and –, which form the melody, are emphasized a little more than the others."[152] Joseph Joachim suggested to Brahms, in their correspondence about the Violin Concerto, that to obviate misunderstanding, he should utilize lines rather than dots under slurs for *portato* in his writing for strings.[153] Brahms stubbornly refused to adopt this into his own notational practice, but belatedly acknowledged the ambiguity for string players by allowing its use in the separate string parts of his later chamber music, while retaining his dots under slurs in the score.[154]

In the later 19th century, explanations in instruction books differ considerably. Louis Schubert's *Violinschule* is even inconsistent between its German, French, and English versions; a literal translation of the German is "broadly

---

[148] Mendel and Reissmann: *Musikalisches Conversations-Lexikon*, xi, 212.
[149] Riemann: *New Pianoforte-School*, 17.
[150] Lavignac et al.: *Encyclopédie de la musique*, pt. 2, 336.
[151] See Ch. 6.
[152] Ferdinand David: *Dur und Moll* op. 39, ii, 3.
[153] For their correspondence on this subject see Clive Brown: 'Joachim's Violin Playing and the Performance of Brahms's String Music' in Michael Musgrave and Bernard Sherman (eds.), *Performing Brahms* (Cambridge, 2003), 48–98.
[154] See Clive Brown, Neal Peres Da Costa, and Kate Bennet Wadsworth: *Performing Practices in Johannes Brahms' Chamber Music* (Kassel, 2015), 7.

staccatoed or *portato*" (*breit gestoßen oder gezogen*), and the French simply reads "broad détaché"[155] (*détaché large*), while the English has: "played staccato with a slight emphasis on each note".[156] Riemann and the *Encyclopédie de la musique* also gave somewhat different descriptions: the former considered it to indicate that the note "is to be held down for its full value (tenuto)",[157] and the latter that the note so marked "ought to be pressed with more firmness than the others".[158]

Consideration of individual instances in which the sign is used reveals some justification for all these interpretations, and also suggests other possibilities. Liszt's employment of the horizontal line in his *Faust-Symphonie* appears to be a *tenuto* instruction rather than an accent (cautioning against matching the detached execution in the strings), though it may also have been intended to counteract the metrical accentuation and obtain equal weight on all four beats (Ex. 3.82a). Where he used it in *legato* passages, however, its function as an accent, implying weight without sharpness of attack, can scarcely be in doubt (Ex. 3.82b–c). Despite Liszt's example, Wagner employed this sign infrequently; indeed, many of its occurrences in his scores seem to result from additions made during publication. On at least one occasion he intended the sign to indicate a discrete *vibrato* (which also has some implication of accent)[159]: Heinrich Porges noted in his account of the rehearsals for the première of the *Ring in* 1876 that at one point in Act III, Scene iii of *Siegfried* "The strokes [lines] above the E and B of 'zitternd' indicate that here Wagner wanted that gentle vibrato—not to be confused with the bad habit of tremolando—whose importance in expressive singing he often spoke of"[160] (Ex. 3.83a). Elsewhere, apart from his use of the horizontal line (instead of the conventional dot) under a slur for *portato*, the sign may sometimes occur in Wagner's scores with a meaning similar to that envisaged by Liszt. According to transcriptions of his instructions at rehearsals of *Parsifal*, he asked at one point that the eighth-notes should be "Very sustained and held [*sehr getragen und gehalten*], not merely slurred, a true portamento" (Ex. 3.83b); and, at a similar passage, "Very dragged [*sehr*

---

[155] The word *détaché*, literally "separated", can also signify well-connected notes, played with separate bows in violin playing (as in Spohr's *Violinschule*).
[156] Louis Schubert: *Violinschule nach modernen Principien* op. 50, 4 vols. (Braunschweig, 1882), i, 12.
[157] Riemann: *New Pianoforte-School*, 17.
[158] Lavignac et al.: *Encyclopédie de la musique*, pt. 2, 335.
[159] See Ch. 16, esp. p. 954.
[160] Heinrich Porges: *Die Bühnenproben zu der Bayreuther Festspielen des Jahres 1876* (Chemnitz and Leipzig, 1881–96), trans. Robert L. Jacobs as *Wagner Rehearsing the "Ring"* (Cambridge, 1983), 109.

*gezogen*], the eighth-note very clear, very distinct, the short note is the main thing" (Ex. 3.83c).[161] Here there are horizontal lines in the 1883 printed edition that are missing from the autograph score. Although they appear under slurs, it seems unlikely that Wagner intended any separation, as would sometimes have been the case with *portato*.

Ex. 3.82 a–c. Liszt: *Eine Faust-Symphonie*, i, "Faust".

Ex. 3.83a Wagner: *Siegfried,* Act III, Scene iii.

---

[161] Richard Wagner: *Sämtliche Werke*, xxx: *Dokumente zur Entstehung und ersten Aufführung des Bühnenweihfestspiels Parsifal*, ed. Martin Geck and Egon Voss (Mainz, 1970), 174.

NOTATION OF ACCENTS AND DYNAMICS 175

Ex. 3.83 b–c. Wagner: *Parsifal*. (*b*) rehearsal letter 45; (*c*) rehearsal letter 48.

In the music of many later 19th-century composers the horizontal line apparently had the function of indicating the slightest degree of separation and/or the slightest degree of expressive weight, but any perceptible element of separation often seems inappropriate. In the theme of Elgar's *Enigma Variations*, for instance (Ex. 3.84a), he evidently considered it a light emphasis, as comparison of the opening of variation XI (Ex. 3.84b) with the passage at bar 6 suggests (Ex. 3.84c). Its accent function seems likely to have been relative rather than absolute and to have been rather to neutralize the metrical hierarchy than to give the note particular prominence.

Ex. 3.84 a–c. Elgar: Enigma Variations op. 36. (*a*) theme; (*b*) variation XI; (*c*) variation XI.

Ex. 3.84 Continued

(b) Allegro di molto

(c)

Tchaikovsky seems sometimes to imply equality of weight together with almost imperceptible articulation (emphasized by his violin bowing in Ex. 3.85a). On other occasions the intention appears to be to obtain a full-length note. In the third bar of Ex. 3.85b, the violins' phrasing should surely match the flute's slur; well-connected separate bows were probably intended to elicit greater power and volume.

Ex. 3.85 a–b. Tchaikovsky: *Symphonie pathétique* op. 74/i.

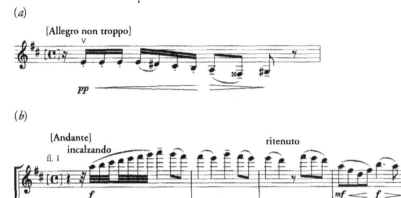

Dvořák often used this sign to indicate a lightly accented, barely detached note, especially in *piano* passages (Ex. 3.86a), but like Tchaikovsky and Elgar he probably used it at times to ensure that the players would give the note its full value (Ex. 3.86b). Sometimes, in the Cello Concerto for instance, there is a suggestion that he may have envisaged an element of agogic accentuation, and perhaps vibrato, in its execution (Ex. 3.86c).

178  CLASSICAL AND ROMANTIC PERFORMING PRACTICE

Ex. 3.86 a–c. Dvořák: (*a*) Violin Sonata op. 57/iii; (*b*) String Quartet op. 105/iv; (*c*) Cello Concerto op. 104/ii.

## NOTATION OF ACCENTS AND DYNAMICS 179

Although Brahms took a stance against adopting horizontal lines for *portato* (or, as he called it, *portamento*), he used them in the Scherzo of his String Sextet op. 36, where they appear to indicate slight weight. The theme sometimes occurs with – on the weak beats, and sometimes with > (Ex. 3.87a–b). A similar interpretation of the (for Brahms) unusual employment of horizontal lines under slurs in the Second Symphony seems probable (Ex. 3.87c). However, Brahms's scepticism about the excessive employment of accent signs is indicated by his remark in a letter of 27 January 1896 to Fritz Simrock, after he had read the proofs of Dvořák's *Te Deum*: "Do those silly accents have to stay on the stressed syllables? Nowadays one often sees that. Since the music stresses the syllables, the markings obviously make no sense whatsoever."[162]

Ex. 3.87 a–c. Brahms: (*a*) String Sextet op. 36/ii; (*b*) String Sextet op. 36/ii; (*c*) Second Symphony op. 73/i.

## The Box (☐)

Among the other accent and expression signs proposed in treatises, the elongated box came closest to gaining currency, but there was no unanimity about its meaning. Herz illustrated this sign in the first quarter of the century,

---

[162] Johannes Brahms: *Briefe an P. J. Simrock und Fritz Simrock*, ed. Max Kalbeck, iv (Berlin 1919), 189.

describing it as a graphic alternative for "*tenuto*, used when a note or chord is to be sustained".[163] Adolf Bernhard Marx, in mid-century, regarded the same sign as indicating a greater degree of accent than dots under slurs: "if the accent should be a stronger heavier one" (Ex. 3.88).[164] This sign was also reproduced in 1879 in the Mendel & Reissmann *Lexikon*, where Marx's instruction was repeated verbatim.[165] But like a number of other theoretical proposals, the sign was not adopted by composers to any significant extent; the horizontal line seems to have been regarded as sufficient for that purpose.

**Ex. 3.88** Marx: *Allgemeine Musiklehre*, 138.

\* \* \*

Most of the signs discussed here are also encountered in combination with slurs. In keyboard playing and, to a large extent, in wind playing the use of a slur in these circumstances usually implies simply that the notes should be less distinctly separated (though in wind playing there may also have been implications for breathing). In string playing the slur is specifically a bowing instruction, but the end effect is much the same. Where such signs appear over successive notes under a slur, however, their function is as much articulation as accent, and it is as articulation marks that they are considered in Chapter 6.

---

[163] Herz: *Méthode*, 17.
[164] Marx: *Allgemeine Musiklehre*, 138.
[165] Mendel and Reissmann: 'Vortrag' in *Musikalisches Conversations-Lexikon*, xi, 212.

# 4
# Articulation and Phrasing

Just as several categories of accentuation were associated with delineating the intended character of a piece of music, so various types and degrees of articulation were discussed by 18th-century and 19th-century musicians. Articulation could be indicated by the composer in the form of rests, or by means of articulation marks; or it might be expected to be provided by performers, based on their experience and musicality. The functions of accentuation and articulation are broadly similar, and are often closely linked, especially in defining musical structure. Articulation operates principally on two levels: the structural and the expressive. At the structural level is the articulation of musical phrases and sections, while, as an expressive resource, appropriate articulation of individual notes and figures is necessary to vivify a musical idea. Throughout this period, composers sought to provide ever more detailed instructions for articulation in their scores, just as they did with accentuation; and, as with accents, the performer's task became increasingly one of accurately executing the composer's markings, rather than recognizing where it was desirable to supplement or modify the musical text. Yet even in the most carefully notated late-19th-century scores, much remained the performer's responsibility.

Music was predominantly perceived as a language, albeit a language that, like poetry, appealed more to the emotion than to the intellect. But the precision with which the language of music expressed the feelings of its creator was considered to be of great importance; Wilhelm Heinrich Wackenroder's fictional creation, the idealistic composer Joseph Berglinger, could hope that at a future time "some person or other will live in whom Heaven has planted such sympathy for my soul that on hearing my melodies he will feel precisely what I felt in writing them—precisely what I so much wanted to put into them".[1] Thus, the separation of phrases and sections was essential to the proper realization of a composer's musical concept, and the

---

[1] Wilhelm Heinrich Wackenroder: *Herzensergiessungen eines kunstliebenden Klosterbruders* (Berlin, 1797), 203.

link between music and rhetoric was constantly cited to illustrate the importance of appropriate punctuation for the lucid delivery of a musical discourse. Mattheson's *Vollkommene Kapellmeister* of 1739, along with other texts from the first half of the 18th century, had dealt with the matter in some detail; and many subsequent discussions during the 18th and 19th centuries employed much the same terminology. In the early 1770s, J. A. P. Schulz introduced his extensive consideration of the subject with the remark that "The phrase divisions are the commas of the melody which, as in speech, should be made apparent by a small pause".[2] Türk, referring to music as the "language of feeling",[3] expanded on this in 1789 with an even closer analogy between language and music, which links the degree of the articulation with its structural function. His account provides a useful digest of the terms used by German theorists:

> A musical **sentence** [**Periode**] (a **section** [**Abschnitt**]), of which there can be several in a piece, would be that which one calls a **sentence** in speech and would be separated from the following by a full stop (.). A musical **rhythm** [**Rhythmus**] can be compared with the smaller speech unit, which one marks with a colon (:) or semicolon (;). The **phrase** [**Einschnitt**[4]], as the smallest unit, would be that which in speech will only be separated by a comma (,). If one wanted to include the **caesura** [**Cäsur**] in this, one would have to compare it with the caesura of a verse.[5]

Musical rhetoric was certainly not merely a feature of Baroque performance that disappeared during the 19th century, although this view became a common misconception during the late 20th century, especially among period instrument performers. If rhetoric weakened as a fundamental driving force in musical performance, it was, like so many aspects of expressive performance, a victim of the 20th-century modernist revolution. The concept of rhetorical or dramatic speech as a model for musical performance remained strong throughout the 19th century. Pierre Baillot observed in 1835: "Notes are used in music like words in speech; they are used to construct a phrase, to create an idea, consequently one should use full stops and commas just as in

---

[2] Schulz: 'Vortrag' in *Allgemeine Theorie*, ii, 1250.
[3] Türk: *Klavierschule*, 332.
[4] *Einschnitt*, literally a cut or incision, was often used to mean not only the division between musical phrases or figures, but also the phrases or figures themselves.
[5] Türk: *Klavierschule*, 343.

ARTICULATION AND PHRASING 183

a written text, to distinguish its sentences and their parts, and to make them easier to understand."[6] Habeneck, a few years later, also introduced the subject by remarking: "In a melody, as in speech, there are sentences, phrases, and figures that make up the phrases."[7] In much the same vein, Charles de Bériot began his discussion of musical punctuation, in his *Méthode de violon* of 1857/8, with the statement: "The object of punctuation in music, as in literature, is to mark the necessary points of repose: we will even add that in music punctuation is more important than in literature because the points of repose are indicated in a more absolute way by the strictness of the time."[8] And in 1905 Andreas Moser could still state that the separation and division of phrases has "just about the same significance for music as articulation and punctuation have for speech".[9]

But this apparent agreement about basic principles may well mask significant differences in practice. The fact that generations of musicians have repeatedly emphasized the importance of musical punctuation for the proper expression of a melody and that they have described that punctuation in similar terms does not mean that a musician of 1780 would have rendered it in the same manner as one of 1880, any more than actors or orators of different generations and traditions would have adopted the same approach to articulation in speech. The vast difference between recent concepts of dramatic declamation and those of the late 19th century, which are preserved in early recordings of celebrated actors, reveals just how fundamentally ideas about such things could be transformed in little more than a century. Quite apart from other considerations, changes in compositional style were accompanied by modified approaches to articulation, as well as to many other aspects of performance. The relationship between rules of correct composition and rules of correct performance, so often emphasized by 18th-century writers,[10] weakened in the 19th century as "unfettered genius"[11] was increasingly seen to override prescriptive aesthetic notions. And though older music continued to be performed, indeed was performed with increasing frequency as the century advanced, there was only limited awareness of historical performance techniques and practices, and little interest in their application. With a few notable exceptions, musicians of successive generations

---

[6] Baillot: *L'art du violon*, 163.
[7] Habeneck: *Méthode*, 107.
[8] Bériot: *Méthode*, iii, 206.
[9] Joachim/Moser: *Violinschule*, iii, 13.
[10] E.g., Türk: *Klavierschule*, VI, §23, 343ff.
[11] Emily Anderson, trans. and ed.: *The Letters of Beethoven* (London, 1961), 1325.

applied contemporary stylistic criteria to all the music in their repertoire. As Beethoven's pupil, Carl Czerny, observed only twenty years after his master's death: "even if it were possible to reproduce his way of playing exactly [. . .] the spiritual conception has acquired a different validity through the changed taste of the times, and must now and then be expressed by other means than were necessary in those days".[12] Almost a century later, Carl Flesch asserted, more forcefully, his conviction that modes of performing older music had to change radically, in line with the massive artistic revolution of the early 20th century.[13]

The vagaries of taste and fashion, as well as changes in compositional style, will certainly have impacted upon the ways in which approaches to articulation evolved. So too will the development of instruments, and it is important to bear in mind that at each stage of their development keyboard instruments, bowed instruments, various kinds of wind instruments, and the human voice have all had their own mechanisms and imperatives, which affect the execution and application of articulation. The means that are available to the organist or harpsichordist to convey phrasing effectively are quite different from those available to pianists, string, woodwind, and brass players, or singers. It is also necessary to remember that great performers, very many of whom were also composers, will have displayed individuality just as much in this area as in others, and that any two artists at a given period may well have adopted quite distinctly personal approaches to articulating the same piece of music, although all these will have been varied reflections of the prevailing aesthetic of that time.

Some of the most obvious differences between periods and performing traditions become apparent on closer consideration; many inevitably remain irrecoverable, for the finer details of performance that distinguish the playing and singing of the most cultivated artists are, as numerous writers explained, not susceptible of verbal description. These refinements certainly cannot be reliably reconstructed from written accounts, however elaborate; they could only have been appreciated through hearing the artists who were felt to represent good taste at any particular period. Nevertheless, early acoustic and piano-roll recordings by some of the great musicians of the 19th century provide us with an invaluable resource for comparing written accounts with performance, sometimes by the people who wrote about it.

---

[12] Czerny: *Pianoforte-Schule*, iv, 34.
[13] Carl Flesch: *Die Kunst des Violinspiels*, 2nd edn, i, 18. See Ch. 1, p. 7, for his words.

The earliest of these recordings provide opportunities to hear artists whose first musical experiences go back beyond the middle of the century, and who were closely associated with the generation of Mendelssohn, Schumann, Wagner, and Berlioz. These include recordings of composers such as Reinecke, Saint-Säens, Joachim, and Grieg performing their own music. The results of the comparison are salutary. It is often difficult to reconcile what was written with what was actually done; but these discrepancies are valuable, because they help to estimate the potential meaning of written accounts from the time before we have any aural evidence of great performers. They also provide a caveat against the assumption that what is not described was not expected. It is a remarkable fact that the celebrated pianist and composer Carl Reinecke, in his many writings about music, never referred to the discretionary arpeggiation of chords, although his recordings show that in his own compositions and those of other composers, from Mozart to Schumann, he used this expressive resource extremely frequently and in many varied ways where it was not marked. Like so many other practices that were obvious, because universally employed and therefore self-evident, it received little attention until changing attitudes towards notation and aesthetics made it controversial.[14]

Despite the incompleteness of theoretical texts, J. A. P. Schulz's discussion of structural articulation provides significant evidence of late-18th-century theories. He began his consideration of the subject by affirming not only that the separation of phrases should occur in the right places, but also that it should be distinctly perceptible, asserting: "The phrase divisions should be marked in the clearest manner and correctly." Nevertheless, it is apparent that Schulz did not regard a real break in the sound as the only method of marking the articulation; he also considered it possible to obtain the same end by a *decrescendo* at the end of a phrase followed by some degree of accentuation at the beginning of the new one; he stated that it could be achieved "if one either shortens the last note of a phrase somewhat, and then firmly begins the first note of the following phrase; or if one lets the volume sink somewhat and then increases it with the beginning of the new phrase."[15] The distinction may have been envisaged as allowing variety appropriate to different circumstances; or perhaps Schulz was thinking of the fundamental differences between various kinds of instruments: keyboard

---

[14] For discussion of improvised arpeggiation see Ch. 13.
[15] Schulz: 'Vortrag' in *Allgemeine Theorie*, ii, 1250.

instruments incapable of dynamic accents such as organ and harpsichord, where the phrase divisions can only be made apparent by separation; clavichord and fortepiano, where subtle degrees of accentuation are also feasible, but where the rate at which the sound decays is largely beyond the control of the player; and bowed instruments, wind instruments, and voice, where bow, tongue, or consonants can be used to produce many different types of articulation, and where controlled *decrescendo* or *crescendo* on a single note is possible.

Unlike Türk, Schulz did not imply a direct relationship between the structural function of articulation and its degree, though he recognized the subtle variety that an experienced artist would give it according to context, noting in a footnote:

> The word "phrase" will be taken here in the widest meaning, in that the *Einschnitts* as well as the *Abschnitts* and sections of the melody will be understood by it. In performance all these divisions will be marked in the same manner; and if great players and singers really observe a shading among them, this is nevertheless so subtle and so complicated to describe that we content ourselves with the mere mention of it.[16]

The rest of his discussion was taken up mainly with the problem of how a performer should recognize the phrase divisions. He conceded that "If the phrase ends with a rest there is no difficulty; the phrase division [*Einschnitt*] marks itself on its own." He also observed that it should not be a problem for the singer to mark the phrase divisions correctly, "because he only has to govern himself by the phrase divisions of the words, above which he sings, with which the phrase division of the melody must exactly accord"; but he acknowledged that difficulties might be encountered in passagework (where the singer had to deliver an extended succession of notes to a single syllable). For instrumentalists he suggested that

> The main rule that has to be taken into account here is this, that one governs oneself by the beginning of the piece. A perfectly regular piece of music observes regular phrases throughout: namely whatever beat of the bar it begins with so begin all its phrases with just the same beat. Therefore,

---

[16] Schulz: 'Vortrag' in *Allgemeine Theorie*, ii, 1250.

in the following pieces the notes marked with o are those with which the first phrase concludes, and those marked with + those with which the new phrase begins: [Ex. 4.1][17]

Ex. 4.1  Schulz: 'Vortrag' in *Allgemeine Theorie*, ii, 1250.

Such symmetry was more characteristic of the lighter Galant style of the mid-18th century than of the emotionally charged and dramatic idioms that were associated with the development of the *empfindsamer Stil*, and what has come to be known as the Viennese Classical style, where movements or sections would be likely to include a variety of contrasting and complementary figures. Recognizing this, Schulz gave an example from the beginning of a C. P. E. Bach sonata (Ex. 4.2), about which he remarked that in such music the player had to recognize phrase divisions "from the character of the melody". But he indicated that with each new idea, just as with the beginning of a piece, the phrasing could be deduced from the placing of the initial part of the phrase. Thus, he warned that "it would be extremely faulty if, for example, one wanted to perform the sixth bar as if the phrase were to begin with its first note, since, in fact, the preceding ends with it, as the eighth-note rest of the preceding bar indicates".[18]

---

[17] Schulz: 'Vortrag' in *Allgemeine Theorie*, ii, 1250.
[18] Schulz: 'Vortrag' in *Allgemeine Theorie*, ii, 1251.

188   CLASSICAL AND ROMANTIC PERFORMING PRACTICE

Ex. 4.2  Schulz: 'Vortrag' in *Allgemeine Theorie*, ii, 1251.

Schulz also remarked that composers sometimes used modified beaming to indicate the beginnings and ends of phrases, and felt that, since it made the phrase divisions very clear, it was to be preferred to continuous beaming in doubtful cases. He observed:

> If, as in the third and fourth examples [of Ex. 4.1], the phrase division falls between eighths or sixteenths, which in notational practice are customarily beamed together, some composers are in the habit of separating those which belong to the preceding phrase from those with which the new one begins by the way they write them, in order to indicate the phrase division all the more clearly, namely therefore: [Ex. 4.3].[19]

Ex. 4.3  Schulz: 'Vortrag' in *Allgemeine Theorie*, ii, 1250f.

This continued to be used by many composers, for instance Schumann (Ex. 4.4), throughout the 19th century.

---

[19] Schulz: 'Vortrag' in *Allgemeine Theorie*, ii, 1250.

Ex. 4.4 Schumann: Second Symphony op. 61/ii.

Observing that this type of notation could not be used with quarter- and half-notes, however, Schulz remarked that in such cases one could "use the little stroke I over the last note of the phrase, as some now and again do".[20] The use of a vertical stroke for this purpose is not unusual in music of the period, but, as Türk was to point out, this employment of the stroke to indicate a shortened and lightened final note could easily be mistaken by less experienced players for the more common type of *staccato* mark, which might imply accent. (See Ex. 4.6.)

Schulz concluded his examination of this subject with some general observations on the importance of correctly articulating phrase divisions, in which he again highlighted the role of accentuation at the beginning of a figure and weakness at the end in clarifying the phrase structure of a piece. (His marking of the beginning of a phrase with +, the same sign that he had elsewhere employed to mark the notes requiring accentuation, is evidently quite deliberate.) His final paragraph shows the close link between phrasing and structural accentuation, and reinforces other writers' remarks about the subordination of purely metrical accentuation to these considerations:

> It is incredible how greatly the melody becomes disfigured and unclear if the phrase divisions are incorrectly marked or, indeed, not marked at all. To convince oneself of this, one ought only to perform a gavotte in such a manner that the phrase divisions at the half-bar are not observed. Easy as this dance is to understand, it will by this means become unrecognizable to everyone. Here again mistakes will most frequently be made in such pieces where the phrases begin in the middle of a bar and indeed on a weak beat; because everyone is, from the beginning, accustomed to mark prominently only the strong beats of the bar on which the various accents of the melody fall, and to leave the weak beats entirely equal as if they were merely passing. In such cases the phrases then become torn apart through this, part of them being attached to the preceding or following, which is just as preposterous as if in a speech one wanted to make the pause before or

---

[20] Schulz: 'Vortrag' in *Allgemeine Theorie*, ii, 1251.

after the comma. In the following example [Ex. 4.5], if the phrase division is marked, the melody is good in itself; if, however, merely the accents of the bar are marked, the melody becomes extremely flat and has the same effect as if, instead of saying: "He is my lord; I am his squire", one wanted to say: "He is my lord I; am his squire."[21]

Ex. 4.5 Schulz: 'Vortrag' in *Allgemeine Theorie*, ii, 1251.

Türk, whose approach shows his intimate knowledge of this and other significant discussions of the subject, made similar points, with some qualifications. Among other things he was particularly insistent, as mentioned above, that the performer should avoid interpreting a vertical stroke that was intended to show the end of a phrase as one that was designed to indicate an accent, commenting:

> Necessary as it is to lift the finger at the end of a phrase, it is nevertheless faulty to perform it in such a manner that the lifting referred to is allied with a violent staccato, as in example a) [Ex. 4.6]. One hears this faulty execution very frequently when the phrase division is indicated by the usual sign for staccato, as at c). For many players have the incorrect idea that a staccato note—as one calls it in artistic language—must always be staccatoed with a certain violence. In order to prevent this faulty performance where possible, and at the same time to make the small, less perceptible articulations recognizable, I have made use of a new sign in my small sonatas [. . .]. This sign, which I simply call the **Einschnitt**, is the one at d).[22]

---

[21] Schulz: 'Vortrag' in *Allgemeine Theorie*, ii, 1251.
[22] Türk: *Klavierschule*, 342.

ARTICULATION AND PHRASING   191

Ex. 4.6 Türk: *Klavierschule*, 342.

When Türk mentioned lifting the finger, he was of course referring to keyboard playing. Schulz, dealing with the matter in a general way, envisaged phrase division being accomplished either through real separation or through demarcation of the phrase by means of accent and *decrescendo*, while Türk mentioned only the former.

One thing to which neither Schulz nor Türk alluded as a factor in the recognition or separation of phrases and figures was the slur. For 18th-century composers the slur was associated far more with the character of a particular musical idea than with structural phrasing. According to some theorists, slurs required not only accentuation (dynamic or agogic) of the initial note but also, especially in keyboard playing, shortening of the final one, but Türk specifically warned against automatically shortening the final note under three- and four-note slurs.[23] Clementi, discussing the realization of appoggiaturas, also envisaged either a full-length note of resolution or a shortened one, giving priority to the former (Ex. 4.7a). Mozart, with typical care, notated a shortened second note in such figures, both for fortepiano and for melody instruments, where he regarded it as essential (Ex. 4.7b).

Ex. 4.7a Clementi: *Introduction to the Art of Playing on the Piano Forte* (London, [1801]), i, 10.

---

[23] See Ch. 2, "Slurred Figures". Also see Ch. 6 for further discussion of slurs and their implications.

Ex. 4.7b Mozart: Piano Trio K. 542/i, (autograph).
[Allegro]

As a means of developing a good sense of phrasing, Türk also recommended not only practising dance pieces, as suggested by Schulz, but also songs by good composers.[24] (In this period Lieder were often printed like keyboard music on two staves with the melody doubled by the keyboard player's right hand throughout, and with the words set between the staves; keyboard players could therefore regulate their phrasing by the punctuation of the text.) Schulz, Türk, and other 18th-century theorists who discussed articulation theoretically were somewhat rigid and simplistic in their approach to phrase construction. They failed almost entirely to take account of, or address issues of, phrase elision and other irregularities that would have disturbed the symmetrical patterns of which they provided examples (though such things were touched upon from the composer's point of view by, among others, Riepel and Koch).[25] Schulz's citation of the C. P. E. Bach sonata was merely a very tentative step in that direction. None of these writers seems to have wanted to explore the circumstances in which composers (or performers) might have wished to create an artistic effect by challenging the listener's expectations. Türk, indeed, appears to have regarded such procedures as illegitimate, for he commented at one point:

---

[24] Türk: *Klavierschule*, 347.
[25] Joseph Riepel: *Anfangsgründe zur musikalischen Setzkunst* (Regensburg, etc., 1752–68); Koch, *Versuch*.

Just as it would be counterproductive if one read on continuously at the end of a phrase, so it would be erroneous if a musician carried on playing connectedly and in a single breath at a point of rest. Consequently, the following manner of performance at a) would be wholly against the musical sense. [Ex. 4.8]

And he observed, before going on to consider the reasons for this in greater detail, that he was convinced his comments could have "some influence on (logically) correct performance".[26]

**Ex. 4.8** Türk: *Klavierschule*, 340.

In fact, however, the phrasing of Türk's examples would depend on the harmonic context, and if one scrutinizes the music of the best composers of the period, who were most fastidious in their markings, instances of just such phrase elision, carefully indicated by the composer, are frequently encountered. In Ex. 4.9a, Mozart initially ended the phrase in bar 4 in the expected way, with a slur from the $a'$ to the $g\sharp'$, but then extended it to the $e''$, thus eliding the phrases. And in Ex. 4.9b, Beethoven similarly elided the phrases with his slur in the fourth bar of the theme. The same thing is found with ever greater frequency in the 19th century (Ex. 4.9c) and was recommended as a strategy for performers by Manuel García, even where nothing had been marked by the composer (see Ex. 4.26).

**Ex. 4.9a** Mozart: Rondo K. 511.

[26] Türk: *Klavierschule*, 340.

Ex. 4.9b  Beethoven: Piano Sonata op. 31/2/iii.

Ex. 4.9c  Chopin: Mazurka op. 6/3.
[Vivace]

Yet in the last quarter of the century, Mathis Lussy seemed still to regard this procedure as illegitimate, and even suggested that composers who indicated such things had simply got their phrasing wrong. He maintained that

> It ought to be an established rule that only such notes as form a musical idea or thought, a section or a rhythm, should be connected by a slur, a curved line or rhythmic connection. Phrasing slurs [*liaisons rythmiques*] should never be placed above notes belonging to two different rhythms, and should never embrace or cover the last note of one rhythm and the first of another.[27]

But this concept of the "phrasing slur" was a relatively recent one in the second half of the 19th century. It was confined largely to piano music, in which a host of new editions of the classics replaced the composer's slurring with the fashionable phrasing slurs.[28] It could not be applied in string music, where the slur indicated bowing, and was also inappropriate in wind-instrument repertoire, where slurring was either connected with breathing or—by analogy with bowing—the articulation of short phrases.

Türk's proposal of new signs for marking phrase divisions and expressive accents, typifies the growing concern, which he shared with C. P. E. Bach, J. F. Reichardt, and many other contemporaries, to find a more explicit means of indicating the articulation that, in practice, the performer had to supply on the basis of experience. Türk's 1783 sonatas had been aimed primarily at amateurs of limited accomplishments, who could not be expected to possess

---

[27] Lussy: *Traité*, 69.
[28] See Ch. 6, "The Long Phrasing Slur".

the skill and judgement of professionals in such matters. The widening market for printed music, for both professional and amateur use, was a significant factor in encouraging this development. The inconsistency of many composers, who relied on the performer's understanding, together with the carelessness of most 18th- and early-19th-century publishers in accurately reproducing the composer's text, frustrated all efforts to ensure that articulation markings were reliable. A writer in 1804, complaining about confusing bowing, observed that "It cannot be denied that the carelessness or haste of the composer is to blame. [...] More often it comes from the engravers. It's all one to them whether the slur is a few notes too long or too short."[29]

Another of Türk's contemporaries, Domenico Corri, who was not only a singer and composer (like Haydn, a pupil of Porpora) but also a publisher, was acutely conscious of the advantages of providing greater guidance in such matters for the predominantly amateur clientele at whom his publications were aimed. He explained that his *Select Collection* of vocal music was intended "to facilitate, and at the same time to render more perfect, the performance of vocal and instrumental music",[30] and he felt that "one of the most important articles in the execution of music (vocal music in particular) is the proper division of the PERIODS; as is evident from hearing good singers often break in upon the sense and the melody, for want of knowing how to take breath in the proper places."[31] In the *Select Collection* he introduced two signs for this purpose. One of these (⁎), which he used in both vocal and instrumental parts, was to mark the phrase divisions of the melody; he instructed that when this was used,

> a Pause is always to be made and breath taken.—The Pause to be about as long as that made by a Comma in reading, and the time taken for it to be deducted from the Note to which the mark is nearest. For example, when before the note; This [Ex. 4.10a] will be nearly equal to this [Ex. 4.10b] and when after the note, This [Ex. 4.10c] equal to this [Ex. 4.10d]. NB. This is likewise applicable to Instrumental Music.

The other (⁎), which applied only to vocal parts, was to indicate points where singers should breathe; but they should "make the pause as imperceptible as

---

[29] Anon.: 'Ueber die heutige verworrene Strichbezeichnung', *Allgemeine musikalische Zeitung*, vi (1803–4), 731f.
[30] Corri: *A Select Collection*, i, 1.
[31] Corri: *A Select Collection*, i, 2.

possible", since these respirations were only "on account of a period being too long, or when particular exertion of the voice is necessary, as before a Cadence &. &."[32]

Ex. 4.10 a–d. D. Corri: *A Select Collection*, i, 8.

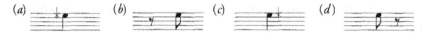

Although Corri did not discuss the principles of phrase division in his introduction, his indications in the music (in so far as the sometimes ambiguous engraving can be relied on) provide useful evidence of his practice. His division of phrases is closely related to the harmonic and periodic structure of the music. In the instrumental parts not all the divisions that might be expected are marked (some perhaps through oversight or careless engraving), but those that are generally occur at obvious breaks in the melody. Where more than one division of the musical text would make musical sense, Corri's choice is naturally determined by the vocal part, even though the instrumental part may precede it. In Giordani's "Sento che in seno" (*Il Barone di Torre Forte*), for instance, the flute part in bars 24–32 is susceptible of being divided in several ways, but the distribution of the words in the vocal part a dozen bars later is the deciding factor (Ex. 4.11a). In Paisiello's "Ti seguirò fedele" a subsidiary articulation comes after the fourth bar in the instrumental parts, the significance of which is only clarified by the vocal entry (Ex. 4.11b); and there is a similar instance in Sacchini's "Rasserena i tuoi bei rai" (*Enea e Lavinia*) in the third bar of the violin part (Ex. 4.11c).

Ex. 4.11 a–c. D. Corri: *A Select Collection*. (*a*), i, 86f; (*b*) i, 19; (*c*) i, 29.

---

[32] Corri: *A Select Collection*, i, 3.

Ex. 4.11 Continued

The positioning of Corri's first sign (✳) in the vocal parts is less predictable than in the instrumental ones; sometimes it may be suspected that the first sign has been printed where the second was intended, but elsewhere it is clear that he used the former not only to mark the principal divisions, but also to indicate breaks, necessary for the articulation of the text, that are inessential to, or sometimes even contrary to, the musical sense, for example in Sacchini's "Dolce speme" (*Rinaldo*) (Ex. 4.12a). In some instances, this relationship of articulation to text means that phrasing divisions in the same passage of music can vary within a song; thus, in Geminiani's "If ever a fond inclination", two versions of the opening melody occur (Ex. 4.12b).

Ex. 4.12 a–b. D. Corri: *A Select Collection.* (*a*) i, 104; (*b*) ii, 5.

The *Select Collection* contains many instances where articulation is obtained by means of shortening an upbeat to a new phrase rather than by curtailing the final note of the preceding phrase. In Giordani's aria "Sento che in seno" (Ex. 4.13a), the time required for the articulation is sometimes taken from the previous note and sometimes from the following. Another illuminating example occurs in "The Soldier Tired" from Arne's *Artaxerxes* (Ex. 4.13b).

Ex. 4.13  a–b. D. Corri: *A Select Collection*. (*a*) i, 88; (*b*) ii, 49.

(a)

(b)

This manner of shortening upbeats for breathing was also recommended by Mary Novello later in the 19th century as the normal procedure for "taking a half breath in the middle of a sentence". She went on to say: "the time of inhalation should be taken from the note which follows respiration, unless the musical phrase requires this note to retain its full value of duration", adding that such breaths ought to be taken before such words as "the", "of", "to", and "and".[33] It is worth noting, however, that this advice seems to be contradicted in the teachings of García, Lablache, Duprez, and Novello's English contemporary John Addison.[34]

While many of Corri's indications for taking breath as imperceptibly as possible occur at places where a subsidiary articulation would make good musical sense, some are found where they might not seem so obvious. A persistent peculiarity is Corri's practice of indicating a breath immediately before a pause bar in which a cadenza is to be executed, even when this is only preceded by a single short, or even very short note. In J. C. Bach's "Nel partir bell'idol mio",

---

[33] Mary Novello: *Voice and Vocal Art* (London, 1856), 11.
[34] John Addison: *Singing Practically Treated in a Series of Instructions* (London, 1850). See also Robert Toft: 'The Expressive Pause: Punctuation, Rests, and Breathing in England 1770–1850', *Performance Practice Review*, vii (1994), 199–232.

from *La clemenza di Scipione*, Corri indicates a breath after the sixteenth-note upbeat even though this has been preceded by a respiration (see Ex. 12.7, bar 36). Often such breaths are indicated even where the upbeat is the first syllable of a word, as in Sacchini's "Se placar non puo quest alma" (*Perseo*) (Ex. 4.14a). Breathing in the middle of a word is also indicated between the anticipation of a note by *portamento* and the note itself, for instance, in Dibdin's "Say little foolish flutt'ring thing" (*The Padlock*) (Ex. 4.14b).

Ex. 4.14 a–b. D. Corri: *A Select Collection*. (*a*) i, 51; (*b*) ii, 22.

(*a*)

(*b*)

In *The Singer's Preceptor*, Corri also considered the more discreet, but nevertheless essential, articulation between words that was to some extent independent of breathing. He observed that in Handel's "Angels ever Bright":

if the first sentence is sung without any separation of the words as written, thus [Ex. 4.15a] the effect would be the same to the Ear as if these two words "bright and" were joined together thus "brightand" whereas, if the word "and" was separated from "bright" by a break as in the following Example, it would preserve the true accent of the words, thus, [Ex. 4.15b] [. A]ll words in repetition as "Sad sad is my breast" ["]Gone gone is my rest" &c should be divided.

My song "Beware of love" affords another instance to prove that the separating [of] words greatly conduces to effect, in the first Verse, which Koyan addresses to his Mother expressive of gratitude, the repetition of the words "no" are sung, thus, [Ex. 4.16a]. In the second Verse, which he addresses to his Sister, conveying a sly caution with some degree of irony, the repetition of the word "Yes" should be sung, thus, [Ex. 4.16b] and the difference of effect demonstrates the advantage produced by separation of words as above remarked; also when the letters k, th, gh & c or any harsh sounding Consonants end a word immediately followed by one beginning with similar letters, great care should be taken to divide those words.[35]

Ex. 4.15  a–b. D. Corri: *The Singer's Preceptor*, 65.

Ex. 4.16  a–b. D. Corri: *The Singer's Preceptor*, 65.

Many 19th-century writers of instrumental and vocal methods contented themselves with general statements about articulating phrase divisions that were not specifically marked by the composer, regarding firm rules or principles as inapplicable to such things, or at least beyond the scope of their treatise. Dotzauer opined that "for the most part the musician must let himself be guided by his correct feelings, although, taken as a whole, there are rules about it, which are concerned with rhythm, phraseology etc. Thus, if certain divisions were not observed, points of repose would be complete lacking, so that the flow of ideas would appear confused."[36] Spohr considered that "the accentuation and separation of musical phrases" were among the distinguishing features of a "beautiful performance style" rather than a merely "correct" one. The difference between these was, in Spohr's opinion, that the former involved "the

---

[35] Corri: *Singers Preceptor*, 65.
[36] Dotzauer: *Violoncell-Schule*, 28.

ability to recognize the character of the piece being performed, seizing its predominant expression and conveying this in performance". And he believed that the things that elevated a correct style into a beautiful style were the product of "a natural gift, which may indeed be awakened and developed, but can never be taught".[37] Hummel, who took a similar view of the division between "correct" and "beautiful" performance,[38] did not discuss phrase division at all in his piano method, though he devoted considerable space to the distribution of expressive accents. Some ten years later Carl Czerny similarly concentrated on the role of accentuation, rather than articulation, in phrasing.[39]

To some extent, changing emphases in the discussion of articulation were connected with changing approaches to notation. Whereas the imprecision of much 18th-century notation often conceals places where a note at the end of a phrase was understood to require a considerably shorter duration in performance than its written length, late-18th-century and 19th-century composers increasingly tended to provide notational clues or instructions to performers that should seldom have left them in doubt about the places where the articulation that was necessary to the proper separation of musical phrases was required. Some writers, however, considered the matter in sufficient detail to provide useful insights into their practice.

The violinist Pierre Baillot, having made the obligatory connection between music and speech, observed that the musical equivalents of punctuation marks are quarter-, eighth-, and sixteenth-note rests, his assumption being that these will have been included by the composer; but he recognized that there were also "light separations, silences of very short duration" that were not always indicated. Like Schulz he admitted two methods of attaining them, though unlike Schulz he seems to have regarded the introduction of an actual silence as the less common means of marking the phrase divisions. He noted: "it is necessary that the performer introduce them, when he sees the need, by allowing the final note of the section of the phrase or of the entire sentence to die away, and that, in certain cases, he even finishes that note a little before the end of its value".[40] However, Baillot's two examples indicate the articulations by means of rests (Ex. 4.17a–b). The first of these, from Viotti's Violin Concerto no. 27, nicely illustrates the limitations of applying Schulz's and Türk's rule about the relationships of phrase divisions to the opening of the melody.

---

[37] Spohr: *Violinschule*, 195.
[38] Hummel: *Anweisung*, 2nd edn, 426ff.
[39] Czerny: *Pianoforte-Schule*, iii, 5ff.
[40] Baillot: *L'art du violon*, 163.

Ex. 4.17 a–b. Baillot: *L'Art du violon*, 163.

The remainder of Baillot's discussion of musical punctuation is concerned with the way in which certain types of phrase ending should be executed. He made the comparison, typical of his countrymen, between the note following an appoggiatura and the mute *e* of the French language. He also commented that where a harmony note occurs on the strong beat at the end of a phrase it should be played "neither with hardness, nor with too much softness unless it is at the end of its value, where it is necessary to allow the sound to die away to announce the end of the phrase or piece".[41] And he made a distinction between endings that required a *rallentando* and a fading-away of the sound, and those where a vigorous execution with marked articulation between the final notes was needed (Ex. 4.18).

Ex. 4.18 Baillot: *L'art du violon*, 164.

[41] Baillot: *L'art du violon*, 163.

In wind playing, Anton Bernhard Fürstenau was naturally concerned with articulation by means of the breathing. He instructed:

> It should be understood that, as a guiding principle, breath is not taken on an inappropriate part of the bar, the time for the breath is taken from the note that precedes it not that which follows it, and that every phrase, every connected idea, should be performed in one breath. If, however, because of the length [of the phrase] this is quite impossible for the player, or can only be achieved with difficulty, he must focus on the larger or smaller parts, the perfect or imperfect cadences, or the caesuras that characterize the musical idea, and breathe in one of these places. (Ex. 4.19)[42]

In the exercises given at the end of his method,[43] Fürstenau meticulously marked the places for breathing, also with the sign !. He dealt with other issues that affect the delivery of a phrase, very similarly to Spohr and other writers of the period, under the heading "Vortrag".[44]

**Ex. 4.19** Fürstenau: *Die Kunst des Flötenspiels*, 11.
Fürstenau's note: NB. Where breath is to be taken, the sign (!) is placed, and the small sections, cadences or caesuras (where breath can be taken if necessary) are marked with a small cross (+).

---

[42] Anton Bernhard Fürstenau: *Die Kunst des Flötenspiels* op. 138 (Leipzig, [1844]), 11.
[43] Fürstenau: *Die Kunst*, 91–112.
[44] Fürstenau: *Die Kunst*, 88–90.

From the mid-19th-century singer's point of view, Manuel García, like Corri, treated phrase division essentially as a matter of breathing; but this was only one of seven elements that made up what he called "the art of phrasing": pronunciation, formation of the phrase, breathing, time, forte-piano, ornaments, and expression. In his consideration of phrase formation, he made the important point that declamatory music or recitative, being musical prose, "pays no regard to the number of bars or symmetry of cadences, or even to regularity of time" and is "wholly influenced by prosodic accents and excitement of passion", whereas in "melodious verse [. . .] there reigns a perfect regularity—required to satisfy the rhythmical instinct". And he observed that "a complete symmetry must be established between the different parts of the melody, and they must be enclosed within certain easily perceptible limits of duration. In this way our ear may unfailingly recognize each element of a phrase".[45] He explained that "Good melodies, like speeches, are divided by pauses, which are regulated [. . .] by the distribution and length of the several ideas composing such melodies";[46] and having observed that the singer should inhale "only during rests that occur simultaneously in words and melody" he remarked:

> These rests may be introduced even where not marked by the composer, either for a better development of ideas, or to facilitate their execution, they serve either to bring out the distribution of ideas more clearly or to facilitate the execution. Breath should not be taken except on the weak accents of a bar, or after the terminal note of a melodic figure; this method enables the singer to attack the next *idea* or *group* at the beginning of its value. Pauses which separate phrases and *semi-phrases*, are of longer duration than those merely separating figures or groups of notes: long rests, therefore should be selected for taking long, full breath; little rests between *figures* admit only of very short breaths, rapidly taken, and, on this account, are termed *mezzi-respiri*. These are seldom indicated; it being left to the singer to insert them when required.[47]

He illustrated this with two examples from Mozart's *Don Giovanni* (Ex. 4.20).

---

[45] García: *École*, ii, 15.
[46] García: *École*, ii, 17.
[47] García: *École*, ii, 18f.

ARTICULATION AND PHRASING    205

Ex. 4.20  García: *École*, ii, 19.

Sometimes, however, García noted, "in order to increase the effect of a phrase, it is allowable to unite its different parts by suppressing pauses which separate them",[48] and he gave an example from Donizetti's *Anna Bolena* (Ex. 4.21), but without indicating where the necessary breath would have to be taken. In cases where a similar effect was achieved by means of a *portamento* he instructed that the breath should be taken immediately after this had been executed, illustrating the point with passages from Rossini (Ex. 4.22). This procedure recalls Corri's indication of a breath after a *portamento* in Dibdin's "Say little foolish flutt'ring thing" (see Ex. 4.15b).

Ex. 4.21  García: *École*, ii, 20.

Ex. 4.22  García: *École*, ii, 20.

[48] García: *École*, ii, 19.

In contrast to the joining of phrases for a particular effect, García noted that short figures, or even successive notes, were sometimes required to be separated, not only between words but also within words, and that this could be done "either by breathing at each beat, or by simply quitting the sound without breathing, which, in some cases, is indispensable".[49] He illustrated this with examples from Pacini's *Niobe* and Meyerbeer's *Il crociato in Egitto* (Ex. 4.23).

Ex. 4.23 García: *École*, ii, 20.

While he agreed with other authorities that, in normal circumstances, breath should not be taken in the middle of a word, or between words intimately connected, he conceded that "In phrases where pauses are badly arranged, an artist may sometimes be obliged to divide a word or sentence, by inhaling; but, in that case, he should disguise the act with such artifice as completely to escape detection." Among the circumstances that favoured imperceptible breathing in the middle of a word was the occurrence of two consonants, "especially if the second consonant be *explosive*". And he recommended breathing through the nose on such occasions (Ex. 4.24). García considered a supplementary breath advisable before a cadenza, when this was preceded by a long note (Ex. 4.25), in which case "a singer must avail himself of the noise made by the accompaniment to inhale".[50] Unlike Corri he does not seem to have regarded it as a general principle to breathe immediately before the pause note of a cadenza.

Ex. 4.24 García: *École*, ii, 21.

---

[49] García: *École*, ii, 20.
[50] García: *École*, ii, 21.

Ex. 4.25 García: *École*, ii, 22.

Another mid-19th-century musician who systematically examined the subject of phrase division, the violinist and composer Charles de Bériot, had close personal connections with García, having been married to his sister, the great singer Maria Malibran. It was perhaps for that reason that Bériot approached the subject of performance style in violin playing very much by analogy with singing. In the section of his *Méthode* entitled "De la ponctuation", Bériot began, after some general introductory remarks, in a rather elementary way, by drawing the violinist's attention to the deleterious effect of abbreviating rests (a problem for inexperienced violinists when practising without accompaniment). He then commented that

> There are, in the body of the phrase, rests of such short duration that they are not always indicated: these little points of repose are not therefore the less necessary to respiration. It is for the judgment of the artist to discern their true places, and to mark them he will let the final note expire a little before its time.

He made no attempt to lay down rules or general guidance as to where such articulation should be introduced, but he gave a series of musical examples of "graduated punctuation in tranquil music" ranging from what he described as "a species of religious music, vague, without order, without rhythm, without words, and so devoid of all punctuation",[51] to the opening theme of the second movement of Mozart's String Quartet in D minor K. 421, in which the articulation was indicated by the composer. This was followed by one of his own *etudes* demonstrating "punctuation in the energetic style", where the division of phrases and figures was again indicated

---

[51] Bériot: *Méthode*, 206f.

throughout by rests and articulation marks.[52] A final set of examples illustrated "breathing rests",[53] first with music in which the composer marked the rests and then with three examples in which Bériot indicated the "breathing rests" by commas (Ex. 4.26). Interestingly, the two Classical examples contain abundant articulations, while the example from his own trio seems to be conceived in a much more *legato* manner, perhaps illustrating a perceived stylistic difference between late-18th-century music and that of his own day, although whether this differentiation accurately reflected a genuine tradition or merely mid-19th-century practice is questionable.

**Ex. 4.26** Bériot: *Méthode*, 210.

A further aspect of Bériot's treatment of articulation comes in the next section of the *Méthode*, which is headed "Syllabation". Here Bériot observed:

> There are rests even slighter than those we have just explained, namely those of syllabation. By this expression we mean the method of separating words and syllables to give them more force and accent in lyrical recitation.

[52] Bériot: *Méthode*, 208.
[53] Bériot: *Méthode*, 210.

These nuances, which are entirely in the spirit of the piece, are so delicate that they cannot be classed in the punctuation. They should be more or less marked according to the sentiment of the song.

Special schools of declamation have been established to teach us to speak well; of lyrical declamation and singing to teach us how to deliver melody. These vocal studies are great helps to the violinist, whose bow should render the accents of the soul.

In music as in literature, these little rests of syllabation cannot be written; the performer should feel them. Hence, we call them the punctuation of sentiment.

The places which these little rests should occupy are indicated in the following examples by a comma. We should notice that their place is chiefly between a dotted note and the short one which follows it.[54]

All three of his examples here are operatic, though the extension to violin music of the French school at this period is not difficult to make (Ex. 4.27).

Ex. 4.27  Bériot: *Méthode*, 211.

A final example, expressive rather than structural, illustrates the subtle flexibility that a musician of the mid-19th century, whether singer or instrumentalist, might have been inclined to introduce into passages of equal-length notes (Ex. 4.28). Bériot's rhythmic treatment of the passage is perhaps

---

[54] Bériot: *Méthode*, 211.

an echo of the French tradition of unequal performance of equal-value notes, which appears, from a number of sources, to have survived in diluted form into the 19th century.[55] Unequal performance of equal-value notes, however, remained a basic element of performance into the early 20th century, as early recordings of older players amply demonstrate, but in ways that have no obvious direct connection with the more rigid principles of French Baroque. The slight hesitation achieved by the articulation is a further refinement that is evidently connected with expressive singing; and this kind of nuance, too, is documented in early recordings. Bériot remarked in his introduction to the example:

> In very soft music the composers do not always mark the long and short notes, for fear that the song should take too rhythmical a form. In such cases they leave to the singer the care of marking the syllables with that infinite delicacy which lends so great a charm. Thus, for instance, if we sung with absolute equality the two eighth-notes which begin each bar of the following Romance, our diction would be flat and cold. But if the composer had written those notes as dotted notes this sweet song would be too jerky in effect and would agree but little with the sentiment of its poem. It is here that a medium form is required, which the feelings alone can understand, and which no sign can express. It is sufficient for the first eighth-note to be a little longer than the second and that the small interval which separates them should be almost insensible.[56]

Ex. 4.28 Bériot, *Méthode*, 211.

---

[55] David Fuller: 'Notes inégales' in Stanley Sadie (ed.), *The New Grove Dictionary of Music and Musicians* (London, 1980), xiii, 423.
[56] Bériot: *Méthode*, 211.

Andreas Moser (a pupil, and later a close colleague of Joseph Joachim), born about the time Bériot's *Méthode* was published, considered the question of articulation at length. His treatment of stylistic issues in performance concentrated even more than those of the mid-19th century on questions of how to approach the music of the past rather than that of his own day; but, despite his considerable historical knowledge,[57] his comments about performance issues in old music seem, on the whole, to reflect late-19th-century practices and techniques of violin playing, rather than those of the periods in which the music was written.[58]

Although he began his discussion of musical articulation with the customary reference to its relationship with speech, Moser brought his own distinct perspective to it. Having observed that a musical idea can consist of as little as two notes, he asked rhetorically how, if the two notes of the figure are not connected by a *legato* slur, one can tell whether they should be articulated or connected when they are not, as in the opening motif of the Allegro vivace of Beethoven's String Quartet op. 59 no. 3 (Ex. 4.29a), unambiguously separated by the composer. He noted that a string player, "who is capable of, and accustomed to accomplish an unnoticeable bow change at the frog",[59] must sometimes forbear from employing this otherwise praiseworthy ability. He observed that the application of this facility in the opening of, for instance, a Handel *bourrée* (Ex. 4.29b) would result in an apparent syncopation rather than an upbeat and instructed the violinist to treat it as if a *staccato* dot were present. In the opening of Tartini's G major Sonata, however (Ex. 4.29c), he observed that "in keeping with the theme's gentle expression, the separation between the first two notes should "hardly, in any case not in an obtrusive manner, come to the notice of the listener".[60] And he noted that the separation should be more or less the equivalent of a pianist playing the same key two or more times in succession (presumably uninterruptedly). These comments about up-beats, which he does not support with any historical evidence, may not have reflected earlier 19th-century practice.

---

[57] Reflected, e.g., in his *Geschichte des Violinspiels* (Berlin, 1923).
[58] Particularly his treatment of bowstrokes (see Ch. 7).
[59] Joachim and Moser: *Violinschule*, iii, 13.
[60] Joachim and Moser: *Violinschule*, iii, 14.

Ex. 4.29 a–c. Joachim and Moser: *Violinschule*, iii, 13.

From this discussion of discrete separation, Moser moved to situations in which he instructed that the violinist should avoid any suggestion of articulation, citing, for instance, a passage in Spohr's Second Concerto, op. 2, where "despite the dot over the highest note in many editions, no gap should intervene between the f‴ and the low b"[61] (Ex. 4.30a). He compared the performer who made a gap to an asthmatic singer, and pointed out that the phrase division (*metrische Einschnitt*) should occur where he had marked the sign ‖. Here, his teaching may be at odds with the composer's expectations, however, since Spohr's original edition (in which his articulation is very carefully indicated) contains the *staccato* mark. In the case of the initial notes of the *Allemand* from Bach's B minor Partita for solo violin (Ex. 4.30b), Moser was concerned that, through the use of a flexible wrist, the player should avoid any hint of a break between the upbeat sixteenth and the four-part chord.

Ex. 4.30 a–b. Joachim and Moser: *Violinschule*, iii, 14.

[61] Joachim and Moser: *Violinschule*, iii, 14.

ARTICULATION AND PHRASING 213

After considering the degree of articulation necessary for the *portato* markings in the first movements of the Mendelssohn and Beethoven violin concertos, Moser referred to the articulation of slurred groups indicated by articulation marks under the last note of the group and remarked that such separation could be facilitated by co-ordinating the use of different strings with the divisions between the figures (Ex. 4.31a). He extended this point, with reference to the relationship between different bowings and fingerings, in the second of the Kreutzer *Études* (Ex. 4.31b), where the phrasing could be reinforced by using the differing tone colours of adjacent strings. With a couple of examples from Viotti he then illustrated the advantages of position changes being synchronized with the divisions between phrases wherever possible (Ex. 4.31c–d).[62]

Ex. 4.31 a–d. Joachim and Moser: *Violinschule*, iii, 14f.

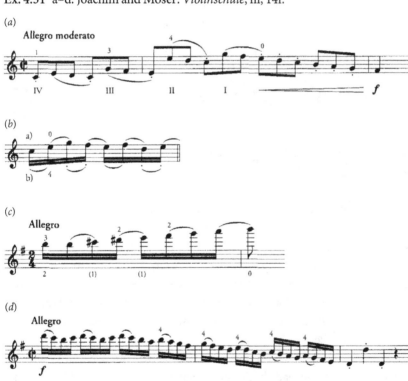

---

[62] Joachim and Moser: *Violinschule*, iii, 15.

Only after reviewing these details of articulation and phrasing did he tackle the question of separating larger melodic units, dealing first with passages in which the composer had indicated the phrase separation. At the opening of Beethoven's String Quartet op. 18 no. 4 (see Ex. 3.25a), he observed that the *staccato* mark in bars 2 and 4 required the type of break "which one called a "sospir" in the 17th and 18th centuries, whose length therefore was that required by a skilful singer for taking breath without disturbing the continuity of a melody as a whole".[63] As illustration of an instance where the composer had not provided the performer with any such guidance he chose one of his few contemporary examples, a melody by Joachim. Here the nature of late-19th-century practice is shown not so much by the one caesura that Moser marked as by those that he failed to indicate; the implication of his example is that the violinist would have been expected to execute all other changes of bow with the seamless *legato* that Moser had earlier referred to as "a violinistic virtue that cannot be highly enough praised"[64] (Ex. 4.32).

Ex. 4.32 Joachim and Moser: *Violinschule*, iii, 15.

Moser, and Joachim himself, would presumably have accomplished all the other phrasing in Joachim's melody by means of dynamic nuance and accent; such an approach is verified by Joachim's own 1903 recording of his Romance in C,[65] where, although it is exquisitely phrased, there are remarkably few perceptible breaks in the sound, except where rests are notated. It is otherwise, however, in Joachim's recordings of two of the Brahms Hungarian dances, where the nature of the piece requires a much more sharply articulated performance.

Moser followed this example with a reference to occasions where a cadenza-like passage leads back into a theme, as in the finale of Beethoven's

---

[63] Joachim and Moser: *Violinschule*, iii, 15.
[64] Joachim and Moser: *Violinschule*, iii, 13.
[65] Issued on CD by Pavilion Records on Opal CD 9851 (see Ex. 12.12).

Violin Concerto (Ex. 4.33), which required a "tension rest" (*Spannungspause*). He conceded, however, that there were many instances where "musical instinct alone is not sufficient to structure phrases appropriately",[66] citing Beethoven's late quartets as especially difficult in this respect. In such circumstances, he suggested, only a basic insight into the rules of phrase structure and the formation of melody could provide clarification.

Ex. 4.33 Joachim and Moser: *Violinschule*, iii, 15.

As a postscript to this section of his discussion of performance matters, Moser referred to orchestral bowing in a manner that again points up the different treatment of vigorous passages and cantabile material. He concurred with the notion of uniform bowing in contexts where there were clear beginnings or ends of a musical phrase, but deprecated the practice in places "which the composer conceived as sustained notes, connected phrases or long-breathed melodies. "In such cases," he believed, "the conductor should leave it to the individual violinist to change the bow as inconspicuously as possible at a point he regards as appropriate. As experience shows that every string player has individual inclinations and habits in this regard, this delegation of fine details creates the illusion of an overall legato, which is unsurpassably beautiful."[67]

\* \* \*

Consideration of the various kinds of articulation that might have been applied to individual notes and phrases, suggests that the mid-18th century's distinction between the appropriate manner of performance for an adagio and that which was required in an allegro[68] began to give way during the late 18th century, and succumbed entirely in the 19th century to a distinction between passages requiring a cantabile performance, in which phrasing was largely a matter of accentuation and dynamic nuance, and those requiring a

---

[66] Joachim and Moser: *Violinschule*, iii, 15.
[67] Joachim and Moser: *Violinschule*, iii, 16.
[68] See Ch. 10.

well-articulated one, where phrases and individual notes might be perceptibly separated from one another. In 19th-century music the performance style appropriate to specific phrases or passages was more dependent on the character the composer conceived for the individual musical idea. There was, in many respects, no longer a meaningful distinction between an *allegro* movement and an *adagio* one. Any single movement might range from the most highly articulated gestures to the most lyrical and connected melody; for this reason, composers who did not want their conceptions to be misunderstood were increasingly obliged to clarify their intentions by means of signs or instructions.

# 5
# Articulation and Expression

The role of articulation in defining musical phrases by means of a perceptible break in the sound or by dynamic nuance is quite distinct from its role in the characterization of musical ideas. A melody or motif acquires much of its expressive impact from the way it is articulated. Attitudes have undoubtedly changed over time, in connection with evolving musical styles; and during the 18th and 19th centuries, composers became increasingly concerned to specify their expectations in their notation. The importance composers attached to differentiated articulation and accentuation for the intended expression of their ideas is indicated by the early introduction and adoption of slurs and, somewhat later, by articulation and accentuation instructions in instrumental music, where they supplied the function that was naturally provided by the words in vocal music: slurs reproduced the effect of melismas on a vowel sound, while unslurred notes corresponded with the effect of syllable change, and accents emphasized the importance of strong syllables.

Whether articulation marks, when these were used, were intended merely to caution the player not to slur, whether they were meant to elicit a sharper and/or shorter *staccato*, similar to the explosive consonant, or whether, indeed, they might have had some other significance is among the most difficult aspects of this thorny subject. Varying theoretical accounts of the functions of dots and strokes, together with divergent, and often inconsistent usage by composers, inevitably led to slurs and *staccato* marks acquiring a complex of meanings, some of which are only tenuously related to their principal purposes.

Before examining what composers may have wanted to convey by using *staccato* marks or slurs, however, it is necessary to consider their intentions when they left the notes without either of these markings. In some cases, it is obvious that unmarked notes were expected to be slurred or articulated, either according to more or less well-understood conventions, or at the will of the performer. In solo parts it was often taken for granted (especially in the 18th and early 19th centuries) that the performer should be substantially responsible for deciding how the music would be phrased and articulated.

Even in orchestral parts, when singers were accompanied, it seems to have been assumed by some 18th-century composers that the phrasing in the orchestra would correspond with that of the vocal line; and in such cases, orchestral string players would ideally have been expected to follow the example of the principal violin and their section leaders. There were undoubtedly many circumstances in which, when neither slurs nor *staccato* marks were present, slurs were implied, or a style of detached performance that is neither slurred nor *staccato* was expected. Furthermore, when *staccato* marks were used, these might often be a warning not to slur, rather than a requirement for a specific style of execution; here too, especially in the 18th century, the tempo and the character of the music are usually more important than the composer's markings. And it is always necessary for the performer to consider whether a specific *non-legato* (or indeed *non-staccato*) style of performance might be required.

## *Staccato,* *Legato,* and *Non-Legato* (or "*Non-Staccato*"?)

In the late 20th century there was a broad consensus that, on the basis of a number of prominent sources, a more highly articulated manner of performing notes with neither slurs nor *staccato* marks was prevalent in the mid-18th century than in the mid-19th century. While this is undoubtedly true in some circumstances, it is far from straightforward. Theoretical sources provide equivocal evidence of the types of articulation available to instrumentalists and singers, and how these were to be executed. In keyboard playing this is linked with the characteristics of the harpsichord and clavichord, and with various phases in the development of the piano. In string playing it is affected by changing designs of bow and the exploration of a wider range of bowstrokes. In wind playing the evolution of the instruments themselves seems to be of less importance, but approaches to wind articulation will have been influenced by general stylistic trends. In singing, the text influences articulation but still leaves much room for differing interpretations. Theoretical sources document divergent practices associated with various schools and traditions, and they catalogue changing conventions over time.[1] As always, however, verbal attempts to describe the

---

[1] For an examination of these and other fundamental notational issues in orchestral practice see Kai Köpp: *Handbuch historische Orchesterpraxis* (Bärenreiter, 2009); rev. French edn, *La pratique d'orchestre historique. Baroque, classique et romantique*, trans. Fabien Roussel (Paris, 2020).

subtleties of performance that distinguish one tradition from another can provide only a pale reflection of aural realities.

Composers' notational practices may sometimes appear to reflect a direct and explicit connection between the written text and the type of execution envisaged. On the other hand, the connection between notation and execution is often unclear, and much may depend on the extent to which the composer relied on the performer's understanding of conventions that applied to particular circumstances and contexts. This is especially important in the music of the second half of the 18th century, when, although theorists liked to link specific performance techniques to distinct notational practices, few composers concerned themselves with that level of detail. As Joseph Riepel remarked in the 1750s, after describing differentiated notational symbols for six types of articulation, each signifying a different execution: "I have included the strokes and dots again only for the sake of explanation; for one does not see them in pieces of music except perhaps sometimes when it is necessary for the sake of clarity."[2] Even this seems to be a rather idealistic statement, to judge from surviving manuscript and printed material, where clarity in this respect is rarely encountered. The engraved parts of Riepel's own Three Violin Concertos op. 1 contain only two of his six differentiated markings: *staccato* strokes, all approximately the same size, and dots under slurs.

Although some later 18th-century composers, and increasingly those of the 19th century, notated articulation with greater frequency, there is still considerable scope for misunderstanding its absence. Where notes were left with neither articulation marks nor slurs in 18th- and early-19th-century music, it is highly probable either that previous slurring or *staccato* was meant to continue, that markings occurring in one part were expected to apply to similar figures in another, that well-known conventions such as the slurring of rapid figures or the application of *portato* to accompaniment figures were taken for granted, or that performers were offered an opportunity to devise their own combinations of slurred and separate notes. At a time when performers routinely made ornamental additions to the composer's texts, improvised slurring and articulation will often have been expected when a succession of unmarked notes occurs in a solo part.[3]

---

[2] Joseph Riepel: *Gründliche Erklärung der Tonordnung* (Frankfurt-am-Main and Leipzig, 1757), 19. For Riepel's symbols see Ex. 6.14.

[3] See Ch. 7, p. 378 and Ex. 7.17 for Ferdinand Kauer's late-18th-century view that the addition of slurring and articulation was a form of improvised ornamentation.

In the music of more fastidious composers, where unmarked notes seem unlikely to imply slurring, the performer is faced with deciding what kind of detached execution to employ. The most difficult matter may often, in fact, be to determine whether, when a *staccato* mark is present, it really indicates a *staccato* execution, merely warns against slurring, or has some other more specialized meaning. Here as elsewhere, contradictions abound, making it difficult to identify any general ruling principles. Knowledge of the evolving performing practices of specific periods and traditions, and those associated with particular composers, is always more important than the actual notation, since much that composers regarded as obvious to the performer was not written down, even by many later 19th-century composers. The use of arpeggiation in piano playing, or of *portamento* and *vibrato* in singing and instrumental performance, are obvious examples; but the execution of detached notes, with or without *staccato* marks, was another crucial area in which the performer was expected to be able to read between the lines of the notation.

Theoretical discussion of the manner of performance appropriate to notes with neither *staccato* marks nor slurs occurs in a significant number of 18th-century German sources. In keyboard playing C. P. E. Bach observed:

> Notes that are neither staccatoed, slurred, nor fully held are sounded for half their value, unless the abbreviation *Ten.* [*Tenuto*] (held)[4] is written over them, in which case they must be held fully. Quarter-notes and eighth-notes in moderate and slow tempos are usually performed in this manner, and they must not be played weakly, but with fire and a very slight accentuation.[5]

Two years later Marpurg similarly advised keyboard players to employ a *non-legato* touch where neither slurring nor *staccato* was indicated, though his description suggests that he regarded this touch as less detached—perhaps much less detached—than Bach did, instructing that it: "consists in very quickly lifting your finger from the previous key just before you touch the next note. This normal procedure is never indicated because it is always assumed."[6]

---

[4] For another implication of the instruction Tenuto see Ch. 3, p. 170.
[5] Bach: *Versuch*, i, 127.
[6] Friedrich Wilhelm Marpurg: *Anleitung zum Clavierspielen der schönen Ausübung der heutigen Zeit gemäss* (Berlin, 1755), 29.

Türk, too, considered that, although the normal style of keyboard playing should be somewhat detached, it should be less so than Bach instructed, stating: "In the case of notes that should be played in the normal way, i.e. neither *staccato* nor slurred, one lifts the finger from the keys a little earlier than the length of the note requires." He repeated Bach's comment that *Ten.* would be written over the note if a full-length performance were required, but argued that his prescription of halving the note value would make no appreciable difference between the normal touch and the *staccato*.[7] Türk suggested that quarter-notes might be shortened to dotted or double-dotted eighths.

For the flute, Quantz specifically limited the wind player's equivalent of the *non-legato* style of performance to notes of a specific value, generally the second fastest type of note in a piece, suggesting, unlike, Bach, that longer note values would be played more connectedly; there is also the implication that, presumably for technical reasons, the fastest notes would not be shortened, or may perhaps have been slurred. He instructed:

> If in an Allegro assai sixteenths are the quickest notes, the eighths must, for the most part, be tongued with a short staccato, while quarters must be played in a singing and sustained manner. But in an allegretto where thirty-second-note triplets occur, the sixteenths must be tipped briefly and the eighths played in a singing fashion.[8]

From the practical viewpoint, since a genuinely detached style of performance is only practicable up to a certain speed, the fastest notes in keyboard music will have been played without any attempt at separation. As will become apparent from examples of composers' practices, it is evident that fast notes in 18th-century string and wind parts that have neither slurs nor articulation marks would also very often have been expected to be played *legato*.

Yet there was a counter-current to the view that certain categories of unmarked notes required a detached, *staccato*, style of performance in keyboard playing. At about the same time as Bach's and Marpurg's treatises, Nicolo Pasquali instructed: "The Legato is the touch that this Treatise endeavours to teach, being a general Touch fit for almost all Kinds of Passages"; and he added that all note that have no marks for other kinds of articulation "must

---

[7] Türk: *Klavierschule*, 356.
[8] Quantz: *Versuch*, 115.

be played Legato, i.e., in the usual Way".[9] Some twenty years later Vincenzo Manfredini observed that

> On the cembalo with hammers, when it is well constructed, the different strength that the so-called chiaroscuro requires can be given to the sounds, if not entirely, at least in some way, and for this reason it is called *Piano-forte*. In order to perform the cantabile as well as possible on these instruments, one must, in touching the keys, press them more or less, as needed, and not strike them, and one must play legato, raising the finger from the key just as one plays the next note, and not before. This must be done not only in cantabile playing, but almost always.[10]

Towards the end of the 18th century an increasing number of authorities suggested that a *legato* style, rather than a *non-legato* or *staccato* one, should be seen as the norm in keyboard playing, and that leaving the notes unmarked was nearly or exactly the same as putting them under continuous slurs. In this context, it is essential to remember that long slurs indicating a general *legato* were very rarely used until after 1800.[11] Nicolas-Joseph Hüllmandel (b. 1751) considered that unless notes were specified as *staccato* "one of the most essential rules" was that, the player should hold down a key "til the next is struck".[12] Milchmeyer, at about the same time, discussed three styles of touch, like Bach, Marpurg, and Türk, but with the important difference that his "normal" style was effectively *legato*, or, at least, as connected as the *détaché trainé* employed by Pierre Rode,[13] the *détaché* described by Spohr,[14] or the passagework of the best Italian singers of the day:

> Now I will distinguish and clearly compare the different **playing styles**, which I take to be three. I call the first the **usual** or natural playing style, the second the **legato**, and the third the **staccato** style. In pieces by good composers, who write music as one should, all notes which do not have dots, strokes, or small slurs over them are in the natural style. To play

---

[9] Nicolo Pasquali: *The Art of Fingering the Harpsichord* (Edinburgh, [c. 1758]), 26.
[10] Vincenzo Manfredini: *Regole armoniche: o sieno precetti ragionati per apprender la musica*, 2nd edn (Venice, 1797), 24f.
[11] See Ch. 6, "Slurs and Articulation".
[12] Nicholas-Joseph Hüllmandel: *Principles of Music Chiefly Calculated for the Piano Forte or Harpsichord* (London, 1796), 20.
[13] Baillot: *L'art du violon*, 109.
[14] Spohr: *Violinschule*, 130 (see Ch. 7).

# ARTICULATION AND EXPRESSION 223

these, one lifts the first finger off the first key when the second has been struck, the finger from the second when the third is played, and so on. Two fingers may never be down at the same time in this usual style of playing in a simple passage [, . . .] The legato playing style [marked by slurs] [. . .] requires a soft and at the same time melting performance. All pianists should in general, according to the requirements of the instrument, choose the legato style, since rapped and at the same time hacked notes certainly do not suit it; rather one should stroke it in a gentle manner. But everything has its exceptions, so, for instance, I do not like this legato style in runs, in chromatic and various other kinds of passage in the bass, because the long resonance of the stronger strings causes unpleasant sounding tones. Such melodies, however, which contain only the true notes of the chord, whether they sound good or bad, are made perfect by this way of playing. It makes the tone of the pianoforte soft and at the same time velvety, and by this means one can sweeten and soften the higher notes of this instrument, which tend towards a certain hardness and dryness. All possible passages, from c over the middle line of the treble stave to the highest notes of the piano can therefore be played in legato style without offending the ear, but the player should only allow himself this if the composer has marked them so. This style requires therefore that one leaves the finger down somewhat longer, and on several notes. See the following examples [Ex. 5.1].

The staccato style, in which one separates the notes from one another, is marked with small dots or strokes over the note, and requires a pianoforte that perfectly damps all notes, particularly the lower bass notes.[15]

Ex. 5.1 Michmeyer: *Die wahre Art*, 6.

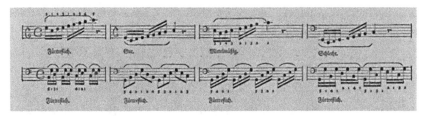

By the early 19th century, the primacy of a genuine *legato* as the "normal" style of keyboard playing was firmly established. In 1801 Clementi published

---

[15] Michmeyer: *Die wahre Art*, 5–7.

his opinion that "When the composer leaves the LEGATO and STACCATO to the performer's taste [i.e., when neither slurring nor staccato is indicated]; the best rule is, to adhere chiefly to the LEGATO; reserving the STACCATO to give SPIRIT occasionally to certain passages and to set off the HIGHER BEAUTIES of the LEGATO."[16] And in the revised eleventh edition of his treatise he seems to have decided that even more emphatic guidance was necessary, changing the phrase "the best rule is to adhere chiefly to the LEGATO" to the more succinct and peremptory "let the LEGATO prevail".

Jean-Louis Adam expressed the same thing in French, in his influential Conservatoire method. As was to become increasingly common for all musical instruments during the 19th century, he drew a parallel with singing, observing: "The sounds must unite and blend into each other if we are to succeed in imitating the legato of the voice"; and, apparently paraphrasing Clementi's recently published book, he continued:

> Sometimes the author indicates the musical phrase that should be slurred, but if he abandons the choice of *legato* or *staccato* to the taste of the performer, it is best to adhere to the *legato*, reserving the *staccato* to make certain passages stand out and to make the advantages of the *legato* felt by means of a pleasant artistic contrast.[17]

Throughout the rest of the 19th century, the view expressed by these writers remained the orthodox one. For instance, in an English version of Henri Herz's *Méthode*, it is stated that slurs indicate "each note being held down its full length, and till the following note is actually struck. This is called the legato style of playing, and is that which is generally used."[18] The passage seems to have been an addition by the translator, for it does not appear in Herz's original text. Indeed, Herz illustrated five different possibilities [Ex. 5.2a], giving no priority to any of them.

> The execution of N°. 1 consists in playing the notes simply, without slurring or separating them. N°. 2 requires lightness: the fingers alone, by withdrawing towards the inside of the hand, produce the soft separation

---

[16] Clementi: *Introduction*, 9.
[17] Adam: *Méthode du piano du Conservatoire* (Paris, 1804), 151.
[18] Henri Herz: *A Standard Modern Preceptor for the Pianoforte* (London, [c. 1840]), 7.

it demands. Nº. 3 is a more pronounced and drier staccato; it is usually used in *forte*, in chords, and for notes that must stand out. It is executed by raising the hand after each note or chord, and by attacking the keys briskly and with elasticity. Nº. 4 indicates legato playing, in which the various notes that make up a phrase must offer only one continuity of sounds blended into each other. Sometimes very legato playing is marked by a double slur ⸺. Nº. 5, used especially in cantabile passages, is rendered by a slight accent on each key: it lends a more penetrating expression to the musical phrase, which is obtained by resting the fingers on the keys, without striking; and by leaving a barely appreciable interval between the notes.[19]

Nº. 1 suggests Milchmeyer's "usual" touch, while Nº. 4 resembles Milchmeyer's "*legato* playing". Herz's double slur for "very legato playing" seems to have been used very rarely indeed; even in Herz's own compositions, it occurs only occasionally, on arpeggiated passages, in which he may have intended the notes to be held down as long as possible (Ex. 5.2b). During the 19th century, many such signs and performance instructions, intended to indicate subtleties of articulation and accentuation, were proposed and sporadically utilized, but with respect to the finer nuances, composers were still reliant on the performer's understanding of musical context, as a host of earlier authors had advised.[20] Indeed, a plethora of signs could be counter-productive.

**Ex. 5.2a**  Henri Herz: *Méthode*, 13.

---

[19] Herz: *Méthode*, 13.
[20] E.g., C. P. E. Bach in the 1750s, Türk in the 1780s, Witthauer in the 1790s, etc.

Ex. 5.2b  Henri Herz: Chant d'amour op. 203, 2.
[Moderato amoroso]

The concern of mid-19th-century pianists with cultivating a *legato* execution as the fundamental basis of their performance style finds its apogee in Sigismond Thalberg's *L'art du chant appliqué au piano* (*The art of singing applied to the piano*). And at the end of the century, Hugo Riemann, in his various editions of the Classics, where *legato* playing is particularly emphasized, reiterated the instruction that "The legato touch should always be used, unless specially marked to the contrary",[21] thus recognizing no separate role for unmarked notes. The pedagogic aims of Riemann's editions necessitated a particularly extensive repertoire of markings to indicate a graduated series of degrees and types of articulation and accent. By that time, many composers' markings were scarcely less prolific, but it is often unclear what they expected their markings to convey.

In string and wind playing, the nature of the instrument gave rise to quite different concerns. On these instruments, it was much more feasible to emulate the human voice. The extent of a seamless *legato* was limited only by the length of the bow or breath. Skilful instrumentalists and singers could produce almost seamless *legato* even between bowstrokes or breaths, but by means of the bow, or the tongue, lips, and chest in wind playing, the instrumentalists could also produce articulation that corresponded closely with the effect of consonants in singing. In the 1980s, Robin Stowell expressed a widespread received opinion when he referred to the "articulated, non-legato stroke of the pre-Tourte bow" and commented that "smooth separate bowings were only rarely used before c. 1760".[22] His familiarity with the source material led him to give a relatively early date for the introduction of smooth, separate strokes, yet even that may be rather too late, especially for string players in Italian traditions. Although Baroque bows may be better suited to executing

---

[21] Schubert: *Moments musicaux*, ed. Riemann (Brunswick, Litolff, [c. 1890]), Preface (copy in the Bodleian Library, Oxford).
[22] Robin Stowell: *Violin Technique and Performance Practice in the Late 18th and Early 19th Centuries* (Cambridge, 1985), 74.

a lively detached on-string stroke than later models, they are in fact, perfectly capable of producing well-connected separate bowstrokes. Most period instrument string players, however, still (2022) assume a pronounced degree of *non-legato* for separately bowed notes in Baroque and Classical repertoire, frequently employing elastic or percussive bowstrokes in the middle or lower half of the bow to achieve it in moderately fast tempos. In many of the contexts where this is commonly used, it undoubtedly runs counter to the expectations of the composer, and the employment of these types of bowstroke in those contexts is unsupported by documentary evidence.[23]

A number of sources contain clear evidence of the use of well-articulated bowstrokes on unmarked notes in particular repertoires and circumstances. In 1776, J. F. Reichardt observed: "In a succession of short accompaniment notes one has to be aware that, if they are written without any markings, as here, they should be played short but not sharply, that is to say, the bow remains resting on the string after the note has been played with a short stroke." He provided a music example of repeated eighth-notes on the same pitch. Then, illustrating the same notes with *staccato* strokes above them, he continued: "but if the bow is to be lifted completely from the string, the usual sign for staccato must first be placed there."[24] He gave no information about the speed of these notes, but his instruction to "lift" the bow suggests a quite moderate tempo. Finally, he gives the example with dots under a slur over groups of four and then eight notes, explaining that this is "the softest, namely, one takes many notes in one bowstroke, without completely connecting them; there remains a little relaxation of the bow between each note."[25]

Reichardt also gave a particularly detailed and lucid account of the relationship between bowstrokes and tempo,[26] from which it is clear that, as the tempo increased, he expected a shorter and sharper execution of *staccato* notes, moving progressively towards the point of the bow. His account made no direct connection between these recommendations and the presence or absence of articulation marks. In assessing the significance of Reichardt's advice, however, it is essential to bear in mind that he was writing about orchestral playing, and also, perhaps, that he was approaching the subject from a north German perspective, strongly influenced by French practice.

---

[23] See Ch. 7.
[24] Reichardt: *Ueber die Pflichten*, 23f.
[25] Reichardt: *Ueber die Pflichten*, 24.
[26] See Ch. 10.

At the time of his treatise, he had just been appointed Kapellmeister to the Francophile Berlin court.

There is much to suggest that there were significant divisions between national and regional practices in string playing in the third quarter of the 18th century, just as there were in keyboard playing, and that there were widely perceived distinctions between what was appropriate in orchestral playing or accompaniment and what was allowable or desirable in solo performance. Quantz's comments on the salient characteristics of French and Italian violinists reveal both types of difference. He observed of accompaniment: "In general it is to be noted that in the accompaniment, particularly in lively pieces, a short and articulated bowstroke, wielded in the French manner, produces a much better effect than a long and dragging Italian stroke."[27] He continued:

> You also find that almost all modern Italian violinists play in the same style, and that as a result they do not show up to the best advantage in comparison with their predecessors. For them the bowstroke, which, like the tongue-stroke on wind instruments, is the basis for lively musical articulation, often serves, like the wind-bag of a bagpipe, only to make the instrument sound like a hurdy-gurdy. [. . .] In the Allegro they consider the sawing out of a multitude of notes in a single bowstroke to be some special achievement.[28]

Quantz referred particularly to the influence of Tartini on Italian violin playing. He appears only to have heard Tartini on one occasion, when he was impressed by his fine tone and technical skill, but considered his music "unvocal"; and it is evident from many other accounts that Tartini and his most faithful disciples were noted not only for their use of slurring, but also for their broad and powerful bowstroke, even on fast-moving notes played with separate bows.[29] Joseph Riepel's mid-18th-century descriptions of a variety of separate bowstrokes, where he linked "long and powerful strokes of the bow" with the performance of *staccato* notes

---

[27] Quantz: *Versuch*, 199.
[28] Quantz: *Versuch*, 312.
[29] For further details on the relationship between articulation, notation, and bowing styles, see Ch. 7.

in concertos,[30] also indicate that broader bowing was regarded as one of the characteristics of solo playing, while, as Quantz suggested, a shorter, more articulated stroke was considered appropriate to accompaniment and ensemble playing.[31]

In singing, where the supremacy of the Italian style was unquestioned, Quantz evidently approved of a smooth and connected manner of performing relatively rapid unmarked notes. In a comment on choral singers in northern Germany he deprecated their disjointed manner of singing passagework and their lack of *legato* in melodies, observing:

> Their disagreeable, forced, and exceedingly noisy chest attacks, in which they make vigorous use of the faculty for producing the *h*, singing ha-ha-ha-ha for each note, make all the passagework sound hacked up, and are far removed from the Italian manner of executing passagework with the chest voice. They do not tie the parts of the plain melody to one another sufficiently, or join them together with appoggiaturas; in consequence, their execution sounds very dry and plain.[32]

There is little to suggest that this type of singing was regarded as stylish. Quantz put it down to the deficient knowledge and taste of most provincial German cantors. In general, the Italian school of singing seems to have cultivated a genuine cantabile style of delivering every type of music. Even in fast music, separation of the notes within a melisma would surely have been exceptional, only to be used when specifically indicated by the composer, either by rests, or by articulation marks (Ex. 5.3a–b). For the sake of expression, of course, it must sometimes have been considered appropriate to deliver a particular phrase in a *staccato* manner; but this, though occasionally marked by careful composers (Ex. 5.4), would normally have been left to the judgement of the singer.

---

[30] See Ch. 6, p. 281.
[31] For his instructions on when the bow should leave the string between successive notes see Ch. 7, p. 357.
[32] Quantz: *Versuch*, 326 (footnote).

**Ex. 5.3a** Perez: *Solimano*, Act I, Scene iv, British Library, London, Add MSS 16093-94; pub. in fac. in the series *Italian Opera 1640–1770* (New York, Garland, 1978).

**Ex. 5.3b** D. Corri: A Select Collection, I, 49.

**Ex. 5.4** Perez: *Solimano*, Act I, Scene vi, British Library, London, Add MSS 16093-94; pub. in fac. in the series *Italian Opera 1640–1770* (New York, Garland, 1978).

As becomes apparent from a closer consideration of string bowing styles, composers' expectations in respect of different modes of articulation can only be appreciated in the light of the influences that moulded their styles, as well as the musicians with whom they worked, or for whom they wrote. Nevertheless, it is evident that there was a greater concern among instrumentalists to emulate a singing style in some quarters than in others. In view of the Italian hegemony in singing, it is not surprising that it should have been Italian musicians (and those most strongly influenced by Italy) who pre-eminently modelled their articulation and expressive delivery on the practices of the best singers, even if, as Quantz complained, Vivaldi, Tartini, and their pupils and colleagues were developing much more instrument-specific figurations, and employing the higher reaches of the fingerboard in ways that went beyond the possibilities of vocal technique.[33] Tension between the advocates of singing styles on instruments and those who admired virtuoso pyrotechnics continued in the following decades. A writer in 1779, having asserted that "The playing style that corresponds most closely to true singing is, probably unquestionably, the most appropriate and best", [34] also went on to disparage the unvocal practices of many virtuosos.

Although 19th-century music tends to be much more explicitly marked in respect of *legato* and various types of articulated execution, there is still considerable scope for misunderstanding a composer's intentions. In the 1820s, for instance, Dotzauer, in his discussion of performance style in general, made clear distinctions between solo playing and accompanying, and between song-like passages and others, saying that if the passage is not song-like and is not otherwise marked it should be played in a detached manner.[35] As an example he gave a passage of eighth-notes, without articulation marks, in a moderato tempo, evidently expecting the type of stroke described in the Paris Conservatoire's violin (1803) and cello (1805) methods, where a well-extended *détaché* bowing, with an abrupt check between each stroke,[36] is described, and he notated its execution in the same way (Ex. 5.5). Yet comparison with a similar example from Spohr's *Violinschule*, which is marked with *staccato* strokes, provides a timely warning that, even in the 1830s, all may not necessarily be as it seems at first sight, for Dotzauer's eighths, without articulation marks, are evidently meant to be played in a more detached style than Spohr's *détaché* eighths with *staccato* strokes, between which no break is to be audible.[37] The notation is often unreliable, for Spohr also marked eighths with *staccato* strokes for a sharply detached *martelé* bowstroke, made near the point of the bow, for which he notated the execution in the same way as Dotzauer's unmarked eighths.[38]

---

[33] Quantz: *Versuch*, 308–11. Quantz refers to "Two celebrated Lombardic violinists" without naming them, but from internal evidence it is clear that he refers to Vivaldi and Tartini.
[34] Anon.: *Wahrheiten die Musik betreffend* [Truths about Music] (Frankfurt a. M., 1779), 69. Kai Köpp, in *Handbuch historische Orchesterpraxis*, has very plausibly identified Ernst Wilhelm Wolf as the author, rather than J. M. Krause (as in some sources).
[35] Dotzauer: *Méthode de violoncelle* (Mainz, [c. 1825]), 56.
[36] Baillot et al.: *Méthode de violon*, 130; *Méthode de Violoncelle*.
[37] Spohr: *Violinschule*, 130.
[38] Spohr: *Violinschule*, 136. See Ch. 7.

Ex. 5.5 Dotzauer: *Méthode de violoncelle*, 56.

One specific place in which late-18th- and early-19th-century musicians seem to have been specially concerned to avoid inappropriate separation was between the first and second notes of a figure where the first note was an anacrusis on a metrically weak beat. This was apparently the case even in the context of a performance style where unslurred notes were generally played in a detached manner. G. W. Fink observed in 1809:

> The weak beats of the bar ought, according to whether they come before a strong or stronger beat, always be tied to some extent to their strong beat as an anacrusis (up-beat), as long as the composer has not specifically prevented this by a dot over the note or by rests. If, however, there is a dot over a note which occupies a weak beat, so, by means of the staccato, it acquires a somewhat greater amount of accent than it would have without it, and thus entails that the following strong beat, particularly if it is the first beat of a new bar, also receives a somewhat sharper accent, assuming that at that place the composer has not also required an exception through a *p* as an extraordinary nuancing expression mark.[39]

Fink's observation about the upbeat being tied to its strong beat is lent support by an instance in pieces written by Haydn for flute clock in the early 1790s and pinned onto the barrels of three surviving clocks by musicians closely associated with the composer. Whereas the majority of separate notes are performed shorter than their written duration, the upbeat in Hob. XIX: 15, which is without *staccato* in the manuscript source (Elßler's *Abschrift*), is lengthened on both of the clocks that play it (Ex. 5.6).[40]

---

[39] Fink: 'Ueber Takt, Taktarten und ihr Characteristisches', *Allgemeine musikalische Zeitung*, xi (1808–9), 229.

[40] *Joseph Haydn: Werke*, XXI, ed. Sonja Gerlach and George R. Hill (Munich, 1984), 20.

Ex. 5.6  Haydn: *Flötenuhrstück* Hob. XIX: 15.

With these caveats about the limitations of relying too greatly on the presence or absence of *staccato* marks, it may be instructive to consider various possible interpretations of unmarked notes in music of the period.

## Unmarked Notes Implying Slurs

It is difficult confidently to identify passages in 18th-century music where slurs, though unmarked, are appropriate, though such passages are undoubtedly frequent. Many composers and copyists were evidently casual about indicating slurs in places where they felt them to be obvious; in the case of very fast notes, especially, they seem often to have marked them only haphazardly or omitted them altogether. They may have considered it more important to indicate where slurring was not intended, which might be achieved by the addition of a few articulation marks at the beginning of a passage, or by the inclusion of a term indicating specific kinds of detached performance. A copyist's score of Piccinni's popular opera *La Ceccina ossia La buona figluola* provides a good example of a situation in which the inclusion of articulation marks on some notes appears to be intended to clarify the extent of an assumed slur. In Ex. 5.7a, the sporadic articulation marks on the eighths in the second violin imply that this note should not be included in the slur that, on account of the thirty-second-notes and the absence of instructions to the contrary, the players would almost certainly have assumed. Later in the aria the copyist occasionally included a slur on these figures (Ex. 5.7b).

Ex. 5.7 a–b. Piccinni: *La Ceccina ossia La buona figluola*, Act I, Scene i, MS score, Conservatorio di musica Luigi Cherubini, Florence; pub. in the series *Italian Music 1640–1770* (New York and London, Garland, 1983).

(a)

(b)

ARTICULATION AND EXPRESSION 235

Instances where accompanying instruments were probably expected to imitate a singer's slurring are especially common in music of this period. In a copyist's score of Umlauf's *Die schöne Schusterin*, probably connected with the 1779 Vienna production, articulation marks are employed to warn that a change of pattern occurs, but the violins seem otherwise intended to match the voice (Ex. 5.8). Here the pattern has been indicated in places, but corroboration of the composer's intention is often absent. Nevertheless, an intention for unslurred performance in passages like Ex. 5.9, from Neubauer's *Fernando und Yariko*, seems highly improbable. And in a passage from André's own edition of his Singspiel *Der Töpfer*, a rare occurrence of articulation marks again provides clues where a not entirely identical relationship with the voice is envisaged (Ex. 5.10).

Ex. 5.8 Umlauf: *Die schöne Schusterin*, no. 2, MS score in Österreichische Nationalbibliothek, Vienna, Mus. HS. 16.481; pub. in fac. in the series *German Opeera 1770–1800* (New York and London, Garland, 1986).

Ex. 5.9 Neubauer: *Fernando und Yariko*, Act I, Scene v, printed full score (Zürich, 1788).

**Ex. 5.10** André: *Der Töpfer*, [no. 4], pp. 39–40, printed full score (Offenbach, [c. 1773]).

Mozart left much less to chance in this respect, and it may be reasonable to assume that in most of his mature compositions for strings, except in cases of evident oversight, the absence of slurs will almost invariably indicate unslurred execution. Haydn was nowhere near so careful, especially before the 1790s; and even in the London symphonies there are many passages where his autographs indicate slurring only in a very spasmodic and general manner, leaving substantial ambiguities. Beethoven, like Mozart a trained violin/viola player, was particularly careful to mark bowing in string parts. Many other prominent composers, however, left numerous ambiguities, being apparently content to entrust the addition of unmarked slurs to the musical instinct of the performers: for instance, Dussek, in his String Quartets op. 60, and Paul Wranitzky, in much of his string chamber music, where occasional slurs are added only when a specific phrasing is required, and articulation marks seem mostly to be included as an instruction not to slur.

In the 19th century, while German composers generally became much more meticulous in such matters, there were still some whose practice was casual enough to provoke doubts about the literalness of their notation. In Weber's scores there are frequent passages where he probably imagined slurring but failed to mark it (Ex. 5.11) and many others where a general *legato* is intimated by a few imprecise and sporadic slurs (Ex. 5.12). It is often not clear, therefore, whether string players were intended to assimilate their bowing to slurs in the wind and vocal parts or whether Weber really wanted strings to play with a separate, probably broad *détaché* bowing, while wind and voices were slurred, for instance in several passages from the E flat Mass (Ex. 5.13). Italian composers, up to at least Verdi's earlier years, were still content to leave much detail of this kind to the instinct or decision of performers.

Ex. 5.11 Weber: *Der Freischütz*, no. 3.

Ex. 5.12 Weber: Mass in E flat J. 224, Credo.

**Ex. 5.13**  Weber: Mass in E flat J. 224, Gloria.

Among composers who marked slurring in orchestral parts, and in chamber music more carefully, there may sometimes have been a deliberate intention to abstain from prescribing details of articulation and slurring in a solo part, perhaps reflecting their awareness of constantly changing performance styles, especially in string playing. A prominent example is provided by Beethoven's Violin Concerto, where the composer seems to have been content to allow Clement, or whoever else performed the work, to decide on patterns of bowing in the passagework. Performance traditions, apparently sanctioned (or at least accepted) by the composer, may be preserved in Jacob Dont's and Ferdinand David's editions of the Concerto,[41] where passages left by Beethoven without slurs or articulation marks receive varied bowings (Ex. 5.14a–b). It can scarcely be doubted that Beethoven envisaged some variety of bowing in these kinds of solo parts; his piano concertos, too, are less meticulously slurred than his piano sonatas. Even where composers provided much more detailed markings, however, it is abundantly clear that many 19th-century soloists did not feel themselves bound to follow them to the letter, and it is probable that few composers would have expected them to do so. Ferdinand David's manuscript bowings in his personal copies of the string quartets and op. 18 String Quintet of his friend and colleague Mendelssohn offer many instructive instances of the type of amplifications and modifications that are likely to have been regarded as legitimate in the mid-19th century.[42] Brahms's correspondence with Joachim provides a revealing glimpse of the composer's perception of the borderline between what was his responsibility and what was best entrusted to the executant.[43]

Ex. 5.14 a–b. Beethoven: Violin Concerto op. 61/i. (*a*) ed. J. Dont; (*b*) ed. F. David.

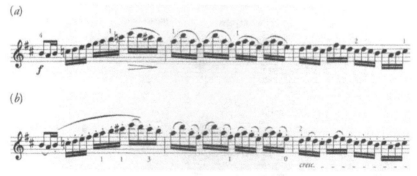

[41] See Clive Brown: 'Ferdinand David's Editions of Beethoven' and Robin Stowell: 'Beethoven's Violin Concerto' in Robin Stowell (ed.), *Performing Beethoven* (Cambridge, 1994), Chs. 6 and 7. Dont claimed in the preface to his edition that his father, first cellist in the Hoforchester, had often played the work with Beethoven and Clement, and had taught the concerto to his son on the basis of that experience. David, though not directly connected with Vienna, was in touch with mainstream traditions of German violin playing of Beethoven's day through his teacher, Louis Spohr.

[42] See https://mhm.hud.ac.uk/chase/view/composer/44/.

[43] See Clive Brown, 'Joachim's Violin Playing and the Performance of Brahms's String Music' in Michael Musgrave and Bernard Sherman (eds.), *Performing Brahms* (Cambridge, 2003), 48–98.

## *Sciolto, Spiccato,* and *Non Legato*

Sometimes, 18th- and 19th-century composers warned players that passages of detached notes required a style of performance that was neither *legato* nor *staccato*. The term most often encountered in this context in the 18th century and early 19th century is *sciolto* (often, but not always, accompanying notes without articulation marks); *spiccato* occurs occasionally (with a meaning different from its later use in string playing), while in the 19th century *non legato* (*non ligato*) is increasingly encountered where the notes have no other markings.

"Sciolto" or its plural "sciolte" was defined in several slightly different ways. Charles Burney gave it as: "unbound, detached, articulate. On the flute and hautbois, every note to be tongued: on the violin, tenor and bass, every note to be bowed, and cut short, as if followed by a rest of half its value."[44] For Burney it seems essentially to have been indistinguishable from *staccato*, for in defining *spiccato* he remarked that it had "nearly the same signification as *sciolto* and *staccato*", adding that "*sciolto* and *staccato* passages require a strong bow to every note".[45] Other writers took a rather different view. Lichtenthal, writing in Italian, described *sciolto* as the "opposite of legato",[46] while Clementi, in the revised eleventh edition of his piano method (it does not appear in the original edition) defined it as "free, neither legato nor staccato".[47] The term "free" (*frei*) was also used by German authors. Koch considered *sciolto* to mean: "free, detached, therefore the notes not bound to one another or slurred, but separated and staccato; at the same time one also understands by it that these staccato notes should be performed with a certain freedom or with the avoidance of any kind of hardness".[48] And Fröhlich, thinking of the violinist, similarly observed that *sciolto* indicated "yet another kind of gentle staccato [...] which means free, detached. It should therefore be played with lightness, without stiffness, but especially with much flexibility of the wrist."[49] Koch's and Fröhlich's definitions seem likely to be close to the intention behind David Perez's use of the term half a century earlier. Perez used a wide range of terms including *staccato, battute,* and *ligato'*. For Perez, therefore, *sciolto* evidently signified a detached execution different from *staccato*. In one passage in his opera *Solimano* (Ex. 5.15) Perez reinforced slurs with *lig*.

---

[44] Charles Burney: 'Sciolto' in Abraham Rees (ed.), *The Cyclopaedia; or, Universal Dictionary of Arts, Sciences, and Literature* (London, 1802–20), xxxiii, no pagination.
[45] Burney: 'Spiccato' in Rees (ed.), *Encyclopedia*, xxxv, no pagination.
[46] Pietro Lichtenthal: 'Sciolto' in *Dizionario e bibliografia della musica*, ii (Milan, 1826), 184.
[47] Clementi: *Introduction*, 11th edn (London, 1826), 9.
[48] Koch: 'Sciolto' in *Musikalisches Lexikon*, 1306.
[49] Fröhlich: *Musikschule*, pt. 4, 49.

[*ligato*], while *sciol.* [*sciolto*] confirmed that the absence of slurs means separate bows, but probably not *staccato* execution (as the simultaneous slurs in the wind instruments on the top two staves suggest). Another informative passage in *Solimano* indicates, perhaps, that Perez was concerned to warn the player not to slur, but did not want to induce a *staccato* attack (Ex. 5.16).[50] Other characteristic occurrences of *sciolto* come in Piccinni's *Catone in Utica*, where *sciolto* invariably occurs in *piano* or *mezza voce* passages, suggesting, maybe, that "any kind of hardness" should be avoided (Ex. 5.17a–b). Somewhat later in the century, Sacchini used *sciolto* in a similar manner, though not always in *piano* (Ex. 5.18). A more unusual use of the term occurs in Paisiello's oratorio *La Passione* of 1782, where the phrase *sciolte stacato* [*sic*] appears to imply a relaxed *portato* (Ex. 5.19). Interestingly, Carl Czerny, in 1839, suggested that since there was no universally recognized Italian term for dots under slurs in piano playing, one might adopt the word *sciolto* to specify it.[51] Mozart's rare employment of *sciolto*, together with articulation marks, in the first movement of the "Haffner" Symphony may, like Perez's use of it, be intended to prevent slurring but avoid a sharp *staccato* (Ex. 5.20).

**Ex. 5.15** Perez: *Solimano*, Act II, Scene xi, British Library, London, Add MSS 16093-94; pub. in fac. in the series *Italian Opera 1640–1770* (New York, Garland, 1978).

[50] For further examples of Perez's bowing indications see Ch. 7, pp. 362–368.
[51] Czerny: *Pianoforte-Schule*, i, 144 (footnote).

ARTICULATION AND EXPRESSION   243

**Ex. 5.16** Perez, *Solimano*, Act III, Scene vi, British Library, London, Add MSS 16093-94; pub. in fac. in the series *Italian Opera 1640–1770* (New York, Garland, 1978).

**Ex. 5.17** a–b. Piccinni: *Catone in Utica*. (*a*) overture; (*b*) Act II, Scene ix.

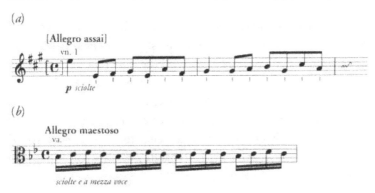

Ex. 5.18  Sacchini, *L'eroe Cinese*, Act I, Scene iv, MS score in Bayerische Staatsbibliothek, Munich, Mus. MS 543; pub. in the series *Italian Opera 1640–1770* (New York and London, Garland, 1982).

Ex. 5.19  Paisiello: *La Passione*, Pt. 2, aria "Ai passi erranti".

Ex. 5.20  Mozart: Symphony No. 35 "Haffner", 1st movement (autograph), Vn 1. [Allegro con spirito]

Some 19th-century examples can be found in music by Cherubini, Spontini, Meyerbeer, and Donizetti. Cherubini's string quartets contain several passages marked *sciolto* or *sciolte*. He used the direction in both *piano* and *forte*, and Fröhlich's definition would be apt in both cases (Ex. 5.21a–b). Examples from Spontini's *La Vestale*, Meyerbeer's *Il crociato in Egitto*, and Donizetti's *Parisina* illustrate its use by younger composers (Ex. 5.22a–c). In these examples Meyerbeer and Donizetti seem to have used *sciolte* in Lichtenthal's sense, merely to confirm that separate notes are really intended in passages that also contain slurs.

ARTICULATION AND EXPRESSION 245

Ex. 5.21 a–b. Cherubni: (*a*) String Quartet no. 2/ii; (*b*) String Quartet no. 5/iv.

(*a*)

(*b*)

246   CLASSICAL AND ROMANTIC PERFORMING PRACTICE

**Ex. 5.22a**  Spontini: *La Vestale* (Paris, Erard, [1808]), Act I, Ballet no. 1.

**Ex. 5.22b**  Meyerbeer: *Il crociato in Egitto*, no. 16 [A major, C Allegro agitato (Più allegro)].

**Ex. 5.22c**  Donizetti: *Parisina*, autograph, Museo Donizettiano Bergamo; pub. in fac. in the series *Early Romantic Opera* (New York and London, 1981).

Definitions of *spiccato* in 18th- and early-19th-century sources agree with J. G. Walther's statement that "one separates the sounds on instruments clearly from each other so that each is heard distinctly".[52] Koch added that it "should indicate a rounded performance in which the notes do not sound blurred or flow into each other."[53] Burney, however, was more specific, stating that it is "nearly of the same signification as *sciolto* and *staccato*; except that, on the violin, when spiccato is written over or under a group of notes, they are to be touched lightly with the vibration of one bow [a gentle slurred *staccato*?]; and sciolto and staccato passages and movements require a strong bow to every note".[54] It is possibly with a distinction similar to Burney's that *spiccato* and *staccato* were both used in the 1780s by Ernst Wilhelm Wolf in

---

[52] Walther: *Musicalisches Lexicon*, 575.
[53] Koch: 'Spiccato' in *Musikalisches Lexikon*, 1422.
[54] Burney: 'Spiccato' in Rees (ed.), *Cyclopaedia*, xxxiii, no pagination.

ARTICULATION AND EXPRESSION 247

his String Quartet op. 3 no. 3 (Ex. 5.23a–b).[55] As late as the 1830s, Carl Gollmick regarded *spiccato* simply as "clearly and neatly separated from one another",[56] while the British author J. A. Hamilton defined it as "Pointedly, distinctly. In violin music, this term implies that the notes are to be played with the point of the bow."[57] Liszt used it in relation to the piano, apparently as a degree of articulation less separated than *staccato*.[58]

Ex. 5.23a  Wolf: Trois Quartetts op. 3, no. 3 in G minor, Vn 1.
[Allegro assai ¢]

Ex. 5.23b  Vn 2.
[Andantino 3/8]

Beethoven seems to have been among the earliest composers to make use of the instruction *non legato* or *non ligato*, but only in his later works, where it occurs in orchestral, keyboard, and string chamber music. He very often used it where a passage was preceded by similar note values with slurs. Its earliest use in the string quartets occurs at bar 20 of the first movement of op. 95, where sixteenths are to be played with separate bows. The autograph shows that this was an afterthought (Ex. 5.24). Whether, in this context, at the extremely rapid tempo called for by Beethoven's metronome mark ($\quarternote$ = 92) the strings have much latitude for differentiating one style of

---

[55] Wolf: Trois Quartetts op. 3 (Speyer, Bossler Conseiller de Brandebourg, n.d.), Plate W. copy in DK Kk. The use of dots and strokes is highly inconsistent in the edition and shows no clear connection with these terms.

[56] Carl Gollmick: *Kritische Terminologie*, 32.

[57] Hamilton: *A Dictionary of Two Thousand Italian, French, German, English, and Other Musical Terms* (New York, 1842), 82 (preface dated "London, March, 1838"). For the use of the term *spiccato* for springing bowstrokes see Ch. 7, p. 410.

[58] Wilhelm von Lenz: *Die großen Pianoforte-Virtuosen unserer Zeit aus persönlicher Bekanntschaft* (Berlin, 1872), 14.

detached bowing from another is a moot point, and it seems likely that the instruction was intended simply to prevent the players from slurring. Other examples where there is a clear intention to prevent slurring can be found in the *Missa solemnis*, in the Piano Sonata op. 111 (Ex. 5.25a–b), and at many points in the last group of string quartets. But the question arises: why did Beethoven not use *staccato* marks to signal that the notes were intended to be separate, as he often did in earlier works and continued to do in late ones? There are very good grounds for thinking that, in the works of this period, he envisaged a specific type of performance when he either wrote *non ligato* or (except where an earlier instruction was obviously intended to continue) left the notes without markings. The first movement of the String Quartet op. 130 is particularly revealing in this respect, for the sixteenths from bar 14 are marked *non ligato* whereas those at bar 64 have *staccato* marks and the instruction *pp ben marcato*; and both passages return with the same markings later in the movement (Ex. 5.26). It is probable that Beethoven wanted a more connected bowstroke in the *non ligato* passage, and this assumption may be strengthened if what is known about the bowing styles of Viennese violinists with whom he worked at that time is taken into account.[59] If this is so, it seems likely that when Beethoven used this instruction in his piano music, he meant the pianist to produce an effect similar to the broad *détaché* of the string player in which each note received a separate bowstroke but without being deliberately shortened. A passage in his Violin Sonata in C minor offers a clue to his understanding of *staccato* marks. In the autograph, at bar 107 the bass is notated as *staccato* eighth-notes, but in the following bar as sixteenth-notes with sixteenth-note rests then, in bars 109–112, reverts to eighth-notes (Ex. 5.27). This is clearly not intended to indicate a different execution from those bars, and evidently arose through oversight (cf. bb. 247–251), but it shows that Beethoven envisaged the eighth-notes with *staccato* marks in that context as equivalent to sixteenths. A similar discrepancy occurs in the piano part of Variation 2 of the second movement of the Violin Sonata op. 47 between the first four bars (eighth-notes with *staccato*) and the rest of the variation (sixteenth-notes with rests) in the copyist's Stichvorlage, but in the first edition of the sonata the first four bars were changed to correspond with the notation in the following bars. This supports the assumption that Beethoven used *non-ligato*, rather than *staccato* marks or the instruction *staccato*, to indicate

---

[59] See Ch. 7, pp. 415–416.

that the notes should not be slurred, but also that they should not be significantly shortened.

**Ex. 5.24** Beethoven: String Quartet op. 95/i.
[Allegro con brio]

**Ex. 5.25** a–b. Beethoven: (*a*) *Missa solemnis*, Dona nobis pacem; (*b*) Piano Sonata op. 111/i.

250   CLASSICAL AND ROMANTIC PERFORMING PRACTICE

Ex. 5.26 a–b. Beethoven: String Quartet op. 130/i.

Ex. 5.27 Beethoven: Violin Sonata op. 30 no. 2/i, bb. 108–9.
[Allegro con brio]

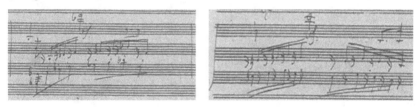

It is unlikely that Beethoven made any clear distinction of this kind in earlier works, where he appears to have been willing to use *staccato* marks as a simple instruction not to slur. There is, nevertheless, the possibility of an intentional distinction as early as, say, the Violin Sonatas op. 30, where notes in the piano part without slurs or articulation marks often correspond with separately bowed notes in the violin part; but the intention is sometimes called into question by the use of articulation marks in the violin part, as, for instance, in bar 28 of the first movement of the G major Sonata op. 30

no. 3—although these may merely have been meant to prevent slurring—or by the frequent absence of markings in the piano part where *legato* seems very likely.

As in Beethoven's late works, Schumann's use of the instruction *non legato*, in the Piano Quintet, for example, implies an execution for the pianist that corresponds with separately bowed passages in the string instruments (Ex. 5.28). Considering Schumann's relationship with Ferdinand David and other violinists of a similar background, the association of such passages with a broad *détaché* bowing is persuasive. The same can be said of later 19th-century uses of the term, where composers were evidently concerned to warn against *legato* in contexts that might otherwise lead players to slur, yet at the same time wished to avoid the danger of encouraging a distinctly *staccato* execution. In Liszt's *Faust-Symphonie*, the instruction appears in conjunction with a *quasi trillo* (Ex. 5.29). Max Bruch used it in his G minor Violin Concerto in a passage that would typically have received a *détaché* bowing, but it is necessary because of the preceding slurs (Ex. 5.30). Saint-Saëns, in his *Danse macabre* op. 40, similarly employed *non legato* after a passage with slurs (Ex. 5.31); the requirement for a broad rather than *staccato* bowing in this instance is suggested by earlier passages of eighths with articulation marks, which appear together with instructions such as *staccato*, *marcatissimo*, or *leggiero*.

Ex. 5.28 Schumann: Piano Quintet op. 44/i.

**Ex. 5.29** Liszt: *Eine Faust-Symphonie*, i, "Faust".

**Ex. 5.30** Bruch: Violin Concerto in G minor op. 26/iii.

**Ex. 5.31** Saint-Saëns: *Danse macabre* op. 40.

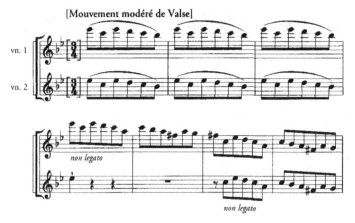

## Implied *Non Legato* or *Non-Staccato*

For every late-18th- or early-19th-century composer who specified *sciolto*, *spiccato*, *non legato*, or something similar where neither a slurred nor *staccato* execution was required, there were many who failed to do so; and it is frequently very uncertain where composers might have envisaged a distinctive execution that was neither *legato* nor *staccato*. In such cases, the terminology *non staccato* might be just as appropriate as *non legato*. Schubert, when he left notes unmarked, often clarified his intentions by instructions such as *staccato* or *sempre staccato*, to save writing dots continuously, or, especially in piano music, by writing *legato* instead of continuing with slurs, but he appears not to have used *non legato* or an equivalent term. That he did, however, sometimes intend a *non legato* or *non-staccato* execution is suggested by many passages in works for piano and strings where slurring, *staccato*, and unmarked separate notes correspond in the keyboard and string parts. There are also passages in Schubert's orchestral music, similar to the ambiguous ones in the Weber's E flat Mass (Exx. 5.12 and 5.13), where slurred wind parts occur simultaneously with separately bowed string parts. But in view of Schubert's usual notational practice, the distinction was almost certainly intended; and in these cases, a broad *détaché* bowing also seems likely (Ex. 5.32).

Ex. 5.32 Schubert: *Alfonso und Estrella*, Act II, no. 22.

By the second half of the 19th century there is little doubt that in almost all cases where a composer wrote separate notes with neither slurs nor articulation marks, these were meant to be detached more by the type of accentuation created by full-length separate bowstrokes than by shortening. This is clearly what is intended by Tchaikovsky in the first movement of the Sixth Symphony, for instance, where he scored upper strings and woodwind in unison for extended passages, the wind with slurs, and the strings with separate bows (Ex. 5.33a). Earlier in the movement where the strings change from passages of mixed slurs and separate bows to a passage that is again in unison with slurred woodwind, he gave the instruction *détaché* to the strings to ensure that they used separate bows. The choice of that term leaves little doubt about the style of bowing required (Ex. 5.33b). It seems possible that the ease with which woodwind instruments could produce a convincing *staccato* was still associated with a greater tendency for them to do so on unslurred notes; perhaps it is significant that at another point in the first movement of the "Pathétique" Tchaikovsky felt it necessary to give the instruction "pesante, non staccato" to the wind, but not to the cellos and basses, who play the same figure (Ex. 5.33c).

Ex. 5.33 a–c. Tchaikovsky: *Symphonie pathétique* op. 74/i.

Ex. 5.33 Continued

(c)

256  CLASSICAL AND ROMANTIC PERFORMING PRACTICE

Brahms, like Tchaikovsky, evidently had a comparable intention when he wrote passages with slurred wind and separate strings, as in the last movement of the Second Symphony (Ex. 5.34). In view of the Viotti School's influence throughout much of Europe in the early 19th century, and its cultivation of broad, singing bowstrokes, it is very plausible that Schubert or Weber conceived a similar effect in analogous circumstances. To suggest, however, that Mozart may have envisaged something of this kind would seem strange to string players brought up in the 20th-century tradition of using short, often elastic bowstrokes for notes of moderate rapidity in this repertoire.[60] Yet a broad *détaché* may well have been in Mozart's mind when he scored and notated a wind and string unison passage in his last symphony (Ex. 5.35). There can be little doubt that the combination of slurred wind and unslurred lower strings was deliberate, for the passage appears in both exposition and recapitulation with the same articulation. The violins, with their repeated notes, were certainly intended to produce a connected sound, and in this context a *staccato* execution in the lower strings seems unlikely. Such passages offer thought-provoking clues to the expectations of late-18th- and early-19th-century composers when they left the notes unmarked.

Ex. 5.34  Brahms: Second Symphony op. 73/iv.

[60] See Ch. 7, pp. 343–44.

Ex. 5.35  Mozart: Symphony no. 41 K. 551/i.

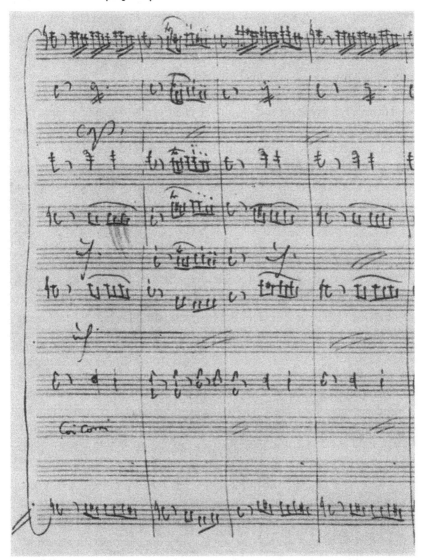

## Heavy and Light Performance

Signs and instructions for articulation and accentuation, even after they became more differentiated and were increasingly used, could only convey limited information. They were in many respects relative to the music's genre and character, and to the composer's choice of metre and note values. Well into the 19th century, performers were expected to interpret the composer's instructions (or lack of them) from their understanding of these other factors, which were partly theorized by German writers in the late 18th and early 19th century as "heavy and light performance".

The nomenclature, and much of its systematized theory, seems to have derived from J. P. Kirnberger and his pupil J. A. P. Schulz, though the ideas dealt with under this heading by these and subsequent theorists were also alluded to in earlier texts. In Kirnberger's *Die Kunst des reinen Satzes* there are many references to the role of metre in determining a heavier or lighter performance style. After stating that longer note values required greater weight and accentuation than shorter ones, he continued: "consequently, a composition that is to be performed with weight and emphasis can only be notated with long note values, and another that is to be performed in a light and playful manner can only be notated with short note values".[61]

These ideas were expounded more extensively by Schulz, who sought to explain the "appropriate lightness and heaviness of performance for the character and expression of the piece". But his comments also indicate that theory was not entirely in line with the practice of the period:

> A great part of the expression depends on this. A piece of grand and pathetic expression must be performed in the heaviest and most emphatic manner: this occurs if every note of it is firmly given and sustained, almost as if **tenuta** were written over it. In contrast, pieces of pleasant and gentle expression are performed more lightly; namely, every note is more lightly given and not sustained so firmly. A wholly merry or dance-like expression can only be obtained through the lightest performance. If this difference in performance is not observed a greater part of the expression is lost in many pieces; and yet it appears as if nowadays little attention is given to this anymore. It is certain that the practice of performing everything lightly and, as it were, playfully has so much gained the upper hand, even having a powerful effect on composition, that people seem no longer to know about any grand and majestic expression in music. One composes for the church as for the theatre, because the true performance of good church music has been lost and no distinction is made between the performance of a church

---

[61] Kirnberger: *Die Kunst des reinen Satzes*, ii, 116.

solo or an opera aria. Instead of the emphatic, earnest performance that touches the heart and soul, everyone strives for the pretty and fashionable, as if music had no other end than to amuse the ear with trifles. Unfortunate is the composer who really has a feeling for the grand and elevated and writes things that ought to be performed heavily; he will not find one in a hundred who knows how to enter into the simplicity of the melody and give due weight to every note. Nor does the vitiated taste find any more pleasure in such things, and considers it pedantry to want to do more than amuse the ear with music.

Like Kirnberger, he explained the role of metre in determining heaviness and lightness, then continued:

In addition, one must note from the character or coherence of the melody such places or phrases which ought to be particularly heavily or lightly performed; the expression will thereby be strengthened and the whole given a pleasant shading. Only in strict fugues and church pieces is this shading dispensed with, for it does not accord well with their dignity and elevation of expression. In such pieces every note, according to the metre, is given with equal firmness and emphasis. As a whole, every metre will be more heavily performed in the church than in the chamber or theatre; also, the very light metres are not found in good church music.[62]

Türk's treatment of the same subject in his *Klavierschule* shows his familiarity with Schulz's account; but he prefaced his discussion with an examination of *staccato*, *portato*, slurring (*legato*), and ties, since he considered that it was principally through the effective use of these means that heavy or light performance style could be achieved. He concurred with Kirnberger and Schulz that "In a heavy performance style everything must be firmly (emphatically) given and held to the full extent of the value of the note", and that a light performance style is achieved "if one gives every note with less firmness (emphasis), and lifts the finger from the key somewhat earlier than the duration of the note specifies". He felt it important, however, to remark that a heavy or light performance style had more to do with sustaining or shortening the notes than with strength or weakness:

---

[62] Schulz: "Vortrag" in *Allgemeine Theorie*, ii, 1253f.

> For in certain cases, e.g. an *Allegro vivo, scherzando, Vivace con allegrezza*, etc., the performance style must certainly be rather light, (short) but at the same time more or less strong; whereas on the other hand a piece of mournful character, for example an *Adagio mesto, con afflizzione*, etc. should certainly be slurred [*legato*] and consequently, so to speak, heavy, but nevertheless not exactly performed strongly. For all that, at any rate, heavy and strong go together in most cases.

He then observed that the heaviness or lightness might be determined:

> 1) from the character and purpose of a piece of music (§ 45.), 2) from the specified tempo, 3) from the metre, 4) from the note values, 5) from the way in which these are employed. Furthermore, the matter of national taste, the composer's style, and the instrument for which a piece of music is written comes into consideration.[63]

He gave lists of performance instructions that might imply heavy, moderately light or very light performance:

> Compositions of a sublime, serious, solemn, pathetic, etc. character must be performed heavily, firmly and powerfully, with strong accentuation, and so on. Among these pieces of music are those which are entitled grave, pomposo, patetico, maestoso, sostenuto, and so on. Pieces of a pleasant, gentle, pleasing &c. character require a somewhat lighter and noticeably weaker performance. Such pieces are usually described as compiacevole, con dolcezza, glissicato, lusingando, pastorale, piacevole and the like. Pieces in which lively, jocular, joyful feelings prevail, e.g. allegro scherzando, burlesco, giocoso, con allegrezza, risvegliato, etc., must be performed quite lightly, while sad and similar emotions especially require slurring and portamento. Compositions of the latter kind are designated by the words: con afflizzione, con amarezza, doloroso, lagrimoso, languido, mesto, etc.

But, in conclusion, he stressed, in bold type: "It goes without saying that in all these cases varied degrees of heavy or light performance must be used."[64]

---

[63] Türk, *Klavierschule*, 358f.
[64] Türk, *Klavierschule*, 359.

In §45 he added: "Pieces written to a serious end, e.g. fugues, well worked-out sonatas, religious odes, and songs etc.* require a far heavier style of performance than certain light-hearted divertimenti, humorous songs, lively dances and so on." [Türk's footnote:] "* If I were not writing primarily for keyboard players, I would include everything that is intended for the church."[65]

Similar principles for violinists, with regard to bowstrokes and the character of the music, were expounded by Löhlein and Reichardt in the 1770s. Reichardt's sensitivity to the implications of metre is also apparent in his compositions.[66] A reviewer of his Lieder collection *Goethe's lyrische Gedichte* vol. 2 (1794) observed of one song: "That Herr R. chose the very appropriate time signature of $\frac{4}{8}$—for which an ordinary song composer would have marked $\frac{2}{4}$—testifies to the author's deep insight and fine feelings. This is not the place to show the real difference between the two time signatures that apparently indicate the same thing [...]. It will be enough here if we say that this time signature requires a very light performance."[67] Such distinctions, however, were already becoming rarer at that time; by 1818 Jérôme-Joseph de Momigny could assert that there was no significant difference between $\frac{4}{8}$ and $\frac{2}{4}$: "The $\frac{4}{8}$ time signature is old-fashioned; we don't even use it anymore, although what it expresses is very commonly used".[68] In fact, late-18th-century French sources seem to have ignored the expressive connotations of metre: Rousseau makes no mention of them in his article "Mesure" (1768) and they are absent from the treatment of metres in the Paris Conservatoire *Principes* (1800).

A somewhat later account of this subject, with the singer in mind, was given by J. F. Schubert, who, while reiterating earlier writers' views, contributed different perspectives. He instructed:

> Heavy performance style is distinguished from light in that the notes are firmly bound to each other, emphatic, and precisely held to the full extent of their value. In a light performance style, on the other hand, the notes are less sustained, less bound together, and are played shorter and with less firmness. Vocal pieces of a pathetic, serious, solemn, and elevated character must be performed with the greatest weight and emphasis. This

---

[65] Türk, *Klavierschule*, 360.
[66] See Ch. 7, pp. 360–61.
[67] Anon.: *Neue allgemeine deutsche Bibliothek*, xli/1 (1798), Anhang (1799), 83f.
[68] Momigny: 'Mesure' in *Encyclopédie méthodique Musique*, ii (Paris, 1818), 139.

genre is commonly given the direction grave, pomposo, maestoso, etc. Pieces with a pleasant, trifling, merry, and lively character require a light performance style. These are commonly headed Allegretto, scherzando, lusingando, etc. The metre also indicates a heavier or lighter performance style. In general one can assume the following rule. The greater the time units (beat divisions) in a piece, the heavier the performance style must be. [...]

A vocal piece with many dissonances demands a heavier performance style than one that consists of fewer dissonances and more consonant harmonies. Fugues, well worked out [contrapuntal] pieces of church music, require a heavy performance style throughout; in general, the performance style in church is, regardless of the metre, heavier than in the chamber or the theatre—The strict [gebunden] (rigorous) style of writing demands a heavier performance style than the unconstrained [frey] (light, galant).* The manner or style of the composer is also to be considered in relation to a heavy or light performance style. Thus, for example, pieces by Mozart require, on the whole, a heavier performance style than those of Haydn. The vocal pieces of the latter must, on the other hand, be more heavily performed than those of Paisiello, Martin, etc. One also often finds that compositions of one and the same master must be differently performed with respect to weight or lightness. Thus, for example, Mozart's *Don Giovanni* requires (on the whole) a heavier performance style than *The Marriage of Figaro*. Salieri's *Axur* must be more heavily performed than *La cifra*.

* [Schubert's footnote] *Gebunden* is the name for the type of writing in which the rules of harmony have been strictly observed by the composer; *frey* the name for the type of writing in which the composer has not bound himself so strictly to the rules of composition and has now and then allowed himself bold turns, surprising entries of foreign, remote keys.

One must also observe from the characteristics of the melody and from the meaning of the text which individual passages should be more heavily or lightly performed than others.

A powerful unison, for example, always demands a heavier performance style in every type of musical composition, as long as the composer has not deliberately specified the contrary. Dotted notes demand, for the most part, a heavier performance style, for example [Ex. 5.36]. [...]⁶⁹

Passagework and ornaments are, without exception, performed lightly.⁷⁰

**Ex. 5.36** J. F. Schubert: *Neue Singe-Schule*, 132.

Gustav Schilling, in the 1840s, was perhaps the last writer to publish substantial discussion of heavy and light performance from the practical rather than historical viewpoint; but his voluminous writings are often merely paraphrases, or even plagiarism of earlier material, and it is questionable whether these concepts significantly influenced many of the younger generation of musicians born during the first half of the 19th century. Some composers, however, including Mendelssohn and Brahms, retained sensitivity to some aspects of these practices, for instance the effects of metre and genre.⁷¹

Performing practices that had previously been associated with the concept of heavy and light performance were usually discussed by German musicians under the general heading *Vortrag* (performance style) in late-18th- and early-19th-century treatises. During the 19th century, the treatment of *Vortrag* changed significantly; writers displayed less and less interest in drawing conclusions about performance style from the types of notes employed, the genre, the type of piece, or the musical context. It became almost an article of faith that, in a new era of individualism, each piece had its own unique demands that could only be indicated by specific instructions from the composer. Thus, in the *Musikalisches Conversations-Lexikon* (1882) the entry for *Vortrag* was strikingly different from that in Sulzer's *Allgemeine Theorie* of just over a hundred years earlier. The *Conversations-Lexikon* considered that *Vortrag* "requires two things above all: the most complete understanding of the performance instructions employed by the creative

---

⁶⁹ See Ch. 14, "Over-Dotting", for information that Schubert includes in this section of his treatise.
⁷⁰ Schubert: *Singe-Schule*, 130–32.
⁷¹ See Ch. 8, pp. 460 and 478, for Mendelssohn's sensitivity to metre and to the tempo of church music.

artist, and the technical skill to execute, on the relevant musical instruments, what they indicate".[72] The rest of the article concerned itself almost entirely with an explanation of signs and performance instructions. By that date, the proliferation of performance instructions had greatly restricted, although not entirely obviated the need for performance choices derived from musical context.

[72] Mendel and Reissmann: 'Vortrag' in *Musikalisches Conversations-Lexikon*, xi (Berlin, 1879), 212.

# 6
# The Notation of Articulation and Phrasing

## Dots and Strokes as Articulation Marks

Since the late 19th century, editors and scholars have devoted much thought to the sorts of theoretical distinctions that were historically made between various forms of articulation marks, illuminating a host of individual views, which, though fairly clear and straightforward in themselves, are frequently incompatible with one another. Theorists and authors of musical instruction books were divided between those who recognized a single form of *staccato* mark and those who advocated two.[1] C. P. E. Bach, whose reputation as a composer made him perhaps the most widely respected of all 18th-century theorists, took the view that only one mark for unslurred *staccato* was necessary; but, stressing that one mark did not mean one kind of execution, he observed that the performer must implement the *staccato* in different ways according to the length of the note, whether it is a half, quarter, or eighth, whether the tempo is fast or slow, and whether the dynamic is *forte* or *piano*.[2] Bach's preference for a single mark was echoed by, among others, Leopold Mozart (1756), Reichardt (1776), Türk (1789), Hiller (1792), Müller (1804), and Spohr (1833).[3] Others, including Quantz (1752), Riepel (1757), Löhlein (1774), Vogler (1778), Koch (1802), Knecht (1803), Adam (1804),[4] and an increasing number of 19th-century authorities, advocated or acknowledged two signs. Hummel (1828) illustrated both dots and strokes as *staccato* signs, but specifically

---

[1] There seems no reason to distinguish between strokes and wedges; the wedge is essentially a printer's convention and, where it has any direct connection with a composer's markings, will normally represent a stroke.

[2] Bach: *Versuch*, i, 125.

[3] Mozart: *Versuch*; Reichardt: *Ueber die Pflichten*; Türk: *Klavierschule*; Johann Adam Hiller: *Anweisung zum Violinspielen für Schulen und Selbstunterrichte* (Leipzig, 1792); Müller: *Klavier- und Fortepiano-Schule*; Spohr: *Violinschule*.

[4] Quantz: *Versuch*; Riepel: *Gründliche Erklärung*; Löhlein: *Anweisung zum Violinspielen*; Georg Joseph Vogler: *Kuhrpfälzische Tonschule* (Mannheim, 1778); Koch: *Musikalisches Lexikon*; Knecht: *Katechismus*; Adam: *Méthode*.

presented them as alternative forms of the same thing.[5] Later in his treatise he exclusively used strokes, perhaps to avoid confusion with dots, which were always used in the context of *portato*. Czerny (1839) similarly made no distinction, but thereafter used only dots.[6] In 1802, Koch argued that, since, in a good performance different degrees of *staccato* were required, there ought to be appropriate signs to specify this, remarking: "It is at least to be regretted that, since two signs are used for this purpose, namely the dot and the small stroke, no agreement has been reached as to which of these two signs should indicate a higher or sharper degree of staccato."[7] By the second half of the 19th century the recognition of two signs with different significance was almost universal; but disagreement about their meaning remained. The majority of 18th- and early-19th-century authors who described both signs favoured the stroke as the sharper and shorter of the two, yet Vogler and his admirer Knecht seem to have wanted it sharper and longer. Gustav Schilling still expressed uncertainty about the significance of the two types of *staccato* mark in 1837.[8] Attitudes differed according to whether the matter was seen primarily from the point of view of keyboard playing, string playing, or wind playing; and there were important differences between French and German musicians, especially about the accent implications of the two kinds of *staccato* mark.[9]

The relationship of theoretical explanations to the practices of specific composers remains highly problematic. There has been little consensus even about identifying which composers used both dots and strokes to mean different things, and which used a single mark with more variable meaning. Many 18th- and early-19th-century manuscript scores seem at first sight to contain both markings, and patterns may apparently emerge, such as dots on a succession of notes in conjunct motion and strokes over isolated notes or successions of disjunct notes. On closer inspection, however, discrepancies become increasingly evident and strengthen doubts about whether a deliberate distinction between two forms of *staccato* mark was intended, leading, perhaps, to the conviction that what initially appeared to be deliberate dots or strokes are rather the product of writing habits or temperament.

---

[5] Hummel: *Anweisung*, 2nd edn, 54.
[6] Czerny: *Pianoforte-Schule*, i, 142.
[7] Koch: 'Abstoßen' in *Musikalisches Lexikon*, 45f.
[8] Gustav Schilling: 'Abstoßen' in *Encyclopädie*, 28f.
[9] See Ch. 3, "The Staccato Mark".

Mozart's practice has been especially controversial, with vehement and sometimes intemperate advocacy on both sides of the issue. Paul Mies argued cogently in 1958 that the marks on unslurred notes in Mozart's autographs, which include every stage between clear dots and long strokes, are a product of his manner of writing and are not intended to represent two distinct signs or different modes of execution.[10] In recent decades, there has been increasing consensus that, whatever their visual form, they are all simply *staccato* marks, and that, independently of variations in their size or shape, they mean whatever Mozart envisaged an articulation mark to signify in that particular context.[11] Some scholars have also distinguished between dots and strokes on unslurred notes in Beethoven, but it is now generally accepted that a single form was intended.[12] Here, judgement is aided by the survival of many corrected copyists' scores and parts, in which, with the exception of corrections to inaccurately notated *portato* (for instance, in the Allegretto of the Seventh Symphony), Beethoven did not concern himself with clarifying any distinction between dots and strokes, despite many inconsistencies on the part of the copyists. One particularly interesting proof copy, corrected by Beethoven, is the piano reduction of the Prometheus music op. 43. At the beginning of the Allegro molto con brio of the overture, the eighths in the violin parts have articulation marks for the first three bars;[13] in the context of early-19th-century practice, musicians might otherwise have assumed that these very rapid notes, which are too

---

[10] Paul Mies: 'Die Artikulationzeichen Strich und Punkt bei Wolfgang Amadeus Mozart', *Die Musikforschung*, xi (1958), 428.

[11] Arguments against two signs have been advanced by: Alfred Einstein and E. Zimmermann, in Hans Albrecht (ed.), *Die Bedeutung der Zeichen Keil Strich und Punkt bei Mozart* (Kassel, 1957); Robert D. Riggs, 'Articulation in Mozart's and Beethoven's Sonatas for Piano and Violin' (diss., Harvard University, 1987); Clive Brown, 'Dots and Strokes in Late 18th- and 19th-Century Music', *Early Music*, xxi (1993), 593–610. Those arguing for two distinct signs included: H. Keller, H. Unterricht, O. Jonas, and A. Kreutz in *Die Bedeutung*; R. Elvers in *Neue Mozart Ausgabe* IV/13/1 (Kassel, 1961), preface, p. x (the *NMA* adopted a consistent, but very dubious policy of attempting to make a distinction between dots and strokes); Frederick Neumann, 'Dots and Strokes in Mozart', *Early Music*, xxi (1993), 429–35.

[12] Mies argued against two marks in Beethoven in *Textkritische Untersuchungen bei Beethoven* (Munich and Duisburg, 1957); see also G. von Dadelsen, ed., *Editionsrichtlinie musikalischer Denkmäler und Gesamtausgaben* (Kassel, 1967). The present author has also taken this view in his editions of Beethoven for Breitkopf & Härtel and Bärenreiter, as has Jonathan Del Mar in his Bärenreiter Beethoven editions. I am grateful to Leonardo Miucci, however, for pointing out that in his very early Piano Quartets (1785) Beethoven experimented with two forms of *staccato* mark.

[13] 1st edn orchestral parts (Leipzig, Hoffmeister & Kühnel), pl. no. 283.

fast to be played *staccato* (except with a *sautillé* bowstroke, which was unknown in Vienna at that time),[14] were meant to be slurred. In the piano reduction Beethoven deleted the articulation marks and wrote a marginal instruction to remove them, almost certainly because he recognized that, for the piano, any kind of genuinely *staccato* execution was impractical at the envisaged tempo.[15]

In Beethoven's own holographs the predominant form is the stroke, and where *staccato* marks over unslurred notes appear to be dots, they may in most cases equally well be interpreted as very small strokes. This is especially evident when they are compared with his *staccato* marks under slurs (for *portato*), which, like Mozart's, are invariably written as unmistakable dots. Beethoven's practice was surely in agreement with the opinion of August Eberhardt Müller, who wrote in 1804 that "it would be best if one used only the little stroke, not the dot, where the notes should be performed staccato; but used the latter only in conjunction with the slur [i.e., *portato*]".[16]

Other important 18th- and 19th-century composers have received less attention in this respect. C. P. E. Bach, having advocated one form in his theoretical writings, appears to have required only one sign in his music. Haydn may, perhaps, have made a distinction between dots and strokes on unslurred notes (and even on notes under slurs)[17] in a few very late chamber works, for instance the op. 77 string quartets, where he experimented with various unusual notational devices, but he seems not to have done so in earlier works. Weber may have intended to use both signs in some instances, but it is by no means clear that the apparent distinctions in most of his autographs are consequential; in *Der Freischütz*, for example, there are quite frequent cases of inconsistency (Ex. 6.1).

---

[14] See Ch. 7 for strong evidence of this.
[15] Beethoven-Haus, Bonn Sammlung H. C. Bodmer, HCB C BMd 1. Online in the Beethoven-Haus Digital Archive.
[16] Müller: *Klavier- und Fortepiano Spiel*, §5, 27 (footnote).
[17] See pp. 328–29.

Ex. 6.1 Weber: *Der Freischütz*, no. 15.

270  CLASSICAL AND ROMANTIC PERFORMING PRACTICE

Schubert was rather more consistent in his employment of two signs, especially in his later works. The orthographic distinction between thin vertical lines and *staccato* marks that correspond with his dots of prolongation is usually quite clear. The passage in Ex. 6.2a recurs with the same obvious strokes in the recapitulation, and the passages with dots are consistent throughout (Ex. 6.2b). In the 1827 1st edition, however, these distinctions were not maintained; dots were printed only under slurs and strokes for *staccato* on separate notes. Schubert's concern to make a difference is demonstrated by a place in the autograph of *Fierrabras*,[18] where he appears to have written dots in the cello and bass part (which was sketched first, together with the vocal parts), but subsequently changed them to strokes to match the other orchestral parts, which he added later. It is also significant that the outer sections of this march consistently have strokes while the gentler middle section has dots throughout.

Ex. 6.2 a–b. Schubert: Piano Sonata in G, D. 894/i.
[Molto Moderato e cantabile]

Cherubini and Spohr were among those who appear to have shown little if any interest in using two marks. It has been argued that Rossini did so, but this remains questionable, at least in all but the last operas. In *Semiramide*, for instance, many pages provide examples of an indiscriminate mixture of dots and strokes as *staccato* marks (Ex. 6.3).

---

[18] No. 3, bar 22.

**Ex. 6.3** Rossini: *Semiramide*, ouverture.
[Allegro vivace]

Among composers born in the 18th century, Meyerbeer certainly seems to have intended two signs in some works, though unlike many German composers he used the dot as his predominant *staccato* mark, employing strokes relatively infrequently. Marschner, too, employed both signs, apparently intentionally.[19] Nevertheless, in almost all cases where the forms of the *staccato* marks range from genuine dots to smaller or larger strokes, it is seldom wholly clear if or where composers intended a distinction between two signs.

In the music of composers born after 1800, both dots and strokes were used with increasing frequency as a means of indicating different types of *staccato* execution. Mendelssohn, however, still seems to have preferred a single sign. Schumann generally used dots, but wrote strokes occasionally, as did Brahms, whose deliberate intention to signify a difference between strokes and dots

---

[19] See Ch. 3, p. 144 for a 19th-century opinion on the meaning of Marschner's *staccato* strokes.

272  CLASSICAL AND ROMANTIC PERFORMING PRACTICE

is attested not only in his scores, but also in a letter to Joachim in 1879.[20] Reger was also among those who undoubtedly wrote both forms of articulation mark intentionally (Ex. 6.4). But ambiguities still abounded at that time, even with composers who generally took care to make their notation as clear and informative as possible. It cannot be assumed, for example, that because composers did something at one period in their lives or, in particular works, the same will have been true at other times, or in other instances.

**Ex. 6.4**  Reger: *Sechs Burlesquen*, no. 4.

[20] See p. 289.

NOTATION OF ARTICULATION AND PHRASING 273

Wagner's practice with respect to dots and strokes is instructive in this respect. In some early autographs he seems exclusively to have employed the dot, while in others he used the stroke (the orthography is not always easy to interpret), but there appears to be no consequential difference. In *Rienzi* and *Der fliegende Holländer*, the predominant form of *staccato* mark is the dot; strokes are used occasionally, but almost entirely on isolated notes, where they may have been intended to indicate an accented execution, or may simply have become a writing habit with no implications for performance. In *Tannhäuser*, however, Wagner adopted the stroke as his principal *staccato* mark, and dots became relatively uncommon. In later works he used dots more frequently, but the stroke remained the predominant *staccato* mark for the rest of his life. In the late autographs at least, there is rarely any ambiguity between the two marks, for while the strokes are clearly vertical lines, the dots tend, like Schubert's, to be elongated somewhat in a horizontal direction, as do his dots of prolongation (Ex. 6.5). In the operas of his middle period, contradictions abound; in the lithographed full score of *Lohengrin*, the copyist frequently wrote strokes where Wagner's autograph contains clear dots (for instance, under the slur in bar 15 of the introduction to Act III). Wagner seems, however, to have been more careful to ensure that an accurate differentiation between dots and strokes was made in the printed scores of his later operas.

**Ex. 6.5** Wagner: *Siegfried Idyll.*
[Ruhig bewegt]

## The Functions of Articulation Marks

Both in theory and in practice, *staccato* marks, or other visually identical marks (whether or not a distinction was made between dots and strokes), signified a number of different things. Some of these were quite specialized and are relatively infrequently encountered outside specific repertoires. In French 18th-century music, for instance, dots and strokes might be used to warn against the application of inequality. Quantz, too, referred to this function of dots and strokes.[21] In such cases, the theory was that the dot merely prevented inequality and the stroke indicated both equality and *staccato*.[22]

An unusual use of the *staccato* mark, which is mentioned by C. P. E. Bach, can be found in the second movement of Beethoven's Violin Sonata op. 30 no. 3 in G major. Throughout the autograph, Beethoven consistently placed a *staccato* stroke not over the first or second note on each appearance of a dotted figure first heard in bar 19, but over the dot of prolongation; the placement is careful and consistent and was included in the 1st edition (Ex. 6.6a–b). The meaning is undoubtedly ♩♫. The same notational device appears in the autograph and copied violin part of the Cavatina in his string quartet op. 130 (Ex. 6.7a–b), though not in the 1st edition. Probably Beethoven used it elsewhere, but not being sought, it has not been noticed.

---

[21] Quantz: *Versuch*, 106.
[22] For a helpful discussion of the problems surrounding inequality in 18th-century music see David Fuller: 'Notes inégales' in the *New Grove Dictionary of Music and Musicians*.

Ex. 6.6a Beethoven: Violin Sonata op. 30/3/ii, (autograph).
[Tempo di Minuetto ma molto moderato e grazioso]

**Ex. 6.6b** Beethoven: Violin Sonata op. 30/3/ii, 1st edn.

**Ex. 6.7** a–b. Beethoven: String Quartet op. 130/v. (*a*) autograph; (*b*) corrected copy.

Beethoven almost certainly derived this notation directly from the passage added in the 1787 edition of C. P. E. Bach's *Versuch*, where positioning a stroke above a dot of prolongation to signify a rest is proposed. Bach first illustrates a turn with its "usual indication" then with its realization, and finally with his "new indication", followed by an alternative notation, with a *staccato* mark over the dot of prolongation to represent the rest (Ex. 6.8). He asserted: "Although these new ways of writing look strange, they are nevertheless necessary. One cannot do too much to indicate the right manner of execution."[23]

**Ex. 6.8** C. P. E. Bach: *Versuch*, 1787, 3rd expanded edn (1787), i, 67.

The use of dots or strokes, apparently to indicate that the notes so marked were not to be slurred, rather than to specify a distinct shortening of the notes, is very common in 18th- and 19th-century music. In many scores of the period these marks are regularly encountered in mixed figures of slurred and separate notes, even if, as was often the case in the second half of the 18th century, the composer hardly ever employed them

---

[23] Bach: *Versuch* 1787, 3rd edn, i, 67.

in other contexts. In such passages they are necessary to the player, as Koch observed, to make clear which notes are slurred and which separate.[24] In these circumstances the notes with articulation marks were evidently not expected to be played shorter or sharper than notes without articulation marks that occurred in close proximity to them, though whether the marked and unmarked notes were meant to be played *staccato*, or whether both were intended to receive some kind of *non-legato* execution, is often unclear. A recognition of this use of *staccato* marks to clarify the articulation in passages of mixed slurred and separate notes evidently lies behind a comment in Bernhard Romberg's 1840 cello method. He cautioned against misinterpreting the marks in this situation, writing: "I must here explain that whenever notes are marked to be played alternately slurred and *staccato*, the *staccato* ones, whether marked with dots or strokes, should never be made with short, hard bowstroke."[25] In other words, those notes will not really be *staccato* in the commonly understood sense of the term, simply, in string playing, executed with separate bows, which could be made either with full-length or shortened strokes. Linked to this usage is the practice of including a few articulation marks at the beginning of a passage but leaving the remainder without, or marking them on a figure of relatively fast-moving notes. In such instances the performer must again decide whether the composer is indicating a distinct *staccato* execution for the passage, or merely cautioning against slurring.

Recognizing the significance of a composer's notation in these situations is difficult and seldom unambiguous. Even the most careful composers of the late 18th century did not always convey their intentions in this respect with absolute clarity. Mozart, even in his late works, sometimes wrote *staccato* marks on a few notes at the beginning of one or two occurrences of a figure, leaving many of its appearances without either slurs or *staccato* marks. A typical example occurs in the final movement of the String Quartet K. 575: the triplet figurations are mostly without *staccato* marks (Ex. 6.9a), but whether this means that they should be performed differently than if he had written them throughout is uncertain. In a couple of places, Mozart added *staccato* marks, but his doing so seems principally to have been prompted by a desire to clarify the extent of a carelessly drawn slur rather than to indicate

---

[24] Koch: 'Abstoßen' in *Musikalisches Lexikon*, 43ff.
[25] Romberg: *Violoncell Schule*, 32.

that the notes so marked required a different type of execution from others (Ex. 6.9b). It may certainly be legitimate to ask whether string players of Mozart's day, employing the types of bowstroke that were familiar to them, would have been prompted to execute fast notes of this kind differently when they had *staccato* marks than when they did not. With most of Mozart's contemporaries, including Haydn, the difficulties posed by incomplete and ambiguous notation are far greater, since they were seemingly much more frequently content to leave many significant decisions about such performance details to the experience or *bon goût* of the executant.

Ex. 6.9 a–b. Mozart: String Quartet K. 575/iv.
[Allegretto]

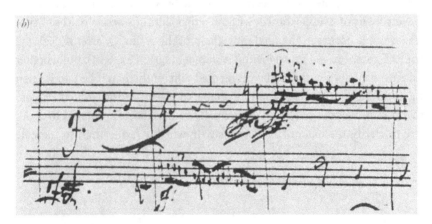

In the first half of the 19th century, as Romberg's comment intimates, the practice of using *staccato* marks to clarify slurring and separation, without necessarily implying *staccato* execution, was remarkably persistent. The first movement of Beethoven's Fifth Symphony provides a good example of a piece in which *staccato* marks first appear in mixed passages of slurred and separate notes, and their lack of additional *staccato* meaning is shown by the fact that they occur only in the part with slurring and cease immediately the slurs finish (Ex. 6.10a). The length of the eighths, and the type of accentuation they require, is clearly independent of the presence or absence of *staccato* marks in this instance. On slower-moving notes the probability that a real *staccato* execution was intended seems greater; thus, although the *staccato* quarter-notes in Ex. 6.10b alternate with slurred pairs, it seems likely that Beethoven wanted them to be played differently from what he would have expected if he had not given them *staccato* marks. This is corroborated by the continuation of the staccato marks throughout the following six bars of separate quarter-notes, and their presence in the instruments that have quarters followed by rests.

Ex. 6.10 a–b. Beethoven: Fifth Symphony op. 67/i.

(a)

(b)

His usage here seems to correspond with Koch's advice about when, in fast movements, composers should employ *staccato* marks:

1) those notes which, without the sign for staccato [Zeichen des Abstoßens], one is accustomed to play in a sustained manner, such as the quarter notes in the following passage; [Ex. 6.11]

2) those notes which the composer believes might not be played *staccato* [Koch's word] by every performer. This includes all notes that do not move very swiftly, especially if they do not follow one another in leaps, but in steps.

Thirdly, he specified passages of mixed slurred and separate notes, to clarify which were slurred and which separate.[26]

Ex. 6.11 Koch: 'Abstoßen' in *Musikalisches Lexikon*, 43f.

Schumann, nearly two generations younger, can be seen to have used a similar cautionary notation from time to time. In the scherzo of the Second Symphony the first violins' theme begins without *staccato* marks on the sixteenths, but in bar 17, following some slurring, the first three separate notes have *staccato* marks (Ex. 6.12), after which the sixteenths continue as before, without *staccato* marks.

Ex. 6.12 Schumann: Second Symphony op. 61/ii, bb. 15–18.

Mendelssohn's music, too, contains these patterns. An example that neatly illustrates the purpose of the mark merely to confirm separation from the slur occurs in his overture *Ruy Blas*, where an isolated mark is found in the parts containing a slur, but not in the parts where there is no slur; this occurs in a passage that has otherwise no hint of *staccato* execution (Ex. 6.13a). It also seems questionable whether the very infrequent articulation marks in the 'Con moto' section of the overture to his oratorio *Paulus* are anything but warnings not to include the marked note in a slur; an isolated dot on an eighth-note in Ex. 6.13b is apparently there to prevent the slur continuing

---

[26] Koch: 'Abstoßen' in *Musikalisches Lexikon*, 44f.

over the bar-line, while at the point where the slurring of the sixteenths ceases, a few articulation marks reinforce the absence of slurs. This practice gradually disappeared, however, during the 19th century, as composers increasingly attributed specific meanings to signs.

Ex. 6.13a  Mendelssohn: *Ruy Blas,* ouverture.

Ex. 6.13b  Mendelssohn: *Paulus,* ouverture.

Most theorists regarded *staccato* marks as primarily instructions for separating, and usually shortening, the notes, but with a subsidiary implication of accent in some cases. How this was to be achieved, and to what degree, depended to a considerable extent on the instrument and the musical circumstances. In string playing, shortening seems often to have been less important than the style of bowstroke. Joseph Riepel considered the matter from the point of view of the string player, and, illustrating three different forms of *staccato* mark (Ex. 6.14), he explains how his imaginary violinist would execute them. He would play the first "with long powerful strokes [of the bow], and this, from time to time, in concertos". The second is "in any case, generally known, but he sometimes makes the notes more, sometimes less staccato." The third is "used only for accompaniment, and he says that, in this case, the bow-hair must touch the strings with no more than a hair's breadth, so that the cantabile *principal* part is clearly heard and is not obscured by so many accompanying instrumentalists." But Riepel admitted that a notational differentiation was very rarely encountered in practice.[27]

---

[27] Riepel: *Gründliche Erklärung*, 15 (see Ch. 5, p. 219).

Ex. 6.14 Riepel: *Gründliche Erklärung*, 19.

Leopold Mozart was less explicit about varieties of *staccato*, saying simply that a composer writes strokes over notes "which he wishes to be played each with a strongly accented bowstroke and separated from one another".[28] (He referred to the dot only under slurs.) Quantz made a clearer distinction than Mozart between circumstances in which the principal purpose of a vertical stroke might be to reduce the length of the note and those in which an accent was also required; his general rule was:

> If little strokes stand above several notes, they must sound half as long as their true value. But if a little stroke stands above only one note, after which several of lesser value follow, it indicates not only that the note must be played half as long, but also that it must at the same time be accented with pressure of the bow.[29]

In addition, however, he recognized a gentler kind of articulation in string playing (marked with dots) that was played "with short bowstrokes and in a sustained manner".[30] Löhlein, also referring to violin playing, mentioned simply that when separate notes have dots one must "separate them by the bowstroke in the aforementioned manner",[31] that is, with normal separate bows (Ex. 6.15a); but for a passage with strokes he instructed: "The quarter-notes over which there are strokes will be played as short as eighths, but sustained with a gentle bow somewhat longer than if they were eighths with eighth-note rests"[32] (Ex. 6.15b). He appears to have been less concerned about the accent implications of the mark than Mozart.

---

[28] Mozart: *Versuch*, 45.
[29] Quantz: *Versuch*, 201.
[30] Quantz: *Versuch*, 194.
[31] Löhlein: *Anweisung*, 32.
[32] Löhlein: *Anweisung*, No. xi, 72.

Ex. 6.15a  Löhlein: *Anweisung zum Violinspielen*, 8, §48, 33.

Ex. 6.15b  Löhlein: *Anweisung*, No. XI, 73.

For keyboard, in the second half of the 18th century, C. P. E. Bach instructed that notes with articulation marks are "always held for a little less than half their notated length",[33] and Türk similarly considered that the finger should be lifted from the key on notes with articulation marks "when almost half the value of the written note is past". Conscious of the strong association between *staccato* and accent, Türk continued: "I should not have to mention that notes that are to be played gently can also be staccato; nevertheless, one hears some players who perform all staccato notes loud without exception, quite in conflict with the correct expression." Echoing and expanding on Bach's opinion, he also cautioned that:

> In the performance of staccato notes one must especially take into account the prevailing character of the composition, the tempo, the prescribed loudness and softness, etc. If the character of a piece is serious, tender, sad, etc. then the notes that are to be played staccato should not be as short as in pieces of a lively, playful, etc. character. In a melodious Adagio, notes that should be given a short, detached execution, should not be made as short as in an Allegro. In *forte* one can generally be given a shorter staccato than in *piano*. Leaping notes are, generally, played with a shorter staccato than intervals that progress stepwise, etc.[34]

Türk was at pains to point out that there were some circumstances in which a note with a *staccato* mark should be shortened, but given absolutely no

---

[33] Bach: *Versuch*, i, 93.
[34] Türk: *Klavierschule*, 353f.

additional accent; for instance, when the mark indicated the end of a phrase at an *Abzug* (see Ex. 4.6) or, more confusingly, when the figure ended with a metrically strong beat (Ex. 6.16).[35]

Ex. 6.16 Türk: *Klavierschule*, 346.

Very similar advice is given in the fifth edition of Löhlein's *Clavier-Schule*, edited and revised by Witthauer in 1791. He observed:

> It is not possible to make a general rule to determine how short the attack on notes that are to be staccatoed should really be, for it depends as much on the length and shortness of the notes as on the faster or slower tempo of the piece and its character. On the whole, you can leave your finger on the key for about half as long as the duration of the staccatoed note requires. A quarter-note, however, in one and the same piece, does not have to be staccatoed as briefly as an eighth- or sixteenth-note: Furthermore, one must see precisely whether the passage or phrase in which one or more staccatoed notes occur, is to be performed *forte*, *mezzo forte*, or *piano*, and then take account of this to make a weaker or stronger attack on the staccato.
>
> It is therefore a great error, which is often committed, if all notes with a staccato mark, are indiscriminately made very short and very strong. Thereby many a piece acquires a totally false and often really barbarous character.[36]

There seems indeed to have been some significant lack of agreement about the accent element in *staccato*, probably dependent on the tradition to which a writer belonged, as well as on the instrument concerned. The author of a British publication, *New Instructions for Playing the Harpsichord, Pianoforte, or Organ etc.* (c. 1790), considered that "Staccato marks ❙❙❙❙ or •••• intimate the Notes must be touched very lightly with taste and spirit,

---

[35] Türk: *Klavierschule*, 342f.
[36] Löhlein, ed. Witthauer: *Clavier-Schule*, 18.

keeping the tone off the Note not above half its natural Length."[37] (On the organ and harpsichord, of course, any degree of percussive accent would have been impossible.) And Weippert's *The Pedal Harp Rotula* (1800) stated simply that strokes or dots show that the notes "must be played in a very distinct manner", giving a musical example in which half of each *staccato* note, of whatever length, is replaced by a rest.[38] In 1801, Clementi, considering the matter in greater detail, referred to differentiated articulation marks only in terms of length. Showing *staccato* strokes, he explained:

> The best general rule, is to keep down the keys of the instrument, the FULL LENGTH of every note; for when the contrary is required, the notes are marked either thus [Ex. 6.17a] called in ITALIAN, STACCATO; denoting DISTINCTNESS, and SHORTNESS of sound; which is produced by lifting the finger up, as soon as it has struck the key: or they are marked thus [Ex. 6.17b] which, when composers are EXACT in their writing, means LESS staccato than the preceding mark; the finger therefore is kept down somewhat longer: or thus [Ex 6.17c] which means STILL LESS staccato: the nice degrees of MORE or LESS, however, depend on the CHARACTER, and PASSION of the piece; the STYLE of which must be well observed by the performer.[39]

Louis Adam's 1804 *Méthode*, in many respects directly indebted to Clementi, allotted specific lengths to the three types of articulation markings, as in Ex. 6.18a–c. This simplistic definition was taken up by many later 19th-century writers.

Ex. 6.17 a–c. Clementi: Introduction, 8.

---

[37] Anon.: *New Instructions for Playing the Harpsichord, Pianoforte or Organ etc.* (London, [c. 1790]), 4.
[38] John Erhardt Weippert: *The Pedal Harp Rotula, and New Instructions for That Instrument* (London, [c. 1800]), 5.
[39] Clementi: *Introduction*, 9.

**Ex. 6.18** a–c. Adam: *Méthode*, 154f.

(a)

(b)

(c)

There was, however, a growing divergence between those (predominantly keyboard players) who focused on the shortening aspect of *staccato* and those who emphasized its accent properties. Fröhlich's treatment of the execution of *staccato* in oboe playing, although employing the same distinctions of strokes, dots, and dots under slurs, contrasts with that of the pianists just mentioned in its explicit combination of shortness and accent. He observed:

> For the sake of clarification for the student, we will give a threefold specification of the types of nuances of the so-called tongue staccato; the first, where the notes are staccatoed very short and with the greatest possible power, is notated as at a); the second, which we could call the soft staccato in contrast to the first, the hardest, in which the staccato is not executed with that force, but where, so to speak, the note receives some check during the staccato itself, is notated as at b); finally the third, yet more gently treated, with its own soft character, which almost depicts the connection between staccato and legato, is shown as at c). [Ex. 6.19][40]

Interestingly, Fröhlich (or rather the author from whose work he extracted his material) did not acknowledge the clarinet to be capable of such a wide range of *staccato* attack as either oboe or bassoon, and no strokes, only dots, occur in the clarinet section of his tutor.

Ex. 6.19 Fröhlich: *Musikschule*, ii, 40.

In fact, among German musicians, while the accent effect of *staccato* was almost universally recognized, there seems to have been considerable doubt about the degree of separation required. A. B. Marx proposed a less extreme shortening of the notes than Adam, regarding the stroke as shortening a note by a half and the dot by a quarter, but, like Witthauer and others, cautioned that "In both cases the exact amount of time that is to be subtracted from their original value remains undecided."[41] Marx's older contemporary J. D. Andersch also seems to have felt that performers should be careful not to make too much separation, for he gave the following

---

[40] Fröhlich: *Musikschule*, pt. 2, 40.
[41] Marx: *Allgemeine Musiklehre*, 84.

definition of "Abstoßen, *Staccare, Détaché*": "Deliver the notes short and somewhat prominently, without, however, making their separation strikingly perceptible to the ear."[42]

In string playing the seeds of confusion over the meaning of the two signs in terms of bowstroke (therefore also of accent, length, etc.) were sprouting vigorously by the 1830s; and agreement over the significance of articulation marks in general can hardly have been helped by Spohr's employment of them in his influential *Violinschule* of 1833 (which used strokes throughout, except under slurs). Having given an exercise consisting of eighths marked with strokes at a tempo of ♩ = 104 (Ex. 6.20), he instructed the pupil that there should be no gap between the notes.[43] Yet, making no notational differentiation, he also used the same strokes in passages where he specified a short, sharp, *martelé* bowstroke, which required both accent and separation.[44]

Ex. 6.20 Spohr: *Violinschule*, 130.

Spohr's pupil Ferdinand David, however, consistently associated wedges with on-string *staccato*, and dots with elastic bowstrokes.[45] Charles de Bériot, at the beginning of his treatise, proposed dots for on-string *martelé* and short *détaché*, and wedges for his version of *grand détaché* in the middle third of the bow;[46] but in his exercises he did not adhere to this distinction, using wedges both for *détaché* and *martelé*.[47] David also employed horizontal lines

---

[42] Johann Daniel Andersch: 'Abstossen' in *Musikalisches Wörterbuch* (Berlin, 1829), 4.
[43] Spohr: *Violinschule*, 130.
[44] Relationships between *staccato* notation and string bowing are further considered in Ch. 7.
[45] David: *Violinschule*, ii, 37f.
[46] Bériot: *Méthode*, 2. Although the *Méthode* was published in three separate volumes, the pagination is continuous through all three.
[47] Bériot: *Méthode*, 80f.

for smoother on-string bowstrokes;[48] Bériot did not include these in his list of signs but used them on a couple of occasions under slurs to indicate a smooth *ondulé* bowstroke.[49]

It is rare to encounter any direct corroboration of individual composers' usages of these signs, but a few scraps of evidence may occasionally be found; for instance, when a composer accompanied particular forms of *staccato* marks with explanatory instructions. Meyerbeer's use of the *staccato* stroke in his Parisian operas certainly seems to have approached the French view of it as light and short in contrast to a heavier and less short dot. This is strongly suggested by a passage in *Les Huguenots* where he gave strokes to the piccolo and dots to the bassoons; evidently not trusting his players to recognize his intentions, he added the supplementary instruction "always *p*. and very detached" under the piccolo part, while for the bassoons he wrote "well-marked and detached" (Ex. 6.21).

Ex. 6.21 Meyerbeer: *Les Huguenots*, no. 4.

Another scrap of evidence, which casts light on Brahms's intentions when he wrote strokes, occurs in a letter to Joachim of 1879,[50] where he comments that instead of Joachim's suggested articulation for a figure in the last movement of his Violin Concerto, with dots under a slur (i.e., the violinist's sharply separated *martelé*-type slurred *staccato*), he would have used "sharp strokes" (*scharfe Strichpunkte*) (Ex. 6.22).[51]

---

[48] David: *Violinschule*, ii, 37.
[49] Bériot: *Méthode*, 118 and 237.
[50] Cited at length below.
[51] Brahms, *Briefwechsel* (Berlin, 1907–22), vi, 146.

Ex. 6.22 Brahms: Violin Concerto op. 77/iii.

In view of the pervasive lack of consensus and consistency about the meaning of *staccato* marks, however, it may seem hopeless, without firm information from composers themselves, or from sources close to them, to determine what they expected them to convey to the performer. Indeed, certainty about a composer's intentions in any given situation is only rarely to be expected. The frustratingly small amount of persuasive evidence for specific usage may, nevertheless, be valuably supplemented by considering the relationship between composers' notational practices and the ways in which they perceived performance style to be dependent on musical context. We can never fully know how accomplished 18th- and 19th-century musicians, with a lifetime's experience, would have understood the notational practices of their time; but the more we are aware of the factors that conditioned their experience, and the more prepared we are to suspend our own preconceptions about what is "musical", the more apt we are to develop fruitful creative intuition for the expectations that lay behind the notation. The inclusion of specific forms of *staccato* marks in music of this period is, therefore, likely to be less reliable, as a guide to the appropriate style of delivery for a specific passage, than an understanding of the technical and stylistic characteristics of vocal and instrumental performance with which composer and performer would have been familiar, and an awareness of the factors that conditioned their responses to different types and genres of music.

## Musical Context as a Guide to Execution

Many clues towards achieving a style of execution closer to what was envisaged by 18th- and 19th-century composers can be found in their attitudes towards musical context. Throughout most of the second half of the 18th century there was a strong connection between the character of the music and the style of execution. An adagio required a more sustained style of performance than an andante, and an andante would not invite as detached a performance as an allegro; a solo part would not be performed in the same style as an accompaniment; church music, chamber music, and opera would each require different approaches; the same music notated in $\frac{3}{2}$ was not expected to elicit the same performance style as it would if it were written in $\frac{3}{8}$, even if it were played at the same tempo; and so on.[52] Consequently, a note, with or without a *staccato* mark, would be played in very different ways in different musical contexts. The nationality and background of the performer would also have a powerful influence on the manner of performance.

Many late-18th-century writers emphasized the necessity of a detached manner of playing in faster movements and a smoother style of performance in adagio, regardless of the speed of the individual notes. The logical conclusion from this is, as Reichardt observed in connection with orchestral playing,[53] that if composers wanted to go against the ruling character of a piece, they would have to indicate it in some way. Instances where such considerations appear to have been taken into account can be found in Mozart and Haydn. In *Don Giovanni*, Don Ottavio's substitute aria "Dalla sua pace" is an Andantino sostenuto, in which players might be expected to have interpreted articulation marks with very little shortening or accent; thus in bar 16, when the music becomes more agitated, Mozart wrote not only strokes over the eighths in the bass, but also the instruction *staccato*, presumably to obtain a more sharply detached execution, which he could perhaps, but more laboriously, have indicated by writing sixteenth-notes separated by rests (Ex. 6.23).

---

[52] The concept of "heavy and light" performance style, which took account of some of these factors, has been considered in Ch. 5.
[53] Reichardt: *Ueber die Pflichten*, 25f. See Ch. 10 for details of Reichardt's view of the ways in which tempo affected the bowstroke.

292  CLASSICAL AND ROMANTIC PERFORMING PRACTICE

**Ex. 6.23** Mozart: "Dalla sua pace" K. 540a (substitute aria for *Don Giovanni*). [Andante sostenuto]

A similar use of the word *staccato* to ensure that the notes will be significantly shortened, and to save the effort of writing rests, can be seen in bar 3 of the Adagio of Haydn's Symphony no. 102. In this example Haydn's inconsistency of notation is particularly revealing: in bar 1 there are eighths with *staccato* marks followed by rests for all the lower strings, but in bar 3 the second violin

NOTATION OF ARTICULATION AND PHRASING 293

has eighths and rests while viola, cello, and bass have quarters with articulation marks and also the word *staccato* (Ex. 6.24). It can hardly be doubted that Haydn wanted the same effect from all the lower strings in bar 3, and it may reasonably be assumed that it was meant to be the same as in bar 1; this being so, there are three different notations in close proximity indicating the same thing.[54] It is surely significant that Haydn appears to have felt that *staccato* marks alone on the quarter-notes would not obtain the required shortening from the players.

Ex. 6.24  Haydn: Symphony no. 102/ii.

The relationship between context and execution continued to be important in the 19th century, but changing stylistic criteria brought about some highly significant shifts of emphasis in the latter part of the 18th century. These were, perhaps, directly influenced by the development of the violin bow and the piano's increasing capability of producing a convincing *legato*, though both these phenomena were themselves driven by the quest for greater sustaining power and tonal variety in instrumental performance. Comparison of Reichardt's account of the types of bowstrokes appropriate to different kinds of music with the treatment of precisely the same matter in Baillot, Rode,

---

[54] A similar instance occurs in his Symphony no. 91. See Ex. 3.51.

and Kreutzer's *Méthode de violon* (1803) and other early-19th-century violin treatises that are apparently indebted to it,[55] as well as cello treatises,[56] illuminates several important differences. In the *Méthode*, the basically *legato* treatment of separate bowstrokes required in adagio is extended, in certain contexts, to allegro and even presto. And in adagio the notes that are marked *staccato* seem to require an even more connected manner than was suggested by Reichardt, the *staccato* element presumably being expressed by accent and nuance, rather than separation. Only in Allegro maestoso is a genuinely detached bowstroke described. This is quite clearly the style of playing adopted by the influential Viotti school and its followers.[57]

In string playing the ability to produce a seamless connection between separate bowstrokes remained a central tenet of teaching throughout the 19th century, as demonstrated by Moser's comments in the treatise he published, together with Joachim, in 1905. But, at the same time, other influences, from Baillot's later practice, from Paganini, and from the Franco-Belgian school, led to the accumulation of further techniques of bowing that widened the string player's range of articulation.[58]

Other instruments and even the voice followed the lead of the violinists. It is well known, for instance, that the development of Liszt's transcendent technique, which depended as much on the variety of sound he was able to elicit from the instrument as from sheer virtuosity, was directly inspired by Paganini's violin playing. And, as the scores of Meyerbeer's Parisian operas indicate, the voice was increasingly often expected to accomplish quasi-instrumental effects. Nevertheless, it remained of paramount importance throughout the 19th century for instruments and piano to emulate the *cantabile* qualities of the human voice. Both Hummel and Spohr in their treatises had recommended listening to great singers as the best way to achieve the refinements of beautiful performance in piano and string playing. Sigismond Thalberg entitled his short treatise *L'art du chant appliqué au piano* (The art of singing applied to the piano), while in Charles de Bériot's *Méthode de violon*, examples of vocal music precede those for the violin throughout his discussion of expressive practices.[59]

---

[55] E.g., the violin method in Fröhlich's *Vollständige Musikschule* (1810–11), Joseph von Blumenthal's *Kurzgefasste theoretisch-praktische Violin Schule* (Vienna, 1811), and Bartolomeo Campagnoli's *Nouvelle méthode de la mécanique du jeu de violon* (Leipzig, 1824), which quote the 1803 *Méthode*'s instructions for bowstrokes almost verbatim. (In some reference works, a date of c. 1797 is given for an original Italian edition of Campagnoli's treatise. This, however, seems never to have existed; if it did, it could certainly not have included the same section on bowstrokes.)

[56] Baillot et al.: *Méthode de violoncelle* (Romberg, Dotzauer).

[57] For the relationship of bowstrokes to tempo see Ch. 10.

[58] For a more detailed consideration of these matters, see Ch. 7.

[59] See Clive Brown: 'Singing and String Playing in Comparison' in Claudio Bacciagaluppi, Roman Brotbeck, and Anselm Gerhard (eds.), *Zwischen schöpferischer Individualität und künstlericher Selbstverleugnung* (Schliengen, Argus, 2009), 83–108.

The signs employed by early-19th-century composers for specifying articulation were too imprecise and too crude, even where differentiated meanings were intended for dots and strokes, to do more than hint at the intended effect, and the practice that began tentatively in the 18th century of providing further written qualifications or other notational clarification became even more necessary. The overture to *Der Freischütz* provides an interesting example of the same form of *staccato* mark serving different functions. In the first four bars of Ex. 6.25a, Weber probably intended the *staccato* marks merely to make clear that the notes in question are unslurred; in woodwind and violins, bars containing mixed slurs and *staccato* marks are followed by a bar of separate eighths with dots in the woodwind, where Weber additionally wrote *stacc:*, presumably to obtain a distinct *staccato* execution in that bar.

Since it appears that many 19th-century string players saw no contradiction in playing faster notes in allegro movements in an essentially connected manner, even if they had dots or strokes on them, composers of that period *needed* to make their intentions clear when they wanted a short, sharp *staccato*. The problem that faced 18th-century composers in slow movements was thus extended to fast movements in the 19th century. The increasingly frequent inclusion of words such as *staccato*, *staccatissimo*, *leggiero*, *marcato*, and so on, in addition to *staccato* marks, testifies to 19th-century composers' concern to clarify their intentions. This passage from *Der Freischütz* neatly illustrates the fact that a careful composer now needed to specify *staccato*, as well as writing *staccato* marks, in contexts where an 18th-century player would naturally have used a detached style of performance (e.g., in an allegro), but where a 19th-century player might tend towards a more connected execution. During the first decades of the 19th century, string instruments seem to have been regarded as being incapable of an effective *staccato* on faster-moving notes. The *martelé* is only practicable up to a certain tempo, and springing bowstrokes, which were already being taught as standard in Franco-Belgian string playing from the 1830s onwards, were widely resisted in Germany into the second half of the century. Weber, who is known to have admired Spohr's playing, was certainly conscious of the distinction between *détaché* and *martelé*, and between the various kinds of articulation available to different instruments. With his customary sensitivity to orchestral effect, he knew how to use it to good purpose. This is well illustrated by another passage from his *Freischütz* overture (Ex. 6.25b). Here the strings have a downward scale of separate eighths without *staccato* marks, which would almost certainly have been played with a *détaché* bowing similar to the one described by Spohr; this is followed by the scale a third higher for wind instruments, where Weber has not only added *staccato* marks but again the verbal instruction. The passage is later repeated with the same markings.

Ex. 6.25 a–b. Weber: *Der Freischütz*, overture.
[Molto vivace]

(a)

NOTATION OF ARTICULATION AND PHRASING 297

**Ex. 6.25** Continued

(b)

Almost every important composer of the early 19th century can similarly be seen to have used *staccato* or other instructions for accent, shortening, or specific styles of performing in allegro movements that a generation earlier might anyway have been expected to be played in a detached manner. Cherubini frequently included the instruction *staccato* with dotted figures in allegro movements, for example in the overture to *Médée* (Ex. 6.26), presumably to achieve the type of detached performance that Mozart had, on occasion, taken great pains to indicate by writing rests in dotted figures in slow movements (Ex. 6.27).

Ex. 6.26 Cherubini: *Médée*, overture.

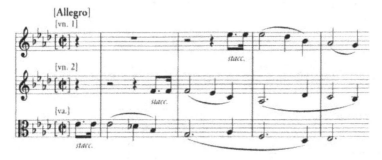

Ex. 6.27 Mozart: Mass in C minor, Qui tollis.

Mendelssohn sometimes juxtaposed notes with articulation marks and others that were shortened by means of rests (Ex. 6.28). In terms of string playing this probably implied a lively on-string bowstroke for the former and a more pronounced separation for the latter, perhaps with a springing bowstroke. Mendelssohn's notation of sixteenth-notes followed by sixteenth-note rests in fast movements[60] seems almost certain to have been linked with

---

[60] E.g., in the Scherzo of the Octet op. 20.

the early-19th-century tendency to employ broad bowstrokes in allegro movements even where *staccato* marks were present.

Ex. 6.28  Mendelssohn: String Quartet op. 13/iii, (autograph).
[Allegro di molto]

## Other Articulation Marks

In addition to the dot and stroke, later 19th-century composers employed other signs as articulation marks. These, like dots and strokes, have already been discussed in the context of accentuation,[61] and they are seldom without an implication of accent. Nevertheless, some theorists treated them primarily as types and degrees of articulation. Towards the end of the century, Riemann gave an extensive list of markings for piano music, some of which were in general use at the time and some of which will scarcely be encountered outside Riemann's editions. It is questionable whether his use of them corresponds with that of all the composers who employed them at that time, but, in view of Riemann's reputation, his definitions may have influenced some of his contemporaries. The list is given here as it occurs in the bilingual preface to his edition of Schubert's *Moments musicaux* op. 94 and two Scherzos (Ex. 6.29).

The last two signs are certainly confined, for the most part, to didactic works, although the comma appears in other editors' instructive editions, for instance, Beethoven's Violin Sonatas edited by Edmund Singer and Wilhelm Speidel (1890). It is interesting to note that although the implication of accent is present in Riemann's definition of the *staccato* stroke, his explanation of the horizontal line and the horizontal line with dot contains no suggestion

---

[61] See Ch. 3.

of added weight. Like Clementi and others, he stated that "The **legato** touch should always be used unless specially marked to the contrary."[62]

Ex. 6.29  Hugo Riemann: Preface to Compositionen von Franz Schubert, *Moments musicaux* op. 94 and two Scherzos.

- ∧ eine geringe **Verlängerung** der Note (agogischer Accent).
- > verstärkte Tongebung (dynamischer Accent).
- – volles Aushalten des Tones bis zum Eintritt des folgenden (Legato-Anschluss).
- ∸ fast volles Aushalten, aber Absetzen vor dem neuen Tone (Non legato, portato).
- . leichtes Absetzen, Halbstaccato.
- ▼ scharfes Abstossen, wirkliches Staccato.
- ⌣ (meist nur nach einer Note mit ∧ ) leichtere Tongebung und unvollkommene Bindung (**Abzug**).
- , (Komma) die Einschaltung einer (meist kurzen) nicht notierten Pause (besonders vor Wiedereintritt eines Thema).
- ⌐∕ **Abbrechen** einer Phrase vor ihrem eigentlichen Ende (worauf meist zurückgegriffen wird).
- ⌐✕ (**Bogenkreuzung**) Zusammenfallen von Ende und Anfang zweier Phrasen (Phrasenverschränkung).

- ∧ a slight **prolongation** in the time of the note.
- > **reinforcement** of the sound.
- – **full holding** of the note until the beginning of the next one (**legato touch**).
- ∸ the note to be held nearly the full length and to be slightly detached from the next one (Non legato, portato).
- . the note to be more detached than ∸ : half staccato.
- ▼ the note to be struck sharply; quite staccato.
- ⌣ a light touch and not quite legato.
- , (comma) indicates a short pause not otherwise marked, especially before the re-entering of a theme.
- ⌐∕ interruption of a phrase before its real end (generally to mark a repetition of some part of the phrase).
- ⌐✕ a double relation (double phrasing) of the notes included within the two slurs (crossing of phrases).

---

[62] Riemann: Preface, *Compositionen von Franz Schubert* (Brunswick, Litolff, [c. 1890]); copy in the Bodleian Library, Oxford, Mus. 118 c. 5. 95(9).

## Slurs and Articulation

The principal meaning of the slur was to signify that the notes within it should be smoothly connected to one another, as in a vocal melisma or a figure performed by a string player in a single, continuous, and even bowstroke. The slur may carry other messages about the execution of the *legato* phrase, which must be deduced partly from the period, background, and notational habits of the composer, and partly from the musical context. It is important, for instance, to determine whether the music is conceived in terms of strings, wind, keyboard, or voice, whether it shows other evidence of having been notated with care, and so on.

Slurs, or signs that are graphically indistinguishable from slurs, however, could signify several quite different things. In vocal music the slur might be used, in its general sense of *legato*, to clarify the grouping of notes on a single syllable (though this was not a consistent convention); but it might also specify a *portamento*, sometimes between notes on different syllables of text.[63] Of course, the same sign connecting two notes at the same pitch usually means a tie, but it may not in all instances indicate a simple prolongation of the note. One persistent curiosity of notation that certainly remained common until the generation of Berlioz and Schumann was the practice, in feminine cadences or similar contexts, of using a two-beat note tied to a one-beat note, instead of a two-beat note with a dot (Ex. 6.30). It seems likely that this notation was intended to warn the performers with the sustained note that they should nuance it in the normal manner required for such cadences. What Beethoven meant by his occasional use of notes that appear to be superfluously tied, for instance in the *Große Fuge* op. 133, the scherzo of the Cello Sonata op. 69, and the Adagios of the Piano Sonatas op. 106, and op. 110, remains controversial; he may perhaps have intended something similar to the shortening and *decrescendo* applied to feminine cadences,[64] but, more probably, he expected a subsidiary stress on the second note. Karl Holz, who played 2nd violin in early performances of the late quartets, questioned the meaning of this notation in one of Beethoven's conversation books, but, of course, we do not have the composer's answer. Where these ties

---

[63] See Ch. 15.
[64] See Emil Platen: 'Zeitgenössische Hinweise zur Aufführungspraxis der letzten Streichquartette Beethovens' in Rudolf Klein (ed.), *Beiträge '76–78: Beethoven Kolloquium 1977; Dokumentation und Aufführungspraxis* (Kassel, 1978), 100–7.

occur in piano parts in opp. 69, 106, and 110, Beethoven marked a 4-3 fingering, surely indicating a repetition of the second note, as explained by his pupil Czerny in relation to op. 69 (Ex. 6.31a):

> The ties in the right hand, and the fingering placed above, here indicate something entirely individual. That is, the second (tied) note is struck again audibly with the 3rd finger, so that it sounds approximately: [Ex. 6.31b] thus the first note (with the 4th finger) very tenuto, and the other (with the 3rd finger) given a short staccato and less accented. And the same throughout. The 4th finger must slide downwards, and make way for the 3rd.[65]

In string parts, a similar effect may be accomplished by means of bow pressure, bearing in mind the string players' practice of emphasizing the strong beat in a syncopation in certain circumstances,[66] or alternatively by changing the finger while continuing the bowstroke without interruption. This practice was described by Spohr as an imitation of the singer's changing a syllable within a single breath.[67]

Ex. 6.30 Sterndale Bennett: Fantasie-Overture *Paradise and the Peri* op. 42.

---

[65] Czerny: *Pianoforte-Schule* iv, 90. Paul Badura-Skoda, 'A Tie Is a Tie is a Tie', *Early Music*, xvi (1988), 84ff, argues against repetition, but Jonathan Del Mar offers cogent arguments to support the repetition of the note in 'Once Again: Reflections on Beethoven's Tied-Note Notation', *Early Music*, xxxii (2004), 7–25.
[66] See Ch. 2, "Syncopation".
[67] See Ch. 15, p. 903.

Ex. 6.31 a–b. Beethoven: Cello Sonata op. 69/ii, in Czerny: *Pianoforte-Schule*, iv, 90. (*a*) piano part; (*b*) execution.

In fact, there was a long tradition, going well back into the 18th century, of composers using slurs (without any other articulation mark) over groups of notes repeated at the same pitch to obtain a very connected *portato*. In 1792, Johann Adam Hiller, explaining the various uses of dots, identified slurred *staccato* and *portato*; he illustrated the latter on repeated notes with dots under a slur (Ex. 6.32a), but observed that "in order not to pile up the signs unnecessarily", the dots could just as well be left out, and provided another example (Ex. 6.32b).[68]

Ex. 6.32 a–b. Hiller: *Anweisung*, 42.

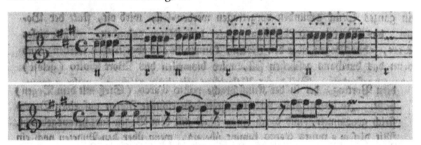

Instances of this notation can be found in works as diverse as Salieri's *Der Rauchfangkehrer* and Wagner's *Parsifal*.[69] From an early stage, successive notes at the same pitch were sometimes included within a slur over a phrase or figure, thus demanding the minutest separation or, more likely only accentuation, to articulate these as repeated notes within the general context of the

---

[68] Hiller: *Anweisung zum Violinspielen*, 42.
[69] See below, "Articulated Slurs".

*legato* phrase, for instance in Beethoven's Fifth Symphony (Ex. 6.33a).[70] In the third movement of the String Quartet op. 95 (Ex. 6.33b) and the Adagio of the Violin Sonata op. 96 (see Ex. 6.40), he may have had Spohr's finger-changing effect in mind (Spohr was in Vienna, and friendly with him at the time he completed the sonata).

Ex. 6.33a Beethoven: Fifth Symphony op. 67/iv.

Ex. 6.33b Beethoven: op. 95/iii autograph. Vn 1.
[Allegro assai vivace ma serioso]

Furthermore, in 18th-century music, the appearance of longer slurs than usual may occasionally be a form of shorthand for the continuation of a slurring pattern already established, for example in Galuppi's *La diavolessa* (Ex. 6.34).

Ex. 6.34 Galuppi: *La diavolessa*, Act I, Scene xi, Österreichische Nationalbibliothek, Vienna, MS 18070.

---

[70] Spohr: *Violinschule*, 176.

## NOTATION OF ARTICULATION AND PHRASING

Apart from the slur's primary meanings, a similar symbol could be used to designate something quite different. In Haydn's string music, for instance, it sometimes identified a passage that should be played on one string (Ex. 6.35). It was also employed to define a triplet or other irregular grouping, often without any implications of slurring. And Berlioz, for instance, used a slur-like sign in horn parts to show the application of hand stopping without change of embouchure.[71] In French and French-influenced 18th-century music a long slur might indicate that the normal inequality did not apply to the notes that were encompassed by it.[72]

Ex. 6.35 Haydn: String Quartet op. 64/4/ii.

### The Nuanced Slur and the Slur as *Legato*

In piano playing there was general agreement throughout the 19th century that slurred pairs should be performed approximately as described in 1804 by Adam:

> when there are only two notes connected together and when the two notes are of the same value or when the second of them has half the value of the first, it is necessary, to express this slur, in the *forte* as well as in the *piano*, to press the finger a little on the first and to lift it on the second, taking away half its value while touching the second more gently than the first. [Ex. 6.36][73]

---

[71] Macdonald: 'Two Peculiarities', 25.
[72] David Fuller: 'Notes inégales' in *New Grove*, xiii, 422.
[73] Adam: *Méthode*, 151.

Ex. 6.36  Adam: *Méthode*, 153.

Sometimes greater shortening of the second note was recommended, for instance by Crelle, who illustrated the second of slurred pairs of sixteenth-notes as thirty-second-notes.[74] And, as the opinions of Hummel, Kalkbrenner (see Ex. 2.1), Czerny, Moscheles, and others indicate, shortening of the final note was also regarded by many 19th-century pianists as appropriate to longer slurred groups.

The detaching of the last note under slurs, particularly in the case of equal pairs where the first note could be seen as an *appoggiatura*, was known in German as the *Abzug*. This term is quite often encountered in late-18th- and early-19th-century writings, and its discussion by various writers offers a useful glimpse of some of the issues surrounding articulation in these circumstances. Late-18th-century views on its execution were neatly summarized by J. F. Reichardt in 1776. He observed:

> The appoggiatura of fixed duration always receives a stronger pressure of the bow than the note itself. It is erroneous, however, if the note after an appoggiatura is for this reason always taken off. One can divide the *Abzug* into the false [*uneigentliche*] and the genuine [*eigentliche*]. In the case of the false *Abzug*, which is appropriate to any note that has an appoggiatura, the bow carries on more weakly, or even remains stationary on the string. In the case of the genuine *Abzug*, which is appropriate to any note that has an appoggiatura and is followed by a rest, the bow is lifted completely from the strings as soon as the note has been faintly heard.
> 
> The lifting of the bow applies to every note that is followed by a rest, with this exception, that a note without an appoggiatura is held for its full value before the bow is lifted; a note with an appoggiatura, however,—like the last syllable in speech—will be heard as extremely short and weak, as long as a rest follows. Since this is the last, and therefore will not be obscured

---

[74] Crelle: *Einiges*, 93.

by any following one, it will always be heard strongly enough. In any case, the appoggiatura will cause the listener to have such a lively expectation of the following note that the smallest touch of the note is sufficient to satisfy him.[75]

This treatment of appoggiaturas became associated, to a considerable extent, with the performance of any paired notes, and to some degree with the execution of other short, slurred groups of notes. But even in the 18th century there were differing opinions about the niceties of performance in these circumstances.

Koch alluded to Reichardt's distinction between the "true" and "false" *Abzug* in his discussion of appoggiaturas: "This soft slurring of the appoggiatura to its following main note is called the *Abzug*, on the execution of which the opinion of musicians is still divided. Some hold namely that, for example, on the keyboard the finger, or on the violin the bow should be gently lifted after the main note; others, however, regard this as unnecessary, so long as a rest does not follow the main note."[76] Later in the 19th century, J. A. C. Burkhard considered that *Abzug* signified

> In general the manner of handling the various refined instruments by the use of the finger for emphasizing and releasing the various notes; or the manner in which the harmony note that follows an appoggiatura is taken off by the bow on string instruments and by the finger on keyboard instruments, whereby one can distinguish between the true and false *Abzug* according to whether the bow or finger is fully lifted from the string as soon as the note has been faintly heard, or goes on more weakly—or remains on the string.[77]

Other definitions of *Abzug* in the first half of the 19th century were given in 1827 by Andersch, who regarded it as denoting "A manner of performance by which one gives the strongest pressure to an appoggiatura, which is attached before a harmony note, and only follows it gently with the latter";[78] and in 1840 Gathy referred to it as "the lifting or drawing away of the bow

---

[75] Reichardt: *Ueber die Pflichten*, 41–43.
[76] Koch: 'Vorschlag' in *Musikalisches Lexikon*, 1721.
[77] Johann Andreas Christian Burkhard: 'Abzug' in *Neues vollständiges musikalisches Wörterbuch* (Ulm, 1832), 7.
[78] Andersch: 'Abzug' in *Musikalisches Wörterbuch*, 5.

from the string on instruments of the violin family, or of the finger from the key or from the hole on keyboard or wind instruments' "[79]

Theoretical discussion of the "true" and "false" *Abzug* may be related to the way these figures were notated in the 18th and 19th centuries. In numerous cases composers took considerable extra trouble to shorten the second note and write a rest. Instances of slurred pairs both with and without a shortened final note (indicated by either a rest or *staccato* mark) are legion in the works of Haydn, Mozart, Beethoven, and Schubert.

Brahms's correspondence with Joachim in 1879, during the composition of his Violin Concerto, provides a revealing late-19th-century perspective on the different attitudes towards the execution of short slurs by a pianist, who was also a great composer, and a violinist with considerable talent in composition. Joseph Joachim, approaching the matter from the point of view of the executant, pointed out the difficulty of deciding whether slurs were an indication for *legato* or for phrasing, observing that it is "tricky to decide with slurs where they merely mean: so and so many notes in the same bowstroke, or on the other hand, where they signify meaningful division of groups of notes, e.g.: [Ex. 6.37a] could just as well sound connected, even when played with different bowstrokes, while on the piano this would have to sound approximately thus in all circumstances: [Ex. 6.37b]."[80]

Ex. 6.37 a–b. Brahms: *Briefwechsel mit Joseph Joachim.*

Brahms disagreed, remarking: "the slur over several notes does not reduce the value of any of them. It signifies *legato*, and one makes it according to groups, phrases, or impulses. Only over two notes does it reduce the value of the last one: [Ex. 6.37c] With longer groups of notes: [Ex. 6.37d] would

---

[79] August Gathy: 'Abzug' in *Musikalisches Conversations-Lexikon*, 2nd edn (Leipzig, 1840), 4.
[80] Andreas Moser (ed.), *Johannes Brahms im Briefwechsel mit Joseph Joachim*, ii (Berlin, 1908), 149.

be a freedom and refinement in performance, which, to be sure, is generally appropriate."

Ex. 6.37 c–d. Brahms: *Briefwechsel mit Joseph Joachim*.

In other words, Brahms regarded the shortening of the last note in pairs as obligatory, whether or not a rest or articulation mark was indicated, and in a longer group as optional. He concluded: "With me such considerations are pointless. But you have the broom in your hand, and we have much to sweep up."[81] Brahms did not concern himself with specifying all the refinements that he might expect the performer to contribute. In his edition of the correspondence, Andreas Moser recalled that Brahms "presupposed an intelligence and a sense of style in the performers which, unfortunately, are not always present, even if the people in question otherwise achieve something technically excellent, indeed outstanding".[82]

There is evidence, despite Brahms's opinion to the contrary (which may, perhaps, have owed something to his antiquarian interests), that even the distinctive execution of slurred pairs was becoming increasingly rare during the 19th century. Mendelssohn in 1845 felt it necessary to point out that these figures would have been given an accent-*decrescendo* treatment in Handel's day, implying that it was no longer automatically customary to perform them in that manner.[83]

In Brahms's music, however, there are many instances where he will have envisaged the traditional nuanced performance of slurred pairs. In the third movement of his String Quartet op. 51 no. 1 (Ex. 6.38a), these are made a feature of the music; and the occurrence of slurred pairs of conjunct descending notes elsewhere in his works seems often to call for a similar treatment, for

---

[81] Moser (ed.), *Briefwechsel mit Joseph Joachim*, ii, 153.
[82] Moser (ed.), *Briefwechsel mit Joseph Joachim*, ii, 147 (footnote).
[83] See Nicholas Temperley, 'Berlioz and the Slur', *Music & Letters*, 1 (1969), 391.

instance in the Adagio of the Clarinet Quintet op. 115 (Ex. 6.38b). In this extremely *legato* context, physical separation is unlikely to have been envisaged, but accent-*decrescendo* on each pair (albeit quite discreet) may well have been. In many other cases in Brahms's string music the degree of accent in slurred pairs seems likely to have been little more than would be achieved by the bow change, for instance in the first movement of the String Quartet op. 67 (Ex. 6.38c). Tempo will often be a deciding factor. In most of these cases, some degree of agogic accentuation of the first note under the slur will surely have been expected and executed by tradition-focused German musicians.

Ex. 6.38a Brahms: String Quartet op. 51/1/iii.

Ex. 6.38b Brahms: Clarinet Quintet op. 115/ii.

Ex. 6.38c Brahms: String Quartet op. 67/i.

The most significant cause of ambiguity in the meaning of the slur, as the Brahms-Joachim correspondence implies, was the tendency to indicate sections of continuous *legato* with a succession of relatively short slurs (usually over a single bar), something technically necessary in string writing, where the bow can only slur a limited number of notes without changing. This was also common in 18th- and early-19th-century keyboard writing, where it remains contentious whether slurs that begin and end at bar lines might have implications for phrasing. Before the end of the 18th century, it is rare to find longer slurs than are practicable in a single bowstroke. This is the case even in wind music, where the breath can sustain a more extended unbroken phrase, or in keyboard music, where the length of a *legato* passage is unlimited, provided that it does not (before the advent of the pedal) contain leaps that go beyond the reach of the hand. The connection between the slur and string bowing remained strong in the minds of 18th-century musicians; Löhlein, for instance, remarked in the 1770s, when explaining the use of slurs and articulation: "The keyboard is not so perfect with respect to expression as string and wind instruments. However, uniform notes can be performed in a variety of ways, and one can imitate some kinds of bowstrokes."[84]

Where 18th- and early-19th-century composers wrote a succession of shorter slurs, it may not be the case that there was an intention to signify expressive accent at the beginning followed by *decrescendo* and shortening of the last note for each slurred group, particularly if the slurs are over a series of whole bars or half bars. Despite the commonly accepted 18th-century convention for the articulated performance of slurred figures in keyboard playing, Türk expressly warned against their separation in circumstances such as Ex. 6.39a, saying that they must not be performed as in Ex. 6.39b.[85]

Ex. 6.39 a–b. Türk: *Klavierschule*. (*a*) p. 341; (*b*) p. 340.

And Czerny, having stated that in piano playing the last of two or three slurred notes required shortening, still felt it necessary in 1839 to state: "when slurs are drawn over several notes, however, although the slurs are not continuous, but are broken into several lines, they are considered as forming but one, and no perceptible separation must take place".[86] He added that where a composer wished a break to occur between slurs he would have to place a dot

---

[84] Löhlein: *Clavier Schule*, i, 69.
[85] Türk: *Klavierschule*, 340f.
[86] Czerny: *Pianoforte-Schule*, i, 143.

or dash over the last note under the slur; but few composers did so, leaving their expectations often unclear.

A further problem concerned the question of whether accent or dynamic nuance (other than *decrescendo*) was permissible within a slur. Theoretical treatment of the subject in the early part of the period appears largely to exclude such possibilities. At the beginning of the 19th century, Koch could still describe the slur exclusively in terms of its basic function of articulating a short phrase or figure with an even *legato*. He maintained that any type of accent or articulation after the first note of a slur was a contradiction of its meaning: "It is an error in the performance of such slurs if, on string instruments, the performer accents the second, or the note which is slurred to the preceding one, with a pressure of the bow or on wind instruments with a fresh pressure of breath; through such an accent the feeling of a renewed attack is to a certain extent aroused, and the real intention and effect of the slur is to a large extent lost."[87] By the time Koch made that statement he was evidently out of touch with the practice of contemporary composers, but it is surprising how long such ideas persisted: the much younger musician Philip Corri could still state in 1810 that "a long slur forbids any emphasis within it".[88]

Clearly, the longer slurs that begin to be found with increasing frequency during the early years of the 19th century, in the works of Beethoven, Clementi, and other composers of their generations, were intended to show that a passage should be continuously *legato*, though not necessarily to forbid accentuation, dynamic shaping, or phrasing; nor were the beginnings and ends of such slurs inevitably meant to be distinguished by, respectively, accent and articulation. Even within shorter slurs, accentuation or dynamic nuance (other than the conventional *decrescendo*) seems often to have been envisaged, though not always indicated. This frequently applies in Beethoven's music, where articulation or accentuation within slurs is sometimes implicit, as in the violin part of the Adagio espressivo of the Sonata op. 96, in bars 9–11 (Ex. 6.40), or the single slur over bars 26–31. Nuancing within slurs is sometimes hinted at, for instance by beaming, or specified by instructions such as <>. There are, in fact, numerous situations in music of this period where an accent-*decrescendo* interpretation of short, slurred groups may not be envisaged.

[87] Koch: 'Legato' in *Musikalisches Lexikon*, 893f.
[88] P. Corri: *L'anima di musica*, 72.

Ex. 6.40 Beethoven: Violin Sonata op. 96/ii.

Beethoven's music provides many challenging examples of slurs that do not conform comfortably to theoretical explanations.[89] Consideration of his autographs together with corrected copyists' scores and parts also provides some valuable lessons about the extent to which we may rely upon his notation as providing accurate and precise information about what he had in mind, reminding us that 20th-century notions of accuracy and completeness can rarely be applied, even to the music of the most conscientious composers of this period. An instructive instance may be taken from the Fifth Symphony. The phrase that begins at bar 64 of the last movement makes its first appearance with viola and clarinet in unison, but with two different patterns of slurring (Ex. 6.41); in subsequent appearances of this frequently recurring phrase, Beethoven predominantly drew the slur from the second note, but sometimes from the first or, ambiguously, from between the first and second notes. In the copied score and parts that Beethoven himself extensively corrected, however, the copyist almost invariably drew the slur from the first note of the figure.

Ex. 6.41 Beethoven: Fifth Symphony op. 67/iv.

Although Beethoven made many changes to the copies in these bars, occasionally adding missing slurs, he did not in any instance attempt to change the beginning of the copyist's slurs from the first to the second note. Had he wanted any kind of expressive accent on the second note of the figure, he would have been bound to do so. (The frequency with which this phrase occurs surely rules out oversight on the composer's part.) The conclusion

---

[89] For examples from his piano music see Rosenblum: *Performance Practices*, 164f.

that Beethoven simply intended to signify a *legato* execution for the whole phrase is almost inescapable. In the case of this four-note phrase, despite the ambiguous beginning of the slur, an accent-*decrescendo* treatment of the whole figure is plausible from the musical point of view, though it can by no means be certain that Beethoven did not conceive of some kind of subsidiary accentuation on the metrically strong third note.

Some composers adopted the practice of eliding slurs in a manner that seems to suggest accentuation within a context of continuous legato. Occasional instances of apparent elision in Beethoven's music seem more likely to result from lengthening a slur to include subsequent notes. Examples where deliberate slur elision seems to be the composer's intention can occasionally be found in Clementi's music,[90] and much more consistently and consequentially in Berlioz's works.[91]

## The Long Phrasing Slur

The confusion between string bowing, the employment of slurs to indicate the articulation of short figures in keyboard or wind writing, and the use of longer slurs to show the extent of a melodic phrase, or simply to signify *legato*, troubled many later 19th-century musicians. Their efforts to make sense of earlier composers' admittedly inconsistent practices added another layer of confusion to the situation, particularly when later editions obscured the original composer's intentions by replacing short slurs on individual figures with long phrasing slurs.

It is not clear to what extent late-19th-century musicians were correct in believing that the slurs employed by earlier composers, particularly in keyboard music, did not adequately represent their musical expectations. It is certainly true that many composers, up to and including Mendelssohn's generation, were far from consistent in this respect. Yet the difficulty seems partly to have arisen from an assumption that slurs, which were merely meant to specify details of *legato* groupings within the larger phrase, were invitations to give the slurred figures a distinctly articulated execution, and thus to distort the contours of the musical structure. This was clearly Karl Klindworth's motivation for modifying the slurring in his edition of Mendelssohn's *Lieder*

---

[90] Rosenblum: *Performance Practices*, 169ff.
[91] See Macdonald: 'Two Peculiarities'.

*ohne Worte*, where he stated in the preface: "Whenever it seemed desirable for the better understanding of the composer's intentions, I have added phrasing slurs, which extend the short bar-sections into melodic phrases. A comparison of the opening of no. 14 in the old with the present edition will serve to illustrate my method of procedure" (Ex. 6.42).[92]

Ex. 6.42 Mendelssohn: *Lieder ohne Worte*, ed. Klindworth, iii.

And, with reference to op. 30 no. 1 in E flat, he observed:

The new phrasing-slurs are intended to preserve the pianist from the error of rendering the melody according to the strict rules of pianoforte playing, which would require that in every group of slurred notes the first is to be accented and the last slightly shortened in value, thus dividing it from the following group. In thinking over the manner in which Mendelssohn may have intended the melody to be played I have imagined the style in which, for instance, a great violinist would render the song thus phrased. He would certainly link the last group of notes played with one bow to the first note of the new bow, without shortening its value, and thus he would logically connect phrase to phrase, so that the melody might appeal to our hearts in a broad and unbroken stream.[93]

Klindworth was only twenty-one years younger than Mendelssohn, and, while it is possible that his understanding of the intentions behind the composer's notation may have been incorrect in some instances, there are no very good grounds for believing that he was fundamentally mistaken about the style in general. If one listens to Joachim's 1903 recording of his own Romance in C, one hears precisely the kind of performance that Klindworth wished the pianist to achieve; and there is no doubt that Joachim's musicianship was

---

[92] Mendelssohn: *Lieder ohne Worte*, ed. Karl Klindworth (London, Novello, 1898), iii.
[93] Mendelssohn: *Lieder ohne Worte*, ed. Klindworth, v–vi.

deeply affected by his early study with Mendelssohn. Whatever Mendelssohn may have intended his slurs to convey, it seems very unlikely that he expected them to be played according to what Klindworth called the "strict rules of pianoforte playing", which had, in any case, already been questioned by Türk (see Ex. 6.39a–b). Klindworth was typical of late-19th-century editors and theorists in believing that most composers employed slurs in a manner that was inadequate to convey their intentions. Lussy, also, criticized the practice of his contemporaries in this respect.[94]

It was Hugo Riemann, however, who made the most sustained effort to find a mode of notating every aspect of phrasing with maximum precision. He laid out his premises in detail in 1884,[95] and over the next decades made practical use of his principles in many editions of late-18th- and 19th-century piano music. As he remarked in the preface to his edition of Schubert's *Moments musicaux* op. 94 and two Scherzos:

> The principal difference between editions with phrasing marks, and others, is in the use of the slur. The curved lines or slurs used to indicate the legato touch (very often in an incorrect manner in Music for the Pianoforte, originating from Violin-bowing) reveal the thematic analysis of a musical work, the union of motives into phrases and the disjunction of phrases from each other; thus supplying a long-felt want of musical Notation, namely, an unequivocal punctuation; enabling the performer (even the least talented) to give a correct interpretation of musical thoughts. This analysis is rendered more detailed and complete by means of the following sign ≣, which shews the extent of the shorter motives contained within a phrase. This sign is sometimes doubled ≣, to point out the principal subdivisions of a phrase; and it is always written obliquely ≣, where it falls upon a bar [line]. This sign by no means indicates a disconnection of the phrase in performance, but is simply intended as an analytical mark; nevertheless, the expression cannot be correct unless the sign is thoroughly understood.

Klindworth's editions and those of many other late-19th-century and early-20th-century editors, including Donald Francis Tovey, were profoundly affected by Riemann's examples, leading to a host of phrased editions,

---

[94] Lussy: *Le Rythme musical*, 66.
[95] Hugo Riemann: *Musikalische Dynamik und Agogik: Lehrbuch der musikalische Phrasierung* (Hamburg, 1884).

some of which have remained in use to the present day. The problem with such editions is that although, in general, they may not radically distort the performance style envisaged by the composer, they will always run the risk of obscuring details. In Klindworth's edition of Mendelssohn's *Lieder ohne Worte*, for example, in the fourth bar of Ex. 6.42, where Mendelssohn marked a slur over all three notes, Klindworth's version may well conceal an intentional connection between the phrase units.[96]

## Articulated Slurs

Articulation marks combined with slurs are directly derived from string-playing techniques. The simultaneous employment of these signs originally signified simply that the specified type of articulation should be produced in a single bowstroke rather than with alternate down- and up-bows. But it was not long before composers began to employ the same notations for other instruments and for vocal music; as with all types of notation that were widely adopted, subtle and not so subtle differences of usage between different instruments and different schools of composers and performers soon emerged.

Another subject addressed in Brahms's correspondence with Joachim illuminates an area in which, by the second half of the 19th century, there were fundamental and deep-rooted contradictions. Their discussion of these issues was prompted when, during work on Brahms's Violin Concerto, Joachim marked some bowings with dots under a slur, which puzzled Brahms. It is clear that they did not disagree on the musical effect of the passage (i.e., a sharp *staccato*), merely on the manner of notating it (see Ex. 6.22). Brahms wrote to Joachim: "With what right, since when and on what authority do you violinists write the sign for portamento (⌢̇) [i.e., *portato*][97]

---

[96] See also Clive Brown: 'Phrasirung' in Heinz von Loesch, Rebecca Wolf, and Thomas Ertelt (eds.), *Geschichte der musikalischen Interpretation im 19. und 20. Jahrhundert*, iii, Aspekte-Parameter (Kassel, 2022), 553–91.

[97] Some 19th-century musicians used the term *portamento* as synonymous with *portato*. Portamento is used throughout this book for the singer's *legato*, or the audible slide between two notes that is sometimes a consequence of *legato*, especially in vocal music and string playing. *Portato* is used to describe all degrees of articulation indicated by dots or lines under slurs, or slurs over a group of notes repeated at the same pitch, which are intermediate between pure *legato* and a sharply detached *staccato*. This is a well-established usage: *portato* notes were defined by Lichtenthal in 1826 as "those which are marked to occur without the bow being raised from the string (Fig. 122) therefore they are neither legato nor detached [*sciolto*], but almost dragged, giving to each note a little stroke of the bow" (*Dizionario*, ii, 128, and fig. 122).

where none is intended? You mark the octave passages in the Rondo (⁀), and I would use sharp strokes | |. Must that be so? Up to now I have not given in to the violinists with their damned horizontal lines ⌒. Why should ⁀ mean anything different to us than it did to Beethoven?"[98] Joachim replied with a detailed account of the origins and meanings of these signs, as he understood them, and remarked that he always cautioned his pupils to consider whether the composers were pianists or string players when deciding how to execute passages designated with dots under a slur. Joachim thought, erroneously, that a divergence of meaning only originated around 1800.[99]

In fact, the meaning of articulation marks under a slur was already a problem in the middle of the 18th century and has continued to cause confusion among performers. The main difficulty is to decide whether the notation indicates either sharply separated notes, more gently emphasized and slightly separated, sometimes almost *legato* notes, or some intermediate degree of articulation; but there is the additional problem in string playing of whether sharp separation, if this was envisaged, was intended to be produced by a firm or elastic bowstroke. Thus, the same notation could indicate every degree of articulation, from a pulsation with hardly perceptible separation, to a flying *staccato*. The range of meanings of dots and strokes under slurs in the mid- and later 18th century is well illustrated by conflicting explanations in treatises.

In 1732, Walther, somewhat vaguely defining *Punctus percutiens*, remarked that in instrumental and vocal music a dot over or under a note means that it is to be played *staccato*, but when in instrumental music (by which he obviously means string music) there is also a slur these notes are "to be executed with a single bowstroke".[100] The implication here is that the notes are still to be performed *staccato*.

Two decades later, C. P. E. Bach, from the clavichord player's point of view, regarded dots under a slur as designating *portato* (*Tragen der Töne*).[101] For German keyboard players of the second half of the 18th century, *portato* seems to have involved a degree of accent on each note, but not perceptible separation. Marpurg described it in the following terms: "If the sign for separation and that for slurring appears together on several notes that follow one another, this signifies that the notes that are thus designated should be

---

[98] Moser (ed.): *Briefwechsel mit Joseph Joachim*, ii, 146f.
[99] Moser (ed.): *Briefwechsel mit Joseph Joachim*, ii, 148ff.
[100] Walther: 'Punctus percutiens' in *Musicalisches Lexicon*, viii, 504.
[101] Bach: *Versuch*, i, 126.

marked with a somewhat stronger pressure of the finger and connected together as in the normal procedure."[102] A generation later, Türk remarked that "the little dot shows the pressure that each key must receive, and through the slur the player will be reminded to hold the note after the pressure until its notated value is fully expired".[103] But when a succession of dots was written over a single note, rather than a group of notes, it signified the clavichord *Bebung* (repeated pressure made without lifting the key, which causes a trembling effect);[104] this could also be indicated by the instruction *tenuto*.[105] Yet five years after the publication of C. P. E. Bach's *Versuch*, Nicolo Pasquali, apparently leaning towards string playing practice, used dots under a slur to indicate a succession of markedly detached notes all to be played *staccatissimo*, "striking every successive Key with the point of one and the same Finger (generally the first)".[106]

At about the same time, Agricola explained the singer's *portato* (though he did not employ the term) in a similar manner to the keyboard *portato* (the text describes it as notated by "little strokes [*Strichelchen*]" under a slur, but the accompanying musical example shows dots); he counselled that such notes "must neither be detached nor attacked, but each note only marked by means of a gentle pressure with the chest".[107] Corresponding descriptions of the performance of *portato* by singers and wind instrument players were given by other writers, for instance, Petri and Lasser.[108] For violinists, Galeazzi provided similar instructions, explaining that *note portate* should be "neither separated nor slurred but almost dragged. They are played in one stroke without lifting the bow from the string, but each note is given a slight accentuation with the bow, which is not done in slurs."[109]

Quantz recognized three types of articulated slur: these were slurs alone, over notes repeated at the same pitch, slurs over dots, and slurs over vertical strokes. The first, which he only mentioned in connection with the flute,

---

[102] Marpurg: *Anleitung zum Clavierspielen*, 29.
[103] Türk: *Klavierschule*, 354.
[104] Bach: *Versuch*, i, 126.
[105] See Ch. 3, p. 170.
[106] Pasquali: *The Art of Fingering the Harpsichord*, 27, and Lesson XIV.
[107] Agricola: *Anleitung zur Singkunst*, 135. Julianne Baird: *Introduction to the Art of Singing by Johann Friedrich Agricola* (Cambridge, 1995), 160, translates this rather differently, interpreting the words "nicht abgesetzt, auch nicht gestoßen" as " [one must] neither separate nor detach [the notes]", omitting the implication of accent in the word "gestoßen".
[108] Johann Samuel Petri: *Anleitung zur practischen Musik, vor neuangehende Sänger und Instrumentspieler*, 2nd edn (Leipzig, 1782); Johann Baptist Lasser: *Vollständige Anleitung zur Singkunst* (Munich, 1798).
[109] Galeazzi: *Elementi*, i, 156.

is produced "by breathing with movement of the chest"; with dots under slurs, he instructs the flautist that "these notes must be pushed out much more sharply, and, as it were, struck with the chest".[110] On the violin, dots under slurs were to be performed "with a short bowstroke and in a sustained manner", while *staccato* strokes under the slur required a more sharply detached bowstroke.[111] Leopold Mozart described Quantz's second and third categories in a similar manner, but in addition he used strokes under a slur encompassing twenty-five sixteenth-notes—clearly, from his description of its execution, this is the classic slurred *staccato*, beginning near the point of the bow. For technical reasons, therefore, his description of its execution by "a quick lift of the bow"[112] means a release of pressure rather than raising it clear of the string. Both these authors illustrated the *portato*, only with dots under a slur, on notes repeated at the same pitch.

Dealing specifically with violin playing, Joseph Riepel described three possible articulation marks under a slur (Ex. 6.43). His explanation of their meaning does not tally with Quantz and Mozart. He instructs: "The first will straightway be attacked very short", by which he may have envisaged a technique resembling the modern slurred *staccato*, which Mozart marked with strokes under the slur. He continues: "The second is longer, so that the violin bow must be raised much higher during the bowing; in order to form a separate bowstroke with each attack, as it were. In the third bar, the bow is almost not lifted at all, but rather it almost represents the sound of a lyre."[113] He also explained that this third type should be made both with an up-bow and a down-bow, leaving it unclear in which direction he expected the first two types to be executed. If he expected them to be made up-bow, as was normal later, it is curious that he did not specify this.

**Ex. 6.43** Riepel: *Gründliche Erklärung*, 16. (The nnn in the third bar is clearly meant to stand for the wavy line used by many composers, with or without a slur, at that time.)

The casualness with which composers used these signs in practice quickly becomes evident on perusal of manuscript or printed music of the period.

---

[110] Quantz: *Versuch*, 65.
[111] Quantz: *Versuch*, 193f.
[112] Mozart: *Versuch*, 128.
[113] Riepel: *Gründliche Erklärung*, 16.

NOTATION OF ARTICULATION AND PHRASING 321

In the autograph of a symphony by Pokorny (a pupil of Riepel), dots under a slur and a wavy line can be seen being employed in close proximity, evidently to mean the same thing (Ex. 6.44).

**Ex. 6.44** Franz Xaver Pokorny: Symphony in C, i, autograph in Fürst Thurn und Taxis Hofbibliothek, Regensburg, Pokorny 7; pub. In fac. In the series *The Symphony 1720–1840* (New York and London, 1984).

Perhaps to ensure that there was no misunderstanding, or possibly to elicit a very smooth *portato*, Anton André chose to mark slurs together with the verbal instruction *portato* (Ex. 6.45).

Ex. 6.45 Johann Anton André: String Quartet op. 14 no. 3 (c. 1801).
[Adagio con moto]

J. F. Reichardt referred in 1776 to sharply separated notes in a single bowstroke and to *portato*, but he made no notational distinction; both are indicated by dots under slurs. His example of *portato*, however, is shown with notes repeated at the same pitch, while his sharply separated notes are shown in melodic figures. He described the *portato* as "the softest" way of executing repeated notes, saying: "one takes several notes in a bowstroke without completely joining them to one another; there remains a small rest in the bow between each note". But he warned against connecting the notes too smoothly, since this would tend to obscure the melodic part;[114] in this he seems not to agree entirely with Mozart, who required merely that the notes "must be differentiated from each other by a little emphasis applied to each note",[115] or Agricola, who wanted no separation. Reichardt also used a wavy-line symbol in his opera *Brenno* (c. 1797), which he does not mention in the 1776 treatise, evidently to signify a string *tremolo* (rapidly repeated notes) with the bow (Ex. 6.46); and he also uses it for timpani rolls in the same opera.

Ex. 6.46 Reichardt: *Brenno*, Act I, Scene iii.

[114] Reichardt: *Ueber die Pflickten*, 24.
[115] Mozart: *Versuch*, 43.

Löhlein's *Anweisung zum Violinspielen* (1774) uses dots under a slur to indicate sharp separation;[116] the text makes no mention of a *portato* execution. In the exercises in chapter XI, however, there are several instances of what, from their context as repeated accompaniment notes at the same pitch, look to be *portato*; these too are simply marked with dots under a slur. Löhlein also employed dots under a slur over a single note to indicate Bebung of the left hand—a violinist's counterpart to C. P. E. Bach's *Bebung* on the clavichord (see Ex. 14.20).[117] But elsewhere the same notation seems to have been used in string music to indicate various kinds of trembling effects with the bow, for instance in Gluck's operas, sometimes in conjunction with the instruction *tremolando*. Whether these effects were a kind of bow vibrato related to *portato* or a technique closer to the modern *tremolo* is unclear. Another possibility is suggested by Galeazzi. He explains that it is executed by "stiffening (so to speak) the nerves of the bow arm and imposing a certain trembling motion which is communicated to the bow, causing it to make a thousand barely perceptible undulations on the string and producing that effect which we call *tremolo*".[118] In his music examples he shows it as a wavy line over halfnotes, but also states that it can be indicated by the word *Tremolo*. Whether, like Reichardt, he envisaged very short alternate down- and up-bows near the point, like the modern orchestral *tremolo* (which seems most likely), or a kind of trembling produced in a single bowstroke, is not clear from his description.

In string music, *portato* rather than *staccato* was generally indicated by the theorists for accompaniment figures where notes were repeated at the same pitch. Indeed, Giuseppe Maria Cambini suggested in about 1800 that this style of bowing should be used whenever "piano", "dolce", or "piano dolce" were written, even though the composer had not specifically indicated a *portato* bowing; and to mark this bowstroke, Cambini used either dots or a wavy line.[119] But as the descriptions of Quantz, Mozart, and Reichardt imply, considerable variation in pressure and separation was current.

A final example from an 18th-century treatise introduces the possibility of executing slurred *staccato* where none seems to be indicated. In 1792, Hiller explained that if dots (without a slur) occur,

> as long as these dots should not merely be strokes, they signify a totally different kind of performance, which in artistic language is called *punto d'arco*

---

[116] Löhlein: *Anweisung*, 32f.
[117] Löhlein: *Anweisung*, 68–70.
[118] Galeazzi: *Elementi*, i, 171 (in the 1817 revision, 193).
[119] Giuseppe Cambini: *Nouvelle Méthode théorique et pratique pour le violon* (Paris, c. 1800), 23.

(attack with the bow).[120] In this case several of the notes thus marked are taken in one bowstroke and brought out shortly by a jerk of the bow. [...] We will clarify the matter with several examples, and note in advance that the *punto d'arco* can most easily be made with the up-bow from the point of the bow to the middle.[121] (Ex. 6.47a)

Ex. 6.47 a–b. Hiller: *Anweisung zum Violinspielen*, 6, §8, 41f.

(a)

(b)

As his example confirms, he is referring to the *staccato* in a single bowstroke at a moderate tempo, which other authors designated by dots under a slur or strokes under a slur. He added that soloists can attempt a much faster version of this bowstroke, which he calls *pikiren*, and illustrates with both dots and slur (Ex. 6.47b).

Hiller, however, also used the notation of dots under a slur to mean *portato*. His statement that the term *punto d'arco* was used to indicate slurred *staccato* even where no slurs were present may cast light on the execution envisaged when the instruction *punto d'arco* occurs in all four parts towards the end of the final movement of Beethoven's String Quartet op. 132 together with *staccato* marks but no slurs.

In 18th-century usage, there was evidently an area of uncertainty about the borderline between *portato* and *staccato*. This is very clearly brought out in Koch's definition of *Piquiren* in 1802:

---

[120] For another, somewhat different, use of the term *punta (punto) d'arco*, which seems also to have been current in the late 18th century and early 19th century see Ch. 7, pp. 368–73.
[121] Hiller: *Anweisung zum Violinspielen*, 41.

With this expression one denotes a particular kind of bowstroke on string instruments by which many stepwise notes following on from one another are detached very short [. . .]; e.g. [Ex. 6.48a] One leaves the performance of running notes in a quick tempo to solo players who have particularly practised this; on notes which are repeated at the same pitch and performed at a moderate tempo, however, one also uses this kind of stroke in orchestral parts; e.g. [Ex. 6.48b].[122]

Ex. 6.48 a–b. Koch: 'Piquiren, Pikkiren' in *Musikalisches Lexikon*, 1155f.

Several of the markings dealt with by 18th-century writers became largely obsolete during the 19th century; the *tremolando* used by Gluck and others and the notation of the *Bebung* with dots under a slur over a single note gradually disappeared from normal usage, as did the employment of the wavy line to indicate *portato*. In Paris, where Gluck's influence remained stronger, these practices seem to have lingered longest. Spontini, who dominated Parisian grand opera during the first decade of the 19th century, used a wavy line in very much the same contexts as Gluck.[123] The use of the wavy line as an indication for *portato* was touched on in 1835 by Baillot, who included Boccherini's works in many of his concerts,[124] and Gluck's *tremolando* was

---

[122] Koch: 'Piquiren, Pikkiren' in *Musikalisches Lexikon*, 1155f.
[123] For further discussion of these signs and their implications see Ch. 15.
[124] Baillot: *L'Art du violon*, 137.

referred to by Berlioz in his *Grand traité* (1843).[125] The wavy line continued to be used in string music to indicate left-hand *vibrato* and *tremolo* with rapid, separate bowstrokes, and on the piano, particularly in vocal scores of operas, to indicate the pianistic equivalent of the *tremolo*. The tendency of composers to use signs haphazardly and inconsistently continued as before, though the possible range of meanings shifted. For instance, while Pokorny had used the wavy line and dots under a slur to mean *portato*, Rossini randomly employed either the wavy line or a figure consisting of three or four diagonal strokes to mean a *tremolo* with separate bowstrokes (Ex. 6.49) in the manner described in the *Principes élémentaires de musique* (c. 1800), where it was observed: "One uses it [the wavy line] normally on a whole-note in the accompaniment parts of an obbligato recitative. The effect of the Tremolo is the same as that produced by a succession of 32nds on the same pitch in a fast movement. Only string instruments and timpani are able to produce the effect of the *tremolo*."[126] Their music example is captioned: "Manner of executing the tremolo" (Ex. 6.50).

Ex. 6.49  Rossini: *Semiramide*, Act II, no. 10.

Ex. 6.50  Gossec et al.: *Principes*, i, 49.

---

[125] Hector Berlioz: *Grand traité d'instrumentation et d'orchestration modernes* op. 10 (Paris, 1843), 19.
[126] Gossec et al.: *Principes*, i. 48f.

In piano methods, the use of dots under a slur to mean *portato* seems to have been generally accepted at the beginning of the 19th century; Adam's explanation of this notation in his *Méthode du piano du Conservatoire* (1802), as signifying that each note was to be sustained for three-quarters of its value,[127] was widely repeated in other piano methods and even, somewhat anomalously, in some string methods. Singing methods and wind tutors also continued to link the notation of dots under a slur with *portato*: for instance, the oboe method in Fröhlich's *Musikschule*, where it is described as having "its own soft character, which forms the transition from separation to slurring".[128] Some authorities, particularly pianists, also stated, like Reichardt, that in passages marked with *portato* notation, each note received a slight emphasis;[129] for violinists, such an effect is a natural outcome of the technique. One implication of this notation, although it is only sporadically mentioned in 19th-century sources, may also have been asynchrony between melody and bass or chordal arpeggiation.[130] Aural evidence of the continuation of this relationship into the early 20th century is preserved in early recordings. The possible range of subtle degrees of accentuation, pressure, separation, and asynchrony or arpeggiation in the execution of passages marked *portato*, therefore, is considerable.

In 19th-century string methods, as in those of the 18th century, this notation is especially ambiguous. Fröhlich, with no apparent sense of inconsistency, used dots under a slur in the violin method section of his *Musikschule* to mean slurred *staccato*, having earlier used them to mean *portato*.[131] Dotzauer, in his 1825 *Méthode de violoncelle*, used dots under a slur only in the context of the firm *staccato*, but in his 1833 *Violoncell-Schule*, he also illustrated a springing *staccato*, in arpeggios across the strings, with the same notation.[132] Spohr's 1833 *Violinschule*, on the other hand, employs dots under a slur solely for the string player's normal slurred *staccato*, but in relation to a down-bow *staccato* he also observed, though only in passing, that "in melodious passages it has a good effect in dragging and gently detaching the notes."[133]

The meaning of dots or strokes under slurs during the late 18th and 19th centuries, therefore, is by no means clear and consistent. In keyboard music it

---

[127] Adam: *Méthode*, 155.
[128] Fröhlich: *Musikschule*, ii, 40.
[129] Czerny, *Pianoforte-Schule*, iii, 24; Hummel: *Anweisung*, i, 64; Starke: *Wiener Pianoforte-Schule*, i, pt. 1, 1; Daniel Steibelt: *Méthode de piano* (Leipzig, [1809]), 57.
[130] See Ch. 14, pp. 833–35.
[131] Fröhlich: *Musikschule*, iii, 48.
[132] Dotzauer: *Méthode de violoncelle*, 27–28; *Violoncell-Schule*, 22.
[133] Spohr: *Violinschule*, 135.

is safe to assume, despite the contrary example from Pasquali, that in the vast majority of instances the intended execution of dots under slurs is some form of *portato*; also in wind music and vocal music this notation will usually indicate *portato*. In string music the situation is much more complex, particularly where the composer was both a keyboard player and a string player, and with the dissemination of an increasingly sophisticated variety of bowings in the 19th century, the range of possible meanings became even wider. In these circumstances, the musical context, considered in conjunction with what is known about a composer's background and training, is the only reasonable guide to understanding the intentions behind these notations.

It may be helpful at this point to consider some specific cases in which one or another interpretation seems to be required. On at least a couple of occasions Haydn used quite distinct strokes rather than dots under slurs. One of these occurs in the autograph score of his Concertante in B flat for violin, cello, oboe, bassoon, and orchestra (1791; Hob. I:105), but his intentions are far from clear. At bars 100f of the first movement, he notated the solo violin part as in Ex. 6.51a. Since he usually wrote unambiguous dots under slurs the use of strokes here implies that he wanted something different from a *portato* bowing, and at first sight it appears likely that he imagined a sharply detached bowstroke, as indicated with this notation by Quantz, Leopold Mozart, and Riepel. But at the parallel passage in the recapitulation (bars 218–19) he gave the figure as it appears in Ex. 6.51b. This leaves it uncertain whether he required a contrast the second time or whether the different notation arose simply from inadvertence and, if the latter, whether he regarded the two forms as having distinct meanings at that stage.

Ex. 6.51 a–b. Haydn: Concertante Hob. I:105.

Ten years later, in the Trio section of the Minuet of his String Quartet op. 77 no. 1, he took care to make a clear notational difference, which suggests very strongly that he was concerned to specify the difference between several sharply detached notes in a single bowstroke and *portato*. In the Eulenburg miniature score, and most editions of the parts, this has uniformly been printed with dots under slurs, but in the autograph Haydn clearly wrote strokes under slurs for the first violin, with its leaping figures, and dots under slurs for the repeated quarter-note accompaniment in the three other parts (Ex. 6.52).

**Ex. 6.52** Haydn: String Quartet op. 77/1/iii.
[Presto]

Haydn's late autographs generally show greater concern for precision in matters of articulation than his earlier ones, and it would be rash to assume that just because in 1800 he used strokes under slurs to indicate *staccato*, passages marked with dots under slurs in his earlier works should never be performed *staccato*, or indeed, since so many of his earlier autographs are missing, that the printed editions faithfully reflect the original notation. Haydn, an active violinist throughout his career, would have been conversant with the use of both notations for a slurred *staccato*. Nevertheless, in most cases the musical context suggests that Haydn used dots under slurs to indicate some kind of *portato*, which would undoubtedly have ranged from very smooth to fairly detached; but lifted or sharply accented bowstrokes rarely seem appropriate.

Mozart, despite his father's distinction between dots and strokes under a slur, seems not to have used the latter at all. In keyboard music he undoubtedly used dots under a slur to indicate *portato*, and in most instances in his string music the context strongly suggests that this is also what he required there; but the possibility remains that he sometimes used this notation in string writing where he wanted a more sharply articulated bowstroke. It is evident from one of his letters that he knew and admired the slurred *staccato*; he described the playing of Ignaz Fränzl to his father in 1777, saying: "He has too a most beautiful clear, round tone. He never misses a note, you can hear everything. It is all clear cut. He has a beautiful staccato, played with a single bowing up or down."[134] It is quite likely that such a *staccato* would have been notated with dots under a slur and it is certainly possible that Mozart might have employed the same notation for this effect. There are places where it appears probable on musical and technical grounds that this was the execution he required. One instance, about which there seems little room for doubt, occurs in the first movement of his Violin Concerto in D K. 211 (Ex. 6.53).

Ex. 6.53 Mozart: Violin Concerto K. 211/i.

[134] Mozart: Letter of 22 November 1777 in *Briefe und Aufzeichnungen* (Kassel, 1962), ii, 137. Translation from Emily Anderson, trans. and ed., *The Letters of Mozart and His Family*, 2nd edn (London, 1966), 384.

On the other hand, there are places where performers commonly play a sharply detached slurred *staccato* but where Mozart probably envisaged a more connected bowstroke, for instance, in the first movement of the String Quartet in D K. 575. At bar 66 he introduced the figure shown in Ex. 6.54a. When he repeated it four bars later, and on all its five subsequent appearances, he wrote the bowing as in Ex. 6.54b. Printed editions generally give the first bowing on all appearances of the figure, but it is arguable that the other bowing reveals Mozart's intentions more clearly. A sharply detached bowstroke would certainly be possible with the first bowing, but the subsequent version makes this much less likely; Mozart would have been well aware that the down-bow produced a different, less crisp *staccato* than the up-bow. In general, musical and technical considerations suggest that Mozart mostly used dots under slurs in his later string music to signify an equivalent of the *portato* that he clearly intended in his keyboard music.

Ex. 6.54 a–b. Mozart: String Quartet K. 575/i.

Beethoven seems consistently to have meant *portato* by dots under a slur in keyboard, wind, and string music. This was surely the significance of his often-quoted letter to Karl Holz on the importance of distinguishing between strokes and dots in copying the autograph of the A minor String Quartet op. 132;[135] the only clear and consistent differentiation in this autograph is between dots under slurs and strokes on unslurred notes. Such an interpretation of that letter is supported by Beethoven's care in correcting copyists' parts of the Seventh Symphony; in the many instances where the copyist had written ⌒, Beethoven painstakingly altered it to ⌒. Despite his frequently chaotic writing in other places, Beethoven invariably wrote dots under slurs with absolute clarity.

---

[135] Anderson: *The Letters of Beethoven*, iii, 1241.

Though Beethoven almost certainly never intended his dots under slurs to indicate a *staccato*, the precise degree of articulation will certainly have been expected to vary according to the musical context. Performers, especially string players, but also wind and keyboard players, have often misunderstood the implication of Beethoven's dots under slurs, and played them in a sharply detached manner. It is probable that this notation was already being misinterpreted by string players in the mid-19th century.

Schubert, like Haydn, Mozart, and Beethoven, was a string player as well as a keyboard player. He grew up during a period when the Viotti school was rapidly gaining dominance, and the slurred *staccato* was an essential part of every aspiring string player's technique. It seems clear that not all the passages that he notated with dots under a slur are meant to be played *portato*. For instance, assuming that the first edition faithfully reflects Schubert's lost autograph, a slurred *staccato* execution is surely indicated in the Menuetto of the String Quartet D. 353 (Ex. 6.55); if this is not Schubert's notation, it merely provides evidence of the 1840 editor's practice.

Ex. 6.55 Schubert: String Quartet D. 353/iii.

When Schubert wrote dots under a slur for arpeggio or scale passages of moderate to rapid velocity it seems possible that he envisaged something on the borderline between *portato* and *staccato*, even when he gave the same notation to string and wind instruments, as in the fourth variation of the Andante of the Octet, or to violin and piano, as in the Andante of the "Trout" Quintet (Ex. 6.56).

NOTATION OF ARTICULATION AND PHRASING 333

Ex. 6.56 Schubert: Piano Quintet "The Trout" D. 667/i.

It is possible in a passage such as this that Schubert was especially concerned to indicate the equality of accentuation (the slight emphasis on each note). A more distinct *staccato* may be appropriate in variation 2 of the Andantino in the "Trout" Quintet; the combination of tempo (probably rather fast),[136] and notation (the *fp* and the separate bow for the first note on

[136] See Ch. 10.

the first appearance of the figure) provide almost a *locus classicus* for slurred *staccato*, though a relatively relaxed rather than extremely crisp *staccato* may be best suited to the context.

Many of Schubert's string-playing associates would certainly have used dots under slurs as a notation for distinctly articulated bowstrokes, as suggested by bowings in manuscript parts of his Sixth Symphony used by members of his circle, dating from between 1825 and 1828, where the triplet sixteenth-notes in the second movement, which are given in Schubert's autograph with dots, were marked (after the parts were written) to be played in groups of three or six to the bow.[137] Composers themselves very rarely notated slurred *staccato* in their orchestral compositions; on occasion, though, dots under slurs were unquestionably used to specify this effect. One example occurs in the first movement of Spohr's Fourth Symphony *Die Weihe der Töne* (Ex. 6.57); another is in the Allegro vivacissimo final movement of Mendelssohn's 'Scotch' Symphony (Ex. 6.58). François-Auguste Gevaert included slurred *staccato* in his 1863 treatise on orchestration, but described it as "very difficult to execute in an orchestra".[138] But in his new treatise on orchestration of 1885, he incorrectly stated: "So far, no one has attempted to use it in the orchestra."[139]

Ex. 6.57 Spohr: Fourth Symphony *Die Weihe der Töne* op. 86/i.

Ex. 6.58 Mendelssohn: Third Symphony op. 56/iv.

---

[137] In the collection of the Gesellschaft der Musikfreunde, Vienna.
[138] François-Auguste Gevaert: *Traité général d'instrumentation* (Paris, 1863), 24.
[139] François-Auguste Gevaert: *Nouveau traité d'instrumentation* (Paris, 1885), 29.

When writing for solo strings, Mendelssohn, also an accomplished violinist/violist, quite frequently used dots under slurs in contexts where he obviously wanted slurred *staccato*, but he also used the same notation for *portato*. A good example of the slurred *staccato* is found in the Scherzo of the Octet (Ex. 6.59a), and this is probably also the bowing required in the last movement of his Piano Trio op. 66, dedicated to Spohr, whose performance of this bowstroke Mendelssohn admired (Ex. 6.59b).[140]

Ex. 6.59 a–b. Mendelssohn: (*a*) Octet op. 20/iii; (*b*) Piano Trio op. 66/iv.

In the last movement of Mendelssohn's Violin Concerto op. 64, the notation is conventionally understood as a slurred *spiccato*, but this surely does not accord with the composer's expectations, since the violinist for whom it was written, Ferdinand David, who used both firm and springing bowstrokes, is documented as having played the dots under slurs in this movement with a firm on-string *staccato*.[141] In the first movement of the

---

[140] See Spohr: *Selbstbiographie*, 2 vols. (Kassel, 1860–61), ii, 203.
[141] See Clive Brown: *Mendelssohn: Performance Practices in the Violin Concerto op. 64 and Chamber Music for Strings / Aufführungspraktische Hinweise zum Violinkonzert op. 64 und zur Kammermusik für Streicher* (Kassel, Bärenreiter, 2018).

336  CLASSICAL AND ROMANTIC PERFORMING PRACTICE

Violin Concerto, the dots under slurs in the wind and solo violin part in the second subject, however, clearly indicate *portato* (Ex. 6.60a–b). Ferdinand David marked the latter passage with lines under slurs in his performing edition (Ex. 6.60c).

Ex. 6.60 a–c. Mendelssohn: Violin Concerto op. 64. (*a*) iii; (*b*) i; (*c*) i.

Even singers could sometimes be expected to execute dots under a slur as sharply articulated notes rather than as *portato*. An interesting example of this can be found in Meyerbeer's *Les Huguenots*, where flute and oboe have a figure of repeated sixteenths, which is immediately answered by the solo soprano in inversion. Both figures are notated with dots and slurs, but Meyerbeer has indicated for the wind instruments "appuyez chaque note" (press each note), and for the voice "saccadé" (jerkily) (Ex. 6.61).

NOTATION OF ARTICULATION AND PHRASING   337

**Ex. 6.61**  Meyerbeer: *Les Huguenots*, no. 7, Andante cantabile ♩ = 69, 12/8.

While most writers before the middle of the 19th century seem to have been relatively unconcerned by the ambiguities of notating *portato*, slurred *staccato*, and slurred *spiccato*, the French violinist Baillot attempted greater precision. For a succession of notes played in a single rebounding bowstroke—a type of bowing discouraged by most German authorities at that time—he proposed strokes or wedges under a slur. He also observed that since dots under a slur could mean both a very smooth *portato* (which he called *ondulation*) and *staccato* (or *détaché articulé*), two other different notations should be used. For *portato* he proposed a sign rather similar to the 18th-century wavy line, confining dots under a slur to the *staccato*. But rather confusingly, he also repeated Adam's formula for the rendition of dots under a slur, and it is not entirely clear from Baillot's account whether he regarded *ondulation* and *portato* as synonymous or significantly different.[142]

Later in the century, with the increasingly widespread concern for notational precision, theorists and composers began to use an augmented range of markings, and some string-playing performer-composers and editors included instructions for signs in their editions. Ferdinand David gave a particularly detailed one in his *Dur und Moll* op. 39 (Ex. 6.62).

Ex. 6.62  Ferdinand David: *Dur und Moll*, op. 39 (Leipzig, Breitkopf & Härtel, [1861]), 4.

| Erklärung der Zeichen. | Explication des Signes. |
|---|---|
| ⊓ Herunterstrich. | ⊓ tirez ⎫ l'archet. |
| V Hinaufstrich. | V poussez ⎭ |
| – liegender ⎫ | – l'archet sur la corde. |
| ' fest abgestossener ⎪ | ' martelé. |
| hpfd. (.) hüpfender ⎬ Strich. | hpfd. (.) sautillé. |
| spgd. (.) springender ⎭ | spgd. (.) sauté. |
| ↳ Mit der Spitze des Bogens aufschlagen. | ↳ frappez la corde de la pointe de l'archet. |
| M In der Mitte ⎫ | M du milieu ⎫ |
| Sp An der Spitze ⎬ des Bogens. | Sp de la pointe ⎬ de l'archet. |
| Fr Am Frosche ⎭ | Fr au talon ⎭ |
| + Pizzicato mit der linken ⎫ Hand. | + pizzicato de la main gauche. |
| ♦   „    „    „  rechten ⎭ | ♦   „    „    „  droite. |
| tr o.N. Triller ohne Nachschlag. | tr o.N. trille sans cadence. |
| g.B. Mit dem ganzen Bogen. | g.B. De toute la longueur de l'archet. |
| ⁓ Behung. | ⁓ Ondulation. |
| ↳— den Finger liegen lassen. | ↳—n'ôtez pas le doigt. |
| ♩—Klang des Flageolettons. | ♩—effet du son harmonique. |
| —lose zu greifende Note. | — doigt effleurant la corde. |
| —fest zu greifende Note. | doigt appuyé. |

[142] Baillot: *L'art du violon*, 268–70.

Some even included a sign for audible sliding (*Rutschen*) (Ex. 6.63).

Ex. 6.63 Edmund Singer (ed.): Beethoven Violin Sonatas (Stuttgart, Cotta, 1887), Violin part, 2.

```
   V    Hinaufstrich.         DREI SONATEN              ,  Zeichen für
   ⌒    Herunterstrich.                                    eine kurze Pause.
   Fr.  Frosch  ⎫            für Pianoforte u. Violine   _  Gehalten.
   Sp.  Spitze  ⎬ des Bogens.           von              Iª  E- ⎫
   M.   Mitte   ⎭                                        IIª  A- ⎬ Saite.
   ⁀    Rutschen (gleiten).      L. VAN BEETHOVEN.       IIIª D- ⎪
 restez in der Lage bleiben.      F. A. Salieri gewidmet. IVª G- ⎭
                                    Op. 12. N.º 1.
```

Yet the association of dots under slurs with *staccato* was so deeply ingrained that even David did not consistently adopt his own criteria for distinguishing between slurred *staccato* and slurred *spiccato* in his numerous editions. Other authors who were undoubtedly influenced by David's theoretical notation of articulation marks, such as Hermann Schröder,[143] followed all his distinctions except the one between slurred *staccato* and *spiccato*. In a further example of inconsistency, David often used lines under slurs for *portato* in his editions but sometimes also retained dots under slurs where *portato* seems to have been intended by the composer. In this case, it is possible that some of David's apparent lack of consistency arose from the fact that he failed to recognize the composer's intention. In his edition of Beethoven's Violin Sonatas, for example, he sometimes used his line-under-slur notation, sometimes retained Beethoven's dots under slurs, and sometimes mixed editorial slurred *staccato* with Beethoven's original *portato* notation.

The horizontal line under a slur to indicate *portato* was adopted by many composers during the second half of the 19th century, including Wagner, Dvořák, and Bruch. Brahms, however, resisted this notation even after his correspondence with Joachim on the subject, and continued to use dots under a slur solely as an indication for *portato*, although he relented somewhat in at least a few late works, retaining his dots under slurs in the score, but permitting them to be replaced by lines in the separate string parts.

Other signs used in conjunction with slurs, such as >>>> and ^^^^, or simply a slur without articulation marks used over notes repeated at the same pitch, were also employed with increasing frequency by many composers during the second half of the century in a search for ever more

---

[143] Schröder: *Die Kunst des Violinspiels* (Cologne, 1887).

precise definition of the type of articulation required. Specific knowledge of a particular composer's background and practice may help to interpret the implications of these markings in individual cases, but even in the later 19th century, inconsistencies abound, and it often remains unclear what composers expected their markings to convey to the performer.

# 7
# Articulation and String Bowing

String instrument bowing techniques and practices are important not only for understanding string playing in its historical context, but also for their relationship with changing attitudes towards articulation and phrasing in general, and are therefore relevant also for performing practices on other instruments. Descriptions of the physical mechanisms required for executing various types of bowing allow a clearer notion of the aural effects they were expected to achieve than is possible with most aspects of keyboard playing, wind playing, or singing. Of course, matching these aural effects to the musical notation of individual composers or schools of performance is more speculative. What is absolutely clear, though, is that bowing techniques, the types of articulation they were able to produce, and the ways in which these have been employed in musical compositions changed radically over the past three centuries and have continued to do so even within living memory. This chapter explores the extent to which changing practices can be reconstructed and offers evidence that may encourage a more historically aware employment of the bow in Classical and Romantic repertoire.

The string player's ability to emulate vocal sounds and practices remained central throughout this period, but virtuosos often sought to develop specifically instrumental effects that went beyond the normal limitations of the human voice. Some of these remained largely confined to virtuoso repertoire, but others became common currency, and composers gradually found a use for them in chamber and orchestral music. As newer practices were disseminated, of course, many performers began to employ them in older repertoire where different types of bowstroke would previously have been used. Awareness of the techniques that were employed at particular times and in particular contexts, therefore, offers a key to understanding composers' stylistic and acoustic expectations.

Major developments in bow design took place during the early part of this period, in response to developments in style and technique (Ex. 7.1). New designs of bow may also, in turn, have prompted experimentation with techniques and types or articulation that would have been less effective with earlier models.

Even after Tourte-style bows became standard during the 19th century, bowing technique continued to change, as did the contexts in which different styles of bowstroke were utilized. By the last quarter of the 19th century, mastery of every type of bowstroke was widely seen as a requirement of professional string playing. This was fostered through the production of study material, and teaching in an expanding network of conservatoires; but even at the end of the 19th century there remained substantial differences between national and regional traditions and individuals. In the 20th century, changing aesthetics led to the marginalization of some bowstrokes and bowing practices that were previously regarded as fundamental, and a progressive normalization of practice internationally. Even the development of the Early Music movement in the 1960s and 1970s scarcely changed this situation, because the bowing practices of most of its practitioners (even with historical bows) were shaped primarily by their modern training. The expansion of period instrument performance into Classical and Romantic orchestral repertoire during the 1980s and 1990s involved the recruitment of many mainstream string players, whose principal concession to historical practice was the use of gut strings. Even into the third decade of the 21st century, many period instrument players have retained the use of shoulder and chin rests and a largely unchanged modern bowing style.

Ex. 7.1 Woldemar: *Grande méthode* (Paris, [c. 1800]) 3. The types of bow that "were in use successively since the origin of the violin" (qui ont été successivement en usage depuis l'origine du Violon). In his *Méthode de Violon par L. Mozart [. . .] redigée par Woldemar*, No. 3 is identified as "Bow of Frantzl senior [Ignaz Fränzl] and Cramer" (Archet par Frantzl pére [*sic*] et Cramer).

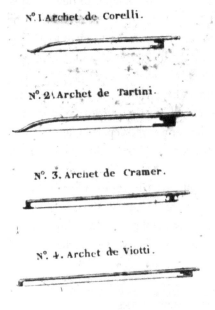

A notable manifestation of the 20th-century style change was the substitution of "thrown" bowstrokes,[1] especially in the lower third of the bow, for *détaché* (in the middle and upper half) or *martelé* (executed near the point).[2] *Martelé*, cultivated since the late 18th century, virtually disappeared from the string player's repertory of bowstrokes during the second half of the 20th century. In the early 1980s, Max Rostal, writing about the performance of Beethoven's Violin Sonatas, noted that its use was "becoming less and less fashionable".[3] A significant factor in these changes was the 20th-century reliance on notation, rather than tradition, in the interpretation of historical repertoire, and the concomitant attribution of specific meanings to particular signs and symbols; *staccato* marks, which had many different implications in previous centuries, became increasingly associated with a single notational meaning—a marked shortening of the note—and often an off-string bowstroke.[4] This historically untenable assumption was manifest, for instance, in Minos Dounias's (1900–1962) advice on performing Mozart's *staccato* marks. Accepting the ill-advised editorial policy of the *Neue Mozart Ausgabe* that Mozart's variously written *staccato* marks should be divided into two categories: strokes (often referred to as wedges) and dots, he referred to instructions in Leopold Mozart's *Versuch*: "Assuming that, for the staccato wedge, the son also requires a short on-the-string stroke, we can presume, for the staccato dot, regardless of whether in *p* or *f*, a more or less elastic, springing bowstroke, which we definitely cannot dispense with in performing Mozart's string music."[5] The interpretation of Mozart's *staccato* marks according to the editor's aesthetic preferences is striking; at no point did Dounias, or apparently any of his contemporaries, question whether this kind of elastic bowstroke was something that Mozart would have known and expected. His advice simply reflected the practice of his own time.[6]

---

[1] See below for Carl Flesch's teaching in this respect.

[2] The widespread use of French terminology reflects the powerful influence of Franco-Belgian traditions of string playing.

[3] Max Rostal: *Beethoven: The Sonatas for Piano and Violin. Thoughts on Their Interpretation* (London, 1985), 137; trans. Anna M. Rosenberg and Horace D. Rosenberg from *Beethoven. Die Sonaten für Klavier und Violine* (München, 1981). Rostal entirely ignored on-string *détaché* in *staccato* passages, frequently recommending *spiccato*, but he still sometimes favoured *martelé* for such passages.

[4] See Ch. 6, "Dots and Strokes as Articulation Marks".

[5] Minos Dounias, ed.: Kirchensonaten, *Neue Mozart Ausgabe*, VI: 16, (1958), ix.

[6] Dounias was a pupil of Andreas Moser, whose endorsement of the appropriateness of springing bowstrokes in Classical repertoire is clearly articulated in volume 3 of the Joachim and Moser *Violinschule*, undoubtedly reflecting the views of his co-author. Moser was well aware, however, that the widespread use of these bowstrokes was a 19th-century development.

Since then, even the choice between a short on-string stroke and a springing stroke has shifted in favour of the latter.

At the time of Dounias's birth, musicians still recognized that the use of springing or thrown bowstrokes in Classical repertoire was a stylistic choice rather than an historically accurate reflection of the composer's expectations. Reinhold Jockish put this very clearly:

> It ought not always to be seen as a sin against the Holy Ghost if occasionally, even in the works of our Classical masters, at the appropriate place, one sometimes introduces a more modern bowing, especially when one is convinced that this will be more likely to fulfil the composer's intentions than his violin-playing contemporaries could have done. In an example from Mozart, it was already demonstrated how, where light grace and sparkling humour predominate in his works, the springing stroke [*Saltatostrich*], which admittedly was not yet known at this master's time, is nevertheless really good to use, indeed according to our present-day taste, is absolutely indispensable.

More specifically, Jockisch added that for a passage in the Finale of Mozart's D minor String Quartet there was "certainly no more appropriate style of bowing than the light, thrown staccato at the frog".[7] A couple of decades earlier, Hermann Schröder had described the springing stroke as "now an indispensable bowing style for every violinist, especially those who have been formed by the newer French school. In the old Italian and particularly in the German school up to L. Spohr, it was less used. On the whole, one played passages suited to these bowstrokes with short, on-string bowing at the point."[8]

## The Action of the Bow Arm

Written descriptions of bowstrokes can be appreciated only in relation to the physical means by which they were executed; posture and the action of

---

[7] Reinhold Jockisch: *Katechismus der Violine und des Violinspiels* (Leipzig, 1900), 141.
[8] Schröder: *Die Kunst des Violinspiels* (Köln, 1887), 72.

joints and muscles, therefore, are a fundamental starting point for understanding the sounds bowstrokes produce. The early 20th century saw major changes in the physical handling of the bow. Friedrich Adolf Steinhausen (1859–1910), a physician and amateur violinist, made considerable impact with his 1903 publication on the physiology of bowing,[9] which went through many editions in the 20th century. Steinhausen's thesis that previous approaches to bowing were based on a fallacious understanding of anatomy was a catalyst for individual teachers to seek what they believed to be new, more physically efficient and effective ways of bowing (though these were not necessarily in conformity with Steinhausen's conclusions). Among the motivations for change may have been a search for greater tonal projection, although whether this was achieved by the physical changes is questionable. Any increases in dynamic potential are probably attributable more to the adoption of synthetic strings, especially the violin's steel E, than to bowing technique.

A few late-19th-century sources, and many early-20th-century ones, provide instructions for the functioning of the bow arm that would have been regarded by earlier pedagogues as seriously faulty. The scroll began to be angled more towards the left (sometimes substantially) and the right upper arm pushed forwards and raised, so that it was held well away from the side of the body, at both the frog and point.[10] In cello playing, the typical upright position of the instrument, which was retained for a while even after the widespread adoption of the end-pin, gave way to a variety of different positions, typically with the scroll of the instrument angled much more sharply towards the player, and the right arm held further from the body. String players began increasingly to bow from the shoulder rather than with the combined action of elbow, wrist, and fingers.

Carl Flesch became the most influential advocate of a fundamentally different bowing technique. He acknowledged that "Steinhausen was the first theoretician who recognized that the sources of strength

---

[9] Steinhausen: *Die Physiologie der Bogenführung auf den Streichinstrumenten* (Leipzig, 1903).
[10] The 19th-century position of the right arm and the angle of the violin was established only towards the end of the 18th century, but this change did not affect the closeness of the right upper arm to the body.

were situated in the upper and lower arm, and who assigned a merely mediatory role to the hitherto immoderately over-estimated wrist and fingers."[11] Flesch stated that the power of the bowstroke derives from "the lower arm, the upper arm and muscles of the back", and that "The transfer of strength occurs most naturally when the elbow part lies *above* rather than *below* the level of the fingers."[12] This was a radical repudiation of previous injunctions that the elbow should never be higher than the wrist.[13] Pre-20th-century cello bowing was characterized by "a raised wrist, a lowered right elbow and a virtually inactive upper arm";[14] but by 1913, Emil Krall could stress that cello bowing required the "*swing* of the whole arm as a unity" and observed that "the smallest movement can only become perfect by this swing" that "must be executed with the whole arm from the shoulder."[15]

Flesch's 1923 *Die Kunst des Violinspiels* contains many photographs, including several that depict "faulty" positions, which correspond closely with illustrations of "correct" positions in pre-20th-century sources, such as Baillot's carefully drawn images (1835), which were reproduced precisely, apart from different clothes and hair styles, by Habeneck (1842), Alard (1844), and Bériot (1858), or those of Spohr (1833) and David (1863). Many 19th- and early-20th-century photographs of violinists in playing positions confirm the accuracy of these drawings. Comparison of these images with Flesch's "faulty" and "correct" positions is instructive. Ex. 7.2a–e compares Flesch's "correct" position of the upper arm in the middle of the bow (c. 45° from the horizontal) with 19th-century violinists' lower elbow (c. 62° for Auer and Baillot). The position of the violin in Flesch's photograph is also significantly further to the left.

---

[11] Flesch: *Die Kunst* (1929), i, 38. Rev. English edn 1939, i, 54.
[12] Flesch: *Die Kunst* (1929), i, 38. Rev. English edn 1939, i, 54.
[13] See below.
[14] George Kennaway: *Playing the Cello, 1780–1930* (Farnham, 2014), 96.
[15] Emil Krall: *The Art of Tone-Production on the Violoncello* (London, 1913), 18.

Ex. 7.2 a–e. In the middle of the bow. (*a*) Carl Flesch (1873–1944): *Die Kunst des Violinspiels* (Berlin, 1923) (the violinist is not Flesch); (*b*) Leopold Auer (1845–1930): *Graded Course of Violin Playing* (New York, 1925); (*c*) Heinrich Dessauer (1863–1917), 1892; (*d*) Heinrich Wilhelm Ernst (1812–1865) photograph ca. 1850; (*e*) Pierre Baillot: *L'art du violon* (Paris, [1835]).

348  CLASSICAL AND ROMANTIC PERFORMING PRACTICE

The contrast is much greater at the extremities of the bow, as shown in Exx. 7.3a–f and 7.4a–f.

**Ex. 7.3** a–f. At the frog of the bow. (*a*) Flesch "correct"; (*b*) Flesch "faulty"; (*c*) Mathieu Crickboom (1871–1947); (*d*) Auer; (*e*) Dessauer; (*f*) Baillot.

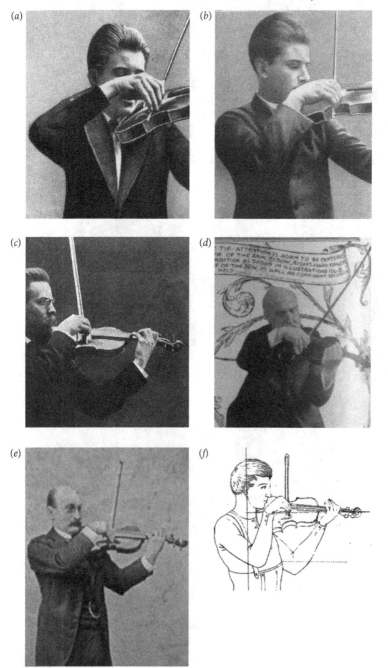

ARTICULATION AND STRING BOWING 349

Ex. 7.4 a–f. At the point of the bow. (*a*) Flesch "correct"; (*b*) Flesch "faulty"; (*c*) Auer; (*d*) Crickboom; (*e*) Dessauer; (*f*) Baillot.

350  CLASSICAL AND ROMANTIC PERFORMING PRACTICE

The high right elbow in Flesch's "correct" positions (Exx. 7.3a and 7.4a) corresponds rather closely with illustrations of "faulty" positions in Leopold Mozart's and Charles de Bériot's treatises (Ex. 7.5a–b), while his "faulty" ones resemble the "correct" ones of the 19th-century violinists.[16]

Ex. 7.5  a–b. Pre-20th-century faulty positions. (*a*) Leopold Mozart: *Versuch*, Fig. III (facing p. 54); (*b*) Charles de Bériot: *Méthode* i, 5 (Fig. 8).

The images are of course affected by the string on which the bow is positioned. An image from Henry Holmes's revised English edition of Spohr's *Violinschule*[17] shows the position of the arm at the point of the bow on all four strings (Ex. 7.6).

---

[16] It is noteworthy, however, that the right arm position of Auer's most prominent pupils, among them Efrem Zimbalist and Jascha Heifetz, resembles the one described by Flesch, while their use of continuous vibrato also violates Auer's vehemently expressed aesthetic (see Ch. 16). For bowing, see for instance the 1926 film of Efrem Zimbalist and Harold Bauer performing the second movement of Beethoven's "Kreutzer" Sonata, https://www.youtube.com/watch?v=wecNrRUZ1yE.

[17] Spohr: *Violin School Revised and Edited with Additional Text by Henry Holmes* (London, 1876).

Ex. 7.6 Spohr, trans. and ed. Henry Holmes: *Violin School* (London, 1878).

With typical 20th-century modernist confidence in the superiority of his own aesthetics and practices over those of the past, Flesch concluded: "It seems as though in the eighteenth century some evil sorcerer had banned the upper arm with a curse destined to endure until the seventh generation: 'Thou shalt not function'".[18] He seems not to have been able to conceive that his distinguished predecessors might have avoided the practices he advocated, not out of ignorance but out of experience and choice.

## The Right Arm in 18th- and 19th-Century Teaching

The passivity of the upper arm and shoulder, and the error of raising the right elbow, was repeatedly insist on in pre-20th-century treatises. Leopold Mozart's injunction was clear: "One must watch the right arm from the shoulder at all times: so that the elbow does not come up too high when

---

[18] Flesch: *Die Kunst*, 39; Rev. English edn, 55.

bowing; but is always held somewhat close to the body."[19] L'abbé le fils instructed: "The forearm only should move, following the wrist in all its operations; the arm as a whole, should only participate in cases where the bow is used from one end to the other."[20] Johann Samuel Petri in 1782, encouraging violinists to keep their chin over the left, not the right of the tailpiece, similarly observed: "The right arm and elbow do not need to be raised upwards to guide the bow, for in this free, natural, and unconstrained position, the flexibility necessary for a light and agile stroke is also preserved."[21] Galeazzi in 1791 was forthright:

> The arm that holds the bow may be allowed to move up or down, but any backwards or forwards movement with the upper arm is completely forbidden, so that the elbow joint must be almost jointless, and must bend easily, since it alone must do all the work, without communicating any movement to the upper part of the arm.[22]

He insisted that if anyone had acquired this fault they should practice against a wall or some other fixed object until they eliminated it. Campagnoli's solution for keeping the student's arm close to the body was a cord attaching the upper-arm to his coat button (Ex. 7.7). His downwards-slanting violin, with the upper left arm resting on the chest, recalls Löhlein's justification of this posture in 1774 "so that in bowing the right elbow remains in its natural position; for if one held it too high one would have to raise the arm with which one bows too high, which is very tiring and causes a forced position and stiff bowstroke".[23]

---

[19] Mozart: *Versuch*, 54.
[20] L'abbé le fils [Joseph-Barnabé Saint-Sevin]: *Principes du violon* (Paris, 1761), 1.
[21] Petri: *Anleitung*, 385.
[22] Galeazzi: *Elementi* (1791), i, 97f.
[23] Löhlein: *Anweisung*, 20.

**Ex. 7.7** Campagnoli: *Nouvelle Méthode* Plate 1.

Spohr, who condemned resting the left arm against the chest, observed like many other violinists and cellists that much string crossing could be achieved simply by movement of the hand. He explained that when crossing between the E to A strings "the elbow can remain unmoving in its position", that on the D string the elbow is "raised a little", and on the G "still more", but that it "must only be raised as much as is absolutely necessary in order to reach the low strings".[24] Baillot was more emphatic:

> Playing with the arm (i.e., with the upper arm and shoulder) is one of the greatest faults one can have. It is necessary constantly to avoid it. When one plays on the low strings, the wrist rises to reach them and the forearm only follows, and this movement is almost imperceptible when one passes quickly from one string to another, as in these passages. [Ex. 7.8][25]

---

[24] Spohr: *Violinschule*, 27.
[25] Baillot: *L'art du violon*, 14.

His music example makes it very clear how different his expectations were from those of the 20th century.

Ex. 7.8 Baillot: *L'art*, 14.

Similar admonitions continued in later Franco-Belgian practice, with Habeneck instructing: "The joints of the wrist and elbow alone must act [...] communicating nothing of their movement to the upper arm or shoulder. This rule is very difficult to observe in the action of changing strings, but it is extremely important never to depart from it."[26] And Bériot: "when the bow is at the point, the elbow may be at wrist level, but never higher than it".[27] He referred the reader to his illustration of a faulty posture (Ex. 7.5b).

Similar directions were given for cellists. Raoul instructed: "The forearm leads the wrist: but it should only lead it and follow it in all its movements. The upper arm should hardly move. This is what must be carefully avoided. As soon as one plays with the arm, one no longer has that beautiful development of the bow, that clearness of sound, that elegance, which is the charm of the execution."[28] Schetky remarked succinctly: "The arm from the Shoulder to the Elbow should move as little as possible. The wrist should act freely and be rather supple."[29] One of the most detailed accounts is provided by Jean-Louis Duport, who gave the following instructions:

> 1) the motion of the fore-arm must almost exclusively be responsible for pushing and pulling the bow throughout its whole length; the upper arm must remain in the same position, except as the wrist approaches the bridge, when the arm makes a small movement to complete the up-bow: the same thing takes place in down-bow, as the forearm extends fully to draw the bow to its point. 2) One must take care to open the elbow well, so that the

---

[26] Habeneck: *Méthode*, 32.
[27] Bériot: *Méthode*, i, 4.
[28] Jean Marie Raoul: *Méthode de Violoncelle* op. 4 (Paris, [1797]), 5.
[29] Johann Georg Christoph Schetky: *Practical and Progressive Lessons for the Violoncello* (London [1813]), 2.

arm may be almost straight when the bow arrives at its point, and not to pull back the upper arm, which makes all the bow's movements heavy, difficult, and constrained; this is known as playing from the shoulder; if, unfortunate, one contracts this habit, it is only the shoulder and very slightly the wrist that acts; the movement of the elbow is eliminated, the smallest things become difficult and very tiring.[30]

Kummer, like Galeazzi and Campagnoli, proposed a physical constraint for the upper arm, instructing that, in crossings between adjacent strings, the wrist joint "must always be the object of the violoncellist's greatest attention, since all turns of the bow should be executed only by means of this joint, without moving the upper arm. In order to acquire this skill, the pupil should study the following examples with all diligence and, when studying them, prevent the right upper arm from moving by leaning it against a table or cabinet."[31]

It is with these physical parameters in mind that the character and execution of the bowstrokes alluded to in 18th- and 19th-century treatises must be understood. Historically plausible bowing is crucial for performers who genuinely want to understand the types of articulation employed by Classical and Romantic string players, and the characteristics of their expressive language. What cannot be achieved with minimal movement of the upper arm will certainly not represent the mainstream practice of the 18th and 19th centuries, nor the sound and style that composers thought they were conveying through their notation. It may also be worthwhile to consider whether, as Flesch believed, the right-arm practices developed in the early 20th century, which are the basis of modern training, resulted in genuine physiological and technical benefits.

## Mid-18th-Century Bowstrokes

These are not documented in sufficient detail to allow more than a fragmentary understanding of their diversity. There was undoubtedly a substantial difference between virtuosos, who sought to impress or even astonish their listeners by their individuality, and the average professional string players

---

[30] Jean-Louis Duport: *Essai sur le doigté du violoncell, et sur la conduite de l'archet* (Paris, [1806]), 159.
[31] Friedrich August Kummer: *Violoncell-Schule für den ersten Unterricht, op. 60* (Leipzig, [1839]), 12.

who formed the bulk of established musical organizations, either as orchestral or chamber musicians. Localized traditions also differed. In the 1750s, for instance, Quantz commented that Italian violinists generally cultivated a more *legato* approach than French and German ones.[32] In view of the consensus about right-arm function, however, it is clear that any succession of shorter notes was normally played in the upper half of the bow. Mid-18th-century sources indicate that successive short notes were predominantly executed about halfway between the middle and point, with shorter or longer strokes, depending on tempo and context. In 1738, Corrette instructed that "To draw the sound from the violin it is necessary to make down- and up-bows with broad strokes of the bow, but in a gracious and agreeable manner. The eighths and sixteenths are played at the tip of the bow. H. J. [Ex. 7.9]."[33] At around the same time, Robert Crome cautioned "take care you don't let your Bow Hand come too near the Fiddle, but rather play with the small end of the Bow, unless it be to lengthen out a long Note".[34]

**Ex. 7.9**  Michel Corrette: *L'École d'Orphée*, 7. The letters A to G in his illustration are connected with the Italian and French bow holds; H to J indicates the place where shorter notes should be played.

[32] See Ch. 5.
[33] Michel Corrette: *L'École d'Orphée, méthode pour apprendre facilement à jouer du violon dans le goût françois et italien avec des principes de musique et beaucoup de leçons* op. 18 (Paris, 1738), 7f. See also p. 34, where he gives further information about bowstrokes.
[34] Robert Crome: *The Fiddle, New Modell'd* (London, [c. 1750]), 34f.

All faster notes were clearly played without raising the bow from the string. Quantz instructed that for a succession of eighth-notes at a tempo of quarter-note = 120, the bow should remained on the string between strokes, while at slower speeds it might be lifted for the sake of articulation, explaining:

> It was said above that the bow must be somewhat raised from the string for notes which have a little stroke over them. I mean this to be so only in the case of notes where there is sufficient time. Thus, in allegro the eighths and in allegretto the sixteenths are excepted from this if many follow one another: for these must certainly be played with a very short bowstroke, but the bow will never be lifted or separated from the string. For if one wanted always to lift the bow as far as is required for the so-called *Absetzen*, there would not be enough time remaining to return it again at the right time, and notes of this sort would sound as if they were hacked or whipped.[35]

Two decades later, J. F. Reichardt, who had just been appointed Kapellmeister in Berlin, succinctly categorized the part and extent of the bow that he recommended for different lengths of notes in his 1776 instructions for orchestral players:

> First long notes, and for these observe equal strength throughout the whole of the bow [Ex. 7.10a], then faster notes, for which one makes a stroke quickly through the whole bow [Ex. 7.10b]; then others, for which one only uses half the bow, from the middle to the point [Ex. 7.10c], and then those that one detaches with the top quarter of the bow. It is best if one takes triplets for these separate bowstrokes to acquire equality in up- and down-bows [Ex. 7.10d].[36]

Ex. 7.10 a–d. Reichardt: *Ueber die Pflichten*, 9f.

(a)

---

[35] Quantz: *Versuch*, 201.
[36] Reichardt: *Ueber die Pflichten*, 9f.

Ex. 7.10 Continued

(b)

(c)

(d)

Reichard also gave clear instructions for the execution of two *staccato* up-bows in succession:

> Then one becomes more accustomed to bowing more than one staccato note on an up-bow—this stroke is indispensable for quick notes that are not to be played sharply but lightly—so one first takes three notes, of which one is bowed down and two up. For this bowstroke, however, one must use little bow, at most an eighth of the whole length of the bow, and that in the region of the third quarter of the bow counted from the hand. [Ex. 7.11][37]

---

[37] Reichardt: *Ueber die Pflichten*, 16f.

Ex. 7.11 Reichardt: *Ueber die Pflichten.*

A few years later, Petri advised how a pupil should be taught good bowing: "One should not let him come too near the middle of the bow, but accustom him only to begin the main notes with a full downbow stroke; to execute the others, however, especially the shorter notes, with the point of the bow (though not all at the extreme end)."[38]

For dotted figures, Reichardt apparently expected a separate bowstroke for each note; but taking the short note in the same bowstroke as the dotted note had been suggested much earlier.[39] Löhlein, having recommended overdotting, observed: "There are only a few violin players who know how to play these kinds of notes well. One can try it out, and first give each note a separate bowstroke, then take them two by two with a long bowstroke, and choose the best way. I, for my part, stick to this last way."[40]

Few authors provide this kind of specific information. Even Leopold Mozart's much fuller discussion of bowing is confined to the dynamic nuancing of long notes and the presentation of various patterns of slurred and separate notes, including the execution of several or many separated notes in a single bowstroke. He gives no clear indication of where in the bow and with what extent of bow the detached notes are to be executed, presumably regarding it as obvious. Joseph Riepel's 1757 treatise goes a step further in identifying a range of different types of bowstrokes for detached notes, either separately or within a slur.[41] Other treatises provide some hints about differing bow management for detached notes, sometimes with separate bows and sometimes under slurs, but it is only possible to speculate how skilled 18th-century string players in different regions and traditions might have responded to the notation of their time.

---

[38] Petri: *Anleitung zur praktischen Musik*, 2nd edn (Leipzig, 1782), 397. The section on violin playing is absent from the first edition of 1767.
[39] E.g., by Corrette (*L'école*, 34) and by Leopold Mozart on several occasions.
[40] Löhlein: *Anweisung*, 84f.
[41] See Exx. 6.14 and 6.43.

Treatises can be misleading as well as informative. Reichardt, for instance, gives much information about how specific patterns of bowing and their concomitant markings should be executed, but his instructions, especially about the significance of *staccato* symbols, are essentially an attempt to standardize inconsistent practice, at least for his Berlin musicians, rather than a reliable reflection of widespread practice. Context, often combined with localized practice, was more important than the notation. Many 18th-century composers failed even to mark unequivocally whether notes should be slurred or detached.[42] Reichardt was clear, however, that "The different character of the pieces also requires different bowstrokes. Thus, the bowstroke in Adagio is very different from that in Allegro, and differs mainly in that it rests more on the strings than that in Allegro." He characterized them as follows:

> In Adagio, nothing but a rest must bring the bow completely off the strings.
> 
> Even in the case of notes that are marked with a stroke (|) for staccato, even for *Abzugs*, it does not have to come completely off the strings in Adagio, but must at least remain resting on them with an eighth of the hair.
> 
> If, however, in a completely contrasting passage, some notes in the Adagio are to be played with a rather sharp staccato, the composer ought really to indicate this with a special sign, or with a word, e.g. furioso (violently) or adirato (angrily).
> 
> In Andante, the bow must have the lightness of the Allegro bow, without its sharpness, and in the *Abzugs* without its speed. In Andante, the above-mentioned bowing, where two notes are given short staccato up-bows, has a very good effect [see Ex. 7.11].
> 
> The same is true for Allegretto: but here, the bow already has a little more liveliness and sometimes also a little sharpness.
> 
> In Allegro, however, the sharpness of the bowstroke on the staccato notes and rapidity in the *Abzugs* is highly necessary.
> 
> Intensified terms, such as Allegro di molto, Allegro assai, Presto[,] Prestissimo, only affect the tempo and change nothing in the character of the bowstroke. For this, a qualification must be added to the term, to determine the character of the piece. Allegro e con brio, Allegro e con spirito, con fuoco, resoluto, etc.

---

[42] See Ch. 6.

> In the same way, terms that reduce the speed of the Allegro, such as Allegro ma non troppo, non tanto, moderato, etc., make no difference to the character of the bowstroke, but only to the tempo. If, however, *cantabile*, *dolce*, or any other designation is used to define the character of the piece more closely, this refers to the bowstroke, which must be gentler and more connected.
>
> In the same way, in slow movements, the terms maestoso, affettuoso, mesto, grave indicate that the longer bowstrokes should have a stronger, more audible accent, and then the notes before the rests must not be cut short, but only gradually fade away.[43]

In addition to these instructions, Reichardt also asserted that in playing three- and four-note chords "every individual chord must be executed down-bow".[44] He referred the reader to Leopold Mozart and Quantz for further information but warned against Quantz's recommendations for frequently retaking down-bows in other circumstances, since "I consider it the violinist's first duty to be able to give equal importance to the up- and down-bows." And he also objected to Quantz's recommendations for heavy metric accents.[45]

Taking account of the constraints imposed on the upper arm and shoulder, Reichardt's detached bowstrokes are executed in the middle or upper third of the bow, with flexible wrist and fingers. The only exceptions he mentions are long notes, chords, and some short notes followed by rests. As with all verbal descriptions of musical effects, however, his instructions provide limited information about the execution of the bowstrokes, and how, in specific instances, a string player might recognize that one or other distinctive use of the bow was expected. A little more insight is provided by performance instructions in music of the period, but their aural implications are often elusive.

The two most common Italian terms for separate bowstrokes are *sciolto* and *staccato*, which some composers certainly used with distinctly different meanings. During the 18th century, and with diminishing frequency into the early 19th century, it was commonly assumed that groups of the fastest note values in a piece would be slurred unless otherwise indicated, and also that

---

[43] Reichardt: *Ueber die Pflichten*, 25–27.
[44] Reichardt: *Ueber die Pflichten*, 12.
[45] Reichardt: *Ueber die Pflichten*, 28.

particular patterns of notes would be slurred. To prevent this, a composer might write articulation marks and/or *sciolto/sciolte*, or *staccato*.[46] The word *staccato*, on the other hand, seems often to have a meaning beyond the employment of articulation marks.[47] The implication of a sharper attack, and perhaps greater shortening of the notes, is evidently intended by Piccinni, in a passage where unmarked eighths and sixteenths were probably expected to be slurred (Ex. 7.12).

**Ex. 7.12** Piccinni: *Alessandro nell'Indie* (1758 version) autograph. Act I, p. 32v.

Some impression of the range of bowing effects that would have been expected from accomplished performers in the second half of the 18th century can be gained from remarkably detailed instructions in operas by Davide Perez (who was also an accomplished violinist), especially *L'isola disabitata* and *Solimano*. In the former he specifies *Arcatte lunghe, Ligato l'arco* (oddly combined with dots, perhaps indicating a well-connected *portato* execution), *ondeggiando l'arco, arco fermo*, and *arco batutto* [sic] (Ex. 7.13a–e). In *Solimano*: *Spiegando l'arco la voce ferma, strappando l'arco, levando l'arco* and *stac. molto* (combined with *con forza spiccate le sillabe* in the vocal part), *in arco spazioso* and *stac. molto* (Ex. 7.13f–m).

---

[46] See Ch. 5, pp. 241–51.
[47] See Ch. 6, pp. 290–93.

ARTICULATION AND STRING BOWING 363

**Ex. 7.13a** Perez: *L'isola disabitata* Act I, overture p. 2r. *Arcatte lunghe* ("Long bows": probably a warning to hold the notes for their full length).

**Ex. 7.13b** Scene ix: Allegro A major p. 135v. *ligato l'arco* ("Connect the bow": probably an instruction to detach but not shorten the notes).

**Ex. 7.13c** Scene xi: Andantino ma con la voce, $\frac{6}{8}$ G major p. 157r. *ondeggiando l'arco* ("Undulate the bow").

364  CLASSICAL AND ROMANTIC PERFORMING PRACTICE

Ex. 7.13d  Scene xi: Poco piu andante $\frac{3}{8}$, 168r. *arco fermo* ("Firm bow").

Ex. 7.13e  Scene xii: Sul cantabile espressivo, E flat, 179r. *arco batutto* ("Beaten or perhaps hammered bow": probably an instruction to use short, sharp *staccato* [? *martelé*]).

**Ex. 7.13f** Perez: *Solimano* Act I, Scene v: Allegro spiegato e maestoso C major, C, 50v. *spiegando l'arco la voce ferma* ("spiegato" is probably related to the modern Italian word "piegato" suggesting to "spread out", therefore an expansive *Allegro*. In the context of double stopping the term is perhaps an instruction to sustain the notes and keep both "voices" firm).

**Ex. 7.13g** Act I, Scene vii: Agitato ne affetuoso 2 flats (g minor) in C. p. 69r *strappando l'arco* ("Tearing or ripping with the bow").

**Ex. 7.13h** Act I, Scene vii: Agitato nel affetuoso, G minor, 73r. *stac. levando l'arco*; *stac. molto* in the bass, where there are dots instead of rests ("*staccato*, lift the bow", in the bass "very *staccato*": the players are instructed to lift the bow clear of the string between the notes.)

**Ex. 7.13i** Act I, Scene vii: Agitato nel affetuoso, G minor, 73v. *à 2. in arco spazioso* ("in pairs with a spacious bow": presumably an instruction to play slurred pairs *f–p* with a well-extended bowstroke).

**Ex. 7.13j** Act I, Scene x: Allegro teatrate, D major, p. 92r. *a punta d'arco* ("at the point of the bow").

**Ex. 7.13k** Act I, Scene x: Allegro teatrate, D major, p. 95r. *puntando l'arco / à puntarle* (*puntando l'arco* suggests a short, sharp bowstroke; *à puntarle* refers to the notes being played *puntando*. The instruction for the oboes: *un fiato se potrà* means "one breath if possible").

**Ex. 7.13l** Act III, Scene i: Lento e sotto voce molto, C major, 2v. *smorzando l'arco* ("let the bowstroke die away").

**Ex. 7.13m** Act III, Scene i: Lento e sotto voce molto, 2v. *ferma ligando si passa l'arcatta* ("connect smoothly if changing bow").

Most of Perez's instructions are unusual, but the instruction *punta d'arco* (sometimes *punto d'arco* in German sources) was quite widely used between 1750 and the 1830s. Generally, the shorter and more delicate the stroke, the nearer the point of the bow; thus Kirnberger, referring to the performance of pieces in $\frac{6}{16}$ time, observed: "On the violin, pieces in this and other similar light time signatures are played only with the point of the bow, whereas in the heavier time signatures a longer stroke and more pressure of the bow is required."[48] Many 18th-century Italian composers and a few Germans included this instruction in their scores, apparently to obtain a lighter stroke than the ordinary detached stroke in the upper half, which might otherwise have been employed. Other examples from between 1760 and 1830 can be seen in Ex. 7.14a–h.

**Ex. 7.14a** Piccinni: *La Ceccina, ossia La buona figliuola* (1760).

**Ex. 7.14b** Cimarosa: *L'amante combattuto dalle donne di punto* (autograph, 1781). Act 2/3 p. 163r. In this example he also uses *sciolte*, evidently to warn against slurring the shorter notes.
[Andante con moto]

---

[48] Kirnberger: *Die Kunst des reinen Satzes*, ii, 120.

**Ex. 7.14c** Rossini: L'*Italiana in Algeri* (1813).

**Ex. 7.14d** Meyerbeer: *Il crociato in Egitto* (1824).

**Ex. 7.14e** Haydn: String Quartet op. 55 no. 1 (1788).

ARTICULATION AND STRING BOWING 371

Ex. 7.14f  Weber: *Der Freischütz* (1821).

**Ex. 7.14g** Beethoven: String Quartet op. 132 (1825).

**Ex. 7.14h** Berlioz: *Symphonie fantastique* (1830).

Since the default manner of performing rapid, separately bowed notes was in the upper third quarter of the bow, it seems clear that *punta d'arco* required a bowstroke nearer than usual to the point of the bow. In 1826, Lichtenthal instructed: "The notes marked with this expression require a particular execution, which consists of striking the string gently with the point of the bow, thus producing a light staccato."[49] And *Busby's Dictionary* explained *colla punta dell'arco* as: "With the end, or with a slight touch of the bow".[50] J. A. Hiller, however, seems to have understood the term (like many German musicians he writes *punto d'arco*) differently, applying it to the up-bow slurred *staccato* at the point of the bow.[51] In one instance, in Cimarosa's *L'amante combattuto*, dots under slurs are combined with *p. stac. a punta d'arco* (Ex. 7.15).

Ex. 7.15 Cimarosa: *L'amante combattuto* (autograph) Act I, p. 184v.
[Allegretto graziosoo (2 flats)]

Although slurred *staccato* near the point of the bow was a basic stroke for all string players, and was taught in violin and cello methods throughout the 18th and 19th centuries,[52] there was a distinction between the rapid slurring of many notes, which, as Hiller pointed out, was "more for the soloist than for the orchestral player",[53] and the articulated slurring of two, or a few more notes at a moderate pace. Spohr later observed that the rapid slurred *staccato* "when well done, is of brilliant effect and one of the principal ornaments of solo playing. However, the ability to do this must be innate, because experience shows that often the most excellent violinists, despite the most diligent practice, never learn it, while other, much lesser violinists can do it immediately without any practice."[54] J. F. Reichardt may have been one of those players who found it challenging, for he recommended that the violinist could fake it by playing a succession of down-up-up strokes.[55] In the

---

[49] Lichtenthal: 'Punta d'arco' in *Dizionario*, ii, 140.
[50] *Thomas Busby's Dictionary of 3000 Musical Terms*, 3rd edn, rev. by J. A. Hamilton (London, [1840]), 40.
[51] Hiller: *Anweisung zum Violinspielen*, 41. See Ch. 6, pp. 323–24.
[52] For example: Corrett: *L'école*, 35; Geminiani: *The Art*, 27; Mozart: *Versuch*, 128; Galeazzi: *Elementi*, i, 157; and all substantial 19th-century methods. In the 20th century it became marginalized and, as Flesch's treatise shows, began to be replaced in earlier music by thrown strokes (see below, pp. 440–41).
[53] Hiller: *Anweisung*, 42.
[54] Spohr: *Violinschule*, 132f.
[55] Reichardt: *Ueber die Pflichten*, 17.

18th century the shorter version, executed as Reichardt explained, around three-quarters of the way towards the point was a very common bowstroke for all string players; there is no evidence that such strokes were made below the middle of the bow during the 18th or early 19th centuries. The notation of other types of articulated slur was very variable,[56] and they were often expected where the composer failed to indicate them.

Looking retrospectively at the changes that had occurred during the previous three or four decades, a writer in 1804 explained that bowing was not so difficult for the older players because they did not have "the quantity of bowing figurations that make our current playing style so difficult". By "bowing figurations", he referred to the varied patterns of separate and slurred notes that had become increasingly fashionable during the last decades of the 18th century. The author stated that in Benda's time, violinists were very skilled at nuancing long notes, but since bowing was not normally indicated, players could detach and slur notes "as it was most convenient and comfortable for them". Later, with Mannheim players and composers, such as Toeschi, Cannabich, and Fränzel, "their bowing indications were already more specific". These players were different from their former Mannheim colleague, Wilhelm Cramer, who moved to London in 1773 and, according to this writer, "was the first to introduce a new, more pleasing style of playing in his concertos. Half and even whole pages full of rolling passages were played staccato. Just as the end of the bow had previously been used to play these rapid notes, so now the middle of the bow was needed. This made them more separate, rounder, in a word, more beautiful." But however neatly Cramer executed this bowstroke (apparently similar to a *sautillé* in which the elasticity of the stick is employed without the bow-hair leaving the string), it seems that many of his imitators were less successful. The writer recalled: "Some, however, also ruined their previously good manner of playing after laborious effort to play with the middle of the bow, through too strong a pressure on the strings. The bow hopped back and forth, and the tone became unpleasant, rough, and scratchy."[57]

The identification of Cramer as the originator of this bowstroke is corroborated by two other late-18th-century sources. C. D. F. Schubart, an accomplished keyboard player who had performed with Cramer, recalled: "His bowstroke is wholly original. He does not do it like other violinists, straight

---

[56] See Ch. 6, "Articulated Slurs".
[57] Anon.: 'Ueber die heutige verworrene Strichbezeichnung', *Allgemeine musikalische Zeitung*, vi (1803–4), 730.

down, but above and away; he makes it short and extremely exact. No-one staccatos the notes with such precision as Cramer."[58] Michel Woldemar (1750–1815) illustrates a *coup d'archet à la Cramer* in his *Grande méthode* (c. 1800) (Ex. 7.16a), noting that it is played with "one bowstroke per note, the first note down-bow, the bow straight on the string about the middle of the stick".[59] And in connection with another illustration of Cramer's style (Ex. 7.16b), he instructed: "This genre requires a lot of neatness, of precision, of exactness, and the first note of the bar is usually forte."[60]

Ex. 7.16 a–b. Woldemar: (*a*) *Grande méthode* 47; (*b*) *Grande méthode* 37.

(*a*)

(*b*)

But the technique was not universally adopted. There is no clear evidence of its having been used by orchestral players, and those soloists who used it seem only to have employed it in solo passagework. Even in that context, it appears to have been controversial and may already have acquired a bad name at an early stage with some musicians. Leopold Mozart wrote to his son in 1778 giving an account of a visit to Salzburg by the violinist Anton Janitsch. He admired many aspects of his playing, describing it as similar to Antonio Lolli's except that he played adagio better. The comparison of Janitsch's

---

[58] Christian Daniel Friedrich Schubart: *Ideen zu einer Ästhetik der Tonkunst* (Vienna, 1806), 139. Posthumously published, but written 1784–85.
[59] Woldemar: *Grande Méthode*, 1st edn (Paris [c. 1800]), 47.
[60] Woldemar: *Grande Méthode*, 37.

playing with that of Lolli is revealing, for a writer in 1799 observed that Lolli's bowing in allegro: "was not the modern use of the bow where it is believed that effectiveness consists of using clipped, hopping strokes and neglects the bow's long melting stroke, which evokes the melodiousness of the human voice. [. . .] Lolly's performance was not like that.—(I am only talking about the Allegro here)."[61] Mozart contrasted Janitsch's style of playing with that of other unnamed violinists, but probably had followers of Cramer in mind, writing: "I'm really not a lover of those frightful tempi where you can barely get everything out with half the tone of the violin, and so to speak, you hardly have to touch the violin with the bow and almost have to play in the air."[62] Everything that is known of the violinists with whom the younger Mozart associated, and whom he admired, argues that he shared his father's preference for the broader style. Rochlitz commented that Mozart specially admired the playing of Johann Friedrich Eck (who had been strongly influenced by Viotti's playing in Paris in the mid-1780s), for its tone, bowing, and command of *legato*.[63]

Cramer's association with the very short, hopping bowstroke, and Woldemar's designation "Cramer" bow for the hatchet-head bow that stood chronologically between what he designated "Tartini" and "Viotti" bows (Ex. 7.1a), is surely not coincidental. Its design was more favourable to an elastic bowstroke in the middle than the former; and although there is no direct evidence that Wilhelm Cramer was really the first to discover the bow's capabilities in this respect, there can be little doubt that he was its most celebrated exponent. Woldemar stated that the "Cramer" bow had been adopted in his day "by most artists and amateurs".[64] His illustration of the "Tartini", with its lightweight tip, corresponds with the bows depicted in Leopold Mozart's (1756) and Löhlein's (1774) treatises, as well as in many other illustrations until the 1770s; for instance, Carmontelle's watercolour of the Mozart family in about 1764. The second, with a more developed head, is much closer to the modern Tourte-style bow, though lighter and shorter; it seems to have evolved as early as the 1750s and was probably used by Mannheim string players, at that time, hence the association of this type

---

[61] Anon.: *Allgemeine musikalische Zeitung*, i (1798–99), 579.
[62] Mozart: *Briefe*, ii, 244.
[63] His forenames are given thus by Gerber (*Lexikon der Tonkunst*), but elsewhere they are given as Friedrich Johann.
[64] Woldemar, *Grande Méthode ou Étude élémentaire pour le violon* (Paris, [c. 1800]), 3.

with Cramer, one of the most celebrated violinists from Mannheim. It seems possible, from what can be seen of the bow on Della Croce's Mozart family portrait of about 1780, that by that date Leopold was using a bow of a transitional type.

During the last three decades of the 18th century there were many variants of the type, to which the "Cramer" and "Viotti" bows belonged; it is possible that some of the bows used by Viotti were of these transitional types, as implied by Baillot's depiction of Viotti's bow as slightly shorter than the later Tourte model (Tourte's earlier bows until the 1790s were somewhat shorter). François Tourte's later model served as the pattern for subsequent bow makers up to the present day, although local variants continued to be made for several decades.

Different bow designs may favour certain types of bowstroke, but it does not necessarily mean that these were all widely exploited.[65] Schubart's observations show that there was great diversity in the bowing styles of celebrated late-18th-century virtuosos. About Tartini's bowing he commented: "the notes are really dragged out of the violin and the bowstroke fully developed. [. . .] The only thing to criticize about the Tartini school is that its majestic sustained bowstroke inhibits velocity in performance and is certainly not suited to winged passages. On the other hand, the pupils of this school are unsurpassably good in the church style, for their bowing has precisely the right degree of power and accent required for the pathetic church style."[66] He remarked that Leopold Mozart "leans towards the Tartini school, though allows the pupil more freedom in bowing";[67] he nevertheless thought that "his bowstroke is too Tartini-like, and not suitable enough for presto".[68] Schubart's descriptions of some of Tartini's most celebrated pupils reveal very different styles from their master. He regarded Domenico Ferrari as "the creator of a new school", observing that his bowstroke was "not the deeply cutting bowstroke of a Tartini, not the majestic and stately employment of the bow, not the pulling out of the notes right down to their roots".[69] And of Nardini he recalled: "His bowstroke was slow and stately; but unlike

---

[65] For further information on bows and their characteristics see Stowell, *Violin Technique*, Ch. 1, where, however, the meaning of the quotation from Woldemar is somewhat obscured—he translates "il se joue un peu détendu" (it is used a little slackly for playing) as "it looks slightly straighter when in use".
[66] Schubart: *Ideen*, 59.
[67] Schubart: *Ideen*, 158.
[68] Schubart: *Ideen*, 298.
[69] Schubart: *Ideen*, 59f

Tartini, he did not tear out the notes by the roots, but kissed only their tips."[70] Leopold Mozart confirms this, writing to his friend Lorenz Hagenauer in 1763 that Nardini "certainly does not play strongly".[71] Schubart noted that Antonio Lolli "not only united the perfections of the Tartini and Ferrari schools, but also found a completely new way. His bowstroke is eternally inimitable."[72] Of Cannabich, he remarked: "it would be extremely difficult to characterize the originality of his bowstroke".[73] These remarks, together with comments about violinists in the Mozart correspondence, reveal great diversity in bowing styles.

In 1791, Galeazzi described the four basic types of bowstroke as *sciolte* (detached), *legate* (slurred), *portate* (gently separated within a slur), and *picchettate* (sharply separated within a slur); but he added a fifth category—*mista* (mixed)—which referred not to the type of bowing, but to the type of passagework, in which separate and slurred notes follow one another in a variety of patterns.[74] Exhaustive examples of these mixed patterns are given by Leopold Mozart,[75] and in numerous 18th- and early-19th-century treatises. This way of playing passages of successive, faster notes remained a prominent aspect of stylish string playing from the middle of the 18th century until at least the 1840s. In the early part of this period, composers often left them with neither articulation marks nor slurs. Where this occurred, some musicians might simply have executed them with normal detached bowstrokes in the middle or upper half of the bow, or perhaps, from the 1770s, exploited the properties of the transitional bow to use a Cramer bowstroke. Others, who were not enamoured of either option, will have employed various patterns of slurred and separate notes where the composer marked nothing. In such cases, improvised bowing patterns could be seen as a form of embellishment. Indeed, Ferdinand Kauer included an illustration of these patterns in the section on ornaments (Verzierungen) in his 1788 cello method, commenting: "The various bow strokes make up the largest part of the ornamentation, such as [Ex. 7.17]."[76]

---

[70] Schubart: *Ideen*, 62
[71] Mozart: *Briefe*, i, 77.
[72] Schubart: *Ideen*, 60.
[73] Schubart: *Ideen*, 137.
[74] Galeazzi: *Elementi*, i, 154.
[75] Mozart: *Versuch*, 130–34.
[76] Ferdinand Kauer: *Kurzgefasste Anweisung das Violoncell zu spielen*, reprint (Vienna, Cappi [c. 1800]), 11. He made a similar observation in his *Kurzgefasste Violin-Schule für Anfänger* c. 1790.

Ex. 7.17  F. Kauer: *Kurzgefasste Anweisung das Violoncell zu spielen*, reprint (Vienna, Cappi [c. 1800]), 11 (first three staves only).

That Kauer, like Paul Wranitzky and other Viennese contemporaries, expected these mostly to be supplied by the performer is evident from the paucity of bowing instructions in his compositions (see, e.g., his Grand Trio).[77]

The perceived need for this kind of "ornamentation", and perhaps dissatisfaction with a growing tendency for string players to choose the Cramer bowstroke for passagework, is suggested by comments in an anonymous publication of 1779, which complained:

> More recent and foreign violinists have made a point of giving each note a separate bowstroke, as short as possible, and have thus completely eliminated any resemblance to true singing from their playing style. The more and faster little bowstrokes these people can produce, the more miracles they believe they are performing. When they play an adagio, they put in so many colourful little notes between the main notes or the melody, each having a very short little bowstroke, that one might always exclaim: "Hey! How quickly the little rabbit runs up the hill, and even more quickly down again!"—This manner of playing, however, receives much applause from the musical rabble, and is therefore not to be entirely rejected.[78]

A couple of years later, Petri alluded to the need for adding slurs where none were notated, observing that in triple metres and for triplets "it is good to divide up the three notes into slurred and separate, and not to get into the habit of fiddling them all away with separate bowstrokes".[79] Criticisms of these

---

[77] Ferdinand Kauer: *Grand Trio a Violino, Viola e Violoncello* (Paris, Imbault, [c. 1790]), https://imslp.org/wiki/String_Trio_in_E-flat_major_(Kauer%2C_Ferdinand).

[78] Anon. (probably Ernst Wilhelm Wolf): *Wahrheiten die Musik betreffend* [Truths about Music] (Frankfurt a. M., 1779), 71f. See also Ch. 5.

[79] Petri: *Anleitung*, 411. By "fiddling away" I have tried to convey the pejorative implications of Petri's term "abzufitscheln".

"fiddling" musicians, as well as Spohr's and Romberg's later condemnation of springing bowstrokes, may well have been based as much on the undifferentiated articulation and limited dynamic range of such bowing practices, used to excess, as on the character of the stroke itself.

More careful composers, of whom Mozart is a prime example, began to mark these mixed patterns explicitly, while others continued to allow much latitude to the performer. Beethoven, in his chamber music, very rarely left his preferred execution in doubt; but he clearly expected soloists in his Violin Concerto to supply the bowings themselves in many passages.[80] Viotti, too, expected the performer to add varied bowings and many other ornamental features in his violin concertos, as is made explicit by André Robberechts's notes on lessons with him in 1816,[81] and also by the editions of Viotti concertos made by Baillot's pupil Charles Dancla.[82] Viotti's disciples Rode, Kreutzer, and Baillot were much more explicit, as were Spohr and an increasing number of younger composers.

## The Impact of Viotti and His Disciples

In 1801, Woldemar, after praising the excellent qualities of mid-18th-century Italian violinists, stated: "but it was reserved for Viotti to eclipse the glory of his predecessors and to become to some extent the leader and model of a new school".[83] An account from 1811 gives a clear and concise description of how one informed contemporary perceived the predominant stylistic criteria that distinguished the string playing of this "new school" from others. Having mentioned several pupils or followers of Viotti who had recently performed in Warsaw, including Rode and the cellist Lamarre, he observed:

> as with painters, one can say that they are all from his school; they play in his spirit, and especially treat their instruments according to his principles, as he himself [Viotti] had taken them from the school of Pugnani and developed them further through his genius. It is known that the most distinctive

---

[80] Beethoven: Violin Concerto, ed. Clive Brown (Wiesbaden, Breitkopf & Härtel, 2012).
[81] See Ex. 13.25b.
[82] See the CHASE website https://mhm.hud.ac.uk/chase/view/work/765.
[83] *Méthode de violon par L. Mozart [...] redigée par Woldemar, élève de Lolli* (Paris, [1801]), 1.

characteristics of this school derive from the following principles: the first is a large, strong, full tone; the second is the combination of this tone with a strong, penetrating, beautifully connected cantabile; the third is variety, charm, light and shade, which must be achieved through the most varied types of bowstrokes.[84]

This style came to exercise such hegemony over European violin playing during the early decades of the 19th century that in 1825 Georg Carl Friedrich Lobedanz could write: "the French school of which Viotti, Baillot, and Rode are the founders [. . .] is distinguished, as is well known, by a characteristic use of the bow, and almost all present-day celebrated violin virtuosos have more or less adopted it".[85] At a similar date, William Gardiner commented that all violinists he had heard, except Wilhelm Cramer's son, Franz, whom he praised for "fullness and firmness of tone, in the old school", were "of the Viotti School".[86]

Giovanni Battista Viotti's performance style began to influence string playing in the 1780s and 1790s. Ange Marie d'Eymar characterized him in 1792 as "a musician who, in composition and in performance, wants to achieve perfection in his art—which means the highest level of perfection; a rare man, a unique artist, the tender and sublime Viotti!"[87] By the end of the 1790s, Viotti's manner of playing, and that of his disciples, was established in Paris as the most admired style. It was also connected with developments in bow making. Woldemar, writing from a Parisian perspective, stated that the recently developed Tourte bow, which was certainly a factor in producing the powerful tone associated with this style, "differs little from Cramer's in respect of the head, but the frog is lower and brought nearer to the button [screw], it is longer and has more hair; it is used a little slackly for playing and is almost exclusively in use today".[88] The adoption of this model elsewhere in Europe was a slower process;[89] Paganini, for instance, whose triumphant concert tours through Europe between 1828 and 1835 exerted a compelling

---

[84] Anon.: *Allgemeine musikalische Zeitung*, xiii (1811), 452.
[85] Anon.: *Cäcilia*, ii (1825), 267.
[86] William Gardiner: *The Music of Nature* (London, 1832), 210 and 216.
[87] A. M. Eymar: 'Anecdotes sur Viotti, précédées de quelques réflexions sur l'expression en musique' (Paris, 1792), 14. Reprinted in *L'esprit des journaux, françois et étrangers*, xii (1798), 100.
[88] Woldemar: *Grande Méthode ou Étude élémentaire pour le violon* (Paris, [c. 1800]), 3.
[89] Kai Köpp: https://tarisio.com/archet-revolutionnaire/kai-koepp-french-or-german-bows-for-beethoven/.

influence on virtuoso technique, still used an older-style bow. Leading string players associated with Mannheim and Munich, however, were almost certainly using Tourte-style bows by the beginning of the century, for when Franz Eck (brother and pupil of the Munich Konzertmeister Johann Friedrich Eck) accepted Spohr as his pupil in 1803 he instructed him to buy a new bow. According to Spohr's diary, this was a genuine Tourte.[90] String players trained in Paris, and German violinists and cellists such as Spohr, the Rombergs, and Dotzauer, as well as many other important teachers, will certainly have encouraged their students to employ Tourte-style bows.

The publication of the highly influential *Méthode de violon par Baillot, Rode et Kreutzer; redigée par Baillot* in 1803 was a key factor in consolidating the idea of a specific Viotti School, which was quickly seen by many as the only legitimate model for aspiring artists. It crystallized trends that were already under way in previous decades, especially in north Italian string playing. The *Méthode*, an instruction book for the Paris Conservatoire, provides a catalogue of the essential bowstrokes required for performing works by Viotti and his followers at that time. Louise Goldberg, in the introduction to her fine translation of Baillot's *L'art du violon*, calls the 165-page 1803 *Méthode de violon* "short and incomplete";[91] but there can be little doubt that the exclusion from the *Méthode* of one or two potential bowstrokes was deliberate. Some bowing practices that had become fashionable for solo violinists during preceding decades were no longer seen as appropriate for performing serious, expressive music. Many of the additional bowstrokes that Baillot included in his *L'art du violon*, thirty years later, probably reflect stylistic developments during the intervening period, not an unintentional omission from the earlier treatise. Baillot himself observed in the introduction to *L'art du violon* that "the more varied resources offered by the violin nowadays required more diversity in the examples",[92] and that Art "whose principles are immutable, is subject to change in its forms over time, which leads to modifications and extensions of technique".[93]

In fact, the 1803 *Méthode* was the most substantial and detailed method of its decade, and early-19th-century professional violinists, regardless of whether they were using the latest Parisian bows, were increasingly expected

---

[90] Spohr: *Tagebuch oder Merkwürdigkeiten einer musicalischen Reise*, Ms. 1802, S. 28–32, http://www.spohr-briefe.de/briefe-einzelansicht?m=1802050629. I am grateful to Carl Goldbach for access to the original diary.
[91] Louise Goldberg: *The Art of the Violin* (Evanston, IL, 1991), xxiii.
[92] Baillot: *L'art du violon*, 3.
[93] Baillot: *L'art du violon*, 7.

to master its bowing practices. The impact of the *Méthode* is attested by its reproduction in translation, in whole or part, during the following years. A German edition was issued soon after the French original, with a second, revised edition in 1806. The *Méthode*'s bowing instructions and music examples were plagiarized at length by the authors of several subsequent methods: Joseph von Blumenthal in Vienna (1811), Franz Joseph Fröhlich in Bonn (1812), John (Jean) Jousse in London (1812), and Bartolomeo Campagnoli in Leipzig (1824). Fröhlich also extended its instructions to the cello, explaining: "The rules given in the Violin School [of Fröhlich's treatise] pp. 23 to 29 all apply to this instrument as well. The teacher should therefore go through them with the pupil, who can also make use of the practice pieces",[94] which, he adds, should be written out in the bass clef.

The instructions in the Paris Conservatoire *Méthode*, its translations and derivatives, together with their notational illustrations and copious exercises, provide the basis for understanding the fundamentals of the bowing style that began to exert ever stronger influence during the first decade of the new century.

In Adagio, where all the sounds must be sustained slowly, the bow will be used from one end to the other, and all the notes will be as smoothly connected as possible. If they must necessarily be played with un-slurred bowing, they will be sustained for their full value, with the same extent of bow. [Ex. 7.18a]

In Allegro maestoso or Moderato assai, where the bow-stroke is quicker and more decided, it is necessary to give the separate notes as much length as possible, from approximately the middle of the bow, so that the sounds are round and that the string vibrates fully. One must also play the down- and up-bows briskly and make a sort of short articulation between each note. [Ex. 7.18b]

In Allegro, the bow stroke will be shorter; one begins the notes about three quarters of the way along the bow, and they are not separated by rests. [Ex. 7.18c]

In Presto, the bow stroke should be even faster and livelier; the detached notes are executed with less bow, also three quarters of the way along the bow, but care must be taken also to use enough bow to make the string

---

[94] Fröhlich: *Musikschule*, iv, 64.

vibrate well, so that the sounds carry as far as possible, that each note comes out clearly, and that the playing can be given power and passion. [Ex. 7.18d]

The more these bows are lengthened, the more effective they will be if they are well managed; but nothing must be exaggerated, and one must seek to regulate the bowing according to the situation. This division of the bow, however, concerns only passagework, and in melodic sections the bow must be lengthened or conserved according to the tempo and the character of the music.

Martelé

This bowing must be made with the point of the bow and articulated firmly: it serves to contrast with the sustained melody, and is very effective when properly employed. [Ex. 7.18e]

One also uses it in triplets. [Ex. 7.18f]

To articulate well without harshness or dryness, it is necessary to mark each note by attacking the string with vivacity and to give enough length to the bow to make the sound round and full. It is also necessary that all the notes are very equal to one another, which one will obtain if one puts more force on the up-bow, which is by nature more difficult to mark than the down-bow.

Staccato or *détaché articulé* is made when one plays several staccato notes in the same bow stroke. Its principle is the same as that of *martelé*, that is, it must be made with the point, without the bow leaving the string, but with this difference, that as little as possible of the bow must be used, if one wants to articulate it well, and that it is necessary to mark the first and the last note firmly. [Ex. 7.18g][95]

**Ex. 7.18** a–g. Baillot et al.: *Méthode*. (*a*) 129f; (*b*) 130; (*c*) 130; (*d*) 130; (*e*) 131; (*f*) 131; (*g*) 131.

(*a*)

[95] Baillot, Kreutzer, and Rode: *Méthode de violon*, 129–31.

ARTICULATION AND STRING BOWING 385

**Ex. 7.18** Continued

(b)

(c)

(d)

(e)

(f)

(g)

The 1804 *Méthode de violoncelle*, which was produced by Baillot and three of his cellist colleagues,[96] provides very similar instructions for bowing but, curiously, unlike the *Méthode de violon*, it prescribes differentiated execution for strokes and dots as articulation marks.[97]

Despite the level of detail in the 1803 *Méthode*, some subtleties of bowing, which undoubtedly characterized the playing of the three authors of the *Méthode de violon* and of their mentor Viotti, will inevitably have lain behind and beyond the written text; and the same is true of the *Méthode de violoncelle*. One of these refinements, not explained before Baillot's 1835 treatise, was the distinction between a *mat* (dry) *Grand détaché* and an *elastique* (elastic) *détaché légere*, both of which were to be executed in the same part of the bow. The principal difference between them, as Baillot explained, is that in the former: "The horsehair of the bow, left on the string, prevents its vibrations from being entirely free, this lack of freedom gives the note made in this way an accent that we could only call a dry accent", while the latter is made "With more play, more bow elasticity than the previous ones, in which we saw that the elasticity was a bit restricted."[98] Neither the 1803 *Méthode*, nor Spohr's 1833 *Violinschule*, draws attention to this distinction, but it seems clear that it was a normal technical detail that would have been made clear in practice. One early-19th-century cello treatise, however, Duport's (1806), alludes to something similar: "There are two kinds of *détaché*, the first one is used when you want to produce volume, and the other one is somewhat elastic and is used for light things. The latter is executed at the three quarters region of the bow towards the tip."[99] In 1816, André Robberechts (1797–1860) wrote in his notes of a lesson with Viotti that a seven-bar passage of separate sixteenth-notes in the Allegro first movement of Viotti's Violin Concerto no. 23 in G (bars 16ff of the first solo) "should be played in the middle of the bow, letting it spring a little".[100] This same passage from Viotti's 23rd Concerto, coincidentally, is given by Baillot in 1835 to illustrate *détaché légere*, in which the elasticity of the stick was utilized without the bow-hair leaving the string.[101] Spohr, too, despite failing to explain this type of stroke in his *Violinschule*, advised a correspondent in 1844 that a passage of separate sixteenths in his

---

[96] Balliot et al.: *Méthode de violoncelle* (Paris, 1804).
[97] See Ch. 6, pp. 293–94.
[98] Baillot: *L'art du violon*, 100 (see Ex. 7.23a and 7.23c).
[99] Duport: *Essai*, 70.
[100] André Robberechts MS notebook, Conservatoire royal de Bruxelles, MS 61.365, p. 197.
[101] Baillot: *L'art du violon*, 99.

Violin Concerto op. 70 (1825), should be "executed with great power in the middle of the bow so that the wood admittedly makes a springing motion, but the hair does not leave the string".[102]

Furthermore, while the Viotti School was seen as highly influential between the 1790s and 1820s, there were also many notable string players whose individuality of style was apparent to contemporaries.[103] A report from Paris of performances there by Bernhard and Andreas Romberg in 1801 indicates that the playing of both cousins (who advertised themselves as brothers) differed from that of the local cellists and violinists. The reviewer remarked that the organizers of a concert series

> engaged the renowned brothers Romberg from Hamburg who gained excellent applause when they made their debut in the first [concert]. This is less surprising in the case of one of these virtuosos, the cellist, since Paris hardly has anyone who could challenge him on this instrument, and on this occasion his reputation was already well established before his arrival here; but it is more surprising in the case of the violinist—here, where there are so many excellent violinists, and where Romberg dares to go against the current fashion with his own manner.[104]

From Andreas Romberg's own carefully bowed, and sometimes fingered compositions, it is impossible to tell what struck the reviewer as different from the prevailing Parisian style. Some contemporary references to string players who did not adopt the Viotti School's priorities suggest the tenacity of other traditions. A writer in 1811,[105] having described the Viotti style, observed: "These principles distinguish this School entirely from Lolly's and the more recent Italian school, which until a few years ago had also become quite dominant in Germany, the merits of which are pleasant tone, great ease and skill, daintiness, gallantry, and many so-called enchantments [*Hexereien*], thus working more on the imagination and captivating it with pleasing things."[106] In Vienna, admiration for the style of performance fostered by Viotti School string players led to dissatisfaction with the stylistic

---

[102] Spohr: autograph letter to Anton Gröber 3 February 1844, in Bibliothek der Tiroler Landesmuseen/Ferdinandeum, Autographen-Sammlung; see www.spohr-briefe.de.
[103] See Clive Brown: 'Leopold Mozart's *Violinschule* and the performance of W. A. Mozart Violin Music' and Clive Brown: *Polarities of Virtuosity*.
[104] Anon.: *Allgemeine musikalische Zeitung*, iii (1800–1), 388.
[105] See above, pp. 380–81.
[106] Anon.: *Allgemeine musikalische Zeitung*, xiii (1811), 452f.

characteristics of even such a brilliant virtuoso as Franz Clement. An 1805 review, for instance, described his style as: "not the marked, bold, strong playing, the moving forceful Adagio, the power of bow and tone that characterize the Rode-Viotti School";[107] in 1813: "his short bow stroke and excessive embellishments [*überhäuften Künsteleyen*], which entirely prevent him from achieving an expressive cantabile, will always exclude him from the rank of *great* violinists";[108] and in 1824: "His method, like the way he wields his bow, is on the whole somewhat outdated."[109] Anton Schindler, too, referred to Clement's "short bowstroke according to the school of the old Italian masters Tartini and Nardini",[110] but like all second-hand stylistic judgements, this is evidently an unreliable oversimplification, for Schubart's comments indicate that even among Tartini's own students, bowing styles were very variable. In contrast, Spohr's playing, modelled at an early stage on Rode's, was seen as exemplary in Vienna, when he performed there in 1812.[111] And when Joseph Böhm wanted to establish himself as a teacher in Vienna in 1816, he felt it helpful to claim to be a pupil of Rode[112] and to teach the principles of the Viotti School.

The growing influence of the Viotti School, and the compositions of its adherents during the first decade of the 19th century, rapidly discredited the vogue for the "Cramer" bowstroke, and the kind of music associated with it. A review of Kreutzer's Violin Concerto op. 12 in 1804 contrasted the style required for that concerto with the performing styles of many established soloists:

> The light performance style, the short bowstroke and the springing bow of most present-day violinists, will not do for the performance of Kreutzer's concertos. What must they do? Change their style of playing? That can't be done so quickly; while they are doing that, Kreutzer's concertos might easily go out of fashion! In any case, the character and individuality of very many players may well be contrary to the performance style required by

---

[107] Anon.: *Allgemeine musikalische Zeitung*, vii (1804/5), 500.
[108] Anon.: *Allgemeine musikalische Zeitung*, xv (1813), 400
[109] Anon.: *Allgemeine musikalische Zeitung*, xxvi (1824), 366f.
[110] Schindler: *Biographie*, 3rd edn (1860), 140.
[111] See, e.g., *Allgemeine musikalische Zeitung*, xv (1813), 115.
[112] Johannes Gebauer has shown convincingly that Böhm could never have had more than a few lessons, within a time span of two weeks, with Rode. Johannes Gebauer: *Der „Klassikervortrag". Joseph Joachims Bach- und Beethovenvortrag und die Interpretationspraxis des 19. Jahrhunderts* (Bonn, 2023), 118f.

Kreutzer's concertos. So they simply ignore it, and, Heaven help us, play Kreutzer's concertos in a light, trifling (perhaps befrilled) manner; the powerful, pathetic, serious Allegro is taken in the fastest tempo; of course the passages that merge into one another, in which the whole bow must be drawn slowly across the string, firmly, powerfully, with complete evenness, without the least wavering, and where the fingers must fall onto the strings with virile strength, are ineffective in a light and rapid style of playing: and then, without more ado, they try to help themselves by playing every passage that cannot be slurred, or that sounds unclear because of the rapid tempo—staccato. Instead of the nuances, that are hidden in Kreutzer's passagework (i.e., instead of hurrying, lingering, bringing out by means of *f* and *p* etc.) they introduce short ornaments; and in places that only produce their effect when played on a single string and which must be executed with an artful use of position changing, they don't even make any attempt to do it, but play the cantabile passages in the position that allows them to make the greatest number of frills; the characteristic fermatas and cadenzas with written-out ornaments in an adagio are altered, usually extended and decked out with arpeggios, double stops, staccato passages and so on; then, in a Rondo every note is played staccato without exception, whether there is a slur over the passage or not, and the tempo here is taken so fast that the accompanying instruments often have difficulty following the soloist. This reviewer, at least, who knows most of the well-known violinists of the present day, has heard three quarters of them do this to Kreutzer concertos.[113]

Other reviews from the same period reveal the pressures on violinists to change their way of playing. At a concert in the Leipzig Gewandhaus in May 1803, for instance, the 23-year-old Paul Emil Thieriot (1780–1831), recently returned home from lessons with Baillot in Paris, "gave indubitable evidence that he has studied in this School with eagerness and sustained application" as he had formerly "worked through Durand's manner".[114] In March 1804 it was observed of an already established violinist, Heinrich Anton Hofmann (1770–1842), "since he heard Herr Rode he seeks with all diligence to model himself on him, and it is astonishing how far he has already succeeded also

---

[113] Anon.: *Allgemeine musikalische Zeitung*, vi (1803–4), 613f.
[114] Anon.: *Allgemeine musikalische Zeitung*, v (1802–3), 585.

in this genre".[115] In the same month, Carl Heroux also played Rode's A minor Concerto in Leipzig and elicited the comment: "He seeks, like almost all the violinists here to study Rode's style, which is certainly praiseworthy, whatever others, accustomed to a less expansive style, may, for easily understood reasons, say against it."[116] Others did not try, or did not succeed in modelling themselves on the Parisian style. Johannes Tollmann, a product of "the school of the truly deserving elder [Ignaz] Fränzl", gave an effective performance of a concerto by Eck, but Rode's D minor Concerto was seen as "less appropriate for his manner of playing".[117] When the Berlin violinist Carl Möser performed in Dresden in 1803, a reviewer noted that he pleased the audience "although he played almost everything with a short bowstroke, his tone is not at all outstanding, his Adagio is cold and extremely embellished etc. It is true, admittedly, that his allegro is fiery, brilliant, and he knows how to overcome tremendous difficulties. But Rode stands much, much higher."[118]

Although Viotti's influence led to an increasing standardization of fundamental techniques, it is also clear that these techniques had their roots in earlier practice. A review of Rode's 7th Violin Concerto in 1803, having described his typical bowing style, continued:

> if the reviewer is not mistaken, this style of playing is by no means new, but rather the older one of Tartini, Pugnani, which, however—in Germany at least—has been less cultivated in recent times, and almost seemed to have been superseded by the endeavour to perform everything as quickly as possible and to dazzle with short and strong staccato passages. [. . .] he must, however, remind those who have adopted this [Rode] style of playing not to neglect the short and strong bowstroke with a half-hopping bow, which in certain passages brings such beautiful clarity and precision, and makes a great deal of effect.[119]

Whether the bowstroke referred to here was the very short Cramer type played with minimal horizontal movement, or more likely the one described by Roberrechts and Spohr, is unclear; but it is evident from many sources that the prejudice against a "light" style of playing, including the Cramer

---

[115] Anon.: *Allgemeine musikalische Zeitung*, vi (1803–4), 415.
[116] Anon.: *Allgemeine musikalische Zeitung*, vi (1803–4), 430.
[117] Anon.: *Allgemeine musikalische Zeitung*, vi (1803–4), 414.
[118] Anon.: *Allgemeine musikalische Zeitung*, v (1802–3), 836.
[119] Anon.: *Allgemeine musikalische Zeitung*, v (1802–3), 664f.

bowstroke, was connected with a change of taste that no longer found the virtuoso compositions of Cramer's generation satisfying. The light bowing style even came to be seen as responsible for engendering meretricious music. As Bernhard Romberg wrote, recalling his youth: "It was formerly the solo bowstroke of sundry virtuosos, who used it in all the passagework, but it never allows a fine playing style, and thus their concertos had so little worth; now one requires more substance, soul, and expression in music."[120] Romberg's opinion tallies with comments in the diary kept by Spohr during his time of study with Franz Eck. Spohr's judgements suggest that many string players who were directly influenced by north Italian practice and its French derivative regarded Cramer's type of elastic bowstroke as unsuitable for music of a higher artistic character. Spohr, undoubtedly reflecting the views of his master,[121] remarked in his diary that while he was in St Petersburg in 1803, he played one of his manuscript duos for two violins (later published as op. 3) with A. F. Tietz (?1742–1810), who performed the passagework "according to the old method with springing bow".[122] He also criticized the style of J. A. Fodor (1751–1828): "He played in a pure and quite accomplished manner, but without warmth and taste. He also lets the bow continually spring in the passagework, which soon becomes unbearable."[123] Ferdinand Fränzl, whom Spohr considered the best violinist in St Petersburg at that time, played the passagework "cleanly and purely", apparently without a springing bowstroke, but was criticized for executing it "always in the middle of the bow and consequently without distinction of *piano* and *forte*".[124]

The Viotti School's broad, singing bowstrokes, and variety of slurred and detached bowing patterns, was espoused by many string players who had been born during the last three decades of the 18th century, and discouraged the cultivation of the Cramer bowstroke, to the extent that there is no firm evidence of its continued use in French and German practice during the following two decades. Tension between established practice and a desire for novelty is, however, inevitable, and it is clear from the difference between the treatment of bowing in the Baillot, Rode, Kreutzer *Méthode* of 1803 and

---

[120] Romberg: *Violoncell Schule*, 109.
[121] Eck, younger brother and pupil of the Munich Konzertmeister, Friedrich Johann Eck, was described by Spohr in his *Selbstbiographie* as a "French" violinist.
[122] Spohr: *Selbstbiographie*, i, 46.
[123] Spohr: Selbstbiographie, i, 48.
[124] Spohr: Selbstbiographie, i, 47.

Baillot's 1835 *L'Art du violon*, that the expectations of at least one of Viotti's direct heirs changed significantly during the three decades that separated these two treatises.

Even during the early decades of the 19th century, a few prominent string players, despite standing somewhat apart from the mainstream of the Viotti School, maintained their prestige. After hearing Bartolomeo Campagnoli perform at the Leipzig Gewandhaus in 1805, Spohr noted in his diary: "I heard the concert-master of the society, Mr Campagnoli, play a concerto by Kreutzer really well. His method, it is true, is of the old school but his playing is pure and finished."[125] In this context, Campagnoli's 1824 *Nouvelle Méthode* is a puzzling source. The frontispiece (Ex. 7.7) shows Campagnoli in clothes of the late 1790s; his posture, with the left upper arm resting against his chest and the downward slope of the violin (viola?), reflects 18th-century sources, such as Löhlein's 1774 treatise, rather than the posture illustrated by Baillot and Spohr. The text is a curious mixture of older and newer techniques. His treatment of bowing, with parallel French and German instructions, includes almost all the original French text from the 1803 *Méthode*, word for word, without acknowledgement;[126] but Baillot's instructions for the slurred *staccato* (which Campagnoli calls *Staccato ou Picchettato*) is followed by two further types of *picchettato*. He explains that the first (the Cramer bowing?) "can be done by detaching the notes with small movements of the wrist and fingers on the bowstick, keeping the arm stiff, making the bow jump on the strings with the greatest ease and always in the middle".[127] The third kind of *picchettato* is clearly a *ricochet* in the middle of the bow. Very exceptionally, however, Campagnoli includes no music example for these bowstrokes in the method, suggesting perhaps that their inclusion was an afterthought, possibly resulting from contact with Paganini, during Campagnoli's visit to Italy in 1816, or even, perhaps, from his awareness of recent trends in Paris.

---

[125] Spohr: *Selbstbiographie*, i, 78.
[126] Campagnoli: *Nouvelle Méthode de la Mécanique Progressive du Jeu de Violon divisée en 5 Parties* op. 21 (Leipzig, [1823]), pt. 5, 16f and 26f. The treatise was announced as newly published in the *Allgemeine musikalische Zeitung* intelligenz Blatt, col. 12 on 7 May 1823. It may well have been mostly written many years before earlier, but its inclusion of bowing instructions from the 1803 Conservatoire *Méthode* shows that it cannot have been published in this form as early as 1797 (as suggested in many reference books, despite the fact that no copy of such a treatise is known).
[127] Campagnoli: *Nouvelle Méthode*, pt. 1, 27.

## A Divergence of Bowing Practices

During the 1820s, the predominance of the bowing practices described in the 1803 *Méthode* began to be challenged by more recent Parisian developments. In 1821, Georg Ludwig Peter Sievers (1775–1830), in one of his regular "Sketches from Paris" in the *Wiener Zeitschrift*, noted that "there are several excellent artists on the violin in Paris, and the newer school of this instrument goes out from here".[128] In his next contribution he reported that Baillot's "*sciolto* (*détaché*), which he always performs with a hopping, never with a firm bowstroke, is the non plus ultra of violin playing in this genre; he plays passages of thirty or forty bars in this manner with such a degree of perfection that the last note has the same aplomb as the first."[129] The tone of Sievers's account makes it evident that he regarded this bowstroke as unusual; he also stated that Baillot extensively used artificial harmonics, but he did not specify in what repertoire. Baillot's exploitation of both these techniques, not mentioned in the 1803 *Méthode*, may suggest that he had been influenced by accounts of Paganini's playing, although he had certainly not heard him at that stage.

Sievers's account may have directly stimulated the emulation of Baillot's "hopping" bowstroke in Vienna because, the following year, Joseph Böhm (1795–1876) experimented with it. The *Wiener Zeitschrift* reported:

> Mr. Böhm, although still a young man, has already achieved a high degree of mastery on his instrument. We do not know whether this artist ever had the opportunity to hear Baillot, and to take him either in whole or in part as a model; all we know is that he succeeded to a rare degree of perfection in imitating the staccato or sciolto, newly invented by this artist (*sons détachés*), which consists in separating the notes not with a horizontal-motion but with a vertical-hopping bow), which, as far as we know, has not until now been used by any German violinist.[130]

At that time Böhm had certainly not had an opportunity to hear Baillot, so he may have developed this bowstroke from Sievers's description.

---

[128] Georg Ludwig Peter Sievers: 'Skizzen aus Paris', *Wiener Zeitschrift*, 22 May 1821, 524.
[129] Sievers: 'Skizzen aus Paris', *Wiener Zeitschrift*, 24 May 1821, 528.
[130] Anon.: *Wiener Zeitschrift*, 23 March 1822, 293. It is possible that this report was, in fact, by Sievers, or had been discussed with him, since at this stage he was certainly in Vienna, writing reports on opera for the *Wiener Zeitschrift*.

Other Viennese violinists quickly adopted it. Böhm's colleague and former pupil Georg Hellmesberger (1800–1873) used it in a concert in 1823, in his "Grandes Variations [...] sur l'Air de Rossini de l'Opera *Zelmira* [...] Oeuvre 10", about which a reviewer noted: "These Variations are very brilliant, particularly the last, with springing bow, which Herr Hellmesberger performed with particular lightness."[131] The following year, when Leopold Jansa (1795–1875) played a set of his own variations, a reviewer praised his "bravura", commenting that "his springing bow was especially excellent".[132] Even the more senior Joseph Mayseder (1789–1863) took it up, as a report from Boulogne in 1835, about the playing of Leonora Neumann (1819–1840) from Vienna, demonstrates; the reviewer remarked, "only from Mayseder have I encountered such a perfect springing bow".[133] Georg Hellmesberger's son Joseph (1828–1893), as leader of the celebrated Hellmesberger Quartet, later made a speciality of springing bowstrokes, causing the Viennese reviewer of a concert in 1860 to praise him because, in Haydn's String Quartet in G op. 54 no. 1, "He abstained this time more than usual from those virtuoso tricks with springing bow and exaggerated nuances."[134]

In their eagerness to adopt the new bowing pioneered by Böhm, however, Viennese performers were untypical of German violinists in general,[135] as later evidence demonstrates. The fact that the reviewer of Böhm's 1822 concert had never heard this kind of bowstroke from a German violinist shows beyond reasonable doubt that for at least a generation it had not been characteristic of Viennese string playing, despite the quite extensive employment of the related Cramer bowstroke by many northern European string players into the early 19th century. How far back the reviewer's experience extended is unknowable, but if it was Sievers it would have been the 1780s. Perhaps the Cramer technique had never been adopted by Viennese string

---

[131] Anon.: [*Wiener*] *Allgemeine musikalische Zeitung*, vii (1823), 152. The Variations can be seen here: https://imslp.org/wiki/Grandes_Variations_sur_Zelmira%2C_Op.10_(Hellmesberger_Sr.%2C_Georg).

[132] Anon.: *Wiener Theater-Zeitung*, xvii (1824), 614. Jansa's own compositions are particularly interesting for the fact that, when he required an elastic bowstroke in his serious chamber music, he marked it with the instruction "spiccato". This occurs, for instance, just once in his String Quartet op. 65 no. 1 (c. 1844), for a 14-bar passage of separately bowed rapid eighth-notes in the scherzo.

[133] Anon.: *Neue Zeitschrift für Musik*, ii (1835), 118.

[134] Anon.: *Deutsche Musik-Zeitung*, i (1860), 94.

[135] Throughout the 19th century, "German" was used for German-speaking people of all nationalities.

players, who were strongly influenced by north Italian traditions stemming from Tartini.

Despite the continuing prestige of the Viotti School, divergent bowing techniques began to be increasingly influential during the 1820s and 1830s. These are reflected in the major treatises. On the one hand, for instance, Dotzauer's *Méthode de Violoncelle / Violonzell-Schule* (Mainz, [1824]) and Spohr's *Violinschule* (Vienna [1833]) are silent about elastic bowstrokes, while Baudiot's two-volume *Méthode de violoncelle* (Paris, [1826/1828]), Guhr's *Ueber Paganinis Kunst die Violine zu spielen* (Mainz [1830]), Mazas's *Méthode de Violon suivi d'un Traité des Sons Harmoniques en simple et double cordes* (Paris, [1831]), Dotzauer's *Violonzell-Schule* (Vienna, [1833]), Baillot's *L'art du violon* (Paris [1835]), and Meerts's *Douze Études* (Mainz [1838]) describe and advocate them.

The translator's preface to Dotzauer's 1824 treatise refers to "changing taste in music" and divides cellists into two types: those who "focus entirely on producing a beautiful sound and acquiring a pure and expressive taste and those "who are naturally inclined to conquer mechanical difficulties". The former, it explains, "were trained in the great style of the old Italians", while the others "played in a less serious, but more brilliant manner", adding: "The one wanted to move, the other to surprise." Referring to Bernhard Romberg (Dotzauer's teacher) as "one of the greatest cellists that ever existed", the translator stated that Dotzauer's treatise is "based fundamentally on the principles of this great artist", and relates this specifically to fingering and bowing.[136] All bowing of faster notes in Dotzauer's treatise is made without the bow leaving the string.[137] In contrast, Charles-Nicolas Baudiot's *Méthode de violoncelle*, published in the same decade, includes a kind of *détaché* "which one makes by letting the bow spring on the string". In 1824, Dotzauer teaches just four bowing actions: *legato*, slurring across the strings, separate *staccato* notes (Ex. 7.19a), and later, *staccato* notes in a single bowstroke, always up-bow except in the case of two-note dotted figures (Ex. 7.19b–c). In the tradition of the 1803 Paris Conservatoire *Méthode*, Dotzauer emphasizes the importance of multifarious mixed bowing patterns, using a schematic representation (Ex. 7.19d), which he also provides for triplet eighth-notes.

---

[136] Dotzauer: *Méthode*, Préface du traducteur, unpaginated.
[137] Charles Nicolas Baudiot: *Méthode de violoncelle* op. 25, 2 vols. (Paris [1820/26]), ii, 62.

Ex. 7.19 a–d. Dotzauer: *Méthode*. (*a*) 10; (*b*) 14; (*c*) 27; (*d*) 19.

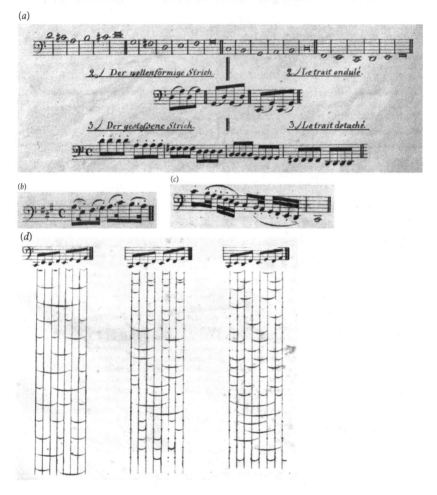

It is illustrative of the changes that took place in bowing during the next few years that Dotzauer's 1833 treatise contains half a page headed "On bowstrokes with a springing bow" describing four types: detached sixteenths in the middle of the bow, eighths a tenth apart where "an intervening string should not be touched", three- and four-note arpeggios across the strings, and *ricochet*. About the last technique, however, he cautions: "The staccato with a springing bow, as opposed to the above-mentioned staccato, which is produced without letting the bow spring, is less to be recommended because it is rarely practical due to its unreliability."[138] It is no coincidence

---

[138] Dotzauer: *Violonzell-Schule für den ersten Unterricht* (Vienna, [1833]), 22.

that this treatise was published in Vienna, where, as many journal reviews show, enthusiasm for these kinds of bowstrokes had been growing since the 1820s.

Spohr's treatment of bowstrokes in his *Violinschule* is more systematic and detailed than any previous string method, but even though it was published in Vienna at the same time as Dotzauer's *Violonzell-Schule*, it makes no mention of a springing bowstroke. From the beginning, Spohr gives precise instructions in the exercises, not only for down- and up-bow, but also, using abbreviations in the text, for length and position in the bow. Since he also gives metronome marks for all the exercises, the speed of the bowstroke is rather accurately specified. After Exercise 50, by which time the student is expected to be able to play up to 7th position, comes a section "On bow management and the various bowstrokes". Spohr assumes that the student will have acquired "correctness in bowing" and can now move on to "dexterity in bowing".[139] After dealing with nuanced *legato*, he continues with instructions for executing "the most usual and effective bowstrokes".[140] These include specific types of detached bowstrokes, as well as mixed patterns of the kind illustrated by Dotzauer. In each case, Spohr indicates numbered bowings above and below the stave to facilitate reference to his verbal instructions. First, for detached notes marked with wedges (Ex. 7.20a) he instructs: "This type of bowstroke (called *détaché* by the French) is made with the longest possible strokes in the upper part of the bow with immobile upper arm. The notes must be completely equal in duration and strength and must follow each other in such a way that no gap is noticeable when the bow is changed."[141] The next twenty examples utilize combinations of slurs and detached notes, involving different lengths of bowstroke that derive from Spohr's *détaché*. At No. 22 Spohr introduces the bowstroke "which is called staccato. It consists of a sharp attack on the notes in a single bowstroke."[142] He confines it to the upper half of the bow, first with two notes, then with increasing numbers in a single bow, the length and exact position of the bow being determined by context (Ex. 7.20b).

---

[139] Spohr: *Violinschule*, 124.
[140] Spohr: *Violinschule*, 130.
[141] Spohr: *Violinschule*, 130.
[142] Spohr: *Violinschule*, 132.

Ex. 7.20  a–f. Spohr: *Violinschule*. (a) 130; (b) 133; (c) 133; (d) 136; (e) 136; (f) 137.

Ex. 7.20 Continued

At No. 1 in Exercise 53 (Ex. 7.20c) he warns that "all notes must be of equal strength and that it is a common, but bad manner of performance always to emphasize the first of three notes". He expects the short notes to be kept quite close to the point of the bow, remarking, "In No. 4, the three slurred notes in the down-bow should be made with as short a stroke as possible, so that they do not have to get too far from the point."[143] He introduces a down-bow *staccato*, but performed from the middle to the point, not from the frog as in Franco-Belgian practice.

In Exercise 54 (Ex. 7.20d), after illustrating four more combinations of slurred and *staccato* notes, he introduces *martelé*, instructing: "the stroke must not be too short, however, because otherwise the notes would become dry and rough. The separation of the notes [Ex. 7.20e] is done by letting the bow stand still on the strings for a moment after each note and thereby immediately inhibiting the vibration of the strongly struck string. The tones must be completely equal in duration and strength."[144] He refers to No. 4 in

---

[143] Spohr: *Violinschule*, 134.
[144] Spohr: *Violinschule*, 136.

Exercise 54 as the "Viotti" bowstroke and later identifies another (Ex. 7.20f) as the "Kreutzer" bowing. He also illustrates the *fouetté*, explaining that the bow "is raised above the string and thrown violently onto it, very close to the point, so that the stick of the bow does not start to tremble. After striking, it is pushed smoothly about 3 inches further."[145] This bowstroke, largely neglected in modern practice, was almost certainly envisaged for the *sfs* in bars 190–94 of the first movement of Mendelssohn's Violin Concerto.

A review of Spohr's *Violinschule* described his careful marking of bow direction and division in the exercises as "an advantage over all other schools, which often do not speak about it at all, or at most in general terms", but it criticized his failure to discuss a bowing, which the French described as: "Very dry (at the frog of the bow)", remarking: "This type of stroke requires its own not insignificant practice, and is frequently used by leading present-day virtuosos, such as Baillot, Molique, Louis Maurer, and Lafont among others."[146] The journal's editor, Gottfried Weber, appended additional comments, including: "In none of our violin schools to date do we find such a comprehensive treatment of everything that a violinist should know and be able to do, with such complete coherence from the basics to the highest level."[147]

When the 42-year-old Frankfurt Kapellmeister Carl Guhr published his treatise on Paganini's violin playing in 1829, he identified six ways in which it "differed from other masters of the violin", the second of these (after scordatura tuning) was "a very idiosyncratic manner of bowing".[148] He explained:

> he knows how to produce the strongest contrasts between *broad legato*, *staccato*, and *springing* notes, the latter in every degree of speed and the most varied characters. [...] In Allegro maestoso he is particularly fond of a bowstroke that differs substantially in execution and effect from that which is indicated in the Parisian violin school [the 1803 *Méthode*] for Allegro maestoso. There it is said: one grasps each struck note with the greatest possible extension and needs half the bow, so that the whole string vibrates properly, and the tone becomes rounded, etc. e.g. [Ex. 7.21]. Paganini, however, allows the bow to make more of a jumping, whipping movement, utilizing almost the middle of it and with only as much length as is

---

[145] Spohr: *Violinschule*, 137.
[146] J. Feski (pseudonym for Eduard Johann Friedrich Sobolewski): in *Caecilia*, xv (1833), 279f.
[147] G. Weber: in *Caecilia*, xv (1833), 282f.
[148] Carl Guhr: *Ueber Paganini's Kunst die Violine zu spielen* (Mainz, [1829]), 4.

necessary to make the string vibrate. He uses this bowing only with half-strong volume, perhaps one degree weaker than mezzo-forte, but then it is also very effective.

The main agent here is the joint of the right hand, while the arm must remain completely still.[149]

Ex. 7.21  Guhr: *Ueber Paganini's Kunst*, 8.

He observed that Paganini rarely used the traditional kind of firm *staccato* from the point of the bow, but that he employed a range of *ricochet* bowstrokes with few or many notes in a single bow. His illustrations of these include the type of springing arpeggios up and down across all four strings, which Paganini employed in the first of his 24 Caprices, and which Mendelssohn was to use in the cadenza of his Violin Concerto.[150]

Although Paganini did not travel north of the Alps until 1828, his reputation and accounts of his techniques were well known before that. He had shared concerts in Italy with Lafont and Lipinsky, and many other violinists would have been aware of his unconventional practices. During a stay of several years in Italy, Jacques-Féréol Mazas became "one of the artists who has studied Paganini's manner the most".[151] Mazas's 1830 *Méthode de violon* included an extensive section on artificial harmonics. During the 1820s he had frequently used these in his concerts, in Paganini's manner, giving rise to criticism of their inappropriate use in places where composers did not intend them. A German reviewer of London concerts in 1822, for instance, objected sarcastically to his performance of a Beethoven string quartet "because he made this great man say so many things that he had certainly never thought of. Beethoven would surely thank him for the harmonics that Mr Mazas thought he should put in every fifth or sixth bar." Mazas's treatise, alongside Guhr's, is also pioneering in its inclusion of springing bowstrokes, and the same reviewer, having complained that French violinists employed

---

[149] Guhr: *Ueber Paganini's Kunst*, 7f.
[150] Guhr: *Ueber Paganini's Kunst*, 9–11.
[151] Anon.: *Revue Musicale*, iv (1830), 39.

"ten times more fiddle and flourish than is necessary", continued: "It is exactly the same with this Mr. Mazas; solidity of playing is completely lacking in him. It is a perpetual jumping around on the strings, without one getting to hear a single full note."[152]

Unlike Dotzauer and Spohr, Mazas dispenses with illustrating all the potential combinations of slurred and separately bowed notes "since they are found in music written for the violin, and especially in modern works, where they are marked with great accuracy". He will, he writes, only indicate those types of bowstroke "that require special study".[153] For the earlier exercises in the *Méthode* he had prescribed a smoothly connected *détaché* with whole bows for long notes, or from the middle to point for shorter ones.[154] He defined the other bowstrokes as: *Martelé*, *Coup d'archet piqué*, *Staccato*. His instructions for *Martelé* correspond with the description in the 1803 Conservatoire *Méthode*. His *Coup d'archet piqué* is the classic slurred *staccato*. The bowstroke he calls *Staccato*, however, encompasses various kinds of springing bowstrokes, both separately bowed and *ricochet*. For the former he instructs: "It differs from the ordinary *détaché* in that the bow, which never leaves the string in the latter, must here, on the contrary, bounce on it, using the middle and giving the least amount of hair possible to each note."[155]

Pierre Baillot's 1835 *L'art du violon*, an updated and greatly expanded version of the 1803 *Méthode*, treats the subject of bowing entirely differently from the earlier treatise and from Spohr's *Violinschule*. His first bowing instructions are for smoothly connected full bowstrokes for long notes, and strokes in the middle third of the bow for shorter ones.[156] Unlike Mazas, he describes a shortened *détaché* bowstroke at an early stage (Ex. 7.22), instructing: "separate each note briskly from point A to point B and stop it neatly, leaving the bow on the string".[157] This serves as a preparation for what he later identifies as *grand détaché*.

---

[152] Anon.: *Allgemeine musikalische Zeitung*, xxiv (1822), 411.
[153] Jacques-Féréol Mazas: *Méthode de violon* op. 34 (Paris, [1832]), 60.
[154] Mazas: *Méthode*, 27.
[155] Mazas: *Méthode*, 62.
[156] Baillot: *L'art du violon*, 14.
[157] Baillot: *L'art du violon*, 17.

Ex. 7.22 Baillot: *L'art du violon*, 17.

Baillot's catalogue of differentiated bowstrokes for successive detached notes is fuller than anything that had preceded this treatise. His analysis of the properties of each region of the bow, and of the various physical movements that can be used to create different types of articulation, is extensive. Each type of bowstroke is shown with specimen music examples, mostly from studies, or French repertoire from Viotti to Bériot, with just a few examples from Haydn and two from Beethoven. His description of *martelé* is similar to Spohr's and Mazas's, but whereas Spohr applies the term *détaché* only to smoothly connected separate bowstrokes in the upper half of the bow, Baillot describes eight different bowstrokes under the general heading *détaché*. He gives the following instructions for seven bowstrokes in which the bow hair does not leave the string:

1. *Grand détaché*. It can only be executed up to a metronome tempo of eighth-note [symbol] = 152,[158] or, for a short time, eighth-note [symbol] = 160. (Ex. 7.23a)

Ex. 7.23a Baillot: *L'art du violon*, 101.

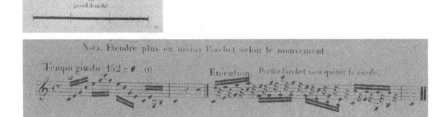

---

[158] In the example, the note value for the metronome mark is misprinted as a quarter, but Baillot's footnote makes it clear that it should be an eighth-note.

2. *Martelé* short sharp strokes and when used at slower tempo, with a bit more length, the bow is stopped and allowed to remain lightly on the string. (Ex. 7.23b)

**Ex. 7.23b** Baillot: *L'art du violon*, 101.

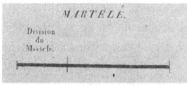

3. *Détaché léger* can be used for faster passages than *grand détaché* (he illustrates it with a passage from Viotti's Violin Concerto no. 24). Its execution is different from the *grand détaché* in that, instead of keeping the bow firmly pressed onto the string after each note one should, "Separate each note by holding the bow very lightly on the string, taking advantage of the elasticity of the stick to give it an imperceptible and slightly elongated bounce."[159] (Ex. 7.23c)

**Ex. 7.23c** Baillot: *L'art du violon*, 108.

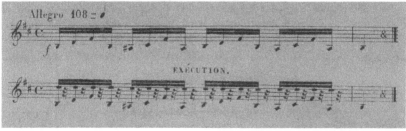

---

[159] Baillot: *L'art du violon*, 108.

4) *Détaché perlé* is used for even faster notes. It is executed like the *détaché léger* but with less bow. He illustrates it with the opening of the final movement of Haydn's String Quartet op. 64 no. 5. (Ex. 7.23d)

Ex. 7.23d Baillot: *L'art du violon*, 108.

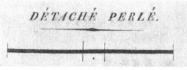

5) *Détaché traîné* or *appuyé* "is played in the middle or at the point of the bow".[160] For the former type, Baillot gives an example from one of his own posthumously published studies, where he states that it should be executed with as little bow as possible. He states that Pierre Rode typically used the type that was played broadly near the point and gives the example of Rode's Caprice no. 10.[161] This helps to explain Spohr's description of *détaché*, since he modelled his own playing on Rode's after hearing him in 1803.

6) *Détaché flûté* is played in the same part of the bow as the previous stroke but very lightly. For this he gives an example from a Boccherini quintet.[162]

7) *Staccato ou détaché articulé* is an on-string slurred *staccato* bowstroke. Baillot's treatment of it is extensive, with many examples. Unlike Spohr, he envisages it occurring in any part of the bow and includes one example of a down-bow slurred *staccato* with twenty-nine notes.[163]

The two springing bowstrokes described by Baillot correspond with those called *Staccato* by Mazas.

1) *Détaché sautillé*, for which he instructs: "Bounce the bow lightly in the same place, leaving the string a little",[164] and gives an example from Paisiello. (Ex. 7.24)

---

[160] Baillot: *L'art du violon*, 109.
[161] Baillot: *L'art du violon*, 110.
[162] Baillot: *L'art du violon*, 110.
[163] Baillot: *L'art du violon*, 102–6.
[164] Baillot: *L'art du violon*, 108.

Ex. 7.24 Baillot: *L'art du violon*, 108.

2) *Staccato à ricochet ou détaché jetté* involves several springing notes in a single bowstroke. He explains that it is usually made down-bow, but can also be made up-bow. He provides one example on pairs of notes where he says Rodolphe Kreutzer employed it in his own 10th Violin Concerto, and also an example from variations by Charles de Bériot including more notes in the bowstroke. For other examples he refers the reader to Guhr's treatise on Paganini.

Another bowing illustrated by Baillot, although not included in his list of specific bowstrokes, does not appear in other methods at that time. It consists of a succession of accented notes on the G-string, played downbow close to the frog. He gives examples from Haydn, Viotti (Ex. 7.25), and his own Violin Concerto no. 2. This is probably the bowstroke that Spohr was criticized for omitting from his *Violinschule*.[165]

Ex. 7.25 Baillot: *L'art du violon*, 93.

Baillot's highly nuanced discussion of bowing was given a more schematic treatment, just three years after the publication of *L'art du violon*, in his pupil Lambert-Joseph Meerts's *Douze Études*, which was designed as an adjunct

---

[165] See above, p. 400. Bériot also describes it (see below, p. 425). In 1929, Carl Flesch (*Die Kunst des Violinspiels*, ii, 57) referred to this bowstroke as "somewhat old-fashioned and hardly used any more in modern works" (etwas veraltet und wird in modernen Werken kaum mehr angewandt).

to his teaching of the beginner classes at the Brussels Conservatoire. Meerts prefaced it with a careful description of his seven basic bowstrokes, which reflect, but differ somewhat from Baillot's.[166] They are described as follows:

1) *Grand détaché.* Unlike Baillot, he instructs that the whole length of the bow should be employed for this stroke and that the initial music examples should sound like the second (Ex. 7.26a)

Ex. 7.26 a–g. Lambert-Joseph Meerts: *Douze Etudes* (Mainz, [1838]), 2–3. (a) *Grand détaché;* (b) *Détaché chantant;* (c) *Détaché martelé;* (d) *Détaché d'avantbras;* (e) *Détaché du milieu;* (f) *Martelé du talon;* (g) un-named.

[166] Lambert-Joseph Meerts: *Douze Études pour le Violon* (Mainz, Schott [1838]), 2f.

**Ex. 7.26** Continued

2) *Détaché chantant*. The "singing *détaché*" is played with full length strokes. He symbolizes this by the rectangle under the note (Ex. 7.26b).

3) *Détaché martelé*. The "hammered *détaché*" is made with the forearm; each note is accented and abruptly stopped without coming off the string (Ex. 7.26c).

4) *Détaché d'avantbras*. The "forearm *détaché*" is made with connected bowstrokes (Ex. 7.26d).

5) *Détaché du milieu*. Meerts instructs that the "*détaché* in the middle" be made by the wrist "in order to give enough vibration to the stick to articulate the note sharply and quickly". He recommends first to practice it on a repeated pitch. This looks at first sight like Baillot's *détaché sautillé*, in which the bow rebounds from the string between notes, but Meerts adds a footnote instructing that "it should also be noted that the hair does not leave the string"[167] (Ex. 7.26e).

[167] Meerts: *Douze Études*, 2.

6) Meerts does not name this bowstroke. He notes that although it "looks very similar to the fifth, it differs totally in its effect, and in the manner of practising it". He instructs that "between each note, the bow must be lifted from the string and allowed to fall back, taking care that it always falls in the same place, and that it is straight on the string".[168] This evidently corresponds with Baillot's *détaché sautillé*, made without participation of the upper arm (now called *spiccato*) (Ex. 7.26f).[169]

7) *Martelé du talon*. Meerts explains that this "*martelé* at the frog" should be practised "not only to be able to use this bow stroke, but also for the capability it gives, to activate all the joints of the arm"[170] (Ex. 7.26g). In this respect, perhaps, he presages the thrown bowstroke and the exercises in Ševčík's op. 2.[171]

Meerts's *Études* went through many editions and served as a foundation for Franco-Belgian bowing technique for the rest of the 19th century.

During the 1820s and 1830s, therefore, Baillot, his pupils, and his younger colleagues in Paris and Brussels were at the forefront of promulgating a new pedagogical approach to bowing technique. By the mid-1830s, Spohr's concept of bowing, which was essentially an elaborated version of what had been taught in the 1803 Paris Conservatoire *Méthode*, would have been seen by Franco-Belgian musicians as incomplete and inadequate for the performance of the new virtuoso repertoire; it is significant that a French edition of Spohr's *Violinschule*, published in the mid-1830s, omits almost all his verbal instructions for bowing in Exercises 52–54, and that its short description of the first bowing in Exercise 52 is completely different (referring only to execution at the point of the bow, with no reference to connecting the notes without a break).[172] His manner of executing bowstrokes, especially his repeated emphasis on remaining in the upper half of the bow, would have seemed far too "Germanic" in Paris and Brussels by the late 1830s.

Resistance to the Franco-Belgian innovations, especially in the performance of Classical repertoire, was strong among German string players, where Spohr's example, and that of his many pupils, remained influential. In

---

[168] Meerts: *Douze Études*, 3.
[169] See below, pp. 437–41, for a later approach to this type of bowstroke.
[170] Meerts: *Douze Études*, 3.
[171] See below, p. 438.
[172] Spohr: *École ou Méthode pour le Violon*, trans. Stephen Heller (Paris: Richault [c. 1833/1835]), 110 (*de la pointe de l'archet*). This French translation was originally produced in separate parts with different plate numbers, some of which were initially published as Études (advertised in the *Revue Musicale* in May 1834). In April 1834, the *Revue Musicale* (p. 128) promised a review of Spohr's "grande méthode", but this seems never to have been published.

Vienna, however, even before Paganini's 1828 visit, musicians and audiences had responded enthusiastically to the newer practices, which are repeatedly mentioned in the Viennese press during the 1840s, but only in relation to virtuoso repertoire. In 1841, Carl Kunt described August Pott (1806–1883) as "one of the leading violinists of the German Spohr school", who will "delight his listeners everywhere with genuine pleasures and, furthermore, with all the fashionable flashy tricks, for which there is so much demand in the great competitive market of the performing arts". As the final piece in his concert Pott performed François Prume's "La melancholie, Pastorale" op. 1, which made a feature of Bériot's recently popularized "Tremolo" bowing.[173] Kunt remarked sarcastically: "*spiccato-arpeggio* and *tremolo*-variations on an original theme, 'The Tremolo' has even been taken up by the shepherds! Where else will this panting, sweat-dripping, monstrous phenomenon go? Is this also a 'pastorale?' God forbid!"[174] The following year, Théodore Hauman (1806–1878) played Bériot's "Le Tremolo" in Vienna, where this bowstroke was described as "continuous *spiccato*".[175] In 1843 "*spiccato*" was mentioned in a review of Theresa Milanollo's playing.[176] In 1844, Prume's "*spiccato*" was described as "pearl-like" (*geperlt*);[177] and in the same year, the Belgian cellist Servais was praised for his "light *staccato* with short springing bowstrokes", for which he held the bow only "with thumb and forefinger".[178]

These practices were still seen during the 1830s and 1840s as innovations. In 1837, the Viennese aesthetician Ignaz Jeitteles remarked that "the newer school has significantly perfected the theory of bowing";[179] and in 1844, Anton Gröber, asking for Spohr's guidance in performing a passage of separate sixteenth-notes in the last movement of his Violin Concerto no. 11 op. 70, inquired whether he should "play it with a firm, on-string bowing, or whether it is allowed to bounce a little according to the modern bowing style".[180]

---

[173] See below, p. 429.

[174] Carl Kunt: *Wiener Zeitschrift* (1841), 1279.

[175] Thalhof: *Österreichisches Morgenblatt* (1842), 569. The term *spiccato* appears to have originated in Vienna, to describe any kind of springing bowstroke. It was only gradually adopted elsewhere. The first uses I have discovered are in the *Wiener Theater Zeitung* (6 May 1833) and the *Allgemeine Musikalische Anzeiger* (30 January 1834), the latter in a review of Ole Bull, which mentions that his bow was "completely different from the usual violin bow and made by Lupot in Paris. In spiccato (springing) it is said to produce the *non plus ultra*."

[176] Thalhof: *Österreichisches Morgenblatt* (1843), 199.

[177] Anon.: *Der Humorist* (1844), 1175.

[178] Anon.: *Signale für die musikalische Welt* (1844), 140. This mode of execution was described by Bériot in violin playing see p. 426.

[179] Ignaz Jeitteles: *Aesthetisches Lexicon* (Vienna, 1837), ii, 188.

[180] Anton Gröber to Louis Spohr, Innsbruck, 8 January 1844. Autograph in Universitätsbibliothek Kassel–Landesbibliothek und Murhardsche Bibliothek der Stadt Kassel (D-Kl), Sign. 4a Ms. Hass. 287. Online at http://www.spohr-briefe.de.

At what point these "modern" bowings began to be used in performing Viennese Classical compositions is uncertain; but by the 1840s, it seems clear that this was becoming a live issue. When the 12-year-old Joseph Joachim, who was practising Paganini at that time, went from Vienna to Leipzig in 1843, he asked Mendelssohn whether it was appropriate to use springing bowstrokes in Classical compositions and reportedly received the answer: "Always, my boy if it is suitable for the particular place and sounds good."[181] It is evident that Joachim, during his early years, had gained the impression that those bowstrokes were not stylistically appropriate in Classical repertoire. Might Joachim's teachers, Böhm and David, both of whom used springing bowstrokes in specific contexts, have eschewed them in Classical chamber music, or might the question have arisen because one or both *did*, sometimes, use them in that repertoire? David's bowing instructions in his printed editions suggests that he did not expect that kind of bowstroke in Classical chamber music; his manuscript markings in copies from which he played show evidence of springing bowstrokes in Baroque and contemporary music (which he often specified either with the annotation *spgd* or *saltato*), but not in Viennese Classical works. In the present state of the evidence, Böhm's practice cannot be ascertained, although Anton Schindler claimed that Böhm regarded them as inappropriate in Classical chamber music. If Böhm did use springing bowstrokes in that repertoire, it was certainly not until after 1822, but some of his pupils, including Joachim, and many of his Viennese colleagues, for instance the Hellmesberger Quartet, employed them in Classical repertoire as early as the 1850s.[182]

In France, it seems clear that string players were already using these types of bowing in "serious" chamber music. The violinist Alexandre Malibran (1823–1867) reported that George Onslow (1784–1853) complained about the inappropriate use of springing bowstrokes in his chamber music, exclaiming: "Ah! the miserable creatures! they spring too much for me, much too much; I almost talk myself to death with the frequent repetition of this warning and they always do it again and again! It is a foregone conclusion, a nail in my coffin."[183] In Germany, in the 1840s and 1850s, however, many German string players had not yet adopted these bowstrokes. Many seem either to have ignored Franco-Belgian technical developments,

---

[181] Andreas Moser: *Joseph Joachim. Ein Lebensbild* (Berlin, 1898), 45. The wording of Mendelssohn's answer was doubtless from Joachim's memory.
[182] These issues are discussed further below, pp. 414–17.
[183] Alexandre Malibran: *Louis Spohr* (Frankfurt am Main, 1860), 208.

or to have failed to master them. When Henri Vieuxtemps visited Berlin in 1846, Friedrich Hieronymus Truhn (1811–1886) wrote a very unflattering comparison of Belgian and German violinists. Having expressed his admiration for "the great reformer of violin playing, the brilliant genius Nicolo Paganini", who "travelled with his magical violin through Germany, France, England and defeated the classic school of the Paris Conservatoire", Truhn asserted: "as far as possible the greatest and most renowned virtuosos adopted his method", and "it is Belgian violinists who have most successfully followed the example of the great Genoese." He identified Charles de Bériot as the creator of a Belgian school and named Vieuxtemps, Artôt, Ghys, Hauman, Prume, Sainton, Stévéniers, and Léonard as its products. Turning to German violinists, he remarked patronizingly that they are mostly "good people who have acquired some proficiency" and that whereas the Belgians "are all more or less real virtuosos, real concert players, one can tell from the first bowstroke of most of the brave German violinists that they are actually very capable orchestral players who have put on solo dress for a particularly festive occasion, have acquired a violin that is as good as possible, but on which they are not yet quite at home, and sometimes miss a little, or even scratch a little at the frog with short chords that cannot be executed with the point of the bow."[184] Truhn's last comment draws attention to the fact that in the mid-19th century, many German violinists retained the older practice of playing most short notes on the string in the upper half of the bow, rather than using elastic bowstrokes.

A couple of years earlier, Wilhelm Happ had written to his former teacher, Spohr, about his experiences in Belgium, explaining how the amateurs "torture themselves with Bériot and Vieuxtemps, and if one doesn't make a fool of oneself with their *sautillés* and *saltandos*, they say one has a stiff arm [. . .]. I have never tackled Bériot, Hauman, or the like, and therefore I lack the coquetry in bowing to play these shallow, insubstantial things to those people's satisfaction."[185] Even in the following decade, on-string bowing, for a succession of fast and moderately fast notes, remained typical of German violinists. In 1851, when Otto von Königslöw (1824–1898), a pupil of Ferdinand David, performed Beethoven's "Kreutzer" Sonata in Paris, Henri

---

[184] (Friedrich) Hieronymus Truhn: 'Henri Vieuxtemps', *Allgemeine musikalische Zeitung*, xlvi (1846), 330f.
[185] Wilhelm Happ an Louis Spohr, Paris, Mittwoch 2. März 1842. Universitätsbibliothek Kassel–Landesbibliothek und Murhardsche Bibliothek der Stadt Kassel (D-Kl), Sign. 4° Ms. Hass. 287 Online at: http://www.spohr-briefe.de/briefe-einzelansicht?&m=1842030240&suchbegriff=happ|#|autoren.

Blanchard (1778–1758), who had studied with Rodolphe Kreutzer, described Königslöw as having "a conscientious German style of playing. His intonation is accurate, his double stops sound good; the bow is kept on the string; his trill is pearly and brilliant; he has a good cantabile; but all this lacks elegance, variety, bow pressure,[186] and that exquisite sensibility that comes from what we call the sixth sense in music: it's teutonic, it's heavy."[187] And in 1853, during a visit to Vienna by the celebrated Müller Quartet,[188] Eduard Hanslick compared their playing with that of the Viennese Hellmesberger Quartet, led at that time by Joseph Hellmesberger Sr. (1828–1893). About Carl Friedrich Müller (1797–1873) he remarked: "His bow has more power, but not the refinement and variety of Hellmesberger's", adding in a footnote: "Like almost all north German violinists, Müller makes no use of a 'springing bow.'" Hanslick's more detailed comparison reveals a substantial stylistic gulf. Having praised Hellmesberger as the more accomplished soloist, he continued:

> On the other hand, Müller's broad, pithy playing and his unerringly chaste artistic sense make him a perfect quartet player, while the more virtuoso Hellmesberger sometimes pushes his personality forward and allows the other three gentlemen to court him musically. The greatest technical advantage of Müller's quartet lies in the equally masculine and purposeful participation of all four voices, which nevertheless pay the utmost attention to the occasions where a momentary retreat of the individual seems appropriate. The Müllers' strong tone and expression give them an advantage over Hellmesberger's ensemble, whose tone often verges on susurration and whose smooth sentimental expression not infrequently blurs the pure contours of musical thought with individual accents, rubatos, and similar refinements. Müller pulls the tone out of his violin by the root, Hellmesberger likes to pluck it at the tip.

He added, probably reflecting a current criticism in Vienna: "To accuse Hellmesberger's quartet of coquetry is going too far."[189]

---

[186] He probably means "subtlety of bow pressure".
[187] Henri Blanchard: *Revue et gazette Musicale*, xviii (1851), 108.
[188] The four Müller brothers from Brunswick formed a quartet in 1830 and began a series of tours that continued until 1855. See Louis Köhler: *Die Gebrüder Müller und das Streich-Quartett* (Leipzig, 1858).
[189] E. H. [Eduard Hanslick]: *Wiener Zeitschrift*, 23 November 1853, p. 1085f.

Strongly divergent styles of bowing undoubtedly co-existed during the middle years of the 19th century. Königslöw, Happ, the Müllers, and many other accomplished German string players, especially Spohr's pupils, who remained true to earlier 19th-century traditions, represented a style that was increasingly regarded as old-fashioned and, by many, as inferior to the newer French and Belgian virtuosity. Already in 1826, Sievers, writing about Alexandre Boucher and Paganini as "charlatans" in violin playing, observed: "The Germans do not possess a single charlatan violinist; that is the reason that none of their violinists have made their mark abroad, e.g. in France and Italy, and that in these lands, especially in France, they even doubt whether there is actually any art of violin playing in Germany."[190] Sievers's comment tallies with the condescending comment of a Parisian critic after a concert given there by Spohr in 1821: "if he stays for a while in Paris he will be able to perfect his taste and then return to form that of the good Germans".[191]

## A Controversy about Bowstrokes in Beethoven

In the 1850s, the question of appropriate bowstrokes for Viennese Classical repertoire remained controversial. It came to the fore in connection with chamber music concerts in Frankfurt am Main, instituted by the Böhm pupil Ludwig Straus (1835–1899). The concerts gave rise to a series of reviews by Beethoven's former associate and biographer Anton Schindler (1795–1864). Schindler, a capable violinist, who had served as Konzertmeister of the orchestra of the Josephstädter Theatre in Vienna during the 1820s, was highly critical of Straus's bowing, which he regarded as totally inappropriate, stylistically, for Classical repertoire.

In his first review, Schindler deplored the execution of the *staccato* eighth-notes in the Presto finale of Beethoven's String Trio op. 9 no. 1 "with a jumping bow at the so-called frog, so that it was absolutely impossible to follow the composition, because attention was solely focused on the virtuoso with his inappropriate *spiccato*". Having asked rhetorically: "Do these recently invented bowstrokes have any justification for being used in the chamber music of the Classics, into which our young virtuosos so often introduce

---

[190] G. L. P. Sievers: 'Schröpfköpfe für Componisten, Operndichter, Sänger und Publicum', *Caecilia*, vii (1829), 248.
[191] Spohr: 'Briefe aus Paris von Louis Spohr. Dritter Brief', *Allgemeine musikalische Zeitung*, xxiii (1821), 181.

them?",[192] he asserted that "dancing about with the bow at the frog" inevitably "results in the most dignified composition being dragged down into the class of ordinary salon music".[193]

In his second article, Schindler criticized Straus's performance of Haydn and Beethoven string quartets, observing: "the usual treatment of the short staccato notes must still be mentioned as particularly annoying. Everything of this sort, however serious, is played with a springing bow and the three colleagues join in with this. Not just individual passages, but entire motifs and movements were performed in this way, e.g. the Allegretto of Beethoven's F major quartet: ♩♩♩♩♩♩♩♩♩♩♩♩♩♩."[194]

For such passages, Schindler evidently envisaged the short on-string bowstrokes that are implied by Ferdinand David's contemporaneous edition (see Ex. 7.27a–b). The categories of detached bowstroke that Schindler considered appropriate in Classical works generally, where Straus and his colleagues were using springing strokes, were the ones designated *détaché* and *détaché léger* by Baillot, whose descriptions of their execution he quotes in his article, from a German translation of Baillot's treatise. It is significant, perhaps, that Schindler writes nothing about the classic *martelé*. Perhaps this too was not a typical bowstroke of Viennese violinists during Beethoven's time in Vienna, although it is described (based on the text in the 1803 Conservatoire *Méthode*) in Joseph von Blumenthal's 1811 Viennese *Violin Schule*[195] and may have been used by some younger players in specific contexts. It was undoubtedly employed by Spohr[196] during his time in Vienna (1812–1815) as second Kapellmeister and Orchesterdirektor at the Theater an der Wien, the orchestra in which Blumenthal played.

In his third article, Schindler returned to the matter of springing bowstrokes, and responded to a comment by a writer in the Viennese *Deutsche Musik-Zeitung* about his condemnation of them in the Allegretto of Beethoven's op. 59 no. 1. The writer agreed with Schindler's general premise, observing: "about the excessive use of the 'springing bow' [...] we are broadly in agreement with Mr. Sch., but with one reservation", and he asserted that the motif from the Allegretto of op. 59 no. 1 "cannot, as we see it, be given

---

[192] Anton Schindler: 'Aus Frankfurt am Main II [Quartett-Spiel]', *Niederrheinische Musik-Zeitung*, vii (1859), 387.
[193] Schindler: *Niederrheinische Musik-Zeitung*, vii (1859), 388.
[194] Schindler: *Niederrheinische Musik-Zeitung*, vii (1859), 62.
[195] Joseph von Blumenthal: *Kurzgefasste theoretisch-praktische Violin Schule*, 19.
[196] E.g., in some passages of the chamber music (opp. 29–35) that he wrote there.

in *piano* in any other way than with a springing bow, although between a 'springing' and 'whipping' bow there is a difference".[197] Schindler's response to this shows that, like many of his contemporaries, he was confused about where the practice of employing springing bowstrokes originated; but his knowledge that it post-dated Viennese practice during most of Beethoven's creative lifetime, and that it was particularly associated with what came to be known as the Franco-Belgian School, is clear. Schindler argued that the Viennese critic "obviously derived this belief from the practice of our time; he is unaware that the Classical period knew nothing about that type of stroke, that it owes its invention only to Mr de Bériot, whose students Haumann, Vieuxtemps, Therese Milanollo and others spread it more widely, and both of the latter also introduced it in quartet playing." And he suggested that "The young critic in the *Deutsche Musik-Zeitung* could easily have enquired about it from old musicians of the imperial city, who heard Schuppanzigh († 1830)".[198] Bowings in annotated editions of op. 59 no. 1 by Ferdinand David and the Hellmesberger Quartet clearly demonstrate that David played the short notes predominantly near the point, while the Hellmesbergers played them near the frog (Ex. 7.27a–b).

Ex. 7.27 a–b. Beethoven op. 59/1/ii. Allegretto vivace e sempre scherzando ♩. = 56. Ferdinand David's bowings compared with the Hellmesberger Quartet bowings, reproduced in the Universal Edition (1901). (*a*) b. 79ff: i. David; ii. Hellmesberger; (*b*) b. 175ff; i. David; ii. Hellmesberger.

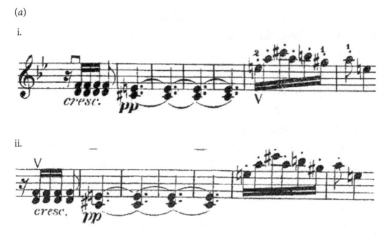

[197] Anon.: 'Zeitungsschau', *Deutsche Musik-Zeitung*, viii (1860), 72.
[198] Schindler: 'Ueber Quartettspiel', *Niederrheinische Musik-Zeitung*, viii (1860), 143.

ARTICULATION AND STRING BOWING 417

**Ex. 7.27** Continued

Many of the bowing instructions in David's numerous editions clearly indicate the use of the upper half of the bow, whereas late-19th-century re-engravings of these editions, still with David's name on the title page, but revised after his death by an un-named editor, include many alterations that facilitate the performance of *staccato* passages near the frog, for instance Ex. 7.28a–b.

**Ex. 7.28** a–b. Beethoven: String Trio op. 9/1/i, Allegro con brio, 55ff. (*a*) Peters pl. no. 4902; (*b*) Peters pl. no. 8942.

Ex. 7.28 Continued

Concerns about springing bowstrokes in Classical repertoire remained a live issue into the 1870s. A reviewer of chamber concerts, including works by Mozart, Beethoven, Schubert, and Mendelssohn, in Strasbourg in 1872 (clearly motivated partly by nationalism, after the German annexation of the city in 1871, following the Franco-Prussian War), reported that "Apart from some mannerisms probably left over from French taste— such as inappropriate use of springing bowings and the like—we were quite pleased with the performances."[199] Andreas Moser's statement that Mendelssohn's advice had freed Joachim "from certain violinistic habits and prejudices, e.g. that springing bowings should not be used in Classical compositions", suggests that there were still German string players in the 1890s who regarded the employment of these bowstrokes in that repertoire as inappropriate.

An interesting pendant to this is provided by an account of the Budapest Quartet's playing in 1927, which caused friction with their new second violinist. The first violinist and cellist "Hauser and Ipolyi did not play spiccato in the customary way of bowing", they did not use "the middle of the bow to create the staccato needed for the execution of fast passages of notes of equal length—as in the scherzo of Beethoven's Quartet in F, Opus 59, No. 1", they employed "very short, incisive strokes with the tip, or point, of the bow".[200] By that date, such an approach seemed unthinkable to most young string players.

---

[199] Anon.: 'Strassburg i. Elsass', *Allgemeine musikalische Zeitung*, vii (1872), 116.
[200] Nat Brandt: *Con Brio: Four Russians Called the Budapest String Quartet* (San Jose, 1993), 41f. The recording can be heard here https://www.youtube.com/watch?v=IurC2218K2Y .

## Orchestral Bowing in the Mid- to Late-19th Century

Schindler concluded his discussion with a warning, which suggests that by 1860 springing bowstrokes, though increasingly heard in Classical chamber music, were still not common in orchestral playing. Having criticized the *Deutsche Musik-Zeitung* for potentially encouraging young violinists to "persist in the wrong use of the bow", he feared that "Perhaps we will still be surprised by seeing the springing bow manifesting its annoying presence in the symphony; indeed, in the fourth movement of the [Beethoven] Symphony in B flat major, the major-key section in the Scherzo of the one in C minor, the Prometheus Overture, but also places in the works of other Classical composers, it would truly produce a diabolical effect."[201] Schindler's "surprise" was nevertheless soon to become a "diabolical" reality.

Lack of co-ordinated bowing in most German orchestras during the 1840s and 1850s meant that some players, who had evidently fallen under Franco-Belgian influence, already began to use springing bowstrokes in some contexts, while others did not. Inconsistent orchestral bowing was complained about as early as 1849, when the virtuoso double-bass player, August Müller (1808–1869), observed:

> Staccatos, for example, are so seldom performed uniformly, and it seems to me that, in this regard, a stricter control on the part of the orchestra directors would be entirely justifiable. Light, playful figures are often taken by one violin player with a springing bow, while another uses a firm bow; this disturbs and damages the effect.[202]

By the 1840s, an expanded repertoire of bowstrokes was evidently beginning to be used, especially by solo players influenced by the most recent trends in Franco-Belgian string playing. Also, with the increase of conservatoire training, bowings that would previously have been the province of the virtuoso were being employed in the orchestra. The meticulously detailed scores of Meyerbeer's Parisian operas show that the composer, perhaps conscious of the growing tendency to employ springing bowstrokes

---

[201] Schindler: *Niederrheinische Musik-Zeitung*, viii (1860), 143.
[202] August Müller: 'Ueber das Wirken des Musikers im Orchester' [About the role of the musician in the orchestra], *Neue Zeitschrift für Musik*, xxxi (1849), 218–19.

420  CLASSICAL AND ROMANTIC PERFORMING PRACTICE

for light *staccato* passages, even in the mid-1830s, felt the need to include instructions where he envisaged a particular style of articulation that would not be achieved by a springing bowstroke (Ex. 7.29a–c).

**Ex. 7.29** a–c. Meyerbeer, *Les Huguenots*, 1st edn score. (*a*) Act II, no. 7, p. 256 "lightly and at the point of the bow"; (*b*) Act II, no. 9, p. 288 "*pp* and at the point of the bow"; (*c*) Act III, no. 16, p. 457 "gentle and at the point of the bow".

In Franco-Belgian practice, however, springing bowstrokes were by no means established as a general orchestral practice in the 1860s.[203] François-Auguste Gevaert, in his 1863 treatise on instrumentation acknowledged only three types of bowing with separate bows: (1) without *staccato* marks,

---

[203] François-Auguste Gevaert: *Traité général d'instrumentation* (Paris, 1863).

which could be used "in all dynamics and all tempos"; (2) with *staccato* dots, adding "In moderate tempos, if you want to obtain great power of sound, you should add: *with the full length of the bow*" and (3) with *staccato* strokes, which he called "The dry détaché".[204] In his 1885 treatise, however, he included the full range of soloist's bowings (except the slurred firm *staccato*) stating that they had "long been introduced into all good orchestras".[205]

Lack of uniform bowing styles in orchestral performance was still a problem in German orchestras in the 1870s; but it is evident that some musicians, perhaps many, no longer regarded springing bowstrokes as inappropriate in Beethoven's orchestral music. After listing deficiencies in performances of works by Wagner and Liszt at the Hamburg Philharmonic Concerts in 1872, a critic complained about conflicting bowing in the string section, in the fugato of the second movement of Beethoven's Seventh Symphony (b. 183ff) where the *staccato* notes "were made by the first violins with a springing bowstroke, by the second violins almost at the point of the bow".[206] Presumably both sections followed the style of their leader. Comments in an 1871 article entitled "Something about the Role of a Concertmaster" demonstrate that stylistic distinctions between later 19th-century repertoire and Classical works were still a controversial matter in this respect:

A person with refined musical taste will certainly be reluctant to have a violin part, which is almost entirely written in the scherzando style, like that of Nicholai's "Merry Wives", performed primarily with short old-fashioned stiff staccato at the tip of the bow, as I heard 8 years ago in Dresden, but will prefer the substitution of the more modern so-called spiccato in the middle of the bow—on the other hand he will know how to prevent this spiccato from being used, as I have unfortunately already heard, in the great, weighty sixteenth-note figure in Gluck's overture to "Iphigenia in Aulis".[207]

Among later composers, who seem not to have expected much if any use of spiccato in their orchestral music, or in his works in general, was Brahms. A violinist in the Frankfurt Museumsorchester (one of the largest in Germany at that time, with which Brahms often worked) recalled: "Brahms

---

[204] Gevaert: *Traité général*, 23. In his 1885 treatise he equated "dry détaché" with "martelé".
[205] Gevaert: *Nouveau traité*, 27.
[206] H-h: 'Hamburg, 9 März', *Musikalisches Wochenblatt*, iii (1872), 128.
[207] A. Ritter: 'Einiges über Concertmeisterthum', *Musikalisches Wochenblatt*, ii (1871), 293.

was rather dismissive of what he jokingly called "conservatory bowstrokes", the virtuoso, lightly thrown ones *à la Paganini*. He loved a tonally beautiful, healthy, virile violin tone."[208]

## The Absorption of Franco-Belgian Techniques into German Practice

Two major mid-19th-century treatises—the *Méthode de violon* (1858/9) by Charles de Bériot (1802–1870) and the *Violinschule* (1863) by Ferdinand David (1810–1873)—demonstrate that essentially the same range of bowstrokes was present in the teaching of the Brussels and Leipzig conservatories by the mid-19th century. Bériot's treatment of bowing encompassed all the techniques employed in Franco-Belgian training, which were being increasingly applied to the full range of concert repertoire. David, while acknowledging the necessity for mastering those techniques, certainly had a different view of the musical contexts in which they should be used. Bériot and David, nevertheless, in common with most pre-20th-century string players, both gave priority to the instrument's vocal qualities.[209] Similar priorities are apparent in *L'art du violoncelle* (1884) by Olive-Charlier Vaslin (1794–1889).

Bériot's initial bowing exercises employ the middle and upper half of the bow. His *grand détaché* was to be executed "in a slow tempo and with sustained bow strokes for the duration of the value of the notes; then [. . .] in a more accelerated movement, with lively bow strokes, from point A to point B, observing a silence between each note"[210] (Ex. 7.30).

Ex. 7.30 Bériot: *Méthode*, i, 30.

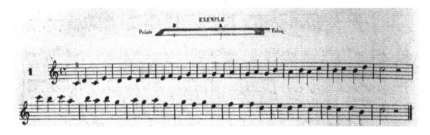

---

[208] Hermann Hock: *Ein Leben mit der Geige. Erinnerungen an Blütezeiten des Musiklebens in Frankfurt am Main* (Frankfurt [1950]), 69f. Hock joined the orchestra in about 1890 and later became its Konzertmeister.
[209] See Brown: 'Singing and String Playing in Comparison'.
[210] Bériot: *Méthode*, i, 30.

ARTICULATION AND STRING BOWING 423

David's early bowing exercises, incorporated into short pieces rather than studies, include more varied rhythms and make considerable use of the point and upper half of the bow, reserving the lower half for more accented, longer notes, or slurred figures (Ex. 7.31a–b).

Ex. 7.31 a–b. David: *Violinschule*. (*a*) i, 34. (For the meaning of the abbreviations see Ex. 7.33.); (*b*) i, 38.

(*a*)

(*b*)

Bériot and David also differ in their treatment of more advanced bowing techniques. Bériot divides his *détaché* bowstrokes into three categories: (1) *Continu* (connected); (2) *Coupé ou mat* (cut off or dry); and (3) *Rebondissent ou élastique* (rebounding or elastic). He normally expected his *détaché continu* to be centred two-thirds of the way towards the point, with more or less breadth according to the note length and volume, and played with "a back-and-forth movement that occurs without interruption between the sounds". He considered it practicable in sixteenth-notes up to a speed of about ¼ =138, explaining, "This *détaché* is the one from which one obtains the greatest power of sound, it allows the stroke to be nuanced by the breadth and pressure graduated according to the force one wants to attain"[211] (Ex. 7.32a). He instructed that the *détaché coupé ou mat* should be played "broadly towards the middle of the bow" and that it was particularly suitable for "grand and majestic passages in concertos, especially where the bow jumps from one string to another"[212] (Ex. 7.32b). His final example of on-string

---

[211] Bériot: *Méthode*, 76.
[212] Bériot: *Méthode*, 80.

separate bowstrokes is the *martelé*, which "differs only from the preceding by its extent. It is made towards the point with a short, sharp and tight wrist action" (Ex. 7.32c).[213] Bériot also includes one other separate bowstroke, not mentioned by David: the succession of down-bows at the frog (*coup d'archet du talon*) mentioned by Baillot,[214] which he illustrates with an example from his 5th Violin Concerto, explaining "This effect is hardly used except on the 4th string and as the termination of a passage in a concerto"[215] (Ex. 7.32d).

**Ex. 7.32a**  Bériot: *Méthode*, ii, 76. *Détaché continu.*

**Ex. 7.32b**  Bériot: *Méthode*, ii, 80. *Détaché coupé ou mat.*

**Ex. 7.32c**  Bériot: *Méthode*, ii, 81. *Martelé.*

---

[213] Bériot: *Méthode*, 81.
[214] See p. 406.
[215] Bériot: *Méthode*, 118.

Ex. 7.32d  Bériot: *Méthode*, ii, 118. *Coup d'archet du talon*.

David describes similar on-string bowstrokes but treats their usage differently. He gives a page of examples, ranging from connected strokes (marked with *tenuto* lines) to separated strokes (marked with *staccato* wedges), but also in combinations of slurred and separate bows, some with varied accentuation (Ex. 7.33).

Ex. 7.33  David: *Violinschule*, ii, 37.

These reflect the typical "Viotti School" bowing patterns that occur in the 1803 Paris Conservatoire *Méthode*[216] and the bowing exercises in Spohr's 1833 *Violinschule*.[217] While Spohr uses the wedge/stroke both for full-length uninterrupted bowstrokes and *martelé*, David makes a notational distinction between separate on-string bowstrokes that are connected uninterruptedly (‿) and those that are shortened (ˌ). Like Spohr, he marks many bowstrokes to be executed close to the point of the bow, whereas Bériot's preference is for all separate strokes except *martelé* (Ex. 7.32c) to be executed more towards the middle. Unlike both Spohr and Bériot, David does not use the term *martelé*, nor describes a specific *martelé* execution, probably expecting the violinist to give the notes with *staccato* strokes a greater or lesser degree of separation and sharpness according to context. Like Spohr and later Joachim, he also includes the *fouetté* (though without naming it), for which he devised a special sign (see No. 12 in Ex. 7.8) that occurs in printed editions of several of his own compositions, and which he wrote by hand into some of his personal copies of other composers' music.[218] This stroke is not mentioned by Bériot, nor, to my knowledge, in any French or Franco-Belgian treatise, despite its French terminology and the fact that the Joachim and Moser *Violinschule* illustrates its use mainly with examples from Rode and Kreutzer.

In their treatment of elastic bowstrokes with separate bows, Bériot and David also differ somewhat. Bériot provides two examples, instructing: "the bow leaves the string after each note by an elastic impulse of the wrist. This *détaché* is made between the 1st and 2nd thirds of the hair at moderate tempo"[219] (Ex. 7.34a). He explains that when the tempo becomes faster the bowstroke naturally moves further towards the point, and that as part of this process the fingers are slightly raised from the bow stick until in the upper part of the bow it is held only by the thumb and index finger (Ex. 7.34b).

---

[216] Baillot et al.: *Méthode*, 132f.
[217] Spohr: *Violinschule*, 130–37.
[218] For David's annotated personal copies see https://mhm.hud.ac.uk/chase/article/uppingham-collection/.
[219] Bériot: *Méthode*, ii, 84.

Ex. 7.34 a–b. Bériot: *Méthode*. (*a*) ii, 84; (*b*) ii, 85.

(*a*)

(*b*)

David, in contrast, divides the elastic bowstrokes into two distinct classes, which he categorizes as "hopping" (*hüpfend, hpfd*) and "springing" (*springend, spgd*). For the former he instructs: "The bow must not leave the string completely; try to make the stick vibrate strongly and play with a very loose wrist, for *forte* in the middle, for *piano* a little more towards the upper half of the bow"[220] (Ex. 7.35a). For the springing bow he instructs that "the bow leaves the string a little between one note and the next; beware of hardness and dryness of tone, which one avoids by letting the bow brush the string a little as it falls".[221] As can be seen from his example (Ex. 7.35b), a slower tempo is implied for this bowstroke, but he gave no further information about the mechanism for its execution. Neither Bériot nor David suggests that the arm is involved in producing these elastic bowstrokes. The wrist alone seems to have been envisaged; they adhere essentially to the principle that the upper arm and shoulder are passive, moving only where absolutely necessary and having no role in the creation of the bowstroke.

---

[220] David: *Violinschule*, ii, 38.
[221] David: *Violinschule*, ii, 38.

**Ex. 7.35** a–b. David: *Violinschule* (*a*) ii, 38; (*b*) ii, 38.

Both Bériot and David describe the traditional, firm on-string *staccato*, most commonly performed up-bow from the point to the middle, as a series of sharp *martelé* articulations, but also performable downbow from the middle, or sometimes from the frog. Both are agreed that it is a fundamental bowstroke for virtuosos. Bériot calls it "the most brilliant and boldest stroke of the violin".[222] And both give similar exercises for practising it (Ex. 7.36a–b). They similarly describe flying *staccato*, involving few or many notes, and the elastic bowstroke for arpeggios of the kind envisaged by Mendelssohn for the cadenza of his Violin Concerto op. 64 and by Schumann and Dvořák in their cello concertos.

[222] Bériot: *Méthode*, 114.

Ex. 7.36a Bériot: *Méthode*, ii, 118.

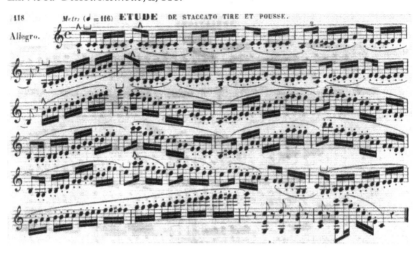

Ex. 7.36b David: *Violinschule*, ii, 40.

In 1840, Bériot had created a sensation through performances of his own composition "Le Trémolo", op. 30 (based on the Andante from Beethoven's "Kreutzer" Sonata op. 47), with a novel bowing, which he calls *ricochet continu* in his *Méthode*.[223] It is a continuous series of very rapid pairs of ricochet notes (Ex. 7.37a). David also illustrates this bowstroke, evidently derived directly from Bériot, as the "Tremolo-Strich" (Ex. 7.37b). It was entirely a virtuoso technique which had limited utility and enjoyed only short-term popularity.[224]

---

[223] Bériot: *Méthode*, 150.
[224] See the Viennese review above, pp. 409–10.

430    CLASSICAL AND ROMANTIC PERFORMING PRACTICE

Ex. 7.37a  Bériot: "Le Trémolo" op. 30, p. 3 [Andante].

Ex. 7.37b  David: *Violinschule*, ii, 38.

Bériot gave a wider range of musical contexts for springing and *ricochet* type strokes than David, mostly in the domain of virtuoso display, but his illustration of one of them anticipates the subsequently widespread use of thrown bowstrokes in the lower half of the bow (Ex. 7.38). Later in the *Méthode*, he includes a similar bowstroke in a short passage in the Allegro maestoso first movement of his Ninth Violin Concerto, explaining: "E. Springing *détaché* in the lower third of the bow" (Ex. 7.39a), whereas, for a passage of *staccato* sixteenths, earlier in the same movement, also marked with dots, he specified: "B broad connected *détaché* 2/3 of the way down the bow"[225] (Ex. 7.39b).

Ex. 7.38  Bériot: *Méthode*, ii, 143. "Study: springing bowstrokes near the frog".

[225] Bériot: *Méthode*, 245.

Ex. 7.39 a–b. Bériot: *Méthode*. (*a*) iii, 245; (*b*) iii, 245.

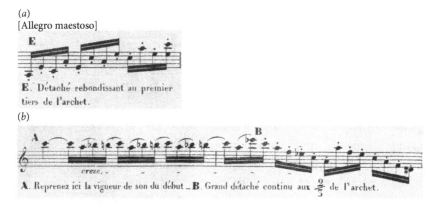

Although both violinists employed and taught a very similar range of bowstrokes, it seems clear that they used them quite differently in practice, partly because they focused on very different repertoires. Vieuxtemps's reminiscences[226] show that Bériot, unlike Baillot, took little interest in German Classical repertoire until relatively late in life. Although he included a few examples from chamber works by Mozart, Haydn, and Beethoven in his *Méthode*, none of them contains passages of successive detached notes. Ferdinand David's many bowed and fingered editions, and annotated personal copies of Classical chamber music, however, are an invaluable resource for evaluating the types of bowstrokes he expected in that repertoire during the mid-19th century: they strongly indicate that he did not envisage springing or thrown bowstrokes.[227] In repertoire in which he wanted off-string strokes, he marked this with either *spgd* or *saltato* (which he clearly regarded as synonymous (Ex. 7.40a–b).

Ex. 7.40a F. David: String Sextet op. 38, 3rd movement Vn 1.
[Allegretto grazioso e vivace (♩ = 100.)]

---

[226] MS Brussels Conservatoire library.
[227] For details of David's Beethoven editions, see Brown: 'Ferdinand David's Editions of Beethoven', in Stowell (ed.), *Performing Beethoven*, 121ff; David's editions and many of his personal copies with manuscript bowing and fingering can be found on the Chase website (https://mhm.hud.ac.uk/chase/), which also contains numerous other violinists' and cellists' 19th-century annotated editions.

**Ex. 7.40b**  F. David: personal annotated copy of Cherubini String Quartet in E flat, 4th movement.
[Allegro assai ♩ =160]

Not only David's markings, but also those of other 19th-century German editors, frequently imply the use of on-string bowstrokes in places where later string players began to use sprung or thrown strokes in the middle or, more frequently, the lower half. These early annotated editions demonstrate that such passages were intended to be played in the upper half with a *détaché*, *martelé*, or slurred *staccato* bowstroke. How little this corresponds with 20th- and early-21st-century practice will be well known to chamber music players who, when sight-reading works by Haydn, Mozart, Beethoven, Mendelssohn, Schumann from these editions, have found themselves caught at the "wrong end" of the bow. Later editions of the same works often reversed these bowings.

Many passages in David's editions of Beethoven, Schubert, and Mendelssohn illustrate his extensive use of the upper half of the bow. In the second movements of Beethoven's string quartets op. 18 no. 4 and op. 59. no. 1, the stroke envisaged by David is mostly to be made between the middle and point of the bow, probably quite close to the point (see Ex. 7.27a–b), though at times he clearly requires the same effect to be produced in different parts of the bow.

In the first movement of Mendelssohn's String Quartet op. 44 no. 3 (Ex. 7.41), David's bowing indicates that the passage of detached eighths in this extract are to be played in the upper half, either *détaché* or *martelé*; the bowings in the Peters *Neu revidierte Ausgabe* facilitate a thrown stroke in the lower half. A passage from David's edition of Schubert's Piano Trio op. 99 shows the use of a slurred *staccato*, followed by a detached bowing near the point for the sixteenths. The Peters *Neu revidierte Ausgabe* implies a light stroke (probably *sautillé*) in the middle of the bow (Ex. 7.42a–b).

ARTICULATION AND STRING BOWING   433

**Ex. 7.41** David's personal copy of Mendelssohn's String Quartets. In the Peters *Neu revidierte Ausgabe* an up-bow is marked at the half bar in line 1 bar 5, leading to a down bow at the beginning of l. 2 b. 2, and l. 5 b. 1 has separate bows, evidently at the frog, since it is followed by the two-bar slur.
[Allegro vivace ♩ =92]

**Ex. 7.42** a–b. (*a*) Schubert, Piano Trio D. 898/i: ed. F. David (Peters pl. no. 4775); (*b*) *Neu revidierte Ausgabe* (Peters pl. no. 10878).

In many places in Beethoven's string music, David used a slurred *staccato* to achieve a sharply separated effect that later violinists almost certainly achieved by means of a springing/thrown stroke in the middle or lower half of the bow, depending on speed and volume (Ex. 7.43). Editions of Classical repertoire by other 19th-century German string players also indicate persistence of a performing tradition in which springing bowstrokes were rarely if ever envisaged.

Ex. 7.43 Beethoven: Piano Trio op. 1/1/iv, ed. F. David (Peters pl. No. 4903).

## Bowstrokes in the Later 19th and Early 20th Centuries

Unequivocal evidence of changing approaches to the execution of detached notes becomes clearer during the last quarter of the 19th century. Schindler's reference to "dancing about at the frog" suggests that some Vienna-trained string players were already using bowstrokes that involved the active participation of the shoulder in the 1850s. An 1879 treatise by Julius Eichberg (1824–1893), who studied at the Brussels Conservatoire in the 1840s, shows that a "thrown" stroke, initiated from the shoulder, had also become an aspect of Franco-Belgian practice; he refers to it as "this important bowing".[228] His graphic illustration and explanation of bowstrokes (Ex. 7.44) differs from Meerts's in its inclusion of a bowstroke "with the arm".

He instructs:

1. Grand Detaché [*sic*]. With the utmost rapidity, from one end of the bow to the other. Do not lift the bow from the string.
2. Singing detaché. (Whole length of bow.) The bow not to leave the strings. Perfect equality of sound, without *cres.* or *dim.*, and no silence between the up and down bow.

---

[228] Julius Eichberg: *Eichberg's Complete Method for the Violin*, rev. edn (Boston, 1879), 59. The only substantial difference from the 1st edn of 1876 is the addition of further exercises.

3. Detaché of the fore-arm. Move the fore-arm independently; use about four inches of the bow, beginning a little above the middle.
4. The Martelé. (Hammered bowing.) Length of bowing about one inch—about 2–3 inches from the top. Each note distinct, short and neat.
5. The springing bow. (With the wrist.) Should be practised with a very flexible wrist, avoiding the least contraction of the muscles of the right arm. [. . .] Place a little above the middle. The springing bow (with the arm) is only used in a very moderate movement. It is made by an elastic and easy motion of the whole arm, avoiding contraction of muscles and stiffness. Place—about the lower third of the bow.[229]

A stroke similar to Eichberg's springing bow with the wrist, was also included by Henry Holmes in his 1878 English edition of Spohr's *Violinschule*, in which he introduced more modern bowings into the original exercises.[230]

Ex. 7.44 Eichberg: *Complete Method for the Violin*, 57.

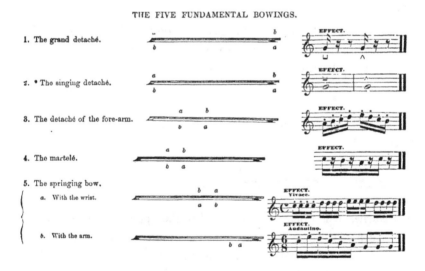

Although a broad range of on- and off-string bowstrokes was established by the early 20th century, terminology remained inconsistent, and individual pedagogues taught divergent approaches to their execution. Hans Sitt, though trained in Prague and teaching at the Leipzig Conservatorium

---

[229] Eichberg: *Complete Method*, 57–59.
[230] *Spohr's Violin School*, ed. Henry Holmes (London, [1878]). E.g., in Spohr's No. 34, 75f.

from 1884 to 1921, seems stylistically closer to Franco-Belgian than to traditional German practice. His *Technical Studies* op. 92, published in 1905, provided a typical Franco-Belgian catalogue of bowstrokes and techniques for their execution. After dealing first with broad *legato* bowing, the text, in German, English, and French, identifies the following categories of detached bowstroke:

1. *Grand détaché*, for which Sitt requires the rapid use of the whole bow, stopping abruptly at the end of each stroke, without the bow ever leaving the string.[231]

| German | English | French |
| --- | --- | --- |
| Der grosse abgestossene Bogenstrich | The broad detached stroke | Le grand détaché |

2. *Martelé*, he explains, can be played at the frog as well as at the point. The bowstroke must be equally crisp and firm in both down and up bow and "is made only with the wrist in combination with the forearm",[232] but requires more pressure on the up-bow than the down-bow.

| | | |
| --- | --- | --- |
| Der gehämmerte (martelé) Bogenstrich | The hammered stroke (martelé) | Martelé[233] |

3. *Détaché*, "using half or also a third of the upper half of the bow, is performed with the forearm",[234] and he comments that, when using the whole bow for longer notes, this bowstroke constitutes the transition from the long *legato* stroke to the detached bowstroke.

| | | |
| --- | --- | --- |
| Der abgestossene (détaché) Bogenstrich | The detached stroke | Détaché |

---

[231] Hans Sitt: *Technische Studien für Violine*, op. 92 (Leipzig, 1905), iv, 21.
[232] Sitt: *Technische Studien*, iv, 24.
[233] He actually names it *Le coup d'archet dit martelé*.
[234] Sitt: *Technische Studien*, v, 3.

4. Sitt notes that mastery of the *martelé* is a precondition for an effective *staccato*, because it is essentially a more or less rapid succession of *martelé* notes in a single bowstroke. He instructs that "it is executed by pressing the index finger on the bow stick while the hand, from the wrist, executes the stroke in the opposite direction without any help from the forearm".[235] He also explains that it can be executed downbow at the frog.

Das Staccato         Staccato            Staccato

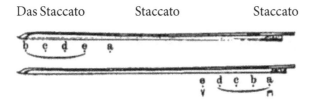

5. Sitt regards *spiccato* as "the first of the springing bowstrokes" He instructs that it "is performed with the arm, just below the middle of the bow, by raising the bow after each stroke and letting it fall back onto the string again. It is the only one of the springing bowstrokes that can be used in slow tempo".[236]

Der geworfene              Spiccato              Spiccato
(Spiccato) Bogenstrich     (The thrown stroke)

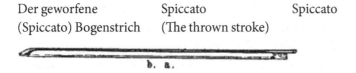

6. In contrast to the *spiccato*, the *sautillé* is used only for rapid notes; it "is executed entirely with the wrist and in the middle of the bow". Sitt points out that "this bowing is generally used in soft passages, but if it should be made a little louder, the movement of the wrist must become correspondingly greater".[237] When faster, the upper middle is used, when slower, the lower middle.

Der kleine hüpfende         The short skipping-bow       Sautillé
(Sautillé) Bogenstrich      (sautillé)

---

[235] Sitt: *Technische Studien*, v, 18.
[236] Sitt: *Technische Studien*, vi, 3. *Spiccato*, executed very much in this manner, can be seen on the 1935 film *Letzte Liebe*, in the short sequence showing Arnold Rosé and his desk partner in a passage from the overture to Mozart's *Don Giovanni*. https://www.fugue.us/Vibrato_History_E.html.
[237] Sitt: *Technische Studien*, vi, 8.

7. Finally, the *ricochet*, made by throwing the bow onto the string in the upper half of the bow, can produce few or many notes in a single bowstroke. (Sitt does not mention Bériot's *tremolo* bowstroke (see Ex. 7.37 a–b).)

| Der geworfene Staccato | The thrown staccato | Ricochet |
| (ricochet) | (ricochet) | |

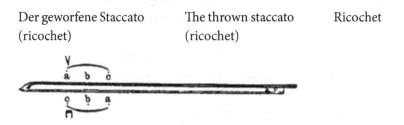

The French terms used by Sitt probably derive from Lambert-Joseph Meerts, of whose *Douze Études* (1838) he made an edition, with German translation, under the title *Die Kunst der Bogenführung* (The art of bowing). It is noteworthy that the bowstrokes described by Joachim/Moser do not include any produced by the arm rather than the wrist and that Sitt's "thrown" *spiccato* is executed only in the middle of the bow. Thrown strokes close to the frog, however, were taught by Ševčík, who associated the dot with on-string "*staccato* or *martelé*" and the stroke or wedge with "thrown *spiccato* or springing *sautillé*".[238] Many of Ševčík's bowstrokes evidently envisaged action from the shoulder. This was the case in early-20th-century cello playing too.[239]

The Joachim and Moser *Violinschule*, published in the same year as Sitt's *Technische Studien*, exposes the rift between traditional German and Franco-Belgian practice that still existed at the beginning of the 20th century. It may, perhaps, be seen as a last-ditch defence. Although it teaches essentially the same categories of bowstroke, its treatment of these, both technically and aesthetically, is quite different. After many exercises with simple on-string bowings, *martelé* and *spiccato* are named and described as the principal types of the "more difficult kinds of bowing".[240] The term *spiccato* is used to encompass all kinds of detached elastic bowstrokes, and the text explains that although, *spiccato* and *saltato* "are not quite exact equivalents in Italian, they

---

[238] Ševčík: *Schule der Bogentechnik* op. 2, ed. Brett (London, 1901), i, 2.
[239] See above, pp. 345–46.
[240] Joachim and Moser: *Violinschule*, i, 116.

nevertheless signify the same thing in violin playing: the use of the springing bow".[241] Moser explains: "In piano the spiccato is executed rather exactly in the middle of the bow; in forte one edges towards the frog."[242] This bowstroke is to be made with "an elastic movement of the wrist";[243] unlike Sitt, no reference is made to the use of the arm. Joachim and Moser do not distinguish between what other treatises call *sautillé*, in which the bow hair does not quite leave the string, and the type of *spiccato* bowstroke, generally employed for less rapid notes, where it does. No mention is made of rebounding or "thrown" strokes near the frog. Exercises for slurred *staccato*, both firm (on-string) and flying (*fliegend/volant*), and the *fouetté*, or "whipped bowstroke",[244] are, however, included.

At first sight, this does not seem very different from Franco-Belgian teaching, although the absence of any reference to bowstrokes initiated from the shoulder is significant. The introductory essay to volume 3, however, presents a strongly contrasting picture. It includes an extraordinary and lengthy diatribe against the stylistically inappropriate performance of German music by Franco-Belgian violinists, including the assertion that their neglect of the vocal aspect

> soon resulted in a complete decline of bowing technique in its classical sense. Modern French violinists have achieved astonishing skill in the use of artificial bowstrokes to achieve virtuoso effects, but their stiff bowing has few of the characteristics necessary for vocal and spiritual aims. Where, however, the means for expression are lacking, because their training has been neglected in this respect, there can be no question of representing musical art-works in the spirit of their creators.[245]

Without recordings of the late-19th-century violinists whom Moser had in mind, it is impossible to know for certain what he and Joachim found offensive in their playing, but some idea of stylistic contrasts during the first decades of the 20th century can be gained from different recordings of the same works. It is instructive, for instance, to compare performances of the

---

[241] Joachim and Moser: *Violinschule*, i, 122. This verbal usage is confirmed by Ferdinand David's manuscript markings (see Ex. 7.40b).
[242] Joachim and Moser: *Violinschule*, i, 122.
[243] Joachim and Moser: *Violinschule*, i, 122.
[244] Joachim and Moser: *Violinschule*, i, 142.
[245] Joachim and Moser: *Violinschule*, iii, 33. (Moser also condemned their use of *vibrato* and *portamento*. See Ch. 16, p. 1008.)

first movement of Mozart's Violin Concerto K. 219 by the Austro-German Marie Soldat (1863–1955), a pupil of August Pott (1806–1883) and Joseph Joachim (1831–1907), and the Franco-Belgian Jacques Thibaud (1880–1953), a pupil of Martin Marsick and Eugène Ysaÿe;[246] or the two middle movements of Beethoven's String Quartet op. 18 no. 5 recorded by the Klingler Quartet, led by the Joachim pupil Karl Klingler (1879–1971), and the Capet Quartet, led by the Paris Conservatoire–trained Lucien Capet (1873–1928).[247] The Capet Quartet's modern-sounding *spiccato* can also be heard, for instance, in their 1928 recording of the scherzo from Schubert's D minor String Quartet, with most of the separate quarter-notes played equally short with an off-string bowstroke,[248] whereas in the 1912 recording by the Klingler Quartet, these notes seem to be played much more on the string with varied length and articulation, probably employing the bowing in Ferdinand David's 1868 edition.[249]

During the following twenty years, Capet and Flesch,[250] building on Ševčík's and Franco-Belgian pedagogy, systematized and promulgated the stylistic bowing practices that were the direct antecedents of later 20th-century string playing. Since at least the middle of the 20th century, the predominant tendency, in many contexts, has been to play moderately fast, separately bowed *staccato* notes with an off-string stroke in the lower half of the bow or even near the frog, mostly with bowstrokes initiated from the shoulder, and to regard all *staccato* notes as requiring a substantially shortened execution.

*Spiccato* and thrown bowstrokes were integral to Carl Flesch's concept of stylish performance, and the theoretical validation of these kinds of bowstrokes in the performance of pre-20th-century repertoire owes much to the prestige of his writing and teaching. He gave instructions to employ them in music by Bach, Mozart, and Beethoven (Ex. 7.45a–f), explaining: "The *Thrown Stroke*, if only because of the frequency of its appearance, is one of the most important aspects of bowing technique; its perfect control is even necessary for the orchestral violinist. It is always used where the tempo indicated by the composer is too slow for the springing bow. It can just as well be

---

[246] Marie Soldat, Odeon, c. 1920, https://www.youtube.com/watch?v=L3G9QxmonP4; Jacques Thibaud 1942 https://www.youtube.com/watch?v=FE0muNoZY7Q.

[247] Klinger Quartet, Odeon 1912, https://www.youtube.com/watch?v=pile0upUa50; Capet Quartet, Columbia 1928. https://www.youtube.com/watch?v=-NA0VHehdBQ.

[248] Capet Quartet Columbia 1928, https://www.youtube.com/watch?v=v8A-jM7lEvc.

[249] The Klingler recording is not currently available online. The David edition can be seen on the CHASE website https://mhm.hud.ac.uk/chase/view/edition/160/.

[250] Lucien Capet: *Le technique supérieure de l'archet* (Paris, 1916); Carl Flesch: *Die Kunst des Violinspiels* (Berlin, 1924/28).

executed in the middle as at the frog or point, although more difficult in the latter case."[251]

**Ex. 7.45** a–f. Flesch: *Die Kunst des Violinspiels*, i, 56. The thrown bowstroke (Der Wurfbogenstrich). (*a*) In the middle; (*b*) In the lower third; (*c*) At the point; (*d*) Very short; (*e*) Moderately lengthened; (*f*) "Thrown staccato" [Wurfstakkato].

(*a*)

(*b*)

(*c*)

(*d*)

(*e*)

(*f*)

The increasing application of these kinds of bowstroke to earlier repertoire, in which they had certainly not been envisaged by the composer, was a gradual process during the 20th century, but by the second half of the century

---

[251] Carl Flesch: *Die Kunst des Violinspiels*, 2nd edn (Berlin, 1928), i, 55f.

they were so firmly established in Baroque, Classical, and Romantic performance that they had become inextricably connected with everyone's expectations for that repertoire.

Mastery of the full range of possible bowstrokes is, of course, essential for all contemporary professional string players, who are not exclusively involved with period instrument performance, and Flesch's approach to bowing (with close parallels in cello playing),[252] together with the exhaustive instructions and exercises of his older contemporary Otakar Ševčík,[253] remains fundamentally unchanged in early-21st-century string teaching. So too, for the most part, does Flesch's conviction that "present-day means of expression" and the cultivation of a style that suits the prevailing tastes of the day are the performer's primary concern.

It is certainly very difficult for musicians who have spent their formative years finely honing all the techniques that are required in modern performance to eschew a large part of them and to use fundamentally different right arm movements when performing older repertoire. Since almost all period instrument performers also initially receive this kind of training on modern instruments, their carefully cultivated modern bowing techniques inevitably underlie their ostensibly historical playing; thus, thrown bowstrokes have frequently been employed also with "period" bows in Baroque and Classical repertoire. To some extent this may reflect passive or active acceptance of the notion that, as Jockisch put it, "a more modern bowing" would be "more likely to fulfil the composer's intentions than his violin-playing contemporaries could have done", but for the most part it seems to have stemmed from an innocent belief that these kinds of bowstrokes, and the very different kinds of articulation they produce, are historically correct in that repertoire.

\*\*\*

Bowing styles are so intimately connected with the physical handling of string instruments that the one cannot be adequately understood without the other. The active employment of the right shoulder was developed extensively during the 20th century to achieve a specific style of bowing. Abundant documentary and aural evidence demonstrates that the action of the right arm in modern string playing, and the acoustic effects of the resulting bowstrokes,

---

[252] See George Kennaway's comprehensive treatment of the subject: *Playing the Cello, 1780–1930* (Farnham, 2014), 63–98.

[253] Especially *School of Bowing Technique* op. 2 and *40 Variations* op. 3 (London, Bosworth, 1905), also arranged for cello by Louis R. Feuillard.

have little connection with 19th-century practice and virtually none with earlier string playing. Stylistic developments in the second half of the 19th century, followed by the technical and aesthetic revolution of the 20th century, transformed the way the notation of pre-20th-century music was understood and interpreted. At the end of the 20th century, the intimate relationship between bowing technique and composers' expectations for the effective realization of their notation was still largely misunderstood or ignored, even within the period instrument community. Attempting to recreate the past, as it really was, is both impossible and, in many respects, undesirable; but the revival and effective utilization of historically verifiable bowing practices offers enticing creative opportunities for string players who seek to deepen their understanding of the expanded range of sound colours and characterization that can be produced with the bow.[254] The rediscovery of historic right-arm techniques provides a powerful tool for innovative artistic exploration of the expectations that lie between the lines of the composer's notation.

---

[254] See Clive Brown: *Classical and Romantic Violin and Viola Playing* (Kassel, Bärenreiter, forthcoming).

# 8
# Tempo

Historical evidence and contemporary experience demonstrate that tempo is among the most variable and contentious issues in musical performance. To a considerable extent the exercise of choice in this, as in other interpretative matters, was seen throughout the period as an essential part of the performing musician's creativity. John Holden put the matter nicely when he observed in 1770:

> it must be acknowledged that the absolute time which ought to be allowed to different pieces, is the most undetermined matter, that we meet with, in the whole science of music. There is one insuperable difficulty, which frustrates all attempts towards regulating this particular, viz. the different humours and tastes of different persons; which are so various, that one person shall think a tune much too quick, for the intended expression, while another thinks it not quick enough.[1]

Nevertheless, for the performer who wishes to approach the composer's expectations as closely as possible, it is important not to misunderstand the workings of the relevant conventions and, through simple ignorance, choose a tempo radically different from that envisaged by the composer. This can all too easily happen when a term such as andante molto or andantino is used by some composers to mean a faster pace than their normal andante and by others a slower one, or when the significance of ¢ for the tempo is unrecognized. It is arguably more fundamental to the integrity of a composition that performers should appreciate the thinking that lay behind the composer's methods of indicating tempo than that they should attempt to achieve specific chronometric tempos (however authentic) in specific cases; indeed, if this more limited end is attained, the likelihood of choosing radically inappropriate speeds is greatly lessened. But in many instances, as becomes apparent on closer investigation, it is by no means straightforward even to

---

[1] Holden: *Essay*, 36.

appreciate the relationship of one tempo to another, especially since tempo is indicated not merely by the Italian term prefixed to the piece, but by a complex of other related factors and conventions that differ from composer to composer, place to place, and period to period.

After the advent of the metronome in the second decade of the 19th century we have a mass of still largely untapped information about the tempo predilections of many major and minor composers, which offers tantalizing possibilities of making better-informed judgements than are possible with the limited evidence for chronometric tempos in the 18th century. But this evidence is by no means easy to interpret. Early metronome marks reveal the last phase of a complicated yet, in the case of some composers, remarkably consistent method of designating tempo. Paradoxically, the availability of the metronome as a means of exactly fixing tempo may have played a part in lessening later 19th-century composers' concerns to indicate their wishes clearly through the old system of relationships between metre, tempo term, and note values, often making it difficult to ascertain their intentions where metronome marks were not supplied. Tradition, after the lapse of a generation or more, is an extremely unreliable guide to such matters. This is demonstrated, for instance, by a comparison of the timings of performances at Bayreuth in Wagner's lifetime with subsequent ones, and by the relationship between metronome marks for Brahms's music provided by musicians who were associated with him (for instance, Joachim's metronome marks for the Violin Concerto or those in early editions of the duo sonatas) and later 20th-century recordings.[2] Even where, as in Beethoven's case, the composer provided metronome marks, these had little posthumous influence.

## Choice of Tempo

Every sensitive musician is aware that the quest for historically appropriate tempos must essentially be concerned with plausible parameters rather than with precisely delineated or very narrowly defined absolute tempos. Many psychological and aesthetic factors, as well as the varying physical conditions in which performance takes place, militate against the notion that a piece

---

[2] See Clive Brown: Brahms Violin Concerto (Kassel, Bärenreiter, 2006); Clive Brown, Neal Peres Da Costa, and Kate Bennett Wadsworth: Brahms Sonatas opp. 38, 78, 99, 100, 108, and 120 nos 1 and 2, and *Performing Practices in Johannes Brahms' Chamber Music* (Kassel, Bärenreiter, 2015).

of music should be rigidly bound to a single immutable tempo. A. B. Marx, having explained the use of metronome marks, observed:

> The performing musician or the director of a major performance must, however, strive to grasp and reproduce the meaning of the composition as deeply and faithfully as possible, therefore it is also incumbent upon him to match the composer's tempo as closely as possible. But ultimately, everything depends on his mood and the way in which the work comes alive in his soul and becomes his own. Only from his animated inner being can it emerge vividly and effectively; performed according to conventional rules, without being felt internally, it remains dead and lacks a lively, invigorating effect. Finally, there are external conditions that cannot possibly be considered in the determination of metronomic tempo. In large ensembles, for example, and in wide spaces, the tempi, especially in figurative movements, must be taken more slowly because the sound spreads more slowly, so that if the movement is too fast, the masses of notes sound confused, even with the most correct execution. Therefore, one must only keep in mind which approximate speed is usually attributed to the various tempo designations in order to understand the terminology; the finer details may and must be left to artistic understanding and feeling at the moment of performance.[3]

This was a view evidently shared by Marx's former friend, Mendelssohn;[4] for it was reported of Mendelssohn that "though in playing he never varied the tempo when once taken, he did not always take a movement at the same pace, but changed it as his mood was at the time".[5] This may well go some way towards explaining Mendelssohn's relative reluctance to supply metronome marks for his own works; the suggestion that he "never varied the tempo when once taken", however, is questionable, as will be discussed later.

Even where a metronome or another method of exact tempo specification had been used to fix the tempo of a particular piece of music, few theorists or composers would have disagreed with Weber's assertion, in a letter accompanying metronome marks for *Euryanthe*, that such means would at best serve to avoid "gross blunders"[6] but are of limited value unless performers

---

[3] Adolf Bernhard Marx: *Allgemeine Musiklehre*, 6th edn (Leipzig, 1857), 102.
[4] The two musicians later fell out over Mendelssohn's refusal to perform Marx's oratorio *Moses*.
[5] George Grove: 'Mendelssohn' in *Dictionary of Music and Musicians*, ii, 299.
[6] Friedrich Wilhelm Jähns: *Carl Maria von Weber in seinen Werken: Chronologisch-thematisches Verzeichniss seiner sämmtlichen Werken* (Berlin, 1871), 374.

feel the rightness of the tempo within themselves. Yet many musicians, including major composers, were insistent that a well-chosen tempo is vital to the effective realization of a piece of music. Although some, like Weber, Mendelssohn, Marx, Wagner, and Brahms, showed a clear awareness of the limitations of the metronome, and were wary of insisting too rigidly on a precise tempo, it cannot be assumed that most composers were happy with the idea that performers should depart radically from their intentions in this respect, any more than they would have been with alterations to the harmony or structure of the music. For this reason, a considerable number of 19th-century composers took great care in assigning metronome marks to their music and insisted upon their validity. In relation to *Aida*, for instance, Verdi wrote in a letter of 10 August 1871: "take care that all the tempos be just as indicated by the metronome".[7]

The divergences of practice in relation to tempo that had helped to convince many musicians of the need for a reliable means of indicating chronometric tempos were scarcely lessened by the adoption of the metronome. The quintessentially Romantic idea, encapsulated in Weber's assertion that the right tempo can only be found "within the sensitive human breast",[8] may be seen as characteristic of an outlook that became stronger during the 19th century. When contemporary art is powerfully in tune with the feelings of an age, the prevalent aesthetic seems to overrule any effective notion of fidelity to the wishes of the original artist. Mozart is relevant to Brahms's and Tchaikovsky's generation not so much as a late-18th-century composer in his own right, but rather as the symbol of a pure beauty for which they nostalgically yearn. For Wagner and his contemporaries, Beethoven's music is seen less as the expression of his own spirit and times than as an anticipation of later musical values.

Such assimilations of past music to present or localized aesthetics begin almost immediately, often indeed within the composer's lifetime. Many of Beethoven's and Schumann's metronome marks, especially those that ask for very fast tempos, were clearly not uncontroversial even among their contemporaries and close associates. An edition of Beethoven's Septet (in a quintet arrangement) published by Schlesinger at about the time of the composer's death[9] gives slower metronome marks for all the movements,

---

[7] Franco Abbiati: *Giuseppe Verdi* (Milan, 1959), iii, 466.
[8] Jähns: *Carl Maria von Weber*, 374.
[9] Copy in the British Library, London.

Table 8.1. Metronome Marks for Beethoven's Septet op. 20

| Movement | MM Beethoven | Schlesinger |
| --- | --- | --- |
| Adagio | ♪ = 76 | — |
| Allegro con brio | 𝅗𝅥 = 96 | 𝅗𝅥 = 84 |
| Adagio cantabile | ♪ = 132 | ♪ = 96 |
| Tempo di Menuetto | ♩ = 120 | ♩ = 92 |
| Andante | ♪ = 120 | ♪ = 96* |
| Scherzo | ♩. = 126 | ♩. = 120 |
| Andante con moto | ♪ = 76 | ♪ = 63 |
| Presto | 𝅗𝅥 = 112 | 𝅗𝅥 = 100 |

* The printed note value is ♩ but the speed of the thirty-seconds demonstrates that this must be a misprint.

and very significantly slower ones for some, than Beethoven himself had given to the work ten years earlier (see Table 8.1).

Anton Schindler, Beethoven's amanuensis and self-declared guardian of his posthumous tradition, felt so strongly about his own notion of the proper tempos for Beethoven's music that he resorted to forging entries in the conversation books to support his view and made the unverifiable assertion, that Beethoven had repudiated a considerable number of his metronome marks in later life. The story about Beethoven losing metronome marks for the Ninth Symphony and replacing them with quite different ones, which has been cited as evidence that his preserved metronome marks lack authority, derives from Schindler and is not supported by any reliable evidence.[10] Schindler's claim that in the letter sent to London in 1827 with metronome marks for the symphony "All the tempos were different, some slower, some faster"[11] than those he gave earlier to Schott is simply incorrect: only one, 66 instead of a mistaken 96 for the initial Presto of the fourth movement, differs. In the case of works for which Beethoven himself provided no metronome marks, the Haslinger edition, initiated shortly after his death, included ones supplied (probably) by his pupil Carl Czerny, which mostly reflect the composer's tempo conception quite closely. Later 19th- and early-20th-century metronome marks for the same works, including some by Czerny, mostly have

[10] For a late-20th-century repetition of the tale see Donington: 'Tempo' in *The New Grove Dictionary of Music and Musicians* (1980), xviii, 675, where it is given without reference to its derivation from Schindler.

[11] Anton Schindler: *Biographie von Ludwig van Beethoven* (Münster, 1840), 220.

slower, sometimes very significantly slower ones.[12] In Schumann's case, discomfort with many of his fast metronome marks, even on the part of his wife, gave rise within a short time of his death to the now discredited rumour that his metronome was faulty; and Clara Schumann altered many of them in her edition of his piano works.[13]

There can be little doubt that through ignoring the implications of a composer's metronome marks, accomplished musicians have frequently committed what the composers themselves would have regarded as, in Weber's phrase, gross blunders. Yet the unquestioning acceptance of metronome marks, even if only as an approximate guide, is also injudicious; for although a composer's metronome marks (or other form of chronometric tempo marking) can give the performer an invaluable message about tempo, they are not without their hazards. It was all too easy for printers, engravers, copyists, or even the composers to make mistakes. Errors in the transmission of metronome marks are far from uncommon; some of these are easily recognizable, yet in numerous instances where a wrong note value or number seems highly probable, the composer's real intention remains unclear. A sizeable number of Beethoven's metronome marks are evidently printing or transcribing errors. In the case, referred to above, of ♩ = 96 instead of 66 at the beginning of the Finale of the Ninth Symphony in the list published by Schott in 1826 and in the subsequent editions, it has been possible to demonstrate the manner in which the mistake occurred.[14] Other metronome marks are so obviously incorrect that they have never caused serious problems, but a few which are almost certainly wrong have continued to mislead modern interpreters, resulting in performances that distort Beethoven's conception.[15] Even a cursory glance at other composers' metronome marks quickly reveals similar mistakes: for instance, the overture to Spontini's *Nurmahal* in the original edition has ♩ = 123 in the score and ♩ = 122 on the index page, but

---

[12] For Czerny's and Moscheles's tempos see Marten Noorduin: *Beethoven's Tempo Indications*, PhD diss., U. of Manchester, 2016. For changing tempos in later editions of works without the composer's metronome marks see Clive Brown: Beethoven Violin Concerto (Wiesbaden, Breitkopf und Härtel, 2012), and Beethoven Sonatas for Pianoforte and Violin, especially the online Performing Practice Commentary co-authored with Neal Peres Da Costa (Kassel, Bärenreiter, 2020).

[13] See D. Kämper: 'Zur Frage der Metronombezeichnungen Robert Schumanns', *Archiv für Musikwissenschaft*, xxi (1964), 141; and B. Schotel: 'Schumann and the Metronome' in A. Walker (ed.): *Robert Schumann: The Man and His Music* (London, 1972), 109ff.

[14] Otto Baensch: 'Zur Neunten Symphonie' in Adolf Sandberger (ed.), *Neues Beethoven-Jahrbuch* (Augsburg, 1925), 145ff.

[15] See Clive Brown: 'Historical Performance, Metronome Marks and Tempo in Beethoven's Symphonies', *Early Music*, xix (1991), 247ff. Marten Noorduin: 'The Metronome Marks for Beethoven's Ninth Symphony in Context', *Early Music*, xlix (2021), 129ff.

since neither of these numbers occurs on the metronome they are probably both misprints for 132.[16] And there are many similar problems with Berlioz's metronome marks.[17]

Nevertheless, most metronome marks will be an accurate record of what composers or editors intended to convey at the time they gave them. Whether they are an accurate record of the tempo at which, in practice, the music was performed or directed is another question. Comparison of late-19th- and early-20th-century composers' metronome marks with recorded performances in which they took part (e.g., Elgar, Richard Strauss, Bartók)[18] show that they often diverged significantly from their own instructions (not only with respect to tempo). It is clear, too, that earlier composers were not consistent in this matter. When Berlioz incorporated several numbers from his *Huit scènes de Faust* into *La Damnation de Faust* he gave them all slower metronome marks than before. And Saint-Saëns recalled that when he heard Berlioz conduct a performance of his *Grande messe des morts*, several of the tempos were quite different from the ones printed in the score: the Moderato ($\boldsymbol{\downarrow}$ = 96) at the beginning of the "Dies irae" was more like an allegro, and the following Andante maestoso ($\boldsymbol{\downarrow}$ = 72), more like a moderato.[19]

Notwithstanding such suggestions of variable practice, 19th-century anecdotes reporting composers' concerns about finding the right tempo for performances of their work abound. Where they appear to have favoured a more *laissez-faire* attitude, as in the case of Weber, Wagner (after *Tannhäuser*), or Brahms, the underlying assumption seems to have been rather that a knowledgeable musician would light upon a tempo within the range envisaged by the composer, than that any tempo, even if chosen by a sensitive artist, would be satisfactory. Wagner, like Weber, clearly regarded metronome marks merely as a starting point, for he observed that it would be a poor state of affairs "if the accompanying metronome marks merely enlighten the conductor and the singers about the tempo; both of them will only unerringly find the correct tempo when they begin to develop a lively sympathy with the dramatic and musical situations, and when that

---

[16] Copy of full score in Bodleian Library, Oxford.
[17] Hugh Macdonald: 'Berlioz and the Metronome' in P. A. Bloom (ed.), *Berlioz Studies* (Cambridge, 1992), 17ff.
[18] E. O. Turner: 'Tempo Variation: With Examples from Elgar', *Music & Letters*, xix (1938), 308–23; Robert Philip: 'The Recordings of Edward Elgar (1857–1934): Authenticity and Performance Practice', *Early Music*, xii (1984), 481–89. Raymond Holden: 'Richard Strauss: The Don Juan Recordings', *Performance Practice Review*, x (1997), 11–30; Marilyn C. Garst: 'How Bartók Performed His Own Compositions', *Tempo*, n.s., clv/12 (1985), 15–21; Robert Philip: *Early Recordings and Musical Style*.
[19] Camille Saint-Saëns: *Musical Memoires*, trans. E. G. Rich (London, 1921), 136f.

understanding allows them to find the tempo as though it were something that did not require any further searching on their part".[20] He had remarked earlier that the composer's greatest concern was "to ensure that your piece of music is heard exactly as you yourself heard it when you wrote it down: that is to say, the composer's intentions must be reproduced with conscientious fidelity so that the ideas contained in it may be conveyed to the senses undistorted and unimpaired".[21] This suggests rather that he was expecting performers to find the *composer's* tempo (variable though that may have been in his own practice), not their own.

Weber's, Wagner's, and Brahms's expectations may not have been too unrealistic while they and the musicians who worked with them were there to provide a yardstick. However, since culture is dynamic and artistic taste is far from universal, the musicianship that results from training and experience within different traditions often leads to quite sharply contrasting notions of the appropriate tempo for particular compositions. The good taste and orthodoxy of one place or time may thus be the "gross blunder" of another, just as much with respect to tempo as to other aspects of performance.

It can be argued that such concerns are irrelevant: dead composers no longer have any rights in their music; it belongs to posterity to treat it however it likes. As the early-20th-century pioneer of the harpsichord revival Wanda Landowska remarked: "If Rameau himself would rise from his grave to demand of me some changes in my interpretation of his *Dauphine*, I would answer, 'You gave birth to it; it is beautiful. But now leave me alone with it. You have nothing more to say; go away!'"[22] Yet some musicians who favour radically different tempos from those indicated by metronome marks or historical evidence do not take that kind of bold stance; they challenge the validity of the evidence. This is nowhere more apparent than in the case of the very rapid tempos in fast movements that seem to have been favoured by many early-19th-century musicians, but which have often run so contrary to later taste. Various theories have been advanced to show that metronome marks are not a correct record of the tempo at which composers wanted their music to be performed. Apart from suggestions that they did not properly know how to use the machine, or that their metronomes were faulty, one author even advanced the bizarre theory that the manner of indicating

---

[20] Wagner: *Ueber die Aufführung des Tannhäuser eine Mittheilung an die Dirigenten und Darsteller dieser Oper* (Zürich, 1852), 26.
[21] Wagner: 'Der Virtuos und der Künstler' in Gesammelte Schriften und Dichtungen (1871), i, 210.
[22] Denise Restout and Robert Hawkins (eds.): *Landowska on Music* (New York, 1965), 407.

metronome markings for faster tempos up to about 1848 has been completely misunderstood, and that they should really be performed at half the speed.[23] Though this theory has attracted a few supporters,[24] it has been ably rebutted by other scholars.[25] Further unequivocal support for the rejection of such ideas can be found in early accounts of how to use metronomes or pendula,[26] and perhaps most explicitly in the method initially adopted for indicating the metronomic tempos in the autograph of Schubert's opera *Alfonso und Estrella*. For instance: for a movement in ¢ the score has "160 = ♩ 2 Striche im Takt", or for a movement in 12/8 "92 = ♪ 12 Striche im Takt".[27]

More reasonable arguments, based on psychological and experiential grounds, might lead to the plausible conclusion that composers' perceptions of tempo in their imagination may have been faster than they would require in performance and that this often results in metronome marks at the upper limits of practicability; but in these cases the margin of error is rarely likely to be enormous, and the metronome marks retain their validity as a guide to the composer's conception.

The important qualification in Marx's comment, quoted earlier, is that "the finer details may and must be left to artistic understanding and feeling". One of the fundamental problems that was explicitly articulated, or that underlay many musicians' comments on tempo, was the degree of deviation from the "ideal" tempo that was possible without altering the intended impact of the music. The acceptable margins of variation cannot be exactly prescribed, but it is obvious to every accomplished musician that, while it would be inartistic to insist on a single immutable tempo for any piece of music in all circumstances, music can be performed at tempos so different from those envisaged by the composer that the character of the composition is completely altered. Thus, Quantz conceded that in applying his instructions

---

[23] Willem R. Talsma: *Wiedergeburt der Klassiker* (Innsbruck, 1980).
[24] E.g., Clemens von Gleich: 'Original Tempo-Angaben bei Mendelssohn' in H. Herrtrich and H. Schneider (eds.), *Festschrift Rudolf Elvers zum 60 Geburtstag* (Tutzing, 1985), 213ff. Wim Winters (various videos online).
[25] E.g., Wolfgang Auhagen: 'Chronometrische Tempoangaben im 18. und 19. Jahrhundert', *Archiv für Musikwissenschaft*, xliv (1987), 40–57. Marten Noorduin: 'Czerny's "Impossible" Metronome Marks', *Musical Times*, cliv (2013), 19–46. Fafner Kr has published online an extensive catalogue of historical timings that fundamentally undermine Winters's double-beat/whole-beat theory: https://www.academia.edu/42802248/Historical_Evidence_of_Tempi_in_the_18_th_and_19_th_Centuries.
[26] E.g., Gesualdo Lanza: *The Elements of Singing* (London, [1809]), and Herz's discussion of metronome marks in *Méthode complète de piano*, 12.
[27] See *Alfonso und Estrella*, ed. Walther Dürr, *Neue Schubert Ausgabe*, II/6 (Kassel, Bärenreiter, 1993), preface, viiff.

to use pulse-rate as a guide to tempo, it would make little difference if an individual's pulse were somewhat faster or slower, but he also stressed:

> We see daily how often tempo is abused, and how frequently the very same piece is played moderately at one time, and still more quickly at another. It is well known that in many places where people play carelessly, a presto is often made an allegretto and an adagio an andante, doing the greatest injustice to the composer, who cannot always be present.[28]

Other 18th-century musicians were more insistent on the necessity for a composer's tempo to be adhered to within a quite narrow margin. Kirnberger, for instance, felt that "Only the person who has composed a piece is able to give the most correct tempo. A small degree more or less can do much damage to the effect of a piece;[29] and he suggested that for greater certainty composers should append to their pieces a note of their duration. A similar recommendation was made by J. A. Scheibe in the same period.[30] There was scarcely a German theorist of the late 18th century who did not stress the importance of finding the right tempo. Among composers and performers, Pisendel was noted for his extraordinary ability to divine a composer's tempo intentions,[31] and Mozart's confident mastery of everything concerning tempo is reflected in his often-quoted letters on the subject. Most accomplished 18th- and early-19th-century musicians would have been confident that they could discern a careful composer's intentions with a high degree of accuracy; but the meaning of the clues and instructions to which they were sensitive were largely forgotten during the 19th century.

## Late-18th-Century and Early-19th-Century Tempo Conventions

During the Classical and early part of the Romantic periods, the determination of tempo was widely acknowledged to depend on a subtle balance and relationship between several basic factors. The most important of these

---

[28] Quantz: *Versuch*, 267f.
[29] Johann Philipp Kirnberger: 'Bewegung' in Sulzer, *Allgemeine Theorie*, i, 157.
[30] Johann Adolf Scheibe: *Ueber die musikalische Composition, erster Theil: Die Theorie der Melodie und Harmonie* (Leipzig, 1773), 299.
[31] See Türk: *Klavierschule*, 113.

were the metre, the tempo term,[32] the note values employed in the piece, the quantity of fast notes that it contained, and the types of figurations in which these notes were used. Additional influences might include such things as the character of the piece and the genre to which it belonged, the harmonic movement, or any close relationship to a specific dance type. All these considerations were intimately related to the speed that competent composers conceived for their music or that well-trained musicians would have chosen for it. Nevertheless, it is evident that there were important variations in emphasis depending on nationality and school, and that individual composers developed their own usages, notably in the matter of metre and tempo terms.

At the beginning of the 17th century, tempo was theoretically determined largely by metre and the so-called principles of proportional notation. During the course of that century, the system of modern time signatures began to emerge, though, as with all evolutionary processes, some elements of the older scheme were retained as anomalous features in the new. The notion of a tactus to which the various metres were related—never very consistent—was already weakening in the early years of the 17th century and by the beginning of the 18th had long ceased to provide an adequate means of indicating tempo. The tactus is still mentioned in a few late-18th-century treatises,[33] but by that stage it had little if any relevance for practical music.

By the middle of the 18th century, the notion of a universal tactus had been effectively displaced by the idea that each metre had a natural rate of motion. This concept of metre seems to have been well established and generally understood in Germany and France; the Italians may have been rather more pragmatic. Few instrumental or singing methods of the period dealt with the tempo implications of metre in any depth, though many alluded to them. Leopold Mozart's account is typical of practical authors, who left the more esoteric aspects of the subject to be imparted to the student by a teacher, or expected an understanding of the refinements of tempo to be absorbed instinctively through experience; he mentioned merely that the various types of metre are "sufficient to show in some degree the natural difference between a slow and a quick melody",[34] without giving any further guidance.

---

[32] The phrase "tempo term" will be used for words like "allegro", "andante", etc., together with their qualifiers ("moderato", "sostenuto", etc.), although in most cases they have connotations of expression as well as tempo.

[33] In Holden's *Essay*, for instance.

[34] Mozart: *Versuch*, 28.

A few 18th-century theorists offered more detailed expositions of contemporary thought on these matters. Perhaps the most comprehensive account was given by J. P. Kirnberger and J. A. P. Schulz, in Kirnberger's *Die Kunst des reinen Satzes*, and in several articles in Sulzer's *Allgemeine Theorie*. Stressing the vital role of metre in determining tempo, Kirnberger observed that the composer (and, presumably, also the performer) must have "a correct feeling for the natural tempo of every metre, or for what is called *tempo giusto*",[35] and he observed that this, like a proper feeling for accentuation and the articulation of phrases, could be attained by the study of all kinds of dance pieces, since each dance has its definite tempo that is determined by the metre and the note values employed in it.

There was no universally recognized chronometric definition of these natural rates of motion of the various metres, and no precisely defined relationship between one metre and another. For 18th-century musicians who were intimately familiar with the speeds of the dance types closely associated with specific metres, it seems probable that this natural tempo, or *tempo giusto*, was not merely a nebulous concept; but in practice there was an abundance of complications. Theorists who wanted to expound a clear and logical system also had to grapple with the difficulties created by the diverse uses that had been made of the most frequently employed metres. For instance, some common dances of radically different kinds, such as the minuet and the sarabande, were written in the same metre, in this case $\frac{3}{4}$, and that led to these metres having more than one natural tempo. Some considered $\frac{3}{8}$ as the proper metre for the minuet, but as John Holden remarked: "we frequently write them in the triple of crotchets, which makes no material difference, because the name itself determines the quickness of the time".[36] In fact, however, by the second half of the 18th century, dances and instrumental pieces of very different tempos were named as minuets.

Duple and quadruple metres, too, appeared in several different guises. According to some writers there were three different kinds of metre with four quarter-notes to the bar (abbreviated hereafter as $\frac{4}{4}$, although this form of the time signature was scarcely used in the 18th and early 19th centuries). The large $\frac{4}{4}$ and the common $\frac{4}{4}$ were described by, among others, Schulz and Türk: these were usually designated by the time signature ¢, but both writers regarded $\frac{4}{4}$ as the proper time signature for the former. Large $\frac{4}{4}$ (explained

---

[35] Kirnberger: *Die Kunst des reinen Satzes*, ii, 106.
[36] Holden: *Essay*, 40.

by some as a substitute for 2/2) required a slow tempo and contained nothing faster than eighths, while common 4/4, which could contain shorter notes, required a faster tempo. In addition, Schulz insisted that a distinction should be made between the common 4/4 and the *zusammengesetzten* (put together) 4/4 (also marked with c), each bar of which, being derived from two joined-up bars of 2/4, had a different accentuation from common 4/4 and required the character of 2/4 in its delivery. Other writers of a more practical bent (particularly in England and France) ignored these theoretical distinctions, recognizing only one type of 4/4 or c, whose character was governed by the musical content and the tempo terms.

Another point, about which the German theorists appear not to have been entirely clear, is whether the quarters in 2/4 were regarded as faster or slower than those in 4/4. Neither Schulz nor Türk is explicit; indeed, in the case of Schulz's *zusammengesetzten* 4/4 they are exactly the same, since he states that, with regard to performance style and motion, the *zusammengesetzten* metres are identical to the simple metres from which they are derived. It follows from this, however, that common 4/4 has a character that is different from 2/4 and *zusammengesetzten* 4/4. But there seem to have been considerable differences of opinion about the relationship of 2/4 to 4/4, since many composers treated the former as if it were really 4/8. Hummel's metronome marks for Mozart symphonies (e.g., no. 36 K425) suggest a steadier interpretation of the quarters in 2/4 than in 4/4 (thus the eighths livelier than the quarters in 4/4); and, somewhat later, Bernhard Romberg, after listing tempo terms with what he regarded as appropriate metronome marks, added: "If all the tempos given here occur [. . .] for pieces written in 2/4 time, the beats must be rather slower than in 4/4 time."[37] In Beethoven's and Mendelssohn's music, metronome marks appear to bear out this view of 2/4 to some extent: compare, for instance, the Allegro c ($\quarter = 80$) in Beethoven's Sixth Symphony op. 68 with the Allegro 2/4 ($\quarter = 126$) of the String Quartet op. 59 no. 1 or the Allegro non troppo c ($\quarter = 92$) of Mendelssohn's *Erste Walpurgisnacht* op. 60 with the Vivace non troppo 2/4 ($\quarter = 126$) in the "Scotch" Symphony op. 56. But in Beethoven's case, and that of other composers, the situation is complicated by a tendency to employ a type of 2/4 with four eighth-note beats in the bar that stands in the same relationship to c as c does to ¢: for example, the 2/4 Adagios in Beethoven's string quartets opp. 18 no. 6 and 59 no. 1 or the first and last movements of op. 18

---

[37] Romberg: *Violoncell-Schule*, 111. See also Peter Williams: 'Two Case Studies in Performance Practice and the Details of Notation, 1: J. S. Bach and 2/4 Time', *Early Music*, xxi (1993), 613ff.

no. 2. The treatment of $\frac{2}{4}$ by later 19th-century composers continued to be variable in this respect; Schumann and Dvořák, for instance, do not seem to have regarded c and $\frac{2}{4}$ as, in themselves, implying any basic difference in the speed of the quarter-notes in relation to the tempo term, but Dvořák quite frequently wrote movements in $\frac{4}{8}$, which have a different character.

In doubtful cases, the note values employed in the piece and its overall musical characteristics were generally expected to provide the necessary clues to decide in which of the metrical sub-types the piece belonged. Despite these complexities, the idea of a *tempo giusto* seems to have played a crucial part in the thinking of many 18th- and early-19th-century musicians. The *tempo giusto* was deemed to be the speed at which a piece in a given metre, containing a certain range of note values, and with a particular character, would be performed, unless made faster or slower by a specific tempo term. At the root of the system, despite all the anomalies, was the idea that, other things being equal, the smaller the denominator in the time signature (i.e., the larger the note values), the slower and heavier the pulse; thus, the same melody notated in $\frac{2}{2}$, $\frac{3}{4}$, and $\frac{3}{8}$ would be performed successively faster and lighter.

But halving the note values did not imply doubling the speed. Schulz explained: "For example, the eighths in $\frac{3}{8}$ metre are not as long as the quarters in $\frac{3}{4}$, but also not as short as the eighths in the latter metre. Therefore, a piece marked *vivace* in $\frac{3}{8}$ time would have a livelier tempo than it would in $\frac{3}{4}$ time."[38] In a similar vein, Koch observed that the same musical phrase notated in $\frac{2}{2}$ and $\frac{2}{4}$ (with halved note values) should be played more slowly in the former than the latter, adding: "and therefore the note values used will, if not in the most exact manner, nevertheless to some extent fix the speed of the movement, and therefore the term that one is accustomed to affix to every movement to designate the speed will be all the clearer." But his following remarks may be taken as a caution against assuming that composers can be relied upon to have observed such principles consistently, for he continued: "In this matter, however, people do not take the hint that the nature of the thing gives us; if it happens from time to time, this is more accidental than intentional, for the use of these two metres in respect of the speed of movement is taken to be wholly arbitrary."[39] He complained that they were often, in fact, employed in a diametrically opposite manner: $\frac{2}{4}$ for slow pieces and (evidently thinking of *alla breve*) $\frac{2}{2}$ for fast ones. He regarded the former

[38] Schulz: 'Vortrag' in Sulzer: *Allgemeine Theorie*, ii, 1253.
[39] Koch: *Versuch*, ii, 292f.

use as less excusable than the latter, since at least writing fast pieces in $\genfrac{}{}{0pt}{}{2}{2}$ had the practical advantage of requiring fewer beams to the notes.

The use of tempo terms to modify the natural rate of motion of a metre had already begun during the 17th century. At first words like *presto*, *adagio*, *vif*, *lent*, *brisk*, *drag*, and so on seem only to have indicated a somewhat slower or faster pace than normal, but a larger number of terms and an extended range of variation gradually evolved, as composers became concerned not only to determine the tempo, but also to govern the expression. The Paris Conservatoire's *Principes élémentaires de musique* (c. 1800) observed:

> Formerly Tempo was determined by the nature of the Metre, that is to say, that such and such a Metre belonged to Slow Tempos; such and such another indicated Moderate Tempos; and Lively Tempos had particular Metres. In a word, the Tempos increased in speed accordingly as the Metres decreased in value. Modern music no longer observes this rule rigorously; and as at present each Metre can be played at three Tempos, that is to say Slow Tempo, Moderate Tempo, and Fast Tempo and their nuances, it follows that the silence of the Metre in this matter has been replaced by terms which indicate the degree of Slowness or Speed which the Tempo should have. This new indication is placed at the head of the piece of music, and at all the places where the Movement changes.[40]

In his discussion of $\genfrac{}{}{0pt}{}{2}{4}$, Schulz considered the theoretical relationship between the tempo terms, the *tempo giusto* of a specific metre, and the note values, explaining:

> It [$\genfrac{}{}{0pt}{}{2}{4}$] is appropriate to all light and pleasant motions of feeling which, according to the quality of the expression, can be softened by *andante* or *adagio* or made even more lively by *vivace* or *allegro*. The particular tempo of this and all other metres is determined by these words and by the types of notes employed.[41]

Schulz's reference to "the types of notes employed" hints at a further subtlety in the system. The relationship between larger note values, and slower and heavier execution applied not only between metres with different

---

[40] Gossec et al.: *Principes*, i, 43.
[41] Schulz: 'Takt' in Sulzer: *Allgemeine Theorie*, ii, 1134.

denominators, but also within the same metre. As already explained, a melody notated in 2/2 that was transcribed into halved note values in 2/4 would, assuming the tempo term remained constant, theoretically be performed somewhat more quickly and more lightly; similarly, if a melody were renotated with halved note values in the same metre, so that two bars of the original version became one of the new version, it too would be played faster and more lightly than before, though not twice as fast. Only if the composer reduced the tempo term, say from *allegro con brio* to *allegro moderato*, would the music be played at the same speed. Such transference from one form of notation to another within the same metre could take place without significant alteration of the pattern of accentuation, since tempo played a large part in determining the frequency and weight of accents. Nevertheless, the different notation, even if the tempo remained the same, would probably have been intended to convey a somewhat different message about the style of performance.[42]

For musicians responsive to these conventions, therefore, larger note values, even within the same metre, implied slower and heavier music. An *allegro* in 2/4 containing a significant number of sixteenths as its fastest notes would, therefore, probably have a quarter-note pulse, and this would be faster and lighter than the half-note pulse of one that contained nothing faster than eighths. Conversely, an *adagio* in 2/4 might have an eighth-note or sixteenth-note pulse, depending on whether its fastest notes were thirty-seconds, or sixty-fourths, as in the *Adagio ma non troppo* of Beethoven's String Quartet op. 18 no. 6. In such cases, it is likely that the choice of metre had consequences not only for tempo but also for character. In that case the relationship that more commonly existed between pieces in different metres would exist between pieces in the same metre.[43] Thus, though the quarter-note pulse of an allegro containing sixteenths in 2/4 might be faster than the half-note pulse of another having only eighths, the quarters in the latter would still be faster than the quarters in the former. But as was normally the case, in practice there would not be a 2:1 relationship. A good example of

---

[42] See Ch. 5, "Heavy and Light Performance".

[43] The recognition of which note value constitutes the pulse unit in these instances depends entirely on the nature of the music. Quantz discussed a type of adagio 2/4 which moves basically in quarters and is performed at twice the speed of one in which there is eighth-note motion. A similar situation seems often to have existed with the true alla breve; it is clear that C was often used when ¢ was really meant, either because a composer regarded the value of the pulse unit as obvious or through inadvertent omission of the vertical bar. The vexed question of alla breve is discussed more fully in Ch. 9, below.

this is provided by the first movement of Beethoven's Fifth Symphony op. 67 and the last movement of his Seventh Symphony op. 92, both of which are Allegro con brio in 2/4: op. 67, with eighths as the fastest notes, has the metronome mark ♩ = 108, while op. 92, with sixteenths, has the metronome mark 𝅗𝅥 = 72.

The tempo terms, the metre, the note values, and the actual speed at which the music should be performed were therefore seen by theorists as necessarily interdependent elements in the system. Considerable evidence can be found to show that many composers during the century between 1750 and 1850 did not merely regard these relationships as purely theoretical. For instance, when Mozart changed the finale of his Quartet in B flat major K. 458 from ¢ (*alla breve*) to 2/4 with halved note values, he also reduced the tempo term from *Presto* to *Allegro assai*; and when Mendelssohn did a similar thing with his *Sommernachtstraum* overture, changing it from ¢ in the orchestral version to c with halved note values in the piano duet version, he altered the tempo term from *Allegro di molto* to *Allegro vivace*. An example of the same principle operating when a piece was re-notated in halved note values without a change of metre is provided by a comparison of the first version of Mendelssohn's Octet with the published version. When he revised the first movement, halving the note values but keeping the metre the same (i.e., two bars of c became one), he altered the tempo term from *Allegro molto e vivace* to *Allegro moderato ma con fuoco*.

Another important constituent of the tempo equation was the quantity of fast-moving notes that a piece contained. After discussing the effect of metre, tempo term, and note values, Schulz went on to explain how this additional factor also exercised an influence on the speed of the pulse unit. He observed: "If the piece is in 2/4, marked with allegro and has few or even no sixteenths, so the beat is faster than if it were filled with them; the same is true of slower tempos."[44]

Among other factors affecting tempo, Schulz pointed out that the time units in uneven (i.e., triple) time were naturally lighter than those in the equivalent even (i.e., duple or quadruple) time; thus the quarters in an *allegro* 3/4 were felt to be somewhat livelier than those in an *allegro* 2/4 or 4/4. John Holden made a similar point, saying, "it is generally agreed, that every mood of triple time ought to be performed something quicker, than the correspondent

---

[44] Schulz: 'Takt' in Sulzer, *Allgemeine Theorie*, ii, 1134.

mood of common time".[45] Holden also drew attention to the convention that tempo was differently perceived in different genres of music, observing that "the real length of the measure ought to be made something more, in Church music; and often much less in Opera music".[46] Türk similarly warned: "An *Allegro* for the church or in sacred cantatas, in an intricate trio, quartet, etc., must be taken in a far more moderate tempo than an *Allegro* for the theatre, or in the so-called chamber style, e.g., in symphonies, divertimenti, etc. An *Allegro* full of sublime, solemnly grand thoughts requires a slower and more emphatic movement than a piece of music with the same heading in which leaping joy is the dominant character, and so on."[47]

These views about tempo are confirmed in many 18th- and early-19th-century sources. J. F. Schubert's *Neue Singe-Schule* (1804), for instance, shows that the ideas on tempo expounded by earlier writers were still seen as valid at that time, and also identifies some of the other things that were felt to have a bearing on tempo:

> The correct tempo or degree of speed cannot be determined by any heading, and can only be gathered from the inner characteristics of a composition itself. So, for instance, an allegro with sixteenths ought not to be performed as quickly as if the fastest passages are only in triplets or eighths. An allegro in church style or in an oratorio must have a slower tempo than an allegro in theatre or chamber style. An allegro where the text has a solemn content and the character of the music is exalted or pathetic must have a more serious motion than an allegro with a joyful text and lightweight music. A well-worked-out allegro with a powerful, full harmony must be performed more slowly than a hastily written allegro with trivial harmony. In an adagio in $\frac{3}{8}$ metre the eighths will be performed more slowly than the eighths in the same tempo in $\frac{3}{4}$ metre. [...]
>
> Differences in compositional style or manner and national taste also necessitate a faster or slower tempo.[48]

There were therefore several less obvious factors that could to some extent affect the choice of tempo term; and these, in combination with the metre and note values, would be expected to convey the correct tempo range to the

---

[45] Holden: *Essay*, 36.
[46] Holden: *Essay*, 27.
[47] Türk: *Klavierschule*, 111.
[48] Schubert: *Singe-Schule*, 124.

performer. Some of them will be considered further in relation to the varied and fluctuating meaning of tempo terms. Clearly the matter was of such complexity that, even when this method of indicating tempo was part of the current performing tradition, only the most gifted and experienced musicians will successfully have found their way through the maze of complications.

## Late-18th-Century Tempo

The extent to which late-18th-century composers were consistent in applying the principles of tempo determination outlined above cannot be objectively assessed. It is reasonable to conclude that Haydn, Mozart, Beethoven and other serious-minded composers tried very carefully to indicate the desired speed by their choice of the appropriate tempo term, in combination with the metre, note values, and other relevant factors. Yet, even if it were possible to determine the internal relationships of Haydn's or Mozart's tempo system with a fair degree of confidence,[49] there would still be insufficient information to do more than speculate about the absolute tempo range they might have conceived for a given tempo formula. No chronometric tempo markings by major composers of the late 18th century are known, and the evidence provided by contemporary and retrospective accounts is frustratingly slender. There are general statements by "ear witnesses": for instance, in 1811:

> I remember very well hearing Mozart and Haydn perform symphonies of their composition in Vienna: they never took their first allegros as quickly as one hears them here [in Leipzig], and probably also now in several German orchestras; the minuets, on the other hand, they both took quickly; Haydn loved to take the finales faster than Mozart—which, of course, emerges from the character and the style of writing of these movements, but is now sometimes forgotten by other directors.[50]

It was also reported just seven years after Mozart's death that he "complained about nothing more vigorously than the 'bungling' of his compositions in public performance—chiefly through exaggerating the rapidity of the tempos". At a rehearsal in Leipzig, he nevertheless insisted upon a tempo for

---

[49] See Neal Zaslaw: 'Mozart's Tempo Conventions', *International Musicological Society Congress Report*, xi (Copenhagen, 1972), 720ff.
[50] Anon.: 'Nachrichten', *Allgemeine musikalische Zeitung*, xiii (1811), 737.

the opening movement of one of his symphonies that drove the orchestral players to the limits of their ability.[51] Perhaps, as he stated afterwards, this was a rehearsal strategy, but it may well be the case that the Viennese *allegro* was already faster in Mozart's day than the north German *allegro*.

References to the tempo of specific pieces by late-18th-century composers often provide only relative information. In Mozart's case, we learn, for instance, that in 1807:

> The addiction to playing musical works ever more quickly is also taking over here in Vienna, so that one often makes a joke and even a merit out of it, e.g. having the symphony "dusted down". Some time ago, for example, a Mozart piano concerto was played twice as quickly as I heard it performed by Mozart himself. [. . .] Now, however, there are also virtuosos who take the opposite extreme; these are the ones who have the so-called grand style (Viotti's school). [. . .] An example I would like to give is that of Lamare [*sic*],[52] who, during his stay in Vienna, played the second movement of the second of Mozart's concertante quartets [K. 589] almost twice as slowly as I heard it played under Mozart's direction.[53]

This writer stressed the need for some form of chronometer, so that the composer could fix tempos precisely.

Local practices were very variable. Gottfried Weber commented that in Paris the *adagio* in the overture to *Don Giovanni* was played a little slower than Mozart had directed it in Prague, while in Vienna it was performed a little faster and in Berlin nearly twice as fast, and that in all three places the *allegro* was given a little faster than Mozart took it.[54] Occasionally the evidence is more precise, such as the plausible assertion that "Ach ich fühl's" from *Die Zauberflöte* was performed under Mozart at a speed in the range ♪ = c. 138–52 (i.e., considerably faster than after his death).[55] Specific and

---

[51] Friedrich Rochlitz: 'Anecdoten aus Mozarts Leben', *Allgemeine musikalische Zeitung*, i (1798–89), 84. The reliability of Rochlitz's retrospective account of Mozart's visit to Leipzig has been doubted since Jahn questioned it in his Mozart biography, but whatever license Rochlitz may have taken in embellishing his recollections, it seems unlikely, from what is known of his profoundly moral character, that he would willfully have invented things that were fundamentally untrue.

[52] The French cellist Jacques Michel Hurel Lamarre (1772–1823), who may well have misunderstood the meaning of ¢ in conjunction with "Larghetto".

[53] Anon.: *Allgemeine musikalische Zeitung*, ix (1806–7), 265f.

[54] Anon.: *Allgemeine musikalische Zeitung*, xv (1813), 306.

[55] Gottfried Weber: 'Ein Zweifel', *Allgemeine musikalische Zeitung*, xvii (1815), 247–49; also in Georg Nikolaus Nissen: *Wolfgang Amadeus Mozart's Biographie* (Leipzig, 1828), 123f.

interesting, but rather less plausible, is the list of metronome tempos given by the ageing Václav Jan Tomášek in 1839 as a supposed record of speeds taken in performances of *Don Giovanni* in Prague in 1791.[56] Comparison of Tomášek's markings with two other sets is interesting: they are fairly consistent with those given in the 1822 publication of the opera by Schlesinger,[57] but both Tomášek and Schlesinger are noticeably different from the chronometric tempos for the opera given by William Crotch in about 1825. Crotch's markings show a clear preference for slower speeds, especially for the sections with faster tempo terms.[58] Hummel's metronome marks for Mozart's last six symphonies and Czerny's similar metronome marks, together with some for his quartets and quintets, certainly preserve an early-19th-century Viennese view of an appropriate tempo for these works, revealing significantly faster tempos for many movements than became customary in the 20th century; whether they preserve the composer's practice is more questionable.[59]

For Haydn, the anecdotes and general comments are supplemented by just a few more precise pieces of information. Among the apparently most authoritative tempos are those reportedly given for Haydn's *Creation* by Salieri (who was involved in the first and many subsequent performances) and by Sigmund Neukomm, Haydn's pupil at the time, who arranged the 1800 vocal score. Neukomm's, although not given until 1832, seem more likely to be closer to Haydn's intentions than the four attributed to Salieri in 1813.[60] In addition, there are metronome marks by Czerny for the twelve London symphonies, which are open to the same objections as those he gave for Mozart's works. The metronome marks for Haydn's string quartets supplied by Karol Lipiński provide a mid-19th-century view; nevertheless, his edition retains the earlier rapid tempos for the minuets and trios.[61] These

[56] See Walter Gerstenberg: 'Authentische Tempi für Mozart's "Don Giovanni"?', *Mozart-Jahrbuch* (1960-61), 58–61.

[57] See Max Rudolf: 'Ein Beitrag zur Geschichte der Tempoabnahme bei Mozart', *Mozart-Jahrbuch* (1976-77), 204–24.

[58] *Don Giovanni* [. . .] *arranged for the piano forte, with an accompaniment for flute or violin* (London, [c. 1825]). The metronome marks up to "Batti batti" are listed in Zaslaw: 'Mozart's Tempo Conventions'.

[59] For Hummel's metronome markings for Mozart symphonies, see R. Munster: 'Authentische Tempi zu den sechs letzten Sinfonien Mozart's?', *Mozart-Jahrbuch* (1962–63), 185ff. For Czerny's metronome marks for Haydn and Mozart, see William Malloch: 'Carl Czerny's Metronome Marks for Haydn and Mozart Symphonies', *Early Music*, xvi (1988), 72–81.

[60] See Nicholas Temperley: 'Haydn's Tempos in *The Creation*', *Early Music*, xix (1991), 235–45; and *Wiener allgemeine musikalische Zeitung*, i (1813), 628.

[61] *Vollständige Sammlung der Quarteten für zwei Violinen, Viola u. Violoncelle von Joseph Haydn. Neue Ausgabe. Revidirt und mit Tempobezeichnung versehen von Carl Lipinski* (Dresden, 1848–52). Copy in the British Library, London, Hirsch III. 266. For a complete list see https://mhm.hud.ac.uk/chase/view/pdf/878/1/.

contradict the Wagnerian assertion that minuets require a stately tempo, which prevailed during much of the 20th century, except in the Joachim tradition.[62]

The key to translating Haydn's and Mozart's tempos into chronometric ones with any degree of confidence, therefore, is missing. It is possible to hypothesize the relationships between them with qualified plausibility, though in the case of the slower tempos the evidence is not unambiguous.[63] With many other late-18th-century musicians, particularly Italian composers working in Italy, there may have been less concern to define the tempo more narrowly than to put it into one of the three, or at best five, main tempo categories. Italian composers working elsewhere in Europe, particularly those involved directly or indirectly with publishing, seem to have been more careful, as performance directions and metronome marks given for their own works (composed towards the ends of their careers) by Mozart's Italian contemporaries Clementi (b. 1752) and Cherubini (b. 1760) suggest.

## Beethoven's Tempo Preferences

Only in Beethoven's case does it become possible to assess with any significant degree of objectivity the extent to which a major composer of the Classical era was consistent in his handling of the theoretical 18th-century tempo equation, and what that meant to him in terms of absolute tempo; for Beethoven gave metronome marks, many of them admittedly retrospective, to a considerable number of important works, the earliest of which were composed around 1800. His musings on the subject of tempo, which he jotted down on a draft of the *minore* section of his song "Klage" WoO. 113 (c. 1790), show that he was aware of the principles that lay behind the Kirnberger–Schulz analysis of the relationship between tempo, metre, tempo term, and note values:

> That which now follows will be sung twice as slowly, *adagio* or, at the most *andante quasi adagio*. Andante in $\frac{2}{4}$ time must be taken much faster than the tempo of the song here. It seems, impossible for the latter to remain in $\frac{2}{4}$ time, because it is much too slow for that. It seems best to set both in ¢ time.

---

[62] E.g., as preserved in the Klingler Quartet's early recordings.
[63] For further discussion of these see Ch. 10.

The first, in E major, must remain in $\frac{2}{4}$ time, otherwise one would sing it too slowly.

Long notes will always be taken more slowly than short ones; e.g. quarters slower than 8ths.

The smaller notes determine the tempo; e.g. 16ths-32nds in $\frac{2}{4}$ time make it very slow.

Perhaps the opposite is also true.[64]

Beethoven's metronome marks suggest that he continued throughout his life to regard this view of tempo as valid, and indicate that he took great care to choose the tempo terms that, in relation to the other relevant factors, most precisely indicated the speed he conceived for his music. This, of course, assumes that, in general, he did not significantly change his mind about the tempos between the period of their composition and the time when he gave them metronome marks. In most cases, pieces are grouped into rather narrow bands, according to the relationship between tempo term, metre, metronome mark, and the fastest note value employed in the music. The distinctions between the three main groups, *adagio*, *andante-allegretto*, and *allegro-presto*, are generally quite sharp. Apparent deviations from a strictly ordered sequence within these groups (when they are not the result of an erroneous marking) are often explained by the quantity and character of the fastest-moving notes in the piece. For the purposes of the present discussion, the quantity of the fastest functional notes in a piece is expressed as a percentage, representing the number of bars containing three or more of the fastest notes in relation to the total number of bars in the piece. This is only one way of calculating that proportion, and inevitably the results are approximate, but other methods that have been considered have been found not to make a significant difference to the result. It is relevant, however, to distinguish in orchestral music between the quantity of bars in which the fastest notes appear as figurations and those in which they are merely used as a *tremolando* effect, since *tremolando* effects are both technically feasible at faster speeds and produce less of a subjective impression of speed on the listener than figurations of notes of the same value. In Tables 8.2–8.4, numbers in brackets represent the percentage of bars in the movement where the fastest notes occur only as *tremolando*. In deciding which note value should be regarded as the fastest, occasional flourishes and purely ornamental

---

[64] Original in the Gesellschaft der Musikfreunde, Vienna, MS Autogr. 9, fol. 2v.

Table 8.2. The Influence of Fast-Moving Notes on Tempo Indication

| Opus | Tempo term | Time Signature | MM | Fastest notes | Approx. % of bars with fastest notes |
|---|---|---|---|---|---|
| 21/iv | Allegro molto e vivace | 2/4 | 𝅗𝅥 = 88 | ♪ | 24 (16) |
| 55/iv | Allegro molto | 2/4 | 𝅗𝅥 = 76 | ♪ | 51 (8) |
| 18/5/i | Allegro | 6/8 | 𝅗𝅥. = 104 | ♪ | 18 |
| 59/2/i | Allegro | 6/8 | 𝅗𝅥. = 84 | ♪ | 58 |

figures, even if written out in large-size notes, are ignored. Naturally, this type of analysis cannot be usefully applied to very short sections.

The modifying effect of this factor can be seen from a comparison of movements, such as the finales of the First Symphony and the Third Symphony or the first movements of the quartets op. 18 no. 5 and op. 59 no. 2, which have the same metre, similar tempo directions, and the same range of note values. The relationship may be shown as in Table 8.2. In other words, the larger quantities of fast-moving notes in op. 55 and op. 59 no. 2 require a slower pulse rate, but in terms of subjective tempo feeling they are equivalent to pieces with faster pulse rates but fewer fast-moving notes.

These relationships can be seen from a different angle in Table 8.3, which compares the first movements of the quartets op. 59 nos. 1 and 3 and the first movement and third movement (trio section) of the Sixth Symphony op. 68. Here the same metres and metronome marks have different tempo terms, but the faster term for op. 59 no. 3 is explained by the fact that the fastest-moving notes are sixteenths as opposed to triplet eighths; and the faster tempo term for the third movement of the Sixth Symphony than for the first movement seems to reflect the much greater quantity of fast-moving notes in the former.

Table 8.3. The Influence of Fast-Moving Notes on Tempo Indication

| Opus | Tempo term | Time Signature | MM | Fastest notes | Approx. % of bars with fastest notes |
|---|---|---|---|---|---|
| 59/1/i | Allegro | ₵ | 𝅗𝅥 = 88 | ♪♪♪ (triplet) | 21 |
| 59/3/i | Allegro vivace | ₵ | 𝅗𝅥 = 88 | ♪ | 34 |
| 68/i | Allegro ma non troppo | 2/4 | 𝅗𝅥 = 66 | ♪ | 26 |
| 68/iii | In tempo d'allegro | 2/4 | 𝅗𝅥 = 132 | ♪ | 60 |

A few cases that initially appear anomalous are elucidated by a closer look at the nature of the music; thus, the first movement of the First Symphony, an Allegro con brio ¢ with a metronome mark of $\dminim = 112$ and sixteenths as its fastest notes, seems as though it ought to have a faster tempo term than the Finale of the Septet op. 20, a Presto ¢, which is also marked $\dminim = 112$ and has triplet eighths as its fastest notes; but the virtuoso triplet figurations in the Septet give a greater subjective feeling of speed than the sixteenths in the symphony, which are *tremolando* with an occasional four-note flourish. Sometimes the relationship between tempo term and metronome mark is also modified by other factors, especially the character of themes or a strong element of contrast (e.g., the first movements of op. 18 no. 4, op. 95, and op. 36), but in the vast majority of cases the margin of variation is relatively small, and the information conveyed by taking into account the factors described by Kirnberger and Schulz defines the actual speed of the music quite narrowly.

The comparison shown in Table 8.4 of all Beethoven's metronomized movements in ¢ metre containing the word *allegro* illustrates the level of consistency of faster tempos in this metre (for slower tempos in most metres the paucity of examples allows only more generalized conclusions). The last two metronome markings indicate that when all the main factors are apparently equal there can be a noticeable difference in speed; but in this case it seems probable that the difference results from the fact that the quartet contains figures of separately bowed sixteenths, while in the symphony, a significant

Table 8.4. Beethoven's Metronome Marks for Movements in ¢ Metre

| Opus | Tempo term | MM | Fastest notes | Approx. % of bars with fastest notes |
| --- | --- | --- | --- | --- |
| 18/4/i | Allegro ma non tanto | ♩= 84 | ♪ | 11 |
| 125/iv | Allegro assai | ♩= 80 | ♪ | 17 |
| 68/iv | Allegro | ♩= 80 | ♪ | 70 (40) |
| 74/i | Allegro | ♩= 84 | ♪ | 19 |
| 67/iv | Allegro | ♩= 84 | ♪ | 39 (24) |
| 59/1/i | Allegro | ♩= 88 | ♫♪ (triplet) | 21 |
| 59/3/i | Allegro vivace | ♩= 88 | ♪ | 34 |
| 95/i | Allegro con brio | ♩= 92 | ♪ | 52 |
| 36/i | Allegro con brio | ♩= 100 | ♪ | 50 (18) |

number of the sixteenths are used in *tremolando* and all the figurations are slurred. The fastest *allegro* marking is, as might be expected, the first movement of the String Quartet op. 59 no. 1, which has triplet eighths rather than sixteenths as its fastest notes, and the slowest, the fourth movement of the "Pastoral" Symphony, has the most sixteenths. The marking for the Allegro assai in the Finale of the Ninth Symphony supports the view that for Beethoven the qualifying term "assai" meant "enough" rather than "very".[65]

The ȼ markings are fairly straightforward; greater problems of reconciling apparent differences are found in other metres. Some of these may merely reveal that Beethoven did not always light upon the combination that most accurately reflected his wishes, that he changed his mind about the speed of a movement between composing it and allotting it metronome marks, or that the metronome marks have been wrongly transmitted.[66]

## The Impact of the Metronome

Many early-19th-century musicians were concerned about finding a method of indicating tempo that would be less easily misunderstood than previous ones, since their own times saw such controversy and confusion in the matter. Earlier devices or methods for indicating tempo chronometrically had failed to gain currency not because of their own deficiencies, but rather, despite the occasional lament on the part of theorists that no such device was readily available, because the need was not sufficiently pressing.[67] The acceptance and rapidly proliferating use of the metronome in the second and third decades of the century was a direct response to changing conditions. Even before the commercial success of Maelzel's metronome had become assured, some composers were attracted by the idea of regularly giving their music chronometric tempo indications by other methods. Gottfried Weber vigorously advocated the use of a pendulum in several articles at about the time of Maelzel's first metronome, and Spohr, among others, adopted Weber's method of indicating tempo by this means before changing to metronome marks around 1820.

---

[65] Advanced, e.g., by Stuart Deas: 'Beethoven's "Allegro assai"', *Music & Letters*, 31 (1950), 333.

[66] For particular examination of two metronome marks in the Ninth Symphony, see Brown: 'Historical Performance', 253ff.

[67] See Rosamond E. M. Harding: *Origins of Musical Time and Expression* (London, 1938); David Martin: 'An Early Metronome', *Early Music*, xvi (1988), 90–92.

The early decades of the 19th century saw gradual but significant changes in composers' approaches towards specifying the tempo of their pieces. To a large extent this was because the fundamental tenets upon which the whole system was founded were breaking down, together with the pan-European aristocratic social system that had prevailed throughout much of the 18th century. The notion that the *tempo giusto* of every metre could be understood by studying all kinds of dance pieces—every dance having its definite tempo, determined by the metre and the note values employed in it—[68] could not survive the disintegration of the social order, with which this aspect of musical culture had enjoyed a symbiotic relationship. The old social order was first weakened, and then then transformed by the French Revolution and the Napoleonic Wars. Drastic social and cultural change, especially relating to the extraordinary growth in numbers and influence of the western-European middle classes, saw the desuetude and gradual disappearance of the repertoire of 18th-century courtly dances, one of the principal yardsticks by which the *tempo giusto* had been measured.

The older system did not break down entirely or immediately, but it seems to have become increasingly unreliable in the hands of composers who lacked a rooted and instinctive feeling for the premises on which it was based. In these circumstances, chronometric tempo measurement, which had failed to take hold in the 18th century despite various perfectly practicable proposals, was seized upon with alacrity by many musicians. It seems quite likely that the widespread adoption of the metronome, which theoretically rendered other means of specifying tempo by the metre-tempo term-note value system redundant, helped to accelerate the decay of the older system. Yet it would perhaps be closer to the mark to attribute the enthusiasm with which so many musicians advocated mechanical means of designating tempo at this time to the recognition that the ever-greater diversity of style and individuality of expression in late-18th-century and 19th-century music made it increasingly difficult to perceive the relationship of a work to the sorts of conventions described by 18th-century theorists. In 1778, Johann Nicolaus Forkel had referred to an article in a Parisian music journal, which mentioned the use of a pendulum to specify tempo. Having observed that Italian tempo terms were a very imprecise way of indicating the tempo, he continued:

> But if, over each piece of music, the composer, by means of numbers, inches, or lines were to specify the required length of a pendulum or

---

[68] Kirnberger: *Die Kunst des reinen Satzes*, ii, 106.

*metrometer*, in order to perform a piece in the best and most appropriate tempo, he would physically determine the tempo—removing the element of chance—and no longer be exposed to the unpleasant situation of seeing his music performed in an incorrect movement, even by the most skilful people, as a result of which it often loses its whole inner value, character and true expression.[69]

Also, as the concept of a canon of great music developed, many composers were attracted to the possibility of fixing this important aspect of their work in a less ambiguous manner. Gottfried Weber's awareness of these issues is suggested by the foreword to his Requiem op. 24 of 1813, in which he provided chronometric markings in pendulum lengths; he recommended that other composers should use this method, since "A piece of music marked in this way brings its own tempo-specifier with it wherever a copy of it goes, and as long as a copy exists, the tempo intended by the composer is immutably and unmistakably prescribed despite all changes of period, fashion, and taste."[70] A similar awareness, expressed in typically Beethovenian style, is apparent in Beethoven's letter to Schott, promising metronome marks for the *Missa solemnis*: "Do wait for them. In our century such indications are certainly necessary [...]. We can scarcely have tempi ordinari any longer, since one must fall into line with the ideas of unfettered genius."[71]

The fact that Beethoven's remark was prompted by correspondence over the publication of the Mass suggests another important impulse behind the growing use of metronome marks: the enormous expansion of publishing during Beethoven's lifetime, catering increasingly for an amateur market, carried with it the expectation that the music would come into the hands of people who had little or no knowledge of this difficult matter. That Beethoven's contemporaries were seriously concerned about a decline in the understanding of tempo conventions by professionals and amateurs alike is corroborated by the increasingly frequent complaints of early-19th-century writers that some music was becoming distorted almost to the point of incoherence by being performed at radically different speeds from those intended by the composer. In 1829, Andersch, having listed various qualifiers for the term Allegro, observed: "Each requires a different tempo, depending

---

[69] Johann Nikolaus Forkel: *Musikalisch-kritische Bibliothek*, i (Gotha, 1778), 259.
[70] Gottfried Weber: *Requiem* (Offenbach am Main, André, [c. 1816]), iii.
[71] Anderson: *The Letters of Beethoven*, 1325.

on how the character of one composition differs from that of another. For this reason, it would be all the more desirable for every composer to indicate the tempo of his music metronomically, and for there to be a metronome in every orchestra. Unfortunately, all too often the correct time measure is missed and thus the character of a composition is distorted."[72]

Early-19th-century comments about circumstances in which there were problems over tempo illuminate national and regional differences, and the application of inappropriate criteria to older music, as well as misunderstandings arising from the performance of music by inexperienced musicians, or those brought up in a different tradition from that of the composer. In 1809, for instance, one writer warned that "German music must not be played in French tempos",[73] and three decades later Bernhard Romberg stated that *allegro* was played faster in Paris than in Vienna and faster in Vienna than in the north of Germany.[74] The critic who had complained in 1807 about tempos in Mozart also lamented that "If this continues, the tempos in Germany will become like our spelling—we will no longer have any rules, so that almost everything will be abandoned to caprice."[75] Thus, although complaints about discrepancies in the treatment of tempo can be found in earlier periods (not everyone, for instance, agreed with Quantz's ideas),[76] the frequency and nature of references to this problem in the early 19th century suggest a much more intractable situation.

Concrete evidence of the way in which the widespread adoption of chronometric tempo measurement delivered the *coup de grâce* to the older system can be found in various early-19th-century discussions of the metronome and its uses. Hummel's brief account is revealing of a new attitude towards indicating tempo. Like Gottfried Weber, he stressed that "To composers it offers the great advantage, that their compositions when marked according to the degrees of the metronome, will be performed in every country in exactly the same tempo; and the effect of their works will not now, as formerly, despite the most carefully chosen musical terms, be lost through hurrying of dragging the tempo." His total abandonment of the older system is indicated by his next sentence: "The long headings become superfluous because the whole time system is divided into three main tempos: the slow, the moderate and the rapid, and thus it is only rarely necessary to add a word to indicate the particular *affect* prevailing in a piece."[77] Maelzel's own table of the

---

[72] Andersch: 'Allegro' in *Musikalisches Worterbuch*, 13.
[73] Anon.: *Allgemeine musikalische Zeitung*, xi (1808–9), 604.
[74] Romberg: *Violoncell Schule*, 110.
[75] Anon.: *Allgemeine musikalische Zeitung*, ix (1806–7), 266.
[76] See Ch. 10, "Allegro".
[77] Hummel: *Anweisung*, 2nd edn, 455.

metronome marks appropriate to slow, moderate, and quick pieces in various metres, which Hummel approvingly includes in his account, immediately implies a coarsening of the subtleties of the older system by making no apparent distinction between the time units in C, ¢, and $\overset{2}{4}$ (Ex. 8.1).

Ex. 8.1 Hummel: *Anweisung*, 1st edn (1827), iii, 440; 2nd edn (1828), 456, Tab. 1. Image from English edition: iii, 67.

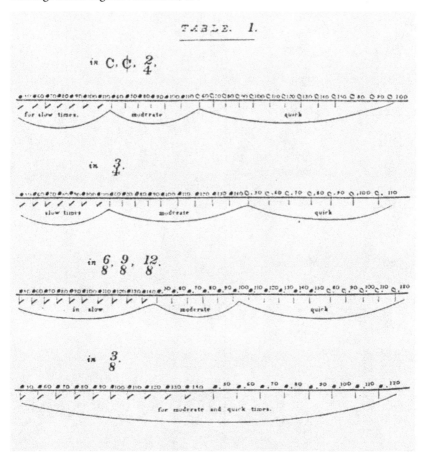

The graduated scale on Maelzel's original metronome listed merely numbers, but it was not long before the scale also included tempo terms, linking a particular word with a rather narrowly circumscribed speed for the beat (Ex. 8.2), thus strengthening the idea that tempo terms were directly related to a particular pulse rate in the music.

One of the other tables reproduced by Hummel purports to show the "inconsistency" of composers in the old system (Ex. 8.3), but in doing so it fails to compare like with like. The metres are muddled (all bars with four quarters are indiscriminately given as C), and a vital element of the tempo equation— the types of notes in the piece—is omitted. Furthermore, the metronome tempos, supposedly given by the composers, are in any case dubious; the three presto illustrations in c metre given for Beethoven do not correspond with any of his markings, and only two of them can be matched with ¢ prestos.

**Ex. 8.2** Metronome scale.

| | | |
|---|---|---|
| 40 | Grave | 42 |
| 44 | Largo | 46 |
| 48 | Larghetto | 50 |
| 52 | Adagio | 54 |
| 56 | | 58 |
| 60 | Andante | 63 |
| 66 | Andantino | 69 |
| 72 | | 76 |
| 80 | Moderato | 84 |
| 88 | | 92 |
| 96 | Allegretto | 100 |
| 104 | | 108 |
| 112 | Allegro | 116 |
| 120 | Vivace | 126 |
| 132 | | 138 |
| 144 | Presto | 152 |
| 160 | | 168 |
| 176 | Prestissimo | 184 |
| 192 | | 200 |
| 208 | | |

Ex. 8.3 Hummel: *Anweisung*, 1st edn (1827), iii, 441; 2nd edn (1828), iii, 457 Tab. 2. Image from English edition: iii, 68.

The result of the tendency illustrated by Hummel's treatment of tempo was that the tempo term came increasingly to be seen as a word that described an aural phenomenon rather than as a single modifying factor in a complex equation. A piece was designated *adagio, andante, allegro,* or *presto* because it was felt to be so. The choice of tempo term and its relation to the envisaged speed of the music seem to have become more subjective, creating very significant problems for performers unfamiliar with the composer's practice when metronome marks were not provided.[78]

## 19th-Century Tempo Conventions

Few composers born after 1800 seem to have shown real understanding of the older system for indicating tempo, though its influence, albeit in a diluted form, may be detected in some aspects of the practice of more conservatively trained or historically aware composers such as Dvořák and Brahms. Mendelssohn's sensitivity to the relationship between tempo term, metre, and note value has already been mentioned; this may be explained by his thorough training under Carl Friedrich Zelter. It is revealing, however, that his exact contemporary and colleague Schumann, whose early musical education was nowhere near as thorough, seems not to have possessed this sensitivity to anything like the same degree, if at all. When Schumann revised his D minor Symphony, for example, he altered the notation of the outer movements: in the first movement he kept the metre the same and halved the note values; in the Finale he changed the metre from $\frac{2}{4}$ to $\frac{4}{4}$ but retained the original note values. In both cases the tempo term in the first version was "Allegro" and in the second version the exact German equivalent *Lebhaft*, indicating in contrast to Mendelssohn's procedure in the *Sommernachtstraum* and Octet, a lack of responsiveness to the old relationship of tempo term, metre, and note values.

Major German theoretical studies from the 1820s onwards scarcely, if at all, allude to that relationship. Gottfried Weber, in his widely disseminated and influential *Versuch einer geordneten Theorie der Tonsetzkunst*, set the pattern for many later theoretical works. Considering the significance of metre, he stressed the effect of different metres and note values on style of performance, but seems entirely to have excluded their direct relationship to tempo. Having observed that $\frac{2}{2}$, $\frac{2}{4}$, and $\frac{2}{8}$ were basically "only different ways of representing one and the same time signature with signs", he continued:

> For this very reason, and since a half note relates to a quarter note in exactly the same way as a quarter note relates to an eighth note, etc., it would

[78] See Ch. 10.

not matter at all which way of writing one chose; every piece of music in $\frac{2}{4}$ time could just as well be written in $\frac{2}{2}$ time as in $\frac{2}{8}$ time, especially since by the tempo markings allegro - adagio, etc., one can sufficiently indicate how quickly the eighth- or quarter- or half-notes are to be taken, so that Allegro $\frac{2}{4}$ would be about as quick and could mean the same as Adagio $\frac{2}{8}$.

By itself, of course, this is also correct: However, it has been agreed that $\frac{2}{2}$ is performed differently from $\frac{2}{4}$ or indeed $\frac{3}{8}$, $\frac{3}{2}$ differently from $\frac{3}{8}$; that is to say, the smaller the notes denoting its units (or in other words, the larger the denominator—the lower number—of the fraction), the lighter and more gently a piece of music is performed, and the larger the note-value, the more weightily and coarsely it is performed; furthermore, the quarter notes in Allegro, for example, are performed very differently from the sixteenth notes in Adagio, although the latter are just as fast as the former.

In this respect, therefore, the difference in time signatures offers the composer a means of indicating the character in which he wishes his piece to be performed; and thus it is important to choose the most appropriate time signature. The older composers were so attached to this that they sometimes used $\frac{2}{16}$ or $\frac{3}{16}$.[79]

For determining tempo, Gottfried Weber, as already mentioned, preferred to rely on chronometric tempo indications, which he included in his own compositions, advocating the use of a simple pendulum rather than a metronome.

With Liszt, and especially Wagner, a move towards simplification in the employment of metres was inevitably related to a change in the significance of note values for tempo. Liszt's *Faust-Symphonie*, with its constant time changes between c ($\frac{4}{4}$), $\frac{2}{4}$, $\frac{2}{4}$, and $\frac{3}{4}$ ("Faust") or between $\frac{2}{4}$, $\frac{6}{8}$, c, $\frac{3}{4}$, and ¢ ("Mephistopheles"), illustrates the imperatives in this music that caused an inevitable reassessment of the implications of metre. The ever-increasing individualism of musical gesture in a single section or movement was seen to be essentially incompatible with the "collectivism" inherent in the old system: the intended expression of the piece could not be adequately conveyed to any extent by the choice of metre; the constantly fluctuating nuances had to be indicated by other means. Liszt's use of c and ¢ is particularly revealing, for the choice of one or other of these metres seems to be

[79] Weber: *Versuch*, i, 95.

directly related to the convenience of the conductor. For greater clarity he even headed the sections in ¢ "Alla breve taktieren" (beat in 2). Wagner, as in so many other respects, followed him in this approach to *alla breve*.[80] Richard Strauss, too, seems largely to have thought of metre in terms of conducting; in *Also sprach Zarathustra*, for instance, he followed an *accelerando* with the instruction "sehr schnell (alla breve)" (very fast (alla breve)) and ten bars later "Ziemlich langsam (in Vierteln)" (rather slow (in quarters)).[81] Coupled with this increasingly "practical" approach to the role of metre went a more subjective employment of tempo terms.[82]

Nevertheless, some of the other considerations, apart from the relationship between metre, note value, and tempo term, which were felt to influence the speed at which a particular piece of music would be performed, retained their validity and even became more pronounced in the 19th century. The slower tempo for church music (which, however, may have been stronger among Protestant and northern musicians than among Catholic and southern ones) is, for example, reflected in the metronome tempos (commented upon adversely by Ferdinand Ries)[83] that Spohr gave for his oratorio *Die letzten Dinge*. It seems also to be a factor in the very slow metronome marks given for Haydn's *Creation* in the Novello edition of 1858. The same appears to be true for much other 19th-century religious music. Mendelssohn's metronome marks for his organ sonatas op. 65 (which may be regarded as falling into the categories both of church music and "strict" music) indicate that in this genre his tempo terms were to be interpreted as slower than they normally were in other types of work (compare, e.g., the Allegro con brio of op. 65 no. 4 at ♩ = 100 with the Allegro vivace in his String Quartet op. 44 no. 3 at ♩ = 92, both in ¢ metre and both containing sixteenths).

The possibility that a tradition of faster tempos for sacred music survived longer in southern Europe, especially in Austria and Italy, may be suggested by an 1844 article, in which the Vienna cathedral Kapellmeister F. S. Hölzl complained about the modern rapid tempo mania, which led to sacred music being performed, in his opinion, much faster than the composers intended. However, his remark that "It may indeed not be an easy task once more to perform at a slower tempo a work that one has performed at the tempo of

---

[80] See Ch. 9.
[81] Miniature score (Leipzig, Eulenburg (EE 3506), n.d.), 94–95.
[82] See Ch. 10.
[83] Cecil Hill, *Ferdinand Ries: Briefe und Dokumente* (Bonn, 1982), 267.

Table 8.5. Hölzl's Metronome Marks for Haydn's "Nelson" Mass

| Movement, tempo term | Time signature | Usual tempo (MM) | Regulated tempo (MM) |
|---|---|---|---|
| Kyrie, Allegro moderato | ¢—♩ | 104 | 92 |
| Gloria, Allegro | ¢—♩ | 116 | 104 |
| Qui tollis, Adagio | ¾—♪ | 108 | 88 |
| Quoniam, Allegro | ¢—♩ | 116 | 104 |
| Credo, Allegro con spirito | ¢—♩ | 92 | 80 |
| Et incarnatus, Largo | ¾—♪ | 96 | 80 |
| Et resurrexit, Vivace | ¢—♩ | 126 | 108 |
| Sanctus, Adagio | ¢—♪ | 104 | 92 |
| Pleni, Allegro | ¾—♩ | 120 | 108 |
| Agnus, Adagio | ¾—♪ | 100 | 80 |
| Dona, Vivace | ¢—♩ | 120 | 100 |

many years standing",[84] and other such comments, indicates that these fast speeds were no recent modern craze in Vienna, but rather the speeds to which everyone was accustomed. He accompanied his comments with a list of metronome marks for Haydn's "Nelson" Mass in which he supplied each movement with the metronome mark for the tempo "to which one is accustomed" followed by "that which I regard as more appropriate for the work", as shown in Table 8.5.

A general preference for slower tempos in the music of the Viennese Classical composers, which was even apparent shortly after Beethoven's death, was clearly prevalent by the 1840s. Eduard Krüger (b. 1807), referring to a performance of the "Eroica" Symphony in Hamburg in 1841, approved of the tempos, as he remembered them. In the following list Krüger's preferred tempos are followed by Beethoven's.

(1) Allegro con brio ♩ = 150, 𝅗𝅥. = 60
(2) Andante con mote ♪ = 66, ♪ = 80
(3) Allegro 𝅗𝅥. = 100, 𝅗𝅥. = 116
(4) Allegro ♩ = 126, 𝅗𝅥 = 76

---

[84] Franz Seraphin Hölzl: 'Einige Bemerkungen über die Regulierung der Tempi für die Kirche', *Allgemeine Wiener Musik-Zeitung*, iv (1844), 334.

Clearly, Krüger was unaware that Beethoven had provided metronome marks,[85] but he knew the ones in Hummel's arrangement for piano, flute, violin, and cello (which are in fact Beethoven's) and particularly criticized those for the Scherzo "which seems to me too fast to the point of indistinctness", and the Finale "which seems appalling and incomprehensible to me". In the same article Krüger listed the tempos he himself had taken for the Fifth Symphony; but for the last two movements (including the final presto) he preferred the ones reportedly taken in Lübeck a couple of years earlier by Wilhelm Friedrich Riem (b. 1779). The metronome marks in the following list are Krüger's, then Riems's (not given for the first two movements), then Beethoven's.[86]

1) Allegro con brio ♩ = 90, -, ♩ = 108
2) Andante con moto ♪ = 66, -, ♪ = 92
3) Allegro ♩. = 110, ♩. = 80, ♩. = 96
4) Allegro ♩ = 90, ♩ = 70, ♩ = 84
   Presto 𝅝 = 90, ♩ = 110, 𝅝 = 112

The later 19th-century tendency to prefer significantly slower tempos in Beethoven than he himself or his most valued associates had provided probably reflected the almost religious veneration with which Beethoven was increasingly viewed. Anton Schindler's unsupported argument that Beethoven later approved slower tempos has been discussed above. Schindler's preference for slower tempos was shared by Wagner, whose powerful influence in this respect was felt well into the second half of the 20th century.

In the later 19th century, a distinct division between German and Italian notions in these matters is revealed by reactions to Verdi's conducting of his *Requiem* in Cologne in 1877, when a critic expressed astonishment at some of the fast tempos. With respect to the "Sanctus" and "Libera me domine" fugues he observed: "both tempos hardly seemed fast enough for the composer. We are not accustomed to such treatment of fugues for voices. Our tempos in the choruses of Bach and Handel allow the somewhat rigid strength of German voices to unfold powerfully and fully."[87]

---

[85] These seem to have been largely unknown until Nottebohm's article in the *Allegemeine musikalische Zeitung*, n.s., v (1870), 138ff.
[86] Eduard Krüger: 'Metronomische Fragen', *Neue Zeitschrift für Musik*, xx (1844), 122.
[87] *Kölnische Zeitung*, no. 141 (22 May 1877), 18; cited in Marcello Conati: *Interviews and Encounters with Verdi*, trans. Richard Stokes (London, 1984), 126.

# 9
# Alla Breve

The question of what Classical and Romantic composers meant when they used ¢, 𝄵, or 2 has caused and continues to cause confusion for performers. Mozart's re-notation of the finale of K. 458 and Mendelssohn's two versions of the *Sommernachtstraum* overture[1] make it evident that these two composers, at any rate, did not regard ¢ as necessarily indicating a literal doubling of speed, as many theorists stated that it should. Not all theorists, however, saw the function of ¢ in the same light, and a variety of apparently contradictory explanations of its significance are found in 18th- and 19th-century theoretical writings.

c and ¢ as indications of metre were direct survivals from the old system of proportional signs. In the 14th and 15th centuries, c was the sign for *tempus imperfecta cum prolatio imperfecta*, while ¢ indicated *proportio dupla* or *diminutio simplex*. Along with other proportional signs, they continued to be used, together with proportions expressed as fractions, during the 16th century. When, during the 17th century, the fractions gradually evolved into modern time signatures, some of the proportional signs were retained with modified meanings. Other signs, such as ○, ⌽, and 𝇋, which also continued to be used alongside the system of time signatures in the 17th century, are only very rarely found in the 18th century, mostly in theoretical works. As a rule, c and ¢ were both used to signify a metre in which each bar contained notes to the value of a whole-note, though ¢ is sometimes found where bars contain notes to the value of a double-whole-note (breve). Already in the 16th century there was ambiguity about whether ¢ indicated that each note should be twice as fast as it would be if the time signature were c or whether it merely indicated that the notes should be somewhat faster than with the other. The same problem bedevilled theorists and performers during succeeding centuries and has continued to challenge modern scholars and performers.

The present discussion will be confined to the use of these two signs for bars containing notes to the value of a whole-note. There are several ways

[1] See Ch. 8, p. 460.

in which these appear to be employed in the music of the Classical and Romantic periods. The most commonly encountered are:

1. the two signs seem to be synonymous;
2. ¢ is twice as fast as c;
3. ¢ is considerably faster but not twice as fast as c;
4. ¢ is somewhat faster than c.

In addition, while most authorities saw c as synonymous with $\frac{4}{4}$ (i.e., four quarter-note time, *Viervierteltakt*, etc., since the time signature $\frac{4}{4}$ was rarely used before the 19th century) and ¢ as synonymous with $\frac{2}{2}$ (i.e., two-half-note time), others either regarded ¢ as another kind of $\frac{4}{4}$ or, while categorizing it as $\frac{2}{2}$, considered it to be different from the time signatures $\frac{2}{2}$ or 2. Explanations of the significance of ¢ from the middle of the 18th century to the end of the 19th century reveal the lack of agreement.

Many writers stated as a firm rule that when ¢ was marked, each note was played twice as fast as when the time signature was c. Quantz commented: "In four-four time it is important to note that if a stroke goes through the c [...] the notes receive a different value, so to speak, and must be played twice as fast as when the c has no stroke through it. This metre is called *allabreve*, or *alla cappella*." And he was insistent that this needed to be stressed, because many people took the wrong speed through ignorance of the meaning of this time signature, which he observed had become "more common in the Galant style of the present day than it was in the past".[2] Despite the latter comment, Quantz was only restating a view of *alla breve* that had been frequently advanced by earlier theorists, including Daniel Merck and Saint-Lambert. Unfortunately, George Houle added another layer of confusion to the question of *alla breve* by consistently and misleadingly translating these authors' instructions to perform it "noch einmal so schnell" and "une fois plus vite" as "half as fast again".[3]

This notional doubling of speed was described by many other writers in the second half of the 18th century, and a considerable number of 19th-century theorists continued to define it in this way. Schulz observed: "The two-two or so-called allabreve metre, whose time units consist of two half-notes, is indicated by the sign ¢ at the beginning of the piece where one also

---

[2] Quantz: *Versuch*, 56.
[3] George Houle: *Meter in Music 1600–1800* (Bloomington, IN, 1987).

takes care to put the heading allabreve. It is performed heavily, but twice as fast as its note values show, and is therefore appropriate for serious and fiery performance, especially for fugues, and in this style and tempo, which is peculiar to it, permits no faster note values than eighths."[4] One of Schulz's German contemporaries who differed from this general view was G. F. Wolf, who stated that the stroke through the c indicated "that the tempo should be taken somewhat faster than it would otherwise be".[5]

In the fifth edition of Löhlein's *Clavier-Schule* (1791) the editor, Johann Georg Witthauer, expanded on earlier editions where ₵ had been mentioned without further explanation, saying that where ₵ or 2 was indicated, the tempo of a piece "is usually taken twice as fast as the value of the notes seems to require".[6] Türk modified his explanation slightly between the first and second editions of his *Klavierschule*: in the 1789 edition he had explained *alla breve* as "every note twice as fast as usual",[7] but in 1802 he changed his definition to "a tempo approximately twice as fast".[8] In the same year as Türk's second edition, H. C. Koch observed that in $\frac{2}{4}$ and $\frac{2}{8}$ metre, "because the half-note is commonly performed as fast as the quarter-note in two-four metre, both are very often called allabreve metres".[9] The following year J. H. Knecht also instructed that in *alla breve* "a half-note moves as fast as a quarter-note in four-four".[10] The description of *alla breve* as twice as fast as $\frac{4}{4}$ is also given by Andersch in 1829, but here the sign for it is given as 2, a Latin Z, or 2, without any mention of ₵.[11]

It may be noted in passing that 2 was used by some 18th-century composers to indicate $\frac{2}{8}$ time and by others, for example Jommelli, to indicate $\frac{2}{4}$. In the latter part of the 18th century and the first half of the 19th, some composers, presumably influenced by earlier French practice, used 2, ϕ, 2, and ₵ for different movements or numbers within the same work, but without any discernible difference of meaning. Examples may be found in Carl Stamitz's six duos op. 27,[12] Spontini's *Fernand Cortez* and *Olympie*, and Meyerbeer's *Les Huguenots* and *Le Prophète*. In the case of Spontini and Meyerbeer, metronome marks leave no doubt about the intended tempo and

---

[4] Schulz: 'Takt' in Sulzer, *Allgemeine Theorie*, ii, 1134.
[5] Georg Friedrich Wolf: *Unterricht im Klavierspiel*, 2nd edn (Halle, 1784), 54.
[6] Löhlein, ed. Witthauer: *Clavier-Schule*, 12.
[7] Türk: *Klavierschule*, 1st edn, 109.
[8] Türk: *Klavierschule*, 2nd edn, 86 (footnote).
[9] Koch: 'Takt' in *Musikalisches Lexikon*, 1481.
[10] Knecht: *Katechismus*, 20.
[11] Andersch: 'Alla breve' in *Musikalisches Wörterbuch*, 12.
[12] Copy in the Bodleian Library, Oxford.

suggest no obvious distinction between these signs and ¢. Other anomalies in composers' uses of such time signatures can easily be found in 19th-century music: Spohr in the overture to *Des Heilands letzte Stunden* used **2** for music with bars containing notes to the value of a double-whole-note; Schubert used ¢¢ (Impromptu in G flat, D. 899 no. 3) and Schumann cc ("Die Löwenbraut", op. 31 no. 1) for bars of that length, while Brahms used ¢ for both $\frac{2}{2}$ and $\frac{2}{1}$ in *Ein deutsches Requiem*. It is not surprising that many examples of this type of essentially antiquarian notation should occur in sacred music.

Some theorists, while implying that the half-note in one time was equivalent to the quarter-note in the other, did not specify an exact relationship. Fröhlich in 1810 equated ¢ with $\frac{2}{4}$, saying that it should be "performed just like the two-four and overall has the same character, with the one difference, that here there are two half-notes and there two quarters, thus each note in this time signature must be performed much faster than it is in the common four-four time".[13] Gustav Schilling in the 1830s maintained that the half-note "does not receive its true value and is only counted like a quarter".[14] Some twenty years later, Carl Gollmick described *alla breve*, or $\frac{2}{2}$, as "an abbreviated $\frac{2}{4}$ metre, with two concentrated beats".[15] Fétis and Castil-Blaze merely took ¢ to signify a bar of two beats.[16] Many mid- to late-19th-century composers seem to have taken a pragmatic and individualistic approach to this matter. As noted in Chapter 8, Liszt and Wagner used it merely to indicate that the music should be conducted in two beats to the bar without any specific connotations of metre or tempo.

For other late-18th and early-19th-century musicians, however, especially in England, the time signature ¢ quite definitely did not signify anything like twice as fast as c. Holden in 1770, discussing "common time", observed that it is notated "when slow, by a large c after the cliff [sic]; when quicker, by the same c with a bar drawn through it". And then, in relation to what he designated *alla breve* ($\frac{2}{1}$) and *alla semibreve* ($\frac{2}{2}$), the former of which he says is properly represented by ¢, he remarked:

> although, in this mood, the notes ought to be made a little shorter than in the other, yet they are not so much shortened as to bring the whole breve

---

[13] Fröhlich: *Musikschule*, pt. 1, 7.
[14] Schilling: 'Takt' in *Encyclopädie*, vi, 569.
[15] Gollmick: 'Alla breve' in *Handlexicon der Tonkunst*, 6.
[16] François-Joseph Fétis: *Traité élémentaire de musique* (Brussels, 1831–32); François Henri Joseph Castil-Blaze: *Dictionnaire de musique moderne* (Paris, 1821).

into the time which a semibreve requires, in the other mood; nor indeed is there any fixt rule for the comparative proportions of the time of a bar, in different moods.[17]

Other English instrumental treatises from the late 18th century show this to be in line with the usual interpretation of ¢ in England. These methods frequently echoed the explanation, attributed to Purcell, of the various signs applied to bars with the value of one whole-note: c for "very slow movement", ¢ "a little faster", and ⌽ "brisk and airy time".[18] A few examples from instruction books published in London during the 1790s may stand for many: Chabran's *Compleat Instructions* gives the time signatures c, ¢, ⌽ and $\frac{2}{4}$, commenting: "the first of them denotes a slow movement, the next a little faster, and the other two brisk and airy movements";[19] in Wragg's *Flute Preceptor*, c, ¢, ⌽ and 2 are listed: "The first of which denotes the slowest sort of Common Time; the second a degree quicker; and the third and fourth marks denote a quick movement."[20] The anonymous author of *Instructions for the Violin*, having discussed c, remarks that "¢ does not differ from the former in point of value it only shows that the time must be played a degree faster than if it had been simply marked thus c";[21] and in *New Instructions for Playing the Harpsichord, Pianoforte or Organ* it is merely observed that one uses "c for slow movements and ¢ or ⌽ for brisker airs".[22] The reference to ⌽ seems to have been pure antiquarianism at this time, for it is not encountered in late-18th-century music. Even ¢ seems to have become much less common in compositions written in England during the early 19th century than it had been in the late 18th century. Dibdin's *Music Epitomized* of 1808 gave only c and $\frac{2}{4}$ as species of common time, though the ninth edition, revised by John Jousse, added ¢ to the list without specifying any difference;[23] Thomas Valentine's *Dictionary*, ignoring continental practice, noted that ¢ signified "a species of quick common time now seldom used".[24] Clementi's treatment

---

[17] Holden: *Essay*, 26.
[18] Henry Purcell [?]: *A Choice Collection of Lessons for the Harpsichord or Spinnet* (London, 1696); introduction unpaginated [p. 4] also included, with attribution to Purcell, in *The Third Book of the Harpsichord Master* (London, 1702).
[19] Francesco Chabran: *Compleat Instructions for the Spanish Guitar* (London, [c. 1795]), 7.
[20] Jacob Wragg: *The Flute Preceptor* (London, [c. 1795]), 8.
[21] Anon.: *Instructions for the Violin by an Eminent Master* (London, [c. 1795]), 6.
[22] Anon.: *New Instructions for Playing the Harpsichord, Pianoforte or Organ* (London, [c. 1790]), 5.
[23] Charles Dibden: *Music Epitomized: A School Book in Which the Whole Science of Music Is Completely Explained [...]* (London, 1808); 9th edn (London, [c. 1820]), 37.
[24] Thomas Valentine: 'Alla breve' in *Dictionary of Terms Used in Music*, 2nd edn (London, 1824), 4.

of time signatures is interesting; the 1801 first edition of his *Introduction to the Art of Playing on the Pianoforte* did not prescribe any difference between ¢ and c, but the revised eleventh edition of 1826 added the following *nota bene*: "A composition marked thus ¢ was ANCIENTLY performed as fast again as when marked thus c, but now ¢ is performed somewhat faster than c."[25]

The 1799 *Principes élémentaires de musique* suggests that in France, too, *alla breve* may no longer have been seen as indicating so fast a tempo as it once had. Here it was explained that the duple metre signified by 2 or ¢ "does not differ in any respect from the quadruple metre $\frac{4}{4}$, often written simply as 4 in French music] with regard to the number of notes which make it up; the only difference which distinguishes it is that one beats it in two because of the rapidity of movement which one formerly used to give to this kind of metre".[26] However, this treatise also shows that the strict *proportio dupla* aspect of *alla breve* could sometimes still be valid, for in some of the exercises later in the volume, 2 is used to specify an exact doubling of tempo from 4 or c and vice versa.[27]

Among 19th-century writers of a more historical bent, particularly in Germany, there was a tendency to retain the notion of *alla breve* meaning that the music should move twice as fast as in c, despite the practical evidence of its contrary use by many composers of the period. Gottfried Weber's account provides a good example of how a desire for a clear and logical exposition of the principles of metre, combined with a knowledge of older theoretical writings, helped to perpetuate this idea. Weber's treatment of the subject shows a mixture of antiquarianism with an attempt to produce order out of the chaos of centuries of inconsistent usage. The antiquarianism is more pronounced in his 1831 3rd edition, from which the following passages are taken, although the content is fundamentally the same. He first considered two half-notes to a bar:

---

[25] Clementi: *Introduction*, 1st edn, 4, and 11th edn, 4.
[26] Gossec et al.: *Principes*, i, 40.
[27] Gossec et al.: *Principes*, ii, 9, ex. 19. The metre changes from 2 ($\frac{2}{2}$) to 4 ($\frac{4}{4}$) with the verbal instruction "ici les noires prennent le mouvement des Blanches. Même mouvement dans les tems. [here the quarters take the speed of halves. The same speed in the tempo]", and a similar change between c ($\frac{4}{4}$) and 2 ($\frac{2}{2}$) takes place in ex. 21 (ii, 11). In these exercises c and 4 are apparently used interchangeably for $\frac{4}{4}$, though it may be possible that 2 is used deliberately rather than ¢ when a real doubling of tempo is intended, despite the description of the two signatures as synonymous in the introduction.

This metre is therefore quite logically called two-two-time. [...]

It is represented by the sign $\frac{2}{2}$; not infrequently also by a large figure 2 with a stroke through it; or also by a c with a perpendicular stroke (a crossed through half circle):

$\frac{2}{2}$,  ¢,  ₵.

The last two signs, however, are frequently used also for the large alla-breve metre [i.e., $\frac{2}{1}$], which we will encounter in § LVII.

The $\frac{2}{2}$ metre is also sometimes called alla-breve metre; although it would be well always to distinguish it from the above-mentioned large, proper alla-breve metre, by the additional expression small alla-breve metre.[28]

Then, discussing two whole notes to the bar, Weber observed:

The sign for this is either $\frac{2}{1}$, or a complete circle with a stroke through it, or a large figure 2, or, even clearer that number, but with a stroke through it:

$\frac{2}{1}$,  Φ,  2,  ¢.

Sometimes it is also indicated by the sign which is more appropriate to the two-two time, ₵; or even by a c without a stroke, which really belongs to four-four time, which we will encounter later.

This species of measure, therefore, is more properly entitled to its name, alla-breve metre, than the previously introduced small one, because a breve just constitutes one bar in this alla-breve metre.[29]

He summarized:

If we review the metres considered so far, we find that all the types of $\frac{2}{1}$, $\frac{2}{2}$, $\frac{2}{4}$ &c. are fundamentally one and the same, though in different forms or modes of presentation, according as whole-notes, half-notes, quarter-notes, &c. are chosen for the designation of the parts of the bar; and so also the different types of uneven metre are properly only varieties of one species, only different ways of representing one and the same thing by signs.[30]

---

[28] Weber: *Versuch einer geordneten Theorie der Tonsetzkunst*, 3rd edn (Mainz, 1830–32), 96f; (in the 1st edn [Mainz, 1817–21], the equivalent passage begins on 91ff); English translation of 3rd edn as *Theory of Musical Composition* (London, 1846), i, 80ff.
[29] Weber: *Versuch*, 3rd edn, 98.
[30] Weber: *Versuch*, 3rd edn, 105.

He then observed that, other things being equal, half-notes would be performed as fast in 𝟤/𝟤 as quarters in 𝟤/𝟦.[31] Later he discussed how the different metres indicated different styles of performance but failed to examine the question of whether this influenced tempo, as Kirnberger, Schulz, and other 18th-century writers had done. Many later German writers reiterated the historically orientated but simplistic description of *alla breve* as doubling the speed of the notes, and this tendency seems not to have been without its effect on composers. Schumann, among others, certainly used ¢ to indicate a speed exactly or approximately twice as fast as c. In his opera *Genoveva*, for instance, when he changed the time signature from ¢ to c at the beginning of no. 17 he instructed "um die Hälfte langsamer" (slower by half), and at the beginning of no. 19, where the time again changes from ¢ to c, he wrote: "Die Viertel etwas langsamer wie vorher die Halben" (The quarters rather slower than the previous half-notes); in neither case was there a new tempo term at the change of time signature.

Clearly, the confusion over this matter ran very deep. There was no theoretical consensus, and usage differed from place to place and from composer to composer. Furthermore, inconsistency or carelessness on the part of composers, copyists, and engravers compounds the difficulty of determining what these signs were intended to convey: there are many instances where composers used c when ¢ would seem to be more appropriate and vice versa. It is also evident that many copyists and engravers were extremely negligent in this matter, for one sign is very frequently found in manuscript copies and printed editions where the composer's autograph clearly has the other. In the printed edition of Anton Eberl's Violin Sonata op. 20 (c. 1802), for example, the first movement has ¢ in the piano part while the separate violin part has c.

Koch had complained about the confusion between the two signatures in the 1780s, recommending that 𝟤 should be used instead of ¢.[32] The continuing prevalence of this sort of discrepancy in the 19th century led Carl Gollmick to observe in 1833, after referring to Beethoven's use of the sign in the Scherzo of the "Eroica" Symphony: "Incidentally, most of the crossed ¢ in more recent compositions are nothing like *Alla breves*, and are to be regarded only as haphazard embellishments of the usual c sign."[33]

---

[31] Weber: *Versuch*, 3rd edn, 106.
[32] Koch: *Versuch*, ii, 295. This use of ¢ and 𝟤 should not be confused with French Baroque practice, where these two signs had theoretically distinct implications.
[33] Gollmick: *Kritische Terminologie* (Frankfurt a. M., 1833), 15.

When the situation is clouded by so much disagreement, it might seem an impossible task to determine with any degree of confidence what kind of distinction composers intended when they used c and ¢, but here metronome marks provide invaluable evidence. The picture that emerges supports all the theoretical approaches to some extent; different composers treated the time signatures in different ways, and while some appear to have been either careless or capricious in their use of them, others seem to have been relatively, though seldom wholly, self-consistent. Despite the exceptions and inconsistencies, an understanding of the basic approach adopted by individual composers can assist in making informed decisions in particular instances.

It seems to have been the case with many continental European composers of the late 18th century and early 19th century, including Haydn, Mozart, Beethoven, Spohr, Schubert, and Mendelssohn, that, though they accepted a notional 2:1 relationship between c and ¢, this was modified in practice by the influence of the note values. Thus, the greater weight of the larger note values in ¢ held back the tempo and prevented it attaining double speed, just as in the case of the relationship between $\frac{2}{4}$ and $\frac{2}{2}$ (¢) illustrated by Mozart's alteration of time signature and tempo term in K. 589. However, the effect of the weight of the note values seems to have been felt more strongly at faster tempos than at slower ones, probably because the larger note values were considered to belong more naturally to slower tempos. In an *adagio* marked with ¢, therefore, the speed of the quarters might be regarded as only slightly less than that of the eighths in an *adagio* marked with c, while in an *allegro* the half-notes of the one would tend to be quite noticeably slower than the quarters of the other; and this would be felt even more strongly in *presto*.

Beethoven's metronome marks suggest that he followed these principles to a considerable extent. For very fast movements, for instance, where the heavier metre offered the greatest resistance to an increase of speed, the distinction between the two metres became somewhat blurred and Beethoven seems to have used ¢ rather inconsistently in relation to the tempo term for these types of movement. The consistency in *allegro* range, on the other hand, is quite striking. It is likely, however, that he did not begin to grasp this notion of *alla breve* until around 1800, and that he may previously have used the time signature ¢ in a more arbitrary manner. This is suggested by the metronome marks he gave for the Finale of the Septet and the first movement of the First Symphony; both movements would fit more logically into the scheme if they were in c metre (see Table 9.1). His comment on the time signature of the Gloria of his Mass in C also suggests a continuing uncertainty in his mind during the first few years of the century. He originally marked the movement ¢ but, as he wrote to Breitkopf & Härtel in 1812, a "bad performance at which they took the tempo too fast" induced him to change it to c; however, he informed them that he had changed it back to ¢, thus making it faster. He clearly recognized on reflection that, although not halving the original tempo, the change of time signature to c would imply much too slow a tempo, for he remarked, "Since I had not seen the Mass for a long time, I noticed it straight away and saw that unfortunately one has to leave such things to chance."[34] Three of Beethoven's slow c movements (the Ninth Symphony op. 125/iii, the String Quartet op. 59 no. 2/ii, and the Seventh Symphony op. 92/i) seem really to have required ¢. (The same is undoubtedly true of several of Mozart's slow movements.[35]) For very fast movements, where the fastest notes were longer than sixteenths, Beethoven usually used ¢ even if they really related more closely to the c scale. Table 9.1 shows the relationship of the movements in ¢ and c to which Beethoven gave metronome marks.

The metronome marks in Schubert's *Alfonso und Estrella*, which, even if not written into the autograph by the composer, almost certainly stem from him, indicate that Schubert, too, shared the concept of ¢ as indicating a speed notionally twice as fast as c; but his sense of the slowing effect of the weightier note values seems to have been less strong than Beethoven's. At slow to moderate tempos, he appears to have regarded the half-note in the one as more or less exactly equivalent to the quarter in the other. The slowing effect of the note values seems to operate, however, in faster movements, though not entirely consistently. The note values employed, and the quantity of fast notes explain discrepancies only to a limited extent (see Table 9.2).[36]

Cherubini's metronome marks in his two Requiems and his string quartets show him to have shared the view of ¢ as indicating a modified doubling of speed. As with other composers, however, the time signatures alone (at least as given in printed editions) cannot be relied on, for the *Allegro agitato* first movement of the String Quartet no. 1 in E flat (♩ = 116) and the Allegro vivace Finale of the posthumous Quartet in F, though evidently *alla breve*, are

---

[34] Beethoven: *Sämtliche Briefe und Auszeichnungen*, ed. Fritz Prelinger (Vienna, 1907), 285. Rosenblum, in her stimulating study (*Performance Practices*, 308), misinterpreted the implications of this letter, apparently failing to appreciate that ¢ was the original marking and assuming that Beethoven meant to slow the tempo down by substituting ¢ for c.
[35] See Uri Toeplitz: 'Über die Tempi in Mozart's Instrumentalmusik', *Mozart-Jahrbuch* (1986), 171ff.
[36] Clive Brown: 'Schubert's Tempo Conventions' in Brian Newbould (ed.), *Schubert Studies* (Aldershot, Ashgate, 1998).

marked ¢; the same is true of "Quam olim Abrahae" in the C minor Requiem, which is headed *Tempo a cappella* (see Table 9.3).

Weber's metronome marks for *Euryanthe* reveal a quite different picture. He seems to have leant towards the English notion of ¢ indicating a tempo only somewhat faster than c, though he used ¢ almost exclusively for fast movements where the difference could in any case be expected to be smaller. He does, however, appear to have marked some slow movements c where the metronome marks indicate that they stand in an *alla breve* relationship to other movements with the same tempo term (compare, e.g., the *largos* nos. 17 and 23b and the overture with the *largos* nos. 17a and 6a in Table 9.4).

Spohr's and Mendelssohn's use of the time signature ¢ seems closer to Weber's than to Beethoven's, Schubert's, and Cherubini's. Schumann's employment of it, however, is in stark contrast with both these approaches. He does not seem to have used ¢ until about 1840, at which time he started to employ several less common time signatures. His first use of ¢, in the *Thematisches Verzeichnis*, is in the String Quartets op. 41. *Drei Gesänge* op. 31 (c. 1840), uses $\frac{2}{8}$ as well as ¢c (for $\frac{4}{2}$); *Myrthen* op. 25/i (1840) uses $\frac{3}{2}$ and $\frac{6}{4}$. In general, as Table 9.5 shows, he seems to have regarded ¢ as indicating literally that half-notes should be seen in the same light as quarter-notes in c. Since Schumann lacked the practical musical apprenticeship enjoyed by many other composers of his generation, this may well have been the result of a reliance on the contemporary theoretical statements of Gottfried Weber and others that he had encountered in his reading.

Some early-19th-century composers were very casual about the use of these time signatures. Spontini's and Rossini's employment of ¢ and 2, mostly without any obvious purpose, has already been alluded to; but their works also include many other pieces, evidently of an *alla breve* type, which have a c time signature. Some movements in c that share the same or similar tempo terms have half-note metronome marks, while others have quarter-note metronome marks with the same or similar numbers; for instance, Spontini gave both the Allegro espressivo agitato in Act I, no. 7 of *Fernand Cortez* and the Allegro agitato assai in Act III, no. 1 of *Olympie* the time signature c, but he fixed the metronome mark for the former at $\goodbreak = 120$ and for the latter at $\goodbreak = 120$.

The use of ¢ and c continued to be very variable in the mid- to late 19th century. Berlioz used ¢ in a few slow and moderate movements but mostly confined it (and occasionally 2 or $\frac{2}{2}$) to allegro movements that would, as his metronome marks indicate, generally have been beaten in two or sometimes one. His c movements are mainly composed with a quarter-note pulse and have quarter-note metronome marks with numbers that are close to those for the half-note pulse in his ¢ movements with similar tempo terms. In quite a few cases, however, movements marked c look as if they should really have been marked ¢. Berlioz does not seem to have had any clearly formulated notion of larger note values implying greater resistance to speed, even at the fastest tempos.

Wagner, like Berlioz, saw things primarily from the practical conductor's viewpoint, though more consistently. He employed c mostly for slow to moderate movements and ¢ for faster ones, perhaps with the implication that c should be beaten in four and ¢ in two (though there appear to be a significant number of occasions on which a metre has been wrongly transmitted or carelessly assigned). In later works his tendency was to use $\frac{4}{4}$ and $\frac{2}{2}$ in the same sense. There is absolutely nothing to suggest that he was influenced by the Kirnberger–Schulz view of the relationship between tempo, metre, tempo term, and note value. The list of numbers in c and ¢ from operas to which Wagner gave metronome marks (Table 9.6) shows graphically how different his approach to this matter was from Beethoven's and Schubert's or even from Schumann's, and indeed from that of many of his younger contemporaries such as Brahms, Tchaikovsky, and Dvořák, who retained the notion that ¢ was twice as fast as c.

## Tables of Metronome Tempos

In the following tables, the term "fastest notes" refers to the fastest functional note values employed in the movement or section (i.e., ignoring tremolando and occasional flourishes or ornamental figures of faster notes). The tables are arranged according to tempo terms, roughly in ascending order of speed, and movements or sections in each column are ranged opposite those with which they have approximately a 2:1 relationship. Entries enclosed in round brackets are very short sections that provide insufficient information to compare them confidently with others. Note values in brackets in the "fastest notes" column indicate that a very small proportion of notes of this value appear in the piece. The letters that follow some of the numbers indicate the order of sections within these numbers of an opera.

**Table 9.1.** The Relationship of ₵ and c Metre in Beethoven's Music

The composer's metronome marks in this table are taken from the symphonies opp. 21, 36, 60, 67, 92, 93, and 125, the string quartets opp. 18 (1–6), 59 (1–3), 74, and 95, the Septet op. 20, and the cantata *Meeresstille und glückliche Fahrt* op. 112. Asterisks indicate movements that appear to have an inconsistent time signature and ought more logically to belong in the other column; these movements are also given, in square brackets, at the appropriate place in the other column.

| ₵ | | | | c | | | |
|---|---|---|---|---|---|---|---|
| Opus | Tempo term | MM | Fastest notes | Opus | Tempo term | MM | Fastest notes |
| [125/iii] | Adagio molto e cantabile | ♩ = 60 | ♫ | | | | |
| [59/2/ii] | Molto Adagio | ♩ = 60 | ♫ | | | | |
| 60/i | Adagio | ♩ = 66 | ♪ | | | | |
| 74/i | Poco Adagio | ♩ = 60 | ♪ | | | | |
| [92/1] | Poco sostenuto | ♩ = 69 | ♫ | | | | |
| 112 | Sostenuto | ♩ = 84 | ♪ | | | | |
| | | | | 21/i | Adagio molto | ♪ = 88 | ♪ |
| | | | | 125/iii* | Adagio molto e cantabile | ♩ = 60 | ♪ |
| | | | | 59/2/ii* | Molto Adagio | ♩ = 60 | ♪ |
| 125/iv | Allegro ma non tanto | 𝅗𝅥 = 120 | ♪ | 92/i* | Poco sostenuto | ♩ = 69 | ♪ |
| 18/3/i | Allegro | 𝅗𝅥 = 120 | ♬ | | | | |
| 18/4/iv | Allegro | 𝅝 = 66 | ♪ | | | | |
| 18/5/iv | Allegro | 𝅝 = 76 | ♪ | | | | |
| 95/iv | Allegro | 𝅝 = 92[a] | ♪ | | | | |
| 59/1/1 | Allegro | 𝅗𝅥 = 88 | ♬ | | | | |
| 60/i | Allegro vivace | 𝅝 = 80 | ♪ | | | | |
| 93/i | Allegro vivace | 𝅝 = 84 | ♬ | 125/iv | Allegro assai | 𝅗𝅥 = 80 | ♪ |
| 18/6/i | Allegro con brio | 𝅝 = 80 | ♪ | 68/iv | Allegro | 𝅗𝅥 = 80 | ♪ |
| | | | | 18/4/i | Allegro ma non tanto | 𝅗𝅥 = 84 | ♪ |

*(continued)*

Table 9.1. Continued

| ₵ | | | | 𝐜 | | | |
|---|---|---|---|---|---|---|---|
| Opus | Tempo term | MM | Fastest notes | Opus | Tempo term | MM | Fastest notes |
| | | | | 74/i | Allegro | 𝅗𝅥 = 84 | ♪ |
| | | | | 67/iv | Allegro | 𝅗𝅥 = 84 | ♪ |
| | | | | 59/3/i | Allegro vivace | 𝅗𝅥 = 88 | ♪ |
| | | | | 95/i | Allegro con brio | 𝅗𝅥 = 92 | ♪ |
| 20/i* | Allegro con brio | 𝅗𝅥 = 96 | ♪ | [20/i] | Allegro con brio | 𝅗𝅥 = 96 | ♪ |
| 21/i* | Allegro con brio | 𝅗𝅥 = 112 | ♪ | [21/i] | Allegro con brio | 𝅗𝅥 = 112 | ♪ |
| 36/iv | Allegro molto | 𝅗𝅥 = 152 | ♪ | | | | |
| 59/3/iv | Allegro molto | 𝅝 = 84 | ♪ | | | | |
| 20/iv | Presto | 𝅗𝅥 = 112 | ♬ | | | | |
| 59/2/iv | Presto | 𝅝 = 88 | ♪ | | | | |
| | | | | 36/i | Allegro con brio | 𝅗𝅥 = 100 | ♪ |
| 67/iv | Presto | 𝅝 = 112 | ♪ | | | | |
| 125/ii | Presto | 𝅝 = 116 | ♩ | | | | |
| 125/iv | Prestissimo | 𝅗𝅥 = 132 | ♪ | | | | |
| 18/4/iv | Prestissimo | 𝅝 = 84 | ♪ | | | | |

[a] The metronome mark for this short section, which concludes the last movement, seems puzzlingly fast for Allegro ₵. It is in a proportional relationship to the preceding [68] Allegretto agitato, itself surprisingly fast at ♩. = 92. In the context of Beethoven's metronome markings as a whole, it seems distinctly possible that in both cases "92" may be a misprint for "72".

Table 9.2. The Relationship of ¢ and c Metre in Schubert's Music

These metronome tempos are all taken from Schubert's opera *Alfonso und Estrella*.

| ¢ | | | | c | | | |
|---|---|---|---|---|---|---|---|
| No. | Tempo term | MM | Fastest notes | No. | Tempo term | MM | Fastest notes |
| 33[a] | Andante | ♩ = 100 | ♪ | 2 | Andante molto | ♪ = 76 | ♪ |
| | | | | (3b | Andante maestoso | ♩ = 52 | ♪) |
| 4 | Andante | 𝅗𝅥 = 58 | 𝅘𝅥𝅯𝅘𝅥𝅯𝅘𝅥𝅯 | 35c | Andante | ♩ = 50 | ♪ |
| | | | | 31 | Moderato | ♩ = 96 | 𝅘𝅥𝅯𝅘𝅥𝅯𝅘𝅥𝅯 |
| | | | | 3a | Andantino | ♩ = 100 | 𝅘𝅥𝅯𝅘𝅥𝅯𝅘𝅥𝅯 |
| | | | | 27a | Allegretto | ♩ = 112 | ♪ |
| | | | | 12 | Andantino | ♩ = 116 | ♪ |
| | | | | 15 | Andantino | ♩ = 120 | 𝅘𝅥𝅯𝅘𝅥𝅯𝅘𝅥𝅯 |
| | | | | 10 | Tempo di marcia | ♩ = 132 | ♪ |
| | | | | 35d | Allegro molto moderato | ♩ = 84 | ♪ |
| 10d | Allegro moderato | 𝅗𝅥 = 116 | ♪ | (6 | Allegro moderato | ♩ = 100 | ♪(♪)) |
| 7a | Allegro moderato | 𝅗𝅥 = 120 | ♪ | 35a | Allegro moderato | ♩ = 120 | ♪(♪) |
| | | | | (34b | Allegro moderato | ♩ = 120 (same music as 35a)) | |
| | | | | 5 | Allegro ma non troppo | ♩ = 126 | ♪ |
| 31a | Allegro | 𝅗𝅥 = 132 | ♪ | 28 | Allegro moderato | ♩ = 132 | ♪ |
| 29 | Allegro assai | 𝅗𝅥 = 138 | ♪ | 16 | Allegro moderato | ♩ = 138 | ♪ |
| 17 | Allegro agitato | 𝅗𝅥 = 144 | ♪ | 1 | Allegro giusto | ♩ = 144 | ♪ |
| 23[b] | Allegro[c] | 𝅗𝅥 = 160 | ♪ | 8a | Allegro giusto[d] | ♩ = 160 | ♪ |
| ov.[e] | Allegro | 𝅗𝅥 = 160 | ♪(♪) | (8 | Allegro[f] | ♩ = 160[g] | ♪) |
| 17b | Allegro molto | 𝅗𝅥 = 160 | ♪ | 9a | Allegro | ♩ = 160 | ♪ |

(*continued*)

496  CLASSICAL AND ROMANTIC PERFORMING PRACTICE

Table 9.2. Continued

| ₵ | | | | C | | | |
| --- | --- | --- | --- | --- | --- | --- | --- |
| No. | Tempo term | MM | Fastest notes | No. | Tempo term | MM | Fastest notes |
| | | | | 18 | Allegro | ♩ = 160 | ♪ |
| | | | | 35b | Allegro | ♩ = 160 | ♪ |
| | | | | 35e | Allegro | ♩ = 160 | ♪ |
| 26 | Allegro molto | 𝅝 = 84 | ♪ | | | | |
| | | | | 22 | Allegro | 𝅗𝅥 = 88 | ♪ |
| | | | | 2b | Allegro | 𝅗𝅥 = 92 | ♪ |
| | | | | 32 | Allegro agitato | 𝅗𝅥 = 104[h] | ♪ |
| | | | | 17a | Allegro assai | 𝅗𝅥 = 104 | ♪ |
| | | | | 33 | Allegro | 𝅗𝅥 = 112[i] | ♪(♫) |
| | | | | 20 | Allegro molto vivace | 𝅗𝅥 = 112 | ♪ |
| | | | | 19 | Allegro molto | 𝅗𝅥 = 112 | ♪ |
| | | | | (10c | Allegro assai | 𝅗𝅥 = 116 | ♪) |
| | | | | 22b | Allegro vivace | 𝅗𝅥 = 120 | ♪ |

[a] Given as C in the 1884–97 *Gesamtausgabe*.

[b] This section and the Allegro of the overture seem out of line with the other ₵ sections; they seem as if they ought to have a faster tempo term. But both are purely orchestral, and this may suggest different criteria for orchestral and vocal music, just as there seems to have been in the case of sacred and secular music.

[c] Originally Allegro moderato, then Allegro ma non troppo, and finally Allegro. The separately bowed sixteenth-note runs in the violins would only be realistic at the original tempo, and Schubert presumably omitted to alter these (by adding slurs) as his conception of the tempo increased.

[d] Originally Mod.to maestoso.

[e] See note 3.

[f] Originally All° mod.to.

[g] Incorrectly given as ♩ = 106 in the score (p. 177) in the *Neue Schubert Ausgabe* and, equally incorrectly, as 100 in the "Quellen und Lesarten" section at the end of the volume (p. 797). It should be 160. Ferdinand Schubert's copy of the opera in the Österreichische Nationalbibliothek also has 160.

[h] The metronome mark is given in Ferdinand Schubert's copy simply as MM 104, without a note value, and the editor of the 1884–97 *Gesamtausgabe* gave it as ♩ = 104. Schubert's autograph, however, clearly has "104 𝅗𝅥".

[i] Given in the score of the *Neue Schubert Ausgabe* as ♩ = 112 (p. 723), though it is referred to in the "Quellen und Lesarten" (p. 825) as 𝅗𝅥 = 112. Ferdinand Schubert's copy has ♩ = 112. The 1884–97 *Gesamtausgabe*, without any known authority, gave it as ₵ = 120. ♩ = 112 would be improbably slow; 𝅗𝅥 = 112, though slightly faster than might be expected, seems likelier to represent Schubert's intentions.

Table 9.3. The Relationship of 𝄵 and 𝄴 Metre in Cherubini's Music

Metronome marks are taken from the Requiem no. 1 in C minor (R1), the Requiem no. 2 in D minor (R2), and the five published string quartets (Q1–Q5).

| 𝄵 | | | | 𝄴 | | | |
|---|---|---|---|---|---|---|---|
| Piece | Tempo term | MM | Fastest notes | Piece | Tempo term | MM | Fastest notes |
| | | | | R1 | Largo | ♩ = 54 | ♪ |
| | | | | R2 | Lento | ♩ = 63 | ♪ |
| R1 | Larghetto sost. | 𝅗𝅥 = 50 | ♪ | | | | |
| R1 | Larghetto | 𝅗𝅥 = 56 | ♪ | | | | |
| | | | | R1 | Sostenuto | ♩ = 60 | ♪ |
| | | | | R1 | Andante | ♩ = 66 | ♪ |
| | | | | R2 | Grave ma non troppo | ♩ = 69 | ♪ |
| | | | | R2 | Andante con moto | ♩ = 88 | ♪ |
| R1 | Allegro maestoso | 𝅗𝅥 = 88 | ♪ (♪) | | | | |
| | | | | R2 | Maestoso | ♩ = 72 | ♪ |
| | | | | R2 | Maestoso | ♩ = 67! [76?] | ♪ |
| R2 | Allegro (più vivo che la prima volta [i.e., Allegro mod.]) | 𝅗𝅥 = 96 | | | | | |
| R1 | Tempo a cappella,[a] poco allegro | 𝅗𝅥 = 120 | ♪ | R2 | Allegro moderato | ♩ = 152 | ♪ |
| | | | | R2 | Vivo | ♩ = 60! [160?] | ♪ |
| Q5 | Allegro vivace[b] | 𝅗𝅥 = 108 | ♪ | Q4 | Allegro maestoso | ♩ = 108 | ♪ |
| Q1 | Allegro agitato[c] | 𝅗𝅥 = 116 | ♪ | | | | |
| Q2 | Allegro vivace | 𝅗𝅥 = 120 | ♪ | Q3 | Allegro comodo | ♩ = 120 | ♪ |
| Q1 | Allegro assai (plus vite encore) | 𝅗𝅥 = 160 | ♪ | Q2 | Allegro | 𝅗𝅥 = 80 | ♪ |

(continued)

Table 9.3. Continued

| ¢ | | | | C | | | |
|---|---|---|---|---|---|---|---|
| Piece | Tempo term | MM | Fastest notes | Piece | Tempo term | MM | Fastest notes |
| | | | | Q3 | Allegro risoluto | 𝅗𝅥 = 88 | 𝅘𝅥𝅯𝅘𝅥𝅯𝅘𝅥𝅯 |
| | | | | Q4 | Allegro assai | 𝅗𝅥 = 88 | 𝅘𝅥𝅮 |

[a] Time signature printed as ₵!
[b] Time signature printed as ₵.
[c] Time signature printed as ₵.

Table 9.4. The Relationship of ¢ and c Metre in Weber's Music

Weber's metronome marks come from *Euryanthe* and from the *Konzertstück* for piano and orchestra J. 282.

| ¢ | | | | c | | | |
|---|---|---|---|---|---|---|---|
| No. | Tempo Term | MM | Fastest notes | No. | Tempo term | MM | Fastest notes |
| | | | | 17 | Largo | ♩ = 50 | 𝅘𝅥𝅮 |
| | | | | 23b | Largo | ♩ = 50 | 𝅘𝅥𝅮 (𝅘𝅥𝅯) |
| | | | | ov. | Largo | ♩ = 52 | ♩ |
| | | | | 17a | Largo | 𝅘𝅥𝅮 = 66 | 𝅘𝅥𝅮 |
| | | | | 6a | Largo | 𝅘𝅥𝅮 = 84 | 𝅘𝅥𝅮 (𝅘𝅥𝅯) |
| | | | | 15 | Adagio non lento | ♩ = 66 | 𝅘𝅥𝅮 |
| | | | | 9a | Andantino grazioso | ♩ = 54 | 𝅘𝅥𝅮 |
| 23 | Maestoso energico ma non troppo | 𝅗𝅥 = 63 | 𝅘𝅥𝅮 | 4 | Maestoso assai | ♩ = 50 | 𝅘𝅥𝅮 |
| | | | | 14c | Maestoso assai | ♩ = 66 | 𝅘𝅥𝅮 (𝅘𝅥𝅯) |
| | | | | 25 | Maestoso con moto | ♩ = 108 | 𝅘𝅥𝅮 |
| | | | | 15a | Moderato | ♩ = 88 | 𝅘𝅥𝅮 |
| | | | | I | Moderato maestoso | ♩ = 92 | 𝅘𝅥𝅮 |
| | | | | 25c | Moderato assai | ♩ = 92 | 𝅘𝅥𝅮 |
| | | | | 5b | Moderato assai | ♩ = 96 | 𝅘𝅥𝅮 |
| | | | | 7 | Moderato assai | ♩ = 104 | 𝅘𝅥𝅮 |
| | | | | 8a | Moderato | ♩ = 100 | 𝅘𝅥𝅮 |
| | | | | 23d | Allegro moderato | ♩ = 104 | 𝅘𝅥𝅮 |

Table 9.4. Continued

| ¢ | | | | c | | | |
|---|---|---|---|---|---|---|---|
| No. | Tempo Term | MM | Fastest notes | No. | Tempo term | MM | Fastest notes |
| | | | | 3 | Allegro | ♩ = 116 | ♪ |
| | | | | 12a | Allegro | ♩ = 120 | ♪ |
| | | | | J. 282 | Tempo di marcia | ♩ = 126 | ♪ |
| | | | | 21a | Allegro non tanto | ♩ = 132 | ♪ |
| | | | | 223a | Allegro moderato | ♩ = 138 | 𝅘𝅥𝅰 |
| | | | | II | Allegro energico | ♩ = 144 | 𝅘𝅥𝅰 |
| | | | | 88b | Allegro fiero | ♩ = 144 | ♪ |
| | | | | 14d | Allegro ma non troppo | ♩ = 144 | ♪ |
| | | | | 16 | Molto passionato | ♩ = 152 | ♪(♪) |
| | | | | 22 | Allegro | ♩ = 152 | ♪ |
| | | | | 23e | Vivace | ♩ = 152 | ♪(♪) |
| | | | | 14e | Con tutto fuoco ed energia | ♩ = 160 | ♪(♪) |
| | | | | 8 | Allegro | ♩ = 160 | ♪ |
| | | | | J. 282 | Allegro passionato | ♩ = 160 | ♪ |
| | | | | 10b | Allegro | ♩ = 160 | ♪(♪) |
| | | | | 20 | Allegro con fuoco | ♩ = 160 | ♪ |
| | | | | 23c | Vivace | ♩ = 160 | ♪ |
| | | | | 4a | Allegro | 𝅗𝅥 = 88 | ♪(♪) |
| | | | | ov. | Allegro marcato, Tempo I assai moderato | 𝅗𝅥 = 88 | 𝅘𝅥𝅰 |
| | | | | 15c | Allegro non tanto | 𝅗𝅥 = 88 | ♪ |
| | | | | ov. | Allegro marcato, con molto fuoco | 𝅗𝅥 = 92 | 𝅘𝅥𝅰 |
| 10 | Allegro con fuoco | 𝅗𝅥 = 92 | ♪ | 6 | Agitato ma non troppo presto | 𝅗𝅥 = 92 | ♪(♪) |
| 13 | Allegro animato | 𝅗𝅥 = 96 | 𝅘𝅥𝅰 | 4b | Con fuoco | 𝅗𝅥 = 96 | 𝅘𝅥𝅰 |
| | | | | 15b | Agitato | 𝅗𝅥 = 96 | ♪ |
| | | | | 25a | Agitato | 𝅗𝅥 = 96 | ♪ |

(*continued*)

Table 9.4. Continued

| ¢ | | | | C | | | |
|---|---|---|---|---|---|---|---|
| No. | Tempo Term | MM | Fastest notes | No. | Tempo term | MM | Fastest notes |
| 14a | Allegro | ♩ = 100 | ♪(♪) | 24 | Con impeto | ♩ = 100 | 𝅘𝅥𝅯 |
| 11a | Con strepito | ♩ = 104 | 𝅘𝅥𝅯(♪) | 3a | Agitato assai | ♩ = 104 | ♪ |
| | | | | 25d | Molto passionato | ♩ = 112 | ♪(♪) |
| | | | | 15d | Presto | ♩ = 116 | ♪ |
| 10d | Vivace feroce | ♩ = 132 | ♪(♪) | | | | |
| 6b | Presto | ♩ = 128 [?138] | ♪ | | | | |

Table 9.5. The Relationship of ¢ and c Metre in Schumann's Music

Schumann's metronome marks are taken from the following works: *Szenen aus Goethes Faust (Faust)*, the symphonies opp. 38, 61, 97, and 120, the Overture, Scherzo, and Finale op. 52, the overtures *Genoveva* op. 81, *Die Braut von Messina* op. 100, *Manfred* op. 115, *Fest-Ouverture* op. 123, and *Hermann und Dorothea* op. 136, the string quartets op. 41 (1–3), and the Piano Quintet op. 44.

| ¢ | | | | c | | | |
|---|---|---|---|---|---|---|---|
| Op. | Tempo term | MM | Fastest notes | Op. | Tempo term | MM | Fastest notes |
| | | | | Faust | Langsam, feierlich | ♪ = 112 | ♪ |
| | | | | 81 | Langsam | ♩ = 50 | ♪ |
| | | | | 120 | Langsam | ♩ = 52 | ♪ |
| | | | | 41/1 | Adagio | ♩ = 54 | ♪ |
| | | | | 123 | Feierlich, doch nicht zu langsam | ♩ = 58 | ♪ |
| | | | | 41/3 | Andante espress. | ♩ = 60 | ♪ |
| | | | | 52 | Andante con moto | ♩ = 60 | ♪ |
| | | | | 115 | Langsam | ♩ = 63 | ♪ |
| | | | | 41/3 | Adagio molto | ♩ = 66 | ♪ |
| 44 | In modo d'una marcia Un poco largamente | ♩ = 66 | 𝅘𝅥𝅯 | 38 | Andante un poco maestoso | ♩ = 66 | ♪ |
| | | | | 128 | Kräftig gemessen | ♩ = 80 | ♪ |
| 100 | Sehr lebhaft | ♩ = 88 | ♪ | | | | |
| 41/1 | Moderato | ♩ = 96 | ♪ | | | | |
| 38 | Allegro animato e grazioso | ♩ = 100 | ♪ | | | | |

Table 9.5. Continued

| ¢ | | | | C | | | |
|---|---|---|---|---|---|---|---|
| 41/3 | Allegro molto vivace | 𝅗𝅥 = 108 | 𝅘𝅥𝅯𝅘𝅥𝅯𝅘𝅥𝅯 | 123 | Lebhaft | 𝅘𝅥 = 108 | 𝅘𝅥𝅮 |
| 44 | Allegro brillante | 𝅗𝅥 = 108 | 𝅘𝅥𝅮 | 136 | Mässig | 𝅘𝅥 = 126 | 𝅘𝅥𝅯𝅘𝅥𝅯𝅘𝅥𝅯 |
| 97 | Lebhaft | 𝅗𝅥 = 120 | 𝅘𝅥𝅮 | | | | |
| 44 | Allegro ma non troppo | 𝅗𝅥 = 126 | 𝅘𝅥𝅮 | | | | |
| | | | | 120 | Lebhaft | 𝅘𝅥 = 126 | 𝅘𝅥𝅮 |
| 81 | Leidenschaftlich bewegt | 𝅗𝅥 = 140 | 𝅘𝅥𝅮 | | | | |
| | | | | 115 | In leidenschaftlichem Tempo | 𝅘𝅥 = 144 | 𝅘𝅥𝅮 |
| 52 | Allegro molto vivace | 𝅗𝅥 = 148 | 𝅘𝅥𝅯𝅘𝅥𝅯𝅘𝅥𝅯 | | | | |
| 41/1 | Presto | 𝅗𝅥 = 160 | 𝅘𝅥𝅮 | | | | |
| 61 | Allegro molto vivace | 𝅗𝅥 = 170 | 𝅘𝅥𝅮 | | | | |

Table 9.6. The Relationship of ¢ and C Metre in Wagner's Music

Metronome marks are taken from *Rienzi* (R), the *Rienzi* ballet music (RB), *Der fliegende Holländer* (H), and *Tannhäuser* (T). In *Rienzi* and *Der fliegende Holländer* the opera is divided into a succession of numbers which run continuously throughout; *Tannhäuser* is divided into acts and scenes. Very many sections include some tremolando in the strings. This has been ignored in calculating the fastest functional note values, as have ornamental flourishes; nevertheless, the fluid nature of Wagner's music makes this factor debatable in many cases. In some instances, the metre is not clear, either because Wagner has not indicated a change from a previous section with four quarter-notes in the bar, or for another reason, but in some cases an intended change has been assumed because of the note content; these sections are marked with a dagger.

| ¢ | | | | C | | | |
|---|---|---|---|---|---|---|---|
| Work | Tempo term | MM | Fastest notes | Work | Tempo term | MM | Fastest notes |
| | | | | TIII,2 | Moderato | 𝅘𝅥 = 46 | 𝅘𝅥𝅯𝅘𝅥𝅯𝅘𝅥𝅯 |
| | | | | TIII,1 | Andante assai lento | 𝅘𝅥 = 50 | 𝅘𝅥𝅮 |
| | | | | H2 | Sostenuto | 𝅘𝅥 = 50 | 𝅘𝅥𝅯𝅘𝅥𝅯𝅘𝅥𝅯 |

(*continued*)

Table 9.6. Continued

| ¢ | | | | C | | | |
|---|---|---|---|---|---|---|---|
| Work | Tempo term | MM | Fastest notes | Work | Tempo term | MM | Fastest notes |
| | | | | TIII,3 | Lento | ♩ = 50 | ♪ |
| | | | | TIII,3 | Lento maestoso | ♩ = 50 | ♬ |
| | | | | H8 | Andante | ♩ = 50 | ♪ |
| | | | | TI,4 | Lento | ♩ = 54 | ♪ |
| | | | | TII,4 | Andante | ♩ = 56 | ♪ |
| | | | | TII,4 | Adagio | ♩ = 58 | ♬ |
| | | | | R4c | Andante energico[†] | ♩ = 60 | ♬ |
| | | | | R1f | Moderato e maestoso | ♩ = 66 | ♬ |
| | | | | H2 | Moderato | ♩ = 66 | ♪ |
| | | | | R6e | Un poco sostenuto[†] | ♩ = 66 | ♪ |
| | | | | Rov | Molto sostenuto e maestoso | ♩ = 66 | ♪ |
| | | | | R13 | Lento | ♩ = 66 | 𝅘𝅥𝅮𝅘𝅥𝅮𝅘𝅥𝅮 |
| | | | | H3 | Lento | ♩ = 66 | ♪ |
| | | | | H6 | Sostenuto | ♩ = 66 | ♪ |
| | | | | H5 | Sostenuto | ♩ = 69 | ♪ |
| | | | | R9d | Maestoso | ♩ = 69 | ♪ |
| | | | | R9b | Andante | ♩ = 69 | ♬ |
| | | | | TIII,3 | Maestoso | ♩ = 69 | ♩ |
| | | | | R4d | Maestoso[†] | ♩ = 72 | 𝅘𝅥𝅮𝅘𝅥𝅮𝅘𝅥𝅮 |
| | | | | TII,4 | Andante[†] | ♩ = 72 | ♪ |
| | | | | R4b | Maestoso[†] | ♩ = 72 | ♬ |
| | | | | R10h | Grave | ♩ = 72 | 𝅘𝅥𝅮𝅘𝅥𝅮𝅘𝅥𝅮 |
| | | | | TI,4 | Andante | ♩ = 76 | 𝅘𝅥𝅮𝅘𝅥𝅮𝅘𝅥𝅮 |
| | | | | TII,3 | Andante | ♩ = 76 | ♪ |
| | | | | R11b | Un poco lento[†] | ♩ = 80 | ♪ |
| | | | | H1 | Moderato | ♩ = 80 | ♩ |
| | | | | H2 | Allegro | ♩ = 80 | ♬ |

Table 9.6. Continued

| ¢ | | | | C | | | |
|---|---|---|---|---|---|---|---|
| Work | Tempo term | MM | Fastest notes | Work | Tempo term | MM | Fastest notes |
| | | | | R12b | Grave | ♩ = 80 | ♪ |
| | | | | H6 | Moderato | ♩ = 80 | ♪ |
| | | | | R10f | Maestoso | ♩ = 84 | ♪ |
| | | | | H3 | Moderato | ♩ = 84 | ♪♪♪ (3) |
| | | | | R5b | Maestoso moderato | ♩ = 88 | ♪ |
| | | | | R6b | Moderato e un poco maestoso† | ♩ = 88 | ♪ |
| | | | | TII,4 | Maestoso | ♩ = 88 | ♪♪♪ (3) |
| | | | | R2e | Maestoso† | ♩ = 80 | ♪♪♪ (3) |
| | | | | TI,3 | Moderato | ♩ = 84 | ♪ |
| | | | | R12a | Un poco maestoso | ♩ = 92 | ♪ |
| | | | | R1b | Maestoso | ♩ = 92 | ♪ |
| | | | | R7a | Allegro maestoso, ma non troppo | ♩ = 96 | ♪ |
| | | | | R11a | Un poco sostenuto | ♩ = 96 | ♪ |
| H3 | Allegro moderato | 𝅗𝅥 = 50 | ♪ | R2b | Allegro non tanto | ♩ = 100 | ♪ |
| | | | | TII,3 | Andante | ♩ = 100 | ♪ |
| | | | | RBe | Allegro maestoso | ♩ = 108 | ♪ |
| | | | | R14a | Moderato e maestoso | ♩ = 108 | ♪♪♪ (3) |
| | | | | TII,4 | Moderato | 𝅗𝅥 = 54 | ♪ |
| | | | | R10b | Allegro energico | ♩ = 112 | ♪ |
| | | | | H6 | Allegro moderato | ♩ = 112 | ♪ |
| | | | | TI,2 | Moderato | 𝅗𝅥 = 58 | ♪♪♪ (3) |
| TII,4 | Moderato | 𝅗𝅥 = 60 | ♪ | RBc | Maestoso | ♩ = 120 | ♪ |

(*continued*)

### Table 9.6. Continued

| Work | Tempo term | MM | Fastest notes | Work | Tempo term | MM | Fastest notes |
|---|---|---|---|---|---|---|---|
| \u00a2 | | | | C | | | |
| TII,4 | Moderato | 𝅗𝅥 = 60 | ♪ | H3 | Animato | 𝅗𝅥 = 60 | 𝅘𝅥𝅰 |
| TII,2 | Moderato | 𝅗𝅥 = 60 | ♪ | H3 | Animato | 𝅗𝅥 = 60 | 𝅘𝅥𝅰 |
| TI,4 | Allegro moderato | 𝅗𝅥 = 60 | 𝅘𝅥𝅰 | TII,4 | Moderato | 𝅗𝅥 = 60 | ♪ |
| H3 | Moderato | 𝅗𝅥 = 60 | ♪ | TII,2 | Allegro moderato | 𝅗𝅥 = 60 | 𝅘𝅥𝅮 |
| | | | | R2a | Agitato | ♩ = 126 | 𝅘𝅥𝅮 |
| | | | | R6a | Moderato | ♩ = 126 | ♪ |
| | | | | H Act II intro. | Allegro vivace | 𝅗𝅥 = 63 | 𝅘𝅥𝅰 |
| TI,2 | Allegro | 𝅗𝅥 = 69 | ♪ | TIII,3 | Allegro† | 𝅗𝅥 = 69 | 𝅘𝅥𝅰 |
| R15b | Molto passionato† | 𝅗𝅥 = 72 | 𝅘𝅥𝅰 | | | | |
| H1 | Allegro con brio | 𝅗𝅥 = 72 | 𝅘𝅥𝅰 | | | | |
| TII,4 | Allegro | 𝅗𝅥 = 72 | 𝅘𝅥𝅰 | | | | |
| TII,3 | Allegro | 𝅗𝅥 = 72 | 𝅘𝅥𝅰 | | | | |
| TI,4 | Allegro | 𝅗𝅥 = 72 | 𝅘𝅥𝅰 | | | | |
| TI,2 | Allegro | 𝅗𝅥 = 72 | 𝅘𝅥𝅰 | | | | |
| H6 | Allegro vivace | 𝅗𝅥 = 72 | ♪ | | | | |
| H3 | Vivace ma non troppo presto | 𝅗𝅥 = 72 | 𝅘𝅥𝅰 | R1e | Allegro | 𝅗𝅥 = 72 | 𝅘𝅥𝅰 |
| H3 | Allegro agitato | 𝅗𝅥 = 76 | ♪ | H5 | Allegro appassionato | 𝅗𝅥 = 76 | ♪ |
| TII,4 | Allegro | 𝅗𝅥 = 76 | 𝅘𝅥𝅮 | R10a | Tempo di marcia | 𝅗𝅥 = 76 | ♪ |
| TI,2 | Allegro | 𝅗𝅥 = 76 | 𝅘𝅥𝅮 | R2C | Allegro | ♩ = 152 | 𝅘𝅥𝅰 |
| TII,4 | Allegro† | 𝅗𝅥 = 80 | ♪ | TIII,3 | Allegro† | 𝅗𝅥 = 80 | 𝅘𝅥𝅮 |
| R10g | Allegro furioso | 𝅗𝅥 = 80 | ♪ | H3 | Allegro | 𝅗𝅥 = 80 | 𝅘𝅥𝅰 |
| TII,4 | Allegro | 𝅗𝅥 = 80 | ♪ | TIII,3 | Allegro | 𝅗𝅥 = 80 | ♪ |
| R6d | Allegro agitato | 𝅗𝅥 = 80 | 𝅘𝅥𝅮 | | | | |

Table 9.6. Continued

| Work | Tempo term | MM | Fastest notes | Work | Tempo term | MM | Fastest notes |
|---|---|---|---|---|---|---|---|
| R3b | Allegro con moto | 𝅗𝅥 = 80 | ♪ | | | | |
| TI,4 | Allegro | 𝅗𝅥 = 80 | ♪ | | | | |
| T ov. | Allegro | 𝅗𝅥 = 80 | ♪ | | | | |
| H8 | Allegro agitato | 𝅗𝅥 = 80 | ♪ | | | | |
| H4 | Allegro con fuoco | 𝅗𝅥 = 80 | ♪ | | | | |
| R9c | Allegro | 𝅗𝅥 = 84 | ♪ | R1c | Allegro | 𝅗𝅥 = 84 | ♪ |
| R ov. | Allegro energico | 𝅗𝅥 = 84 | ♫₃ | | | | |
| H2 | Molto passionato | 𝅗𝅥 = 84 | ♪ | | | | |
| TII,4 | Allegro | 𝅗𝅥 = 84 | ♪ | | | | |
| H8 | Molto agitato | 𝅗𝅥 = 84 | ♪ | | | | |
| R14b | Con spirito | 𝅗𝅥 = 84 | ♪ | | | | |
| H5 | Allegro con fuoco | 𝅗𝅥 = 84 | ♪ | | | | |
| R10c | Agitato | 𝅗𝅥 = 88 | ♪ | | | | |
| TII,1 | Allegro | 𝅗𝅥 = 88 | ♫₃ | | | | |
| R1a | Allegro animato | 𝅗𝅥 = 88 | ♪ | | | | |
| R11c | Allegro† | 𝅗𝅥 = 88 | ♫₃ | | | | |
| H Act III intro. | Allegro molto | 𝅗𝅥 = 88 | ♪ | | | | |
| R2d | Allegro con brio | 𝅗𝅥 = 88 | ♪ | | | | |
| R8a | Molto agitato | 𝅗𝅥 = 88 | ♪ | | | | |
| H ov. | Vivace | 𝅗𝅥 = 92 | ♫₃ | | | | |
| H8 | Feroce | 𝅗𝅥 = 92 | ♫₃ | | | | |
| R6f | Allegro agitato | 𝅗𝅥 = 92 | ♪ | | | | |
| R9e | Vivace | 𝅗𝅥 = 92 | ♪ | | | | |
| R12c | Allegro molto | 𝅗𝅥 = 96 | ♪ | | | | |

(*continued*)

Table 9.6. Continued

| ¢ | | | | C | | | |
|---|---|---|---|---|---|---|---|
| Work | Tempo term | MM | Fastest notes | Work | Tempo term | MM | Fastest notes |
| R15a | Con impeto | ♩=96 | ♪ | | | | |
| H6 | Allegro molto | ♩=96 | ♪ | | | | |
| TII,4 | Allegro† | ♩=100 | ♪ | | | | |
| TII,2 | Allegro | ♩=100 | ♪ | | | | |
| H7 | Molto vivace | ♩=100 | ♪ | | | | |
| H4 | Prestissimo possibile | ♩=100 | ♪ | | | | |
| R4a | Allegro con fuoco | ♩=104 | ♫₃ | | | | |
| R10e | Allegro molto | ♩=104 | ♪ | | | | |
| R9a | Molto agitato | ♩=104 | ♫₃ | | | | |
| TI,4 | Allegro | ♩=108 | ♪ | | | | |
| R10i | Allegro molto | ♩=116 | ♪ | | | | |
| R16 | Molto passionato | ♩=120 | ♪ | | | | |
| TI,1 | Allegro molto | ♩=132 | ♫₃ | | | | |

# 10
# Terms of Tempo and Expression

As the connotations of metre for tempo weakened during the 17th and 18th centuries, the Italian directions, which began increasingly often to be affixed to the beginning of a piece, became more important for determining tempo. Concomitantly, with the proliferation of these terms, a lack of consensus about their meaning also became apparent. Although there was no significant disagreement about the fact that *adagio*, *andante*, *allegro*, and *presto* indicated a series of progressively faster speeds, that pieces marked *largo*, *lento*, *grave*, and *larghetto* were all slower than those marked *andante*, or that *adagissimo* implied a slower tempo than *adagio* and *prestissimo* a faster one than *presto*, there were many points of detail upon which composers' practices were at odds with one another.

A particular problem with these terms was that they served a dual purpose; in the earlier part of the period composers tended to use them as much to prescribe the appropriate mood or style as to designate the tempo. As Koch observed at the turn of the century, they could be used "merely to indicate the tempo, or merely the style of performance, or both at the same time".[1] Thus, while there was seldom doubt about the general tempo region to which the most commonly employed terms belonged, there was often a significant lack of agreement about precisely how they stood in relation to each other, or, in the case of qualifying terms, how, if at all, these might affect the tempo indicated by the principal term. An additional matter, about which there were considerable differences between regions, individuals, and generations, was the absolute degree of momentum implied by the most common principal terms, particularly *andante* and *allegro*. There has been a widely held view that *andante* meant something more active to late-18th- and early-19th-century musicians than it did a few decades later, and there is evidence to suggest that, in some places at least, early-19th-century composers and performers saw *allegro* as indicating a substantially faster tempo than did those of the mid- to late 19th century.

---

[1] Koch: 'Adagio' in *Musikalisches Lexikon*, 63.

Theorists, trying to make sense of a host of evident discrepancies in practice, chose several different courses. Some, particularly in the 18th century, regarded many of these terms as primarily describing expression, or signifying a particular mode of execution, rather than tempo; some grouped them in broad categories; some explicitly recognized divergent usages; others simply contented themselves with prescribing a hierarchy of tempo terms without comment. A few writers attempted to fix chronometric tempos or tempo ranges for the various terms; in most cases, however, these provide little useful information, since by giving nothing but tempo term and metronome mark, they failed to compare like with like.

The confusion and complexity that cloud this matter at every stage may be illustrated by the contrasting approaches of two British writers, William Crotch and John Jousse, in the early 19th century. Crotch proposed the following list of tempo terms in ascending order of speed: *grave, largo, larghetto, adagio, lento, andante, allegretto, allegro, vivace, alla breve, presto, prestissimo*; but he admitted that there were those who regarded *adagio, lento, andante, alla breve*, and *vivace* "rather as terms of expression and taste, than of time". He further observed that some considered *adagio* to indicate a slower tempo than *largo* and that others thought *andantino* called for a slower one than *andante*.[2] Jousse's *A Compendious Musical Grammar* (1825), an English translation of Bonifazio Asioli's *Principj elementari di musica*, nicely illustrates the gulf which separated British and Continental musicians in this matter. Asioli's list gave the order: *largo, grave, larghetto, adagio, andantino, il tempo giusto, tempo di minuetto, andante, allegretto, allegro, presto, prestissimo*, but Jousse appended a footnote: "The above description, which the French have adopted, is according to the Italian school; in England the following order is generally adopted: 1) Grave 2) Adagio 3) Largo 4) Larghetto 5) Andante 6) Andantino 7) Maestoso 8) Allegretto 9) Allegro 10) Vivace 11) Presto 12) Prestissimo."[3]

In this respect, as in many others, the last decades of the 18th century and the first of the 19th were a period of transition. Conservative writers in the 1770s could still adhere primarily to the notion of these conventional Italian words as terms of expression, with a secondary connotation for tempo. Löhlein in 1774, for instance, explained that they were intended "to indicate

---

[2] Crotch: 'Remarks on the Terms at Present Used in Music, for Regulating the Time', *Monthly Magazine*, viii (1800), 941–43.
[3] Jousse: *A Compendious Musical Grammar*, iii.

the ruling character [Affekt] of a piece",[4] and he listed them with more or less literal translations into German, which, in many cases, do not refer directly to speed. In his subsequent discussion of the meaning the performer should derive from them, he focused largely on aspects of performance style rather than tempo. He discussed, for instance, how the bowstroke should vary in a "joyful" Affekt, explaining that "in this manner one seeks to define every degree of joy by means of the performance style".[5] Yet his manner of cataloguing the terms provides an unstated, albeit partial, hierarchy of speed; the first three categories imply a progressive increase of speed while the fifth, eighth, and ninth (with the exception of *mesto*) suggest a progressive decrease of speed; the relative speeds of the fourth, sixth, and seventh categories are less clearly implied. The ambiguous position of *allegro furioso* evidently results from the difficulty of using *allegro* as a term for fast music that was not in any way joyful.[6] A decade after the appearance of Löhlein's treatise, Türk commented on the absurdity of the literal meaning of *allegro furioso* as "cheerfully angry" and suggested that *allegro* should be regarded merely as meaning "brisk" (*hurtig*) rather than "merry" or "cheerful" (*munter, lustig*).[7]

Löhlein's list reads as follows:

**A moderate joy** is expressed, for example, by:
*Vivace*, merry, lively.
*Allegro*, cheerful, joyful.
**A joy, which has more exuberance:**
*Allegro assai*, cheerful enough.
*Allegro di molto*, very cheerful.
*Presto*, quick.
**An extravagant joy:**
*Prestissimo*, the quickest.
**An angry exuberance:**
*Allegro furioso*, brisk and vehement.
**A moderated joy, that has more calmness:**
*Allegro moderato*, moderate.
*Tempo giusto*, at an appropriate pace.
*Poco allegro*, somewhat cheerful.

---

[4] Löhlein: *Anweisung zum Violinspielen*, 104.
[5] Löhlein: *Anweisung zum Violinspielen*, 107.
[6] Löhlein: *Anweisung zum Violinspielen*, 105f.
[7] Türk: *Klavierschule*, 108.

*Allegretto*, somewhat less cheerful.
*Scherzante*, funny, joking.
*Molto andante*, at a strong pace.

**Magnificence:**
*Maestoso*, splendid, proud.

**Tenderness:**
*Affetuoso*, with feelings.
*Cantabile*, singing.
*Arioso*, aria-like.

**Calmness:**
*Andante*, walking.
*Andantino*, or poco andante, at a gentle walking pace.
*Larghetto*, somewhat spacious.

**Sadness:**
*Mesto*, sad.
Adagio, slow.
Largo, spacious.
Lento, lazy, slack.
*Grave*, ponderous.

It is not difficult to see how such lists, even where a definite hierarchy of speed was not intended, could give rise to confusion when, on the one hand, writers such as Quantz appeared to link Italian terms to precise chronometric tempos and, on the other, Kirnberger and Schulz were advocating a system in which the "tempo" term played a crucial role in a complex equation that was intended to allow the speed of a piece to be determined as closely as possible. There can be little doubt that although many late-18th-century musicians had a definite idea about the order of quickness or slowness indicated by specific terms, they were by no means in agreement about it. Furthermore, as Türk observed, "composers themselves are not all of the same opinion as to the determination of the tempo and the terms used for it; for one understands by *allegro* a far greater degree of speed than another".[8]

The distinction between terms that primarily designated speed and those that denoted a type of expression or style of performance is much more apparent in Türk's treatise than in Löhlein's, but towards the end of the 18th century, and in the 19th, there was a tendency to attribute definite tempo implications also

---

[8] Türk: *Klavierschule*, 111 footnote.

to words or phrases such as *maestoso, sostenuto, con spirito, vivace*, or *con brio* when these were combined with another term, or to try to assign a definite tempo region to terms that clearly described character, like *amoroso*. This tendency is apparent in Domenico Corri's list, from the early 1780s, of "words used to expr[e]ss the time, arranged progressively from the slowest to the most rapid movement".[9]

\* \* \*

The following consideration of individual tempo terms is intended to be illustrative rather than exhaustive, but it identifies some of the ambiguities that affect those most commonly used during the period under consideration. Of course, as in so many aspects of performing practice, generalized conclusions, though they may alert musicians to areas of uncertainty, are of only limited value. There is scope for several major studies of the attitudes and practices of individual composers, and schools of composers, towards tempo in the 19th century, for which the (as yet) scarcely investigated evidence of metronome marks in the works of individual composers who frequently used them (other than Beethoven) would provide a mass of invaluable evidence. The present discussion attempts to draw general, and in some cases specific, conclusions from composers' metronome marks; but the correlation between a metronome mark, a tempo term, and the speed of the music is not a simple one, hence the fallacy of theorists attempting to link terms with particular tempo ranges. The musical content within any given metre is so variable, in terms of density, texture, frequency of harmony change, and so on, that a metronome mark (linked to a particular note value) and the tempo term alone can be seriously misleading; and even when other factors are considered, the rationale behind the choice of term and chronometric tempo is not always easy to appreciate.

## Slow Tempo Terms

Löhlein, having included these terms in the general category "Sadness", made no significant reference to tempo in his description of the performance style appropriate to them. He observed:

---

[9] Corri: *A Select Collection*, i, 10.

Sadness, as a main category of feeling, has various grades, the differences between these grades must therefore also be considered in their execution. *Larghetto, adagio* depicts more a peaceful, thoughtful and pleasant state of mind than a sad one; for that reason one must not perform it so heavily as if it were the sad *Affekt*. However, *mesto, largo, lento*, already signify a suffering *Affekt*, and must be performed with a heavy and sustained bowstroke, one note joined to the other and well-supported. One must also put oneself into a sad *Affekt* if one wants to perform these melodies well, in accordance with their character. *Grave* requires even more sustaining of the bow and the tone than the previous kinds. Also, with respect to the composition it must have a slow and heavy movement, consisting of long notes and strong harmonies.[10]

In the same decade, Reichardt made very similar associations between different types of bowstroke in string playing and the terms *Adagio, Andante, Allegretto,* and *Allegro*, but associated the terms more directly with tempo rather than expression.[11] These comments from the 1770s reflect similar remarks in Quantz's and Leopold Mozart's treatises of twenty years earlier, but there is every reason to believe that some such considerations continued to be relevant to later generations. Reichardt did not expunge or modify these passages in Löhlein's treatise when he produced a new edition of it in the 1790s. The account of bowstrokes in the 1803 Paris Conservatoire *Méthode de violon*, which is repeated more or less verbatim in other treatises into the 1820s, makes similar points about the relationship of bow length and articulation to particular terms, although there is a greater emphasis on broadness and *legato* even in faster tempos.[12] The growing tendency of composers to mark their requirements more clearly, and their partiality for including music of an *andante* or *adagio* character in *allegro* movements, and so on, meant, however, that in the 19th century such distinctions became gradually less clear-cut than formerly, because the term that headed the beginning of the movement was increasingly unlikely to provide an appropriate characterization for the whole of it.

The connotations for tempo of the principal terms that were employed in slow pieces were very variable, since these words were, and remained, as

---

[10] Löhlein: *Anweisung zum Violinspielen*, 108f.
[11] Reichardt: *Ueber die Pflichten*, 25ff. See Ch. 7, pp. 360–61, for Reichardt's instructions.
[12] For the text of the Paris *Méthode* see Ch. 7, pp. 383–84.

Crotch had observed, essentially "terms of expression and taste". Also, since slow tempos were not as frequently used as moderate and fast ones, there was less opportunity for them to acquire a generally recognized order of speed. The quotations above demonstrate that different composers and theorists adopted irreconcilably different approaches. Sandra Rosenblum identified the following writers as propounding the view that *largo* indicated a slower tempo than *adagio*: Brossard, L. Mozart, Rousseau, Kirnberger, Lorenzoni, Türk, Galeazzi, Dussek, F. P. Ricci (J. C. Bach), Milchmeyer, Koch, Hummel, and Czerny.[13] To this list may be added Campagnoli, Crotch, Asioli, Adam, E. Miller, and Arrey von Dommer. In support of the opposite view, she lists Purcell, Malcolm, Gassineau, Quantz, C. P. E. Bach (commenting on Berlin practice), J. Hoyle, Vogler, Busby, Clementi, Mason, Knecht, and Cramer. These may be supplemented by Fröhlich, Dibdin, and Jousse (on British practice). The list could be lengthened indefinitely.

Not all musicians, however, were constant in their allegiance. Jousse, for instance, seems later to have shifted his ground towards the majority view, for whereas the early editions of Dibdin's *Music Epitomized* (1808) defined *adagio* as meaning "one degree faster [than grave] but always elegant and graceful", and *largo* and *lento* as "something faster than adagio", the ninth edition, revised by Jousse, defines *adagio* as "one degree faster [than *grave*] but very expressive", and *largo* as "slow and in an extended style".[14] Many authors frankly acknowledged areas of disagreement. John Holden gave the following explanation of *largo*:

> Large or ample. A slow movement. There are different explanations given to this word. Some will have it, a large, and frequently, unrestricted measure, slower than Adagio; others, more conformably to its modern acceptation, define it, a slow Andante; but not so slow as Adagio; and in this sense Largo, as compared with Andante, is like an ample stride compared with an ordinary step. The diminutive Larghetto is smaller or less ample; and therefore denotes a movement something quicker.[15]

Some theorists avoided the problem by grouping terms together without explicitly ranking them within each group in order of speed. Domenico Corri regarded *grave*, *largo assai*, and *largo sostenuto* as indicating "very slow and

---

[13] Rosenblum: *Performance Practices*, 313f.
[14] Dibdin: *Music Epitomized*, 1st edn, 63; and 9th edn, 39.
[15] Holden: *Essay*, 36.

with a certain gravity of expression", while he bracketed *largo*, *lento*, and *adagio* together as meaning "slow and with ease".[16] Carl Gollmick, towards the middle of the 19th century, adopted a similarly judicious standpoint, tacitly recognizing that most of these terms often applied less to speed than to character,[17] while Mathis Lussy, whose approach illustrates the decay of the Classical tempo conventions discussed in the two previous chapters, bracketed *largo* and *adagio* together as indicating slow tempos within a suggested metronome range of 40–60.[18] But, as will be apparent from the following pages, many composers gave numbers outside this range for music marked with those terms.

*Grave*, too, was often seen rather as a description of character than of tempo. Holden explained it as "A slow and solemn manner. Some authors define it as slower than Adagio; others a degree quicker than Adagio; but it ought probably, to be considered rather as a particular manner, than a mood of time."[19] Leopold Mozart's explanation of *grave* also emphasizes its character and prescribes a particular style of performance; he observed that it should be played "sadly and seriously, and therefore very slowly. One must, indeed, indicate the meaning of a piece before which the word *Grave* is marked, by means of long, rather heavy and solemn bowing and by means of consistent prolonging and maintaining of the various notes."[20]

A. F. C. Kollmann considered *grave* to signify a kind of *alla breve* in reverse, explaining that whereas in *alla breve* every note should be "as fast again as otherwise", when music is marked *grave* one should play "every note as slow again as otherwise";[21] and he went on to observe that *grave* is used with $\frac{4}{4}$ as a substitute for $\frac{4}{2}$, which is difficult to read, and that in that case every quarter-note "should be expressed slow and heavy like a minim".[22] Mozart's and Kollmann's descriptions should alert us once again to the very definite notions that obtained in the late 18th and early 19th centuries about the distinct performance styles appropriate to different types of pieces, which could be indicated by metre, by the note values employed, by the choice of such terms as *grave*, and so on.[23] Of authors who proposed a definite tempo

---

[16] Corri: *A Select Collection*, i, 10.
[17] Gollmick: *Kritische Terminologie*, 5ff.
[18] Lussy: *Traité*, 161.
[19] Holden: *Essay*, 41.
[20] Mozart: *Versuch*, 49.
[21] Kollmann: *An Essay*, 72.
[22] Kollmann: *An Essay*, 74.
[23] See Ch. 5, "Heavy and Light Performance".

relationship between *grave* and other terms, Crotch, Dibdin, Hummel, and Czerny regarded it as indicating a slower tempo than that implied by *largo* and *adagio*. Some of the writers who considered *adagio* to indicate a slower tempo than *largo*, for instance Vogler, Knecht, Clementi, and Lanza, placed *grave* between them, while Hüllmandel listed them, in ascending order, *largo, grave, adagio*,[24] as, much later, did Mendel;[25] and Dommer gave the order *largo, grave, lento, adagio*.[26]

The significance of *lento* was equally unclear. Some 18th-century authors, such as Quantz, Löhlein, and Miller,[27] seem to have regarded it as indicating a very slow tempo; many failed to include it in their lists, while others such as Crotch and Campagnoli saw it as meaning only moderately slow. A few 19th-century composers used it largely as a qualification to other terms (e.g., *adagio non lento*), but it is not always quite certain whether they considered it to mean "slow" in the general sense or whether, unlikely as it seems, they intended to modify the main term in the direction of another term that was seen as having a definite relationship to it.[28]

The relatively small number of examples makes it difficult to determine the usages of major composers with any degree of confidence. It has been suggested, on the basis of *Die sieben letzte Worte*, that Haydn regarded *largo, lento, grave*, and *adagio* as signifying progressively faster tempo terms.[29] This does not seem, however, to have been the view of Haydn's contemporary Crotch, for in 1800 he gave the following tempos (in pendulum lengths, converted here to the nearest metronome mark) for movements from *Die sieben letzte Worte*: no. 4, Largo ⅔, ♪ = 120, no. 5, Adagio ¢ ♪ = 126, no. 6, Lento ¢ ♪ = 152.[30] The slower tempo for the Largo is to some extent counteracted by a greater number of sixteenth-notes than in the Adagio, though its opening certainly seems more expansive; the Lento, on the other hand, with some quite active sixteenth-note figurations, seems to have greater animation at Crotch's speed. Karol Lipinski apparently considered Haydn's *largo* faster than his *adagio*, for in his metronome marks for the complete Haydn

---

[24] Hüllmandel: *Principles of Music*, 8.
[25] Mendel and Reissmann: 'Tempo' in *Musikalisches Conversations-Lexikon*, x (1878), 138ff.
[26] Dommer: 'Tempo' in *Musikalisches Lexikon*, 830.
[27] Edward Miller: *The New Flute Instructor or the Art of Playing the German Flute* (London, [c. 1799]).
[28] See below for Berlioz's curious use of "adagio un poco lento" and "andante un poco lento".
[29] Isidor Saslov: 'Tempos in the String Quartets of Joseph Haydn' (diss., Indiana University, 1969), 57f.
[30] Crotch: 'Remarks'.

String Quartets,[31] he gave ♪= 80 for the *Largo cantabile* of op. 54 no. 3 and ♪=72 for the *Adagio cantabile* of op. 55 no. 1, even though both of them have many thirty-second-notes and the former even has a substantial number of sixty-fourth-notes.

For Mozart the situation is similarly unclear; terms like *Andante un poco adagio* (Piano Sonata K. 309) do not necessarily indicate that he regarded *adagio* as indicating a faster tempo than *largo*, since *adagio* in this sense could merely have been used, like *lento*, with its generalized meaning of slow. However, it seems highly probable that Mozart, like his father, regarded *largo* as having a greater implication of slowness than *adagio*, and several factors, such as the alteration of the second movement of the String Quartet K. 465 from *Adagio* to *Andante cantabile*, suggest that Mozart did not consider *adagio* to imply a very slow tempo (since there is every reason to believe that he regarded *andante* as indicating a fairly flowing tempo). In addition to its connotations of speed, however, *adagio* will certainly have had implications of style that also relate to the use of *cantabile* with *andante*.

It seems likely that Beethoven, too, along with his younger contemporaries Hummel and Czerny, regarded a very slow tempo as appropriate for *largo*. This is suggested by his metronome mark of ♪ = 76 for the Largo in the Piano Sonata op. 106, whose fastest notes are thirty-seconds. However, he may also have considered *adagio* as indicating a rather slower speed than Mozart; the ⅔ *Adagio ma non troppo* of the String Quartet op. 18 no. 6, containing thirty-seconds and a few sixty-fourth triplets, has the marking ♪ = 80, and the ⅔ *Adagio molto e mesto* of op. 59 no. 1, containing thirty-seconds and a few sixty-fourths, has ♪ = 88.

Metronome marks indicate continuing disagreement among 19th-century composers about the tempo relationships between these directions. On the strength of metronome markings in the original editions of *Le siège de Corinthe*, *Le comte Ory*, *Moïse*, and *Guillaume Tell*, Rossini seems to have used the terms *adagio*, *lento*, and *largo* without any clear order of slowness among them, though his use of the French term *lent* suggests, curiously, that he regarded this as slower than the other three. His older Italian contemporary, Spontini, rarely used terms slower than *andante* or *andantino* (with various qualifiers). In the operas *Fernand Cortez*, *Olympie*, and *Nurmahal*, to which he gave metronome marks, *largo*, *lento*, and *grave* do not occur, and

---

[31] Carl Lipinski, ed.: *Vollständige Sammlung der Quartetten [. . .] von Joseph Haydn [. . .] Revidiert und mit Tempobezeichnung versehen*, 3 vols (Dresden, Wilhelm Paul, [1848–52]).

there is only one *adagio*—in *Fernand Cortez*—which is in 3/4 with a metronome mark of ♪ = 88 and movement mainly in eighths, though with some sixteenths;[32] an *Andantino passionato* in the same opera,[33] which has similar note values and is also in 3/4, is only slightly faster at ♪ = 96; and a 3/4 *Andante sostenuto* in *Olympie*, admittedly with more sixteenth-note movement, has a slower metronome mark of ♪ = 76.[34]

In *Euryanthe*, Weber used *largo* much more frequently than *adagio*; he did not use *lento* alone, but employed it as a qualifying term in the expressions *adagio non lento* and *larghetto non lento*, apparently to warn against too slow a tempo. There is no clearly discernible difference in the implications for tempo of *largo* and *adagio* (though the sample is too small to be certain of his intentions). In Weber's case, as in so many others, it may be more appropriate to consider the terms *largo* and *adagio* as indicating a different character rather than a different speed. Spohr left many more metronome marks for his works, and it is clear that, for him, *largo* implied something slower and more expansive than *adagio*. His normal term for his slow movements, however, was *adagio*, or *adagio molto* (he did not use *lento*). *Largo* appears only six times among the movements with metronome marks (and very rarely elsewhere), and of these six, four *largos* occur in the opera *Pietro von Abano*, and are very slow; so, too, is the opening *largo* section of his Fourth Symphony *Die Weihe der Töne*, which is meant to evoke the "deep silence of nature before the birth of sound". Spohr very rarely used *grave* alone as a tempo term, though he used it quite often in the expression *andante grave*, which indicated a slower tempo than *andante*.

Berlioz's metronome marks present a particularly inconclusive picture. *Adagio*, *largo*, and *lento* seem to apply to the same tempo area without any obvious hierarchy, though, if anything, it seems that he regarded *adagio* as indicating a somewhat slower tempo than *largo* and *lento*. Berlioz's use of *lento*, both as an absolute tempo term and as a qualifying term, in such phrases as *un poco lento* and *non troppo lento* complicates the situation. Comparison of the 6/8 *Lento quasi Adagio*, no. 33 in *Les Troyens* (♪ = 120), with the 6/8 *Adagio*, no. 48 in the same opera (♪ = 96),[35] and the *adagios* in the *Symphonie fantastique* (♪ = 84) and the *Reverie et caprice* (♪ = 88), all of

---

[32] Spontini: *Fernand Cortez*, Act I, no. 3.
[33] Spontini: *Fernand Cortez*, Act II, no. 3.
[34] Spontini: *Olympie*, Act III, no. 5.
[35] It is wrongly given as ♪ = 48 in D. Kern Holoman: *Catalogue of the Works of Hector Berlioz, Hector Berlioz: New Edition of the Complete Works*, xxv (Kassel, etc., 1987). Holoman's numberings for Berlioz's works are henceforth prefixed with H.

which are comparable in terms of their note values, appears to indicate that he regarded *adagio* as indicating a slower tempo than *lento*. The ⁹⁄₈ *Adagio un poco lento e dolce assai* (♪ = 96) of the orchestrally accompanied version of his song "Le Spectre de la rose" (H. 83b), which was given as *Andante un poco lento e dolce assai* with the same metronome mark in its original version with piano accompaniment (H. 83a), could be interpreted in a similar sense only in the unlikely circumstances that, in the former, *un poco lento* were taken to suggest a slightly faster speed than the principal tempo term and, in the latter, a slower one! In this context it is interesting, though hardly enlightening, that Domenico Corri, who bracketed together *Adagio* and *Lento* as "slow and with ease" followed these with a category of "not so slow" terms which included *Lento Andante* and *Lento Adagio*.[36]

The metronome marks in Wagner's earlier operas also indicate inconsistency in the use of slow tempo terms (which for Wagner and many other composers of his and subsequent generations included *andante*). The third act of *Tannhäuser* contains the following markings: *Andante assai lento* c ♩ = 50, *Andante maestoso* ¾ ♩ = 50, *Lento* c ♩ = 60, *Moderato* ♩ = 46, *Lento* c ♩ = 50, and *Lento maestoso* c ♩ = 50. In all of these, the note content and character of the music gives little if any clue to the rationale behind the union of these tempo terms with the specified speed. Metronome marks in Verdi's music suggest that, like Spohr and several other composers, he used *largo* for pieces in which longer note values predominated (generally quarters and eighths and occasionally triplet eighths), while he reserved *adagio* for pieces with more florid melodic lines, often including sixteenths. In common time both markings are most often used in the range ♩ = 50–66, with occasional pieces outside that range. Dvořák's use of *lento* is worthy of note: there can be little doubt that he regarded it as indicating a slower tempo than *andante con moto*, yet the metronome marks he gave to two movements from his string quartets to which he affixed these terms appear at first sight to indicate the opposite (Ex. 10.1a–b). Both are in ⁶⁄₈ with predominantly eighth and sixteenth movement; the *Lento* (op. 96) is marked ♪ = 112 and the *Andante con moto* (op. 51) ♪ = 100. The *Lento* also has many more sixteenths than the *Andante con moto* as well as a considerable number of bars containing thirty-second-note figures (the *Andante con moto* has some thirty-seconds, but fewer). Despite these factors, superficially indicating that the *Lento* is faster than the *Andante con moto*, this is not, arguably, how these two movements feel in

---

[36] Corri: *A Select Collection*, i, 10.

TERMS OF TEMPO AND EXPRESSION 519

**Ex. 10.1** a–b. Dvořák: (*a*) String Quartet op. 96/ii (Berlin, Simrock, 1894); (*b*) String Quartet op. 51/iii (Berlin, Simrock, 1879).

performance. The principal melodic line of the *Lento* is more expansive, the fundamental harmonic movement is slower, and the movement will tend for much of the time to be felt in two beats to the bar, while the *Andante con moto* appears more frequently to move in six notes to the bar. Nevertheless, there does not seem to be much difference in tempo between these movements. The distinction is much more one of character; and that character distinction will be emphasized if something like the types of performance style appropriate to these tempo terms (greater weight and *sostenuto* for the *Lento*, and a lighter less sustained execution for the *Andante*) are applied in this instance, as Dvořák almost certainly intended they should be.

Examinations of other composers' tempo terms and metronome marks reveal a similarly baffling picture, and it is scarcely surprising that many theorists were unable to offer any confident explanations of these words in terms of absolute tempo. The impression is inescapable that, regarding speed alone, though not perhaps expression and execution, a neutral word meaning "slow" would have conveyed as much information to the performer; it is certainly the case that, without their metronome marks, many of these movements would be taken at significantly different speeds by musicians unacquainted with their composer's practice.

## Intermediate Tempo Terms

*Larghetto* was almost universally understood to indicate a faster tempo than *largo*. (An exception to this occurs in Lanza's *The Elements of Singing*, where for sixteenths in *larghetto* a pendulum length of 7 inches is suggested and for *largo* 6 inches, i.e., *larghetto* MM c. 144 and *largo* MM c. 152).[37] But beyond that, there was considerable disagreement about its relation to the other terms. For those musicians, such as Holden, Lussy, and others, who regarded *largo* as requiring a faster tempo than *adagio*, *larghetto* naturally formed the bridge between the slow tempos and the moderate ones. Yet the idea that *larghetto* indicated the fastest of the slow tempos is also encountered among those who believed *largo* to mean "very slow"; thus, Koch described the tempo of *larghetto* as "usually similar to that of andante",[38] while Fröhlich also categorized it as "almost like andante".[39] And about 1800 the *Principes*

---

[37] Gesualdo Lanza: *The Elements of Singing* (London [1809]), 19.
[38] Koch: 'Larghetto' in *Musikalisches Lexikon*, 890.
[39] Fröhlich: *Musikschule*, i. 51.

*élémentaire de musique*, which included *largo* in the slowest of its five tempo groups, put *larghetto* in the middle group along with *andante* and *allegretto*.[40] Löhlein, who similarly considered it to be the slowest of the moderate terms, regarded its performance style as tending more towards that appropriate for the slower tempos.[41] A few musicians, however, such as Campagnoli and Bernhard Romberg, who regarded *largo* as among the slowest tempo terms, considered *larghetto* to imply a slower pace than *adagio*,[42] and it also appears in this position on the tabulation of the metronome.

Here, too, composers' practices seem to have been variable. It has been claimed that Mozart regarded *larghetto* as indicating a slower tempo than *adagio*,[43] but this seems unlikely in view of the discrepancies between the tempo terms in some of his later works and the entries in his autograph *Verzeichnüss*, where the *Andante* in Davide Penitente K. 469 was entered as *Larghetto*, the *Larghetto* of the Lied K. 468 as *Andantino*, the *Larghetto* of the aria K. 489 as *Andante*, and the *Larghetto* of the String Quintet K. 593 as *Adagio*. This suggests that for Mozart, *larghetto* signified a tempo somewhere between *adagio* and *andante*, but that, in terms of speed, the differences were not very marked. It also implies, perhaps, that for Mozart, as for many other 18th-century composers, *adagio* was not regarded as indicating a very slow tempo.

Beethoven's treatment of *larghetto* also suggests that he regarded it as the bridge between *andante* and the slower tempo terms, but seemingly closer to *andante* than to *adagio* (which for him may have signified a somewhat slower tempo than for Mozart). Beethoven chose the tempo terms *larghetto* and *andante con moto* respectively for the closely analogous slow movements of the Second and Fifth symphonies, both of which are in $\frac{3}{8}$ with thirty-seconds as their fastest notes, but he later gave them the same metronome mark ($\flat$ = 92). To some extent the difference in the terms is explained by the fact that when performed at the same speed as the *Larghetto* of the Second Symphony, the *Andante con moto* of the Fifth Symphony may *seem* faster, because of its slightly greater number of thirty-seconds; but the metronome marks may also indicate that by the time Beethoven fixed them, more than a decade later, he conceived the tempo of the *Larghetto* of the earlier symphony as being

---

[40] Gossec et al.: *Principes*, i, 43.

[41] See below, "Andante and Andantino".

[42] Campagnoli: *Nouvelle méthode*, v, 10; Romberg: *Violoncell Schule*, 111 (Largo MM 50, Larghetto MM 56, Adagio MM 60).

[43] Toeplitz: 'Über die Tempi', 183. This is not shared, however, by Zaslaw, 'Mozart's Tempo Conventions', and Jean-Pierre Marty: *The Tempo Indications of Mozart* (New Haven, 1988).

faster than he had originally done. This is perhaps supported by his changing the tempo term to *Larghetto quasi andante* in his piano trio arrangement of the Second Symphony; however, this designation, too, confirms the position of *larghetto* as indicating a tempo only just slower than *andante*.

In Weber's *Euryanthe*, sections marked *larghetto* generally contain rather more active music than those marked *largo* and *adagio*, thus making them seem subjectively faster. However, the metronome marks are within the same range as those for the term *largo*. But direct comparison is impossible since all the *largos* are in ¢, while all but one of the *larghettos* (also the metronomized *Larghetto ma non troppo* from the *Konzertstück* J. 282) are in $\frac{3}{4}$; the other *larghetto* is in $\frac{6}{8}$. In Spohr's music, *poco adagio* and *larghetto* share the same metronome mark range; but as in Weber's case, movements marked *larghetto*, the bulk of which (twenty-three out of thirty-one) are in triple or compound metre, tend to have a more flowing character. Spontini similarly favoured the combination of $\frac{3}{4}$ and *larghetto* in *Fernand Cortez*, *Olympie*, and *Nurmahal*. With a tempo range of ♩ = 50–54, Spontini's $\frac{3}{4}$ *larghettos* in these operas have a distinctly slower pulse than his $\frac{3}{4}$ *andantes*.

Berlioz, too, used *larghetto* most often in triple or compound metres. Of fourteen *larghettos* in his works only three are in ¢, and they have a tempo range that makes them, in general, a little faster than his *adagios*, but by their metronome range and note values alone they are scarcely distinguishable from his *andantes*. Indeed, many of the *andantes* are slower than the faster *larghettos*. All the $\frac{3}{4}$ *larghettos* have a quarter-note pulse within a range from 48 for *Larghetto un poco lento* and 54 for *Larghetto sostenuto* to 76 for *Larghetto espressivo*; the simple *larghettos* are in the range ♩ = 56–72. His $\frac{3}{4}$ *adagios* are in the range ♩ = 44–58 while his $\frac{3}{4}$ *andantes*, with and without qualifying terms, are in the range ♩ = 50–69.

Dvořák rarely used *larghetto*, but when he did, in the *Stabat mater* op. 58 and the Symphonic Variations op. 78, he used it for movements with the unusual time signature $\frac{4}{8}$, which he also employed with *largo*, *adagio*, and *andante*. The two above-mentioned *larghettos* are not only faster than the *largos* and *adagios*, but, with the metronome marks ♪ = 104 and ♪ = 66 respectively, they are also faster than the only $\frac{4}{8}$ *andante* (♪ = 92) from "Legendy" op. 59; all three movements have sixteenths as their fastest notes (op. 78 even having occasional thirty-seconds).

Löhlein prescribed the following performance style for the group of terms from *andante* to *larghetto*, which he considered to share the general characteristic of "calmness":

Calmness is performed with a restrained and calm bowstroke, certainly not too powerful, but also not weak; and if passages occur which depart somewhat from calmness, and approach the brilliant or even the pathetic, then the performance must be regulated in that direction: for just as in certain situations in speech the content often requires animation in the voice, so is it in music, and a piece that always flows along uninterruptedly and restfully in a monotone tires the listener and makes for boredom. This applies to the words *andante*, *andantino*, *poco andante*. *Larghetto* however approaches still more to peaceful rest.[44]

Reichardt's view of Andante seems to have been more active.[45]

Interestingly, the Paris Conservatoire's *Méthode de violon*, and those who plagiarized it, failed to specify a particular style of performance for *andante* (which was relatively infrequently used by composers associated with the Viotti school). They went straight from discussing the bowstroke appropriate to music marked *adagio* to that required when the terms *allegro maestoso* and *moderato assai* were used—tempo terms that for them seem to have occupied a similar tempo area to the Classical *andante* (see, e.g., Spohr's metronome mark of ♩ = 88 for the *Allegro moderato* first movement of Rode's Seventh Violin Concerto, which he had heard the composer perform).[46]

The nature of the relationship between *andante* and *andantino*, with respect to tempo, was subject to frequent theoretical discussion and disagreement. Some composers and theorists regarded *andantino* as meaning slower than *andante*, others as faster; as is the case with the slower tempo terms, some appear to have made less a distinction of speed than of character. The problem hinged on the fact that *andante* was ranked with neither the slow nor the fast tempo terms, and so, in contrast to *largo–larghetto* and *allegro–allegretto*, it was unclear which way the diminutive should modify it. Those who considered *andante* to signify a rather spacious tempo tended to see *andantino* as indicating a faster one, and those who regarded it as signifying a brisker tempo were inclined to take the opposite view.

The stylistic connotations of *andante*, as clear, even, distinct, and well separated, were often independent of any explicit notion of tempo until well into the middle of the 18th century; Quantz, for instance, observed that if instead of sustaining the dotted notes in an *adagio* one were to replace the

---

[44] Löhlein: *Anweisung zum Violinspielen*, 108.
[45] Reichardt: *Ueber die Pflichten*, 26. See Ch. 7.
[46] Spohr: *Violinschule*, 198. (Spohr heard Rode perform the work in 1803.)

dot with a rest, the *adagio* would be transformed into an *andante*.[47] These stylistic considerations remained an important aspect of the meaning of *andante* throughout the 18th century, but from at least the middle of the century onwards it was also generally accepted that it indicated a tempo somewhere between *adagio* and *allegretto*. Leopold Mozart stated that its meaning, *gehend* in German (which can be translated into English as "going" or, more specifically, "walking"), demonstrates "that one must leave the piece to its natural course; especially when one adds *ma un poco Allegretto*",[48] suggesting that he saw it as tending rather towards a brisk stride than a leisurely stroll. Fifty years later, Knecht defined *andante* as "walking or step by step, (that is to say, all sounds should be performed finely, equally, clearly, and well separated from each other)" and *andantino* as "walking somewhat". But, recognizing that his view was not universally shared, he continued: "Some composers are of the opinion that *andantino* must go somewhat faster than *andante*; but since the former is the diminutive of the latter, the contrary is true: *andantino* relates to *andante* like *allegretto* to *allegro*. Despite this, however, some composers take it in the first sense as 'going somewhat faster than *andante*'."[49] John Holden's earlier definition shows how two musicians, even when they agreed about the meaning of the word *andante* itself, could interpret the effect of the diminutive element quite differently. Holden explained: "*Andante*, walking. A regular, distinct and moderate movement. The diminutive *Andantino* is somewhat quicker than *Andante*, as if it were to be measured by a little mincing step."[50]

It seems probable that during the 18th century, in Germany and Italy at any rate, the faster interpretation of *andante* and the slower one of *andantino* was the more widespread. C. D. F. Schubart, for instance, referred to *andante* as a tempo "that kisses the borderline of *Allegro*".[51] And it has been persuasively argued that Mozart regarded *andante* as indicating a faster tempo than *andantino*.[52] But during the 19th century, as *andante* was increasingly seen to signify a rather steadier tempo, the faster view of *andantino* gradually gained ground. C. W. Greulich still maintained in his *Kleine practische Clavierschule* that *andantino* indicated a slower tempo than *andante* and,

[47] Quantz: *Versuch*, 194.
[48] Mozart: *Versuch*, 49.
[49] Knecht: *Katechismus*, 4th edn (1816), 39.
[50] Holden: *Essay*, 41.
[51] Schubart: *Ideen*, 360.
[52] Max Rudolf: 'Ein Beitrag'; Nikolaus Harnoncourt: *Der musikalische Dialog* (Salzburg, 1984), 127ff.; Zaslaw: 'Mozart's Tempo Conventions'.

like Knecht, acknowledged: "by a few composers a faster tempo than *andante* is indicated by *andantino*".[53] J. A. Gleichmann, reviewing Greulich's tutor, commented: "This, however, is not only done by some composers, but it is quite rightly assumed to be so", and his justification shows Knecht's observation about *allegretto* and *allegro* being turned on its head, for he continued: "the diminutive of andante (andantino) is analogous to that of largo (larghetto), and just as it indicates a less slow tempo here, it also indicates a less slow one there".[54] To this remark the journal's editor, Gottfried Weber, possibly recalling Knecht's view, merely appended the comment: "-? Allegretto -?"

Carl Gollmick's explanation in 1833 illustrates the growing tendency to regard *andante* as indicating a distinctly slow tempo:

> *Andante* belongs decidedly to the slower *tempi* and is more strictly defined only by the term walking. In this sense, regarded and translated as slow, the prefixes of *più* / more *andante* and *meno* / less *andante* are no longer doubtful; *più Andante* is thus taken slower, *meno Andante* faster than *Andante*; while, if one translates *andante* as walking, these prefixes obtain precisely the opposite meaning. [. . .] For this reason, the controversy over "andantino" still remains undecided.[55]

He cited Rousseau (*Dictionnaire de musique*, 1773), Türk (*Clavierschule*, 1789), Sommer (*Fremdwörterbuch*, 1828), and Nicolo (*Notice sur le métronome de J. Maezel*) as favouring the slower conception of *andantino*, and Wolf (*Musicalisches Lexicon*, 1787), Koch (*Musikal. Lexicon*, 1802), Petri (*Handbuch der Fremdwörter*, 1823), and Häuser (*Musikal. Lexikon*, 1828) as opting for the faster one.

The depth of confusion at that time is well illustrated by W. N. James's statement in 1829 that the Italians interpreted *andantino* to mean faster than *andante*,[56] whereas only three years earlier John Jousse, in his annotated translation of Asioli's *Principi*, had given the Italian view of *andantino* as indicating a slower tempo than *andante* and the English as indicating a faster one.[57] Searches through other authorities from the end of the 18th century

---

[53] Quoted in *Caecilia*, xiv (1832), 268.
[54] J. A. Gleichmann: *Caecilia*, xiv (1832), 268.
[55] Gollmick: 'Andante' in *Kritische Terminologie*, 7.
[56] William Nelson James: *The Flutist's Catechism* (London, 1829), 43.
[57] Jousse: *A Compendious Musical Grammar*, iii.

and the beginning of the 19th century reveal, in addition to those authors who judiciously acknowledged the lack of consensus, a more or less balanced weight of dogmatic authority on either side of the question.[58]

In Rossini's music, to judge by the metronome marks, *andante* and *andantino* seem to signify little obvious difference in speed, though in many instances sections marked *andantino* have a very slightly slower pulse. However, as far as such a restricted sample can show, the treatment of the two terms appears closely related to the metre with which they are coupled: in ¢ the pulse in *andantino* is equivalent to a slow *andante*, but there are faster-moving notes in the *andantino* sections; in the four operas with metronome marks mentioned above (*Le siège de Corinthe*, *Le comte Ory*, *Moïse*, and *Guillaume Tell*), there are five 2/4 *andantes*, all of which have an eighth-note pulse between 56 and 84, while a single *andantino* has a quarter-note pulse of 60 but fewer fast-moving notes. In 6/8, 3/8, and 3/4 there is no obvious difference in tempo between the two terms, but it may be significant that most of his *andantinos* are in these metres, while a considerably greater proportion of andantes are in ¢ and 2/4. Spontini certainly seems to have regarded *andantino* as implying a tempo on the slow side of *andante*, but in *Nurmahal*, for instance, there is no obvious difference of tempo between the Andantino malinconico no. 16 (♩ = 50), the Andantino sostenuto no. 27 (♩ = 48), the Andante poco sostenuto no. 18 (♩ = 50), and the Andante un poco sostenuto no. 21 (♩ = 48), all of which are in ¢ metre and have similar note values.

It seems possible that the notion of *andantino* as indicating a gentler (i.e., somewhat more leisurely) style of performance than *andante* remained stronger in Italy than elsewhere. Verdi may have employed it in this sense. In *Il trovatore*, for instance, there is a 3/8 Andante with the metronome mark ♪ = 76 (no. 3) and a 3/8 Andantino with similar note values and melodic profile marked ♪ = 72 (no. 14); in *Rigoletto*, on the other hand, there is a 3/8 Andantino (no. 5), similarly with sixteenths, that is marked ♪ = 92. For a faster *andante* Verdi often used *andante mosso*; for example, the 3/8 Andante mosso in no. 10 is marked ♪ = 120, thus occupying a place almost exactly halfway between his *andante* and *allegretto* (all three 3/8 allegrettos in *Il trovatore*, nos. 4, 5, and 14, are marked ♩. = 60).

---

[58] *Andantino* faster than *andante*: Anon.: *New Instructions for Playing the Harpsichord*, 36; Castil-Blaze: 'Andante' in *Dictionnaire*. Andantino slower than *andante*: Busby: 'Andante' in *A Complete Dictionary of Music* (London, 1806); Milchmeyer: *Die wahre Art*, 52; Valentine: 'Andante' in *Dictionary*.

During the course of the 19th century, however, as a slower notion of *andante* gained ground in Germany and France, *andantino* was more often defined as faster. An English version of Fétis and Moscheles's *Méthode des méthodes de piano* stated that that *andantino* should strictly mean a slower tempo than *andante*, but that in common usage it meant faster, adding, with dubious justification: "for which we have the authority of Mozart and the practice of modern composers".[59] In 1857, Carl Gollmick resolved the indecision in his earlier book by coming down firmly on the side of *andantino* indicating a faster tempo than *andante*, stating that it meant "less andante, somewhat faster, the fastest grade of the slow tempos and bordering on the allegretto".[60]

Because of its ambiguity, Beethoven rarely used the term *andantino*. In a letter to Thomson about Scottish songs, he commented on the disagreement saying: "Andantino sometimes approaches an Allegro and sometimes, on the other hand, is played like Adagio".[61] But when he did use the term, as in many of the songs he arranged for Thomson, he clearly favoured the faster meaning, as his employment of such terms as *andantino più tosto allegretto* testifies. Spohr, in line with the predominant German practice, appears to have regarded *andantino* as indicating a somewhat more active tempo than *andante*, though both terms seem to imply roughly the same tempo area in his music. This is illustrated by comparison of three $\frac{6}{8}$ numbers in his opera *Jessonda*, the *Andantinos* in nos. 7 and 10 (♩ = 58 and ♩ = 50) and the *Andante* no. 20 (♩ = 52); nos. 7 and 20 have similar note values, though the music is slightly more active in no. 7, while no. 10 has considerably more sixteenth-note movement than the other two. Interesting light on Spohr's notion of the meaning of *andante* and *andantino* is shed by three holographs of the song "Nachgefühl": the original of 1819 was marked *Moderato*, while a copy written for an album in 1834 is headed *Andante* and another, published as a facsimile in 1839, has the direction *Andantino*. A further peculiarity of Spohr's use of these tempo terms is that his *andantinos*, like his *larghettos* and like Rossini's *andantinos*, occur mainly in $\frac{6}{8}$ with a few in $\frac{2}{4}$, $\frac{3}{8}$, and $\frac{9}{8}$; none of Spohr's *andantinos* are in ₵, whereas his use of the term *andante* occurs principally in ₵ and $\frac{3}{4}$.

Berlioz, too, favoured *andantino* for certain metres and *andante* for others; almost all occurrences of the former are in $\frac{3}{4}$ and $\frac{6}{8}$, while *andante*

---
[59] Fétis and Moscheles: *Complete System of Instruction for the Piano Forte* (London, [1841]), 5.
[60] Gollmick: *Handlexikon der Tonkunst*, i, 10.
[61] Letter of 19 February 1813, in Anderson, *The Letters of Beethoven*, 406.

is frequently found in ¢. The tempo range for his *andantinos* is considerable and does not show any clear preference for a faster or slower conception than for movements marked *andante*. In fact, his use of the term seems to bear out Beethoven's observation of several decades earlier. In $\frac{3}{4}$ metre, Berlioz ranges from *Andantino quasi allegretto* (♩ = 108) in the romance "Le Matin" of around 1850 (H. 125) to *Andantino quasi adagio* (♩ = 50) in the Te Deum of 1848–49 (H. 118). When he revised the ballade "La morte d'Ophélie" (H. 92a) in 1848 (H. 92b) he altered the tempo term from *Andante con moto quasi allegretto* to *Andantino con moto quasi allegretto* ($\frac{6}{8}$), keeping the same metronome mark of ♩ = 63. This suggests that for Berlioz, as probably for other composers at that time, the difference in the significance of *andantino* and *andante* was rather one of character than tempo; probably the diminutive suggested something more lightweight. In 1829, Andersch speculated that those who first employed the term intended it to convey "not the degree of speed, but only less weight and significance, or a lighter, less serious content" than *Andante*.[62]

Schubert, who, unlike Beethoven, frequently used the tempo direction *andantino*, undoubtedly intended it to indicate a tempo considerably faster than that indicated by *andante*. In *Claudine von Villa Bella*, no. 6 is marked *Andantino quasi allegretto*, and the same direction is given for no. 2 in *Die Freunde von Salamanka*. The second movement of the Piano Sonata op. 164 is marked *Allegretto quasi andantino*. In the autograph of *Fierrabras*, no. 2 originally bore the heading *Allegretto*, but Schubert subsequently replaced this with *Andantino*. These and other similar instances suggest that he regarded *andantino* as having a tempo between *andante* and *allegretto*. Five numbers in *Alfonso und Estrella* have the heading *Andantino*, and for all of these there are quite strikingly brisk metronome marks, which seem well into the region of the tempo normally associated with *allegretto*. Taking account of the note values employed and the metre ¢, the *Andantinos* nos. 3a, 12, and 15, with metronome marks ♩ = 100, 116, and 120 respectively, all seem faster than the *Allegretto* (¢) no. 27a at ♩ = 112.

Composers within the Franco-German sphere of influence generally adopted the faster conception of *andantino* during the 19th century, but there are many inconsistencies. Meyerbeer's notion of *andantino* as faster than *andante* is indicated by such markings as *Andantino quasi allegretto* in *Les Huguenots* (nos. 1c and 9); but it is difficult to see clearly from the metronome

---

[62] Andersch: *Musikalisches Wörterbuch*, 17.

marks what Meyerbeer had in mind, since although the note content of the two numbers is comparable, they are marked ♩ = 66 and ♩ = 104 respectively. A similar movement that is headed simply *Andantino* (no. 5) has the metronome mark ♩ = 84, and many numbers in the same opera with the headings *poco andante, andante,* and even *andante sostenuto* are within the same range. Perhaps Meyerbeer's cosmopolitan musical experience (in Germany, Italy, and France) led him to use these terms inconsistently. In any case, it certainly seems that his intended tempo cannot easily be determined from the combination of metre, tempo term, and note values.

Brahms, judging from the use of such terms as *Allegretto grazioso (quasi andantino)* for the third movement of his Second Symphony, may be supposed to have seen *andantino* as signifying a tempo somewhat faster than *andante*; but his heading *Allegretto grazioso (quasi Andante)* for the final movement of the Violin Sonata op. 100 suggests that he may have made little if any tempo distinction between *andante* and its diminutive, except perhaps in character; Eduard Hanslich's review of the premiere of the sonata, before publication, indicates that at that stage the movement was headed *Andante grazioso (quasi Allegretto)* and the lost Stichvorlage reportedly had another deleted tempo marking.[63] Dvořák used directions such as *Allegro ma non troppo, quasi andantino* and *Un poco allegretto e grazioso, quasi andantino* ("Legendy" op. 59) or *Andante con moto, quasi allegretto* (*Stabat mater* op. 58), which indicate that he saw *andantino* along with *andante con moto* as meaning a more lively tempo than *andante*. His metronome marks, however, also suggest that these terms had subjective implications, rather than a narrowly defined or clearly conceived role in determining the tempo. Many other composers (e.g., C. G. Reissiger in his piano trios) used these two words in a similarly ambiguous manner in relation to *allegretto* or other terms indicating moderately fast speeds.

## *Andante* as a Relative Tempo Direction

One of the more important problems for the performer, rising from the lack of consensus about whether to regard *andante* as tending more towards the fast or the slow tempos, is, as Gollmick observed, the meaning of terms such

---

[63] See Brahms, Violin Sonata op. 100, ed. Clive Brown and Neal Peres Da Costa (Kassel, Bärenreiter, 2015), xviii.

as *più andante* and *andante molto* (or *molto andante*). If *andante* is taken literally to mean "walking" or "going", such phrases ought to imply a faster tempo, while *meno andante* and *poco andante* should imply a slower one, and this is undoubtedly how they were used by many composers, especially in the 18th century. A classic example of where *molto andante* has caused confusion occurs in the finale of Act II of Mozart's *Figaro*, where Susanna unexpectedly emerges from the countess's dressing room. (In the autograph score Mozart wrote Andante di molto above the score and Molto Andante below). Here musical sense may support the notion that the tempo should be relatively rapid, for Susanna's triplets lose their effect of pertness (suppressed laughter?) if taken too slowly. Other interpretations may be possible; David Fallows suggests that the direction *Molto Andante* is "surely used to denote an extremely controlled and ironically measured tempo contrasting with the preceding *allegro*".[64] But an early recognition that a rapid tempo was intended here is shown by the change of tempo direction in two editions of the opera from the early 1820s: the Schlesinger edition designated it *Allegro [sic] con moto*, and the Simrock edition *Andante con moto*, both giving it the metronome mark ♪ = 120.[65]

It is clear that Beethoven also kept the literal meaning of *andante* in mind when using such expressions, for in the variation movement of op. 109 he wrote: *Un poco meno andante ciò è un poco più adagio come il tema (Etwas langsamer als das Tema)*, which translates as "A little less Andante, that is a little slower than the theme (Somewhat slower than the theme)". His inclusion of the qualification in German, however, makes it clear that here, as in the case of *andantino*, he was well aware of the possibility of ambiguity. Schubert, however, as his fast conception of *andantino* might suggest, seems to have taken the opposite view. The *Andante molto* (**c**) from *Alfonso und Estrella* (no. 2), with the metronome mark ♪ = 76, is notably slower than his other *andantes* in **c** metre in that opera.

There remains also the possibility that some composers may not have intended the various qualifying words to have a significance for tempo. Rossini, for instance, headed a number in *Le siège de Corinthe* with the term *Andante assai*,[66] but the given metronome mark does not show that he wanted it faster or slower than other *andantes* in the same metre ($\frac{2}{4}$) to which he also

---

[64] Fallows: 'Andante' in *New Grove*, 1st edn, i, 397; 2nd edn, 608.
[65] Max Rudolf: 'Ein Beitrag zur Geschichte der Temponahme bei Mozart', *Mozart Jahrbuch* (1976–77), 209.
[66] For ambiguities in the meaning of "assai" see Deas: 'Beethoven's "Allegro assai"', *Music & Letters*, xxxi (1950), 333ff.

gave metronome marks. It seems possible that here, and perhaps with other composers too, the intensification applied more to the character of firmness and distinctness that still remained widely associated with the term in the early years of the 19th century, as Knecht's description (above) indicates.

Brahms may have inclined to a somewhat brisker notion of *andante* than some of his contemporaries, since he used the word *gehend* (walking, going) as the equivalent when he gave German tempo directions, though his idea of walking was probably more like strolling, as in Gollmick's 1857 definition: "In a moderated step and calm movement",[67] than Knecht's interpretation, with its implications of a brisk walk. In Brahms's music, however, *più andante* could sometimes mean "faster" and sometimes "slower", since he clearly saw it as occupying a definite central tempo area. This is shown, for example, by his employment of the sequences *Adagio–Più andante* in the finale of his First Symphony to indicate an increase in speed and, in his *Liebeslieder-Walzer* op. 39, *Vivace* (no. 6)—*poco più andante* (no. 7) to obtain a slower tempo.

Dvořák, although he does not seem to have regarded *andante* as calling for an especially slow tempo, clearly considered *poco andante* to mean a speed somewhat faster than that normally indicated by *andante*, indeed, apparently faster than the tempo implied by *andante con moto*. This is suggested by comparisons of, for instance, the 2/4 *Andante con moto* Dumka of the String Quartet op. 51 (♩ = 63), which contains sixteenths, with the 2/4 *Poco andante* from the Humoresques op. 101 (♩ = 72), which has sixteenths, triplet sixteenths, and a few thirty-seconds, or the *Poco andante* in the Symphonic Variations op. 78 (♩ = 80), which has triplet eighths.

## The Changing Connotations of "*Andante*" for Tempo and Performance

Metronome marks suggest varying 19th-century attitudes towards appropriate speeds for *andante*; and evidence from theorists indicates considerable differences of opinion. Gesualdo Lanza gave c. 60, as does the calibration on the metronome, but in 1840 Bernhard Romberg suggested 80, and a generation later Mathis Lussy proposed 72–84.[68] Of course, these pure numbers are of very limited value since they have no relationship to metres or note values

---

[67] Gollmick: 'Andante' in *Handlexicon der Tonkunst*, i, 10.
[68] Lanza: *Elements of Singing*, 19 (he gave his measurement in pendulum inches); Romberg: *Violoncell Schule*, 111; Lussy: *Traité*, 161.

(except in Romberg's case, where the 80 refers to quarter-notes in $\frac{4}{4}$) and they tell us nothing about the type of music envisaged.

Composers' metronome marks, some of which have been considered above, are more interesting. Beethoven's *andantes* are generally very active. The $\frac{2}{4}$ *Andante cantabile* of op. 18 no. 5 is marked ♪ = 100 and has a substantial number of thirty-seconds, making it faster, note for note, than the $\frac{2}{4}$ *Allegretto* in the Seventh Symphony op. 92 at ♪ =76. Comparison of the $\frac{2}{4}$ *Andante con variazioni* of the Septet op. 20 at ♪ = 120 (with thirty-seconds) with the $\frac{2}{4}$ *Allegretto con variazioni* of the String Quartet op. 74 at ♩ = 100 (with sixteenths) reveals little difference between the implications for tempo of the two terms. The $\frac{3}{8}$ *Andante scherzoso quasi allegretto* of the String Quartet op. 18 no. 4 and the $\frac{3}{8}$ *Allegretto vivace e sempre scherzando* of the String Quartet op. 59 no. 1 both have sixteenths as their fastest notes and received the same metronome mark (♩. = 56); the *Allegretto* has only a few more sixteenths than the *Andante*. The $\frac{3}{8}$ *Andante cantabile con moto* of the First Symphony, which contains some triplet sixteenths, is scarcely slower at ♪ = 120. Beethoven's metronome mark certainly indicates that this movement should be played at a considerably faster speed than it was normally performed for most of the 20th century. The same is true of the $\frac{3}{8}$ Andante con moto of the Fifth Symphony, which has many thirty-seconds and a metronome mark of ♪ = 92.

For Mendelssohn, *andante* still seems to have indicated a relatively flowing tempo. The *Andante con moto tranquillo* (c) in the D minor Piano Trio op. 49, with the metronome mark ♩ = 72, contains many sixteenths, which, despite the broad character of the main theme, do not give it the feel of a slow movement. A similar situation obtains in the *Andante maestoso* (c) no. 3 in *Die erste Walpurgisnacht* at ♩ = 80, where an expansive melodic line is accompanied by continuous sixteenths. When a rather slower metronome mark is indicated, as in the *Andante* (c) of the String Quartet op. 44 no. 2 (♩ = 60), whose beginning has a more sustained character, Mendelssohn's concern that it should not be taken like an *adagio* is shown by his appended instruction: "Dieses Stück darf nicht schleppend gespielt worden" (this piece should not be played sluggishly). But although Mendelssohn clearly did not want his *andantes* to be taken too slowly, there seems to be no direct evidence that he associated them with the 18th-century notion of a "well separated and distinct" performance style. Yet perhaps there was still an element of lightness in his choice of the term; if this were borne in mind it might avoid the more unctuous interpretations of numbers such as "If with all your hearts ye truly seek me" / "So ihr mich von ganzem Herzen suchet" ($\frac{3}{4}$ *andante con moto*, ♩ = 72) in *Elijah*.

The style of writing employed in Schumann's *andantes* seems, in most instances, entirely to preclude the characteristics formerly associated with the term. His *andantes* often feel distinctly closer to *adagio*, though in general those with metronome marks have only a slightly slower pulse than Mendelssohn's. The *Andante con moto* (♩) that opens the Overture, Scherzo, and Finale op. 52, for instance, has a metronome mark of ♩ = 60, but it moves mostly in *legato* eighths. It feels slower, subjectively, than the introduction to the overture to *Genoveva* (♩ = 50), which is marked *Langsam* (literally "slow", and usually regarded as an equivalent of *adagio*),[69] and contains *legato* sixteenths in comparable figurations to the eighths in op. 52. Similarly, the initial *Langsam* of the overture *Manfred* (♩ = 63), also with *legato* sixteenths, feels rather faster than the op. 52 *Andante*.

In Wagner's earlier operas *andante* is rather uncommon. Where it does occur, the metronome marks range in ¾ from ♩ = 50 to ♩ = 80 and in common time from ♩ = 50 to ♩ = 76 and even, in one case, to an anomalous ♩ = 100 (*Tannhäuser*, Act II, Scene iii). The characters and textures of these *andantes* differ considerably from one another, and it is difficult to see any consistent motivation for Wagner's choice of this term rather than another. Some, like Erik's Cavatina from *Der fliegende Holländer* (♩ = 50), are decidedly slower in effect than any of Mendelssohn's *andantes*. A revealing example occurs in *Tannhäuser* Act II, Scene iv, where, at Elisbeth's words "Der Unglücksel'ge" the music is marked c *Andante* ♩ = 56: the vocal line is sustained in quarters and eighths with the occasional anacrustic sixteenth, and, apart from some *tremolandos*, the accompaniment is in long note values with periodic interjections of an accelerating repeated-note figure in the bass (Ex. 10.2a); after a while there is a *poco ritard.* to ♩ = 50, then after another six bars the tempo term changes to *Adagio* with the metronome mark ♩ = 58 and the music becomes slightly more active, though it is essentially the same material as at the beginning of the preceding *Andante* (Ex. 10.2b).

Wagner made no use of the term *gehend* after abandoning Italian directions in his later operas; any movements that might have been marked *andante* were almost certainly designated *langsam* (slow) or *mäßig* (moderate), the latter of which, as discussed below, could also in its Italian form, *moderato*, mean something very slow to Wagner.

---

[69] The equivalence of German and Italian tempo terms in the 19th century was by no means clear, however, as the inconsistent "translation" of German terms into Italian ones in many 19th-century editions indicates.

Ex. 10.2 a–b. Wagner: *Tannhäuser*, Act II, Scene iv.

## Moderately Fast Tempo Terms

Around 1780, Domenico Corri bracketed *allegretto, poco allegro, maestoso*, and *moderato* together as "a Small degree Slower than Allegro".[70] This certainly represents their usage by many composers during the next century, but there were numerous subtle variants and individual usages.

[70] Corri: *A Select Collection*, i, 10.

## *Moderato* and *Allegro Moderato*

These terms were not generally regarded by 18th-century writers as indicating a distinct performance style, but for musicians associated with the Viotti school of string players, they were, together with *maestoso*, particularly cultivated and are often found for the opening movements of concertos. The Paris Conservatoire's *Méthode* and its plagiarists required as broad a bowstroke as possible from the middle of the bow towards the point in *Allegro maestoso*, or *Moderato assai*, and, when playing passages of sixteenths, with a small gap between the notes resulting from the liveliness of the stroke.[71] But their view of these terms was not universally shared.

The tempo significance of *moderato* was particularly subject to disagreement. W. N. James stated that the French regarded *allegretto* as indicating a tempo slower than *moderato*, "though the time is certainly faster than the latter movement".[72] It is not clear, however, what French source he had in mind, for the *Principes élémentaires de musique* puts *moderato* in the second slowest of its five groups of tempo terms, that is, slower even than *larghetto* and *andante*.[73] That interpretation of the term perhaps reflects Rousseau's use of the French word *modéré* as the equivalent of the Italian *adagio* in his 1768 dictionary. Most authorities did not regard *moderato* as so slow (though Rousseau's equivalent perhaps suggests a flowing *adagio*); but a certain amount of confusion arose from the fact that some composers seem to have used *moderato* and *allegro moderato* as two separate tempo terms, while others apparently regarded them as synonymous. A. E. Müller, in 1804, saw *Tempo giusto* as "approximately like Moderato in tempo, usually lighter in expression",[74] and in descending order of speed, placed it between Moderato and Maestoso. Campagnoli gave the ascending order, *allegretto, allegro moderato, allegro maestoso, allegro*;[75] Marx *allegretto, moderato, allegro*;[76] Mendel/Reissmann *andante, andantino, moderato, allegretto*;[77] Dommer *andante, moderato, maestoso, andantino, allegretto*.[78] Composers sometimes seem to have designated a slower tempo with *moderato* and at other times used it

---

[71] Baillot et al.: *Méthode de violon*, 130. See Ch. 7, p. 383, for the full quotation.
[72] James: *The Flutist's Catechism*, 42.
[73] Gossec et al.: *Principes*, i, 43.
[74] Müller: *Klavier- und Fortepiano-Spiel*, 298.
[75] Campagnoli: *Nouvelle méthode*, v, 10.
[76] Schilling: 'Tempo' in *Encyclopädie*, vi, 600f.
[77] Mendel and Reissmann: 'Tempo' in *Musikalisches Conversations-Lexikon*, x, 138f.
[78] Dommer: 'Tempo' in *Musikalisches Lexicon*, 830.

as a qualifier to *allegro* for movements that are well into the *allegro* range. Schubert's only metronomized *moderato*, no. 31 in *Alfonso und Estrella*, is in c metre with the marking ♩ = 96, and its fastest notes are triplet eighths; his *allegro moderatos* in the same metre (nos. 6, 16, 28, and 34a) are marked ♩ = 100, 138, 132, and 120 respectively. The slower marking for no. 6 may be explained by the continuous thirty-second-note *tremolos* in the accompaniment; the others contain sixteenths with some faster notes. However, the opera also contains one *Allegro molto moderato* in c metre (no. 34d), which at ♩ = 84 is slower than no. 31. But the sample of Schubert's markings is too small to suggest any firm conclusions.

Metronome marks given by other composers indicate variability of practice. Rossini's suggest that he may sometimes have used *moderato* to indicate a slower pace than would have been implied by *allegro moderato*, but he was far from consistent. Weber's employment of *moderato* and *allegro moderato* in *Euryanthe* suggests that for him they shared the same tempo region; the *Moderato assai* no. 7 and the *Allegro moderato* no. 23d, for instance, both in c metre, have an identical metronome mark (♩ = 104) and similar note values. Spohr's metronome marks, too, reveal no obvious distinction between the two terms. Verdi's designation of successive sections in no. 9 of *Il trovatore* as *Moderato* and *Allegro moderato maestoso*, to both of which the metronome mark ♩ = 96 was allotted, indicates that he made no distinction of tempo. Berlioz, on the other hand, seems generally to have meant a decidedly slower tempo by *moderato*, and, again contrary to James's contention about French practice, his *allegretto* appears normally to have indicated a faster tempo than his *moderato*.

In the case of many other composers, where sufficient data exists to hazard a conclusion, *allegretto* and *moderato* appear to have suggested a similar tempo range; the choice of term may well have been connected with character rather than tempo, as the example from Verdi's *Il trovatore* suggests. In this context it is interesting to note, once again, that several composers favoured particular terms for particular metres. Spohr, for instance, scarcely if ever used *allegretto* for pieces in c, whereas he freely used it for pieces in 6/8; in contrast, he often used *moderato*, *allegro moderato*, or *allegro ma non troppo* for pieces in c, but scarcely if ever for pieces in 6/8. Berlioz, too, showed a preference, albeit less marked, for the association of *allegretto* with compound metres and *moderato*, *allegro moderato*, or *allegro non troppo* with common time. Rossini scarcely ever used *allegretto* for movements in c metre, but frequently did so for those in 3/4, whereas his sections marked *allegro moderato* are almost invariably in c metre.

Wagner, like Berlioz, evidently intended *moderato*, in some cases, to indicate a slower tempo than *allegro moderato*, but in others apparently regarded the two terms as synonymous. His fastest *moderato* at ♩ = 126 (*Rienzi*, no. 6) is, in fact, slightly more rapid than his fastest *allegro moderatos* at ♩ = 120 (*Tannhäuser*, Act I, Scene iv, and Act II, Scene ii), but his slowest *allegro moderato* (*Der fliegende Holländer*, no. 3), which is given in ¢ metre, is marked ♩ = 50. In *Der fliegende Holländer* he twice marked successive sections in the same metre *Moderato* and *Allegro moderato*. In one of these (no. 6) there is no doubt about the relationship, for he indicated ♩ = 80 for the *Moderato* and ♩ = 112 for the *Allegro moderato*, both in common time. In the other, from no. 3, the situation seems to be reversed, for the *Moderato* is marked ♩ = 60 and the *Allegro moderato* ♩ = 50; but the presence of sextuplet eighths and a few sixteenths in the latter, together with a decidedly more active vocal line, gives an impression of somewhat greater speed. *Moderato*, used on its own, is perhaps Wagner's most flexible marking in the operas up to *Tannhäuser*, for he gave it metronome markings in c ranging from ♩ = 46 (his slowest c marking: slower than for *andante, lento, sostenuto, adagio,* and *grave*) to ♩ = 126. At both ends of the scale, the music moves in quarter notes. It may be reasonable to assume that he conceived a similar flexibility in terms of tempo for the German equivalent *mäßig*, which occurs very frequently in his later operas.

## Maestoso

Löhlein considered that *maestoso* or *pomposo*

> Requires a firm tone, that is well-sustained and well-articulated. It is mostly expressed in figures where the first note is long and the second short, or, to put it more clearly: where after the first, third, fifth note, etc. there are dots. The former overtures always began with such movements. Nowadays marches, in particular, but also from time-to-time other musical pieces, still have these figures.[79]

Reichardt regarded *maestoso* as one of the terms that, along with *affettuoso, mesto,* and *grave*, might be appropriate for slow tempos, requiring long, sustained bowstrokes, and stronger, more expressive accents.[80]

---

[79] Löhlein: *Anweisung zum Violinspielen*, 12, §90, 107.
[80] Reichardt: *Ueber die Pflichten*, 27.

The association of *maestoso* with music of a majestic, processional character meant that it was preeminently employed in common time, though it is occasionally found in other metres. It occurs most frequently as a qualification to *andante* and *allegro*, but, especially in the 19th century, is quite often found as a term on its own. Its effect on the tempo of an *allegro* seems always to be a moderating one; its effect on that of an *andante*, however, is more variable and is probably linked to some extent with a composer's feeling about the tempo area appropriate to that term. Mozart almost certainly intended *andante maestoso* to be slower than his normal *andante*.[81] Beethoven gave metronome marks to only two tempo directions that include the term *maestoso*, both in the Ninth Symphony. The 3/4 *Maestoso* has quite a stately pulse at ♩ = 60 but contains many thirty-seconds. The *Andante maestoso* in 3/2, which is marked ♩ = 72, has eighths as its fastest notes and seems similar to the 3/4 *Andante moderato* (♩ = 63, with sixteenth-note movement); but the *Andante maestoso* has a greater feeling of speed at that tempo, and, taking the metre into account, it seems clear that Beethoven saw this tempo marking as the faster of the two.

Some composers, probably including Beethoven, evidently felt that *maestoso* itself occupied a particular niche in the tempo hierarchy and that the effect of its attachment to another term depended on whether the tempo indicated by the main term was slower or faster than the tempo area appropriate to *maestoso* alone. For Spontini it apparently occupied a distinct place between *andante* and *allegro*. His metronome marks indicate that he regarded *andante maestoso* as signifying a faster tempo than *andante*, while he, like other composers, regarded *maestoso* or *allegro maestoso*, as indicating a quite distinctly slower tempo than *allegro*. For Spohr, on the other hand, *maestoso* seems, as with Mozart, always to have had a restraining effect on the principal tempo term, and thus he undoubtedly used *andante maestoso* to specify a slower tempo than *andante*. The sections in ₵ metre marked *andante maestoso* in *Jessonda* (no. 1) and in the Fourth Symphony op. 86, with the metronome marks ♩ = 56 and ♩ = 60 respectively, equate closely with sections also in ₵, marked *andante grave* in the Third Symphony op. 78 and the Concertino op. 79, to which Spohr likewise gave the metronome marks ♩ = 56 and ♩ = 60 respectively. Movements in the same metre which he marked *andante*, however, are generally in the region of ♩ = 76–92.

---

[81] Jean-Pierre Marty: *The Tempo Indications of Mozart* (New Haven, 1988), 84ff. Although Marty's arguments are largely subjective, his instinct seems very plausible in this case.

Weber's use of *maestoso* in *Euryanthe* is very varied, ranging from the extremes of *Maestoso assai* ¢ ♩ = 50 (no. 4), with eighth-note movement and a few figures consisting of a dotted-eighth and a sixteenth, to *Maestoso energico ma non troppo* ¢ ♩ = 63 (no. 23) with sixteenth-note movement. In between come a *Moderato maestoso* ¢ at ♩ = 92 (no. 1) and a *Maestoso* 3/4 at ♩ = 96 (no. 1), both with sixteenths. Two other short sections, a *Maestoso assai* ¢ at ♩ = 66 and a *Maestoso con moto* ¢ at ♩ = 108, both have primarily eighth-note movement.

Rossini, like many other composers, appears to have felt that *allegro maestoso* and *allegro moderato* indicated a similar speed, and perhaps differed significantly only in expression, though he may have considered the former to be a little slower, perhaps about ♩ = 120, with the central range of the latter being ♩ = 120–132 (both assuming sixteenth-note movement). *Maestoso* and *moderato* by themselves probably signified something rather slower, perhaps ♩ = 92 and 100 respectively with similar note content. Rossini's pieces in ¢ and 2/4 fit into the same range as those marked simply *andante*.

Mendelssohn's metronome marks suggest that he may have seen *maestoso* alone as occupying a similar tempo area to *andante* (in ¢ with sixteenth-note movement ♩ = 60–80, though a *Maestoso* in *Antigone* has the faster metronome mark ♩ = 92) and that the effect of the term *maestoso* in combination with *andante* was rather one of expression than speed. The metronome marks for his *Andante maestoso* ¢ music in *Antigone* and *Die erste Walpurgisnacht* indicate, taken in conjunction with other musical factors, a similar speed to music designated *andante*, with perhaps a tendency to be slightly faster. In *Antigone*, however, the 6/8 *Andante con moto maestoso* (♪ = 138) feels somewhat slower than the 6/8 *Andante con moto* in the same work, which is not only given a marginally higher metronome mark (♪ = 144), but also has some faster-moving notes.

*Maestoso* had a scarcely less extended meaning for Wagner than *moderato*. His fastest use in ¢ metre (in which he chiefly employed it) in the three operas with metronome marks is ♩ = 120 (in the *Rienzi* ballet music), and his slowest ♩ = 69 (in *Rienzi*, no. 9 and in *Tannhäuser*, Act III, Scene iii). Like *allegro moderato* and *moderato*, *allegro maestoso* is found only in the upper part of the range, the lowest being an *Allegro maestoso ma non troppo* (♩ = 96) in *Rienzi*, no. 7.

## Allegretto

Reichardt considered the character of *allegretto* to be similar to that of *andante*, but requiring somewhat livelier articulation.[82] Löhlein approached the question from the opposite angle and considered that, along with *allegro moderato*, *tempo giusto*, and *poco allegro*, "in keeping with its character, it should be played with a gentler and more connected bowstroke than the completely joyful [i.e., *allegro*]. But it must not be sleepy, rather it must hold to the mean between cheerful and moderate."[83]

The relationship of *allegretto* to slower tempo terms has frequently been touched on above, and it only remains to make one or two general points here. Some composers particularly associated *allegretto*, like many other tempo terms, with specific metres, or avoided using it in some metres. Among the *allegrettos* to which Beethoven gave metronome marks, for instance, there are none in c or ¢; all occur in $\frac{2}{4}$, $\frac{6}{8}$, and $\frac{3}{8}$. Berlioz's *allegrettos* are preponderantly in the latter metres, especially $\frac{6}{8}$, though there is also a group in $\frac{3}{4}$. Rossini too avoided c and ¢, and had a marked tendency to apply this term to movements in $\frac{3}{4}$. Spontini, on the other hand, seems to have been quite happy to use *allegretto* for music in c; *Olympie* alone contains five of them. Dvořák was especially fond of writing $\frac{2}{4}$ *allegrettos*.

*Allegretto* normally indicated a tempo somewhat slower than would have been signified by *allegro*, but its closeness to *allegro* may have depended on the composer's view of that tempo term. Mozart seems not to have regarded the difference between *allegro* and *allegretto* as very great, for on two occasions he entered a work which he had marked *allegretto* in the score as *allegro* in his *Verzeichnüss*. Nevertheless, for many composers in the 19th century, *allegretto* evidently indicated a quite significantly less rapid tempo than *allegro*, but the practice of some—Berlioz for example—was very erratic; sometimes *allegretto* was intended to specify a slower and sometimes a faster tempo than *allegro*.[84] This ambiguity of the term for French composers may be reflected in Mathis Lussy's observation that "some take *Allegretto*, the diminutive of *Allegro* for its augmentative, and render it by a quicker tempo instead of a slower one".[85]

---

[82] Reichardt: *Ueber die Pflichten*, 26.
[83] Löhlein: *Anweisung zum Violinspielen*, 107.
[84] Macdonald: 'Berlioz and the Metronome'.
[85] Lussy: *Traité*, 156.

## Fast Tempo Terms

Löhlein and Reichardt were essentially agreed about the need for a well-articulated bowstroke in music marked with *allegro* and closely related tempo terms. Löhlein taught that:

> The joyful [i.e., *allegro, vivace, presto*, etc.] is performed with a cheerful, lively and articulated bowstroke, and as this passion becomes more moderate, e.g. with the words *moderato, allegretto, poco allegro*, one must also reduce the liveliness of the stroke and move towards calmness. In contrast, with the words *allegro assai, allegro di molto*, which signify greater abandon, the bowstroke, must also be taken more fleetingly and shorter. In this manner one seeks to define every degree of joy through the performance style.[86]

A rather different view of the matter, stressing the connectedness and breadth of the *allegro* bowstroke, is found in the early-19th-century string methods that were influenced by the approach of the Viotti school.[87]

### *Vivace*

Before examining what 18th- and 19th-century composers may have understood in terms of chronometric tempo by *allegro, presto*, and so on, it will be useful to consider this associated tempo word, which was used in several different ways. *Vivace* is frequently encountered both as a term on its own and as a qualifier of *allegro*. During the earlier and mid-18th century it sometimes had a slower connotation than it later acquired. It was described by Leopold Mozart, along with *spiritoso*, as "the median between quick and slow";[88] but, in 18th-century England at any rate, it was used by some composers to indicate a relatively slow tempo.[89] Löhlein's list of terms (above) implies that he regarded it as indicating a slower tempo than *allegro*. Koch's definition of *vivace*—"lively, designates as much a lively tempo as a quick one, and

---

[86] Löhlein: *Anweisung zum Violinspielen*, 107.
[87] See Ch. 7 for Reichardt's and Baillot's descriptions of the allegro bowstroke.
[88] Mozart: *Versuch*, 48f.
[89] Charles Cudworth: 'The Meaning of "Vivace" in Eighteenth-Century England', *Fontes artis musicae*, xii (1965), 194.

light, flowing performance style"[90]—suggests that this signification of *vivace* survived to some extent into the early years of the 19th century; elsewhere in his dictionary Koch included *vivace* just before *allegro* in the fourth of his five tempo categories (reckoning from slow to fast).[91] But during the late 18th century and the 19th century it seems to have been used much more, either alone or in the phrase *allegro vivace*, to indicate a tempo not only livelier but also faster than that indicated by an unqualified *allegro*. As early as the 1780s, Domenico Corri regarded *vivace*, along with *allegro con brio*, as meaning "sprightly and a degree quicker" than *allegro*. Jousse, in English usage (it was not given in Asioli's original Italian), listed it between *allegro* and *presto*,[92] as, much later in the 19th century, did Mendel[93] and Dommer,[94] while Marx placed it after *allegro, con brio*, and *animato*.[95]

Metronome marks indicate that Beethoven's *allegro vivace* is normally rather faster than his simple *allegro* but not as fast as his *allegro con brio*. When Schubert added *vivace* to *allegro*, however, it seems to have signified a considerably faster pulse: most of the ¢ allegros in *Alfonso und Estrella* are marked $\downarrow$ = 160, while the two numbers in that metre marked *allegro vivace* (no. 22b) and *allegro molto vivace* (no. 20) are marked $\downarrow$ = 112 and $\downarrow$ = 120 respectively. But these movements have nowhere near so many sixteenths. Spohr's metronome marks suggest that he used *vivace* alone to indicate a somewhat faster tempo than when he used the term *allegro vivace*. For many later 19th-century composers it was seen, either alone, or in combination with *allegro*, as indicating a faster tempo than solely *allegro*; but a few, for instance Dvořák, may have regarded *vivace* alone as calling for a slower tempo than *allegro vivace*.

## Allegro

At the beginning of the 19th century there was undoubtedly a tendency for some composers and performers to prefer very fast speeds. How far this tendency goes back into the 18th century and which composers may have favoured it is difficult to determine. Certainly, Quantz's chronometric tempos

---

[90] Koch: 'Vivace' in *Musikalisches Lexikon*, 1699.
[91] Koch: 'Zeitmaaß' in *Musikalisches Lexikon*, 1755.
[92] Jousse: *A Compendious Musical Grammar*, III.
[93] Mendel and Reissmann: 'Tempo' in *Musikalisches Conversations-Lexikon*, x, 130.
[94] Dommer: 'Tempo' in *Musikalisches Lexikon*, 830.
[95] Schilling: 'Tempo' in *Encyclopädie*, vi, 600.

seemed very fast to other contemporaries. Only two years after the appearance of Quantz's treatise, C. P. E. Bach, who spent many years as his colleague in Berlin, commented on the fact that in Berlin in 1753 "adagio is performed far slower and allegro far faster than is customary in other places".[96] Türk, too, gave his opinion that the difference between *adagio assai* and *allegro assai* in Quantz's scheme was too great.[97]

Information about Mozart's preferences, as outlined earlier, is ambiguous, and it is difficult to say whether his pupil Hummel's tempos for his works represent Mozart's own ideas or a more recent preference for faster tempos. Rochlitz's anecdote about Mozart's visit to Leipzig in 1789 suggests that he might sometimes take his own *allegros* rather quickly.[98]

There was undoubtedly controversy in the early years of the 19th century about excessively rapid speeds, yet there were important crosscurrents in this respect. Many Viennese and Parisian musicians appear to have favoured very fast tempos; Friedrich Guthmann, however, complained vigorously in 1805 about what he perceived as an almost universal tendency to adopt very fast speeds, "especially the intemperate haste in the so-called minuets of symphonies and in the Allegro of overtures [first movements of symphonies?]."[99] On the other hand, the newer French school of string players, inspired by Viotti, and their German followers (including Spohr) were noted for their very expansive *allegros*, at least in their concertos (as Guthmann also acknowledged), though these are very often explicitly marked *moderato, allegro moderato*, or *allegro maestoso*.

Metronome marks offer the possibility of examining the basis of such claims, though the question of what *allegro*, alone or in its various combinations, meant to late-18th-century and 19th-century composers in terms of absolute tempo is difficult to determine, for many additional factors affect subjective perceptions of speed. The matter is further complicated because, while some composers frequently used simply *allegro*, or combined this with a limited number of terms that appear to have quite precise relationships, others, particularly Italian composers, employed a wide range of different expressions.

The present discussion will be confined to movements marked c and ¢ (in general, the quarter-notes in $\frac{3}{4}$ were expected to be somewhat faster than in

---

[96] Bach: *Versuch*, ii, 304.
[97] Türk: *Klavierschule*, 111f.
[98] See pp. 462–63 and footnote 51.
[99] Guthmann: 'Ueber die allzugrosse Geschwindigkeit des Allegro, und überhaupt über das eingerissene unmässige Eilen', *Allgemeine musikalische Zeitung*, vii (1804–5), 775.

544  CLASSICAL AND ROMANTIC PERFORMING PRACTICE

those metres). It is clear that there were considerable differences in the perception of *allegro* during the 19th century, but that some composers did indeed have a marked predilection for extremely fast *allegros*. In the work of those composers to whom metre still seems to have been a significant factor, the fastest tempo is almost invariably found in c (or dubious ¢) movements, with sixteenths as their fastest notes, rather than in genuine ¢ movements with eighths. This is not surprising if one bears in mind the notion that larger note values had a greater resistance to speed than smaller ones.

Beethoven's fastest movements of this kind are those marked *allegro con brio*. (His movements marked *allegro molto*, *presto*, and *prestissimo* all have the time signature ¢, having eighths as their fastest notes, or in one case [the Septet op. 20] triplet eighths, and do not achieve as rapid an absolute tempo.) The speediest of all, in terms of the velocity of the fastest functional notes,[100] in this case sixteenths, are the *Allegro con brio* first movements of the First and Second symphonies at ♩ = 112[101] and ♩ = 100 respectively (though in the case of the First Symphony most of the sixteenths are repeated notes or short slurred scale passages). A more breathless effect may be created by the slightly slower first movement of the String Quartet op. 95 at ♩ = 92 because of the proportion of separately bowed sixteenths and the more angular patterns in which they occur. The fastest functional notes in these movements move, therefore, at between 736 and 896 notes per minute (hereafter npm). Some of Schubert's fastest movements seem, based on the metronome marks in *Alfonso und Estrella*, to be equally rapid, with the fastest functional notes in *allegro assai* and *allegro molto* in the dizzying range of 832–896 npm. In the movements marked simply *allegro* by both these composers, the fastest notes are never slower than 640 npm; in Beethoven's case they reach 676 npm in the last movement of the Fifth Symphony op. 67 and the first movement of the String Quartet op. 74, and in Schubert's case 736 npm in no. 2 of *Alfonso und Estrella*, though only for a few bars. Cherubini's use of *allegro*, in the few works to which he gave metronome marks, matches Beethoven's and Schubert's; in the Second String Quartet a movement headed *Allegro* has its fastest notes at 640 npm, but his most rapid metronome tempo, with

---

[100] The expression "functional notes" is taken here to exclude tremolando or ornamental flourishes.
[101] As explained in Ch. 9, the ¢ time signatures for this movement and the Allegro con brio of the Septet op. 20, which also has sixteenths, seem anomalous, and both movements give the impression they should really be in c.

its fastest notes attaining 704 npm, was given to a movement in the Fourth String Quartet marked *Allegro assai*.

Rossini's, Spontini's, Mendelssohn's, and Verdi's rapid movements attain a similar range, yet they do not quite reach the fastest speeds in Beethoven and Schubert (except in the case of some of Mendelssohn's piano figurations). In Rossini's fastest movements in the operas *Le siège de Corinthe*, *Le comte Ory*, *Moïse*, and *Guillaume Tell*, sometimes marked *Allegro vivace* but most just *allegro*, and with an utterly inconsistent mixture of c and ¢, the fastest notes reach 836 npm; the slowest *allegro vivace* has them at 640 npm. The range for *allegro* alone is enormous: 504–836 npm. Spontini, unlike Rossini, was particularly fond of combining *allegro* with other terms, and *allegro* on its own appears very infrequently. His markings in the operas *Fernand Cortez*, *Olympie*, and *Nurmahal* range from *Allegro nobile* at 448 npm (*Nurmahal*, no. 8) through *Allegro giusto* at 528 npm (*Fernand Cortez*, Act III, no. 4) and *Allegro agitato espressivo* at 768 npm (*Olympie*, Act I, no. 4) to *Allegro vivace assai* at 816 npm (*Fernand Cortez*, Act I, no. 6). In Mendelssohn's *Allegro assai appassionato* (Piano Trio op. 49 and String Quartet op. 44 no. 2), *Allegro vivace* (String Quartet op. 44 no. 3 and Cello Sonata op. 45), *Allegro assai* (Cello Sonata op. 45), *Molto allegro vivace* (String Quartet op. 44 no. 1), and *Molto allegro con fuoco* (String Quartet op. 44 no. 3) the fastest notes move at between 704 and 800 npm. An astonishing 1,344 npm is reached in the piano figurations in the *Allegro vivace* of the op. 3 Piano Quartet.

Verdi often expressed his liking for fast tempos. In relation to the Viennese première of *Ernani*, for instance, he wrote to Leon Herz in 1844: "I caution [you that] I do not like slow tempos; it is better to err on the side of liveliness than to drag."[102] And he made similar comments in connection with *Don Carlos* in 1869.[103] It is not surprising, therefore, to find that his tempos are among the fastest in the later 19th century. Movements marked simply *allegro* may be found with their fastest notes in the range 480 npm (*Rigoletto*, no. 10) to 672 npm (*Il trovatore*, no. 14), while in movements marked *allegro assai mosso* (*Il trovatore*, no. 9), *allegro assai vivo* (*Rigoletto*, no. 7, *Il trovatore*, nos. 11 and 13), and *allegro vivo* (*Il trovatore*, no. 8) they occupy the region 672 to 832 npm. Meyerbeer sometimes demanded rather quick speeds. His *allegro con spirito* in *Les Huguenots* varies from 576 npm (no. 6) to 736 npm

---

[102] G. Morazzoni: *Verdi: Lettere inedite* (Milan, 1929), 27.
[103] A. Damerini: 'Sei lettere inedite di Verdi a J. C. Farrarini', *Il pianoforte*, vii (August–September 1926), letter no. 3.

(no. 12), but these are his fastest tempos. Weber specified ♩ = 132 for a *Vivace feroce* (𝄵) in *Euryanthe* (no. 10), which contains a few slurred sixteenth-note runs, making a rate of 1,056 npm, but on the whole his tempos seem more moderate than those of Beethoven and Schubert. Nevertheless, his *vivace*, *allegro con fuoco*, and *allegro* sometimes involve movement at between 640 and 736 npm, though his *allegro* movements can sometimes be as slow as 464 npm.

Composers who do not seem to have required such extremes of tempo when they marked their music *allegro* include Clementi, Spohr, Wagner, and Dvořák. Clementi, however, did specify some fairly rapid speeds for movements with sixteenths. In the *Allegro* of the Piano Sonata op. 50 no. 1 the sixteenths move at 640 npm, and the *Allegro ma non troppo ma con energia* of op. 50 no. 2 contains triplet sixteenths moving at 576 npm and thirty-seconds at 768 npm. Spohr seldom required very fast tempos; his *allegro molto* rarely approaches 872 npm, and his average *allegro vivace* is around 552 npm. But the complicated nature of many of his figurations often makes the music seem faster. In Wagner's most rapid *allegro* tempos in *Tannhäuser* (marked 𝄵), the fastest notes reach 608 npm, and in one *allegro* in *Rienzi* they attain 676 npm, but such velocity is rare, and his *allegros* are often very much slower. Dvořák's *allegro con brio* and *allegro agitato*, his fastest tempos in c metre, reach only 552 npm, though in an *allegro con brio* 𝄵 (Hussite Overture op. 67), triplet eighths attain 720 npm.

## Other Terms Affecting Tempo and Expression

To survey all the various tempo and expression words employed during this period, many of which present no significant problems, is beyond the scope of this book, but a few quite common terms, primarily of expression, which could also affect tempo, warrant consideration.

### Amoroso

When appended to a tempo word, this term sometimes implied a broadening of the tempo. Woldemar described *andante amoroso* as meaning "slower than the ordinary andante".[104] It certainly seems to have had this meaning for

---

[104] Woldemar: *Grande méthode*, 1st edn, 33.

Spontini. The *Andantino amoroso* (no. 5) in *Nurmahal* belongs, together with such expressions as *andante sostenuto* and *andantino melancolico*, among the more leisurely *andantinos* and *andantes* for which he gave metronome marks. Spontini often appears, however, also to have used the word in a more purely expressive sense in such phrases as *Andante amoroso un poco mosso* (*Nurmahal*, no. 13) and *Allegro amoroso agitato* (*Olympie*, Act II, no. 4).

When used as a term of expression, *amoroso* or *con amore* may also have encouraged tempo flexibility. *Con amore* and occasionally *amorosamente* (in "Le retour à Paris") was often employed by Dussek, along with a substantial vocabulary of other terms, in contexts where an influence on tempo seems likely to have been envisaged (e.g., in his String Quartets op. 60, in the *Allegro grazioso* of no. 1, and the *Adagio pathetico* of no. 2). Carl Czerny's employment of an even richer vocabulary of such terms in his compositions may also have been connected with the subtle changes of tempo that he regarded as necessary "in almost every line" of an effective performance.[105]

## *Animato; Animoso, Con anima*

These terms might literally be translated as "spirited / with spirit" and seen as essentially synonymous. Gollmick, however, insisted that they did not convey the same thing, translating *animato* / *animoso* into German as "regsam, beherzt, belebt" (lively, spirited, animated) and *con anima* as "seelenvoll" (soulful).[106] Koch suggested that *animoso* (he did not include *animato*), spirited, animated, would imply, according to context, "sometimes a more, sometimes a less accentuated performance style".[107] It seems clear that *Animato* will often have been expected to encourage an increase in tempo, even though this is not mentioned in most musical dictionaries. Lichtenthal, however, states: "In the middle of a composition, it indicates a faster movement than what was established in the beginning", he also notes that "The expression *più animato* indicates not only a greater degree of speed, but also of energy, and more distinct pronunciation of sounds, almost as

---

[105] Czerny: *Pianoforte-Schule*, iii, 24. See Clive Brown: 'Czerny the Progressive' in Leonardo Miucci, Claudio Bacciagaluppi, Daniel Allenbach and Martin Skamletz (eds.), *Beethoven and the Piano. Philology, Context and Performance Practice* (Schliengen, 2023).
[106] Gollmick: *Kritische Terminology*, 10 and 29.
[107] Koch: 'Animoso' in *Musikalisches Lexikon*, 146.

if arising from a more fiery soul."[108] An 1828 review of Chelard's *Macbeth* contains the comment: "Finally, with the third scene, the fatalistic hero of the play appears, immediately betraying his restlessness, his stricken mind, in the various changes of the so frequently broken time measure, in these animato's, meno mosso's; the frequent rallentando's and stringendo's."[109] The term *più animato* is unmistakably used to indicate increase of tempo, and similarly, in many contexts, *con anima*, as in the first movement of Brahms' Violin Sonata op. 78, where it is followed by *sostenuto* and then *calando* and *in tempo*.

Another implication of *con anima*, or *animato* for pianists may have been a more prominent use of un-notated arpeggiation, as suggested by P. A. Corri.[110]

## Cantabile

*Cantabile* was employed as a tempo direction in its own right, both as a modifier of tempo, and as a term of expression. Domenico Corri placed it in his third group of tempo terms along with *larghetto*, regarding it as faster than *adagio* but slower than *andantino*.[111] Koch, too, explained that *cantabile*, used as a tempo direction, indicating a moderately slow tempo.[112] Campagnoli, however, who regarded the term *larghetto* as signifying a slower tempo than *adagio*, saw it as even slower, placing it between *grave* and *larghetto*,[113] and the *Principes élémentaires de musique* put it in the slowest tempo category along with *grave*, *largo*, and *adagio*.[114] When used in conjunction with other terms it seems, like *sostenuto*, sometimes to have indicated a modification of the tempo and at other times, as its literal meaning in Italian suggests, simply to have specified a singing style of performance. That Mozart may have considered *andante cantabile* to indicate a slower tempo than *andante* is implied by his modification of the tempo term of the slow movement of his String Quartet K. 465 from *Adagio* to *Andante cantabile*.

---

[108] Lichtenthal: 'Animato' in *Dizionario*, i, 35.
[109] Anon.: *Allgemeine musikalische Zeitung*, xxx (1828), 597.
[110] See Ch. 14, p. 849.
[111] Corri: *A Select Collection*, i, 10.
[112] Koch: 'Cantabile' in *Musikalisches Lexikon*, 299.
[113] Campagnoli: *Nouvelle méthode*, v, 10.
[114] Gossec et al.: *Principes*, 43.

When it is used in the middle of a movement, it may often have implied a somewhat slower tempo. Anton André used the term frequently (e.g., in his string quartets opp. 14 and 15) in places where a tempo implication seems probable. An instance in the third volume of his *Lieder und Gesänge* (rev. edn), where he supplied metronome marks and many performance instructions indicating tempo flexibility,[115] provides a clear example (Ex. 10.3). Where he wanted only the expressive aspect, he wrote *cantabile ma l'istesso movimento* in "Sensucht", the first song of the first volume of his *Lieder und Gesänge*.

Beethoven, too, in the String Quartet op. 59 no. 1, evidently conscious that performers might regard *cantabile* as a modifier of tempo, not only marked ♪ = 88 for the *Adagio molto e mesto* at the beginning of the third movement, but also repeated the same metronome mark later at the section marked *molto cantabile*.

In any case, *cantabile* was certainly intended to convey a singing style of performance. Reichardt instructed that in an *allegro*, where the string player's bowstroke was normally lively and well-marked, *cantabile* was among the terms that required "gentler and more connected" bowing.[116]

According to some English writers, *cantabile* could also have a more specialized meaning in the late 18th century and early 19th century: the introduction of extempore ornamentation. In 1771, Anselm Bayly complained that "What are called *cantabiles* betray in general such a want of invention, and absurdity of application, that they make the hearer sick before they are half finished."[117] Sometimes, as an anonymous author observed around 1790, the term *cantabile* "when set at the conclusion of an air signifies an extempore cadence";[118] and still, in 1818 Richard Mackenzie Bacon could refer to "that degree of ornament which is essential to the CANTABILE".[119] Dibdin, too, maintained in the first edition of his *Music Epitomized* that it indicated the "introduction of extempore ideas gracefully"; this was changed by Jousse in the ninth edition to the simple definition "in a singing style", perhaps indicating that, despite Bacon's comment, the earlier definition was by that time regarded as obsolete.[120]

---

[115] See Ch. 11, pp. 597-99.
[116] Reichardt: *Ueber die Pflichten*, 27.
[117] Anselm Bayly: *A Practical Treatise*, 65.
[118] Anon.: *New Instructions for Playing the Harpsichord* (London, c. 1790), 36.
[119] Richard Mackenzie Bacon: 'On the Structure of the Italian Opera', *Quarterly Musical Magazine and Review*, i (1818), 37.
[120] Charles Dibdin: *Music Epitomized: A School Book in Which the Whole Science of Music Is Completely Explained*... 1st edn (London, 1808), 67; 5th edn (c. 1818), 66.

Ex. 10.3 Anton André: Lieder und Gesänge vol. 3, p. 12.

## Diminuendo

Although the terms *decrescendo* and *diminuendo* are conventionally taken simply as instructions to become gradually quieter, a few early-19th-century sources suggest a distinction between the two. The term *decrescendo* seems primarily to have indicated a decrease of volume; *diminuendo*, on the other hand, was described by several writers as affecting tempo. Türk and Czerny included it among the terms that indicated relaxation of tempo;[121] and it was defined by Junghanss as "decreasing, diminishing, in the strength of the sound, or also decreasing in tempo. >—", whereas he confined *decrescendo* to a decrease in dynamic.[122] Carl Gollmick, too, made this distinction, commenting: "*Decrescendo* refers more to the diminution of the tone in continuous passages, while *diminuendo* already expresses more of a diminution in passion." Gollmick, who taught piano to Spohr's daughters, referred specifically to Spohr's use of *dim.*, immediately following *decresc.*, in

---

[121] Türk: *Klavierschule*, 371; Czerny: *Pianoforte School*, iii, 21. See Ch. 11, pp. 583 and 596–97.
[122] Johann Christian Gottlieb Junghanss: *Pianoforte-Schule* (Vienna, [c. 1820]), 41.

his opera *Faust*, which he had performed as timpanist under the composer's direction in Frankfurt in 1818, "with the intention of making the power disappear to the last breath". He observed, too, that "*dim.* is also used mostly for short passages, as well as often for hesitating; *decresc.* and *dim.* are therefore not quite synonymous".[123] François Habeneck in 1842 associated the term, and also the symbol, with a relaxation of tempo; in his list of performance instructions, he included: "*Dim.* > Diminishing the intensity of the sound and sometimes of the tempo".[124] A Viennese review of a pianist in 1847 included the comment "the performance was highly disgusting in its mannerism. No bar, I would rather say no note, is heard without a *ritardando, smorzando, diminuendo*, and whatever all these individual means of emotional expression may be called."[125]

Among composers who undoubtedly distinguished between *decrescendo* and *diminuendo*, and treated the latter as an instruction to relax tempo as well as volume, was Schubert. Walther Dürr noted in the general preface to volumes of the *Neue Schubert Ausgabe*: "As a rule Schubert distinguished clearly between the indications *ritardando* (becoming slower), *decrescendo* (becoming softer) and *diminuendo* (becoming slower and softer). The latter is frequently followed, as is *ritardando*, by *a tempo*."[126]

This usage is found particularly in Viennese compositions. Early examples occur in E. A. Förster's String Quartets op. 7 of 1794 (Ex. 10.4a) and also at the end of the first movement of his String Quintet op. 20 (c. 1801). Anton André, whose firm had published Förster's op. 7, similarly employed both *decrescendo* and *diminuendo*, for instance in his String Quartet op. 15 no. 1 of about 1802 (Ex. 10.4b). Nikolaus von Krufft employed it repeatedly, from his Piano Sonata op. 4, dedicated to Beethoven (c. 1802), to his later String Quartets, Violin Sonata, and 24 Preludes and Fugues (after 1810). Franz Weiss (who played viola in Schuppanzigh's quartet) used *decrescendo* and *diminuendo* in this sense in his String Quartet op. 9 (Ex. 10.4c), but evidently experimentally, since he did not use it in his other string quartets. Ignaz

---

[123] Gollmick: *Kritische Terminologie*, 3. The printed vocal score and other surviving sources of Spohr's *Faust* do not contain these markings, but they may well have been present in the performance material from which Gollmick played.

[124] Habeneck: *Méthode*, 116.

[125] Ph. .s.: 'Privat-Konzert der Pianistin Emelie Stiller', *Wiener allgemeine Musik-Zeitung*, vii (1847), 203.

[126] Neue Schubert Ausgabe. See also Dürr: 'Notation und Aufführungspraxis. Artikulation und Dynamik bei Schubert' in Helga Lühning (ed.): *Musikedition. Mittler zwischen Wissenschaft und musikalischer Praxis* (Tübingen 2002), 313ff.

**Ex. 10.4a** A. E. Förster [sic]: String Quartet op. 7 no. 1 in A major, 1st movement (manuscript copy from 1794). The same initials (A, E, instead of E. A.) and 'dynamic' markings are present in the published edition (Offenbach: Johann André).

[Allegro vivace]

**Ex. 10.4b** Johann Anton André: String Quartet op. 15 no. 1/iii.

[Adagio con moto quasi andantino]

**Ex. 10.4c** Franz Weiss: String Quartet op. 9, 1st movement.

[Allegro spirituoso (*sic*)]

Moscheles, in his Studies op. 70 (c. 1827), also used both *decrescendo* and *diminuendo* purposefully.

It is impossible to tell what relationship there may have been between *diminuendo, calando, smorzando, perdendosi, ritardando, rallentando*, and other terms that possibly implied relaxation of tempo (several of which were often used in the same composition). For some composers, these may have represented not only different types of expression, but also different degrees of tempo relaxation. What may have lain behind Beethoven's adoption of *diminuendo* rather than *decrescendo* around 1805 is unclear, but it may suggest that he thought *diminuendo* better to express a subtle relaxation of tempo, which he may almost always have associated with decreasing volume. A couple of exceptional occurrences of *decrescendo* in the Piano Sonatas opp. 109 and 110 may have been to avoid slackening of tempo, which would fit their musical contexts.

The potential connotations of *crescendo, decrescendo* and *diminuendo*, and their graphic representation by < and >, is discussed further in Chapter 11.

## *Dolce*

Apart from its literal meaning of sweet, gentle, soft, *dolce* may sometimes have been employed as a specific dynamic level. Milchmeyer (1797) placed it between *p* and *mf*, and explained that it "indicates a discourse, of which the characteristic is gentleness, tenderness, and serves for the expression of melancholy, love, and rapture".[127] *Dolce* may also have encouraged a broadening of tempo. It is possible that this was partly implicit in Clementi's rather curious definition of the term as "SWEET, with TASTE; now and then SWELLING some notes". It is reported that Brahms envisaged a relaxation of tempo in passages marked *dolce*. William Primrose reported: "[Sir Charles] Stanford was a friend of Brahms, and it was he who brought to my attention the fact that when Brahms writes the word *dolce* he means not only all that it connotes but indicates a slightly slower pace as well. If you examine the Brahms works where this word occurs, you will note that the music lends itself very well to this admonition."[128]

---

[127] Milchmeyer: *Die wahre Art*, 49.
[128] Primrose: *Memoirs* (London, 1978), 169.

The instructions *dolce* and *dolcissimo* may also have had connotations in string playing, both for bowing and for *vibrato*. Reichardt included it along with *cantabile* (above) as a term for gentler, more connected bowing. Something similar seems still to have been envisaged for this term at the end of the 19th century. Ferdinand David's pupil August Wilhelmj explained how to produce the effect of *dolce* and *dolcissimo*:

> If the Bow is placed at a great distance from the Bridge (and therefore almost over the fingerboard—"sur la touché"), while the Bow moves at a considerable speed, so without pressure, the result is a tone of little intensity, but of clarinet like sweetness and much carrying power. This is known as Dolce. As a special effect it is most valuable. [...] Dolcissimo is merely the same mechanical device carried to an extreme.[129]

Marion Ranken described a similar bowstroke as characteristic of Joachim's playing, but related it to *pianissimo* rather than *dolce*:

> a *pianissimo* passage following on a merely *piano* one was seldom played simply *more piano*, with a smaller tone, but it was nearly always given a different character as well: That is to say, very usually, as soon as the *pp* sign occurred, instead of using *less* bow, one played with about double as much as before, drawing the bow lightly and swiftly across the strings at the top end of the fingerboard. [...] The above quality of tone comes out best on the two lower strings.[130]

She associated *dolce* primarily with a more frequent use of *vibrato*, recalling that in passages marked *dolce*: "a free use was usually [often] made of the *vibrato*, producing thus the sweetness that the word *dolce* indicates".[131]

*Dolce* was also another of the terms associated by P. A. Corri with greater use of improvised piano arpeggiation.[132]

---

[129] August Wilhemj and James Brown: *A Modern School for the Violin*, 6 pts. (London, 1899–1900), pt. 2b, vii.
[130] M[arion] R[anken]: *Some Points of Violin Playing and Musical Performance as Learnt in the Hochschule für Musik (Joachim School) in Berlin during the Time I Was a Student There, 1902-1909* (Edinburgh, 1939), 18.
[131] M. R[anken]: *Some points of Violin Playing*, 19. In her personal copy (kindly made available to me by Job ter Haar) she amended the printed version "use was usually made" to "use was often made".
[132] See Ch. 14, "Arpeggiation".

## Espressivo

Most sources that list the term among other performance instructions give nothing more than a literal statement that passages marked thus should be performed expressively. A few, however, hint at ways in which that expressiveness might be achieved. Clementi explained: "CON ESPRESSIONE, or CON ANIMA, with expression; that is, with passionate feeling; where every note has its peculiar force and energy; and where even the severity of time may be relaxed for extraordinary effects."[133] Czerny explicitly included *espressivo* in his list of circumstances that invite relaxation of tempo, with the comment that this should occur "almost always where the composer has marked an *espressivo*".[134] Czerny's comment is supported by some of Beethoven's markings. In the last movement of the Violin Sonata op. 96, for instance, *espressivo* (b. 97) is followed five bars later by *a tempo*. Similarly in the second movement of the Piano Sonata op. 109, *un poco espressivo* and later *p. espressivo* are both followed four bars later by *a tempo*. André's *Lieder* provide evidence that he too saw *espressivo* as moderating tempo (see Ex. 11.5).

An article in the Parisian journal *Le pianist*, probably by the editor Charles Chaulieu (b. 1788), associated *espressivo* with *tempo rubato*.

> Dussek—who greatly loved rubato, even though he never wrote the word in his music—Dussek had tried to render it visible by way of syncopation, but even when one faithfully performed this syncopation, one did not even come close to his mellow and delicious way of playing. He gave up the idea himself and was happy just to write *espressivo*. Happy are those who heard him perform his music! Happier even are those who could imitate him.[135]

In string playing the term may have been associated with a particular kind of intense tone, at least in Brahms's circle. Marion Ranken recalled:

> in *piano espressivo* sections, the *vibrato* (if used at all) was used sparingly and not in a way to interfere with the intensity of the tone i. e. there was no movement of the hand big enough to produce perceptible waves of sound

---

[133] Clementi: *Introduction*, 14.
[134] Czerny: *Pianoforte-Schule*, iii, 26.
[135] Anon.: 'J. L. Dussek' in *Le pianiste*, v (1834), 78.

and often all that it consisted in was a slight movement of the tip of the finger which helped to intensify the tone and expression.[136]

The implication that Brahms associated *espressivo* with intense bowing is strengthened by a recollection by the conductor Max Fiedler (1859–1939) that "In a rehearsal conducted by Brahms, he criticized the rendition of a *piano espressivo* passage, with the words: 'no, gentlemen, a juicy *piano*! Just not so colourless! Think of *mezzoforte*!'"[137]

P. A. Corri also associated *con espressione* with the employment of broad, un-notated arpeggiation. In this context, it is noteworthy that a century later, at the marking *espressivo* in Carl Reinecke's piano transcription of the Vorspiel to Act 5 of his opera *Manfred*, which he recorded on piano roll in 1905, he begins to arpeggiate much more broadly.

## *Morendo, Smorzando, Perdendosi, Calando*

Although all these terms have been commonly associated with relaxation of tempo, they are also suggestive of distinctive modes of expression, and evidently had quite particular connotations for individual composers. This was evidently the case with Dussek as the successive employment of the first three of these instructions in his Piano Sonata "Le retour à Paris" demonstrates (Ex. 10.5); and similar uses in close sequence are found in other early-19th-century music.

**Ex. 10.5** Dussek: "Le retour à Paris" op. 64 (in other sources op. 70 or 71).

[Finale: Scherzo Allegro con spirito]

---
[136] M. R[anken]: *Some Points of Violin Playing*, 19.
[137] Gaston Roman Dejmek: *Max Fiedler: Werden und Wirken* (Essen, 1940), 224. I am grateful to Johannes Leertouwer for alerting me to this quotation.

## Sostenuto

Sostenuto was sometimes used alone as a rather imprecise tempo direction, sometimes in conjunction with another tempo term, and sometimes as a term of expression. It appears as a tempo term in several lists. In the *Principes élémentaires de musique* it is in the second slowest tempo category between the largo-adagio group and the andante-allegretto group. Marx, however, listed it after *andante* and *andantino*, but before *andante con moto*. For Beethoven it seems to have signified a tempo somewhat, but not much, faster than he might have intended by *adagio*, to judge by his metronome marks for the *Sostenuto* in op. 112 (♩ = 84), where movement is largely in quarter-notes and the *Poco sostenuto* in op. 92 (♩ = 69), which includes a significant number of sixteenths. Spontini employed *sostenuto* and *poco sostenuto* with a similar meaning in *Olympie* and *Fernand Cortez*, in a somewhat slower tempo range than Beethoven (♩ = 50–63, with movement generally in eighths), and for him it seems to have been virtually synonymous with *andante sostenuto*. Wagner used *sostenuto* as a tempo term in its own right in *Der fliegende Holländer*, for sections to which he gave metronome marks comparable to the generally rather slow *andantes* (*andante* ₵ ♩ = 50–76; *sostenuto* ₵ ♩ = 50–69).

Brahms also used *sostenuto* as a tempo term: an instance is the *Un poco sostenuto* which opens his First Symphony. This, however, led to confusion with his employment of the very similar term *Poco sostenuto*, in a quite different sense, for the last seventeen bars of the first movement. In October 1881 he wrote to his publisher, Simrock, requesting him to change *Poco sostenuto* to *Meno allegro* since, he observed, "people always take the tempo of the introduction".[138] But the change was never made, though Brahms himself pencilled it into his own copy. Elsewhere, Brahms frequently used *sostenuto* and *poco sostenuto* in the sense of *meno mosso* or *allargando*, for instance in the last four bars of the third movement of his Second Symphony. At the beginning of the development section of the first movement of his G major Violin Sonata he wrote *poco a poco più sostenuto*; the fact that in this case he required a slower tempo, not merely a different expression, is demonstrated by the direction *poco a poco tempo I°* just before the recapitulation. And similar instructions to return to the original tempo are found in much earlier works, for instance towards the end of the first movement of the 1854 version of the B major Piano Trio. J. A. Fuller Maitland identified this usage of

---

[138] *Johannes Brahms Briefwechsel*, ed. Max Kalbeck (Tutzing, 1974), x, 192.

*sostenuto* with what he called the "romantic" school, but it was certainly used in the same sense at an early stage in the 19th century.[139]

Spontini clearly understood *sostenuto*, when appended to other tempo terms, to mean slower, hence in *Olympie*, Act II, no. 4, he headed the section *Andante espressivo sostenuto* with the metronome mark ♩ = 56; later in the number he wrote *Meno sostenuto* and gave the metronome mark ♩ = 72. In Berlioz's music, too, the term is used, in combination with *adagio, larghetto,* and *andante*, to indicate slower tempos than usual. Spohr employed the tempo term *andante sostenuto* on a couple of occasions (the male-voice part-songs op. 44 no. 1 and op. 90 no. 4), in both cases with metronome marks that equate with those he gave for movements headed *adagio*. Mendelssohn, on the other hand, does not seem to have used it in this way, but rather as an expression marking, perhaps calling for extremely *legato* execution. His use of the term in the Second Symphony (Lobgesang) op. 52, for instance, appears not to have been intended to affect the speed. He gave the same metronome mark (♪ = 100) to the *Andante* and to the *Andante sostenuto assai*, both of which movements are in $\frac{2}{4}$ and contain similar note values.

---

[139] John Alexander Fuller Maitland: 'Sostenuto' in H. C. Colles (ed.), *Grove's Dictionary*, 3rd edn (London, 1927), v, 81f.

# 11
# Tempo Modification

A degree of deviation from mechanical adherence to a constant beat is inevitable in a musically effective performance of any reasonably extended piece, even if the performer's primary intention is to adhere strictly to the initial tempo.[1] Departures from an unyielding observation of the beat, when they do not merely arise from lack of skill or negligence, will be the natural outcome of a musician's deliberate or subconscious response to the expressive content of the music.

During the 20th century, as more than a hundred years of recordings demonstrate, attitudes towards tempo modification changed radically.[2] In the first decades of the century, although there was considerable diversity, the notated text was often treated with substantial freedom of rhythm and tempo, ranging from extensive modifications of the pulse to subtler but noticeable fluctuations, which nevertheless remain closely centred on the prevailing tempo term. Later practice was increasingly characterized by steadiness of tempo, with noticeable deviation restricted mostly to occasional, slight relaxations at expressive points. As in so many areas of musical performance during the 20th century, the overall trend was towards a much more objective treatment of the notated text. In the first decades of the 21st century, mainstream orthodoxy still permitted very little flexibility of tempo in Classical and Romantic repertoire, where the text contains no explicit instruction to the contrary, and demanded a high degree of precision in executing the composer's notated rhythms. These requirements were reinforced by conservatoire teaching and the demands of auditions and competitions. Even in the world of period instrument performance, close adherence to similar norms remained the general rule. Although a limited amount of temporary relaxation of tempo was still tolerated at the ends of phrases or sections, the expressive use of *accelerando* remained very rare.

---

[1] The word *tempo* is used here with the dual sense inherent in the German word *Bewegung*, so that the phrase *tempo modification* encompasses both localized departures from mathematical observance of the note values in one or all parts and more extended alterations to the speed of the beat.

[2] Robert Philip: *Early Recordings and Musical Style* (Cambridge, 1992).

Throughout the Classical and Romantic periods, in contrast, there was a general recognition (as there had also been in the Baroque) that, if certain aesthetic borderlines were not crossed, holding back some notes or passages, and hurrying others was not merely permissible, but was an indispensable adjunct of sensitive and effective performance. C. P. E. Bach's list of the essential attributes of good performance concludes with "holding back, and pushing forward", and he commented: "whoever either does not use these things at all, or uses them at the wrong time, has a bad performance style".[3] The important questions that exercised musical authorities, therefore, were where, how, and to what extent such flexibility should be introduced. This was often highly controversial. At one extreme were musicians who believed that this expressive resource should be used sparingly and subtly, while at the other were those who introduced frequent and substantial tempo modifications. There is abundant evidence that examples of both these extremes could have been heard in professional performances throughout the period; but the balance between them did not remain constant; at different times and in different places influential opinion and practice varied significantly. Of course, in the period before recording, it is virtually impossible to know what was considered subtle and what was considered extreme. Early recordings can sometimes by paired with written advice given by performers in which words like "imperceptible" are used in connection with tempo modification, when the recordings demonstrate a degree of flexibility that does not seem at all imperceptible to early-21st-century ears.[4]

During the 18th and early 19th centuries, most of those who wrote about performance were in favour of a restrained employment of tempo flexibility where it was not marked by the composer (except in certain specific types of pieces such as fantasias or recitative). But, of course, their concept of restraint may well have been what more recent musicians would have characterized as license. Where flexibility was felt to be appropriate, particular emphasis was often laid on the use of specialized techniques of *tempo rubato*, which did not obviously disturb the underlying unity of tempo. Exceptions to this general rule seem largely to have been confined to a few individuals and schools of solo instrumentalists and singers. In the second half of the 19th century, a more pronounced degree of tempo modification,

---

[3] Bach, *Versuch*, i, 117.
[4] See Neal Peres Da Costa: *Off the Record* (Oxford, 2012).

in a wider range of musical genres, was sanctioned by influential sections of the musical élite, while some of the older established techniques of *tempo rubato* seem to have been less widely cultivated as the century drew to its close. During those years, the employment of more conspicuous tempo modification, which affected the steadiness of the beat, spread increasingly from solo and small ensemble performance to orchestral performance, encouraged by the advocacy of "interpretative" conducting by Wagner and his disciples. The influence of this approach, forcefully advanced in Wagner's polemical writings, was closely tied to the growing prestige of the New German School (*neudeutsche Schule*), and in due course made itself felt in France, Italy, and elsewhere.

Despite the evidence for significant modification of the beat by individual musicians during the 18th century, there is little to suggest that musicians in general explicitly challenged the notion that the beat should remain fundamentally steady unless the composer decreed otherwise. In the 19th century, on the other hand, the promotion of such ideas, and their practice as a matter of conviction by leading musicians of the day, provoked strong reactions from those who remained true to the older aesthetic, espoused most notably perhaps by Mendelssohn and his circle. It is questionable, however, whether musicians schooled in the modernist aesthetics of the 20th century would have regarded Mendelssohn and his followers as strict in tempo and rhythm. One of the most important of his admirers, Joseph Joachim, made recordings in 1903 that demonstrate his very notable elasticity of pulse and rhythm, which nevertheless retains a close relationship with the fundamental tempo. Joachim's pupil and biographer, Andreas Moser, reported specifically that he derived this aspect of his playing from Mendelssohn.[5]

The tension between these two approaches, and the strength of feeling it generated, may partly be explained by an apparent discrepancy between theory and practice among the champions of freedom of tempo. Although most of those who supported this approach, including Wagner, were insistent in their theoretical or polemical writings that tempo modification should be employed with discretion, it is evident from documentary evidence that one person's discretion was another's excess.

---

[5] See below, pp. 612–13.

## Types of Tempo Modification

There are various distinctly different ways in which, where no modification of tempo has been indicated by the composer, the note values, or the beat, can be manipulated by the performer for expressive purposes. These fall into two basic categories: one involves genuine alteration of the tempo; the other, which is intimately related to improvisation and embellishment, causes a redistribution of note values and accents in an individual strand of the music, but leaves the regularity of the beat fundamentally undisturbed. C. P. E. Bach described and recommended both types, though he considered each of them to be appropriate to different circumstances. Having warned that added embellishments should not unintentionally disrupt the pulse, he observed:

> Often, however, one can purposefully commit the most beautiful offences against the beat, but with the distinction that, if one is playing alone or with a few people who have good judgment, it is permissible to make an impact on the tempo as a whole, for the accompanying players, instead of letting themselves be led astray, will be far more likely to become alert, and will enter into our intentions; if, however, one is playing with a larger accompanying body, and if indeed the latter consists of a mixture of people of unequal accomplishment, one can only make a change that goes against the regular distribution of the bar in one's own part, for the basic pulse must be kept absolutely steady.[6]

The term *rubato* has been used to describe both these types of tempo modification since the end of the 18th century, although it was predominantly employed at that time to designate techniques of Bach's second kind. During the 19th century, the expression *rubato* was increasingly invoked to describe his first type, but general acceptance of that meaning was slow to develop. An early instance of a definition that might imply the first kind of tempo modification is found in Thomas Busby's 1786 *Dictionary*, where *rubato* is explained as "An expression applied to a time alternately accelerated and retarded for the purpose of enforcing the expression";[7] but this is ambiguous and could perhaps refer to fluctuation within a steady beat. Türk, however, acknowledged, in a gloss on the index entry for *Tempo rubato* in his

---

[6] Bach: *Versuch*, i, 120.
[7] Thomas Busby: 'Tempo rubato' in *A Complete Dictionary of Music* (London, [1801]), no pagination.

*Klavierschule*, that some considered the use of *accelerando* and *ritardando* to be covered by this expression. Yet most dictionaries and treatises continued to use the term in its traditional sense right through the 19th century; thus, *rubato* and *tempo rubato* were defined by James Alexander Hamilton in the 1830s as stealing from one part of the bar to give back elsewhere "so that the time of each bar is not altered in the aggregate", and this definition was still reproduced in the 1882 revised edition of *Hamilton's Dictionary*.[8]

The history of tempo modification between the mid-18th century and the beginning of the 20th century reveals many different approaches and aesthetic attitudes, as well as changing notions of where one or the other type might be most appropriate. The principal techniques and practices may be categorized as follows:

1. The classic *tempo rubato* occurs when the accompaniment (or in the case of a keyboard instrument, usually the left hand) remains steady, while the melodic line is modified.
   (a) A single note, or rest, may be lengthened where it has a particular expressive or structural function, and the time that is lost will be regained by hurrying the immediately following notes.
   (b) The relationship of the melodic line to the bass is modified throughout a phrase, an extended passage, or even a whole movement. This technique, involving syncopation, was widely used, particularly in the 18th century, to create a special effect or to vary a passage on repetition. It required skill and understanding of the rules of composition on the part of the performer not to produce inappropriate harmonic clashes with the bass, though the retardation and anticipation of essential harmony notes. Even when the technique was employed by experts, it will sometimes have caused effects that would not normally have been written down.
   (c) In addition to, or instead of redistribution of the note values, embellishments in the form of *fiorituras* might be added to the melodic line in such a way that it appears to be rhythmically independent of the accompaniment. The employment of this technique can be traced from C. P. E. Bach and Franz Benda to Dussek,

---

[8] Hamilton: 'Tempo rubato' in *A Dictionary of Two Thousand [. . .] Musical Terms*, 4th edn (London, [1837]); and *Hamilton's Dictionary of Musical terms. New Edition [. . .] Enlarged* (London, [1883]) (copies in the Bodleian Library, Oxford).

Chopin, and beyond, though with the passage of time, as with many of the above-mentioned *tempo rubato* practices, it became a resource for the composer rather than for the performer.
2. Modification of the basic pulse of the music either momentarily or for a more extended period, for dramatic, expressive or structural purposes.
   (a) This can occur on the small scale as the lengthening, without restitution, of a single beat or rest.
   (b) There can be a gradual slowing down or speeding up of the pulse over several beats or bars.
   (c) It can involve the adoption of a slower or faster basic tempo for a whole phrase or section, either abruptly or preceded by a *ritardando* or *accelerando*. In such cases the change of speed can either be slight, and scarcely perceptible to the casual listener, or can result in the establishment of an unmistakably different tempo.

## Modification of Tempo over a Steady Beat

During the 19th century, growing emphasis on tempo modification that necessitated an alteration of the basic pulse was accompanied by correspondingly less focus on the types of *tempo rubato* that were obtained without significant disturbance of a regular beat. Many 18th- and early-19th-century accounts, however, suggest that, until at least the 1830s, *tempo rubato* in its various forms was still widely regarded as the most legitimate method of achieving tempo flexibility. Some writers, even in the early 19th century, seem not to have recognized any other kind of tempo modification as desirable.

Applied to a single note or a group of notes that were slightly longer or shorter than their written length, subtle flexibility might be present for much of the time in the performance of a sensitive musician without noticeably disturbing the regularity of the beat, but this was not normally identified specifically as *tempo rubato*.[9] The term was generally understood to mean a more radical reorganization of the note values, a redistribution of accentuation, or even the addition of rhythmically free embellishment, any of which could be introduced as a variant to the notated text. *Tempo rubato*, under the name *rubamento di tempo*, was explained by Pier Francesco Tosi's translator, J. E.

---

[9] This is considered further in Ch. 14.

Galliard, in 1742 as "when the Bass goes an exactly regular Pace, the other Part retards or anticipates in a singular Manner, for the Sake of Expression, but after a Time return to its Exactness, to be guided by the Bass".[10] Leopold Mozart, like other 18th-century writers, elaborated on this manner of "postponing or anticipating the notes" against a steady accompaniment, apparently referring primarily to note redistribution, but he remarked in a footnote that an effective *tempo rubato* was "more easily demonstrated than described".[11]

J. A. P. Schulz's discussion of the subject in the 1770s provides a good example of the widespread view that this was the most artistic manner of obtaining flexibility of tempo in performance, though it also confirms that real alteration of the pulse was often encountered, and that accompanying parts sometimes failed to accommodate it. Schulz observed:

> Singers and players often introduce a holding-back or a pressing-forward which the composer has not marked, and these are certainly often of very good effect. But whoever does this must have an adequate knowledge of harmony, so that he does not go against the rules of strict composition. In addition, one must be aware whether the other accompanying parts allow such alterations in the movement. If the violins or flutes accompany the principal part in unison, it can neither delay nor hurry, since it would only make seconds with the other parts.
> 
> One should not confuse the so-called dragging and hurrying, which results from a real lack of feeling for the true tempo, with the appropriate and expressive holding-back and pressing-forward; for these are real and serious errors, which ruin the whole harmony of a piece.[12]

Some musical authorities continued to take a very hard line on the matter into the 19th century, requiring an extremely restrained approach. In 1804, Louis Adam, for instance, asserted:

> One of the first qualities that is required in musical performance is to observe the beat; without this there would be nothing but indecision,

---

[10] Tosi: *Opinioni de'cantori antici e moderni, o sieno Osservazioni sopra il canto figurato* (Bologna, 1723), trans. and ed. Galliard as *Observations on the Florid Song; or, Sentiments on the Ancient and Modern Singers* (London, 1742), 156.
[11] Mozart: *Versuch*, 263.
[12] Schulz: 'Verzögerung' in Sulzer, *Allgemeine Theorie*, ii, 1237.

vagueness, and confusion. It is necessary, therefore, that the pupil habituates himself to play exactly in time and endeavours to keep the same tempo from beginning to end of a piece. It is not permissible to alter the beat unless the composer has indicated it, or the expression demands it; still it is necessary to be very sparing of this resource. [. . .] Doubtless expression requires that one holds back or hurries certain notes in the melody, but these rallentandos should not be continual throughout a piece, but only in those places where the expression of a languid melody or the passion of an agitated melody requires a rallentando or a more animated tempo. In this case it is the melody that must be changed and the bass should strictly mark the beat.[13]

Thus, Adam limited his acceptance of unspecified tempo modification to occasional places where "the expression demands it"; while, for the most part, he required it to take place within the framework of a stable tempo, that is, as *tempo rubato* in the strictest sense of the term.

A somewhat more relaxed attitude, which nevertheless indicates that the basic pulse was expected to remain essentially constant, can be found in a reissue, much altered and expanded, of Leopold Mozart's *Violinschule*, published in 1804. The anonymous reviser, J. C. W. Petiscus, commented:

An appropriate hurrying and holding-back is a helpful adjunct of expression, if it is applied with taste and in the right place. In order to strengthen the effect of his playing it may be permissible that the solo player performs the lyrical passages in his piece somewhat slower, but seeks to give the passagework more life and strength through a slight hurrying of the tempo. We are only talking, however, about a small, imperceptible alteration of the tempo. What is even more permissible, however, for the sake of expression and is often of very beautiful effect, is a slight alteration of the individual beats without displacing the bar as a whole. The player may dwell somewhat longer than written on the most important, emphatic notes; the thus modified time is regained by hurrying on the following notes. It is understood that also this expressive hesitating and hurrying must be introduced rarely and with taste. It is no more permissible for it really to displace the beat than it is for it to confuse the [musical] ideas. Finally, it should not

---

[13] Adam: *Méthode*, 160.

occur too often, so that it does not degenerate into an affectation and lose its effect.[14]

Türk, too, had stressed the necessity of employing the latter kind of expressive lingering as an adjunct of fine performance, cautioning: "It is understood that the following note loses as much of its value as the accented note receives from it."[15] In both Türk's and Petiscus's treatises, the explanation of the appropriate circumstances in which expressive lingering might be employed correspond closely with those usually given for the application of expressive accent.[16]

A generation later, Spohr in his *Violinschule* described this type of expressive lingering in his explanation of how Rode's Seventh Concerto should be performed (see Ex. 12.10). A similar procedure is evidently intended to be applied, probably together with vibrato, in many of Rode's own Caprices in instances where he marks notes with the sign <>. A passage from Rode's Third Caprice (Ex. 11.1) was described thus in the Joachim and Moser *Violinschule*:

Here the vibrato necessitates not only a slight lingering on the notes marked < >, but the bow should also support the trembling by a soft pressure on the string. The time lost on the vibrated note must be regained from the notes that follow, so that the proceeding takes place without in any way interrupting the rhythmic flow of the passage.[17]

Ex. 11.1 Rode: Third Caprice, in Joachim and Moser: *Violinschule*, iii, 7.

Joseph Joachim's and Marie Soldat's recorded performances show that, along with more obtrusive modifications of tempo, they continued to employ this type of *rubato*; and similar practices are a prominent feature of Carl

---

[14] Anon [Johann Conrad Wilhelm Petiscus]: *Violinschule oder Anweisung die Violine zu spielen von Leopold Mozart. Neue umgearbeitete und vermehrte Ausgabe* (Leipzig, [1804]); repr. edn (Leipzig, 1817), 68.
[15] Türk: *Klavierschule*, 339.
[16] See Ch. 2.
[17] Joachim and Moser: *Violinschule*, iii, 7.

Reinecke's recordings. Indeed, even in the later 19th century many writers who discussed expressive lingering, both on notes and rests, emphasized the necessity of regaining the lost time. But in practice there was often a combination of quasi *tempo rubato* and tempo flexibility; and this may have been increasingly envisaged during the 19th century.

*Tempo rubato* could, however, involve a more radical redistribution of the note values during an extended passage. In its most straightforward form this might amount to little more than simple syncopation; and it is shown thus by, among others, Marpurg, Agricola, Hiller, Lasser, Koch, and Türk. Koch and Türk elaborated the idea of *tempo rubato* as being essentially confined to a regular cross-rhythm or displacement of the metrical accent, and as such it came to be regarded primarily as a resource for the composer. Indeed, Koch declared in 1808 that the improvisatory *tempo rubato* as used by Franz Benda in the Adagios of his sonatas and concertos was as good as obsolete and that, where it was still used, it was much more unobtrusively employed than formerly. He suggested that this development was no bad thing:

> partly because modern composers work out in full the adagio movements of their concertos, not at all representing them only as skeletons like the old composers who left their elaboration to the solo player; partly and especially also because the quest for imitation easily oversteps the bounds beyond which this type of performance sinks into ridiculousness and nonsense.[18]

In fact, however, many performers of Koch's generation, and younger, continued to advocate and employ *tempo rubato*, though always with the warning that it should be tastefully and sparingly introduced. Two years after the publication of Koch's article the veteran singer Domenico Corri defined *tempo rubato* as

> a detraction of part of the time from one note, and restoring it by increasing the length of another, or vice versa; so that whilst a singer is, in some measure, singing ad libitum, the orchestra, which accompanies him keeps the time firmly and regularly. Composers seem to have arranged their works in such a manner as to admit of this liberty, without offending the laws of harmony: one caution, however, becomes highly necessary; namely that this grace, or licence, is to be used with moderation and discretion, in

---

[18] Koch: 'Ueber den technischen Ausdruck Tempo rubato', *Allgemeine musikalische Zeitung*, x (1807–8), 518f.

order to avoid confusion; for too frequent a use of Tempo Rubato, may produce *Tempo indiavolato*.[19]

Spohr, although he gave only one specific example of *tempo rubato* in his *Violinschule*, later warned that orchestral players should not try to follow a soloist's *tempo rubato*, which suggests that he did not consider it unusual in concertos.[20] At about the same time, Baillot described Viotti's *tempo rubato* (which he called *temps dérobé*) and attempted to notate two examples of his use of it, warning, however, that "Up to a certain point this device can be notated, but like all impassioned accents it will lose much of its effect if it is executed in cold blood."[21] Baillot's examples show less a redistribution of notes, than a redistribution of accent and articulation (Ex. 11.2a–b).

**Ex. 11.2** a–b. (*a*) Viotti: Violin Concerto no. 19 in Baillot: *L'art du violon*, 136f; (*b*) Viotti: Violin Concerto no. 18 in Baillot: *L'art du violon*, 137.

---

[19] Corri: *The Singers Preceptor*, 6.
[20] Spohr: *Violinschule*, 249. See above.
[21] Baillot: *L'art du violon*, 136.

A few examples in which composers wrote out an elaborate *tempo rubato* of this kind nicely illustrate the effect of more flexible and radical note redistribution. The second movement of Haydn's String Quartet op. 54 no. 2 provides a particularly extended and subtle example, showing how an adept late-18th-century exponent of the art might have applied a combination of rhythmic redistribution and melodic embellishment to the whole of an Adagio (Ex. 11.3).

**Ex. 11.3** Haydn: String Quartet op. 54/2/ii.

**Ex. 11.3** Continued

**Ex. 11.3** Continued

Ex. 11.3 Continued

Mozart's piano music contains several revealing examples of the type of *rubato* he might have introduced into his own performances to vary the repetitions of a melody, in accordance with the principle referred to in an often-cited passage from his letter of 1777 where he reported that the people in Augsburg could not grasp the fact that in an Adagio, when he executed *tempo rubato* with the right hand, the left stayed firmly in tempo, because with them, the left hand always followed the right.[22] The difference between the autograph and the Artaria first edition of the Piano Sonata K. 332 is particularly revealing, for in preparing the work for publication, Mozart evidently decided to include a stylized version of the kind of ornamentation and *rubato* that, in his own performance, he might have introduced on repetitions of the theme (Ex. 11.4a–b). And the A minor Rondo K. 511 incorporates written-out variants that reflect this practice (Ex. 11.5a–b).[23] The Cavatina from Beethoven's String Quartet op. 130 contains a shorter passage illustrating how he might perhaps have envisaged the use of the technique at moments of special expressiveness (Ex. 11.6).

---

[22] Mozart: *Briefe*, ii, 83.
[23] Rosenblum: *Performance Practices*, 379–80.

Ex. 11.4 a–b. Mozart: Piano Sonata K. 332/ii. (a) autograph; (b) 1st edn.

Ex. 11.5 a–b. Mozart: Rondo K. 511. (a) 5ff; (b) 85ff.

Ex. 11.6 Beethoven: String Quartet op. 130/v.

On occasion, later 19th-century composers incorporated the stylized, syncopated *tempo rubato* into their music. Good examples are to be found in Liszt's *Canzonet napolitana*, in which for the first sixteen bars the right hand is a sixteenth-note behind the left (Ex. 11.7), and the fourth piece from Schumann's *Noveletten* op. 21, where a theme is varied in this way on its repetition (Ex. 11.8).

Ex. 11.7 Liszt: *Canzona napolitana.*

Ex. 11.8 Schumann: *Noveletten* op. 21/4.

Yet, despite the neat and convenient notation of *tempo rubato* by many writers as simple syncopation or displaced accent, it seems clear that the rhythmic displacement practised by the best players and singers was, as Baillot's caveat suggests, considerably more complex. Perhaps the most subtle attempts to notate *tempo rubato* are to be found in the works of Chopin, who was celebrated for his mastery of the type of keyboard *tempo rubato*, practised by Mozart, in which the left hand remained in time while the right hand anticipated or retarded the notes of the melody. Chopin employed intricate, carefully elaborated notation to convey the free and improvisatory impression that his performances conveyed; indeed he was criticized in a Parisian review of his Nocturnes op. 15 in 1834 for his affectation in writing his music "almost as it should be played"; the reviewer went on to remark that, in any case, it was not possible to notate adequately "this swaying, languid, groping style, this style which no known arrangement of note values can well express".[24] Since Chopin expected ornaments, as a matter of course, to be executed on the beat, he often used small notes, additional to the time of the bar, to indicate displacement of the melody from the bass, as in the Nocturne op. 15 no. 2 (Ex. 11.9a–b).

Ex. 11.9 a–b. Chopin: Nocturne op. 15 no 2. (*a*) b. 1; (*b*) b. 9.

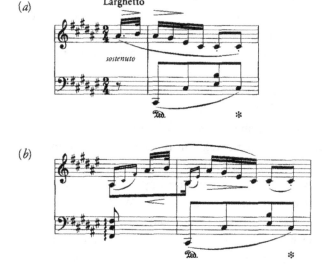

---

[24] *Le Pianiste*, i/5 (March 1834), 78, cited in Richard Hudson, *Stolen Time: A History of Tempo Rubato* (Oxford, 1994), 190.

Among 19th-century performers who appear to have continued the practice of this art in a more elaborate form were the violinist Paganini and the singer Manuel García (1775–1832), Rossini's first Almaviva in *Il barbiere di Siviglia*. García's son (also Manuel) cited an example of his father's style of employing *tempo rubato*, which is especially instructive, since he attempted to notate it much more literally than was usual. Garcia's account indicates how, in Italian opera, *tempo rubato* remained a significant means of expression well into the 19th century Having prefaced his remarks by the statement that "Instead of slowing down the tempo, one should have recourse to the tempo rubato", he continued:

By tempo rubato is meant the momentary increase of values, which is given to one or several sounds, to the detriment of the others.

This distribution of notes into long and short, breaks the monotony of regular movements, and gives greater vehemence to bursts of passion. Ex. [Ex. 11.10a]

To make tempo rubato perceptible in singing, the accents and tempo of an accompaniment should be strictly maintained. The singer is then at liberty to increase and decrease the note values alternately to give certain phrases an entirely now aspect. Accelerando and rallentando require the voice and accompaniment to work together to slow down or speed up the tempo. It is therefore a serious mistake to use a rallentando in the penultimate bar, instead of the tempo rubato, as for example in (A) [Ex. 11.10b];

In the first way, while aiming for enthusiasm, one simply falls into awkwardness and heaviness.

This prolongation is usually conceded to appoggiaturas, to notes placed on long syllables, and those which are *naturally prominent in the harmony*, or to those that are meant to stand out. In all such cases, the time lost must be regained by accelerating other notes. This is one of the best means for giving colour to melodies. Ex. [Ex. 11.10c]

Two artists of a very different kind, García (my father) and Paganini, excelled in the use of tempo rubato, applied *by phrase*. While the tempo was regularly maintained by the orchestra, they would abandon themselves to their inspiration, and only coincided with the bass when the chord changed, or else at the very end of the phrase. An excellent perception of *rhythm*, and great aplomb on the part of the musician, however, are requisite for the adoption of this method. This procedure can hardly be used except in passages where the harmony is stable, or only slightly varied. Apart from these exceptions it would be very harsh on the ear, and would be very difficult for the performer. Here, however, is a successful application of this difficult method. [footnote: "This passage offers an approximate example of the use which the author's late father made of the tempo rubato"]: [Ex. 11.10d]

The tempo rubato is also useful in in another respect: for preparing a trill; it facilitates the trill by allowing its preparation to be taken from the value of the preceding notes. Ex. [Ex. 11.10e] Employed indiscriminately, and with affectation, tempo rubato destroys all balance, and tortures the melody.[25]

Ex. 11.10 a–e. García: *École*, ii, 24f. In (*a*) he also gives examples from Mozart: *Figaro* and Zingarelli: *Romeo*. In (*c*) he also gives an example from Donizetti: *Anna Bolena*.

[25] García: *École*, ii, 24f.

**Ex. 11.10**  Continued

(e)

## Tempo Rubato as Arhythmical Embellishment

A somewhat different type of *tempo rubato* goes back at least to C. P. E. Bach, who used this term to describe an irregular number of notes performed independently above a regular bass; Ex. 11.11, from his Sechs Sonaten [...] mit veränderten Reprisen, illustrates the sort of situation to which he refers. Illustrations of similar procedures can be found in the embellishments that Bach's Berlin colleague Franz Benda introduced into his own violin sonatas.[26] This sort of thing was sometimes written out, but it seems much more often to have been introduced in the form of improvised ornamentation.

**Ex. 11.11**  C. P. E. Bach: *Sechs Sonaten [...] mit veränderten Reprisen* Wq. 50/4/i. [Allegretto grazioso]

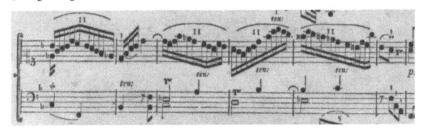

Examples similar to Bach's and Benda's are also preserved as additions to the original text of Viotti's slow movements, which he is known to have embellished lavishly in this manner; some are found as pencilled additions

---

[26] Staatsbibliothek zu Berlin–Preußischer Kulturbesitz, Mus.ms. 1315/15.

by the composer himself, while others are suggested by elaborations of the melodic line in editions by his pupils and followers (Ex. 11.12).[27]

Ex. 11.12  Viotti: Violin Concerto no. 27/ii, in Chappell White, ed., *Recent Researches in the Music of the Pre-Classical, Classical, and Early Romantic Eras*, v (Madison, WI, 1976).

In the piano music of Dussek, Field, Hummel, Chopin, and others such things may well have occurred as improvised additions in performances by the composers themselves, but they are also frequently indicated in the notation. The well-known description of Chopin's *tempo rubato*—"Fancy a tree with its branches swayed by the wind; the stem represents the steady time, the moving leaves are the melodic inflections. This is what is meant by *Tempo* and *Tempo rubato*"[28]—seems neatly to describe the effect appropriate to many passages in Chopin's works (Ex. 11.13).

Ex. 11.13  Chopin: Impromptu op. 36 no. 2 1st edn.
[Andantino]

---

[27] See Ch. 13. Robberechts's manuscript. Other published examples may be found in Baillot's *L'art du violon*, 159 (also in Stowell, *Violin Technique*, 351), and in Ferdinand David (ed.), *Concert-Studien für die Violine. Eine Sammlung von Violin-Solo-Compositionen berühmter älterer Meister, zum Gebrauch beim Conservatorium der Musik in Leipzig* (Leipzig, Bartholf Senff, n.d.), i.

[28] Edward Dannreuther: *Musical Ornamentation* (London, 1893–95), ii, 161. Richard Hudson, in his wide-ranging and informative study *Stolen Time*, 191ff, gives other versions of this statement from Chopin's contemporaries together with descriptions of his treatment of tempo rubato.

The two principal types of *tempo rubato*, the one consisting of a redistribution of note values and the other involving the performance of *fioriture* that were rhythmically independent of a regularly moving bass, represent, in some sense, two quite distinct techniques. In the hands of the most accomplished artists, however, the distinction became blurred, since, as can be seen from García's examples, redistribution of notes and accents and addition of ornamentation seem often to have been used in combination. Henri Herz, apparently oblivious of the use of *tempo rubato* by his contemporary Chopin, provides some interesting insights into Dussek's employment of the technique, but certainly implies that it was encountered much less frequently towards the middle of the 19th century than formerly:

> A too exact and uniform tempo at times produces monotony. Each melodic phrase needs to be slower than the brilliant passage which follows it; sometimes even the double character of the accompaniment and the melody requires a different rhythmic effect from each hand. Thus, while the right hand seems to lose itself in frivolous variations, the left, accenting the offbeats in the bass, follows it in heavy steps and with syncopated notes. This case, like all those where the expression is complex, requires not only hands which are perfectly independent from one another, but also, so to speak, a different soul in each of them. It is thus that Dussek spread a hazy and melancholy atmosphere over certain passages, by letting the right hand sing in a vague and careless manner, while the left performed arpeggios strictly in time. I do not know why this manner of phrasing, formerly so widespread, has now fallen into oblivion.[29]

## Modification of the Basic Pulse

Many 18th-century musicians besides C. P. E. Bach discussed the types of tempo modification that involved a real disturbance of the basic pulse, and a few of the more pedagogically minded or meticulous ones attempted to indicate it graphically. Türk proposed several symbols for tempo modification in the *Vorrede* of his *Sechs leichte Klaviersonaten [. . .] erster Theil* published

---

[29] Herz: *Méthode*, 20.

in 1783 (Ex. 11.14a–d), and Georg Friedrich Wolf included these symbols in the second edition of his keyboard method in 1784.[30] Curiously, however, having provided symbols for *accelerando* and abrupt changes to a faster tempo, Türk made no use of them in the sonatas.

Ex. 11.14 a–d. Türk: *Sechs leichte Klaviersonaten* (Leipzig and Halle, 1783), erster Theil, Vorrede.
(*a*) Passages getting gradually slower; (*b*) Single ideas that should be played more slowly; (*c*) Passages getting gradually faster; (*d*) Single ideas that should be played more quickly.

Türk's consideration of tempo modification is among the most detailed late-18th-century treatments of the subject. Having stated that "It is difficult to determine all the situations in which accelerating or retarding can take place",[31] he suggested that *accelerando* could be effective: for the most powerful places "in pieces which have a character of vehemence, anger, rage, fury and the like"; for single motifs "which are repeated more powerfully (usually higher)"; "occasionally when gentle feelings are interrupted by a lively passage"; or "for a motif that should unexpectedly arouse a violent emotion"[32]

He considered that *tardando* could produce a telling effect: "in exceptionally tender, languishing, sad passages in which the feeling is, so to speak, concentrated on a single point" (perhaps Ex. 11.15 furnishes an example of what he meant); before certain pauses "as if the strength is gradually exhausted"; in "places which, towards the end of a piece (or section), are marked with *diminuendo, diluendo, smorzando*, and the like"[33]; for lead-in figures, not only when they are written in small notes or explicitly *senza tempo*, but also "when the composer has kept to the normal method of writing", for which he gave his examples marked a); or for "a languid idea on its repetition", as in his example b) (Ex. 11.16).[34]

---

[30] Wolf: *Unterricht*, 2nd edn, 85f.
[31] Türk: *Klavierschule*, 371.
[32] Türk: *Klavierschule*, 371, §66.
[33] Türk: *Klavierschule*, 371, §67.
[34] Türk: *Klavierschule*, 372, §69.

Ex. 11.15 Türk: *Sechs leichte Klaviersonaten*, erste Theil, 17.
[Allegro con spirito ¢]

Ex. 11.16 Türk: *Klavierschule*, 372.

He also proposed that an abrupt change of speed could sometimes be appropriate. For instance, a somewhat slower tempo could be adopted: for "a tender, moving passage between two lively, fiery ideas" (as in Ex. 11.17); or, he suggested, "in general, holding back may be most appropriate in slow-moving passages". This advice seems rather vague, but Ex. 11.18 from his *Sechs leichte Klaviersonaten* may indicate the type of passage he had in mind.[35]

Nevertheless, Türk recommended, like Bach, that such things should be attempted only "when playing alone or with very alert accompanists".[36] In the 1802 revision of his treatise he added: "But here I remind you again that the movement should hardly be changed noticeably when you hesitate or when you accelerate. For it has a bad effect, and is generally very detrimental to unity, when one almost passes over from Allegro into an Adagio, or the reverse."[37]

---

[35] Türk: *Klavierschule*, 372, §68.
[36] Türk: *Klavierschule*, 371, §65.
[37] Türk: *Klavierschule*, 2nd edn, 417.

**Ex. 11.17** Türk: *Sechs leichte Klaviersonaten*, erster Theil, 10.
[Presto assai ¢]

**Ex. 11.18** Türk: *Sechs leichte Klaviersonaten*, erster Theil, 22.
[Moderato e con afflizione 2/4]

Türk clearly believed that this type of tempo nuancing was a legitimate, indeed necessary, aspect of cultivated performance. In his *Vorrede*, having proposed his signs for tempo modification, he remarked that "almost every idea requires its individual expressive delivery".[38] But, in agreement with the general view, he acknowledged that tempo flexibility was something to be used judiciously with respect to its degree, except in such things as fantasias, preludes, and caprices, where the notation itself often indicates a requirement for substantial freedom of pulse. Türk's remarks also imply that, in practice, more extreme modifications of the tempo than would have been approved of by the majority of accomplished musicians were often to be heard; but, of course, too much or too little will have been relative to 18th-century expectations, which were almost certainly very different from those of the later 20th and early 21st centuries, when, except for expressive *ritenuto* on very short figures, any kind of noticeable tempo variation, especially *accelerando* in places where the composer did not indicate it, has been strongly discouraged.

Tempo fluctuations that some highly accomplished musicians regarded as excessive, were not confined to performances by less experienced, or amateur musicians; they were also associated with soloists of distinction and reputation. After a visit to Salzburg in 1778 by the violinist Anton Janitsch and the

---

[38] Türk: *Sechs leichte Klaviersonaten*, erster Theil, Vorrede, [2].

cellist Joseph Reicha, for instance, Leopold Mozart described their playing in a letter to his son, praising many aspects of their performance; but, in conformity with his warning against the wilful treatment of tempo in his *Violinschule*,[39] he remarked: "Both, however, have Becke's fault of dragging the time, holding back the whole orchestra by a wink and by their movement, and then returning to the original tempo."[40] Since Janitsch and Reicha were employed at the Oettingen-Wallerstein court, this suggests the possibility of localized practices, but it seems likely that such habits were, and remained, widespread.

Discussion of tempo modification involving alteration of the pulse of the music was prominent in music journals and instruction books during the first few decades of the 19th century, suggesting that the appropriateness, or otherwise, of this expressive resource was very much a live issue. Writers were generally concerned to caution restraint. In 1804, Friedrich Guthmann aimed his article "On Deviation from the Beat" specifically at amateur musicians. He explained:

> By deviation from the beat, I mean the localized hurrying and hesitating which the player allows himself out of feeling or principle without the composer having clearly indicated it. Not unreasonably one asks: should this deviation from the beat be allowed? I say: Yes! [. . .] Every fine art loves a certain freedom—certainly not religious, but also not constrained by rules. In the latter case this would cease entirely. All too often one sacrifices the end to the means. The beat is the means by which we express our feelings more freely and better. It should not, however, inhibit them. Our feeling can indeed—so to say—overflow, but not cascade over—their rise and fall is so gradual, the rapid or slow flight of fancy depends so much on the spiritual content of the music being played—that one certainly cannot indicate all this with notes and words, let alone prescribe it definitively.—While speaking, the narrator becomes now more ardent, now more serious; the subject fills his soul more and more the longer he deals with it; his words become quieter and louder, his language becomes passionate—he speaks from heart to heart. So does the [musical] performer. He begins rather calmly, the musical subject interests him, animates him increasingly, his feelings resonate more deeply and strongly—is it to be wondered at if he gradually hurries or hesitates without being aware of it himself? Would it be right, would it be more effective if he did not do it? Indeed, the best dancer is not he who calculates his steps mathematically and timidly, who cannot

---

[39] See esp. Mozart: *Violinschule*, 262.
[40] *Mozart Briefe und Auszeichnungen*, ii, 244.

sometimes gracefully make a small deviation and variation. (Of course, I speak about solo playing and singing!)

He was at pains to point out, however, that a distinction needed to be made between this type of artistically effective flexibility and mere unrhythmicality, asserting:

> This deliberate deviation from the beat must, however, be distinguished from the unsteadiness that results either from undisciplined emotions, or from inattention. One should not believe that a beautiful performance style requires arbitrary, unmotivated swaying back and forth in the tempo, or, like the clumsy actor, making movements that are useless and that have no purpose.—Passions in music—as in life—must be controlled if they are to be useful, not harmful. Through much study, combined with an internal feeling for the pulse of the music, one will get to the point of giving every passage its appropriate tempo.—The controlled sentiment must, as it were, only shimmer through, not burst forth impetuously. [...] The overall tempo must remain constant, even if it deviates in individual passages. Where a theme is presented from different angles, one can also modify the tempo a little, according to circumstances, without its being specifically indicated.[41]

The following year, Guthmann contributed an article about an imaginary piano performance in which:

> Like flashes of lightning, one heard here and there unexpected but very well calculated accentuations, which gave the thoughts that were presented more novelty and interest, facilitated their understanding, and kept the soul in a state of excitement. No note was blurred or meaningless. Although the virtuoso deviated noticeably from the tempo in individual passages, sometimes more, sometimes less, the main character of the movement always shone through, and these deviations only served to make it shine more brightly on all sides. What was most peculiar was that one almost forgot that he had deviated; one said to oneself, conscious of the deviation, that this passage could be performed in this way and no other![42]

---

[41] Friedrich Guthmann: 'Ueber Abweichung vom Takte', *Allgemeine musikalische Zeitung*, vii (1804–5), 347–49.
[42] Guthmann: 'Das Konzert auf dem Fortepiano. Eine Phantasie', *Allgemeine musikalische Zeitung*, viii (1805–6), 398.

Shortly afterwards, G. W. Fink addressed the issue in the same journal. In a series of articles on dynamic and articulation markings he touched upon the subject of holding back or hurrying the tempo on short phrases, single bars, or individual beats. He observed:

> It would be extremely pedantic if anyone were to venture to rob the player of this freedom, which, applied with taste, is able to invest the simplest ideas with a splendid, exalted spirit (as the sensitive singer, Mlle Jagemann, as Sextus in Titus [*La clemenza di Tito*], does at the often-repeated words "That is more than the pains of death"). I treasure and love this manner of performance, just as I and anyone else who is receptive to beauty must treasure and love it. But the finer and tenderer something is, the more it can be spoiled.[43]

And he went on to warn against over-frequent use, which he believed would seriously weaken the effect.

In fact, even allowing for the exaggeration to which writers, seeking to make a point, are prone, many sources indicate that around 1800 exaggerated changes of tempo where none were indicated by the composer had become endemic to the extent that this style of performance was beginning to be accepted as normal, at least by a considerable portion of the concert-going public. In 1799, a report on a concert given by the horn-playing Brün brothers in Hamburg mentioned, as if it were something remarkable, that they kept regular time during their concerto performance, noting: "So, for example, they never beat time—it was also not necessary, for they themselves kept the tempo very exactly; therefore they were also so well accompanied, as certainly no ever-so-efficient time beater has been, or will be accompanied here."[44]

Carl Cannabich (1771–1806), who was appointed Hofmusikdirektor in Munich around that time, seems to have been responsible for encouraging substantial tempo flexibility there, which many years later still remained a prominent feature of performance style in Munich. A writer in 1819 lamented, "they didn't give it up, the new taste was established, even after the death of the founder they thought of nothing better". And he complained that even when a fine singer tried to employ what he regarded as better practices, "the beat, tempo, expression, declamation, cantabile had become pedantic

---

[43] Gottfried Wilhelm Fink: 'Ueber Takt, Taktarten, und ihr Charakteristisches', *Allgemeine musikalische Zeitung*, xi (1808–9), 230.

[44] Anon.: 'Briefe über Tonkunst und Tonkünstler', *Allgemeine musikalische Zeitung*, i (1798–99), 622.

terms: an eternal ritardando, accelerando, which they mistakenly called tempo rubato, had taken their place".[45]

In 1802, Koch commented sarcastically that if musicians had difficulty accompanying a performer who made much use of tempo flexibility, they could "console themselves with the dictum in the improved edition of the musical-catechism, that true expression does not always lie within the limits of the beat, but often requires sometimes more fire, sometimes more moderation in the performance.—Thus, arbitrary treatment of tempo gradually becomes the order of the day."[46] Koch's cautious statement that a specific tempo should be maintained "without very noticeable deviation", however, makes clear that he did not expect it to be adhered to rigidly.[47] At about the same time, referring specifically to pianists, Louis Adam approved of what he regarded as appropriate tempo modification but observed: "Some have made it fashionable not to play in time, and perform every type of music like a fantasia, prelude, caprice. They believe thus to give more expression to a piece, and they change it in such a manner as to make it unrecognizable."[48]

Another opponent of obtrusive tempo flexibility was J. F. Reichardt. His critique of the twenty-one-year-old Louis Spohr's performances in Berlin in 1805 contained the suggestion that

> he ought not to allow himself to make such radical changes of tempo for every cantabile passage that alternates with virtuoso sections, according to the habit of newer virtuosos that has become so fatally fashionable. It is not merely a gradual holding back of the tempo, which is so beneficial to beautiful expression and so natural to sensitive performance, and which can easily and gracefully be led back into the actual movement of the piece to which even the greatest singers and masters of earlier times, who excelled precisely in beautiful and sensitive performance, conscientiously limited themselves; it is the exaggeration, the caricature of that beauty. From the first note of such a passage, Herr Spohr changes the tempo completely, and changes it again in the livelier, difficult passages according to the nature of the figures; so that such an Allegro has three or four different tempi.[49]

---

[45] Anon.: *Allgemeine musikalische Zeitung*, xxi (1819), 886.
[46] Koch: 'Concert' in *Musikalisches Lexikon*, 352.
[47] Koch: 'Zeitmaaß' in *Musikalisches Lexikon*, 1756.
[48] Adam: *Méthode*, 160.
[49] Reichardt: 'Concert des Herrn Louis Spohr und der Demoiselle Alberghi', *Berlinische musikalische Zeitung*, i (1805), 95.

Reichardt's description of Spohr's playing at that time suggests that it reflected the practice of his teacher Franz Eck, with whom he studied until 1803, and therefore almost certainly that of Eck's elder brother and teacher Friedrich Johann Eck, who was also Carl Cannabich's teacher, and predecessor as Hofmusikdirektor in Munich. Franz Eck's likely freedom of tempo is also suggested by Spohr's account of his time as his pupil, where he commented that by leading the orchestra with which Eck played in Ludwigslust, he was able to ensure more effective accompaniment of Eck's concerto playing, which he "knew well", relating that the orchestra "followed me willingly so that the solo player's performance was made much easier".[50]

Spohr's playing was profoundly influenced by Reichardt's criticism. He recalled: "I was obliged to confess that, yielding to my depth of feeling, I had perhaps, held back in the cantabile too much, and in the passagework and other more impassioned places, carried away by my youthful fire, I had hurried too much. I therefore determined to correct such blemishes in my execution without diminishing its force of expression, and by constant attentiveness I succeeded."[51] In later accounts of Spohr's playing, inappropriate tempo modification was not an issue; but his continuing employment and teaching of tempo flexibility and *tempo rubato* is shown in his 1833 *Violinschule*, by his inclusion of "hurrying the tempo in fiery and powerfully passionate passages, as well as holding back in those that have a tender or melancholy-mournful character", which he included among the features that he associated with "beautiful performance".[52] Also by his advice to quartet players to accommodate themselves to "the small fluctuations of tempo, that may be introduced by the first violinist".[53]

Other soloists, however, continued to allow themselves to be influenced by the "fatally fashionable" habit of extensive tempo flexibility, apparently in considerable numbers. In 1808, the reviewer of some fugal quartets by Gassmann and Monn, commenting that fugues above all require a very strict observance of the beat, digressed to remark:

> Now, however, it is known that the majority of those musicians who particularly dedicate themselves to the performance of solo parts have for a long time dealt very wilfully with the tempo, and that they are ever more inclined to shake off the yoke of the beat. However, it is absolutely inappropriate

[50] Spohr: *Selbstbiographie*, i, 32.
[51] Spohr: *Selbstbiographie*, i, 87.
[52] Spohr: *Violinschule*, 196. See below p. 617 for Spohr's use of tempo flexibility in conducting. For further consideration of the concept of "beautiful performance" (schöner Vortrag) see Ch. 13, pp. 802–07.
[53] Spohr: *Violinschule*, 247.

in the performance of fugue to justify the wavering back and forth of the tempo, which is offensive to every uncorrupted feeling and cultured ear, with the indeed customary but very unsustainable gloss that a perfected expression is thereby obtained.[54]

To this statement the editor, Friedrich Rochlitz, appended a comment in which, having averred that, in his opinion, this now widespread habit had arisen simply from careless self-indulgence during private practice, he stated:

> The pretence that expression might gain from holding back or pushing forward the tempo, is, except in very rare cases, nothing more than a pretence, intended only to throw sand in the eyes of the listeners and make it necessary for the accompanists to give way, so that, if all the parts do not give way simultaneously, which in many cases is not possible, one can blame the offense against the beat, which is one's own fault, on the accompaniment. Unfortunately, fashion still allows this to the singer or solo player; unfortunately, the result is that orchestral playing becomes ever more discredited, and the result of this common procedure is that the honour of orchestral players is often offended in public music-making. Are authorities against this misuse required? Well then: Mozart played to a nicety in time, Ph. Em. Bach did so too, and Clementi, Romberg, and Rode still do it! [...] Although there may occasionally be a few places in a solo part which, through a somewhat increased or decreased rapidity of movement, not merely appear to gain in expression, but actually do so: at least these cases cannot be anything like as frequent, nor as bad, as when a so-called piquant solo player deviates from the beat; and with a sudden jerking and twitching, a sudden alteration of the tempo, perhaps to the extent of a third, if not a half, such as one now not infrequently hears, can and must never be tolerated anywhere.[55]

There can be little doubt that despite respected authorities constantly warning about the dangers of excessive tempo modification, an ever-increasing number of solo players and singers went far beyond what many other distinguished musicians would have regarded as tasteful. By the 1830s there are signs that, as Koch had feared a generation earlier, this sort of thing had become so general that it was perceived by the public as the norm. In 1833 J. F. E. Sobolewski observed:

---

[54] Anon.: *Allgemeine musikalische Zeitung*, x (1807–8), 438.
[55] Anon.: *Allgemeine musikalische Zeitung*, x (1807–8), 438f (editor's footnote)

*Ritardando* and *accelerando* alternate all the time. This manner has already become so fixed in the minds of the musical public that they firmly believe a *diminuendo* must be slowed down and a *crescendo* speeded up; a tender phrase (e.g., in an allegro) will be performed more slowly, a powerful one faster. At times this kind of treatment may well be applicable; but how to determine where requires very deep insight into the composition and very correct feeling. Furthermore, the compositions of the older composers tolerate this type of treatment extremely rarely, and the newer ones are well enough endowed with markings of this kind! In these, on the other hand, one misses the exalted calm, in which the older composers distinguished themselves.[56]

It is in the light of such comments that Spohr's response to Reichardt's review, and his advice about appropriate tempo flexibility in his 1833 *Violinschule*, must be evaluated. One aspect of Sobolewski's argument, however, reveals the growing tendency to regard the music of the past in a light that is very different from what 18th- and early-19th-century sources indicate. This idealistic "classicization" of the earlier "great" composers was to become increasingly strong over time, as all memory of how the music had actually been performed faded from living memory.

In the 1840s, Czerny explicitly stated that Beethoven's music should be performed according to the improved taste of the day, not as it was played in the composer's own time.[57] Like Sobolewski, he warned against excessive tempo fluctuation, employing the term *tempo rubato* in the looser sense that was by that time accepted in common parlance (indeed coming to be seen as the primary meaning of the expression). He complained:

the *tempo rubato* (i.e., the improvisatory holding back or acceleration of the tempo) is now often used to the point of caricature. How often have we heard in recent times that, for example, in the performance of a Hummel concerto, already in the first movement (which consists of only one tempo) the first part is Allegro, the middle melody Andante, the following passage Presto. Hummel himself performed his compositions in such a steady tempo that one could almost always have set the metronome to beat along with it.[58]

---

[56] J. Feski (pseudonym of Johann Friedrich Eduard Sobolewski): 'Wildlinge', *Caecilia*, xv (1833), 270.
[57] Czerny: *Pianoforte-Schule*, iv, 34.
[58] Czerny: *Pianoforte-Schule*, iv, 31.

Despite such accounts, and Rochlitz's references to C. P. E. Bach, Mozart, Rode, and Clementi playing strictly in time, it is impossible to believe that it would really have been possible to let the metronome even approximately beat time to their playing. Bach had identified tempo flexibility as an essential aspect of fine performance, and there is every reason to believe that this was shared by all gifted musicians of the 18th and 19th centuries; it was merely a matter of degree.[59] Czerny's exaggeration is contradicted by Hummel himself, who stated: "Many persons still erroneously imagine, that, in applying the metronome, they are bound to follow its equal and undeviating motion throughout the whole piece, without allowing themselves any latitude in the performance for the display of taste or feeling."[60] Hummel provided numerous specific examples in his own Concerto in A minor op. 85, where, despite the absence of instructions in the published edition, tempo modification was expected. In a footnote, however, he instructed that the holding back "must take place almost imperceptibly, and not be carried to excess, so that the difference between the holding-back of the tempo, and the pushing forwards may never appear too striking in relation to the original tempo"[61] (Ex. 11.19a–f).

Ex. 11.19 a–f. Hummel: *Anweisung*, 1st edn (1827), 419ff; 2nd edn (1828), iii, 429ff.
(*a*) From here in a moderate tempo; (*b*) Somewhat held back and in a singing style; (*c*) Somewhat forward-moving; (*d*) The middle section somewhat held back and with tender feeling; (*e*) Faster and spirited; (*f*) Giving way somewhat in preparation for the cadence.

(*a*)

---

[59] See above, p. 562.
[60] Hummel: *Anweisung*, 2nd edn, iii, 455.
[61] Hummel: *Anweisung*, 2nd edn, iii, 433 (footnote).

594  CLASSICAL AND ROMANTIC PERFORMING PRACTICE

**Ex. 11.19** Continued

(b)

(c)

(d)

(e)

(f)

Nevertheless, Czerny advocated flexibility of tempo; and perhaps his conception of appropriate flexibility was greater than Hummel, since he evidently perceived Hummel's playing as "metronomic". His notion of excess—if his reference to Allegro, Andante, and Presto was not a gross exaggeration—suggests that he was warning against something much more conspicuous than Hummel's recommendations. He remarked that "Tempo is just as infinitely divisible as dynamics" and explained:

> It is true that each piece of music must be performed at the tempo prescribed by the author and set by the player at the beginning, as well as strictly in time and with unwavering tempo to the end. But notwithstanding, there are very often, in almost every line, individual notes or passages where a small, often hardly noticeable lingering or acceleration is necessary to beautify the performance and increase interest. It is the great art of the good player to make these partial deviations in a tasteful and comprehensible manner, while firmly keeping the underlying pulse, and it is only through refined sensitivity, much attentive practice, and hearing good artists on all instruments, but especially great singers that it can be acquired.[62]

These sources make it clear that there were distinct polarities during the 18th and early 19th centuries. But before considering the growing influence of the opposite approach as an alternative orthodoxy, in theory as well as practice, it will be helpful to consider the circumstances in which early-19th-century musicians may have regarded tempo modification, whether subtle or more pronounced, as appropriate and effective.

Theorists constantly stressed the importance of knowing where, how, and to what extent tempo modification would be suitable. While recognizing that such things must ultimately be left to the sensitivity of a cultivated musician, a few attempted to provide specific guidance. Among these was the mathematician and musician August Leopold Crelle. In 1823, having stated that strict tempo is an essential aspect of music, he went on to identify situations in which he regarded speeding up and slowing down to be appropriate. He linked tempo flexibility with many aspects of performance, including articulation and accent markings. After describing the three principal categories of articulation marks—strokes, dots, and dots under slurs—and explaining the extent to which these affected the length of the note (in the same terms as Adam),[63] he observed: "Apart from this, however, these signs also have

---

[62] Czerny: *Pianoforte-Schule*, iii, 24.
[63] See Ch. 6, p. 327.

significance for the tempo of performance. The staccato [i.e., with strokes] hurries rather than drags. In the case of notes with dots, however, this is rather reversed and even more so if the dots are under slurs."[64] He further observed that "As a general rule, one can assume that all strong notes, except in special circumstances, do not hurry."[65] and, discussing phrasing, he asserted that the end of a phrase "decreases in strength and increases in speed."[66]

Crelle's recommendations for expressive performance have some aspects in common with Kalkbrenner's. Crelle's comment that strengthened notes do not hurry is essentially in agreement with Kalkbrenner's view that "when a frequent change of harmony occurs, or modulations succeed each other rapidly, the tempo must be retarded", and the traditional view that "all notes foreign to the key, and those which bear accidentals, should be well marked". But Kalkbrenner disagreed with Crelle's dictum that the ends of phrases should hurry, stating: "all terminations of melodic phrases should be retarded".[67]

Czerny, with characteristic thoroughness, gave a much fuller list of circumstances that invite modification of the tempo. His recommendations are partly related to structural features in the music, though for him, unlike Crelle, the major factor is the emotional or expressive content of the passage. He stated: "Not only each piece of music as a whole, but each individual passage either really expresses some particular feeling, or at least allows such a feeling to be put into it through the performance." He then explained that these feelings could include "gentle persuasion, quiet doubts or indecisive pacing, tender lamentation, calm devotion, transition from an excited state to a calm one, deliberate or pensive calm, sighs and grief, whispering a secret, saying goodbye, and countless other states of this kind. [. . .] And in such cases, a little holding back (*calando, smorzando,* etc.) is usually appropriate."[68] On the other hand: "Sudden cheerfulness, hasty or curious questions, impatience, erupting in anger, strong resolve, unwilling reproaches, high spirits and mood, fearful flight, sudden surprise, transition from a calm state to an excited one, etc. In such cases, the pushing and hurrying of the *tempo* (*accelerando, stringendo,* etc.) is natural and in its

[64] Crelle: *Einiges*, 92f.
[65] Crelle: *Einiges*, 61.
[66] Crelle: *Einiges*, 54f. Nicholson's instructions for the application of trembling effects to final notes provide an interesting parallel. See Ch. 16, p. 974.
[67] Kalkbrenner: *Méthode*, 12.
[68] Czerny: *Pianoforte Schule*, iii, 24, §4.

place."[69] Structurally, he explained that slowing down occurs on the return of the principal subject, on notes that lead to the subdivisions of a melody, on long notes strongly accented, in the transition to a different tempo, after a fermata, on the *diminuendo* of a quick lively passage, where the ornamental notes cannot be played a *tempo giusto*, in a well-marked *crescendo* serving as introduction or wind-up to an important passage, in capricious or fantastic passage, to bring out their character, almost always when the composer marks the passage *espressivo*,[70] and at the end of a trill or cadence.[71] He also observed that an *accelerando* is required in an ascending phrase and expresses passion and agitation.

A few 19th-century composers took the view, like Türk in the previous century, that they ought to convey their intentions for tempo modification more fully, although they all seem to have accepted that they could do no more than provide hints since, as Czerny had pointed out, there was scarcely a line of music that did not invite some degree of tempo flexibility. The places where composers definitively demanded flexibility could, of course, be indicated by words that specifically required it, or by more ambiguous terms, such as *smorzando* and *calando*, which were widely associated with relaxing, or, like *agitato*, with enlivening.[72] Mostly, these terms were used sparingly, but a few composers experimented with giving more detailed directions.

Composer and publisher Anton André (1775–1842) evidently took the view that composers could and should make their intentions clearer in this respect. Already in his String Quartets opp. 14 and 15 he included more explicit indication of tempo flexibility than was common (Ex. 11.20a–b).

Ex. 11.20a  Anton André: String Quartet op. 14 no. 1/i.
[Allegro brioso]

---

[69] Czerny: *Pianoforte Schule*, iii, 24, §5.
[70] Beethoven certainly used it in this way. See Ch. 10, p. 555.
[71] Czerny: *Pianoforte Schule*, iii, 25f.
[72] See Ch. 10, pp. 546–58, for other terms that might imply tempo flexibility.

**Ex. 11.20b** Anton André: String Quartet op. 15 no 1/ii. Both *sostenuto* and *dim.* may be employed to relax tempo.
[Adagio con moto quasi Andantino]

Later, he employed many more tempo modifying instructions in his *Lieder und Gesänge*, published in four volumes. In volume 1 he supplied verbal instructions, some of which are clearly intended as tempo modifiers even when that is not their obvious meaning, since they are followed by *in tempo* or *Tempo 1mo*. These include *tenuto*; *poco a poco morendo*; *tenuto e lento*; *espressivo*; *accelerando*; *poco a poco piu vivace*; *ritard*; *Tenuto e ritard*; *tenuto e diminuendo*; *stringendo*; *poco ritard—poco a poco il Tempo 1mo*; *marcato*; and *espressivo e cantabile*.

In volume 2 André devised a scheme rather like Türk's *accelerando* and *ritardando* markings. In the preface (*Vorbericht*) to volume 3 (1818), he explained:

> To the remarks on the performance of these songs, which are printed in the second volume, I add: that the signs ⟨⟩ and ⟨⟩, if they are above the uppermost vocal line and below the piano part at the same time, apply to all verses; if they are only single, then they also only apply where they occur. Incidentally, these signs, as well as all others concerning the performance, are to be regarded only as indications, which every tasteful singer and accompanist on the pianoforte will know how to interpret according to the circumstances.[73]

The original edition of volume 3 contains no metronome marks, but these were added in a subsequent impression (Ex. 11.21).

---

[73] Anton André: *Lieder und Gesänge*, Heft 3 (Offenbach, 1818), [3].

TEMPO MODIFICATION 599

Ex. 11.21 André: *Lieder und Gesänge*, vol. 3.

In 1826, Fanny Mendelssohn (later Hensel) wrote a piano piece in which she experimented with using the dynamic signs ⟨ and ⟩ to signify tempo modification, which may already have been implicit in them at an earlier date. In a footnote she explained, "This piece must be performed with much variation of *tempo*, but always gentle and without disorderliness. The signs ⟨ ⟩ stand for *accelerando* and *ritardando*" (Ex. 11.22).[74]

[74] Fanny Mendelssohn: autograph of piano piece, Allegro ma non troppo, '20th February 1826 nach Mitternacht'. Staatsbibliothek zu Berlin, MA Ms 35.

Ex. 11.22 Fanny Hensel: Allegro ma non troppo, "20th February 1826 nach Mitternacht".

This association between *crescendo/accelerando* and *diminuendo/ritardando* probably reflects a looser connection between these terms and signs that was often envisaged by composers and understood by performers in other music of this period.[75] Even before Fanny Mendelssohn's explicit use of these signs with that meaning, it seems likely that they were sometimes—perhaps often—associated with tempo flexibility. The combination ⤚⤙ may already have begun to acquire an implication of lingering at the beginning of the century. This is made explicit in Prosper Josef Mosel's Grand Trio op. 3, published in Vienna around 1807 (Ex. 11.23a–b).

Ex. 11.23 a–b. Prosper Joseph Mosel: Grand Trio in D major op. 3, c. 1807 (Vienna: Johann Traeg, pl. no. 311). (*a*) 2nd movement; (*b*) 3rd movement.

(*a*)
[Andante]

(*b*)
[Adagio Cantabile]

Mosel's usage here may well be relevant to our understanding of the employment of these signs by Beethoven and other contemporaries. Ignaz Moscheles, for instance, apparently associated them with tempo fluctuations. In his verbal introduction to No. 5 of his Studies op. 70 (c. 1827), a seventy-two-bar Allegretto agitato con passione, he stated that it required "a frequent wavering in the pulse, accelerating and returning to the original tempo".[76] It contains twenty-five "hairpin" markings, only two

---

[75] For relaxation of tempo indicated by *diminuendo* in Schubert and earlier Viennese composers, see Ch. 10, pp. 550–53.

[76] Moscheles: Etudes pour le piano forte [...] op. 70, 29. A characteristic performance of the piece can be heard on a 1905 piano roll made by Gustav Lazarus https://youtu.be/7cmu-ZN9VRg. I am grateful to Sebastian Bausch for drawing my attention to this recording.

of which occur in the twenty-five-bar middle section, marked *calmato e cantabile*.

By the end of the 19th century, the association of ‹ and › with tempo modification was well established. Brahms's use of them in this sense is well supported, not only by early recordings of his music by people associated with him, but also by documentary evidence.[77] Richard Scholz's *Die Vortragskunst in der Musik* (1892) links these signs explicitly with tempo modification. He refers to "Pushing forwards (accelerando and stringendo mostly associated with ‹ )" and notes that "all prominent melody notes in passage, for instance, will be lengthened (usually marked with < >, <, or +)."[78] In the Joachim and Moser *Violinschule*, too, < > is given as an indication both for vibrato and lingering (see Ex. 11.1).

Liszt attempted to introduce specific symbols for *accelerando* and *ritardando*. In the first version of the piano piece "Au bord d'une source", in *Album d'un voyageur* (composed 1837–8) he included signs for a

Ex. 11.24a  Liszt: "Au bord d'une source", 1842.

---

[77] David Hyun-Su Kim: 'The Brahmsian Hairpin', *19th-century Music*, xxxvi (2012), 45–57. Brown, Peres Da Costa, and Bennett Wadsworth: *Performing Practices in Johannes Brahms' Chamber Music* (Kassel, Bärenreiter, 2015).

[78] Richard Scholz: *Die Vortragskunst in der Musik mit besonderer Berücksichtigung des Violinvortrages. Katechismus für Lehrende und Lernende*, 2nd ed. (Hannover, [1892]), 28f.

"*crescendo* of tempo" and a "*decrescendo* of tempo", together with another sign for lingering less long than the normal fermata sign (Ex. 11.24a). He also used these signs in his *Grandes Études*, composed around the same time; but he later decided to abandon them. In his revision of the *Grandes Études* (in a copy of the 1st edition) for publication as *Études d'exécution transcendante* (1851), he deleted the signs (Ex. 11.24b), and they were also omitted in the revision of "Au borde d'une source" in *Années de pèlerinage* (1855).

Ex. 11.24b  Liszt: *Études d'exécution transcendante*, 1851. Engraver's copy with Liszt's autograph revisions.

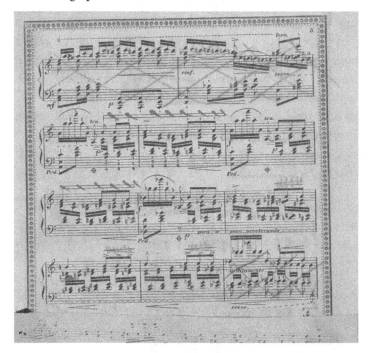

Liszt nevertheless remained concerned about these issues, and in the published edition (1871) of his Missa Solennis, he included the letters R and A to indicate *ritardando* and *accelerando*. An obituary in 1886 noted "there is something very important for the correct performance of Liszt's works: an extremely elastic tempo, not an arbitrary *tempo rubato*, but a good separation of contrasting periods, small, barely noticeable *ritardandos* and *accelerandos*".[79] What a writer in 1886 might have meant by "barely noticeable" remains speculative.

---

[79] S-t.: 'Ein Requiem für Liszt und Liszt's Requiem', *Neue Zeitschrift für Musik*, lxxxii (1886), 418.

Some mid-19th-century pedagogic sources also provide insights into circumstances in which tempo flexibility might have been employed. Adolph Kullak, who had studied with both Czerny and Liszt, published a treatise on the aesthetics of piano playing in 1861. He deals with the rationale for, and application of, un-notated tempo flexibility, and is in no doubt that these things are expected in an artistic performance.[80] He makes the point that the opportunities for *rallentando* are more frequent than for *accelerando* but that both are necessary, and gives examples of places where these might be introduced, many from Beethoven. He does not engage with contemporaneous controversies, but his standpoint seems closer to the Mendelssohnian ethos than the Wagnerian. Regarding *accelerando*, he remarks, citing Beethoven's Bagatelle op. 33 no. 1 as an example, that it is often implied by the alternation of "brilliant with calm", and that the former might appropriately encourage "a slight hint of acceleration". Among other circumstances are passages in which a motive is repeated. He uses Beethoven's op. 33 no. 2 to illustrate this, explaining: "The acceleration, however, must not continue in uninterrupted progression; this would again be monotonous; where a phrase of 8 bars is concerned, a rallentàndo of the same figures is added towards the end. The passage is therefore performed in this way: [Ex. 11.25a]."[81]

Ex. 11.25a Beethoven: Bagatelle op. 33 no. 2 in Kullak: *Aesthetik*, 326. [Scherzo Allegro]

Referring to Bach preludes and Mendelssohn *Lieder ohne Worte* (e.g., op. 85 no. 1), he remarks that "In general, where a piece involves the repetition of a figuration, it will be difficult to do without accelerando and rallentando."[82]

---

[80] Adolph Kullak: *Die Aesthetik des Klavierspiels* (Berlin, 1861); Ch. 16, "Das Accelerando und Rallentando".
[81] Kullak: *Aesthetik des Klavierspiels*, 325.
[82] Kullak: *Aesthetik des Klavierspiels*, 327.

His discussion specifically focuses on the relationship of tempo and dynamic change:

> Hurrying and holding back correspond to each other like crescendo and decrescendo; in the first of these natural relations, the concept of increase has the crescendo and the accelerando as the natural means of its expression; the calming has the decrescendo and the rallentando, and both will often unite.—The pushing of the feeling out of the chest, the vehemence of its movement is naturally expressed in the former, its calm breathing out in the latter. Wherever there is any deeper emotion, both are to be found in the performance, whereby—as noted earlier—the principle of alternation is by no means to be rejected as a motive for this type of performance, even in the most spiritual sense.
>
> It will hardly be possible to think of an adagio where this would not be indispensable.[83]

To illustrate this, he offers an example from the Adagio of Beethoven's Sonata op. 10 no. 1 (Ex. 11.25b), which he follows with the observation that "The accelerando can also be connected with the decrescendo, and the rallentando with the crescendo"[84], which recalls Ferdinand Ries's recollection of Beethoven's sometimes holding back the tempo during a *crescendo* with striking effect.[85]

Ex. 11.25b  Beethoven: op. 10 no. 1 in Kullak: *Aesthetik*, 327.
[Adagio molto]

---

[83] Kullak: *Aesthetik des Klavierspiels*, 327f.

[84] Kullak: *Aesthetik des Klavierspiels*, 328. Examples from later 19th-century composers were added in a posthumous 2nd edn, available online at http://www.koelnklavier.de/quellen/kullak/kap16-8.html.

[85] F. G. Wegeler and Ferdinand Ries: *Biographische Notizen über Ludwig van Beethoven* (Coblenz, 1838), 106.

## The Endorsement of Conspicuous Tempo Modification

Twenty-one years before Kullak's treatise and a year after Czerny's *Pianoforte-Schule* appeared in print, Anton Schindler had published quite different views about tempo modification. Schindler, whose desire to be seen as the only true disciple of Beethoven made him jealous of those whose claims to know and understand Beethoven were better than his, criticized Czerny's notion of tempo. He attacked not only Czerny's recommendations for absolute tempos (i.e., his metronome marks for the sonatas)[86] but also his rather cautious attitude towards flexibility of tempo.[87] In his assertions about Beethoven's requirements for the proper performance of his music, Schindler was the most insistent, and perhaps the most influential advocate of substantial tempo modification in the first half of the 19th century.

He asserted: "Whatever I myself heard Beethoven perform was, with few exceptions, always free from all constraints of time; a 'tempo rubato' in the true sense of the word"; and he reported "that he only adopted this freer manner of performance in the first years of the third period of his life, and that he totally departed from the earlier, less nuanced one".[88] His statement about Beethoven's earlier practice is highly questionable; having first come to Vienna in 1813, he could not have had first-hand experience. He nevertheless claimed that Beethoven applied this freer performance style retrospectively to earlier works. In relation to the first movement of the Piano Sonata op. 14 no. 2, Schindler promulgated the notion of two principles, which characterized the performance style (including tempo), describing them as an interaction between a "pleading" (bittende) one and a "resisting" (widerstrebende) one. In his account of Beethoven's rubato in the first movements of the two op. 14 Sonatas, he referred to changes of tempo that sometimes reduced the initial Allegro to Andantino or Andante, thus unmistakably describing very conspicuous fluctuations.[89] Schindler concluded his claims about Beethoven's expectations with the statement:

> But I must, in all seriousness, guard against any accusations that these hints are my invention. The performance of the Beethoven quartets by

---

[86] Schindler: *Biographie von Ludwig van Beethoven*, 1st edn, 216.
[87] For a thoughtful discussion of the conflicting approaches of Czerny and Schindler, see Rosenblum, *Performance Practices*, 387ff.
[88] Schindler: *Biographie*, 228.
[89] Schindler: *Biographie*, 230f.

Schuppanzigh and the other three initiates clearly showed how Beethoven had his music performed when he could influence it personally; and whoever did not have the opportunity to hear those performances may quite wrongly be sceptical about how this way of changing the pace of the tempo at the appropriate place makes the most difficult music become an intelligible language, even for lay people.[90]

The reliability of his claims about Beethoven's intentions in general were seriously and persuasively questioned in the 20th century; and it has been shown that he provided false evidence for some of these claims by forging entries in Beethoven's conversation books.[91] Nevertheless, his testimony that Beethoven worked in detail on the performance of his quartets with Schuppanzigh and his colleagues is unambiguously confirmed by other sources. An 1837 obituary of the cellist Joseph Linke, who played in the quartet from 1808, stated:

> as if by a magnet he was drawn to Vienna, where he arrived in 1808 and was so happy to find a gracious and friendly welcome in the house of the then Imperial Russian Ambassador, Prince Rasumoffsky. It was there that Beethoven, a darling of the art-loving prince, met him; there Schuppanzigh and Weiss [viola] became his inseparable colleagues; and because that master musician first rehearsed almost all his newly completed chamber works with the princely ensemble, indicating performance style, tempo, bowstrokes, all nuances and shadings with pinpoint accuracy, it explains how these quartet players were able to achieve such widespread celebrity performing Beethoven's compositions.[92]

Schuppanzigh remained closely connected with Beethoven's chamber music from op. 18 to op. 135, and it was probably his return to Vienna in 1823, after seven years of concert touring, that prompted Beethoven's renewed engagement with quartet composition after a thirteen-year gap.[93]

---

[90] Schindler: *Biographie*, 242.

[91] See, e.g., Dagmar Beck and Grita Herre: 'Einige Zweifel an der Überlieferung der Konversationshefte' in Harry Goldschmidt, Karl-Heinz Köhler, and Konrad Niemann (eds.), *Bericht über den Internationalen Beethoven-Kongress . . . 1977 in Berlin* (Leipzig, 1978), 257–74; and also Peter Stadlen: 'Schindler's Beethoven Forgeries', *Musical Times*, cxviii (1977), 551, and 'Schindler and the Conversation Books', *Soundings*, vii (1978), 2–18.

[92] Anon.: *Allgemeine musikalische Zeitung*, xxxix (1837), 440.

[93] John M. Gingerich: 'Ignaz Schuppanzigh and Beethoven's Late Quartets', *Musical Quarterly*, xciii (2010), 450–513.

The unsatisfactory premier of Beethoven's op. 127 caused a temporary break with Schuppanzigh, but not his colleagues. The fact that Beethoven regularly took part in the quartet's rehearsals and continued to do so for the late quartets makes it evident that their manner of performance reflected his expectations. Sir George Smart who attended a rehearsal for op. 132, led by Schuppanzigh in 1825, noted that Beethoven "directed the performers, and took off his coat the room being warm and crowded. A staccato passage not being expressed to the satisfaction of his eye, for alas, he could not hear, he seized Holz's violin and played the passage a quarter of a tone too flat."[94] Smart heard Schuppanzigh and his colleagues play the quartet again, together with the Piano Trios op. 70 and op. 97 with Carl Czerny, and noted that "Beethoven was seated near the pianoforte beating time during the performance of these pieces."[95] Another account from 1825 demonstrates that tempo flexibility was indeed a prominent, though not uncontroversial, aspect of Schuppanzigh's quartet performances:

> The quartet entertainments have almost completely ceased, even those given by Schuppanzigh left us cold in the end, which probably resulted partly from the fact that newly rehearsed works went rather badly for lack of rehearsals, while the older ones, despite their admirable ensemble, lost more than they gained through too much caprice [Willkürlichkeit] and too frequent use of *tempo rubato*.[96]

This account makes interesting comparison with another obituary of Linke by someone who knew him:

> He was a close friend of Beethoven, who wrote a lot for him. His way of performing his compositions was also unique, and, so far, I have not heard a cellist with this conception, which was sometimes flattering, sometimes repulsive, capricious, passionate & c., in short, completely in keeping with the humoristic requirements, and thus reflected Beethoven's fundamental style [Manier]. This style became too one-sided after Beethoven's death and often lapsed into distortion.[97]

---

[94] H. Bertram Cox: *Leaves from the Journals of Sir Georg Smart* (London, 1907), 109.
[95] Cox: *Leaves from the Journals*, 114. It seems very unlikely that Beethoven would have beaten time throughout if he merely expected a steady tempo.
[96] Anon.: 'Wien im Jahre 1825', *Cäcilia*, iii (1825), 246.
[97] Anon.: *Neue Zeitschrift für Musik*, vi (1837), 130.

This may suggest that the stylistic features complained of in the 1825 account became even more pronounced in later years.

Despite the unreliability of Schindler's comments as firm evidence of the extent and character of Beethoven's own practice or intentions, therefore, it seems likely that Beethoven did, indeed, expect substantial un-notated tempo flexibility for an effective performance. Joseph Fischhof (1804–1857), a piano professor at the Vienna Conservatorium, who organized the publisher Artaria's collection of Beethoven manuscripts, reported that: "On the autograph of the song 'Nord oder Süd' [. . .] one can clearly read his [Beethoven's] remark: '100 according to Mälzl [sic], but this can only apply to the first bars, because sentiment also has its pulse, this cannot, however, be expressed by this number (i.e., 100).'"[98] Fischhof concurred, remarking that keeping rigidly to a tempo was unsatisfactory, "because the lively interaction, the declamation, the passionate nuance, the occasional upsurge, as well as the laws of intensification, through which the higher level of artistic performance has a ravishing effect, make it impossible to hold on to it anyway".[99]

Thus, although the extent to which Schindler's account genuinely represents Beethoven's conception of tempo flexibility remains questionable, it undoubtedly reflected an aspect of musical performance in his lifetime that was rapidly gaining ground among prestigious and increasingly influential musical authorities. More celebrated musicians than he, such as Franz Liszt (who was, perhaps significantly in this respect, a pupil of Carl Czerny) and Richard Wagner, became powerful advocates, practically and theoretically, of more lavish employment of tempo flexibility than was favoured by other contemporaries; and Schindler's widely believed testimony that this approach had been sanctioned by Beethoven undoubtedly played a part in encouraging a more widespread acceptance of its orthodoxy.

The growing influence of these ideas, promulgated by Schindler and championed by Wagner, can be seen in the writings of the Swiss musician Mathis Lussy (who worked principally in Paris). Lussy referred directly to Czerny's instructions, objecting that they were both vague and misleading. His discussion of tempo modification reflects the shift of emphasis towards a more obtrusive use of this resource. Lussy's comments, like Kullak's, explicitly identify rhythmic flexibility and tempo modification with expressive

---

[98] Joseph Fischhof: 'Einige Gedanken über die Auffassung von Instrumentalcompositionen in Hinsicht des Zeitmaaßes, namentlich bei Beethoven'schen Werken', *Caecilia*, xxvi (1847), 94.

[99] Fischhof: 'Einige Gedanken', *Caecilia*, xxvi (1847), 87.

performance, but they also indicate that many musicians still chose to use this resource more sparingly than he considered appropriate. He observed that two schools existed, the tone of his comments leaving no doubt as to his own allegiance:

> One demands a uniform rate of time, without *accelerando* or *ritardando*; the other, on the contrary, is accustomed to quicken and slacken with every rhythm, every change. The first regards regular and mechanical precision as the height of perfection; the second will alter the time at every phrase, and will not feel anything objectionable in the constant irregularity. Now we have observed that the warmest partisans of the uniform and regular rate of time are precisely those who have no feeling for expression.

He went on to admit, however, that not every piece required or tolerated the same degree of tempo modification:

> In Prestos, Allegros, Galops Valses etc. it seems natural to keep up a uniform rate, only slackening with the loss of power and impetus, or when there is an evident change of structure. And in slow expressive pieces, such as Nocturnes, Rondos, Reveries, Andantes, Adagios, Romances etc. it seems equally natural to modify the time. In such pieces there should be *accelerandos* and *ritardandos* according to every change of feeling, and whenever the expressive structure of the phrases, or their motion up or down seems to require them.[100]

Lussy's characterization of musicians playing with "regular and mechanical precision" is undoubtedly an exaggeration, but it is clear that there was a well-recognized distinction between the slight flexibility that was always expected to be present in a sensitive performance by skilled musicians, and more major disturbances of the rhythmic flow, such as pronounced *rallentando* at the ends of sections and conspicuous alternation between slower and faster tempos, where the composer had not indicated them.

The development of a repertoire that contained an increasing proportion of established masterpieces from different periods and traditions fostered differing approaches to appropriate performing practices. Among these was

---

[100] Lussy: *Traité*, 115f.

a widely held belief, whether historically justified or not, that the music of different eras required different approaches to tempo. Thus, for instance, Manuel García stated: "The compositions of Haydn, Mozart, Cimarosa, Rossini &c., demand great exactitude in their rhythmic movements. Any change in the values must, without altering the movement of the beat, be a result of the use of the *rubato tempo*";[101] on the other hand, "Donizetti's music—and above all Bellini's contains a great number of passages, which without indications either of *rallentando* or *accelerando*, require them to be employed."[102]

By the time Lussy published his influential book, the dividing lines between two strands in 19th-century music had been drawn. On the one hand were the supporters of classical restraint and on the other of romantic freedom, often identified as the "New-German School". Mendelssohn and Wagner began to be seen as the opposite poles and, in the polemics of the mid-19th century, it is often difficult to separate reality from propaganda. Mendelssohn's strictness of tempo may well have been exaggerated by opponents of Wagner's theories and practices. Sir George Grove, for instance, assembled information that emphasized Mendelssohn's treatment of the notation as rather literal in respect of tempo:

> Strict time was one of his hobbies. He alludes to it, with an eye to the sins of Hiller and Chopin, in a letter of May 23, 1834, and somewhere else speaks of "nice strict *tempo*" as something particularly pleasant. After introducing some *rallentandos* in conducting the introduction to Beethoven's second symphony, he excused himself by saying that "one could not always be good,"* and that he had felt the inclination too strongly to resist it. In playing, however, he never himself interpolated a *ritardando* or suffered it in anyone else.** It specially enraged him when done at the end of a song or other piece. "Es steht nicht da!" ["It is not there"] he would say; "if it were intended it would be written in—they think it expression, but it is sheer affectation."***[103]
>
> \* Kellow Pye.
> \*\* Hans von Bülow.
> \*\*\* Mrs Moscheles and W. S. Rockstro.

---

[101] García: *École*, ii, 22.
[102] García: *École*, ii, 23 (footnote).
[103] Sir George Grove: 'Mendelssohn' in *Dictionary of Music and Musicians*, ii, 299.

Such accounts give the impression of an approach that might justify the maintenance of very regular tempos as historically based, which became dominant during the second half of the 20th century; but other accounts indicate something quite different. In fact, an objective view of historical evidence strongly indicates that the art of employing constant, but subtle, tempo and rhythmic flexibility, while never losing sight of the fundamental tempo of a movement, seems to have remained an ideal for all those musicians, such as Spohr, Mendelssohn, Reinecke, Joachim, Brahms, and many others, who throughout the century represented the "classical" strand in musical composition and performance. The difference between the two polarities was one of degree rather than kind.

Although the language employed by those who championed the "classical" approach seems often to imply strictness in the realization of musical notation, other evidence suggests that the strictness of those "classical" musicians was relative rather than absolute, sometimes providing tantalizing glimpses of practices that were so fundamental and self-evident that they were rarely mentioned. Grove's comment on Mendelssohn's maintenance of "strict time", written at a time when Wagner's authority had sanctioned much more extensive tempo modification, evokes a quite different impression from Joachim's assertion in 1905, in his introduction to Mendelssohn's Violin Concerto (which he had studied with the composer), that Mendelssohn, "who so perfectly understood the elastic management of time as a subtle means of expression, always liked to see the uniform *tempo* of a movement preserved as a whole".[104] And Joachim's biographer, Andreas Moser, also stated (evidently reflecting his subject's own words) that "Joachim's unrivalled rubato playing primarily derived from the example of Mendelssohn, who knew how to lead from one subject to another without doing the slightest violence to the passage in question."[105] Some impression of what that implied in practice can be gained from the tempo and rhythmic flexibility in Joachim's 1903 recordings, those of his pupil Marie Soldat (c. 1920),[106] the pre-1920 recordings of the Klingler Quartet, the 1905–6 piano rolls made by Carl Reinecke, who had

---

[104] Joachim and Moser: *Violinschule*, iii, 228f.
[105] Andreas Moser: *Joseph Joachim: Ein Lebensbild* (Berlin, 1898), 45.
[106] See Johannes Gebauer: *Der "Klassikervortrag": Joseph Joachims Bach- und Beethovenvortrag und die Interpretationspraxis des 19. Jahrhunderts*. Veröffentlichungen des Beethoven-Hauses Bonn, Beethoven Interpretationen Band 1, ed. Kai Köpp (Bonn, 2024).

been a protégé of Mendelssohn and Schumann during the 1840s, and those of Czerny's pupil Theodor Leschetizky.[107]

## Tempo Flexibility in Orchestral Performance

The same principles that applied to solo playing and singing certainly applied also to playing in small ensembles, especially in passages where an individual instrument was dominant. Spohr referred to it in connection with quartet playing,[108] and it is evident that Schuppanzigh's quartet, an ensemble of skilled musicians, could, as C. P. E. Bach had explained, successfully collaborate in making real alterations to the pulse of the music.

In an orchestra, individual string players could not modify the time at will. Many 18th-century and early-19th-century writers specifically made this obvious point. Reichardt instructed that "it is the orchestral player's duty to keep to the *tempo* in the most exact manner once it has been set by the leader".[109] Accompanying a singer or instrumental soloist's flexibility, however, depended on the skill of the leading violinist and the alertness of the individual orchestral musicians since it must often have been necessary to modify tempo to accommodate soloists. Spohr's account of his leading an orchestra in accompanying Franz Eck's concerto playing provides a concrete example.[110] And in the late 18th century, Francesco Galeazzi, who had extensive experience as concertmaster of an orchestra in Rome, alluded to the alertness and flexibility needed by the members of an orchestra with respect to aspects of performance that were not indicated in their performing parts, instructing: "It is the duty of every orchestral player to keep his ear attuned to the ensemble, in order to slur, if the others slur, to detach if the others detach, to increase or relax the tempo if the others (and especially the first violin) do so."[111]

That the ideal orchestral performance, theoretically at least, was not necessarily expected to involve regularity of tempo is demonstrated by

---

[107] An essential aspect of this flexibility was the free but subtle treatment of note lengths and rhythms, which is considered further in Chs. 13 and 14.
[108] Spohr: *Violinschule*, 247. See above, p. 590.
[109] Reichardt: *Ueber die Pflichten*, 78.
[110] See above, p. 590.
[111] Galeazzi: *Elementi*, i, 210.

Carl Ludwig Junker's 1782 book on the duties of a Kapellmeister or Music Director. Discussing how tempo should be handled, he remarked:

> Now another interesting question arises? "How? Is every piece, every allegro, every adagio, bound to a completely uniform tempo? Must every piece, right to the end, be performed in the same tempo, which never approaches either greater speed or slowness? Or may this tempo, even in the middle of the piece, be somewhat altered, may it be accelerated, may it be retarded?" To accept the former would mean to deprive musical art of its most powerful means of emotion, and to think of it as having no relation to the fluctuations of passionate feeling. To affirm the latter in principle would be to tear the stream from its banks, cause a thousand disorders, and to deprive music of its truth. But we can accept the last sentence if it is qualified; the musician, the solo singer, limits it. There is no passion whose momentum always remains the same; it flows through various modifications of emotion. It is true, that the composer can express these modifications better and more completely through his composition, through the various types of colouring, than the director can through alterations of pace; but it is equally true that both, composer and performer, must work hand in hand, and that alterations of pace remain necessary, as a subsidiary art.[112]

The absence of an independent, time-beating, conductor in purely orchestral music, and the customary divided direction in the theatre (the *maestro al cembalo*, or time-beating director being primarily concerned with the singers, while the first violinist was responsible for the orchestra), militated against controlled manipulation of the beat for interpretative purposes. This situation persisted well into the 19th century in many places; direction by an independent time-beater in purely orchestral music at the Gewandhaus concerts in Leipzig, for instance, did not become usual until Mendelssohn's arrival in 1834. Furthermore, in performances of orchestral music during the late 18th century and early 19th century it seems unlikely that much planned use of unwritten *rallentando* or *accelerando* can have been expected, since the necessary conditions to rehearse it were rarely present. In addition, the repertoire of 18th- and early-19th-century orchestras consisted largely of new or unfamiliar music, which they generally had to perform after minimum

---

[112] Carl Ludwig Junker: *Einige der vornehmsten Pflichten eines Kapellmeisters oder Musikdirektors* (Winterthur, 1782), 36f.

rehearsal. Thus, Reichardt stressed that "the orchestral violinist must often play everything that is put before him at first sight";[113] and for the same reason Anton Reicha recommended that in orchestral pieces the composer should not write anything higher than f² for the violins.[114]

But there is evidence that in rare circumstances, with an orchestra of highly trained musicians, the effective accompaniment of a solo instrumentalist or singer could be very successful. A visitor to Vienna in 1790 observed of the opera orchestra at the Hoftheater: "Such order rules here, such a rare unanimity of ensemble, depending not merely on the beat, and such an equal and unanimous feeling in the subtleties of expression, that no orchestra in Europe, even though it might surpass it in detail, surpasses it as a whole."[115] After discussing the relative merits and demerits of the orchestras in London, Paris, Naples, and Munich, he described the marvellous flexibility of the Vienna orchestra in a performance of Salieri's *Axur*, during which he observed:

> On this occasion I noticed a manner and method of expressing the dying fall of passion which were till then unknown to me. As the storm of passion gradually sank to exhaustion and the most violent agitation gave way to milder feelings, so the orchestra allowed the beat to relax in the most perfect accord with the singers and the melodies to ebb away more and more slowly, as the mood was intended to become more and more gentle. When the passion grew again, so the pulse became more impetuous and emphatic, and they also accelerated the flow of the melody with rare unanimity of ensemble. This kind of performance arouses delight.[116]

The rarity of this type of performance is evident from the fact that this experienced and musically aware traveller considered it to be exceptional; but, theoretically at least, a good 18th-century orchestra must have been expected to follow a soloist's deviations from strict tempo, if only to avoid an embarrassing breakdown in the performance.

Expectations for controlled tempo flexibility in orchestral playing, not only to follow a soloist, seems to have been growing during the early 19th century.

---

[113] Reichardt: *Ueber die Pflichten*, 70.
[114] Anton Reicha: *Cours de composition musicale*, trans. and ed. Carl Czerny as *Vollständiges Lehrbuch der musikalischen Composition* (with parallel Fr. and Ger. text) (Vienna, 1834), i, 3, 303.
[115] Anon. [Carl Ernst Philipp von Reitzenstein]: *Reise nach Wien* (Hof, Vienna, 1795), 253.
[116] Anon. [Reitzenstein]: *Reise*, 256.

In 1803, the author of a journal article stated that "appropriate hurrying (accelerando) and hesitating (ritardando)" was a necessary skill for a good opera orchestra.[117] Even without a separate conductor, tempo flexibility was increasingly expected. In the same year, the journal reported that the Leipzig Gewandhaus Orchestra, which performed instrumental music under the directorship of the principal violinist until Mendelssohn's time, "gains increasingly through the inclusion of young, skillful men and through playing together frequently, so that even in symphonies or other full-voiced pieces, for example, without visible or audible hints from the director, it can perform passages where the expression is enhanced by deliberately slowing down or speeding up the tempo without the slightest hesitation, and faultlessly."[118]

The desire for greater tempo flexibility also encouraged the development of conducting technique. Weber was concerned that his metronome marks for *Euryanthe* should not induce the conductor to keep rigidly to an unvarying beat. In his accompanying instructions he was explicit about his requirement for real modification of the tempo, though without excess:

> The beat (the tempo) should not be a tyrannical and inhibiting one, or a driving mill-hammer, it must rather be to the piece of music what the pulse beat is to the life of mankind. There is no slow tempo in which passages might not occur that encourage a quicker pace in order to combat the feeling of dragging.—There is no presto which does not also in contrast require calm performance in some passages, in order not to take away the means of expression through excessive hurrying. But for heaven's sake, no one believes himself entitled to that madcap style of performance, which distorts individual bars arbitrarily and creates a sensation in the listener that is just as unbearably embarrassing as when he sees a juggler violently contorting all his limbs. Moving forward in tempo, just as much as holding back, must never create the feeling of lagging, pushing or violence. In musical-poetic terms, therefore, it can only be done periodically and in phrases, conditioned by the passionate nature of the expression.[119]

A few years later, Spohr, discussing the duty of the orchestral violinist, remarked, apparently in contrast to Weber's aesthetic: "The distribution of the notes in the bar according to their duration, must, in orchestral playing,

---

[117] Anon.: 'Was soll man von dem Musikdirektor eines Operntheaters verlangen?' *AmZ* 6(1803–4), 172.
[118] Anon. [?Friedrich Rochlitz]: 'Musik in Leipzig', *AmZ* 6(1803–4), 201.
[119] Quoted in Friedrich Wilhelm Jähns: *Carl Maria von Weber* (Berlin, 1871), 374.

be extremely strict, otherwise no precise unity among the performers would be possible. Consequently, lingering on one or several notes (the *tempo rubato*), which is often of such great effect in solo playing, cannot be permitted here."[120]

Spohr's use of the term *tempo rubato*, however, refers to the original meaning of the term, which he had discussed in his annotated version of Rode's Seventh Concerto.[121] In purely orchestral music, Spohr certainly envisaged tempo modification, for he also noted: "With respect to tempo, the orchestral player must be guided entirely by the conductor, whether leading or time-beating. It is also his duty frequently to cast a glance at him, so that he not only always adheres strictly to the tempo, but also immediately follows when it is somewhat held back or accelerated."[122]

What Weber may have had in mind as a "madcap style of performance", or Spohr may have meant by "slight deviations from the tempo", was obviously related to the normal expectations of the time, and it is quite likely that what Weber or Spohr considered moderate or "slight" would have seemed quite substantial to an early-21st-century musician, accustomed to a very close adherence to the composer's specified tempo throughout a section or movement. Spohr, as a conductor, certainly employed more tempo flexibility than was normal in some other places, for instance London, where concerts were still given with minimum rehearsal in the mid-19th century. After an extended visit there in 1843, he wrote to his former pupil and friend Moritz Hauptmann:

> All the things that the orchestra had played many times went splendidly. The greatest sensation, however, was made by the *Freischütz* overture. This had hitherto been a bit pompous and carried out in strict rhythm—I took it, as you know it from our theatre, now quickly, now slowly, and the orchestra followed excellently. This was so impressive that the next morning all the newspapers were full of it.[123]

Since Spohr was among those who favoured a more restrained approach to tempo modification in general, and since he was in any case among the earliest effective baton conductors, there will have been no significant discrepancy between what he sought to achieve as a soloist and as a conductor, though

---

[120] Spohr: *Violinschule*, 248.
[121] See below, pp. 816–25.
[122] Spohr: *Violinschule*, 249.
[123] Spohr, letter of 6 October 1843, in La Mara: *Classisches und Romantisches aus der Tonwelt* (Leipzig 1892), 136f; online in *Spohr Briefe* http://www.spohr-briefe.de/briefe-einzelansicht?&m=1843100603.

naturally the subtleties of expression that he aimed for in violin playing could not so easily be attained by an orchestra. To a musician like Liszt, whose solo performances apparently involved much greater and more pervasive manipulation of the tempo, the conventional orchestral performance in the first half of the 19th century, which allowed limited flexibility, seemed far from satisfactory. Hence his statements in the foreword to his symphonic poems about freeing performance from the "mechanical, fragmented up and down playing in strict time, which is still usual in many places".[124] The difference between his approach and Spohr's is nicely suggested by their very different styles of conducting, which must have made a striking contrast when they were joint conductors of the great Beethoven Festival at Bonn in 1845. Spohr was noted for his extremely calm and dignified presence on the rostrum, but the English conductor Sir George Smart, in his diary of the festival, referred to Liszt as conducting "with much twisting of the person".[125]

The gradual development of conducting technique during the early 19th century did not immediately encourage conductors to manage their orchestras as the more wilful soloists managed their instruments. Many musicians continued to believe that the ideal in orchestral performance was steady maintenance of the tempo throughout a movement with only subtle nuances at important points. A writer, probably Schumann, in 1836 recommended that a conductor should beat only at the beginning of a movement or at tempo changes, though he conceded that it might be helpful to beat regularly in very slow tempos.[126] This seems to have been close to the practice adopted by Mendelssohn, although it is evident that Mendelssohn did not want absolutely regular tempo in orchestral music, despite Wagner's insinuations,[127] for Hans von Bülow, who in his youth observed Mendelssohn's conducting, vividly recalled his masterly performance of Schubert's great C major Symphony, in which Mendelssohn's "sensitive elasticity" and "ingenious tempo nuances" made a deep and lasting impression on him.[128]

In 1840, Schindler had conceded that "it goes without saying that in orchestral music in general it is not permissible [he seems really to mean

---

[124] Franz Liszt: 'Vorwort' in *Symphonische Dichtungen für grosses Orchester*, i (Leipzig, 1857), no pagination.
[125] Smart Papers, British Library, London, Dept. of Manuscripts, vi, 16.
[126] Anon.: *Neue Zeitschrift für Musik*, iv (1836), 129.
[127] Richard Wagner: 'Ueber das Dirigieren', *Neue Zeitschrift für Musik*, lxv (1869), 405ff.
[128] Hans von Bülow: 'Lohengrin in Bologna. Kein Leitartikel, sondern ein vertrauliches Gespräch (im australischen Style), durch diplomatische Indiskretion in die Öffentlichkeit gebracht', *Signale für die Musikalische Welt*, xxx (1872), 24f. His comments here call into question Sir George Grove's account of Bülow's testimony. (See above p. 611.)

'practicable'] to change the tempo so often as in chamber music",[129] but he went on to suggest that a much greater degree of tempo modification was appropriate in the performance of Beethoven's symphonies than had hitherto been the case. He argued that the tradition of "in tempo" performance, which, he asserted, had been prevalent in Beethoven's Vienna, was simply a consequence of circumstances; that, if Beethoven could have had his own orchestra for unlimited rehearsal, he would certainly have wanted the symphonies performed in a more flexible manner.[130] Schindler's specific suggestions, purportedly coming from Beethoven himself, are interesting because they prefigure the kind of treatment that Wagner and his disciples were later to give to the symphonies, convinced that this was what the composer had really wanted. In the "Eroica", for instance, Schindler claimed that the passage beginning at bar 83 of the first movement (Ex. 11.26a) should be played somewhat more slowly until the following *pp* (Ex. 11.26b), where "by means of a gently held accelerando it hurries into the original tempo of the movement, which is finally attained with the phrase in B flat major *f*".[131]

**Ex. 11.26** a–b. Beethoven: "Eroica" Symphony op. 55/i in Schindler: *Biographie von Ludwig van Beethoven*, 239.
[Allegro con brio]

Most notably, he attributed to Beethoven the expression "thus fate knocks at the door" as an explanation of the opening gesture of the Fifth Symphony, and claimed that at each of its appearances it should be much slower than the rest: "♩ = 126, approximately an Andante con moto".[132] His most detailed

---

[129] Schindler, *Biographie von Ludwig van Beethoven*, 1st edn, 235.
[130] Schindler, *Biographie*, 242f.
[131] Schindler, *Biographie*, 239.
[132] Schindler, *Biographie*, 241.

example of tempo modification in the symphonies is the Larghetto of the Second Symphony; this gives a clear idea of the extent to which Schindler believed such flexibility of tempo was apposite (Ex. 11.27).

Ex. 11.27 Beethoven, Second Symphony op. 36/ii in Schindler, *Biographie von Ludwig van Beethoven*, 237.
[Larghetto]

Whether Classical period composers, and Beethoven in particular, would have welcomed more tempo flexibility in orchestral performance than circumstances generally allowed has been controversial. Schindler's assertions that Beethoven desired such flexibility in his orchestral music has often been dismissed as another expression of Schindler's own preferences, which he sought to validate by falsified accounts of Beethoven's practice and statements. Without giving credence to any specific instance described by Schindler, however, a review of the concert on 8 December 1813, at which the Seventh Symphony and *Wellingtons Sieg* were performed by an exceptionally large orchestra containing many of the finest musicians in Vienna, provides solid evidence that Beethoven did, indeed want tempo flexibility in orchestral performance. It is also evident that Beethoven had an unusually generous amount of time to influence the performance; Spohr, who participated next to Schuppanzigh on that occasion, recalled in 1840, in a letter to Robert Schumann: "I played in the first performance of this symphony and took part in 4 or 5 rehearsals under Beethoven's own direction."[133] The 1813 reviewer specifically referred to tempo flexibility, writing:

Both compositions were performed by Vienna's most excellent musicians (around 100 in number) under Mr v. Beethoven's overall direction, and Mr. Schuppanzigh's direction from the first violin, with such expression, power, and precision, that the former confessed, with the most heartfelt emotion, that it was the *non plus ultra* of art, and that the orchestra completely satisfied his every requirement in executing his compositions. Truly the greatest praise an orchestra has ever earned, if one takes into account the difficulties—certainly motivated by tremendous effects—of a Beethovenian movement and this great master's equally strict demands with regard to execution! But it was also strange to see how, feeling the importance of the undertaking, everyone worked together with zeal and love for the esteemed composer, how he led the performance of his works in transfigured delight, how every expression in the piano and forte, in the accelerando and ritardando, passed from him to each individual artist, who contributed with eager attention, so that the ideal of Beethoven's creation, so to speak, emerged from it.[134]

---

[133] Letter of 25 November 1840 in *Spohr Briefe* (online), http://www.spohr-briefe.de/briefe-einzelansicht?&m=1840112511. Spohr's text was published in the *Neue Zeitschrift für Musik*, xiii (1840), 180. The article was a response to Anton Schindler's criticism of his tempos in a performance of Beethoven's Seventh Symphony at the Aachen Festival of 1840.

[134] Anon.: 'Große musikalische Akademie', *Wiener allgemeine musikalische Zeitung*, i (1813), 749f.

Here, the reviewer is evidently concerned with tempo flexibility by the whole orchestra, but it is highly likely that Beethoven will also have expected tempo and rhythmic flexibility where individual wind instruments had genuine solo passages. This is strongly suggested by Ignaz von Seyfried's recollection that "With regard to the expression of the smaller nuances, the even distribution of light and shadow, as well as an effective *tempo rubato*, he was very precise, and gladly discussed it individually with everyone without being reluctant to share his thoughts with them."[135]

This manner of orchestral performance may indeed have been exceptional, since Seyfried also remarked that Beethoven's manner of rehearsing was not always very effective; but the 1813 review certainly lends support to Schindler's assertion that Beethoven ideally wanted tempo flexibility in the execution of his orchestral music as well as in his chamber and solo works. How much, and what kind of *rubato* Beethoven desired at various stages of his development remains unclear. The review also suggests that Schindler, whose close contact with Beethoven was confined to his final years, was incorrect in his limitation of this practice to Beethoven's "third period", although it is possible that Beethoven favoured more frequent and extensive flexibility in his later years.[136] Curiously, Schindler seems not to have been aware of Beethoven's use of tempo flexibility in the December 1813 concert, despite his claim, in published criticism of Spohr's 1840 performance of Beethoven's Seventh Symphony, to have taken part in that performance. In fact, it is highly implausible that he played in the 1813 concert, which occurred shortly after his move to Vienna; had he done so it is very unlikely that he would not have mentioned it in support of his claim that Beethoven wanted tempo flexibility in his orchestral works.

Wagner asserted in 1869 that, in orchestral performances, "modification of tempo" was something "not merely entirely unknown to our conductors but, precisely because of that ignorance, treated with foolishly dismissive contempt".[137] He later remarked that it was not surprising that Beethoven's "Eroica" Symphony made a poor impression when played in strict time by the pupils at the Prague Conservatoire under Dionys Weber; observing that at that time "it was nowhere played any differently",[138] he asserted that it was

---

[135] Ignaz von Seyfried: *Ludwig van Beethoven's Studien im Generalbasse, Contrapuncte und in der Compositionslehre* (Vienna, 1832), Anhang, 18f.
[136] Schindler: *Biographie*, 228.
[137] Wagner: 'Ueber das Dirigieren', *Neue Zeitschrift für Musik*, lxv (1869), 439.
[138] Wagner: 'Ueber das Dirigieren', *Neue Zeitschrift für Musik*, lxvi (1870), 4.

only when the symphony was performed on the piano, with the proper flexibility of tempo, that people began to appreciate the true import of the music. As with Schindler, however, Wagner's veracity in matters of fact, is not always trustworthy, especially when he sought to validate his own agenda.

Wagner argued that each section of a movement had its own appropriate tempo, and believed that the fundamental *adagio* element in lyrical melody should be emphasized. He claimed that he expected this to take place only in a discreet manner, but accounts of performances conducted by him suggest that, in fact, his modifications of tempo were extreme. During his conductorship of the Philharmonic Society in London in 1855, one of the most frequent complaints against him concerned his distortion of tempo. Henry Chorley described Wagner's conducting of a Beethoven symphony as "full of [...] ill measured rallentandos",[139] while Henry Smart objected to his tempos in every respect:

> Firstly he takes all quick movements faster than anybody else; secondly he takes all slow movements slower than anybody else; thirdly he prefaces the entry of an important point, or the return of a theme—especially in a slow movement—by an exaggerated ritardando; and fourthly, he reduces the speed of an allegro—say in an overture or the first movement—fully one-third, immediately on the entrance of its cantabile phrases.[140]

Despite much criticism, however, Wagner's growing prestige among a significant portion of his contemporaries, and the influence of his writings, together with the adulation accorded to his aesthetic ally, Liszt, legitimized and encouraged, indeed glamorized, an approach to tempo modification in orchestral performance that had previously been resisted by most musical authorities. A particularly clear and informative account of the change that took place in the second half of the 19th century is contained in Heinrich Ehrlich's record of a discussion with the eighty-four-year-old Verdi in 1897. In reply to Verdi's enquiries about the "new school of German conductors", Ehrlich replied that they

> are orchestral virtuosi, highly gifted, with a thorough musical education; the instrument they play is the orchestra and they have developed its technique to an extent hitherto unknown and impose their individual

---

[139] *Athenaeum* (17 March 1855), 329.
[140] *Sunday Times* (17 June 1855), 3.

interpretations on a great variety of works. They are the precise opposite of the conductors of former generations, whose overriding concern was to play everything accurately and scrupulously in time. This endeavour led with rare exceptions to mechanical routine. Operas and symphonies were sung and performed correctly; the most popular singers were allowed to take liberties with the tempi, but the conductor resisted their temptations. Today the opposite applies. The young conductors, who all follow Richard Wagner's example and teachings, do not hesitate to change the tempo of an aria or any piece of music, according to how they see fit. [. . .] They make the most intensive and detailed study of operas and orchestral works, and are able to throw into bold relief, in the most masterly fashion, beautiful and interesting moments that until then have gone unnoticed, and thus obtain remarkable effects [. . .] yet during their performances of orchestral works the audience will often attend more to the orchestra's virtuosity and the conductor's individuality than the sequence of ideas in the work itself.

Verdi concurred, and remarked that after hearing a virtuoso performance of Beethoven's First Symphony in Paris he had similarly felt that

> everything sounded so beautiful, that sometimes you only seemed to hear the sound and not the composition itself—and it occurred to me that the essence of the work of art was more obscured than emphasized. Moreover, what you were just telling me about German conductors and their arbitrary treatment of tempi—that is beginning to spread rapidly in Italy too; it is almost comic to observe how many of our young conductors endeavour to change the tempo every ten bars or introduce completely new nuances into every insignificant aria or concert piece.[141]

The consequences of the theoretical and practical legitimizing of substantial tempo modification can be heard in recording, by Nikisch, Fürtwängler, Mengelberg, and others made during the first half of the 20th century, which contrast with those of other conductors, such as Weingartner, who explicitly adopted what they saw as a more "classical" approach.

This tendency, however, was by no means unchallenged during the later decades of the 19th century. When Hans von Bülow visited Vienna in 1884 with the Meiningen Orchestra, which he had trained to follow his every

---

[141] Ehrlich: 'Beim 84 jährigen Verdi', *Deutsche Revue* (Stuttgart), xxii/2 (1897), 325ff., quoted in Conati: *Interviews and Encounters with Verdi*, 294–95.

inflection, his use of tempo modification, explicitly identified as representative of Wagnerian principles, was controversial. Gustav Dömpfe, a strong supporter of Brahms, observed:

> Countless of his well-considered tempo modifications would have a much more pleasant effect if reduced somewhat, because they would hardly be noticeable, and the conductors who have learned, or will learn from Bülow without bias—we wish him many more—will undoubtedly reduce them and thus derive pure profit from many of his experiments.
>
> But we found the maltreatment, scarcely classable as mere exaggeration, of the "Egmont" overture, which Bülow smashed as if with a clumsy hammer by a truly crude change of tempo when introducing the second theme, utterly reprehensible—a tastelessness which we would never have attributed to Bülow, and which still shows him today in the fetters of the New German School, those fetters which he wore throughout his life and which in our eyes are his undoing.[142]

He went on to remark sarcastically that Bülow derived this manner of conducting the piece directly from Wagner's "discovery" in *Ueber das Dirigieren* that this was the proper way of performing the overture.

Brahms's collaboration with the Meiningen Orchestra, first with Bülow and later, more comfortably, with Fritz Steinbach, and his misgivings about Hans Richter's tendency towards minimal tempo flexibility, show him to have pursued a "middle way" in this respect.[143] This middle way was evidently located somewhere within the broad spectrum of approaches to orchestral tempo flexibility in the late 19th century, which is clearly demonstrated by early recordings, ranging, for instance, from the Wagnerian/Bülow tempo flexibility of Nikisch's 1913 recording of Beethoven's Fifth Symphony to the much stricter though still flexible tempos of the 1910 recording of the work by the Großes Odeon-Streich-Orchester, Berlin, with an un-named conductor.

---

[142] G[ustav] Dömpke: 'Feuilleton. Concerte', *Wiener allgemeine Zeitung* (29 November 1884, Nr. 1707), 2.

[143] See Johannes Leertouwer: *Re-inventing the Nineteenth-Century Tools of Unprescribed Modifications of Rhythm and Tempo in Performances of Brahms's Symphonies and Concertos* (diss., University of Leiden, 2023), online at https://scholarlypublications.universiteitleiden.nl/handle/1887/3511968.

The accompanying recordings, especially those from 2021 and 2022, represent a major advance in exploring the interpretative possibilities offered by currently neglected expressive "tools" in orchestral playing that were regarded as integral to an effective performance of that repertoire. Leertouwer's demonstration that Brahms's preferred manner of performance had already been forgotten by the 1920s ties in with Richard Barth's similar remarks about the chamber music. See Brown et al.: *Performing Practices in Johannes Brahms' Chamber Music*, 33f.

# 12
# Notated Ornaments

In the matter of ornament notation, the musical archaeologist is working in extensively excavated ground. The finds are abundant, but their identification and ordering are by no means straightforward; much of the information derived from them is confusing, contradictory, and often controversial. Considerable scholarly attention has been focused on ornament signs in the music of the early part of the period, and on theorists' accounts of the realization of ornaments; but these durable survivals, like the artefacts from an excavation, represent only a relatively small proportion of what once existed. The ephemeral nature of the aural experience has left us with mere traces of evidence that are not easy to interpret. In the first half of the period especially, a mass of ornamentation was associated with the performance of all sorts of contemporary music, and only a small proportion of it was indicated by means of ornament signs; yet its absence from the musical text does not by any means imply its absence from a good performance. As C. P. E. Bach observed: "although pieces in which all ornaments are indicated need give no trouble, pieces in which, on the other hand, little or nothing is marked, must be supplied with their ornaments in the usual way".[1]

To ornament the music of the period convincingly it is important to understand not only the types of ornament that are stylistically appropriate, but also the perceived function of ornaments at that time; this is nicely summed up by Schulz, who observed that

> They give the notes on which they are introduced more accent, or more charm, set them apart from the others and, in general, introduce variety and to some extent light and shade into the melody. They are not to be seen merely as something artificial, for feeling itself often generates them, since even in common speech abundance of feeling very often brings forth a change of tone and a lingering on accented syllables which is similar to ornaments in the melody. Sensitive feelings lead to accents of many kinds

---

[1] Bach: *Versuch*, i, 55.

being made on notes that express especially strong passions. This undoubtedly gave rise to the different ornaments in singing.[2]

Aesthetics changed during the 19th century, and a greater proportion of concrete evidence survives; yet even here the relationship between what was written and what was expected to be performed often remains equivocal.

In the late 18th century and early 19th century, ornaments were frequently marked in a very casual manner. Different notations were sometimes employed in close proximity for what appears to be envisaged as the same ornament, or the same sign was used with obviously different meanings; in my translations, therefore, the original-language terms for ornaments will be used where there might be any ambiguity about their implications. During the course of the 19th century almost all ornaments, apart from trills and mordents,[3] came to be notated either in normal note values, or indicated in small notes that are not counted in the value of the bar. Sometimes even trills were written out fully: Beethoven and other pianist composers had notated continuous trill-like figures in certain contexts, where they were an integral part of the texture, and trill effects were occasionally written out in the later 19th century (Ex. 12.1a–d).

**Ex. 12.1a** Liszt: Hungarian Rhapsody no. 19 (1885), (autograph). p. 7.

[2] Schulz: 'Manieren (Musik)' in Sulzer: *Allgemeine Theorie*, ii, 741.
[3] The term *mordent* is generally used in English for a three-note ornament (main note–upper auxiliary–main note or in the 18th century often with the lower auxiliary). Many other terms for the upper *mordent* are encountered in the historical literature, including *Mordant* (French and German), *Pralltriller*, and *Schneller*.

Ex. 12.1b Liszt: *Eine Faust-Symphonie*, i, "Faust".

Ex. 12.1c Tchaikovsky: Fifth Symphony op. 64/ii.

Ex. 12.1d Tchaikovsky: Sixth Symphony op. 74/iii.

In his String Quartet op. 106, Dvořák evidently felt it necessary to spell out the trill at the opening of the first movement because he wished it to be without a turn (which was still widely regarded as an essential element of the ornament whether notated or not), but having made his intentions clear he used the conventional *tr* at the recapitulation (Ex. 12.2).

Ex. 12.2 Dvořák: String Quartet op. 106/i.

Many composers continued to employ turn signs, but this ornament, too, was written out with increasing frequency in the second half of the 19th century. The progression is nicely illustrated by Wagner, who went from using a sign for connecting turns (in the operas up to *Tannhäuser*) to writing out his turns either in small or normal notes (e.g., in *Tristan und Isolde*), to consistently notating them in full-size notes in his last operas. Brahms used the turn sign in his Sextet in G (though he wrote the ornament out in full at one point in the first movement), and it occurs from time to time in his later music, for instance, in the first movement of the C major Piano Trio op. 87. Some composers in the late 19th century such as Dvořák continued to use turn signs occasionally,[4] but many others did not employ them at all.

## *Appoggiaturas* and *Grace-Notes*

The employment of small notes, extra to the value of the bar, was a feature of musical notation throughout the period; but the types of small notes used, and their meanings, changed with time. Until the early decades of the 19th century, small notes, occurring singly, were widely employed to mean several very different things. There was, and is no universally, or even generally agreed terminology for specifying their various functions. The Italian term *appoggiatura* was often applied to any of these single small notes, though it was also used in more specialized, often contradictory senses. In Germany, small notes associated with the note they precede were commonly known

---

[4] A late example occurs in the second movement of the String Quartet op. 106.

as *Vorschläge* (singular *Vorschlag*), and those associated with the note they follow *Nachschläge* (singular *Nachschlag*); in England they were usually referred to by the general term *graces*, with a profuse array of qualifying words; while in France a range of expressions, including *accent, appuy, coulé,* and *port de voix*, were employed to describe their various functions.[5] The Italian word *acciaccatura* was sometimes applied to the very short *appoggiatura* instead of to the more specific keyboard ornament where two notes are sounded simultaneously; already at the beginning of the 19th century the distinction seems to have become somewhat blurred, for Koch, describing the difference between the *acciaccatura* and the short *appoggiatura*, commented: "The distinction between the two consists merely in the fact that in the case of the acciaccatura the little note is performed more simultaneously [*sic*] with the main note than in the case of the short appoggiatura."[6]

In the ensuing discussion of single-note ornaments that are a second above or below the following note, the term *appoggiatura* will be used for one that is connected to the note that follows, from which it takes its value; the term *anticipatory-note* will be used for one taking a significant part of the value of the note that precedes it. The term *grace-note* will be used to describe a very short ornament that barely removes anything from the value of the notes between which it stands, and which is so fleetingly heard that the ear may not register whether it comes with or slightly before the beat;[7] the term's employment here carries no necessary implication of pre-beat performance as it does when used by some 20th-century writers.[8] These basic categories cannot be regarded as entirely exclusive, for borderlines are often blurred in performance, especially over the question of when an ornamental note is so short that it may be perceived as a *grace-note* rather than an *appoggiatura* or *anticipatory-note*.

Many 18th-century and early-9th-century theorists attempted to clarify distinctions between different types of single-note ornaments, to suggest ways of linking their appearance with their function, and to adduce rules for determining what they were intended to convey in any specific set of

---

[5] For further information on nomenclature see *New Grove*, 2nd edn (London, 2001), xviii, art. 'Ornaments', esp. 133–742.

[6] Koch: 'Acciacatura', *Musikalisches Lexikon*, 56.

[7] This use of *grace-note* conforms with the definition in the *Oxford English Dictionary* (Oxford, 1933) of "additional notes introduced into vocal or instrumental music, not essential to the harmony or melody" (vi, 326).

[8] Frederick Neumann: *Ornamentation and Improvisation in Mozart* (Princeton, 1986); Rosenblum: *Performance Practices*.

circumstances; but the haste or negligence of composers and copyists, and the lack of any universally accepted or recognized notational principles for these ornaments, seems to have made the interpretation of them quite as troublesome to many musicians at that time as it has to their successors. Most performers of contemporary music during this period would undoubtedly have been content to follow their instincts, which were conditioned by their training and experience. During the 19th century, however, as earlier music constituted an increasing proportion of the repertoire, the correct interpretation of ornaments became a musicological matter, rather than a living tradition.

In the 18th century, theorists periodically urged composers to minimize ambiguity by writing *appoggiaturas* with their intended value or even as full-size notes; Türk, for instance, advised that all *appoggiaturas* should be written as full-size notes, leaving the small ones for *grace-notes*.[9] During the late 18th century these recommendations, and their acceptance by composers, gradually become more frequent.[10] Changing attitudes, and the concerns that lay behind them, are illustrated by a passage that appears for the first time in the fifth edition of Löhlein's *Clavier-Schule*; the editor, Witthauer, having urged composers to indicate the length of *appoggiaturas*, concluded: "How many pieces would then, at least with respect to the Vorschläge, be less badly performed, and how much trouble would be spared to the beginner!"[11] By the early decades of the 19th century the practice of indicating *appoggiaturas* in normal notes was increasingly being adopted, and the use of single small-note ornaments became progressively more restricted, so that by the 1830s composers very rarely employed them except as *grace-notes*. Carl Czerny's commentary on a section dealing with ornamentation in his translation of Reicha's *Cours de composition* is among the last admonitions on this subject, and his concern seems primarily to be focused on the confusion that was engendered by these signs in the performance of older music. He observed that it is much better if the composer writes all embellishments, slow *Vorschläge*, *appoggiaturas*, etc. everywhere in a definite manner, where there obtains the slightest doubt over their execution, adding, "Many, often

---

[9] Türk: *Klavierschule*, 203.
[10] Quantz, who, unlike C. P. E. Bach, did not advocate the practice of showing a precise value for *appoggiaturas*, still used an eighth-note indiscriminately for almost all of them in his *Versuch,* but according to Edward R. Reilly (Quantz, *On Playing the Flute*, 91) his *Sei duetti* op. 2 of 1759 began to show a change of attitude.
[11] Löhlein, ed. Witthauer: *Clavier-Schule*, 25.

very unpleasant-sounding mistakes by the performer (particularly in piano music) are thereby avoided. The former customary manner of writing the ornament sign for Mordents, Doppelschlags, Pralltrillers [sic], etc. is all too obviously imprecise, frequently quite unknown to many players, and often abandons the most beautiful ornaments to tasteless caprice."[12] But, as earlier comments indicate, uncertainty about the significance of such ornaments was scarcely less widespread during the period in which their use was current notational practice.

Until the habit of notating *appoggiaturas* with small notes was abandoned, the problem of how to recognize when they were meant to indicate *grace-notes*, rather than *appoggiaturas* or *anticipatory-notes*, was particularly vexatious. Nevertheless, there was broad agreement about many of the circumstances in which small notes were unlikely to indicate anything other than *grace-notes*. Perhaps the most comprehensive examination of contexts for *grace-note* interpretation is Türk's, which seems to have provided the basis for similar accounts by Witthauer, J. F. Schubert, A. E. Müller, F. J. Fröhlich, and others. Türk explained that this type of performance applied to small notes:

1) Which stand before a note that is repeated several times (c, c, c &c.):
2) Before a note (particularly a short one) after which several of like duration follow one another:
3) Before notes which should be performed short (staccato):
4) Before leaping intervals:
5) At the beginning of a movement, or an individual idea and, similarly after a rest:
6) Before syncopations . . .:
   (Often the appoggiaturas before notes after which syncopations follow, as at a), fall under this rule.)
7) If a similar pattern is previously required:
8) Before dotted notes in rather fast tempo a), particularly between leaps b):
9) Before breaks between phrases [Einschnitten] a),* particularly when monotony [. . .] might result from a rather slow appoggiatura in this case, as at b):

---

[12] Anton Reicha: *Cours de composition*, trans. and ed. Carl Czerny as *Vollständiges Lehrbuch der musikalischen Composition* (Vienna, [1832]), ii, 537.

* [Türk's footnote] There are frequent exceptions to these two rules, e.g. in slow tempo, or when an ornament (over the main note) follows after the appoggiatura.

10) If the melody rises a step, and then goes back to the previous note:*

Further situations in which he considered a *grace-note* to be likely, but not certain, were:

11) Before several slurred rising or falling seconds:
    The Vorschläge at c, according to some, should rather be performed long, namely an eighth. [Türk also quotes Agricola's edition of Tosi (p. 72) suggesting that the Vorschläge at e should be performed somewhat longer than a normal short one, but not too long.]
12) Before falling thirds:
    [Türk discusses whether, as some teach, when three occur successively, the third should also be short, but concludes that this is usually not the case. At b) he recommends that the Vorschläge should be performed in an ingratiating manner, and recalls that Bach wants them to take at least a third of the value of the following note in an Adagio. He identifies the style of performance at e) and f) as French and observes: "I would rather advise against the last two realizations, than recommend them in German compositions, because one cannot know whether the composer presupposed the French style or the so-called Lombard taste."]
13) Before two-note figures:
    [Türk points out that c) would be incorrect, except if it went with triplets in another part, as at d).]
14) Before triplets and other three-note figures:
    [Türk explains that b) not c) is the correct treatment of a), although Marpurg recommended c); but he concedes that when groups of three and four notes are mixed it might sound better to use the "incorrect" realization (as in his examples d)–k), but not in l)–m)]
15) Before a note after which two of half its length follow:
    [for Türk's qualifications about such notes see p. 653]
16) If the pitches indicated by the small notes are not diatonically related to the following main note:

634  CLASSICAL AND ROMANTIC PERFORMING PRACTICE

17) If the independently entering appoggiaturas are separated from the main note by more than a second or make a leap to it:
[He explains that his proposed realizations are too short for *appoggiaturas* and too long for *grace-notes*, but that except in fast and fiery contexts, he would execute them as in the final example.][13]

Ex. 12.3 Türk: *Klavierschule*, 220–2, §21 (1–10), §23 (11–17).

[13] Türk: *Klavierschule*, 220–27. In the 1802 revised edition, Türk made a few changes, partly for clarification and partly to reflect changing practice. In 2 he omitted the third example and provided the following tempo markings for the 1st, 2nd 4th, 6th, and 7th examples: Allegro, Andante, Moderato, Allegro, Moderato. Most significant, perhaps, he moved 9 and 10 to the category where a *grace-note* seems likely, but not certain. About 9 he explained: "However, according to present taste, at least in a), a long appoggiatura is more usual, and with regard to singing &c. also more appropriate, than a short one"; and for 10: "Immediately before a cadence, as here in b), an appoggiatura of this kind has been used for some time in modern compositions, and, moreover, it is often performed in a noticeably pronounced or prominent manner." Türk: *Klavierschule* (Neue vermehrte und verbesserte Ausgabe, 1802), 253f.

NOTATED ORNAMENTS 635

Ex. 12.3 Continued

**Ex. 12.3** Continued

Ex. 12.3 Continued

Türk confessed that in all these circumstances some theorists and some composers held a different opinion. In such doubtful cases, many theorists took refuge in appealing to experienced performers to rely on their taste, to be aware of the character of the whole piece and of the individual sections; or, in the case of singers, to take account primarily of the text.

During the early 19th century, as the practice of writing out *appoggiaturas* in normal notes became more common, these sorts of comprehensive lists were no longer felt to be so necessary, at least for the performance of the contemporary music that formed the bulk of the repertoire. It is symptomatic of this change of practice and attitude that, in 1810, Philip Corri's focus was principally on the *short appoggiatura (grace-note)* and its execution; reversing the procedure of Türk and his followers, he gave several examples of how to perform the short variety and then observed: "Note: the Appoggiatura is always to be played short, as above, except in the following instances."[14] He then considered a few situations in which the long species might be encountered (Ex. 12.4).

Ex. 12.4 P. A. Corri: *L'anima di musica*, 14.

One of the latest repetitions of the gist of Türk's instructions, which was clearly intended, at least in part, as a guide to performing contemporary music, occurs in the 1830s in Schilling's *Encyclopädie*. The author felt that, despite the widespread adoption of the notation of *grace-notes* by means of a small stroke through the tail of the note, there was still occasional ambiguity. By that stage, though, the main purpose of the list was to assist performers in interpreting the older music that constituted an ever-increasing proportion of the contemporary repertoire. By the end of the 19th century, treatises such as Dannreuther's *Musical Ornamentation* approached the subject from a much more obviously historical viewpoint.

## The *Appoggiatura*

If the performer resolved that a small note was intended to signify an *appoggiatura* rather than a *grace-note*, there remained the problem of deciding what its duration should be. The matter was obfuscated, both during the period of their general use and, later, by the existence of two widely disseminated, but sometimes incompatible, guidelines for determining their length. On the one hand was a series of not entirely consistent prescriptions for deciding what proportion of the value of the main note should be given to the *appoggiatura* in any given circumstances: on the other was the idea that the notational value of the small note would show the approximate value that the composer intended it to receive.

---

[14] P. A. Corri: *L'anima di musica*, 14.

The theory promulgated by Tartini, Quantz, Leopold Mozart, C. P. E. Bach, and others in the mid-18th century, that an *appoggiatura* should normally take half of a binary main note and two-thirds of a ternary main note, was widely repeated by 18th- and 19th-century authors. Some musicians (including Francesco Galeazzi[15] and Bernhard Romberg[16]), however, taught that before a ternary note the *appoggiatura* should take only a third of its value; others (for instance, Clementi)[17] allowed it to take either one-third or two-thirds of a dotted note according to context. A further principle, for what is sometimes called an *overlong appoggiatura*, was expounded by C. P. E. Bach, Leopold Mozart, and Quantz and followed by many other German theorists in the 18th century: this proposed that where a small-note *appoggiatura* stood before a tied note or one followed by a rest, it took the whole value of the note before which it stood (Ex. 12.5). It was admitted, however, that the resolution onto a rest might not always be permitted by the harmony.

Ex. 12.5

Other rules may be found in the works of individual theorists. A late authority, Baillot, instructed that, in realizing the *appoggiature préparée*, where a small-note *appoggiatura* was preceded by a normal note at the same pitch, the *appoggiatura* should be half the length of the preparatory note and, as an example of where this rule would operate, he gave the opening of Mozart's D major String Quartet K. 575, but with all three small notes incorrectly shown as quarters (Ex. 12.6).[18] Yet, whatever general rules were expounded, these musicians would almost certainly have agreed with C. P. E. Bach that the theoretical length of *appoggiaturas* must sometimes be modified for the sake of expression or to avoid corrupting the purity of the voice-leading.[19]

Ex. 12.6 Mozart: String Quartet K. 575/i, in Baillot: *L'art du violon*, 74.

---

[15] Galeazzi: *Elementi teorico-pratici di musica, con un saggio sopra l'arte di suonare il violino annalizzata, ed a dimostrabili principi ridotta*, 2 vols. (Rome, 1791–96), i, 2, 15.
[16] Romberg: *Violoncell Schule*, 39.
[17] Clementi: *Introduction*, 10.
[18] Baillot: *L'art du violon*, 74. Mozart's original has an eighth (originally a quarter) in the third bar and a sixteenth in the fourth bar. Early editions have very various note lengths differing from Mozart's autograph.
[19] Bach: *Versuch*, i, 68.

A convention similar to the *overlong appoggiatura*, apparently unremarked by theorists of the day, seems also to have been widely observed by late 18th- and early-19th-century composers: this was that when a small-note *appoggiatura* occurred, at the interval of a second above or below, before a pair of notes of the same length and the same pitch, the *appoggiatura* was to be conceived as taking the whole value of the initial note, not merely a proportion of it (Ex. 12.7).

Ex. 12.7

This convention was certainly employed by Haydn. In a letter of 1768 he explicitly stated that the notation shown in Ex. 12.8a should be rendered as in Ex. 12.8b not as in Ex. 12.8c.[20]

Ex. 12.8 a–c. Haydn: "Applausus" letter (1769), quoted in Landon: *Haydn at Eszterháza*, 147.

It is probable that this was also intended by J. C. Bach; certainly Domenico Corri considered it to have this meaning, and realized it thus in his version of Bach's "Nel partir bell'idol mio" (see Ex. 13.3, bars 18, 31, 33, 76, 78, etc.). Later examples of the use of *appoggiaturas* in this manner can be found in Schubert. Where two syllables of this kind occur in his vocal music, he generally indicated the desired *appoggiatura* with a small note before the first of the pair, but wrote the small note with only half the intended value of the *appoggiatura*. There are many occurrences of this notation in his late opera *Fierrabras* (Ex. 12.9). The intended realization is made clear by numerous occasions on which the orchestral parts have the same figure fully written out (Ex. 12.10).

---

[20] H. C. Robbins Landon: *Haydn at Eszterháza 1766–1790* (London, 1978), 147.

Ex. 12.9 a–c. Schubert: *Fierrabras*, no. 4.

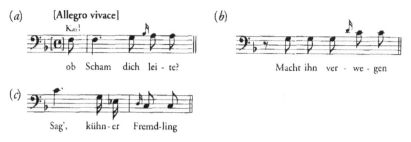

Ex. 12.10 Schubert: *Fierrabras*, no. 10.

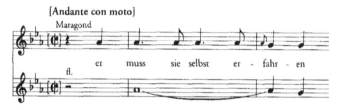

If Schubert required the figuration that his *appoggiaturas* seem to indicate, he wrote it in full (Ex. 12.11). Where *appoggiaturas* occur before single syllables (or in instrumental parts before single notes), however, he generally gave them the value with which he intended them to be performed (Ex. 12.12); but since he did not use small half-notes this is not the case before longer notes (Ex. 12.13).

Ex. 12.11 Schubert: *Fierrabras*, no. 10.

Ex. 12.12 Schubert: *Fierrabras*, no. 10.

Ex. 12.13 Schubert: *Fierrabras*, no. 17.

Ernest Walker believed that this notational habit in Schubert's music was peculiar to him and not mentioned in theoretical writings.[21] The practice, however, was evidently widespread, and examples may also be found in Weber's music. At least one late-19th-century writer, Franklin Taylor, recognized and described the convention.[22]

The problem with the rules advanced by theorists was not only that they disagreed among themselves, but also that, where persuasive evidence exists to show how *appoggiaturas* were intended to be realized in specific instances, even the rules about which most of the theorists agreed seem to have had a rather tenuous relationship with many composers' and performers' practices. This is particularly the case with *appoggiaturas* before notes of longer duration than quarters.

The practice of giving a small-note *appoggiatura* the approximate value intended for its realization offered a potentially much more reliable means of avoiding confusion. C. P. E. Bach observed in 1753: "people have recently begun to indicate such appoggiaturas according to their true value".[23] Although this was true of a few composers, the practice was certainly not widespread at that stage; and even where composers did begin to use different lengths of small notes for their *appoggiaturas*, it would be rash to assume that these always represented the desired length, or that they might not admit of equally acceptable alternative solutions, with respect to either length or embellishment. Nevertheless, during the second half of the 18th century, composers began increasingly to use differentiated note values for

---

[21] Walker: 'The Appoggiatura', *Music & Letters*, v (1924), 121–44.
[22] Grove: 'Appoggiatura' in *Dictionary*, 1st edn, i, 78.
[23] Bach: *Versuch*, i, 63.

small notes and to write many of their longer *appoggiaturas* in normal notation, to convey to the performer their preferred approximate duration for the dissonance (it was approximate because by convention the *appoggiatura*, like all expressive notes, required a degree of metrical freedom in its execution).

A progression from undifferentiated to varied small-note *appoggiaturas* can be traced in the music of major composers of the Classical period. Gluck used small eighths for *appoggiaturas* of all lengths and types in his earlier operas (in *Semiramide riconosciuta* [1748], for instance), and the actual performing lengths of these small notes are governed by no discernible rules; sometimes they evidently obey the rule to take half the note (Ex. 12.14a) but they seem never to follow the two-thirds or longer rule, and appear most frequently to be intended to be short (Ex. 12.14b). The only guiding principle for interpreting these notes appears to have been confidence in the musical instinct—*le bon goût*—of the performer.

**Ex. 12.14** a–b. Gluck: *Semiramide riconosciuta*. (*a*) Act II, Scene vi; (*b*) Act I, Scene iv. Österreichische Nationalbibliothek, Vienna, Cod. mus. 17.793.

In his later operas, especially those written for Paris, Gluck differentiated the values of small notes.

Haydn began increasingly to notate small notes in a more differentiated manner from about 1762.[24] In works after this date the value of the small

---

[24] See Laslo Somfai: 'How to Read and Understand Haydn's Notation in Its Chronologically Changing Concepts', in Eva Badura-Skoda (ed.), *Joseph Haydn: Bericht über den internationalen Joseph Haydn Kongress, Wien [...] 1982* (Munich, 1986), 25.

note is likely to be a useful indicator of how it was expected to be realized; but there remained habitual oddities, such as his use of a small sixteenth note in the pattern shown in Ex. 12.15, where something shorter is clearly meant (either a thirty-second or a *grace-note*).

Ex. 12.15

Mozart already began to use small notes of different values in very early works. At first, he employed half, quarter, eighth, sixteenth, and occasionally thirty-second small notes, but after about 1780 he stopped using small half-notes, and wrote out his longer *appoggiaturas* as normal notes. Neither Haydn nor Mozart seems to have used dotted small notes (which are extremely rare anywhere in 18th-century music). In most cases where *appoggiatura* treatment is called for in Mozart's music, the length of the small note is likely to be a useful guide to its duration, though it should not be regarded as enjoining a rhythmically exact execution, or precluding some form of nuanced or embellished performance. In view of his obvious care in specifying different values for small notes, however, it is difficult to see the logic of suggestions such as those in some of the *Neue Mozart Ausgabe* volumes, for instance in the Violin Sonata in E minor K. 304, where a different notational value for the resolution is suggested (Ex. 12.16).

Ex. 12.16   Mozart: Violin Sonata K. 304/i, piano part (*Neue Mozart Ausgabe*).

Many other late-18th-century composers, for instance J. F. Reichardt and G. J. Vogler, similarly adopted the practice of differentiating the values of their *appoggiaturas*; but many, probably the majority, were much more casual, and there is every reason to suspect that Italian composers, especially, were extremely indifferent in this matter.

It is clear from a mass of manuscript and printed music by minor figures, as well as from reiterated complaints about the difficulties presented to less experienced players by this notation, that considerable scope for misunderstanding remained throughout the 18th century. This was true not only in compositions, but also in instruction books, where a more consistent approach might have been expected. Löhlein's widely disseminated *Clavier-Schule* and *Anweisung zum Violinspielen*, for instance, contain many ambiguous small notes in the musical exercises; hence Witthauer's comments (above) in the fifth edition of the *Clavier-Schule* in 1791 and J. F. Reichardt's similar remarks in the fourth edition of the *Anweisung zum Violinspielen* in 1797. Reichardt observed of one of Löhlein's examples, where small eighth-notes were employed: "but this manner of writing is not the most correct one; for most people will, in accordance with the convention, execute the eighth-note appoggiatura as an eighth. A short appoggiatura of this kind [he evidently means a *grace-note*] should reasonably be designated by a sixteenth or thirty-second".[25]

Despite the ambiguities resulting from the custom of using small notes for *appoggiaturas*, there were undoubtedly factors, apart from force of habit, that favoured its survival into the 19th century. In an age when the addition of improvised ornaments was endemic, the notation of the *appoggiatura* as a small note would, as Leopold Mozart observed, warn the player or singer against distorting the harmony by the addition of inappropriate embellishments to notes that were already ornamental.[26] More importantly, writing an *appoggiatura* in this manner encouraged the executant to give it a particular style of performance, and a greater degree of rhythmic freedom than it might have received if written in precise note values. Many comments from the period suggest that this was the case. John Holden remarked: "The appoggiatura should always be tied to one of the principal notes; and, though we are not strictly obliged to give it just the time which its figure would require, yet whatever length of time is bestowed on it, must be, as it were, borrowed from the principal note with which it is tied."[27] Forty years later, Anton Reicha would write that one could either indicate a particular figure with *appoggiaturas* or normal notes (Ex. 12.17a), but observed that

---

[25] Löehlein, ed. Reichardt: *Anweisung zum Violinspielen*, 44.
[26] Mozart: *Versuch*, 195.
[27] Holden: *Essay*, 39.

in the first case: "one may perform them with a greater or lesser value according to the character of the piece", and gave three alternative possibilities (Ex. 12.17b).

Ex. 12.17 a–b. Reicha: *Cours de composition musicale* (Paris, [1818]), 85.

He explained that when appoggiaturas are written as normal notes, "they should be performed with the value prescribed by the composer",[28] but this comment certainly implied something more flexible to him and his contemporaries in 1818 than it does to most musicians at the beginning of the 21st century. Domenico Corri's *The Singers Preceptor*, published just eight years before Reicha's treatise, contains the comment: "The length of time given to Graces, tho' in general marked, yet never can be given so accurately as to direct the true expression of the words, which must be therefore regulated by the judgement, taste and feeling of the Singer,"[29] and as Corri's earlier *Select Collection* clearly demonstrates, similar flexibility extended to many other notes (see Chapter 13).

There is every reason to believe that a similar attitude was taken in instrumental performance, as implied by C. P. E. Bach's comment about modifying the length of *appoggiaturas* for the sake of expression. Michel Woldemar, in his revision of Leopold Mozart's *Violinschule* (which, in fact, has only a tenuous relationship with the original), gave several examples of how to perform *appoggiaturas*, remarking that the small note requires half the value of the following note, never more, but sometimes less.[30] He included two

---

[28] Anton Reicha: *Cours de composition musicale* (Paris, [1818]), 85.
[29] D. Corri: *Singers Preceptor*, 32.
[30] Woldemar: *Méthode de violon par L. Mozart*, 30.

examples from the original edition but realized them differently from Mozart (Ex. 12.18a–b).

**Ex. 12.18** a–b. (*a*) Woldemar: *Méthode de violon par L. Mozart*, 30; (*b*) Mozart: *Versuch*, ix, §3, 194f.

It seems likely, in fact, that *appoggiaturas* were very often executed shorter than is suggested by many ornament tables and theoretical guidelines, though without being performed as short as *grace-notes*. A passage from an *opera buffa* by Gassmann, *L'opera seria*, in which a Kapellmeister instructs the orchestra how to play his music, is instructive: the orchestra parts have Ex. 12.19a, and the singer's demonstration is notated as in Ex. 12.19b.

**Ex. 12.19** a–b. Gassmann: *L'opera seria*, Act II, Scene vi, MS score in Österreichische Nationalbibliothek, Vienna, ms. no. 177775; pub. in fac. in the series *Italian Opera 1640–1770* (New York and London, Garland 1982).

Much later, in two posthumously published violin sonatas, probably composed in the early 1790s, by Beethoven's Viennese rival Anton Eberl, there is similar evidence of a shorter realization than might be expected in the different notation employed for a unison passage between violin and piano in the Rondo of his Violin Sonata op. 49 (Ex. 12.20a), though this may perhaps be taken as notation for a *grace-note* rather than an *appoggiatura*. In contrast, an *appoggiatura* in the violin part of the Rondo of his Violin Sonata op. 50

is given a longer realization in the piano part than its apparent value, but a shorter one than might be expected from the "two-thirds of a dotted note" rule (Ex. 12.20b).

**Ex. 12.20** a–b. Eberl, Violin Sonata. (*a*) op. 49/iii; (*b*) op. 50/iii.

When a singer or solo instrument and an accompaniment part were in unison, it was not uncommon for composers to include small-note *appoggiaturas* in the solo part and to write the ornament in full-size notes in the accompaniment, as in the examples from Eberl and the passages from Schubert's *Fierrabras* cited above. Such instances provide useful indications of the duration envisaged for the *appoggiatura*. But this cannot be relied on in all cases, especially with small sixteenth-notes, where, as in the example from Eberl's Sonata op. 49, the choice between a *grace-note* and a literal sixteenth is often unclear.

While unison passages shed light on the length of *appoggiaturas*, they do not necessarily prove that a performance in which the soloist delivers the *appoggiatura* in complete synchronization with the orchestra was what the composer wanted or how accomplished singers of the day would actually have executed them. Corri's *Select Collection*, which, as far as the notation of the period allowed, purports to give the ornaments as they might have been rendered, provides examples (Ex. 12.21). Corri's collection also includes interesting instances of less predictable realizations of *appoggiaturas*, which indicate that the use of a single small note might well have been understood to allow a variety of more elaborate realizations.[31]

---

[31] See Ex. 13.4, bb. 33, 47, etc.; Ex. 12.73a for Leopold Mozart's examples of the *appoggiatura* combined with an extempore turn.

Ex. 12.21 D. Corri, *A Select Collection*, I, 6.

The pervasiveness of this kind of ornamental treatment in different times and schools is suggested by Pierre Baillot's examples, half a century later, of very similar methods of varying an *appoggiatura*: the *appoggiatura* in Ex. 12.22a might be realized as in Ex. 12.22b–d.

Ex. 12.22 a–d. (*a*) Notated appoggiatura; (*b*), (*c*), and (*d*) realizations in Baillot: *L'art du violon*, 74f.

One aspect of the execution of *appoggiaturas*, on which there was general agreement, was that they should be smoothly connected to their main notes,[32]

---

[32] E.g., Türk: *Klavierschule*, 218; Joseph Gehot: *A Treatise on the Theory and Practice of Music together with the Scales of Every Musical Instrument* (London, 1784), 3; Löhlein: *Clavier-Schule*, 5th edn, 25; Romberg: *Violoncell Schule*, 39.

and that the *appoggiatura* received the greater stress, the main note being phrased off and sometimes shortened. Some writers of string, wind, and singing methods, however, suggested that this should generally be a very different kind of emphasis from the simple accent that would be given to the same figure written in normal notes. According to several authors,[33] where time allowed, as Tromlitz explained, the player should "sound the appoggiatura softly, allow it to grow in strength, and slur it to the following note very softly, allowing it to decrescendo at the same time".[34] This treatment of the *appoggiatura* is explicitly shown in many of the exercises in Campagnoli's *Nouvelle méthode*, where the notation (illustrating a rare employment of a dotted *appoggiatura*) sometimes also indicates a longer *appoggiatura* than might be expected (Ex. 12.23a–c).

Ex. 12.23 a–c. Campagnoli: *Nouvelle méthode*. (*a*) ii, 38; (*b*) ii, 39; (*c*) ii 43.

Koch's consideration of *appoggiaturas*, and the reason for writing them with small notes, neatly synthesizes the views of many of his contemporaries. He observed that many dissonances are

---

[33] Giuseppe Tartini: *Traité des agréments de la musique*; ed. E. R. Jacobi (Celle, 1961), 66; Quantz: *Versuch*, 8, §4, 78; Jean Baptiste Cartier, *L Art du violon ou collection choisie dans les sonates des écoles italienne, françoise et allemande précédée d'un abrégée des principes pour cet instrument* (Paris, [1798]), 4.

[34] Tromlitz: *Unterricht*, 242.

distributed properly in the bar and indicated in normal notes. The reason why this does not likewise happen with the appoggiatura, has its origin in the particular and exceptional way the appoggiatura is performed. That is to say, it is agreed that in delaying a melodic main note by means of the appoggiatura, one should markedly bring out the appoggiatura itself with a particular accent, or sound it with a certain rapid swelling of the strength of the note: and then slur the following melodic main note to it softly or with decreased strength.[35]

With the demise of the small-note *appoggiatura* and the growing precision of composers' notation, any such special treatment was more likely to be indicated by signs; and the persistence of this style of performance for written-out *appoggiaturas* in the 19th century is attested, for instance, by dynamic markings, similar to those used by Campagnoli, on *appoggiaturas* in the Largo of Mendelssohn's String Quartet op. 12, and in many Lieder by his teacher Zelter. Later in the 19th century, Charles de Bériot seems to describe a related procedure when he instructs: "In order to render the appoggiatura well, we must press softly with the bow on the long note, making it vibrate with the finger when the expression admits, and letting the sound expire on the final note, represents the mute E [in the French language], with as much purity as elegance."[36]

For keyboard players, this kind of nuanced performance was obviously not possible; and in their discussion of *appoggiaturas* most writers of keyboard methods mentioned simply that the small note requires greater emphasis than the main note.[37] But it is evident from occasional examples that, at least in the 19th century, there might be circumstances in which this rule of emphasizing the *appoggiatura* did not operate. In an editorial note to his translation of Reicha's *Cours de composition*, Carl Czerny gave an example of ornaments and their resolutions in which he showed the main note with the accent (Ex. 12.24).[38] Naturally, individual cases were likely to be conditioned by their particular contexts, and where, as in the vast majority of cases, the small-note *appoggiatura* is dissonant, the usual convention of stressing dissonances would apply; Czerny did not indicate the harmony in

---

[35] Koch: 'Vorschlag' in *Musikalisches Lexikon*, 1721. (See Ch. 6 for Koch's and other writers' further views on the performance of the *Abzug* in such instances.)
[36] Bériot: *Méthode*, 187.
[37] E.g., Türk: *Klavierschule*, 217; Löhlein, *Clavier-Schule*, 5th edn, 25.
[38] Reicha, ed. Czerny: *Cours de composition/Vollständiges Lehrbuch*, 537.

his example, but, whatever the harmony, it appears that in this instance he felt that the principle of displacement of accent by a syncopation overrode that of accenting an *appoggiatura*.

Ex. 12.24 Reicha, ed. Czerny: *Cours de composition/Vollstandiges Lehrbuch*, i, 537.

It was probably the association of dissonance with a stronger accent than usual that led Philip Corri to state that though figures like Ex. 12.25 were to be performed as four equal notes, the first of the group received more accent if it was written in this manner rather than with full-size notes.[39]

Ex. 12.25 P. A. Corri: *L'anima di musica*, 14.

Like so many rules in instruction books, this offered only rough guidance to the inexperienced player, for while in many cases the small note was dissonant, this was not always so. Philip Corri's treatment of these figures may indicate a change of attitude around the beginning of the 19th century, as comparison with Türk's discussion of the matter implies. Türk explained that (according to generally accepted theory) the *appoggiatura* in figures such as Ex. 12.3 (15) required a short (i.e., *grace-note*) performance; but he felt that this was frequently unsatisfactory, remarking:

> With these and similar figures [Ex. 12.26] almost all music teachers require, indeed, that the appoggiaturas should be short, as at b); and in various cases, if, for example, single figures of this kind occur, as at c) below, or when several similar figures follow immediately one after another, as at d) etc., this realization may be good and necessary on harmonic grounds. Yet still I cannot convince myself that this rule should apply so generally and in

---

[39] P. A. Corri: *L'anima di musica*, 14.

NOTATED ORNAMENTS 653

every instance. If one makes the appoggiatura short in example e), after the preceding and following four-note figures, the flow of the melody seems to me to become, at the same time, limping.

Also, I have heard only few tasteful, practical musicians realize passages like f) as at g), but many more as at h).

Although the realization at g) may be commoner than that at h), I desire that the latter should be used in my works, except where in individual cases other rules are against it.[40]

**Ex. 12.26** Türk: *Klavierschule*, 225.

Türk's preferred realization of such figures, with equal notes and an accent, appears to reflect an approach that was gaining ground in the 18th century and which, by the time of Philip Corri's treatise of 1810, had become the standard method. By that date, too, the use of a small note in notating these figures was becoming increasingly uncommon. Interestingly, Philip Corri's

---

[40] Türk: *Klavierschule*, 225f.

approach was somewhat at odds with his father's more varied treatment of figures of this kind in vocal music. In an aria from J. C. Bach's *La clemenza di Scipione*, for instance, Domenico Corri rendered the notation in two different manners (see Ex. 13.3, bb. 22 and 29).

There were also circumstances in which some musicians, principally singers, seem to have regarded it as stylish to reverse the usual dynamic pattern for *appoggiaturas*; this was when they were taken from the semitone below. In 1810, Domenico Corri explained that in such cases, one should "Take the Grace softly and force it into the Note."[41] Some thirty years earlier he had given similar instructions in the preface to *A Select Collection*. Corri's extensive annotations to the pieces in that collection provide some interesting practical illustrations of where this technique might be applied (Ex. 12.27), and all of them indicate that despite the reversed dynamic, the second note was still shortened.

Ex. 12.27 D. Corri: *The Singer's Preceptor*, 32.

Gesualdo Lanza was also quite explicit about performing the rising *appoggiatura* in this manner. He observed of long *appoggiaturas* in general that they "should be sung much stronger than the note which follows them", but his examples show the realization of a rising *appoggiatura* with a *crescendo* to the note of resolution and a shortening of that note (Ex. 12.28).[42] Somewhat later he observed: "The under appoggiatura generally rises and the upper diminishes in strength."[43] However, many other musicians evidently performed rising *appoggiaturas*, whether written in normal notation or indicated by small notes, in a similar manner to falling ones. Leopold Mozart, for example, instructed that they must still be performed stronger than the main note.[44]

Ex. 12.28 Lanza: *The Elements of Singing*, i, 68.

[41] D. Corri: *The Singers Preceptor*, 32.
[42] Lanza: *Elements of Singing*, i. 68.
[43] Lanza: *Elements of Singing*, i, 82.
[44] Mozart: *Versuch*, 208.

Another practice, peculiar to many early-19th-century French violinists, seems to have been the habit of ending phrases, even, apparently, after a falling *appoggiatura*, with an accent and trembling effect. This mannerism, however, was regarded as ugly by some German musicians. A Viennese writer in 1813, noting this habit in Pierre Rode's playing, remarked: "Whether Herr Rode's mannerism, or rather that of the new French school, of accentuating the last note of a passage with a powerful Tremolando is an essential aspect of a brilliant performance style, would still have to be proved in accordance with the principles of musical aesthetics."[45] Seven years later Spohr, referring to Charles Lafont's playing, also deprecated the bringing out of the last note of a phrase by means of reinforced pressure and rapid, accented up-bow, even when a note comes on a weak beat, which, he reported, was common to all French violinists. And he added: "It is incomprehensible to me how this unnatural accentuation, which sounds just as if a speaker were to stress the weak final syllables particularly strongly, could have come about. If singing had always been taken as a model for the performance of cantabile (as I believe every instrumentalist should do), then one would not have gone astray in this manner."[46] A generation later Charles de Bériot instructed that, when one or more ornamental notes occur between the *appoggiatura* and its resolution, the note of resolution should be played with a separate bow, though he did not call for an accent on the final note.[47]

## The *Grace-Note*

The matter of whether *grace-notes* should precede or coincide with the beat was already controversial in the 18th century and has remained so until the present day. The belligerent positions adopted by some 20th-century scholars, combined with the disagreements of 18th- and 19th-century writers, fuelled a heated debate that sometimes tended to obscure rather than clarify the issue.

There is abundant evidence that either conception of the rhythmic placement of *grace-notes* would have found partisans at any stage during the period. Some musicians would perhaps have taken a dogmatic stand on one side of the argument, while many would have been more flexible, favouring one or the other interpretation according to context. Even among those who

---

[45] Anon.: *Wiener allgemeine musikalische Zeitung*, i (1813), 48.
[46] Spohr: 'Briefe aus Paris von Louis Spohr', *Allgemeine musikalische Zeitung*, xxiii (1821), 191.
[47] Bériot: *Méthode*, 187.

admitted both possibilities there would doubtless have been disagreement in specific instances; but this simply illustrates the diversity and mutability of musical taste. In very many cases, though, the problem is essentially an illusory one, for *grace-notes* will often be performed so rapidly that their precise relationship to the beat, which may itself be flexible, is virtually incapable of being distinguished either by the listener or, frequently, by the performer.

General rules for an appropriate style of *grace-note* performance in any given period are impossible to formulate. During the Classical period, however, it is evident that the vast majority of writers who addressed the problem favoured an on-beat conception (i.e., beginning the *grace-note* simultaneously with the bass note) in most, if not all, circumstances. Some writers described a type of single-note ornament, principally in the context of *tierces coulées*, which could be regarded either as an *anticipatory note* or pre-beat *grace-note*, and internal evidence suggests that composers sometimes used small notes with this meaning in other contexts (see below); but Milchmeyer's *Die wahre Art das Pianoforte zu spielen* (1797), which was very severely criticized for its treatment of ornaments in a review in the *Allgemeine musikalische Zeitung*, was among the few late-18th-century sources unequivocally to recommend a pre-beat conception of *grace-notes* as the norm. There appears to have been greater diversity of opinion in the 19th century, especially about the placement of ornaments of more than one note; yet many musicians of standing seem still to have regarded it as good practice to consider single *grace-notes* as occurring on the beat in most cases, and many of them recommended the same treatment for ornaments of several notes. Throughout the century, German writers continued to advance the traditional view.[48] Performers and composers were probably more pragmatic, though the majority, especially in the German sphere of influence, apparently continued predominantly to envisage single *grace-notes* as coinciding with the beat. This is clearly demonstrated by late-19th-century annotated editions of earlier piano music that include realizations of the ornaments. Examples may be found in the editions of Sigmund Lebert and Immanuel von Faisst, for instance (Ex. 12.29, but see the accent on the main note).[49]

[48] Schilling, Dommer, Paul, Mendel.
[49] E.g., Beethoven, Sonata op. 2 no. 3 (Hamburg, Schuberth, 1891).

Ex. 12.29 Beethoven: Sonata op. 2 no. 3, ed. S. Lebert and I. von Faisst.

Hugo Riemann's editions provide similar examples (Ex. 12.30a–b), though unlike the majority of his contemporaries, Riemann appears in general to have favoured an accented performance of the *grace-note*).

Ex. 12.30 a–c. Schubert: (*a* and *b*) *Moment musical* in A flat op. 94 no. 2, ed. H. Riemann; (*c*) *Moment musical* in A flat op. 94 no. 2, in Dannreuther, *Musical Ornamentation*, ii, 131.

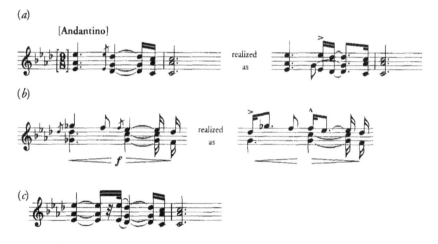

The treatise *Musical Ornamentation* by Edward Dannreuther, a practising concert pianist, who was a friend of Wagner, Tchaikovsky, and other prominent musicians of the period, pursues its historical survey right up to the practices of Dannreuther's own day and also confirms the continuing strength of an on-beat, generally unaccented, conception of *grace-notes* among his contemporaries. In individual instances, however, there always remained the possibility of disagreement. Dannreuther, for instance, considered that the *short appoggiatura* in bar 3 of Schubert's A flat *Moment musical* op. 94, which Riemann would have executed on the beat, "is meant for a Nachschlag"[50] and illustrated it as in Ex. 12.30c.

---

[50] Dannreuther: *Musical Ornamentation*, ii, 131.

Some 19th-century musicians, however, were much more inclined to regard *grace-notes* as quite definitely preceding the beat. An English edition of the Fétis and Moscheles treatise on piano playing was specific about a change in practice during the 19th century: "Acciaccaturas, slides and groups of two or three notes are placed immediately before the principal note. In the old school it was understood that they should share in the time of the principal note, but they are now to be played quickly and lightly before the time of the large note" (Ex. 12.31).[51] The contemporary Belgian violinist Charles de Bériot specified that small notes should precede the beat when they occurred "at the beginning of a piece or a phrase. These, far from having a sense of weight, serve only as a preparation, to give more force to the note which marks the strong beat of the bar."[52] (Ex. 12.32) But he remained silent about *grace-notes* in other contexts.

Ex. 12.31 Fétis and Moscheles: *Complete System*, 6.

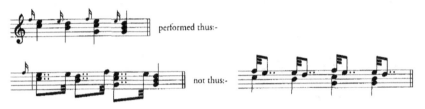

Ex. 12.32 Bériot: *Méthode*, 204.

Practices in this matter seem not only to have been affected by individual preferences, but may also, to some extent, have been specific to particular instruments, especially in the later 19th century. The German violinist Andreas Moser, writing at the beginning of the 20th century, supported a pre-beat conception in many situations, arguing that the approach was largely determined by the nature of different instruments. He observed that "even today the most contradictory opinions exist among practical musicians."[53]

---

[51] Fétis and Moscheles: *Complete System*, 6. (This statement is not present in the original *Méthode des Méthodes*.)
[52] Bériot: *Méthode*, 187.
[53] Joachim and Moser: *Violinschule*, iii, 28.

He noted that keyboard players still tended to favour placing *grace-notes* firmly on the beat while the majority of singers and string players anticipated them, and he suggested that this had been the case continuously since the middle of the 18th century. There is little firm historical evidence to support Moser's claim for practices before his own day, but it probably reflects the views of his teacher and colleague, Joseph Joachim, whose practical experience, and association with the leading musicians of the day in Vienna and Leipzig stretched back to the 1840s.

Some of the argument that has led, perhaps, to an over-reaction against the on-beat conception of the *grace-note* is worthy of closer examination. Much of it may derive from a conception of metrical regularity that developed only during the 20th century. Frederick Neumann, in his extensive studies of ornamentation,[54] advanced the opinion that an accent or *staccato* on the main note before which a *grace-note* stands precludes its performance on the beat; he felt that the rhythmic displacement of the accent, which would arise from following the instructions laid down by Leopold Mozart, Koch, Türk, and others for a softer rendering of the *grace-note* than the main note, would weaken the accent or *staccato* and thus the rhythmic structure. He also, in contrast to Lebert and Faisst (see Ex. 12.29), regarded a "Lombard" rhythm with the dynamic soft–loud as scarcely feasible, especially in fast music. With respect to theoretical prescriptions that the long note should bear the accent in such figures, he argued:

> Apart from the sense of affectation emanating from a routinely applied reverse dynamic pattern, it is for a simple reason highly improbable that anybody, including the authors themselves, followed this prescription with any degree of consistency. Such reverse dynamics are feasible only in a slow tempo, before single, long principal notes. The faster the tempo, the less feasible they become. We never find Mozart, nor presumably any other classical master, combining his frequently spelled-out "Lombard" rhythm [Ex. 12.33a] with reverse dynamics [Ex. 12.33b], not even in slow tempos. The very point of the Lombard rhythm is the snap effect produced by the accentuation of the short note.[55]

---

[54] Neumann: *Ornamentation in Baroque and Post-Baroque Music* (Princeton, 1978), and *Ornamentation and Improvisation in Mozart*.
[55] Neumann: *Ornamentation and Improvisation*, 9.

Ex. 12.33 a–b. Neumann: *Ornamentation and Improvisation*, 9.

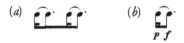

His argument is only valid, however, if the Lombard rhythm is performed strictly as notated in a fairly steady tempo and with a very powerful attack on the first note followed by an abrupt *piano*. In practice, the slighter the dynamic contrast between the two notes, or the more the initial note of the figure is shortened, the more prominently the second note will appear to bear the accent. A number of theorists of the period who specifically discussed the accentuation of Lombard rhythms considered that they would normally have the stress on the dotted note. Discussion of Lombard rhythms in Neumann's terms is scarcely relevant, since, with a very rapidly delivered *grace-note*, not only is it virtually impossible to give the small note more accent than the following one, but also the ear no longer perceives a distinct Lombard rhythm even if the *grace-note* coincides exactly with the bass. Even in written-out Lombard rhythms, as in the Trio section of the Minuetto in Mozart's D minor String Quartet K. 421, the initial note can sound like a *grace-note* when it is played very short, a practice that seems to have been preserved throughout the 19th century in some traditions.[56]

Some of the confusion seems to arise from the very reliance on ornament tables, of which Neumann was rightly so suspicious. The sections on "Graces" in Domenico Corri's *A Select Collection* (c. 1782) and *The Singers Preceptor* (1810) provide good examples of the caution that is necessary. In the latter he illustrated his discussion of the "Leaping Grace" with what is apparently a conventional Lombard rhythm (Ex. 12.34):[57] in the former he instructed that this grace was "to be taken softly and to leap into the note rapidly".

Ex. 12.34 D. Corri: *The Singer's Preceptor*, 32.

Corri's fuller verbal description in the earlier publication demonstrates that the rhythmic pattern of the example in the later work was not to be taken literally:

[56] See Ch. 2, pp. 44–45.
[57] D. Corri: *Singers Preceptor*, 32.

They are not to be considered as forming any part of the air; but are only intended to give to certain notes a particular emphasis or expression. The execution of them, therefore, ought to be so rapid, that, while the effect is felt, the ear shall yet be unable to determine the character of the sounds or to distinguish them from the predominant note[;] by no effort whatever indeed can they be rendered totally imperceptible, or if they could they would not then exist. But the more imperceptible they are, the more happy is the execution, the more perfect the union, and the more delicate the effect, whereas, by an execution that renders them distinctly perceptible, they would lose their nature and instead of the adventitious graces now under consideration, become part of the melody itself.[58]

All the graces to which Corri applied this description were unequivocally conceived as taking place on the beat; he described anticipating and connecting graces quite separately. The continuity of an on-beat style of performance for *grace-notes* of this kind in Corri's own family is attested to by Philip Corri's discussion of them (for which he uses the term *appoggiatura*): "The general fault is playing the Appoggiatura before the bass."[59] This, of course, like similar remarks by other writers, makes it clear that many people at the time did indeed play these notes distinctly before the beat.

Whatever support individual preference for a pre-beat conception of *grace-notes* may receive from negative evidence, the fact remains that in the late 18th century and early 19th century most of the leading musicians of the day who expressed themselves on the subject were strongly opposed to it. One of the alterations that J. F. Reichardt made in the fourth edition of Löhlein's *Anweisung zum Violinspielen*, in 1797, for instance, concerns this matter. Earlier editions contained the passage and realization as shown in Ex. 12.35a, but Reichardt changed the realization to Ex. 12.35b. The evident objection of Reichardt and many other musicians and teachers in the 18th and 19th centuries to the concept of pre-beat performance of small notes, even in such instances of *tierces coulées*, may well have reflected their concern to ensure that *grace-notes* created the effect so clearly described by Domenico Corri and were not given greater length than they required.

---

[58] D. Corri: *A Select Collection*, 8.
[59] P. A. Corri: *L'anima di musica*, 13.

**Ex. 12.35** a–b. Löhlein: *Anweisung zum Violinspeilen.* (*a*) 1st edn, 44; (*b*) 4th edn, ed. J. F. Reichardt.

There is a good deal of musical common sense in this approach, for when *grace-notes* are conceived as preceding the beat there is a real danger that they will be performed somewhat longer and more lazily—thus giving the effect of *anticipatory notes*—than if they are thought of as coinciding with it. On the other hand, the laboured rendition that *grace-notes* sometimes receive when performers are anxious to leave no doubt that they are executed on the beat (often with an attempt to give them a greater accent than the main note) seems equally contrary to their nature. Neumann's arguments notwithstanding, it seems clear that in the case of the short *appoggiatura* there was no requirement that it should really be louder than its main note. A sharper attack on the *grace-note*, as recommended by C. P. E. Bach, or a more caressing one, as suggested by Leopold Mozart, has little to do with the player's or listener's perception of metric or expressive accent. This misconception of the *grace-note* was undoubtedly encouraged in later 20th-century performance by the idea that they are executed with a deliberate rhythm in the manner that many musical examples, such as those in Corri's *Singer's Preceptor*, seem to imply. This was another manifestation of the modern, literal approach to musical notation, which, especially in its strict observance of notated rhythm, would have been quite alien to an 18th-century musician. At that time Ex. 12.36a could, in some circumstances, just as well mean Ex. 12.36b, c, or even d, according to context.

**Ex. 12.36** a–d.

Taken in conjunction with verbal descriptions, the sense in which these graphic illustrations are to be understood becomes quite clear. A *grace-note* (*kurzer Vorschlag*) should, as Schilling's *Encyclopädie* commented in the 1830s, "always be rendered as short as possible, for which reason, doubtless, they are also called pinched *Vorschläge*"; in addition it confirmed the view that they ought to be essentially accentless, commenting: "the short

V[orschläge] finally give the main note an even greater, stronger accent than it actually possesses in itself, and must therefore be performed as lightly as clarity allows";[60] but no doubt was entertained about their placement on the beat, for the writer asserted: "All Vorschläge, without exception, fall in the time of their main note."[61]

The concept of an extremely light and rapid performance of *grace-notes* is, in fact, implicit in almost all instructions for their execution throughout the Classical and Romantic periods. Reichardt referred to "very short appoggiaturas, which one adds to notes without them seeming to lose any of their value".[62] Koch similarly observed that such notes are "slurred so fast to the main note that, as a result, the latter seems not to lose the slightest part of its value".[63] Both these writers specified performance on the beat. Baillot, apparently envisaging pre-beat performance, characterized the *grace-note* (which he called the *appoggiature rythmique*) as being played "briskly and almost on the main note", adding, "In animated movements one naturally makes it faster than in slow movements: however, it always retains a certain speed which distinguishes it from melodic small notes."[64] Spohr, writing a couple of years earlier and requiring on-beat performance, instructed in the typical German way that it "deprives the note before which it stands of scarcely any of its value. With this note it is quickly and lightly connected in one bow."[65] Moser, too, emphasized the light, fleeting nature of this ornament, saying that "a note that has an extremely short, often immeasurable duration, cannot have any good claim to special accentuation";[66] and, cutting the Gordian knot of pre- or post-beat performance (despite his own preference for the former), he observed: "Its duration should be as short as possible, i.e., not revealing whether the time necessary for its execution was taken from the following main note of the preceding one."[67] This accords perfectly with Joachim's performance of *grace-notes* in his 1903 recording of his Romance in C, which is very rapid, so that it is impossible to say whether they fall on or before the beat, especially since the beat itself is quite fluid.

The impression gained from these and numerous other 18th- and 19th-century descriptions is that, regardless of whether the writers thought they were performing *grace-notes* on or before the beat, they were very closely in

---

[60] Schilling: 'Vorschlag' in *Encyclopädie*, vi, 803.
[61] Schilling: 'Vorschlag' in *Encyclopädie*, vi, 802.
[62] Reichardt: *Ueber die Pflichten*, 41.
[63] Koch: 'Vorschlag' in *Musikalisches Lexikon*, 125f.
[64] Baillot: *L'art du violon*, 75.
[65] Spohr: *Violinschule*, 170.
[66] Joachim and Moser: *Violinschule*, iii, 29.
[67] Joachim and Moser: *Violinschule*, i, 145.

agreement about their effect. Arguments for real anticipation of a *grace-note*, on the grounds that the principal notes of a chord should be sounded together on the beat, also reflect a misconception of 18th- and 19th-century attitudes. In a period which favoured three- and four-part chords in orchestral string writing (usually executed *divisi* in recent times, but certainly intended to be "broken") and when frequent unnotated arpeggiation was recommended and employed by keyboard players, it seems highly improbable that the very slightly staggered accentuation that might result from the introduction of a *grace-note* with the beat would have been regarded as disturbing. Concern for absolute regimentation in such matters (largely a product of recording) has been the norm only since the middle of the 20th century.

There is little firm information about attitudes towards the performance of *grace-notes* by the major composers of the Classical period: three musical clocks, two dated (1792 and 1793) and one undated (c. 1796), however, illustrate how contemporary musicians closely associated with Haydn realized his ornaments. The barrels of the clocks were apparently pinned either by Joseph Niemecz, who was both librarian and cellist at Eszterháza and, probably, Haydn's composition pupil, or by his assistant Joseph Gurk. They realized the ornaments on these mechanical instruments in a variety of ways, and comparison with the surviving autographs, and copies by Haydn's amanuensis Johann Elßler, shows conclusively that whoever pinned the barrels did not recognize any one immutable method of executing particular ornament signs or small notes. The editors of these "Flötenuhrstücke" in *Joseph Haydn Werke* have this to say about the performance of the *grace-notes*:

> Unfortunately, it is not possible to determine, either through listening or through measuring the impressions from the cylinders, whether the organ-builder took the value of a grace-note from the following or preceding note or whether, perhaps, he placed it in between [*sic!*]. Performance on the beat, however, seems to predominate.[68]

What is abundantly clear about these *grace-notes* is that—in agreement with the instructions of Reichardt, Koch, Corri, Baillot, Spohr, Schilling, Moser, and many others—they are rendered very fleetingly.

Most of the time, 19th-century composers, like their 18th-century predecessors, were content to rely on the performer's taste and skill in the execution of *grace-notes*. In a significant number of instances, though,

---

[68] *Joseph Haydn Werke*, xxi, 66.

the more painstaking among them were concerned to indicate special requirements. Some pianist composers, including Chopin, Schumann, and Alkan, periodically specified the performance of *grace-notes* before the beat by the positioning of the small note (Ex. 12.37a–b).

Ex. 12.37a Schumann: Noveletten op. 21/3.

Ex. 12.37b Alkan: *Douze Études*, no. 10.

Schumann also employed this form of notation in his string writing (Ex. 12.38).

Ex. 12.38 Schumann: String Quartet op. 41/1/iv (violin 1).

Berwald, a violinist, carefully marked accents on some of the *grace-notes* (apparently to be played on the beat) in the Finale of his Quartet in A minor

(1849), whereas elsewhere in the same movement he put accents on the main notes (Ex. 12.39).

Ex. 12.39 a–b. Berwald: String Quartet in A minor, iv.

Some late-18th- and early-19th-century composers occasionally used single small notes that did not fit into the conventional categories of *grace-notes*, *anticipatory notes*, or *appoggiaturas*. Such small notes, which often stand for short notes of precise value, were a form of shorthand, generally employed to avoid notational complications that would not only have been troublesome to write, but might also have appeared confusing to the performer. These "pseudo-grace-notes" may involve performance either on or before the beat. Haydn's string quartets op. 76 no. 1 and op. 76 no. 4 and Mozart's Duo for violin and viola K. 423, for instance, contain examples of small notes standing for normal notes on the beat (Ex. 12.40a–c).

Ex. 12.40 (a) Haydn, String Quartet op.76/2/i; (b) Haydn, String Quartet op. 76/4.i; (c) Mozart, Duo K. 423/ii.

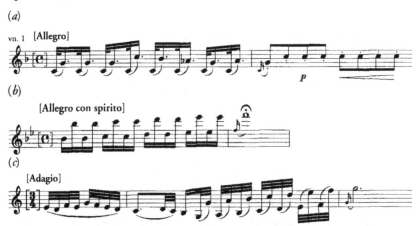

NOTATED ORNAMENTS 667

An example of similar notation indicating a note before the beat occurs in Beethoven's Violin Sonata op. 12 no. 1; comparison with the corresponding passage in the recapitulation clarifies its meaning (Ex. 12.41).

Ex. 12.41 a–b. Beethoven: Violin Sonata op. 12/1/i. (*a*) 63ff; (*b*) 188ff.

In later works, too, Beethoven occasionally used this kind of shorthand where a precise rhythmic placement of the note would make the music look unduly complicated and distort the clarity of the phrasing (Ex. 12.42). Like so much else in the music of the Classical period, instances of this kind are recognizable not so much by the notational symbols employed as by their musical context.

Ex. 12.42 Beethoven: Rondo op. 51/1.

## Anticipatory Notes

Despite the strictures of most German theorists, there were some single small-note ornaments which, like the two-, three-, or occasionally four-note *Nachschlag* (most commonly occurring after a trill), were definitely conceived as belonging to the time of the note they follow. Among them were *tierces coulées*, which were difficult to distinguish by their context from *appoggiaturas* or *grace-notes* and, presumably, often taken in different senses by different musicians, as the example from Reichardt's edition of Löhlein's *Anweisung zum Violinspielen* (Ex. 12.35) implies. The same kind of *appoggiatura* or *grace-note* was considered by Türk, who illustrated both ways of realizing it, depending on whether the composer expected a French or a *Lombard* style.[69] Other ornaments that presupposed anticipation were connected with particular types of portamento (*cercar della nota, port de voix*) and are considered in that context in Chapter 15.

## The Trill

Trills and turns are closely related ornaments, involving, for the most part, a number of auxiliary notes decorating the main harmony note with notes a second above and below. Some ornaments that share many of the characteristics of trills and turns may involve notes that are further than a second from the main note; and a variety of inconsistent names and signs may be found in those 18th- and 19th-century writings that attempt to categorize the numerous forms these ornaments could take. The variants described by theorists provide a useful digest of typical patterns, but linking these formulas with the practice of individual composers and their ornament signs requires circumspection. It is important, once again, to remember that even where the composer has notated an ornament with small notes, or in those relatively rare instances where we can confidently associate a composer's ornament sign with a particular pattern of notes, there may, depending on the musical circumstances, be more room for flexibility and initiative on the performer's part than is commonly believed. Composers would certainly have regarded some realizations of their ornament notation as inappropriate,

---

[69] Türk: *Klavierschule*, 223. See above, p. 633 and Ex. 12.3(12).

but this does not mean, especially in the late 18th century and early 19th century, that they would necessarily have considered a single realization to be the only possibility with regard either to rhythm or the pattern of notes employed. As in other aspects of notation, later 19th-century composers were often more prescriptive, and where a precise rendition of an ornament was considered integral to their musical intentions, they tended to write the ornament out in full, at least on its first appearance.

It will be useful initially to consider these types of ornament independently of the notations employed to indicate them in the music of the period, and to look in a general way at contexts and situations in which 18th- and 19th-century musicians believed them to be appropriate. A comprehensive survey of the relationships between signs and particular patterns of notes is beyond the scope of this chapter, but a few of the most commonly encountered problems will be illuminated by examples and extracts from music and writings of the period.

In its simplest form, a turn consists of four notes: the normal turn (Ex. 12.43a) and the inverted turn (Ex. 12.43b). It may also have five notes (Ex. 12.44a–b).

Ex. 12.43 a–b.

(a)   (b)

Ex. 12.44 a–b.

(a)   (b)

If further repetitions of the main note and its upper auxiliary are added, these turns will be heard as trills. Trills, turns, and associated ornaments tend to function as accents when they occur at the beginning of a strong beat, and as connecting figures when they occupy a weak beat. On long notes, of course, the repetitions of the main note and its upper auxiliary, which differentiate the trill from the turn, are necessary to fill out the note; on short notes the rapidity of the music or the expression aimed at by the performer will determine whether a simple turn (which can be seen as synonymous with a short trill) or a more extended trill is employed.

## Trill Beginnings

Much attention has been focused on the way trills were expected to be performed in the second half of the 18th century and early years of the 19th century, when they were a much more common feature of musical compositions than they later became. Discussion has focused particularly on the extent to which performers and composers at that time accepted the apparently rigid prescription by Quantz, Marpurg, C. P. E. Bach, L. Mozart, and the vast majority of other 18th- and early-19th-century theorists, that the trill should (almost) invariably begin with the upper auxiliary, and especially that the upper note should fall on the stronger part of the beat. There can be little doubt that the treatise writers, who were mostly also composers, usually, if not always, envisaged an upper-note, on-beat beginning to trills in their own music, but the practice of major composers is by no means clear-cut.

The issue was already a matter for discussion during the 18th century, and the employment of both types of trill beginning is amply documented.[70] Koch, for example, wrote: "The majority hold, with C. P. E. Bach, that the beginning of the trill must be made with the upper auxiliary; others, however, that one should always begin it with the main note."[71] In a footnote he referred to Tromlitz, who was one of the few treatise writers to support the latter view. Tromlitz's argument, however, had more to do with the prominence of the main note during the trill, for almost all his examples are preceded either by the note above or the note below the trilled note; for trills that begin after a silence, he proposed either a trill preceded by a *grace-note* from above, or one beginning on the main note (in that order).[72] J. F. Reichardt strongly advocated the upper-note start, but his comment in the 1770s that it should begin with the upper note, "not as many mistakenly believe with the note itself",[73] also reveals the diversity of 18th-century practice.

Those who advocated an upper-note start as the rule during the second half of the 18th century were undoubtedly, as Koch remarked, in the majority;

---

[70] See Neumann, *Ornamentation in Baroque and Post-Baroque Music*.
[71] Koch: 'Triller' in *Musikalisches Lexikon*, 1589.
[72] Tromlitz: *Unterricht*, 271–74.
[73] Reichardt: *Ueber die Pflichten*, 45f.

but Koch expressed no preference and observed that it was scarcely a matter of much importance whether the trill began one way or the other, since there was no audible difference after the initial note had been sounded. Despite Marpurg's remark that "The trill has its origin in the connected appoggiatura from above to below, and is thus basically nothing but a series of falling appoggiaturas reiterated with the greatest rapidity,"[74] it seems highly unlikely that this view, emphasizing the dissonance of the auxiliary throughout the length of the trill (which, in any case, would only have been obvious in a rather slow trill), was significant in the late 18th century. Leopold Mozart, after giving examples of trills beginning with a long *appoggiatura*, wrote: "If, however, a passage begins with a trill, the appoggiatura will hardly be heard, and it is in such cases nothing more than a strong initiation of the trill."[75] He did not, like Tromlitz, offer the option of beginning such trills on the main note. In a heavily revised 1804 reissue of Mozart's treatise, the second clause was modified to "a short Vorschlag [grace-note] will be made which is really the beginning of the trill."[76]

The trill was overwhelmingly seen as an embellishment in which the harmonic and melodic primacy of the main note remained distinct. Domenico Corri acknowledged two principal manners of performing a trill (in English usage "shake") in singing, remarking that some recommended "a close rapid shake, giving a brilliancy and shortness to the upper Note", while others, including himself (following his master Porpora), required it with "equality of notes, distinctly marked and moderately quick. Also that the Note which bears the Shake ought to be the most predominant, and if the auxiliary Note is too closely blended the principal cannot be sufficiently distinguished."[77] In his publications, Domenico Corri appears to envisage some cadential trills beginning with the main note, others with the upper note. Philip Corri, however, in *L'anima di musica*, published in the same year as his father's *Singers Preceptor*, instructed, "The turn and sometimes the first note of the shake is written (tho' it is understood without it)", observing that the figures in Ex. 12.45a "would be played alike", and added "Sometimes the shake

---

[74] Friedrich Willhelm Marpurg: *Anleitung zum Clavierspielen, der schönern Ausübung der heutigen Zeit gemäße entworfen* (Berlin, 1755), 53.
[75] Mozart: *Versuch*, 223.
[76] Mozart, ed. Petiscus: *Violinschule* (Leipzig, 1804), 57.
[77] D. Corri: *The Singers Preceptor*, 30.

begins with an inverted turn [Ex. 12.45b] Hence the shake must begin either above or below, and end on the principal note, but never begin on the principal note."[78]

Ex. 12.45 a–b. P. A. Corri: *L'anima di musica*, 18f.

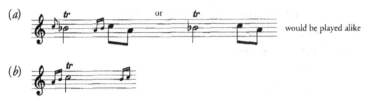

On the other hand, Domenico Corri's younger son Haydn Corri gave examples of trills beginning on the main note; but, eschewing dogmatism, he added the following *nota bene*:

> When a perfect shake is obtained there are many very elegant additions, as the preparing note and the closing ornament, but this I leave to the taste of the Master, as there are too many for imitation in a work founded upon brevity. Also it would appear presumptuous, were I to dictate which was most graceful as that is all matter of opinion.[79]

Scholarship has produced an impressive body of evidence and argument to support the view that there was far greater diversity of practice than the most frequently cited sources might suggest, and that the supposed hegemony of the "*appoggiatura* trill" in the late 18th century is a fiction. Further examples of late-18th-century sources that demonstrate theoretical support for main-note starts, and are not cited by Neumann or others, can be found in English instruction books. The anonymous *Instructions for the Violin by an Eminent Master* shows the trill beginning on the main note.[80] J. Mc Kerrell's *A Familiar Introduction to the First Principles of Music* gives further examples of trills starting on the note (Ex. 12.46).[81]

---

[78] P. A. Corri: *L'anima di musica*, 18f.
[79] Haydn Corri: *The Delivery of Vocal Music* (London, 1823), 5.
[80] Anon, *Instructions for the Violin* (London, [c. 1795]), 17.
[81] Mc Kerrell: *A Familiar Introduction* (London, [c. 1800]), 3.

Ex. 12.46 Mc Kerrell: *A Familiar Introduction*, 3.

During the 19th century an increasing number of treatise writers, including composers of importance, such as Hummel and Spohr, stated that trills should normally begin with the main note, and that composers who required an alternative beginning should indicate this. It is more likely, however, that such statements are evidence of the growing opinion that musical notation should be a more specific representation of the composer's expectations, than a reflection of normal contemporary practice. It is even unlikely that they reflect the notational practice or performing practices of these composers themselves, at least in their earlier works.[82] There is also no good reason to imagine that experienced early-19th-century performers would have felt inhibited from varying their trill beginnings (or endings), nor that most composers would have wished to interdict a reasonable degree of licence in the matter.

Whatever may have been the views and practices of individual composers, it seems certain that performers employed trills beginning from the note above, the main note, or the note below as it suited their musical purpose. Despite the apparently prescriptive teaching of some theorists, there are abundant indications in others of an acceptance that the execution of trills, like other ornaments, would be left to the taste of the performer, especially since few composers took the trouble to spell out their requirements clearly. In 1770, John Holden, for instance, whose musical examples show trills beginning on the main note, some with and some without a concluding turn, remarked: "Sometimes the shake is not begun until one half of the note be sung plain. These and other such varieties are

---

[82] This is demonstrably the case with Carl Czerny. See Clive Brown: 'Reading between the Lines of Beethoven's Notation' in *Beethoven Violin Sonatas* (Kassel, Bärenreiter, 2020), xxiv. See also below, pp. 679–83.

generally left to the performer's choice, being all indiscriminately marked in the same manner"[83] (Ex. 12.47).

Ex. 12.47 Holden: *Essay*, 39.

Much the same attitude is apparent in Baillot's treatment of the matter some sixty years later when he offered the performer a choice of four possibilities for the execution of trill beginnings (Ex. 12.48). Like Holden and Haydn Corri, he considered the executant's choice to be determined by taste, though in contrast with his German contemporaries, he observed that a trill beginning with the upper auxiliary "is that which one most often uses".[84] Younger authors of French treatises generally agreed with Hummel, Spohr, and Czerny in giving primacy to a main-note trill unless the composer indicated otherwise.[85]

Ex. 12.48 Baillot: *L'art du violon*, 78.

Despite all the evidence for diversity of practice, the question of stylistic propriety in the execution of trill beginnings in earlier music occupied the minds of some late-19th-century musicians of a theoretical bent who failed, however, to appreciate earlier, less prescriptive attitudes towards notation. The pianist Franklin Taylor noted in the first edition of *Grove's Dictionary*

---

[83] Holden: *Essay*, 39.
[84] Baillot: *L'art du violon*, 78.
[85] E.g., Herz: *Méthode* (1838); Habeneck: *Méthode* (1842); Bériot: *Méthode* (1857/8).

that beginning the trill with the main note was the "manner most shakes in modern music are executed". He went on to suggest that, historically, composers' methods of notating a trill that was required to begin from below will reveal whether they intended a normal trill to start with the upper auxiliary or the main note (Ex. 12.49a–c):

> From a composer's habit of writing the lower prefix with one, two or three notes, his intentions respecting the beginning of the ordinary shake *without* prefix, as to whether it should begin with the principal or subsidiary note, may generally be inferred. For since it would be incorrect to render Ex. 32 or 33 in the manner shown in Ex. 36, which involves the repetition of a note, and a consequent break of legato—it follows that a composer who chooses the form Ex. 32 to express the prefix intends the shake to begin with the upper note, while the use of Ex. 33 shows that a shake beginning with the principal note is generally intended.
>
> That the form Ex. 31 always implies the shake beginning with the principal note is not so clear (although there is no doubt that it usually does so) for a prefix is possible which leaps from the lower to the upper subsidiary note. This exceptional form is frequently employed by Mozart, and is marked as in Ex. 37 [. . .]. Among later composers Chopin and Weber almost invariably wrote the prefix with two notes (Ex. 32); Beethoven uses two notes in his earlier works (see op. 2 no. 2, Largo bar 10), but afterwards generally one (see op. 57).[86]

Ex. 12.49 a–c. Taylor: 'Shake' in Grove, *Dictionary*.

---

[86] Taylor: 'Shake' in *A Dictionary of Music and Musicians*, 1st edn (1883), iii, 483.

The violinist Andreas Moser, having quoted C. P. E. Bach's comment that since all trills begin with the upper auxiliary note it is unnecessary to indicate it unless an appoggiatura is intended, observed, with dubious historical justification: "Apparently this remark is occasioned by the special approach of the Mannheim School, where the practice obtained only to begin the trill with the upper auxiliary if this were specifically required by a grace-note." He identified the strongest support for the upper-note trill as being in north Germany, though C. P. E. Bach's authority gave the doctrine wider currency, and remarked: "the powerful influences which stemmed from the Viennese masters of instrumental music seem finally to have broken its hegemony".[87] The basis for Moser's assertions about Mannheim and Vienna are unclear. His unsupported reference to Mannheim practice probably relates to his erroneous identification of Spohr as a product of that school (evidently on the basis of his studying with Franz Eck, whom Spohr himself describes, however, as a "violinist of the French School").[88] His authority for Viennese practice was presumably Joachim, who would have acquired his impressions from his studies there with Joseph Böhm (b. 1795) and Georg Hellmesberger (b. 1800) in the 1840s. By the time Joachim came to Vienna, however, Hummel (1828), Spohr (1833), and Czerny (1839), all in treatises issued by the Viennese publisher Haslinger, had asserted the principle that a trill began with the main note unless otherwise specified. Moser evidently assumed that these treatises reflected an established Viennese practice and that composers from Haydn to Schubert would normally (unless an alternative was notated) have expected their trills to begin on the main note.[89]

Direct information about the intentions of major composers of the Classical period is rare. In Joseph Haydn's case the *Flötenuhrstücke* indicate a lack of rigidity in the execution of the ornament. Many trills begin with the main note. Especially instructive are pieces that appear on more than one clock; here there is frequent disagreement about the realization of trills and other ornaments. In these duplicated pieces, the undated clock almost exclusively begins trills on the main note (exceptions occur only in Hob. XIX: 13 and, once, in Hob. XIX: 16). Much of the time, the other clock is in agreement, but it sometimes has an upper-note start where the undated clock begins with the main note. None of these upper-note starts appears

---

[87] Joachim and Moser: *Violinschule*, iii, 20.
[88] Spohr: *Selbstbiographie*, i, 22.
[89] See also Franz Kullak: *Beethoven's Piano Playing with an Essay on the Execution of the Trill* (New York, 1901).

to precede the beat. In other instances, one clock may have a turn at the end of the trill while the other carries on to the end with repetitions of the main note and its upper auxiliary. Another interesting point is that where a passage recurs within a piece, a clock may execute a trill differently on the repetition (in Hob. XIX: 18 the trill in bar 1 begins with the upper note but in the repetition of the passage at bar 33 it starts with the main note; in Hob. XIX: 18 the trill in bar 26 is longer than that in bar 2). None of these variant versions derives support from the notation of the surviving autographs or copies, and few consistencies of practice emerge. Both the undated clock and the 1793 clock agree in adopting an upper auxiliary start in an ascending chain of trills (Hob. XIX: 13, bars 21–22), but even here they differ on whether the trills should conclude with a turn. Frederick Neumann argued that since the 1792 and 1793 clocks were made while Haydn was away from Austria and the undated clock was probably made after his return in 1796, the versions on this clock, which has a greater preponderance of main-note starts to trills (as well as pre-beat ornamentation), probably indicate Haydn's preferred treatment.[90] Another tenable explanation would be that the third clock was pinned by Niemecz's assistant, Gurk, and therefore indicates a difference in practice between these two musicians.[91] Far more important is the evidence for diversity. Niemecz's evident musical abilities and the closeness of his association with Haydn may suggest that the composer's own attitudes in this matter were not inflexible, but it seems clear that he grew up with the view that most trills began from above. Mozart too will certainly have been schooled in that doctrine, as exemplified in his father's *Violinschule*. Whether, in their own practice, they and their Viennese contemporaries took a more flexible view is indeterminable, but it is probable that there were some specific musical circumstances in which a main-note beginning to the ornament was deemed more effective. In any case, there can be little doubt that musicians at that time regarded prescribed ornamentation as advisory rather than prescriptive and were accustomed to vary or supplement it according to their own sense of good taste.

Haydn's increasingly detailed performance instructions in later works and Mozart's even fuller guidance for the performer were untypical of Viennese composers, but Beethoven went further in his concern to specify

---

[90] Neumann: 'More on Haydn's Ornaments and the Evidence of Musical Clocks' in *New Essays on Performance Practice* (Ann Arbor, 1989), 105–19.
[91] See *Joseph Haydn Werke*, XXI, ix.

performance details. His almost unprecedented notational care and his subsequent status in the highest tier of the musical Pantheon led during the 19th century to a growing tendency to regard his notation as definitive. His treatment of trills has given rise to substantial scholarly disagreement, as 20th-century musicians and musicologists became increasingly influenced by the idea that musical notation was a definitive repository of the composer's intentions.[92] Exaggerated and misconceived veneration for his text already gave rise to absurdities in the later 19th century when, for instance, in the absence of any additional small notes many musicians were persuaded to play his trills with neither an initial appoggiatura nor a concluding turn. With respect to the trill beginning, Czerny's instructions, since he was Beethoven's student and friend, have often been assumed to reflect his master's practice.[93] In his 1839 *Pianoforte Schule*, Czerny began his instructions for the execution of trills (more detailed than those of Hummel and Spohr) with several music examples, all showing trills starting on the main note, then continued:

The trill can begin in three ways, i.e.:

a) With the main note. This happens if the trill is preceded either by no note or by one that is different from the main note, and therefore on another key. (Ex. 12.50a)
b) With the auxiliary. This must happen when the main note of the trill immediately precedes it (Ex. 12.50b)
c) With the note below, i.e.: (Ex. 12.50c):

This can occasionally be allowed if the trill is rather long, and one wants particularly to emphasize it.

If the composer specifically shows, with a small note, how it should begin, one must, as always, obey.[94]

---

[92] E.g., in the exchange of views between William S. Newmann and Robert Winter (see bibliography).

[93] Czerny's status as an authority for Beethoven's practice in general has been questioned, however, by James Parakilas and George Barth in *Beyond the Art of Finger Dexterity. Reassessing Carl Czerny*, ed. David Gramit (Rochester, 2008). See also Clive Brown, 'Czerny the Progressive'.

[94] Czerny: *Pianoforte-Schule*, i, 130f.

Ex. 12.50 a–c. Czerny: *Pianoforte-Schule*, i, 17, §4, 130f.

While Beethoven, like many of his contemporaries, undoubtedly envisaged some trills, in particular circumstances, as beginning with the main note, it is clear that Czerny's attitude had changed over the years, reflecting his intention to move with the times. During Beethoven's lifetime he evidently began many trills from the auxiliary. In the late 1820s, Czerny made an extensively revised edition of A. E. Müller's treatise on piano playing,[95] in which he left Müller's treatment of ornaments indicated by small notes largely unchanged, merely adding a couple of footnotes suggesting that some of them were better indicated by full-size notes; but he made substantial changes in the section on ornaments indicated by signs. He retained Müller's introductory paragraph to the section on trills almost unaltered, except that where Müller wrote: "its execution begins always with the higher of the two notes (the auxiliary)",[96] Czerny substituted "its execution begins normally, as a rule, with the higher

---

[95] Müller's treatise was nominally the sixth edition of Georg Simon Löhlein's 1773 *Klavierschule*, but was in fact an entirely new treatise, hence its full title: *G. S. Löhleins Klavierschule, oder Anweisung zum Klavier- und Fortepiano-Spiel nebst vielen praktischen Beyspielen und einem Anhang vom Generalbasse. Sechste Auflage, ganz umgearbeitet und sehr vermehrt von A. E. Müller* (Leipzig, 1804). Czerny's revision was published as *Große Fortepiano Schule von Aug. Eberh*[d] *Müller [. . .] Achte Auflage mit vielen neuen Beispiele und einem vollständigen Anhang vom Generalbass versehen von Carl Czerny* (Leipzig, c. 1830).

[96] Müller: *Klavier- und Fortepiano Spiel*, 38f.

of the two notes (the auxiliary)", adding: "But it can also begin with the lower and occasionally with the addition of an even lower note."[97] Both editions began with the same example (Erstes Beyspiel), but Czerny added two new ones (Ex. 12.51). All but one of Czerny's subsequent music examples show an upper-note start; the exception is a chain of descending trills, which like the first of Czerny's additional examples (Zweytes Beysp.) involves the trill being preceded by a main-note one step higher.[98]

Ex. 12.51 Müller, ed. Czerny: 222.

In this treatise, therefore, Czerny only cautiously indicated the possibility of beginning a trill with the main note in one specific circumstance. Other Viennese sources from Beethoven's later years suggest that upper-note trill beginnings were still typical. Joseph von Blumenthal's 1811 *Violin Schule* presented an upper-note start initially, before illustrating one from the main note and one from the note below.[99] In a practice piece for trills, in his *100 Übungsstücke*, however, published at about the same time as Czerny's edition of Müller's treatise, Blumenthal writes out all the trills in full, giving them either an upper note start or, twice, one from below the main note.[100] August Swoboda's 1826 *Allgemeine Theorie der Tonkunst*, published in Vienna, gives trills starting from above and below but none from the main note.[101] In contrast to Domenico Corri, however, he asserted that "in performance, the higher note must be given more strongly than the lower one".[102] As late as 1840, Bernhard Romberg gave no alternative to a trill beginning with the upper auxiliary; and where a trilled note is preceded by the note

---

[97] Müller, ed. Czerny: *Große Fortepiano-Schule*, 222.
[98] Müller, ed. Czerny: 224.
[99] Joseph von Blumenthal: *Violin Schule* (Vienna, [1811]) Table XXIII, Fig. 10.
[100] Blumenthal, *100 Übungsstücke für zwey Violinen. Zum Studium der mechanischen Behandlung der Violine* op. 42 (Vienna, [1828–29]), Book 6, no. 99.
[101] Swoboda: *Allgemeine Theorie*, 45–48.
[102] Swoboda: *Allgemeine Theorie*, 46.

above, he instructed: "If the note with which the trill is to be made is already there, in order to be able to start the trill well, one must first insert the lower note before it"[103] (Ex. 12.52).

Ex. 12.52 Romberg: *Violoncell Schule*, 80.

Two of Czerny's arrangements of Beethoven's Violin Sonata op. 47, from the 1820s, one of the second movement for solo piano,[104] and the other of the whole sonata for piano duet,[105] clearly demonstrate that his teaching in 1839 was at odds with his understanding of Beethoven's expectations during the composer's lifetime, and with his own earlier practice. His fingerings and annotations in these arrangements make it abundantly clear that he expected almost all the trills to begin with the upper note. In Ex. 12.53a the trill starts with the upper auxiliary despite the octave leap. In Ex. 12.53b, the fingerings indicating upper-auxiliary beginnings for all the trills except the first one in bar 26, which, as in Czerny's illustration of a main-note start in his edition of Müller, is preceded by the note above (see Ex. 12.51); and to make his intention clear in this instance, Czerny precedes the trilled note with a grace-note on the same pitch. This treatment also corresponds with Bernhard Romberg's instruction for a trill in these circumstances (see Ex. 12.52). In Ex. 12.53c, in the solo transcription, Czerny gives fingerings for a succession of upper-auxiliary beginnings, even for the trill preceded by the note above; comparison with the duet transcription suggests that he took these upper-auxiliary beginnings for granted. In the duet version, however, he marked

---

[103] Romberg: *Violoncell Schule*, 80.
[104] *Variations brillantes tirées de l'Oeuvre 47 / de Louis van Beethoven. arrangées pour le Piano-Forte seul par Charles Czerny. Vienne Cappi et Diabelli* [c. 1823].
[105] *Grand duo brillant pour le Piano Forte à quatre mains, arrangé d'après la Sonate de L. van Beethoven, Oeuv 47, par Charles Czerny. Vienne chez Ant. Diabelli et Comp.* [c. 1825].

the turns, which he had omitted in the other transcription, but not for the trill that is followed by another a step below, which reflects his teaching on successive descending trills.

**Ex. 12.53a** i. Beethoven: 1st edition piano part 1st movement b. 221f; ii. Czerny: piano duet transcription, Primo; iii. Czerny: piano duet transcription, Secondo.

**Ex. 12.53b** Czerny: piano solo transcription 2nd movement b. 23ff.

**Ex. 12.53c** 2nd movement b. 145ff; i. Solo transcription [i and ii]; ii. Duet transcription [iii and iv].
Primo.

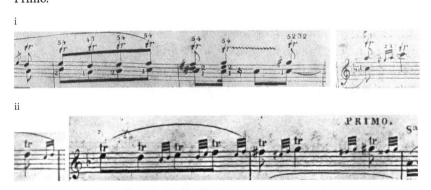

Ex. 12.54, from one of his own serious works, the 6th Piano Sonata op. 124, composed around the same time as these arrangements, shows how Czerny took upper-auxiliary beginnings for granted during the 1820s, only marking the upper-note start (in the final bar of the example) when an accidental was necessary.

Ex. 12.54  Czerny: Piano Sonata no. 6 op. 124.

On occasion, however, Beethoven apparently required a main note start, as suggested by his fingering for the first of the "Kleinigkeiten" he provided for vol. 3 of Friedrich Starke's *Wiener Pianoforte-Schule* (Ex. 12.55).

Ex. 12.55  F. Starke: *Wiener Piano-forte-Schule*, iii, 71.

Later 20th-century authors, writing primarily about Mozart, suggested various criteria for deciding on the appropriate treatment of trills in Classical repertoire,[106] which can, to varying extents, be supported by theoretical writings; but it may be legitimate to maintain a degree of scepticism about assuming too readily that what seems musical and tasteful to us in these

---

[106] Eva and Paul Badura-Skoda: *Mozart-Interpretation* (Vienna and Stuttgart, 1957), trans Leo Black as *Interpreting Mozart on the Keyboard* (London, 1962), 111–16. F. Neumann: *Ornamentation and Improvisation in Mozart*, 114. See also the first edition of this book, 497.

matters would necessarily have done so to musicians of previous generations. Changing taste affected every aspect of musical performance, but especially the execution of ornaments. As Fétis observed in 1840: "I do not think I need speak here of the ornaments in piano music of the present time, which will perhaps be modified within ten years, or replaced by others."[107]

## Trill Endings

Trill beginnings received more extensive attention in modern scholarship than trill endings, although, arguably, the latter have a much more prominent impact on the character of the ornament. During the second half of the 18th and the first half of the 19th centuries, few musicians were in any doubt that (except in a few specific contexts discussed below) trills must have some kind of ornamental ending, whether notated or not. In the mid-18th century, this might sometimes have been merely an anticipation of the note that follows the trill, as illustrated in the second example from Holden (Ex. 12.47), or as notated in Anton Bemetzrieder's *New Lessons* (Ex. 12.56);[108] but this type of ending seems already to have been less usual than the two-note turn, and by the end of the century it was clearly unfashionable. Hummel, in 1828, referred to it as "a false Nachschlag, which, however, is rarely used anymore".[109]

Ex. 12.56 Bemetzrieder: *New Lessons*, 14.

Numerous treatises asserted the principal that a turn (usually of two notes) was a necessary part of the ornament, for example:

C. P. E. Bach (1752), keyboard: "The trill on a note that is somewhat long, regardless of whether it proceeds up or down, always has a turn."[110]

---

[107] Fétis and Moscheles: *Méthode des méthodes* (Paris, [1840]), 75.
[108] This possibility is also given by Leopold Mozart (*Versuch*, 220) as the first of two "most usual and natural" (gewöhnlichsten und natürlichsten) endings, the second of which is the normal two-note turn.
[109] Hummel: *Anweisung*, 2nd edn, 395.
[110] Bach: *Versuch*, 1st edn, i, 74.

Reichardt (1776), strings: "The trill often has a Nachschlag,[111] which in orchestral parts is normally written out, but sometimes omitted. In this case one should see that at least every trill on a long note has a Nachschlag."[112]

Tromlitz (1791), flute: "Two small notes are appended at the end of every trill", adding "This is what we call the Nachschlag, which every trill must have."[113]

Anon (c. 1795), violin: "a shake should never be finished without [a turn]".[114]

Alexander (1802), cello: "At the end of every trill, the Nachschlag, which is often shown, must always follow."[115]

Koch (1802), general: "Onto the trill [. . .] two notes are finally added, which are a necessary part of this ornament."[116]

Hummel (1828), piano: "Every proper trill must have a Nachschlag, even if this is not notated; but if the shortness of the trill or the next sequence of notes does not allow it, it is not a trill, but only a trilled note, and must not be designated by the tr. sign."[117]

Czerny (c. 1830), piano: "Since the Nachschlag rounds off and completes the trill, it is to be accepted as a rule, according to current taste, and also to be used where the composer failed to indicate it."[118]

Czerny (1839), piano: "Although these final notes are usually added, they also have to be added where this is not the case."[119]

Fürstenau (1844), flute: "Every proper trill, to be complete, must, as a rule, have a so-called Nachschlag, which connects it to the following note."[120]

Alard (1844), violin: "The trill should always have an ending, it is not complete without it."[121]

---

[111] The English equivalent "turn" is used to refer both to the two-note termination to a trill called "Nachschlag" in German and also for the four- or five-note ornament called "Doppelschlag" in German. In the following discussion "after-notes" will be used as the equivalent of "Nachschlag", and "turn" will be reserved for the "Doppelschlag", except of course in quotations, where the meaning will be clear from the context.
[112] Reichardt: *Ueber die Pflichten*, 46.
[113] Tromlitz: *Unterricht*, 272.
[114] Anon.: *Instructions for the Violin by an Eminent Master*, 17.
[115] Joseph Alexander: *Anweisung zum Violoncellspiel* (Leipzig, [1802]), 34.
[116] Koch: *Musikalisches Lexikon*, 1590.
[117] Hummel: *Anweisung*, 2nd edn, 394.
[118] Müller, ed. Czerny: *Anweisung*, 223.
[119] Czerny: *Pianoforte-Schule*, i, 130.
[120] Fürstenau: *Kunst des Flötenspiels*, 49.
[121] Jean Delphin Alard: *École du violon Méthode complète et progressive à l'usage du Conservatoire* (Paris, 1844), 30.

686  CLASSICAL AND ROMANTIC PERFORMING PRACTICE

Some of these statements, and those of many other writers, make it clear that there were various situations in which concluding after-notes were not, however, expected. A few gave examples of alternative signs that might be used in these circumstances.[122] Others specified where, even when a composer designated the ornament as *tr*, after-notes might exceptionally be omitted. Among such instances identified by Fürstenau, for instance, was very short trills, where it would be very difficult to execute them.[123] In such cases a performer might employ the shortest alternation of a main note with its upper neighbour (*Mordent, Mordant,*[124] *Pralltriller, Schneller*), consisting of three notes; when not indicated by small notes, this was often marked ⁕, but sometimes *tr*. Furthermore, after-notes were often omitted on longer trills in certain circumstances, of which the most common was an unbroken succession of trills. Hummel gives a clear account of early-19th-century practice, explaining: "The so-called chain trill comprises an uninterrupted series of conjunct or disjunct notes; the Nachschlag is then only appended to the last note of the trill chain." But he added: "Upwards, however, if the tempo allows, the Nachschlag can occur after each note: but then it has to be specially indicated"[125] (Ex. 12.57).

Ex. 12.57  Hummel: *Anweisung*, 2nd edn, 395.

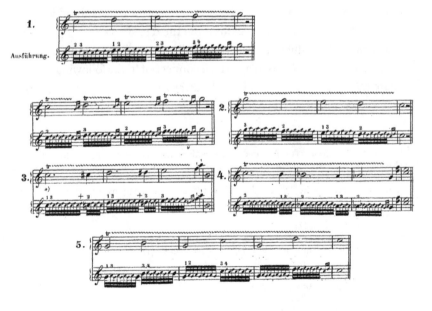

---

[122] E.g., Clementi: *Introduction*, 11; Müller: *Anweisung*, 39.
[123] Fürstenau: *Kunst des Flötenspiels*, 49.
[124] In Baillot, Rode, Kreutzer: *Méthode*, 127, however, *Mordant* is used for an ornament of more notes. In some sources it is used for a rapid alternation of the main note with the note below.
[125] Hummel: *Anweisung*, 2nd edn, 395.

In a short chapter "On false trills or trilled notes" he explained: "These notes are trilled throughout their entire value, but are by no means to be confused with the true trill, since a) because of the tone sequence, b) because of the short duration of the note, they do not allow a Nachschlag"[126] (Ex. 12.58).

Ex. 12.58 Hummel: *Anweisung*, 2nd edn, 397.

Czerny gave very similar instructions for pianists, and early-19th-century string treatises also provided much the same advice about the circumstances in which the otherwise obligatory after-notes were not appropriate. In the middle years of the century, however, the ground was shifting in the treatment of trill endings towards the principle that had been established by Hummel for their beginnings. Already in the late 1830s, Henri Herz expressed this view, stating: "The small notes which, sometimes, precede the conclusion of the trill, are called *termination*. The termination is not an essential part of the trill, as some authors maintain, but purely optional: thus, when it is wanted, it is up to the composer to indicate it, as he must also do for the small notes with which the trill can begin."[127] The idea that composers were expected to make their intentions as clear as possible through the notation became increasingly influential in the mid-19th century and encouraged many later musicians to apply such principles anachronistically to earlier repertoire.

A classic example of this tendency is the trill that begins Beethoven's Violin Sonata op. 96, which the composer probably expected to be executed with an upper-note start and a pair of after-notes, but which almost all later 19th- and 20th-century performers began with the main note and, increasingly, ended without after-notes. Different approaches to the after-notes were taken by three pupils of Joseph Böhm in Vienna: Jacob Dont (b. 1815), Edmund Singer (b. 1830), and Joseph Joachim (b. 1831). Dont's edition marked the after-notes on each occurrence of the figure;[128] Singer stated in his 1887 edition,

---

[126] Hummel: *Anweisung*, 2nd edn, 397.
[127] Herz: *Méthode*, 68.
[128] No copy of Dont's original edition, published in 1883, has yet been located, but the early-20th-century Universal Edition contains a violin part "bezeichnet von Jac. Dont," which was evidently based on his 1883 edition. I am grateful to Kai Köpp for drawing my attention to the Universal Edition.

at the beginning of the sonata, that "All the trills in this movement are to be executed without a Nachschlag;"[129] while Joachim's edition includes no after-notes, his 1905 *Violinschule* contains a footnote referring to "the much-disputed theme", asserting that the trill must have "a proper Nachschlag if the theme is not to forfeit its natural charm".[130]

Terminations other than the simple anticipation of the next note or the normal pair of after-notes were sometimes indicated. The most common of these (Ex. 12.59a), already illustrated by Leopold Mozart (Ex. 12.59b), was evidently widely used and sometimes notated in compositions.

Ex. 12.59a Spohr: *Violinschule*, 155.

Ex. 12.59b Mozart: *Versuch*, 224.

Until at least the middle of the 19th century, however, in certain musical genres and traditions, individual performers devised and employed more elaborate after-notes, especially for cadential trills. In 1811, John Jousse gave

---

[129] Edmund Singer and Wilhelm Speidel: Sonaten für Pianoforte und Violine von Ludwig van Beethoven (Stuttgart, Cotta, 1887), "Sämtliche Triller in diesem Satz sind ohne Nachschlag auszuführen."

[130] Joachim and Moser: *Violinschule*, i, 164. For a more detailed discussion of the trill in Beethoven's op. 96, see Clive Brown and Neal Peres Da Costa: *Beethoven Sonatas for Pianoforte and Violin. Performing Practice Commentary* (online).

examples of highly decorative endings, which, he remarked, "are become very fashionable" (Ex. 12.60).[131]

Ex. 12.60 Jousse: *Theory and Practice of the Violin*, 47.

Baillot's examples of terminations for trills indicate the most usual variants of the normal ending (Ex. 12.61); but he also included forty-eight more elaborate endings in his instructions for the embellishment of pauses (Ex. 12.62). There were, therefore, as many views about the endings of trills as about their beginnings, and here, too, it seems unlikely that experienced executants would have been greatly inhibited by the composer's notation in varying the endings as they saw fit. Until well into the 19th century, most composers were remarkably casual about indicating their trills.

Ex. 12.61 Baillot: *L'art du violon*, 78.

---

[131] John Jousse: *Theory and Practice of the Violin*, 47.

690 CLASSICAL AND ROMANTIC PERFORMING PRACTICE

Ex. 12.62 Baillot: *L'art du violon*, 171f.

A nice, but by no means unusual, example of notational inexactitude in this respect can be found in the printed orchestral parts of Anton Flad's Oboe Concertino in C (c. 1800); in the opening tutti the solo oboe and the first violin are in unison throughout, but the trills are notated quite differently (Ex. 12.63). Despite three different ways of showing the trills, it seems likely that a trill beginning with the upper note and ending with after-notes was envisaged in each case.

Ex. 12.63  A. Flad: Concertino in C, i.

In general, however, it seems likely that in ensemble playing, and in most normal circumstances, trills would usually have concluded with the familiar two-note pattern. When composers in the later part of the 19th century quite definitely did not want this, they would certainly have had to indicate it, as Dvořák did at the beginning of his String Quartet op. 106 (see Ex. 12.2). Brahms was careful in his compositions to indicate the after-notes to his trills, both with and without accidentals, and where, in the solo part of his Violin Concerto he wanted no after-notes (first movement b. 144), he left them out; but the work's dedicatee, Joseph Joachim, in his edition of the solo part in his *Violinschule*, still felt it necessary to add the instruction "ohne Nachschlag".

* * *

Another aspect of trill performance—speed and dynamics—was discussed in some treatises. There was general agreement that the alternation of the notes in most trills should be regular, that the speed of the trill should be dictated not only by the tempo in which it occurred—faster in Allegro and slower in Adagio—but more especially by the character of the passage; and some suggested that trills on lower pitches should be slower than those on higher ones.[132] Many agreed that there were circumstances in which the alternations in a trill might get faster. Czerny also suggested that a trill might begin rapidly and get slower in some circumstances,[133] but Spohr condemned that practice.[134] The idea that longer trills might be given a kind of *messa di voce* treatment, becoming faster and louder towards the middle and slower and softer towards the end, was more generally recommended.[135] Kalkbrenner

---

[132] E.g., L. Mozart: *Violinschule*, 220f, and many later writers.
[133] Czerny: Pianoforte-Schule, i, 132.
[134] Spohr: *Violinschule*, 156.
[135] E.g., Türk: *Klavierschule*, 254; Müller: *Klavier- und Fortepiano Spiel*, 39; Müller, ed. Czerny: *Große Fortepiano-Schule*, 223; Spohr: *Violinschule*, 156; Baillot: *L'art du violon*, 79f.

seems to expect it in most trills, marking almost all his examples < >.[136] This practice seems to have been widespread, but perhaps became unfashionable in the later 19th century, since the Joachim and Moser *Violinschule* remarks that "It is an annoying habit of many violinists to let every longer trill crescendo towards the middle."[137]

### The Turn (*Doppelschlag*)

#### Accenting Turns

The expressive effect of the turn depends on its position in relation to the note it ornaments, on its rhythmic configuration, and on the speed at which it is executed. The relationship between the turn that embellishes the beginning of a beat and the trill has always been close. C. P. E. Bach considered that the two ornaments were interchangeable in many instances, but since, for him, the turn was principally an accenting ornament at the beginning of a note, he advised that they should not normally be used on long notes, because these would remain "too empty".[138] His examples of turns show that only at a very fast tempo might the notes of the turn be even (Ex. 12.64).

Ex. 12.64 C. P. E. Bach: *Versuch*, Table V, fig. L.

Leopold Mozart used the term *Mordent* for a similar pattern of notes (and the inverted form), but his explanation of its performance, influenced by Italian practice, differed from Bach's, for he considered that "the stress falls

---

[136] Kalkbrenner: *Méthode*, 32.
[137] Joachim and Moser: *Violinschule* i, 165.
[138] Bach: *Versuch*, i, 87. In his example (Ex. 12.65), the abbreviations stand for *adagio* and *moderato*. Note that the lowest note is a double sharp (it was misprinted as a sharp in the first edition of this book).

on the note itself, while the mordant, on the contrary, is slurred quite softly and very quickly on to the principal note"[139] (Ex. 12.65). He was particularly emphatic about the speed of the ornament. For Mozart this was essentially an improvised embellishment, to be applied where a note required special liveliness.

Ex. 12.65 Mozart: *Versuch*, 244.

Domenico Corri, from the singer's point of view, gave a somewhat different explanation of its execution, instructing that "The Ascending Turn, begins softly, and encreases [sic] its strength as it rises, then gently again sinks into the note" (Ex. 12.66a), while "The Descending Turn, begins strong, and decreases its strength as it falls, then rises into the note strong again" (Ex. 12.66b).[140]

Ex. 12.66 a–b. D. Corri: *A Select Collection*, i, 8.

Corri, Nicolo Pasquali, Justin Heinrich Knecht, and other writers also, however, illustrated these kinds of turn with a longer first note, suggesting, perhaps, a degree of agogic accent (Ex. 12.67a–b).[141]

Ex. 12.67 a–b.

---

[139] Mozart: *Versuch*, 244.
[140] D. Corri: *A Select Collection*, i. 8.
[141] D. Corri: *The Singers Preceptor*; Pasquali: *The Art of Fingering the Harpsichord* (Edinburgh, [c. 1760]); Knecht, *Kleine theoretische Klavierschule für die ersten Anfänger* (Munich, [1799]).

Yet another explanation of their execution was given in the 19th century by García, who categorized them as "Mordant (*Grupetto*)", instructing: "The grupetto can be obtained by a *sforzando* on the first of the three notes that make it up, attacking freely, boldly, so that it stands out over the preceding and following notes. The stress given to this note should carry off the two others that follow."[142] García considered this form of turn (Ex. 12.68a) the most common ornament after the *appoggiatura* and evidently regarded what he called *mezzi-grupetti* and double *appoggiaturas* as ornaments closely related in their musical function (Ex. 12.68b).

Ex. 12.68 a–b. García: *École*, 1st edn, i, 51.

Most authors stated that these types of turn should be performed quickly; but a variety of speeds, depending on context, might certainly have been employed by musicians throughout the period. An example from the 18th century illustrates how, even with the same notation, two turns might be differently executed in close proximity: Löhlein gave realizations indicating varied treatment of on-beat turns (Ex. 12.69).

Ex. 12.69 Löhlein: *Anweisung zum Violinspielen*, 48.

In the 19th century, however, just as there was a greater tendency for trills to begin with the principal note, there is evidence that in some circumstances performers may have been inclined to start these turns with the main note. Baillot, for example, suggested realizing the sign in the Allegro of Mozart's Violin Sonata K. 379 as in Ex. 12.70, though it seems more likely that Mozart intended something like his father's *mordant* or García's *sforzando* turn, beginning from the note above.

---

[142] García: *École*, 1st edn, i, 51. "Mordant" was translated as "Turn" in García's *New Treatise* (1858), 33.

Ex. 12.70 Baillot: *L'art du violon*, 84.

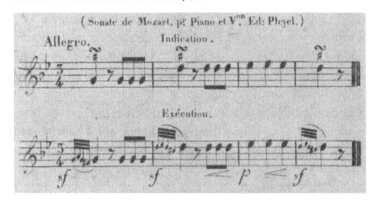

Baillot's instinct to begin such figures with the main note was evidently shared by his younger colleague Charles de Bériot, who similarly illustrated the resolution of a turn sign, in almost identical circumstances; but he also stated: "This figuration is called *mordant* and is used only in fast movements on short notes. It is indicated either by this abbreviation ∾ or by *tr* placed above the note."[143] His example shows that he regarded these turns as beginning on the main note, but the trill with an upper-note start (Ex. 12.71), like C. P. E. Bach's *presto* turn.

Ex. 12.71 Bériot: *Méthode*, iii, 188.

Various kinds of turn, along with other short ornaments, would have been added at will in the performance of 18th-century and early-19th-century music and remained appropriate as improvised embellishment in some later 19th-century repertoires, especially Italian vocal music. With respect to their positioning on or before the beat, many of the same factors apply as in the case of the *grace-note*: most authorities favoured on-beat performance, but some advocated pre-beat performance.

---

[143] Bériot: *Méthode*, 188.

## Connecting Turns

The form of turn for which Leopold Mozart used the conventional German term *Doppelschlag* was clearly considered by him as a connecting ornament, whose principal function was as an extempore embellishment to an *appoggiatura* (Ex. 12.72a),[144] and the same usage was still recommended in the 19th century by Campagnoli.[145] In the revised 1787 edition of his *Versuch*, however, Mozart added an example illustrating it as a simple connection between two notes, perhaps indicating that this type had grown in popularity during the intervening thirty years (Ex. 12.72b).[146] Both these patterns were standard in the late 18th century, varying slightly from author to author in their exact rhythmic configuration and placement (see, e.g., Ex. 12.69).

**Ex. 12.72** a–b. Mozart: (*a*) *Versuch*, 1st edn (1756), 214; (*b*) *Versuch*, 3rd edn, 217.

---

[144] Mozart: *Versuch*, 215.
[145] Campagnoli: *Nouvelle méthode*, 43. See Ex. 12.23c.
[146] Mozart: *Versuch*, 3rd edn, 217.

In the 18th century, it seems to have been generally accepted that the connecting turn would be performed rapidly, and this remained true for many 19th-century musicians, for instance Spohr, who instructed that "the turn is always played quickly, whether in slow or quick tempo".[147] García took a similar view of all types of turn (*Mordant*), whether accented, connecting, or anticipatory. He explained and exemplified the three types thus in the 1840 first edition of his treatise:

> It can 1) attack the sound, 2) occupy the middle of it, 3) finish it. In the first case, it must be played in the first instant of the note's value. Example: [Ex. 12.73a]
>
> In the second case, the note is first laid down, and, in the middle of its duration, the mordant is executed. Example: [Ex. 12.73b]
>
> In the third case, the note should be completed with the mordant. Example: [Ex. 12.73c]
>
> The special character of the mordant is that it is fast and incisive, so it should be confined to the value of a sixteenth note at n° 100=♪ on the Maëlzel metronome.[148]

**Ex. 12.73** a–c. García: *École*, 1st edn, i, 51f. (*a*) Unidentified embellished recitative; (*b*) Mozart: *Don Giovanni*, Act. 1 no. 12 Andante grazioso, "Batti. Batti"; (*c*) Cimarosa: *Il matrimonio segreto* Act 2 (no. 13), Andante sostenuto, Pria che spunti.

(*a*)

(*b*)

---

[147] Spohr: *Violinschule*, 169.
[148] García: *École*, i, 1st edn, 51f.

**Ex. 11.73** Continued

(c)

In the 1856 revised one-volume edition,[149] the English translation as *García's New Treatise*,[150] and subsequent reprintings of the original two-volume version, he gave different examples for the first two, and simplified the third one (Ex. 12.74a–c), perhaps reflecting changing taste: for instance, in the performance of recitative, in increasing resistance to added ornamentation in Mozart, and in standardized execution of turns.

**Ex. 12.74** a–c. García: *Nouveau traité sommaire de l'art du chant* (Paris, 1856), 39.

(a)

(b)

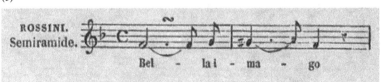

[149] García: *Nouveau traité sommaire de l'art du chant* (Paris, 1856), 39.
[150] García: *García's New Treatise on the Art of Singing* (London, [1858]), 33.

Ex. 11.74 Continued

(c)

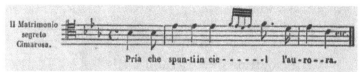

García made another informative comment about this ornament: "As it comprises solely the combination of appoggiaturas below and above the main note, the rule established for appoggiaturas must be applied to it, which prescribes that a semitone should always be placed between the small note below and the large note; from this it follows, as the Conservatoire's *Méthode de chant* observes, that the turn cannot exceed a minor third without losing its grace and lightness."[151]

There was a growing tendency towards the middle of the 19th century to execute some connecting turns in a more leisurely manner. A. B. Marx thought that they should be "performed in moderately fast or even fast tempo",[152] but a generation later Dannreuther recorded:

> The turn in Bellini's cantilena, both andantino and largo, was sung in a very broad way, so the notes formed part of the principal phrase, just as it is now to be found written out and incorporated in Wagner's *Tristan*. The ornamental notes, resembling a turn at the end of a long breath, were always given piano, diminuendo, leggiero as in Chopin. [Ex. 12.75].[153]

Ex. 12.75 Bellini: *I Puritani*, in Dannreuther: *Musical Ornamentation*, ii, 141.

In Joachim's C major Romance, the composer performs the turns in bars 7 and 98 as five equal notes commencing at the beginning of the bar, rather than starting halfway through the first note as suggested by most 19th-century

---

[151] García: *École*, 1st edn, i, 51.
[152] A. B. Marx: 'Doppelschlag' in Schilling, *Encyclopädie*, ii, 461.
[153] Dannreuther: *Musical Ornamentation*, ii, 141.

theorists. His pupil, Marie Soldat, executed the turns in the Adagio of Spohr's Ninth Violin Concerto and Beethoven's F major Romance more slowly than is suggested by Spohr's advice.

## The Notation of Turns and Trills

Most of the instructions about ornaments in theoretical writings were less an objective record of contemporary notational practice than an essentially vain attempt to produce order out of the chaos of conflicting signs and practices. Composers were remarkably casual about how they indicated ornaments, and where evidence exists to show what individual composers meant by their signs, this frequently appears to be different from the realizations proposed in standard theoretical writings. Even when composers complained about engravers failing accurately to transcribe the signs they had written (as Haydn did to Artaria), it is clear from numerous instances in their own autographs that they were often not at all consistent in their employment of them. Bernhard Romberg confessed to a laxity in the use of signs for standard and inverted turns, which was probably typical of many composers' attitudes; having illustrated ∾ for a turn from above and ⸺ for an inverted turn, Romberg commented: "There are however some composers (among whom I include myself) who write in such haste that they do not take the trouble to mark this ornament in such a way as to show whether they intend it to be made from above or below."[154] Spohr followed Hummel in giving ⸺ for a normal turn and ∾ for an inverted turn,[155] in contrast to most writers, who employed these signs in the opposite sense. But in his autographs Spohr does not seem to have adopted his own recommendations. In the works of his Vienna period (1812–15) he invariably notated turns, like Pleyel, as ✚;[156] and in the year of Hummel's treatise he was still using the same notation,[157] though in all cases the first editions printed the normal turn sign ∾. In a copy of his song "Nachgefühl" written in an album in 1834, just after the publication of the *Violinschule*, Spohr indicated what was evidently meant to be a direct turn with the sign he had recommended in his treatise, but when

---

[154] Romberg: *Violoncell Schule*, 84.
[155] Spohr: *Violinschule*, 156ff.
[156] See, e.g., the autographs of op. 29 no. 2 and op. 30 shown in facsimile in *The Selected Works of Louis Spohr*, ed. Clive Brown, vol. ix, no. 2 (New York, Garland, 1988).
[157] See the autograph of op. 82 no. 2 in the same publication.

NOTATED ORNAMENTS 701

he prepared another copy of this song for publication as a facsimile in the *Allgemeine musikalische Zeitung* in 1839, he employed the conventional direct turn sign (Ex. 12.76a–b).

Ex. 12.76 a–b. Spohr: "Nachgefühl" WoO. 91, autographs.

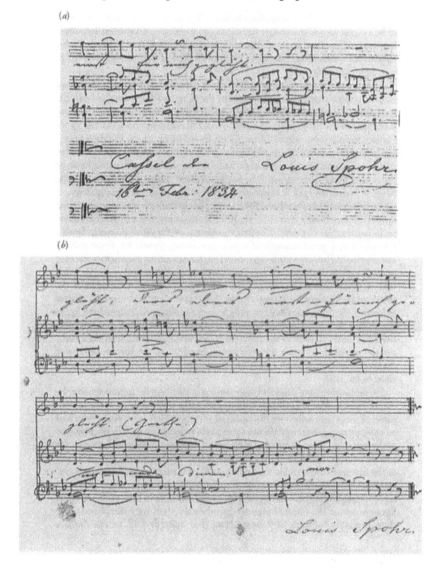

An interesting, more general case-study is provided by late-18th- and early-19th-century employment of the signs and formulas shown in Ex. 12.77.

These often seem to have been used synonymously, sometimes in close proximity in the same piece of music, with the meaning shown in Ex. 12.78.

Ex. 12.77 a–f.

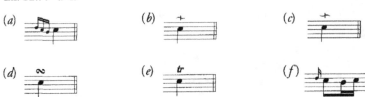

Ex. 12.78

Haydn, for instance, employed several of the forms shown in Ex. 12.77a–f with apparently identical meanings (Ex. 12.79a–c).

Ex. 12.79 a–c. Haydn: (a) String Quartet op. 54/2/i; (b) String Quartet op. 64/2/i; (c) String Quartet op. 64/6/iii.

(a)

(b)

(c)

He was certainly not alone in this; his pupil Pleyel used them in a similar manner and with similar meanings. Comparison of different notations in Pleyel's own edition of his twelve string quartets (in four books of three quartets) of 1787, dedicated to the King of Prussia, is instructive.[158] In many places in these quartets *tr* seems to be used as a shorthand for Ex. 12.77a, as in (Ex. 12.80a–b). The first movement of the third quartet in book 3 provides a very good example of how cautious one should be about making assumptions of pre-beat performance for such ornaments, even before *staccato* notes; for while the first violin has three small notes, the second violin, in thirds with it, simply has *tr* (Ex. 12.80c). The synonymity of these notations and the turn sign is suggested by such passages as Ex. 12.80d, where the first violin has a turn sign on the initial appearance of the figure, then *tr* on its subsequent appearance; and when viola and cello play the figure in thirds later in the movement, the viola has a turn (without the vertical line) while the cello has *tr*. Ex. 12.80e shows apparent equivalence between the notations in Ex. 12.77a and 12.77f.

Ex. 12.80 a–e. Pleyel: *Douze Nouveau Quatuors / DÉDIÉS / A sa Majesté / Le Roi de Prusse. / Composés par / Ignace Pleyel / Nouvelle Edition [...]* (Paris, Pleyel, [c. 1805]). (*a*) book 1/3/i; (*b*) book 2/3/ii; (*c*) book 3/3/i; (*d*) book 2/2/iii; (*e*) book 3/2/i.

[158] Pleyel: *Douze Nouveaux Quatuors* (Paris, Pleyel, [c. 1805]).

**Ex. 11.80** Continued

Further examples of this kind of inconsistent notation for ornaments may be drawn from numerous printed editions and manuscript sources of the period; some of them may reflect an intention to vary ornamentation at the return of an earlier passage, but most do not seem likely to have any such implication. Often these alternative methods of notation offer clues to the types of ornamentation the composer may have imagined. Comparison of Mozart's draft of the first movement of his Violin Sonata K. 306 with the final version (1778) appears to show different methods of notating the same ornaments. In bar 18 both versions have the notation shown in Ex. 12.81a. In bars 40ff the same figure occurs in the finished manuscript while the draft has a simplified notation, probably meaning the same thing (Ex. 12.81b–c). In the draft, a connecting turn is shown at bars 36f as in Ex. 12.81d, while in the final version it is fully written out as in Ex. 12.81e.

Ex. 12.81 a–e. Mozart: Violin Sonata K. 306/i.

In Clementi's Piano Sonata op. 40 no. 1, as in many examples from Haydn, a turn is written first as three small notes, then as ∞ (Ex. 12.82a–b).

Ex. 12.82 a–b. Clementi: Piano Sonata op. 40 no. 1, printed edn (London, Clementi, [1802]).

Wenzel Müller, in *Das Sonnenfest der Braminen*, employed a somewhat differently notated version of this ornament and abbreviated it later as *tr* (Ex. 12.83).

Ex. 12.83 Müller: *Das Sonnenfest der Braminen*, no. 11.

Süssmayr's opera *Der Spiegel von Arkadien* presents another example of the interchangeability of the accenting turn or mordent, written this time as three notes, and the short trill beginning from above (Ex. 12.84).

Ex. 12.84 Süssmayr: *Der Spiegel von Arcadien*, no. 5.

As an abbreviation for the same figure, Salieri used ✚ rather than *tr* in his Singspiel *Der Rauchfangkehrer*; in this case the synonymity of the two signs is confirmed by a passage in which the flute is written one way and the oboe the other (Ex. 12.85a). In the same number of the opera Salieri employed the sign ✚ together with notation clearly indicating a turn of four equal notes (Ex. 12.85b).

Ex. 12.85 a–b. Salieri: *Der Rauchfangkehrer*. (*a*) Act I, no. 6; (*b*) Act II, no. 5.

This convention was not apparently confined to Viennese composers, for Weber employed it in *Der Freischütz* (Ex. 12.86), though perhaps he derived it from his brief period of study with Michael Haydn.

Ex. 12.86 Weber: *Der Freischütz*, no. 2, (autograph)
[poco più moderato (following Allegro 6/8)]

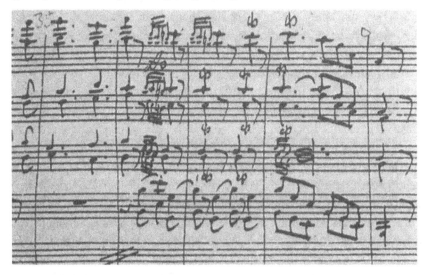

Theorists gave several quite incompatible explanations of the sign ᛭ or ᛭ (often impossible to distinguish from ∿ in manuscript sources). Cartier regarded ᛭ as a trill with after-notes, whereas *tr* was a simple trill without after-notes;[159] and Philip Corri saw the line through the middle as a sign that the ornament should be a "close turn" (i.e., with an accidental before the first or third notes).[160] Also with respect to accidentals in turns, Reichardt rather confusingly suggested the signs in Ex. 12.87.

Ex. 12.87 Reichardt: *Ueber die Pflichten*, 57.

Notational inconsistencies of this sort may lie behind the ambiguity of the accidentals in some of Beethoven's turns, for example in the *Chorfantasie* op. 80, where a turn sign in bar 33 with a sharp followed by a natural sign above it almost certainly indicates a turn with a sharpened under-note;[161] or

---

[159] Cartier: *L'art du violon*, 4.
[160] P. A. Corri: *L'anima di musica*, 16.
[161] Beethoven: *Chorfantasie* op. 80, ed. Clive Brown (Wiesbaden, Breitkopf & Härtel, 1993), 4 and 64f.

in the "Kreutzer" Sonata op. 47, where the turn added to the violin's g♯¹ in the *Stichvorlage* at bar 95 of the first movement (the turn is absent from the autograph fragment) has a pair of sharp signs beneath it, evidently signifying an f𝄪,[162] while at the recapitulation (b. 416) the sign after the violin's c♯¹ is written with a sharp above it, signifying a b♯¹.

Many later 19th-century musicians seem to have found the use of a semitone between the main note and its lower neighbour in such circumstances distasteful. A footnote to b. 95 in a late-19th-century edition op. 47 states: "Here, and similarly in the later parallel passage, we have to suggest that the player use a simple ♯ instead of the 𝄪, which might sound a bit too harsh for some ears."[163] That it did not sound harsh to 18th- and early-19th-century ears is indicated by C. P. E. Bach's examples, the Paris Conservatoire's *Principes*, Beethoven's practice, and García's instructions.

Mendelssohn's notation in some early works provides enlightening comparisons between trill signs and turns. In the Scherzo of the Octet for Strings op. 20, he first wrote the ornament at bar 95, as in Ex. 12.88a, but later changed it to Ex. 12.88b; on all subsequent occurrences of the figure, he followed the trill with written-out after-notes. In his own piano duet arrangement of the Octet this bar occurs as in Ex. 12.88c, and the notes marked *tr* in this passage in the autograph score are all written as similar four-note turns in the piano arrangement. Where the string version has Ex. 12.88d, the piano duet has an inverted turn, or three-note trill, beginning on the main note Ex. 12.88e.

Ex. 12.88 a–e. Mendelssohn: Octet op. 20/iii.

---

[162] The first edition, confusingly, gives a sharp above and a sharp below at 95, and a sharp above at 416. Ferdinand David's 1868 edition gives 𝄪 at 95. The Beethoven *Gesamtausgabe* (Henle) erroneously gives it as f♯¹.

[163] Beethoven: Violin Sonata op. 47, ed. Edmund Singer and Wilhelm Speidel (Stuttgart, Cotta, 1887), piano part, 5.

In his almost contemporaneous opera *Die Hochzeit des Camacho*, he again used different notation in his full score (Ex. 12.89a) and in the piano part of the published vocal score (Ex. 12.89b). At bar 202 of the Finale of his op. 6 Piano Sonata he wrote a trill in the autograph (Ex. 12.90a), but at this point in the first edition, and elsewhere where a similar figure occurs in the autograph, it is written as four sixteenths (Ex. 12.90b).

Ex. 12.89 a–b. Mendelssohn: *Die Hochzeit des Camacho*, no. 14. (*a*) autograph; (*b*) vocal score.

Ex. 12.90 a–b. Mendelssohn: Piano Sonata op. 6/iv. (*a*) autograph; (*b*) 1st edn.

Apart from the evidence of inconsistent notation, such examples lend support to the idea that those composers regarded accenting ornaments of this kind as coinciding with the beat rather than preceding it, and that they retained a fairly strong notion of an upper-note start to trills. It would, however, be contrary to the spirit of 18th- and 19th-century performance to conclude from this that a metrically regimented or uniform execution of ornaments in these or similar circumstances was envisaged; the rhythmic placement, in particular, may be subject to many subtle variations depending on context and the effect desired by the performer. There is no reason to suppose, for instance, that the turn signs and trill signs in the piano part of Beethoven's *Chorfantasie* op. 80 (Ex. 12.91a) should not be capable of a variety of different realizations. In bar 63 any of the forms shown in Ex. 12.91b–f) seem plausible. In relation to the last of these examples, it is interesting to note that Karl Klindworth suggested a similar approach to the inverted turn in Mendelssohn's *Lieder ohne Worte* no. 2 (Ex. 12.92).

Ex. 12.91 a–f. Beethoven: *Chorfantasie* op. 80.

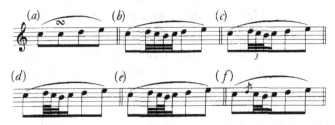

Ex. 12.92 Mendelssohn: *Lieder ohne Worte* op. 19/ii, ed. Klindworth.

## Direct and Inverted Turns

At the end of the 19th century, Dannreuther, discussing the notation of turns, emphatically asserted that "with Hummel, as with all contemporary instrumentalists and vocalists ∞, when connecting one note with another, meant a turn from above, and nothing else".[164] The remark by Bernhard Romberg quoted above shows that this was not true of at least one important musician among Hummel's contemporaries, as do the inconsistencies in Spohr's notation of turns. Other information from the mid-19th century indicates that Romberg's apparent willingness to leave the choice to the performer was by no means eccentric. Adolf Bernhard Marx considered that "The turn from below is mostly explicitly written out with notes; but one can also introduce it at the sign ∞, if a gentler, more pensive expression is aimed at; and in this case it will be executed more slowly." He also felt, like Romberg, that the turn from below was generally more appropriate where the melody falls, and, referring to both forms of turn, continued:

> It is left to the taste of the performer to introduce this often very graceful ornament, which at the same time wreathes and seeks the main note, even where it is not marked. But one should be sparing and thoughtful about it,

---

[164] Dannreuther: *Musical Ornamentation*, ii, 174.

since a mass of such small figures easily becomes fussy and obscures and disturbs the deeper meaning and character of the melody.[165]

Among major composers of the second half of the 19th century in whose music the turn (either written out or indicated by a sign) played an important part was Wagner. His practice in this matter, and how his instructions were interpreted by leading contemporaries, nicely illustrates the flexibility which persisted even in that period of ever-increasing prescriptiveness in notation. In his operas up to *Lohengrin*, Wagner used a variety of conventional ornament signs; in the later operas, with very few exceptions other than his trills (which according to Dannreuther were normally meant to start on the main note),[166] he dispensed with signs, and either indicated his ornaments with small notes or incorporated them into the musical text in normal-size notes. In the overture to Raupach's *König Enzio* of 1832, Wagner employed the turn sign ∞. In *Rienzi*, *Der fliegende Holländer*, and *Tannhäuser* he regularly used the sign ✣ for turns. He does not seem to have employed a different sign to indicate an inverted turn, but in his later works, where the turns are written out, some begin from above and others from below. The *Vorspiel* to *Götterdämmerung*, for instance, has inverted turns and direct turns closely juxtaposed. A written-out inverted turn also occurs in the 1855 version of his *Faust* overture; this example is particularly interesting, since in the 1844 version of the overture the turns are indicated by Wagner's usual turn sign. Whether Wagner originally envisaged an inverted turn in the *Faust* overture is open to question.

How Wagner wished the turn signs in his earlier operas to be interpreted was by no means clear even during his own lifetime. In Liszt's piano versions of the Prayer from *Rienzi* and the March from *Tannhäuser* (Act II, Scene iv), the turn signs are realized as direct turns. Hans von Bülow, however, apparently without any authority from the composer, insisted for a while on the Meiningen Orchestra performing many of the turns in *Rienzi* and others of Wagner's earlier operas as inverted turns. This was subject to considerable controversy in the late 19th century, but though Bülow later changed his mind, other conductors adopted the habit. Dannreuther reported that at Munich in the 1890s, for instance, the inverted turn was routinely used in

---

[165] A. B. Marx: 'Doppelschlag' in Schilling, *Encyclopädie*, ii, 462.
[166] Dannreuther: *Musical Ornamentation*, ii, 172.

*Rienzi*.[167] This practice was perpetuated by Karl Klindworth's vocal score, in which the signs are realized as inverted turns. Wagner himself seems to have added to the confusion over the meaning of his turn signs, for when present at rehearsals of *Tannhäuser* in Vienna in 1875, he asked the conductor, Hans Richter, to take the turns (marked by the sign for a normal turn) that follow the words "So stehet auf!" in Act II, Scene ii, as inverted turns. In the revised vocal score of *Tannhäuser* (1876), prepared by Joseph Rubinstein under Wagner's direct supervision, however, these turns were written out as normal turns, and they also appear thus in Klindworth's vocal score.

[167] Dannreuther: *Musical Ornamentation*, ii, 174.

# 13

# Improvised Ornamentation and Embellishment

Documentary and aural sources demonstrate unambiguously that throughout this period, musical notation in European art music was viewed as indicative rather than prescriptive. During the 18th and early 19th centuries, the ornamentation and embellishment of all kinds of music by performers was endemic and, in many respects, fundamental to the aesthetic experience of composer, performer, and listener alike. As the tendency for composers to specify their requirements with greater precision increased, performers gradually became inclined to observe the letter of the notation more closely than their predecessors and began to be seen as interpreters, rather than the composer's creative equals; the rapidity with which these changes occurred, however, differed according to genres and localized traditions. Change was slower in vocal music, especially opera, and more rapid in German chamber music, but even at the end of the 19th century, musicians still understood that, in contemporary works, as well as in older music, some deviation from the literal signification of the notation was necessary to convey the affective, dramatic, or expressive intentions that were inherent, though not explicit in the composer's text. Nevertheless, in the second half of the century, substantial differences of attitude existed between those who took a more literal approach to the notation and those who considered it their duty to interpret it more freely. Joseph Joachim, for instance, stated that the Belgian virtuoso Henri Vieuxtemps, "like most violinists of the Franco-Belgian School in recent times adhered too strictly to the lifeless printed notes when playing the classics, not understanding how to read between the lines".[1]

Joachim's attitude is in line with that of other German musicians. In 1883, Otto Klauwell observed:

---

[1] Andreas Moser: *Joseph Joachim. Ein Lebensbild*, 2nd edn, 2 vols. (Berlin: Verlag der Deutschen Brahms-Gesellschaft, 1908–10), ii, 292.

A musical work of art does not function like a machine, the parts of which can be illustrated in their nature and their mutual interaction through words and pictorial signs in the most precise way; it is more like an animated organism whose largely unpredictable living conditions cannot be measured precisely and thus not symbolized by visible signs.

He concluded, like Joachim, that the flexibility necessary for fine performance "is, of course, only to be read between the lines".[2] And Klauwell's teacher, Carl Reinecke, writing about Beethoven performance in the 1890s, similarly observed that, even though Beethoven had specified numerous expressive nuances in his Piano Sonata op. 111, "there still remains much to be read between the lines which no composer can convey by signs, no editor by explanations".[3]

From the modern perspective, these statements could refer simply to the expressive flexibility that occurs in any performance by sensitive musicians, even if they strive to be faithful to the notated text. Yet, as recordings of Joachim and Reinecke demonstrate, their "reading between the lines", both in Classical repertoire and their own compositions, reveals a relationship with the notation that is very different from later 20th- and early-21st-century mainstream practice. To what extent recordings of musicians born in the first half of the 19th century preserve aspects of practice that pre-date their own lifetimes must remain speculative, but their deviations from the literal meaning of the notation often reflect instructions in earlier treatises, and it seems clear that their attitudes to the text were far closer to those of the 18th century than early-21st-century performers' perceptions and practices are to theirs.

\* \* \*

In the following discussion, "ornamentation" will refer to the addition of notes to the composer's text, either in the form of standard ornaments such as appoggiaturas, trills, and turns, or in improvised ornamental figurations (*fioriture*). "Embellishment" will refer to all other conspicuous additions or alterations to the text that do not involve extra notes, such as sliding and trembling effects, various kinds of asynchrony, as well as improvised flexibilities of tempo, rhythm, and dynamics; these are examined more

---

[2] Otto Klauwell: *Der Vortrag in der Musik* (Berlin and Leipzig, 1883), 2.
[3] Carl Reinecke: *Die Beethoven'schen Clavier-Sonaten*, 2nd edn (Leipzig, 1897), 126.

specifically in other chapters, but will be referred to here in their broader aesthetic context. In the case of both ornamentation and embellishment, the term "improvised", as employed here, is not intended to apply only to additions and alterations to the notated text that were created spontaneously during the act of performance (though some of them undoubtedly were). A certain amount of preparation and pre-planning will undoubtedly have occurred, especially in the case of more elaborate ornamentation, but gifted executants will surely have varied aspects of ornamentation and embellishment in successive performances of the same work.

## Improvised Ornamentation in 18th-Century Theory and Practice

In the second half of the 18th century, it was a common assumption that, in many genres of solo music, composers would entrust ornamental elaboration to performers, who would employ it in a manner that displayed their own abilities to best advantage. Even where the composer included signs or notated ornaments, it was understood that performers were at liberty to substitute others that might suit them better. In 1771, for instance, Anselm Bayly, writing primarily, but not only, for singers, observed:

> Many composers insert appoggiaturas and graces, which indeed may assist the learner, but not a performer well educated and of a good taste, who may omit them as he shall judge proper, vary them, or introduce others from his own fancy and imagination. [. . .] The business of a composer is to give the air and expression in plain notes, who goes out of his province when he writes graces, which serve for the most part only to stop and confine the invention and imagination of a singer. The only excuse a composer can plead for this practice, is the want of qualifications in the generality of singers.[4]

For Charles Burney, the individuality of a singer's ornamentation of the given notation was a vital part of the musical experience. In 1778 he commented that "La Bernasconi" "has no great voice, but she has a very elegant style of singing, and many embellishments and refinements that are wholly new here".[5] And three years later he remarked approvingly of Teresa

---
[4] Bayley: *A Practical Treatise*, 47f.
[5] Alvaro Ribeiro SJ (ed.): *The Letters of Dr Charles Burney* (Oxford, 1991), i, 264f.

Maddalene Allegranti: "Indeed she seems to me original—her graces and embellishments do not appear to have been copied from any other singer, or to have been mechanically taught by a master."[6] The continuation of improvised ornamentation well into the 19th century, even in some genres of instrumental music, is suggested by the cellist J. J. F. Dotzauer's comment in the 1820s: "There are a mass of ornaments which fashion and the humours of virtuosos have increased to such a number that suitable names have not even been found for them."[7]

Although mid-18th-century sources demonstrate that ornamentation of the composer's text was an essential aspect of skilled solo performance, less-accomplished musicians frequently employed it incorrectly in relation to the harmony or, in the opinion of treatise writers and critics, in inappropriate contexts, inartistically, or excessively. Francesco Geminiani, in the introduction to his discussion of "all the Ornaments of Expression, necessary to the playing in a good taste",[8] criticized the musician who "thinks of nothing so much as to make continually some Passages or Graces, believing that by this Means he shall be thought to be a good Performer".[9] His discussion shows, however, that he expected performers to be capable of improvised ornamentation. In his Example 19, for instance, he demonstrated "how a single Note (in slow Time) may be executed with different Ornaments and Expressions".[10] And referring to the *appoggiatura* from above he remarked that "it may be added to any Note you will",[11] or of the *Close Shake* that "it should be made use of as often as possible".[12]

C. P. E. Bach, too, was clear that the ability to employ free ornamentation effectively was one of the chief requisites of a good musician. He began the Preface to his 1760 *Sonates pour le clavecin avec des reprises variées* with the statement: "When we make a repeat nowadays, and reproduce something, it is indispensable to make changes in it. This is expected of all those who are charged with the execution of any work." Having drawn attention to the deficiencies of performers who failed to ornament well, he continued: "Nevertheless, and despite the difficulties and abuses, well-made

---

[6] Ribeiro (ed.): *The Letters of Dr Charles Burney*, i, 334, "Graces" was a typical English expression for ornaments.
[7] Dotzauer: *Méthode de violoncelle*, 40.
[8] Geminiani: *The Art of Playing on the Violin* (London, 1751), 6.
[9] Geminiani: *The Art*, 6.
[10] Geminiani: *The Art*, 8.
[11] Geminiani: *The Art*, 7.
[12] Geminiani: *The Art*, 8. See also Ch. 16, pp. 986–87.

ornamentation always retains its value." He referred to the first volume of his own *Versuch* for guidance, where he had also warned against ineptitude and excess.[13] Finally, he explained:

> In the composition of these Sonatas, I was primarily thinking of those beginners and amateurs, who, because of their age, or their occupations, have neither the time nor the patience to devote themselves to rather intensive practice. I wanted to provide them with an easy means of obtaining for others the satisfaction of incorporating some changes in the pieces they perform, without their needing to invent them themselves, or to rely on others to prescribe things for them, which they would only memorize with great effort.[14]

Quantz explained that there were differences between French and Italian practice in the performance of *adagio* movements, noting that the former "requires a neat and connected performance of the melody, and decoration with the standard ornaments, such as, whole and half trills, mordants, turns, *battemens, flattemens*, and so on, but otherwise no extensive passagework or substantial addition of improvised ornamentation". The latter required that the performer should "try not only to execute these little French decorations, but also extensive invented ornaments that must, however, fit with the harmony".[15]

Leopold Mozart discussed *appoggiaturas* at length, in relation to their notation, and concluded that these were ornaments "that the composer must notate, or at least should and can, if he optimistically hopes for a good performance of his written pieces". But he pointed out that there are related ornaments, "which are rarely or never indicated by the composer. Thus, these are decorations that the violinist, according to his own healthy judgment, must know how to apply in the right place."[16] After an extensive discussion of trills, he devoted a chapter to improvised ornaments, but cautioned; "You need all these decorations only if you are playing a solo; and there very

---

[13] W. J. Mitchell, reflecting the aesthetics of the mid-20th century, commented, in a footnote in his English translation of Bach's treatise, that the practice of adding free embellishment "was changing about 1750 to the modern method, whereby the composers specified every last detail and the performer, hopefully speaking, follows orders". *Essay on the True Art of Playing Keyboard Instruments* (London, 1949), 80. This is clearly a distortion of the historical reality and a misinterpretation of complaints about misuse.

[14] C. P. E. Bach: Sonates Pour le Clavecin avec des reprises variées Wq. 50 (Berlin, 1760), Préface.

[15] Quantz: *Versuch*, xiv, 136.

[16] Mozart: *Versuch*, ix, 205.

moderately, at the right time, and only to vary a few passages that occur repeatedly one after another." Perhaps surprisingly, he also felt it necessary to warn: "but one should beware of adding any improvised ornamentation when several people are playing the same part".[17] He was not the last musician to do so. Reports show that Italian orchestral players were still committing this offense in the second decade of the 19th century.[18]

## Vocal Ornamentation

For singers, the art of spontaneous improvised ornamentation was particularly important. Tosi stated in the introduction to his 1723 singing treatise:

> Although a singer may have fundamental intelligence, and be capable of executing every difficult composition easily, and, moreover, has an excellent voice which he employs with skill, he nevertheless does not deserve to be called an outstanding master if he lacks the ability to introduce ornamentation on the spur of the moment.[19]

This statement was retained unchanged, without any qualifications, by Agricola in his 1757 translation and commentary.

Hiller's books on "correct" singing (1774) and "refined" singing (1780) make it clear that, half a century after the publication of Tosi's treatise, improvised ornamentation remained an essential art. In his treatise on "correct" singing, Hiller stated: "It is not my present intention to teach improvised ornamentation; I save this topic for part two of this work."[20] He nevertheless gave extensive exercises for the kinds of figures (*passaggi*) that would be needed for this art, as well as for the conventional smaller ornaments, since the techniques for executing them effectively required much practice. In his second book, Hiller dealt with improvised ornamentation at length, providing extended examples. Two years earlier, in a publication of Six Italian Arias "with the manner of singing and ornamenting them",[21] he had illustrated elaborate ornamentation, above the original notation, in arias by Hasse (Ex. 13.1a–b), Anfossi, Sacchini, Graun, and Majo.

---

[17] Mozart: *Versuch*, 251.
[18] Spohr: *Selbstbiographie*, i, 330f.
[19] Tosi: *Opinioni*, 2f.
[20] Johann Adam Hiller: *Anleitung zum musikalisch-richtigen Gesang* (Leipzig, 1774), 13, §1, 175.
[21] Johann Adam Hiller: *Sechs italienische Arien verschiedener Componisten, mit der Art sie zu singen und verändern* [Six Italian arias by various composers with the way to sing them and vary them] (Leipzig, 1778).

**Ex. 13.1** a–b. Hiller: *Sechs italienische Arien*. (*a*) Hasse: *Leucippo*, "Per me vivi, amato Bene" [Lento c]; (*b*) Hasse: *Solimano*, "Or di contento in lagrime" [Allegro non troppo ¢].

(*a*)

(*b*)

By the end of the century concerns about inappropriate or unskilful improvised ornamentation seem to have been growing. Not only was it criticized in the increasingly influential musical press, but also warned against in treaties that taught its technical and artistic employment. In 1804, Johann Friedrich Schubert began his consideration of improvised ornamentation with the warning:

> Taste has introduced a number of standard and improvised ornaments by which a piece of music can be embellished, and its expression heightened. But they must be applied appropriately and chosen with consideration for their diversity. A singer therefore does not have the privilege of applying them arbitrarily wherever it occurs to him; only where the composer has left a place, and where the character of the piece and the harmony permit them, are they appropriate. In any case, too frequent use of them is in bad taste. A singer who introduces an ornament of whatever kind, on every note that is not very rapid, certainly has no fine feeling and no pure taste.

Evidently feeling that this warning was not strong enough, he added a lengthy footnote:

> The addiction to ornament, to embellish, to dress up everything with ornaments and to make changes, has become so widespread today that a budding singer cannot be sufficiently warned against this dangerous urge. It is not uncommon for singers who claim to be virtuosos, to dress up their songs with a host of standard and improvised ornaments that do not even fit the harmony, let alone the content of the text and the character of the music. It is carried to the extent that one believes one is hearing a free fantasy instead of an aria, and the harmonic accompaniment seems to be something separate, which has no connection with the principal part.
> 
> If, in addition, in every vocal piece, a singer always uses the same ornaments, which he has picked up from others, or learned mechanically from his singing teacher, one is seized with displeasure and cannot resist denying the perpetrator any pretentions to musical knowledge or taste.
> 
> Every music director and singing teacher should try to persuade his singers and pupils that virtuosity does not consist in unnatural changes to the melody, or incessantly sliding down by semitones, turning the singing into disgusting wailing, but in a performance corresponding to the content of the text and the character of the music.[22]

[22] Schubert: *Singe-Schule*, 135.

Despite such warnings, the ability to employ improvised ornamentation continued to be seen as an essential qualification for all professional singers. Having acknowledged the merits of its tasteful use, Schubert noted: "It is merely a question of where ornaments and embellishments are appropriate and where they are objectionable." He identified the following conditions for including them:

> First: every alteration must be appropriate to the meaning of the text and the character of the music.
> Secondly: ornaments must be placed on significant words.
> Thirdly: the same ornaments must not be used too often.
> Fourthly: the beat must not be affected at all by the change, but most carefully observed.
> Fifthly: the additions must be clear to the listener and be performed with ease, informality, precision, and clarity, so that it is impossible to tell whether they are the work of the composer or the interpreter.
> Sixthly: the ornamentation must not impair the clarity of the words, or the punctuation and declamation.
> Seventhly: the additions must fit with the harmony of the accompaniment and must not produce incorrect part-writing.[23]

Finally, he explained that no ornament was permitted in unison, in a choir, or when the voice was a subsidiary part of the texture. In contrapuntal writing and canons, he did not entirely rule out the use of standard ornaments, although he forbade melismatic ornamentation.

Maria Pellegrini Celoni's 1810 singing treatise is more practical than polemic. Having described various appropriate ornaments, she warned, like many earlier writers, that "A good singer must not, however, abuse them",[24] but asserted, like Tosi, that "he will never rise from the common sphere if he does not know how, according to his own abilities, to vary and ornament a piece of music".[25] She gave copious examples of ornamental figurations, which singers could practise to provide themselves with suitable patterns for decorating longer note values (Ex. 13.2a), or to vary a repetition of the same melodic material (Ex. 13.2b–d).

---

[23] Schubert: *Singe-Schule*, 136f.
[24] Maria Pellegrini Celoni: *Grammatica o siano regole di ben cantare* (Leipzig, 1810), 29.
[25] Pellegrini Celoni: *Grammatica*: 40. The parallel German text translates "a suo talente" with "mit eignem guten Geschmack und Talent" (with his own good taste and talent).

722 CLASSICAL AND ROMANTIC PERFORMING PRACTICE

Ex. 13.2 a–d. Pellegrini Celoni: *Grammatica*. (a) p. 41; (b–d) p. 42f.

IMPROVISED ORNAMENTATION AND EMBELLISHMENT 723

Ex. 13.2 Continued

(c)

(d)

Drawing attention to the ornamental requirements of the various types of aria that had become fashionable since Hiller's time, she stated that the Cavatina, which unlike the *da capo* aria, has no repetition, can be ornamented from the beginning "with supreme judgement and great expression", and that the increasingly popular Rondos "have several repeated sections and it is therefore necessary to adorn them, and sometimes to change them in various graceful ways, in order to increase their original beauty". She advised, however, that ensemble numbers,

> duets, terzetts, quartets etc. must be sung as they are written; it is permissible to vary a few small things in the solos; since in the remainder it is necessary to preserve unity, and to be attentive to the forte, the piano, and pianissimo; cantabile, legato, and staccato; and this is the requisite expression, which

I mentioned above, and which is absolutely necessary in ensemble pieces, in which appoggiaturas, trills, and turns are still permitted, but always with appropriate moderation.[26]

The latter exception echoes J. F. Schubert's proscription of melismas, but not standard ornaments in ensemble.

While treatise writers provided descriptions and exemplars of good practice, with the occasional music example, Domenico Corri, a pupil of the renowned Neapolitan singing teacher Nicola Porpora, took a different approach in his innovative *Select Collection*, published in the early 1780s (with subsequent volumes in 1795 and in 1810), which was aimed especially at students and amateur musicians. He began his preface: "When a person has purchased a book, would it not appear very extraordinary if he should be under the necessity of applying to a master of language to correct the orthography, and to distinguish the members of every sentence by proper stops, in order to render the author's meaning intelligible? Just such an absurdity appears in written music, vocal music in particular." The manner of writing it, he added, "is quite insufficient to express the meaning, spirit, and peculiar delicacy of the composition".[27] Having explained his system of performance markings, he continued:

> either an air, or recitative, sung exactly as it is commonly noted, would be a very inexpressive, nay, a very uncouth performance; for not only the respective duration of the notes is scarcely hinted at, but one note is frequently marked instead of another [...] in consequence of which the singer

---

[26] Pellegrini Celoni: *Grammatica*, 46f. The Italian phrase "e necessario di andare uniti", translated here as "to preserve unity", is given in the parallel German translation as "ist es nothwendig, das Uebrige ohne Verzierung zu singen" (it is necessary to sing the remainder without ornament). The term "spianare", translated here as "cantabile", is given in German as "Aufziehen der Stimme". Peter Lichtenthal's *Dizionario* of 1826 defines it thus in the article "Canto" (i, 127): "The so-called Canto spianato, or Cantabile (the particular qualities of which, in addition to the features described above, are: the perfect art of modulating the sound, performing the phrases of the song, the graces and the figures with expression, and with that nobility which distinguishes this character from all the others) it allows few ornaments, and these must be carried out in a broad, sustained, dignified manner, without being heavy, or losing their elegance, lightness, and expression." I have translated "mordenti" ("Doppelschlag" in the German text) as "turn", but it probably refers here to the rapid two- or three-note ornament preceding the main note from the note below to the note above (see Ex. XX for Corri's notation of this ornament).

[27] D. Corri: *Select Collection*, i, 1.

is misled, by being made to sing a wrong note; or (unless he be a master of the science) he must be reduced to the alternative of either singing the notes just as they are expressed, or of making them worse should he attempt to vary them.[28]

He then tackled the issue of additional ornaments:

> We are now to take notice of the principal refinements in song; such as cadences [*cadenzas*], divisions [*fioriture*], and all those intervening ornaments, the proper use of which alone can give to song its highest degree of grace and elegance. These ornaments, to the great disadvantage of composition, have never yet been written down. The Author has introduced into this work such as he judged proper, (and has distinguished them by notes of a smaller size than those which constitute the original melody). As the invention of such ornaments is attended with difficulty, and as it is of great importance to know where and in what measure to introduce them, and where their application would be improper, the advantage of having them written down must be evident. At the same time, he hopes none of his readers have so much misunderstood him, as to conceive, he means these ornaments which he offers to the Public, as those only which can or ought to be made use of: Even within the limits of the strictest propriety, there is still left a very considerable latitude for the exertions of taste and fancy.

Corri saw his additions as making it possible for someone "ignorant of the Italian, French, or any other particular style of singing" to "sing all the music contained in this Collection with a degree of grace and expression, of which, without help of the additional signs made use of, he would have no idea". He believed that by this means "he will of course become familiar with a good manner of singing, and he will apply these graces with success to other music, and find himself greatly assisted towards inventing new ones himself".[29]

---

[28] D. Corri: *Select Collection*, i, 2.
[29] Corri: *Select Collection*, i, 4.

His additions to the original texts include signs for breathing, accents, *crescendo*, and *diminuendo*, short ornaments, written out in small notes (among which were some to indicate different kinds of *portamento*), as well as written-out *fioriture*. What he did not mention in his preface are many small alterations of rhythm, especially when a specific melodic passage is repeated, which become evident when Corri's version is compared with the text from which it was drawn, for instance in his version of the aria "Nel partir bell'idol mio" from J. C. Bach's 1778 opera *La clemenza di Scipione* (Ex. 13.3). In this example, which compares Corri's text with that of the original edition, the small notes are given exactly as in Corri's edition, some with two and some with three flags. It is questionable whether a distinction was intended in most cases, for in his instructions (where the small note has two flags) he taught that they should be "so rapid that, while the effect is felt, the ear shall yet be unable to determine the character of the sounds or to distinguish them from the predominant note".[30] Corri's specific instruction for the "Grace of more intervals" (e.g., in b. 1), which in his *Singer's Preceptor* (1810) he called the *leaping grace*, was that it "is to be taken softly, and to leap into the note rapidly". The grace "close after the note"—as at the ends of bars 70 and 93—called the *anticipation grace* in the *Singers Preceptor*, was "to show that the time necessary for its execution is to be deducted from the last part of that note", and he advised that "in executing it, it is necessary to swell the note into the Grace, and the Grace must melt itself again into the note following".[31] For the "Turn Grace" (Hiller's *Doppelschlag*)—for example, in bar 2—he instructed that it should be "taken strong, and melted into the note". His two signs for breathing meant either a gap "about as long as that made by a Comma in reading"—as in bar 2—or a gap that is to be made "as imperceptible as possible"—as in bar 12. The sign above the fourth note of bar 4 is an accent.[32]

---

[30] Corri: *Select Collection*, i, 8 (for the full quotation see Ch. 12, p. 661).
[31] For further discussion of these types of vocal *portamento*, see Ch. 15.
[32] Corri: *Select Collection*, i, 8.

**Ex. 13.3** J. C. Bach: "Nel partir bell'idol mio", D. Corri: *A Select Collection*, i, 90–94.

**Ex. 13.3 Continued**

[2] in Corri

## Ex. 13.3 Continued

## Ex. 13.3 Continued

**Ex. 13.3** Continued

In his much later *Singers Preceptor* (1810), Corri complained about "the abuse of ornament", considering it to be "of recent date". He observed: "within my memory, those famous singers Farinelli, Cafarello, Geziello, Pacchiarotti, Millico, Aprile, David, Raff and others of the first eminence, sung compositions with little ornament, exerting their talents, on the parts appointed to them; nor were they permitted to introduce, at random, any graces, ornaments etc., as caprice directed, but in such places only as the composer had allotted".[33] And he added that the talent of these singers was principally shown by their *portamento di voce*.[34] His earlier publications certainly suggest a more retrained approach to improvised ornamentation than some other late-18th-century sources, but from a 21st-century perspective, he changed the musical text very extensively and indicated features, such as different types of *portamento* and rhythmic modification, that are very rarely shown so clearly in other pedagogic material.

Whether the amount of improvised ornamentation in opera had increased in the last decades of the 18th century, as Corri's statement suggests, or whether early-19th-century complaints about it arose rather from changing taste than an increase in ornamentation is indeterminable. Anton Reicha, in his *Traité de mélodie* of 1814, was among those who expressed substantial reservations, commenting:

> Singers, at the period of this decadence, only want songs to embroider: and one might say that for almost forty years [i.e., as far back as Reicha, born in 1770, could remember] we have lived in the period of musical embellishment, of which the three arias we have cited may henceforth provide an idea, and serve as a tradition for the history of this art; for it may be presumed that this manner of singing, as a result of the abuse to which it leads, will pass out of fashion, or at least be restrained within reasonable bounds, employing these airs very rarely, and suiting them to an excellent voice very capable of performing them; finally, entrusting them only to singers of exquisite taste, and only in appropriate circumstances. In that case one might see them as a special genre and distinguish them from others by calling them *airs à broder*.[35]

Reicha's examples of *da capo* arias of this kind, by Cimarosa, Giordanello, and Lamparelli, illustrate extensive added ornamentation, both for the first and second appearances of the initial section (Ex. 13.4).

---

[33] Corri: *Singers Preceptor*, 3.
[34] For the potential implications of this term, see Ch. 15.
[35] Reicha: *Traité de mélodie*, 69.

Ex. 13.4 Reicha: *Traité de mélodie*. Plates A5, 40f.

These *da capo* arias, however, were different from other aria types in more recent operas, in which, nevertheless, ornamentation of a less elaborate kind was still envisaged. Regarding improvised ornamentation in general, Reicha posed the rhetorical question, whether composers could not prescribe all the required decoration: his response was *yes* for instrumental music but *no* for vocal music, since he believed that "what a composer writes for his voice, or with his voice, never suits the talent nor the voice of a skilled singer.

Consequently, *prescribed* ornaments are almost always badly executed."[36] Much the same reasoning was offered two decades later by Isaac Nathan, a pupil of Domenico Corri, who observed:

> The same execution [of improvised ornaments], that would from one singer afford pleasure, might from another, excite disgust: the compositions of old masters have no written cadences to a repeated passage, doubtless for this very reason: but it is understood, and indeed expected, that a singer of talent should display his own taste by the introduction of such fanciful and graceful ornaments, as may be best calculated to exhibit his own voice to advantage, and impart full and judicious effect to the composition.[37]

He praised the faultless improvised ornamentation of Gertrud Elisabeth Mara, a pupil of J. A. Hiller, whom he must have heard in her old age, and enthused at length about the "splendid ascensions, turns, and descents of voice" of Maria Malibran, concluding: "The preceeding [sic] remarks have shewn, that the brilliant effect of a musical production must not only depend upon its correct execution, but on the grace and congruity of all its embellishments, without which little or no variety can be given to the repetition of the same passage. [. . .] But the selection of ornaments suited to the subject is the great test of the musician."[38]

The persistence of substantial improvised ornamentation in opera during the 1830s is indicated in a treatise by Heinrich Ferdinand Mannstein (b. 1806), who designated it as "one of the most difficult things in the whole art of singing",[39] because each vocal genre required a different approach. Having noted that ornamentation was subject to changes in taste and that it was impossible to specify where a particular type might most effectively be introduced, he suggested guidelines that are very little different from J. F. Schubert's, three decades earlier:

> Every decoration should fit the words, the character of the music, and always fit the situation of the person portrayed by the singing, and it should

---

[36] Reicha: *Traité de mélodie*, 69.

[37] Isaac Nathan: *Musurgia Vocalis. An Essay on the History and Theory of Music, and on the Qualities, Capabilities, and Management of the Human Voice*, 2nd edn (London, 1836), 262f.

[38] Nathan: *Musurgia Vocalis*, 267f. Nathen's encomium on Malibran was evidently written before her untimely death after an accident in Manchester in 1836, the year Nathan's treatise was published.

[39] Heinrich Ferdinand Mannstein [pseudonym for Steinmann]: *Das System der grossen Gesangschule des Bernacchi von Bologna* (Dresden and Leipzig, [1835]), 60.

be harmonically correct. It should also be executed so that one does not hear the hardship and effort it cost the singer to learn it, and to be always true to this principle, ornaments that are uncomfortable should be avoided. [. . .] The singer must diligently practice decorating melodies, to acquire the ability to apply them everywhere with ease and elegance, but only apply them very selectively so as not to commit the musical crime of overwhelming a melody of beautiful and noble simplicity with inappropriate ornamentation.[40]

To help the singer avoid these pitfalls, he explained the appropriate treatment for various vocal genres. He regarded *Cantabile*, always in slow tempo, as the highest perfection of vocal music, requiring perfect *portamento* and "decorations, which should only infrequently be introduced, all having a dignified character, combining grace and loveliness". *Cadenze* and *Fermate* in general, however, provided an opportunity for singers to display "all artistry and imagination".[41] In arias, the style of singing depended on genre. An *Allegro* should be "furnished with lively and powerful ornaments". In an *Andante* the ornamentation should be "light and pleasing", while agitato arias "admit only a few brilliant ornaments".[42] He advised that "the performance of the *Rondo* presents great difficulties", because it involves frequent repetition of the same material, but it also offered the singer "a broad field for brilliantly displaying his creative imagination and taste. To deserve the name of a singer, he must adorn each repetition of the recurring stanza with ingenious and graceful ornamentation, without violating the basic harmony, in such a way that with every repetition the listener believes he is hearing a new composition."[43] In a prayer (*Preghiera*), "any decoration would be merely ridiculous",[44] while a *Romance* required "an undecorated but intimate and moving performance".[45] In a *Lied*, however, "when several verses are sung one after the other and to the same melody, each can be decorated with small, pleasing ornaments, to avoid monotony".[46] His recommendations for recitative are given below. A revised second edition was published in 1848, but no changes were made to this section.

---

[40] Mannstein: *Das System*, 60f.
[41] Mannstein: *Das System*, 62f, §2.
[42] Mannstein: *Das System*, 63, §3.
[43] Mannstein: *Das System*, 63f, §4.
[44] Mannstein: *Das System*, 64, §5.
[45] Mannstein: *Das System*, 64, §6.
[46] Mannstein: *Das System*, 64, §7.

Manuel García's immensely detailed singing treatise offers abundant evidence that, despite changes of taste, improvised ornamentation and embellishment, sometimes very extensive, was still expected in almost all genres and repertoires of solo vocal music in the middle years of the century.[47] Like Reicha, some thirty years earlier, he gave specimen examples of ornamented arias, in operas by Cimarosa, Crescentini, Morlacchi, and Rossini (*Semiramide*), but, in addition, he included many verbal instructions for their expressive delivery. He prefaced these with the statement:

> So far, we have presented only isolated precepts; we have enumerated the various elements of performance: we will examine these parts in their relation to the whole. To understand fully all the resources of knowledgeable practice, it would be necessary carefully to analyse a series of masterpieces, under the direction of a consummate artist: we do not pretend to replace this skilful master here. In the guidance accompanying these pieces, which are offered for pupils to study, we do not hope always to determine the best ways of performing the melody, or even fully to reveal our own way of feeling it. We seek only to explain, through a few examples, how the student can apply the various principles posed by this method in performance, and in what frame of mind he should approach the study of any piece.[48]

In the arias, the variation of repeated figures, the use of *portamento* (with slurs and small notes), as well as breathing, and many expressive practices are lavishly indicated. In García's examples, trembling effects, signified by *tremolo*, *tremblé*, or by various signs, are very rarely envisaged, which corresponds with his severe warnings, in the earlier part of the treatise, against overusing these effects (Ex. 13.5a–c). The employment of the occasional *vibrato* of intensity, but little, if any *tremolo* of pitch, was certainly envisaged within the context of a generally steady sound.[49]

---

[47] García: *École*, ii, 82.
[48] García: *École* ii, 82–105. Sarah Potter's impressive experimental recreation of 19th-century voice production, ornamentation, and embellishment, closely based on García's annotations of the arias by Cimarosa (*Il sacrificio d'Abramo*), Crescentini (inserted into Zingarelli's *Romeo e Giulietta*), and Morlacchi (*Teobaldo ed Isolina*), can be heard in CD4 of her PhD thesis *Changing Vocal Style and Technique in Britain during the Long Nineteenth Century*, University of Leeds, 2014 (online at https://etheses.whiterose.ac.uk/8345/).
[49] See Ch. 15.

**Ex. 13.5** García: *École* (García's verbal instructions are given in English in Sarah Potter's dissertation). (*a*) Cimarosa: *Il sacrificio d'Abramo*, ii, 83f; (*b*) Crescentini: insertion aria in Zingarelli: *Romeo e Giulietta*, ii, 95; (*c*) ii, 97.

Ex. 13.5 Continued

(c)
[Andante sostenuto]

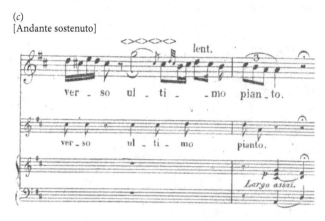

García's specimens of ornamented arias were omitted from the single-volume French edition of 1856 and the revised English version of his treatise, first published in 1858. This may have been for lack of space, but was perhaps a response to the fact that by the 1850s, this repertoire had largely disappeared from the operatic stage, because in the fifth edition of the original French two-volume treatise (Paris, Heugel, 1863) these examples were also omitted. By that date, too, the legitimacy of *elaborate* improvised ornamentation was becoming more questionable.

## The Performance of Recitative

Secco recitative, like *da capo* arias, became increasingly uncommon as a compositional form during the first half of the 19th century, and traditional ways of performing it were gradually forgotten or abandoned. By the early 20th century, its performance, as with so many aspects of older music, had been reduced to a dry routine in which the notation was followed rather precisely. Even in the late 18th century, in some traditions, recitative had begun to be performed in a less dramatic manner. Domenico Corri noted that in Britain "it is seldom considered in any other light than as a mere foil to the succeeding air". Yet Corri regarded it as "beyond a doubt, the highest species of vocal music".[50] It may well be that, despite the flexibilities that have been explored since the 20th-century rise of interest in early music performance,

---

[50] D. Corri: *Select Collection*, i, 2.

we are still far from appreciating the dramatic liberties that were expected during the 18th and early 19th centuries.

In fact, recitative was one of the genres in which notation and performance were most sharply at odds with each other. This was greatest in *recitativo secco*. *Recitativo accompagnato*, which in various modified forms, and without being specifically identified as such, can be found throughout the 19th century, was expected to be delivered more literally, but still with freedoms and conventions that involved substantial departures from the strict meaning of the notation.

There were conflicting views about whether different manners of singing recitatives should be adopted in theatre, church, and concert-hall. Corri considered that in the sacred recitative "A noble simplicity should govern throughout, corresponding with the sublime character of the words, in Church music, ornaments ought not to be used; every note should begin softly, and swell into a fine, well supported sound, decreasing it again in the same proportion." The theatrical recitative he divided into two categories:

The Serious
This should be a graceful, dignified, imitation of speaking, delivered with emphatic expression, and accompanied with appropriate action; ornament very sparingly used, for narrative should always be perspicuous, and such Recitative ought to be supported with strength and precision: in a soliloquy, or Instrumented Recitation, or where the words are intended to move the passions, a Performer should remember that the whole combination of gesture, look, and inflexion of voice, must contribute their various powers to convey the sentiment or feeling he would express.

The Comic
This differs from the serious only by requiring more free familiar delivery approaching still more nearly to speaking; yet in Compositions of this character there often occur passages that require energy and pathos of expression, equally as the Serious.

The concert recitative he regarded as including "all other descriptions of Recitative", and he believed that it "admits of more ornament than either of the preceding, as not being so narrative, or requiring the accompaniment of action".[51] Other authorities did not draw such clear distinctions or, in

---

[51] D. Corri: *The Singers Preceptor*, 71.

the case of Mancini, for instance, disagreed with the idea that church, theatre, and chamber recitative each automatically required a different style of performance.[52]

Most writers laid particular emphasis on the delivery of *secco* recitative like dramatic speech, and the importance of never being constrained by the notated rhythms. Schulz, explained that

> Recitative is distinguished from true song by the fact that a note should never, not even at perfect cadences, be sustained noticeably longer than it would be in declamation. [. . .] One can imagine the recitative as a brook that now flows gently, now rushes between stones, now plunges over cliffs. In the same recitative peaceful, merely narrative passages occur from time to time; a moment later, however, powerful and extremely pathetic passages.[53]

Koch shared the view that "with respect to the duration of the individual syllables, the recitative should be performed just like a speech", but he observed that this was by no means a universal practice, noting:

> In some regions of Germany, the rural cantors and schoolmasters have the habit of performing the recitative in their church music in a measured tempo and teaching this manner to their singing pupils; by this means it acquires a modification that is wholly against its nature, and many passages in it get an extraordinary hardness and sound extremely nonsensical.[54]

Despite the concept that recitative was essentially declamation, there was general acceptance that some ornamentation was appropriate, but as Schulz explained, only with discretion and only from skilled singers:

> A singer of feeling does not fail, here and there, where the emotional context allows beauty, to introduce trembling and sliding effects [*Schwebungen und Ziehungem*], also appoggiaturas (hardly trills), which however, look very silly on paper, and which no singer who is not a born and professional singer can well accomplish. For mediocre singers, simple declamation, where one note is set to one syllable, makes a better effect.[55]

---

[52] See W. Crutchfield, 'Voices' in Howard Mayer Brown (ed.), *The New Grove Handbook of Performance Practice: Music after 1600* (London, 1989), 296.
[53] Schulz: 'Recitativ' in *Allgemeine Theorie*, ii, 943.
[54] Koch: 'Recitativ' in *Musikalisches Lexikon*, 1232 footnote.
[55] Schulz: 'Recitativ' in *Allgemeine Theorie*, ii, 947.

His contemporary J. A. Hiller provided more specific instructions for how a recitative might be ornamented with *appoggiaturas* (which, though not notated, were essential for a "correct" performance) and, occasionally, other small ornaments, explaining: "Recitative permits only a few vocal ornaments, inverted mordents (*Pralltriller*) very seldom, mordents just occasionally; definitely not full trills. Appoggiaturas, however, are good, and often a great help to singers who are not skilled enough at hitting their notes."[56] He illustrated this with a nineteen-bar passage, demonstrating his conception of how "a few vocal ornaments" might be appropriately applied, which however contains nineteen *appoggiaturas* from above, five from below, and three of the two-note ornament he calls *Doppelvorschlag* (Ex. 13.6).

**Ex. 13.6**  Hiller: *Anleitung zum musikalisch-richtigen Gesang*, 205f.

[56] Hiller: *Musikalisch-richtigen Gesang*, 202.

**Ex. 13.6** Continued

Many similar recommendations were made a generation later by A. F. Häser, who advised that, in general, there should be "almost no ornaments at all", but in accompanied recitative, he allowed that "in very passionate passages, and also at the end, there can admittedly be exceptions, though it is advisable even in these instances to make use of *portamento*, *messa di voce*, and rarely introduced, not over-elaborate coloratura". With respect to appoggiaturas, however, he was at pains to point out, as earlier writers had often done, that the pitches of some notes in recitative should not be sung as notated:

> The recitatives of all older composers and of most modern ones are so written that the individual notes, at least on the strong beats, mostly lie in the harmony. Since this sort of recitative, performed exactly as it is written, appears rather stiff and awkward, it is the responsibility of the singer, particularly on several identical notes following immediately after one another, to bring more flow into the melody by means of appoggiaturas and other small ornaments. It goes without saying that knowledge of harmony and declamation is necessary for this.[57]

[57] A. F. Häser: *Caecilia*, x (1829), 154.

IMPROVISED ORNAMENTATION AND EMBELLISHMENT 743

In the mid-1830s, Mannstein reiterated the teaching that recitative should for the most part be "simple and unadorned", but in melodic passages he explained that *portamento* and some ornamentation might be introduced. He illustrated this in several examples from Mozart, Spontini, and Rossini, indicating *portamento* by a slur between syllables, and in several examples including much more elaborate *fioriture* than his verbal text might have suggested (Ex. 13.7). In *parlando* sections, too, he explained that the recitative required "melodic and metric alterations",[58] and at cadences the introduction of the traditional notes a semitone, tone, third, etc. higher, before the harmonic resolution.

Ex. 13.7 Mannstein: *Das System*, 73.

[58] Mannstein: *Das System*, 61, §1.

**Ex. 13.7** Continued

In the following decade, García also provided revealing music examples to convey his conception of expressive performance in recitative, showing not only the notes but also including detained verbal instructions in the examples (Ex. 13.8).

**Ex. 13.8** Cimarosa: *Il sacrificio d'Abramo* in García: *École*, ii, 82f.
[Largo espressivo]

While treatise writers displayed individual approaches to the ornamentation and embellishment of recitatives in general, there was virtually no disagreement about the melodic changes that were necessary at cadences. In almost all cases where a pair of notes of the same pitch occur with a strong–weak placement, the singer would have been expected to modify the first of them, as illustrated in the examples from Mannstein and García.

Most authorities, however, were against the practice of embellishing so-called masculine endings. J. A. Hiller allowed it,[59] but his contemporary Schulz considered that this would be "Very halting and repugnant."[60] A generation later, J. F. Schubert similarly condemned this practice on the grounds that "the delivery thereby becomes dull, the flow of the text is pulled up and comes to a feeble conclusion".[61] In one circumstance, however, an appoggiatura on a masculine ending was generally seen as necessary: that was when the preceding note was a third higher, as illustrated by Schulz (Ex. 13.9) and exemplified by García (Ex. 13.8, in the ninth bar on p. 83).

Ex. 13.9 Schulz: 'Recitativ' in *Allgemeine Theorie*, ii, 943.

The necessity to modify the notation of "blunt endings" in this manner, and indeed in many other subtle ways, was recognized throughout the 19th century and applied not only to earlier music but also to recitative-like passages in later 19th-century music. This remained especially true of Italian music and music in the Italian tradition. Lichtenthal's statement in 1826 that "The Italian school makes the appoggiatura so familiar to the singers that composers dispense entirely from writing them in recitatives"[62] was undoubtedly still valid for the next generation of musicians. The tradition remained so strong that composers could only be certain that appoggiaturas would not be added if they specified this clearly in the music. Thus Verdi. In the Scena, terzetto e Tempesta (no. 13) in *Rigoletto*, instructed, "This recitative should be performed without the customary appoggiaturas."

---

[59] Hiller: *Anweisung zum musikalisch-zierlichen Gesang*, 101.
[60] Schulz: 'Recitativ' in *Allgemeine Theorie*, ii, 951.
[61] Schubert: *Singe-Schule*, 142.
[62] Lichtenthal: 'Appoggiatura' in *Dizionario*, i, 40.

The addition of such appoggiaturas became a matter of controversy during the 20th century. There was a tendency, for many years, to omit them, particularly in Germany, and deliver all recitatives exactly as they were notated. During the last quarter of the 20th century, it was increasingly acknowledged that, in virtually all such cases, appoggiaturas should be added not merely in recitatives but also, frequently, in arias.[63] The matter was not uncontroversial, but the arguments of those who claimed that the practice is not adequately supported by evidence are unconvincing. Seen in the light of the predominant late-18th- and 19th-century attitude towards the relationship of notation and performance, it is likelier that simply adding the conventional appoggiaturas would be erring on the side of caution, and that greater freedom and adventurousness in the rendition of recitative, as García's examples suggest, would be closer to the spirit of the time.

## Recitative Accompaniment

In the early part of the period recitatives would normally have been accompanied by a keyboard instrument (organ in church music and harpsichord in theatre and chamber), sometimes with one or more melody instruments on the bass-line. By the last decades of the 18th century, the harpsichord began to be superseded by the fortepiano in many places. But before the turn of the century, the direction of opera was increasingly being entrusted to the violin rather than to the keyboard in many parts of Europe, and in some theatres, this meant the total disappearance of the keyboard instrument from the pit. A writer in 1799 observed that "If one wants to get rid of the harpsichord *qua* keyboard instrument, so one at the same time banishes its substitute, the pianoforte, and makes use of the violin to direct, as is now becoming ever more common."[64] Coupled with this tendency was the practice of accompanying recitatives in the theatre with only a cello, a cello and bass, or occasionally, strange as it may seem, with a violin. The same writer in the *Allgemeine musikalische Zeitung* observed:

---

[63] Will Crutchfield: 'The Prosodic Appoggiatura in the Music of Mozart and His Contemporaries', *Journal of the American Musicological Society*, xlii (1989), 229–74. A telling example of where, at the beginning of the 20th century, the modification was recognized as appropriate, and where not, can be heard in Lilli Lehman's 1907 recording: https://www.youtube.com/watch?v=mwzBNafRLws.

[64] Anon.: 'Bruchstücke aus Briefen an einem jungen Tonsetzer', *Allgemeine musikalische Zeitung*, ii (1799–1800), 17.

If one wants to attain these important goals by giving the chords on the violoncello, as in some places, or on the violin, as in others: so one has the disadvantage—leaving aside the question of whether the necessarily skilled men may well not be easy to find everywhere—that the chords on the former are too dull and transitory, and perform the necessary service neither for the singer nor hearer; the chords of the latter, however, sound too high and pointed, and repulsively offend the ear, particularly in the accompaniment of tenor and bass voices.[65]

The cello, as the principal accompaniment instrument for recitative, seems nevertheless to have been growing in favour at that time. Among notable exponents of this practice was J. G. C. Schetky, whom the writer of the above article admitted to be highly effective at it, noting that he always gave the singers their note at the top of the arpeggiated chord.[66] Schetky's own treatise includes instructions for the accompaniment of recitative that confirm this account; he advised: "In Recitative the Violoncellist should fashion the Chords in such a manner that the highest note is the Singer's next one and should be struck as soon as the Singer has pronounced the last word viz [Ex. 13.10]."[67]

Ex. 13.10 Schetky: *Practical and Progressive Lessons*, 38.

[65] Anon.: 'Bruchstücke', *Allgemeine musikalische Zeitung*, ii (1799–1800), 18f.
[66] Anon.: 'Bruchstück', *Allgemeine musikalische Zeitung*, ii (1799–1800), 35.
[67] Johann Georg Christoph Schetky: *Practical and Progressive Lessons for the Violoncello* (London, [1813]), 38. Similar advice had already been given in Ferdinand Kauer's *Kurzgefasste Anweisung das Violoncell zu Spielen* (Speyer, 1778) repr. (Vienna [c. 1800]), 12, together with examples of appropriate chords. The annotations provided by Jean-Pierre Duport in the manuscript parts used by King Friedrich Willhelm II of Prussia for accompanying recitative on the cello, however, do not follow the principle of always including the singer's next note at the top of the chord. (I am grateful to Alexander Nicholls for this information.)

In England the practice was continued by the cellist Robert Lindley, who was regularly partnered by Domenico Dragonetti on the double bass. This form of accompaniment, usually by a cellist alone, was widespread throughout Europe. Instructions for the performance of recitatives by cellists were given in the Paris Conservatoire's *Méthode de violoncello* and in Fröhlich's *Vollständige Musikschule*. In 1811, Gottfried Weber expressed his opinion that it was generally better to accompany recitative in this manner than with the fortepiano, because he considered that even the best fortepiano cannot sound good against an orchestra, and he suggested that if the cellist could not perform it from the figured bass the director should write it out.[68] In 1831, he referred to this type of cello accompaniment again, as something that was employed from time to time in Italian opera;[69] and it appears to have survived in Italy as late as the 1870s.[70] Mendelssohn dispensed with keyboard accompaniment of recitative in his 1841 performance of Bach's *St Matthew Passion* in Leipzig; the Bodleian Library, Oxford, possesses a bass part used for that performance in which the accompaniments are scored for double bass with two solo cellos playing chords to provide the harmony (the organ part in this performance material contains no music for the recitatives). Other examples of accompaniment of this kind occur in Meyerbeer's Parisian operas, in this case, with his usual attention to detail, written out in full (Ex. 13.11).

There was considerable confusion in the early 19th century about several aspects of recitative accompaniment. This undoubtedly resulted, to some extent, from the growing notion that there should be a closer correspondence between what composers wrote and what executants performed. Many old-established conventions were being superseded, and doubt arose about how to interpret the notation in older music, as well as which conventions might have been adopted by contemporary composers. Articles in the *Allgemeine musikalische Zeitung* in 1810 and 1811 reveal significant differences of opinion about whether the accompanying chords in recitative should be sustained, when notated

---

[68] G. Weber: 'Begleitung des Recitativs', *Allgemeine musikalische Zeitung*, xiii (1811), 96f.
[69] G. Weber: 'Ueber das sogennanten Generalbassspielen', *Caecilia*, xiii (1831), 145ff.
[70] See Claudio Bacciagaluppi: 'Die »Pflicht« des Cellisten und der Generalbaß in der Romantik', in Claudio Bacciagaluppi, Roman Brotbeck, Anselm Gerhard (eds.), *Spielpraxis der Saiteninstrumente in der Romantik* (Schliessen, 2011).

750  CLASSICAL AND ROMANTIC PERFORMING PRACTICE

Ex. 13.11  Meyerbeer: *Les Huguenots*, no. 27.

as long notes, or cut short. There was already uncertainty about what was intended in the recitatives of Haydn's *Die Schöpfung* only a decade after the work had been written. A correspondent remarked that Hasse and Graun intended the notes to be played short (as they usually were), and that this was confirmed by the practice of the Dresden and Berlin orchestras, which they had trained; he added that Hiller, who was a pupil of Hasse, also did this in Leipzig. Only when Hasse wrote *ten. (tenuto)* did he require the bass notes to be sustained. On the other hand, the writer implied that orchestras in Italy, Vienna, and Munich sustained the notes. He also illuminated another doubt about the performance of recitative that seems to have arisen around that time: whether in a secco recitative any accompaniment other than the bass note was required. His conclusion reveals the rapidity with which musical conventions were changing in the early 19th century. "Certainly for a hundred years there has been no doubt about the best manner of accompanying recitative: however, it may well be possible that in the present revolutionary times one may also in this matter do and require the opposite of what was formerly recognized as good and correct."[71] Gottfried Weber responded that it was necessary to be familiar with individual composers' practices: that some composers adopted the convention of always writing long notes, while others, for example his own teacher G. J. Vogler, wrote the notes as they wished them to be played. On the question of accompanying recitative only with a bass-line in *Die Schöpfung*, Weber merely expressed astonishment that there should be any doubt, since Haydn would hardly have wasted time writing figures above the bass if he had not wanted a chordal accompaniment.[72]

At that time, there was a general feeling that the accompaniment to *secco* recitative should be as simple and unobtrusive as possible. A Viennese writer in 1813 observed that "far from marking this accompaniment in a brilliant fashion, it should be made scarcely noticeable, and should bring out the designed effect, with magical power, unnoticed". The writer added, however, perhaps supporting a Viennese tendency to sustain the bass notes: "at times when the recitative is more passionately expressed and

---

[71] Anon.: 'Welches ist für die Bässe die beste und zwechkmässigsten Art, das einfache Recitativ zu begleiten?', *Allgemeine musikalische Zeitung*, xii (1809–10), 974.
[72] G. Weber: 'Begleitung des Recitativs', *Allgemeine musikalische Zeitung*, xiii (1811), 93–98.

therefore takes on a more inward, moving character, a simple accompaniment in sustained notes may be used to effect".[73] Gottfried Weber also took the view that the accompaniment should be unobtrusive and for this reason felt that figures were better than a written-out accompaniment.[74] In the light of this evidence, the widespread late-20th- and early-21st-century tendency for keyboard players to supply embellishments in recitative seems questionable.

There was also some lack of consensus about what should happen when the entry of the voice coincided with the final note of the accompaniment (particularly in orchestrally accompanied recitative), or when the accompaniment was notated to begin at the same time as the singer's final note, whether the music should be performed literally as written or whether overlap should be avoided. Quantz considered overlap to be not only proper, but also necessary in some instances.[75] Haydn, on the other hand, was quite specific in performance instructions for his "Applausus" Cantata in 1768: "In the accompanied recitatives you must observe that the accompaniment should not enter until the singer has quite finished his text, even though the score shows the contrary." Probably the practice outlined by Haydn was the normal one, at least in Italian and Italian-influenced traditions, for Domenico Corri, in the 1780s, was also quite specific about avoiding overlap, illustrating the relationship between notation and performance in such instances as in Ex. 13.12.

Ex. 13.12 Corri: *Select Collection*, i, 3.

Once again Meyerbeer provides an illuminating perspective on the practice in the 19th century. His later operas, written for Paris, contain recitative passages where he carefully warns the performers that the accompaniment should commence after the singer has finished (Ex. 13.13a–b).

---

[73] Anon.: 'Ueber das Rezitativ', *Wiener allgemeine musikalische Zeitung*, ii (1813), 14f.
[74] G. Weber: 'Ueber das sogennanten Generalbassspielen', *Caecilia*, xiii (1831), 145ff.
[75] Quantz: *Versuch*, 272.

Ex. 13.13 a–b. Meyerbeer: (*a*) *Les Huguenots*, no. 22; (*b*) *Le Prophète*, no. 28 (supplément pour abréger le trio qui precède).

(*a*)

(*b*)

## Improvised Ornamentation in Songs

García's ornamentation, more obviously connected with the expression of the text than with vocal display, seems closer to the "small, pleasing ornaments" that Mannstein considered appropriate in *Lieder*. Songs, especially strophic songs, were undoubtedly expected to receive a similar type of treatment to the more modestly ornamented arias. Domenico Corri had already presented many examples of ornamented songs in his *Select Collection* from the 1780s and 1790s. In his 1810 treatise, he included one of Haydn's Canzonettas, which provides a typical example of the types of adaptations to the original text he considered appropriate in songs, comprising *portamento* effects in bars 1–3 and 15, dynamic shadings, perhaps also connected with *vibrato* of intensity, especially <>, and added-note ornamentation where a melodic phrase is repeated (Ex. 13.14a–b).

Ex. 13.14 a–b. (*a*) The original edition (London: Corri, Dussek & Co. [1795]); (*b*) Haydn: Canzonetta "She never told her love" in Corri: *The Singer's Preceptor* (London [1810]), ii, 32.

(b)

Compelling evidence of a similar approach to the performance of Schubert's *Lieder* within his closest circle is provided by Johann Michael Vogl's notation of ornament in songs he performed with the composer.[76] Walther Dürr demonstrated beyond reasonable doubt that the ornamentation notated by Vogl was entirely congruent with Viennese practice.[77] Schubert's friend Eduard von Bauernfeld recalled that "Small alterations and embellishments, which this skilful singer, a past master of effect, allowed

---

[76] Examples of Vogl's ornamentation are preserved in "Lieder von Franz Schubert und Reichardt verändert von M. Vogl". In *Wittezeck-Spaun*, Gesellschaft der Musikfreunde. Vienna, Austria, and in an edition of *Die schöne Müllerin* published by Diabelli shortly after Schubert's death.

[77] Walther Dürr: 'Schubert and Johann Michael Vogl: A Reappraisal', *19th-Century Music*, iii (1979), 126–40. Despite this evidence, improvised ornamentation in Schubert's music, including his songs, remained a controversial issue during the 1990s; for instance, David Montgomery: 'Modern Schubert Interpretation in the Light of the Pedagogical Sources of His Day', *Early Music*, xxv (1997), 100–18. The stance expressed by Montgomery, among others, may be seen as part of a last-ditch defence of the historically untenable "textual literalism" mentality, which propagates the unsophisticated view that departures from the literal meaning of the notation are only justifiable if they can be supported by clear and specific historical evidence. This article was ably rebutted by Eric Van Tassel: ' "Something Utterly New": Listening to Schubert Lieder. 1: Vogl and the Declamatory Style', *Early Music*, xxv (1997), 702–14, and by Robert Levin: 'Performance Prerogatives in Schubert', *Early Music*, xxv (1997), 723–27, as well as by Levin and Dürr: in "Correspondence", *Early Music*, xxvi (1998), 533–35. More recently there has been growing engagement with Vogl's ornamentation in Schubert's *Lieder*; for instance, Joseph R. Matson: 'Johann Michael Vogl's Alterations to Schubert's "Die Schöne Müllerin" ' (diss., University of Iowa, 2009); Olivia Claire Sanders Robinson: 'Towards a Declamatory Performance in Schubert Lieder' (diss., Edith Cowan University, Western Australia, 2020).

himself, received the composer's consent to some extent, but not infrequently gave rise to friendly controversy."[78] Schubert may not always have been convinced by particular instances, but it is a failure of historical understanding and imagination to believe that he did not expected an accomplished singer to add standard ornaments, or even to introduce melismas, alter pitches, and modify rhythms (especially to characterize the text in successive verses of strophic songs). Later rejection of any ornamentation—for instance, by Schubert's friend Leopold von Sonnleithner in 1857[79]—reveals more about changing taste during the 19th century than about earlier practice.

Although many operatic singers were castigated for their excessive employment of ornamentation, this was never the case with Vogl, who was consistently praised for putting his vocal skills entirely at the service of dramatic characterization.[80] There is no ambiguity about Schubert's appreciation of Vogl as a collaborator in the performance of his songs, for he wrote enthusiastically to his brother Ferdinand in 1825: "The manner in which Vogl sings and I accompany, how we appear in such a moment to be *one*, is something quite new and unheard of for these people."[81]

That Vogl's artistry as a lyrical and dramatic singer was regarded as a model of tasteful restraint is made clear in an essay by one of the most prominent Viennese champions of classical singing, Ignaz von Mosel. Posing the rhetorical question "What is method, what is art?", Mosel challenged the prevailing idea that "method", by which he evidently means style and technique, consists in making florid ornaments. He condemned the type of singer "who never sings anything longer than, occasionally, a quarter-note, more usually turning everything into sixteenths, or, if possible, dividing the composer's original melody into thirty-seconds or even smaller note-values, not leaving a bar unchanged, making any existing ornamentation even more elaborate". He complained that such singers would use "the same flourishes, twenty times in a single evening", whatever the emotion behind

---

[78] Otto Erich Deutsch: *Schubert: Die Dokumente seines Lebens* (Kassel, 1964), 314.
[79] Otto Erich Deutsch: *Schubert: Die Erinnerungen seiner Freunde* (Leipzig, 1957), 130f, 135ff.
[80] The fullest account of Johann Michael Vogl's musicianship, drawing upon numerous contemporary reviews, and his relationship with Schubert, is given in Andreas Liess: *Johann Michael Vogl. Hofoperist und Schubertsänger* (Graz and Köln, 1954).
[81] Deutsch: *Schubert: Dokumente*, 314.

the words, taking no account of "whether these so-called coloraturas fit with the accompanying chords or create the most offensive dissonance".[82] In contrast, Mosel identified the following qualities of fine singing: perfect clarity in articulating the text, perfect breath control, correct intonation, dynamic flexibility, and fine cantabile. Finally, he praised the singer who "introduces pleasing variety by decorating the simple melody, when it returns one or more times in its original form, not with unbridled imagination, nor an addiction to impress through mechanical skill, but with understanding, feeling, and taste". Mosel believed that "often the expression can be enhanced and the effect intensified by adding a single appoggiatura, a nicely rounded mordant, or sometimes an ornament of three, four, or, at most, six notes, always with a new and graceful shape, always pure and clear in execution, always appropriate to the meaning of the text, the character of the song and the singer, and always fitting with the harmony."[83] He concluded his article: "I dare to assert that the most excellent dramatic singer of the present day is the one who combines Italian method with German art; and whoever wants to convince himself of the truth of this assertion should go and hear our Vogl perform the roles of Almaviva [Mozart: *Figaro*], Orestes [Gluck: *Iphigenie auf Tauris*], the patriarch Jacob [Méhul: *Joseph*], Creon [Cherubini: *Medea*], Astyages [Mosel: *Cyrus und Astyages*], and above all the prophet Daniel [Weigl: *Baal's Sturz*]!"[84]

Although Mosel's remarks are specifically about operatic singing, there is no reason to doubt that the same aesthetic principles were expected in performing songs, which were equally concerned with the effective delivery of a text that was intended to convey expression or drama. Indeed, Mannstein's comment about the ornamentation of *Lieder* demonstrates that even in the 1830s, improvised vocal ornamentation was not confined to the operatic stage. Vogl's preserved ornamentation of Schubert songs fits precisely with Mosel's concept of sensitive elaboration, which reveals "understanding, feeling, and taste".

---

[82] Ignaz von Mosel: 'Ueber die gewöhnliche Anwendung der Wörter: Methode und Kunst, auf die Leistungen der dramatischer Sänger', *Taschenbuch für Schauspieler und Schauspielfreunde: auf das Jahr 1821 [...]*, hrsg. Von Lembert (Vienna, 1821), 38f.
[83] Mosel: 'Ueber die gewöhnliche Anwendung', 40.
[84] Mosel: 'Ueber die gewöhnliche Anwendung', 43.

The strophic song "Jägers Abendlied" is among those ornamented by Vogl. His changes are varied in each of the three verses (Ex. 13.15a). An example of Vogl's approach to a more dramatic, almost operatic, song is provided by "Antigone und Oedip", which Schubert dedicated to him (Ex. 13.15b).

Ex. 13.15a  Schubert: "Jägers Abendlied" with ornamentation by Vogl.

Ex. 13.15b  Schubert: "Antigone und Oedip" with ornamentation by Vogl.

## Changing Attitudes towards Vocal Ornamentation

The skills and musicality required to ornament music tastefully in the spirit of Mosel's aesthetics were very considerable. Nathan, having castigated singers for a whole host of deficiencies in this respect, commented: "From this wanton abuse the ornamental style of singing has in all ages, but of late years in particular, become censured."[85] Similar condemnation of incompetent or stylistically questionable ornamental practices during the late 18th century and the early 19th century has sometimes been misinterpreted as evidence that ornamentation was neither envisaged nor desired by the composers in whose music it was employed.[86] Certainly, 19th-century

---

[85] Nathan: *Musurgia Vocalis*, 263.
[86] E.g., Beverley Jerold: 'How Composers Viewed Performers' Additions', *Early Music*, xxxvi (2008), 95–109.

composers became increasingly concerned to restrict, or even prohibit, the use of improvised ornamentation in their vocal music; and changing attitudes towards the relationship between composer and performer began to be projected backwards onto the older repertoire that had retained its place in concert hall and opera house. By the early-20th century the unhistorical conviction that composers notated precisely what they wanted to hear was firmly entrenched, even to the extent of ignoring all the implied *appoggiaturas* in recitative.[87] More recently, early-19th-century objections to the decoration of arias in *Figaro* and *Die Zauberflöte* by the bass I. L. Fischer (who had been the first Osmin in *Die Entführung*) have been cited in support of the contention that improvised ornamentation "should be strongly discouraged for all [Mozart's] operas starting with *Idomeneo*, and all arias after approximately 1780".[88] Critics of Fischer, however, took him to task not because he added ornamentation, but because he added it unskilfully. In 1802 a reviewer complained about his treatment of "In diesen heil'gen Hallen" (*Die Zauberflöte*), where the harmony was complex and where Mozart had in any case written many notes;[89] yet three years earlier, criticizing the same piece, a reviewer merely asked that he employ "somewhat fewer ornaments".[90] The fact that Fischer's use of ornaments, despite his distinguished career, was by no means exemplary is confirmed by a report from Hamburg of his elaboration of a *fermata* in Haydn's *Die Schöpfung*. Having condemned a French singer's harmonically false ornaments in the same work, the reviewer observed: "The lack of thorough knowledge and the concomitant French levity could at least explain this; but how astonished I was when I heard the German singer who has been famous for more than 30 years do the following [Ex. 13.16] and introduce several similar ornaments and decorations, to which our knowledgeable audience listened with deep rapture and rewarded with loud applause."[91]

---

[87] Winton Dean noted in 1977 that "the ungrammatical omission of this feature is still not unknown", in 'The Performance of Recitative in Late Baroque Opera', *Music & Letters*, lviii (1977), 392.
[88] Neumann: *Ornamentation and Improvisation in Mozart*, 239.
[89] Anon.: *Allgemeine musikalische Zeitung*, v (1802–3), 174.
[90] Anon.: *Allgemeine musikalische Zeitung*, i (1798–99), 32.
[91] Anon.: 'Briefe über Tonkunst und Tonkünstler', *Allgemeine musikalische Zeitung*, iv (1801–2), 14f.

Ex. 13.16 *Allgemeine musikalische Zeitung*, iv (1801/2), 15.

Other complaints about improvised ornamentation from the same journal are revealing both of attitudes and of the types of interpolation that were common. In a report from Hamburg in 1799 a reviewer commented of Madam Righini that

> her singing was clean and correct throughout; also she rarely made superfluous ornaments and decorations, and when one heard them, they nevertheless fitted with the harmony and the accompaniment. How much good that did me, and how I rejoiced over it! for the following examples may prove how right are my frequent complaints about the widespread mania for making bad and often harmonically quite incorrect decorations and alterations which are not only tolerated by music directors, but even, to judge by the loud applause of the public, are regarded as the *non plus ultra* of art.

The reviewer then gave several examples from Mozart operas. Herr Rau, as Tamino in *Die Zauberflöte*, sang ornamentation as in Ex. 13.17, and he added sarcastically that "Herr Krug, as Sarastro in the first aria of Act 2, always introduced the following excellent appoggiatura" (Ex. 13.18), before continuing: "All this cannot in any way be compared with the ornamentation of a fermata in the last duet of Mozart's opera *Così fan tutte* by which Mad. Lange [Mozart's sister-in-law and former pupil!] was able to gain equally universal and loud applause. This went as follows: [Ex. 13.19]."[92]

---

[92] Anon.: 'Briefe über Tonkunst und Tonkünstler', *Allgemeine musikalische Zeitung*, i (1798–99), 604f.

Ex. 13.17 *Allgemeine musikalische Zeitung*, i (1798–99), 605.

Ex. 13.18 *Allgemeine musikalische Zeitung*, i (1798–99), 605.

Ex. 13.19 *Allgemeine musikalische Zeitung*, i (1798–99), 606.

Many critics, however, also praised beautiful ornamentation; and all these sources can only be understood in the context of their own time, not of ours, which has been so strongly influenced by the notion of the inviolability of a great composer's notation. When Handel, Gluck, Haydn, Mozart, Beethoven, Rossini, Verdi, Berlioz, or Wagner condemned performers' improvised ornamentation, or implied that their music should be performed as it was notated, they undoubtedly meant something quite different from each other and from musicians whose experience post-dates the 20th-century modernist revolution. Neumann's contention that all ornamentation in Mozart's later operas should be "strongly discouraged" might arguably be applied more legitimately to the "abuse" of Mozart's notation by those 20th- and early-21st-century singers whose unhistorical *continuous vibrato* has often turned every sufficiently long note into a flaccid trill, occasionally wider than a whole tone.[93]

In 1814, Friedrich Rochlitz wrote: "An operatic piece is intended to express what this or that particular character feels in this or that situation, and, by expressing these feelings, seeks to arouse the audience's empathy. So, as far as ornamentation is concerned, it depends on what kind of character it is, and what kind of situation." Then, having condemned the ornamentation of Sarastro's "In diesen heil'gen Hallen" "with conceited fripperies and elegant flirting flourishes" (which he had probably experienced), he continued:

> But let us also not forget the opposite! There sits a young prince, idle, lost in dreamy enjoyment, and his imagination conjures up the picture of his beloved. He directs a song to her, in which this picture is embellished more and more gracefully with each stanza. The composer treated this effusion as a Rondo, on the subject: she is beautiful [. . .]. This subject, as is normal in a Rondo, returns repeatedly. Nothing can be more natural here than that the singer, having first expressed it as simply as those words, always paints it anew, and always richer and more graceful, closer and closer to his heart, and consequently to that of the listener[.][94]

Curiously, Rochlitz's description does not correspond with Tamino's "Dies Bildniss ist bezaubernd schön", which is neither strophic nor a Rondo.

---

[93] Genuine 'historical' trills can be heard to perfection in several of Adelina Patti's recordings, e.g., Bellini's "Ah, non credea".
[94] R. [Rochlitz?]: 'Beytrag zur Lehre von den Verzierungen', *Allgemeine musikalische Zeitung*, xvi (1814), 129.

There is much evidence of changing attitudes towards improvised vocal ornamentation during the second and third decades of the 19th century, but also a continuing belief that it was appropriate or even necessary in many circumstances. A writer in 1812, praising Antonio Brizzi's ornamentation in Paër's *Achille*, observed: "Compositions from the current German school (in which I count the works of Mozart, Haydn, van Beethoven, and Cherubini) tolerate less improvised decoration than those that are closer to the Italian style." Even in German school compositions, however, he believed that, when prominent solos occurred,

> the singer has a free field to paint a meaningful phrase, an important word, either expressing it with a simple and long-lasting *messa di voce*, or with an impressive coloratura; here the individuality of the performing artist has free play, and here it would be unjust to prevent him from expressing himself one way or another according to his feelings and his individual artistic ability, as long as the way he chooses does not clash with the situation and the purpose of the drama as a whole.[95]

Even some Italian composers attempted to restrict the singer's freedom. Rossini began to notate ornaments more fully than had previously been common in Italian opera; but he was probably prompted less by concern about performers altering and adding to his musical text than by incorrect or inappropriate ornamentation on the part of inept or tasteless performers; in fact, his notated ornaments may rather be to indicate of where it is appropriate, than to prescribe specific notes. Even in Verdi's generation, it is clear that opera composers did not expect the singer to execute written-out ornamental passages literally; they provided them rather as a guide to length and correct positioning.[96] Thus, although writers and musicians, throughout the Classical period, had inveighed against unskilful ornamentation, such comments should not be taken to mean that these writers advocated none, or even very little. As Reicha remarked:

> One should not confound something with the abuse that is made of it; for there is always a great difference between the two. It is necessary also to

---

[95] Anon.: *Allgemeine musikalische Zeitung*, xiv (1812), 543f.
[96] David Lawton: 'Ornamenting Verdi Arias: The Continuity of a Tradition' in Alison Latham and Roger Parker (eds.), *Verdi in Performance* (Oxford, 2001), 49–80.

distinguish between a singer of talent who embellishes a melody with a flexible and pleasant voice, and with exceptional tact and exquisite taste, with those bad mimics and pitiful caricatures who make something worse of it. And if the former, in addition, is intelligent enough to introduce his embellishments appropriately, one should not confuse him with the latter who use them indiscriminately.[97]

In a few cases, the examples of ornamented vocal music provided by Reicha and others can be supplemented with examples supplied by composers themselves. Salieri pencilled some ornamentation into the vocal line in a copy of his *Venti otto divertimenti vocali*;[98] in no. 2, for instance, he amended the printed text from Ex. 13.20a to Ex. 13.20b.

Ex. 13.20 a–b. Salieri: *Venti otto divertimenti vocali*, no. 2.

(a)

(b)

Mozart's ornamented versions of arias by himself and J. C. Bach, intended to assist an inexperienced singer, are readily available.[99] Evidence of a contemporaneous tradition of ornamentation in *Die Zauberflöte* is contained in a string quartet arrangement that was published shortly after Mozart's death, which the title page, albeit questionably, attributed to Mozart himself (Ex. 13.21a–c).[100]

---

[97] Reicha: *Traité de mélodie*, 66.

[98] Salieri: *Venti otto divertimenti vocali* (Vienna, [c. 1803]); copy in the British Library Shelfmark K.7.C.26.

[99] See, e.g., *New Grove*, 1st edn, ix, 46, 'Improvisation', §1, 3. An example of embellishment indicated by Haydn, in *Il ritorno di Tobia*, is also given there on p. 45.

[100] *Die Zauberflöte*. Grand opéra, arrangé pour deux violons, alto & basse, par l'autheur, Mr W. A. Mozart (Berlin, Amsterdam, J. J. Hummel [1793]).

# 766 CLASSICAL AND ROMANTIC PERFORMING PRACTICE

Ex. 13.21 a–c. Comparison of the vocal part in the 1st edition vocal score (Simrock, 1793) with the violin part of a string quartet arrangement (J. J. Hummel in Berlin, [1793]) plate number 831, the title page of which states: Arrangé pour deux violons, alto & basse par l'autheur Mr W. A. Mozart.

Much later, Meyerbeer's acquiescence in the modification of display passages in his operas is implied by his own practice of providing different versions. This is nicely illustrated by comparison of a transposed version of the Page's aria from *Les Huguenots* with the original (Ex. 13.22).

**Ex. 13.22** Meyerbeer: *Les Huguenots*, no. 6b.
Transposed in the German version from MS in the Meyerbeer Archiv,
Staatliches Institut für Musikforschung Preussische Kulturbesitz, Berlin.
Original French version from the printed Full Score (Paris, Schlesinger, 1836).

How far such examples might encourage a modern performer to depart from the notated text is a matter of taste and artistry, as it was in Mozart's and Meyerbeer's time, as well as for later generations.

Nevertheless, 19th-century retrospective, unverifiable reports of Haydn's and Mozart's condemnation of singers ornamenting their parts, and Weber's reliably documented distaste for it,[101] undoubtedly reflect changing attitudes. By the 1830s and 1840s a widespread prejudice was developing against the addition of ornaments where the composer had not indicated them, particularly in music that was increasingly coming to be seen as "classical". This strengthened over the following decades, although there were still contrary opinions. In 1854, Henry Chorley, as well as confirming that Viennese singers were still employing improvised ornamentation in Mozart, advocated a broader view, asserting:

> That the Vienna tradition of singing Mozart's operas does not bind the vocalist to a bald and literal enunciation of the text and nothing but the text, we have had proofs in the singing of Madam van Hasselt-Barth, Madam Jenny Lutzer, and, most recently, Mdlle. Zerr—all vocalists formed in Mozart's own town, and who may naturally be supposed to possess some idea of the manner of executing his operas, sanctioned and provided for by himself. But this newly fashioned edict, in command of an utterly and servile plainness, which, if carried out, would utterly destroy all the singer's individuality in art, seems to me to receive contradiction from the music of Mozart itself—even if we had not tradition to confirm us—even if we did not know that Mozart wrote for singers, who were nothing without their changes and their closes. That to apply ornament unsparingly would be an insolence—that to employ it out of place and out of style is a musical offence, to be repudiated by all musical people—are facts which by no means imply that to apply and employ it *at all* are cardinal sins. It is the promulgation of such a canon by modern Pedantry, which has caused one-half of the transgressions found so nauseous by severe folks and purists who are never so complacent as when they can "make *those* singers keep in their right places". Without some discretionary taste, delicately and scientifically exercised by the *Susanna*, the *Zerlina*, the *Fiordiligi*, and the *Pamina*, of Mozart's operas, I am satisfied that no performance of his music is classical—otherwise in conformity with his intentions.[102]

Referring to ornamentation in the vocal music of Gluck and Beethoven, however, he added, with dubious historical justification, especially with respect to the former, that "the addition of even an appoggiatura would be intolerable". This is perhaps surprising, since Chorley, who had been on friendly terms with Mendelssohn, went on to state:

---

[101] John Warrack: *Carl Maria von Weber* (Cambridge, 1968), 207.
[102] Henry Chorley: *Modern German Music* (London, [1854]), ii, 376f.

Mendelssohn [...] wrote so as to allow no space or exercise of fancy for the vocal embroiderer; and thus, to alter or add to his music, would be to injure it, by showing an arrogant disloyalty to the master's wishes and meanings. Nevertheless, I well recollect the quiet smile of pleasure with which even Mendelssohn used to receive a shake [trill] exquisitely placed in the second verse of his delicious "Frühlingslied" (Op. 47); and it must not be forgotten, by all who desire to see the question fairly argued out, and illustrated by facts, not dogmas, that the first singer of *Elijah* in Mendelssohn's *Oratorio*— Herr Staudigl—was sanctioned, in one of the finest pieces of dramatic *recitative* which the work contains, to heighten the effect, by substituting one note for another—the upper G flat, I mean, in place of D flat—in the scene with Baal's priests, on the last repetition of the words "Call him louder."[103]

Had Mendelssohn lived to complete his planned opera for Jenny Lind, whom he very deeply admired, he might well have allowed her scope for her renowned fertility of invention.[104]

In fact, as late as the 1860s, Ferdinand Sieber (whose father had been a pupil of Aloysia Lange, and later a member of Spohr's opera company in Kassel) still taught that improvised *fioriture* are "left to the choice, or rather, to the taste of the singer who, when a melody repeatedly occurs without changes, may decorate it with these kinds of flourishes to protect it from monotony and uniformity." He then gave the following question and answer:

**Is it permitted to add a series of notes to a composer's piece of music at will, since it can be assumed that the composer himself would have notated variations and added ornamentation had it been his intention to make the melody appear differently when it was repeated?**

In the classical works of Bach, Handel, Gluck, and Beethoven etc. any such addition would be offensive; on the other hand, Mozart's works, which are far more in line with the demands of artistic singing and actually blossomed on the basis of Italian melodies, but even more so all the works of the Italians themselves, allow such ornamentation. While we may permit ourselves to interpolate the most substantial passagework into the opera arias of Italian composers, and to change runs and so on at will, as it fits the individual gifts of each voice—we will do well in the case of Mozart,

---

[103] Chorley: *Modern German Music*, ii, 377.

[104] For examples of her *fioriture* see *Jenny Lind: A record and analysis of the "Method" of the late Madam Jenny Lind-Goldschmidt by W. S. Rockstro together with a selection of cadenze, solfeggio abellimenti, etc.* [...] edited by Otto Goldschmidt (London, 1894).

Haydn, Weber, Spohr et al. only to limited ourselves to the interjection of small *fioriture*, which occur inconspicuously and do not impair the charm of the melody.[105]

It is noteworthy that by this date, Handel, whose works would certainly have invited ornamentation in the mid-18th century, could be seen as too "classical" to permit it, while more recent repertoire by major German composers, whose performing traditions were still in living memory, allowed it! In the 1870s, William Cusins observed, in relation to the disjunction between Handel's notation and his expectations for its performance: "At this time we are so accustomed, and rightly, to play everything as it is written, that we are falling into the error of supposing that music of the last century is to be treated in a like manner; but as Mr G. A. Macfarren, in a note to me, aptly puts it, 'the modern system of literal exactitude, at the cost of spiritual fidelity, ignores tradition, and stiff and clumsy are the results.'"[106]

By the end of the century, improvised ornamentation in the vocal music of all the composers mentioned by Sieber would have been almost unthinkable, although, as early recordings demonstrate, it was still a living tradition into the early 20th century. Sir Charles Santly (b. 1834) included ornaments in his recording of "Non più andrai" from Mozart's *Figaro*, and the treatment of some of Rossini's arias by late-19th-century singers, whose performances are preserved on early recordings, indicates that the tradition of individual and often substantial improvised ornamentation and embellishment in that repertoire was far from defunct, even in the generation after Rossini's death. The cavatina "Una voce poco fa" from *Il barbiere di Siviglia* (1816) is typical of the type of early-19th-century display piece that lent itself admirably to the inventive ornamentation cherished by 19th-century singers and audiences alike. In the performance of such long-established repertoire pieces, an element of tradition undoubtedly crept in, so that one might expect to find correspondences between the interpretations of different artists; but the desire for individuality was just as important, if not more so, even to the extent that many 19th-century singers were renowned for their fertility of invention in elaborating the same aria differently on different occasions.[107]

---

[105] Ferdinand Sieber: *Katechismus der Gesangkunst* (Leipzig, 1862), 95f.
[106] William George Cusins: *Handel's Messiah. An Examination of the Original and of Some Contemporary MSS* (London, 1874), 24.
[107] See Austin Caswell: 'Mme Cinti-Damoreau and the Embellishment of Italian Opera in Paris 1820–45', *Journal of the American Musicological Society*, xxviii (1975), 459–92.

Recordings of "Una voce poco fa" by three great sopranos born during the second half of the 19th century reveal consistency in the choice of places that invited elaboration and in some traditionally sanctioned changes, but they also show how other passages were regarded as an opportunity for the singer to introduce the types of ornamentation that displayed the individuality of their voices and technique to the best advantage.[108] Late-20th-century treatment of this repertoire was very different; it was rare to hear more than one or two very minor conventional modifications and departures from Rossini's notated text.

Verdi's comment in a letter to Tito Ricordi in 1871: "I want only one creator and am satisfied if what is written is simply and correctly executed" seems like a clear repudiation of traditional practice; yet despite complaining "the trouble is that this is never done",[109] he remained greatly enthusiastic about the performances of many of the singers with whom he worked, who certainly treated his text freely. Some of these singers can be heard, alongside numerous of their contemporaries, on early recordings, performing Verdi's music with many deviations from his written text.[110] Whether ornamentation of the kind that is preserved on these recordings (which is undoubtedly less elaborate than it would have been in earlier generations) was enjoyed, merely tolerated, or even detested by the composer does not alter the fact that it was a pervasive, if often contentious, aspect of 19th-century musical experience.

## Improvised Ornamentation in 18th- and Early-19th-Century Instrumental Music

Treatises from the middle years of the 18th century show that improvised ornamentation was envisaged in solo instrumental genres. Warnings against its overuse were common. In the 1770s, J. A. P. Schulz advised that all ornaments not indicated by the composer and all changes to entire phrases "can only be added in certain pieces where they really serve to beautify the expression". In

---

[108] Compare, e.g., recordings of the aria by Marcella Sembrich (1858–1935), Luisa Tetrazzini (1871–1940), and Amelita Galli-Curci (1882–1963).

[109] Desmond Shawe-Taylor: 'Verdi and His Singers' in *Overture Opera Guides. Simon Boccanegra* (London, 2011), 31.

[110] Will Crutchfield: 'Vocal Ornamentation in Verdi: The Phonographic Evidence', *19th-century Music*, vii (1983), 3–52.

some compositions that have a "tender, pleasing, lively character or expression",[111] he explained that ornamentation could be essential, but that it required skill, taste, and knowledge of harmony to avoid faulty ornamentation, and that it was vital to know where it was inappropriate. Johann Samuel Petri, in the 1782 edition of his *Anleitung zur praktischen Musik*, explained that ornaments are partly indicated, by signs, partly by small notes, and "partly they are also not prescribed at all".[112] He clarified their function by analogy with painting: "Forte and piano are the landscape painter's foreground, middle and background, ornaments are his colouring and the delicacy of his brush, while the shape of the melody is equivalent to the boldness and relaxation of his expression."[113] His explanation of how to execute thirteen different types of ornament, concludes with the statement:

> Finally, there are all variations of the notes by the addition of improvised appoggiaturas or after-notes, inverted mordents, schneller, turns, etc., which a composer is unwilling to write out completely for each main voice. Every practical musician has his favourite ornaments and does not like to have too much constraint imposed on him. This is alright, only if he knows how to judge the content of a piece of music correctly and is neither too meagre nor too liberal with his ornaments.[114]

Much later in the book, at the end of the section on violin playing, he wrote:

> Since in an Adagio only the main notes of the melody are written down, but the ornaments and transitions from distant notes to other distant notes are not written down, a difficult question arises: how is a naked Adagio to be treated so that it does not offend the ears by its nakedness? Only listening can help. Let a master play an Adagio several times, and notice a few passages where a *groppo*, *tirata*, etc. can be added, and at the same time notice that too much frippery can make the Adagio somewhat too colourful, just as it would sound too bare and dull without decorations.

For further elucidation he recommended "diligent practice of Haydn's, Seifert's, Ditter's, Hofmann's, Filz's and similar trios and quartets".[115]

The final decades of the 18th century and the first decades of the 19th century saw a progressive decrease in improvised ornamentation of instrumental

---

[111] Schulz: in Sulzer *Allgemeine Theorie*, ii, 1257.
[112] Petri: *Anleitung*, 2nd edn, 149.
[113] Petri: *Anleitung*, 150.
[114] Petri: *Anleitung*, 156.
[115] Petri: *Anleitung*, 413f.

IMPROVISED ORNAMENTATION AND EMBELLISHMENT 773

music. Changing tastes and attitudes during the later 18th century are indicated by the final item in the first edition of Michel Woldemar's *Grand Méthode* (Ex. 13.23) containing his *Grand Adagio Moderne* in which the expression is produced by dynamic nuance (*sons filés*) "serving as a sequel to Tartini's variation and Nardini's embroidered Adagios".[116] A growing emphasis on *sons filés* was a particular feature of the influential Paris Conservatoire methods that were produced during the first decade of the 19th century.

**Ex. 13.23** Michel Woldemar: *Grande Méthode*, 1st ed. (Paris [c. 1799]), 63. This item was omitted from the 2nd edn of c. 1800. (Copy online from the Library of Congress.)

[116] Michel Woldemar: *Grande Méthode*, 1st edn (Paris [c. 1798]), 63. Copy in the British Library.

774  CLASSICAL AND ROMANTIC PERFORMING PRACTICE

It is probably the case that Woldemar derived his knowledge of Tartini's and Nardini's ornamentation from J. B. Cartier's *L'art du violon*, published in 1798, which included very similar terminology. Cartier's treatise, based on his own extensive collection of music manuscripts, includes an ornamented version of an Adagio by Nardini (Ex. 13.24a) and an appendix illustrating seventeen possible variants of one by Tartini (Ex. 13.24b).

Ex. 13.24 a–b. Cartier: *L'art du violon*. (*a*) Nardini: Adagio, 202; (*b*) Tartini: Adagio. No page number (following 287).

(*a*)

Ex. 13.24 Continued

(b)

Pierre Baillot's change of attitude between the 1803 *Méthode de violon* and his 1835 *L'art du violon* is instructive. In the former he made conventional warnings against tasteless ornamentation, but no recommendations about the repertoires in which it was appropriate, concluding: "Good taste dictates that the ornaments be used wisely, and especially that we derive them from the melody's true expressive character."[117] In the later treatise, he provided an entirely new text for the section on ornaments. Taking account of developments, especially his own engagement with Viennese classical repertoire, he wrote, though with questionable historical accuracy:

> towards the end of the last century Haydn, Mozart, and later Beethoven, determined their intentions by noting the melodies as they wanted them to be performed, at least as to the notes, leaving, in general, almost nothing in this regard to the arbitrariness of the performer: little by little, this usage

[117] Baillot et al: *Méthode*, 139.

has spread; for some years, composers have finally sought not to omit anything that could make their thoughts more precise.[118]

He instructed that certain types of melodies, which he illustrated with examples from concertos by Viotti, Kreutzer, Rode, and himself, should be played without ornament and shaped by dynamic nuance. He nevertheless stated, in relation to the Adagio from Viotti's Violin Concerto no. 3, that ornamentation was needed "because, if it is natural and necessary, in general, to add some ornamentation to a passage which is repeated twice, there is all the more reason to vary one whose contours are the same six times in a row".[119] Baillot's example of appropriate ornamentation in that movement also included extensive cadenza passages where Viotti marked a *fermata*. In view of Baillot's close relationship with Viotti, his ornamental additions plausibly reflect the composer's expectations, but they differ substantially from another source that is much more directly connected with Viotti's teaching. A notebook kept by the Belgian violinist André Robberechts (b. 1797), one of Baillot's former students, contains accounts of lessons with Viotti himself, which combine verbal instructions with handwritten copies of the music he was studying with him. He dated his first lesson, on Viotti's 3rd Violin Concerto, 20 September 1816. On 24 September he recorded his "Third lesson with the good and Great Viotti" (Troisieme lecon du bon et Grand Viotti). After writing out an alternative manner of performing a passage in the first movement, he notated a heavily ornamented version of the Adagio, bars 12–26, followed by the instruction *ad libitum* just before the first *fermata*, then bars 29–37 and 39. Ex. 13.25 presents Viotti's un-ornamented original, in Massart's edition,[120] Robberecht's manuscript, and Baillot's ornamented version.

---

[118] Baillot: *L'art du violon*, 156f.
[119] Baillot: *L'art du violon*, 158.
[120] In 1850, an edition of all twenty-nine of Viotti's Violin Concertos, edited by Lambert Massart, was published. (see https://mhm.hud.ac.uk/chase/view/edition/1075/). It reproduced only the unadorned notation of the original editions, with minimal corrections and performance markings. The preface remarked: "It is also known that when a passage was performed several times, Viotti varied the bowstrokes and even the notes. Mr. Massart also refrained from making any indications of this nature; this is a matter of taste, which we merely wished to mention." Viotti's Violin Concertos remained compulsory examination pieces at the Paris Conservatoire until 1853, and were also frequently set for examination after that date. There is little doubt that, in preparing their students for examination at that time, the teachers at the Conservatoire would have taught them appropriate ornamentation and embellishment.

**Ex. 13.25** a–c. Viotti: Violin Concerto no. 3. (*a*) Massart's edition; (*b*) Robberechts's notebook ("modern" pagination 192); (*c*) Baillot: *L'art du violon*, 159.

(*a*)

(*b*)

**Ex. 13.25** Continued

(c)

Several editions of Viotti's most celebrated Violin Concerto no. 22 in A minor were published in the later 19th century. Ferdinand David, in 1856, provided elaborate ornamentation for the Adagio on a stave above the plain text, adding a footnote: "Since Viotti used to decorate his Adagios in various ways when they were publicly performed, the editor has elaborated this movement for that purpose."[121] Twenty years later, Charles Dancla made editions of twelve of the concertos, including no. 22, with a preface beginning:

> For a long time, I had in mind the project of making a new edition of Viotti's Sonatas and his best Concertos. Recollection of the lessons and advice of

[121] Ferdinand David: *Concert-Studien für die Violine*, vol. i "Viotti" (Leipzig, [1856]), 38, https://mhm.hud.ac.uk/chase/view/pdf/2030/38/#page.

my illustrious master Baillot, and the valuable indications he gave me on this subject, which he himself had received from Viotti, enabled me to know the tradition of this great master, and provided me with the means of being able, in my turn, to pass it on to students who did not, like me, have the advantage of drawing from this pure source![122]

His editions contain not only extensive alternatives for ornamenting and embellishing the original text, both in fast and slow movements, but also detailed fingering, with many verbal indications of expression, and styles of bowstroke (Ex. 13.26a–b).

Ex. 13.26 a–b. Viotti: (*a*) Concerto 22, ed. Charles Dancla (Paris, 1874); (*b*) Concerto 24, ed. Charles Dancla (Paris, 1876).

[122] Charles Dancla (ed.): *Oeuvres Choisies de Viotti—Concertos* (Paris, 1874–78), Preface, https://mhm.hud.ac.uk/chase/view/work/765.

780  CLASSICAL AND ROMANTIC PERFORMING PRACTICE

Ornamented editions of no. 22 were later issued by Joseph Joachim (1905) and Emil Sauret (1917).

While Ferdinand David's ornamentation of Viotti's Concerto clearly belonged to a well-known tradition, which was still seen as valid into the early 20th century, his employment of ornamentation in "classical" repertoire, such as Beethoven's Violin Concerto, rapidly came to be seen as illegitimate during the 19th century. Evidence of David's practice in Beethoven's Concerto is contained in his personal copy of the first edition (a reprint from the late 1820s), probably reflecting his 1834 performance in Dorpat (now Tartu, Estonia). Ex. 13.27 shows examples of added trills (staves 4–5) and changes of *appoggiaturas* to *Schneller* (stave 5).

Ex. 13.27  Beethoven: Violin Concerto. Ferdinand David's personal copy (British Library, Music Collections Tyson P.M.46.[1.].
[Allegro non troppo]

Although David's additional slurs mostly correspond with those in his 1865 edition of the Concerto, and are representative of the types of slurring and articulation in subsequent editions, well into the 20th century, the added ornaments were not included in his edition. There is evidence that, as late as the 1840s, limited interpolation of standard ornaments, such as short trills and turns into recent repertoire, was not entirely unthinkable—as Chorley's reference to Mendelssohn's *Frühlingslied* suggests—but by the 1860s, when David's edition was published, added ornaments in an edition of Beethoven's music would have been very contentious. It is likely, however, that most musicians of Beethoven's time, and the composer himself, would have had no objection to skilfully added "standard" ornaments in such circumstances, or even occasional small *fioriture*, for instance, in the repetition of the exposition of a sonata-form movement, or a Rondo where the principal theme was repeated unchanged. One instance that indicates Beethoven's awareness of this, is the instruction *semplice* at bar 38 of the Adagio in his Sonata op. 96, on the return of the principal theme in the violin part. If the instruction were intended to elicit a "simple" style of performance, it would be at odds with the expressive intensity of the melody; if, however, it was a warning not to ornament the melody—since improvised ornamentation would have been normal, according to long-standing practise when something is repeated—it would make perfect sense. The rarity of *semplice* in analogous circumstances in Beethoven's works, suggests that he generally expected, or at least tolerated sensitive ornamentation in such situations. That the term *semplice* might be understood at that time as a warning not to ornament is shown by its definition in Burkhard's 1832 musical dictionary, as "simple, without ornamentation".[123]

In 1846, Carl Czerny admonished that "In the performance of his [Beethoven's] works (and, in general, those of all classical authors)[124] the player ought absolutely not to permit himself any change to the composition, any addition, any abbreviation."[125] This, however, was certainly not his opinion during Beethoven's lifetime. An often-mentioned incident, assigned by Czerny himself to "about 1812" in his account of it (published in 1845), but probably referring to a performance in February 1816, was Beethoven's condemnation of his ornamentation of the piano part of his Quintet op. 16. This incident cannot, however, be taken as evidence that Beethoven rejected tasteful improvised ornamentation in appropriate circumstances. Czerny himself admitted that his changes were not modest, recalling: "with youthful

---

[123] Johann Andreas Christian Burkhard: 'Vortrag' in *Neuestes vollständiges musikalisches Wörterbuch* (Ulm, 1832), 372. einfach, ohne Verzierung.
[124] The term "classical" (klassisch) was used here with the general meaning of "serious", as in the modern term "classical music", rather than specifically of composers in the Viennese Classical style, a distinction that was not yet current.
[125] Czerny: *Pianoforte-Schule*, iv, 34.

recklessness I allowed myself many an alteration—elaboration of the passagework, use of the higher octave etc."[126] The very fact that Czerny, after studying with Beethoven since 1801, dared to add *any* ornamentation in his presence, shows beyond reasonable doubt that he was not expecting Beethoven disapproval; he just went much too far on that occasion, thus prompting Beethoven's angry response, and his comment in a letter written the following day: "you must excuse a composer who would rather have heard his work played exactly as it was written".[127]

Many later 19th-century composers made similar remarks, although abundant evidence can be adduced to show that they were perfectly willing to accept appropriate changes by the performer. Ferdinand Ries, writing in the 1830s, stated that Beethoven was not lavish in his addition of ornaments, but that he sometimes improvised them.[128] Comments by Crelle in 1823 show not only that the practice of improvised ornamentation was current, but also the growing opinion that performers ought to subordinate themselves to a serious composer's notation in this respect, even to the extent of eschewing improvised ornamentation entirely:

> The ornaments are always secondary things. They should never extend to substantial changes in melody and harmony. They should not go beyond what the good composer prescribes, and should only be performed in such a way that they do not obscure the melody anywhere. The correct composer writes exactly what he wants. Had he wanted this or that ornament, he would certainly have hinted at it, and it is again presumptuous when every performer believes he can improve the works of great masters.[129]

Czerny's final comment about the 1816 incident was that Beethoven's reaction "cured my addiction to allowing myself to make changes in performing his music, and I wish it would have the same influence on all pianists",[130] which indicates both that Czerny often made extempory embellishments during Beethoven's lifetime, and that the practice was still current in 1840s Vienna, even though opinion was increasingly turning against it. Czerny's Viennese contemporary Ignaz Jeiteles, in 1837, still envisaged either changing old and unfashionable notated ornaments for others, or adding ornaments where none were notated, observing that in the latter case "the artist must possess

---

[126] Alexander Wheelock Thayer: *Ludwig van Beethovens Leben*, 3rd edn (Leipzig, 1917), iii, 548.
[127] Beethoven: *Briefe*, no. 902.
[128] Franz Gerhard Wegeler and Ferdinand Ries: *Biographische Notizen ueber Ludwig van Beethoven* (Coblenz, 1838), 107.
[129] Crelle: *Einiges*, 99f.
[130] Czerny: in 'Beethoviana', *Allgemeine Wiener Musikzeitung*, v (1845), 450.

taste and appropriate proportionality, or be guided by a good master. In addition, ornaments, which like all forms of decoration, are subject to fashion, quickly become outdated, and only novelty and taste can add zest."[131]

Czerny's earlier practice, at least as far as he was prepared to commit it to paper, is documented in two transcriptions of Beethoven's "Kreutzer" Sonata op. 47, which he made and published during Beethoven's lifetime, some years after the incident with op. 16. Ornamented passages, according with the often-stated principle that an exact repetition should be varied, occur in Variation 2 of the Andante (Ex. 13.28a–c); and in the first movement, the violin's accompaniment to the second part of the lyrical theme at bars 107–16 and 428–37—a simple transposition in Beethoven's original—is varied by Czerny on its return (Ex. 13.29a–c).

Ex. 13.28 a–c. Beethoven: Op. 47 Andante con variazioni, Variation 2. (*a*) Variation 2, bb. 19–27, 1st edn violin part; (*b*) Czerny: piano solo transcription; (*c*) Czerny: piano duet transcription (primo).

(*a*)

(*b*)

[131] Ignaz Jeiteles: 'Manier' in *Aesthetisches Lexikon. Ein alphabetisches Handbuch zur Theorie der Philosophie des Schönen und der schönen Künste* (Vienna, 1837), ii, 57.

Ex. 13.28 Continued

(c)

Ex. 13.29 a–b. Czerny: piano duet transcription (primo). (*a*) bb. 107–16; (*b*) bb. 428–37.

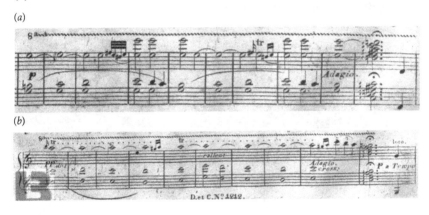

Among other "additions" to Beethoven's text, which Czerny allowed himself in his transcriptions of op. 47, was the elaboration of *fermata* signs in the Andante. Curiously, perhaps, he did not ornament the *fermata* at b. 27 of the first movement, where George Bridgetower is known to have done so (to Beethoven's delight);[132] but both of Czerny's 1820s transcriptions contain a *cadenza* in the Andante: a different one in each (Ex. 13.30).

---

[132] For a full account of this see *Beethoven Violin Sonatas*, ed. by Clive Brown (Kassel, 2020), vol. ii, Introduction, vi–vii = Einführung, xli–xlii.

IMPROVISED ORNAMENTATION AND EMBELLISHMENT   785

**Ex. 13.30a** Beethoven: Violin Sonata op. 47, ed. Clive Brown (Kassel, Bärenreiter, 2020). Andante con variazioni, bb. 192–96.

**Ex. 13.30b** Czerny: solo piano transcription, bb. 190–96.

**Ex. 13.30c** Czerny: piano duet transcription (primo), bb. 190–96.

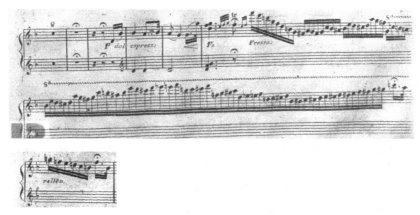

It seems likely therefore that Beethoven expected elaboration of these *fermata* signs, possibly envisaging a *cadenza* for violin as well as piano in this sonata *scritta in uno stile molto concertante, quasi come d'un concerto*. In both transcriptions Czerny omitted Beethoven's arpeggio on the dominant chord of C major, replacing it in the piano solo transcription with an extended version of the arpeggio followed by rapid scales, while in the piano duet transcription he may have imagined a longer violin cadenza, since this is written entirely in the treble register, beginning from the violin's trilled f$^2$. In both transcriptions, Czerny also altered the preceding violin melody, apparently imitating the use of sliding effects by the violinist in the upbeats to bars 194 and 196; and in the duet transcription he added further ornamentation to the violin's melody.

That Carl Czerny's aesthetic changed substantially between the 1820s and the 1840s is demonstrated by his edition (c. 1830) of Müller's widely admired 1804 piano method.[133] Czerny made very many alterations to Müller's text and included much additional material. Having explained his amendments with regard to fingering and other aspects of technique in his preface to the new edition, Czerny continued: "Likewise, in the chapter on ornamentation and performance style, the changed and, I believe, very refined taste of our time had to be taken into account."[134] In that chapter he included many additions and removed many parts of Müller's original, but he made only minor changes to Müller's introductory paragraph on improvised ornaments (*willkührliche Verzierungen*). Significantly, he retained Müller's statements that this "is left more to the feeling and taste of the player. [. . .] only those who understand composition and are trained artists are allowed to add anything that is not prescribed" and "that such ornaments must neither violate the beat, nor the character of the piece, which is why they must sometimes be performed more, sometimes less quickly, sometimes more often, sometimes more sparingly, in order to give the melody more flow and closer connection".[135]

Another passage from Müller's original text, which Czerny retained, reiterates the traditional wisdom that an accomplished performer was expected to modify the repetition of a phrase or melody:

---

[133] August Eberhard Müller's treatise was nominally the sixth edition of Georg Simon Löhlein's 1773 treatise, but was in fact an entirely new treatise, hence its full title: *G. S. Löhleins Klavierschule, oder Anweisung zum Klavier- und Fortepiano-Spiel nebst vielen praktischen Beyspielen und einem Anhang vom Generalbasse. Sechste Auflage, ganz umgearbeitet und sehr vermehrt von A. E. Müller* (Leipzig, 1804).

[134] Czerny (ed.): *Große Fortepiano Schule von Aug. Eberh.$^d$ Müller [. . .] Achte Auflage mit vielen neuen Beispielen und einem vollständigen Anhange vom Generalbass versehen von Carl Czerny* (Leipzig [c. 1830]), iv.

[135] Müller: *Anweisung zum Klavier- und Fortepiano-Spiel*, 6, §27, 45f.; with insignificant, cosmetic changes in Czerny (ed.): *Große Fortepiano Schule von Aug. Eberh.$^d$ Müller*, iii, 8, §27, 228.

For this purpose, it will be very beneficial if the teacher plays to the student the pieces, which—for the sake of mechanically correct playing—he has already learned; not only with regard to its character as a whole, but also to draw his attention to details, which the teacher will be able to play so much more beautifully.—Thus, at the right time, he can show him, for example, how to decorate one and the same melodic passage, especially when it is frequently repeated, with free ornamentation or to alter it in various ways, partly to avoid monotony and partly, in this manner, to make the passage pleasanter and more distinctive for the listener.[136]

Despite growing discomfort with improvised ornamentation in German instrumental music, it was still not unthinkable in the 1840s. Carl Maria von Weber's friend Anton Bernhard Fürstenau, in *Die Kunst des Flötenspiels* (1844), recommended: "the appropriate application of the various ornaments for accenting and connecting the notes, as well as of ornamentation, which can also be of great use in a melodic passage, if it recurs frequently—partly to prevent potential monotony, partly to make the same passage more pleasant and impressive for the listener".[137] Like Müller and Czerny, he stressed that these must be well executed and avoid any offence against the rules of harmony.

That improvised ornamentation was indeed still a living tradition in the 1840s is demonstrated by Berlioz's experience during his visit to Dresden in 1843, where he conducted his *Symphonie fantastique* with the court orchestra.

> The first oboe has a fine tone, but an old-fashioned style, and an irritating mania for trills and mordents. He gave himself terrible liberties, more especially in the solo at the beginning of the *Scène aux champs*. At the second rehearsal I expressed my detestation of these melodic tricks pretty sharply, and he abstained from them at subsequent rehearsals. But this was only a deception, and on the day of the concert, the perfidious oboe, knowing that I could not stop the orchestra and remonstrate with him in public and before the Court, recommenced his little villainies, giving me at the same time a cunning look that almost laid me flat with indignation and fury.[138]

---

[136] Czerny (ed.): *Große Fortepiano Schule von Aug. Eberh.ᵈ Müller*, 234.
[137] Fürstenau: *Die Kunst*, 89.
[138] Hector Berlioz: *Mémoires* (Paris, Calmann Lévy, 1897), 71.

By the 1850s, however, such practices were becoming almost unthinkable in most instrumental contexts. Charles de Bériot, in his 1858/9 *Méthode de Violon*, discussing *fioriture*, remarked:

> The melody which is best adapted to the type of ornaments we are discussing here is that which aims to please by its amiable, flowery, and graceful style, and of which the accompaniment is light and simple in harmony. But all melody that contains a very pronounced sentiment, whether profound, solemn, or serious, and of which the accompaniment produces complicated harmony, excludes, in part, all kinds of ornament.
>
> Hence it comes about that German music, more bound by harmony than Italian music, lends itself less to ornamentation. In proportion as this harmonic complexity has won over all the modern schools, ornamentation has become rarer, while the old melody, more simply accompanied, lends itself more advantageously to it.
>
> These changes are due more to progress than to fashion. It is for the performer to accept these diversities of expression, and to adapt his playing with discrimination, only ornamenting music of which the character is suitable: that is a matter of taste.[139]

## The *Fermata*

One of the areas in which improvised ornamentation retained its validity throughout the period, although with increasing limitations, especially in instrumental music, was the *fermata* (*corona*, pause) that signified a *cadenza*. This was not, however, the only function of the conventional sign: it could indicate several different things in the music of this period. These different functions were not generally distinguished by any graphic difference in the sign, though some composers adopted the practice of writing an elongated *fermata* over a passage of several notes where these were either to be ornamented or performed *ad libitum* (see below). The various ways in which the sign might be used can be illustrated by a few theoretical discussions and practical examples.

---

[139] Bériot: *Méthode*, 189.

C. P. E. Bach wrote:

> At times one makes a fermata for expressive reasons, without anything being indicated. Apart from this, there are three circumstances in which these fermatas occur. One pauses either over the penultimate note, or over the last bass note, or over a rest after this bass note. To be correct this sign should always be indicated at the point at which one begins to make the fermata and, at best, once again at the end of the fermata.
>
> Fermatas over rests occur mostly in Allegro, and are performed quite simply. The other two kinds are commonly found in slow and expressive pieces, and must be ornamented, or one would be guilty of naivety. In any case, therefore, elaborate ornamentation can rather be left out in other parts of a piece than here.[140]

Türk, in his usual painstaking manner, discussed the contemporary usage of the sign, as it was known to him, in exhaustive detail. He observed that it could indicate "a pause with or without arbitrary ornamentation", or an elongated rest. The length of time for which a *fermata* should be held would be conditioned by "whether one is performing alone or with others; whether the piece has a lively or sad character; whether the *fermata* is to be ornamented (i.e., beautified with improvised additions) or not, etc." Other things being equal, Türk recommended that in slow music it should be approximately twice its written length, but in fast tempo this would be too short; thus, if it were a quarter-note he recommended making it four times its length, though with longer values he felt that twice the length should be enough. If the *fermata* were over a short rest in fast tempo, a pause of three or four quarter-notes length would probably suffice, and if it were in slow tempo, twice the given length. He suggested that the rest after a *fermata*, whether it too had a *fermata* sign or not, would be lengthened. Commenting on the use of the sign to indicate a final *cadenza*, Türk observed that "if one does not wish to make a *cadenza*, one holds the note a little and finishes with a trill approximately as long again as the written value requires".[141] Where the sign was merely used to indicate the end of a piece or section, Türk called it an end-sign and warned, particularly in songs with several verses or *da capo* pieces, against making an inappropriate pause (Ex. 13.31).

---

[140] Bach: *Versuch*, i, 112.
[141] Türk: *Klavierschule*, 121.

Ex. 13.31 Türk: *Klavierschule*, 121.

He pointed out that many such signs could be misleading and recommended that the only sure way for a composer to distinguish between an end-sign and a *fermata* was to use the notation shown in Ex. 13.32, 1) and 2), but not that in 3), since then "a novice [. . .] might play on after a short delay, as now and then happens"; he instructed that: "In such cases one plays the note that follows the end-sign each time without delaying the beat, and only in the last verse does the end-sign apply."[142]

Ex. 13.32 Türk: *Klavierschule*, 121.

Türk later discussed the ornamentation of a *fermata*, giving examples.[143] For those "that come here and there, particularly in expressive pieces, where a suitable ornament can be of good effect", he proposed the following rules:

1. "Each ornamentation must be appropriate to the character of the piece." (He warned against lively passages in a sad adagio.)
2. "The ornamentation ought, strictly speaking, only to be based on the given harmony." (He conceded that "in general one is not so exact about following this second rule. But one takes care to avoid actual modulations into other keys".)
3. "The ornamentation ought not to be long; one is, however, unrestricted in respect to the beat."[144]

His examples offer varied treatment for given musical situations, of which Ex. 13.33 provides a representative selection.

---

[142] Türk: *Klavierschule*, 123.
[143] Türk: *Klavierschule*, 299–304.
[144] Türk: *Klavierschule*, 301.

Ex. 13.33 Türk: *Klavierschule*, 301f.

Koch, too, regarded the ornamentation of a *fermata* as optional, writing: "In the performance of a solo part one has the freedom to decorate the sustained note of fermatas with improvised ornaments, or to make a transition from the fermata to the following phrase."[145] And J. F. Schubert admitted a

---

[145] Koch: 'Fermate' in *Musikalisches Lexikon*, 566.

*portamento* alone as a substitute for the usual type of ornamentation in certain cases (see Ex. 15.15).

Domenico Corri, in his *Select Collection*, offered his reader indicative alternatives at points in the music where he considered ornamentation necessary. The examples in his publications provide many interesting and useful models. All of them conform to the often-stated rule that ornamented *fermate* in arias should not exceed what is possible in a single breath. A couple of typical examples appear in Ex. 13.3 above. Very occasionally he seems to have felt that the context called for something more elaborate, as in the case of arias by Giordani and Sacchini (Ex. 13.34).

Ex. 13.34 a–b. D. Corri: *A Select Collection.*(*a*) i. 4: Hasse: *Artaserse*, adapted by Giordani; (*b*) i. 74: Sacchini: *Creso*.

IMPROVISED ORNAMENTATION AND EMBELLISHMENT 793

The Paris Conservatoire's *Principes élémentaires de musique* gave a particularly succinct account of how to recognize whether a *fermata* should be elongated or ornamented or, in some cases, whether it implied neither type of treatment:

> When this fermata is placed on a note, as in the following examples [Ex. 13.35a] it indicates that one should stop on this note and that one may pause there for as long as desired, but without introducing any embellishment or ornament. In this case the fermata is called a pause [*Point de Repos*]. One also calls it a pause when one employs the following style [Ex. 13.35b]. In this case one may add some ornamentation to the note on which the pause is placed. The fermata used in the following example is called a stopping or suspending point [POINT D'ARRET, ou de SUSPENSION. Ex. 13.35c]. In this circumstance one should certainly not prolong the note on which the fermata occurs, rather one should quit it crisply as soon as it is attacked.[146]

Ex. 13.35 a–c. Gossec et al.: *Principes*, i, 45.

How widely this convention of the *point d'arrêt, ou de suspension* was recognized by composers of the period is unclear, but it is certainly true to say that most modern performers in these circumstances would sustain

---

[146] Gossec et al.: *Principes*, i, 45.

the final note with the *fermata* rather than quitting it crisply. The *Principes* concluded by identifying the circumstances, recognizable by the harmonic context and the final trill, in which a *fermata* was used to indicate a full cadenza.

These instructions, which are almost certainly a good guide for early-19th-century French practice, may also be relevant to late-18th-century German usage. Haydn, in op. 64 no. 2, uses what to all intents looks like a *point d'arrêt*, except that he includes the instruction *tenuto*, perhaps to counter the player's natural instinct to quit the note too quickly (Ex. 13.36). On the other hand, the addition of *tenuto* might have been meant to warn the players not to make any ornamentation, or perhaps to make some form of trembling effect.[147]

Ex. 13.36 Haydn: String Quartet op. 64/2/iv.

In op. 77 no. 1 there are two *fermata* signs that may also be of this kind (Ex. 13.37). In the *Adagio*, significant elongation seems unlikely; it would be more plausible in the *Presto* Menuetto, possibly implying a short break at the end of the bar; but Haydn's intention is unclear.

---

[147] See Ch. 16 (Swoboda: *Allgemeine Theorie*).

IMPROVISED ORNAMENTATION AND EMBELLISHMENT 795

Ex. 13.37 a–b. Haydn: String Quartet op. 77/1. (*a*) ii; (*b*) iii.

A *fermata* sign may sometimes have been used simply for *tenuto*, with no implication of holding the note longer or affecting the tempo. An unusual employment of signs that resemble a *fermata*, though with a stroke rather than a dot under the curved line, occurs in the finale of Mozart's E flat String Quartet K. 428, where they are first given together with *ten*. (Ex. 13.38). Their unusual form suggests that his intention may have been to achieve an accented performance by means of a *staccato* stroke, but also to prevent the notes from being shortened.[148]

Ex. 13.38 Mozart: String Quartet K. 428, Allegro vivace.

In late-18th- and early-19th-century music, when a *fermata* sign was written in a lengthened form to indicate that a group of notes in a vocal part should be sung without constraint of tempo (perhaps *ritardando*), it may often have encouraged ornamentation. In such cases it would frequently appear in the same form in the accompanying parts, to alert the instrumentalists to follow the singer (Ex. 13.39a–b).

Ex. 13.39a Salieri: *Der Rauchfangkehrer*, Act III, no. 15.

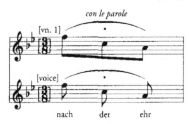

---

[148] See also Ch. 3, "The *Staccato* Mark".

**Ex. 13.39b** Vogler: *Der Kaufmann von Smyrna*, no. 2, Hessische Landes- und Hochschulbibliothek, Darmstadt, mus. ms. 1090.

Perhaps Anton André's symbols for *ritardando* and *accelerando* were connected with this usage.[149] Mozart's employment of this type of *fermata* has been extensively discussed by, among others, Frederick Neumann, who gives a useful account of its probable treatment, vitiated only by the persistent representation, in his realizations, of pairs of notes on the same pitch without any appoggiatura or related ornamentation.[150]

A good example of *fermata* ornamentation supplied by the composer occurs in the autograph of Weber's *Der Freischütz*, in the insertion aria no. 13, where Weber wrote out a *fioritura*, apparently as an afterthought (Ex. 13.40).

**Ex. 13.40** Weber: *Der Freischütz*, no. 13, autograph.

---

[149] See Ch. 11, p. 598.
[150] Neumann: *Ornamentation and Improvisation*, 218ff.

A little later in the 19th century, Pierre Baillot gave the following categorization of these signs, apparently based on the *Principes élémentaires de musique*:

1. a *point de repos* "On which one adds nothing";
2. a *point de repos* (*point d'orgue*) "After which one may make a little figuration between the *point d'orgue* or *point de repos* and the note that follows"
3. a *point d'arrêt* or silence "after which [sic] it is necessary to quit the note".

Diverging from the *Principes*, however, he further observed:

> One cannot recommend too much to remain on these *points d'arrêt* or *silences* all the time that is necessary for their effect. In order that the *silence* contrasts with the motion that precedes it, a certain length is required for it to be felt; reason will have it so, but sentiment does more; for it knows at the appropriate moment how to make eloquence felt: "the genius of the musician subjects the entire universe to his art, it paints all pictures in sound and makes silence itself speak." (J. J. Rousseau)[151]

Baillot initially illustrated what he meant by his second type of *fermata* with an example from Haydn's String Quartet op. 9 no. 2 (Ex. 13.41a) where he added suitably restrained ornamentation, presumably bearing in mind the much more florid elaboration provided by the composer on the final repetition of the melody (Ex. 13.41b).

**Ex. 13.41a** Baillot: *L'art du violon*, 165.

---

[151] Baillot: *L'art du violon*, 165.

Ex. 13.41b  Haydn: String Quartet op. 9/2/iii.

His catalogue of *points d'orgue*, for which he provided sixteen pages of music examples, was organized under ten headings, though only the first two ("Suspensions or turns on the tonic"[152] and "Slightly extended *points d'orgue* or turns on the dominant to approach the final cadence"[153]) dealt with short, ornamented *points d'orgue*; the rest were more developed *candenze*.

A. F. Häser, a slightly younger German contemporary of Baillot, cautioned that although the decoration of *fermata* signs in solo playing or singing was frequent, they should not be ornamented if they were there to express such emotions as "astonishment, or expectation, or exhaustion".[154] In singing he considered that the text should be the main guide, and that if the vowel were inappropriate for vocalizing, this might determine whether or not to include ornamentation. Haydn Corri, however, gave instructions for modifying the vowel in such instances.[155] García, too, referring both to the ornamentation of *fermata* signs and to virtuoso figuration in general, observed that "the master and singer are at liberty to add,—if the sense allows it,—one or other of the monosyllables, *ah!*, *no*, *si*, either to increase the number of syllables or to substitute for others".[156] Häser also gave five different ways of nuancing an unornamented *fermata* (Ex. 13.42). He commented that those marked 1 and 2 were rare, that 3 was the most usual, and that 4 was also not uncommon, while 5 was at least as rare as 1 and 2. His final observation reveals the growing expectation that the composer's intentions should be made more explicit and respected more punctiliously, for he felt that although performers must rely upon their taste in deciding how to execute a *fermata* for which the composer had not specified the manner of performance, it was necessary, in order to banish uncertainty, to mark anything except 3.[157]

---

[152] Baillot: *L'art du violon*, 167.
[153] Baillot: *L'art du violon*, 169.
[154] A. F. Häser: 'Fermate' in Schilling (ed.), *Encyclopädie*, ii, 679.
[155] Haydn Corri: *The Delivery of Vocal Music Simplified* (Dublin, 1826).
[156] García: *École*, ii, 14.
[157] Häser: 'Fermate' in Schilling (ed.), *Encyclopädie*, ii, 677–79.

Ex. 13.42 Häser's dynamic treatment of *fermata* signs.

1. $\bar{\bar{o}}$  2. $\overset{<}{o}$  3. $\overset{>}{o}$  4. $\overset{<>}{o}$  5. $\overset{><}{o}$

## Improvised Embellishment: Correct and Beautiful Performance

In mid- to late-19th-century practice, although major elaboration, which substantially changed the shape of the melodic line, was increasingly confined to specific genres of music and to individual circumstances, there was still an expectation that skilled performers would modify the written text in a multitude of less obtrusive ways, which, even though they involved deviations from the strict meaning of the notation, were regarded as necessary adjuncts of an artistic performance, rather than unwarranted violations of the composer's intentions. Domenico Corri's opinion that a piece of music performed exactly as it is written would be a poor if not a "very uncouth performance" was widely shared by solo singers and instrumentalists for more than a century afterwards. The fact that composers expected much "reading between the lines" in performance is beyond dispute, but understanding what this involved, and how it was expected to be applied at different periods, can only be explained verbally in the most general terms. Yet, if we want to free ourselves from the 20th-century fallacy that respect for the composer's intentions in performance requires a very close adherence to the notated text, it is certainly necessary to understand, as far as possible, what kind of liberty was envisaged, why it was regarded as necessary, and in what circumstances it was expected to be employed.

Treatises dealt primarily with technical issues, and although they sometimes allow more general conclusions about the broader relationship between notation and performance to be drawn from them, their musical examples, given in conventional notation, perpetuate the impression of a more intimate connection between the notated text and its realization in sound than was surely the case. Few writers attempted to deal in depth with disparities between the written score and an artistic performance. Most merely allude to it in a generalized way. Rousseau, in his 1768 *Dictionnaire*, for instance, made the briefest reference to these issues in the article "Execution", referring specifically only to tempo flexibility:

the spirit depends more on taste than notation, nothing is as rare as good execution. Reading the notes exactly is no great merit, the performer must enter into all the ideas of the composer, and feel—and make the hearer feel—the fire or pathos of the expression. [. . .] In French music the leader must be particularly careful to press and relax the time according to the taste of the melody, the power of voice, and the gesticulation of the singer; the other parts must consequently be extremely careful in following him.[158]

Around the same time, J. A. P. Schulz considered more fully how artistic performers were expected to modify and embellish a written text, without necessarily introducing additional ornamental notes. In his article on performance (*Vortrag*), he employed the term "good performance" (*guter Vortrag*) to describe one that was both accurate and expressive. He observed that "it is expression alone that distinguishes the master from his pupil in performing the same piece, the great virtuoso from the mediocre", adding: "It is easy to understand that this is not just about reading the notes correctly. The signs that indicate the expression of a piece are very few and indefinite." Like later musicians who tackled these issues he observed that

It would be a foolish undertaking to specify in which way the performance must differ, in order to depict every character and especially every expression exactly, since the young artist of feeling can, in a few minutes, get a clearer idea of this through listening to well-performed pieces than through any verbal description, even of exhaustive length.[159]

He nevertheless identified three elements that were essential to expressive performance: correct tempo, the appropriate heavy or light performance style for the character and expression of the piece,[160] and suitable dynamic variation. He discussed each in turn; but recognizing the inadequacy of words, he concluded:

Nothing more definite can be said about this: whoever wishes to develop this aspect of expression must listen, feel, and learn. [. . .] This and everything

---

[158] Jean-Jacques Rousseau: *Dictionnaire de Musique* (Paris, 1768), 209. This was also included in vol. i of the *Encyclopédie méthodique musique* (Paris, 1791), 526, and Charles Burney's article 'Execution in *Musical Performance*' in Rees: *Cyclopedia*, xiii (London, 1806), unpaginated.

[159] Schulz: 'Vortrag' in *Allgemeine Theorie*, ii, 1252f.

[160] For discussion of "heavy and light performance" see Ch. 5.

else, by means of which the artist gives expression to his performance, if he possesses the other skills, is subject to a single rule: he must immerse himself in the feeling [Affect] of the piece. Only then, when he has well understood the character of the piece, and feels his whole soul permeated by its expression, will he achieve his aim, by using these means, and a thousand other subtleties that are impossible to describe, which often elevated the expression beyond the composer's expectations; they will come to him by themselves while playing or singing. The notes will mean the same to him as the words do to an inspired speaker; not so much as signs for what he should play, but as combinations of notes that evoke an expressive image for him, which he wants to make as perceptible to his listeners as to himself. He will slur some notes, detach others; make some tremble, keep others steady; now lowering the tone, now increasing it. He will feel where he is to hold a note beyond its length and hurry others after it; he will accelerate or hold back wherever it strengthens the expressiveness: his instrument or throat will produce louder, moving plaintive sounds and progressions in a sad adagio, and proclaim joy in every note of a cheerful allegro. Which sensitive listener will not be irresistibly carried away by that kind of performance of an expressive piece?[161]

His catalogue of the practices necessary for artistic performance concludes with "Beauty" [Schönheit]. He explained that this "aims to add refinements, independent of clarity and expression, which give the performance as a whole greater charm; or by the introduction of ornaments into the melody, which are appropriate to the character and expression of the piece".[162] Among these beauties he also included beautiful tone, spontaneity and facility, decorous posture, and minimal bodily movement.

Towards the end of the 18th century, some German authors developed the terminology "*richtige Vortrag*" (correct performance) and "*schöne Vortrag*" (beautiful, or fine performance) to explain the distinction between a conscientiously accurate reproduction of the notation and one in which the performer modified and elaborated it, to convey its expressive and emotional content to the listener. Most of those who employed this, or

---

[161] Schulz: 'Vortrag' in *Allgemeine Theorie*, ii, 1255.
[162] Schulz: 'Vortrag' in *Allgemeine Theorie*, ii, 1256. For "ornaments" he uses the word *Verzierungen*, which could apply both to ornamentation with added notes or to the trembling and sliding effects designated in this chapter as embellishments.

similar, terminology were themselves composers, who evidently expected the notation of their own works to be understood in this way. A. E. Müller (b. 1767) used "correct" and "beautiful" to distinguish more succinctly between the mechanical and aesthetic aspects of musical performance, explaining:

> The character that has been put into the piece of music by the composer, must naturally be put into it by he who performs it. He must therefore
> 
> (a) be able to play the piece accurately, in respect of its literal meaning, or in respect of that which can be exactly conveyed by notes and signs: then his performance will be (mechanically) correct. He must also however
> (b) grasp the character of the piece correctly and precisely, put himself into the feeling of the piece, and modify his playing accordingly; he must, for instance, distinguish throughout all his playing between a merry Allegro that is virile and one that is humorous, even if both are written in exactly the same tempo, with the same time signature etc.—in the type and degree of *forte* and *piano*, in the touch and consequently the tone, which he draws from the instrument, in his way of handling passagework, full chords etc.: only then will his performance be (aesthetically) beautiful.[163]

With his reference to the treatment of chords as an aspect of beautiful performance, Müller probably alluded to expressive arpeggiation.[164]

First, he detailed the abilities required for "mechanically correct" performance: a good musical ear and the greatest possible technical proficiency, the correct execution of notated ornaments, and meticulous observation of notated slurs and articulation. He advised, however, that the student should be given "only such pieces in which all these things are more fully marked than in many of the most recent compositions" and instructed that at this stage the teacher should "allow him no improvised ornamentation".[165] Beautiful, expressive performance required additionally "a sensitive and correct feeling, supported and firmly founded in healthy aesthetic judgment—or taste" and "a not insignificant knowledge of the rules of harmony, or of thoroughbass." With regard to the former, he explained: "It may be charitable

---

[163] Müller: *Amweisung zum Klavier und Fortepiano Spiel*, 9, §2, 295.
[164] See Ch. 14, "Arpeggiation".
[165] Müller: *Anweisung*, 296, §4.

to presuppose that everyone has such feeling and taste, but experience shows that this is far from being so" and asserted: "whoever does not possess them can, with all diligence and all skill, get no further than mechanically correct performance—they can become a useful orchestral player, a useful chorister, which is valuable, but it is not art." On the other hand, while "feeling and taste cannot be given, they may well be awakened and cultivated where nature has laid the foundations," so that, with the right training, the player will be able "always to find the character of the piece of music by himself and without long reflection or even calculation [. . .] and will then be able unfailingly to play the piece with true, expressive, beautiful performance."

At this point, as with so many treatises, Müller stopped short of trying to describe in detail the ways in which a beautiful performance might differ from a merely correct one, simply recommending that the teacher should let the pupil "frequently, where possible, always hear good music, also well performed", but, like Schulz, he mentioned some types of deviation from the literal meaning of the notation that would be appropriate. Having explained how teachers might show their students where improvised ornamentation should be employed, he suggested that they might demonstrate:

> furthermore, how one lingers longer on some notes, such as on the main notes of a phrase, indeed also on a sequence of several notes—rather like one can deliver a sentence in declamation—slower for greater effect, or also, according to the content, faster but more marked, than the tempo that is taken for the whole piece. He also makes him aware of the difference in the performance of a piece of music set at a slow or rapid tempo—how and why, in the former, the notes must be more connected, and how they must be performed heavily rather than detached; how and why dissonances should as a rule be emphasized more than consonances etc.[166]

In conclusion, he reiterated his insistence that knowledge of harmony was essential, remarking: "Beautiful performance allows the player a great deal of freedom with the work that he is performing, even inducing him to make major or minor changes to it: this is not possible without precise knowledge and skill in the secure application of at least the principal rules of harmony or figured bass. One must know the rule exactly everywhere, and be able

---

[166] Müller: *Anweisung*, 297, §5.

to obey it, before one can dare to rise above it."[167] All these passages from Müller's text were retained, a quarter of a century later, in Carl Czerny's substantially revised edition.

Johann Nepomuk Hummel's 1828 piano method also employed the terminology "correct" and "beautiful" performance. He explained that the former "concerns the mechanism of playing, as far as it can be indicated by musical notation"; the latter he described vaguely and ambiguously as concerning "what is rounded off, what is appropriate to each piece of music, to each part of it, to what is tasteful and pleasant, especially in the ornaments, which can only be hinted at".[168] He, too, asserted that beautiful performance could not be adequately described in words: it required an innate gift that could only be developed effectively by hearing excellent performers. His characterization of the deficiencies of those who were not gifted with inherent musical feeling and taste, however, is instructive:

> In recent times, some have tried to compensate for what they intrinsically lacked in beautiful performance and expression with various external things, to conceal this deficiency in their playing by a parody of these qualities—among these are, especially in piano playing: twisting the body, raising the arms, deliberate changes in facial expressions; a ringing in the ears produced by the constant use of the pedals; deliberate distortion of tempo, often ad nauseam, (*tempo rubato*); garnishing melodic passages with a superfluity of notes, so that eventually the melody and the character are changed beyond recognition.[169]

Later, he briefly enumerated some of the un-notated features that belonged to a truly beautiful performance style. These included subtlety of touch and dynamics; awareness of the differences in style required by the character and emotional content of the music, and the distinct requirements of Allegro and Adagio, which involved an appropriate degree of tempo flexibility; the proper execution of ornaments and the appropriate addition of improvised ornamentation in Adagio, noting that "it must be used without exaggeration and in the right places".[170] Finally, he observed (like many other authors at this period) that unless the composer marks it otherwise, ascending passages

---

[167] Müller: *Anweisung*, 300.
[168] Hummel: *Anweisung*, 2nd edn, 426, §1.
[169] Hummel: *Anweisung*, 2nd edn, 426, §3.
[170] Hummel: *Anweisung*, 2nd edn, 428.

will normally be *crescendo* and descending ones *decrescendo*. In extracts from his own Concerto op. 85 he provided examples of tempo modification and discussed expressive accentuation and pedalling.[171] Apart from his observation that on the Viennese pianos "full chords are mostly performed in very rapid arpeggio",[172] he wrote nothing about *expressive* arpeggiation or asynchrony, although these were certainly regarded as an aspect of beautiful performance in piano playing throughout the 19th century.[173]

For violinists, Spohr too believed that beautiful performance—if the player had a natural aptitude for it—was best acquired by frequently hearing "good music and excellent singers and virtuosos",[174] but he gave a rather more extended catalogue than Hummel of the acquirements needed for "correct" and "beautiful" performance on string instruments:

> Correct performance requires: 1) pure intonation, 2) precise division of the notes according to their length, 3) keeping strict time without hurrying or holding back 4) strictly observing all the notated nuances of strong and weak, and also 5) correct execution of the various styles of bowstroke, slurs, turns, trills etc.
>
> Beautiful performance requires, in addition to the foregoing technical skills: 1) finer shadings of bowing, in respect of tone from strong, even rough, to soft and fluty, and the appropriate accentuation and articulation of musical phrases, 2) the higher positions, which are used not for the sake of convenience or ease of playing, but for expression and tone, which includes sliding from one note to another, as well as changing fingers on a single note, 3) the *Bebung* [trembling] in its four categories; 4) the hurrying of tempo in fiery and strongly passionate passages, as well as holding back in those of a tender or melancholy-mournful character.[175]

Spohr's comments about tone and phrasing might just as well apply to good practice at any period, but his requirements for sliding effects, selective and ornamental trembling effects, and tempo modification reveal substantial differences from more recent mainstream practice. In every respect, though, his expectations were undoubtedly different from conventional

---

[171] See Ch. 11, pp. 593–94.
[172] Hummel: *Anweisung*, 2nd edn, 454.
[173] See Ch.14; also Neal Peres Da Costa: *Off the Record*.
[174] Spohr: *Violinschule*, 196.
[175] Spohr: *Violinschule*, 195f.

early-21st-century understanding of the messages 18th- and 19th-century composers expected their notation to convey to the performer. That those expectations remained substantially the same for the rest of the 19th century, despite evolving technical practices and tastes, is strongly suggested by the fact that his instructions for the employment of *portamento* and *vibrato* were quoted at length in the 1905 Joachim and Moser *Violinschule*.

Anton Bernhard Fürstenau, writing for flautists, made a further terminological distinction, observing:

> Playing can generally be called correct if it reproduces faithfully what is prescribed by the composer through notes, symbols, and verbal instructions. This includes correctly fingering and producing the right notes; accurate time-keeping in general, such as correctly placing the constituents of the individual bars, precise observation of the time value of the individual notes and rests.

In addition, he explained:

> For correct playing in a higher sense—artistically correct playing—the following are also necessary (things that might often be thought of as different from an accurate realization of the composer's instructions, but without which, perhaps, the performance cannot claim to be called "good"): that all rough, uneven, indistinctness, furthermore such small imperfections of intonation, which are occasionally still possible, even with the most correct fingering, and can only be remedied by means of special techniques, are avoided, that all notes respond equally well, that more difficult passages in the music do not sound less fluent than easier passages, that breath is not taken at the wrong time, in short, that everything has been eliminated that makes an unpleasant or at least uncomfortable impression on the educated ear.[176]

In orchestral playing, he added, "where the entire effect intended by the composer can only be based on the exact ensemble of the individual parts, each correct in itself, absolutely nothing else remains to be desired in performance". Crucially, however, he continued: "Disregarding those special

---

[176] Fürstenau: *Die Kunst*, 88.

circumstances, however, and focusing primarily on solo playing, this is by far not enough, but only forms the basis for the higher, true art of performance."[177] His next section begins with the statement: "This higher art consists in giving the playing charm, character, and expression, and thereby elevating the correct performance to a beautiful one."[178] Apart from finer subtleties of tone production, dynamic nuance, accentuation, and phrasing, which would be typical of artistic performance at any period, he specified the modification of note lengths, hurrying and relaxing the tempo of individual phrases, variety of articulation and slurring, the introduction of appropriate ornamentation, under which he doubtless included two different techniques for producing trembling effects, and the means of achieving audible slides, which he had discussed earlier in the treatise.[179]

A grey area exists between what Fürstenau identified as "correct performance in a higher sense" and "beautiful performance". The properly trained student was certainly required to know about aspects of notation that were conventionally understood to require something different from their literal meaning, and to conform to those conventions. In the 18th and early 19th centuries, these would have included such things as recognizing the contexts in which the first of a pair of notes on the same pitch should be replaced by an *appoggiatura* a tone higher, where dotted rhythms required over- or under-dotting, and awareness of such general conventions as *crescendo* on rising figurations and *decrescendo* on falling ones, or the nuanced performance of slurs. In singing, the techniques of *portamento*, in its sense of *legato* as well as the audible connection of notes, will have been taught; and in string playing the latter will have been practised as an essential element of expressive position changing. Young keyboard players will certainly not have been instructed to play all chords firmly together, since in many contexts arpeggiation and asynchrony were normal; if anything, they might have been taught to play the notes of a chord simultaneously as a special technique. Similar aesthetics were expounded in articles for the *Encyclopädie* edited by Gustav Schilling,[180] which, together with earlier treatises, provided the basis for his 1843 book on performance.[181] Although these distinctions were not so systematically developed in other languages, the ideas that lay behind them

---

[177] Fürstenau: *Die Kunst*, 89, §147.
[178] Fürstenau, *Die Kunst*, 89, §148.
[179] See Chs. 14 and 15.
[180] Schilling (ed.): *Encyclopädie*, 6 vols and 2 supplements (1835–1842).
[181] Gustav Schilling: *Musikalische Dynamik oder die Lehre vom Vortrage in der Musik* (Cassel, 1843).

were clearly international. In French, for instance, Pierre-Joseph-Guillaume Zimmermann stated succinctly: "It is the soul, the sensitivity, the distinction, the nobility of style, which reveal the great pianist. Merely playing correctly is like talking well to say nothing."[182]

Distinctions between the mechanical and the spiritual, or aesthetic aspects of performance remained a live issue in books and articles on musical performance during the later 19th century.[183] In the early 1860s, Adolph Kullak argued that

> In the whole teaching of performance, conceptual intuition is important; it is no longer sufficient to stipulate that the player should heed the composer's terms and perform them accordingly. He should help create and feel with the latter, and although he is not equal to him in terms of productive imagination, he should show himself to be equal to him in terms of aesthetic judgement.[184]

At about the same time, Arrey von Dommer recognized that the aesthetics of performance differed according to "the period in which a work was created" and "the individuality of the particular composer"; but his conception was strongly conditioned by mid-19th-century notions of the performer's subsidiary status. He asserted that the executant's "activity is not independent production but reproduction [. . .]. He must view his task objectively: relate to the work, not the work to himself." He nevertheless believed that "Although only reproducing the musical work, he is also its co-creator" and concluded: "From all this it follows that it is not enough for the performer to execute his dynamic shadings and degrees of strength, types of bowstroke, and any other attributes of expressive performance, precisely according to the composer's instructions; he can do all this quite correctly as prescribed, and yet appear sober, dry, and cold." Furthermore, he argued that although correct technique was a primary consideration, "the cultured listener will

---

[182] Pierre-Joseph-Guillaume Zimmermann: *Encyclopédie du pianist compositeur* (Paris, 1840), ii, 58.

[183] Hugo Riemann, in his *Lexikon* (article: 'Ausdruck') lists the following, which he considered the best in recent times: Adolph Kullak, *Aesthetik des Klavierspiels* (Berlin, 1861), Mathis Lussy, *Traité de l'expression musicale* (Paris, 1873), Otto Klauwell, *Der Vortrag in der Musik* (Berlin and Leipzig, 1883), Hugo Riemann, *Musikalische Dynamik und Agogic* (Hamburg, 1884), Adolph J. Christiani, *Das Verständnis im Klavierspiel* (Leipzig, 1886), Karl Fuchs, *Die Zukunft des musikalischen Vortrags* (Danzig, 1884), Karl Fuchs, *Die Freiheit des musikalischen Vortrags* (Leipzig, 1885), Franz Kullak: *Der Vortrag zu Ende des 19. Jahrhundert* (Leipzig, 1897).

[184] Kullak: *Aesthetik*, 315.

nevertheless be much more able to forget small mechanical defects in a spiritually significant conception and performance than to allow even the most brilliant technique to compensate for spiritual poverty".[185]

The primacy of the composer and the authority of the text, however, became increasingly predominant towards the end of the century. In contrast to earlier treatments of "Performance" (*Vortrag*) in German literature, the article in the Mendel/Reissmann *Lexikon* is almost entirely about how to understand and execute the composer's instructions and symbols.[186] Without the evidence of early recordings, it would be easy to imagine from the written evidence that something close to modern literalism in performance had already developed by 1900. In fact, recordings, most strikingly those of the oldest celebrated 19th-century musicians, reflect many of the freedoms in performance that are mentioned in 18th- and early-19th-century sources and, in general, a lack of inhibition in "reading between the lines" of the notated text.

Careful comparison of the instructions given by Corri, and other writers of the late 18th century and early 19th century, with recorded performances by singers and instrumentalists trained during the middle of the 19th century, offers some vital clues to interpreting the necessarily ambiguous verbal and graphic attempts to explain the practices that late-18th- and early-19th-century musicians associated with "beautiful" performance. It seems likely, for instance, that many of the so-called graces that Domenico Corri described and illustrated were still used—though perhaps to a lesser extent, and probably not in quite the same manner—by singers who were born in the generation after his death. Vocal effects quite different from those employed by singers who came to maturity in the early 20th century can be heard from one of the oldest great singers to make recordings, Adelina Patti (b. 1843). Her approach to different repertoires reveals fascinating stylistic distinctions. In Mozart and Bellini, for instance, she frequently used a sliding effect that resembles Domenico Corri's description of the "leaping grace", which Nicolo Vaccai and Manuel García already regarded as old-fashioned before the middle of the century. Ex. 13.43 offers a speculative representation of Patti's recording of Mozart's "Voi che sapete" as Corri might have notated it in his *Select Collection*.[187]

---

[185] Dommer: 'Vortrag' in *Musikalisches Lexikon*, 955f.
[186] Mendel and Reissmann: 'Vortrag' in *Musikalisches Conversations-Lexikon*, xi (1879), 211–22.
[187] See Exx. 13.4 and 13.9.

**Ex. 13.43** Mozart: *Le nozze di Figaro*, "Voi che sapete", recorded by Adelina Patti in 1905. Original text (lower stave) and emulation of Corri's notational practice in his *Select Collection* (upper stave).

812  CLASSICAL AND ROMANTIC PERFORMING PRACTICE

**Ex. 13.43** Continued

In her recordings of later repertoire, she uses the "leaping grace" effect much less; she more often employs the type described by Corri as the "anticipation grace", which connects one syllable with another, as well as the pervasive, but subtly varied *portamento* which Corri regarded as "the perfection of vocal music".[188]

The "leaping grace" can also be heard prominently in recordings by one younger singer, the castrato Alessandro Moreschi (b. 1858). His performances, though artistically undistinguished and technically limited, provide insight into the traditions of the castrati, who were confined to sacred music as a result of their exclusion from operatic repertoire soon after Meyerbeer's *Il crociato in Egitto* (1824). In Moreschi's performances, the frequent use of sliding ornaments comparable to Corri's suggests the preservation of older practices among the castrati, who may well have clung to the style and methods employed during the period of their final ascendancy in the 18th century. Rossini's use of slurs across syllables, as shown in Mannstein's treatise (Ex. 13.7, above) indicates *portamento di voce*, and it is notable that Moreschi here introduces very frequent instances of both kinds of Corri's graces. Ex. 13.44 provides a few bars from Moreschi's recording, also notated as Corri might have presented it.[189] Patti's and Moreschi's recordings give a tantalizing glimpse of what, in aural terms, Corri's notational conventions may have been intended to convey.

---

[188] D. Corri: *The Singers Preceptor*, 3.
[189] A similar transcription of the whole piece was included in the 1st edition of this book.

**Ex. 13.44** Rossini: *Petite messe solennelle*, "Crucifixus", bars 5–16. Recorded by the castrato Alessandro Moreschi in 1904.
Original text (lower stave) and emulation of Corri's notational practice in his *Select Collection* (upper stave).

**Ex. 13.44** Continued

It is evident from comparison of these stylized transcriptions with Ex. 13.3 that, apart from their similarity in respect of the graces, many of the slight and not so slight changes of rhythm and pitch, which may at first seem merely capricious, are also paralleled in Corri. Sliding and trembling effects are considered in more detail in Chapters 15 and 16, but it may be appropriate to draw attention here to the frequent employment of the former (corresponding, again, with what is implied in Corri and other late-18th-century sources) and the discreet and varied use of the latter during the 19th century, which on the earliest recordings is perceived more often as a fluctuation of intensity than of pitch, and in Patti's case is often undetectable to the ear.

Vocal music may have exhibited the most extreme manifestations of artistic freedom in the late 18th century and 19th century. This was partly because of long-standing Italian traditions of vocal virtuosity, but more importantly, as extensive ornamentation became increasingly unfashionable, it was explicitly a dramatic art, in which expressive nuance, together with rhythmic and tempo flexibility, was essential for conveying the emotional and dramatic implications of the verbal text. A similar approach was by no means excluded from the performance of instrumental music. Music for string instruments, which allowed the closest approach to the 18th- and 19th-century instrumentalist's ideal of emulating the human voice, provides some illuminating examples. Comparison of the original text of Rode's Seventh Violin Concerto with Spohr's version, included in the final section of his 1833 *Violinschule*, reveals many deviations, the reasons for which are partly explained in Spohr's accompanying commentary and partly passed over in silence. Since Spohr had heard the concerto performed by its composer in 1804 and had, by his own admission, striven to perform it as much like Rode as he was able, it is tempting to believe that Spohr's text furnishes hints of how Rode himself might have played it at that time; but it is probably more representative of Spohr's own manner. In any case, Rode himself almost certainly varied his performance considerably with the passage of time.

Another performing edition of Rode's Seventh Concerto, edited by Spohr's pupil Ferdinand David, includes the note: "The markings and ornaments are precisely those which the composer was wont to employ in performance of this concerto, and the editor thanks his late friend Eduard Rietz, one of Rode's most outstanding pupils, for the information."[190] David's version is quite different from Spohr's with respect both to notes and to bowing, though much of the fingering is similar. Perhaps it represents Rode's later conception of the piece, when Rietz studied with him in the 1820s. Spohr's and David's versions of the first movement of the concerto are compared with the text of the original edition in Ex. 13.45. Spohr marked four types of *tremolo* with different forms of wavy line,[191] indicating fast (b. 3), slow (not included in this extract), accelerating (b. 5), and decelerating (b. 37). The following aspects of performance are indicated by notational changes or added instructions in Spohr's and David's texts:

[190] Ferdinand David, ed.: *Concert-Studien für die Violine*, no. 7, 20.
[191] See Ch. 16, pp. 994–95.

1. Rhythmic modification/agogic accent/*tempo rubato*.
    Spohr: bars 16–19, 25, 28, and 30.
    Spohr's commentary [*Violinschule* p. 199] reads: "The second half of the 28th and 30th bar must be so played as slightly to augment the duration of the first notes beyond their exact value, compensating for the time thus lost, by a quicker performance of the following notes. (This style of playing is called *tempo rubato*). But this acceleration of the time must be gradual, and correspond with the decrease of power."
    Spohr: bars 31–34, 58, and 60
    Spohr's commentary [p. 201] reads: "In the 58th and 60th bar, the ninth note, the *g*, should be dwelt upon a little, and the lost time regained by increasing the rapidity of the following notes."
    Spohr: bars 66, 71, 81, and 83
    Spohr's commentary [p. 203] reads: "The last two eighths of the 81st and 83rd bar are to be slightly prolonged, yet so as not to occasion any marked difference in the time."
    David: bars 4, 12, 16, 17, 31, 33, 80–82, 83–85.
2. Accent.
    Spohr: bars 10, 11, 15, 22, 26, 42, 44, 51, 66, 67, 69, 77.
    David: bars 14, 22, 42, 44, 60, 80–85, 90, 91.
3. Articulation.
    Spohr: bars 5, 13, 31–34, 80, 82.
    David: bars 5, 13, 85.
4. Embellishment (added notes).
    Spohr: bars 40 and 48 ("leaping grace"), 69, 77, 92.
    David: bars 3, 7, 25, 50, 69, 74, 75.
5. Realization of Rode's small notes as *appoggiaturas* or *grace-notes* (where different from Rode's notation or from each other).
    Appoggiaturas:
    Spohr: bars 8, 11, 21, 42, 77, 79, 85.
    David: bars 6, 11, 14, 21, 42, 77, 85.
    Grace-notes:
    Spohr: bars 6, 14, 52, 54.
    David: bars 8, 52, 54, 79.
6. Trembling effects (not specifically marked by David).
    Spohr: bars 3, 5 (accelerating), 11, 13, 21, 22, 24, 26, 37 (decelerating), 43, 44, 52, 58, 60.
    David: bar 44? (<>).
7. Sliding effects, implied by fingering or specified by Spohr's commentary.

Spohr: bars 5, 13, 36, 40, 48, 68, 69, 76, 77, 79, 90.
David: bars 5, 13, 36, 68, 69, 76, 77, 79. (The shifts in 68, 69, 76, and 77 occur between different notes in Spohr's and David's versions.)

**Ex. 13.45** Rode: Violin Concerto no. 7 in A minor, i, first solo section. Text of the first edition (bottom stave) compared with the versions by Ferdinand David (c. 1856) and Spohr (1833).

Ex. 13.45 Continued

**Ex. 13.45** Continued

Ex. 13.45 Continued

822 CLASSICAL AND ROMANTIC PERFORMING PRACTICE

Ex. 13.45 Continued

IMPROVISED ORNAMENTATION AND EMBELLISHMENT 823

Ex. 13.45 Continued

824  CLASSICAL AND ROMANTIC PERFORMING PRACTICE

Ex. 13.45 Continued

Ex. 13.45 Continued

Interestingly, a review of a performance of the concerto by a Russian violinist, Raczynski, in 1818, which referred to his "tasteless additions" and cited the opening of the first movement as an example,[192] indicates that some of the embellishment preserved in David's edition had become "traditional" at an early stage (Ex. 13.46). (The tied notation and accents in the first, second, and fifth bars, however, are meant to illustrate Raczinski's "poor management of the bow", also referred to in the review.)

Ex. 13.46 *Allgemeine musikalische Zeitung*, xx (1818), 317.

Some early recordings provide aural evidence of the discrepancy between text and performance, which confirms the testimony of Spohr's and David's editions of Rode's concerto, but at the same time indicates the inadequacy of notation to convey the subtleties that were essential for a "beautiful" performance. For late 19th-century string playing, in the spirit of the 19th-century classical German string-playing tradition, those of Joseph Joachim, Marie Soldat, and the Klingler Quartet are of particular relevance. Joachim, a student of Joseph Böhm in Vienna and Ferdinand David in Leipzig, was widely seen as the "High Priest" of Classical violin playing in the second half of the 19th century. His five recordings, made in 1903, when he was seventy-two, include two pieces of solo Bach, two of his own arrangements of Brahms's Hungarian dances, and his own Romance in C major. Of these pieces, the Romance is closest to the mainstream 19th-century Classical chamber music tradition, and the one which offers the best possibility to imagine how he

---

[192] Anon.: *Allgemeine musikalische Zeitung*, xx (1818), 317.

might have treated the musical texts of his mentors Mendelssohn and Schumann, and his friend Brahms. His performance of his own composition demonstrates that he regarded substantial deviation from the notated text as perfectly legitimate, indeed necessary.[193]

Other especially revealing examples of this style are the recordings of Bach, Mozart, Beethoven, and Spohr by Marie Soldat (b. 1863), who studied with August Pott (b. 1806), a pupil of Spohr in 1820, before becoming one of Joachim's most faithful students and one of Brahms's favourite violinists. Her recording of the Adagio from Spohr's Ninth Violin Concerto, which she regularly performed throughout her concert career, closely reflects Spohr's own performance instructions in the annotated edition he included in his 1833 *Violinschule*. She adopted most of Spohr's *portamento* fingerings, her use of left-hand trembling was just as sparing as his markings suggest (though not always in the same places); and her freedom of rhythm and tempo closely resembles Joachim's.[194] The Klingler quartet recordings, particularly those from the second decade of the century, offer revealing aural impressions of the types of rhythmical flexibility that were regarded as essential components of the German classical performance tradition.

The 1912 recordings of Eugène Ysaÿe (b. 1858) provide similar insights into string playing in a late 19th-century Franco-Belgian tradition, where a more or less continuous, but very narrow and subtle *vibrato* was becoming characteristic of the sound. His and Marie Soldat's recordings of Schumann's "Abendlied" reveal fundamental differences between Franco-Belgian and German string playing styles on the cusp of a revolution in taste that was to extinguish both of them. His recording of his own "Rêve d'enfant" provides a compendium of characteristic sliding effects, following the fingering in his 1901 edition.

Many similar things would undoubtedly also have been heard in solo performance on wind instruments, although their capacity to execute

---

[193] The 1st edition of this book contains a transcription of Joachim's recording, compared with the original text, which indicates, a far as notation can, its deviations from that text. In the 1990s, when the book was written, the Internet had not yet made such sources freely available. The transcription has been omitted in this edition, because listening to the recordings in conjunction with the original texts (available online) is certainly the best way to appreciate their profound difference from later 20th-century, much more literal, responses to musical notation.

[194] See Clive Brown: 'Marie Soldat-Roeger and the Twilight of a Nineteenth-Century German School of Violin Playing' in *Im Schatten des Kunstwerks II. Theorie und Interpretation des musikalischen Kunstwerks im 19. Jahrhundert. Wiener Veröffentlichungen zur Theorie und Interpretation der Musik*, vol. ii (Wien, Praesens Verlag, 2014), 179–210.

*portamento* was more limited. In piano playing, *tempo rubato* in the strict sense, tempo flexibility, and modifications of notated rhythms were naturally employed in similar ways. Even though the piano provided less scope for emulating many vocal embellishments, some keyboard players were noted for the vocality of their playing. This became increasingly possible as the sustaining power of the instrument was improved, and was enhanced by the idiomatic keyboard techniques of arpeggiation and vertical asynchrony, which were widely applied where they were not indicated in the notation,[195] partly as a means of achieving a fuller, more cantabile effect, and partly for emulating the kinds of expressive gestures that could be obtained by means of sliding and trembling effects in singing, on string instruments and, to various degrees, on wind instruments. As Sigismond Thalberg explained in the introduction to his *L'Art du chant appliqué au piano* (The art of singing applied to the piano): "As the piano cannot, *rationally* speaking, reproduce the melody in its most perfect form, that is to say the faculty of sustaining the sounds, it is necessary by dint of skill and art to overcome this imperfection, and succeed not only in producing the illusion of *sustained* and *prolonged* sounds, but also that of swelling sounds." One of the means of doing this, he explained, was arpeggiating chords.[196]

Alongside Patti's, Joachim's, and Soldat's recordings, those of Carl Reinecke (1824–1910), made on Welte and Hupfeld piano rolls in 1905–6, offer some of the most revealing aural evidence of mid-19th-century practice.[197] Greatly admired as a composer and pianist, Reinecke became a major figure in Leipzig music-making, a chamber music partner of Ferdinand David and Joseph Joachim, and, like them, closely connected with Mendelssohn and Schumann. Like Joachim's and Soldat's recordings, they exemplify a concept of *rubato* that, without ever losing touch with a consistent underlying tempo, involved licence to alter rhythms substantially, within the framework of correct harmony and essential melodic contours which was becoming increasingly rare in the playing of younger musicians. Reinecke's performances of

---

[195] For the relationship of notated arpeggiation to improvised arpeggiation see Ch. 14, pp. 852–57.
[196] Thalberg, *L'art du chant appliqué au piano* op. 70 (Paris, Heugel, [1853]), no pagination, 1st page of text, following Préface des Éditeurs.
[197] Early recordings by leading representatives of other traditions reveal both similarities and differences, which it is beyond the scope of this book to discuss. Much has been written about early recordings since the publication of Robert Philip's seminal studies, both in print and online, which offers abundant material for further study. The recordings discussed here, however, represent the final phase of a tradition of performance, with its roots in 18th-century practice, that was virtually extinct at the time they were made.

Mozart were widely and deeply admired; in 1893 he was described as "one of the finest players of Mozart's concertos", and "thoroughly conversant with the best traditions of Mozart playing, which, through the persistent neglect of present-day players, are in danger of being lost".[198] In 1896, Heinrich Schenker observed: "He is now the only pianist who, equipped with historical awareness, is able to perform Mozart's works as they might have sounded 110 or 120 years ago."[199] And just after he died, it was stated: "His pianoforte playing belonged to a school now almost extinct. Grace and neatness were its characteristics, and at one time Reinecke was probably unrivalled as a Mozart player and accompanist."[200]

In the light of 20th-century practice, Reinecke's Mozart playing may shock. "Grace and neatness" are terms that would hardly be applied to it according to modern understanding of those words. His playing has no connection with what later became established as stylish in Classical repertoire, such as disciplined rhythms and tempo, crystal-clear textures, and avoidance of arpeggiation and asymmetry except where it is specified in the notation, which became typical of the Mozart playing of pianists and fortepianists from Arthur Rubinstein to Malcolm Bilson. Yet all Reinecke's liberties with the text correspond closely with practices that are described in late-18th-century sources. In 19th-century repertoire, including Beethoven, Field, Schumann, and his own compositions, Reinecke's rhythmic freedom closely resembles Joachim's, while the independence of his right and left hands reflects Joachim's relationship with his chamber music partners. It is impossible to capture the flexibility of Reinecke's or Joachim's freedoms in notation; they must be heard to appreciate their subtle complexity. Nevertheless, a couple of short extracts from Reinecke's edition of the Larghetto from Mozart's Piano Concerto K. 537, compared with an approximate transcription of his Welte Piano roll recording of the piece, makes clear the width of the gulf between what he expressed in notation and how, in practice, he understood Mozart's notation (Ex. 13.47).[201]

---

[198] Anon.: 'Letter from Leipzig', *Monthly Musical Record*, xxiii (1893), 152.
[199] Heinrich Schenker: 'Zur Mozartfeier', *Die Zeit*, no. 82, 25 April 1896, 60.
[200] Anon [? D. F. Tovey]: 'Reinecke, Carl Heinrich Carsten' in *Encyclopædia Britannica*, 11th edn, xxiii (Cambridge, 1911), 56.
[201] His Welte recording can be heard, together with scrolled text on Robert Hill's 2014 YouTube posting: https://www.youtube.com/watch?v=ADxuDONsguY.

**Ex. 13.47** a–b. Mozart: Piano Concerto K. 537, Larghetto. (*a*) i. Reinecke's edition, bb. 21–25; ii. Reinecke's performance (approximately notated) on 1905 Welte piano roll; (*b*) bb. 38–43; i. Text; ii. Performance.

**Ex. 13.47** Continued

The historical context for his employment of vertical asynchrony, which can only be hinted at in a transcription, is considered further in the following chapter.

# 14

# Asynchrony, Arpeggiation, and Flexible Rhythm

## Asynchrony

Strict vertical synchrony, or in plainer language "exact togetherness", based on the literal meaning of the score, which became an essential feature of accomplished classical music performance during the 20th-century,[1] would, in most contexts, have been regarded as unmusical in earlier centuries. Throughout the Classical and Romantic periods, it was deemed appropriate only for students who had not yet gained the ability to perform rhythmically in a steady tempo. As gifted students progressed towards mastery, and learned to use the expressive practices that were associated with beautiful, artistic performance, they would have begun to discover asynchrony as an inevitable consequence of many of those practices.

Synchrony is so deeply engrained in the training of contemporary musicians, and so strongly reinforced by the experience of the recording studio, that it takes a powerful leap of imagination to appreciate the ways in which, historically, asynchronous techniques were conceived and employed as a means of communicating the character or emotional content of a composition to the listener. The lack of coincidence between melody and bass that can be heard so often in early recordings of 19th-century pianists was increasingly disparaged in the early 20th century and came to be seen, from a false historical perspective, as a tasteless product of decadent Romanticism. Neal Peres Da Costa has persuasively shown, however, that such practices belong to a continuous tradition, documented as early as the 17th century in French harpsichord music by symbols such as slanting lines, or Couperin's

---

[1] The terms "strict" and "exact" in this context are not meant in a scientific sense but in an aural one. As studies have shown, what seems to the human ear to be synchronous can often be shown, by scientific measurement, not to be. See, e.g.: Eric Clarke: 'Expression in Performance: Generativity, Perception and Semiosis' in John Rink (ed.), *The Practice of Performance* (Cambridge: Cambridge University Press, 1995), 21–54.

*suspension* symbol.[2] Couperin explained: "On the occasions when the bowed instruments swell their notes, the *Suspension* of those of the harpsichord seems, (by a contrary effect) to produce the desired result on the ear";[3] and he made it clear that the length of "the silence that precedes the note on which it is marked should be regulated by the performer's taste".[4] Marpurg, in 1755, reproduced Couperin's *suspension* sign,[5] referring to this and all ornaments that involve "shortening, lengthening, anticipation, and suspension of a main note" as "wavering ornaments".[6] The invention of signs to designate specific practices makes it clear that performers were using those practices. The fact that the signs were rarely if ever employed by most 18th-century composers certainly cannot be taken as evidence that the practices themselves were seldom used, since improvised ornamentation was endemic in most genres of composition. The ways in which these and similar performing practices were employed, how often, and in what contexts, must nevertheless remain entirely speculative. What is not speculative is that skilful employment of these practices was an essential, not an optional aspect of artistic performance, without which the composer's expectations would not have been fulfilled. This was just as true of the 19th century as it was of the 18th, the only difference being the ways the techniques were executed and utilized, which related closely to changes in compositional style. Comparison of the scant 19th-century written information about these practices with the aural evidence of early recordings demonstrates the extent to which words and signs are very poor, often entirely misleading descriptors of how musicians actually performed.

One frequently encountered 18th- and 19th-century notation that has a verifiable connection with asynchrony between bass and melody in keyboard writing, however, is dots under slurs, usually referred to as *portato* or, sometimes by pianists, as *portamento*. At the very start of the 19th century, Louis Adam, calling it *notes portées*, observed that it "contributes much to the expression of the melody, and is sometime made with a little delay of the note, which one can illustrate thus: [Ex. 14.1]".[7] Francesco Pollini, in 1811, gave analogous instructions, evidently derived from Adam, with a similar

---

[2] Neal Peres Da Costa: *Off the Record*, 57ff.
[3] François Couperin: *L'art de toucher le Clavecin* (Paris, 1716), 16.
[4] Couperin: *L'art*, 18.
[5] Marpurg: *Anleitung*, Table II no. 49.
[6] Marpurg: *Anleitung*, 40.
[7] Adam: *Méthode*, 155.

music example, which was also reproduced in Pietro Lichtenthal's 1826 *Dizionario*.[8]

Ex. 14.1 Adam: *Méthode*, 156.

Evidently related to this practice was the association of *portato* notation with arpeggiation in 19th-century piano playing. Moscheles illustrated an arpeggiated performance of *portato* chords in his Studies op. 70 (Ex. 14.2). Having explained that articulation marks applied equally to melodic lines and chords, he continued: "If, therefore, the double notes or chords are marked with dots and slurs at the same time, they must be given delicately in an arpeggiated manner and with the same value that staccato requires under a slur."[9]

Ex. 14.2 Moscheles: *Studien für das Pianoforte* op. 70, 9.

The studies, first published in 1827, were reprinted and republished in new editions throughout the 19th century, always retaining these instructions in the preface (where this was included).[10] In the light of the earlier association between *portato* and asynchrony, it is beyond reasonable doubt that Moscheles's explanation described a generally understood practice, and that the inclusion of his instructions in the many new editions of his studies will have reinforced that association. It can scarcely be doubted that Brahms's frequent use of similar *portato* notation in his piano writing, for instance at the beginning of the Cello

---

[8] Pollini: *Metodo per clavicembalo* (Milan, 1811), 59; Lichtenthal: 'Staccato' in *Dizionario*, ii, 216.
[9] Moscheles: *Studien* op. 70, 9.
[10] Neal Peres Da Costa identifies Gordon Saunders's 1899 edition as the last to include these instructions.

Sonata op. 38 and the Violin Sonata op. 78, signified obligatory, rather than optional asynchrony. Unlike the various signs that denoted the arpeggiation of individual chords, however, *portato* notation, which also had implications for note-length and/or accentuation, never achieved universal acceptance as specifically requiring asynchrony.[11] Moscheles's explanation was omitted in Franklin Taylor's 1915 edition of the studies, when attitudes towards arpeggiation were becoming increasingly negative. Thereafter, the use of *portato* notation to signify the performance of chords "delicately in an arpeggiated manner" was rapidly forgotten.

Some degree of asynchrony between bass and melody in keyboard playing for expressive purposes was probably, as with many ubiquitous practices, regarded as so normal, that relatively few pedagogues discussed it, except when moved to do so by what they perceived as its inappropriate use. Even Carl Czerny, in his extraordinarily detailed *Pianoforte-Schule* did not write about it, although he felt it necessary to give detailed instructions for the appropriate use of improvised arpeggiation. In the preface to Sigismond Thalberg's 1853 *L'art du chant appliqué au piano*, however, the fifth of his twelve techniques for achieving vocal effects on the piano makes it clear that asymmetry of this kind was not only a widespread practice in piano playing, and a valuable expressive tool, but also that it was often, he felt, employed excessively and badly. In fact, he begins his brief consideration with condemnation of its abuse:

> It is essential to avoid the ridiculous bad taste of making an exaggeratedly long delay between playing the bass and the melody-note, thus producing continuous syncopation effects throughout the piece. In a slow melody written in long notes, it is a good effect, especially at the opening of each bar or the beginning of each section of a phrase, to play the melody-note after the bass, but only with an almost imperceptible delay.[12]

In the same decade, the Lebert and Stark piano method briefly mentioned this practice as one of the ways to emphasis an important melody note, remarking: "One may, therefore, and in most cases should begin the melody imperceptibly later than the accompaniment, which creates a kind of arpeggio."[13]

---

[11] See Ch. 6, "Articulated Slurs".
[12] Thalberg: *L'art du chant appliqué au piano*, unpaginated [2].
[13] Sigmund Lebert and Ludwig Stark: *Grosse theoretisch-praktische Klavierschule* (Stuttgart, 1858), iii, 3.

The fact that Thalberg associated this practice with making the piano sing is significant. A decade earlier, Manuel García had discussed various circumstances in which singers might attack a note after the accompaniment. For instance, when an awkward syllable comes on a high note "one can try preceding the high-pitched notes with an ascending *port de voix*",[14] which his illustration (Ex. 14.3a) shows as delaying the high note slightly by means of *portamento* executed on the beat. In Ex. 14.3b, where a breath is necessary, "one does not breathe until after having executed the *port de voix*; then one attacks the following note".[15] In Ex. 14.3c, when a *forte* phrase is followed by its repetition *piano*, "it is necessary to separate it from the *forte* by a slight rest, attacking the note immediately after the bass".[16]

Ex. 14.3 a–c. García: *École*. (*a*) ii, 13; (*b*) ii, 20; (*c*) ii, 33.

(*a*)

(*b*)

(*c*)

---

[14] García: *École*, ii, 13.
[15] García: *École*, ii, 20.
[16] García: *École*, ii, 33.

García also provided examples where a note is sung earlier than it is notated; for instance, when a *forte* phrase follows a *piano* one (Ex. 14.4).

Ex. 14.4  García: *École*, ii, 31f.

Other such examples, which might also be seen as a kind of *tempo rubato*, are illustrated in García's treatise.

Early recordings provide abundant instances of such practices. The frequent occurrence of a delayed melody note in piano playing, its varied use, and its declining incidence over time have been amply demonstrated by Peres Da Costa in his commentary on recordings of twenty-five pianists born between 1824 and 1895.[17] Much more rarely, the melody note might precede its bass note. As García's examples suggest, a singer or instrumentalist might anticipate the accompaniment, often, but not exclusively, on strong entries. Karl Klingler documented specific instances where Joseph Joachim did this; and Johannes Gebauer has illustrated it in his graphic analysis of Joachim's 1903 recording of his own Romance in C.[18] It can also be heard very prominently in the solo entries after rests in bars 69–72 of Beethoven's F major Romance, in Marie Soldat's c. 1920 recording, where she comes in almost an eighth-note in advance of the beat. Many other instances can be found in early recordings.

Substantial asynchrony in ensemble playing, for instance string quartets, is likely to have been pervasive in the 18th and early 19th centuries, and, as recordings demonstrate, it continued into the early 20th century in some traditions. When the players were accomplished professional musicians, this will have resulted not from inadequate rehearsal, but from prioritizing

---

[17] See Peres Da Costa: *Off the Record*, 45–50.
[18] Gebauer: *Der Klassikervortrag*, 241.

individuality of melody above scrupulously co-ordinated ensemble. In 1826, Lichtenthal observed:

> If the beat is always kept with extreme exactness, a perfect ensemble is necessarily achieved. But such a symmetrical and square performance lacks magic. The yoke that is imposed on us by the beat should be decked with flowers, and from time to time we should free ourselves from it with felicitous licence.[19]

A review from the middle of the century suggests that, for some cultivated listeners, too much precision of ensemble in chamber music was not entirely satisfactory. When the Müller String Quartet, one of the early travelling professional quartets, performed in Leipzig in 1862, a correspondent to the *Atheneum* commented: "Their rendering of the andante in Haydn's 'Kaiser Quartett' was especially masterly; but still I feel that, on the whole, too much is sacrificed by them to achieve perfection in ensemble-playing"[20].

Some of the greatest musicians, at the end of the 19th century, were notable for their freedom from the strict constraints of the beat, while at the same time preserving the overall sense of steady tempo. Joseph Joachim, who admired Spohr's quartet playing for this quality,[21] must often have been out of vertical alignment with the bass in his own ensemble playing. Julius Levin recalled in the 1920s: "One of Joachim's partners told me confidentially: 'playing with the "old man" is damned difficult. Always a different tempo and a different accent.'"[22] It is also clear that, when a pianist like Reinecke played chamber music, the vertical asynchrony in his own playing must have affected the whole ensemble. The crucial issue was how such freedom was to be exercised. Under Joachim's aegis, the artistic application of techniques that inevitably resulted in vertical asynchrony was taught at the Berlin Hochschule until the early years of the 20th century.[23]

---

[19] Lichtenthal: 'Esecuzione' in *Dizionario*, i, 258.
[20] Anon.: *Athenaeum*, No. 1830, November 22 (1862), 668. The quartet comprised four sons of Carl Müller the 1st violinist of the original Müller Quartet (also four brothers).
[21] Andreas Moser: *Joseph Joachim. Ein Lebensbild*, 2nd edn, ii, 292.
[22] Julius Levin: 'Adolf Busch', *Die Musik*, xviii (1925/1926), 746.
[23] Some of its characteristics are described by Joachim's pupil Karl Klingler, who taught there, in his essay 'Vom musikalischen Einfall und seiner Darstellung', in Marianne M. Klingler and Agnes

It was described in detail by Marion Ranken, who studied there from 1902 to 1909:[24]

> In long florid passages such as occur so often in slow movements of Haydn or Mozart quartets, when the first violin wanders about meditatively (probably in demi-semiquavers) above an accompaniment of quavers in the under parts, there seemed in Joachim's playing to be no attempt at exact "ensemble" between the two, that is to say the quavers, which in this case took on themselves the role of the "beat," moved along unconcernedly in strict time while the demi-semiquavers moved as unconcernedly up above, without any attempt to synchronise regularly with the beat (four into each quaver), but with free and gracious lines, only making sure to arrive at certain given points at the right moment and together. [...] There was no sense of there being any anxiety in his mind about keeping in with the rest of the quartet, or that any of them made an undue effort to keep together but, instead of the mechanical ensemble and "fitting in" of the present day, one had an ensemble of spirit—a sense that one common objective bound them all together, and that they all meant to reach the goal in company.[25]

This freedom was not confined to the leading melodic voice in the ensemble, but also employed in the other parts where the character of a phrase encouraged or required it. Ranken described at length that she was taught how, in performing the opening of the first movement of Schubert's A minor String Quartet, all the members of the ensemble could shape their parts freely, yet without losing the sense of coherence within an overall steady tempo. She concluded her detailed account:

> Should anyone at this point have had the pedantry as well as the courage during a lesson of this nature in the Hochschule to call the whole argument

---

Ritter (eds.), „Über die Grundlagen des Violinspiels" und nachgelassene Schriften (Hildesheim, 1990), 109–43.

[24] For a complete online copy of her book see https://josephjoachim.com/2020/11/17/marion-bruce-ranken-some-points-of-violin-playing-and-musical-performance/ on Robert W. Eshbach's "Joseph Joachim" website.

[25] Ranken: *Some Points of Violin Playing*, 79.

in question on the grounds "that the composer had not written it down like that," I think that (after the fury and the damning had subsided) the answer would have been something like this: "Very well, if that is your opinion, can you tell me in what other way Schubert could have written it down if he *had* wished you to play it in *my* way?"[26]

Later, she remarked: "Klingler said to me recently [i.e., in the 1930s] when discussing the 'faultless ensemble playing' which gets so much praise from the musical critics nowadays: 'As a matter of fact, I personally do not want that sort of ensemble, but if I put this in print I should only be misunderstood.'"[27]

## Arpeggiation

The asynchronous execution of many chords was common in piano playing until the early 20th century. During the first decades of the century, however, the increasing predominance of misconceived ideas about the relationship between composers' intentions for their notation and their expectations for its realization led to any kind of asynchrony being regarded as permissible only in places where it was explicitly indicated by signs. Through a fundamental misunderstanding of historical practice, the existence and use of these signs came to be seen as evidence that, where it was not specifically marked, arpeggiation was a violation of the composer's intentions. As suggested earlier, however, the existence of signs merely proves the existence of the practices, not the extent to which they were employed.

Various means, however, were sporadically used to indicate arpeggiation in the music of the period, included a vertical wavy or curved line, various forms of hooked straight lines, a slanting line through the chord, and the indication of the arpeggiation with small notes. Mozart, for instance, sometimes used a wavy line and sometimes small notes; in his Violin Sonata K. 306 he employed one form in the initial draft of the first movement (Ex. 14.5a) and the other in the final version (Ex. 14.5b).

---

[26] Ranken: *Some Points*, 82f. For a stimulating, richly illustrated account of this aspect of Joachim's and his circle's practice, see Johannes Gebauer: *Der Klassikervortrag*, 202–57.
[27] Ranken: *Some Points*, 119.

Ex. 14.5 a–b. Mozart: Violin Sonata K. 306/i. (*a*) Draft; (*b*) Final version.

(*a*)

(*b*)

Different signs were described by mid-18th-century theorists for specialized treatments of arpeggiation. Marpurg gave examples of strokes through the stem below the chord indicating normal upwards arpeggio (Ex. 14.6a), and through the stem above the chord for a downwards arpeggio (Ex. 14.6b), as well as a range of arpeggiations,[28] including additional ornaments, such as Ex. 14.6c.

Ex. 14.6 a–c. Marpurg: *Anleitung*. (*a*) Table V no 16; (*b*) Table V no. 17; (*c*) Table V nos. 18–19.

(*a*)

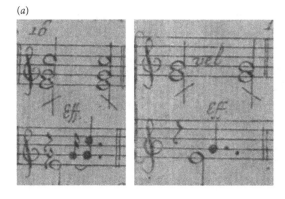

---

[28] Marpurg: *Anleitung*, Table V, nos. 18–29.

Ex. 14.6 Continued

(b)

(c)

These are oriented towards French practice (he used the signs in Ex. 14.6a and b in his *Pièces de Clavecin* of around 1740, but apparently not in "German" repertoire).

Löhlein in 1765 illustrated not only the conventional wavy line, but also different signs for arpeggio from top to bottom (Ex. 14.7a) and from bottom to top (Ex. 14.7b). The wavy line appears in some of Löhlein's published works from the 1760s but not, to my knowledge, the other signs.

Ex. 14.7 a–b. Löhlein: *Clavier Schule*, 70.

(a)  (b)

Clementi explained that where a grace-note or acciaccatura was required before one note of the arpeggio, this might be indicated by a slanting line below the note to which the ornament should be added. He instructed that

(Ex. 14.8a) should be performed as in Ex. 14.8b.[29] This notation, however, was also used to indicate normal arpeggiation without an added grace-note, for instance by J. B. Cramer.[30]

Ex. 14.8 a–b. Clementi: *Introduction*, 9.

Most of the signs indicating special arpeggio effects, which were illustrated by theorists, seem scarcely to have been used in compositions. Even those indicating a normal ascending arpeggio, which gained wider currency, were used relatively infrequently. As with all ornaments in this period, there is no reason to think that composers troubled to mark every place where they might have expected, or been happy to have heard some form of arpeggiation, or that they specified every aspect of its performance, since it was essentially an expressive embellishment. In fact, there is powerful evidence to suggest that in harpsichord, clavichord, and piano playing during the 18th and 19th centuries, the arpeggiation of chords, either rapidly or more broadly, was pervasive and normal.[31] Arpeggiation (*Brechen*) was one of the items in C. P. E. Bach's short list of generally un-notated practices that were necessary for stylish performance.[32] In organ playing during the Classical period, on the other hand, it was not normally expected. Bach instructed that "arpeggiation is not used at all on the organ".[33] This is confirmed in German practice by Adlung's comment on the appropriate techniques for keyboard instruments with plucked or struck strings: "Playing on such stringed instruments is different from playing on the organ: one must make more of

---

[29] Clementi: *Introduction*, 9.
[30] Cramer: *Instructions for the Pianoforte*, 42. The interchangeability of symbols is also indicated by notation in the first edition of Beethoven's A minor Violin Sonata, where the spreading of the violin's three-part chord in bar 164 is indicated by a slanting line through the chord in the 1st edition, but as a vertical wavy line in the c. 1830 Haslinger edition (although the arpeggio instruction was omitted from all later editions until my Bärenreiter edition of 2020).
[31] Since the original publication of this book, an increasingly rich fund of evidence has been unearthed by Anselm Gerhard, Neal Peres Da Costa, Sebastian Bausch, and others (see bibliography).
[32] Bach: *Versuch*, i, 117.
[33] Bach: *Versuch*, ii, 316.

an effort to arpeggiate the notes and the like, rather than striking the keys together or too slowly."[34] One of Samuel Wesley's letters confirms that a similar view was current in the early 19th century (see below). Czerny, too, giving instructions for performing fugues on the piano, stated that arpeggiation must be avoided in contrapuntal writing, explaining: "in this respect the fortepiano is to be handled just like the organ, where all chords and harmonies are struck firmly together".[35] Arpeggiation on the organ, however, appears to have been used by 17th- and early-18th-century French organists, who included signs for arpeggiation in their ornament tables,[36] and by 17th-century Italian organists.[37] In the later 19th century it was used on the organ by César Franck.[38]

Although there is limited written evidence about when, where, and how pianists were expected to execute chords in arpeggio, this can certainly not be interpreted as indicating that the normal rule was for the notes of a chords to be played simultaneously unless otherwise indicated.[39] Indeed, the silence of so many theorists and treatise writers on this matter might suggest that the norm was to arpeggiate most chords to some extent, and that it was therefore superfluous to mention it. Sometimes, perhaps for the sake of less sophisticated players and amateurs, composers took the trouble to mark places where the use of arpeggiation was particularly necessary. Clementi, for instance, when reissuing some of his piano sonatas in London editions added many more arpeggio signs than had been present in the original Viennese editions.[40] And Haydn marked much more arpeggiation in his London keyboard compositions than in his earlier Viennese ones. Comparison of the

---

[34] Jakob Adlung: *Musica mechanica organoedi. Das ist: Gründlicher Unterricht von der Struktur, Gebrauch und Erhaltung, etc. der Orgeln, Clavicymbel, Clavichordien und anderer Instrumente*, ii (Berlin, 1768), 112, §522.
[35] Czerny: *Die Kunst des Vortrags*, 128.
[36] David Ponsford: *French Organ Music in the Reign of Louis XIV* (Cambridge, 2011), 87.
[37] Luigi Ferdinando Tagliavini: 'L'arte di »non lasciar vuoto lo strumento«. Appunti sulla prassi cembalistica italiana nel Cinque e Seicento', *Rivista italiana di musicologia*, x (1975), 375.
[38] Hyun Jyung Seoh: *Articulation and Arpeggiation in the Prélude, Fugue et Variation, Op. 18, and Pastorale, Op. 19, by César Franck (1822–1890)* (DMA diss., University of Houston, 2016), 18. Maurice Emmanuel: *César Franck: Etude Critique* (Paris: Laurens, 1930), stated "he was more pianist than organist" (p. 101) and remarked that "He played a little too much like a pianist on the keyboards of his "Cavaillé-Coll" [organ], and was not afraid to arpeggiate chords" (p. 107f). Il était plus pianiste qu'organiste. Il jouait un peu trop du piano sur les claviers de son «Cavaillé-Coll» [organ], et ne craignait pas d'arpéger des accords.
[39] See below (pp. 852–53) for Czerny's problematic statement that playing chords together is the rule and arpeggiation the exception.
[40] Anselm Gerhard: 'Willkürliches Arpeggieren—ein selbstverständliches Ausdrucksmittel in der klassisch-romantischen Klaviermusik und seine Tabuisierung im 20. Jahrhundert', *Basler Jahrbuch für historische Musikpraxis*, xxvii (2003), 123–34.

autograph of the E flat Sonata (Hob. XVI:52) with the 1799 Breitkopf und Härtel edition shows that he added many additional arpeggiation signs for the publication.

The unreliability of drawing conclusions from negative evidence is strikingly illustrated by early recordings, most tellingly those of the oldest major musician to make them, Carl Reinecke (1824–1910). He was not only a distinguished composer, concert pianist, conductor, and teacher, but also a prolific author of publications on piano performance, but he never wrote anything about arpeggiating chords where it was not indicated. Most remarkably, it is absent from his book on performing Beethoven's Piano Sonatas, or in his recommendations for the revival of performing practices in Mozart's Piano Concertos.[41] His silence about this practice might easily have been taken as very strong evidence that Reinecke did not regarded un-notated arpeggiation as proper in that repertoire, or indeed in any other, were it not for his many 1905/6 Welte and Hupfeld piano roll recordings, including works by Beethoven and Mozart, in which the majority of chords receive some kind of tight or, often, expansive arpeggiation. In fact, playing a chord exactly together seems like a special effect in Reinecke's playing. Since Reinecke was regarded by contemporaries as an upholder of tradition, and his style was characterized as graceful and neat,[42] the importance of his recordings for understanding the characteristics of early- to mid-19th-century pianism is crucial.

There is no good reason to believe that what we hear from the eighty-one-year-old Reinecke represents something significantly different from how he played when he was a protégé of Mendelssohn and a valued colleague of Schumann in the 1840s and 1850s, when Liszt, too, praised his playing, in the Parisian journal *La musique* in July 1849. The absence of any yet discovered criticism of Reinecke's arpeggiation, even in his later years, when the practice was coming under increasing scrutiny, is very significant; if his use of it had been regarded as inappropriate, or stylistically questionable, it would certainly have been deplored by reviewers. In fact, reviews of Reinecke's playing during the first twenty years of his career indicate that he was seen from the start as a "classical" pianist. In 1845, after he played Hummel (Septet), Beethoven (op. 47), Mendelssohn (op. 62, no. 2) and some of his own compositions, a reviewer commented that the twenty-one-year-old Reinecke

---

[41] See Bibliography.
[42] See Ch. 13, pp. 828–31.

belongs to the small number of piano virtuosos in whom the spiritual element is the predominant one. Poetic conception, lively imagination, combined with the gift of perfectly conveying what he feels and thinks to others, gives his playing deeper content and charm. In addition, he easily overcomes all the technical difficulties that have been developed in recent times, and has a secure and strong mastery of the instrument. Thus, we heard from him a technically and spiritually perfect performance.[43]

After he performed Beethoven's C minor Piano Concerto in Hamburg in 1852, a reviewer noted that Reinecke "proves himself to be an excellent pianist who has not only acquired the self-evident technical skill and dexterity, but also the analogous solidity of performance style, which is necessary for the execution of classical masterpieces".[44] In Paris the previous year, there had been criticism of his overuse of the pedal, but in other respects his playing was praised as "crisp and bright; it has power in the sound, a rare quality among pianists".[45] In Frankfurt, performing Beethoven and Chopin, it was reported that he "demonstrated in his achievements a solid pianist, well trained in every respect",[46] while in Kassel, it was said: "He plays with such delicacy and elegance, without in any way coquetting with modern virtuosity, that his performance was a real joy to the hearts of the really musical audience."[47] He clearly did not belong in the company of "the newer players, who endlessly break the chords",[48] who were criticized in the same journal a few years earlier. On his first visit to England in 1869 his playing of his own F♯ minor Concerto was characterized as "brilliant and fluent, and his expression at once natural and unaffected".[49] He was reported to have played the Larghetto of Mozart's "Coronation" Concerto, one of the pieces he recorded in 1905, "with natural, unobtrusive expression";[50] and in another journal, the whole concerto with "remarkable precision and rhythmical expression".[51] By the time of his death in 1910, his style of playing was seen not only as "graceful and neat", but also as "virtually extinct".[52] These accounts convey

---

[43] L. R.: *Allgemeine musikalische Zeitung*, xlvii (1845), 122.
[44] Anon.: 'Dur und Moll', *Signale für die Musikalische Welt*, x (1852), 103.
[45] Anon.: 'Matinées et soirées musicales', *Revue et Gazette Musicale*, viii (1851), 108.
[46] F. J. K.: *Süddeutsche Musik-Zeitung*, viii (1859), 16.
[47] Anon.: *Süddeutsche Musik-Zeitung*, xi (1862), 78.
[48] Ernst: 'Aus Hamburg', *Süddeutsche Musik-Zeitung*, i (1852), 87.
[49] Anon.: 'Crystal Palace Concerts', *The Musical World*, xlvii (1869), 303.
[50] Anon.: 'Music and the Drama', *The Athenaeum*, Issue 2165 (1869), 578.
[51] Anon.: 'Concerts', *The Orchestra*, xii(1869), 68.
[52] *Encyclopædia Britannica*, 11th edn, 56. See Ch. 13, pp. 828–29 for full quotation.

something very different from the impression the unprepared modern listener derives from hearing Reinecke's recordings for the first time. By conventional modern criteria, they are neither graceful nor neat, and certainly not what has come to be seen as classical.

Reinecke's playing style offers valuable clues to the interpretation of the fragmentary written evidence. J. B. Cramer, for instance, offered only a brief comment on chord playing: "Chords can be played in two different ways, first in an abrupt manner striking all the Notes at once, which is done chiefly at the end of a piece or a sentence, 2dly in Arpeggio sounding successively the Notes of which the chord is composed." Cramer's limitation of the first kind of execution, mostly to the final chord of a melodic unit or a piece, strongly suggests that the second manner was the usual way of playing chords. His illustration of arpeggio chords seems to indicate a very leisurely spreading (Ex. 14.9), but he followed this with a *nota bene*: "The notes of a Chord are played with more or less velocity, as the character of the piece requires."[53]

Ex. 14.9 Cramer: *Instructions*, 42.
The curious appearance of one wavy line among the curved lines is surely a printer's error, since Cramer explained the three ways of marking arpeggio—these two and a slanting line through the chord—as equivalents.

The question again arises: Why, if it was usual to spread chords, should it be necessary sometimes to mark this with a sign? Two treatises by Philip Anthony Corri that discuss arpeggiation (which, with his Italian background, he calls "appoggiando") cast light on this paradox. In the first of these, *L'anima di musica* (1811), he gave Ex. 14.10a, commenting:

> Observe that in the above Example, the longer notes only, are to be played appoggiando; those that are equal are to be struck together, tho' not staccato; and the end of the tie must have the cadence or fall, that is; to be touched lightly.

---

[53] Cramer: *Instructions for the Pianoforte* (London, 1812), 42.

But if on the contrary, all the chords are played appoggiando, without distinction, the Time and Metre would be so confused and disguised that no air or melody could be discoverable, and therefore, it should be remember'd that where notes or chords are of equal length, in succession, they should all be played together.*[Corri's footnote] There is an exception which I shall next explain. [His explanation is the one given in the paragraph below beginning "There are occasions..."]

To prove what I have just asserted play the foregoing Example with all the notes appoggiando and without emphasis—Judge then which is the most pleasing style; the 1st at No 1—monotonous without expression, the 2nd at No 2 with proper expression—or the 3rd as just directed, with an excess of expression.

The latter style is two [sic] often adopted by those who affect to play with Taste and who from ignorance of its effects, distort and disfigure the melody so hideously that no one can make it out; I therefore recommend the appoggiando to be used cautiously and sparingly.

Ex. 14.10 a–c. P. A. Corri: *L'anima di musica*, 75.

Ex. 14.10 Continued

(c)

There are occasions where the appoggiando may be used, altho' it be not for emphasis, for instance;—in a slow strain, the long chords are to be sustained, tho' there are many of the same quality, yet their harmony is better heard, and produces more effect by being touch'd appoggiando, (As the Minims in the following Ex [14.10b]:) but then observe that the Crotchets that follow, being shorter, ought to be played together as a relief to the other style.—Example.

Further Examples, shewing that the appoggiando should be used on the long chords; and also on shorter ones, where brilliancy is required to be given, touching them as nearly as possible together.— [Ex. 14.10c]

When the words "con Espressione, con Anima, or Dolce etc." are mark'd at a passage, it signifies that the appoggiando must be particularly and often used, and made as long as possible.

Corri followed this with further examples from Cramer, Clementi, and Dussek. He then warned of some circumstances in which arpeggiation should generally be avoided, for instance, a succession of octaves, which "must never be played appoggiando, but always together unless they are very long notes, or have emphasis".[54] Where the arpeggiation occurred in livelier contexts, he included it among what he called the "forcing or leaning Graces", instructing that it should "always be played very swiftly with Emphasis and exactly with the Bass [Ex. 14.11]".[55]

Ex. 14.11 P. A. Corri: *L'anima di musica*, 15.

[54] P. A. Corri: *L'anima di musica*, 76t.
[55] P. A. Corri: *L'anima di musica*, 15.

Corri's discussion of arpeggiation in his slightly later book on preluding elucidates his comments in the earlier treatise. Here he makes it evident that his use of the term *appoggiando* relates only to chords that are quite broadly spread, and does not even apply to chords marked with a conventional arpeggiation sign:

> Chords that are long and which conclude the Prelude (as at 1st Prelude Page 22 [Ex. 14.12]) should not be struck together, but by a long extended Appoggiando (see * at the bottom of Page 1 [where he explains "Appoggiando signifies; playing a chord in a leaning or slanting direction so that the notes are heard successively"]).
>
> Those Chords that begin any run or passage (as the Chord marked *sf* in the same Prelude Page 22) should have emphasis, and should be played more together, and with more firmness; When there are several Chords together (as the beginning of the same Prelude Page 22 [where wavy-line arpeggiation signs are marked]) they should be played almost together and not Appoggiando.[56]

Ex. 14.12  P. A. Corri: *P. A. Corri's Original System of Preluding* (London, [1814]), 22.

Frequent arpeggiation was clearly normal in piano playing in England. In 1824, William Sheppard stated: "In *slow* movements it is better to spread the chords whether they are marked or not."[57] The ubiquity of this practice during the early decades of the 19th century is confirmed by Samuel Wesley in 1829, in a letter in which he discussed the difference between playing the piano and playing the organ. He observed that pianists "do not put down the Keys simultaneously *which on the Organ should always be done*, but one after another, beginning at the lowest note of the Base".[58]

---

[56] Philip Anthony Corri: *P. A. Corri's Original System of Preluding* (London, [1814]), 4.
[57] William Sheppard: *A New Pianoforte Preceptor* (London, 1824), 55.
[58] British Library Add 31764, f. 28. I am indebted to Dr Philip Olleson for kindly drawing my attention to this letter.

There is every reason to believe that an asynchronous execution of most chords was normal on the European continent, too, but the fragmentary written evidence alone provides only hints of what was regarded as good practice. In 1828, Hummel stated that arpeggiation was particularly necessary on Viennese action pianos, because

> They allow neither a powerful attack by striking of the keys with the whole weight of the arms, nor a ponderous touch: the power of the sound must be produced solely by the speed of the finger. Full chords are, for example, mostly broken very quickly and are far more effective than if the notes were played together with the same degree of strength.[59]

He wrote nothing about the *expressive* use of arpeggiation, but in France, at around the same time, Frédéric (Friedrich) Kalkbrenner, discussing expression, stated: "In passages in double notes, octaves, or chords, long notes should be arpeggiated, those preceding them should not";[60] and he gave an example in which arpeggiation was shown on all first beats of the bar except the final chord, which recalls Cramer's instruction for synchronous chords at the ends of phrases and sections.

In the light of P. A. Corri's more detailed explanation and Reinecke's recordings, however, it is unclear whether nominally un-arpeggiated chords were really played exactly together, or rather like Corri's "almost together and not Appoggiando" chords. Similarly, when Kalkbrenner stated that in piano arrangements of orchestral music it is necessary to "suppress arpeggiation", because "the greatest merit of an orchestra consists in its ensemble",[61] it remains uncertain what he envisaged, especially since the precision of modern orchestral ensemble is unlikely to have been a characteristic even of the famed Conservatoire orchestra at that time. They would certainly not, for instance, have expected strings to divide three- and four-part chords between adjacent players, as—aiming for meticulous synchrony—became the usual orchestral practice during the 20th century. Furthermore, Reinecke, playing his own piano reduction of the orchestral Vorspiel to Act 5 of his opera *König*

---

[59] Hummel: *Anweisung*, iii, II, 4, §3, 454. The section on Viennese pianos was not included in the contemporaneous English edition, presumably because these instruments were virtually unknown there.
[60] Kalkbrenner: *Méthode* (Paris [1831]), 12.
[61] Kalkbrenner: *Méthode*, 12.

*Manfred*, after a couple of synchronous bars, used almost continuous arpeggiation where none was marked, but of a very varied character.

Kalkbrenner also stated: "The high notes of the piano should never be attacked in a sudden or hard way, the effect of the percussion, which is heard more at the top should be hidden as much as possible."[62] Perhaps, without mentioning it explicitly, he had arpeggiation in mind here too, for a few years later Pierre-Joseph-Guillaume Zimmermann, discussing tone quality, recommended: "Always, to avoid dryness, I recommend arpeggiating the chords, especially in the upper part of the piano and particularly in the forte."[63] In a section headed "Style", Zimmermann explained: "The dissonances, the appoggiaturas, the syncopations, the sensitive notes, are emphasized a little more than the note on which they resolve; in music, this second note is rather like the silent *e* [in the French language]. When these notes, which receive the musical accent, are accompanied by a chord, the chord is arpeggiated"[64] (Ex. 14.13). This practice is pervasive in Reinecke's playing.

**Ex. 14.13** P.-J.-G. Zimmermann: *Encyclopédie du pianiste compositeur*, ii, 59.

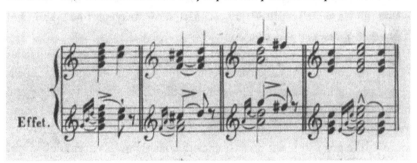

Carl Czerny's immensely detailed piano method treats arpeggiation more systematically than any other. His motivation seems partly to have been to counteract what he considered an insufficiently varied use of arpeggiation as an expressive resource. He was concerned that "Some players accustom themselves so much to arpeggiating chords, that they are absolutely incapable of striking full chords or even double notes firmly and together; though the latter is the rule, while the former constitutes the exception."[65] His reference

---

[62] Kalkbrenner: *Méthode*, 12.
[63] Zimmermann: *Encyclopédie du pianiste compositeur*, ii, 58.
[64] Zimmermann: *Encyclopédie*, ii, 59.
[65] Czerny: *Pianoforte-Schule*, iii, 40.

to a "rule" appears to be the first suggestion of this kind, and a symptom of the growing tendency to attribute a more precise meaning to notation than it had possessed until then. Like Hummel's prescription that trills begin on the main note unless the composer indicates an alternative,[66] it was clearly not a statement of the *status quo*, but an attempt to lay down a rule where none had previously existed. Czerny's next sentence nevertheless acknowledged that he expected much improvised arpeggiation where it was not prescribed by a sign: "The exception (namely arpeggiation), however, can so frequently be used effectively, that we only need to show where the one is more appropriate than the other."[67] First he explained that chords should normally be played firmly in the following circumstances:

(1) When they are very short, unless they are "specifically marked" to be arpeggiated (Ex. 14.14a).

Ex. 14.14 a–f. Czerny: *Pianoforte-Schule*, iii, §5, 41f.

(a)

(b)

(c)

[66] See Ch. 12.
[67] Czerny: *Pianoforte-Schule*, iii, 40.

Ex. 14.14 Continued

(d)

(e)

(f)

(2) When they are to be played with great force, "especially when they begin or end a piece or a phrase", explaining, in contrast to Hummel, that this is "always more effective since arpeggiation takes away and diminishes a good part of the forte." He added that composers should indicate it when they want such chords arpeggiated (Ex. 14.14b).

Whether this reflects the growing power of the piano since Hummel's time, ten years earlier, or simply a divergence of taste, is debatable.

(3) In contrapuntal passages, chords "must always be struck with strict firmness, and only sometimes can arpeggiation be permitted on a longer, full chord, on which a particular emphasis falls". In his example (Ex. 14.14c), he instructed, "Only the 3 chords marked +, (the last in any case) allow a moderate arpeggiation, which however may not interrupt the legato."[68]

---

[68] Czerny: *Pianoforte-Schule*, iii, 41.

He then explained cases in which arpeggiation was necessary:

(1) "On all slow and sustained chords that form a melody." In his example (Ex. 14.14d), he explained that only the last chord should be played together (again recalling Cramer's instruction) and that the others should be arpeggiated so that "the upper melody note never gets out of tempo".
(2) Like Zimmermann, he instructed that when a longer chord is tied to a shorter one only the first should be arpeggiated (Ex. 14.14e), especially when the shorter one is *staccato*, and he again marked the arpeggiated chords with + (Ex. 14.14f).
(3) Finally, he clarified that chords do not only have to be arpeggiated very quickly, but in all degrees of speed, even to the point that each individual note of the chord might be "like a quarter-note in slow tempo".[69]

Two of the circumstances in which Czerny regarded arpeggiation as normal—chords accompanying a melody and a long chord followed by shorter ones—were also mentioned in 1850 by Francesco Tomicich, in a book intended for elementary tuition in piano playing.[70]

Czerny returned to the subject of arpeggiation in 1846, expressing concern that those who exclusively devote themselves to the modern style of playing are unable to perform a fugue properly. And he attributed this largely to the fact that "In the modern style, all passages in many parts are now invariably played in arpeggio; and so greatly is this the case, that many pianists have almost forgotten how to strike chords firmly." Referring to a music example showing a succession of full half-note chords, he continued: "Some otherwise really good players would not be able to perform the following passage quite firmly, that is, to strike all the notes of each chord exactly together."[71] In fugue playing, Czerny regarded arpeggiation as self-evidently entirely inappropriate, though he conceded that "In the free style of playing this may often be really good."[72] Whether his prohibition of arpeggiation in

---

[69] Czerny: *Pianoforte-Schule*, iii, 41f.

[70] Francesco Serafino Tomicich: *Il fanciullo triestino al piano-forte o sia Metodo elementare pel piano-forte compilato sulle opere dei migliori autori* (Trieste, 1850), 13. Quoted by Anselm Gerhard in '»You do it«', 164.

[71] Czerny: *Pianoforte-Schule*, iv, 159.

[72] Czerny: *Pianoforte-Schule*, iv, 160. Czerny writes "Im galanten Spiel", which is translated in the contemporaneous English edition as "In the free style of playing".

such circumstances can be taken as evidence that he required absolute vertical synchrony, however, is questionable.

In 1853, Sigismond Thalberg, in the seventh of his twelve recommendations for making the piano sing, also echoed Czerny's recommendation for chordal accompaniment of a melody, instructing: "The chords that support a melody on the highest note should always be arpeggiated, but VERY TIGHT, almost TOGETHER, and the melody note should be given more weight than the other notes of the chord."[73] He regarded this treatment as so natural that he introduced a sign: [, which he placed before chords that should be played strictly together; but this appears very infrequently in his arrangements of vocal music. Underlying Thalberg's discussion of asynchrony between bass and melody, and the related practice of arpeggiation, is a strong implication that in common with many of his contemporaries he regretted that these practices, although a valuable means of expression, were often employed tastelessly.

A few years later, Adolph Kullak's comment on Thalberg's instructions suggests that taste was beginning to change in this respect:

> If a cantabile part is accompanied by another in the same hand, then, according to Thalberg, the arpeggiation of the double-note chords supporting the cantabile note should be the means to give the cantabile part the necessary emphasis. It cannot be denied that in this way the melody can be brought out better. Nevertheless, it is indispensable to practise emphasizing the cantabile note while simultaneously playing two or more notes. Aside from the usefulness of such study, it also mitigates the monotony caused by continually arpeggiating a lengthy cantabile movement. The latter would, for example, be intolerable in the first part of Beethoven's C sharp minor sonata, if the player wanted always to play the melody after the accompaniment.
>
> The best thing to do here is to reserve the arpeggiation only for the more important places. The middle movement of the Sonata *pathétique* op. 13. would make an excellent study in this respect.[74]

Among the few later 19th-century sources to discuss arpeggiation in some detail is Otto Klauwell's 1883 *Der Vortrag in der Musik*. Having stated that

---

[73] Thalberg: *L'art du chant appliqué au piano*, unpaginated [2].
[74] Kullak: *Ästhetik des Klavierspiels*, 331.

it "is in general a bad habit" to arpeggiate chords when it is not specified by the composer, he continued: "We have already seen that a great many small changes in tempo and dynamics, even if they could be indicated, as well as the use of the pedal, which will be discussed in detail later, are left to the insight of the player in many places where it is indispensable; in the same way, there are also numerous cases where the breaking of a chord even though it is not indicated is permitted, or even required." He then identified circumstances in which arpeggiation would be needed:

(1) "for greater fullness of sound", giving as an example a chord under a *fermata*, as in bar two of Schumann's "Träumerei", or, in contrast to Cramer, at the end of many pieces; but he qualified this by the observation that in *pp*, as at the end of Chopin's Nocturne op. 9 no. 2, an unbroken cord "often has a more beautiful effect".[75]
(2) On loud or *sf* chords, giving examples from Schubert's Piano Sonata op. 164 and the first of Mendelssohn's Zwei Klavierstücke WoO. 19.
(3) On accented dissonances, for which he gave an example from the second movement of Beethoven's Piano Sonata op. 81a.
(4) For high passages against a low bass, for which he provided an example from the third movement of Schumann's Phantasie op. 17.

As with P. A. Corri's distinction between "appoggiando" and less broadly spread asynchronous chords, it is unclear whether Klauwell really expected most of the chords that were not included in the above categories to be together in the modern sense, especially since he had studied in Leipzig with Reinecke.

Despite the warnings of treatise writers, it is evident that, at the end of the 19th century, arpeggiation in many contexts, especially on slow-moving chords, was so normally envisaged that if composers specifically required chords to be played strictly together, they would need to indicate it. Thus in 1895, the American pianist and composer Edward MacDowell, who had studied in Paris and Frankfurt, employed Thalberg's sign in "Starlight" from *Sea Pieces* op. 55, with an explanatory footnote (Ex. 14.15).

---

[75] Klauwell: *Der Vortrag in der Musik*, 101f.

Ex. 14.15  Edward MacDowell: *Sea Pieces* op. 55 no. 4, "Starlight".

*) Chords marked ⌈ are not to be rolled.

Hans von Bülow was among the later 19th-century pianist who cautioned against what he considered to be improper use of improvised arpeggiation, especially in Beethoven. His attitude was undoubtedly connected with an increasing, but fallacious, belief in the literalness and inviolability of Beethoven's notation, which was occasioned by the gradual extinction of a direct connection with the performing traditions of Beethoven's own time, and the misleading revisionist instructions of Carl Czerny and others. It is not clear, however, what Bülow understood by the term *arpeggiation*; in all likelihood, like Corri, he would not have regarded slight, but perceptible, asynchrony as arpeggiation. In the case of Mendelssohn's piano music, Bülow, who had received instruction from the composer on one occasion in the mid-1840s, stated in the foreword to his 1880 edition of Mendelssohn's *Rondo capriccioso* op. 14 that the composer "hated all arbitrary arpeggiation", adding, "There is not a single arpeggio mark in Op. 14 despite the 'brilliant' notation." He supported his statement with reference to the introductory section of Mendelssohn's *Capriccio brillant* op. 22, where arpeggio is specified for the first three sixteenth-note chords, followed by rests, which occur on almost every beat for ten bars, and which accompany a right-hand melody from bar 5. By his reference to this passage, Bülow tacitly suggested that arpeggiation was only appropriate where Mendelssohn indicated it. What he failed to acknowledge, however, was that in op. 22, without the indication to arpeggiate, players might assume, in accordance with Czerny's first "rule" (see Ex. 14.11a), that the chords were to be played strictly together, which Mendelssohn evidently did not want. Bülow also stated: "If you want to play Mendelssohn properly, you have to play Mozart beforehand."[76] One

---

[76] Hans von Bülow: *Ausgewählte Schriften. 1850–1892* (Leipzig, 1911), ii, 206.

might legitimately speculate what he had in mind as fine Mozart playing, since his older contemporary, Carl Reinecke, a guardian of tradition, used so much asynchrony in performing it. In this context, it is also significant that it was Mendelssohn who gave Reinecke the opportunity to make his first important public appearance, in a Leipzig Gewandhaus concert on 16 November 1843, playing Mendelssohn's own *Serenade und Allegro giocoso* op. 43, which he would hardly have done if he found Reinecke's playing in poor taste. One other point about the *Rondo capriccioso*, not mentioned by Bülow, is the *portato* notation in the opening bar, which Mendelssohn, as a pupil (in 1824) and later a close friend of Ignaz Moscheles, surely understood as indicating asynchrony. Perhaps Mendelssohn employed improvised arpeggiation more sensitively than many of his contemporaries, but that he, or Bülow, generally played with strict vertical synchrony is implausible.

Among later 19th-century musicians who certainly used improvised arpeggiation freely was Johannes Brahms, just nine years younger than Reinecke. The virtuoso pianist Moritz Rosenthal, who was close to Brahms in the composer's later years, told his pupil Charles Rosen, "You know, Brahms let me play [his music] however I wanted [...]. He never told me I was wrong or that what I had done was incorrect. 'I have a different idea of the piece,' he would say, and he would play it for me. It was a wonderful experience."[77] He also told Rosen that "Brahms arpeggiated all the chords when playing the piano".[78] Whether or not that was an exaggeration, it certainly indicates that Brahms's arpeggiation seemed unusually extensive in the later 19th century; perhaps that he used it significantly more than Reinecke. While no criticism of Reinecke's arpeggiation has yet come to light, it was suggested in 1865 that Brahms used it excessively. After he performed his First Piano Concerto in Karlsruhe, a critic commented: "As a performer, H[er]r Brahms proved to be a very capable virtuoso; there is only one thing we would like to note in his playing: the incessant breaking of the chords at slower tempos."[79] In fact, however, since Brahms included the instruction *molto dolce ed espress.* at the first solo entry in the Adagio, he almost certainly intended this as an

---

[77] Charles Rosen and Catherine Temerso: *The Joy of Playing, the Joy of Thinking: Conversations about Art and Performance* (Paris, 2016), 8.

[78] Charles Rosen: *Critical Entertainments* (Cambridge, MA, 2000), 178 (footnote).

[79] Anon [Heinrich Kroenlein]: *Karlsruher Zeitung*, no. 265, 9 November 1865, unpaginated, [1]. See also Frithjof Haas, *Zwischen Brahms und Wagner: Der Dirgent Hermann Levi* (Zurich and Mainz, 1995), 106; and Richard Hudson: *Stolen Time: The History of Tempo Rubato* (Oxford, 1994), 333.

instruction to arpeggiate freely, despite the occasional marking of individual chords with an arpeggio sign.

An important issue arises from Brahms's evident practice in the Adagio of his First Piano Concerto: what is the significance of a composer's arpeggio markings if improvised arpeggiation was expected to be used freely? Reinecke's recording of his piano arrangement of the Vorspiel to Act V of his opera *König Manfred*[80] is particularly revealing in this respect, and offers evidence of an explicit connection between the instruction *espressivo* and broader arpeggiation, as instructed by Philip Corri almost a century earlier. Reinecke included just three arpeggiation signs in the whole piece: two in bar 26 and another in bar 50. In the first two bars, he plays the bass octaves together or almost together; from bar 3 he begins to use more noticeable, but still tight asynchrony, especially to characterize accents, and in bar 11 to executes successive chords marked *portato* also with tight asynchrony. From bar 13, however, where *espressivo* is marked, he begins to arpeggiate the four- and five-part chords much more luxuriantly. In bars 26 and 50, the chords with notated arpeggiation are not distinguishably different (indeed the second one in 26 is tighter than most). Perhaps he regarded those arpeggiations as obligatory, while the others were discretionary; what is absolutely clear, however, is that his notation does not convey his aural conception. As with Joachim, performing his own Romance in C, or Saint-Saëns, Grieg, Mahler, Debussy (all of whom employed asynchrony to a greater or lesser extent), and many other composers performing their own works, the disparities between text and performance are striking. Saint-Saëns is a particularly interesting case, since he spoke strongly against improvised arpeggiation, yet did it frequently himself.

Periodically, throughout the 19th century, arpeggiation was perceived as excessive and was criticized as a "modern" abuse; but this certainly does not mean that composers expected every chord, unless preceded by an arpeggiation sign, to be played precisely together. Such an approach would certainly have been considered inartistic. The synchronous performance of all chords not marked to be arpeggiated that became obligatory during the 20th century was another result of the misguided piety that confused composers' intentions for their notation with their expectations for its performance. Reinecke's very extensive but subtly varied use of asynchrony, which surely

---

[80] Welte piano roll. The piano score is online at https://s9.imslp.org/files/imglnks/usimg/1/11/IMSLP134675-PMLP133318-Reinecke_-_Konig_Manfred_Op93_VS_rsl2.pdf.

reflects to a considerable extent the predominant style of the early to mid-19th century, was clearly regarded as a model of classical sobriety.

The continuing use of unwritten asynchrony and arpeggiation in piano performance, into the first half of the 20th century, though with decreasing frequency, is abundantly documented in recordings.[81] Peres Da Costa tellingly observes that these recordings preserve the remains of "a practice that had already passed its zenith. In this light it is significant that Reinecke, the oldest recorded pianist, uses it most."[82] Peres Da Costa also provides a helpful summary of the varied ways in which early recorded pianists employed arpeggiation:

> On early recordings, pianists arpeggiate chords in either hand, or in both together. And most commonly, the notes are played from the lowest to the highest note. In some cases, the notes in both hands are spread simultaneously; in others, the spread commences with the lowest note in the left hand and proceeds continuously to the highest note in the right hand. The aural effect is that sometimes the highest note in the chord (the melody note) is aligned with the pulse; the accompanying note or notes anticipate it. At other times, the lowest note in the chord is aligned with the pulse, delaying the arrival of the highest note. When arpeggiation occurs in conjunction with dislocation of the hands or tempo modification, it is not always easy to discern where any of the notes lie in relation to the pulse. In these cases, the practice contributes to a sense of ambiguity, softening the edges of the rhythm and texture.[83]

## Rhythmic Flexibility

Many instances of the fluid relationship between the literal meaning of the musical notation, and the ways in which 18th- and 19th-century performers might have been expected to interpret it have been frequently touched upon in preceding chapters. In solo performance and chamber music, Classical

---

[81] Arpeggiation and extensive asynchrony between the hands is abundant, for instance, on piano rolls by Saint-Säens (b. 1835), Carl Reinecke (b. 1824), and Theodor Leschetizky (b. 1830), available on CD Archiphon-106. See also Robert Philip: *Early Recording and Musical Style: Changing Tastes in Instrumental Performance 1900–1950* (Cambridge, 1992).
[82] Peres Da Costa: *Off the Record*, 187.
[83] Peres Da Costa: *Off the Record*, 101f.

and Romantic notions of musical rhetoric undoubtedly excluded the idea that notated rhythms should, in general, be immune from expressive manipulation, though in particular contexts a degree of strictness may have been required for the envisaged effect. Musical figures involving pairs of notes (with or without dots of prolongation), or figures with an upbeat were particularly prone to be modified in performance. Some of this modification might occur at the instinct of the performer; but there were several circumstances in which specific types of rhythmic alteration appear to have been customary, or even obligatory, and others where, by convention, composers employed misleading notation.

## Dotted Notes and Triplets

The question of whether a dotted rhythm was intended to be assimilated to a simultaneous triplet rhythm in another part was not uncontentious in the second half of the 18th century, as the move towards greater precision in notation began to gather pace. Many writers of instruction books in that period showed their awareness that composers notated the phrase shown in Ex. 14.16a as in Ex. 14.16b; and some asserted unreservedly that when triplets and dotted figures occurred together, the latter should be played with a triplet rhythm.

Ex. 14.16 a–b.

This was stated in the first edition of Löhlein's *Clavier-Schule* in 1765,[84] but criticism by Agricola, who observed that "This is true only in the utmost speed,"[85] led to the revised text in the 1773 edition of Löhlein's treatise: "If triplets occur in fast tempo against dotted notes, they will be distributed as follows [Ex. 14.17]:

---

[84] Löhlein: *Clavier-Schule*, 70.
[85] Agricola: 'Kurze Nachrichten von den schönen Künsten', in F. Nicolai (ed.), *Allgemeine deutsche Bibliothek*, x/1 (1769), 242f.

Ex. 14.17 Löhlein: *Clavier-Schule*, 2nd edn (1773), 68.

Otherwise, the sixteenth must really be played, in accordance with its duration, after the last note of the triplet."[86]

It seems very rarely, if ever, to have occurred to 18th- and early-19th-century composers, certainly before the 1830s, to use the notation shown in Ex. 14.16a for unequal triplet rhythms, even in slow pieces. I have been unable to find any 18th-century examples. Despite Agricola's comment, they conventionally used dotted figures. Indeed, given Agricola's contact with J. S. Bach, his statement seems more like wishful thinking than a documentation of accepted 18th-century practice, since Bach routinely employed dotted figures where a 2:1 ratio was expected, even in compound meters such as $\frac{9}{8}$ (e.g., in the autograph manuscript of the cantata "Unser Mund sei voll Lachens" BWV 110, c. 1725). C. P. E. Bach, in his treatment of *Vortrag*, stated: "Since triplets have begun to be used frequently in so-called common or $\frac{4}{4}$ metre, as well as in $\frac{2}{4}$ or $\frac{3}{4}$ metre, one finds many pieces which, instead of being notated in these metres, might often be more conveniently set in $\frac{12}{8}$, $\frac{9}{8}$, or $\frac{6}{8}$. One would then distribute the notes against the other part as shown in Fig. XII [Ex. 14.18]."[87]

Ex. 14.18 C. P. E. Bach: *Versuch*, 1st edn, Table VI, Fig. XII.

---

[86] Löhlein: *Clavier-Schule*, 2nd edn (Leipzig and Züllischau, 1773), 68.
[87] Bach: *Versuch*, i, 128f. The passage is retained unchanged in the 1787 3rd edn.

Bach's example shows that dotted figures and pairs of equal notes in these contexts could both indicate a 2:1 ratio. Marpurg, a couple of years later, explained that this was "always" (allezeit)[88] to be done in such circumstances, giving examples both of equal notes and dotted notes against triplets in 4/4 indicating the same as the passage written in 12/8 (Ex. 14.19).

Ex. 14.19  Marpurg: *Anleitung*, Table 1, Exx. 42a & b, 43.

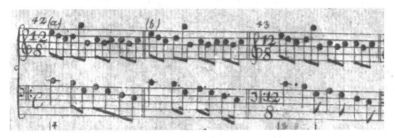

Many cases occur in Haydn, in passages such as Ex. 14.20, from the last movement of the String Quartet op. 74 no. 2, especially since this is a Presto, or in the first movement of op. 77 no. 1 (Ex. 14.21).

Ex. 14.20  Haydn: String Quartet op. 74/2/iv.

---

[88] Marpurg: *Anleitung*, 24.

Ex. 14.21  Haydn: String Quartet op. 77/1/ii.

But in the first movement of op. 74 no. 3 (Ex. 14.22), assimilation was almost certainly not envisaged, and Haydn may, on the contrary, have expected over-dotting to emphasize the difference between the triplets and the dotted figure, since he marked the dotted motif to be played *sul' una corda* and probably saw it as a sliding effect of the "anticipation grace" type.[89]

Ex. 14.22  Haydn: String Quartet op. 74/3/i.

[89] See Ch. 13, p. 726.

Assimilation of the dotted rhythm to a triplet was certainly intended by Haydn's pupil Pleyel in his 1787 Prussian quartets when, for instance, he gave the double-stop shown in Ex. 14.23 to the cello.

Ex. 14.23 Pleyel: Prussian Quartets, book 3/2/i.

There are also instances in Beethoven's mature music where the dotted notation was surely expected to stand for a 2:1 ratio (Ex. 14.24), but also many others where perhaps the notes were not intended to coincide exactly.

Ex. 14.24 Beethoven: String Quartet op. 59/2/ii.

In the Piano Trio op. 97, we see him inconsistently struggling towards a more precise notation, resulting in curious anomalies (Ex. 14.25a–b).

ASYNCHRONY, ARPEGGIATION, AND FLEXIBLE RHYTHM  867

Ex. 14.25 a–b. Beethoven: Piano Trio op. 97 Andante Cantabile, b. 172ff.
(*a*) Autograph; (*b*) Breitkopf & Härtel Gesamtausgabe.

(*a*)

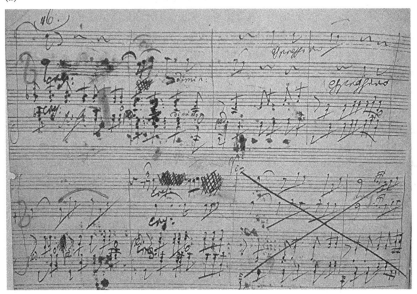

(*b*)

Since, in the first edition, there was no published score, and none of the performers could see what the others were playing, it is almost certain that the strings would have assimilated their eighths (whether triplets or not) and the cello's sixteenth to the triplets in the piano part, and in bars 186–90, their dotted rhythms, which was surely what Beethoven envisaged; of course, always bearing in mind that the modern concept of perfect vertical synchrony was not expected.

Assimilation was clearly envisaged in many instances by Schubert, even in his last works, as the notation of passages in the piano part of *Winterreise* demonstrates (Ex. 14.26a–b).

Ex. 14.26 a–b. Schubert: *Winterreise*. (*a*) No. 4: "Erstarrung"; (*b*) No. 6: "Wasserflut".

But in his case, too, there are ambiguous situations where assimilation may not always be appropriate, for example in the first movement of the Piano Trio in B flat (Ex. 14.27) where the dotted figures will probably have been executed with various ratios according to context by the performers, who could each see only their own part.[90]

---

[90] The string parts were not included with the piano part in editions at that time.

Ex. 14.27  Schubert: Piano Trio op. 99/i.

Composers born in the 19th century were much less likely to adopt this type of ambiguous notation. Mendelssohn and Schumann, for instance, sometimes employed modern triplet notation in such circumstances (Ex. 14.28a–b), although Mendelssohn could still use rhythms more impressionistically (Ex. 14.27c).

Ex. 14.28a  Mendelssohn: "Italian" Symphony op. 90/iv.

Ex. 14.28b  Schumann: Second Symphony op. 61/ii.

Ex. 14.28c  Mendelssohn: *Lied ohne Worte* op. 85 no. 1.

870 CLASSICAL AND ROMANTIC PERFORMING PRACTICE

Examples from Berlioz and, especially, Brahms show these composers using modern notation for uneven triplets and apparently making a deliberate feature of the contrast between the triplet and the dotted figures (Ex. 14.29a–b).

**Ex. 14.29a**  Berlioz: *Romeo and Juliet* op. 17 pt. 2.

Ex. 14.29b Brahms: Second Symphony op. 73/ii.

Not all 19th-century music in which a distinction between triplet figures and dotted figures seems intended, however, would appear to have been understood in that sense by contemporary performers. In "Ah non credea", from the beginning of the finale of *La sonnambula*, Bellini employed a mixture of triplets and normal dotted figures over an accompaniment of almost continual triplets, and he even used the notation shown in Ex. 14.16a on a couple of occasions. But when Adelina Patti recorded the piece in 1905, she assimilated all the dotted figures to the accompanying triplets, including not only figures of a dotted eighth and sixteenth, but also those of a dotted quarter and eighth (Ex. 14.30). It is noteworthy, too, that she several times sang the rhythm of Ex. 14.16a in places where Bellini notated a pair of equal eighths, recalling C. P. E. Bach's instruction in Ex. 14.18.

**Ex. 14.30** Bellini: *La sonnambula*, Act II Finale, "Ah non credea" (bottom stave) and Adelina Patti's interpretation (employing Corri's "leaping" and "anticipation grace" notation).

A similar disregard for the literal meaning of dotted figures can be demonstrated in at least one instance of an important later 19th-century composer performing his own music. In Edvard Grieg's Humoresque op. 6 no. 2, which he recorded in 1903, two bars of dotted eighth-sixteenth figures are followed by two bars of triplets with a similar melodic outline and the same bass line as the preceding bars; this pattern is then repeated a minor third lower (bb. 21–28). Grieg clearly plays the dotted figures in bars 21–22 and 25–26 in triplet rhythm.

## Over-Dotting

The question of whether dotted figures should be over-dotted was often addressed by theorists. Leopold Mozart instructed that "One always does better if one plays the note after the dot somewhat late." He also remarked that when dotted notes are followed by two short ones within a slur: "One must always rather hold the dot longer than too short."[91] Agricola similarly advised: "The short notes that follow a dot, especially sixteenths or thirty-seconds, also the eighths in allabreve, whether in slow or fast tempos, and whether there is one or more of them, are always executed very rapidly and at the very end of their duration: the one before the dot, on the other hand, is held correspondingly longer."[92] Both of these musicians also applied the same principle to reverse dotted figures. Mozart stated: "If the second note is dotted, then the first must be quickly slurred onto the dotted note, but the dotted note must not be accented, but played warmly sustained with a gentle decrescendo."[93] Agricola specified that in these figures the first note should be "as short as possible".[94] Mozart and Agricola also recommended the same for dotted figures in which there were several short notes. Agricola illustrated both types (Ex. 14.31a–b).

Ex. 14.31 a–b. Agricola: *Anleitung*, 134.

(a)

[91] Mozart: *Versuch*, 144f.
[92] Agricola: *Anleitung*, 133f.
[93] Mozart: *Versuch*, 145.
[94] Agricola: *Anleitung*, 133f.

Ex. 14.31 Continued

(b)

A similar treatment of short-long dotted figures is recommended in Dotzauer's 1825 *Violoncell-Schule*, where he instructed that "the sixteenth-note before the dotted eighth should be treated as if it were a *grace note* [*Vorschlag*]".[95] (For discussion of accentuation in reverse dotted figures see below.)

Instructions for long-short over-dotting occur in other 18th- and early-19th-century treatises. Löhlein stipulated without qualification in his *Clavier-Schule* that the one should "hold the dot approximately half as long again as it should be according to the notation",[96] and he applied the same principle where a rest took the place of the dot, giving the examples in Ex. 14.32a–b.

Ex. 14.32 a–b. Löhlein: *Clavier-Schule*, 69.

(a)

(b)

[95] Dotzauer: *Violoncell-Schule*, 19.
[96] Löhlein: *Clavier-Schule*, 69.

In his *Anweisung zum Violinspielen* he explained: "If there are many dotted figures in a sad and, in any case, moderate and pathetic melody, the rule of performance style demands that one lengthens the dot by half its worth and performs the following note that much shorter."[97] He applied this to an Adagio in F sharp minor (no. XVI) and a Maestoso in D major (no. XVIII), which he described as having a type of melody "peculiar to marches".[98] At the beginning of the 19th century, J. F. Schubert recommended similar over-dotting in vocal music, in the context of "heavy and light performance style", also where a rest took the place of a dot, noting: "in passionate passages the note with the dot will always be held longer than its value and the following note will be performed that much shorter".[99]

It was not uncommon for 18th-century composers to employ dots in a very imprecise manner. Examples of this may be found, for instance, in Clementi's music. In *La Chasse* op. 16 and the Sonata in F op. 26 he used a single dot to lengthen a note by less than half its value. In the Sonata in G op. 40 no. 1 a dot lengthens the note by two-thirds, but in the second movement of the same Sonata a double dot is used for the same purpose (Ex. 14.33a–b).

Ex. 14.33 a–d. Clementi. (*a*) *La Chasse* op. 16, 1st edn, p. 3; (*b*) Piano Sonata op. 26/iii; (*c*) Piano Sonata op. 40/1/i; (*d*) Piano Sonata op. 40/1/ii.

---

[97] Löhlein: *Anweisung zum Violinspielen*, 30.
[98] Löhlein: *Anweisung zum Violinspielen*, 84.
[99] Schubert, *Singe-Schule*, 131.

**Ex. 14.33** Continued

Some 18th-century composers, however, including Mozart, more frequently differentiated between single and double dots, and, in many cases, they took trouble to indicate rests instead of dots (see Ex. 6.26). Yet it seems rather unlikely that Mozart would have expected a rhythmically precise performance of the dotted figures rather than an over-dotted one in such contexts, for instance, in the first section of his Adagio and Fugue, with its strong resemblance to the old French overture (Ex. 14.34). He may well have felt that a double dot would elicit too sharp an effect and, following his father's advice that it was "always better" to leave the dot somewhat later than its notated length, preferred to trust the performer to find the right rhythmic relationship.

**Ex. 14.34** Mozart: Adagio and Fugue K. 546.

ASYNCHRONY, ARPEGGIATION, AND FLEXIBLE RHYTHM 877

An increasing number of later composers, from Beethoven onwards, seem to have differentiated between various treatments of such figures. In the movement of the String Quartet op. 59 no. 2 where assimilation to triplets was certainly envisaged (see Ex. 14.24), Beethoven uses three different notations for a dotted figure with a sixteenth as the second note, evidently to achieve varied articulation (Ex. 14.35a).

Ex. 14.35 a–b. Beethoven: (*a*) op. 59/2/ii, 1st edn; (*b*) op. 59/2/ii, b. 29ff. [Molto adagio]

Such care over details might argue that everything should be performed as exactly as possible in such cases; it may even be taken as an argument against the assimilation of the triplets, but this would be to ignore the overwhelming evidence for a substantial degree of rhythmic freedom as an essential element of beautiful performance. Here, and in passages such as Ex. 14.35b, performers of Beethoven's time would probably have over-dotted everything, sometimes more and sometimes less.

Some 19th-century writers continued to recommend over-dotting in particular cases, for instance the mathematician and musician August Crelle in 1823, who believed that "In any case, insofar as it is appropriate to the emotional character [*Affecte*], the performance gains if one makes the long notes even longer." He gave an example of single dotted figures performed with double dots, but observed: "If, however, the composer writes in a very correct manner one must play the passage just as it is written."[100] He did not explain, though, how one was expected to know whether the composer writes in a very correct manner.

At about the same time, Franz Schubert made an interesting distinction in *Alfonso und Estrella* between his notation for orchestral instruments and for solo singers. The instruments have double-dotted figures while the voices are left with single dots, but it is implausible that he intended them to perform the rhythms differently; he evidently expected the singers to over-dot in this type of passage and spared himself the trouble of indicating it, but took the precaution of warning the orchestra (Ex. 14.36a). A similar instance occurs in his last completed opera, *Fierrabras* (Ex. 14.36b).

Ex. 14.36 a–b. Schubert. (*a*) *Alfonso und Estrella*, no. 10; (*b*) *Fierrabras*, no. 6 (Scene xii).

[100] Crelle: *Einiges*, 77.

Ex. 14.36 Continued

(*b*)

In Rossini's music, too, there is sometimes a lack of correspondence between the dotted rhythms of the accompaniment and those of the singer, for instance in the aria "Ah si per voi già sento nuovo valor" from *Otello*, as illustrated by García, where the singer would surely over-dot, while the orchestra needed to be alerted to this (Ex. 14.37).

Ex. 14.37 García: *École*, ii, 22.

In similar pieces of a martial or majestic character it seems clear that the convention of over-dotting remained strong throughout the 19th century, especially in the Italian operatic repertoire. But it was not only in such genres of music, where composers conventionally left much in the way of detail to be supplied by the performer, that the practice persisted. Even a composer whose notation might be expected to have been particularly exact could, as late as the 1880s, call for performers to apply over-dotting. According to Heinrich Porges, Wagner intervened at one point during a rehearsal of

*Parsifal* (Ex. 14.38) to request: "hold the quarter with the dot longer; the sixteenth can then be somewhat shorter".[101]

**Ex. 14.38** Wagner: *Parsifal*, rehearsal number 74.

Early recordings demonstrate the widespread survival of the practice of over-dotting into the 20th century. In some recordings of Classical repertoire, it corresponds closely with the historical evidence. In recordings of Mozart (Minuets from K. 421 and 428) by the Klingler Quartet, for instance,

---

[101] Porges in the piano score which he used during rehearsals for the première of *Parsifal*, quoted in Martin Geck and Egon Voss, eds., *Richard Wagner: Sämtliche Werke*, xxx: *Dokumente zur Entstehung und erster Aufführung des Bühnenweihfestspiels Parsifal* (Mainz, 1970), 179.

over-dotting is pervasive, also when the dotted note is followed by two faster notes (e.g., K. 428 bars 12, 14, and 15).

Despite the rarity of instructions to over-dot as a matter of course in later 19th-century documentary sources, recordings also demonstrate that the practice remained strong in early-20th-century performances of Romantic repertoire. As Robert Philip remarked, early recordings "demonstrate that the reason why most writers did not comment on the interpretation of dotted rhythms is that the practice of overdotting was universal in the early 20th century."[102] He provided many examples from recordings made in the 1920s and 1930s (pre-1920s recordings were still much less accessible when Philip's book was written, and the Klingler Quartet recordings seem not to have been available to him). His examples also chart the gradual adoption of a much stricter approach to rhythm during those decades.[103] Over-dotting and the related hurrying of up-beat figures can frequently be heard in orchestral recordings of Elgar's music conducted by the composer. In the case of his 1926 recording of the "Enigma" Variations, his satisfaction with the places where these practices occur prominently is demonstrated by his own comments.[104]

Even stronger evidence that later 19th-century composers not only acquiesced in the flexible treatment of dotted figures, but in fact expected it, is contained in a 1933 review by Marion Margaret Scott, in *The Musical Times*. Referring to a performance of Brahms's G major Violin Sonata op. 78 by Isolde Menges (b. 1893) and Harold Samuel (b. 1879), she drew attention to their rhythmically exact execution of dotted rhythms in the Adagio. Scott, who knew Clara Schumann's pupil Fanny Davies personally, had probably been present at a concert given by Marie Soldat and Fanny Davies during Soldat's last concert tour to London in 1930; in any case, she had evidently heard Soldat's performance of the sonata, for, having commented in her review of the 1933 performance that "one might occasionally disagree with a fresh interpretation put on a familiar passage", she continued:

> As an example of disagreement, one may cite the treatment of the middle section of the Adagio in the G major Violin and Pianoforte Sonata. The tradition for this passage is to lengthen by a little the dotted quavers and

---

[102] Philip: *Early Recordings*, 76.
[103] Philip: *Early Recordings*, 77–93; and 'Traditional Habits of Performance in Early Twentieth-Century Recordings of Beethoven' in Stowell (ed.), *Performing Beethoven*, 198–99.
[104] Philip: *Early Recordings*, 81f.

correspondingly shorten the semiquavers—a tradition followed by Madam Marie Soldat—who (I have been told) was Brahms's favourite violinist for his sonatas. Its effect was noble and incisive. Miss Menges and Mr Harold Samuel, on the contrary, hewed out the notes at their exact face value till this admirer of theirs mentally trotted alongside saying *one*-two-three-*four*, *one*-two-three-*four*.[105]

Soldat had, indeed, often played Brahms's sonatas with him, so there can be little doubt that her over-dotting reflected the composer's own treatment of that passage.

Similar flexibility was evidently inherent in the performance of short-long pairs of notes (Lombard rhythms or scotch snaps). The preservation of 18th-century practice into the early 20th century in such figures is demonstrated by Karl Klingler's performance in the Trio section of his recording of the Menuetto from Mozart's String Quartet in D minor K. 421. He played the sixteenths much shorter than written, as instructed by Leopold Mozart, Agricola, and Dotzauer.[106] They sound almost as if they were notated as *grace-notes*, and so light that it almost creates an effect of pre-beat performance. This manner of performing Lombard rhythms seems not to have been confined to the German tradition, for a similar execution can be heard in the 1920 recording by the Flonzaley Quartet (whose members were strongly connected with Franco-Belgian practice), where Alfredo Betti also shortened the first note, though not quite as much as Klingler. By the time the Amadeus Quartet made their 1954 recording, the tradition had been forgotten, or rejected, and the unhistorical modern orthodoxy of rhythmic exactness established.

## Agogic Nuance

During the second half of the 20th century, when conventions of performance prioritized a stricter adherence to the composer's text than had ever existed before, anything but a *literally* imperceptible deviation from notated rhythms came to be seen more as a lapse of taste or attention than an artistic choice. The question of where formal inequality and agogic accentuation

---

[105] M. M. R. [Marion Margaret Scott]: *The Musical Times*, lxxiv (1933), 548.
[106] See also p. 660.

were inherent in the notation, therefore, became a battleground, especially in "early music" performance and scholarship.[107] This often focused on the circumstances in which French *inégale* might be appropriate, for instance in J. S. Bach's music, assuming that the guidelines offered by treatise writers really represented what they appear to describe, rather than being a vain attempt to reduce the subtleties of artistic performance to a set of rules.

Since the first edition of this book was written, the increasing availability of early recordings, and their rapidly burgeoning study, has revealed even more clearly the immensity of the gulf between what theorists wrote and what performers did. The recordings demonstrate unequivocally that documentary information about how and where apparently equal notes might have been performed unequally is a very inadequate, indeed misleading, guide to the complexities of rhythmic flexibility in performance as it was practised during the later 19th century (and surely also in earlier periods). As discussed in Chapter 2,[108] documentary sources make clear that the lengthening of melodically or harmonically important notes remained an aspect of beautiful performance throughout the period under consideration, though not in the rather mechanistic manner implied by French theory or in Quantz's *Versuch*, which, like all attempts to describe performance in words, sought to impose order on practices that will have been infinitely varied and flexible. Treatises, even the most ambitious ones, were aimed primarily at educating students and amateurs in the basic requirements of notation and technique and, if they mentioned rhythmic flexibility at all, it was only in the most generalized terms. As Löhlein, at the end of his chapter on "correct note-reading", remarked: "One could still say much more in this chapter, but that is not appropriate in a book of this kind. Perhaps I have already done too much. But in any case, beauty in the arts cannot be entirely determined by rules."[109] Much the same was acknowledged in treatises by A. E. Müller, Hummel, Spohr, and many others, who saw aural experience as the only sure means of acquiring beauty of performance. Some later 19th-century writers, most notably Lussy and Riemann, tried to describe these and other expressive practices in greater detail, or even, in Riemann's case, to prescribe them in editions; but their words and symbols fail to prepare us for the richness and complexity of the practices revealed by early recordings. Aural experience of

---

[107] See, e.g., Frederick Neumann: 'The French "Inégales", Quantz, and Bach', *Journal of the American Musicological Society*, xviii (1965), 313–58.
[108] See Ch. 2, "Agogic Accent".
[109] Löhlein: *Clavier-Schule*, 70.

great performers from the period before recording is, of course, irrevocably lost to us, but knowledge of the situations in which notation was, by convention, meant to convey something beyond its literal meaning can at least free us from the erroneous 20th-century notion that a performance faithful to the score is faithful to the composer's expectations for its performance.

Alongside the flexibility of rhythm that was expected in the execution of dotted figures, successive notes of equal value were also subject to certain generally understood principles during the Classical period. The most significant of these were that *staccato* marks encouraged equality and that the first note of slurred pairs and short slurred figures implied a somewhat longer duration than the written value, which was balanced by a slight hurrying of the following note or notes. Leopold Mozart, for instance, stated that the performance of slurred groups *always* involved inequality. He instructed: "The first of two notes in one bowstroke is accented more strongly, also held slightly longer; the second, however, is slurred on to it very quietly and rather late".[110] Later he reiterated even more emphatically:

> The first of two, three, four, or even more notes, slurred together, must at all times be stressed more strongly and sustained a little longer; those following must diminish in volume and be slurred on somewhat later, but this must be carried out with such good judgment that the bar-length is not altered in the smallest degree. The somewhat longer duration of the first note must, by an appropriate placement of the notes that are slurred on to it a little more quickly, be made not only acceptable to the ear, but also quite pleasant.[111]

Eight decades later, Bartolomeo Campagnoli included a succinct paraphrase of Mozart's instructions in his *Nouvelle Méthode* of 1824, instructing: "The first of two, three or four slurred notes must always be accented and sustained somewhat, and the others follow somewhat later, whereby the tone also decreases without, however, interrupting the uniformity of the tempo."[112]

Even though there seem to be no comparable mandatory directives in later 19th-century sources, it would not be safe to assume that this practice has no relevance beyond the mid-18th century, or applies only to performing

---

[110] Mozart: *Versuch*, 123.
[111] Mozart: *Versuch*, 145.
[112] Campagnoli: *Nouvelle Méthode*, v, 19, §60.

practices during the Classical period. Later writers occasionally alluded briefly to rhythmic flexibility in similar contexts. Moscheles in the 1820s observed that, in *legato* passages, the first note of each group of four sixteenths or three triplet eighths might receive both accent and lengthening.[113] And Charles de Bériot in the 1850s explained that a composer might write successive eighths when a delicate inequality was needed, because they "do not always mark the long and short notes, for fear that the melody would take too rhythmical a form".[114] There is, in fact, clear evidence that closely related practices in the treatment of notes of nominally equal value continued into the early 20th century. Karl Klingler, writing in the middle years of the 20th century about the performance of Rode's Caprices, referred to the unequal performance of notes of the same value, commenting that it "did not need to be explained to the average musician from Rode's time until the turn of the twentieth century. Today, however, it has evidently been forgotten that, with such notes of nominally equal value, an agreeable, imperceptible hastening that makes up for what was lost, was self-evident."[115] Although this passage does not refer specifically to the execution of short slurred figures, the early-20th-century recordings of the Klingler Quartet demonstrate unequivocally that in the performance of music by Mozart and Beethoven, Karl Klingler's execution of slurred pairs of equal-length notes and other short slurred figures corresponds closely with Leopold Mozart's and Campagnoli's instructions for rhythmical nuance. Klingler's unequal slurs (surely reflecting the practice of his master, Joachim, with whose quartet he had played viola just a few years earlier) are particularly prominent in the Menuetto from Mozart's E flat major String Quartet K. 428, which has many slurred pairs. The degree of inequality in his execution of these figures is extremely varied, according to metrical, harmonic, and structural context. How close this manner of performance may have been to that of Mozart's time is indeterminable, but there can be little doubt that it reflects long-standing practice. Another of Joachim's pupils, Marie Soldat, plays slurred pairs even more unequally in her recording of the first movement of Mozart's A Major Violin Concerto K. 218. The connection of both these musicians with Joachim, whose mentors Joseph Böhm, Ferdinand David, and Mendelssohn linked him, at one remove, with Beethoven, Spohr, and Zelter, suggests continuity

---

[113] Moscheles: *Studien* op. 70, 5. See Ch. 2, p. 69.
[114] Bériot: *Méthode*, 232. See Ch. 4, p. 207, for the full quotation.
[115] Karl Klingler: 'Anmerkungen an Hand der 24 Capricen von Pierre Rode' in „*Über die Grundlagen des Violinspiels*", 171.

of tradition in this respect. None of Joachim's five recordings provides an opportunity to hear his execution of such figures in Classical repertoire, but his very flexible treatment of notated rhythms in general is suggestive. In the Mozart recordings of Carl Reinecke, too, the unequalizing of slurred pairs and short figures is pervasive, and his immensely varied nuancing of long and short may provide a persuasive model for executing such figures in Classical works. In Reinecke's many recordings of later repertoire, including his own compositions, the rhythmic flexibility is—like Joachim's—freer, tied more to phrasing within the context of an overarching *legato*. These features are less pronounced in recordings by younger players, but still, in numerous recordings made before 1930, notably different from later practice. Even in orchestral performance, where wind instruments had solos, they exercised their soloist's prerogative to modify notated rhythms. One among many passages of this kind occurs in the second movement of Beethoven's Fifth Symphony, in Nikisch's 1913 recording with the Berlin Philharmonic Orchestra, where at bars 127–42, clarinet, bassoon, flute, and oboe employ subtle and not so subtle rhythmic flexibility. And even as late as 1933, in John Barbirolli's recording of Tchaikovsky's *Swan Lake* Ballet Suite, the oboe soloist in No. 1 (probably Léon Goossens) plays with striking rhythmic flexibility.

\* \* \*

The practices discussed in this chapter were connected both with "correct" and "beautiful" performance. As part of the former, students will have been expected, once they had gained a certain degree of fluency, to recognize that important melodic notes were often expected not to be precisely synchronous with the accompaniment; that, in certain contexts, dotted rhythms were required to be performed differently from their notional value; and that equal value notes were to be played unequally. As talented students progressed, they will have understood that these deviations from strict observance of the notated text were an essential component of effective characterization and emotional expression, and will have learned, from the experience of hearing accomplished performers, how they could be employed artistically. There can be no doubt that, like their Baroque predecessors, Classical and Romantic composers, from Haydn, Mozart, and Beethoven to Brahms, Mahler, and Elgar, expected and required performers to exercise these rhetorical artistic freedoms, without which the spirit of the music could not be conveyed to the listener. During the 20th century such practices, although rooted in long-standing traditions of performance, were gradually forgotten. In fact, their employment was actively suppressed, as the composer's score came increasingly to be seen as literal and prescriptive—in a way that the composers never envisaged—rather than flexible and indicative. Even in the 1930s, some musicians, such as Fanny Davies and Marie Soldat, remained true to the older conception of notation, while younger performers put their faith in the authority of the text. At that stage, there were still critics of the literalist mentality. Not only did Marion Margaret Scott criticize the strict realization of Brahms's dotted rhythms, she also, in the same article, wrote condescendingly about a performance by violinist Frederick Grinke (1911–1987) and pianist Dorothy Manly, noting that it "pleased by its modest competence. Neat as to technique, the players had so eliminated all superfluity from their performance that their Mozart sonata struck one as less interesting than they or it deserved to be." In the second half of the 20th century, however, the older practices slipped inexorably from living memory. Even in the 1980s, early recordings, if they were heard at all, seemed bizarre or even laughable to most musicians. It is only during the last twenty-five years that their large-scale rediscovery and study has provided a musical Rosetta Stone to unlock forgotten meanings in pre-modern notation.

# 15
# Sliding Effects

Sliding effects in musical performance are documented as early as the 17th century, for instance in Giovanni Doni's reference to "the continuous raising and lowering of the voice which imitates the sound of a bowed violin string when the finger is simultaneously moved down".[1] Abundant written evidence, from the 18th century to the present day, much of it expressed in trenchant language, documents changing aesthetic and technical opinions, making it clear that the employment of these effects has varied greatly over time and in differing traditions of performance.

## Terminology

The Italian term *portamento*, or *portamento di voce*, literally "carrying" or "supporting" the voice, was recognized internationally in musical terminology, although not always with the same signification. A direct equivalent in French was *port de voix*; in German *Tragen der Stimme*, more commonly *Tragen der Töne*, *Tragen des Tones*, or sometimes naturalized as *Portament*. Other words that either indicated or implied an audible slide in German, French, Italian, and English were *ziehen*,[2] *durchziehen*, *durchschleifen*, *durchtragen*, *glisser*, *glissando*, *strascinando*, *drag*, or *dragg*,[3] *glide*, *slide*, *slur*. In piano music, *portamento* could be used to mean the same as *portato*, for example by Brahms,[4] and it is still occasionally used in that sense. Expressions, such as *cercar della nota*, *messa di voce crescente*, or *messa di voce decrescente*, were used, in relation to vocal music, to describe various ways of connecting

---

[1] Giovanni Battista Doni: *Trattato della musica scenica* (c. 1635–39) (Rome, 2018), 134.
[2] *Ziehen* is used by C. P. E. Bach as an equivalent to *legato*. In later sources, for instance an account of native singing in the Polynesian Marquesas Islands (*Allgemeine musikalische Zeitung*, vii [1805], 269) it is explicitly used to describe an audible slide.
[3] John Galliard: *Observations on the Florid Song* (London, 1743).
[4] Brahms: *Briefwechsel*, vi, 146.

notes at different pitches; but as with so much terminology, the usage of these phrases by different authors is often inconsistent.

*Glissando*, invented in the first half of the 19th century by "italianizing" the French *glisser*, apparently to describe the effect of sliding the back of the fingers on the piano,[5] has also been used to characterize sliding effects on other instruments and sometimes in singing. In the 20th century, *portamento* and *glissando* were sometimes differentiated, as in a 1929 reference to "The glissando of string instruments or the singer's portamento".[6] Around the same time, the third edition of *Grove's Dictionary* gave four possible meanings for *Glissando*: (1) sliding with the back of the finger on the piano; (2) a similar effect on the harp; (3) on strings, "a prolonged *portamento*"; (4) on the trombone, "much used in music of the "Jazz" type".[7] Sometimes they were used synonymously, as in an article from 1941.[8] Continuing confusion over the implications of these terms, inevitably reflecting the complexity of their historical usage, is revealed by Internet searching; in 2015, for instance, an enigmatic response to the question "What is the difference between portamento and glissando?": "Glissando is a discrete portamento whereas portamento is a continuous glissando."[9]

## Types of Vocal *Portamento* and Their Execution

During the 18th and 19th centuries, *portamento* had two basic connotations; both implied a smooth connection of one sound with another, but this connection could either be seen simply as *legato* or as a linking of different notes by a more or less rapid audible slide through the intervening pitches. J. B. Lasser ambiguously defined *Tragen der Stimme* in singing as "to drag [*schleifen*] one note into the other without stopping, without hearing anything empty in between; this happens when you let the previous note sound until the next one responds, with alternating strength and weakness of the notes themselves".[10] He also used *messa di voce crescente* and *messa di voce*

---

[5] Czerny: *Pianoforte-Schule*, ii, 23.
[6] Siegfried Nadel: 'Hugo Riemann und Karl Stumpf', *Zeitschrift für Musik*, xcvi (1929), 383.
[7] H. C. Colles: 'Glissando' in *Grove Dictionary*, 3rd edn (London, 1928), ii, 397.
[8] See below, pp. 951–52.
[9] Stack Exchange, Music Practice & Theory (2014–2015): 'What Is the Difference Between Portamento and Glissando?', https://music.stackexchange.com/questions/27056/what-is-the-difference-between-portamento-and-glissando [accessed 21 June 2022].
[10] Lasser: *Vollständige Anleitung zur Singkunst*, 154. The German word *schleifen* need not necessarily describe an audible slide.

*decrescente*, however, unambiguously to signify audible sliding. Domenico Corri, writing in English, gave a definition of *portamento di voce* (which he regarded as "the perfection of vocal music") that comprises both a dynamic effect and an audible liaison: "the swelling and dying of the voice, the sliding and blending one note into another with delicacy and expression".[11] The former effect—the *messa di voce* on a single note—which involves no sliding was often seen as an important aspect of *portamento*, for example by J. F. Schubert (b. 1770), who simply stated: "This is the basis of *portamento di voce*" (Ex. 15.1).[12]

Ex. 15.1 J. F. Schubert: *Singe-Schule*, 23.

Where *portamento* or other terms were explicitly used for sliding effects in vocal music, there were fundamentally three ways in which these were executed:

(1) an uninterrupted connection between two notes at different pitches sung to the same syllable;
(2) a connection from a very short lower note (generally not notated) to a higher one on the same syllable;
(3) a connection between two notes on different pitches and different syllables, made by sliding rapidly from the note of the first syllable to sound the pitch of the note for the following syllable just before pronouncing it.

The relationship of the first type to simple *legato* was equivocal, since a true *legato* in singing, especially between distant intervals, is scarcely possible without some degree of audible connection, so the issue of whether the slide should be virtually imperceptible, or expressive, was a matter of technique and taste. This seems to have been taken for granted in many treatises. Corri referred to that kind of *portamento* as if it were a normal component of fine singing, but also, like Galliard, he used the term *drag*, probably to describe an intensified version of the ordinary *portamento*. This is implied

---

[11] D. Corri: *Singer's Preceptor*, 3.
[12] Schubert: *Singe-Schule*, 23.

by his observation: "Singers are of too [sic] sorts, those of Taste, and those of Knowledge; the attention of the former is entirely given to Graces, as dragging, shakes, turns, &. at every note." His immediately preceding paragraph included the warning that "as too much Honey will be apt to cloy, so too much of the Italian Taste of dragging Notes as if from the very bottom of the Stomach, may too much resemble that retrograde motion it is sometimes subject to, and which would be indelicate to express in broader terms."[13] J. F. Schubert, who discussed expressive sliding between two notes under the term *cercar della nota*, perhaps when it was more prominent than the normal *portamento*, described it as a practice "which is now common", consisting of "a gentle imperceptible raising and lowering of the voice from one tone to another", as when a violinist "draws together two different notes with one finger on a string, and melts them into each other". He gave examples, without words, on various intervals ascending and descending, including semitones, and signified the slides with slanting lines, explaining in a footnote that no sign existed for "melting the notes into each other" (Ex. 15.2).[14]

Ex. 15.2 Schubert: *Singe-Schule*, 57.

The other two procedures are more technical in their execution and therefore more frequently described by theorists. In the early 1780s, Corri included examples of the second and third techniques in the introductory "Explanation of the Graces" in his *Select Collection*. He specified them with grace notes, explaining that their execution "ought to be so rapid that, while the effect is felt, the ear shall yet be unable to determine the character of the sounds or to distinguish them from the predominant note[;] by no effort whatever indeed can they be rendered totally imperceptible, or if they could, they would not then exist. But the more imperceptible they are, the more

---

[13] D. Corri: *Singer's Preceptor*, 63.
[14] Schubert: *Singe-Schule*, 57.

happy is the execution, the more perfect the union, and the more delicate the effect"[15] (Ex. 15.3a).

Ex. 15.3a  Domenico Corri: *A Select Collection*, i, 8.

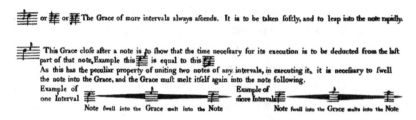

In his later *Singer's Preceptor*, he called these the *leaping grace* and the *anticipation grace*, and provided additional information about their execution (Ex. 15.3b).

Ex. 15.3b  Corri: *The Singer's Preceptor*, 32.

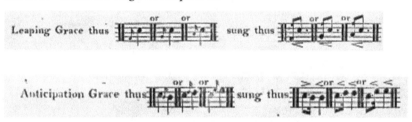

For the *leaping grace*, which takes place with the syllable of the note it precedes, he explained: "the strength necessary to its execution must be regulated more or less according to the distance of the Intervals".[16] It could be used to connect the pitches of two notes but was more often employed simply as an ornament, with the *grace-note* theoretically belonging to the harmony of the following note, with which it was connected. J. F. Schubert gave a single illustration of this in his discussion of ornaments. His example of three successive uses of the ornament, however, has no parallel in Corri (Ex. 15.4).

---

[15] D. Corri: *Select Collection*, i, 8.
[16] D. Corri: *Singer's Preceptor*, 32.

Ex. 15.4 J. F. Schubert: *Singe-Schule*, 54.

The *anticipation grace*, which takes place with the syllable of the note it follows, was always carried to the pitch of the note it preceded, but it did not have to be consonant with the harmony of the note from which it took its value.[17] In the *Select Collection*, Corri illustrated only rising versions of this ornament, but in the *Singer's Preceptor* he instructed: "In descending, drop the Grace into the Note [i.e., *decrescendo*], and in ascending, swell the Note into the Grace." For the *anticipation grace*, the *portamento* could be either rapid or drawn out; for the *leaping grace*, it seems invariably to have been executed rapidly. Here, as elsewhere, dotted rhythm representations need not be taken literally; the short note would almost certainly have been made much shorter in most instances.[18] This is implied by many verbal descriptions of the execution of *portamento*, for instance, that of G. G. Ferrari in 1818: "In carrying the voice from one note to another, the second must receive a slight intonation, previous to being articulated."[19] At about the same date as Corri's *Select Collection*, J. C. F. Rellstab illustrated a *cercar della nota* similarly to Corri's *anticipation grace*.[20]

Not all tutors from this period concurred with the dynamic indications proposed by Corri. J. F. Schubert, who included similar figures in his treatment of ornaments (*Manieren*), considered that "If afternotes [*Nachschläge*] of this kind are to produce the desired effect the main note should be strongly attacked and the afternote slurred very gently and weakly to the preceding note, particularly downwards. Only in vocal pieces of a fiery, vehement character would I, now and then, allow the rising afternote, but never the falling one, to be given more accent than the main note" (Ex. 15.5).[21]

---

[17] Fröhlich provided exercises in which the small note is shown at different pitches from the one that follows, but these were exercises for pitching the intervals rather than instructions for performance.
[18] See Ch. 14.
[19] Giacomo Gotifredo Ferrari: *Breve trattato di canto italiano* (London, 1818), cited by W. Crutchfield in 'Portamento' in *The New Grove Dictionary of Opera*, iii, 1070.
[20] See Ex. 15.20.
[21] Schubert: *Singe-Schule*, 56.

**Ex. 15.5** J. F. Schubert: *Singe-Schule*, 56.

Fröhlich, on the other hand, who in the main poached his text directly from Schubert (including the above passage),[22] illustrated the *portamento* both upwards and downwards with *messa di voce* inflexions (Ex. 15.6).

**Ex. 15.6** Fröhlich: *Musikschule*, 36.

He also observed: "The portamento on a descending interval must be taken somewhat faster, as is marked by the little note at the fall of the octave, so that no wailing, instead of singing, results and the unbearable drawling will be avoided. The more distant the interval, therefore, the faster it must be performed in descending."[23] Later in the same treatise, where Schubert's text was reproduced almost verbatim, this type of treatment was advocated also for rising *portamento*.

Two decades later, Nicola Vaccai, having illustrated *portamento*, in a similar manner to Corri's *anticipation grace* (Ex. 15.7a), included the *leaping grace* as a second kind of *portamento* (Ex. 15.7b), but described it as "less used".[24] Nevertheless, this kind of *portamento* can be heard in early recordings, especially those of Adelina Patti (b. 1843) and Alessandro Moreschi (b. 1858).[25] In modern singing, a related effect, usually seen simply as bad singing, is commonly described in English as *scooping*.

**Ex. 15.7** a–b. Nicola Vaccai: (*a*) *Metodo pratico di canto Italiano*, 27; (*b*) *Metodo*, 29.

---

[22] Fröhlich: *Musikschule*, i, 58.
[23] Fröhlich: *Musikschule*, i, 36.
[24] Vaccai: *Metodo pratico di canto Italiano* (London, 1834), 27, 29.
[25] See Ch. 13, pp. 811–15.

Ex. 15.7 Continued

Ambiguity about the aural effects encompassed by the term *portamento* is found in many 19th-century sources. J. A. Hamilton defined it, similarly to Corri, as "The manner of sustaining and conducting the voice. A gliding from one note to another."[26] In the same decade, however, in a treatise supposedly based on the teaching of Antonio Maria Bernacchi (1685–1756), by Heinrich Ferdinand Mannstein, a pupil of J. A. Miksch (b. 1765), through whom he was somewhat implausibly seen as "a grandson of this splendid school",[27] gave a much more detailed description of the various practices that might be subsumed under that term. He first illustrated conjunct (Ex. 15.8a) and disjunct notes (Ex. 15.8b) and, seeming to make no meaningful distinction between *legato* and *portamento*, commented: "These two methods of carrying the notes are referred to in Italian as: *Cantar legato, leger i tuoni*, and in German it can best be described as *getragen singen* [*chanter legato* in the parallel French translation]."

Ex. 15.8 a–d. Mannstein: *Das System der grossen Gesangschule des Bernacchi von Bologna*, 26–28. (*a*) A smooth succession of slurred notes in conjunct motion, 26; (*b*) The connection of disjunct notes sung to the same syllable, 27; (*c*) The connection of disjunct notes sung to different syllables, 28; (*d*) A musical ornament that is almost always regarded as portamento, 27.

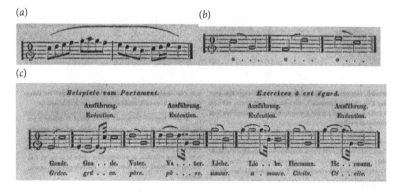

---

[26] J. A. Hamilton: *A Dictionary of Two Thousand Italian, French, German, English, and Other Musical Terms* (London, 1838), 69.
[27] Gottfried Weber: 'Das System der grossen Gesangschule des Bernacchi von Bologna, dargestellt von H. F. Mannstein', *Caecilia*, xvii (1835), 257.

Ex. 15.8 Continued

(d)

He remarked that this is

> in the real Italian school of singing, the one and only *Portamento di voce*. The second type of legato, like the portamento, consists in allowing the voice to glide from the end of the first note to the second note via the tones in between This bond must þe so delicate that the two separate notes almost seem to the ear to be merged into one. But this end can only be achieved if no intermediate note is detected; neglecting this rule would make legato and portamento similar to yawning or wailing.

He also explained that "it can only be carried out by anticipation of the second tone (anticipation), which, however, may not amount to more than a thirty-second part of its value" (Ex. 15.8c).

In a footnote, he added: "If the anticipation is long, the portamento creates a musical ornament that is almost always regarded as portamento E.g. [Ex. 15.8d]."[28]

Significantly, perhaps, he made no reference at all to Vaccai's second type, which seems by this date to have been very much out of fashion.

Continuing disagreement about the terminology for various kinds of vocal sliding effects continued into the middle of the century. Ferdinand Sieber stated:

> There is hardly a vocal ornament about which there are such different and frequently erroneous views than the portamento. It is sometimes confused with the simple binding of the notes (cantar lagato [sic]), sometimes with the swelling of the note and its return to piano (messa di voce), sometimes with passing through intermediate notes (strascinare la voce)—and yet it is none of these.
>
> The art of singing understands portamento as the process whereby the singer connects two notes with different words or syllables, which

---

[28] Mannstein: *Das System*, 26–28.

follow each other up or down at any intervallic distance, so that the note belonging to the second syllable is sung on the vowel of the first syllable. As can be seen from this, the portamento is nothing but a kind of anticipation (Vorausnahme) of a following note on the preceding syllable, which aims to connect two syllables and notes seamlessly.—Of course, this anticipation may only be made fleetingly and not rob the first note of more than the value of 1/16th of its duration.[29]

In the 1870s, Heinrich Ruff, borrowing a definition from a recently published treatise,[30] defined vocal *legato* as "joining two notes by moving from one to the other, so that all conceivable pitches are heard".[31] On instruments, however, *legato* (Mannstein's first kind of *portamento*) can certainly be executed with no break in sound, but also no audible connection.

## Types of Instrumental *Portamento* and Their Execution

### String Instruments

String treatises were slow to explain the means of executing expressive position changes, or indeed the mechanisms for any kind of position changing. *Portamento* is scarcely touched upon in the 1803 Paris Conservatoire *Méthode*,[32] although all its authors, especially Rode, employed it frequently as a prominent expressive resource; Baillot's musical contribution to the *Méthode*, 50 Études sur la gamme, however, contains passages that require *legato* changes between positions and one (N° 25 on p. 146) is evidently a study in *portamento*.[33] Their cellist compatriot, Jean-Louis Duport, having condemned the use of the same finger for semitone steps in playing scales, conceded: "It is true that one can make two notes with the same finger a little slowly; one can even pass from an interval of a third, a fourth, a fifth, etc., by

---

[29] Ferdinand Sieber: 'Das ABC der Gesangskunst. Ein kurzer Leitfaden beim Studium des Gesanges', *Neue Zeitschrift für Musik*, xxxv (1851), 108f.

[30] Thuiskon Hauptner: *Ausbildung der Stimme* (Leipzig, 1876).

[31] Heinrich Ruff: 'Das Portamento im Gesange. Ein Versuch zur Klarstellung dieses Begriffs', *Musikalisches Wochenblatt*, ix (1878), 147.

[32] A short reference is made in the section on ornaments to composers using grace-notes to indicate "PORTAMENTO ou PORT DE VOIX", but with no explanation of how it might be executed. Baillot et al: *Méthode*, 126.

[33] See Ex. 15.28c, where he gives a fingered version of this study in his 1835 *L'art du violon*.

sliding the same finger strongly, and this produces a very good effect"[34] (Ex. 15.9). But he did not discuss the matter further.

**Ex. 15.9** Duport: *Essai*, 17.

Not until the 1820s, with Dotzauer's *Méthode de violoncelle*, is there a fuller explanation of how the hand might be shifted expressively when successive notes were to be taken by different fingers. Dotzauer alluded to the vocal origin of *portamento* and observed: "if the slide [*Ziehen*] happens in a way that does not sound like wailing, it has a very pleasant effect".[35] In his treatment of ornaments, he gave the examples shown in Ex. 15.10. The first, which like Duport's illustration, involves slides with a single finger is self-explanatory; for the others, Dotzauer explained:

> In example N°. 2, the slide is introduced four times with different fingers. From B to G the first finger remains firmly down on the string during the slide approximately until E, and since the slide cannot continue from the E to the G the fourth finger must come down on the G so much the faster after this E. It is the same with the following C to G and C sharp to G; however, with the D to B one substitutes the third finger for the second during the slide: and it is the same with the next example from B to F. In examples 3 and 4 the rules already given are to be used. In the fourth example the third finger substitutes for the fourth and goes onto the A, and in the second bar the first finger slides from E downwards to B.[36]

**Ex. 15.10** Dotzauer: *Méthode de violoncelle*, 46.

---

[34] Duport: *Essai sur le Doigté du Violoncelle*, 17.
[35] Dotzauer: *Méthode*, 45f. The French translation says "if it is applied with taste and rarely...". For the German noun and verb *Ziehen/ziehen*, the French translation uses *glissement* and *glisser*.
[36] Dotzauer: *Méthode*, 46f.

Ex. 15.10 Continued

In this type of *portamento* the aim seems to have been to give the impression that the glide, like the singer's, continued all the way between the two notes; but practical experiment shows that the various methods of executing these kinds of shifts can produce subtly different expressive effects.

Spohr, whose violin playing was repeatedly praised for its vocality, is explicit about the emulation of the singer's *portamento*. He observed that "The violin has, among other advantages over keyboard and wind instruments, the ability convincingly to imitate the human voice's characteristic gliding from one note to another, both in soft and passionate passages."[37] He left discussion of this aspect of position changing until the student had already been introduced to playing in all parts of the fingerboard, before explaining, in a commentary on his practice piece No. 50:

> If two notes that lie at a distance from each other are to be connected in a single bowstroke [. . .] then the leap from one note to the other cannot be made without the sliding of the hand being audible. In order not to degenerate into unpleasant wailing, it must be done in the following way: Move the finger of the first note until the finger of the second note can fall into place, [. . .] thus, the first finger from *e* to *b* [Ex. 15.11a], and only then let the fourth finger come down on the high *b*; similarly in the 11th bar, with the second finger from *e* to *b* [Ex. 15.11b], whereupon the little finger falls on the high *b*. This must be done as quickly as possible, so that the gap from the small to the highest note [. . .] is not noticed and the listener's ear is deceived into believing that the whole space from the low to the high note is evenly covered by the sliding finger.[38]

---

[37] Spohr: *Violinschule*, 126.
[38] Spohr: *Violinschule*, 120.

**Ex. 15.11** a–c. Spohr: *Violinschule*, 120. (*a*) Example showing the execution of Exercise No. 50, b. 9; (*b*) Example showing the execution of Exercise No. 50, b. 11; (*c*) The "faulty" method.

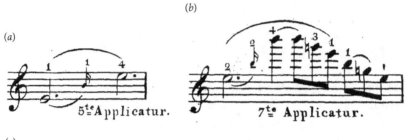

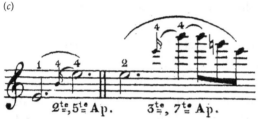

This procedure was clearly intended to emulate Mannstein's disjunct notes sung to a single syllable. Spohr warned, however: "For such leaps, some violinists (in contravention of the above rule) slide with the finger that takes the high note and therefore play in the following manner: [Ex. 15.11c]. Since, however, the unpleasant wailing cannot be avoided with this method, it must be rejected as faulty."[39]

In Exercise 51 (intended primarily for bowing) Spohr provided further examples of the "correct" method of sliding, both up and down (Ex. 15.12).

**Ex. 15.12** a–b. Spohr: *Violinschule*, 126, No. 51, b. 13. (*a*) Notation; (*b*) Execution.

---

[39] Spohr: *Violinschule*, 120. It is noteworthy, however, that, as shown by Dotzauer's examples in Ex. 15. 10 (i.e. $d^1$ to $b^1$ and b to $f^1$ in No. 2, and $d^1$ to $a^1$ in No. 4), cellists endorsed this method in some instances. The same practice is also described in Davydov's *Violoncell-Schule* (Leipzig [1888]), 70.

Ex. 15.12 Continued

(b)

He did not explain the use of this procedure for *portamento* connections between bowstrokes, although he certainly expected these in many cases, as fingerings in the instructive version of his Ninth Violin Concerto indicate (Ex. 15.13a–b). He provided no instructions for executing *portamento* with the same finger between slurred notes, presumably because this was obvious.

Ex. 15.13 a–b. Spohr: *Violinschule*: Spohr Ninth Violin Concerto op. 55. (*a*) Adagio, p. 228; (*b*) Adagio, p. 231.

In violin music, a figure resembling Corri's *leaping grace* often occurs without any *portamento*, and this version of the ornament is frequently used on instruments that have more limited possibilities for *portamento* or, like the keyboard, none. But sometimes Spohr supplied this type of figure with a *portamento* fingering (Ex. 15.14).

Ex. 15.14 a–b. Spohr: *Violinschule*: Spohr Ninth Violin Concerto. (*a*) Allegro, p. 222; (*b*) Adagio, p. 230.

(*a*)

(*b*)

Other passages show that he also expected *portamento* from and to harmonics (Ex. 15.15) and to an open string.

Ex. 15.15 a–c. Spohr: *Violinschule*, 127: No. 51. (*a*) Notation; (*b*) Execution; (*c*) Spohr: *Violinschule*, 202: Rode Seventh Violin Concerto.

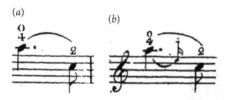

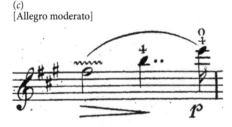

In his annotations to Rode's Seventh Violin Concerto he explained his fingering for the opening of the Adagio (Ex. 15.16): "The gentle gliding from one note to the next must not only take place upwards, as in the first bar from *g* to *e*, but downwards, as in the same bar from *c* to the open *e* and in the following bar from *g* to *b*."[40]

[40] Spohr: *Violinschule*, 209.

Ex. 15.16 Spohr: *Violinschule*, 209: Rode Seventh Violin Concerto. [Adagio]

He probably also envisaged occasionally making a *portamento* from an open string, as illustrated by his pupil Ferdinand David (see Ex. 15.47) and utilized quite often by Charles de Bériot (see Ex. 15.40c).

In his treatment of ornaments, following his discussion of the vocal origin of left-hand *Bebung* (trembling), Spohr explained one further effect that could be obtained by sliding fingers. He likened this embellishment to the effect of a singer "separating two notes on the same pitch in a single breath, by pronouncing a new syllable"[41] (Ex. 15.17a). But he instructed that despite the sliding of the finger, the "guide notes" (indicated in Ex. 15.17b) should not be heard.

Ex. 15.17 a–b. Spohr: (*a*) *Violinschule*, 175; (*b*) *Violinschule*, 176.

Pierre Baillot's almost contemporaneous *L'art du violon* includes *ports de voix* in the section on ornaments (*Agrémens du chant*). His descriptions differ from Spohr's in several respects. He stated that there are "two ways of carrying the voice [*de porter la voix*] or the sounds"[42] and began with simple *legato*, performed without any shifting of the left hand, therefore no possibility of sliding (Ex. 15.18a).

[41] Spohr: *Violinschule*, 175.
[42] Baillot: *L'art du violon*, 75.

**Ex. 15.18a** Baillot: *L'art du violon*, 75.

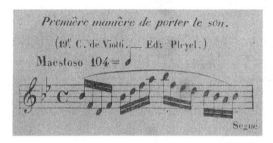

His second type of *portamento* is produced by sliding fingers, and he gave three of this type. The first is the common practice of sliding a single finger (Ex. 15.18b).

**Ex. 15.18b** Baillot: *L'art du violon*, 76.

The other two relate more directly to illustrations of vocal *portamento* than Spohr's. One of these reflects Corri's *anticipation grace* and Vaccai's first type (see Ex. 15.7a), but his music example is curious since it appears to involve a change of bow where the original notation is slurred (Ex. 15.18c).

**Ex. 15.18c** Baillot: *L'art du violon*, 76.

He seems really to have intended this bow change, however, since he illustrates it also in an example from Mozart's String Quintet K. 515 (Ex. 15.18d).

Ex. 15.18d Baillot: *L'art du violon*: Mozart, String Quintet K. 515, 76. (Mozart's tempo marking is Allegro, but in the edition published by Imbault in Paris it is Mod^to.)

The other procedure resembles Corri's *leaping grace* and Vaccai's second type (see Ex. 15.7b), but he provides no example of its employment in compositions (Ex. 15.18e).

Ex. 15.18e Baillot: *L'art du violon*, 76. This example is a truncated version of the one given in the 1803 *Méthode*, but with additional dynamic indications.

Just as this type of *portamento* was becoming less common in singing by the 1830s, it may also have been decreasing in violin playing as an improvised ornament, although, as the examples from Spohr's *Violinschule* demonstrate, similar effects continued to be notated by composers. Other treatises do not illustrate it in the form depicted by Baillot. But Manuel García's critical comment in the late 1840s, that the *leaping grace* type of *portamento* remained too popular with French singers, may suggest that French string players also continued to use a related effect. In another example, Baillot indicates something similar to Spohr's method in Ex. 15.11, but he does not mention sliding the finger all the way to the new position (although that must surely have occurred), and he appears not to have expected the ear to be deceived into hearing a continuous slide, since he instructed: "drag the first finger a little, barely touching the *b* sharp, and bring the sound directly to the *g*, which should crescendo" (Ex. 15.18f).[43]

---

[43] Baillot: *L'art du violon*, 76.

**Ex. 15.18f** Baillot: *L'art du violon*, 76: Viotti Violin Concerto no. 18, first movement.

Perhaps he expected a pronounced slide at the beginning followed by a very rapid and virtually inaudible continuation of the sliding finger to $d^3$.

Baillot, like Spohr, also gave instructions for changing fingers on the same note within a smooth bowstroke, with a similar warning against allowing the intervening small notes to be heard.[44]

Analogous *portamento* effects were certainly used in classical guitar playing. Theoretical treatment is lacking in 19th-century guitar treatises, but in Giuliani's "Variations sur l'Air favori de la Molinara" op. 4, an effect similar to Corri's *leaping grace* is marked with the instruction *striciando* (dragging) (Ex. 15.19).

**Ex. 15.19** Mauro Giuliani: "Variations sur l'Air favori de la Molinara" op. 4, Variation 5 (Vienna, Haslinger [c. 1820]).

---

[44] Baillot: *L'art du violon*, 153.

## Wind Instruments

Wind instruments also imitated vocal *portamento*, especially during the late 18th century and first half of the 19th century, although, except in the case of the trombone, possibilities were more limited by technical considerations than in singing and string playing. A common method was to slide fingers to or from open holes in various ways.[45] Fröhlich borrowed instructions from J. G. Tromlitz's 1791 *Unterricht* to explain that it can be produced "if you gradually pull your finger away from the hole, or slide it on, or cover it gradually from the side, and open it in the same way".[46] Some mid-19th-century flute methods provided fingering charts for producing these effects: Fürstenau illustrated only groups of rising and falling semitones,[47] while Charles Nicholson gave rising figures spanning as much as a 6th. Nicholson instructed that the *glide* "when judiciously introduced, has a most beautiful effect: it is produced by drawing the fingers off the holes instead of lifting them, by which means two or more notes with a continuity of tone may be exquisitely blended [. . .]. The highest note where the glide is marked should generally be forced."[48] John Clinton gave a similar chart (Ex. 15.20).[49] Nicholson and Clinton used double slurs to indicate the glide; Fürstenau notated it with a triple slur. Nicholson had already explained gliding in his *Preceptive Lessons* of 1821[50] and used double slurs in some of the practice pieces;[51] but this sign seems not to have gained currency.

---

[45] Three variants of this method are identified by Anne Pustlauk: *The Simple System Flute between 1790 and 1850, Its Performance Practice and Chamber Music Repertoire with Pianoforte and/or Strings* (PhD diss., Vrije Universiteit Brussel, 2016), 70.
[46] Fröhlich: *Musikschule*, pt. 2, 87.
[47] Fürstenau: *Die Kunst*, 85.
[48] Charles Nicholson: *A School for the Flute* (London, [1836]), ii, 70.
[49] John Clinton: *A School or Practical Instruction Book for the Boehm Flute* (London, [1846]), 73.
[50] Charles Nicholson: *Preceptive Lessons for the Flute* (London, [1821]), 5.
[51] Also in his *Appendix to Nicholson's Preceptive Lessons* (London, [1825]).

Ex. 15.20 John Clifton: *A School or Practical Instruction Book*, 73.

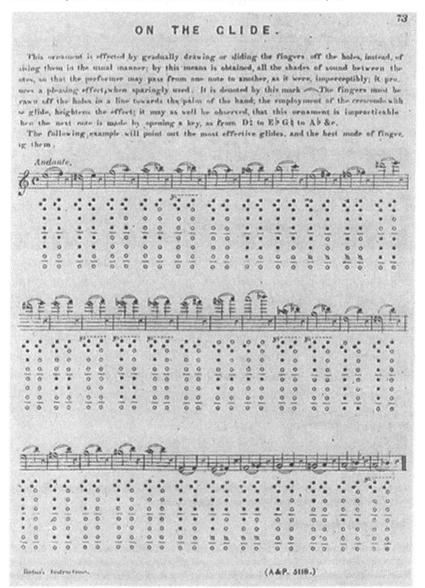

An 1828 review of William Nelson James's *A Word or Two on the Flute* by Carl Augustin Grenser (first flute of the Leipzig Gewandhaus Orchestra) provides a revealing glimpse of attitudes towards this practice. In relation to James's discussion of the glide, Grenser observed that "The effect of this adornment is extraordinarily flattering and beautiful; but, like the tremolo

[*Bebung*], it must be used with caution and only sparingly." His further comments imply that, as suggested by Tromlitz's warnings (see below), these gliding effects had previously been used more frequently by wind players. He observed:

> in Germany where this embellishment has already passed through the period of misuse, and is only still practised here and there by individuals as an ornament, we know how to appreciate it. Originally, this gliding through the pitches probably arose from the well-meant intention of coming closer to imitating the human voice. However, since an artist only rarely succeeded in producing the barely noticeable passing from one tone to another, just as softly, or even close to it on an instrument, it was often more reminiscent of certain animal voices, which are not among the more pleasant ones, and thus they failed to achieve what they intended.

He pointed out that the worst effects were produced when flautists tried to imitate other flautists' sliding effects, and most successful where they directly tried to imitate singers; but he also considered that "the imitation of the human voice in this respect is easier to make on bowed than on wind instruments and therefore more often and more successfully on the latter than on the former".[52] In the later 19th century, progressively more complex key systems inhibited woodwind instruments' potential for trembling effects with the finger.

That these effect were successfully achieved on other wind instruments is indicated by Grenser's remark that the most effective use of the ornament he had heard from wind players was from the flautist Fürstenau and the oboist Friedrich Eugen Thurner.[53] This suggest that other methods may have been used, since the holes of the oboe are rather small for an effective finger *portamento*.[54] One bassoon method proposes that the effect can be achieved with the tongue: "The tonguing that executes the repetition of the two notes that make the *portamento* must be achieved by making it strike the palate without touching the reed."[55] Sliding effects can, in fact, be produced by a variety of means that may well have been used in the 19th century without being

---

[52] Carl Augustin Grenser: 'Für Flötenspieler bemerkenswerther Stellen aus dem Buche *A Word or Two on the Flute by W. N. James*', *Allgemeine musikalische Zeitung*, xxx (1828), 115.

[53] Grenser: 'Für Flötenspieler [...]', 115.

[54] Pustlauk: *The Simple System Flute*, 73. Áurea Domínguez Moreno: *Bassoon Playing in Perspective. Character and Performance Practice from 1800 to 1850* (PhD diss., University of Helsinki, 2013), 194f.

[55] Jean-Baptiste-Joseph Willent-Bordogni: *Méthode complète pour le basson* (Paris, 1844), 77.

described. In the 20th and early 21st century, when *portamento* on wind instruments has been largely confined to popular music and avant-garde repertoire, "A variety of explanations and methods have been suggested for producing it. All involve lip pressure, oral cavity shape, throat opening, tongue position, air pressure, and fingers, although in various hierarchical positions of importance."[56]

## Sliding Effects in Late-18th- and Early-19th-Century Practice, and Their Reception

Audible slides in singing have unquestionably been used since pre-history. In 18th-century vocal training, they will have been one category among many expressive practices that were only occasionally specified. While they were used by all skilled singers, the manner and extent to which they employed them, and the contexts in which they did so, are insufficiently documented to gain a clear conception of the practice. Pier Francesco Tosi's treatise of 1723 makes various references to connecting pitches artistically. John Galliard's English translation of it in 1743 includes the terms *glide* and *slur*, inconsistently used for Tosi's single word *scivolo* (literally: slide); for Tosi's *stracinar* (literally: drag) Galliard uses *dragg*. Agricola in his German translation and commentary utilizes the terms *gestossen, geschleift*, and *Ziehen* as translations of Tosi's *battuto, scivolato*, and *stracino*.[57] Galliard evidently made a distinction (perhaps between simple *legato* and an audible slide) not present in Tosi's original, when he referred to "a certain Gliding, by the Masters called a Slur; the Effect of which is truly agreeable when used sparingly".[58] But Agricola provides music examples illustrating this paragraph, showing groups of slurred notes in conjunct motion, which implies an interpretation of Tosi's meaning different from Galliard's. Tosi's use of *stracino* suggests a more intense descending slide. Evidently, there were contexts in which such embellishments were especially appropriate. Tosi advised, for instance, that in a Siciliano "Glidings and Draggs are Beauties" (Galliard's translation).[59]

---

[56] E. Michael Richards: *The Clarinet of the Twenty-First Century. New Sonic Resources Based on Principles of Acoustics*, 1992/2009, Ch. 4, https://userpages.umbc.edu/~emrich/clarinet21.html [accessed 20 June 2022].

[57] Pier Francesco Tosi: *Opinioni de' cantori antichi e moderni* (Bologna, 1723).

[58] John Galliard: *Observations on the Florid Song*, 4, §5, 53. Galliard's *Glidings* is here a translation of Tosi's *un certo sdruccioloso liscio* (literally: a certain slippery smoothness), which he equates with *scivolo* Tosi: *Opinioni* 31. in Agricola, *Singkunst*, 126, *schlupfrige Glatte*.

[59] Galliard: *Observations*, 58; Tosi: *Opinioni*, 34: *lo Scivolo, e lo Strascino delizie*; Agricola: *SingkunstI*, 133: *das Schleifen und Ziehen aber Schönheiten*.

Since these sliding effects were almost exclusively seen as optional ornaments, their use is rarely indicated in musical notation. In the later decades of the century, however, a few sources offer more explicit information about the contexts in which vocal embellishments of this type were implied. J. C. F. Rellstab discussed the discretionary use of the *cercar la nota*. In an example from Graun's aria "Ihr weichgeschafne Seele", he commented that "every good singer" would use it in a passage of this kind" (Ex. 15.21a) and notated the ornament as a dotted figure (Ex. 15.21b).[60] Here, as elsewhere, the rhythmic representation is undoubtedly indicative rather than prescriptive.

Ex. 15.21 a–b. Rellstab: *Versuch über die Vereinigung*.

Only from the 1780s, with Domenico Corri's *Select Collection*,[61] is there abundant evidence of where and how sliding effects may have been employed expressively by a distinguished singer and teacher. Corri's *Select Collection* is unique in the quantity of music—ranging from operatic arias to simple songs—which is provided with such detailed performance information. His annotations suggest that the *leaping grace* may have been more extensively used in the 18th century than the *anticipation grace*; the latter occurs relatively seldom, while the former is very frequently encountered. Corri's later publications, however, reverse this situation, implying that, by the beginning of the 19th century, the popularity of the *leaping grace* was already diminishing in favour of the *anticipation grace*. As mentioned above, this is borne out by the expressed preferences of later writers. A few examples offer insights into the contexts in which Corri expected these two types of sliding effects to be used (Ex. 15.22a–f).[62] Others can be seen in Ex. 13.4.

---

[60] Johann Carl Friedrich Rellstab: *Versuch über die Vereinigung der musikalischen und oratorischen Declamation* (Berlin, [1786]), 37.

[61] Domenico Corri: *A Select Collection of the Most Admired Songs, Duetts, &c*, Vols. i–iii [c. 1783], Vol. iv (1795).

[62] The original texts of the arias and songs, on which Corri based his performing versions, have been collected and published together with the whole of the *Select Collection* and his 1810 treatise as *Domenico Corri's Treatises on Singing: A Select Collection of the Most Admired Songs, Duetts, etc. and the Singer's Preceptor: A Four-Volume Anthology*, ed. C. R. F. Maunder (New York and London: Garland, 1995).

Ex. 15.22a  (*leaping grace*) i, 3: Giordani (Hasse): *Artaserse*.
[Andante]

Ex. 15.22b  (*leaping grace*) i, 23: Gluck: *L'Olimpiade*.
[Andantino]

Ex. 15.22c  (*leaping grace*) i, 42: Gluck: *Orfeo*.
[Andante]

Ex. 15.22d  (*anticipation grace*) i, 17: Rauzzini: *L'ali d'amore*.
[Larghetto]

Ex. 15.22e  (*anticipation grace*) i, 32: Giordani: *La marchesa Giardinera*.
[Andante]

Ex. 15.22f  (*anticipation grace*) i, 42: Gluck: *Orfeo*.

Even in simple songs, like Haydn's Canzonettas, Corri envisaged expressive *portamento*, as shown by comparison of the original London edition, published by Corri at the time of Haydn's second visit to London, with the version in the second volume of his *Singer's Preceptor*, which contains three occurrences of the *anticipation grace* in the first three bars (see Ex. 13.9). Interestingly, Haydn, like Corri, had studied with the celebrated Neapolitan singing teacher Nicola Porpora.

In the second half of the 18th century, string players began to use sliding effects with increasing frequency. The major mid-18th-century treatises do not discuss them explicitly, but because they are a natural outcome of position changing, they had probably been employed as an artistic effect ever since string players began to make regular use of shifting. They are implied by a few fingerings in treatises, for instance Leopold Mozart's (Ex. 15.23).[63]

Ex. 15.23 Mozart: *Versuch*, 178.

A comment in Burney's *General History* indicates that by the 1770s, sliding effects in violin playing were already quite widespread; he observed that Geminiani "was certainly mistaken in laying it down as a rule that 'no two notes on the same string, in shifting, should be played with the same finger'; as beautiful expressions and effects are produced by great players in shifting, suddenly from a low note to a high, with the same finger on the same string".[64]

By the last quarter of the 18th century, sliding effects were a prominent feature in the technique of a growing number of string players, and, occasionally, fingerings were included by composers, as in Lolli's Sonata op. 9, no. 4 (Ex. 15.24).

Ex. 15.24 Antonio Lolli: Sonata op. 9 no. 4 (c. 1785).

---

[63] See also Ex. 16.30.
[64] Charles Burney: *A General History of Music from the Earliest Ages to the Present Period* (London, 1776–89), ii, 992.

Several of Haydn's string quartets also include instructions for sliding, where a special effect was intended, often humorous or picturesque, as in the minuets of op. 33 no. 2 and op. 64 no. 6 (Ex. 15.25a–b) or, as in the "gypsy" finale of op. 76 no. 2, an allusion to folk music (Ex. 15.25c).

Ex. 15.25a  Haydn: op. 33/2/ii (Paris, Sieber).
[Scherzo Allegro]

Ex. 15.25b  Haydn: op. 64/6/iii. (autograph).
[Menuetto Allegretto]

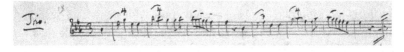

Ex. 15.25c  Haydn: op. 77/2/iv, 1st edn (London, Longman, Clementi).
[Presto]

Haydn's *una corda* markings, which also call for audible position changing, seem usually to have a more expressive or characterful purpose, for instance, in op. 17 no. 2 (1771), op. 20 no. 3 (1772), op. 50 no. 5 (1787), and op. 74 no. 3

(Ex. 15.25d–g). In op. 64 no. 6 there is an evident analogy with Corri's *leaping grace*, and in op. 74 no. 3 with his *anticipation grace*.

**Ex. 15.25d** Haydn: op. 17/2/iii. It seems probable that Haydn expected the first six bars to be played on the A-string also with *portamento* in the falling slurred pairs.

**Ex. 15.25e** Haydn: op. 20/3/1 (London, Blundell).
[Allegro con spirito]

**Ex. 15.25f** Haydn: op. 50/5/iv, 1st edn (Vienna, Artaria).

**Ex. 15.25g** Haydn: op. 74/3/i, Hummel (Berlin, 1797).
[Allegro]

Sliding fingerings of this kind, as well as the vocal *portamento*, which they emulated, must certainly have been familiar to members of Haydn's Esterházy musical establishment even before Nicola Mestrino was employed there between 1780 and 1785; but it seems very likely that *prominent* portamento was already an aspect of Mestrino's playing when he arrived there.[65] In any case, by the time of his move to France, he was certainly using sliding effects extensively. After he performed in Paris at the beginning of 1787, the *Mercure de France* commented: "The connoisseurs found his style new, full of expression and sensibility."[66] Michel Woldemar, a pupil of Antonio Lolli, who evidently heard Mestrino's performance of his Third Violin Concerto, provided a musical example from it in his *Grande Méthode* (Ex. 15.26), followed by the explanation: "One sees from the preceding example that Mestrino was only able to perform this piece by means of the enharmonic scale, that is to say, by quarter-tones, just as all these slides from one note to another are notated, and since these intervals are so small that the ear cannot distinguish them he made almost all of them with the same finger."[67]

Ex. 15.26  Woldemar: *Grande méthode*, 1st edn, 34; 2nd edn, 43.

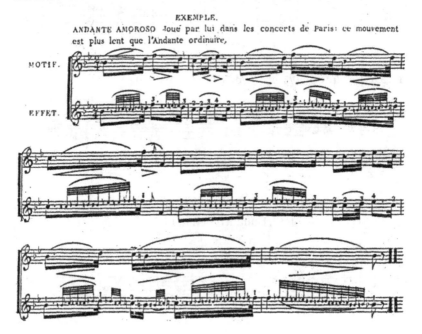

[65] Mestrino and Domenico Dragonetti practised together in their youth in Venice, and both were associated with the use of expressive portamento, which Dragonetti employed to great effect when playing Beethoven's op. 5 cello sonatas (at original pitch) with the composer in 1797 (see below).
[66] *Mercure de France*, 6 January 1787.
[67] Woldemar: *Grande Méthode*, 1st edn, 34.

In the introduction to his treatise Woldemar had stated that this "enharmonic scale" distinguished the Italian style from that of the French and Germans, asserting that it

> was formed, with as much sensitivity as grace, by means of the chromatic or rather the enharmonic, which is nothing more than a slur from one note into another through the inflexion of the voice. This style, so touching, has triumphed over the other two in this century of enlightenment, and Italian music, based on that of the Greeks, which they derived from the Egyptians, the first scholars in the world—this music so delicious and so touching has become the universal language of all musicians.[68]

In his slightly later *Méthode de violon par L. Mozart*, which has little connection with Leopold Mozart's original, Woldemar's explanation was even more explicit, for he observed: "The enharmonic genre may only be explained by the slur, for it is formed from immeasurable intervals, though to reduce them in principle one divides them into quarter-tones."[69] Woldemar's account of Mestrino's use of *portamento* is corroborated by Mestrino's own *Douze Grands Solo* [*sic*] (Ex. 15.27), which include many fingerings and *una corda* instructions that required changes of position within slurs.

Ex. 15.27 Mestrino: Douze Grands Solo [*sic*] no. 1.
[Maestoso]

Another string player working in Paris at that time, Giuseppe Cambini, who will certainly have known Mestrino, associated *portamento* specifically with Haydn's music. In his *Méthode de violon* he took a theme by Haydn and presented three successive versions: the first (Ex. 15.28a), with no markings except a slur in the last bar, he regarded as suitable only for inducing peasants to dance, but certainly not what Haydn envisaged; in the second (Ex. 15.28b), he added a mixture of slurs and *portato* markings, which "must have made

---

[68] Woldemar: *Grande Méthode*, 1st edn, 1. This sentence is equally tortuous in the original. For a translation of a more extensive section of this introduction see the first edition of this book, p. 561f.

[69] Woldemar: *Méthode de violon par L. Mozart redigée par Woldemar, élève de Lolli* (Paris, 1801), 56f.

young women smile", but even played like this, he explained, "the composer's aim is not yet fulfilled".[70] His third version (Ex. 15.28c), with fingering, involves slurred changes of position, and he asserts: "See, this is what I'm sure the author wanted: to interest, move, and affect the listener."[71] He then indicates that it was in this style that he had played quartets of Boccherini and Haydn with the three admired Italian string players: Manfredi, Nardini, and Boccherini.

Ex. 15.28 a–c. Cambini: *Méthode*, 21f.

(a)

(b)

(c)

These sources hint at what Haydn had in mind when he wrote *una corda*, or marked shifts of position within slurs. In Vienna, where Italian influence was strong, it seems likely that this style of string playing, emulating the best Italian singers' *portamento*, was already well known by the 1770s, even before it made an impact in Paris. Numerous instances in Mozart's string chamber music suggest that he, as well as many of his Viennese contemporaries, will have envisaged this vocal style in *cantabile* or impassioned contexts. The aesthetic issue is where and in what manner such sliding effects will have been envisaged and might be effectively emulated by 21st-century musicians.

The use of sliding effects in singing, string playing, and wind playing seems to have become increasingly fashionable during the last decades of the 18th century and the first decades of the 19th century. As is usual with

---

[70] Giuseppe Maria Cambini: *Nouvelle Méthode* (Paris, c. 1795), 21.
[71] Cambini: *Méthode*, 22.

stylistic changes, the growing establishment of sliding effects as a prominent expressive resource led to increasing complaints about their misuse, which may sometimes document genuinely unmusical or unskilful employment of them, or sometimes merely reflect resistance to change. In 1791, Tromlitz, despite describing how to produce a sliding effect (*Durchziehen*) in flute playing, was uncomfortable about its use; he explained his inclusion of this technique in his treatise, "because it has become so fashionable nowadays", but warned that it should be used very rarely "if it is not to arouse disgust", adding: "people do it ten times in one movement, and wail down and up at every opportunity, so that it is hardly bearable". "I call it a monstrosity", he asserted: "that's what it is in the hands of most of our so-called concert players".[72]

The impetus for a greater use of sliding effects in string playing seems to have been encouraged particularly by representatives of the increasingly admired Viotti School. It became a distinctive feature in the playing of Viotti's admirers and disciples, despite the fact that Viotti himself seems to have been more sparing in its use. Baillot, in *L'art du violon*, writing from firsthand experience, recalled that Viotti often liked to keep the left hand in a single position (although he gave examples of *portamento* in Viotti's 18th and 22nd Concertos), while his pupil Rode made a feature of shifting up and down a single string "which favoured *port-de-voix* in graceful melodies" (Ex. 15.29a). Kreutzer, too, liked to change position frequently, and Baillot provided an example with "an expressive fingering that should not be changed" (Ex. 15.29b). He concluded: "it is best to finger one's own music, to suit the type of expression one wants to give it", and he offered a fingered version of one of his own studies that had previously been included in the 1803 *Méthode de violon*, but without fingering (Ex. 15.29c).[73]

Ex. 15.29 a–c. Baillot: *L'art*, 149. (*a*) Kreutzer; (*b*) Rode; (*c*) Baillot (The instructions for which strings to use are present in the version published in the 1803 *Méthode*, but not the fingering).

(*a*)

---

[72] Tromlitz: *Unterricht*, 264.
[73] Baillot: *L'art du violon*, 149.

Ex. 15.29 Continued

Many examples of Rode's sliding effects are also detailed in Spohr's *Violinschule*, in his annotated solo part of Rode's Seventh Violin Concerto (for a telling example, see Ex. 15.16 and Ex. 13.45).

This use of sliding effects as an expressive resource, which was retrospectively documented in Baillot's *L'art du violon*,[74] was quickly taken up by younger players. Spohr recalled how hearing Rode in 1803 transformed his way of playing, and his later so greatly admired use of a vocal style of *portamento* was part of this transformation. In 1805, Reichardt, who, like many of the older generation remained uncomfortable with the increasing prevalence of sliding effects, even in solo playing, criticized Spohr's adoption of Rode's "constantly sliding the hand up and down on a string in order to give the notes the greatest possible connection and fusion, and to breathe into the string the sighing sound of a passionate voice".[75] Three years later, another writer, in Prague, after praising Spohr's ravishing performance in an Adagio, continued: "one could call him unsurpassable in this genre, if he did not often disturb us in this enjoyment, and sometimes quite unpleasantly, by an embellishment that is used far too

---

[74] Baillot: *L'art du violon*, 75–78.
[75] Reichardt: 'Concert des Herrn Louis Spohr und der Demoiselle Alberghi. Im Saale des Königl. Nationaltheaters, am 3ten März', *Berlinische Musikalische Zeitung*, i (1805), 95.

often—by sliding up and down with one and the same finger at all possible intervals—by the artificial miaow as one might call it, if it did not sound teasing".[76] In the same year, however, another reviewer noted the importance of *portamento* to the proper performance of Spohr's compositions and drew attention to his careful marking of the necessary fingerings, remarking:

> The execution of the notes, which are to be performed well in the manner of vocal portamento, makes it necessary to change the position of the left hand far more often than would otherwise be necessary. [...] This characteristic position changing is what now makes the performance of his solo parts especially difficult for other violin players who have not yet accustomed themselves to his style.[77]

Many more string-playing composers at this time began to mark fingerings, especially where expressive shifting was intended. Among Spohr's older contemporaries to do so were Andreas Romberg (Ex. 15.30a) and Ferdinand Fränzl (Ex. 15.30b).

Ex. 15.30a  Andreas Romberg: String Quartet op. 59/1/i.

Ex. 15.30b  Ferdinand Fränzl: String Trio op. 17/1/ii.

---

[76] Anon.: *Allgemeine musikalische Zeitung*, x (1807–8), 313.
[77] Anon.: *Allgemeine musikalische Zeitung*, xi (1808–9), 183.

During the first three decades of the century, as more musicians employed sliding effects, criticism continue in the press. In 1811 a singer was warned: "She might, however, beware of the *maniera smorfiosa* (that sliding down from one interval to another), which is wrongly mistaken for the real *portamento*, in which the second note of the interval is only slightly anticipated and tied to the first one without one hearing any intermediate note. (Our singers use this *cercar della nota* too often!)"[78] Two years later, August Ferdinand Häser observed:

> Just as *portamento* is considered in Italy to be one of the first requirements of a good singer, so it is strictly distinguished from the disgusting, distressing sliding (similar to the sliding on string instruments through the gradual shifting of the finger), which some singers mistakenly consider to be *portamento*. This dragging (*tirare*) and, if it is very conspicuous, this wailing (*urlare*), which is called *maniera affettata, smorfiosa*, to use a delicate term, is rarely tolerated for long.[79]

This suggests that, by curious reversal, the string player's *portamento*, which sought to emulate the singer's, was now inducing vocalists to make their *portamento* more pronounced.

As late as 1823, A. L. Crelle, a mathematician and keyboard player, registered his objection to *portamento* by singers and violinists in terms that seem to propose its total abolition.[80] But by that stage, many admired performers were using these sliding effects as an essential element of their style, and many more composers had begun to regard them as a valuable expressive tool. Among these was Beethoven. An article written five years after his death by the English composer and pianist Cipriani Potter, who was on friendly terms with Beethoven during his eight-month stay in Vienna in 1817–18, related a conversation in which Beethoven told him that Domenico Dragonetti's extraordinary bass playing had "led him to imagine [...] those slidings upon one string which impart so beautiful and spiritual a character to his chamber music."[81] Ignaz Schuppanzigh, the violinist who

---

[78] Anon.: *Allgemeine musikalische Zeitung*, xiii (1811–12), 257.
[79] August Ferdinand Häser: 'Mittheilungen über Gesang und Gesangsmethode. 2: Verbindung der Register der Stimme. Portamento di voce. Athemnehmen,' *Allgemeine musikalische Zeitung*, xv (1813), 167.
[80] Crelle: *Einiges*, 88.
[81] C. [Cipriani Potter]: 'Dragonetti', *The Court Magazine and Belle Assemblée*, i (1832), 74. Potter's authorship is confirmed by details in other articles written by C. for this magazine, which correspond with his known activities.

worked most closely with Beethoven throughout his time in Vienna, played many of his sonatas with him and premiered most of his string quartets, certainly employed sliding effects. This is confirmed by a comment written by Beethoven's teenage nephew, Carl, in one of his uncle's conversation books in 1824: "What I noticed among Schuppanzigh's peculiarities is that he slides from one note to the other with the finger on the string; for example, when he plays the notes [Ex. 15.31a], one hears the intervening notes [Ex. 15.31b] quickly joined together like an indistinct scale. Is that right?"[82]

Ex. 15.31 a–b. Beethoven: conversation book.

We do not know what Beethoven answered, but in view of Potter's report he presumably reassured Carl, who at that stage probably had limited experience of professional performances, that it was a perfectly normal expressive device when sensitively employed. The cellist Joseph Linke, too, who worked closely with Schuppanzigh and Beethoven, "delighted especially through his beautiful *portamento*" in a concert at the Theater an der Wien in 1819.[83] Other string players working in Beethoven's Vienna, such as the three Blumenthal brothers: Joseph, Casimir, and Leopold, Joseph Mayseder, and Joseph Böhm, employed *portamento* regularly, as demonstrated by their fingerings in editions of their own music.

Many early-19th-century string players were praised for their skilful and effective use of *portamento*. Sometimes a reviewer wanted more of it, as in the case of violinist L. W. Maurer: "His *portamento* is beautiful and vocal: but one wishes he would use it more frequently."[84] Even the Viennese contrabass player Johann Hindle was praised for his handling of the instrument because "he understands how to draw forth its commanding tone powerfully and also tenderly, with expressive, sustained *portamento*, and overall to sing on it".[85] And Jacques-Féréol Mazas was lauded in Berlin for his "beautiful *portamento* and genuine *legato*".[86] Praise for some string players' sliding

---

[82] *Ludwig van Beethovens Konversationshefte*, ed. Karl-Heinz Köhler, Grita Herre, and Peter Pötschner (Leipzig, 1970), v, 134.
[83] S . . . r: 'Wiener-Bühnen', *Allgemeine musikalische Zeitung* [Wien], iii (1819), 640.
[84] Anon.: *Allgemeine musikalische Zeitung*, xxii (1820), 49.
[85] Anon.: *Allgemeine musikalische Zeitung* [Wien], v (1821), 253.
[86] Anon.: *Allgemeine musikalische Zeitung*, xxv (1823), 185f.

effects, however, did not mean that opinions were united about everyone's use of it. In 1833, Elisabeth Filipowicz wrote to her former teacher, Spohr, from Paris after hearing Paganini: "I cannot understand why there are people who consider that his Adagio on the G string moves them to tears. His constant sliding with the finger brings forth a wailing that makes me laugh."[87] Clearly Paganini's use of it was very different from Spohr's. Singers too were criticized for unskilful or tasteless *portamento*. In Eleonora Zrza's performance, for instance, "connoisseurs still very much missed the correct use of a beautiful *portamento*, in place of which she produced a dragging that was offensive to every educated ear".[88] A. F. Häser, despite his earlier more negative comments, nevertheless expressed the view that was to remain dominant throughout the century:

> Portamento makes the singing highly attractive and is an important means of expression; but used constantly, it creates monotony and weakness. One should get accustomed therefore to alternately carrying and connecting the notes and then again to take them afresh without holding them and sliding them, since nothing is more necessary than to give the song variety though differing ornaments.[89]

Composers only rarely indicated *portamento* explicitly, and when they did, just as with arpeggiation signs in keyboard music, there is no reason to believe that they meant it to be used only in those places. In some contexts, however, they clearly regarded it as obligatory. In string music this could easily be shown by fingerings, but occasionally, where fingerings were not given, it might be required by a verbal instruction, as in Anton André's String Quartet op. 14 no. 3 (Ex. 15.32).

Ex. 15.32 Johann Anton André: String Quartet op. 14/3/ii.
[Adagio con moto]

In vocal music, an audible connection between notes was often specified by slurs. During the 18th century and much of the 19th, these were not written as a matter of course over melismas in vocal music. They were sometimes

---

[87] Elisabeth Filipowicz letter of 2 June 1833, *Spohr Briefe*.
[88] Anon.: *Allgemeine musikalische Zeitung*, xxiii (1821), 430f.
[89] August Ferdinand Häser: *Versuch einer systematischen Uebersicht der Gesangslehre* (Leipzig [1822]), 74.

included to clarify the disposition of syllables and sometimes to indicate phrasing or breathing in long melismas, but composers employed them intermittently and haphazardly in these contexts. Where they are found between notes on different syllables, however, they were certainly intended to elicit audible sliding. Examples can be found, for instance, in operas from Rossini to Wagner (Ex. 15.33a–e),[90] occasionally with an additional instruction as in *Les Huguenots* (Ex. 15.33d), where Meyerbeer made his intention (which involved a "leaping grace" type of *portamento*) quite clear by the grace-note.

Ex. 15.33a Rossini: *Semiramide*, no. 3 (autograph p. 120).

Ex. 15.33b Spohr: *Jessonda*, no. 18.

Ex. 15.33c Meyerbeer: *Les Huguenots*, no. 3.

Ex. 15.33d Meyerbeer, *Les Huguenots*, no. 24.

[90] For Moreschi's use of *portamento* in similar circumstances in the "Crucifixus" from the *Petite Messe solonnelle*, see Ch. 13.

Ex. 15.33e  Wagner, *Tristan und Isolde*, Act II, Scene ii.

The usage of a slur between syllables to indicate a *portamento* of the anticipation grace type is made explicit in Charles de Bériot's vocally inspired *Méthode de violon* (Ex. 15.34).

Ex. 15.34  Bériot: *Méthode*, 214.

Sometimes, where this procedure could not be used—or simply as an alternative—a verbal instruction might be supplied (Ex. 15.35).

Ex. 15.35a  Meyerbeer: *Les Huguenots*, no. 10.

Ex. 15.35b  Wagner: *Der fliegende Holländer*, no. 29.

## Sliding Effects in the Orchestra

In 1776, J. F. Reichardt, writing about string playing, had asserted:

> Shifting with a finger through various positions is absolutely forbidden to the orchestral player, although it is sometimes permitted for soloists. It takes much delicacy to make it bearable to a fine ear; as it is done by most violinists, it sounds exactly like the sighs of a despairing tomcat on the

doorstep of his half-deaf beloved. Even if done in the very best manner, though, one could not tolerate it from two at the same time; it is therefore doubly forbidden for the ripienist.[91]

Despite Reichardt's strictures, however, string players were certainly using sliding effects in orchestral playing in the later 18th century. A reviewer of operas at the Magdeburg theatre in 1798 noted:

> The theatre here supports 10 players of its own who all individually play splendidly, but on account of their dissimilar performance styles they do not form a good ensemble. This applies notably to the violinists.—So, for example, in a symphony I heard one of these players, instead of taking the third, D-F sharp, as two separate quarter-notes, slide from the D to the F sharp. Certainly, the higher note is easier to find in this way, but does this sort of aid, which is over-used to the extent of nausea by the majority of violinists, belong in a piece where there are 3 or 4 players to a part? I have now noticed this embellishment, which is so disfiguring in tutti passages, in the orchestras of many places.[92]

The reviewer also complained about excessive, and presumably unskilful, use of sliding effects by the prima donna, Toscani, remarking: "like the above-mentioned violinist, without even once singing differently, she constantly slides through the intervening notes on rising or falling fourths, fifths, or sixths, and since she does this incessantly, with her in any case piping voice, a dreadful miaow arises out of what is supposed to be an Italian ornament."[93]

Various references to a *maniera smorfiosa* around 1810 connect with Antonio Salieri's use of the term in his condemnation of what he regarded as an inappropriate use of sliding effects by orchestral string players. As Imperial Kapellmeister, responsible for the Viennese court theatres, he was particularly concerned about its growing employment in orchestras. In 1811 he complained publicly:

> For some time now, an effeminate and ridiculous manner of handling their instrument has crept into the playing of various weak solo violinists,

---

[91] Reichardt: *Ueber die Pflichten*, 35.
[92] Anon.: 'Ueber den Zustand der Musik in Magdeburg', *Allgemeine musikalische Zeitung*, i (1798–99), 461.
[93] Anon.: 'Ueber den Zustand', 463f.

which the Italians call *maniera smorfiosa*, and which consists in an abuse of shifting the fingers up and down on the strings.

This feeble and childish manner has, like an infectious disease, also spread to some orchestral players, and what is most ridiculous, not only to otherwise good violinists, but also to violists and even contrabassists. Such a manner, especially in a full orchestra, must inevitably—because a tolerated evil always gets worse—transform it from a harmonious body into a collection of whining children or meowing cats.[94]

And he insisted that the directors of the Imperial Opera would make it their duty to stamp it out. He implausibly attributed the increasing use of sliding effects to Antonio Lolli's humorous "Cat Concerto", complaining that Lolli's joke had led to a fashion that had been adopted not only by violinists and cellists but also singers.[95] This too suggests that he referred to something more prominent than the traditional vocal *portamento*. The ineffectiveness of Salieri's intervention, however, is evidenced by a similar diatribe, which he first issued as a pamphlet in 1814.[96]

In his general dislike of more prominent sliding effects than had previously been deemed stylish, however, Salieri was swimming against the tide. This is documented by Fröhlich's advice in 1811:

> Oboists, clarinettists, bassoonists can read the article about *portamento* [*Durchziehen*] in the flute school and apply it to their instruments. Horn players, trombone players should try to imitate the singing voice as much as possible through diligent study. But this is something for people who want to appear as up-to-date artists.[97]

By this stage, it seems very likely that some wind players will have used sliding effects not only as an expressive resource in solo repertoire, but also in solo passages of orchestral works. Certainly, wind players in the best orchestras still considered it legitimate to add ornaments, even in the 1840s, as Berlioz's complaint about a Dresden oboist demonstrates.[98]

---

[94] Antonio Salieri: Letter in Italian to the editor of the *Allgemeine musikalische Zeitung*, published in a German translation, xiii (1811), 207f.

[95] Salieri: Letter, 209.

[96] Antonio Salieri: 'Der musikalischen Dilettanten-Gesellschaft in Wien von dem Unterzeichneten', *Gesellschaftsblatt für gebildete Stände*, v (1815), 425f.

[97] Fröhlich: *Musikschule*, i, 58.

[98] See Ch. 13.

Authorities such as Spohr in 1833[99] and Gassner in 1844[100] insisted that orchestral string players should not add improvised ornaments, among which *portamento* was included. Spohr nevertheless certainly envisaged it in his orchestral music, but presumably only where he indicated it by the inclusion of fingering (Ex. 15.36a–b), or where the director encouraged it.

Ex. 15.36 a–b. Spohr: Fifth Symphony op. 102. (*a*) 1st movement; (*b*) 2nd movement.

Meyerbeer, too, occasionally called explicitly for sliding effects in the orchestra, as when he instructed in the score of *L'Etoile du nord* "slide with the same finger".[101] But it seems highly likely that by the middle years of the century it was becoming an established and accepted practice in many orchestras, not only where specifically indicated, but often at the discretion of individual players. This was undoubtedly hastened by the proliferation of conservatoire training, which prepared violinists to be soloists, even though their careers would mostly be spent as orchestral players. By the late 19th century, it was certainly possible for an orchestral string section to play like a soloist, as Hans von Bülow's work with the Meiningen Orchestra demonstrated, and it seems very likely that many later 19th-century composers, including Brahms, with whom Bülow collaborated, would have envisaged *portamento* at appropriate places in their orchestral music. A particularly revealing example of the effect a composer might expect in this respect is provided by Elgar's 1914 recording of an orchestra version of his "Salut d'amour", in which many of his own *portamento* fingerings, from the original solo violin

---

[99] Spohr: *Violinschule*, 249.
[100] F. S. Gassner: *Dirigent und Ripienist* (Karlsruhe, 1844), 52f.
[101] Meyerbeer: *L'Etoile du nord*, Full score (Paris, Brandus, 1854), 184.

version, are observed by the whole violin section.[102] Mahler indicated it specifically in the string parts of his orchestral scores by slanting lines, and clearly regarded it as an essential feature in his musical conception, but by the 1930s, his instructions in this respect were already being ignored, as the 1938 recording of his Ninth Symphony by the Vienna Philharmonic Orchestra demonstrates, in which the very numerous *portamento* indications are almost entirely ignored.[103]

## Sliding Effects in the Later 19th Century

By the 1840s, sliding effects were established as an essential attribute of beautiful performance; but the question of their tasteful employment remained a live issue. In singing, theorists and critics continued to insist on a clear distinction between the delicate audible connection associated with classic *portamento di voce*, the more pronounced, but still appropriate sliding that was associated with the expression of emotion, and the abuse of the embellishment, either through inappropriate technique, poor placement, or too frequent use. Not until the later 19th century, with the aid of recordings by artists born before 1850, can we begin to grasp what cultivated musicians at that time might have regarded as the aural distinction between tasteful and excessive *portamento*.

Manuel García's treatment of sliding effects in his *École* reflects the importance they were perceived to have in beautiful singing during the mid-19th century. He uses the term *Port de voix* (*Portamento di voce*) exclusively to designate expressive sliding:

> The *portamento* may encompass from a semitone to the full extent of the voice. It takes its value from the last portion of the note one leaves. The speed depends on the tempo of the phrase to which it belongs.
> 
> It can go from weak to strong,
> from strong to weak.

---

[102] https://www.youtube.com/watch?v=HlVVB_0ezDc.

[103] The highly effective employment of orchestral string *portamento* in present-day performances of this repertoire has been demonstrated in the pioneering recordings of Brahms orchestral works by Johannes Leertouwer (https://brahms.johannesleertouwer.nl/), and of Mahler's Ninth Symphony by Philipp von Steinaecke (https://www.youtube.com/watch?v=haHc6A47mkQ), of which a CD recording is due to be published in 2024.

It can be normal, or weak, or strong.

It can be performed in these different ways, either up or down.

The *portamento* will help to equalize the registers, timbres, and strength of the voice.

The voice will only touch the actual note by emphasizing the *portamento* itself.[104]

García makes a distinction between *portamento* (*Sons portés*) and *legato* (*Sons liés*), providing a graphic illustration of the two procedures (Ex. 15.37).

Ex. 15.37 García: *École*, i (1840), 15; i (1847), 31.

He illustrates both types of *portamento* referred to by Corri, Vaccai, and others but discourages the use of the second type (see Ex. 15.7b), asserting: "The *portamento* is executed by carrying the voice with the syllable which one is going to leave, and not, as it is too often done in France, with the following syllable taken by anticipation."[105] As an example, he gives a phrase from Cimarosa's *Sacrifizio d'Abraham*, first with the "correct" method and secondly with the "incorrect" method of singing it (Ex. 15.38a).

He had previously illustrated "correct" *portamento* with a music example showing how his father, who premiered the role of Count Almaviva in Rossini's *Il barbiere di Sevilla* in 1816, used it in that opera (Ex. 15.38b).

Earlier in the treatise, however, he had recommended the second method as an aid to pronouncing the syllable of a high note (Ex. 15.38c); but here, he contradicts his own advice.

Using the same passage from Donizetti's *Lucia di Lammermoor*, he warns that pupils are too easily tempted to adopt the former method, even though "There is another procedure that has the same advantages without the same drawbacks" (Ex. 15.38d).

---

[104] García: *École*, i, 1st edn, 14; 2nd edn, 29.
[105] García: *École*, ii, 28.

He also gives an example to illustrate how "Some singers, either from negligence or lack of taste, are not merely content to increase the number of *ports de voix*; they make the mistake of taking them all from below with the second syllable taken in anticipation. The result of this method is to spoil the attack on the second note and thus the rhythm; the melody, weakened in this manner, becomes nauseatingly languid" (Ex. 15.38e).[106]

Ex. 15.38  a–e. García: *École*. (*a*) ii, 28; (*b*) ii, 28; (*c*) ii, 13; (*d*) ii, 28; (*e*) ii, 28.

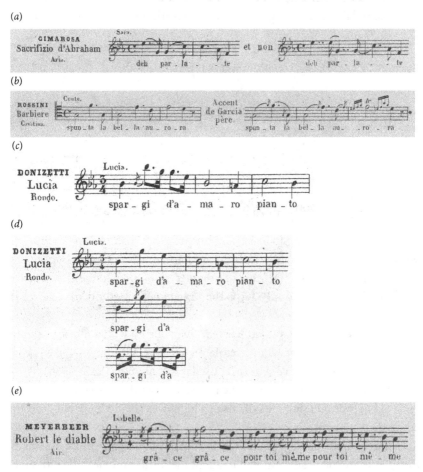

García's strictures, together with his example from Meyerbeer's *Robert le diable* (though obviously exaggerated), clearly represent a further stage in the preference for Vaccai's first type over the "less used" second type, while at the same time suggesting that the second type was still frequently heard.

[106] García: *École*, ii, 28.

Despite García's disapproval, the continued use of the *leaping grace* type of *portamento*, in very much the sorts of contexts illustrated by Corri, is attested by its occurrences in Adelina Patti's 1905 recordings.[107] But these occur mostly in her performances of earlier repertoire, from Mozart to Bellini, apparently revealing stylistic sensitivity to music of different periods. It is surely not coincidental that she is one of the oldest female singers on record, and that in recordings of younger singers this embellishment is rare, if not entirely absent. Its pervasiveness in recordings made by the much younger papal castrato Alessandro Moreschi in 1902–4, probably reflects his training in a tradition of singing that had been faithfully preserved among the Papal castrati in Rome after they disappeared from the operatic stage in the early 19th century.[108]

Charles de Bériot, who wrote the most detailed Franco-Belgian violin treatise of this period (1857/1858), had been married to García's sister, Maria Malibran, and, according to Heinrich Heine, it seemed "as if the soul of his deceased wife sat in his violin and sang".[109] His treatment of *portamento* (as of *vibrato* [*sons vibrés*]) has much in common with his brother-in-law's, and he begins his discussion of these practices with examples of their appropriate use in vocal music.[110] In common with other 19th-century musicians, he devotes more space to sliding than to trembling effects, with six pages on the former and three on the latter. His treatment of sliding effects is particularly informative because he uses differentiated graphic symbols (Ex. 15.39), which he first employs in musical extracts to demonstrate "incorrect" use of sliding in violin playing (Ex. 15.40a), "correct" use in singing (Ex. 15.40b), and "correct" use in violin playing (Ex. 15.40c).

Ex. 15.39 Bériot: *Méthode*, 215. Rapid *port-de-voix*; soft *port-de-voix*; dragged *port-de-voix*.

---

[107] See Ch. 13.
[108] Meyerbeer's *Il crociato in Egitto* (1824) was the last important opera to contain a major castrato role.
[109] Heinrich Heine: *Heinrich Heine's sämmtliche Werke*, xi (Hamburg 1874), 334.
[110] See Clive Brown: 'Singing and String Playing'.

934 CLASSICAL AND ROMANTIC PERFORMING PRACTICE

**Ex. 15.40** a–c. Bériot: *Méthode*. (*a*) 217. "Bad prosody, poor changes of position, abuse of the *port-de-voix*, counter to the sense of the music"; (*b*) 218. "After the examples we have just given, taken from melodies whose severe style includes the least amount of dragging of the sounds, we classify here in a graduated order the various genres of song in which the *port-de-voix* is not only permitted, but indispensable for rendering all the affectionate, plaintive, or painful expressions of the feelings of the soul"; (*c*) 219. "Examples of violin music corresponding to those on the preceding page".

(*a*)

**Ex. 15.40** Continued

(b)

**Ex. 15.40** Continued

(c)

Bériot's example of appropriate sliding effects at the beginning of the Adagio of Beethoven's String Quartet op. 59 no. 1 suggests that there was broad agreement between Franco-Belgian and German musicians about the appropriate placement of audible slides at this stage in the 19th century: comparison with the fingering in Ferdinand David's bowed and fingered edition shows *portamento* shifts in the same places (Ex. 15.41).

Ex. 15.41a Bériot: *Méthode*, 229.

Ex. 15.41b David: Beethoven String Quartets, p. 60.

Early recordings indicate more pervasive use of sliding effects. In the first six bars of this movement, for instance, the first violinist of the Budapest String Quartet made three additional, very prominent slides their 1929 recording. An increasingly extensive employment of heavy sliding by string players may well have contributed significantly to its almost total rejection in the later 20th century.

Bériot makes no reference to the mechanism by which the slides should be achieved, making it unclear whether, except in the case of single-finger shifts, he countenanced sliding with the finger that was to take the target note, in the manner condemned by Spohr. Bériot's fingerings do not, in general, suggest that procedure, but in the annotated version of his Ninth Violin Concerto, which concludes the *Méthode*, there is one example that explicitly requires it (Ex. 15.42a), and there are several resembling the *leaping grace*, which reflect the kind of vocal *portamento* generally deprecated, but occasionally recommended by García (Ex. 15.42b).

Ex. 15.42 a–b. Bériot: *Méthode*. (a) 244. Allegro 1st solo bb. 4–6. "Carry the sound with the little finger to the high A with vivacity and force; then descend to the E with the same finger with a soft *port-de-voix*. E affectionate *port-de-voix* descending from B to F♯ without affectation in the slide";
(b) 250 Adagio, bb. 8–11. The first ascending phrase with soft and tender expression growing gradually in intensity until letter C.

(a)

Ex. 15.42 Continued

(b)

Portamento of the former type was evidently not uncommon among Franco-Belgian violinists of the next generation, for in the 1880s Hermann Schröder explained: "It would be an offense against aesthetic rules if the finger of an upper note went down early and slid up to it, or vice versa, causing a wailing effect. Unfortunately, one often hears this bad habit, and even from leading virtuosos." In a footnote he added: "In the French school in particular [. . .] this perverse mannerism is often popular and common, but we, however, absolutely cannot approve of it."[111]

Treatises provide glimpses of the difference between aesthetic theory and practical music-making. Many writers sought to defend the aesthetic they had grown up with against the practices of younger musicians who were the harbingers of change. Bériot warned: "Almost all violinists who use *port-de-voix* too frequently, abuse *son vibré* (*vibrato*); the one fault inevitably leads to the other. The affectation that results from the employment of these elements makes the artist's playing mannered, exaggerated, for it gives a piece more expression than is consistent with truth."[112] The disjunction between theory and practice, in string playing as well as singing, which these admonitions suggest, is also clear from reviews of performers whose playing was seen either to offend against aesthetic orthodoxy or to affirm it. Violinist Georg Hänflein was criticized in 1873 for his "all-too-frequently used *glissando* (which he really cannot have got from his master Joachim!)".[113] Cellist Leopold Grützmacher (b. 1835) was taken to task for his "excessive use of *glissando*", and the critic added: "This mannered 'sliding' from one note to another is just as blameworthy as the singer's too frequent use of the *portamento*, and decidedly tasteless."[114] Leopold's more celebrated brother Friedrich Grützmacher (b. 1832) seems not to have been criticized for abuse of *portamento*, although

---

[111] Schröder: *Die Kunst des Violinspiels*, 33.
[112] Bériot, *Méthode*, 220.
[113] Anon.: *Neue Berliner Musikzeitung*, xxvii (1873), 380.
[114] Anon. [Max Ehrenfried]: *Neue Berliner Musikzeitung*, 29 (1875), 243.

his editions contain concrete evidence that he used it freely; this is shown not only by fingerings, but also the instruction *gliss*. in places where a sliding effect cannot be clearly indicated by the fingering, for instance, to or from an open string (Ex. 15.43a–b). He also employed sliding effects after a rest, or a *staccato* note, presumably in a manner similar to Corri's *leaping grace*, a practice that would only rarely have been considered acceptable in German violin playing (Ex. 15.43c–d).[115] Since he was often praised for his classical performing style, however, and even hailed as the Joachim of the cello, it seems likely that his use of sliding effects and trembling effects was regarded as a model of tastefulness.[116]

**Ex. 15.43** a–d. Mendelssohn: Cello Sonatas, ed. Friedrich Grützmacher (Leipzig, 1878). (*a*) op. 58 [Allegro assai vivace]; (*b*) op. 58 [Adagio]; (*c*) op. 45 [Andante]; (*d*) op. 45 [Allegro vivace].

[115] Grützmacher's edition of Mendelssohn's Cello Sonatas is described on the title page as "Precisely marked in the tradition of the composer. (Nach dem Tradition des Componisten genau bezeichnet), a phrase that also occurs on the title pages of David's editions of his master Spohr's violin concertos. See CHASE.

[116] See Kate Bennett Wadsworth: *"Precisely marked in the tradition of the composer": The Performing Editions of Friedrich Grützmacher* (PhD thesis, University of Leeds, 2017).

940  CLASSICAL AND ROMANTIC PERFORMING PRACTICE

Another 19th-century violinist, the Böhm pupil Edmund Singer (b. 1831), in his edition of Beethoven's Violin Sonatas, indicated sliding effects with slanting lines in places where the fingering might not clearly show it (Ex. 15.44).

Ex. 15.44  Beethoven: Violin Sonata op. 24, Rondo, Allegro ma non troppo, ed. Edmund Singer (Stuttgart, 1887).

Fingerings in Ferdinand David's numerous annotated editions of violin and chamber music (published between 1843 and 1873) provide similarly clear evidence of his expectations for sliding effects; and his surviving personal copies contain his even more detailed handwritten fingering and bowing, which shows extensive use of them. Sometimes he included a verbal reminder, such as *rutschen* [slide], that it should be employed in places where it might not be expected, for instance between notes marked with *portato* lines (Ex. 15.45).

Ex. 15.45  Heinrich Biber: Sonata in C minor in Ferdinand David's personal performing copy of his *Hohe Schule des Violinspiels* (Leipzig, 1867). [Passacaglia A tempo moderato]

More generally, it is the fingering alone that indicates a sliding effect, since almost all position changes within *legato* were expected to be heard to some extent. Where the position changes are technically unnecessary, they imply a particularly expressive *portamento*, as in many places in David's personal copies of Mendelssohn's String Quintet op. 18, and String Quartets opp. 12,

13, and 44 nos. 1–3, some of which he undoubtedly played with the composer taking the viola part (Ex. 15.46a–b).

**Ex. 15.46a** Ferdinand David's copy of Mendelssohn's String Quintet op. 18 (containing alterations in the composer's hand in red, with performance markings by David in blue) (Staatsbibliothek zu Berlin) [Larghetto].

**Ex. 15.46b** Mendelssohn String Quartet op. 44 no. 3. David's fingering. [Allegro vivace]

As Grützmacher's *gliss.* instructions involving open strings indicate, it is not always clear from the fingering alone that a sliding effect was envisaged; but many string players undoubtedly made sliding effects in those contexts. As mentioned above, Spohr, in his *Violinschule*, described a slide to an open string in Rode's Seventh Violin Concerto, which he may well have observed in Rode's playing, when he heard him in 1803. Ferdinand David, in the context of an exercise demonstrating the mechanism for shifts at all intervals from seconds to tenths, included instructions for slides from and to open strings, with the final position of the shifting finger indicated by a small thirty-second-note (Ex. 15.47).

Ex. 15.47 Ferdinand David: *Violinschule*, ii, 33.

*) Bei diesen Stellen setze man den ersten Finger hinter den Sattel und ziehe ihn bis zur kleinen Note herauf.
*Put down the first finger behind the nut and draw it up to the small note.*

There are several examples of slides from open strings, too, in Bériot's *Méthode* (see Exx. 15.39 and 15.40c), and the same procedures are also described in the Joachim and Moser *Violinschule* in 1905.

At this stage of the 19th century there was probably little difference between the fingering practices of German and Franco-Belgian players. Comparison of the fingering in Ferdinand David's published edition of Mendelssohn's Violin Concerto with Hubert Léonard's fingering in the proof copy, from which he played it, with the composer at the piano, before publication, reveals remarkable similarities, especially in the placing of expressive shifts.[117] The only difference in the opening theme of the Andante is that in bars 13–14 Léonard indicates the position change between the first and second notes, while David makes it between the second and third; both shift 1-1 between the third and fourth notes in bar 9, 3-3 between the fourth and fifth notes in bars 13–14, and 4-4 between the fourth and fifth notes in bar 15 (Ex. 15.48a–b); both shift up the A-string to the harmonic on the first note of bar 10.

---

[117] See Clive Brown: Mendelssohn Violin Concerto (Kassel, Bärenreiter, 2018).

Ex. 15.48 a–b. Mendelssohn: Violin Concerto op. 64, Andante. (*a*) Léonard's proof copy (Brussels Conservatoire library); (*b*) David's edition (Leipzig, Breitkopf & Härtel, 1865).

David's pupil Robert Heckman, who was certainly familiar with the Leipzig traditions of chamber music performance, made an edition of Schumann's three String Quartets op. 41 in 1887, in which very similar sliding fingerings abound (Ex. 15.49).

Ex. 15.49 Schumann: String Quartet op. 41 no. 3.

Warnings against the abuse of both sliding and trembling effects persisted into the first decade of the 20th century. While the admonitions against too frequent employment of trembling effects must be seen, with hindsight, as a rear-guard action against a practice that was being used with increasing frequency and intensity,[118] the teaching of *portamento* was concerned with practices that were still regarded, universally, as a major factor in beautiful,

---

[118] See Ch. 16.

expressive performance. The concerns of critics and treatise writers were primarily focused on the appropriate execution and placement of sliding effects.

The section on *portamento* in the Joachim and Moser *Violinschule* shows that emulation of vocal practice still lay at the heart of 19th-century string playing. They echo a comment about the use of ornaments in instrumental playing that had been made more than a century earlier: "The embellishment which corresponds most closely to true singing is unquestionably the most appropriate and best."[119] The first paragraph of Moser's text includes the statement:

> As a means of expression borrowed from the human voice [...] the application and execution of portamento will naturally be subject to the same rules that apply to "the art of beautiful singing". Portamento performed on the violin between two notes under the same bowstroke thus corresponds to the connection of two notes on the same text-syllable in singing, and the portamento with simultaneous change of bow and [left-hand] position to the situation in which a singer wants to create a connection, for the sake of musical expression, where a new syllable comes on the second note. This advice is all the more important because the clear remembrance of the origin and meaning of a 'practice' will best protect the pupil from its misuse.[120]

Spohr's example of "correct" *portamento* is given, but his "incorrect" type is not mentioned, presumably because it was regarded as unthinkable in the context of German practice (see Flesch's comments, below); and Spohr's changing of fingers on a note within a single bowstroke is also given. Much of the article deals with special cases, involving shifts to and from natural harmonics and open strings. One example contains a shift from $c^2$ to an $a^2$ harmonic in Joachim's arrangement of Brahms' Second Hungarian Dance (Ex. 15.50a), which can be heard very prominently on Joachim's 1903 recording.

Particularly interesting is the analysis of a descending octave shift between bowstrokes in Beethoven's F major Romance op. 50, with four "faulty" methods of executing it, which "one unfortunately hears very often" (Ex. 15.50b). The "correct" one, which is only acceptable if it "does not at all impinge on the listener's consciousness",[121] can be heard on the recording of the Romance by Marie Soldat (one of Joachim's most faithful students, whose style was considered very similar to his),[122] where, to

---

[119] Anon [G. F. Wolf?]: *Wahrheiten die Musik betreffend*, 69.
[120] Joachim and Moser: *Violinschule*, ii, 92.
[121] Joachim and Moser: *Violinschule*, ii, 94.
[122] Clive Brown: 'Marie Soldat-Roeger and the Twilight of a Nineteenth-Century German School of Violin Playing' in *Im Schatten des Kunstwerks*, 179–210.

modern ears, unaccustomed to 19th-century expectations, the shift is quite noticeable.

Ex. 15.50 a–b. Joachim and Moser: *Violinschule*. (*a*) ii, 93; (*b*) ii, 94.

(*a*)

(*b*)

Although Joachim himself was perceived to be much less lavish with *portamento* than many of his contemporaries, his bowed and fingered editions of music from Bach to Brahms in volume 3 of the *Violinschule* contain frequent *portamento* fingerings, very similar to those in Ferdinand David's many editions. These fingerings were considered anathema by the middle of the 20th century. Later editions provided very different, often quite convoluted ones, designed solely to avoid shifting. A telling example is the second movement of Brahms's Violin Sonata in A major op. 100, where the composer clearly expected the kind of vocal *portamento* that is indicated by fingerings in all the early editions of the Sonata up to the 1920s, which were replaced in later editions by fingerings that avoided shifts as much as possible.[123]

Carl Flesch, a champion of *continuous vibrato*, still regarded *portamento* as an essential aspect of expressive violin playing. The susceptibility to sensuality that attracted him to Kreisler's *vibrato* seems also to have manifested itself in a lavish exploitation of sliding effects that would certainly have been deplored by Joachim, both for their quantity and the manner of

---

[123] In many of the 19th- and early-20th-century editions on the CHASE website, which were obtained from conservatoire libraries, the pervasive replacement of the printed fingerings with "clean" modern ones, is very instructive of this change of taste.

execution. This was already coming under increasing critical scrutiny during Flesch's own lifetime; his use of *portamento* was criticized in 1914 when he played Beethoven's Violin Concerto in New York. A report of his performance included the comment: "He lacks an innate feeling for rhythm and is afflicted with a marked tendency to slide from note to note in 'glissando' or 'portamento.'"[124] Flesch's recordings, as well as his writings, show that he and many of his contemporaries often used the "French" *portamento* condemned by so many German musicians from Spohr onwards. Motivated by the modernist tendency to reject the received wisdom of the past, he was just as critical of the old German tradition of "correct" *portamento* as he was of its approach to *vibrato*, and sought in his treatises to legitimize theoretically the type condemned by Spohr. He identified two forms of *portamento*: A—"connected to the beginning note [*Anfangsnote*]" and E—"executed with the ending finger [*Endfinger*]" (Ex. 15.51).

Ex. 15.51 Flesch: *Die Kunst*, i, 30.

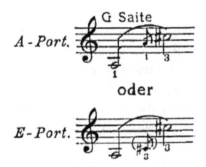

He commented:

If we consult the best-known violin schools on this point, up to the beginning of the 20th century, we will find that all authors without exception recognize the A-Portamento as the only road to salvation, whereas the E-Portamento is cursed as a diabolical manifestation of bad taste. [...]

In the portamento question there is a gap between theory and practice that cannot be bridged. In fact, there is not one of the great violinists

---

[124] Anon.: *New York Times*, 23 January 1914, 5.

of our time who does not use the E-portamento more or less often. Its rejection therefore leads to the condemnation of all modern violin playing and its most outstanding representatives, starting with *Ysaye* [*sic*], and probably not even the most indomitable reactionary will go that far.[125]

Flesch also identified what he called *Phantasie-Portamenti*, of which he specifically approved the type illustrated in Ex. 15.52 that resembles the similar type of cellists' *portamento* described by Dotzauer and Davydov among others (see above).

Ex. 15.52 Flesch: *Die Kunst*, i, 34.

Recordings support Flesch's claims. Joachim and Marie Soldat, for instance, employ Flesch's A-Portamento as their standard method of shifting. Recordings of younger string players in the first half of the century contain very many examples of E-Portamento, although Ysaÿe scarcely used the latter on his 1912 recordings. Comparison of three recordings of the violin arrangements of Schumann's "Abendlied" provides revealing examples of the types of A-, E-, and *Phantasie-portamento* illustrated by Flesch. Spectrograms of bar 7 as recorded by Marie Soldat (c. 1920), Manuel Quiroga (1928), and Eugène Ysaÿe (1912) show them (in that order) very clearly. On these recording, too, the difference between Soldat's almost unnoticeable *vibrato*, Ysaÿe's almost continuous but narrow *vibrato*, and Quiroga's slower, broader *vibrato* are obvious (Ex. 15.53).[126]

---

[125] Carl Flesch: *Die Kunst des Violinspiels* (Berlin, 1923), 30.
[126] See Johannes Gebauer: 'Die Joachim-Tradition. Methodische Ansätze der Interpretationsforschung' in Thomas Gartmann and Michaela Schäuble (eds.), *Beiträge der Graduate School of the Arts* 2 (Bern, 21–35), https://boris.unibe.ch/120740/1/181105_GSA2_eVersion.pdf, 2018, 31–34. For further discussion of these spectrograms, reproduced here with his kind permission [accessed 9 November 2020].
  The violin arrangements of this piece can be accessed at https://imslp.org/wiki/12_Klavierst%C3%BCcke_f%C3%BCr_kleine_und_gro%C3%9Fe_Kinder%2C_Op.85_(Schumann%2C_Robert).

**Ex. 15.53** Sonic visualiser images from recordings of Schumann's 'Abendlied' by (from top to bottom): Marie Soldat c. 1920: Classic German *portamento* with starting finger; Manuel Quiroga 1928: "French" *portamento* with ending finger; Eugène Ysaÿe 1912: "Fantasie" *portamento* with both fingers. (Reproduced by kind permission of Johannes Gebauer.)

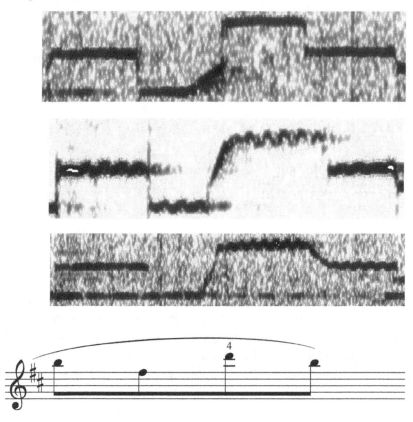

In the truncated version of Elgar's Violin Concerto, which Marie Hall recorded under the direction of the composer in 1916, there are many sliding effects from both soloist and orchestra. The *portamento* implied by Elgar's fingering in the soloist's second bar in the Andante (Ex. 15.54) is performed very strikingly with a slow slide of the first finger up the G-string. The same *portamento*, though still obvious, is much less prominent on Yehudi Menuhin's 1932 recording with the composer, but in later recordings, including Menuhin's in 1966, it is executed in an extremely discreet manner.

Ex. 15.54 Elgar: Violin Concerto op. 61/ii.

Early-20th-century recordings of singers reveal a similar picture. An audible connection between notes in *legato*, and abundant expressive slides, remains prominent in the singing of all of them. To modern ears, Patti's *portamento* seems very prominent, but in 1878, it was held up as a model of discretion and good taste by Heinrich Ruff, who stated that "the fragrance and magic of her cantilena is based on the subtleties of her portamento, through which she moves so ethereally lightly from step to step". He also associated its beauty with her restraint in the use of *vibrato* or *tremolo*:

> When Madam Patti intones the "ah fors' e lui" in the Andantino of the "La Traviata" aria, everyone involuntarily holds their breath as if they had to bring the beating of the heart into 3/8 time. The much-discussed bel canto of the Italians was nothing other than this portamento, to which the fine shading from the piano to the mezzo forte was added. Any trembling was of course out of the question; the calm of the breath is a main condition of beautiful song for all times.[127]

Patti did not record this aria, but the artistry of her *portamento* and the subtlety of her *vibrato*, ranging from imperceptible to delicately or passionately expressive, are consistently displayed in her many 1905–6 recordings. The documented admiration of her artistry by Rossini, Berlioz, Verdi, Tchaikowsky, and numerous other knowledgeable contemporaries provides a corrective to J. B. Steane's later 20th-century perception that "certain features of Patti's style at this date simply were not musical".[128] Most importantly, 19th-century accounts show that Patti's use of sliding and trembling effects (which in the late 20th century still seemed so alien to most listeners

---

[127] Heinrich Ruff: 'Das Portamento im Gesange. Ein Versuch zur Klarstellung dieses Begriffs', *Musikalisches Wochenblatt*, ix (1878), 146f.
[128] John Barry Steane: *The Grand Tradition. Seventy Years of Singing on Record* (Portland, 1974), 15.

that it often prompted laughter when I played it during lectures) was then considered exceptionally beautiful.[129] Much the same could be said of the mismatch between Joseph Joachim's tremendous reputation as a great violinist and musician, and the impression created on late-20th-century ears by his recordings, which even in the 1990s were similarly inclined to provoke incredulity and even ridicule.

This gap in perception can only be explained adequately by the magnitude of the transformation that occurred when many members of a younger generation of artists, like Flesch, sought to distance themselves deliberately and assertively from former traditions and practices. Artistic development was no longer a dialogue with the past, leading to gradual evolution, but a fundamental rejection of previously cherished principles and practices. The force of this revolution was so powerful that previous criteria of taste came to seem not merely old-fashioned, but totally alien to performers and listeners of later generations, who had not experienced it directly in their formative years. People brought up in cultured musical environments, whose memories extend back no further than the 1930s, such as J. B. Steane (b. 1928), have tended to regard any kind of noticeable sliding effects as distinctly distasteful. This acquired tastelessness of *portamento* in classical performance undoubtedly owes much to its prominence in the kinds of popular music that began to challenge classical music's cultural predominance during the early 20th century, and were subsequently perceived by many as its cultural equal. The author of an article "*Neue Klänge in der Musik. Der Jazz als Vorbild*" in 1930 enthused about the use of *portamento* by jazz musicians:

> The saxophone vibrates and always hangs like a veil over the sound of the jazz orchestra, enveloping it in a soft mass, so to speak. Characteristic of jazz is vibrato and the vocal-like portamento with which the jazz saxophonist intertwines the tones of a melody. Dragging from one tone to another, which is strictly forbidden in classical and romantic orchestral music and is regarded as utterly tasteless, is a feature of beauty in jazz. A good saxophone player can pull through the entire scale in a glissando without one being able to distinguish between the individual notes.[130]

---

[129] See Roger Freitas: 'Singing Herself: Adelina Patti and the Performance of Femininity', *Journal of the American Musicological Society*, lxxi (2018), 287–369.

[130] Anon.: 'Neue Klänge in der Musik. Der Jazz als Vorbild', *Neues Wiener Journal*, 2 April 1930, 8.

By that time, the sensitivity of classical musicians to this association had already made an impact. In 1929, Carl Flesch asked rhetorically: "And what would our old master [Joachim] say about the latest developments in the field of portamenti initiated by the saxophone in jazz music, a clumsy distortion that transforms and parodies the originally noble, expression-intensifying goal of connecting the notes, into a ridiculous, lascivious whimpering?"[131] A decade later he revised his positive evaluation of a type of *portamento* developed by Jacques Thibaud, which he had described as *Phantasie-Portamento* in the German editions of his *Kunst des Violinspiels* (Ex. 15.55).[132] In the 1939 revised English translation he added: "In the meanwhile [...] this portamento has become, alas, the indispensable requisite of every jazz musician."[133]

Ex. 15.55 Flesch, *Die Kunst*, i, 34.

Numerous reviews in musical journals during the 1930s and 1940s reveal growing criticism of sliding effects in classical singing and string playing. When it was combined with an increasingly broad *continuous vibrato*, it had a very different effect than when it was associated with pitch-steady tone and occasional very narrow *vibrato*. By that stage, the new style of *continuous vibrato* was too deeply embedded in the modernist aesthetic to be abandoned, despite its exploitation by "popular" musicians. Sliding effects, however, was strongly associated not only with the increasingly disparaged performing practices of 19th-century classical music-making, but had also been enthusiastically adopted and developed in "jazz"; in this context, it became increasingly problematic for "classical" musicians who, for whatever reason, sought to disassociate themselves from "popular music". The perceived need for a style that was entirely free from sliding effects is nicely illustrated by an article on the new approach to cello fingering pioneered by Wilhelm Lamping:

> The glissando, the necessity for which has been made into a virtue with very questionable success, can now be dispensed with entirely. The violoncellist

[131] Flesch: *Die Kunst* (1928), ii, 183.
[132] Flesch: *Die Kunst*, 1st edn, i, 34.
[133] Flesch: *The Art of Violin Playing* (New York, 1939), i, 34.

therefore has the option of deleting the portamento as a means of expression from his musical breviary. If a healthy feeling stirs in him, he quickly decides to do so. Tasteful musicians, insofar as they are not prompted by some sort of egocentric reasons to oppose it, usually realize quickly that playing that has been freed from any sentimentality by Lamping's instructions is very beneficial for works of all styles, and confirm it without reservation. Since warmth and intensity of expression can be achieved in any desired degree without the use of portamento—all wind instruments can prove this convincingly—the violoncello is now able to achieve a healthy, genuinely German style of performance, and to ban from the concert halls a means of expression, that is used particularly abundantly in the lower regions of musical culture.[134]

The undertones of cultural ideology in this article are suggestive; but prejudice against sliding effects was certainly not confined to the Third Reich. Various other reasons than cultural bias, or the incompatibility of *portamento* with *continuous vibrato*, have been suggested to account for the sharp decline in the use of sliding effects that occurred in the mid-20th century; these include the perceived inappropriateness, after the horrors of the early 20th century, of some forms that may have associations with the comforting effect of lullabies, described as "motherese" (2006),[135] or the impact of recording.[136] Whatever the complex motivations that led to 20th-century changes in taste, the result was that, in this respect, as in so many others, Classical and Romantic composers' expectations for the realization of their notation in sound were misunderstood in ways they would probably have regarded not only as incorrect, but also as fundamentally detrimental to the integrity of their musical intentions.

---

[134] Gerhard Weckerling: 'Wilhelm Lampings neue Violoncelltechnik', *Zeitschrift für Musik*, cviii (1941), 238.
[135] Daniel Leech-Wilkinson: 'Portamento and Musical Meaning', *Journal of Musicological Research*, xxv (2006), 233–61.
[136] Mark Katz: 'Portamento and the Phonograph Effect', *Journal of Musicological Research*, xxv (2006), 211–32.

# 16
# Trembling Effects

During the past three centuries, attitudes towards the use of trembling effects in musical performance, where these are not specified in the notation, have fluctuated between outright condemnation and enthusiastic espousal. Numerous terms, in several languages, have been used historically to describe a variety of trembling effects, many of which were entirely different from the practices now conventionally associated with the term *vibrato*, which since at least the 1920s has been conventionally regarded as a trembling of pitch, and an intrinsic aspect of tone quality, rather than an ornamental gesture. Some practices described by other terms may be regarded as antecedents of the 20th-century *continuous vibrato*; but probably none of them, either in the way they were produced or their artistic application, could be considered congruent with the *vibrato* that began to be taught in mainstream vocal and instrumental tuition during the 20th century.[1]

## The Notation of Trembling Effects

Although trembling effects, like other optional ornaments or embellishments, were usually left to the discretion of the performer, various signs were proposed and sporadically employed to signify them. The most common were dots under a slur, or a wavy line, both of which could have other meanings. These are quite often encountered in 18th-century orchestral scores,[2] but are seldom marked in solo music. As Petri remarked, in connection with the *Bebung* (notated with dots under a slur): "It is mostly not marked, but occurs merely in performance. Occasionally, however, one finds

---

[1] Since writing the first edition of this book, it has become clear to me that the word *vibrato* is used to describe so many different types of trembling effect, that I decided to use italics throughout (except of course in quotations where italics were not used). I also use italics for the 20th-century concept of *continuous vibrato*, which, apart from its continuity, has also changed its character over the past century.

[2] For its use by Gluck and other 18th-century composers as a symbol for trembling of intensity (especially with the bow) see Ch. 6.

it, for the sake of beginners who do not yet know where they should introduce ornaments."[3] In the 19th century, dots and a slur became increasingly rare as a notation for trembling effects, whereas the wavy line became more strongly connected with them, including timpani rolls. But the wavy line as an instruction to use left-hand trembling on string instruments is rarely found outside textbooks. Spohr included it in a few of his later publications (see Ex. 16.35), in all of which its relative infrequency is noteworthy. Wagner used it in *Siegfried* together with the instruction "with trembling voice" (Ex. 16.1).[4] And Joachim employed it in some of his arrangements of Brahms's Hungarian Dances.

Ex. 16.1  Wagner: *Siegfried*, Act I, Scene iii. Full score 1st edn, p. 105.

In the 1830s, >>>> or ~~~~ were given as indicating "the vibration or close shake".[5] Here the former notation seems likely to have been associated with the series of small accents which are apparent in a trembling of intensity, while the wavy line might imply a more connected trembling, either of intensity or pitch. Examples of similar notation can be found in Meyerbeer's scores, but as with numerous notational matters at this period, there are inconsistencies. The notation shown in Ex. 16.2a occurs in an early Italian copyist's score of *Il crociato in Egitto*, while in the printed vocal score of the same work (overseen by the composer) this is given as Ex. 16.2b.[6]

Ex. 16.2  a–b. Meyerbeer: *Il crociato in Egitto*. (*a*) MS full score, no. 9; (*b*) Printed vocal score (Paris, Pacini, [c. 1826]), no. 8.

In *Les Huguenots* >>>> again seems to be used to indicate a trembling effect in a passage for solo viola (Ex. 16.3).

---

[3] Johann Samuel Petri: *Anleitung zur praktischen Musik*, 1st edn (Lauban, 1767), 32.
[4] Wagner: *Siegfried*, Act I, Scene 3. Full score, 1st edn, p. 105.
[5] J. A. Hamilton: *Dictionary*, 88.
[6] MS score copy in the archives of Teatro La Fenice, Venice; pub. in fac. in the series *Early Romantic Opera* (New York and London, Garland, 1979), 459; vocal score (Paris, Pacini, [c. 1826]), 107 (copy in Bodleian Library, Oxford).

Ex. 16.3 Meyerbeer: *Les Huguenots*, Full score, 1st edn, no. 2, p. 84. The o over f♯[1] is evidently a misprint.

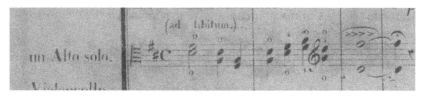

The sign <>, which is evidently related to the traditional *messa di voce*, may often have been used over a single note to imply a trembling effect at its apex. It is present in Baillot's *L'Art du violon*, together with a wavy line, in an example from Viotti's Violin Concerto no. 19 (Ex. 16.4).

Ex. 16.4 Baillot: *L'art du violon*, 138.

Campagnoli, too, used it frequently in his *Nouvelle méthode*, where he linked it specifically though not exclusively with what he variously designates as *balancement, ondegiamento* [sic], *tremblement*, and *Bebung*.[7] It is also equated explicitly with left-hand *vibrato* in the Joachim and Moser *Violinschule*, where Moser explained: "The vibrato, however, plays its role as a seasoning [Würzemittel] not only in slow pieces on notes of longer duration, but also in the fleeting course of passages that are to be played rapidly. Rode made a specialty of this, and not infrequently required it in his compositions by marking <>, even on thirty-second-notes and sixty-fourths."[8] He followed this with an example of its use on selected sixteenths in Rode's Third Caprice (see Ex. 11.11). The sign is frequent throughout Rode's caprices and elsewhere in his music; it is not widely found elsewhere on single notes in early-19th-century music, but it occurs relatively often in the music of Zelter, his pupil Mendelssohn (whose close friend and violin teacher, Eduard Rietz, was a pupil of Rode), Schumann, and Brahms. In the music of all these composers, it seems probable that, whatever else it might

---

[7] Campagnoli: *Méthode*, pt. 2, 62, and pt. 5, 29.

[8] Joachim and Moser: *Violinschule*, iii, 7. The English equivalent of this passage in the bilingual original edition of the *Violinschule* translates Moser's "auf Tönen langer Dauer seine Rolle als Würzemittel" as "employed for the beautifying of notes of longer duration": an important difference between "spice" and "beauty" which illuminates very different aesthetic attitudes.

be intended to convey, such as a gentle dynamic accent, agogic accentuation,[9] arpeggiation in piano writing,[10] or, in some contexts a sliding effect, the use of this sign in many circumstances may well have been expected to encourage expressive trembling.

Trembling effects could also be specified by verbal instructions. These are found occasionally, even as late as the first half of the 20th century, both in solo and orchestral music. In the 19th century and even the early 20th century, therefore, if a composer required it in the orchestra, it needed to be specified; and from at least the 1840s, the word *vibrato*, in contexts that evidently indicate a left-hand trembling effect, occurs occasionally in printed music. Ex. 16.5 offers examples from Loewe, Wagner, and Elgar.[11] In the 18th and early 19th centuries, however, as demonstrated below, the word may have an entirely different implication when it occurs in orchestral scores.

**Ex. 16.5** a–d. *Vibrato* in orchestral music. (*a*) Loewe: *Die Festzeiten* op. 66, fac. edn of autograph (Mainz, Schott, 1842), p. 27; (*b*) Wagner: *Siegfried*, Act III, Scene iii; (*c*) Wagner: *Parsifal*, following rehearsal number 191; (*d*) Elgar: Second Symphony op. 63/ii.

---

[9] See Ch. 3.
[10] See Ch. 13.
[11] For the increasing use of *vibrato* by orchestral players see below.

Ex. 16.5 Continued

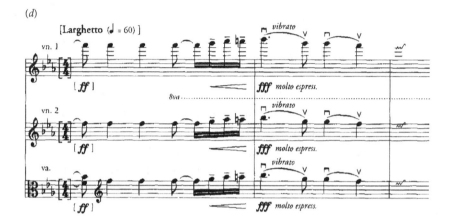

## Terminology and Types of Trembling Effects

Discussion of *vibrato*, now universally understood as an essentially continuous oscillation of pitch, of variable rapidity and amplitude, is complicated by semantic difficulties, which have led to substantial conceptual problems. In the late 20th and early 21st centuries, the term *vibrato* has been employed indiscriminately in print and online in connection with a range of historical trembling effects, most of which certainly had little or no aural resemblance to modern *continuous vibrato*. Many different terms were used during the 18th and 19th centuries to describe the various kinds of wavering that are now generally subsumed in the word *vibrato*, and some of these were also used to characterize a range of different practices. Thus, *tremolo* could mean a trembling effect (either of pitch or intensity) on a single sustained note, rapid repetition of notes on the same pitch, or rapid alternation of notes at different pitches (e.g., on the piano). In Germany, until the middle of the 19th century, *Tremolo* and *Bebung* were the terms most commonly used to signify trembling effects (in 1756, Leopold Mozart had used *Tremulant* and *Tremoleto*; Löhlein in 1774 employed the term *ondeggiamento* as well as *Bebung*). In England, too, *tremolo* was frequently used (equivalent terms, such as *close shake*,[12] *dumb shake*, and *sweetenings*, gradually dropped out of usage in the 19th century). In French, *ondulation*, *tremblement*, and, pejoratively, *chevrottement* were employed. Charles de Bériot's *Méthode de violon* (1858) used the term *sons vibrés* (translated literally in the original English-language edition as "vibrated sounds") for left-hand trembling effects, while Hermann Schröder's *Die Kunst des Violinspiels* (1887), under the main heading *Bebung*, gave the alternative terms *Tremolando, Vibrato, Balancement*. But most of these terms could also have been applied to techniques that would not be called *vibrato* in modern terminology.

Before the middle of the 19th century, the instruction *vibrato* occurs occasionally in a musical context, but primarily to signify some kind of accentuation or articulation. *Vibrato* and *vibrato assai* appear in this sense as performance directives in instrumental music by G. J. Vogler, on short *piano* or *pianissimo* notes, usually with articulation marks. In one case Vogler used it, apparently, in contrast to *sciolto* (Ex. 16.6a) and in another as a qualification of *sciolto* (Ex. 16.6b).

Ex. 16.6 a–b. Vogler: Symphony in C, Scala. Autograph Badische Landesbibliothek Karlsruhe. Don Mus.Ms. 1968. (See also facsimile extract from a Vogler Symphony in G, in Brown: *Classical and Romantic*, 1999, 518.) (a) *vibrato molto*; (b) *Sciolte e vibrato assai*.

(a)

---

[12] *Shake* remined the common English term for a trill into the early 20th century.

Ex. 16.6 Continued

(b)

This usage may correspond with C. F. D Schubart's late-18th-century definition of *vibrato* as "Here, the notes are not pulled out by the root, but only tickled at their tips."[13] In 1823, however, a revised edition of Thomas Busby's dictionary explained *vibrato* as: "A term used in Italian opera, to signify that at the note or passage, to which it refers, the voice is to be thrown out, in a bold heroic style."[14] And in 1826, Lichtenthal defined *vibrato* simply as "strongly marked"; he made a distinction between this and *Vibrazione di voce*, the next entry in his dictionary, which he defined as "Part of the execution of the *messa di voce*, taken from the middle to the end".[15] *Vibrato*, *vibrate*, or even *vibratissimo* occur frequently in the scores of early-19th-century Italian operas. Most circumstances in which they are used, in works by Rossini and Meyerbeer for instance, suggest the forceful delivery of a note or group of notes, which may of course have involved an element of trembling, but certainly not *vibrato* in the modern sense. Other definitions carry more connotation of a repeated pulsating effect either of dynamic or pitch, while still implying accentuation. J. A. Hamilton gave the definition of *vibrato* or *vibrante* as "With a strong, vibrating quality of tone";[16] and this was echoed

---

[13] Schubart: *Ideen*, 366. Although published in 1806, this was written before 1791. The sentence was later used (without attribution) in the *Wiener allgemeine musikalische Zeitung*, i (1813), 435.

[14] Thomas Busby: *A Dictionary of Music, Theoretical and Practical 5th Edition, with Additions and Improvements* (London, 1823), 183.

[15] Lichtenthal: 'Vibrato' in *Dizionario*, ii, 281.

[16] J. A. Hamilton: 'Vibrato' in *Dictionary*, 93

a generation later by John S. Adams, who defined it as "with much vibration of tone".[17] These explanations recall Leopold Mozart's analogy between *tremolo* and the effect of striking a slack bass string or bell.[18] Such effects were regarded as occurring only in specific circumstances on isolated notes.

The connection between accent and vibration was widely felt to be a close one. As early as the mid-18th century, William Tans'ur had rather oddly defined "Accent" as "a sort of *wavering* or *quivering* of the *Voice*, or *Instrument*, on certain *Notes*, with a *stronger* or *weaker Tone* than the rest, &c. to express the *Passion* thereof; which renders *Musick* (especially *Vocal*) so very agreeable to the Ear, it being chiefly intended to *move* and *affect*".[19] A century later, in the English translation of Mathis Lussy's treatise on musical expression, it was noted: "The longer a note, especially if it is the first of the bar, the more it must be accented. It is on these notes that singers and violinists produce the effect called vibrato" (Lussy's original does not include the second sentence);[20] and later, the translator again added the word "vibrato" to Lussy's text: "If a long note follows by exception several short ones, it acquires great force, and will produce a crescendo, a vibrato" (Ex. 16.7).[21] Here the association between function and terminology is more explicit, for Lussy's example includes the sign <>, long associated in singing with *messa di voce*, and, as already shown, widely used in the 19th century where a trembling effect on string instruments seems to have been envisaged. Probably this use of the term "vibrato" referred to a trembling effect with little or no perceptible fluctuation of pitch (see below).

Ex. 16.7 Lussy: *Musical Expression*, 130.

The association of *vibrato* with accent continued until the middle decades of the 19th century. Gottfried Weber explained: "Vibrato: This word (literally translated: hurled, or swinging) is sometimes used to indicate the violent

---

[17] John S. Adams: 'Vibrato' in *5000 Musical Terms* (Boston, 1851), 106.
[18] Mozart: *Versuch*, 238.
[19] William Tans'ur: *A Musical Grammar and Dictionary*, 3rd edn (London, 1756), 29.
[20] Lussy, trans. M. E. von Glehn: *Musical Expression, Accents, Nuances, and Tempo, in Vocal and Instrumental Music* (London and New York, [1892]), 33; Lussy: *Traité*, 3rd edn, 25.
[21] Lussy: *Musical Expression*, 129; *Traité*, 3rd edn, 95.

ejection of a note, and in so far is synonymous with Fortzando or Sfortzato;— but sometimes also to describe the whirring, as it were, oscillating striking of fast notes and the like. e.g. [Ex. 16.8]."[22]

Ex. 16.8 G. Weber: *Allgemeine Musiklehrer*, cxci.

Weber clearly considered that *vibrato* and *tremolo* had different primary meanings but were related. For *tremolo* he gave the German equivalent *Bebung*, and explained it as:

that particular pulsating or wave-like recurring decrease and increase in the strength of a sustained sound, which is sometimes also associated with a change in the type of sound or tone colour, and even with an imperceptible rise and fall in pitch, a pulsating, a rocking and fluttering of the note, which gives it a charm of its own, by which it differs (as Sulzer so aptly expresses it) from a uniformly held tone in much the same way as in the visual arts so-called soft contours and wavy lines differ from stripes or hard outlines drawn with compass and ruler. 2.) The word *tremolo* is sometimes used as synonymous with *rollo* [i.e., rapid note repetition on timpani, strings or piano],—3.) sometimes also perhaps for *vibrato*.[23]

Carl Gollmick more succinctly acknowledged a connection between the two terms, defining "Tremolo / Tremolando / Vibrato" as "trembling, shaking"[24]. Later, however, he gave the definition: "Vibrato, undulating, 1) similar to tremolo; 2) to eject a sound violently, then the same as sfz and ∧ . Therefore vibrate: swing, tremble."[25]

An Italian review of the child prodigy pianist Alfred Jaell in 1843 commented: "Il tocco di lui, al par del suo carrattere, e deciso e vibrato",[26] which was translated shortly afterwards into German as "Sein Anschlag,

---

[22] Gottfried Weber: *Allgemeine Musiklehrer zur Selbstunterricht für Lehrer und Lernende. Dritte . . . Auflage, vermehrt mit einer Erklärung aller in Musikalien vorkommenden italiänischen Kunstwörter* (Mainz, 1831), cxci.
[23] Weber: *Allgemeine Musiklehrer*, clxxxix.
[24] Gollmick: *Kritische Terminologie*, 30.
[25] Gollmick: *Handlexicon der Tonkunst*, i, 96.
[26] Anon.: *Gazzettino musicale di Milano*, ii (1843), 220.

ganz zusagend seinem Character, ist bestimmt und klangvoll (*vibrato*)".[27] The fact that the translator felt the need to include the Italian word in brackets suggests its ambiguous implications at that time. On the piano, of course, no oscillation of pitch or intensity could be artificially produced, but on string and wind instruments, trembling effects could be achieved by a variety of technical means, and the association with accent remained strong. Spohr, for instance, identified left-hand *tremolo* as particularly appropriate "for bringing out powerfully all notes marked *fz* or >".[28]

From the 1840s onwards, the word *vibrato* was increasingly employed in the international press specifically to describe a trembling effect. In Vienna the tenor Enrico Buonfigli was encouraged to improve his voice by undertaking studies that "will help to develop that vibrato, which is so frequently required by present-day maestros in dramatic performance".[29] In Paris, a review of violinist Théodore Hauman (b. 1808) reported: "He has deployed and displayed in this piece all the violin's expansive and exuberant sensibility, *il suono vibrato* [*the vibrato sound*], the musical and dramatic vocal tremor [literally: hiccup] of Italian singers."[30] In London it was observed of Italo Gardoni (b. 1821) in a production of Bellini's *La sonnambula*: "He uses the 'voce vibrato' very constantly, a plan of singing which to us appears likely to destroy the sustaining power of the voice, although admissible enough in some passages."[31]

By the middle of the 19th century, *vibrato* and *tremolo* were the most frequently employed terms for vocal and instrumental trembling effects, although *Bebung* continued to be used regularly in German. At that time, they were predominantly applied to contrasting techniques. During the early 19th century, *tremolo* was increasingly used in an instrumental context to describe rapid note repetition, which Gottfried Weber had identified in 1831 as a potential meaning for both *vibrato* and *tremolo*. Charles de Bériot's virtuoso violin piece *Le Trémolo* op. 30, based on the theme of the second movement of Beethoven's "Kreutzer" Sonata op. 47, in which he introduced a novel technique of very rapid, continuous flying *staccato* of two or three notes on a single

---

[27] Js. C . . . : 'Alfred Jaell', *Allgemeine Wiener Musik-Zeitung*, iv (1844), 12. "His touch, quite in keeping with his character, is determined and sonorous (*vibrato*)."

[28] Spohr: *Violinschule*, 175.

[29] Anon.: *Wiener Zeitschrift für Kunst, Literatur, Theater und Mode*, Nr. 205, 24 December 1840, 1638.

[30] Henri Blanchard: 'Concert donnée par M. Hauman', *Revue et Gazette musicale de Paris*, vii (1840), 604.

[31] Anon.: *The Literary Gazette*, no. 1574 (1847), 237.

pitch in each bowstroke,[32] created a sensation on its numerous performances by the composer before publication in 1840, and afterwards by many other violinists. It spawned other compositions, including piano pieces, with *tremolo* in the title. At the same time, *tremolo* continued in use, especially in singing, as a term for the pitch oscillation that became an integral aspect of 20th-century *vibrato*. During the mid- to late-19th century and into the early 20th, a distinction was commonly made in singing between *vibrato* as an oscillation of intensity without any perceptible pitch fluctuation, and *tremolo* as an oscillation of pitch, although it is not always clear from the context whether these two terms are being used synonymously or with differentiated meaning.

The confusion in terminology is demonstrated in numerous sources at that time. For instance, a French text explained: "The *flatté* was what the singers of today call *vibrato*, with the difference that this effect, which consists in giving several attacks with the throat on a single note and at the same pitch, was only executed gently, while today it is generally made powerfully"; and "The *balancement* was a tighter *flatté*, and in short represented nothing more than the *tremolo* of the stringed instruments. It is indicated by a wavy line ~~~~~~."[33] Fétis, discussing musical expression, also equated the singer's *vibrato* of intensity with the string player's left-hand *vibrato*, in which, however, the pitch element was expected to be almost imperceptible[34] (see below). In 1889, Harry Collings Deacon defined vocal *vibrato* as "an alternate partial extinction and reinforcement of the note", in contrast to *tremolo*, which was "an undulation of the notes, that is to say, more or less quickly reiterated departure from true intonation".[35] This widely accepted distinction persisted into the 20th century in singing. In 1900 *Der Humorist* cautioned: "Miss Domenego must be careful not to increase the vibrato to the point of tremolo on the sustained notes."[36] And in 1921, soprano Elisabeth Mattei was warned: "The vocal vibrato runs the risk of becoming a tremolo."[37]

But Deacon also noted that "the instrumental tremolo [i.e., rapid repetition of a note with separate bowstrokes] is more nearly allied to the vocal

---

[32] See Ch. 7, pp. 429–30.

[33] Adrien de la Fage: 'De l'ancien goût du chant en France', *Revue et Gazette Musicale de Paris*, xxiv (1857) 36.

[34] François-Joseph Fétis: 'De l'expression en musique', pt. 2 in *Revue et Gazette musicale de Paris*, xxvi (1859), 215.

[35] Harry Collings Deacon: 'Tremolo' in Sir George Grove (ed.), *A Dictionary of Music and Musicians*, iv (London, 1889), 166f.

[36] Anon.: *Der Humorist*, 1 November 1900, 3.

[37] Walther Hirschberg: *Signale für die musikalische Welt*, lxxix (1921), 44.

vibrato. Indeed, what is called 'vibrato' on bowed instruments is what would be 'tremolo' in vocal music."[38] The following year, however, another writer remarked: "I am, of course, perfectly well aware, although the two terms are now used in an identical sense, that theoretical writers discriminate between the tremolo and vibrato, the difference in which is even more strongly marked in instrumental music."[39] Thus, the 19th-century distinction between *vibrato* and *tremolo* in singing only gradually disappeared during the early decades of the 20th century, but by the second half of the century, *vibrato* was almost universally understood in all contexts as an obvious oscillation of pitch. Perhaps for this reason, Robert Donington misleadingly subverted the historical usage in his *Interpretation of Early Music*, by defining vocal "tremolo" as "a fluctuation of intensity" and "vibrato," as "a fluctuation of pitch".[40] This confusing terminology also appears in scientific papers, for instance: "a cyclic variation in the loudness, which in music is generally called tremolo; [. . .] a cyclic variation in pitch, generally called vibrato".[41] In recent decades, *tremolo* has generally been applied in singing to any kind of "defective vibrato" (as well as to rapid repetition of a single note in instrumental practice). By a curious reversal, therefore, the 19th-century defect of too much pitch variation became the 20th-century defect of too little. In modern usage, as one Internet site puts it, "A tremolo is a vibrato that is too fast and varies too little in pitch."[42]

The terminological situation is complicated, therefore, by the fact that, in contrast to the singer's *vibrato* of intensity and *tremolo* of pitch, *vibrato*, rather than *tremolo*, became increasingly the norm to designate left-hand trembling of pitch in string playing during the second half of the 19th century. This probably occurred because *tremolo* was widely used to describe the string-player's rapid note repetition, used as an orchestral effect; but perhaps also because left-hand trembling effects were generally made with very narrow pitch variation, and therefore aurally resembled the singer's *vibrato* of intensity rather than *tremolo* of pitch. In the 1830s, Marc Colombat, a French doctor specializing in vocal problems, referred to the vibration of the singing voice that produces "those kinds of sonorous ripples [. . .] which give

---

[38] Deacon: 'Tremolo' in Grove, *Dictionary*, iv, 166.
[39] Anon.: 'Vocalists and Wobblers', *The Magazine of Music*, vii (1890), 135.
[40] Robert Donington: *The Interpretation of Early Music* (London, 1963), 164.
[41] Nevill Horner Fletcher: 'Vibrato in Music', *Acoustics Australia*, xxix (2001), 97.
[42] Claudia Friedlander: 'The Liberated Voice. Revolutionizing Vocal Technique with Timeless Wisdom' (2012), https://www.claudiafriedlander.com/the-liberated-voice/2012/05/vibrato-hell.html [accessed 12 March 2022].

it a flute-like sound of the type that our celebrated violinists draw from their instruments by a kind of trembling which they communicate to the strings by pressing on them, more or less, with the tip of the fingers".[43] Colombat's perception of "pressing" on the string is suggestive of the visual effect, with very little participation of the wrist. Although the string player's old-fashioned finger *vibrato*, by its very nature, slightly affects the pitch of the note, the amplitude was normally so narrow that pitch fluctuation was virtually undetectable. Spohr insisted that "the deviation from true pitch should be scarcely perceptible to the ear".[44] Baillot's graphic illustration of left-hand trembling indicates the minimal pitch disturbance that he expected (Ex. 16.9).

Ex. 16.9 Baillot: *L'art*, 138.

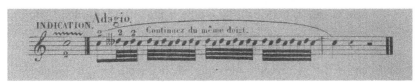

Hermann Schröder, in the 1880s, still instructed that "One moves the finger that presses the string quickly up and down without essentially departing from the real position of the note."[45] The predominance of this technique is corroborated by early recordings, in which the *vibrato* of the oldest string players has very narrow amplitude, and by critiques such as those of Carl Flesch (b. 1873), one of the leading promoters of 20th-century *continuous vibrato* with substantial pitch fluctuation, who recalled that "in 1880 the great violinists did not yet make use of a proper vibrato but employed a kind of *Bebung*, i.e., a finger vibrato in which the pitch was subjected to only quite imperceptible oscillations."[46]

By the later 19th century, therefore, the term *vibrato* had become strongly associated with trembling effects in string playing, but it certainly did not apply only to a single technique. This is nicely demonstrated by the section on "Vibrato" in an 1895 treatise, *Le virtuose moderne* (the modern virtuoso) by Luis Alonso (b. 1865) who gained a first prize for violin "*avec plus grande distinction*" (with the greatest distinction) in 1885 at the Brussels

---

[43] Marc Colombat de l'Isère: 'Mécanisme de la voix', pt. 2, *Revue Musicale*, viii (1834), 324.
[44] Spohr: *Violin School*, 175.
[45] Hermann Schröder: *Die Kunst des Violinspiels*, 26.
[46] Carl Flesch: *The Memoirs of Carl Flesch*, ed. H. Keller and C. F. Flesch, trans. Hans Keller (London, 1957), 120.

Conservatoire.[47] He began: "The vibrato is a major thing for a virtuoso"; but, identifying five types, he disapproved of the three that most closely relate to modern vibrato:

> There are several vibratos: finger vibrato, wrist vibrato (or a sort of regular swaying of the hand), nervous vibrato (which comes from the left arm) vibrato by attraction or sympathy, and bow vibrato.
>
> The first is done by stopping the string with a finger to which an upper finger must be added to simulate a trill without the latter touching the string; this primitive vibrato is no longer used, only Italian players still do it.[48]
>
> The vibrato of the wrist is usually too slow. It produces a kind of goat-like sound similar to that of street singers.
>
> The arm vibrato is unbearable, it is a nervous, stiff vibrato, similar to a false chromatic trill, it would be difficult in a large hall to distinguish the note on which one is vibrating, it assaults your hearing and when the violinist plays in the high register and especially in double stops, it is with delight that one sees the end of the piece approaching.
>
> The vibrato by sympathy or attraction is soft, pearly, superb, but it can only be used when one finds a note doubled by an open string or on a harmonic note making the octave. [Ex. 16.10]
>
> The vibrato of the bow is very elegant and is rarely used because it is hardly heard, but it produces its visual effect, its elegance; it is a kind of serpentine slur.[49]

Ex. 16.10  Alonso: *Le virtuose moderne*, iv.

---

[47] Brussels Conservatoire, unpublished records, no. 1758. I am grateful to Richard Sutcliffe for help in finding this material.
[48] This method is, in fact, still recommended in Francesco Sfilio: *Nuova Scuola Violinistica Italiana* (Varese: Zecchini, 2002), 58. This publication has been compiled from material originally written by Sfilio between 1935 and 1937. I'm grateful to Fernando Caida Greco for alerting me to this publication.
[49] Luis Alonso: *Le virtuose moderne sur le violon* (Paris, [1895]), iv.

The two effects that elicited Alonso's enthusiasm would hardly be classed as *vibrato* nowadays, though both seem to have been practised for much of the period under consideration. It is, in fact, significant that Alonso preferred these two, both of which consisted of trembling without pitch fluctuation, and furthermore made no objection to his first kind—which would also cause almost no pitch variation—except that the technique was "primitive".

Other sources also indicate that, although the use of trembling effects was increasing significantly during the second half of the 19th century, there remained a clear distinction between trembling that affected the dynamic steadiness of the note and that which changed its pitch. The circumstances in which the trembling of pitch was approved by musical authorities and critics, and probably the extent to which it was used by most performers, were much more circumscribed than those in which trembling of intensity was regarded as acceptable. This is made absolutely clear in relation to string playing.

## Sympathetic Trembling on String Instruments

Many methods fail to describe Alonso's fourth kind of *vibrato*, but his liking for it does not seem to have been eccentric at that time, either in Franco-Belgian or in German practice, for in 1887 it was also described by Hermann Schröder as the third of three kinds of *Bebung*:

(1) *Bebung* with oscillation of the left hand, to which he devoted nineteen lines and a music example from Spohr (see below);
(2) *Bebung* as an orchestral *tremolo*, with fast, repeated bowstrokes, which he covered in six lines and a music example;
(3) *Bebung* "Through phenomenal sound effects" (*durch phänomenale Klangwirkungen*) to which he devoted nearly three pages, with many music examples. He explained "This preferable, most clearly appealing *Bebung*, is known to most violinists as *vibrato* or *vibration*. In practice, this phenomenon has not yet been exploited, because of its weak and unreliable response, but on any good violin, passages resembling the following example should not fail to have a highly individual effect: [Ex. 16.11]."[50]

---

[50] Schröder: *Die Kunst des Violinspiels*, 27.

Ex. 16.11 Schröder: *Die Kunst*, 27.

His reference to "most violinists" suggests that this effect was quite widely familiar, if not widely exploited. It is also clear that it was not a new practice in the late 19th century. J. A. C. Burkhard referred to it in 1832 under the name *Glockenton*, explaining: "Bowing the note of an open string while quickly and gently touching a lower open string with the finger gives the special tone which is called a *Glöchchen (Glockenschlag)*."[51] Eight years earlier, Dotzauer discussed this effect at some length, in his *Méthode de violoncelle*. Having referred to it as the *Pochen* (knocking, throbbing, pulsation) as one of three possible ways of producing trembling effects, he explained its properties in more detail in a section on *Mitklingen der Töne* (resonating sounds). More than thirty years earlier, Francesco Galeazzi, too, referred to this effect on the violin, without giving it a name, explaining that some players "with a finger placed on the octave below [the note that is being bowed] make a kind of trill with a third finger, raising and lowering the finger alternately with speed, and leaving the resonant octave now free and now covered, resulting in a sound that is somewhat intermittent and of a curious effect, which, as long as it is not abused, is sometimes not displeasing."[52]

## Trembling Effects with the Bow

Alonso's fifth type of *vibrato*, with the bow, though discreet in its result, was much more frequently described than his fourth type and was probably part of the expressive resources of most 18th- and 19th-century solo players, although not all major treatises refer to it as an embellishment.[53] Bowed

---

[51] Burkhard: 'Violine' in *Wörterbuch*, 356.
[52] Galeazzi: *Elementi*, 1st edn (1796), ii, 170.
[53] Whether an account given in 1799 of J. C. Schetky's playing refers to this technique is difficult to determine, but it contains one of the earliest references specifically to *vibrato* in relation to bowing. Having described his distinctive manner of holding the bow, the writer continued: "With this bowhold Schetky made staccato upwards and downwards, but in Adagio he drew the tone out of his instrument as one presses the sweet oil from the ripe olive, and in Allegro there was such dexterity in going over the strings that one would have needed ten eyes to notice his viprato [sic], although one only needed one ear for it." *Allgemeine musikalische Zeitung*, ii (1799–1800), 34.

trembling effects on a single pitch go back to the early history of the violin family, and are closely related to *portato*, being the most extremely *legato* form of that technique.[54] As a class of techniques it is implied by various types of notation on short notes repeated at the same pitch (which are also used over groups of notes at different pitches), including slurs, slurs over dots slurs over wavy lines, or wavy lines alone;[55] the last three are sometimes also used over a single longer note.

Bailleux in his *Méthode raisonné* of 1779 gives two types of trembling effect, both of which he regards as varieties of *balancement*. The first, made by "small movements" of the left hand, he also calls *flatté*. The second, marked with dots under slurs, he equates, with the Italian *tremolo*, stating that it "produces the effect of the tremulant of the organ", and notes that it is made "in a single bowstroke, without leaving the string", which indicates a pulsation without breaks in the sound (Ex. 16.12).[56] Since Bailleaux includes this in his treatment of ornaments (*agréments*), it is clear that it is not merely a bowing technique, but an expressive resource.

**Ex. 16.12** Antoin Bailleaux: *Méthode raisonné à apprendre le violon* (Paris, 1779), 11.

There seems to be no sharp distinction, however, between the manner of executing Bailleux's *balancement* and the effect that Joseph Riepel indicated two decades earlier by a wavy line under a slur for notes in conjunct motion, in which "the bow is hardly raised at all, rather it almost represents the song of a lyre".[57]

In the 18th and 19th centuries, not only was the *Bebung* on the clavichord normally indicated by dots under a slur,[58] but also left-hand *vibrato* was frequently indicated in the same manner.[59] In all these cases there is an implication of a regular, perceptible pulsation in the sound, but to what extent any of them were expected to indicate more than the slightest unsteadiness of pitch

---

[54] For the 17th-century antecedents of this practice see Stewart Carter: 'The String Tremolo in the 17th Century', *Early Music*, xix (1991), 43–58.
[55] See Ch. 6.
[56] Antoin Bailleaux: *Méthode raisonné à apprendre le violon* (Paris, 1779), 11.
[57] Riepel: *Gründliche Erklärung*, 17. See Ch. 6, p. 320.
[58] Also sometimes by the instruction *tenuto*. See below.
[59] See, e.g., Ex. 14.13.

is questionable. References to the tremulant on the organ, as Bailleaux's account shows, cannot be taken as evidence of a trembling of pitch, although they might certainly imply an extended passage of tremulousness rather than the embellishment of occasional single notes.

Despite Bailleaux's inclusion of the left-hand *flatté*, the seminal Conservatoire *Méthode de violon*, published a quarter of a century, later makes no reference to a left-hand trembling effect, referring only to one made by the bow. This was included in the context of dynamic nuances on sustained notes, especially as a means of intensifying a *messa di voce*. The authors advised: "One can nuance the sounds [*on peut filer les sons*] in another manner by a sort of undulation of the bow. It is sometimes used on *tenutos* and *fermatas*, but this manner of nuancing the sounds should be used rarely. The composer indicates it by this sign ~~~~~~~ (Ex. 16.13).[60]

Ex. 16.13 Baillot et al., *Méthode de violon*, 137.

Mention of an "undulating motion" seems clearly to link this description with the "serpentine slur" of Alonso, but the distinction between that kind of *bow vibrato* and *portato* is not always clear. When, for instance, the notation of dots under a slur is encountered, the temptation might be to make a distinct separation of the sound, though in many instances, this may not be what was intended. Two English translations of the *Méthode* were published in the 1820s—one retained the original wavy line,[61] while the other replaced it with dots.[62]

At about the same time as the publication of the conservatoire *Méthode*, Michel Woldemar issued a second edition of his *Grande Méthode* (with a revised title). His first edition had made no mention of any kind of trembling effect, but in the second he added a section on a "Serpentine Bowstroke", with a graphic illustration of its execution (Ex. 16.14), explaining: "This

---

[60] Baillot et al.: *Méthode de violon*, 137.
[61] R. Cocks and Co's improved and enlarged Edition of the Celebrated Method for the Violin by Rode, Kreutzer and Baillot, trans. J. A. Hamilton (London, Cocks, [1828]), 17.
[62] Rode, Baillot, & Kreutzer's Method of Instruction for the Violin, edited by Baillot (London, Boosey, [1823]), 15.

bowstroke is made by turning the bow-stick alternately towards the fingerboard and the bridge, moving it at nine lines [*lignes*] from the bridge and the same from the fingerboard."[63] Perhaps this effect was retained in French practice throughout the 19th century.

Ex. 16.14 Woldemar: *Grande méthode*, 2nd edn, 56.

Dotzauer, in his bilingual *Méthode de violoncelle*, saw *Bebung* with the bow as virtually interchangeable with left-hand trembling, which again suggests how very little pitch variation was expected in the latter. He observed: "Many solo players are accustomed to perform sustained notes with *Bebung* (i.e., *Tremolo*), that is, the finger rocks back and forth [the French version adds "with little velocity" avec peu de vitesse]; and many seek to produce the same effect by means of the bow, which might be roughly notated: [Ex. 16.15]."

Ex. 16.15 Dotzauer: *Méthode*, 47.

At this point the French version continued with another comment missing from the German: "It is composed of many nuanced sounds [*sons filés*], of which one makes the *forte* apparent at the beginning of each beat or half-beat."[64]

Although little is written about ornamental trembling effects with the bow during the succeeding decades, Alonso's treatise indicates that it was not

---

[63] Michel Woldemar: *Grande méthode, ou, étude élémentaire pour le Violon, contenant un grand nombre de Gammes, toutes les Positions du Violon, et leur doigter; tous les Coups d'Archet anciens et Nouveaux* [;] *l'Echelle enharmonique* [;] *Moderne fugues, des Exemples d'après les plus grands Maitres &c. . . Seconde Edition Augmenté de 15 leçons Faciles* (Paris, [c. 1803]), 56. Lignes were a pre-revolutionary measure (12 ligne to one pouce). Nine ligne corresponds with about 2.3 cm, which indicates that Woldemar's fingerboard was already as long as a modern fingerboard.

[64] Dotzauer: *Méthode*, 47.

entirely obsolete. In any case, composers' *portato* notation (with dots or accent signs under slurs) may often elicit an effect of this kind; these notations will frequently have been expected to involve pressure rather than separation in the bowstroke, or for wind players and singers, pulsation from the chest without interruptions in the breath.

## Pulsating Effects on Wind Instruments

For wind instruments, there were several ways of producing the kinds of pulsation without noticeable pitch variation that string players could achieve by sympathetic vibrations, bowing, or very tight left-hand finger action. For the flute, Quantz referred to a method of performing repeated notes that were notated solely with a slur, "by means of exhalation, with chest action"[65] (the contemporaneous French translation adds that this should be done without employing the tongue).[66] A similar technique was described by Delusse, which he designates *Tac aspiré*, explaining: "This is done solely by the action of the lungs, articulating the syllable *HU*. It is also designated by small dots under a slur, on the notes that require it; but it is never used except in slow & tender movements."[67] He also referred to a faster version, also coming from the lungs, "which the Italian call *Tremolo*".[68] The only form of *Bebung* for the flute discussed by A. E. Müller in the early 19th century was evidently a similar effect:

> The *Bebung* will be specified by the Italian word: *Tremolo* (trem.) or by more or fewer dots over a note, according to whether this ornament [*Manier*] should be performed faster or slower: e.g. [Ex. 16.16a–b]. On the flute this embellishment [*Verzierung*] can only be produced by a moderate increase and decrease of wind pressure, which would have to be specified thus in the notation; e.g. [Ex. 16.16c]. By means of a small movement of the chin the performance of this ornament becomes easy.[69]

---

[65] Quantz: *Versuch*, 65.
[66] Quantz: *Essai d'une methode* [sic] *pour apprendre à jouer de la flute traversiere* [sic] (Berlin, 1752), 66.
[67] Delusse: *L'art de la flute traversiere* (Paris, 1760), 4.
[68] Delusse: *L'art*, 9.
[69] A. E. Müller: *Elementarbuch für Flötenspieler* (Leipzig, [1815]), 31.

Ex. 16.16 a–c. Müller: *Elementarbuch für Flötenspieler*, 31.

Müller's account, particularly the third music example, links its effect closely with the string player's bow *tremolo* as described by Dotzauer, while his final comment recalls Hiller's remarks about Carestini (see below). His discussion solely of this type suggests comparison with the *bow vibrato* of the 1803 Paris Conservatoire *Méthode*.

Similar trembling effects, produced by the chest, without pitch variation, were also employed on brass instruments, since these were incapable of producing a finger *vibrato*. Its use by trumpeters is dealt with in Altenburg's 1795 treatise, where his illustration of the execution of the *Bebung* or *Schwebung*, marked like the clavichord *Bebung* (Ex. 16.17), is explained as "a sustained strengthening and weakening of a particular note",[70] which again puts it in the same category as the devices described by Müller, Dotzauer, and others. Such devices in wind playing had antecedents going back at least two centuries.[71]

Ex. 16.17 Altenburg: *Versuch*, 118.

The most common type of trembling technique for wind instruments that was described during the second half of the 18th century and the first half of the 19th (though perhaps not the most commonly employed) was produced by making a trill-like motion over an open hole. Quantz was among many who mentioned this *Bebung* (*flattement* in the French version) in the context of the *messa di voce*, instructing that it should be made "by the nearest open hole", but warned: "the tone does not become higher or lower during the increase

---

[70] Johann Ernst Altenburg: *Versuch einer Anleitung zur heroisch-musikalischen Trompeter- und Pauker-Kunst* (Halle, 1795), 118.

[71] See Bruce Dickey: 'Untersuchung zur historischen Auffassung des Vibratos auf Blasinstrumenten', *Basler Jahrbuch für historische Musikpraxis*, ii (1978), 88ff.

and decrease, (which fault could arise from the characteristic of the flute)".[72] With the same technique, however, John Gunn, designating it *sweetening* and *flattement*, envisaged pitch fluctuation, explaining that it is "made by approaching the finger to the first or second open hole, below the proper note that is sounded and moving it up and down over the hole, approaching it very near each time, but never entirely upon it; thus occasioning an alternate flattening and sharpening of the note".[73] A generation later, Carl Almenräder described the same procedure on the bassoon, noting that it was an effect imitated from string instruments; he nevertheless warned that the sustained note must not become sharper or flatter as a result, merely change its colour.[74]

On wind instruments, therefore, trembling effects could be made either with the finger or the breath, just as string players could use either right or left hands. Descriptions of trembling effects made with the breath, and their artistic use are increasingly encountered in 19th-century flute methods. It is difficult, however, to determine to what extent this involved fluctuations of pitch, and to what extent they reflected the finger techniques. Nicholson in his 1836 *School* described "Vibration" as "an Embellishment deserving the utmost attention of all those who are anxious to become finished performers on the Flute". He echoed Leopold Mozart, likening the Vibration to "the beats, or pulsations of a Bell, or Glass", but went further in drawing the conclusion that the pulsations must get faster. He gave three ways of achieving trembling effects: "by the breath—by a tremulous motion of the Flute, and by the Shake [trilling over an open hole]". He envisaged various combinations of these methods but saw them all as contributing to the same musical effect. In relation to a music example (Ex. 16.18), he explained: "When the Vibration becomes too rapid to continue the effect with the breath, a tremulous motion must be given to the Flute with the right hand, the lips being perfectly relaxed, and the tone subdued to a mere whisper."[75] He made no reference to pitch fluctuation.[76]

Ex. 16.18 Nicholson: *School for the Flute*, ii, 71.

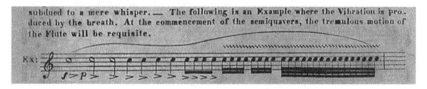

---

[72] Quantz: *Versuch*, 140.
[73] John Gunn: *The Art of Playing the German Flute* (London, [1793]), 18.
[74] Carl Almenräder: *Die Kunst des Fagottblasens, oder, Vollständige theoretisch praktische Fagottschule* (Mainz, 1843), 69.
[75] Charles Nicholson: *A School for the Flute* (New York, [1836]), ii, 71.
[76] Nicholson: *School for the Flute*, ii, 71.

Trembling with the finger remained a standard part of the flautist's technical equipment for at least the first half of the 19th century. Like Nicholson's *School*, two substantial treatises from the mid-1840s contain charts showing the required fingering to produce the Vibration. John Clinton explained the intended effect: "The beats (which are made with the finger in a similar manner to the movement in the shake [trill]) may be commenced slowly, but with firmness (or even, force) then gradually increased in rapidity, and the force (or strength) of the beats, gradually lessened." He gave a detailed chart of how this "Vibration" could be obtained, marking the position of the trilling finger ∼ (Ex. 16.19), and concluded: "For the first four notes, the Vibration (if required) can only be produced by a tremulous action of the flute, at the Embouchure, which however cannot be recommended for the lowest notes; it however may be applied to the middle and upper notes with good effect, if skilfully managed."[77]

**Ex. 16.19** Clinton: *A School or Practical Instruction Book*, 72.

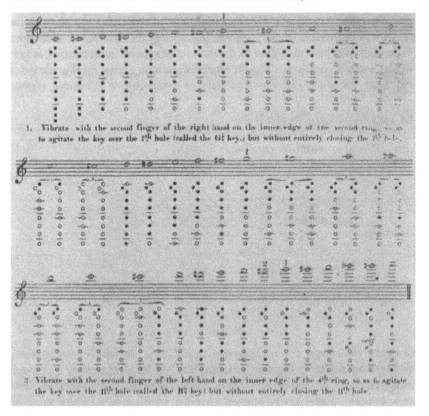

[77] Clinton: *A School or Practical Instruction Book*, 72.

Anton Bernhard Fürstenau gave a similar chart, but quite different instructions. He considered the breath and finger techniques as separate, not only in their methods of execution, but also in their expressive functions. The *Bebung* (with the breath) he regarded as an emulation of the singer's tremulousness when moved by powerful emotion, and acknowledged that "This ornament, which suits and is particularly employed on string instruments, can also be advantageous in flute playing". He recommended "rapid and successive pressures from the lungs" as the best means of executing it, but conceded that it might also be done by a trembling movement of the chin.[78] He provided examples marked with wavy lines to show where he considered it appropriate (Ex. 16.20).

Ex. 16.20 Fürstenau: *Die Kunst*, 81.

He did not, on the other hand, see the finger technique, *Klopfen*, as an emotionally expressive ornament, but a decorative one, resembling "a strongly struck bell",[79] and associated it exclusively with dynamic nuances, explaining that with &lt; the finger movements should begin gradually and get faster, but with &gt; become progressively slower, and with &lt;&gt;, faster then slower. He marked it with a different sign in his examples of its artistic use (Ex. 16.21).

Ex. 16.21 Fürstenau: *Die Kunst*, 83

Similar practices were common on oboe, clarinet, and bassoon during the first half of the 19th century.[80]

---

[78] Fürstenau: *Die Kunst*, §136, 79.
[79] Fürstenau: *Die Kunst*, §138, 81.
[80] Moreno: *Bassoon Playing in Perspective*, 212–15.

## Vocal Trembling Effects

A difference between *expressive* and *decorative* trembling, which Fürstenau's distinction throws into sharp relief, runs through the whole history of these techniques. Tartini began his consideration of *tremolo* with the statement: "This kind of ornament by its nature is better suited to instruments than to voices",[81] adding that if it was sometimes encountered from a singer, this was merely a peculiarity of that specific voice. There is no suggestion that either he or Leopold Mozart, who incorporated Tartini's instructions into his own treatise, regarded the *tremolo* as having anything to do with emotion, nor that they expected any noticeable fluctuation of pitch. Tartini is quite specific about always maintaining mathematically strict intonation, and concerned to avoid destabilization of pitch, "even imperceptibly",[82] when performing a *messa di voce*.

Despite Tartini's assertion that *tremolo* was an instrumental practice, similar ornamental pulsating effects were certainly used by 18th-century singers, as they had been in previous generations. W. A. Mozart, writing to his father from Munich in 1778, described and objected to Joseph Meissner's "bad habit of making his voice tremble at times, turning a note that should be sustained into distinct quarters, or even eighths—and this I could never endure in him". He contrasted this with "the natural quivering of the voice at moments of emotion".[83] Here we have a clear tension between *decorative* and *expressive* trembling, which is perhaps indicative of the aesthetic changes that were taking place during the later 18th century. Nevertheless, even after Mozart's death, the same kind of trembling ornament was still being taught. The Austrian singer Johann Baptist Lasser, just five years older than Mozart, explained in his 1798 treatise that a *Bebung* is produced: "if, on a whole-note, one allows four quarters or eight eighths to be clearly heard by means of a slight pressure while it is being sustained" (Ex. 16.22).[84]

Ex. 16.22 Lasser: *Vollständige Anleitung*, 158.

---

[81] Giuseppe Tartini: *Traité des agrémens de la musique* (Paris, 1770), 27.
[82] Tartini: *Traité*, 30.
[83] W. A. Mozart: letter of 12 June 1778, *Briefe und Auszeichnungen*, ii, 378.
[84] Lasser: *Vollständige Anleitung*, 154.

Whether such effects in singing were produced by the chest, as suggested by Agricola in 1757 (using almost exactly the same terms as Quantz used for the flute),[85] or by the throat, as instructed by others, was evidently variable. J. A. Hiller observed in 1780 that the *Bebung*

> consists in not holding a long tone steadily, but allowing it to weaken and strengthen somewhat, without its thereby becoming higher or lower. On string instruments, it is most easily done by a back-and-forth rocking of the fingers that stop the strings. For the singer it is more difficult if he wants to produce it purely with the *throat*; some make it easier for themselves by the motion of the jaw. Carestini did it often, and always with good success.[86]

It may be noted in passing that Hiller's comparison of the singer's *Bebung*, without variation of pitch, with left-hand *Bebung* on string instruments once again indicates that the latter was not expected to produce any perceptible pitch fluctuation.

The continuation of techniques similar to Tartini's *tremolo*, Hiller's and Lasser's *Bebung*, Nicholson's *Vibration*, and Fürstenau's *Klopfen*, in 19th-century singing is attested by diverse sources, though these particular techniques may have been less commonly employed during the later decades of the century. In 1890, Deacon observed that the alternate partial extinction and reinforcement of the note, which he called *vibrato*,

> seems to have been a legitimate figure, used rhythmically, of the fioritura of the Farinelli and Caffarelli period, and it was introduced in modern times with wonderful effect by Jenny Lind in "La figlia del reggimento". In the midst of a flood of vocalization these groups of notes occurred [Ex. 16.23a] executed with the same brilliancy and precision as they would be on the pianoforte thus—[Ex. 16.23b].[87]

Ex. 16.23 a–b. Deacon: 'Tremolo' in *Grove*, iv, 167.

(a)

---

[85] Agricola: *Anleitung zur Singkunst*, 135.
[86] Hiller: *Anweisung zum musikalisch-zierlichen Gesang* (Leipzig, 1780), 75f.
[87] Deacon: 'Tremolo' in Grove, *Dictionary*, iv, 166.

Ex. 16.23 Continued

(b)

The influential treatise on singing by Manuel García, Jenny Lind's teacher, contains particularly detailed descriptions of similar techniques as they would have been used by singers of the Swedish Nightingale's generation, and it is evident from his account that there were many subtle variations in the ways different singers employed them. The first type described by García is designated "Swelled Sounds with Inflexions or Echoed Notes (Flautati)", and seems to refer to what was frequently designated *vibrato* at this time. He explained:

> They consist of a uniformly continued series of small, swelled sounds, multiplied to as great an extent as the breath will allow.[1] These inflexions may be applied in different ways; that is, they may be of equal duration and power; may follow an increasing or decreasing progression; and so on. Great singers usually employ them according to the following method:—they first hold out a sustained sound with a third of the breath, which sound is followed by another of less power and duration; after which follows a long succession of echoes, becoming weaker as they approach the end—the last, indeed, can scarcely be heard. The throat must contract and dilate with elasticity at each inflexion.[2]
>
> 1. Some authors call this *making the voice vibrate* (Italian, *vibrar di voce*), and indicate this effect by syncopated notes:—[Ex. 16.24a]
>
> 2. Velluti put it this way: *the echo becomes a flute and the throat is fully opened to achieve it.* [Ex. 16.24b]
>
> Echoed notes must be executed from weak to strong.[88]

Ex. 16.24 a–b. García: *École*, i (1840), 45; i (1847), 64.

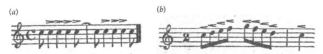

---

[88] García: *École*, i, 45; 2nd edn, i, 61.

The second type, which he referred to simply as "Repeated Notes", seems from his description closer to a trembling of pitch, though García dealt with pitch *tremolo* as such at a later point in his treatise and in a rather different manner, treating it not as a decorative ornament but as an expression of uncontrollable emotion, noting that when agitation "is produced by grief so intense that it completely overwhelms us, the organ experiences a kind of wavering which is communicated to the voice. This wavering is called *tremolo*."[89] The distinction between the technique described here and *tremolo* is made clear by García's insistence that the "repeated notes" should not be a "mere trembling of the voice" but a regular and controlled pulsation, in other words, a decorative effect. He explained:

> Notes repeated while remaining on the same vowel, constitute a variety of sustained sounds; but, in this case, the voice performs without interruption a series of percussions, in order to subdivide the note which at first would have been a sustained one. Each percussion is effected by the larynx rising or falling, as in the act of executing the shake [trill]. These movements are slight and rapid; moreover, the note should be pinched by a sort of appoggiatura of less than a quarter of a tone below, for each repetition. One should carefully avoid aspirating different articulations in the same breath and executing them with a trembling or goat-like effect [*chevrottement*] of the voice. The percussions not being perceptible and pleasing unless produced by light voices, are only suitable for women; and to produce a fine effect, they should never exceed four sixteenth-notes to each beat of 100 on Maelzel's Metronome; their succession also should always be smooth and delicate.[90]

## Speed and Amplitude

Ideas about the speed of the pulsations in trembling effects varied from time to time, instrument to instrument, and performer to performer. Evidence

---

[89] García: *École*, ii, 53.
[90] García: *École*, i, 45. The sentence beginning "One should carefully avoid" in the above translation is given in the English edition of 1855 simply as "These articulations must neither be aspirated, nor a mere trembling of the voice."

as firm as Garcia's is exceptional; nevertheless, some tentative conclusions about broad trends may be elicited from references to the technique in contemporary instruction books or descriptions.

There were, of course, always faster and slower trembling effects, depending on context, but in the 18th century, trembling effects seem to have been generally quite slow, while in the 19th century, evidence points towards a faster norm, which prevailed until the development of a slower *continuous vibrato* with wider pitch fluctuation in the 20th century. Changing taste around 1800 is implied by warnings, such as Baillot's in 1835, to "avoid giving the vibrato a slackness that would make the playing old-fashioned".[91] More concrete are the numerous 18th-century sources that specify the number of oscillations to be made on a note, either in the context of general instruction or in specific musical instances. Leopold Mozart, giving the illustration in Ex. 16.25 for three different manners of producing a left-hand *Tremulo* [sic], observes: "The larger strokes can represent eighths, the smaller sixteenths, and as many strokes as there be, so often must the hand be moved";[92] but he does not specify a tempo for his whole-notes.

Ex. 16.25  Mozart: *Versuch*, 239.

Der langsame.

Der anwachsende.

Der geschwinde.

His other music examples, based on Tartini's treatise, strongly suggest a rather leisurely tempo (Ex. 16.26), as does his insistence on the regular distribution of metrical stress in the trembling.

---

[91] Baillot: *L'art du violon*, 139.
[92] Mozart: *Versuch*, 239.

Ex. 16.26 Mozart: *Versuch*, 240.
(Mozart's instruction: "In the two examples in No. 1 the strong part of the movement falls always on the note marked by the numeral 2, for it is the first note of the whole or half-quarter-note. In example No. 2, on the contrary, the stress falls, for the same reason, on the note marked with the numeral 1".)

Interestingly, his description of this technique on the violin seems intended to produce an effect very like the one that his son condemned in the singing of Meissner twenty years later. This may indicate that, in practice, Leopold Mozart's left-hand movements were freer than his account suggests; but it may also indicate the differing aesthetic attitudes of father and son.

Like Leopold Mozart, many 18th-century writers, especially of the older generation, linked the form of the graphic signs that were occasionally used to designate trembling effects with the number of pulsations required. Marpurg instructed that for *Bebung* on the clavichord, "One takes care always to set as many dots over the note as movements of the finger should be made." Heinrich Christoph Koch, a musician of great experience, was in no doubt that composers who employed this notation intended it in that sense, for, having remarked that the introduction of the *Bebung* was usually left to the performer, he added: "Various composers, however, are accustomed to mark it with dots over the note, and indeed with as many dots as movements should be made with the finger."[93] One of the latest to repeat this, more or

---

[93] Koch: 'Bebung' in *Musikalisches Lexikon*.

less literally, is Justin Heinrich Knecht in 1816, explaining *Bebung* as "A slow trembling motion on one and the same note which is produced by the breath in singing and wind playing, by means of the tip of the finger on strings. One indicates the same by as many points or little dots [*Düpschen*], which are set over a long note, as movements should be made, as, for example [Ex. 16.27]."[94]

Ex. 16.27 Knecht: *Katechismus*, 53.

In practice, even if the number of dots in this rarely encountered notation was meant only roughly to indicate the frequency of pulsations, a very measured movement is implied. Löhlein, for instance, indicated a *Bebung* in one of the practice pieces in his *Anweisung*. His commentary makes it clear that this is a *Bebung* with the left hand, but since it immediately follows a *portato* with the bow, it may well be meant to continue with similar, or slightly faster pulsations of the left hand (Ex. 16.28).

Ex. 16.28 Löhlein, *Anweisung zum Violinspielen*, 68.

Many 19th-century accounts imply a faster basic trembling effect. In Petiscus's 1804 updated version of Leopold Mozart's violin school, the replacement of Mozart's section on *Tremolo* begins with the explanation that the ornament is "a quick up and down movement of the finger pressed on the string".[95] Another difference from the original is that he specifically required players to be able to decrease as well as increase its speed. Baillot's illustration of the effect of the *ondulation* (Ex. 16.9), too, suggests something very much quicker than Leopold Mozart's, despite his verbal description of

---

[94] Knecht: *Musikalischer Katechismus*, 4th edn (Freyburg, 1816), 53.
[95] Anon. [Johann Conrad Wilhelm Petiscus]: *Violinschule oder Anweisung die Violine zu Spielen von Leopold Mozart*, 59. This appeared in an unauthorized reprint by Cappi (Vienna, [1806]) and was reprinted by Peters in 1817. I am grateful to Axel Beer for this information.

it as a more or less moderate movement. In fact, his example of *ondulation* as performed by Viotti (see Ex. 16.4) indicates it as thirty-second-notes at a tempo of ♩ = 104 (Ex. 16.29), though he stressed that the oscillation should not be precisely measurable.[96]

**Ex. 16.29** Baillot, *L'art du violon*, 138.
Illustrating the execution of the first bar of the preceding example from Viotti's Nineteenth Violin Concerto.

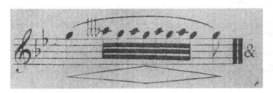

Bernhard Romberg's instruction is unequivocal; for him the oscillations of the *Bebung* are made with "very rapid movement".[97] But Baillot's account, like most other important ones in the 19th century,[98] also stressed that the player should be able to vary the speed of the *ondulation* according to the musical context.

Different performers would undoubtedly have treated trembling effects differently in differing contexts, as they would the performance of trills and other ornaments. This often depended on the relationship between speed and dynamic nuance in the execution of these ornaments. Leopold Mozart instructed that in performing a *messa di voce* type of bowstroke the player should make a left-hand trembling effect: "very slowly at the weak part of the sound, moving somewhat more quickly with the strong part".[99] Later, giving the example of the note before a *cadenza*, which he marked with an accelerating *tremolo* (Ex. 16.30), he instructed: "one must begin the stroke softly and gather strength towards the middle, in such fashion that the greatest strength falls at the beginning of the more rapid movement; and at last the stroke must finish softly again".[100]

---

[96] Baillot: *L'art du violon*, 138.
[97] Romberg: *Violoncell Schule*, 85.
[98] E.g., those of Spohr, Bériot, and Schröder.
[99] Mozart: *Versuch*, 103.
[100] Mozart: *Versuch*, 242.

Ex. 16.30 Mozart: *Versuch*, 141.

While Spohr, who associated *tremolo* with emotion, prescribed accelerating for *crescendo* and decelerating for *decrescendo*,[101] Mozart may have envisaged an effect more like the one described by Charles Nicholson, accelerating the trembling effect with *decrescendo*. In his *Preceptive Lessons for the Flute* of 1821, Nicholson explained this effect with the same analogy as Leopold Mozart, observing: "Vibration on the flute ought to resemble that of a Bell or Glass, the beats or pulsations of which are never rapid at first, but are governed by the strength of the Tone; for example, if your tone is full and strong, the beat should be slow, but gradually increased in proportion as you diminish the Tone—thus (Ex. 16.31)."[102]

Ex. 16.31 Nicholson: *Prescriptive Lessons*, 5.

A further point about the execution of trembling effects, on which there seems to have been very diverse opinions, was whether the pulsation should occupy the whole length of the note to which it was applied. Some authors,

---

[101] Spohr: *Violinschule*, 175.
[102] Charles Nicholson: *Prescriptive Lessons for the Flute* (London, [1821]), 5.

since they gave no instructions to the contrary, imply that this should be so, and indeed in the case of an effect that is closely related to *portato*, where little or no pitch variation is envisaged, this would seem to be the expected procedure. In the case of trembling that involved any element of pitch instability, however, there was considerable concern that it should not detract from accuracy of intonation, and several authoritative musicians recommended that a portion of the vibrated note should be pure. Baillot required that the beginning and end of the note should, as a rule, be free of *ondulation* (see Ex. 16.29).[103] Bernhard Romberg taught that "it should be made only at the beginning of the note, and ought not to be continued throughout its whole duration".[104]

## Changing Aesthetics in the Musical Application of Trembling Effects

### The Late 18th and Early 19th Centuries

In the middle of the 18th century, extensive ornamentation of the notated text was expected of solo singers and instrumentalists,[105] and trembling effects were perceived as ornaments. Studies of wind instrument tablatures from the late 17th century, and tutors from the early 18th century, suggest that many players left few notes of any length without some kind of ornamentation.[106] Francesco Geminiani's advice to use a trembling effect (*close shake*) where no other ornament is appropriate belongs in this context. He included the *close shake* in his "Ornaments of Expression necessary to the playing in a good Taste" and recommended its use "as often as possible" on notes where other ornaments were impractical. His statement that "it only contributes to make their Sound more agreeable"[107] is an isolated 18th-century association of the effect with tone enhancement. Interestingly, Geminiani considered that, whereas in violin playing the *close shake* could "be made on any Note whatsoever," in flute playing "it must only be made on long Notes".[108] The

---

[103] Baillot: *L'art du violon*, 138.
[104] Romberg: *Violoncell Schule*, 85.
[105] See Ch. 11.
[106] See Dickey: 'Untersuchung zur historischen Auffassung des Vibratos auf Blasinstrumenten', 88ff.
[107] Geminiani: *The Art*, 8.
[108] Francesco Geminiani: *Rules for Playing in a True Taste* (London, 1748), Preface.

reason for this was undoubtedly that the flautist's trembling effect, by trilling the finger over an open hole, could scarcely be used, from a technical point of view, except on longer notes. It was left to the French flautist Charles Delusse, who reproduced Geminiani's recommendations for the *close shake* in an almost verbatim translation, to devise a means of imitating this ornament on the flute, by rolling the instrument between finger and thumb while playing the note in the normal way, which he called *tremblement flexible*.[109]

In the same decade as Geminiani's treatise, Leopold Mozart posed a clear challenge to Geminiani's aesthetic, which was evidently shared by many of his contemporaries, complaining about violinists "who constantly tremble on every note".[110] And his argument that *tremolo* must be employed only in such places where Nature herself might produce it pointed the way towards later attitudes, rather than Geminiani's more stylized notion that it could represent affliction, fear, dignity, majesty, etc., which seems at odds with his recommendation to use it as often as possible to make the sound more agreeable. A few years later, Löhlein cautioned, from a somewhat different angle, against frequent use of the ornament. Like Mozart, he likened it to the vibrations of a bass string or a bell:

> Therefore, one must not be so liberal in its use: for if one applies it too often, as some do, the listener will feel a sympathetic anxiety, because he believes that this perpetual tremor comes from an attack of cold fever that is now afflicting the player. It therefore belongs only to notes that last for a long time, and especially to final notes. This tremor must be appropriate to the content of the piece. In a slow tempo, it must be slow, but in a fast movement, it must also be fast. Some have the laudable practice of trembling on the open strings. This is something worse than bad, and belongs in the alehouses.[111]

Geminiani's recommendations to employ trembling effects frequently were suppressed in later 18th-century editions of his treatise,[112] and in 1777 his pupil, Robert Bremner, argued that *tremolo* is only admissible "for the sake of variety" on a long note in a solo melody, but not in ensemble, where "every

---

[109] Delusse: *L'Art*, 9.
[110] Mozart: *Versuch*, 238f.
[111] Löhlein: *Anweisung zum Violinspielen*, 51.
[112] See Roger Hickman: 'The Censored Publications of *The Art of Playing on the Violin* or Geminiani Unshaken', *Early Music*, xi (1983), 73–76.

note should be as void of ornament as if produced by an open string".[113] The view that *tremolo* was detrimental in ensemble playing seems to have been generally acknowledged. Reichardt's 1776 treatise on orchestral playing did not mention it at all. In these and many other accounts from the Classical period, trembling effects are seen primarily as extemporary ornaments in solo playing, although their connection with particular kinds of expression is often acknowledged. Carl Friedrich Cramer, commenting on Bremner's *Preface* in 1783, observed: "as far as vocal performance and the expression of passionate sensation is also a model and ideal for the instrument—as much as the indeterminacy of mere notes without words allows—it follows irrefutably that the instrumentalist not only *may*, but also *must* use it in places where the voice would cause the tremor".[114] The reaction against *tremolo*, therefore, was not against a technique that was used to colour the tone continuously, but reflected a growing rejection of excessive ornamentation and a move towards an aesthetic in which directness of utterance was prized above artifice.

Many musicians and connoisseurs in the late 18th century and early 19th century saw expressiveness and emotional truth as higher virtues than the display of dexterity and ingenuity. Such a view was entirely in tune with the spirit of an age that was influenced by Rousseau to prize sincerity and naturalness above elaboration and artificiality. It is noteworthy that the strongest reactions against trembling techniques imply a general rejection of what John Gunn referred to as "graces of the finger", while the texts that support their moderate and proper use seem often, explicitly, or implicitly, to link them with the expression of natural emotion. The mass of evidence does not support Robert Donington's contention that something like *continuous vibrato*, in the modern sense, has been a common aspect of string playing at least since Geminiani. His assumption that Geminiani's description "corresponds to modern usage"[115] is untenable, and his statement that "[Leopold] Mozart preferred a more selective but still fairly continuous vibrato"[116] has absolutely no foundation in anything written by or about Leopold Mozart.

---

[113] Bremner: 'Some Thoughts on the Performance of Concert Music' (Preface to J. G. C. Schetky's op. 6). See Zaslaw: 'The Compleat Orchestral Musician', *Early Music*, vii (1979), 48 and 53.
[114] Carl Friedrich Cramer: *Magazin der Musik*, I (1783), 1217.
[115] Donington: 'Vibrato' in *New Grove*, 1st edn, xix, 697.
[116] Donington: *Early Music*, xvi (1988), 571, in his review of Greta Moens-Haenen's impressive study *Das Vibrato in der Musik des Barock* (Graz, 1988). Since then, a great deal of nonsense has been written about the use of *vibrato* in pre-20th-century music, some of it of a polemic nature unworthy of serious scholarship.

Although some degree of extemporary melodic ornamentation continued in instrumental playing at least until the 1840s, and even later in singing, the Classical aesthetic of beauty laid greater stress on nuancing the sound (*sons filés*) than on any kind of discretionary ornamentation.[117] In the 1790s, Gunn confirmed this change of taste, observing: "The performers of the *old school* had much more of what may be called the *graces of the finger*, than the modern, which cultivates more the expression and powers of the bow, and the management of *tone*." Reporting that many old ornaments had been abandoned, he added: "Among these was the dumb shake on stringed instruments, corresponding to what the French call *Flattement* on the flute, [...] producing a trembling palsied expression, inconsistent with just intonation, and not unlike that extravagant trembling of the voice which the French call *chevrotter*, to make a goat-like noise; for which the singers of the Opera at Paris have so often been ridiculed."[118]

Michel Woldemar's *Grande méthode*, published at the end of the 18th century, confirms this change of taste. It illustrates three alternative treatments of a melody: "*Grande broderie*" (Tartini) with elaborate ornamentation; "*Broderie légere*" (Nardini), lightly embellished; and "*Sons filés*", the unadorned melody with dynamic inflexions, which he calls "Grand Adagio Moderne".[119] This method makes no mention of trembling effects in relation to *sons filés*, or in any other context. In his 1801 radical revision of Leopold Mozart's *Versuch*, Woldemar omits all Mozart's treatment of *tremolo*; here too he advises that one should "*filer les sons*".[120] Only in the second edition of his *Grande méthode*, as mentioned above, did he include a kind of *bow vibrato*. Similarly, the highly influential 1803 Paris Conservatoire *Méthode de violon* by Baillot, Rode, and Kreutzer ignored left-hand trembling effects and, like Mozart's *Versuch*, focused on various kinds of treatment that can be given to sustained notes, either performing them with a firm and equal bowstrokes (*sons soutenus*), an increasing dynamic (*sons enflés*) marked <, a diminishing dynamic (*sons diminués*), marked >, and nuanced (*sons filés*) marked <>.[121]

A significant number of sources around 1800 cautioned against abusing trembling effects. Tromlitz warned: "One does not do it with the breath on the flute, it does not make a good effect, it wails, and whoever does it spoils

---

[117] See Ch. 13.
[118] Gunn: *The Art of Playing the German Flute*, 18.
[119] Woldemar: *Grande Méthode*, 1st edn (Paris, c. 1800), 63. This section is missing in the 2nd edn. See Ch. 13, Ex.13.23.
[120] Woldemar: *Méthode de violon par L. Mozart*, 79.
[121] Baillot et al.: *Méthode*, 135ff.

the chest and ruins his whole playing, for he loses firmness and is consequently unable to hold a firm and pure note; he makes everything come from his chest in a trembling manner."[122] Francesco Galeazzi asserted that left-hand *tremolo* "should be entirely banned from music by anyone equipped with good taste";[123] he did not even discuss the selective use of this effect for expressive purposes. In singing, too, *Bebung*, as a stylized trembling ornament, seems to have become relatively uncommon around the turn of the century. Lasser, having explained how to produce it, added: "I heard it from a singer, from whose throat I really liked it, but it's not something for everyone".[124] Among those who actively discouraged it was Johann Friedrich Schubert. Having illustrated and discusses all the major ornaments, from *appoggiaturas* to trills, Schubert, who was also a violinist, concluded with a discussion of *Bebung*, which offers a revealing glimpse of changing attitudes and contrasting practices, both in singing and string playing, around the turn of the century:

> Finally, I would like to mention an ornament that was a beauty in the past, but is now never heard any more from a tasteful singer: It is the *Bebung* (French: *balancement*, Italian: *tremolo*), which consisted in a wavering or wobbling of a long note. Anyone with an educated ear will admit that this ornament, if often heard, must arouse disgust; nevertheless, it has been preserved among violinists up to the present time, and skilful virtuosos not infrequently regale us with this ornament on every note that is long enough to permit it, in every piece of music, without exception, in which they let themselves be heard. Even those virtuosos who have been educated in a school where a beautiful, firm, equal tone alternating with f and p is a basic rule, are not free from this tasteless ornament.* My intention is in no way to teach violinists better, but only to warn the singing pupil, when he hears a singer or violinist who has adopted this ornament (even if it is one of the greatest virtuosos), not to adopt it. I would allow the violinist a *Bebung* on a long, isolated note only very rarely, but the singer never; the latter can give his sustained notes more modification and variety than the violinist.
>
> * [Schubert's footnote] The use of this ornament is a matter of taste, and there is certainly no evidence that could be used to condemn this ornament

---

[122] Tromlitz: *Unterricht*, §4, 239.
[123] Galeazzi: *Elementi*, 1st edn (1791), 171; 2nd edn (1817), 193.
[124] Lasser: *Vollständige Anleitung*, 154.

completely. I am happy to refrain from imposing my judgement on those who disagree with me; but this much is certain, that among ten musical connoisseurs and experts, there are perhaps not two who unreservedly approve of this ornament. The violinists, to whatever mast they may have nailed their colours, can have nothing to say here, since one's own feeling is never an unimpeachable judge, especially when a longstanding habit has formed it.[125]

A reviewer of Schubert's treatise, noting that singers use *Bebung* in inappropriate places, and badly executed, added his personal opinion "that he can, at best, only approve of this ornament—even the proper one—at fermatas, in certain cases, but otherwise finds it tasteless if the aforementioned passionate expression does not justify its use on a very long note, towards the end of it".[126] By the beginning of the 19th century, therefore, there was an overwhelming consensus, among those who set themselves up as musical authorities, that trembling effects, if used at all, should be employed only with great discretion. Nevertheless, as continuing complaints about overuse demonstrate, some, perhaps many performers continued to use them more extensively than these connoisseurs considered appropriate. Fröhlich incorporated large portions of Schubert's *Singe-Schule* into his *Vollständige Musikschule* with few alterations. In the section on ornaments, however, he omitted Schubert's diatribe against the use of the *Bebung*, replacing it with a very short comment, which like others from the first half of the 19th century suggests not only that trembling effects were no longer fashionable, but also perhaps that repeated criticism had led to them being decreasingly employed: "As for the almost obsolete ornament—the *Bebung*—which consists of a hovering or swaying of a long tone, which is marked with . . . or ~~~, it is not to be recommended to the singer, since it is only rarely performed well, and he has other and more telling means of expression than this dangerous ornament".[127] It may also be indicative of changing taste in such matters that the only feature in the playing of the almost legendary Viotti that came in for criticism when he gave one of his rare public performances in Europe in the late 1790s was his "somewhat strong *tremolando*".[128]

---

[125] Schubert: *Singe-Schule*, 68.
[126] Anon.: *Allgemeine musikalische Zeitung*, vii (1804–5), 60.
[127] Fröhlich: *Musikschule*, i, 65.
[128] Anon.: 'Briefe über Tonkunst und Tonkünstler', *Allgemeine musikalische Zeitung*, i (1798–99), 762.

Other treatises from the first forty years of the 19th century also note that trembling effects were being used less than formerly. In England, John Jousse (b. 1760), in his *Modern Violin Preceptor* (c. 1805), merely described the mechanism of the *close shake* in a single sentence without commenting on its use. In his later *Theory and Practice of the Violin*, a short section is entitled "Of the Tremolo or Close Shake. (It is become obsolete)"; this is followed solely by a nine-line, unacknowledged, quotation from Bremner's 1777 "Some thoughts on the performance of Concert Music".[129] In 1817, Charles J. Smyth observed: "A good portamento implies also that the notes be properly *sustained*. He who sings *tremulously*, and makes that kind of *close shake*, which old-fashioned violin and bass players were so fond of, fails egregiously as to portamento."[130] A couple of years later, A. F. Häser (b. 1779), under the heading "Vocal errors" warned:

> Quivering of the voice, tremolo, which some singers portray as a means of higher expression, is only repugnant, a sign of a weak chest, and lack of the strength to sustain a note, therefore one often hears it from old, but otherwise very worthy artists; with beginners, it generally comes from the fact that they still do not know enough to master the voice and do not know how to breathe deeply enough at the right time. Where it therefore takes place, one tries to prevent it by diligently sustaining individual notes, by singing very slow scales and by breathing properly at the right time, otherwise it will easily become a habit.[131]

In string playing, as J. F. Schubert's comments suggest, a certain amount of ornamental *tremolo* was accepted. Bernhard Romberg (b. 1767), in his very brief treatment of left-hand *tremolo*, commented:

> Rarely introduced, and executed with much power of the bow, it gives the tone fire and life; however, it should only be done at the beginning of the note and not for the entire duration of the note. In the past, no one could sustain a note, however short, without constantly shaking with the finger, and it became a truely miserable kind of music.[132]

---

[129] Jousse: *Theory and Practice of the Violin* (London, 1811), 48.
[130] Smyth: *Six Letters on Singing* (Norwich, 1817), 4f.
[131] August Ferdinand Häser: 'Fehler der Stimme', *Allgemeine musikalische Zeitung*, xxiv (1822), 38.
[132] Romberg: *Violoncell Schule*, 85.

Romberg's pupil J. J. F. Dotzauer (b. 1783) also considered trembling effects old-fashioned. After discussing how trembling effects with the left hand or bow were used by many soloists on sustained notes—to which his French translator added in parentheses "especially Italian professors"—he cautioned: "Although these ornaments are not to be completely rejected, it is not recommended to use them too often, since the ability to maintain a beautiful, pure, level tone, stronger or weaker depending on the circumstances, is independent of these tricks, which good taste only very rarely finds admissible."[133] His 1833 *Violoncell-Schule* mentions only the left-hand technique, commenting briefly: "Shaking or trembling on a long note with your finger is certainly an old ornament [*Manier*]; rarely used, however, and in the appropriate place—which is a matter of good taste—it should not be completely discarded."[134] It is nevertheless clear that some string players still made more use of trembling effects than the cognoscenti considered appropriate; or perhaps, as later evidence suggests, a resurgence of interest in trembling effects among younger performers was beginning to make itself felt in the 1830s. A reviewer of Dotzauer's *Violoncell-Schule*, having quoted the above passage, commented: "May these remarks by a celebrated master not go unnoticed. Particularly in Vienna the *tremolo* is much too often used."[135]

Two major violin treatises of the 1830s, Spohr's and Baillot's, which include substantial discussion of left-hand trembling effects, contain no references to contemporaneous overuse, perhaps indicating that, at that stage, an aesthetic of pure, tremor-free sound in string playing, enlivened by an occasional trembling effect, was a widely acknowledged ideal. Both instruct that these effects should be used only sparingly, for the expressive characterization of specific notes. There is no reason to doubt that the recommendations of these leading performers and teachers reflected their own practice; and it was reported by Joseph Joachim that the playing of their younger contemporary Bernhard Molique (b. 1802), who studied with Spohr and Rovelli, "was without any vibrato whatsoever".[136] Spohr includes *tremolo* in his treatment of ornaments; Baillot, however, though he includes *ports de voix* among melodic ornaments (*Agréments du chant*), discusses *ondulation* (both of the bow

---

[133] Dotzauer: *Méthode*, 47.
[134] Dotzauer: *Violoncell-Schule*, 28.
[135] Anon.: *Allgemeine musikalischer Anzeiger*, vi (1834), 22.
[136] Samuel B. Grimson and Cecil Forsyth, *Modem Violin-Playing* (New York, 1920), 34.

and of the left-hand) in a section on *Son* (sound/tone), perhaps presaging an incipient division between German and French practice that was to widen during the 19th century. He nevertheless demanded the greatest discretion in its use, explaining that it "gives the sound of the instrument a close analogy with the human voice when it is strongly touched with emotion. This type of expression is very powerful, but if frequently used it would have only the dangerous disadvantage of making the melody unnatural and depriving the style of that precious naivety which is the greatest charm of art and recalls it to its primitive simplicity."[137] He concluded his survey of the ways in which the *ondulation* could be produced, and the circumstances in which it was appropriate, by requiring the player to "avoid making a habit of vibration of the hand, which must be employed only when the expression renders it necessary and, furthermore, conforming with all that has been indicated in order to prevent its abuse".[138]

Spohr marks it with four different types of wavy line: fast, speeding up, slow, and slowing down, of which the first two are the most frequent. These are included in practice pieces Nos. 65 and 66, as well as in his annotated versions of Rode's Seventh Violin Concerto and his own Ninth Violin Concerto op. 55 in Part 3 of the *Violinschule*.

It is clear from both these major treatises that the trembling effect is a contrast to the normal steady tone, and Baillot even instructs: "so that the ear does not suffer, and we are immediately consoled, it is necessary to begin and end by sounding the exact, pure note".[139] Like Baillot, Spohr characterizes it as resembling the effect "when the singer sings while moved by passion";[140] and both insist that it should be used only in such circumstances. Spohr's marking of places where he regarded *tremolo* as appropriate shows how sparingly he expected it (Ex. 16.32).[141]

---

[137] Baillot: *L'art du violon*, 138.
[138] Baillot: *L'art du violon*, 139.
[139] Baillot: *L'art du violon*, 138.
[140] Spohr: *Violinschule*, 175.
[141] Marie Soldat's recording of the Adagio from Spohr's Ninth Concerto (c. 1920) contains similarly sparing use of *vibrato* and expressive *portamento* fingering, similar but not identical to Spohr's markings in his version in the *Violinschule*.

Ex. 16.32 a–b. Spohr: *Violinschule*; (a) Rode: Seventh Violin Concerto, 198; (b) Spohr: Ninth Violin Concerto, 228.

Similar comments and warnings against overuse were made in wind methods that mention trembling effects. Fürstenau, in 1826, also compared the flautist's use of *Bebung* with that of the singer and warned in strong terms that it should be introduced only if confined to a single note, and then with only three or four wavering motions.[142] In his later treatise of 1844, his illustrations of where to use the *Bebung* and *Klopfen* show how infrequently he expected them. In Ex. 16.20, he even gave alternative places to introduce the *Bebung*, instructing either here, or here above the wavy lines. Other flute methods in the first half of the century reiterated Fürstenau's admonition, in more or less strong language, that trembling effects (both produced by the breath and the fingers) should be used very sparingly.[143] As the addition of keys on wind

---

[142] Fürstenau: *Flöten-Schule* (Leipzig, [1826]), 79.

[143] Charles Nicholson: *Complete Preceptor for the German Flute* (London, [c. 1816]); Nicholson: *A School for the Flute* (New York, [1836]); Charles Weiss: *A New Methodical Instruction Book for the Flute* (London, [c. 1821]); James Alexander: *Complete Preceptor for the Flute* (London, [c. 1821]); Thomas Lindsay: *The Elements of Flute Playing* (London, [1828]); John Clinton: *A School or Practical Instruction Book for the Boehm Flute* (London, [1846]).

instruments increasingly limited the possibilities for trembling effects with the finger, players will certainly have continued to make trembling effects with the breath, but in mid-century there were still influential musicians who considered them inappropriate or even unfeasible on wind instruments. In 1863, Moritz Hauptmann, Thomascantor in Leipzig, stated in an article on acoustics that "a vibrated wind note is just as impossible as a vibrated harmonic [on string instruments], and in this sense the wind instruments lack a means of expression that only the string instruments, violin, viola, and violoncello, have in common with the voice".[144] Hauptmann's statement was directly challenged two years later by Arrey von Dommer, who asserted that trembling effects were possible and effective on many wind instruments.[145] Nevertheless, Hauptmann's comment suggests that he had not observed it in the Dresden Hofkapelle (where he served from 1812 to 1815), nor in the Kassel Orchestra (where he served under his former violin teacher, Spohr, from 1822 to 1842) nor in the Leipzig Gewandhaus Orchestra during the following twenty years, nor from any wind soloists. A growing tendency to use trembling effects in wind playing later in the century, however, is implied by the fact that Carl Reinecke felt it necessary to instruct in the Più lento quasi Andante of the Intermezzo of his 1882 Flute Sonata op. 167 that it should be played "without any trembling [Bebung] in tone".[146]

Despite criticisms of performers using trembling effects too frequently, there is nothing to suggest that trained singers or instrumentalists would have indulged in anything like continual trembling, except perhaps as a joke. An ear-witness of Paganini's playing in Italy, probably Cipriani Potter, who certainly heard him there in 1818, reported in 1821 that the violinist had "studied the odd as well as the delightful", and after describing his left-hand pizzicato, recalled "He produces another singular, and at the same time whimsical effect by a close tremolo, which he maintains during the whole of a short air; it resembles the crazed and trembling voice of an old woman, and its merits may be estimated by this circumstance, that every person laughs very heartily during the performance."[147] Nevertheless, after Paganini came north of the Alps in 1828, he was perceived to use considerably more *tremolo* in his playing than was normal at that time. His example was blamed for

---

[144] Moritz Hauptmann: 'Klang', *Jahrbuch für musikalischen Wissenschaft*, i (1863), 22.
[145] Dommer: 'Bebung, *Tremolo*' in *Musikalisches Lexikon*, 100.
[146] Carl Reinecke: Flute Sonata "Undine" op. 167 (Leipzig: Robert Forberg, [1882] Plate no. 2987), score p. 15.
[147] Anon.: *The Kaleidoscope*, 1821, 200.

encouraging its increasing employment. In 1842, H. F. Chorley, reviewing the singing of Giorgio Ronconi (1810–1890), referred to "the tremulous tone of the present mode (Paganini's solitary and worthless legacy to Art)".[148]

Although there was evidently some disjunction between theory and practice, the extent of which is impossible to determine, the last decade of the 18th century and the first thirty or forty years of the 19th century seems to have been a period in which trembling effects were less esteemed and less frequently used than either before or after, while sliding effects followed an opposite trajectory.[149]

## The Mid-19th Century

By the 1840s it is evident that, in both singing and instrumental playing, trembling effects were being gradually rehabilitated as an ancillary attribute of beautiful performance, but with the expectation that they should be sparingly and tastefully employed. In singing they were still seen, theoretically, as appropriate only occasionally, as an intensification of emotion. Many singers, however, were increasingly perceived to make excessive and unmusical use of them, and were frequently criticized for it. Christian Wilhelm Häser in 1841 implied that some singers may have seen trembling effects as an adjunct of *portamento* (probably in the sense of nuancing a note <>)—a combination that Charles Smyth had explicitly rejected—commenting:

> As for the *tremolo* while sustaining a note, which some singers cultivate and want to use as if it were a special ornament, there is no denying that a certain gentle and quiet tremor or vibration of the note (like the *vox humana* in an organ), the *timbre* of the French, is pleasant to the ear in expressive places, if it doesn't happen too often and is kept in bounds; only this should not be confused with *portamento*.[150]

In the middle years of the century, singers were often praised for resisting a growing tendency to use trembling effects frequently and without sufficient

---

[148] Chorley: *The Athenaeum*, 1842, 348.
[149] See Ch. 15.
[150] Christian Wilhelm Häser: 'Aphorismen', *Jahrbücher des deutschen National-Vereins für Musik und ihre Wissenschaft*, iii (1841), 248.

expressive motivation. Looking back in the 1880s, Deacon (b. 1822), who, in youth, had studied singing in Milan, reported that *tremolo*, by which he meant wavering of pitch, is "the abuse of a means of expression or effect, legitimate if used only at the right time and place, and in the right way. It assumed the character of a vocal vice about 40 years ago, and is supposed to have had its origin in the vibrato of Rubini, first assuming formidable proportions in France, and then quickly spreading throughout the musical world."[151] Deacon's reference to Rubini's *vibrato*, which he defined as a trembling of intensity, not pitch, is significant, because *vibrato*, in this sense, though often criticized as excessive, was by no means so severely condemned as *tremolo* (trembling of pitch), when inappropriately introduced. The teasing review, already quoted, of Hauman's violin playing in 1840 demonstrates not only the inconsistent terminology for trembling effects, but also makes absolutely clear that even at that time, Rubini's trembling effect was perceived as an oscillation of intensity, not pitch. Having mentioned Hauman's use of *il suono vibrato*, Blanchard referred mockingly to: "all the tremor or tremolo invented by Rubini, imitated by Batta on the cello [. . .], perfected by de Bériot, and which we do not despair of seeing introduced into piano teaching and reduced to mathematical proportions by Kalkbrenner".[152] Here, by *tremolo*, he evidently refers specifically to rapid note repetition of a single pitch with the bow, as in Bériot's *Le Trémolo* op. 30 or with the fingers in piano music. Blanchard's comments also confirm that he saw this type of *vibrato/tremolo* as deriving from Rubini's influence. Other accounts, too, demonstrate concern about a recently increasing abuse of trembling effects in singing. A report from Prague in August 1839 expressed approval because: "Mr Steinmüller makes less frequent misuse of the modern sin of *tremolo* than some more famous singers."[153]

Deacon's attribution of the spread of trembling effects in singing directly to Rubini's influence has often been repeated in later accounts, but this is certainly an oversimplification. In 1842, Fridolin von Wend, reviewing the singing of Madam Hoffmann in Graz, described "a certain excessive sliding of the notes, combined with strong tremolo", which he categorized as "a

---

[151] Deacon: 'Tremolo', in *Grove* (London, 1889), iv, 166.
[152] Henri Blanchard: 'Concert donnée par M. Hauman', *Revue et Gazette musicale de Paris*, vii (1840), 604.
[153] Bohemia: 'Nachrichten von fremden Bühnen', *Der Sammler* (1839), 416.

stereotypical fault of the Italian method",[154] and in a subsequent review he criticized her "incessant Tremolo".[155] Later in the season he remarked:

> The Tremolo is a mistaken belief, held by an Italian school that certainly has nothing in common with that of the great Bernacchi. Well applied it has a ravishing effect; once it has become a prevailing characteristic of the sound, it sins against the art of singing and against artistic genius by abolishing the definiteness and regular oscillation of the note, clouding the clarity of the musical figure, especially at a fast pace, and, with its stupid obligato wailing, perverts and destroys the character of the composer's conception of the piece.[156]

Another review from this period specifies the Bergamo tenor school of Marco Bordogni (b. 1789) as a source of the habit: "Tremolo in the voice and *Coloratura cavalletta* are unfortunately the main mistakes of this singing master, which he moreover maintains to be a great beauty in singing."[157] Significantly, Rubini had begun his career as a violinist and chorister at the theatre in Bergamo.

This "modern sin" quickly became associated with France as well as Italy. Abuse of trembling effects attracted less attention from the press in string playing than in singing, but there is solid evidence that the 1840s also saw its increase, especially among some French and Belgian string players. Cellist Alexandre Batta was warned: "even his friends would like him not to be so fond of *the vibrato sound, like the singing of an old woman*".[158] In 1846, in contrast, a reviewer in Leipzig commented approvingly on the playing of Belgian violinist Hubert Léonard (b. 1819): "The avoidance of everlasting trembling, which, as an excessive exuberance of feeling, almost all young virtuosos from the West [i.e., Paris and Brussels] believe they have to use to excess, is praiseworthy."[159] Léonard's detailed MS fingering in a proof copy of Mendelssohn's Violin Concerto, from which he played, with the composer at the piano, before the work's publication, contains extensive use of open strings and harmonics

---

[154] Fridolin, Freiherr von Wend: *Allgemeine Wiener Musik-Zeitung*, ii (1842), 195.
[155] Wend: *Allgemeine Wiener Musik-Zeitung*, ii (1842), 247.
[156] Wend: *Allgemeine Wiener Musik-Zeitung*, ii (1842), 575.
[157] Johannes Heitmann: 'Dresden im Dezember 1839', *Jahrbücher des deutschen National-Vereins für Musik und ihre Wissenschaft*, ii (1840), 21.
[158] Henri Blanchard: 'Matinées et soirées musicales. Le jeune Filtsch.—M. Batta.—M. Géraldy', *Revue et Gazette musicale de Paris*, x (1843), 150.
[159] Anon.: *Allgemeine musikalische Zeitung*, xlvii (1845), 263f.

on long notes, which confirm this reviewer's comments.[160] Heinrich Wilhelm Ernst's violin playing in 1848, however, elicited the criticism that "the elegiac is distorted by the false French romantic habit of eternal morbid vibrato, reminiscent of old men or old women, against which true feeling must protest". Henri Vieuxtemps's playing, on the other hand, was praised by this reviewer because "all these deficiencies fall away; he uses vibrato and tremolando only very sparingly, where the spirit of the piece demands it".[161]

The international activities of Italian opera singers were an important factor in spreading the contentious practice throughout Europe. Some critics accepted it, but others continued to complain vociferously over the following decades, especially when the *vibrato* of intensity became the *tremolo* of pitch. Deacon recalled: "In some cases this [*tremolo*] has been cultivated (evidently) to such an extent as to be utterly ludicrous. Ferri, a baritone, who flourished about 35 years ago, gave four or five beats in a second, of a good quarter tone, and this incessantly."[162] In fact, on Nicola Ferri's first appearance in England in 1861, a reviewer had castigated him as

> another example of what singers come to who abandon the legitimate school of singing for the modern system of "shouting." [. . .] What is the result? Every note becomes a shake [trill] through the incessant "vibrato," which is either a defect or a weakness. Owing to this the intonation suffers materially, as instead of one note, two or three are distinctly audible. We are quite aware that other singers, even of repute, indulge in the same failing, but we never heard it carried to such an excess, and think the example of Signor Ferri may prove a warning to those who have fallen into the same error.[163]

Among the singers of repute whom the reviewer may have had in mind at that time was the *tenore robusto* Enrico Tamberlik (b. 1820), who appeared regularly in London from 1850. The early reviews recognized his great talent. One reviewer, however, complained on his first appearance about his "excessive use of the *voce vibrato*", adding that it "is a fine quality in a singer, but it is possible to abuse it to a pitch of unpleasantness to the listener";[164] and

---

[160] See Clive Brown: *Performance Practices in the Violin Concerto op. 64 and Chamber Music for Strings of Felix Mendelssohn Bartholdy* (Kassel, Bärenreiter, 2018).
[161] Robert Saxo: 'Petersburger Musikleben, 1846–1848', *Neue Zeitschrift für Musik* (1848), 80.
[162] Deacon: 'Tremolo' in Grove, *Dictionary*, iv, 167.
[163] Anon.: 'Royal Italian Opera', *The London Review*, iii (1861), 520.
[164] Anon.: 'Royal Italian Opera', *Literary Gazette*, 6 April 1850, 251.

a subsequent review commented, "More evenness, and less of the *vibrato*, would render him a great singer."[165] Over the next few years, Tamberlik's use of *vibrato* continued to be controversial, often condemned by critics, but clearly tolerated, or even enjoyed by some of the public. In 1852 a critic remarked: "Signor Tamberlik's voice was in excellent condition while the richness of his tones, accompanied by that peculiar 'vibrato,' which, after some discussion, has been accepted, not merely as a peculiarity, but (when under entire control, as now), a beauty, gave additional effect to his large and finished style of phrasing, leaving the ear and the judgment equally satisfied."[166] Another journal in 1853 described how "his magnificent *vibrato* soared triumphantly over chorus and orchestra"[167] and in 1855 reported how his "large phrasing and the passionate vibrato were welcomed with satisfaction by the regular opera-goers".[168] On the other hand, a later reviewer remarked: "If he could but get rid of his inveterate habit of delivering every passage with what is technically termed 'the vibrato,' he would double the estimation in which he is justly held as one of our greatest artists."[169] And another commented: "It is greatly to be regretted that the otherwise beautiful singing of this great tenor is often destroyed by his incessant 'vibrato,' which at times becomes so strong as to endanger not only his individual success, but that of the opera."[170] Without aural evidence it is impossible to appreciate the characteristics of Tamberlik's *vibrato*, but recordings of Francesco Tamagno (b. 1850), widely regarded as his successor, reveal an almost constant rapid *vibrato* of intensity, mostly with little or no perceptible fluctuation of pitch.

Complaints about the excessive employment of vocal *vibrato*, seen sometimes as an Italian, and sometimes a French practice, persisted in the British press during the middle decades of the 19th century, with comments such as: "that fatal *vibrato*, which is the Nemesis of so many dramatic vocalists of the present era";[171] or condemnation of "the prevailing *vibrato* epidemic".[172] One reviewer referred to a soprano possessing "the *vibrato* in all the perfection of its ugliness", adding that she "has evidently taken special pains to cultivate the nuisance".[173] Another, in 1865, castigated "the prevalent transalpine

[165] Anon.: 'Royal Italian Opera', *Literary Gazette*, 27 April 1850, 299.
[166] Anon.: 'Royal Italian Opera', *The Musical World*, xxx (1852): 215.
[167] Anon.: 'Royal Italian Opera', *The Leader*, iv (1853), 381.
[168] Anon.: 'Royal Italian Opera', *The Leader*, vi (1855), 381.
[169] Anon.: 'Royal Italian Opera', *The Saturday Review*, xi (1861), 449.
[170] Anon.: 'Royal Italian Opera', *The London Review* ii (1861), 540.
[171] Anon.: 'Royal Italian Opera', *The Musical World*, xl (1862), 356.
[172] Anon.: 'Royal Italian Opera', *The Theatrical and Musical Examiner*, 9 August 1862, 503.
[173] Anon.: *The Reader*, vi (1865), 580.

vice of the last ten years, the *vibrato*".[174] In 1864, Mademoiselle Brunetti was praised because she "dispenses with the exasperating *vibrato* which most French vocalists mistake for taste—but which is about as much taste as a six-guinea harmonium can afford with the expression stop [tremulant] pulled out".[175] Another critic referred to "the quavering vice called by Italians the *vibrato*".[176] A report from the 1870s perceived it as a widespread continental disease, attributing it to singers "who have [...] been submitted to the Italian school of Verdi's imitators, to the French school as represented by Meyerbeer and Halevy, &c., or to the German school of the *Zukunft*".[177]

The employment of trembling effects, and concern about their inartistic use, seems to have reached a new peak around the 1870s, at least in London, prompting the complaint: "the evil [...] has extended very considerably into the instrumental world of music. Solo players on the violin have not been permitted its exclusive use, but all members of the stringed family freely employ it. The various kinds of wind instruments are following suit: from the gentle flute to the brazen ophicleide, all seem afflicted with the senseless wobble."[178] Looking back in 1904, James Swinburne pointedly identified this trend as predominantly French. He recalled that a keyboard operated string-playing machine he heard at the Paris Exhibition of 1878 was

> not playing the music in French. I must digress to explain what I mean by playing in French. In 1878 the crime of producing everything tremolo was especially French. All the singers sang tremolo and every instrument that could play tremolo did so; even the cors de chasse played in this hysterical way. The tremolo microbe got out all over the world, and everybody sings tremolo now and plays tremolo when he can; so playing in French has, in 1904, no distinct meaning.

Continuing sarcastically, he added: "Perhaps if I talked of playing with expression it would be clearer, for tremolo performers are always said to perform with so much expression."[179]

---

[174] Anon.: 'Mdlle. Ilma de Murska', *The Reader*, v (1865), 635.
[175] Anon.: 'Covent Garden', *The Orchestra*, ii (1864), 695.
[176] Anon.: *The Theatrical and Musical Examiner*, 23 April 1864, 265.
[177] Anon.: 'Crystal Palace Concerts', *The Musical World*, lvi (1878), 245.
[178] Anon.: *The Musical Standard*, ix (1875), 84.
[179] James Swinburne: 'Expression by Machinery', *Musical Opinion and Music Trade Review*, xxviii (1905), 278.

Criticism of vocal *vibrato*, and more particularly *tremolo*—and resistance to it—seems to have been particularly strong in Britain. Scrutiny of English-language journalism suggests a vigorous and temporarily successful rear-guard action against excessive *vibrato/tremolo* in singing in the late 19th century.[180] A writer in 1890 claimed: "England has for forty years and more been the one country in the world where the tremolo is a bar to artistic success", naming "Adelina Patti, Nilsson, Albani, and Trebelli [. . .] and such comparatively new celebrities as Jean and Edouard de Reszké, Nordica, De Lussan, and M'Intyre" as "free from the defect". The writer continued: "It was really lamentable last week to hear in 'Les Huguenots' three such excellent new vocalists as the soprano, Madam Tetrazzini; the tenor, M. Ybos; and the baritone, M. Dufriche; all three sound and intelligent artists, possessed of capital voices [. . .] practically singing away their chances of fame, by adopting a mannerism condemned alike by the artistic feelings of audiences and by common sense."[181] This kind of attitude may have been encouraged by the presence in London of Manuel García, who taught at the Royal Academy of Music from 1848 to 1895. In his highly influential *École de García* he had made it clear that trembling of pitch, which he includes under the heading "Émotion de la voix", should be used only to express very powerful emotions, adding:

> In these specific circumstances, its use must be regulated with taste and moderation; as soon as its expression or duration is exaggerated, it becomes tiring and unattractive. Apart from the special cases we have just mentioned, one must be careful not to alter the firmness of the sound in any way, because repeated use of the tremolo makes the voice unsteady. [. . .] Some singers believe, wrongly, that they are making their voice more vibrant by this means, and, like many violinists, seek to increase the strength of their instrument by the undulation of the sound.[182]

Like so many other 19th-century authorities, García's brother-in-law Charles de Bériot also equated vibrated sounds [*sons vibrés*] with "the emotion of the soul conveyed through the voice". He considered that it was "an

---

[180] Richard Bethell: 'Vocal Vibrato in Early Music', www.york.ac.uk/music/news-and-events/events/conferences/nema/bethell/#chapter3, 2009 [accessed 25 June 2022].
[181] Anon.: 'Vocalists and Wobblers', *The Magazine of Music*, vii (1890), 135.
[182] García: *École*, ii, 54. See above, pp. 979–80, for García's instructions for trembling effects in which the pitch should not be affected.

accomplishment with the artist who knows how to use it with effect, and to abstain from it when that is necessary: but it becomes a fault when too frequently employed", stating, "The voice of the singer, like the fine quality of tone in the violinist, is impaired by this great fault." In common with Spohr and Ferdinand David, Bériot uses several forms of wavy lines to indicate different intensities (speeds) of trembling. In his *Méthode de violon* of 1858/9, before discussing how the *sons vibrés* might effectively be used, he provided vocal and violin examples in which no vibrated sounds at all should be heard, and some where they might be used selectively, remarking: "Almost all violinists who use *port-de-voix* too frequently, abuse *sons vibrés*; the one fault inevitable leads to the other. The affectation that results from the employment of these elements makes the artist's playing mannered, exaggerated, for it gives a piece more expression than is consistent with truth."[183]

Although trembling effects were clearly employed to a significant extent by many later 19th-century string players, it was certainly not yet regarded as a continuous colouring to the sound, even in Franco-Belgian violin playing, as Alonso's treatise of 1895 demonstrates. In more than twenty Franco-Belgian violin methods examined, from Mazas in 1832 to Léonard in 1877, only four mention left-hand trembling. Charles Dancla deals with it in four and a half lines and one music example.[184] J. Blanc mentions it simply in connection with a single note in a music example (Ex. 16.33), for which he instructs: "Press the finger as well as the bow strongly on the string while giving the hand a soft but rapid tremor without changing the position. This tremor augments the vibration of the string and communicates more intensity to the sound."[185]

Ex. 16.33 Blanc: *Grande méthode*, 107.

[183] Bériot: *Méthode*, 220.
[184] Charles Dancla: *Méthode élémentaire et progressive pour violon* op. 52 (Paris, [1855]), 42.
[185] J. Blanc: *Grande méthode complète et raisonnée pour le violon* op. 9 (Paris, 1846), 107.

A similar isolated example occurs in Hermann Schröder's *Preis-Violinschule* (Ex. 16.34) where a footnote explains: "Vibration of the note due to trembling movement of the left hand, whereby the base of the index finger must be removed as far as possible from the neck of the violin, i.e., the hand momentarily adopts an abnormal position."[186]

Ex. 16.34 Schröder: *Preis-Violinschule*, 66.

Ferdinand David similarly instructed that "the first finger must leave its usual place on the neck of the violin", adding that only the finger making the *vibrato* must be on the string.[187] Dancla, too had observed that, to produce the effect it was necessary to "keep the other fingers lifted".[188] These instructions, which require an exception to the standard 18th- and 19th-century practice of keeping the fingers down unless it was absolutely necessary to lift them, go against the normal requirements of modern practice, in which, to facilitate *continuous vibrato*, only a single finger is normally down at any one time. Clearly, since in 19th-century practice an unusual physical position was required to produce the *vibrato*, a continuous effect could not have been envisaged.

Among the treatises that ignore *vibrato* entirely are the *Méthode théorique et pratique de violon* (1842) by François Habeneck (1781–1849) and the *École du violon, méthode complète et progressive* (1844) by Jean Delphin Alard (1815–1888), Baillot's successor at the Paris Conservatoire. The fingerings in Alard's annotated editions of violin music demonstrate that he expected little use of this embellishment; in the Beethoven violin sonatas, he marked many open strings and natural harmonics on long melodic notes;[189] and the same is true of Ferdinand David's editions. Hubert Léonard, whose sparing use of *vibrato* was noted in 1845, is also silent about

---

[186] H. Schröder: *Preis-Violinschule*, 2nd edn (Leipzig, 1894), 66.
[187] Ferdinand David: *Violinschule*, ii, 43.
[188] Dancla: *Méthode*, 42.
[189] Published in the 1860s. See Clive Brown and Neal Peres Da Costa: *Beethoven Violin Sonatas Performing Practice Commentary* (Kassel, Bärenreiter, 2020), https://www.baerenreiter.com/en/shop/product/details/BA9014/.

it in his *École Léonard pour le violon* (a collection of seven publications from the 1860s).

Vehement warnings against excessive use of trembling effects are found in almost all later 19th-century string treatises that make any mention of them; but numerous references to string players, even from German traditions, indicate that some were using these effects far more than treatises recommended. In 1859, F-J. Fétis complained in an article on musical expression:

> The instrumentalists also have their favourite formulas. Just as the singers have vibrato of the voice, the violinist and the cellist have vibrato of the finger on the string; and some have made such a habit of it, that it has become as difficult for them, I would say almost as impossible, to produce a pure sound, rather than the effect of a broken voice, as it would be for most singers to make a sound that is not like a bleating goat.[190]

This increase in *vibrato/tremolo* usage may have been one of the reasons Spohr chose to indicate *tremolo* with wavy lines in printed editions of his violin music published during the 1850s, beginning with his String Quintet op. 144 and his Violin Duets opp. 148, 150, and 153 (Ex. 16.35).[191] Trembling effects, indicated by wavy lines, are also occasionally handwritten into surviving personal performing copies belonging to Spohr's pupil Ferdinand David (Ex. 16.36). The wavy lines in Ex. 16.36a are the only ones in the whole piece.

Ex. 16.35  Spohr: Violin Duet op. 153, 1st edn (Leipzig, 1856).

---

[190] François-Joseph Fétis: 'De l'expression en musique', *Revue et Gazette musicale*, xxvi (1859), 215.
[191] This notation was so little understood in the early 21st century that a recording of the Duet op. 153 in 2006, using *continuous vibrato*, executed all the wavy lines as trills.

Ex. 16.36a  Beethoven: Romance in G op. 40. F. David's personal copy with his own annotations.

Ex. 16.36b  Biber: Sonata in C minor no. 1 in F. David, ed.: *Die Hohe Schule des Violinspiels*. F. David's personal copy with his own annotations.

There is substantial evidence of diverse approaches among prominent performers during the second half of the century, the French cellist A-J. Franchomme (b. 1808) was praised on a visit to London in 1856 because he "carefully abstains from all abuse of the tremolo and of the exaggerated expression which are the distinguishing features in most modern violoncello playing".[192] In 1871, however, the respected German cellist Bernhard Cossmann, who had spent years in Paris, was taken to task because he "cultivates the vice of many violoncellists (and also violinists)—an almost uninterrupted use of vibrato. It is regrettable that he lets himself be controlled by a mannerism, which most greatly impacts on the effect of the performance."[193] What this critic perceived as "an almost uninterrupted use of vibrato" is, of course, unknowable; such things are always relative, so it would be reasonable to assume that Cossmann used more than was deemed tasteful, but as early recorded evidence suggests, it is highly unlikely that it was an effect that corresponded closely with what has commonly been understood as *continuous vibrato* since the middle years of the 20th century. Certainly, the cellist Alfredo Piatti, who played in Joachim's and Wilma Norman Neruda's string quartets in London, maintained a tradition of using trembling effects as an occasional ornament. This is confirmed by many contemporary accounts,[194] among which is violinist Edmund Fellowes's

---

[192] Anon.: *Weekly Chronicle and Register*, 3 May 1856.
[193] Anon.: *Allgemeine musikalische Zeitung*, neue Folge 1871, 764.
[194] George Kennaway: *Playing the Cello*, 2010, 137f.

statement, recalling his experiences in the late 1870s: "Piatti was a very fine artist of the traditional classical school. [. . .] Nor had it then become the custom to use the left arm and wrist in the manner of modern 'cellists to produce a tremolo or vibrato effect."[195]

The short section "Vibrato" in the Joachim and Moser *Violinschule* consists mostly of a quotation from Spohr's *Violinschule*, concluding with the injunction: "its habitual use—especially in the wrong place—cannot be warned against strongly enough! A tasteful violinist, with healthy sensitivity will always regard the steady tone as normal, and apply the vibrato only where the demands of expression indicate it from inner necessity."[196] Moser's introductory essay to volume 3 of the *Violinschule* contains a lengthy diatribe against Franco-Belgian violinists, among other things because

> In order not to seem uninteresting, where the inner feeling failed or, if it was there, could not express itself because of bad habits, they employed, instead of natural vocal expression, that flickering tone caused by unpleasant vibrato, which, in association with mostly wrongly executed portamento, is the mortal enemy of all music-making.[197]

Evidence that musicians in the Joachim tradition preserved elements of this approach into the 1920s can be found in editorial fingering by Ossip Schnirlin (a Joachim pupil) in editions of 19th-century chamber music, as well as in his three-volume *Der neue Weg zur Beherrschung der gesamten Violinliteratur* (The new way to master all the repertoire of the violin), with extensive bowed and fingered extracts. His fingering in Brahms's String Quartet op. 51 no. 2, for instance, still shows extensive use of natural harmonics and open strings (Ex. 16.37a–b). Such fingerings are only rational in contexts where *vibrato* was expected to be used selectively.

Ex. 16.37 a–b. Schnirlin: *Der neue Weg*, 142.

(a)

[195] Edmund Fellowes: *Memoirs of an Amateur Musician* (London, 1946), 18f.
[196] Joachim and Moser, *Violinschule*, ii, 96a.
[197] Joachim and Moser, *Violinschule*, iii, 34.

Ex. 16.37 Continued

(b)

In the pedagogy of solo violin playing, during the first two decades of the 20th century, there was a transitional period between *selective* and *continuous vibrato* use, as well as a transition from very narrow, fast *vibrato* to a much wider and slower oscillation of pitch. Mathieu Crickboom (b. 1871), for instance, who owed much to Ysaÿe's frequent though not entirely continuous employment of a mostly narrow *vibrato*, was still in touch with the 19th-century aesthetic of judicious use. After quoting Spohr's instructions, he continued:

> Furthermore, the *vibrato* must continually relate to the expression and the style of the phrase we interpret, it must become a vibration as natural as the beating of our arteries. Almost non-existent, as if interior, in calm and placid melodies, it should increase in speed and intensity as the musical phrase expresses more and more passionate feelings.

He instructed that "The inner vibration of the finger is communicated to the hand and never concerns the arm", and concluded with the hope that he had convinced the student that

> the *vibrato* is a marvellous means of expression, employed indiscriminately it can also deprive the playing of all accuracy and proportion. Charles de Bériot was of our opinion, since he wrote fifty years ago: "In the artist dominated by the fever of producing effect, the *vibrato* is no more than a convulsive movement which distorts the accuracy of intonation and makes it fall into ridiculous exaggeration!" What would our great violinists say today?[198]

The removal of the last sentence from a later edition of his treatise testifies to the rapid ascendency of the newer *continuous vibrato* aesthetic.

---

[198] Mathieu Crickboom: *Le Violon théorique et pratique*, 5 vols (Brussels, 1917–23), v, 133.

By the time the original edition of Crickboom's treatise was in print, Siegfried Eberhardt (b. 1883) had already published *Der beseelte Violin-Ton*, which was also issued in English translation in 1911 as *Violin Vibrato*. The title of the German edition—*Der beseelte Violin-Ton* (Soulful Violin Tone)— already suggests that the new aesthetic is focused on the quality of the sound rather than an emotional enhancement of specific expressive gestures in the music. From this point on, *vibrato* was increasingly seen as an essential and continual element of tone quality on string instruments. In opposition to the traditional view that fine tone was created by bowing, Eberhardt asserted that a correctly made *vibrato* was fundamental—that the bow was dependent on the left hand, which was in turn dependent on the *vibrato*.[199] This view was shared by many musicians born in the last decades of the 19th century. Another early-20th-century publication, exclusively on *vibrato*, calls it "by far the most enchanting of violin tones".[200]

Fritz Rau's 1922 sixty-seven-page book on violin *vibrato* embodies the early-20th-century aesthetic that beautiful tone and expression were achieved through the combination of *continuous vibrato* and frequent *portamento*. He asserted:

> Only when the vibrato comes in does the mechanical disappear, the rigidity of the sound dissolves, and you feel the inner acceptance of the artist, the playing begins to warm up, acquires a lively character, becomes animated. In addition to the portamento, vibrato is precisely the factor to which the stringed instruments owe their high expressiveness.[201]

Unlike Crickboom, Rau and most later pedagogues required the participation of the arm in producing *vibrato*.

Carl Flesch, who become one of the leading protagonists of this approach to *vibrato*, accused Eberhardt of plagiarism, asserting that his book contained "my ideas about left-hand technique printed word for word".[202] In *Die Kunst des Violinspiels* (1923, 35ff), however, Flesch provided his own detailed exploration of the physical mechanisms and aesthetic use of *vibrato*. He was forthright in criticizing the *vibrato* practices of the 19th century, as represented by Joseph Joachim, Arnold Rosé, and his teacher Jakob Grün,

---

[199] Siegfried Eberhardt: *Der beseelte Violin-Ton* (Dresden, 1910), 23.
[200] Petrowitch Bissing: *Cultivation of the Violin Vibrato Tone* (Chicago, 1914), 10.
[201] Fritz Rau: *Das Vibrato auf der Violine* (Leipzig,1922), 33.
[202] Flesch: *Mémoires*, 242.

as well as many other more conservative contemporaries, as technically and aesthetically inadequate. He recalled that the old school favoured: "a kind of extremely narrow trembling, which apparently no longer corresponds with the taste of present-day leading representatives of our instrument—the current speed of the individual vibrato vibrations has become incomparably slower than 40 years ago".[203] His conception derived from developments in the employment and physical execution of *vibrato* by late-19th-century Franco-Belgian violinists, but most particularly from its use by the Paris-trained Fritz Kreisler, whose sound, as Flesch experienced it in 1895, was a revelation—"one of the strongest impressions in my life"—which, with his modernist attitude towards "progress", he regarded as heralding a new, more advanced phase of artistic development. He described Kreisler's *vibrato* as "an unrestrained orgy of sinfully seductive sounds, depravedly fascinating, whose sole driving force appeared to be a sensuality intensified to the point of frenzy".[204] In his pedagogic writing, however, Flesch remained conscious of a tension between theory and practice: "From a purely theoretical point of view, vibrato should only be used as a means of increasing expressive intensity where the expression of feeling is musically justified. However, if we look at the well-known violinists of our time, we have to realize that almost everyone uses an uninterrupted vibrato."[205] And in 1931:

> The pure sound is theoretically also possible without vibrato, but for the listener it sounds empty and expressionless except in the case of neutral or supernatural complexes of sensations. [. . .] The vibrato in passage-work, which was mainly introduced by Kreisler, is one of the most important achievements of the modern violinist's art. One can disagree about the aesthetic justification of this practice. In any case, it is certain that it corresponds to the taste of the times and that it is already considered an essential part of our art.[206]

The self-confident notion, that modern taste should trump tradition, and therefore the composer's expectations, was typical of the 1920s. A succession of letters to the editor of *The Musical Times* in 1925, extending over

---

[203] Flesch: *Die Kunst des Violinspiels*, 2nd edn, i, 26.
[204] Flesch: *Mémoires*, 118.
[205] Flesch: *Die Kunst*, 2nd edn, i, 24.
[206] Carl Flesch: *Das Klangproblem im Geigenspiel* (Berlin, 1931), 12.

several issues under the general heading "The Lure of Vibrato", debated the propriety of *continuous vibrato* in singing. It began with a correspondent's objection to "the incessant *tremolo* on every note and word", which he saw as "monotonous and unmusical".[207] A subsequent letter, responding in support of *tremolo*, asserted: "Modern modes of expression imperatively demand modern methods of voice-production. [. . .] vocalisation follows the law of progress in common with other arts and sciences."[208] The 1925 issues of the journal contain other discussions of *vibrato*, most of which express concern about its increasing pervasiveness.

Among the last prominent rejections of *continuous vibrato* in string playing was Leopold Auer's lengthy diatribe against it in *Violin Playing as I Teach It*:

> violinists who habitually make use of the device—those who are convinced that an eternal *vibrato* is the secret of soulful playing, of piquancy in performance—are pitifully misguided in their belief. [. . .] No, the *vibrato* is an effect, an embellishment; it can lend a touch of divine pathos to the climax of a phrase or the course of a passage, but only if the player has cultivated a delicate sense of proportion in the use of it. [. . .] The excessive *vibrato* is a habit for which I have no tolerance, and I always fight against it when I observe it in my pupils—though often, I must admit, without success. As a rule I forbid my students using the *vibrato* at all on notes which are not sustained, and I earnestly advise them not to abuse it even in the case of sustained notes which succeed each other in a phrase.[209]

It is noteworthy that Auer's most distinguished students, who included Jascha Heifetz, Mischa Elman, and Efrem Zimbalist, were all enthusiastic exponents of *continuous vibrato*. Auer also condemned the overuse of *portamento*, but his own recordings, made in old age (1920), do not entirely correspond with his strictures, with respect to either *portamento* or frequency of *vibrato*, although the latter is certainly intermittent and, where present, very narrow.

---

[207] H. J. King: *The Musical Times*, lxvi (1925), 539.
[208] W. E. Bell-Porter: *The Musical Times*, lxvi (1925), 1021.
[209] Leopold Auer: *Violin Playing as I Teach It* (London, 1921), 59f.

By the 1930s, Kreisler's style, with "continual, most intensive vibrato (even in runs)"[210] had become the standard for string players. In Kreisler's own words:

> The vital fact about vibrato is that it should be *continuous*; there must be *no break in it whatever*, especially at the moment of proceeding from one note to another [...] there is nothing so deadly or ruinous to an expressive phrase as the sound of a cantabile slow passage in which one or two notes are partly or wholly devoid of vibrato.[211]

The rapid impact and consequences of this approach is nicely summarized by Boris Schwarz (b. 1906): "The French vibrato of the later nineteenth century, pioneered by Ysaÿe and then Kreisler, became wider and used more abundantly. The violin became a much more sensuous-sounding instrument, and the public loved it. Soon, a violinist with the old-style vibrato had no chance of being successful."[212]

Among the last opponents of the use of *continuous vibrato* in string playing were some of the pupils of Joseph Joachim and his colleagues at the Berlin Hochschule für Musik. Aural evidence can be heard not only in Joachim's own recordings, but also, most tellingly, in those of Marie Soldat (b. 1863) and, to a lesser extent, Karl Klingler (b. 1879). In 1939, Marion Ranken recalled Joachim's use of almost totally *vibrato*-free, but intense tone for "deep" passages in Beethoven, stating: "once having heard them played so, the sickly wobble of most modern playing, in such places, becomes very painful".[213]

In singing, Lilli Lehmann (born 1848) had condemned *tremolo* utterly in 1902, warning: "Even the vibrato, to which full voices are prone, should be nipped in the bud, for gradually the tremolo and later something even worse is developed from it."[214] Sir Henry Wood was among the last prominent musicians to condemn the vocal *tremolo*. In 1927 he wrote about how its use had increased during his lifetime.[215] He complained that it "reaches the audience as out-of-tuneless", adding that anyone teaching "the octave duet

---

[210] Flesch: *Die Kunst*, 1st edn, i, 4 (footnote).
[211] Lionel Tertis: *Beauty of Tone in String Playing* (London, 1938), 12 (Kreisler's foreword).
[212] Boris Schwarz: *The Great Masters of the Violin* (New York, 1983), 286.
[213] M[arion] R[anken]: *Some Points of Violin Playing*, 13.
[214] Lilli Lehmann: *Meine Gesangkunst* (Berlin, 1902), 25, trans. Richard Aldrich as *How to Sing* (New York, 1902), 174.
[215] Henry Wood: *The Gentle Art of Singing* (Oxford, 1927), iv, 87.

for soprano and mezzo soprano, Agnus Dei in Verdi's *Requiem*, to singers of whom one has a decided tremolo and the other a true even, still tone, will understand why. It is impossible to get the octaves to sound in tune. The voice with the tremolo never blends in with the still tones of the other. The sharpness and flatness of the tremolo become clear." He still believed that he could explain "fairly clearly why it exists, and how it can be cured."[216]

With the increasing 20th-century cultivation of *vibrato/tremolo* as an essential aspect of tone quality, wind players, who had long used these practices as embellishments, began to develop techniques for a more continual *vibrato*, such as "oscillation in lung pressure produced by periodic contraction of muscles of the torso [...] variation in the aperture of the glottis, oscillation in lip shape or position produced by changes in lip or jaw muscle tension [...] oscillation of the tongue or jaw muscles to change vocal tract resonances".[217] Despite the comment of Swinburne and others about the use of *vibrato* in France, wind instrument *vibrato* on early orchestral recordings from before the Second World War, where it can be detected at all, is generally sporadic and very narrow. Certainly, in England, it was not readily accepted in the early years of the 20th century. Léon Goossens (b. 1897), a pioneer in the use of continuous vibrato on the oboe, recalled that when he joined the Queen's Hall Orchestra, "I suffered a great deal of abuse and jibing from other players at this time for persisting with my own concept of a beautiful oboe sound incorporating vibrato as an essential aspect of its singing quality."[218] By the middle of the century, however, woodwind *vibrato* of fairly narrow amplitude (approximately 1/8th of a tone for flutes and somewhat under a 1/4 of a tone for oboe and bassoon) was normal except for clarinettists.[219] In the 19th century, Brahms's favourite clarinettist Richard Mühlfeld apparently employed *vibrato* selectively.[220] Some French clarinettists in early-20th-century orchestral recordings used a fast tremor and some solo clarinettists, for instance, employed slower *vibrato* (e.g., Reginald Kell and Jack Brymer); but in classical music clarinettists have generally eschewed it entirely, or used it very occasionally, while clarinettists in jazz and popular music employed

---

[216] Wood: *The Gentle Art*, iv, 55.
[217] Joe Wolfe, Neville Horner Fletcher, and Jordan Smith: 'Interactions between Wind Instruments and Their Players', *Acta Acustica United with Acustica*, ci (2015), 214.
[218] Léon Goossens and Edwin Roxburgh: *Oboe* (London, 1977), 87.
[219] Neville Horner Fletcher: 'Vibrato in Music', *Acoustics Australia*, xxix (2001), 101.
[220] Clive Brown and Neal Peres Da Costa: *Brahms Sonaten für Clarinette und Klavier* (Kassel, 2015), Preface/Vorwort, xi/xxxix.

it freely, which was probably a factor in discouraging classical clarinettists from doing it. The same distinction between classical and popular music is largely true for brass instruments, although in some 20th-century classical music traditions, *vibrato* has occasionally been used by them.[221]

The gap between theory and practice in the employment of trembling effects had certainly been widening during the second half of the 19th century, but even where performers were using it frequently, it seems clear that it rarely involved more than a very small fluctuation of pitch, and that it was generally performed with more rapid oscillations than later 20th-century *vibrato*. The early decades of the 20th century were the tipping point, when theory and critical reception began to reflect practice, and to create not only new criteria for an artistic use of *vibrato*, but also new techniques for producing it. Until the 1920s, a distinction between the use of *vibrato* in solo and ensemble playing seems to have been preserved by older players, at least in the German tradition. Cellist Julius Klengel (b. 1859) and violinist Arnold Rosé (b. 1863) made both solo and quartet recordings and used *vibrato* more prominently in the former than the latter. One remarkable example can be heard in the 1926 Gewandhaus Quartet recording of Beethoven's String Quartet op. 131; spectrogram images of the cello and viola duet in the 4th movement, bars 98–105, confirm the aural impression that Klengel uses no *vibrato* at all, while Carl Herrmann (b. 1876) uses it on every note. Very soon, however, that distinction disappeared, and more or less *continuous vibrato* became obligatory.

In orchestral string playing, there was a period of transition, probably between the 1890s and 1940s, in which the use of prominent *continuous vibrato* gradually replaced a basically *non-vibrato* manner of performance. By the 1890s there was clearly tension between younger and older players in this respect. Hermann Hock (b. 1870), who joined the Frankfurt Museumsorchester as a second violin in about 1890 and was later Konzertmeister, recalled that in his early years in the orchestra:

> the modern tone of the younger generation of violinists, i.e. their more singing violin tone produced by a vibrato, was very beneficial to the orchestra, it was a style of playing which the old school of violinists did not yet know at that time: a slight sideways back and forth movement of the

---

[221] For an informative survey of wind instrument *vibrato* in early recordings see Robert Philip: *Early Recordings and Musical Style* (Cambridge, 1992), 109–40.

finger of the left hand placed on the fingerboard, while at the same time a casual shaking of the loosened wrist took place. [...] I remember very well that the technically excellently trained, often virtuoso older gentlemen in the first violins of our orchestra tried to ridicule the vibrato of their younger colleagues, which was still unknown to them, by exaggerating the swinging movement of the left hand to such an extent that the playing became a pure caricature. Insightful, progressive-minded colleagues, on the other hand, endeavoured to adopt our more relaxed style of playing for their own benefit as a new means of expression, which has found its way into all orchestras over time.[222]

A preference for more limited *vibrato* usage in orchestral than solo playing evidently lingered into the 1930s. The 1935 film *Letzte Liebe* contains a short scene featuring the Vienna Philharmonic Orchestra performing a passage from the overture to Mozart's *Don Giovanni*, which reveals two out of five visible violinists using hardly any *vibrato*, one of whom is the leader, Arnold Rosé (b. 1863).[223] Rosé, who belonged to the same generation as Hock, was probably one of the younger players of the 1890s who used more *vibrato* than his older colleagues, but by the end of his time in the orchestra an even more continuous and pronounced *vibrato* was becoming normal among the next generation of string players. Hock, writing in the 1940s, deplored this change, remarking: "Unfortunately, however, today's vibrato has taken on such a nervous character, even among many of our soloists, that it has more a disturbing than an enhancing effect on the tone production."[224]

The documentation of *vibrato* usage in the 20th century not only in written accounts, but also in recorded sound, allows instructive comparison. It illustrates that words do not always prepare us for what we hear; different speeds, degrees of pitch variation, and fluctuations of intensity in *vibrato* usage have strongly characterized musicians of various schools and successive generations in a manner that would be difficult if not impossible to extrapolate from the written record. In the study of earlier periods, when the aural resource is not available, it is therefore necessary to accept that,

---

[222] Hermann Hock: *Ein Leben mit der Geige* (Frankfurt, 1950), 70f.
[223] Tomoyuki Sawado: *History of Vibrato Usage in Orchestral Performance*, online: https://www.fugue.us/Vibrato_History_E.html.
[224] Hock: *Ein Leben*, 71.

however much information is assembled and whatever patterns of change are identified, we are still far from knowing what kinds of sounds would have been considered tasteful and beautiful by our forebears. Yet much can be learned from careful scrutiny of 18th- and 19th-century accounts and, at the very least, it is possible to appreciate, in this as in other aspects of performance, the extent to which composers, performers, and audiences of past generations did not share the aesthetic predilections of their 20th- and 21st-century successors.

\* \* \*

# Bibliography

ABBIATI, FRANCO: *Giuseppe Verdi*, 4 vols. (Milan, 1959).
ADAM, JEAN LOUIS: *Méthode du piano du Conservatoire* (Paris, 1804).
ADAMS, JOHN S.: *5000 Musical Terms* (Boston, 1851).
ADDISON, JOHN: *Singing Practically Treated in a Series of Instructions* (London, 1850).
ADLUNG, JAKOB: *Musica mechanica organoedi. Das ist: Gründlicher Unterricht von der Struktur, Gebrauch und Erhaltung, etc. der Orgeln, Clavicymbel, Clavichordien und anderer Instrumente*, 2 vols. (Berlin, 1768).
AGRICOLA, JOHANN FRIEDRICH: *Anleitung zur Singkunst* (Berlin, 1757). Revised translation of Tosi's *Opinioni*. Also trans. and ed. Julianne C. Baird as *Introduction to the Art of Singing by Johann Friedrich Agricola* (Cambridge, 1995).
ALARD, JEAN DELPHIN: *École du violon Méthode complète et progressive à l'usage du Conservatoire* (Paris, 1844).
ALBRECHT, HANS, ed.: *Die Bedeutung der Zeichen Keil Strich und Punkt bei Mozart* (Kassel, 1957).
ALEXANDER, JAMES: *Complete Preceptor for the Flute* (London, [c. 1821]).
ALEXANDER, JOSEPH: *Anweisung zum Violoncellspiel* (Leipzig, [1802]).
ALMENRÄDER, CARL: *Die Kunst des Fagottblasens, oder, Vollständige theoretisch praktische Fagottschule* (Mainz, 1843).
ALONSO, LUIS: *Le Virtuose moderne* (Paris, [1895]).
ALTENBURG, JOHANN ERNST: *Versuch einer Anleitung zur heroisch-musikalischen Trompeter und Pauker-Kunst*, 2 vols (Halle, 1795).
ANDERSCH, JOHANN DANIEL: *Musikalisches Wörterbuch* (Berlin, 1829).
ANDERSON, EMILY, trans. and ed.: *The Letters of Beethoven* (London, 1961).
ANDERSON, EMILY, trans. and ed.: *The Letters of Mozart and his Family*, 2nd edn (London, 1966).
ANDRÉ, (JOHANN) ANTON: 'Bemerkungen über den Vortrag meiner Lieder und Gesänge.' (Offenbach, 1822). Preface to later reissues of his *Lieder und Gesänge*.
ANON.: *A Choice Collection of Lessons* (London, 1696); repr. with attribution to Purcell in *The Third Book of the Harpsichord Master* (London, 1702).
ANON.: 'Einiges über die Pflichten des Violoncellisten als Orchesterspieler und Accompagnateur', *Allgemeine musikalische Zeitung*, lviii (1841), 129ff.
ANON. [WILLIAM CRAWFORD HONEYMAN]: *Hints to Violin Players* (Edinburgh, [c. 1885]).
ANON.: *Instructions for the Violin by an Eminent Master* (London, [c. 1795]).
ANON.: *New Instructions for Playing the Harpsichord, Pianoforte or Organ etc.* (London, [c. 1790]).
ANON.: 'Noch etwas vom Kurköllnischen Orchester', *Musikalische Realzeitung* (Speier, 1791), Nr 47, 373ff.
ANON. [CARL ERNST PHILIPP VON REITZENSTEIN]: *Reise nach Wien* (Hof, 1795).
ANON.: 'Ueber die heutige verworrene Strichbezeichnung', *Allgemeine musikalische Zeitung*, 6 (1803–4), 731f.
ANON. [WILLIAM CRAWFORD HONEYMAN]: *The Violin: How to Master It. By a Professional Player* (Edinburgh, [1882]).

ANON. [JOHANN CONRAD WILHELM PETISCUS]: *Violinschule oder Anweisung die Violine zu spielen von Leopold Mozart. Neue umgearbeitete und vermehrte Ausgabe* (Leipzig [1804]); repr. edn Leipzig, 1817).

ANON. [JOHANN CONRAD WILHELM PETISCUS]: *Violinschule oder Anweisung die Violine zu spielen von Leopold Mozart. Neue umgearbeitete und vermehrte Ausgabe* (Vienna, [c. 1805]). (Unauthorised edition).

ANON. [ERNST WILHELM WOLF?]: *Wahrheiten die Musik betreffend* (Frankfurt a. M., 1779).

ASIOLI, BONIFAZIO: *Principj elementari di musica* (Milan, 1811); trans. and ed. John Jousse as *A Compendious Musical Grammar in which the Theory of Music is Completely Developed, in a Series of familiar Dialogues written by Bonifacio Asioli* (London, [1825]).

AUER, LEOPOLD: *Violin Playing as I Teach It* (London, 1921).

AUHAGEN, WOLFGANG: 'Chronometrische Tempoangaben im 18. und 19. Jahrhundert', *Archiv für Musikwissenschaft*, 44 (1987), 40–57.

BACCIAGALUPPI, CLAUDIO: 'Die »Pflicht« des Cellisten und der Generalbaß in der Romantik' in Claudio Bacciagaluppi, Roman Brotbeck, and Anselm Gerhard (eds.), *Spielpraxis der Saiteninstrumente in der Romantik* (Schliessen, 2011), 138ff.

BACH, CARL PHILIPP EMANUEL: *Versuch über die wahre Art das Clavier zu spielen*, vol. i (Berlin, 1753, rev. 2nd edn 1787), vol. ii (Berlin, 1762, rev. 2nd edn 1797); fac. repr. of 1st edn, incl. revs., of 1787 as a separate section (Leipzig, 1787); trans. and ed. William J. Mitchell as *Essay on the True Art of Playing Keyboard Instruments* (New York, 1949).

BADURA-SKODA, EVA and PAUL: *Mozart-Interpretation* (Vienna and Stuttgart, 1957); trans. Leo Black as *Interpreting Mozart on the Keyboard* (London, 1962).

BADURA-SKODA, PAUL: 'A Tie Is a Tie is a Tie', *Early Music*, 16 (1988), 84.

BAENSCH, OTTO: 'Zur Neunten Symphonie' in Adolf Sandberger (ed.), *Neues Beethoven Jahrbuch* (Augsburg, 1925), 145ff.

BAILLEUX, ANTOINE: *Méthode raisonné à apprendre le violon* (Paris, 1779).

BAILLOT, PIERRE MARIE FRANÇOIS DE SALES: *L'Art du violon: Nouvelle méthode* (Paris, [1835]). Trans. Louise Goldberg: *The Art of the Violin* (Evanston, IL, 1991).

BAILLOT, PIERRE MARIE FRANÇOIS DE SALES, LEVASSEUR, JEAN HENRI, CATEL, CHARLES-SIMON, and BAUDIOT, CHARLES-NICOLAS: *Méthode de violoncelle et de Basse d'Accompagnement* (Paris, [1804]).

BAILLOT, PIERRE MARIE FRANÇOIS DE SALES, RODE, PIERRE, and KREUTZER, RODOLPHE: *Méthode de violon* (Paris, [1803]).

BAILLOT, PIERRE MARIE FRANÇOIS DE SALES, RODE, PIERRE, and KREUTZER, RODOLPHE: *Rode, Baillot, & Kreutzer's Method of Instruction for the Violin*, edited by Baillot (London, Boosey, [1823]).

BAILLOT, PIERRE MARIE FRANÇOIS DE SALES, RODE, PIERRE, and KREUTZER, RODOLPHE: *R. Cocks and Co's improved and enlarged Edition of the Celebrated Method for the Violin by Rode, Kreutzer and Baillot*, trans. J. A. Hamilton (London, Cocks, [1828]).

BARTH, GEORGE: 'Carl Czerny and Musical Authority: Locating the "Primary Vessel" of the Musical Tradition' in David Gramit (ed.), *Beyond the Art of Finger Dexterity. Reassessing Carl Czerny* (Rochester, 2008), 125ff.

BAUDIOT, CHARLES NICOLAS: *Méthode de violoncelle* op. 25, 2 vols. (Paris, [1820/26]).

BAUER-LECHNER, NATALIE: *Erinnerungen an Gustav Mahler* (Leipzig, Wien, Zürich, 1923).

BAYLY, ANSELM: *A Practical Treatise on Singing and Playing with Just Expression and Real Elegance* (London, 1771).

BECK, DAGMAR, and HERRE, GRITA: 'Einige Zweifel an der Überlieferung der Konversationshefte' in Harry Goldschmidt, Karl-Heinz Köhler, and Konrad Niemann (eds.), *Bericht über den Internationalen Beethoven-Kongress . . . 1977 in Berlin* (Leipzig, 1978), 257ff.

BEETHOVEN, LUDWIG VAN: *Ludwig van Beethoven. Briefwechsel Gesamtausgabe*, 7 vols. (Munich, 1996–1998).

BEETHOVEN, LUDWIG VAN: *Ludwig van Beethovens Konversationenshefte*, ed. Karl-Heinz Köhler, Grita Herre, Peter Pötschner, 5 (Leipzig, 1970).

BEMETZRIEDER, ANTON: *New Lessons for the Harpsichord* (London, 1783).

BENNETT WADSWORTH, KATE: *"Precisely marked in the tradition of the composer": The Performing Editions of Friedrich Grützmacher* (PhD thesis, University of Leeds, 2017).

BÉRIOT, CHARLES DE: *Méthode de violon* (Mainz, [1857–1858]): 1st edn. Also pub. with parallel Ger. and Fr. text; and with parallel Eng. and Fr. text (both of which have same layout and pagination).

BERLIOZ, HECTOR: *Grand traité d'instrumentation et d'orchestration modernes* op. 10 (Paris, 1843).

BERLIOZ, HECTOR: *Mémoires* (Paris, Calmann Lévy, 1897).

BETHELL, RICHARD: 'Vocal Vibrato in Early Music', www.york.ac.uk/music/news-and-events/events/conferences/nema/bethell/#chapter3 2009 [accessed 25 June 2022].

BISSING, PETROWITCH: *Cultivation of the Violin Vibrato Tone* (Chicago, 1914).

BLANC, J.: *Grande méthode complète et raisonnée pour le violon* op. 9 (Paris, 1846).

BLUMENTHAL, JOSEPH VON: *Kurzgefasste theoretisch-praktische Violin Schule* (Vienna, [1811]).

BRAHMS, JOHANNES: *Briefwechsel*, 16 vols. (Berlin, 1907–22).

BRANDT, NAT: *Con Brio: Four Russians Called the Budapest String Quartet* (San Jose, New York, Lincoln, Shanghai, 1993).

BREMNER, ROBERT: 'Some Thoughts on the Performance of Concert Music', pub. as preface to J. G. C. Schetky, *Six Quartettos for Two Violins, a Tenor, and Violoncello op. VI To which are prefixed some thoughts on the performance of concert-music by the publisher* (London, R. Bremner, [1777]).

BROWN, CLIVE: 'Bowing Styles, Vibrato and Portamento in Nineteenth-Century Violin Playing', *Journal of the Royal Musical Association*, cxiii (1988), 97ff.

BROWN, CLIVE: 'Czerny the Progressive' in Leonardo Miucci, Claudio Bacciagaluppi, Daniel Allenbach and Martin Skamletz (eds.), *Beethoven and the Piano. Philology, Context and Performance Practice* (Schliengen, Argus, 2023) (*Musikforschung der Hochschule der Künste Bern*, 16 [2023], 15ff.

BROWN, CLIVE: 'Dots and Strokes in Late 18th- and 19th-Century Music', *Early Music*, 21 (1993), 593–610.

BROWN, CLIVE: 'Ferdinand David's Editions of Beethoven' in Robin Stowell (ed.), *Performing Beethoven* (Cambridge, 1994), 117ff.

BROWN, CLIVE: 'Historical Performance, Metronome Marks and Tempo in Beethoven's Symphonies', *Early Music*, xix (1991), 247ff.

BROWN, CLIVE: 'Joachim's Violin Playing and the Performance of Brahms's String Music' in Michael Musgrave and Bernard Sherman (eds.), *Performing Brahms* (Cambridge, 2003), 48ff.

BROWN, CLIVE: 'Leopold Mozart's *Violinschule* and the Performance of W. A. Mozart's Violin Music' in Thomas Steiner (ed.), *Cordes et claviers au temps de Mozart / Strings and Keyboard in the Age of Mozart* (Lausanne, 2010), 23ff.

BROWN, CLIVE: 'Marie Soldat-Roeger and the Twilight of a Nineteenth-Century German School of Violin Playing' in Dieter Torkewitz (ed.), *Im Schatten des Kunstwerks II. Theorie und Interpretation des musikalischen Kunstwerks im 19. Jahrhundert. Wiener Veröffentlichungen zur Theorie und Interpretation der Musik II* (Wien, Praesens Verlag, 2014), 179ff.

BROWN, CLIVE: *Mendelssohn: Performance Practices in the Violin Concerto op. 64 and Chamber Music for Strings / Aufführungspraktische Hinweise zum Violinkonzert op. 64 und zur Kammermusik für Streicher* (Kassel, Bärenreiter, 2018).

BROWN, CLIVE: 'Phrasierung' in Heinz von Loesch, Rebecca Wolf, and Thomas Ertelt (eds.), *Geschichte der musikalischen Interpretation im 19. und 20. Jahrhundert*, iii Aspekte-Parameter (Kassel, Bärenreiter, 2022), 553ff.

BROWN, CLIVE: 'Polarities of Virtuosity in the First Half of the Nineteenth Century' in Andrea Barizza and Fulvia Morabito (eds.), *Nicolò Paganini. Diabolus in Musica* (Turnhout, 2010), 22ff.

BROWN, CLIVE: 'Reading between the Lines of Beethoven's Notation' in *Beethoven Sonatas for Pianoforte and Violin* (Kassel, Bärenreiter, 2020); with associated online Performing Practice Commentary co-authored with Neal Peres Da Costa (access by clicking 'Extras' https://www.baerenreiter.com/en/shop/product/details/BA9036/).

BROWN, CLIVE: 'Schubert's Tempo Conventions' in Brian Newbould (ed.), *Schubert Studies* (Aldershot, Ashgate, 1998), 1ff.

BROWN, CLIVE: 'Singing and String Playing in Comparison' in Claudio Bacciagaluppi, Roman Brotbeck, and Anselm Gerhard (eds.), *Zwischen schöpferischer Individualität und künstlerischer Selbstverleugnung* (Schliengen, 2009), 83ff.

BROWN, CLIVE: 'String Playing Practices in the Classical Orchestra', *Basler Jahrbuch für historische Musikpraxis*, xvii (1993), 41ff.

BROWN, CLIVE: 'Vibrato und Portamento' in Heinz von Loesch, Rebecca Wolf, and Thomas Ertelt (eds.), *Geschichte der musikalischen Interpretation im 19. und 20. Jahrhundert*, iii Aspekte-Parameter (Kassel, Barenreiter, 2022), 629ff.

BROWN, CLIVE, ed.: Beethoven Violin Concerto (Wiesbaden, Breitkopf & Härtel, 2012).

BROWN, CLIVE, ed.: Brahms Violin Concerto (Kassel, Bärenreiter, 2006).

BROWN, CLIVE, PERES DA COSTA, NEAL, and BENNETT WADSWORTH, KATE: *Performing Practices in Johannes Brahms' Chamber Music* (Kassel, Bärenreiter, 2015).

BROWN, HOWARD MAYER, ed.: *The New Grove Handbook of Performance Practice: Music after 1600* (London, 1989).

BÜLOW, HANS VON: 'Lohengrin in Bologna. Kein Leitartikel, sondern ein vertrauliches Gespräch (im australischen Style), durch diplomatische Indiskretion in die Öffentlichkeit gebracht', *Signale für die Musikalische Welt*, xxx (1872), 17ff.

BÜLOW, HANS VON: *Ausgewählte Schriften, 1850–1892* (Leipzig, 1911).

BURKHARD, JOHANN ANDREAS CHRISTIAN: *Neues vollständiges musikalisches Wörterbuch* (Ulm, 1832).

BURNEY, CHARLES: *A General History of Music from the Earliest Ages to the Present Period*, 4 vols. (London, 1776–89).

BUSBY, THOMAS: *A Complete Dictionary of Music* (London, 1806).

BUSBY, THOMAS: *A Dictionary of Music, Theoretical and Practical 5th edition, with Additions and Improvements* (London, 1823).

BUSBY, THOMAS: *A Dictionary of Three Thousand Musical Terms Ancient and Modern, Foreign and English including all that are to be found in the works of Bellini, Bertini,*

Chopin . . . *Rossini, Spohr, Thalberg, and other composers of the present day. With descriptions of the various voices and instruments*, 3rd edn, rev. J. A. Hamilton (London, [1840]).

*Cäcilia* [from 1826, vol. 5, *Caecilia*]: *Eine Zeitschrift für die musikalische Welt*, ed. Gottfried Weber, 27 vols. (Mainz, Brussels, and Antwerp, Schott, 1824–48).

CALLCOTT, JOHN WALL: *A Musical Grammar* (London, 1806).

CAMBINI, GIUSEPPE MARIA: *Nouvelle méthode théorique et pratique pour le violon* (Paris, [c. 1795]).

CAMPAGNOLI, BARTOLOMEO: *Nouvelle méthode de la mécanique du jeu de violon* (Leipzig, 1824).

CARTER, STEWART: 'The String Tremolo in the 17th Century', *Early Music*, xix (1991), 43ff.

CARTIER, JEAN BAPTISTE: *L'Art du violon ou collection choisie dans les sonates des écoles italienne, françoise et allemande précédée d'un abrégée des principes pour cet instrument* (Paris, [1798]).

CASTIL-BLAZE, FRANÇOIS HENRI JOSEPH: *Dictionnaire de musique moderne* (Paris, 1821).

CASWELL, AUSTIN: 'Mme Cinti-Damoreau and the Embellishment of Italian Opera in Paris 1820–45', *Journal of the American Musicological Society*, xxviii (1975), 459ff.

CHABRAN, CARLO FRANCESCO: *Compleat Instructions for the Spanish Guitar* (London, [c. 1795]).

CHORLEY, HENRY FOTHERGILL: *Modern German Music* (London, [1854]).

CHRISTIANI, ADOLPH J.: *Das Verständnis im Klavierspiel* (Leipzig, 1886).

CLARKE, ERIC: 'Expression in Performance: Generativity, Perception and Semiosis' in John Rink (ed.), *The Practice of Performance* (Cambridge, Cambridge University Press, 1995), 21ff.

CLEMENTI, MUZIO: *Introduction to the Art of Playing on the Pianoforte* (London, 1801); 11th edn (1826).

CLINTON, JOHN: *A School or Practical Instruction Book for the Boehm Flute* (London, [c. 1850]).

CONATI, MARCELLO: *Interviews and Encounters with Verdi*, trans. Richard Stokes (London, 1984).

COOK, NICHOLAS: *Beyond the Score: Music as Performance* (Oxford, 2013).

CORRETTE, MICHEL: *L'École d'Orphée, méthode pour apprendre facilement à jouer du violon dans le goût françois et italien avec des principes de musique et beaucoup de leçons* op. 18 (Paris, 1738).

CORRI, DOMENICO: *A Select Collection of the Most Admired Songs, Duetts, &c.*, 3 vols. (Edinburgh, [c. 1782]).

CORRI, DOMENICO: *The Singer's Preceptor* (London, 1810).

CORRI, HAYDN: *The Delivery of Vocal Music* (London, 1823).

CORRI, HAYDN: *The Delivery of Vocal Music Simplified* (Dublin, 1826).

CORRI, PHILIP ANTHONY: *L'anima di musica* (London, 1810).

CORRI, PHILIP ANTHONY: *P. A. Corri's Original System of Preluding* (London, [1814]).

COX, H. BERTRAM: *Leaves from the Journals of Sir Georg Smart* (London, 1907).

CRAMER, CARL FRIEDRICH: 'Einige Gedanken über Aufführung von Concertmusik', *Magazin der Musik*, i (1783), 1213ff.

CRAMER, JOHN BAPTIST: *J. B. Cramer's Instructions for the Piano Forte* (London, [c. 1812]).

CRAMER, JOHN BAPTIST: [Anon.] *Praktische Pianoforte Schule... von J. B. Cramer. Neueste umgearbeitet und vervollständigste Ausgabe* (Leipzig [c. 1872]).

CRELLE, AUGUST LUDWIG: *Einiges über musikalischen Ausdruck und Vortrag* (Berlin, 1823).

CRICKBOOM, MATHIEU: *Le Violon théorique et pratique*, 5 vols (Brussels, 1917–23).

CROME, ROBERT: *Fiddle, New Modell'd or a useful Introduction for the Violin [...]* (London, [c. 1750]).
CROTCH, WILLIAM: 'Remarks on the Terms at Present Used in Music, for Regulating the Time', *Monthly Magazine*, viii (1800), 941ff.
CRUTCHFIELD, WILL: 'The Prosodic Appoggiatura in the Music of Mozart and His Contemporaries', *Journal of the American Musicological Society*, xlii (1989), 229–74.
CRUTCHFIELD, WILL: 'Vocal Ornamentation in Verdi: The Phonographic Evidence', *19th-century Music*, vii (1983), 3–52.
CRUTCHFIELD, WILL: 'Voices' in Howard Mayer Brown (ed.), *The New Grove Handbook of Performance Practice after 1600* (London, 1989).
COUPERIN, FRANÇOIS: *L'art de toucher le Clavecin* (Paris, 1716).
CUDWORTH, CHARLES: 'The Meaning of "Vivace" in Eighteenth-Century England', *Fontes artis musicae*, xii (1965), 194f.
CUSINS, WILLIAM GEORGE: *Handel's Messiah: An Examination of the Original and of Some Contemporary MSS* (London, 1874).
CZERNY, CARL: *Chapter 1 to Czerny's Royal Pianoforte School. Being the Second Supplement by the Author* (London, [1846]).
CZERNY, CARL: *Die Kunst des Vortrags der älteren und neueren Klavierkompositionen* (vol. iv of *Vollständige . . . Pianoforte-Schule* op. 500) (Vienna, 1846); trans. John Bishop as *The Art of Playing the Ancient and Modern Piano Forte Works* (London, [1846]).
CZERNY, CARL: *Vollständige theoretisch-practische Pianoforte-Schule* op. 500, 3 vols. (Vienna, 1839); vol. iii, *Von dem Vortrage*, pub. in fac. (Wiesbaden, Breitkopf & Hartel, 1991); trans. as *Complete Theoretical and Practical Piano Forte School* op. 500, 3 vols. (London, [1839]).
CZERNY, CARL, ed.: A. E. Müller: *Große Fortepiano Schule von Aug. Eberhd Müller [. . .] Achte Auflage mit vielen neuen Beispiele und einem vollständigen Anhang vom Generalbass versehen von Carl Czerny* (Leipzig, c. 1830).
CZERNY, CARL, ed.: Anton Reicha: *Cours de composition musicale*, as *Vollständiges Lehrbuch der musikalischen Composition* (with parallel Fr. and Ger. text), 4 vols. (Vienna, [1832]).
DADELSEN, G. VON, ed.: *Editionsrichtlinie musikalischer Denkmäler und Gesamtausgaben* (Kassel, 1967).
DAMERINI, A.: 'Sei lettere inedite di Verdi a J. C. Ferrarini', *Il pianoforte* (August–September 1926).
DANCLA, CHARLES: *Méthode élémentaire et progressive pour violon* op. 52 (Paris, [1855]).
DANNELEY, JOHN FELTHAM: *Dictionary of Music* (London, 1825).
DANNREUTHER, EDWARD: *Musical Ornamentation*, 2 vols. (London, 1893–95).
DASCHAUER, ANDREAS: *Kleines Handbuch der Musiklehre* (Kempton, 1801).
DAVID, FERDINAND: *Violinschule* (Leipzig, [1863]).
DAVID, FERDINAND, ed.: *Concert-Studien für die Violine. Eine Sammlung von Violin-Solo-Compositionen berühmter älterer Meister, zum Gebrauch beim Conservatorium der Musik in Leipzig*, 3 vols. (Leipzig, Bartholf Senff, n.d.).
DAVID, FERDINAND: *Die hohe Schule des Violinspiels* (Leipzig, [1867]).
DAVIES, FANNY: 'Some Personal Recollections of Brahms as Pianist and Interpreter' in *Cobbett's Cyclopedic Survey of Chamber Music* (London, 1929), i, 182ff.
DEAN, WINTON: 'The Performance of Recitative in Late Baroque Opera', *Music & Letters*, lviii (1977), 389ff.
DEACON, HARRY COLLINS: article 'Tremolo' and 'Vibrato' in Sir George Grove (ed.): *A Dictionary of Music and Musicians*, 4 vols. iv (London, 1890).

Deas, Stuart: 'Beethoven's "Allegro assai"', *Music & Letters*, xxxi (1950), 333ff.
Dejmek, Gaston Roman: *Max Fiedler: Werden und Wirken* (Essen, 1940).
Delusse, Charles: *L'Art de la flute traversière* (Paris, [c. 1761]).
Del Mar, Jonathan: 'Once Again: Reflections on Beethoven's Tied-Note Notation', *Early Music*, xxxii (2004), 7ff.
Deutsch, Otto Erich: *Schubert: Die Erinnerungen seiner Freunde* (Leipzig, 1957).
Deutsch, Otto Erich: *Schubert: Die Dokumente seines Lebens* (Kasel, 1964).
Dibdin, Charles: *Music Epitomized: A School Book in which the Whole Science of Music is Completely Explained*... (London, 1808); 9th edn, rev. J. Jousse (London, [c. 1820]).
Dickey, Bruce: 'Untersuchung zur historischen Auffassung des Vibratos auf Blasinstrumenten', *Basler Jahrbuch für historische Musikpraxis*, ii (1978), 77ff.
Dommer, Arrey von: *Musikalisches Lexicon auf Grundlage des Lexicon's von H. Ch. Koch* (Heidelberg, 1865): alternative title-page: *H. Ch. Koch's Musikalisches Lexicon. Zweite durchaus umgearbeitet und vermehrte Auflage von Arrey von Dommer*.
Doni, Giovanni Battista: *Trattato della musica scenica* ([c. 1635–39]/Rome, 2018).
Dont, Jacob: *Zwölf Uebungen aus der Violinschule von L. Spohr mit Anmerkungen, Ergänzungen des Fingersatzes der Bogen-Stricharten und der Tonschattierungszeichen* (Vienna, 1874).
Dotzauer, Justus Johann Friedrich: *Méthode de violoncelle/Violonzell-Schule* (Mainz, [1824]).
Dotzauer, Justus Johann Friedrich: *Violoncell-Schule für den ersten Unterricht* op. 126 (Vienna, [1833]).
Dounias, Minos, ed.: W. A. Mozart Kirchensonaten, *Neue Mozart Ausgabe*, VI: 16 (Kassel, 1957), viiff.
Droopoulou, Loukia Myrto: *Dynamic, Articulation and Special Effect Markings in Manuscript Sources of Boccherini's String Quintets* (diss., University of York, 2008).
Duport, Jean-Louis: *Essai sur le doigté du violoncelle et sur la conduite de l'archet* (Paris, [1806]).
Dürr, Walther: 'Notation und Aufführungspraxis. Artikulation und Dynamik bei Schubert' in Helga Lühning (ed.), *Musikedition. Mittler zwischen Wissenschaft und musikalischer Praxis* (Tübingen, 2002), 313ff.
Dürr, Walther: 'Schubert and Johann Michael Vogl: A Reappraisal', *19th-Century Music*, iii (1979), 126ff.
Eberhardt, Siegfried: *Der beseelte Violin-Ton* (Dresden, 1910); trans. as *Violin Vibrato: Its Mastery and Artistic Uses* (New York, 1911).
Edwards, F. G.: 'George P. Bridgetower and the "Kreutzer" Sonata', *Musical Times*, xlix (1908), 308.
Ehrlich, Heinrich: 'Beim 84jährigen Verdi', *Deutsche Revue* (Stuttgart), 22/2 (1897), 325ff.
Eichberg, Julius: *Eichberg's Complete Method for the Violin* (Boston, 1876); rev. edn (Boston, 1879).
Emmanuel, Maurice: *César Franck: Etude Critique* (Paris, Laurens, 1930).
Escudier (frères): *Dictionnaire de musique théorique et historique* (Paris, 1854).
Eymar, Ange Marie: 'Anecdotes sur Viotti, précédées de quelques réflexions sur l'expression en musique' (Paris, 1792).
Faisst, F.: 'Mozart's Don Giovanni' [ed. Bernhard Gugler], *Neue Berliner Musikzeitung*, xxiv (1870), 113ff and 129ff.
Fellowes, Edmund: *Memoirs of an Amateur Musician* (London, 1946).

FERRARI, GIACOMO GOTIFREDO: *Breve trattato di canto italiano* (London, 1818).
FÉTIS, FRANÇOIS-JOSEPH: *Manuel des principes de musique* (Paris, 1864).
FÉTIS, FRANÇOIS-JOSEPH: *La musique mise à la portée de tout le Monde* (Paris, 1830), 2nd edn (Paris, 1834).
FÉTIS, FRANÇOIS-JOSEPH: *Traité élémentaire de musique* (Brussels, 1831–32).
FÉTIS, FRANÇOIS-JOSEPH, and MOSCHELES, IGNAZ: *Méthode des méthodes de piano* (Paris, [c. 1840]); trans. as *Complete System of Instruction for the Piano Forte* (London, [1841]).
FINK, GOTTFRIED WILHELM: 'Accent' in Gustav Schilling (ed.), *Encyclopädie der gesammten musikalischen Wisenschaften* (Stuttgart, 1835), i, 35ff.
FINK, GOTTFRIED WILHELM: 'Ueber Takt, Taktarten, und ihr Charakteristisches', *Allgemeine musikalische Zeitung*, xi (1808–9), 193ff, 209ff, 225ff.
FISCHHOF, JOSEPH: 'Einige Gedanken über die Auffassung von Instrumentalcompositionen in Hinsicht des Zeitmaaßes, namentlich bei Beethoven'schen Werken', *Caecilia*, xxvi (1847), 84ff.
FLEMING, JAMES M.: *The Practical Violin School for Home Students* (London, 1886).
FLESCH, CARL: *The Art of Violin Playing*, 2 vols. (New York, 1939). Rev. English edn.
FLESCH, CARL: *Die Kunst des Violinspiels*, i (Berlin, 1923); trans. as *The Art of Violin Playing* (London, 1924).
FLESCH, CARL: *Die Kunst des Violinspiels*, ii (Berlin, 1928)
FLESCH, CARL: *Die Kunst des Violinspiels*, 2nd ed., i (Berlin, 1929)
FLESCH, CARL: *The Memoirs of Carl Flesch*, ed. H. Keller and C. F. Flesch, trans. Hans Keller (London, 1957).
FLETCHER, NEVILLE HORNER: 'Vibrato in Music', *Acoustics Australia*, xxix (2001), 97ff.
FOSTER, RONALD: *Vocal Success* (London, 1934).
FRAMERY, NICOLAS ETIENNE, GINGUENÉ, PIERRE LOUIS, MOMIGNY, JEROME JOSEPH DE, and PANCKOUCKE, CHARLES-JOSEPH, eds: *Encyclopédie Méthodique. Musique*, i (Paris, 1791).
FRAMERY, NICOLAS ETIENNE, GINGUENÉ, PIERRE LOUIS, and MOMIGNY, JEROME JOSEPH DE: *Encyclopédie Méthodique. Musique*, ii (Paris, 1818).
FREITAS, ROGER: 'Singing Herself: Adelina Patti and the Performance of Femininity', *Journal of the American Musicological Society* lxxi (2018), 287ff.
FRIEDLANDER, CLAUDIA: 'The Liberated Voice. Revolutionizing Vocal Technique with Timeless Wisdom' (2012), https://www.claudiafriedlander.com/the-liberated-voice/2012/05/vibrato-hell.html [accessed 12 March 2022].
FRÖHLICH, FRANZ JOSEPH: *Vollständige theoretisch-praktische Musikschule* (Bonn, 1810–11).
Fuchs, Karl: *Die Freiheit des musikalischen Vortrags* (Leipzig, 1885).
Fuchs, Karl: *Die Zukunft des musikalischen Vortrags* (Danzig, 1884).
FULLER, DAVID: 'Notes inégales' in Stanley Sadie (ed.), *New Grove Dictionary of Music and Musicians*, xiii, 420.
FULLER MAITLAND, J. A.: 'Sostenuto' in H. C. Colles (ed.), *Grove's Dictionary*, 3rd edn (London, 1927).
FÜRSTENAU, ANTON BERNHARD: *Flöten-Schule* (Leipzig, [1826]).
FÜRSTENAU, ANTON BERNHARD: *Die Kunst des Flötenspiels* (Leipzig [1844]).
GALEAZZI, FRANCESCO: *Elementi teorico-pratici di musica, con un saggio sopra l'arte di suonare il violino annalizzata, ed a dimostrahili principi ridotta*, 2 vols. (Rome, 1791–96). 2nd edn (Ascoli, 1817).

GALLIARD, JOHN: *Observations on the Florid Song; or, Sentiments on the Ancient and Modern Singers* (London, 1742). Rev. translation of Tosi's *Opinioni*.
GARCÍA, MANUEL PATRICIO RODRIGUEZ: *École de Garcia. Traité complet de l'art du chant*, i (Paris, 1840), revised edn (Paris, 1847) and ii (Paris, 1847). Rev. single volume edition as *Nouveau traité sommaire de l'art du chant* (Paris, 1856), trans. as *Garcia's New Treatise on the Art of Singing* (London, [1858]).
GARDINER, WILLIAM: *The Music of Nature* (London, 1832).
GARST, MARILYN M.: 'How Bartók Performed His Own Compositions', *Tempo*, n.s., clv/12 (1985), 15ff.
GASSNER, F. S.: *Dirigent und Ripienist* (Karlsruhe, 1844).
GATHY, AUGUST: *Musikalisches Conversations-Lexikon Encyklopädie der gesammten Musik-Wissenschaft für Künstler, Kunstfreunde und Gebildete* (Leipzig, Hamburg, and Itzehoe, 1835); 2nd edn (Hamburg, 1840); 3rd edn (Berlin, 1871).
GEBAUER, JOHANNES: *Der "Klassikervortrag": Joseph Joachims Bach- und Beethovenvortrag und die Interpretationspraxis des 19. Jahrhunderts*, Veröffentlichungen des Beethoven-Hauses Bonn, Beethoven Interpretationen Band 1, ed. Kai Köpp (Bonn, 2024).
GECK, MARTIN, and VOSS, EGON, eds.: *Richard Wagner: Sämtliche Werke*, xxx: *Dokumente zur Entstehung und ersten Aufführung des Bühnenweihfestspiels Parsifal* (Mainz, 1970).
GEHOT, JOSEPH: *A Treatise on the Theory and Practice of Music together with the Scales of Every Musical Instrument* (London, 1784).
GEIRINGER, KARL: *Joseph Haydn* (Potsdam, 1932).
GEMINIANI, FRANCESCO: *The Art of Playing on the Violin* (London, 1751).
GEMINIANI, FRANCESCO: *Rules for Playing in a True Taste* (London, 1748).
GERHARD, ANSELM: 'Willkürliches Arpeggieren—ein selbstverständliches Ausdrucksmittel in der klassisch-romantischen Klaviermusik und seine Tabuisierung im 20. Jahrhundert', *Basler Jahrbuch für historische Musikpraxis*, xxvii (2003), 123ff.
GERHARD, ANSELM: '»You do it!« Weitere Belege für das willkürliche Arpeggieren in der klassisch-romantischen Klaviermusik' in Claudio Bacciagaluppi, Roman Brotbeck, and Anselm Gerhard (eds.), *Zwischen schöpferischer Individualität und künstlerischer Selbstverleugnung* (Schliengen, 2009), 159ff.
GERSTENBERG, WALTER: 'Authentische Tempi für Mozart's "Don Giovanni"?', *Mozart-Jahrbuch* (1960–61), 58ff.
GINGERICH, JOHN M.: 'Ignaz Schuppanzigh and Beethoven's Late Quartets', *The Musical Quarterly*, xciii (2010), 450f.
GLEICH, CLEMENS VON: 'Original Tempo-Angaben bei Mendelssohn' in H. Herrtreich and H. Schneider (eds.), *Festschrift Rudolf Elvers zum 60 Geburtstag* (Tutzing, 1985), 213ff.
GOLLMICK, CARL: *Kritische Terminologie* (Frankfurt-am-Main, 1833).
GOLLMICK, CARL: Handlexikon der Tonkunst (Offenbach am Main, 1857).
GOOSSENS, LÉON, and ROXBURGH, EDWIN: *Oboe* (London, 1977).
GOSSEC, FRANÇOIS-JOSEPH, AGUS, JOSEPH, CATEL, CHARLES-SIMON, and CHERUBINI, LUIGI: *Principes élémentaires de musique Arrètés par les Membres du Conservatoire, pour servir à l'étude dans cet établissement [,] suivis de solfèges* (Paris, An VIII [1799]).
GREULICH, CARL WILHELM: *Kleine practische Clavierschule zum Selbstunterricht* (Berlin, [c. 1831]).
GRIMSON, SAMUEL B., and FORSYTH, CECIL: *Modern Violin-Playing* (New York, 1920).
GROVE, SIR GEORGE, ed.: *A Dictionary of Music and Musicians* (London, 1879–89).
GUHR, CARL: *Ueber Paganini's Kunst die Violine zu spielen* (Mainz, [1829]).
GUNN, JOHN: *The Art of Playing the German Flute* (London, [1793]).

GUNN, JOHN: *The Theory and Practice of Fingering the Violoncello* (London [1789]).
GUTHMANN, FRIEDRICH: 'Das Konzert auf dem Fortepiano. Eine Phantasie', *Allgemeine musikalische Zeitung*, viii (1805–6), 396ff.
GUTHMANN, FRIEDRICH: 'Ueber Abweichung vom Takte', *Allgemeine musikalische Zeitung*, vii (1804–5), 347ff.
GUTHMANN, FRIEDRICH: 'Ueber die allzugrosse Geschwindigkeit des Allegro, und überhaupt über das eingerissene unmässige Eilen', *Allgemeine musikalische Zeitung*, vii (1804–5), 773ff.
HABENECK, FRANÇOIS: *Méthode théorique et pratique de violon* (Paris, [1842]).
HAMILTON, JAMES ALEXANDER: *A Dictionary of Two Thousand Italian, French, German, English and other Musical Terms*, 4th edn (London, 1837); 5th edn (New York, 1842); rev. as *Hamilton's Dictionary of Musical Terms. New Edition . . . Enlarged* (London, [1882]).
HANSLICK, EDUARD: *Geschichte des Concertwesens in Wien* (Vienna, 1869).
HARDING, ROSAMOND E. M.: *Origins of Musical Time and Expression* (London, 1938).
HARNONCOURT, NIKOLAUS: *Der musikalische Dialog* (Salzburg, 1984).
HÄSER, AUGUST FERDINAND: *Versuch einer systematischen Uebersicht der Gesangslehre* (Leipzig [1822]).
HAUPTMANN, MORITZ: *Die Natur der Harmonik und der Metrik* (Leipzig, 1853).
HAUPTNER, THUISKON: *Ausbildung der Stimme* (Leipzig, 1876).
HEINE, HEINRICH: *Heinrich Heine's sämmtliche Werke*, xi (Hamburg, 1874).
HERZ, HENRI: *Méthode complète de piano* op. 100 (Mainz and Anvers, 1838).
HERZ, HENRI: *A New and Complete Pianoforte School* (London, [c. 1838]).
HERZ, HENRI: *A Standard Modern Preceptor for the Pianoforte* (London, [c. 1840]).
HICKMAN, ROGER: 'The Censored Publications of *The Art of Playing on the Violin* or *Geminiani Unshaken*', *Early Music*, xi (1983), 71ff.
HILL, CECIL: *Ferdinand Ries: Briefe und Dokumente* (Bonn, 1982).
HILLER, JOHANN ADAM: *Anleitung zum musikalisch-richtigen Gesang* (Leipzig, 1774)
HILLER, JOHANN ADAM: *Anweisung zum musikalisch-zierlichen Gesang* (Leipzig, 1780).
HILLER, JOHANN ADAM: *Anweisung zum Violonspielen für Schulen und Selbstunterrichte* (Leipzig, 1792).
HILLER, JOHANN ADAM: *Sechs italienische Arien verschiedener Componisten, mit der Art sie zu singen und verändern* (Leipzig, 1778).
HOCK, HERMANN: *Ein Leben mit der Geige. Erinnerungen an Blütezeiten des Musiklebens in Frankfurt am Main* (Frankfurt [1950]).
HOFFMANN, KURT: *Johannes Brahms in den Erinnerungen von Richard Barth* (Hamburg, 1979).
HOLDEN, JOHN: *An "Essay" towards a Rational System of Music* (Glasgow, 1770).
HOLDEN, RAYMOND: 'Richard Strauss: The Don Juan Recordings', *Performance Practice Review*, x (1997), 11ff.
HOULE, GEORGE: *Metre in Music 1600–1800* (Bloomington, IN, 1987).
HUDSON, RICHARD: *Stolen Time: The History of Tempo Rubato* (Oxford, 1994).
HÜLLMANDEL, NICHOLAS-JOSEPH: *Principles of Music Chiefly Calculated for the Piano Forte or Harpsichord* (London, 1796).
HUMMEL, JOHANN NEPOMUK: *Ausführliche theoretisch-practische Anweisung zum Piano-Forte-Spiel*, 3 vols. 1st edn (Vienna, 1827) 2nd edn (Vienna, 1828); trans. as *A Complete Theoretical and Practical Course of Instructions, on the Art of Playing the Piano Forte*, 3 vols. (London, [1828]).

JÄHNS, FRIEDRICH WILHELM: *Carl Maria von Weber in seinen Werken: Chronologischthematisches Verzeichniss seiner sämmtlichen Compositionen* (Berlin, 1871).
JAMES, WILLIAM NELSON: *The Flutist's Catechism* (London, 1829).
JEITELES, IGNAZ: *Aesthetisches Lexikon. Ein alphabetisches Handbuch zur Theorie der Philosophie des Schönen und der schönen Künste*, 2 vols (Vienna, 1837).
JEROLD, BEVERLEY: 'How Composers Viewed Performers' Additions', *Early Music*, xxxvi (2008), 95ff.
JOACHIM, JOSEPH, and MOSER, ANDREAS: *Violinschule*, 3 vols. (Berlin, 1905).
JOCKISCH, REINHOLD: *Katechismus der Violine und des Violinspiels* (Leipzig, 1900).
JOUSSE, JOHN: *A Compendious Musical Grammar*. See Asioli.
JOUSSE, JOHN: *The Modern Violin Preceptor* (London, [c. 1805]).
JOUSSE, JOHN: *The Theory and Practice of the Violin* (London, 1811).
JUNGHANSS, JOHANN CHRISTIAN GOTTLIEB: *Theoretich-praktische Pianoforte-Schule* (Vienna, [1820]).
JUNKER, CARL LUDWIG: *Einige der vornehmsten Pflichten eines Kapellmeisters oder Musikdirektors* (Winterthur, 1782).
KALKBRENNER, FRÉDÉRIC: *Méthode pour apprendre le piano-forte à l'aide du guide mains* op. 108 (Paris, [1831]); trans. and ed. as *Complete Course of Instruction for the Piano Forte* (London, [c. 1835]).
KÄMPER, D.: 'Zur Frage der Metronombezeichnungen Robert Schumanns', *Archiv für Musikwissenschaft*, xxi (1964), 141ff.
KATZ, MARK: 'Portamento and the Phonograph Effect', *Journal of Musicological Research*, xxv (2006), 211ff.
KAUER, FERDINAND: *Kurzgefasste Anweisung das Violoncell zu spielen* (Speyer, 1778), repr. (Vienna, Cappi, [c. 1800]).
KAUER, FERDINAND: *Kurzgefasste Violin-Schule für Anfänger* (Vienna, [1787]).
KENNAWAY, GEORGE: *Playing the Cello, 1780–1930* (Farnham, 2014).
KIM, DAVID HYUN-SU: 'The Brahmsian Hairpin', *19th-Century Music*, xxxvi (2012), 45ff.
KIRNBERGER, JOHANN PHILIPP: *Die Kunst des reinen Satzes in der Musik*, i (Berlin and Königsberg, 1774), ii, pts 1–3 (Berlin and Königsberg, 1776–79); trans. David Beach and Jurgen Thym as *The Art of Strict Musical Composition* (New Haven and London, 1982). See also Sulzer.
KLAUWELL, OTTO: *Der Vortrag in der Musik: Versuch einer systematischen Begründung desselben zunächst rücksichtlich des Klavierspiels* (Berlin and Leipzig, 1883); trans. as *On Musical Execution: An Attempt at a Systematic Exposition of the Same, Primarily with Reference to Piano-playing* (New York, 1890).
KLINDWORTH, KARL: 'Preface' and 'Explanatory Notes' in Mendelssohn's *Lieder ohne Worte* (London, Novello, 1898).
KLINGLER, KARL: *„Über die Grundlagen des Violinspiels" und nachgelassene Schriften*, ed. Marianne M. Klingler and Agnes Ritter (Hildesheim, 1990).
KNECHT, JUSTIN HEINRICH: *Kleine theoretische Klavierschule für die ersten Anfänger* (Munich, [1799]).
KNECHT, JUSTIN HEINRICH: *Knechts allgemeiner musikalischer Katechismus* (Biberach, 1803); 4th edn (Freyburg, 1816).
KOCH, HEINRICH CHRISTOPH: *Musikalisches Lexikon* (Frankfurt-am-Main, 1802).
KOCH, HEINRICH CHRISTOPH: 'Ueber den technischen Ausdruck Tempo rubato', *Allgemeine musikalische Zeitung*, x (1807–8), 518f.

Koch, Heinrich Christoph: *Versuch einer Anleitung zur Composition* (Rudolstadt and Leipzig, 1782–93).
Kogel, G. F.: Preface to Heinrich Marschner, *Hans Heiling*, full score, ed. Kögel (Leipzig, Peters, [c. 1880]).
Kollmann, August Frederic Christopher: *An Essay on Musical Harmony* (London, 1796).
Köpp, Kai: *Handbuch historische Orchesterpraxis* (Bärenreiter, 2009); rev. French edn *La pratique d'orchestre historique. Baroque, classique et romantique*, trans. Fabien Roussel (Paris, 2020).
Krall, Emil: *The Art of Tone-Production on the Violoncello* (London, 1913).
Kramer, Richard: 'Notes to Beethoven's Education', *Journal of the American Musicological Society*, xviii (1975), 75ff.
Kullak, Adolph: *Die Aesthetik des Klavierspiels* (Berlin, 1861); posthumous 2nd edn (Berlin, 1876).
Kullak, Franz: *Beethoven's Piano Playing with an Essay on the Execution of the Trill* (New York, 1901).
Kullak, Franz: *Der Vortrag zu Ende des 19. Jahrhundert* (Leipzig, 1897).
Kummer, Friedrich August: *Violoncell-Schule für den ersten Unterricht*, op. 60 (Leipzig, [1839]).
Kürzinger, Ignaz Franz Xaver: *Getreuer Unterricht zum Singen mit Manieren, und die Violin zu spielen* (Augsburg [1763]).
L'abbé le fils [Joseph-Barnabé Saint-Sevin]: *Principes du violon* (Paris, 1761).
La Mara [Marie Lipsius]: *Classisches und Romantisches aus der Tonwelt* (Leipzig 1892).
Landon, Howard Chandler Robbins: *Haydn at Eszterháza 1766–1790* (London, 1978).
Lanza, Gesualdo: *The Elements of Singing* (London, [1809]).
Lasser, Johann Baptist: *Vollständige Anleitung zur Singkunst* (Munich, 1798).
Lavignac, Albert, and Laurencie, Lionel de la: *Encyclopédie de la musique et dictionnaire du Conservatoire* (Paris, 1920–31).
Lawton, David: 'Ornamenting Verdi Arias: The Continuity of a Tradition' in Alison Latham and Roger Parker (eds.), *Verdi in Performance* (Oxford, 2001), 49ff.
Lebert, Sigmund, and Stark, Ludwig: *Grosse theoretisch-praktische Klavierschule*, 3 vols. (Stuttgart, 1858).
Lee, Douglas: 'Some Embellished Versions of Sonatas by Franz Benda', *Musical Quarterly*, xii (1976), 58ff.
Leech-Wilkinson, Daniel: 'Portamento and Musical Meaning', *Journal of Musicological Research*, xxv (2006), 233ff.
Leertouwer, Johannes: *Re-inventing the Nineteenth-Century Tools of Unprescribed Modifications of Rhythm and Tempo in Performances of Brahms's Symphonies and Concertos* (diss., University of Leiden, 2023).
Lehmann, Lilli: *Meine Gesangkunst* (Berlin, 1902). Trans. Richard Aldrich as *How to Sing* (New York, 1902).
Lenz, Wilhelm von: *Die großen Pianoforte-Virtuosen unserer Zeit aus persönlicher Bekanntschaft* (Berlin, 1872).
Levin, Julius: 'Adolf Busch', *Die Musik*, xviii (1925/1926), 744ff.
Levin, Robert: 'Performance Prerogatives in Schubert', *Early Music*, xxv (1997), 723ff.
Lichtenthal, Pietro: *Dizionario e bibliografia della musica* (Milan, 1826).
Liess, Andreas: *Johann Michael Vogl. Hofoperist und Schubertsänger* (Graz-Köln, 1954).
Lindsay, Thomas: *The Elements of Flute Playing* (London, [1828]).
Liszt, Franz: Preface to *Liszts Symphonische Dichtungen für grosses Orchester*, 3 vols. (Leipzig, Breitkopf & Härtel, [1856]).

LOCKNER, LOUIS PAUL: *Fritz Kreisler* (London, 1951).
LÖHLEIN, GEORG SIMON: *Anweisung zum Violinspielen, mit pracktischen [sic] Beyspielen und zur Uebung mit vier und zwanzig kleinen Duetten erläutert* (Leipzig and Züllichau, 1774); 4th edn, rev. Johann Friedrich Reichardt (Leipzig and Züllichau, 1797).
LÖHLEIN, GEORG SIMON: *Clavier-Schule, oder kurze und gründliche Anweisung zur Melodie und Harmonie, durchgehends mit practischen Beyspielen erkläret* (Leipzig and Züllichau, 1765); 2nd edn, *Georg Simon Löhleins Clavier-Schule*... (Leipzig and Züllichau, 1773); rev. and enlarged 5th edn, ed. Johann Georg Witthauer (Leipzig and Züllichau, 1791); 6th edn, *G. C. [sic] Löhleins Klavierschule oder Anweisung zum Klavier- und Fortepiano- Spiel umgearbeitet und sehr vermehrt von A. E. Müller* (Jena, 1804): for the alternative title of 6th edn see Müller below.
LUSSY, MATHIS: *Le Rythme musical, son origine, sa fonction et son accentuation* (Paris, 1883).
LUSSY, MATHIS: *Traité de l'expression musicale: Accents, nuances et mouvements dans la musique vocale et instrumentale* (Paris, 1874); 6th edn (Paris, 1892); trans. M. E. von Glehn as *Musical Expression, Accents, Nuances, and Tempo, in Vocal and Instrumental Music* (London, [c. 1885]), also (London and New York, [1892]).
M. R. [MARION BRUCE RANKEN]: *Some Points of Violin Playing and Musical Performance as learnt in the Hochschule für Musik (Joachim School) in Berlin during the time I was a Student there.* (Edinburgh, 1939).
MACDONALD, HUGH JOHN: 'Berlioz and the Metronome' in P. A. Bloom (ed.), *Berlioz Studies* (Cambridge, 1992), 17.
MACDONALD, HUGH JOHN: 'Two Peculiarities of Berlioz's Notation', *Music & Letters*, 1 (1969), 25ff.
MACKINLAY, MALCOLM STERLING: *García the Centenarian and His Times* (Edinburgh, 1908).
MALIBRAN, ALEXANDRE: *Louis Spohr* (Frankfurt-am-Main, 1860).
MALLOCH, WILLIAM, 'Carl Czerny's Metronome Marks for Haydn and Mozart Symphonies', *Early Music*, xvi (1988), 72ff.
MANFREDINI, VINCENZO: *Regole armoniche: o siene Precetti ragionate* (Venice, 1775); 2nd edn (Venice, 1797).
MANNSTEIN [pseudonym for Steinmann] HEINRICH FERDINAND: *Das System der grossen Gesangschule des Bernacchi von Bologna* (Dresden and Leipzig, [1835]).
MARPURG, FRIEDRICH WILHELM: *Anleitung zum Clavierspielen der schönen Ausübung der heutigen Zeit gemäss* (Berlin, 1755); 2nd edn (Berlin, 1765; fac. New York, 1969).
MARPURG, FRIEDRICH WILHELM: *Kritische Briefe über die Tonkunst* (Berlin, 1760-64).
MARTIN, DAVID: 'An Early Metronome', *Early Music*, xvi (1988), 90ff.
MARTY, JEAN-PIERRE: *The Tempo Indications of Mozart* (New Haven and London, 1988).
MARX, ADOLF BERNHARD: *Allgemeine Musiklehre: Ein Hülfsbuch für Lehrer und Lernende in jedem Zweige musikalischer Unterweisung* (Leipzig, 1839); trans. A. H. Wehrhan as *A Universal School of Music* (London, 1853); 6th edn (Leipzig, 1857).
MARX, ADOLF BERNHARD: *Die Musik der neunzehnten Jahrhunderts und ihre Pflege: Methode der Musik* (Leipzig, 1855), trans. August Heinrich Wehrhan as *The Music of the Nineteenth Century and its Culture* (London, 1854).
MATSON, JOSEPH R.: 'Johann Michael Vogl's Alterations to Schuberts "Die Schöne Müllerin"', (diss., University of Iowa, 2009).
MAZAS, JACQUES FÉRÉOL: *Méthode de violon* op. 34 (Paris, [1832]).
MC KERRELL, J.: *A Familiar Introduction to the First Principles of Music* (London, [c. 1800]).
MEERTS, LAMBERT-JOSEPH: *Douze Études pour le Violon* (Mainz, Schott [1838]).
MENDEL, HERMANN, and REISSMANN, AUGUST: *Musikalisches Conversations-Lexikon* (Berlin, 1870-).

MIES, PAUL: 'Die Artikulationzeichen Strich und Punkt bei Wolfgang Amadeus Mozart', *Die Musikforschung*, xi (1958), 428ff.

MIES, PAUL: *Textkritische Untersuchungen bei Beethoven* (Munich and Duisburg, 1957).

MIES, PAUL: 'Ueber ein besonderes Akzentzeichen bei Johannes Brahms' in Georg Reichert and Martin Just (eds.), *Bericht über den internationalen musikwissenschaftlichen Kongress Kassel 1962* (Kassel, 1963), 215ff.

MILCHMEYER, JOHANN PETER: *Die wahre Art das Pianoforte zu spielen* (Dresden, 1797).

MILLER, EDWARD: *The New Flute Instructor or the Art of Playing the German Flute* (London, [c. 1799]).

MIUCCI, LEONARDO: 'Beethoven's pianoforte damper pedalling: a case of double notational style', *Early Music*, XLVII (2019), 371ff.

MIUCCI, LEONARDO: ed. Beethoven, Ludwig van: Three Quartets for Pianoforte, Violin, Viola and Violoncello WoO 36 (Kassel, Bärenreiter, 2020).

MOENS-HAENEN, GRETA: *Das Vibrato in der Musik des Barock* (Graz, 1988).

MONTGOMERY, DAVID: 'Modern Schubert Interpretation in the Light of the Pedagogical Sources of His Day', *Early Music*, xxv (1997), 100ff.

MORAZZONI, G.: *Verdi: Lettere inedite* (Milan, 1929).

MORENO, ÁUREA DOMÍNGUEZ: *Bassoon Playing in Perspective. Character and Performance Practice from 1800 to 1850* (PhD diss., University of Helsinki, 2013).

MOSCHELES, IGNAZ: *Studien für das Pianoforte* op. 70 (Leipzig, Probst, [1827]).

MOSCHELES, IGNAZ: See also Fétis.

MOSEL, IGNAZ VON: 'Ueber die gewöhnliche Anwendung der Wörter: Methode und Kunst, auf die Leistungen der dramatischer Sänger', *Taschenbuch für Schauspieler und Schauspielfreunde: auf das Jahr 1821* [...] hrsg. Von Lembert (Vienna, 1821), 38ff.

MOSER, ANDREAS: *Geschichte des Violinspiels* (Berlin, 1923).

MOSER, ANDREAS: *Joseph Joachim. Ein Lebensbild* (Berlin, 1898); trans. Lilia Durham as *Joseph Joachim* (London, 1901). *Joseph Joachim. Ein Lebensbild*, 2nd edn, 2 vols. (Berlin: Verlag der Deutschen Brahms-Gesellschaft, 1908–10).

MOSER, ANDREAS: *Violinschule*: See Joachim.

MOZART, LEOPOLD: *Versuch einer gründlichen Violinschule* (Augsburg, 1756); 3rd edn (Augsburg, 1787); trans. Editha Knocker *A Treatise on the Fundamental Principles of Violin Playing*, 2nd edn (Oxford, 1951): including the additions and changes in the 1787 edn as well as the whole of the original text. See also Anon.

MOZART, WOLFGANG AMADEUS: *Briefe und Aufzeichnungen* (Kassel, 1962).

MOZART, WOLFGANG AMADEUS: *The Letters of Mozart and his Family*, trans. and ed. Emily Anderson, 2nd edn (London, 1966).

MÜLLER, AUGUST: 'Ueber das Wirken des Musikers im Orchester', *Neue Zeitschrift für Musik*, xxxi (1849), 218f.

MÜLLER, AUGUST EBERHARDT: *Elementarbuch für Flötenspieler* (Leipzig, [1815]).

MÜLLER, AUGUST EBERHARDT: *G. S. Löhleins Klavierschule oder Anweisung zum Klavier- und Fortepiano Schule [. . .] ganz umgearbeitet und sehr vermehrt* (Jena, 1804) (entirely rewritten, but nominally 6th edn of Löhlein's *Klavierschule*); revised Carl Czerny as *Große Fortepiano Schule von Aug. Eberhd Müller [...] Achte Auflage mit vielen neuen Beispiele und einem vollständigen Anhang vom Generalbass versehen von Carl Czerny* (Leipzig, c. 1830).

MUNSTER, R.: 'Authentische Tempi zu den sechs letzten Sinfonien W. A. Mozart's?', *Mozart-Jahrbuch* (1962–63), 185ff.

NATHAN, ISAAC: *Musurgia Vocalis. An Essay on the History and Theory of Music, and on the Qualities, Capabilities, and Management of the Human Voice*, 2nd edn (London, 1836).

NEEFE, CHRISTIAN GOTTLOB: in *Magazin der Musik*, i (1783), 377.

*Neue Zeitschrift für Musik*, ed. Robert Alexander Schumann, Franz Brendel, et al. (Leipzig, 1834–1928).
NEUMANN, FREDERICK: 'Dots and Strokes in Mozart', *Early Music*, xxi (1993), 429ff.
NEUMANN, FREDERICK: 'The French "Inégales", Quantz, and Bach', *Journal of the American Musicological Society*, xviii (1965), 313ff.
NEUMANN, FREDERICK: *New Essays on Performance Practice* (Ann Arbor, 1989).
NEUMANN, FREDERICK: *Ornamentation and Improvisation in Mozart* (Princeton, 1986).
NEUMANN, FREDERICK: *Ornamentation in Baroque and Post-Baroque Music* (Princeton, 1978).
*The New Grove Dictionary of Music and Musicians*, ed. Stanley Sadie (London, 1980).
*The New Grove Dictionary of Opera*, ed. Stanley Sadie (London, 1992).
NICHOLSON, CHARLES: *Complete Preceptor for the German Flute* (London, [c. 1816]).
NICHOLSON, CHARLES: *Preceptive Lessons for the Flute* (London, [1821]).
NICHOLSON, CHARLES: *A School for the Flute*, 2 vols (New York, [1836]).
NISSEN, GEORG NIKOLAUS: *Wolfgang Amadeus Mozart's Biographie* (Leipzig, 1828).
NOORDUIN, MARTEN: *Beethoven's Tempo Indications* (PhD diss., University of Manchester, 2016).
NOORDUIN, MARTEN: 'The Metronome Marks for Beethoven's Ninth Symphony in Context', *Early Music*, xlix (2021), 129ff.
NOVELLO, MARY: *Voice and Vocal Art* (London, 1856).
PARAKILAS, JAMES: 'Playing Beethoven His way: Czerny and the Canonization of Performance Practice' in David Gramit (ed.), *Beyond the Art of Finger Dexterity. Reassessing Carl Czerny* (Rochester, 2008), 108ff.
PASQUALI, NICOLO: *The Art of Fingering the Harpsichord* (Edinburgh, [c. 1760]).
PAUL, OSCAR: *Handlexikon der Tonkunst* (Leipzig, 1873).
PELLEGRINI CELONI, MARIA: *Grammatica o siano regole di ben cantare* (Leipzig, 1810).
PERES DA COSTA, NEAL: *Off the Record* (Oxford and New York, 2012).
PETISCUS, JOHANN CONRAD WILHELM: See Anon. 1804.
PETRI, JOHANN SAMUEL: *Anleitung zur practischen Musik, vor neuangehende Sänger und Instrumentspieler*, 1st edn (Lauban, 1767); rev. 2nd edn (Leipzig, 1782).
PHILIP, ROBERT: *Early Recordings and Musical Style: Changing Tastes in Instrumental Performance 1900–1950* (Cambridge, 1992).
PHILIP, ROBERT: 'The Recordings of Edward Elgar (1857–1934): Authenticity and Performance Practice', *Early Music*, xii (1984), 481ff.
PLATEN, EMIL: 'Zeitgenössische Hinweise zur Aufführungspraxis der letzten Streichquartette Beethovens's' in Rudolf Klein (ed.), *Beiträge '76-98: Beethoven Kolloquium 1977; Dokumentation und Aufführungspraxis* (Kassel, 1978), 100ff.
POLLINI, FRANCESCO: *Metodo per clavicembalo* (Milan, 1811).
PONSFORD, DAVID: *French Organ Music in the Reign of Louis XIV* (Cambridge, 2011).
PORGES, HEINRICH: *Die Bühnenproben zu der Bayreuther Festspielen des Jahres 1876* (Chemnitz and Leipzig, 1881–96); trans. Robert L. Jacobs as *Wagner Rehearsing the "Ring"* (Cambridge, 1983).
POTTER, SARAH: *Changing Vocal Style and Technique in Britain during the Long Nineteenth Century* (PhD thesis, University of Leeds, 2014), (online at https://etheses.whiterose.ac.uk/8345/).
PRIMROSE, WILLIAM: *Memoirs* (London, 1978).
PUSTLAUK, ANNE: *The Simple System Flute between 1790 and 1850, Its Performance Practice and Chamber Music Repertoire with Pianoforte and/or Strings* (PhD diss., Vrije Universiteit Brussel, 2016).

QUANTZ, JOHANN JOACHIM: *Versuch einer Anweisung die Flöte traversiere zu spielen* (Berlin, 1752); trans. Edward R. Reilly as *On Playing the Flute* (London, 1966).
RANKEN, MARION: See M.R.
RAOUL, JEAN MARIE: *Méthode de Violoncelle* op. 4 (Paris, [1797]).
RAU, FRITZ: *Das Vibrato auf der Violine* (Leipzig, 1922).
REES, ABRAHAM, ed.: *Cyclopaedia* (London, 1819).
REICHA, ANTON: *Cours de composition musicale* (Paris, [1818]).
REICHA, ANTON: *Cours de composition musicale*, trans. and ed. Carl Czerny as *Vollständiges Lehrbuch der musikalischen Composition* (with parallel Fr. and Ger. text), 4 vols. (Vienna, [1832]).
REICHA, ANTON: *Traité de Mélodie* (Paris, 1814).
REICHARDT, JOHANN FRIEDRICH: *Ueber die Pflichten des Ripien-Violinisten* (Berlin and Leipzig, 1776).
REINECKE, CARL: *Die Beethoven'schen Clavier-Sonaten. Briefe an eine Freundin* (Leipzig, 1895); 2nd edn (Leipzig, 1897).
REITZENSTEIN, CARL ERNST PHILIPP VON: See Anon.
RELLSTAB, JOHANN CARL FRIEDRICH: *Versuch über die Vereinigung der musikalischen und oratorischen Declamation* (Berlin, [1786]).
RESTOUT, DENISE, and HAWKINS, ROBERT: *Landowska on Music* (New York, 1965).
RIBEIRO, ALVARO, SJ, ed.: *The Letters of Charles Burney* (Oxford, 1991).
RICHARDS, E. MICHAEL: *The Clarinet of the Twenty-First Century. New Sonic Resources Based on Principles of Acoustics*, 1992/2009, Chapter 4, https://userpages.umbc.edu/~emrich/clarinet21.html [accessed 21 June 2022].
RIEMANN, CARL WILHELM JULIUS HUGO: 'Der Ausdruck in der Musik', *Sammlung musikalische Vorträge*, i, no. 50 (Leipzig, 1883).
RIEMANN, CARL WILHELM JULIUS HUGO: *Musikalische Dynamik und Agogik: Lehrbuch der musikalische Phrasierung* (Hamburg, 1884).
RIEMANN, CARL WILHELM JULIUS HUGO: *Musik-Lexikon* (Leipzig, 1882); 5th edn (1900).
RIEMANN, CARL WILHELM JULIUS HUGO: *New Pianoforte-School/Neue Klavierschule*, 12 pts. (London, [1897–1910]).
RIEPEL, JOSEPH: *Anfangsgründe zur musikalischen Setzkunst* (Regensburg etc., 1752–68). *Gründliche Erklärung der Tonordnung* (Frankfurt-am-Main and Leipzig, 1757).
RIES, FERDINAND: See Wegeler.
RIGGS, ROBERT D.: 'Articulation in Mozart's and Beethoven's Sonatas for Piano and Violin' (diss., Harvard University, 1987).
RITTER, A.: 'Einiges über Concertmeisterthum', *Musikalisches Wochenblatt*, ii (1871), 291ff.
ROBBERECHTS, ANDRÉ: MS notebook, Conservatoire royal de Bruxelles, MS 61.365.
ROBINSON, OLIVIA CLAIRE SANDERS: 'Towards a Declamatory Performance in Schubert Lieder' (diss., Edith Cowan University, Western Australia, 2020).
ROCKSTRO, WILLIAM SMYTH: *Jenny Lind: A Record and Analysis of the "Method" of the Late Madam Jenny Lind-Goldschmidt [. . .] together with a Selection of Cadenze, Solfeggio, Abellimenti, etc. [. . .] edited by Otto Goldschmidt* (London, 1894).
ROMBERG, BERNHARD HEINRICH: *Violoncell Schule* (Berlin and Posen, 1840); trans. as *A Complete Theoretical and Practical School for the Violoncello* (London, 1840).
ROSEN, CHARLES: *Critical Entertainments* (Cambridge, MA, 2000).
ROSEN, CHARLES, and TEMERSO, CATHERINE: *The Joy of Playing, the Joy of Thinking: Conversations about Art and Performance* (Paris, 2016).

ROSENBLUM, SANDRA, P.: *Performance Practices in Classic Piano Music* (Bloomington and Indianapolis, 1988).

ROSTAL, MAX: *Beethoven: The Sonatas for Piano and Violin. Thoughts on Their Interpretation* (London, 1985); trans. Anna M. Rosenberg and Horace D. Rosenberg from Beethoven. *Die Sonaten für Klavier und Violine* (München, 1981).

ROTHSCHILD, FRITZ: *The Lost Tradition: Musical Performance in the Time of Mozart and Beethoven* (London, 1961).

ROUSSEAU, JEAN JACQUES: *Dictionnaire de musique* (Paris, 1768).

RUDOLF, MAX: 'Ein Beitrag zur Geschichte der Temponahme bei Mozart', *Mozart-Jahrbuch* (1976–77), 204ff.

SAINT-SAËNS, CAMILLE: *Souvenirs* (Paris, 1900); trans. E. G. Rich as *Musical Mémoires* (London, 1921).

SASLOV, ISIDOR: 'Tempos in the String Quartets of Joseph Haydn' (diss., Indiana University, 1969).

SAURET, EMILE: *Gradus ad Parnassum du violiniste* op. 36 (Leipzig, [c. 1890]).

SAWADO, TOMOYUKI: *History of Vibrato Usage in Orchestral Performance*, https://www.fugue.us/Vibrato_History_E.html.

SCHEIBE, JOHANN ADOLF: *Ueber die musikalische Composition, erster Theil: Die Theorie der Melodie und Harmonie* (Leipzig, 1773).

SCHENK, ERICH: 'Zur Aufführungspraxis des Tremolo bei Gluck' in Joseph Schmidt-Görg (ed.), *Anthony von Hoboken: Festschrift zum 77. Geburtstag* (Mainz, 1962).

SCHETKY, JOHANN GEORG CHRISTOPH: *Practical and Progressive Lessons for the Violoncello* (London, [1813]).

SCHILLING, GUSTAV, ed.: *Encyclopädie der gesammten musikalischen Wissenschaften* (Stuttgart, 1835–38).

SCHINDLER, ANTON: *Biographie von Ludwig van Beethoven* (Münster, 1840) 3rd expanded edition in 2 vols (Münster, 1860).

SCHOLZ, RICHARD: *Die Vortragskunst in der Musik mit besonderer Berücksichtigung des Violinvortrages. Katechismus für Lehrende und Lernende*, 2nd edn (Hannover, [1892]).

SCHÖNBERG, ARNOLD: Serenade op. 24 (Copenhagen and Leipzig, W. Hansen, 1924), preface.

SCHOTEL, B.: 'Schumann and the Metronome' in A. Walker (ed.), *Robert Schumann: The Man and His Music* (London, 1972); rev. 2nd edn (1976), 109ff.

SCHRÖDER, HERMANN: *Die Kunst des Violinspiels* (Cologne, 1887).

SCHRÖDER, HERMANN: *Preis-Violinschule* [...] *verbesserte und vermehrte Ausgabe* (Leipzig, 1894). Original edition (Köln, 1880).

SCHUBART, CHRISTIAN DANIEL FRIEDRICH: *Ideen zu einer Ästhetik der Tonkunst* (Vienna, 1806).

SCHUBERT, FRANZ: Impromptus, ed. Hugo Riemann (Henry Litolff Verlag, n.d.).

SCHUBERT, JOHANN FRIEDRICH: *Neue Singe-Schule oder gründliche und vollständige Anweisung zur Singkunst* (Leipzig, [1804]).

SCHUBERT, LOUIS: *Violinschule nach modernen Principien* op. 50 (Brunswick, [1883]); trans. T. Baker as *Violin Method in Accordance with Modern Principles* (New York, n.d.).

SCHULZ, JOHANN ABRAHAM PETER: See Sulzer.

SCHWARZ, BORIS: *The Great Masters of the Violin* (New York, 1983).

SEOH, HYUN JYUNG: *Articulation and Arpeggiation in the Prélude, Fugue et Variation, Op. 18, and Pastorale, Op. 19, by César Franck (1822–1890)* (DMA diss. University of Houston, 2016).

ŠEVČÍK, OTAKAR: *Schule der Bogentechnik* op. 2 (Leipzig, 1895); ed. Brett (London, 1901).

ŠEVČÍK, OTAKAR: *Schule der Violine-technik* op. 1 (Leipzig, 1881).

SEYFRIED, IGNAZ VON: *Ludwig van Beethoven's Studien im Generalbasse, Contrapuncte und in der Compositionslehre* (Vienna, 1832).
SFILIO, FRANCESCO: *Nuova Scuola Violinistica Italiana* (Varese, Zecchini, 2002).
SHAWE-TAYLOR, DESMOND: 'Verdi and His Singers' in *Overture Opera Guides. Simon Boccanegra* (London, 2011), 26ff.
SHEPPARD, WILLIAM: *A New Pianoforte Preceptor* (London, 1824).
SIEBER, FERDINAND: *Katechismus der Gesangkunst* (Leipzig, 1862).
SINGER, EDMUND, and SPEIDEL, WILHELM (eds): Sonaten für Pianoforte und Violine von Ludwig van Beethoven (Stuttgart, Cotta, 1887).
SITT, HANS: *Technische Studien für Violine* op. 92 (Leipzig, 1905).
SMART, SIR GEORGE: Papers, British Library Dept, of Manuscripts, Add. 41771-9.
SOMFAI, LASLO: 'How to Read and Understand Haydn's Notation in its Chronologically Changing Concepts' in Eva Badura-Skoda (ed.), *Joseph Haydn: Bericht über den Internationalen Joseph Haydn Kongress, Wien . . . 1982* (Munich, 1986), 23ff.
SPOHR, LOUIS: *Louis Spohr Lebenserinnerungen*, ed. F. Göthel (Tutzing, 1968).
SPOHR, LOUIS: *Louis Spohr's Selbstbiographie*, i (Cassel and Göttingen, 1860), ii (Cassel and Göttingen, 1861) trans. as *Louis Spohr's Autobiography* (London, 1865).
SPOHR, LOUIS: *Tagebuch oder Merkwürdigkeiten einer musicalischen Reise*, Ms. 1802, http://www.spohr-briefe.de/briefe-einzelansicht?m=1802050629.
SPOHR, LOUIS: *Violinschule* (Vienna, [1833]); trans. John Bishop as *Louis Spohr's Celebrated Violin School* (London, [1843]); trans. Stephen Heller as *École ou Méthode pour le Violon* (Paris, [c. 1833/1835]); *Spohr's Violin School*, ed. Henry Holmes (London, [1878]).
STADLEN, PETER: 'Schindler and the Conversation Books', *Soundings*, vii (1978), 2ff.
STADLEN, PETER: 'Schindler's Beethoven Forgeries', *Musical Times*, cxviii (1977), 551ff.
STARKE, FRIEDRICH: *Wiener Pianoforte-Schule* (Vienna, 1819).
STEANE, JOHN BARRY: *The Grand Tradition. Seventy Years of Singing on Record* (Portland, 1974).
STEIBELT, DANIEL: *Méthode de piano* (Leipzig, [1809]).
STEINHAUSEN, FRIEDRICH ADOLF: *Die Physiologie der Bogenfuehrung auf den Streichinstrumenten* (Leipzig, 1903).
STOWELL, ROBIN: *Violin Technique and Performance Practice in the Late-Eighteenth and Early-Nineteenth Centuries* (Cambridge, 1985).
STOWELL, ROBIN, ed.: *Performing Beethoven* (Cambridge, 1994).
STRAETEN, EDMUND VAN DER: *The Romance of the Fiddle: The Origin of the Modern Virtuoso and the Adventures of His Ancestors* (London, 1911).
STRUNK, OLIVER: *Source Readings in Music History* (New York, 1952).
SULZER, JOHANN GEORG, ed.: *Allgemeine Theorie der schönen Künste*, 2 vols. (Leipzig, 1771–74), 2nd rev. edn (Leipzig, 1792–94): contains many articles on music by Johann Peter Kirnberger and Johann Abraham Peter Schulz; the former wrote articles from A to R and the latter those from S to Z as well as assisting with and editing earlier articles.
SWOBODA, AUGUST: *Allgemeine Theorie der Tonkunst* (Vienna, 1826).
TAGLIAVINI, LUIGI FERDINANDO: 'L'arte di »non lasciar vuoto lo strumento«. Appunti sulla prassi cembalistica italiana nel Cinque e Seicento', *Rivista italiana di musicologia*, x (1975), 360ff.
TALSMA, WILLEM: *Wiedergeburt der Klassiker* (Innsbruck, 1980).

TANS'UR, WILLIAM: *A New Musical Grammar, and Dictionary: or, A General Introduction to the Whole Art of Music* 3rd edn (London, 1756).

TANS'UR, WILLIAM: *A New Musical Grammar: or The Harmonical Speculator, with Philosophical Demonstrations on the Nature of Sound* (London, 1746).

TARTINI, GIUSEPPI: *Traité des agréments de la musique*, ed. E. R. Jacobi (Celle and New York, 1961).

TAYLOR, FRANKLIN: articles 'Appoggiatura', 'Phrasing', and 'Shake' in Sir George Grove (ed.): *A Dictionary of Music and Musicians*, 4 vols. (London, 1879, 1880, 1883, 1890).

TEMPERLEY, NICHOLAS: 'Berlioz and the Slur', *Music & Letters*, l (1969), 388ff.

TEMPERLEY, NICHOLAS: 'Haydn's Tempos in *The Creation*', *Early Music*, xix (1991), 235ff.

TERTIS, LIONEL: *Beauty of Tone in String Playing* (London, 1938).

THALBERG, SIGISMOND: *L'Art du chant appliqué au piano* op. 70 (Paris, [1853]).

THAYER, ALEXANDER WHEELOCK: *Ludwig van Beethovens Leben*, 3 Vols (Berlin, 1866–79).

TOEPLITZ, URI: 'Über die Tempi in Mozart's Instrumentalmusik', *Mozart-Jahrbuch* (1986), 171ff.

TOFT, ROBERT: 'The Expressive Pause: Punctuation, Rests, and Breathing in England 1770–1850', *Performance Practice Review*, vii (1994), 199ff.

TOMICICH, FRANCESCO SERAFINO: *Il fanciullo triestino al piano-forte o sia Metodo elementare pel piano-forte compilato sulle opere dei migliori autori* (Trieste, 1850).

TOSI, PIER FRANCESCO: *Opinioni de' cantori antici e moderni, o sieno Osservazioni sopra il canto figurato* (Bologna, 1723). See also Galliard and Agricola.

TROMLITZ, JOHANN GEORG: *Ausführlicher und gründlicher Unterricht die Flöte zu spielen* (Leipzig, 1791); trans. and ed. Ardal Powell as *The Virtuoso Flute-Player* (Cambridge, 1991).

TÜRK, DANIEL GOTTLOB: *Klavierschule oder Anweisung zum Klavierspielen für Lehrer und Lernende mit kritischen Anmerkungen* (Leipzig and Halle, 1789); 2nd enlarged edn (Leipzig and Halle, 1802).

TURNER, E. O.: 'Tempo Variation: With Examples from Elgar', *Music & Letters*, xix (1938), 308ff.

VACCAI, NICOLA: *Metodo pratico di canto italiano per camera* (London, 1832).

VALENTINE, THOMAS: *Dictionary of Terms Used in Music*, 2nd edn (London, 1824).

VAN TASSEL, ERIC: '"Something Utterly New": Listening to Schubert Lieder. 1: Vogl and the Declamatory Style', *Early Music*, xxv (1997), 702ff.

VOGLER, GEORG JOSEPH: *Kuhrpfälzische Tonschule* (Mannheim, 1778).

WACKENRODER, WILHELM HEINRICH: *Herzensergiessungen eines kunstliebenden Klosterbuders* (Berlin, 1797).

WAGNER, RICHARD: *Gesammelte Schriften und Dichtungen*, 10 vols., 2nd edn (Leipzig, 1887–88); ed. and trans. William Ashton Ellis as *Richard Wagner's Prose Works*, 8 vols. (London, 1892–99).

WAGNER, RICHARD: *Sämtliche Werke*, xxx: *Dokumente zur Entstehung und ersten Aufführung des Bühnenweihfestspiels Parsifal*, ed. Martin Geck and Egon Voss (Mainz, 1970).

WAGNER, RICHARD: *Ueber die Aufführung des Tannhäuser eine Mittheilung an die Dirigenten und Darsteller dieser Oper* (Zürich, 1852).

WALKER, ERNEST: 'The Appoggiatura', *Music & Letters*, v (1924), 121ff.

WALTHER, JOHANN GOTTFRIED: *Musicalisches Lexicon* (Leipzig, 1732).

WARRACK, JOHN: *Carl Maria von Weber* (Cambridge, 1968).

WASIELEWSKY, J. W. VON: *Das Violoncell und seine Geschichte* (Leipzig, 1889).

WATKIN, DAVID: 'Beethoven's Sonatas for Piano and Cello: Aspects of Technique and Performance' in Robin Stowell (ed.), *Performing Beethoven* (Cambridge, 1994), 89ff.

WEBER, GOTTFRIED: *Allgemeine Musiklehre zum Selbstunterricht für Lehre und Lernende* (Darmstadt, 1822).

WEBER, GOTTFRIED: *Allgemeine Musiklehrer zur Selbstunterricht für Lehrer und Lernende. Dritte . . . Auflage, vermehrt mit einer Erklärung aller in Musikalien vorkommenden italiänischen Kunstwörter* (Mainz, 1831).

WEBER, GOTTFRIED: *Versuch einer geordneten Theorie der Tonsetzkunst* (Mainz, 1817–21); trans. J. F. Warner as *Theory of Musical Composition*, 2 vols. (London, 1846).

WEGELER, FRANZ GERHARDT, and RIES, FERDINAND: *Biographische Notizen über Ludwig van Beethoven* (Koblenz, 1838).

WEIPPERT, JOHN ERHARDT: *The Pedal Harp Rotula, and New Instructions for That Instrument* (London, [c. 1800]).

WEISS, CHARLES: *A New Methodical Instruction Book for the Flute* (London, [c. 1821]).

*Wiener allgemeine musikalische Zeitung*, ed. Ignaz von Schönholz, 1 vol. (Vienna, 1813).

WILHEMJ, AUGUST, and BROWN, JAMES: *A Modern School for the Violin*, 6 pts. (London, 1899–1900).

WILLENT-BORDOGNI, JEAN-BAPTISTE-JOSEPH: *Méthode complète pour le basson* (Paris, 1844).

WILLIAMS, PETER, 'Two Case Studies in Performance Practice and the Details of Notation, 1: J. S. Bach and 2/4 Time', *Early Music*, xxi (1993), 613ff.

WINRAM, J.: *Violin Playing and Violin Adjustment* (Edinburgh and London, 1908).

WOLDEMAR, MICHEL: *Grande méthode ou étude élémentaire pour le violon* (Paris, [c. 1800]), 2nd edn (Paris, [c. 1803]).

WOLDEMAR, MICHEL, ed.: *Méthode de violon par L. Mozart rédigée par Woldemar, élève de Lolli* (Paris, 1801).

WOLF, GEORG FRIEDRICH: *Kurzer aber deutlicher Unterricht im Klavierspiel* (Göttingen, 1783).

WOLF, GEORG FRIEDRICH: *Kurzgefasstes muskalisches Lexikon* (Halle, 1792).

WOLF, GEORG FRIEDRICH: *Unterricht in Klavierspielen. Zweite, ganz umgearbeitete Ausgabe* (Halle, 1784).

WOLF, GEORG FRIEDRICH: *Unterricht im Klavierspiel. Dritte, verbesserte und vermehrte Auflage* (Halle, 1789).

WOLFE, JOE; FLETCHER, NEVILLE HORNER; and SMITH, JORDAN: 'Interactions between Wind Instruments and Their Players', *Acta Acustica United with Acustica*, ci (2015), 211ff.

WOOD, SIR HENRY: *The Gentle Art of Singing* (Oxford, 1927).

WRAGG, J.: *The Flute Preceptor* (London, c. 1795).

ZASLAW, NEAL: 'The Compleat Orchestral Musician', *Early Music*, vii (1979), 46ff.

ZASLAW, NEAL: 'Mozart's Tempo Conventions', *International Musicological Society Congress Report*, xi (Copenhagen, 1972), 720ff.

ZASLAW, NEAL: 'The Orchestral Musician Completed', *Early Music*, viii (1980), 71f.

ZEHETER, MATTHÄUS, and WINKLER, MAX: *Vollständige theoretisch-praktische Generalbass- und Harmonielehrer* (Nördlingen, 1845).

ZIMMERMANN, PIERRE JOSEPH GUILLAUME: *Encyclopédie du pianiste compositeur*, 3 vols. (Paris, [1840]).

# Index

*For the benefit of digital users, indexed terms that span two pages (e.g., 52–53) may, on occasion, appear on only one of those pages.*

Abschnitt  182, 186
Abstossen  279, 280f, 287–88
Abzug  283–84, 306, 307–8
accelerando  559, 562–63, 578, 582–83, 585, 588–89, 592, 596–97, 601, 602–3, 610
accent abbreviations
   *ffp*  81
   *mfp*  81
accent / accentuation  7, 185–86, 189, 200–1, 217, 299, 303–4, 960
   agogic  61–71, 166–67, 693, 817
   expressive  9, 20–21, 23–35, 36–37, 134
   grammatical  9–10
   metrical  10, 15–22, 23, 36, 37, 49–50, 98–99
   oratorical  9, 23, 25, 36, 70
   pathetic  9, 23, 36
   percussive  72–74
   rhetorical  9
   rhythmic  134, 135–36
   structural  9, 18, 31–32, 37, 86
accent signs
   ◀  135–36
   |  137–47
   ^  36, 70–71, 102–3, 135–36, 152, 961
   ʌ  143
   >  107, 110, 135–36, 147, 961–62
   v  135–36
   <>  110–11, 172, 567, 955, 960
   +  135–36
   >>>>  339–40, 954
   ^^^^  339–40
   ⸺  134–35
   ⸺  135–36
   ☐  179–80
   - ⸗ ⸗  169–79, 339

acciaccatura  629–30, 658, 842–43
accompaniment figures  20–21
Adagio / *adagio*  360, 379, 383, 389–90, 489, 512–14, 521–22, 623, 717, 772
Adam, Jean Louis  224, 265–66, 285, 305, 327, 565–66, 589, 833–34
Adams, John S.  959–60
Addison, John  198
Adlung, Jakob  843–44
*affetuoso*  361
*agitato*  597
agogic accent  62, 65, 68–71. See also inequality / *agogic*
Agricola, Johann Friedrich  137, 319, 322, 568, 718, 761, 862, 910, 978
*Airs à broder*  732
Alard, Jean Delphin  346, 685, 1005–06
Albani, Emma  1003
Alexander, Joseph  626
Alkan, Charles-Valentin
   Douze Études  664–65
*alla breve / alla cappella / alla semibreve.* See metre
Allegranti, Teresa Maddalene  715–16
*allegretto*  523–24, 540
*allegro*  383, 489, 523–24, 735
*allegro assai*  541
*allegro con brio*  544–45
*allegro maestoso / allegro moderato*  383, 400–1, 535
*allegro vivace*  541–42
Almenräder, Carl  973–74
Alonso, Luis  965–67, 970, 1004
Altenburg, Johann Ernst  973
Amadeus Quartet  882
*amoroso (con amore, amorosamente)*  510–11, 546–47

*anacrusis. See* upbeat / Auftakt
*andante* 507, 516, 523–33, 735
*andante amoroso* 546–47
*andante cantabile* 548
*andante grave* 517
*andante molto* 444–45, 529–30. *See also molto andante*
*andantino* 444–45, 523–29
Andersch, Johann Daniel 287–88, 307–8, 471–72, 483, 527–28
André, Johann
  *Der Töpfer* 235
André, (Johann) Anton 797
  *Lieder und Gesänge* 170–71, 549, 555, 598
  String Quartets op. 14/15 322, 549, 551–53, 597, 924
*animato* (*animoso, con anima*) 547–48, 849
anticipation grace. *See* Sliding effects
anticipatory note 630, 662, 666, 668–69
Apold, Felix 4n.5
*Appoggiando. See* arpeggiation (piano)
*appoggiatura* 306, 629–30, 631–32, 639–40, 661, 662, 666, 668, 670–71, 717–18, 723–24, 740–42, 759–60
  prosodic 3
*appoggiature préparée* 639
*appoggiature rhythmique* 663
Arne, Thomas
  *Artaxerxes* 198
arpeggiation (piano) 169, 220, 327, 554, 556, 803
articulation
  expressive 181
  structural 181, 185–86
articulation marks 595–96
Artôt, Alexandre Joseph 411–12
Asioli, Bonifazio 38–39, 42, 77–78, 110, 508
asynchrony 3, 714–15, 805–6, 808–9, 827–29, 832–40
Auer, Leopold 347f, 348f, 349f, 1012

Bach, C. P. E. 45–46, 169–70, 187, 194–95, 220, 265–66, 268, 274, 276, 283, 318–19, 323, 542–43, 560, 562, 563–64, 591, 593, 626, 639, 642–43, 670, 684, 692, 708, 789–39, 843–44, 863

Sechs Sonaten . . . mit veränderten Reprisen 580, 716–17
Sonaten für Kenner und Liebhaber 169–70
Bach, J. C. 640
  *Cefalo & Procris* 53, 86–87, 115
  *La clemenza di Scipione* 198–99, 640, 726
  *L'Endimione* 115
Bach, J. S. 440–41, 480, 769–70, 863, 882–83
  B minor Partita for solo violin 212
  *St. Matthew Passion* 749
Bacon, Richard Mackenzie 549
Bailleux, Antoin 969
Baillot, Pierre 51–52, 79–80, 138, 139–40, 182–83, 201–2, 294, 325–26, 338, 346, 353–54, 377, 380, 381, 389–90, 393, 400, 569, 639, 649, 663, 674, 689, 694, 775, 897–98, 903–6, 919, 955, 964–65, 981, 983–84, 985–86, 993–94
  *L'art du violon* 382, 386–87, 391–92, 395, 402–7
  Violin Concerto no. 2 406
*balancement* 955–56, 963, 969
Barbirolli, John 884–86
Baroque 209–10, 226–27
Barth, Richard 7–9
Bartók, Bella 450
bassoon 973–74, 976
Batta, Alexandre 999–1000
*battemen* 717
*battute* 241–42
Baudiot, Charles-Nicholas 395
Bauer-Lechner, Natalie 7–9
Bauernfeld, Eduard von 755–56
Bausch, Sebastian 601n.76
Bayly, Anselm 549, 715
beaming 52–53
beautiful performance (*schöner Vortrag*) 4–5, 7, 36–37, 80, 200–1, 886–87
*Bebung* 323, 903, 908–9, 953–54, 955–56, 957–58, 961, 967, 976, 989–90, 995–96
  clavichord *Bebung* 169–70, 318–19, 982–83

Beethoven, Carl van 922–23
Beethoven, Ludwig van 3–4, 30–31, 77–78, 91–92, 98–99, 101, 107, 118–19, 147, 236, 247–51, 267–68, 308, 312–14, 380, 418, 432, 447–50, 456–57, 465–69, 489–90, 521–22, 527, 540, 542, 553, 592, 601–2, 618–19, 675, 677–78, 680–81, 764, 768, 769–70, 775–76, 922–23
  Bagatelle op. 33 604
  Cantata *Meeresstille und glückliche Fahrt* op. 112 493*t*
  Cello Sonata op. 69 301–2
  *Chorfantasie* op. 80 53–54, 148, 707–8, 709
  "Egmont" overture 625
  Die Geschöpfe von Prometheus op. 43 267–68, 419
  *Große Fuge* op. 133 301–2
  "Klage" WoO. 113 465
  Mass in C 489–90
  *Missa solemnis* 121, 247–49, 471–72
  'Nord oder Süd' WoO. 148 609
  Piano Concerto no. 3 846–47
  Piano Sonata op. 2 no. 3 657*f*
  Piano Sonata op. 10 no. 1 605
  Piano Sonata op. 13 856
  Piano Sonata op. 14 no. 2 606
  Piano Sonata op. 26 118–19
  Piano Sonata op. 27 no. 2 856
  Piano Sonata op. 31 no. 2 193
  Piano Sonata op. 53 118–19, 143
  Piano Sonata op. 81a 857
  Piano Sonata op. 106 301–2, 516
  Piano Sonata op. 109 530, 553, 555
  Piano Sonata op. 110 301–2, 553
  Piano Sonata op. 111 247–49, 714
  Piano Trio op. 1 no. 1 434*f*
  Piano Trio op. 70 608
  Piano Trio op. 97 608, 866
  Quintet for piano and wind op. 16 781–82
  Romance in F op. 50 699–700, 837, 945*f*
  Rondo op. 51 667*f*
  Septet op. 20 143, 447–48, 468, 489–90, 532
  String Quartet op. 18 no. 2 456–57
  String Quartet op. 18 no. 4 101, 432, 468, 532
  String Quartet op. 18 no. 5 82, 439–40, 467, 532
  String Quartet op. 18 no. 6 456–57, 459–60, 516
  String Quartet op. 59 no. 1 415, 432, 456–57, 467, 516, 532, 549, 936
  String Quartet op. 59 no. 2 467, 489–90, 866, 877
  String Quartet op. 59 no. 3 82, 211, 467
  String Quartet op. 74 532, 544–45
  String Quartet op. 95 118–19, 247–49, 303–4, 468, 544–45
  String Quartet op. 127 82, 121
  String Quartet op. 130 247–49, 274, 573
  String Quartet op. 131 82, 101, 148, 1015
  String Quartet op. 132 121, 324, 331, 372*f*, 608
  String Quartet op. 135 118–19, 148, 167
  String Trio op. 9 no. 1 414–15, 489–90
  Symphony no. 1 op. 21 467, 532, 544–45, 623
  Symphony no. 2 op. 36 468, 521–22, 544–45, 611, 619–20
  Symphony no. 3 (Eroica) op. 55 467, 479, 480, 488, 618–19, 622–23
  Symphony no. 4 op. 60 419
  Symphony no. 5 op. 67 53–54, 279, 303–4, 313, 419, 459–60, 468, 480, 521–22, 532, 544–45, 619–20, 625, 884–86
  Symphony no. 6 (Pastoral) op. 68, 456–57, 467
  Symphony no. 7 op. 92 267–68, 421, 459–60, 489–90, 532, 621
  Symphony no. 9 (Choral) op. 125 448–49, 468–69, 489–90, 538
  Violin Concerto op. 61 239–40, 780, 780*f*, 945–46
  Violin Sonata op. 12 no. 1 667
  Violin Sonata op. 24 118–19, 940*f*
  Violin sonata op. 30 no. 2 82, 247–49
  Violin Sonata op. 30 no. 3 250–51, 274
  Violin Sonata op. 47 247–49, 412–13, 429, 681–82, 707–8, 783–84

Beethoven, Ludwig van (*cont.*)
   Violin Sonata op. 96  303–4, 312, 555, 687–88, 781
   Violin Sonatas  339, 343–44, 922–23, 940, 1005–06
   *Wellingtons Sieg* op. 91  621
Bellini, Vincenzo  149, 610–11
   *La Sonnambula* "Ah non credea"  810, 871–72, 962
   *I Puritani*  699*f*
Bell-Porter, W. E.  3–4
Bemetzrieder, Anton  684
Benda, Franz  374, 563–64, 568, 580
Bennett, William Sterndale  302*f*
   *The Naiads*  82
Bériot, Charles de  38–39, 72–74, 182–83, 207–10, 288–89, 294, 346, 354, 406, 411–12, 422–31, 651, 655, 658, 695, 884–86, 903, 926, 933–37, 957–58, 1003–04
   Ninth Violin Concerto  430, 937
   *Le Tremolo*  409–10, 429, 962–63
Berlin  411–12, 463–64, 838–39
Berlioz, Hector  98–99, 184–85, 301–2, 305, 314, 517–18, 522, 527–28, 536, 540, 928, 949–50
   *La Damnation de Faust*  450
   *Grande messe des morts*  450
   *Grand traité d'instrumentation et d'orchestration modernes*  325–26
   *Huit scènes de Faust*  450
   "*Le Matin*"  527–28
   *La mort d'Ophélie*  527–28
   *Reverie et caprice*  517–18
   *Romeo and Juliet* op. 17  870
   "Le Spectre de la rose"  517–18
   *Symphonie fantastique*  372*f*, 517–18
   *Te Deum*  527–28
   *Les Troyens*  163, 517–18
Bernacchi, Antonio Maria  895
Bernasconi, Antonia  715–16
Berwald, Franz
   String Quartet in A minor  665–66
Betti, Alfredo  882
Biber, Heinrich  940*f*
Bilson, Malcolm  829
Blanc, J.  1004
Blanchard, Henri  412–13, 997–98

Blumenthal, Casimir von  923
Blumenthal, Joseph von  382–83, 415, 680–81, 923
Blumenthal, Leopold von  923
Boccherini, Luigi  115, 325–26, 405, 917–18
Böhm, Joseph  387–88, 393, 411, 676, 687–88
Bordogni, Marco  999
Boucher, Alexandre  414
bowing. *See* string bowing
Brahms, Johannes  34–35, 36–37, 38–39, 77–78, 126–27, 156, 168–69, 171, 239–40, 263, 271–72, 308–11, 317–18, 421–22, 450–51, 476, 529, 553, 555, 556, 602, 612, 625, 859–60, 888–89, 955–56
   Alto Rhapsody op. 53  104
   Cello Sonata op. 38  834–35
   Cello Sonata op. 99  104
   Clarinet Quintet op. 115  126–27, 145, 149, 309–10
   Double Concerto op. 102  126–27
   *Ein deutsches Requiem* op. 45  104, 483–84
   Horn Trio op. 40  171
   Hungarian dances  944, 953–54
   Liebeslieder-Walzer op. 39  531
   Piano Concerto no. 1  859–60
   Piano Quintet op. 34  104
   Piano Sonata op. 1  104, 126–27, 149
   Piano Trio in B major op. 8  557–58
   Piano Trio op. 87  126–27, 629
   Scherzo op. 4  104
   Serenade op. 16  104
   String Quartet op. 51 no. 1  309–10
   String Quartet op. 51 no. 2  56, 1008
   String Quartet op. 67  309–10
   String Quintet op. 88  104
   String Quintet op. 111  104
   String Sextet op. 18  104
   String Sextet op. 36,  179, 629
   Symphony no. 1 op. 68  145, 531, 557–58
   Symphony no. 2 op. 73  97, 179, 256, 529, 557–58, 870
   Symphony no. 3 op. 90  104
   Symphony no. 4 op. 98  104

*Triumphlied* op. 55  104
Variations on a Theme of Haydn op. 35  104
Violin Concerto op. 77  172, 289, 445, 691
Violin Sonata op. 78  547–48, 557–58, 834–35, 881
Violin Sonata op. 100  529, 945
breathing (singing)  726
Bremner, Robert  987–88, 992
Bridgetower, George Polgreen  784
Brizzi, Antonio  764
Brossard, Sébastien de  512–13
Bruch, Max  339
  Violin Concerto op. 26  168, 251, 965–66
Bruckner, Anton  156
  Symphony no. 3 WAB103  164–65
Brussels (Conservatoire)  406–7, 409, 422, 434
Brymer, Jack  1014–15
Budapest String Quartet  418, 937
Bull, Ole  410n.175
Bülow, Hans von  618, 624–25, 711–12, 858–59, 929–30
Buonfigli, Enrico  962
Burkhard, Johann Andreas Christian  307, 781, 968
Burney, Charles  15–16, 21–22, 241–42, 246–47, 715–16, 913
Busby, Thomas  138, 372–73, 562–63, 959–60

*cadenza* (*cadence*)  725, 734, 735, 776, 784–86, 788–89, 984
Cafarello (Caffarelli), Gaetano Majorano  731–32, 978
*calando*  78–79, 553, 556, 596–97
Callcott, John Wall  14–16, 53–54
Cambini, Giuseppe Maria  323, 917–18
Campagnoli, Bartolomeo  167, 352, 355, 382–83, 392, 508, 512–13, 520–21, 535–36, 548, 649–50, 696, 884, 955–56
Cannabich, Carl  374, 588–89, 590
Cannabich, Christian  377–78
*cantabile*  361, 516, 548, 554, 723–24, 735, 756–57
Capet, Lucien (Capet Quartet)  439–40

caprice  589
Carestini, Giovanni  973, 978
Cartier, Jean Baptiste  707, 774
Castil-Blaze, François Henri Joseph  15–16, 484
Catel, Charles-Simon  13n.13
Cavatina  723
*cercar della nota / cercar la nota*  668, 888–89, 890–91, 911, 922
Chabran, Francesco  485–86
chaconne  15–16
Chélard, Hippolyte André Jean Baptiste
  *Macbeth*  547–48
Cherubini, Maria Luigi Carlo Zenobio  98–99, 147, 270, 465, 764
  *Anacreon* overture  115
  *Medée* overture  298
  Requiem in C minor  107, 490–91, 497*t*
  Requiem in D minor  497*t*
  String Quartet no. 1 in E flat  107, 432*f*, 490–91
  String Quartet no. 2 in C  544–45
  String Quartet no. 4 in E op. posth.  544–45
  String Quartet no. 5 in F op. posth.  490–91
  String Quartets  244, 497*t*
*chevrottement*  957–58, 980
Chopin, Frédéric François  98–99, 563–64, 577, 611, 664–65, 675
  Impromptu op. 36 no. 2  581*f*
  Mazurka op. 6 no. 3  193
  Nocturne op. 9 no. 2  857
  Nocturnes op. 15  577
Chorley, Henry Fothergill  623, 767–68, 996–97
chromatic notes  46–47
church music style  739, 740
Cimarosa, Domenico  610–11, 732, 736
  *L'amante combattuto*  369*f*, 372–73
  *Il matrimonio segreto*  697*f*
  *Il sacrificio d'Abramo*  745*f*, 932*f*
clarinet (*vibrato*)  976
Classical / Viennese Classical  21–22, 28, 187, 226–27, 344, 409–10, 411, 414, 418, 421, 431, 465, 513–14, 621, 643, 667, 764, 767–68, 775, 781–82, 829, 843–44, 884

Clementi, Muzio 117, 191, 223–24, 241–42, 284–85, 299–300, 312, 314, 465, 485–86, 546, 553, 555, 591, 593, 639, 656, 842–43, 844–45
  *La Chasse* op. 16  875
  Piano Sonata op. 26  875
  Piano Sonata op. 40 no. 1  705, 875
  Piano Sonata op. 50 no. 1  546
  Piano Sonata op. 50 no. 2  546
Clinton, John  907
close shake. *See* Trembling effects
Colombat, Marc  964–65
*contra-tempo*  60
*corona*  788. *See also fermata*
correct performance (*richtiger Vortrag*),  7, 36–37, 200–1, 886–87
Corrette, Michel  355–56, 359n.39
Corri, Domenico  60, 68, 135–36, 199, 510–11, 513–14, 517–18, 534, 541–42, 548, 568–69, 646, 654, 660, 671–72, 693, 738–39, 754, 810, 889–90
  *A Select Collection*  195–99, 640, 648, 654, 724, 752, 792, 792f, 891–92, 911
Corri, Haydn  672, 799
Corri, Philip Anthony  40–41, 49, 60, 152, 312, 548, 554, 556, 637–38, 652, 671–72, 707, 847–50
Cossmann, Bernhard  1007–08
*coulé*  629–30
Couperin, François  832–33
Cramer, Carl Friedrich
  *Magazin der Musik*  169–70, 987–88
Cramer, François (Franz / Francis)  381
Cramer, John Baptist (Johann Baptist)  117, 129, 842–43, 847
Cramer, Wilhelm
  bowstroke  374, 381–82, 388, 390–91, 394–95
Crelle, August Ludwig  27–28, 38–39, 59–60, 69, 306, 595–96, 782, 878, 922–23
*crescendo*  76, 78–79, 111–23, 592, 726
  "hairpin"  149, 599
Crescentini, Girolamo  736
Crickboom, Mathieu  348f, 349f, 1009
Crome, Robert  355–56

Crotch, William  463–64, 508, 512–13, 515–16
Cusins, William  770
Czerny, Carl  3–4, 21–22, 38–39, 43, 49, 102–3, 125–26, 161–62, 171, 183–84, 200–1, 241–42, 265–66, 301–2, 306, 311–12, 448–49, 463–65, 547, 550–51, 555, 592–95, 596–97, 608, 631–32, 651–52, 676, 677–83, 685, 691–92, 781–87, 804–5, 835, 843–44, 852–56
  *Grande fantaisie en forme de Sonate*, opp. 143, 144, 145  103
  *Grand Polonaise Brillante* op. 118  103
  *Huit Nocturnes Romantiques*, op. 604 no. 1  103
  Piano Sonata op. 7  103
  Piano Sonata op. 57  103
  Piano Sonata op. 124  103, 683
  *Sonate Militaire et Brillante* op. 119  103

*da capo*  732
Dancla, Charles  380, 778, 1004, 1005
Dannelley, John Feltham  111–12
Dannreuther, Edward  638, 657f, 699, 710
David, Ferdinand  139, 172, 239–40, 251, 288–89, 335–36, 346, 412–13, 415–16, 422–34, 439–40, 778, 780, 816, 903, 936, 940, 1005–06
  *Dur und Moll* op. 39  172, 338
  *Die hohe Schule des Violinspiels*  34–35
David, Giacomo  731–32
Davies, Fanny  104, 169, 881, 886–87
Davydov, Karl  900n.39, 947
Deacon, Harry Collings  963, 978, 997–98, 1000
Debussy, Claude  860
*decrescendo*  78–79, 550–51
Delusse, Charles,  972, 987
Dessauer, Heinrich  347f–49f
*détaché*. *See* string bowing
Dibdin, Charles  485–86, 513, 549
  *The Padlock*  198–99, 205
*diluendo*  583
*diminuendo*  76, 78–79, 550–51, 583, 592, 596–97, 598, 726
  "hairpin"  550–51, 599
*dolce / dolcissimo*  323, 361, 553, 849

INDEX 1045

Domenego, Melanie 963
Dommer, Arrey von 16–17, 24–25, 70, 74, 124, 139, 535–36, 541–42, 809–10, 995–96
Dömpfe, Gustav 624–25
Doni, Giovanni Battista 888
Donington, Robert 448n.10, 963–64, 988
Donizetti, Gaetano 610–11
   *Anna Bolena* 123, 205, 836*f*
   *Lucia di Lammermoor* 932*f*
   *Parisina* 244
Dont, Jacob 140, 239–40, 687–88
*Doppelschlag* 696
*Doppelvorschlag* 741
Dotzauer, Justus Johann Friedrich 38–39, 42–43, 150–51, 200–1, 231, 327, 395–97, 715–16, 762–63, 898, 947
   *Glockenton* 968, 971, 993
Dounias, Minos 343–44
Dragonetti, Domenico 749, 922–23
Duport, Jean-Louis 354–55, 386–87, 897–98
Duport, Jean-Pierre 748n.67
Duprez, Gilbert 198
Durand, Auguste Frédéric (Duranowski, August Fryderyk) 389–90
Dürr, Walther 551, 755–56
Dussek, Jan Ladislav 123, 147, 236, 547, 555, 563–64, 581–82
   Piano Sonata op. 64 'Le retour à Paris' 117, 547, 556
   String Quartet op. 60 no. 1 117
   String Quartet op. 60 no. 2 91–92, 547
Dvořák, Antonín 98–99, 156, 339, 456–57, 476, 518–20, 522, 529, 540, 542, 546, 691
   Cello Concerto op. 104 177, 428
   *Humoresques* op. 101 531
   Hussite Overture op. 67 546
   *Legendy* op. 59 522, 529
   *Stabat mater* op. 58 529
   String Quartet op. 51 518–20, 531
   String Quartet op. 80 145
   String Quartet op. 96 164–65, 518–20
   String Quartet op. 105 177
   String Quartet op. 106 163–65, 628
   Symphonic Variations op. 78 531
   *Te Deum* op. 103 179
   Violin Sonata op. 57 163, 177
dynamic instructions 75, 80–81
   *forte assai* 111–12
   *fortissimo* 75
   *più forte* 77–78
   *poco forte* 75, 77–78

Eberhardt, Siegfried 1010
Eberl, Anton 107
   Violin Sonata op. 20 488
   Violin Sonata op. 49 647–48
   Violin Sonata op. 50 647–48
Eck, Franz 381–82, 390–91, 590, 613, 676
Eck, Johann Friedrich 375–76, 381–82, 389–90, 590
Ehrlich, Heinrich 623
Eichberg, Julius 434
*Einschnitt* 182, 186, 190, 212
Elgar, Edward (William) 274, 450
   *Enigma Variations* op. 36 175, 881
   Salut d'amour op. 12 929–30
   String Quartet op. 83 168
   Symphony no. 1 op. 55 146–47
   Symphony no. 2 op. 63 956*f*
   Violin Concerto op. 61 948
   Violin Sonata op. 87 168
Elman, Mischa 1012
Elßler, Johann 232, 630
embellishment 378, 562, 564–65, 570, 580–82, 642–43, 671–72, 689, 692–93, 695–96, 713–831, 843–44, 903, 909, 920–21, 927, 930, 932–33, 944, 968–70, 972, 974, 1005–06, 1012
*Empfinsamer Stil* 187
*Encyclopédie de la musique et dictionnaire du Conservatoire* 139–40, 166–67, 172–73
Ernst, Heinrich Wilhelm 347*f*, 999–1000
*espressivo / con espressione* 555, 596–97, 598, 849
Eymar, Ange Marie, comte d' 381–82

Faisst, Immanuel von 656
Fallows, David 529–30
Farinelli (Carlo Broschi) 731–32, 978
*fatto voce* 77–78
Fellowes, Edmund 1007–08

*fermata* 596–97, 602–3, 735, 759–61, 776, 784, 788–800, 857. *See also corona*; pause
  *point d'arrêt* 793, 798
  *point de repos* 793, 798
  *point d'orgue* 799
Ferrari, Domenico 377–78
Ferri, Nicola 1000
Feski, J. *See* Sobolewski, Eduard Johann Friedrich
Fétis, François-Joseph 124, 140, 484, 527, 658, 683–84, 963, 1006
Fiedler, Max 556
Field, John 581
Filipovicz, Elisabeth 923–24
Fink, Gottfried Wilhelm 16–17, 24–25, 156–57, 232, 588
*fioritura* 563–64, 725–26, 743, 769, 781, 788
Fischer, I. Ludwig 759–60
Fischhof, Joseph 609
Flad, Anton
  Oboe Concertino in C 690
*flattemen / flattement / flatté. See* Trembling effects
Fleming, James M. 139
Flesch, Carl 3–4, 7, 183–84, 345–46, 347*f*, 348*f*, 349*f*, 350, 351, 355, 440–42, 945–46, 950, 951, 965, 1010–11
Flonzaley Quartet 882
flute playing 203
Fodor, Josephus Andreas 390–91
Forkel, Johann Nicholaus 470
Förster, Emanuel Aloys
  String Quartets op. 7 551–53
  String Quintet op. 20 551–53
*forzato / forzando / fz/ fzp* 77–78, 86, 98–99, 961–62. *See also sforzando / sforzato / sf / sfz / sfp*
*fouetté. See* string bowing
Franchomme, Auguste-Joseph 1007–08
Franck, César 843–44
Franco-Belgian string playing 4–5, 294, 295, 399, 409–10, 411–12, 415–16, 419–20, 422, 434, 435–36, 438–40, 827, 882, 936, 938, 942, 1008, 1010–11
Fränzl, Ferdinand 390–91
  String Trio op. 17 921

Fränzl, Ignaz 330, 374, 389–90
Friedrich II, King of Prussia 63–64
Friedrich Wilhelm II, King of Prussia 748n.67
Fröhlich Franz Joseph 124, 139, 241–42, 286–87, 327, 382–83, 484, 520–21, 749, 894, 907, 928, 989–90
Fürstenau, Anton Bernhard 203, 685, 807, 907, 909–10, 976, 995–96
Fürtwängler, Wilhelm 624

Galant style 187
Galeazzi, Francesco 110–11, 167, 319, 323, 351–52, 355, 378, 613, 639, 968, 989–90
Galliard, John Ernest 564–65, 910
Galuppi, Baldessare 78–79
  *Anfione* 113–14
  *Antigone* 77–78
  *La diavolessa* 304
García, Manuel (junior) 21–22, 47, 60, 64–65, 69, 193, 198, 204–6, 578, 610–11, 694, 697, 736, 744, 754, 799, 810, 836, 837, 879, 905–6, 930–33, 979–80, 1003
García, Manuel (senior) 578
Gardiner, William 381
Gardoni, Italo 962
Gassmann, Florian 590
  *L'opera seria* 647
Gassner, Franz Xaver 929
Gathy, August 123, 307–8
Gebauer, Johannes 837, 948*f*
*gehend (andante)* 523–24, 531, 533
Geminiani, Francesco 134, 716, 913, 986–87, 988
  "If ever a fond inclination" 197
Gevaert, François-Auguste 334, 420–21
Ghys, Joseph 411–12
*gigue* 63–64
*giocoso* 260
Giordanello (Giuseppe Giordani) 732
Giordani, Tommaso
  *Artaserse* (adapted from Hasse) 792, 911
  *Il Barone di Torre Forte* 196
  *La marchesa Guardinera* 911
  "Sento che in seno" 198

Giuliani, Mauro
 "Variations sur l'Air favori de la
  Molinara" op. 4  906
Gleichmann, Johann Andreas  524–25
glide. *See* Sliding effects
*glissando*. *See* Sliding effects
*Glockenschlag*. *See* Trembling effects
*Glockenton*. *See* Trembling effects
Gluck, Christoph Willibald von  323, 325–26, 768, 769–70
 *Ihiginea in Aulis*  421
 *L'Olimpiade*  911
 *Orfeo ed Euridice*  80–81
 *Semiramide riconosciuta*  75, 643, 911
Goldberg, Louise  382
Gollmick, Carl  102–3, 129–30, 152, 161–62, 221, 488, 513–14, 525, 527, 550–51, 961
Goossens, Leon  1014–15
*grace-note*  630–34, 655–67
*grand détaché*. *See* string bowing
Graun, Carl Heinrich  749–51, 911
*grave*  261–62, 361, 514–16, 517
Grenser, Carl Augustin  908–9
Greulich, Carl Wilhelm  524–25
Grieg, Edvard,  184–85, 860
 Humoresque op. 6 no. 2  872–73
Grinke, Frederick  886–87
Gröber, Anton  410
Grove, Sir George  611
Grün, Jakob  1010–11
*grupetto*. *See* ornaments / ornamentation
Grützmacher, Friedrich  938–41
Grützmacher, Leopold  938–39
Guhr, Carl  395, 400, 406
Gunn, John  973–74, 988
Gurk, Joseph  664, 676–77
Guthmann, Friedrich  543, 586–87

Habeneck, François  16–17, 182–83, 346, 354, 550–51, 1005–06
Halévy, Jacques François Fromental Elias  139–40, 1001–02
Hall, Marie  948
Hallé, Wilma. *See* Neruda, Wilma Norman
Hamilton, James Alexander  169–70, 246–47, 562–63, 895, 959–60

Handel, George Frederic  199, 211, 309, 480, 769–70
Hänflein, Georg  938–39
Hanslick, Eduard  412–13, 529
Happ, Wilhelm,  412–13
harp  284–85
harpsichord  747, 832–33
Haselt-Barth, Maria Wilhelmine  768
Häser, August Ferdinand  742, 799, 922, 924, 992
Häser, Christian Wilhelm  997
Hasse, Johann Adolf  718, 749–51
 *Leucippo*  719f
 *Solimano*  719f
Hauman, Théodore  409–10, 411–12, 415–16, 962, 997–98
Hauptmann, Moritz  16–17, 617, 995–96
Haydn, Joseph  53–54, 98–99, 135–36, 147, 195, 236, 262, 277–78, 305, 308, 330, 406, 415, 462, 464–65, 489, 610–11, 643–44, 700–1, 702, 764, 769–70, 775–76, 844–45
 'Applausus' Cantata  640, 752
 *Armida*  86–87
 Canzonnettas  912–13
 Concertante in B flat (Hob. I: 105)  328
 *Flötenuhrstücke*  232–33, 664, 676–77
 "Nelson" Mass  478–79
 Piano Sonata Hob XVI:52  844–45
 *Die Schöpfung (The Creation)*  464–65, 478, 749–51, 759–60
 *Die sieben letzte Worte*  515–16
 String Quartet op. 9 no. 2  798
 String Quartet op. 17 no. 2  914–15
 String Quartet op. 17 no. 4  86–87
 String Quartet op. 20 no. 3  914–15
 String Quartet op. 33 no. 2  914
 String Quartet op. 50 no. 5  914–15
 String Quartet op. 54 no. 1  394
 String Quartet op. 54 no. 2  702f
 String Quartet op. 55 no. 1  370f
 String Quartet op. 55 no. 2  570
 String Quartet op. 64 no. 2  702f, 794
 String Quartet op. 64 no. 6  702f, 914
 String Quartet op. 71 no. 2  116
 String Quartet op. 74 no. 2  864
 String Quartet op. 74 no. 3  864, 914–15
 String Quartet op. 76 no.1  666

Haydn, Joseph (*cont.*)
  String Quartet op. 76 no. 2  914
  String Quartet op. 76 no. 4  666
  String Quartet op. 77 no. 1  328–29, 794, 864
  String Quartets op. 77  268
  Symphony no. 91  140
  Symphony no. 102  141–42, 292–93
  Symphony no. 104  150–51
Haydn, Michael  706
heavy and light performance  45–46, 79
Heckmann, Robert  943
Heifetz, Jascha  1012
Heine, Heinrich  933
Hellmesberger, Georg
  Grandes Variations  394
Hellmesberger, Joseph Sr.  394, 412–13
Hellmesberger Quartet  411, 412–13, 415–16
Herrmann, Carl  1015
Heroux, Carl  389–90
Herz, Henri  48, 123, 161–62, 169–70, 179–80, 224–25, 582, 687
Herz, Leon  545–46
Hiller, Ferdinand  611
Hiller, Johann Adam  265–66, 303, 323, 372–73, 568, 718, 726, 741, 746, 978
Hindle, Johann  923–24
Hock, Hermann  1015–16
Hoffmann, Ernst Theodor Amadeus  68–69
Hofmann, Heinrich Anton  389–90
Holden, John  18–19, 444, 454n.33, 455, 460–61, 484, 513, 514, 523–24, 645–46, 673–74
Holmes, Henry  350, 435
Holz, Carl  301–2, 608
Hölzl Franz Xaver  478–79
Houle, George  482
Hüllmandel, Nicolas-Joseph  222
Hummel, Johann Nepomuk  19, 21–22, 28–29, 38–39, 49, 59, 107, 135–36, 152, 156–57, 200–1, 265–66, 294, 306, 463–64, 472–73, 480, 543, 581, 592, 673, 674, 676, 684, 685, 686, 700–1, 710, 805, 851
  Piano Concerto in A minor op. 85  593–95, 805–6

inequality / *agogic*  62, 63–64, 65, 274, 305, 817, 882–83, 884–86
  *notes inégales*  882–83

Jaell, Alfred  961–62
James William Nelson  525–26, 535–36, 908–9
Janitsch, Anton  375–76, 585–86
Jansa, Leopold  394
jazz  4, 65–66, 889, 950, 951, 1014–15
Jeitteles, Ignaz  782–83
Joachim, Joseph  2, 4–5, 38–39, 70–71, 172, 184–85, 239–40, 271–72, 289, 308, 317–18, 411, 418, 439–40, 464–65, 554, 561, 612, 658–59, 676, 687–88, 713, 838–39, 949–50, 951, 953–54, 993–94, 1007–08
  recordings  567–68, 826–27, 829, 944, 1010–11, 1013, 1016–17
  Romance in C major  315–16, 663, 699–700, 837
Joachim, Joseph and Moser, Andreas
  *Violinschule*  139, 426, 438–39, 567, 602, 691–92, 806–7, 944, 1008
Jockisch, Reinhold  344, 442
Jommelli, Niccolò  483–84
  *Demofoonte*  112
  *L'Olimpiade*  112
Jousse, John  49–50, 382–83, 485–86, 508, 513, 525–26, 541–42, 549, 688–89, 992
Junghanss, Johann Christian Gottleib  550–51
Junker, Carl Ludwig  613–14

Kalkbrenner, Frédéric (Friedrich)  38–39, 43, 47–48, 59, 306, 596, 691–92, 851, 852
Kauer, Ferdinand  378
Kell, Reginald  1014–15
Kirnberger, Johann Philipp  13–14, 258, 368–69, 453, 454–55, 510
Klauwell, Otto  4–5, 713–14, 856–57
Klengel, Julius  1015
Klindworth, Karl  314–15, 316–17, 709
Klingler, Karl  837, 840, 884–86, 1013
The Klingler String Quartet  44–45, 439–40, 612–13, 826–27, 880–81, 882, 884–86

Knecht, Justin Heinrich 44–45, 49–50, 123–24, 138, 265–66, 483, 523–24, 693, 982–83
Koch, Heinrich Christoph 9, 19, 21–22, 23–24, 36, 61–63, 102–3, 111–12, 123–24, 134–35, 192, 241–42, 246–47, 265–66, 276–77, 279–80, 307, 312, 324, 457–58, 483, 488, 507, 520–21, 541–42, 547–48, 568, 589, 650, 663, 670, 685, 740, 982–83
Kogel, Gustav Friedrich 144
Kollmann, Augustus Frederick Christopher 514–15
Königslöw, Otto von 412–13
Köpp, Kai 381n.89
Krall, Emil 345–46
Kreisler, Fritz 945–46, 1010–11, 1013
Kreutzer, Rodolphe 380, 919
   Kreutzer bowing 399–400
   Violin Concerto no. 10 406
   Violin Concerto op. 12 388
Krufft, Nikolaus von
   Piano Sonata op. 4 551–53
   Preludes and Fugues 551–53
   String Quartets 551–53
   Violin Sonata 551–53
Krüger, Eduard 479
Kullak, Adolph 604, 809, 856
Kummer, Friedrich August 355
Kunt, Carl 409–10
Kürzinger, Ignaz 44–45

L'abbé le fils. *See* Saint-Sevin, Joseph-Barnabé
Lablache, Luigi 198
Lafont, Charles Philippe 400, 401–2, 655
Lamarre, Jacques Michel Hurel 380, 463
Lamparelli, Innocente 732
Lamping, Wilhelm 951
Lange, Aloysia 769
Lanza, Gesualdo 520–21, 531–32, 654
*larghetto* 513, 520–23, 548
*largo* 512–13, 514–20
Lasser, Johann Baptist 319, 568, 977, 989–90
Lebert, Sigmund 656, 835

*legato* 40–43, 173–74, 207–8, 215, 218–33, 241–42, 259–304, 308, 309–10, 355–56, 378, 395, 400–1, 512, 808–9, 854, 884–86, 890–91, 895–96, 897–98, 903, 910, 923–24, 940–41, 949, 968–69
*leggiero* 251, 295, 699
Lehmann, Lilli 1013–14
Leipzig (Gewandhaus /Conservatorium) 389–90, 392, 422, 435–36, 462, 615–16, 658–59, 908–9, 943
*lento* 514–20
Léonard, Hubert 411–12, 942, 999–1000, 1004, 1005–06
Leschetizky, Theodor 612–13
Levin, Julius 838–39
Lichtenthal, Pietro 241–42, 317n.97, 372–73, 547–48, 746, 833–34, 837–38, 959–60
Lieder (embellishment of ) 549, 598, 735, 754–56, 757
Lind, Jenny 769, 978
Lindley, Robert 749
Linke, Joseph 607, 923
Lipiński, Karol (Carl) 401–2, 464–65, 515–16
Liszt, Franz 34–35, 98–99, 130–31, 161–62, 246–47, 294, 421, 484, 617–18, 623, 711–12, 845
   *Album d'un voyageur* 602–3
   *Années de pèlerinage* 131, 602–3
   *Canzona napolitana* 575
   *Études d'execution transcendante* 602–3
   *Faust-Symphonie* 97, 173–74, 251, 477–78, 628f
   *Grandes Études* 602–3
   *Harmonies Poetiques et Religieuses* 131
   Hungarian Rhapsody no. 19 627f
   *Missa Solennis* 603
Lobedanz, Georg Carl Friedrich 381
Loewe, Carl
   *Die Festzeiten* 956
Löhlein, Georg Simon 15–16, 38–39, 68, 261, 265–66, 282, 310–11, 323, 352, 359, 376–77, 392, 508–9, 511, 520–21, 522, 537, 540, 541, 645, 661, 694, 842, 874–75, 883–84, 957–58, 983, 987

Lolli (Lolly), Antonio 375–76, 387–88, 862, 928
   Sonata op. 9, no. 4 913
"Lombard" rhythm 44–45, 659, 668, 882
London (Philharmonic Society) 617, 623
Luchesi, Andrea 118–19
*lusingando* 260
Lussan, Zelie de 1003
Lussy, Mathis 9–10, 34–35, 41, 49, 194, 315–16, 513–14, 531–32, 540, 609–11, 960
Lutzer, Jenny 768

MacDowell, Edward 857
Macfarren, George Alexander 770
Maelzel, Johann Nepomuk 469, 472–73
*maestoso* 361, 510, 537–39
Mahler, Gustav 7–9, 36–37, 860, 929–30
Maitland, John Alexander Fuller 557–58
Malibran, Alexandre 411–12
Malibran, Maria 207, 734, 894
Mancini, Giambattista 739–40
Manfredini, Vincenzo 221–22, 917–18
*maniera smorfiosa*. *See* Sliding effects
Manly, Dorothy 886–87
Mannheim 77, 118–19, 374, 376–77, 381–82, 676
Mannstein, Heinrich Ferdinand (pseudonym for H. F. Steinmann) 734, 743, 754, 895–96, 900
Mara, Gertrud Elisabeth 734
*marcatissimo* 251
*marcato* 247–49, 295, 598
Marpurg, Friedrich Wilhelm 62–63, 220, 318–19, 633, 670–71, 841–42, 864, 982–83
Marschner, Heinrich August 34–35, 271
   *Hans Heiling* 144
Marsick, Martin 439–40
*martelé*. *See* string bowing
Martín y Soler, Vicente 262
Marx, Adolph Bernhard 12, 15, 171, 179–80, 287–88, 446, 452–53, 535–36, 541–42, 557, 699, 710
Marxsen, Edouard
   Capriccio op. 47 126–27
*mäßig*. *See* moderato

Mattei, Elisabeth 963
Mattheson, Johann 181–82
Mattioli, Gottlob Cajetano 77–78
Maurer, Ludwig Wilhelm 400, 923–24
Mayseder, Joseph 394, 923
Mazas, Jacques Féréol 395, 401–2, 405, 923–24, 1004
McKerrell, J. 672
Meerts, Lambert-Joseph 395, 406–9, 438
Méhul, Étienne Nicolas
   *Joseph* 756–57
Meiningen Orchestra 624, 625, 711–12, 929–30
Meissner, Joseph 977, 982–83
Mendel, Hermann and Reissmann, August
   *Musikalisches Conversations-Lexikon* 41, 139, 172, 179–80, 535–36, 541–42, 810
Mendelssohn-Bartholdy, Fanny (later Hensel) 599
Mendelssohn Bartholdy, (Jacob Ludwig) Felix 30–31, 34–35, 36–37, 98–99, 168, 184–85, 263, 271–72, 309, 315–16, 418, 432, 446, 476, 489, 491, 545, 561, 611, 618, 749, 858–59, 955–56
   *Antigone* 539
   *Capriccio brillant* op. 22 858–59
   Cello Sonata op. 45 545, 939*f*
   Cello Sonata op. 58 939*f*
   *Die erste Walpurgisnacht* op. 60 456–57, 532, 539
   *Elijah* 532, 769
   *Die Hochzeit des Camacho* 709
   Italian Symphony 869
   *Lieder ohne Worte* 314–15, 316–17, 604–5, 709, 869
   Octet for Strings op. 20 335, 460, 708
   organ sonata op. 65 no. 4 478
   *Paulus* 280–81
   Piano Quartet op. 3 545
   Piano Sonata op. 6 709
   Piano Trio op. 49 95, 532, 545
   Piano Trio op. 66 335
   *Rondo capriccioso* op. 14 858–59
   *Ruy Blas* 280–81
   *Serenade und Allegro giocoso* op. 43 858–59

INDEX 1051

*Sommernachtstraum* overture 103 460, 481
String Quartet op. 12 651
String Quartet op. 13 298–99
String Quintet op. 18 239–40, 940–41
String Quartet op. 44 no. 1 545
String Quartet op. 44 no. 2 532, 545
String Quartet op. 44 no. 3 432, 478, 545
String Quartets 239–40, 940–41
Symphony no. 2 (Lobgesang) op. 52, 558
Symphony no. 3 op. 56 334, 456–57
Violin Concerto op. 64 335–36, 399–400, 401, 428, 563, 942, 999–1000
Zwei Klavierstücke WoO. 19 857
Mengelberg, Willem 624
Menges, Isolde 881
Menuhin, Yehudi 948
Merck, Daniel 482
*messa di voce* 167, 742, 764, 970, 973–74, 984
  *crescente* 889–90
  *decrescente* 889–90
*mesto* 361
Mestrino, Nicola 915–16
  *Douze Grands Solo* [sic] 917
*Méthode de violon* (Baillot, Rode, Kreutzer) 293–94, 382–83, 391–92, 395, 512, 523, 535, 970, 989
*Méthode de violoncelle* (Baillot, Levasseur, Catel, Baudiot) 386, 749
metre 454–60. *See also proportio dupla*; proportional signs
  *alla breve* 457–58, 460, 477–78, 482–83, 514–15
  *alla cappella* 482
  *alla semibreve* 484
  ₵ 444–45, 465, 472–73, 477–78, 481–92
  𝄵 483–84, 485–86
  ₵₵ 483–84
  c 472–73, 477–78, 481–82, 485–86, 489–92
  $\frac{2}{4}$ 481
  $\frac{2}{2}$ 481, 482, 486
  $\frac{4}{4}$ 486
  $\frac{2}{1}$ 483–84
  $\frac{3}{2}$ 457–59, 482
  $\frac{2}{4}$ 455–56, 458–59, 465, 516, 532
  $\frac{2}{8}$ 476
  $\frac{2}{16}$ 477
  $\frac{3}{2}$ 457, 538
  $\frac{3}{4}$ 455, 457
  $\frac{3}{8}$ 455, 457, 509, 521–22, 526, 532
  $\frac{3}{16}$ 477
  $\frac{4}{2}$ 455–56, 483, 514–15
  $\frac{4}{4}$ 455–56, 482
  $\frac{4}{8}$ 456–57, 522
  Z 483
  zusammengesetzten metre 455–57
metronome 397, 445–52, 469, 483–84, 508, 592–93, 598, 616, 697, 980
Meyerbeer, Giacomo (Jakob Liebmann Beer) 110, 147, 271, 294, 528–29, 545–46, 959–60, 1001–02
  *Il crociato in Egitto* 206, 244, 370f, 813, 954
  *L'Étoile du nord* 929–30
  *Les Huguenots* 92, 151, 157, 289, 336, 419–20, 528–29, 545–46, 749, 752, 766–67, 925f, 926f, 954, 1003
  *Le Prophète* 157, 483–84, 752
  *Robert le diable* 932f
*mezza voce* 77–78, 241–42
*mezzo forte* 75, 77–78, 284, 400–1, 949
Mies, Paul 267–68
Miksch, Johann Aloys 895
Milchmeyer, Johann Peter 15–16, 21–22, 40–41, 102–3, 111–12, 129, 222–23, 553, 656
Millanolo, Theresa 409–10, 415–16
Millico, Giuseppe 731–32
minuet 455
Mitchell, William J. 717n.13
*Mitklingen der Töne*. *See* Trembling effects
*moderato* 535–37. *See also allegro maestoso / moderato*
*moderato assai* 383, 523, 535
Molique, Bernhard 400, 993–94
*molto andante* 510, 529–30. *See also andante molto*
Momigny, Jérôme-Joseph de 261
Monn, Georg Mathius 590

*mordent / mordant* 627n.3, 631–32, 686, 692–93, 694–95, 697, 705, 741, 756–57, 772, 787
*Pralltriller* 741
*morendo* 78–79
Moreschi, Alessandro 813, 894, 932–33
Morlacchi, Francesco 736
Moscheles, Ignaz 38–39, 306, 527, 551–53, 658, 858–59, 884–86
  Studies op. 70 69, 601–2, 834
Mosel, Ignaz von 756–57
Mosel, Prosper Josef 601
Moser, Andreas 169, 182–83, 211–15, 294, 309, 418, 439–40, 561, 612–13, 658–59, 663, 676
Möser, Carl 389–90
Mozart, Leopold 14, 20, 27, 38, 46–47, 48–51, 52, 65–68, 137, 148, 265–66, 282, 319–20, 322, 343–44, 351–52, 359, 359n.39, 361, 375–76, 377–78, 454–55, 514, 523–24, 541–42, 564–65, 585–86, 639, 645–46, 654, 670–71, 688, 692–93, 696, 717–18, 873, 884, 913, 957–58, 959–60, 977, 981–82, 983–85, 987, 988
Mozart, Wolfgang Amadeus 28–29, 30–31, 91–92, 98–99, 100, 147, 184–85, 191, 236, 262, 267–68, 298, 308, 330, 343–44, 380, 418, 440–41, 447, 462–64, 489, 521, 524–25, 538, 540, 543, 573, 577, 610–11, 644, 676–77, 764, 767–68, 775–76, 797, 810, 977
  Adagio and Fugue K. 546 876
  *Così fan tutte* 761
  *Davide Penitente* K469 521
  *Don Giovanni* 89, 100, 133, 141–42, 204, 262, 291, 463–64, 696*f*, 1016
  Duo for violin and viola K. 423 666
  "Haffner" Symphony 241–42
  *Idomeneo* 759–60
  Lied zur Gesellenreise K468 521
  *Le nozze di Figaro* 262, 529–30, 759–60
    'Voi che sapete' 810–12
  Piano Concerto K. 537 829
  Piano Sonata K. 309 516
  Piano Sonata K. 332 573
  Rondo in A minor K. 511 193, 573
  String Quartet K. 421 44–45, 207–8, 344, 660, 880–81, 882, 884–86
  String Quartet K. 428 795–96, 880–81
  String Quartet K. 458 460, 481
  String Quartet K. 465 516, 548
  String Quintet K. 515 904–5
  String Quartet K. 575 89, 277–78, 331, 639
  String Quartet K. 589 100, 463, 489
  String Quintet K. 593 521
  Symphony no. 35 K. 385 241–42
  Symphony no. 36 K. 425 456–57
  Symphony no. 38 K. 504 29*f*
  Symphony no. 41 K. 551 141–42, 256
  Violin Concerto no. 4 in D K. 211 330
  Violin Concerto no. 5 in A K. 219 439–40, 884–86
  Violin Sonata K. 304 644
  Violin Sonata K. 306 704, 840
  Violin Sonata K. 379 694
  Violin Sonata K. 454 28–29, 29*f*
  *Die Zauberflöte* 463–64, 759–60, 761, 763, 765, 766*f*
    "Ach ich fühl's" 463–64
    "In diesen heil'gen Hallen" 759–60
Mühlfeld, Richard 1014–15
Müller, August 419
Müller, August Eberhardt 58–59, 111–12, 123–24, 265–66, 268, 535–36, 786–87, 802–3, 972
Müller, Carl Friedrich 412–13
Müller, Wenzel
  *Das Sonnenfest der Braminen* 705
The Müller String Quartet 412–13, 838
Munich (München) 381–82, 588–89, 711–12
musical clocks 598, 676–77

*Nachschlag* (*Nachschläge*) 657, 668, 685, 686
Nardini, Pietro 377–78, 387–88, 772–74, 917–18
Nathan, Isaac 733–34, 759–60
Neefe, Christian Gottlob 77–78
Neruda, Wilma Norman (Lady Hallé) 1007–08
Neubauer, Franz Christoph
  *Fernando und Yariko* 235
Neukomm, Sigmund 464–65

Neumann, Frederick 659–60, 672, 676–77, 759–60, 762–63, 797
Neumann, Leonora 394
New German School (*neudeutsche Schule / Zukunft*) 560–61, 611, 625, 1001–02
Nicholai, Otto 421
Nicholson, Charles 907, 974, 985
Niemecz, Joseph 664, 676–77
Nikisch, Arthur 624, 625, 884–86
Nilsson, Christina (Christine), Countess de Casa Miranda, 1003
*non legato* (*non ligato*) 217–18, 221, 222, 226–27, 241, 247–53
*non-staccato* 217–18, 253–56
Nordica, Lillian 1003
Norman-Neruda. *See* Neruda, Wilma Norman
Novello Mary 198

oboe 976
*ondeggiamento* 955–56, 957–58
ondulation 338, 957–58, 983–84, 993–94
Onslow, George 125–26, 411–12
orchestral playing 334, 357–61, 373–74, 419–22, 560–61, 609–10, 611, 618, 622–23, 624–25, 807–8, 884–86, 1015
organ 843–44, 850, 969–70
ornaments / ornamentation 714–38, 772, 775–76. *See also* embellishment; *grace-note*; trill, shake, trille; turn / Doppelschlag / Nachschlag; *appoggiatura*

Pacchiarotti, Gasparo 731–32
Pacini, Giovanni
 *Niobi* 206
Paër, Ferdinando
 *Achille* 764
Paganini, Niccolo 294, 381–82, 392–93, 400–2, 411–12, 414, 421–22, 578, 923–24, 996–97
Paisiello, Giovanni 262, 405
 *La Passione* 241–42
 *Ti seguiro fedele* 196
Paris 381–82, 392–93, 400–1, 409, 412–13, 414, 463–64, 472, 543, 624, 772–73, 917–18, 923–24, 1007–08

*parlando* 743
Pasquali, Niccolo 221–22, 318–19, 327–28, 693
passagework 21–22, 63–64, 69, 186, 222, 229, 239–40, 263, 375–76, 378–79, 384, 388–89, 390–91, 566–67, 590, 717, 769–70, 781–82, 803, 1011
*passaggi* 718
*pastorale* 260, 409–10
Patti, Adelina 810, 871–72, 894, 932–33, 1003
Paul, Oscar 16–17
pause 583, 689, 788, 789, 793. *See also fermata*
Pellegrini Celoni, Anna Maria 721
pendulum (to specify tempo) 469, 470–71, 477, 515–16
*perdendosi* 553, 556
Peres Da Costa, Neal 449n.12, 832–33, 837, 861
Perez, Davide 362
 *L'isola disabitata* 362
 *Solimano* 230f, 241–42, 362
Petiscus, Johann Conrad Wilhelm, 566–67, 983–84
*petit chapeau. See* accent signs
Petri, Johann Samuel 17, 79, 319, 351–52, 359, 379–80, 771–72, 953–54
pf 77–78
Philip, Robert 881
phrasing slur 194, 314–17
*piacevole* 260
Piani, Giovanni Antonio 147
*pianissimo* 75, 554
*piano* 75
*piano assai* 75
piano playing 3, 38–39
piano roll 1, 184–85, 828–29
Piatti, Alfredo 1007–08
*Picchettato. See* string bowing
Piccini, Niccola 100
 *Alessandro nell'Indie* 361–62
 *Catone in Utica* 241–42
 *La Ceccina ossia La buona figluola* 233, 369f
*piquiren / pikiren. See* string bowing
Pisendel, Georg Johann 453
Pleyel, Ignaz Joseph 123, 125–26
 Prussian quartets 702–3, 866

*Pochen. See* Trembling effects
*poco forte* 75, 76–78, 102–3, 112
Pokorny, Franz Xaver 320–21, 325–26
Pollini, Francesco 833–34
*pomposo* 261–62, 537
'Popular music' 4, 1014–15
Porges, Heinrich 173–74, 879–80
Porpora, Nicola 195, 671–72, 724
*portato* 173–74, 179, 219, 241–42, 259, 265–66, 267–68, 303, 319–20, 325–26, 378, 833–34, 971–72, 983, 985–86
*port-de-voix. See* Sliding effects
Pott, August 409–10, 439–40
Potter, Cipriani 922–23, 996–97
Prague 435–36, 463–64
Pralltriller. *See mordent / mordant*
Preghiera 735
*presto* 383–84, 489
Primrose, William 553
*Principes élémentaires de musique* 15–16, 17, 261, 325–26, 458, 486, 520–21, 535–36, 548, 557, 708, 793
*proportio dupla* 486
proportional signs 454
Prume, François 411–12
  *La melancholie Pastorale* op. 1 409–10
Puccini, Giacomo
  *Tosca*, 133
Pugnani, Gaetano 380–81, 390
*Punctus percutiens* 318
*punta d'arco / punto d'arco* 323–24, 368–69
Purcell, Henry 484–85

Quantz, Johann Joachim 18–19, 20, 27, 46–47, 63–64, 65, 68, 221, 228–29, 230–31, 265–66, 274, 282, 319–20, 355–57, 361, 452–53, 459n.43, 472, 482, 510, 523–24, 542–43, 639, 717, 752, 883–84, 972
Quiroga, Manuel 947

Raff, (Joseph) Joachim
  *Phantasie fur Pianoforte* op. 119 123
*rallentando* 202, 553, 578, 604–5, 610–11, 614–15
Ranken, Marion Bruce 554, 555, 838–40, 1013

Raoul, Jean Marie 354
Rau, Fritz 1010
Rauzzini, Vananzio 911
recitative 738–53
  accompaniment of 747–53
  *recitativo accompagnato* 739
  *recitativo secco* 738–39
recording(s) 1, 3, 7–9, 70–71, 184–85, 559, 561, 567–68, 612–13, 624, 625, 663–64, 770–71, 810, 826–29, 832–33, 837, 845, 861, 880–81, 883–84, 894, 932–33, 937, 947, 952, 965, 1013
Reger, Max
  *Sechs Burlesquen* op. 58 271–72
Reicha, Anton 4–5, 614–15, 645–46, 732–34, 764–65
Reicha, Joseph 585–86
Reichardt, Johann Friedrich 18–19, 63–64, 68, 76–79, 102–3, 111–12, 123–24, 134–35, 194–95, 226–28, 265–66, 291, 293–94, 306, 322, 357–59, 360–61, 373–74, 512, 523, 537, 540, 549, 554, 589, 613, 614–15, 644–45, 661, 663, 670, 685, 707, 920–21, 926–27, 957–58
  *Ariadne auf Naxos* 125
  *Brenno* 134–35, 322
  *Goethe's lyrische Gedichte* 261
  *Piano Sonata in F minor* 125
Reinecke, Carl 4–5, 184–85, 556, 612, 838–39, 858–61
  *Flute Sonata* op. 167 "Undine" 995–96
  *Piano Concerto No. 1* op. 72 846–47
  piano roll recordings 567–68, 612–13, 714, 828–29, 845
  Vorspiel to Act 5 of *König Manfred* 851–52, 860
Reissiger, Carl Gottlob 529
Reissmann, August. *See* Mendel, Hermann and Reissmann, August
Reitzenstein, Carl Ernst Philipp von 615
Rellstab Johann Carl Friedrich 80–81, 911
Reszke, Édouard de 1003
Reszke, Jean 1003
*rf* 123–29. *See also rinforzando / rinf / rf, / rfz. / rfp*
rhetoric 182–83

Richter, Jean Paul 68–69
Richter, Hans 625, 711–12
*richtiger Vortrag. See* correct performance
*ricochet. See* string bowing
Ricordi, Tito 771
Riem, Wilhelm Friedrich 480
Riemann, Hugo 9–10, 13, 34–35, 62, 70–71, 111–12, 139, 155–56, 166–67, 172–73, 226, 299, 316, 657, 809n.183
Riepel, Joseph 192, 219, 228–29, 265–66, 281, 320, 359, 969
  Violin Concertos op. 1 219
Ries, Ferdinand 478, 605, 782
Rietz, Eduard 816, 955–56
Righini, Henriette 761
*rinforte* 111–12
*rinforzando / rinf / rf / rfz / rfp* 76–77, 78–79, 80–81, 102–3, 110–33
*rinforzato* 102–3, 111–12, 123–24, 130
*ritardando* 553, 562–63, 588–89, 591, 601, 602–3, 610
*ritenuto* 585
Robberechts, André 380, 386–87, 390–91, 776
Rochlitz, Friedrich 375–76, 543, 591, 763
Rode, Pierre 167, 222, 380, 381, 387–88, 389–90, 405, 591, 593, 655, 884–86, 919
  Caprice no. 3 169, 955–56
  Caprice no. 10 405
  Violin Concerto no. 1 389–90
  Violin Concerto no. 7 70–71, 389–90, 523, 567, 617, 816, 920, 941, 994
*rollo* 961. *See also* Trembling effects
Romance 735
Romberg, Andreas 381–82, 387–88
  String Quartet op. 59 no. 1 921
Romberg, Bernhard Heinrich 21–22, 47, 51–52, 276–77, 379–80, 381–82, 387, 390–91, 395, 456–57, 472, 520–21, 531–32, 639, 680–81, 700–1, 710, 984, 985–86, 992
Ronconi, Giorgio 996–97
Rondo 723, 735, 763, 781
Rosé, Arnold 1010–11, 1015, 1016
Rosen, Charles 859–60
Rosenblum, Sandra 512–13

Rosenthal, Moritz 859–60
Rossini, Gioacchino Antonio 147, 491, 516–17, 527, 536, 539, 540, 610–11, 764, 813, 949–50, 959–60
  *Il barbiere di Siviglia* 932*f*
  "Una voce poco fa" 770–71, 837*f*
  *Le comte Ory* 526, 545
  *La gazza ladra* 156, 205, 836*f*
  *Guillaume Tell* 123, 526, 545
  *L'Italiana in Algeri* 370*f*
  *Moïse* 526, 545
  *Otello* 879
  *Petite messe solennelle* "Crucifixus" 162
  *Semiramide* 270, 325–26, 698*f*, 736, 925*f*
  *Le Siège de Corinthe* 526, 530–31, 545
  *Tancredi* 743*f*
Rostal, Max 343–44
Rousseau, Jean Jacques 15–16, 261, 525, 535–36, 798, 800, 988
Rovelli, Pietro 993–94
*rubato. See tempo rubato / rubato*
Rubini, Giovanni Battista 997–98
Rubinstein, Arthur 829
Rubinstein, Joseph 711–12
Ruff, Heinrich 897, 949

Sacchini, Antonio Maria Gaspare 100, 241–42
  *Creso* 792*f*
  *Enea e Lavinia* 196
  *Perseo* 198–99
  *Rinaldo* 197
Saint-Lambert, Michel de 482
Sainton, Prosper 411–12
Saint-Saëns 184–85, 450, 860
  Album our Piano op. 72 129
  Danse macabre op. 40 251
  Piano Quintet op. 14 129
  Six Bagatelles op. 3 129
Saint-Sevin, Joseph-Barnabé (L'abbé le fils) 351–52
Salieri, Antonio 464–65, 927
  *Axur* 262, 615
  *La cifra* 262
  *Der Rauchfangkehrer* 81, 91–92, 303–4, 706, 796
  *Venti otto divertimenti vocali* 765

*saltato / saltado. See* string bowing
Samuel, Harold  881
Santley, Sir Charles  770–71
Sauret, Emile  139–40
*sautillé*  374, 405, 408, 412–13, 432, 437.
    *See* string bowing
Scheibe, Johann Adolf  453
Schenker, Heinrich  828–29
Schetky, Johann Georg Christoph  354, 748, 968n.53
Schilling, Gustav
    *Encyclopädie der gesammten musikalischen Wissenschaften*  263, 265–66, 484, 638, 662–63, 808–9
Schindler, Anton  387–88, 411, 414–16, 419, 434, 448–49, 480, 606–7, 618–19
*Schneller*  627n.3, 686, 772, 780
Schnirlin, Ossip  1008
Scholz, Richard  98–99, 161–62
Schönberg, Arnold
    Serenade op. 24  146–47
schöner Vortrag. *See* beautiful performance
Schröder, Hermann  339, 344, 938, 957–58, 965, 967, 1005
Schubart, Christian Daniel Friedrich  374–75, 377–78, 524–25, 959–60
Schubert, Franz Peter  91–92, 98–99, 109, 147, 149, 308, 332, 432, 489, 528, 551
    *Alfonso und Estrella* D. 732  152–53, 253, 451–52, 490, 528, 535–36, 542, 544–45, 878
    "*Antigone und Oedip*" D. 542  758
    *Claudine von Villa Bella* D. 239  528
    *Fierrabras* D. 796  270, 528, 530, 640–41, 878
    *Die Freunde von Salamanca* D. 326  528
    Impromptu D. 899 no. 3  483–84
    "*Jägers Abendlied*" D. 368  758
    *Lieder*  755–57
    Moment musical op. 94, no. 2 (D.780)  299, 657
    Octet D. 803  332
    Piano Sonata op. 164 D.537  528, 857
    Piano Sonata D. 894  270
    Piano Trio op. 99 D.898  152–53, 432, 868
    Symphony no. 8 D.759  152–53
    Symphony no. 9 D.944  618
    String Quartet D. 353  332
    String Quartet D. 804  839
    String Quartet D. 810  439–40
    String Trio D. 581  56
    "Trout" Quintet D. 667  332
    *Winterreise* D. 911  868
Schubert, Johann Friedrich  18, 20, 21–22, 45–47, 48, 61, 68–69, 135–36, 156–57, 261, 461, 720–21, 724, 746, 791–92, 875, 890–91, 892, 893–94, 989–91
Schubert, Louis  139, 172–73
Schulz, Johann Abraham Peter  7–9, 10–11, 13–14, 15, 25–26, 32–33, 51, 52–53, 75, 79, 137, 181–82, 185–90, 191, 201, 258–59, 454–56, 457–58, 460, 482–83, 510, 565, 626–27, 740, 746, 771–72, 801–2
Schumann, Clara  43, 448–49
Schumann, Robert  34–35, 36–37, 98–99, 110, 130, 156, 184–85, 271–72, 301–2, 447–49, 456–57, 618, 955–56
    "*Abendlied*"  827–28, 947
    *Album für die Jugend* op. 68  144, 162–63, 171
    *Die Braut von Messina* op. 100  500*t*
    Carneval op. 9  130
    Cello Concerto op. 129  428
    Concert ohne Orchester op. 14 (Dritte grosse Sonate)  130
    *Drei Gesänge* op. 31  491
    *Fest-Ouverture* op. 123  500*t*
    *Genoveva* op. 81  488, 500*t*, 533
    *Hermann und Dorothea* op. 136  500*t*
    *Kinderszenen* op. 15
        "Träumerei"  857
    Lied op. 101/4  168
    "Die Löwenbraut" op. 31 no. 1  483–84
    *Manfred* op. 115  500*t*
    *Myrthen* op. 25/1  491, 533
    *Noveletten* op. 21  575, 664–65
    Overture, Scherzo and Finale op. 52  500*t*, 533

Phantasie op. 17  857
Piano Trio op. 80  92
Piano Quintet op. 44  56, 251, 500*t*
String Quartet op. 41 no. 1  665
String Quartet op. 41  491, 500*t*, 943
Symphony no. 1 op. 38  93–94, 500*t*
Symphony no. 2 op. 61  162–63, 188, 280, 500*t*, 869
Symphony no. 3 op. 97  144, 162–63, 171, 500*t*
Symphony no. 4 op. 120  93–94, 476, 500*t*
*Szenen aus Goethes Faust* WoO. 3  500*t*
Violin Sonata op. 105  82
Violin Sonata op. 121  82, 162–63
Schuppanzigh, Ignaz  107, 415–16, 606–8, 621, 922–23
Schwarz, Boris  1013
*sciolto / sciolte*  241–47, 253, 345, 369*f*, 378, 393, 958
scordatura  400
"scotch snap". *See* 'Lombard' rhythm
Scott, Marion Margaret  881, 886–87
*semplice*  781
Servais, Adrien-François  409–10
Ševčík, Otakar  140, 438, 439–40, 442
Seyfried, Ignaz von  622
Sfilio, Francesco  966n.48
*sforzando / sforzato / sf / sfz / sfp*  80–81, 86, 98–99, 694
  dolce *sfz*  157
  poco *sfz*  157
shake. *See* trill, shake, trille
Sheppard, William  850
Siciliano  910
Sieber, Ferdinand  769, 896
Sievers, Georg Ludwig Peter  393, 394–95, 414
Singer, Edmund  299–300, 339*f*, 687–88, 940
Sitt, Hans  435–36
Sliding effects  740, 785–86
  anticipation grace  661, 726, 813, 904–5, 911
  glide  888–89, 899, 907–9, 910
  leaping grace  660, 726, 810, 905, 911
  portamento  3–4, 169, 173–74, 179, 198–99, 205, 220, 317–18, 726–32, 736, 742–43, 778–79

*portamento di voce*  731–32, 813, 888–90
*port-de-voix*  629–30, 668, 888–89, 930–31, 993–94
  slur  301–2
  *Tragen der Töne*  318–19, 888–89
  *ziehen*  888–89
slur / slurring  37–46, 180, 191, 217, 301–17
  double slur  224–25
Smart, Sir George  608, 617–18
*smorzando*  78–79, 553, 556, 583, 596–97
Smyth, Charles J.  992, 997
Snart, Henry  623
Sobolewski, Eduard Johann Friedrich (alias J. Feski)  591–92
Soldat, Marie  70–71, 881, 886–87
  recordings  567–68, 612–13, 699–700, 826–27, 837, 947, 994n.141, 1013
Sonnleithner, Leopold von  755–56
*sons filés / son filé*  971, 989
*sons vibrés*. *See* Trembling effects
*sostenuto*  557
Speidel, Wilhelm  299–300
*spiccato*. *See* string bowing
Spohr, Louis  3–4, 34–35, 36–37, 98–99, 147, 200–1, 222, 231, 265–66, 270, 288, 294, 302, 303–4, 344, 346, 353, 373–74, 379–80, 381–82, 387–88, 390–91, 405, 409, 414, 415, 469, 489, 491, 517, 522, 527, 536, 542, 543, 546, 569, 589, 612, 613, 616–18, 621, 655, 663, 673, 676, 691–92, 697, 700–1, 710, 769–70, 806–7, 899–903, 920–21, 923–24, 929, 937, 944, 953–54, 961–62, 964–65, 985, 993–94, 1009
  Concertante WoO. II (1803)  153–54
  Concertino op. 79  538
  *Faust*  92, 95, 109, 160–61, 550–51
  *Des Heilands letze Stunden*  483–84
  *Jessonda*  527, 538, 925*f*
  *Die letzten Dinge*  478
  "Nachgefühl"  527, 700–1
  *Pietro von Abano*  517
  Sechs Gesänge op. 44 no. 1  558
  Sechs Gesänge op. 90 no. 4  558
  String Quartet op. 82 no. 2  109

Spohr, Louis (*cont.*)
   String Quintet op. 144  1006
   Symphony no. 3 op. 78,  538
   Symphony no. 4 "Die Weihe der
      Töne"  334, 517, 538
   Symphony no. 5 op. 102  929*f*
   Violin Concerto no. 2 op. 2  212
   Violin Concerto no. 8 "Gesagsszene"
      op. 47  3–4
   Violin Concerto no. 9 op. 55  699–700, 994
   Violin Concerto no. 11 op. 70  386–87,
      410
   Violin Duos opp. 148, 150, 153  1006
   *Violinschule*  70–71, 327, 386–87, 395,
      397–400, 435, 567, 590, 816
Spontini, Gasparo Luigi Pacifico  325–26,
      516–17, 522, 538, 540, 545, 546–47
   *Fernand Cortez*  483–84, 491, 516–17,
      545, 557
   *Nurmahal*  449–50, 526, 545, 546–47
   *Olympie*  483–84, 491, 516–17, 540, 545,
      546–47, 557–58
   *La Vestale*  244
*staccatissimo*  295
*staccato / stoccato*  259, 295–99, 361–62,
      395, 400–1, 402
   slurred *staccato* (*détaché articulé / festes
      staccato / coup d'archet piqué*) (*see*
      string bowing)
   *staccato* mark  137–47, 217–19, 220,
      343–44, 373–74, 384, 401, 402,
      428, 432, 437
Stanford, Sir Charles  553
Starke, Friedrich  107, 835
Staudigl, Joseph  769
Steane, John Barry  949–50
Steinbach, Fritz  625
Steinhausen, Friedrich Adolf  344–46
Steinmann, Heinrich Ferdinand. *See*
      Mannstein, Heinrich Ferdinand
Stowell, Robin  226–27
Straus, Ludwig  414
Strauss, Richard  274, 450
   *Also sprach Zarathustra*  477–78
string bowing
   *détaché*  231, 236, 247–49, 251, 253–54,
      343–44, 386–87, 393, 395, 402,
      432, 436

*détaché appuyer ou trainé*  222, 405
*détache chantant*  408, 434
*détaché continu*  423–24
*detaché d'avant bras*  408, 435
*détache du milieu*  408
*détache flûté*  405
*détaché léger*  386–87, 404
*detaché martelé* (*see below martelé*)
*détaché mat / coupé*  423–24
*détaché perlé*  405
*détaché rebondissant ou
      élastique*  423–24
*détaché sautillé* (*see below sautillé*)
*fouetté*  399–400, 426, 438–39
*grand détaché*  402, 407, 422, 434, 436
*hüpfend*  427
*martelé*  289, 295, 343–44, 384, 399–
      400, 402, 404, 415, 424*f*, 426, 432,
      435, 436, 438–39
*martelé du talon / coup d'archet du
      talon*  409, 423–24
*picchettato*  378
*piquiren / pikiren*  324
*ricochet / jetté /* flying staccato  392, 401,
      402, 406, 428–29, 430, 438
*saltato / saltado*  344, 412–13, 431
*sautillé*  374–75, 405, 408–9, 412–13,
      432, 437, 438–39
slurred *staccato*  319–20, 324
*spiccato*  241–47, 253, 338, 343n.3,
      409–10, 414–15, 421–22, 426, 437,
      438–41
springing bowstrokes / *springend*  343–
      44, 401–2, 405–6, 412–13, 418–19,
      427, 430, 435
string bowing in orchestral playing  357–
      61, 419–22
*stringendo*  596–97
Stuttgart  77
Sulzer, Johann Georg. *See* Schulz, Johann
      Abraham Peter
Süssmayr, Franz Xaver  147
   *Der Spiegel von Arkadien*  141–42, 705
sweetenings. *See* Trembling effects
Swinburne, James  1002
Swoboda, August  111–12, 170–71,
      680–81
syncopation  49–52

INDEX 1059

*Tac aspire.* See Trembling effects
tactus 454–55
Tamagno, Francesco 1000–01
Tamberlik, Enrico 1000–01
Tans'ur William 960
Tartini, Giuseppe, 228–29, 230–31,
 377–78, 390, 394–95, 639, 772–
 74, 977
 bow 376–77
 G major Sonata 211
 School 387–88
Taylor, Franklin 43, 642, 674–75,
 834–35
Tchaikovsky, Pyotr Illyich 949–50
 Swan Lake op. 20 884–86
 Symphony no. 5 op. 64 628*f*
 Symphony no. 6 op. 74 56, 177, 253–54,
 628*f*
*tempo giusto* 454–55, 457, 458, 470, 508,
 535–36, 540, 596–97
*tempo indiavolato* 569
*tempo rubato / rubato* 49–50, 560–61,
 562–65, 588–89, 592, 603, 606,
 608, 616–17, 622, 837
*temps dérobé* 569
*tenuta* 258–59
*tenuto* 169–70, 179–80, 220, 598, 749–51,
 794, 970
Tetrazzini, Luisa 1003
Thalberg, Sigismond 226, 294, 827–28,
 835, 856
Thibaud, Jacques 439–40
Thieriot, Paul Emil 389–90
thrown bowstroke 343–44, 434, 437,
 440–41, 442
Thurner, Friedrich Eugen 909–10
*tierce coulée* 656, 661, 668
Titz (Tietz), Anton Ferdinand 390–91
Toeschi, Carlo Giuseppe 374
Tollmann, Johannes 389–90
Tomášek, Václav Jan 463–64
Tomicich, Francesco 855
Tosi, Pier Francesco 137, 564–65, 718,
 910
Tourte, François 376–77, 381–82
Tovey, Donald Francis 316–17
*Tragen der Töne.* See Sliding effects
Trebelli-Bettini, Zelia 1003

Trembling effects 156, 740
 *continuous vibrato* 945–46, 947, 951,
 952, 953, 957–58, 965, 988, 1005,
 1007–08, 1009, 1011–16
 dumb shake 957–58
 *flatté* 963, 969, 970
 *flattemen / flattement* 717, 973–74, 989
 *Glockenschlag* 968
 *Glockenton* 968
 *Klopfen* 976, 995–96
 *Mitklingen der Töne* 968
 *ondeggiamento* 955–56, 957–58
 *ondulation* 957–58, 993–94
 *Pochen* 968
 *rollo* 961
 *sons vibrés / son vibré* 938–39, 957–58
 sweetenings 957–58, 973–74
 *Tac aspiré* 972
 *tremblé* 736
 *tremblement / tremamblement
 flexible* 955–56, 986–87
 tremolo, tremulo, tremolando,
 tremoletto 322, 325–26, 466–67,
 816, 908–9, 957–58, 959–60, 963,
 989–90, 991, 992
 tremolo 736, 949, 961, 962–63, 977
 tremolo bowing 409–10
 Vibration 974
 *vibratissimo* 959–60
 Vibrato 3, 220, 325–26, 555–56, 651,
 949, 955–1017
 bow vibrato 966, 968–72, 983,
 993–94, 997–98
 in cello playing 992–93, 997–98, 1015
 close shake 957–58, 986–87, 992
 close tremolo 996–97
 dumb shake 957–58, 989
 in orchestral playing 956, 995–96
 in singing 173–74, 949, 973, 997–98,
 1000–04, 1011–12, 1013–14
 in violin / viola playing 891–92,
 938–39, 943–44, 945–46, 955–56,
 962–63, 967, 981–84, 993–94,
 997–98, 999–1000, 1004–07,
 1008–11
 in wind playing 995–96, 1002, 1014–15
 vibrato (of intensity) 736
 *vibrato assai* 958

trill, shake, trille 579, 596–97, 627, 668–
　　92, 705, 707, 708–9, 723–24
　beginnings 670–84
　endings 3, 668, 684–92
　shake 957–58, 975
　speed and dynamics 691–92
Tromlitz, Johann Georg 649–50, 670, 685,
　　907, 989–90
Trommelbass 20
Truhn, Friedrich Hieronymus 411–12
Türk, Daniel Gottlob 15–16, 25–28, 30–31,
　　31*f*, 36, 38–41, 41*f*, 45–47, 48, 52–
　　53, 64, 77–78, 135–36, 137, 156–57,
　　181–82, 189, 190–93, 194–95, 201,
　　221, 259–61, 265–66, 283, 311, 315–
　　16, 455–56, 460–61, 483, 508–9,
　　525, 542–43, 550–51, 562–63, 567,
　　568, 582–85, 632–38, 652, 789
　*Sechs leichte Klaviersonaten* 36, 135–36,
　　582–83
turn / Doppelschlag / Nachschlag 692–
　　700, 723–24. *See also* trill, shake,
　　trille: endings
　accenting turns 692, 705, 709
　close turn 707
　connecting turn 696–700
　direct turn 700–1, 710–12
　*Doppelschlag* 685n.111, 692–700
　double appoggiatura 694
　*grupetto / mezzo grupetto / mordant* 694
　inverted turn 669, 671–72, 692–93,
　　700–1, 708, 709, 710–12
　*mezzo-grupetto* 694
　speed 697, 699
　turn grace 726

Umlauf, Ignaz
　*Die schöne Schusterin* 235
upbeat / Auftakt 16–17, 27, 28–30, 48,
　　198–99, 211–12, 232, 861–62
Urtext 3, 7

Vaccai, Nicola 810, 894
Valentine, Thomas 485–86
Vaslin, Olive-Charlier 422
Velluti, Giovanni Battista, 979
Veracini, Francesco 134, 147

Verdi, Giuseppe 114, 110, 151, 236, 518–
　　20, 545–46, 623, 771, 949–50
　*Aida* 446–47
　*Don Carlos* 545–46
　*Messa per Rossini* 160–61
　Requiem 160–61, 480, 1013–14
　*Rigoletto* 526, 545–46, 746
　*Il trovatore* 526, 536, 545–46
*vibrazione di voce* 959–60
Vienna / Viennese 379, 409–10, 412–13,
　　434, 462, 463–64, 472, 543, 551–
　　53, 615, 618–19, 647–48, 655,
　　658–59, 676–77, 711–12, 751–52,
　　755–56, 782–83, 927
Viennese Classical. *See* Classical /
　　Viennese Classical
Vieuxtemps, Henri 411–12, 415–16, 431,
　　713, 999–1000
Viotti, Giovanni Battista (Jean
　　Baptiste) 375–76, 380–92, 406,
　　569, 983–84
　Viotti bowing 399–400
　School 256, 380, 382, 386–88, 391–92,
　　395, 463, 535, 541, 543, 919
　Violin Concerto no. 3 776
　Violin Concerto no. 19 955
　Violin Concerto no. 22 778
　Violin Concerto no. 23 386–87
　Violin Concerto no. 27 201, 580–81
*vivace* 508, 510–11, 541–42
Vivaldi, Antonio 230–31
Vogl, Johann Michael 755–58
Vogler Georg Joseph 138, 147, 150–51,
　　265–66, 644, 749–51
　*Lampedo* 42
　*Der Kaufmann von Smyrna* 796
　Symphony in C 958
Vorschlag (Vorschläge) 629–30, 631–32,
　　662–63
Vortrag 45–46, 203, 263–64, 801, 802–3,
　　810, 863

Wackenroder, Wilhelm Heinrich 68–69,
　　181–82
Wagner, (Wilhelm) Richard 34–35, 98–
　　99, 146–47, 152, 156, 184–85, 220,
　　339, 421, 445, 450–51, 464–65,

477–78, 480, 484, 518–20, 546, 560–61, 609–10, 611, 622–23, 629
*Faust* overture 711
*Der fliegende Holländer* 273, 533, 537, 557, 711, 926f
*Götterdämmerung* 711
*König Enzio* 711
*Lohengrin* 273, 711
*Parsifal* 149, 166–67, 173–74, 303–4, 879–80, 956f
*Rienzi* 273, 537, 539, 546, 711
*Siegfried* 166–67, 173–74, 953–54, 956f
*Siegfried Idyll* 273
*Tannhäuser* 273, 450–51, 518–20, 533, 537, 539, 546, 711
*Tristan und Isolde* 629, 925f
*Ueber das Dirigieren* 625
*Die Walküre* 166–67
Walker, Ernest 642
Walther, Johann Gottfried 137, 246–47, 318
Weber, Carl Maria von 34–35, 110, 147, 236, 447, 450–51, 545–46, 642, 675, 769–70
 E flat Mass 56, 86, 236
 *Euryanthe* 446–47, 491, 498t, 517, 522, 536, 539, 545–46, 616
 *Der Freischütz* 86–87, 150–51, 152, 268, 295, 371f, 617, 706, 797
 Konzertstück 498t, 522
Weber, Dionys 622–23
Weber, Gottfried 19, 20, 58–59, 62–63, 400, 463–64, 469, 476, 486–88, 524–25, 749–52, 960–61
 Requiem op. 24 471

Weigl, Joseph
 *Baal's Sturz* 756–57
Weingartner, Felix 624
Weippert, John Erhardt 284–85
Weiss, Franz 107
 String Quartet op. 9 551–53
Wend, Fridolin von 998–99
Wesley, Samuel 843–44, 850
Wilhemj, August 554
Willent-Bordogni, Jean-Baptist-Joseph 909n.55
Witthauer, Johann Georg 284, 483, 631–32, 645
Woldemar, Michel 374–75, 380, 381–82, 646–47, 772–74, 970–71, 989
Wolf, Ernst Wilhelm 379n.78
 String Quartet op. 3 no. 3 246–47
Wolf, Georg Friedrich 36, 111–12, 135–36, 156–57, 482–83, 582–83
Wood, Sir Henry 1013–14
Wragg, Jacob 485–86
Wranitzsky, Paul 236, 379

Ysaÿe, Eugène 439–40, 947, 1009
 "Rêve d'enfant" op. 14 827

Zelter, Carl Friedrich 476, 955–56
 Lieder 651
Zerr, Anna 768
Ziehen. *See* Sliding effects
Zimbalist, Efrem 1012
Zimmermann, Pierre-Joseph-Guillaume 808–9, 852
Zrza, Eleonora 923–24